P9-ARO-629

THE
COLLINS
POCKET
GREEK
DICTIONARY

GREEK·ENGLISH ENGLISH·GREEK

Harry T. Hionides

New Edition by/Νέα Έκδοση
Niki Watts, Helen George-Papageorgiou

COLLINS
London and Glasgow

First published in this edition 1988

© **William Collins Sons & Co. Ltd. 1988**

ISBN 0 00 433208 3

Harry T. Hionides

new edition by/νέα έκδοση
Niki Watts, Helen George-Papageorgiou

consultant/σύμβουλος
Roger Green

editorial staff/εκδοτικό προσωπικό
Jeremy Butterfield, Val McNulty, Susan Dunsmore

489.3321
Hio

442373
CALVIN PARK BRANCH

CAT'D
19 89

Conditions of Sale
This book is sold subject to the condition that it shall not,
by way of trade or otherwise, be lent, re-sold, hired out or
otherwise circulated without the publisher's prior consent
in any form of binding or cover other than that in which it
is published and without a similar condition including this
condition being imposed on the subsequent purchaser.

ISBN 0 00 433209 1 Special edition for Greece and Cyprus

Printed in Great Britain
Collins Clear-Type Press

ΕΙΣΑΓΩΓΗ

Ο χρήστης που επιθυμεί να διαβάσει και να καταλάβει Αγγλικά θα βρει σ' αυτό το λεξικό έναν περιεκτικό και σύγχρονο κατάλογο λέξεων, καθώς και σημαντικό αριθμό φράσεων που χρησιμοποιούνται σήμερα. Επίσης θα βρει σε αλφαβητική σειρά τους κύριους ανώμαλους τύπους με παραπομπή στο βασικό τους τύπο, καθώς και μερικές από τις συνηθέστερες συντομογραφίες, αρκτικόλεξα και γεωγραφικές ονομασίες.

Ο χρήστης που επιθυμεί να εκφραστεί και να επικοινωνήσει στα Αγγλικά θα βρει όλους τους τρόπους χρήσης των βασικών λέξεων. Όπου μια λέξη έχει πολλές σημασίες, οι αντίστοιχες μεταφράσεις δίνονται κατά σειρά προτεραιότητας ανάλογα με τη συχνότητα των Ελληνικών εννοιών,

INTRODUCTION

The user whose aim is to read and understand Greek will find a comprehensive and up-to-date wordlist which includes the most common scientific and technical terms. The official ("monotonic") accent system has been used throughout, and a high proportion of Demotic words and Demotic versions of words which also have Katharevousa forms have been included.

The user who wants to communicate and express himself in Greek will find clear and detailed treatment of all the basic words, with numerous indicators pointing to the appropriate translation and helping him to use it correctly.

ABBREVIATIONS

επίθετο	**a**	adjective
συντομογραφία	**abbr**	abbreviation
επίρρημα	**ad**	adverb
γεωργία	**AGR**	agriculture
ανατομία	**ANAT**	anatomy
αρχαιολογία	**ARCH**	archaeology
αρχιτεκτονική	**ARCHIT**	architecture
αστρονομία	**ASTR**	astronomy
επίθετο	**attr**	attributive
αυτοκίνητο	**AUT**	automobile
αεροπορία	**AVIAT**	aviation
βιβλικός	**BIBL**	biblical
βιολογία	**BIOL**	biology
βοτανική	**BOT**	botany
Αγγλισμός	**Brit**	British usage
ξυλουργική	**CARP**	carpentry
χημεία	**CHEM**	chemistry
κινηματογράφος	**CINE**	cinema
σύνδεσμος	**cj**	conjunction
κοινός	**col**	colloquial
περιληπτικός	**collect**	collective
εμπορικός	**COMM**	commercial
συγκριτικός	**comp**	comparative
σύνθετος	**compd**	compound
ηλεκτρονικοί υπολογιστές	**COMPUT**	computers
υποκοριστικό	**dim**	diminutive
διπλωματία	**DIP**	diplomacy
εκκλησιαστικός	**ECCL**	ecclesiastical
οικονομία	**ECON**	economics
ηλεκτρισμός	**ELEC**	electricity
ειδικά	**esp**	especially
επιφώνημα	**excl**	exclamation
θηλυκό	**f**	feminine noun
μεταφορικά	**fig**	figuratively
οικονομία	**FIN**	finance
γεωγραφία	**GEOG**	geography
γεωλογία	**GEOL**	geology
γραμματική	**GRAM**	grammar
κυνήγι	**HUNT**	hunting
απρόσωπο	**impers**	impersonal
απαρέμφατο	**infin**	infinitive
επιφώνημα	**interj**	interjection
αμετάβλητος	**inv**	invariable
ανώμαλο	**irreg**	irregular
γλωσσολογία	**LING**	linguistics
κυριολεκτικός	**lit**	literal
λογοτεχνία	**LITER**	literature
αρσενικό	**m**	masculine noun
μαθηματικά	**MATH**	mathematics
μηχανισμός	**MECH**	mechanical

ιατρική	**MED**	medical
στρατιωτικός	**MIL**	military
μουσική	**MUS**	music
ουσιαστικό	**n**	noun
ναυτικός	**NAUT**	nautical, naval
ουδέτερο	**nt**	neuter
αριθμός	**num**	numeral
απαρχαιωμένος	**old**	old-fashioned
εαυτός	**o.s.**	oneself
κοινοβούλιο	**PARL**	Parliament
μετοχή	**part**	participle
υποτιμητικός	**pej**	pejorative
προσωπικός	**pers**	personal
φιλοσοφία	**PHIL**	philosophy
φωνητική, φωνολογία	**PHON**	phonetics
φωτογραφία	**PHOT**	photography
φυσική	**PHYS**	physics
πληθυντικός	**pl**	plural
ποίηση	**POET**	poetry
πολιτική	**POL**	politics
κτητικός	**poss**	possessive
μετοχή αορίστου	**pp**	past participle
κατηγορούμενο	**pred**	predicative
πρόθεση	**prep**	preposition
τυπογραφία	**PRINT**	printing/typography
αντωνυμία	**pron**	pronoun
αόριστος, παρατατικός	**pt**	past tense
σήμα κατατεθέν	Ⓡ	registered trademark
ραδιοφωνία	**RAD**	radio
σιδηρόδρομος	**RAIL**	railways
θρησκεία	**REL**	religion
σχολείο	**SCH**	school
ενικός	**sing**	singular
λαϊκός	**sl**	slang
κάποιος	**s.o.**	someone, somebody
κάτι	**sth**	something
υπερθετικός	**sup**	superlative
τεχνικός	**TECH**	technical
τηλεπικοινωνίες	**TEL**	telecommunications
υφαντά	**TEX**	textiles
θέατρο	**THEAT**	theatre
τηλεόραση	**TV**	television
πανεπιστήμιο	**UNIV**	university
Αμερικανισμός	**US**	American usage
ρήμα	**v**	verb
ρήμα αμετάβατο	**vi**	intransitive verb
ρήμα μεταβατικό	**vt**	transitive verb
ρήμα μεταβατικό και αμετάβατο	**vti**	transitive and intransitive verb
ζωολογία	**ZOOL**	zoology

ΣΥΝΤΟΜΟΓΡΑΦΙΕΣ

athletics, sport	αθλητ	αθλητικά
aviation	αερο	αεροπορία
accusative	αιτ	αιτιατική
intransitive verb	αμ, αμετ	ρήμα αμετάβατο
anatomy	ανατ	ανατομία
negative	αρνητ	αρνητικός
architecture	αρχιτεκ	αρχιτεκτονική
astronomy	αστρον	αστρονομία
see (cross-reference)	βλ	βλέπε
botany	βοτ	βοτανική
geography	γεωγρ	γεωγραφία
geometry	γεωμ	γεωμετρία
grammar	γραμμ	γραμματική
religion	εκκλ	εκκλησιαστικός
commerce	εμπόρ	εμπόριο
adjective	επίθ	επίθετο
adverb	επίρ	επίρρημα
exclamation	επιφ	επιφώνημα
zoology	ζωολ	ζωολογία
electricity	πλεκ, πλεκτ	πλεκτρισμός
medicine	ιατρ	ιατριλή
et cetera	κτλ	και τα λοιπά
mathematics	μαθημ	μαθηματικά
mechanical	μηχαν	μηχανισμός
figuratively	μεταφ	μεταφορικά
music	μουσ	μουσική
nautical, naval	ναυτ	ναυτικός
law	νομ	νομική
economics	οικ, οικον,	οικονομικά
noun	όνομ, ουσ	όνομα, ουσιαστικό
plural	πλ	πληθυντικός
politics	πολιτ	πολιτική
preposition	πρόθ	πρόθεση
e.g. (for example)	π.χ.	παραδείγματος χάρη
military	στρατ	στρατιωτικός
conjunction	σύνδ	σύνδεσμος
technical	τεχν	τεχνολογία
telecommunications	τηλεπ	τηλεπικοινωνίες
printing, typography	τυπογρ	τυπογραφία
philosophy	φιλοσ	φιλοσοφία
photography	φωτογρ	φωτογραφική
chemistry	χημ	χημεία

PRONUNCIATON OF MODERN GREEK

Each letter in Greek nearly always represents the same sound. The few exceptions are listed below on page viii. The pronunciation system used in the text (given in brackets after each Greek main entry) transcribes the letters of Greek into the English alphabet, with one special character used to represent a less obvious sound. A list of sounds which the English alphabet is used to represent is given below. When you read out the pronunciation you should sound the letters as if you were reading an English word.

GREEK LETTER		CLOSEST ENGLISH SOUND	SHOWN BY	EXAMPLE	PRONOUNCED
A	α	hand	a	άνθρωπος	anthropos
B	β	vine	v	βούτυρο	vooteero
Γ	γ	see page viii	g	γάλα	gala
		yes	y	για	ya
Δ	δ	this	ð	δάκτυλος	ðakteelos
E	ε	met	e	έτοιμος	eteemos
Z	ζ	zone	z	ζώνη	zonee
H	η	meet	ee*	ήλιος	eeleeos
Θ	θ	thin	th	θέατρο	theatro
I	ι	meet	ee*	ίππος	eepos
K	κ	key	k	και	ke
Λ	λ	log	l	λάδι	laðee
M	μ	mat	m	μάτι	matee
N	ν	not	n	νύχτα	neehta
Ξ	ξ	rocks	ks	ξένος	ksenos
O	o	cot	o	όχι	ohee
Π	π	pat	p	πόλη	polee
P	ρ	carrot see page viii	r	ρόδα	roða
Σ	σ,ς	sat	s	σήμα	seema
T	τ	top	t	τράπεζα	trapeza
Y	υ	meet	ee*	ύπνος	eepnos
Φ	φ	fat	f	φούστα	foosta
X	x	see page viii	h	χάνω χέρι	hano heree
Ψ	ψ	lapse	ps	ψάρι	psaree
Ω	ω	cot	o	ώρα	ora

* The letter *i* is used to represent the "ee" sound a) when two such sounds occur together; b) when "ee" is followed by "e"; c) before a stressed vowel e.g.

ικανοποίηση	eekanop*i*eesee
βίαιος	v*i*eos
κριός	kr*i*os

COMBINATIONS OF LETTERS

The combinations of letters shown below are pronounced as listed.

GREEK LETTERS	CLOSEST ENGLISH SOUND	SHOWN BY	EXAMPLE	PRONOUNCED
ει	meet	ee	είδος	*ee*ðos
οι			οίκοι	*ee*kee
αι	met	e	αίμα	*e*ma
ου	food	oo	που	p*oo*
μπ	beer	b	μπύρα	*b*eera
	or amber	mb	κάμπος	ka*mb*os
	or ample	mp	σύμπαν	see*mp*an
ντ	door	d	ντομάτα	*d*omata
	or bent	nt	συναντώ	seena*nt*o
	or bend	nd	πέντε	pe*nd*e
γκ, γγ	good	g	γκάζι	*g*azee
	or angle	ng	Αγγλία	a*ng*leea
γξ	links	ks	σφιγξ	sfee*nks*
τζ	friends	dz	τζάμι	*dz*amee

The pairs of vowels shown above are pronounced separately if the first has an acute accent (´) or the second a dieresis (¨); e.g.

παιδάκι	peðakee	παϊδάκι	pa*ee*ðakee
καιρός	keros	Κάιρο	ka*ee*ro

Some Greek consonant sounds have no English equivalent. The υ of the groups αυ, ευ and ηυ is generally pronounced *v*.

GREEK LETTER	REMARKS	EXAMPLE	PRONOUNCED
Ρ, ρ	slightly trilled *r*	ρόδα	ro*ð*a
Χ, χ	like *ch* in *loch*	χάνω	*h*ano
	or like a rough *h*	χέρι	*h*eree
Γ, γ	like a rough *g*	γάλα	*g*ala
	or like *y*	για	*y*a

STRESS

All Greek words of two or more syllables have an accute accent which indicates where the stress falls. For instance, άγαλμα is pronounced a*galma* and αγάπη is pronounced a*gapee*.

ΑΓΓΛΙΚΗ ΠΡΟΦΟΡΑ

Φωνήεντα και δίφθογγοι		Σύμφωνα	
	Αγγλικό παράδειγμα		Αγγλικό παράδειγμα
ɑː	father	b	bat, baby
ʌ	but, come	d	mended
æ	man, cat	f	fine, raffle
ɔ	father, ago	g	get, big
ɜː	bird, heard	dʒ	gin, judge
ɛ	get, bed	ŋ	sing
ɪ	it, big	h	house, he
iː	tea, see	j	young, yes
ɒ	hot, wash	k	come, mock
ɔː	saw, all	l	little, place
ʊ	put, book	m	ram, mummy
uː	too, you	n	ran, nut
aɪ	fly, high	p	pat, pope
aʊː	how, house	r	red, tread
ɛɔ	there, bear	s	sand, yes
eɪ	day, obey	t	tab, strut
ɪɔ	here, hear	v	vine, river
ɔʊ	go, note	z	rose, zebra
ɔɪ	boy, oil	ʃ	she, machine
ʊɔ	poor, sure	tʃ	chin, rich
		w	water, which
		ʒ	vision
		θ	think, myth
		ð	this, the

Το σημείο * σημαίνει ότι το τελικό 'r' δεν προφέρεται στα Αγγλικά εκτός αν η λέξη που ακολουθεί αρχίζει με φωνήεντο. Το σημείο ['] καθορίζει την τονιζόμενη συλλαβή.

GREEK-ENGLISH
ΕΛΛΗΝΙΚΑ-ΑΓΓΛΙΚΑ

Α, α

α-, αν- (negative particle) in-, un-, il-, ir-, -less.

αβαθής [avathees] shallow.

αβάπτιστος [avapteestos] unbaptised.

αβάσιμος [avaseemos] groundless || (υποψία) unfounded.

αβάστακτος [avastaktos] unbearable || (δύναμη) uncontrollable.

άβατος [avatos] inaccessible || untrodden.

άβγαλτος [avgaltos] inexperienced.

αβγό, το [avgo] egg.

αβγολέμονο, το [avgolemono] sauce or soup with eggs and lemon.

αβέβαιος [aveveos] doubtful || uncertain.

αβίαστος [aveeastos] unforced, natural.

αβίωτος [aveeotos] unbearable, intolerable.

αβλαβής [avlavees] (έντομο κτλ) harmless.

αβοήθητος [avoeetheetos] without help.

άβολος [avolos] inconvenient || (κάθισμα κτλ) uncomfortable.

άβυσσος, η [aveesos] abyss.

αγαθός [agathos] good, kind || (αφελής) naive || (τίμιος) honest.

άγαλμα, το [agalma] statue.

άγαμος [agamos] unmarried, single.

αγανακτώ [aganakto] be irritated.

αγανάκτηση, η [aganakteesee] indignation, anger.

αγάπη, η [agapee] love, affection.

αγαπημένος [agapeemenos] dear, beloved || (πράγμα) favourite.

αγαπητός [agapeetos] βλ αγαπημένος.

αγαπώ [agapo] love || (μου αρέσει) like.

αγγαρεία, η [angareea] chore || drudgery.

αγγείο, το [angeeo] vase || (πήλινο) pot || (ανατ) blood vessel.

αγγειοπλαστική, η [angeeoplasteekee] pottery.

αγγελία, η [angeleea] announcement || (εμπορ) advertisement.

αγγελιαφόρος, ο, η [angeleeaforos] messenger || (στρατ) orderly.

αγγελικός [angeleekos] angelic(al).

αγγέλλω [angelo] announce, declare.

άγγελμα, το [angelma] message, notice.

άγγελος, ο [angelos] angel.

αγγίζω [angeezo] touch.

Αγγλία, η [angleea] England.

αγγλικά, τα [angleeka] English (language).

αγγλικός [angleekos] English.

Αγγλίδα, η [angleeδa] Englishwoman.

Άγγλος, ο [anglos] Englishman.

αγγούρι, το [angouree] cucumber.

αγελάδα, η [ayelaδa] cow.

αγέλαστος [ayelastos] morose, sullen.

αγέλη, η [ayelee] herd || (προβάτων) flock || (λύκων) pack.

αγένεια, η [ayeneea] rudeness.

αγενής [ayenees] rude, impolite.

αγέραστος [ayerastos] ever young.

αγέρωχος [ayerohos] haughty, arrogant.

αγιάζι [ayazee] hoarfrost, cold || (αύρα) breeze.

αγιάζω [ayazo] (γίνομαι άγιος) become a saint.

αγιασμός, ο [ayasmos] blessing with holy water.

αγιάτρευτος [ayatreftos] incurable.

αγίνωτος [ayeenotos] (φρούτο) unripe, raw.

άγιος [ayos] holy || (πρόσωπο) saint.

αγκαζάρω [angazaro] reserve, book || hire.

αγκαζέ [angaze] arm in arm || (πιασμένο) engaged, taken, occupied.

αγκάθι, το [angathee] thorn, prickle.

αγκαλιά, η [angalia] embrace || (επιρ) armful.

αγκαλιάζω [angaliazo] embrace, hug.

αγκίδα, η [angeeδa] splinter, thorn.

αγκινάρα, η [angeenara] artichoke.

αγκίστρι, το [angeestree] hook.

αγκομαχώ [angomaho] gasp, pant.

αγκύλες, οι [angeeles] brackets.

άγκυρα, η [angeera] anchor || **σηκώνω ~** weigh anchor.

αγκυροβολία, η [angeerovoleea] mooring.

αγκυροβολώ [angeerovolo] anchor, drop anchor.

αγκώνας, ο [angonas] elbow.

αγναντεύω [agnantevo] see from a distance.

άγνοια, η [agneea] ignorance.

αγνός [agnos] chaste, modest.

αγνοώ [agnoo] be ignorant of || (περιφρονώ) ignore.

αγνωμοσύνη, η [agnomoseenee] ingratitude.

αγνώμων [agnomon] ungrateful.

αγνώριστος [agnoreestos] unrecognizable.

άγνωστος [agnostos] unknown || (ουσ) stranger.

άγονος [agonos] infertile, barren || ~ **γραμμή** unprofitable shipping line.

αγορά, η [agora] (το μέρος) market || (η πράξη) purchase.

αγοράζω [agorazo] purchase, buy.

αγοραίος [agoreos] for hire || (μεταφ) vulgar, common.

αγορανομία, η [agoranomeea] market inspection police.

αγοραπωλησία, η [agorapoleeseea] transaction.

αγοραστής, ο [agorastees] buyer, purchaser.

αγορεύω [agorevo] make a speech || (με στόμφο) harangue.

αγόρι, το [agoree] boy, lad.

άγουρος [agouros] unripe, green, sour.

αγράμματος [agrammatos] illiterate, uneducated.

άγραφος [agrafos] unwritten.

αγριάδα, η [agriaδa] fierceness, savageness.

αγριεύω [agrievo] be infuriated, become angry.

αγρίμι, το [agreemee] wild animal || (μεταφ) rude fellow.

άγριος [agreeos] wild || savage.

αγροίκος [agreekos] coarse, unrefined.

αγρόκτημα, το [agrokteema] farmland.

αγρός, ο [agros] field || country.

αγρότης, ο [agrotees] farmer || peasant.

αγροφυλακή, η [agrofeelakee] agrarian police.

αγρυπνώ [agreepno] stay awake, lie awake || (επαγρυπνά) be watchful.

αγύμναστος [ageemnastos] untrained, unexercised.

αγχιστεία, η [anghisteea] relationship by marriage.

αγχόνη, η [anghonee] gallows, hanging.

άγχος, το [anghos] anxiety.

άγω [ago] lead, conduct, guide.

αγωγή, η [agoyee] breeding, conduct || (νομ) lawsuit.

αγώγι, το [agoyee] fare.

αγωγός, ο [agogos] conductor || (σωλήνας) pipe, conduit.

αγώνας, ο [agonas] struggle, fight || (αθλητ) game, contest || **αγώνες** πλ games, sporting events.

αγωνία, η [agoneea] agony || anxiety.

αγωνίζομαι [agoneezome] struggle, fight, strive.

αγωνιστής, ο [agoneestees] contestant, fighter || (πολιτ) militant.

αγωνιώ [agoneeo] be in agony || be anxious.

αγωνιώδης [agoneeoδees] anxious, troubled.

αδαής [aδaees] inexperienced, unfamiliar (with).

αδάμαστος [aδamastos] untamed || (λαός) unconquered || (θάρρος) unbroken.

άδεια, η [aδeea] leave, permission || (γάμου κτλ) licence, permit.

αδειάζω [aδeeazo] empty || (ευκαιρώ) have time.

άδειος [aδeeos] empty, unoccupied.

αδέκαστος [aδekastos] incorruptible || (αμερόληπτος) impartial, unbiased.

αδελφή, η [aδelfee] sister.

αδέλφια, τα [aδelfeea] πλ brothers, brother and sister.

αδελφικός [aδelfeekos] (αγάπη) brotherly || (φίλος) dear.

αδελφός, ο [aδelfos] brother.

αδένας, ο [aδenas] gland.

αδέξιος [aδekseeos] awkward, clumsy.

αδέσμευτος [aδesmeftos] (μεταφ) under no obligation || (χώρα) non-aligned.

αδέσποτος [aδespotos] stray, without an owner.

άδηλος [aδeelos] uncertain, doubtful || **άδηλοι πόροι** invisible income.

αδήλωτος [aδeelotos] undeclared.

ʹΑδης, ο [aδees] Hell || Hades.

αδηφάγος [aδeefagos] voracious || (μεταφ) greedy.

αδιάβαστος [aδiavastos] (βιβλίο) unread || (μαθητής) unprepared.

αδιάβατος [aδiavatos] impassable.

αδιάβροχο, το [aδiavroho] raincoat.

αδιάθετος [aδiathetos] (υγεία) unwell || (κεφάλαιο) unspent.

αδιαίρετος [aδieretos] indivisible || undivided.

αδιάκοπος [aδiakopos] uninterrupted, continuous.

αδιάκριτος [aδiakreetos] imperceptible || (χαρακτήρας) indiscreet.

αδιάλλακτος [aδialaktos] implacable, uncompromising.

αδιάλυτος [aδialeetos] indissoluble, undissolved.

αδιάντροπος [aδiantropos] brazen || (ενέργεια) impudent.

αδιαπέραστος [aδeeaperastos] impenetrable.

αδιάρρηκτος [aδeeareektos] unbreakable || (μεταφ) indissoluble.

αδιάσπαστος [aδiaspastos] unbroken || inseparable.

αδιάφορος [aδiaforos] indifferent.

αδιαχώριστος [aδeeahoreestos] inseparable.

αδίδακτος [aδeeδaktos] untaught.

αδιέξοδος, η [aðieksoðos] impasse || (δρόμος) cul de sac, dead end.

αδικία, η [aðeekeea] injustice, wrongdoing, offence.

άδικος [aðeekos] unjust, unfair || **έχω άδικο** I'm in the wrong.

αδικώ [aðeeko] do wrong || (κάποιον) be unjust to.

αδιόρθωτος [aðeeorthotos] irreparable || (χαρακτήρας) incorrigible.

αδίστακτος [aðeestahtos] unhesitating, resolute.

άδολος [aðolos] guileless, innocent.

άδοξος [aðoksos] inglorious.

αδούλευτος [aðouleftos] unwrought, raw || (αγρός) uncultivated.

αδράνεια, η [aðraneea] inertia || (μεταφ) indolence.

αδράχτι, το [aðrahtee] spindle.

αδύνατος [aðeenatos] thin || (δεν γίνεται) impossible.

αδυναμία, η [aðeenameea] (πνεύματος) deficiency || (σώματος) weakness.

αδυνατώ [aðeenato] be unable to.

αδυσώπητος [aðeesopeetos] relentless, implacable.

άδυτο, το [aðeeto] (εκκλ) sanctuary.

αειθαλής [aeethalees] evergreen.

αεικίνητος [aeekeeneetos] in perpetual motion.

αείμνηστος [aeemneestos] late, fondly remembered.

αεράμυνα, η [aerameena] air defence.

αεραγωγός, η [aeragogos] air duct.

αέρας, ο [aeras] air, wind.

αερίζω [aereezo] ventilate, air.

αερισμός, ο [aereesmos] ventilation, airing.

αέριο, το [aereeo] gas.

αεριούχος [aereeouhos] aerated, gaseous.

αεριστήρας, ο [aereesteeras] ventilator.

αεροδρόμιο, το [aeroðromeeo] airport.

αερόλιθος, ο [aeroleethos] meteorite.

αερολιμένας, ο [aeroleemeenas] airport.

αεροπλάνο, το [aeroplano] aeroplane.

αεροπορία, η [aeroporeea] air force.

αεροπορικώς [aeroporeekos] by air.

αερόστατο, το [aerostato] balloon.

αετός, ο [aetos] eagle || (μεταφ) clever person || (χαρτσετός) kite.

αζήτητος [azeeteetos] unclaimed || (εμπορ) not in demand.

άζυμος [azeemos] unleavened.

άζωτο, το [azoto] nitrogen.

απδής [aeeðees] loathsome, sickening.

απδία, η [aeeðeea] disgust, loathing.

απδιάζω [aeeðeeazo] feel disgust for, loathe.

αηδόνι, το [aeeðonee] nightingale.

αήττητος [aeeteetos] undefeated, unbeatable.

αθανασία, η [athanaseea] immortality, eternity.

αθάνατος [athanatos] immortal, deathless.

αθέατος [atheatos] invisible, unseen.

άθελα [athela] unintentionally.

αθέμιτος [athemeetos] illegal, unlawful.

άθεος [atheos] godless || (ουσ) atheist.

αθεόφοβος [atheofovos] impious || (ουσ) rogue.

αθεράπευτος [atherapevtos] incurable || (μεταφ) incorrigible.

αθετώ [atheto] break one's word, violate.

άθικτος [atheektos] untouched, unharmed.

αθλητής, ο [athleetees] athlete.

αθλητικός [athleeteekos] athletic || (σώμα) robust.

αθλητισμός, ο [athleeteesmos] athletics.

άθλιος [athleeos] wretched, miserable.

άθλος, ο [athlos] feat, exploit.

αθόρυβος [athoreevos] quiet, silent.

άθραυστος [athravstos] unbroken || (αντικείμενο) unbreakable.

άθρησκος [athreeskos] irreligious.

αθροίζω [athreezo] add up, count || (στρατ) gather, assemble.

άθροισμα, το [athreesma] sum, total.

αθυμία, η [atheemeea] dejection, depression.

αθυρόστομος [atheerostomos] indiscreet, impertinent.

αθώος [athoos] innocent.

αθωώνω [athoono] acquit, exonerate.

αίγλη, η [eeglee] splendour || (ονόματος κτλ) grandeur, glory.

αιγόκλημα, το [egokleema] honeysuckle.

Αίγυπτος, η [eeyeptos] Egypt.

Αιγύπτιος, ο [eeyepteeos] Egyptian.

αιγυπτιακός [eeyepteeakos] Egyptian.

αιθέριος [ethereeos] ethereal, essential.

αιθήρας, ο [etheeras] (χημ) ether || air.

αίθουσα, η [ethousa] large room, hall || (σχολική) schoolroom.

αίθριος [ethreeos] clear, bright || (καιρός) fair.

αίμα, το [ema] blood.

αιματηρός [emateeros] bloody, bloodstained.

αιματοχυσία, η [ematoheeseea] bloodshed.

αιμοβόρος [emovoros] bloodthirsty || (μεταφ) ferocious, cruel.

αιμοδοσία, η [emoδoseea] blood donation.

αιμομιξία, η [emomeekseea] incest.

αιμορραγία, η [emorayeea] haemorrhage.

αιμοσφαίριο, το [emosfereeo] blood corpuscle.

αίνιγμα, το [eneegma] enigma, riddle.

άιντε [aeede] (έπιφ) come now!, come on!

αίρεση, η [eresee] heresy.

αιρετικός [ereteekos] heretical.

αισθάνομαι [esthanome] feel.

αίσθημα, το [estheema] sensation, feeling || αισθήματα πλ feelings.

αισθηματικός [estheemateekos] sentimental.

αίσθηση, η [estheesee] sense, sensation.

αισθητικός [estheeteekos] aesthetic || ο ~ beautician.

αισθητός [estheetos] perceptible, noticeable.

αισιόδοξος [eseeoδoksos] optimistic.

αίσχος, το [eshos] shame, disgrace.

αισχροκέρδεια, η [eshrokerδeea] profiteering.

αισχρολογία, η [eshroloyeea] obscenity, filthy talk.

αισχρός [eshros] shameful, infamous.

αίτηση, η [eteesee] application, petition, request.

αιτία, η [eteea] cause, reason, motive.

αιτιατική, η [eteeateekee] (γραμμ) accusative (case).

αίτιο, το [eteeo] cause || (εγκλήματος) motive.

αιτιολογία, η [eteeoloyeea] explanation || (οίκον) particulars.

αίτιος [eteeos] responsible.

αιτώ [eto] request (κάτι) || αιτούμαι beg (κάτι).

αιφνιδιασμός, ο [efneeδeeasmos] surprise.

αιχμαλωτίζω [ehmaloteezo] capture || (μεταφ) captivate.

αιχμάλωτος, ο [ehmalotos] captive, prisoner.

αιχμή, η [ehmee] (βελόνας) point || (βέλους) head.

αιώνας, ο [eonas] age, century.

αιώνιος [eoneeos] eternal || perpetual.

ακαδημία, η [akaδeemeea] academy.

ακαθαρσία, η [akatharseea] filth, dirt.

ακάθαρτος [akathartos] dirty, filthy.

ακάθεκτος [akathektos] unrestrained, unchecked.

ακαθόριστος [akathoreestos] undefined.

ακακία, η [akakeea] (δένδρο) acacia.

άκακος [akakos] harmless, innocent.

ακαλαισθησία, η [akalestheeseea] lack of taste.

ακάλεστος [akalestos] uninvited.

ακαλλιέργητος [akalyergeetos] uncultivated || (άνθρωπος) uncultured.

ακαμάτης, ο [akamatees] loafer.

άκαμπτος [akamptos] unbending.

ακανθώδης [akanthoδees] thorny, prickly.

ακανόνιστος [akanoneestos] unregulated || (σχήμα) irregular || (σφυγμός) uneven.

ακαριαίος [akareeayos] instantaneous.

άκαρπος [akarpos] unfruitful || (μεταφ) fruitless.

ακατάβλητος [akatavleetos] indomitable || (χρέη) unpaid.

ακατάδεκτος [akataδektos] disdainful, haughty.

ακατάληπτος [akataleeptos] incomprehensible.

ακατάλληλος [akataleelos] unsuitable, unfit.

ακαταλόγιστος [akatalogeestos] not responsible (for) || irrational.

ακατανόητος [akatanoeetos] inconceivable, unintelligible.

ακατάπαυστος [akatapavstos] unceasing, endless.

ακατάστατος [akatastatos] untidy || (καιρός) changeable.

ακατοίκητος [akateekeetos] uninhabited.

ακατόρθωτος [akatorthotos] unfeasible, impossible.

ακέραιος [akereos] integral, whole || (τίμιος) upright || ~ αριθμός integer.

ακεφιά, η [akefia] dejection, gloom.

ακίνδυνος [akeenδeenos] safe, harmless.

ακίνητος [akeeneetos] immovable || (περιουσία) estate, property.

άκλιτος [akleetos] indeclinable.

ακμάζω [akmazo] flourish, thrive.

ακμαίος [akmeos] vigorous, sturdy || (γερός) robust.

ακμή, η [akmee] height, peak || (ιατρ) acne.

ακοή, η [akoee] hearing || εξ ακοής by hearsay.

ακοινώνητος [akeenoneetos] unsociable || (εκκλ) not having taken first communion.

ακολασία, η [akolaseea] debauchery, excess.

ακολουθία, η [akoloutheea] retinue, suite || (εκκλ) church service || κατ' ~ν in consequence.

ακόλουθος [akolouthos] (ουσ) attendant || (στρατ) attaché || (επίθ) following, next.

ακολουθώ [akoloutho] follow.

ακολούθως [akolouthos] consequently, afterwards || ως ~ as follows.

ακόμα [akoma] yet, more || ~ και even if.

ακονίζω [akoneezo] sharpen, whet.

ακόντιο, το [akonteeo] javelin, dart.

άκοπος [akopos] not cut || (εύκολος) easy || (ξεκούραστα) untiring.

ακόρεστος [akorestos] insatiable.

ακουμπώ [akoumbo] lean.

ακούραστος [akourastos] indefatigable, unwearied.

ακούρδιστος [akourðeestos] not tuned || (ρολόι) not wound up.

ακούσιος [akouseeos] unintentional || involuntary.

ακουστικό, το [akousteeko] (τηλεφ) receiver.

ακουστικός [akousteekos] acoustic.

ακουστός [akoustos] famous, celebrated.

ακούω [akouo] hear, listen to || (εισακούω) obey.

άκρα, η [akra] end, tip, extremity.

ακραίος [akreos] extreme, utmost.

ακρατής [akratees] intemperate, incontinent.

ακράτητος [akrateetos] impetuous, rash, unrestrained.

άκρη, η [akree] βλ άκρα.

ακριβά [akreeva] dearly.

ακρίβεια, η [akreeveea] (ωρολογίου) accuracy, precision || (μεταφράσεως κτλ) exactness || (τιμής) costliness.

ακριβής [akreevees] exact || (ωρολόγιο κτλ) accurate || (υπολογισμός) correct || (σε ραντεβού) punctual.

ακριβός [akreevos] dear, expensive.

ακριβώς [akreevos] precisely, accurately.

ακρίδα, η [akreeða] locust, grasshopper.

ακρόαση, η [akroasee] hearing, listening || (συνάντηση) audience, interview.

ακροατήριο, το [akroateereeo] audience.

ακροατής, ο [akroatees] listener || (πανεπιστημίου) auditor.

ακροβάτης, ο [akrovatees] acrobat.

ακρογιάλι, το [akroyalee] seashore.

ακρόπολη, η [akropolee] acropolis || citadel.

ακρωτηριάζω [akroteereeazo] maim, mutilate.

ακρωτήριο, το [akroteereeo] cape, promontory.

ακτή, η [aktee] shore, beach, coast.

ακτίνα, η [akteena] ray, beam || (ελπίδος) gleam || (ενεργείας) range || (τροχού) spoke || (κύκλου) radius.

ακτινοβολία, η [akteenovoleea] radiation.

ακτινογραφία, η [akteenografeea] X-ray.

ακτινοθεραπεία, η [akteenotherapeea] radiotherapy.

ακτοπλοΐα, η [aktoploeea] coastal shipping.

άκυρος [akeeros] invalid, void.

ακυρώνω [akeerono] nullify, invalidate || cancel.

αλάβαστρο, το [alavastro] alabaster.

αλάδωτος [alaðotos] (φαγητό) without oil.

αλαζονεία, η [alazoneea] arrogance, boastfulness.

αλάθητος [alatheetos] infallible.

άλαλος [alalos] speechless, dumb.

αλάνθαστος [alanthastos] infallible, certain.

αλάργα [alarga] far off.

αλάτι, το [alatee] salt || αλατιέρα saltcellar.

αλατίζω [alateezo] salt.

Αλβανία, η [alvaneea] Albania.

αλβανικός [alvaneekos] Albanian.

Αλβανός, ο [alvanos] Albanian.

άλγεβρα, η [alyevra] algebra.

Αλγερία, η [alyereea] Algeria.

Αλγερινός, ο [alyereenos] Algerian man || α~ (επιθ) Algerian.

αλγερίνικος [alyereeneekos] Algerian.

αλέθω [aletho] grind.

αλείβω [aleevo] coat, smear, rub.

αλείφω [aleefo] βλ αλείβω.

αλεξικέραυνο, το [alekseekeravno] lightning conductor.

αλεξιπτωτιστής, ο [alekseeptoteestees] parachutist.

αλεξίπτωτο, το [alekseeptoto] parachute.

αλεπού, η [alepou] fox || (μεταφ) sly person.

άλεσμα, το [alesma] grinding.

αλέτρι, το [aletree] plough.

αλεύρι, το [alevri] flour.

αλήθεια, η [aleetheea] truth || (επιρ) really, indeed.

αληθεύω [aleethevo] be true.

αληθινός [aleetheenos] real, genuine, true.

αλησμόνητος [aleesmoneetos] unforgettable.

αλήτης, ο [aleetees] vagabond, vagrant.

αλιεία, η [alieea] fishing || fishery.

αλιεύς, ο [alievs] fisherman.

αλιεύω [alievo] fish (for).

αλκοολικός [alkooleekos] alcoholic.

αλκυόνα, η [alkeeona] kingfisher, halcyon.

αλλά [ala] but, however, yet.

αλλαγή, η [alayee] change || variation.

αλλάζω [alazo] change, alter.

αλλαντικά, τα [alanteeka] πλ sausages.

αλλεπάλληλος [alepaleelos] repeated, successive.

αλλεργία, η [aleryeea] allergy.

αλληλεγγύη, η [aleelenyiee] mutual help, solidarity.

αλληλένδετος [aleelenðetos] interdependent, bound together.

αλληλογραφία, η [aleelografeea] correspondence.

αλλοδαπός, ο [aloðapos] foreigner, alien.

αλλοίθωρος [aleethoros] cross-eyed.

αλλοίμονο [aleemono] (επιφ) oh dear!

αλλοιώνω [alleeono] alter, change.

αλλοιώς [alios] otherwise, in a different way.

αλλοίωση, η [aliosee] change, alteration || (τροφίμων) adulteration.

αλλοιώτικος [alioteekos] different, unlike || (πρόσωπο) odd, strange.

αλλόκοτος [alokotos] queer, strange, odd.

άλλος [alos] (an)other, else || (επόμενος) next || (διαφορετικός) different || (επί πλέον) more || **κάθε άλλο!** anything but!

άλλοτε [allote] formerly || sometime.

αλλού [alou] elsewhere.

άλλωστε [aloste] besides, on the other hand.

άλμα, το [alma] jump, leap || ~ **τώδης** by leaps and bounds.

άλμη, η [almee] brine, pickle.

αλμυρός [almeeros] salty || (μεταφ) costly.

άλογο, το [alogo] horse || **αλογόμυγα** horsefly.

αλοιφή, η [aleefee] ointment.

αλουμίνιο, το [aloumeeneeo] aluminium.

άλσος, το [alsos] grove, thicket.

αλύγιστος [aleeyeestos] inflexible.

αλύπητος [aleepeetos] pitiless, cruel.

αλυσίδα, η [aleeseeða] chain.

άλυτος [aleetos] (που δεν ελύθη) unsolved || (δεν μπορεί να λυθεί) unsolvable.

άλφα, το [alfa] the letter A.

αλφάβητο, το [alfaveeto] alphabet.

αλώνι, το [alonee] threshing floor || **αλωνίζω** thresh || (σκορπώ) scatter.

άλωση, η [alosee] fall, capture, conquest.

άμα [ama] as soon as || (εάν) if.

αμαζόνα, η [amazona] amazon.

αμάθεια, η [amatheea] ignorance, illiteracy.

αμαθής [amathees] ignorant, illiterate.

αμάν [aman] (επιφ) for heaven's sake!

αμαξάς, ο [amaksas] coachman, cab driver.

αμάξι, το [amaksee] carriage || (αυτοκίνητο) car.

αμαξοστοιχία, η [amaksosteeheea] train.

αμαρτάνω [amartano] sin.

αμαρτία, η [amarteea] sin || **είναι ~ απ' το Θεό** it's a pity!

άμαχος [amahos] non-combatant.

άμβωνας, ο [amvonas] pulpit.

αμέ [amme] (επιφ) why not? || of course!

αμείβω [ameevo] reward, compensate.

αμείλικτος [ameeleektos] implacable, inexorable.

αμείωτος [ameeotos] undiminished.

αμέλεια, η [ameleea] negligence, carelessness.

αμελής [amelees] negligent || (μαθητής) lazy.

αμελώ [amelo] neglect.

άμεμπτος [amemptos] irreproachable, blameless.

αμερικάνικος [amereekaneekos] American.

Αμερικανός, ο [amereekanos] American.

Αμερική, η [amereekee] America.

αμέριμνος [amereemnos] carefree, heedless.

αμερόληπτος [ameroleeptos] impartial.

άμεσος [amesos] direct, immediate.

αμέσως [amesos] at once, immediately.

αμετάβλητος [ametavleetos] unchanged || immutable.

αμετάκλητος [ametakleetos] irrevocable.

αμεταχείριστος [ametaheereestos] unused, new.

αμέτοχος [ametohos] exempt, not participating in.

αμέτρητος [ametreetos] countless, immeasurable.

αμήχανος [ameehanos] perplexed, embarrassed.

αμηχανία [ameehaneea] perplexity, confusion.

αμίαντος, ο [ameeantos] asbestos.

αμίλητος [ameeleetos] silent, quiet.

άμιλλα, η [ameela] emulation, rivalry.

αμίμητος [ameemeetos] inimitable.

άμισθος [ameesthos] unsalaried, without pay.

άμμος, η [ammos] sand.

αμμουδιά, η [amouðia] sandy beach.

αμμώδης [amoðees] sandy.

αμμωνία, η [amoneea] ammonia.

αμνησία, η [amneeseea] amnesia.

αμνηστία, η [amneesteea] amnesty.

αμνός, ο [amnos] lamb.

αμοιβαίος [ameeveyos] mutual, reciprocal.

αμοιβή, η [ameevee] reward, recompense.

άμοιρος [ameeros] unfortunate, destitute.

αμόνι, το [amonee] anvil.

άμορφος [amorfos] shapeless.

αμόρφωτος [amorfotos] uneducated, unrefined.

αμπαζούρ, το [ambazour] lampshade.

αμπάρι, το [ambaree] storeroom || (ναυτ) hold.

αμπέλι, το [ambelee] vine || vineyard.

αμπραγιάζ, το [ambrageeaz] clutch.

άμπωτη, η [ambotee] ebb tide.

αμυγδαλές, οι [ameegðales] πλ tonsils.

αμύγδαλο, το [ameegðalo] almond.

αμυδρός [ameeðros] dim, faint.

άμυλο, το [ameelo] starch.

άμυνα, η [ameena] defence.

αμφιβάλλω [amfeevalo] doubt.

αμφίβιος [amfeeveeos] amphibious.

αμφίβολος [amfeevolos] doubtful, dubious.

αμφίεση, η [amfiesee] dress, attire, clothing.

αμφιθέατρο, το [amfeetheatro] amphitheatre.

αμφίρροπος [amfeeropos] undecided, in the balance, wavering.

αμφισβητώ [amfeesveeto] dispute.

αμφορέας, ο [amforeas] amphora, pitcher.

αμφότεροι [amfoteree] πλ both.

αν [an] if, whether || ~ **και** although, though.

ανά [ana] along, over || ~ **εις** one by one || ~ **την πόλη** through the city.

αναβαίνω [anaveno] βλ **ανεβαίνω**.

αναβάλλω [anavalo] put off, postpone, delay.

ανάβαση, η [anavasee] ascent.

αναβολή, η [anavolee] postponement, adjournment.

αναβρασμός, ο [anavrasmos] agitation, excitement || fermentation.

ανάβω [anavo] light || (φως κτλ) turn on, switch on || (θυμώνω) get provoked.

αναγγέλλω [anangelo] announce, make known.

αναγγελία, η [anangeleea] announcement, notice.

αναγέννηση, η [anageneesee] revival, renaissance.

αναγκάζω [anangazo] force, compel.

αναγκαίος [anangeyos] necessary, essential, needed.

αναγκαστικός [anangasteekos] compulsory || (προσγείωση κτλ) forced.

ανάγκη, η [anangee] need, necessity, want.

ανάγλυφο, το [anagleefo] bas-relief.

αναγνωρίζω [anagnoreezo] recognize || (παραδέχομαι) admit.

αναγνώριση, η [anagnoreesee] recognition, acknowledgement.

ανάγνωση, η [anagnosee] reading.

αναγνώστης, ο [anagnostees] reader.

αναγούλα, η [anagoula] nausea, disgust.

ανάγω [anago] raise || (μετατρέπω) reduce, convert.

ανάγωγος [anagogos] ill-bred, ill-mannered.

αναδάσωση, η [anaðasosee] reafforestation.

αναδιοργανώνω [anaðeeorganono] reorganize.

αναδιπλασιασμός, ο [anaðeeplaseeasmos] (γραμμ) reduplication.

ανάδοχος, ο [anaðohos] godparent, sponsor.

αναδρομικός [anaðromeekos] retroactive, retrospective.

αναζητώ [anazeeto] search for, seek.

αναζωογονώ [anazoogono] revive, invigorate.

αναζωπυρώ [anazopeero] relight, rekindle || (μεταφ) revive.

ανάθεμα, το [anathema] curse || (εκκλ) excommunication.

αναθέτω [anatheto] commission, entrust || (αφιερώνω) dedicate.

αναθεώρηση, η [anatheoreesee] revision, review.

αναθυμίαση, η [anatheemeeasee] stench, exhalation, fumes.

αναίδεια, η [aneðeea] impudence.

αναιδής [aneðees] impudent, shameless.

αναίμακτος [anemaktos] bloodless.

αναιμία, η [anemeea] anaemia.

αναίρεση, η [aneresee] refutation.

αναισθησία, η [anestheeseea] unconsciousness || (μεταφ) insensibility.

αναισθητικό, το [anestheeteeko] anaesthetic.

αναίσθητος [anestheetos] insensitive || (στους πόνους) unconscious, insensible || (ασυγκίνητος) unmoved.

ανακαινίζω [anakeneezo] renovate, renew.

ανακαλύπτω [anakaleepto] discover, detect.

ανακαλώ [anakalo] recall || (άδεια, διάταγμα) repeal, abrogate || (διαταγή κτλ) cancel, withdraw || (υπόσχεση) retract.

ανακατώνω [anakatono] mix, stir || (συγχέω) confuse.

ανακάτωμα, το [anakatoma] mixing || (φασαρία) confusion || (στομάχου) nausea.

ανακεφαλαίωση, η [anakefaleosee] recapitulation.

ανακηρύσσω [anakeereeso] proclaim, declare.

ανακινώ [anakeeno] stir up || (μεταφ) bring up, raise.

ανάκληση, η [anakleesee] revocation, recalling.

ανακοινώνω [anakeenono] announce.

ανακοπή, η [anakopee] checking || (νομ) reprieve || (ιατρ) heart failure.

ανακουφίζω [anakoufeezo] relieve, alleviate, lighten.

ανακριβής [anakreevees] inaccurate.

ανάκριση, η [anakreesee] interrogation, inquiry.

ανακριτής, ο [anakreetees] examining magistrate.

ανάκτορο, το [anaktoro] palace.

ανακωχή, η [anakohee] armistice, truce.

αναλαμβάνω [analamvano] undertake || recover.

ανάλατος [analatos] (μεταφ) dull.

ανάληψη, η [analeepsee] (εργασίας) resumption, undertaking || (του Χριστού) ascension.

αναλλοίωτος [analeeotos] unchanging, constant, unaltered.

αναλογία, η [analoyeea] relation, proportion, ratio || portion.

αναλογικός [analoyeekos] proportionate.

ανάλογος [analogos] proportionate || (μαθημ) proportional.

αναλόγως [analogos] proportionately, according to.

ανάλυση, η [analeesee] analysis.

αναλυτικός [analeeteekos] analytical || detailed.

αναλφάβητος [analfaveetos] illiterate, ignorant.

αναμένω [anameno] wait for, expect.

ανάμεσα [anamesa] in between, among.

αναμεταξύ [anametaksee] between, among || στο ~ in the meantime, meanwhile.

αναμιγνύω [anameegneeo] mix, blend || implicate.

ανάμικτος [anameektos] mixed.

ανάμιξη, η [anameeksee] mixing, interfering.

άναμμα, το [anama] lighting || (προσώπου) inflammation || (έξαψη) excitement || (μοτέρ κτλ) ignition.

αναμμένος [anamenos] alight, burning.

ανάμνηση, η [anamneesee] recollection, memory.

αναμονή, η [anamonee] expectation, waiting.

αναμφισβήτητος [anamfeesveeteetos] indisputable, unquestionable.

ανανάς, ο [ananas] pineapple.

ανανεώνω [ananeono] renew, renovate.

ανανέωση, η [ananeosee] renewal, renovation.

ανάξιος [anakseeos] unworthy, unfit, inefficient.

αναπαράσταση, η [anaparastasee] representation || (εγκλήματος) reconstruction.

ανάπαυλα, η [anapavla] respite, rest.

ανάπαυση, η [anapavsee] rest, repose || (στρατ) stand easy!

αναπαυτικός [anapavteekos] comfortable, restful.

αναπαύομαι [anapavome] rest, relax.

αναπηδώ [anapeedo] jump up, leap up, start.

ανάπηρος [anapeeros] disabled || (διανοητικώς) deficient.

ανάπλαση, η [anaplasee] reforming, remodelling.

αναπληρώνω [anapleerono] replace || substitute || refill.

αναπνέω [anapneo] breathe.

αναπνοή, η [anapnoee] breath, breathing, respiration.

ανάποδα [anapoda] backwards || (μέσα έξω) inside out, topsy-turvy.

αναποδιά, η [anapodia] reverse, bad luck || contrariness.

αναποδογυρίζω [anapodogeereezo] turn upside down.

ανάποδος, [anapodos] reversed || (άνθρωπος) difficult, cantankerous.

αναπόφευκτος [anapofevktos] inevitable, unavoidable.

αναπτήρας, ο [anapteeras] cigarette lighter.

ανάπτυξη, η [anapteeksee] development || (εξήγηση) explanation.

αναπτύσσω [anapteeso] unfold, develop || (λόγο) expound, explain.

αναρίθμητος [anareethmeetos] countless, innumerable.

ανάρπαστος [anarpastos] quickly bought up.

ανάρρωση, η [anarrosee] convalescence, recovery.

αναρχία, η [anarheea] anarchy.

αναρχικός [anarheekos] anarchical || (ουσ) anarchist.

αναρωτιέμαι [anarotieme] ask o.s., wonder.

ανάσα, η [anasa] breath, breathing || rest, respite.

ανασηκώνω [anaseekono] lift up, raise.

ανασκαφή, η [anaskafee] excavation.

ανάσκελα [anaskela] on one's back.

ανασκόπηση, η [anaskopeesee] review, weighing up.

ανασταίνω [anasteno] revive, restore to life.

ανασταλτικός [anastalteekos] restraining, holding back.

ανάσταση, η [anastasee] resurrection.

ανάστατος [anastatos] in disorder, agitated, excited.

αναστατώνω [anastatono] disturb, upset.

αναστέλλω [anastelo] stop, stay, suspend.

αναστενάζω [anastenazo] sigh, groan.

αναστηλώνω [anasteelono] restore, erect.

αναστήλωση, η [anasteelosee] restoration, erection.

ανάστημα, το [anasteema] height, stature.

αναστολή, η [anastolee] reprieve || suspension || restraint.

ανασυγκρότηση, η [anaseengroteesee] reconstruction.

ανασύρω [anaseero] raise, pull out, pull up, draw up.

αναταράσσω [anataraso] stir up, upset.

ανατέλλω [anatelo] (ήλιος) rise || appear.

ανατίμηση, η [anateemeesee] price rise || revaluation.

ανατινάζω [anateenazo] blow up || spring up.

ανατίναξη, η [anateenaksee] explosion.

ανατοκισμός, ο [anatokeesmos] compound interest.

ανατολή, η [anatolee] east || (ήλιου) sunrise || 'Απω 'Α~ Far East || Μέση 'Α~ Middle East.

ανατολικός [anatoleekos] eastern || oriental.

ανατομία, η [anatomeea] anatomy.

ανατρέπω [anatrepo] upset || (βάρκα κτλ) overturn, capsize.

ανατρέφω, [anatrefo] rear, bring up, raise.

ανατρέχω [anatreho] refer back to, go back to.

ανατριχιάζω [anatreeheeazo] shiver, shudder.

ανατροπή, η [anatropee] upset, overthrow || (νομ) refutation, reversal.

ανατροφή, η [anatrofee] upbringing, breeding.

ανάτυπο, το [anateepo] offprint, reprint.

άναυδος [anavδos] speechless, dumbfounded.

αναφέρω [anafero] mention, cite || report || relate.

αναφλέγω [anaflego] inflame, ignite.

ανάφλεξη, η [anafleksee] combustion, ignition.

αναφορά, η [anafora] report || (αίτηση) petition.

αναχαιτίζω [anaheteezo] check, restrain || (επίθεση) repel.

αναχρονισμός, ο [anahroneesmos] anachronism.

ανάχωμα, το [anahoma] mound, bank, dyke.

αναχώρηση, η [anahoreesee] departure.

αναχωρώ [anahoro] leave, depart, go.

αναψυκτικά, τα [anapseekteeka] πλ refreshments.

αναψυχή, η [anapseehee] recreation.

ανδρεία, η [anδreea] bravery, valour.

ανδρείος [anδreeos] brave, courageous.

ανδρικός [anδreekos] manly, virile, male.

ανεβάζω [anevazo] raise, lift up || (θέατρο) put on.

ανεβαίνω [aneveno] ascend, climb, go up.

ανέβασμα, το [anevasma] going up || lifting || (έργου) production.

ανεβοκατεβαίνω [anevokateveno] go up and down || (τιμές) fluctuate.

ανέγγιχτος [anengeehtos] untouched, new.

ανέγερση, η [aneyersee] erection || (σήκωμα) getting up.

ανειλικρινής [aneeleekreenees] insincere || false.

ανέκαθεν [anekathen] always, ever, from the beginning.

ανέκδοτο, το [anekδoton] anecdote, funny story.

ανεκμετάλλευτος [anekmetalevtos] unexploited.

ανεκτικός [anekteekos] tolerant, patient, indulgent.

ανεκτίμητος [anekteemeetos] priceless, inestimable.

ανεκτός [anektos] bearable, tolerable.

ανέκφραστος [anekfrastos] inexpressible, indescribable || (ηθοποιός) expressionless || (βλέμμα) vacant.

ανελλιπής [aneleepees] flawless || (οργάνωση) complete || (φοίτηση) continuous.

ανέλπιστος [anelpeestos] unexpected || (γεγονός) unforeseen.

ανεμίζω [anemeezo] ventilate, air || (σίτο) winnow.

ανεμιστήρας, ο [anemeesteeas] fan, ventilator.

ανεμοβλογιά, η [anemovloya] chickenpox.

ανεμόμυλος, ο [anemomeelos] windmill.

άνεμος, ο [anemos] wind.

ανεμοστρόβιλος, ο [anemostroveelos] whirlwind.

ανεμπόδιστος [anemboδeestos] unhindered, unimpeded.

ανεμώνα, η [anemona] anemone.

ανένδοτος [anenδotos] unyielding, inflexible.

ανενόχλητος [anenohleetos] undisturbed.

ανεξάντλητος [aneksantleetos] inexhaustible.

ανεξαρτησία, η [aneksarteeseea] independence.

ανεξάρτητος [aneksarteetos] independent.

ανεξέλεγκτος [anekselengtos] unconfirmed || (δαπάνη κτλ) unexamined.

ανεξήγητος [anekseeyeetos] inexplicable.

ανεξίτηλος [anekseeteelos] indelible.

ανεπαίσθητος [anepestheetos] imperceptible, slight.

ανεπαρκής [aneparkees] insufficient, inadequate.

ανέπαφος [anepafos] untouched, intact.

ανεπηρέαστος [anepeereastos] unaffected, uninfluenced.

ανεπιθύμητος [anepeetheemeetos] undesirable.

ανεπίσημος [anepeeseemos] unofficial.

ανεπιτυχής [anepeeteehees] unsuccessful.

ανεπιφύλακτος [anepeefeelaktos] unreserved.

ανεπτυγμένος [anepteegmenos] (άνθρωπος) cultured || (σωματικώς) developed.

άνεργος [anergos] unemployed, idle.

ανέρχομαι [anerhome] ascend, climb || (λογαριασμός) amount to.

άνεση, η [annese] ease, comfort.

ανεστραμμένος [anestramenos] reversed, inverted.

άνετος [anetos] comfortable, easy.

άνευ [anev] without.

ανεύθυνος [anevtheenos] irresponsible.

ανεφάρμοστος [anefarmostos] inapplicable || (μη εφαρμοσθείς) unapplied.

ανέφικτος [anefeektos] unattainable, impossible.

ανεφοδιάζω [anefodeeazo] provision, restock.

ανέχομαι [anehome] tolerate.

ανεψιά, η [anepsia] niece.

ανεψιός, ο [anepsios] nephew.

ανήθικος [aneetheekos] immoral, corrupt.

άνηθο, το [aneetho] dill, anise.

ανήκουστος [aneekoustos] unheard of, incredible.

ανήκω [aneeko] belong (to).

ανήλικος [aneeleekos] under age || minor.

ανήμερα [aneemera] on the same day.

ανήμπορος [aneemboros] indisposed.

ανησυχία, η [aneeseeheea] uneasiness, concern.

ανήσυχος [aneeseehos] uneasy, anxious.

ανησυχώ [aneeseeho] be anxious, be worried.

ανήφορος, ο [aneeforos] uphill road || ascent.

ανθεκτικός [anthekteekos] endurable, resistant.

ανθίζω [antheezo] blossom, flourish.

ανθίσταμαι [antheestame] resist, oppose.

ανθοδέσμη, η [anthodesmee] bouquet, nosegay.

ανθοδοχείο, το [anthodoheeo] flowerpot, vase.

ανθολογία, η [antholoyeea] anthology.

ανθοπώλης, ο [anthopolees] florist.

άνθος, το [anthos] flower.

άνθρακας, ο [anthrakas] coal || (ιατρ) anthrax.

ανθρακικός [anthrakeekos] carbonic.

ανθρακωρυχείο, το [anthrakoreeheeo] coalmine.

ανθρωπιά, η [anthropia] civility || good breeding.

ανθρώπινος [anthropeenos] human.

ανθρωπιστής, ο [anthropeestees] humanist.

ανθρωποκτονία, η [anthropoktoneea] homicide.

ανθρωπολόγος, ο [anthropologos] anthropologist.

άνθρωπος, ο [anthropos] man, person.

ανθρωπότης, η [anthropotees] mankind, humanity.

ανθυγιεινός [antheeyeeinos] unhealthy, unwholesome.

ανία, η [aneea] boredom, weariness, ennui.

ανίατος [aneeatos] incurable.

ανίδεος [aneedeos] unsuspecting || ignorant.

ανικανοποίητος [aneekanopieetos] unsatisfied.

ανίκανος [aneekanos] incapable, unable, unfit || impotent.

ανισόρροπος [aneesoropos] unbalanced.

άνισος [aneesos] unequal, uneven.

ανίσχυρος [aneesheeros] powerless, weak, feeble.

ανίχνευση, η [aneehnevsee] tracking, searching.

άνοδος, η [anodos] ascent, accession.

ανοησία, η [anoeeseea] folly, foolishness, nonsense.

ανόητος [anoeetos] foolish, silly, absurd.

ανόθευτος [anothevtos] unadulterated, pure.

άνοιγμα, το [aneegma] opening, aperture.

ανοίγω [aneego] open || (βρύση) turn on || (σύρτη) draw || (ομπρέλλα) put up || (φώτα κτλ) turn on, switch on || (συζήτηση) open, broach || (χάρτη) unfold || (χορό) lead, open || (πηγάδι) dig || (κουρτίνες) draw || (για χρώμα) fade.

ανοίκιαστος [aneekeeastos] unlet, unrented.

ανοικοδομώ [aneekodomo] rebuild.

ανοικτός [aneektos] open || (επί χρωμάτων) light.

άνοιξη, η [aneeksee] spring, springtime.

ανοιχτόκαρδος [aneehtokarðos] open-hearted, cheerful.

ανοιχτοχέρης [aneehtoherees] open-handed, magnanimous.

ανομβρία, η [anomvreea] drought.

ανόμοιος [anomeeos] dissimilar, unlike.

ανοξείδωτος [anokseeðotos] stainless, rustproof.

ανοργάνωτος [anorganotos] unorganized.

ανορεξία, η [anorekseea] loss of appetite || (μεταφ) half-heartedness.

ανορθογραφία, η [anorthografeea] misspelling.

ανοσία, η [anoseea] immunity.

άνοστος [anostos] insipid, unsavoury || (μεταφ) ugly, disagreeable.

ανοχή, η [anohee] forbearance, tolerance || **οίκος ανοχής** brothel.

ανταγωνίζομαι [antagoneezome] compete, vie (with).

ανταγωνισμός, ο [antagoneesmos] competition, contest, rivalry.

ανταλλαγή, η [antalayee] exchange.

αντάλλαγμα, το [antalagma] thing exchanged, recompense.

ανταλλακτικό, το [antalakteeko] spare part, refill.

ανταλλάσσω [antalaso] exchange.

ανταμείβω [antameevo] reward, recompense.

ανταμώνω [antamono] meet, join.

αντάμωση [antamosee] : **καλή ~** goodbye, farewell.

αντανάκλαση, η [antanaklasee] reflection.

αντανακλώ [antanaklo] reflect.

αντάξιος [antakseeos] worthy, deserving.

ανταποδίδω [antapoðeðo] return, repay.

ανταποκρίνομαι [antapokreenome] be like, correspond to, respond, suit.

ανταπόκριση, η [antapokreesee] correspondence || (εφημερίδας) dispatch.

ανταποκριτής, ο [antapokreetees] correspondent, reporter.

ανταρσία, η [antarseea] rebellion, revolt, mutiny.

αντάρτης, ο [antartees] rebel, insurgent, guerrilla.

άντε [ante] (επιφ) come on!, get a move on!

αντένα, η [antena] aerial, antenna.

αντεπίθεση, η [antepeethesee] counterattack.

αντεπιτίθεμαι [antepeeteetheme] counterattack.

άντερο, το [antero] intestine.

αντέχω [anteho] endure, hold firm, last.

αντζούγια, η [andzouyeea] anchovy.

αντηλιά, η [anteelia] glare.

αντηχώ [anteeho] resound, echo.

αντί [antee] instead of, in exchange for || (τιμή) for || **~ για** instead of || **~ να** instead of.

αντιαεροπορικός [anteeaeroporeekos] anti-aircraft.

αντιγραφή, η [anteegrafee] copy, copying.

αντίγραφο, το [anteegrafo] copy, transcript.

αντιγράφω [anteegrafo] copy, imitate || (στο σχολείο) crib.

αντίδι, το [anteeðee] endive.

αντίδικος, ο [anteeðeekos] opponent.

αντίδοτο, το [anteeðoto] antidote.

αντίδραση, η [anteeðrasee] reaction, opposition.

αντιδραστικός [anteeðrasteekos] reactionary, reactive.

αντιδρώ [anteeðro] react, counteract, oppose.

αντίδωρο, το [anteeðoro] (εκκλ) holy bread.

αντίζηλος [anteezeelos] rival.

αντίθεση, η [anteethesee] contrast || opposition.

αντίθετος [anteethetos] contrary, opposite.

αντίκα, η [anteeka] antique.

αντικαθιστώ [anteekatheesto] replace, substitute || relieve.

αντικανονικός [anteekanoneekos] irregular, against the rules.

αντικατάσταση [anteekatastasee] replacement || substitution.

αντικαταστάτης, ο [anteekatastatees] substitute || successor.

αντίκειμαι [anteekeeme] be opposed to.

αντικειμενικός [anteekeemeneekos] objective.

αντικείμενο, το [anteekeemeno] object, thing || topic.

αντικλείδι, το [anteekleeðee] passkey.

αντικοινωνικός [anteekeenoneekos] unsocial.

αντικρούω [anteekrouo] oppose, refute.

αντίκρυ [anteekree] opposite, face to face.

αντικρύζω [anteekreezo] face, front || meet.

αντίκτυπος, ο [anteekteepos] repercussion, effect, result.

αντίλαλος, ο [anteelalos] echo.

αντιλαμβάνομαι [anteelamvanome] understand || perceive, notice.

αντιλέγω [anteelego] object, contradict.

αντιληπτός [anteeleeptos] perceptible || understandable.

αντίληψη, η [anteeleepsee] understanding, opinion || quickness of mind.

αντιλυσσικός [anteeleeseekos] anti-rabies.

αντιμετωπίζω [anteemetopeezo] confront, face.

αντιμέτωπος [anteemetopos] face to face, facing.

αντιναύαρχος, ο [anteenavarhos] vice-admiral.

αντίο [anteeo] (επιφ) goodbye!

αντιπάθεια, η [anteepatheea] antipathy, aversion.

αντιπαθητικός [anteepatheeteekos] repulsive, repugnant.

αντιπαθώ [anteepatho] dislike.

αντίπαλος, ο [anteepalos] adversary, opponent || (στρατ) enemy.

αντιπερισπασμός, ο [anteepereespasmos] distraction || (στρατ) diversion.

αντίποινα, τα [anteepeena] πλ reprisals.

αντιπολίτευση, η [anteepoleetevsee] opposition.

αντίπραξη, η [anteepraksee] opposition, thwarting.

αντιπρόεδρος, ο [anteeproeðros] vice-president, deputy chairman.

αντιπροσωπεία, η [anteeprosopeea] representation || delegation.

αντιπροσωπεύω [anteeprosopevo] represent, stand for.

αντιπρόσωπος, ο [anteeprosopos] representative || (εμπορικός) agent.

αντίρρηση, η [anteereesee] objection, contradiction.

αντισηπτικός [anteeseepteekos] antiseptic.

αντισταθμίζω [anteestathmeezo] balance || (μηχανική) compensate.

αντίσταση, η [anteestasee] resistance, opposition.

αντιστέκομαι [anteestekome] resist, oppose.

αντίστοιχος [anteesteehos] corresponding, equivalent.

αντιστράτηγος, ο [anteestrateegos] lieutenant-general.

αντιστρέφω [anteestrefo] invert, reverse.

αντίστροφος [anteestrofos] reverse, inverse.

αντισυνταγματικός [anteeseentagmateekos] unconstitutional.

αντιτίθεμαι [anteeteetheme] be opposed.

αντίτιμο, το [anteeteemo] value, price.

αντιτορπιλλικό, το [anteetorpeeleeko] destroyer.

αντίτυπο, το [anteeteepo] copy.

αντίφαση, η [anteefasee] contradiction, discrepancy.

αντιφάσκω [anteefasko] contradict o.s.

αντίχειρας, ο [anteeheeras] thumb.

αντλία, η [antleea] pump.

αντλώ [antlo] pump, draw (off) || derive.

αντοχή, η [antohee] endurance, strength, resistance.

άντρας, ο [antras] man || husband.

αντρίκιος [antreekeeos] βλ **ανδρικός**.

αντρόγυνο, το [antroyeeno] married couple.

αντωνυμία, η [antoneemeea] pronoun.

ανύπανδρος [aneepanðros] unmarried, single.

ανύπαρκτος [aneeparktos] non-existent.

ανυπαρξία, η [aneeparkseea] non-existence, lack.

ανυπολόγιστος [aneepoloyeestos] incalculable.

ανύπομονος [aneepomonos] impatient, anxious.

ανυπόπτος [aneepoptos] unsuspecting || not suspect.

ανυπόστατος [aneepostatos] groundless, unfounded || unsubstantial.

ανυπότακτος [aneepotaktos] insubordinate || (λαός) unsubdued.

ανυπόφορος [aneepoforos] intolerable.

ανυψώνω [aneepsono] raise || (μεταφ) praise, elevate, extol.

άνω [ano] up, above || ~ **κάτω** in confusion, upset || (μέρος) above, over.

ανώδυνος [anoðeenos] painless.

ανωμαλία, η [anomaleea] irregularity, unevenness || anomaly.

ανώμαλος [anomalos] (επιφάνεια) irregular, uneven || (άνθρωπος) erratic, eccentric.

ανώνυμος [anoneemos] anonymous || ~ **εταιρεία** limited company.

ανώτατος [anotatos] supreme, uppermost.

ανώτερος [anoteros] superior, higher, upper || ~ **χρημάτων** above money.

άξεστος [aksestos] uncouth, rough, unpolished.

αξέχαστος [aksehastos] unforgotten || unforgettable.

αξία, η [akseea] worth, value, price.

αξιαγάπητος [akseeagapeetos] amiable, lovable.

αξιέπαινος [akseepenos] praiseworthy, laudable.

αξίζω [akseezo] be worth, cost || merit || **αξίζει να τιμωρηθεί** he deserves to be punished.

αξίνα, η [akseena] pickaxe.

αξιοθαύμαστος [akseeothavmastos] wonderful, admirable.

αξιοθέατος [akseeotheatos] worth seeing || **τα αξιοθέατα** the sights.

αξιοθρήνητος [akseeothreeneetos] lamentable, deplorable.

αξιόλογος [akseeologos] remarkable || distinguished.

αξιόπιστος [akseeopeestos] trustworthy, reliable.

αξιοπρεπής [akseeoprepees] dignified, decent.

άξιος [akseeos] capable || deserving || worthy, worth.

αξιοσημείωτος [akseeoseemeeotos] noteworthy, notable, remarkable.

αξιότιμος [akseeoteemos] estimable, honourable.

αξιωματικός, ο [akseeomateekos] officer.

άξονας, ο [aksonas] axis || axle, pivot, shaft.

αξύριστος [akseereestos] unshaven.

άοπλος [aoplos] unarmed.

αόριστος [aoreestos] invisible, indefinite || (γραμμ) aorist.

άοσμος [aosmos] odourless, scentless.

απαγγελία, η [apangeleea] recitation, declamation || diction.

απαγόρευση, η [apagorevsee] prohibition.

απαγορεύω [apagorevo] prohibit, forbid.

απαγωγή, η [apagoyee] abduction || (παιδιού) kidnapping.

απάθεια, η [apatheea] indifference, apathy.

απαισιόδοξος [apeseeoδoksos] pessimist.

απαίσιος [apeseeos] frightful, sinister, horrible.

απαίτηση, η [apeteesee] claim || demand.

απαιτητικός [apeteeteekos] demanding, exacting, importunate.

απαιτώ [apeto] claim, demand, require.

απαλλαγή, η [apalayee] deliverance || release || dismissal.

απαλλάσσω [apalasso] deliver, free || (καθήκοντα) relieve.

απαλλοτριώ [apalotreeo] expropriate, alienate.

απαλός [apalos] soft || gentle.

απάνθρωπος [apanthropos] inhuman, cruel.

άπαντα, τα [apanta] πλ complete works.

απάντηση, η [apanteesee] reply, answer, response.

απαντώ [apanto] answer, reply || meet.

απάνω [apano] up, above || upstairs || ~ **κάτω** approximately || **από πάνω** on top, from above || **έως** ~ to the top || ~ **που** at the moment when || ~ **από**

above, more than || ~ **σε** at the moment of.

απαράδεκτος [aparaδektos] unacceptable, inadmissible.

απαραίτητος [apareeteetos] indispensable.

απαράλλακτος [aparalaktos] identical || unchanged.

απαράμιλλος [aparameelos] unrivalled, incomparable, peerless.

απαρατήρητος [aparateereetos] unnoticed, unobserved.

απαρέμφατο, το [aparemfato] (γραμμ) infinitive.

απαρηγόρητος [apareegoreetos] inconsolable.

απαριθμώ [apareethmo] enumerate, count.

απαρνούμαι [aparnoume] renounce, deny, disavow, disown.

απαρτίζω [aparteezo] form, constitute.

απασχόληση, η [apasholeesee] occupation.

απασχολώ [apasholo] occupy, busy.

απατεώνας, ο [apateonas] cheat, deceiver, swindler.

απάτη, η [apatee] deceit, fraud || illusion.

απατηλός [apateelos] deceptive, false, fraudulent.

απατώ [apato] deceive, cheat, defraud.

απεγνωσμένος [apegnosmenos] desperate.

απειθαρχία, η [apeetharheea] insubordination, lack of discipline.

απεικονίζω [apeekoneezo] represent, portray, depict.

απειλή, η [apeelee] threat, menace.

απειλητικός [apeeleeteekos] threatening.

απειρία, η [apeereea] inexperience || (μέτρο) infinity, immensity.

άπειρος [apeeros] inexperienced || (αριθμός) infinite, boundless.

απέλαση, η [apelasee] deportation, expulsion.

απελευθερώνω [apeleftherono] set free, emancipate.

απελευθέρωση, η [apeleftherosee] liberation, emancipation.

απελπίζομαι [apelpeezome] despair.

απελπισία, η [apelpeeseea] despair || **είναι** ~ it's hopeless!

απέναντι [apenante] opposite.

απεναντίας [apenanteeas] on the contrary.

απένταρος [apentaros] penniless, broke.

απέραντος [aperantos] immense, boundless, endless.

απεργία, η [aperyeea] strike.

απερίγραπτος [apereegraptos] indescribable.

απεριόριστος [apereeoreestos] unlimited.

απεριποίητος [apereepieetos] neglected, untidy.

απερίσκεπτος [apereeskeptos] thoughtless, foolish, heedless.

απερίσπαστος [apereespastos] undistracted.

απέριττος [apereetos] simple, plain, concise.

απεσταλμένος, ο [apestalmenos] envoy, minister, delegate.

απευθύνομαι [apeftheenome] apply, appeal, address.

απεχθάνομαι [apehthanome] detest, abhor.

απεχθής [apehthees] odious, repulsive, detestable.

απέχω [apeho] abstain || be distant, be far from.

απήχηση, η [apeeheesee] effect || echo.

άπιαστος [apeeastos] not caught || intact, intangible.

απίθανος [apeethanos] unlikely, improbable.

απίστευτος [apeestevtos] unbelievable, incredible.

απιστία, [apeesteea] infidelity || incredulity.

άπιστος [apeestos] unbelieving || faithless, infidel.

απιστώ [apeesto] be unfaithful.

άπλα, η [apla] spaciousness.

απλά [apla] simply.

άπλετος [apletos] abundant.

απλήρωτος [apleerotos] unfilled || unpaid.

απλησίαστος [apleeseeastos] unapproachable.

άπληστος [apleestos] insatiable, greedy, avid.

απλοϊκός [aploeekos] naïve, simple.

απλός [aplos] simple || (εισιτήριο) single || (ντύσιμο) plain.

απλότητα, η [aploteeta] simplicity, naivety, plainness.

απλούστατα [aploustata] simply.

άπλυτος [apleetos] unwashed || **τα άπλυτα** dirty linen.

άπλωμα, το [aploma] spreading, unfolding || (χεριών) stretching || (ρούχων) hanging out.

απλώνω [aplono] spread, stretch || (ρούχα) hang out.

απλώς [aplos] simply, merely, plainly.

άπνοια, η [apneea] lack of wind.

από [apo] from, of || by || through || than || ~ **καιρού σε καιρόν** from time to time || ~ **φόβο** out of fear || ~ **μνήμης** by heart || ~ **τον ίδιο δρόμο** by the same road || ~ **το παράθυρο** through the window || **ξέρω περισσότερα ~ σένα** I know more than you || (προθ) **μέσα ~** out of || **πριν ~** before.

αποβάθρα, η [apovathra] pier, wharf.

αποβάλλω [apovalo] reject, expel, dismiss || (μωρό) miscarry.

απόβαση, η [apovasee] disembarkation, landing.

αποβιβάζω [apoveevazo] disembark, unload.

αποβλέπω [apovlepo] consider || aim at, look forward to || regard.

αποβολή, η [apovolee] dismissal || (μωρού) miscarriage, abortion.

αποβραδίς [apovradees] yesterday evening, since last night.

απογειώνομαι [apoyeeonome] take off.

απογείωση, η [apoyeeosee] takeoff.

απόγεμα, το [apoyema] afternoon.

απόγνωση, η [apognosee] despair, desperation.

απογοήτευση [apogoeetevsee] disappointment, disillusionment.

απογοητεύω [apogoeetevo] disappoint, disillusion.

απόγονος, ο [apogonos] offspring, descendant.

απογραφή, η [apografee] (πληθυσμού) census || (εμπορ) inventory.

αποδεικνύω [apodeekneeo] prove, demonstrate.

αποδεικτικό, το [apodeekteeko] certificate.

απόδειξη, η [apodeeksee] proof || receipt.

αποδεκατίζω [apodekateezo] decimate.

αποδεκτός [apodektos] acceptable || accepted.

αποδέχομαι [apodehome] accept || admit.

απόδημος [apodeemos] living abroad, migrant.

αποδίδω [apodeedo] give back, return || (τιμές) grant, award || (κάτι σε κάτι) attribute || (ελευθερία) restore || (μετάφραση) express || (έργο) produce.

αποδοκιμάζω [apodokeemazo] disapprove of || demonstrate against.

αποδοκιμασία, η [apodokeemaseea] disapproval, rejection || booing.

απόδοση, η [apodosee] (επιστροφή) return, repayment || (μηχανής κτλ) efficiency, capacity || (εργοστασίου) output || (της γης) yield, produce || (έργου) rendering.

αποδοχή, η [apodohee] acceptance || acceptation || **αποδοχές** πλ salary, fees.

απόδραση, η [apodrasee] escape.

αποδυτήριο, το [apodeeteereeo] changing room.

αποζημιώνω [apozeemeeono] compensate, indemnify.

αποζημίωση, η [apozeemeeosee] compensation, indemnity.

αποθαρρύνω [apothareeno] discourage.

απόθεμα, το [apothema] deposit || stock, reserve.

αποθέωση, η [apotheosee] apotheosis || (μεταφ) rousing reception.

αποθηκεύω [apotheekevo] store up.

αποθήκη, η [apotheekee] storage room, storehouse, warehouse.

αποθρασύνομαι [apothraseenome] become arrogant.

αποικία, η [apeekeea] colony, settlement.

αποκαθιστώ [apokatheesto] rehabilitate, restore || (κόρη) marry.

αποκαλύπτω [apokaleepto] disclose, unveil, reveal.

αποκάλυψη, η [apokaleepsee] revelation || (θρησκεία) Apocalypse.

αποκαρδιωτικός [apokarðeeoteekos] disheartening.

αποκατάσταση, η [apokatastasee] restoration, resettlement || (κόρης) marriage.

απόκεντρος [apokentros] outlying, remote, out-of-the-way.

αποκέντρωση, η [apokentrosee] decentralization.

αποκεφαλίζω [apokefaleezo] decapitate, behead.

αποκήρυξη, η [apokeereeksee] denunciation, proscription.

αποκηρύσσω [apokeereeso] renounce, disavow || proscribe, outlaw.

αποκλεισμός, ο [apokleesmos] exclusion, blockade, boycott.

αποκλειστικός [apokleesteekos] exclusive.

αποκλείω [apokleeo] exclude || debar || boycott || **αποκλείεται** it's out of the question.

αποκληρώνω [apokleerono] disinherit.

αποκλίνω [apokleeno] lean, diverge, incline.

αποκοιμίζω [apokeemeezo] lull to sleep.

αποκοιμούμαι [apokeemoume] fall asleep.

αποκομίζω [apokomeezo] carry away || derive.

απόκομμα, το [apokoma] press-cutting || (κομμάτι) bit.

αποκοπή, η [apokopee] cutting off || amputation.

απόκρημνος [apokreemnos] precipitous, steep, abrupt.

αποκριές, οι [apokries] πλ carnival.

αποκρίνομαι [apokreenome] answer, reply.

απόκρουση, η [apokrousee] repulsion || (κατηγορίας) refutation.

αποκρούω [apokrouo] repulse || reject.

αποκρύπτω [apokreepto] conceal, hide, cover.

απόκρυφος [apokreefos] secret || (εκκλ) apocryphal.

απόκτηση, η [apokteesee] acquisition.

αποκτώ [apokto] obtain, get || (παιδί) have.

απολαβή, η [apolavee] gain, profit, income.

απολαμβάνω [apolamvano] gain, earn || (διασκεδάζω) enjoy.

απόλαυση, η [apolavsee] enjoyment.

απολίθωμα, το [apoleethoma] fossil.

απολογία, η [apoloyeea] defence, plea, excuse.

απολογισμός, ο [apoloyeesmos] financial statement, account, report.

απολογούμαι [apologoume] justify o.s., apologize.

απολύμανση, η [apoleemansee] disinfection.

απόλυση, η [apoleesee] release || dismissal.

απολυτήριο, το [apoleeteereeo] discharge certificate || (σχολείου) school leaving certificate, diploma.

απόλυτος [apoleetos] absolute || (αριθμός) cardinal.

απολύτως [apoleetos] absolutely || entirely.

απολύω [apoleeo] release || (διώχνω) dismiss || (από το στρατό) discharge.

απομακρύνω [apomakreeno] remove, send away, keep off.

απόμαχος, ο [apomahos] veteran, pensioner.

απομεινάρια [apomeenaria] πλ remains, left-overs, remnants.

απομένω [apomeno] remain, be left || (κατάπληκτος) be left speechless.

απομίμηση, η [apomeemeesee] imitation, copy.

απομνημονεύματα, τα [apomneemonevmata] πλ memoirs.

απομονώνω [apomonono] isolate || (ηλεκτ) insulate.

απονέμω [aponemo] bestow, allot || confer, award.

απονομή, η [aponomee] award.

αποξενώνω [apoksenono] alienate, estrange.

αποξήρανση, η [apokseeransee] draining, drying.

απόπειρα, η [apopeera] attempt, trial.

αποπεράτωση, η [apoperatosee] completion.

αποπλάνηση, η [apoplaneesee] seduction || (φωτός) aberration.

αποπλέω [apopleo] set sail, sail away.

απορία, η [aporeea] doubt || uncertainty, perplexity.

άπορος [aporos] needy, poor.

απορρέω [aporeo] flow, stem (from), emanate.

απόρρητος [aporeetos] secret.

απορρίματα, τα [aporeemata] πλ rubbish, refuse.

απορρίπτω [aporeepto] cast off || (προσφορά κτλ) reject, refuse || (στις εξετάσεις) fail.

απορροφώ [aporofo] absorb.

απορρυπαντικό, το [aporeepanteeko] detergent.

απορώ [aporo] be at a loss, wonder, be surprised.

απόσβεση, η [aposvesee] extinguishing || (χρέους) liquidation (of debt).

αποσιωπητικά, τα [aposeeopeeteeka] πλ points of omission.

αποσιωπώ [aposeeopo] hush up, pass in silence.

αποσκοπώ [aposkopo] aim, have in view.

απόσπασμα, το [apospasma] extract, excerpt || (στρατ) detachment || **εκτελεστικό** ~ firing squad.

αποσπώ [apospo] detach, tear || (στρατ) detach.

απόσταξη, η [apostaksee] distillation.

αποστασία, η [apostaseea] revolt, defection || apostasy.

απόσταση, η [apostasee] distance || remoteness.

αποστειρώνω [aposteerono] sterilize.

αποστέλλω [apostelo] dispatch, send, transmit.

αποστερώ [apostero] deprive.

αποστηθίζω [aposteetheezo] learn by heart.

απόστημα, το [aposteema] abscess.

αποστολέας, ο [apostoleas] sender, shipper.

αποστολή, η [apostolee] sending, consignment || (εμπορική κτλ) mission.

αποστομώνω [apostomono] silence.

αποστράτευση, η [apostratevsee] demobilization.

απόστρατος, ο [apostratos] retired officer, ex-serviceman, veteran.

αποστρέφω [apostrefo] avert, turn away.

αποστροφή, η [apostrofee] repugnance, aversion, abhorrence.

απόστροφος, η [apostrofos] apostrophe.

αποσύνθεση, η [aposeenthesee] decay, decomposition || disorganization.

αποσύρω [aposeero] withdraw || retract.

αποταμιεύω [apotamievo] save, put aside || (τρόφιμα) lay up.

αποτελειώνω [apoteleeono] complete || finish off.

αποτέλεσμα, το [apotelesma] result, effect || **αποτελεσματικός** effective.

αποτελούμαι [apoteloume] consist of, be composed of.

αποτεφρώνω [apotefrono] reduce to ashes, burn down.

απότομος [apotomos] sudden, abrupt || (στροφή) steep, sheer || (τρόπος) curt, gruff.

αποτραβιέμαι [apotravieme] withdraw, give up.

αποτρέπω [apotrepo] avert, turn aside, ward off.

αποτρόπαιος [apotropeos] abominable, hideous, horrible.

αποτροπή, η [apotropee] averting, warding off, dissuasion.

αποτσίγαρο, το [apotseegaro] cigarette end, stub, fag end.

αποτυγχάνω [apoteenghano] fail, fall through, miss.

αποτυπώνω [apoteepono] impress, imprint.

αποτυχία, η [apoteeheea] failure, reverse.

απουσία, η [apouseea] absence || **απουσιάζω** be absent.

αποφασίζω [apofaseezo] decide, resolve, determine.

απόφαση, η [apofasee] decision, resolution || (νομ) verdict || **το παίρνω** ~**ν** make up one's mind.

αποφασιστικός [apofaseesteekos] decisive, determined.

αποφέρω [apofero] yield, bring in || produce.

αποφεύγω [apofevgo] avoid, keep clear of || (κάπνισμα κτλ) abstain from.

απόφοιτος [apofeetos] school leaver || university graduate.

αποφυγή, η [apofeeyee] avoidance, evasion.

αποφυλακίζω [apofeelakeezo] release from prison.

απόφυση, η [apofeesee] excrescence || protuberance.

αποχαιρετίζω [apohereteezo] wish goodbye, bid farewell.

αποχαιρετισμός, ο [apohereteesmos] farewell, goodbye.

αποχέτευση, η [apohetevsee] draining, drainage.

απόχρωση, η [apohrosee] shade, tone || (χρώματος) fading.

αποχώρηση, η [apohoreesee] withdrawal, retirement, departure.

αποχωρητήριο, το [apohoreeteerio] W.C., lavatory || (στρατ) latrine.

αποχωρίζομαι [apohoreezome] part with, be separated from.

αποχωρισμός, ο [apohoreesmo] separation, parting.

αποχωρώ [apohoro] withdraw, retire, leave.

απόψε [apopse] tonight, this evening.

αποψινός [apopseenos] tonight's.

άποψη, η [apopsee] view, sight || (μεταφ) view, idea.

άπρακτος [apraktos] unsuccessful || unachieved.

απραξία, η [aprakseea] inactivity || (οικ) stagnation, standstill.

απρέπεια, η [aprepeea] indecency, bad manners.

απρεπής [aprepees] indecent, improper, unbecoming.

Απρίλης, ο [apreelees] April.

απρόβλεπτος [aprovleptos] unforeseen, unexpected.

απροετοίμαστος [aproeteemastos] unprepared, unready.

απροθυμία, η [aprotheemeea] reluctance, hesitancy.

απρόθυμος [aprotheemos] unwilling, reluctant, hesitant.

απρόοπτος [aprooptos] unforeseen, unexpected.

απρόσβλητος [aprosvleetos] unassailable || invulnerable.

απροσδόκητος [aprosδokeetos] unexpected, unforeseen, sudden.

απρόσεκτος [aprosektos] inattentive, careless, remiss.

απροσεξία, η [aproekseea] inattention, inadvertence.

απρόσιτος [aproseetos] inaccessible, unapproachable.

απροστάτευτος [aprostatevtos] unprotected || forlorn.

απρόσωπος [aprosopos] impersonal.

αποχώρητο, το [aprohoreeto] limit, dead end.

άπτερος [apteros] wingless.

απτόητος [aptoeetos] undaunted, intrepid.

απύθμενος [apeethmenos] bottomless.

απωθώ [apotho] repel, repulse, thrust back || (μεταφ) reject.

απώλεια, η [apoleea] loss || (θάνατος) bereavement.

απώλητος [apoleetos] unsold.

απών [apon] absent, missing.

απώτατος [apotatos] furthest, remotest, most distant.

απώτερος [apoteros] farther, further || ~ σκοπός ulterior motive.

άρα [ara] so, thus, therefore, consequently.

άρα [ara] I wonder if, can it be that?

αραβικός [araveekos] Arabian, Arabic.

αραβόσιτο, ο [aravoseeto] maize, corn.

άραγε [araye] is it?, can it be?, I wonder if.

άραγμα, το [aragma] anchoring, mooring.

αραδιάζω [araδeeazo] put in a row, line up || (ονόματα κτλ) enumerate.

αράζω [arazo] moor, anchor, drop anchor.

αραιός [areos] sparse, scattered || (επισκέψεις) infrequent, rare.

αραιώνω [areono] (σάλτσα κτλ) thin down || (γραμμές κτλ) spread out || (επισκέψεις) lessen, cut down.

αρακάς, ο [arakas] (common) pea.

αράπης, ο [arapees] negro, dark person || (φόβητρο) bogey.

αραπίνα, η [arapeena] negress, dark woman.

αράχνη, η [arahnee] spider || cobweb.

'Άραβας, ο [aravas] Arab.

αργά [arga] slowly || late.

αργαλειός, ο [argalios] loom.

αργία, η [aryeea] holiday, closing day || idleness.

άργιλλος, η [aryeelos] clay.

αργοκίνητος [argokeeneetos] slow-moving, sluggish.

αργομισθία, η [argomeestheea] sinecure.

αργοπορία, η [argoporeea] slowness, delay.

αργός [argos] slow || idle, inactive.

αργόσχολος [argosholos] idle, unoccupied.

αργότερα [argotera] later, then.

άργυρος, ο [aryeeros] silver.

αργώ [argo] be late || (μαγαζί) be closed.

άρδευση, η [arδevsee] irrigation.

'Άρειος [areeos] : ~ Πάγος Supreme Court.

αρεστός [arestos] agreeable, pleasing, gratifying.

αρέσω [areso] please, delight, like || μου αρέσει I like it.

αρετή, η [aretee] virtue.

αρετσίνωτος [aretseenotos] unresinated.

αρθρίτιδα, η [arthreeteeδa] arthritis.

αρθρογράφος, ο [arthrografos] journalist.

άρθρο, το [arthro] article, clause, term.

άρθρωση, η [arthrosee] articulation, joint || good articulation.

αρίθμηση, η [areethmeesee] numbering, counting, pagination.

αριθμητική, η [areethmeeteekee] arithmetic.

αριθμός, ο [areethmos] number.

αριθμώ [areethmo] count, enumerate.

άριστα [areesta] very well || (βαθμολογία) excellent.

αριστερά [areestera] left hand || (επιρ) on the left, to the left.

αριστερός [areesteros] left, left-handed || left-wing.

αριστοκρατία, η [areestokrateea] aristocracy.

αριστούργημα, το [areestouryeema] masterpiece.

αρκετά [arketa] enough, sufficiently.

αρκετός [arketos] enough, sufficient, adequate.

αρκούδα, η [arkouða] bear.

αρκτικός [arkteekos] Arctic, northern.

αρκώ [arko] be enough, suffice || **αρκεί να** as long as.

αρλούμπα, η [arloumba] foolish talk, nonsense.

άρμα, το [arma] chariot || (στρατ) ~ **μάχης** tank.

αρματώνω [armatono] arm || equip.

αρμέγω [armego] milk || (μεταφ) fleece.

Αρμένης, ο [armenees] Armenian.

αρμενίζω [armeneezo] set sail, sail.

άρμη, η [armee] brine.

αρμόδιος, ο [armoðeeos] qualified, competent || propitious.

αρμοδιότης, η [armoðeeotees] province, jurisdiction.

αρμόζω [armozo] fit || befit, be becoming, be proper.

αρμονία, η [armoneea] harmony, concord.

αρμός, ο [armos] joint.

αρμοστής, ο [armostees] high commissioner, governor.

αρμύρα, η [armeera] saltiness.

αρμυρός [armeeros] salty.

άρνηση, η [arneesee] refusal || denial || negation.

αρνί, το [arnee] lamb || (μεταφ) docile person.

αρνούμαι [arnoume] refuse, deny, decline || disown.

άροτρο, το [arotro] plough.

αρουραίος, ο [aroureos] field mouse, rat.

άρπα, η [arpa] harp.

αρπαγή, η [arpayee] rapine || rape || stealing.

αρπάζομαι [arpazome] take hold of || come to blows.

αρπάζω [arpazo] grab, snatch || steal, pinch || (ευκαιρία) seize || (λέξεις) catch, pick up.

αρπακτικός [arpakteekos] greedy || (ζώο) rapacious, predatory.

αρραβώνες, οι [aravones] engagement.

αρραβωνιάζω [aravoneeazo] betroth (old), engage.

αρραβωνιαστικιά, η [aravoneeasteekia] fiancée.

αρραβωνιαστικός, ο [aravoneeasteekos] fiancé.

αρρενωπός [arenopos] manly, masculine.

άρρην [areen] male.

αρρωσταίνω [arosteno] make sick || fall ill.

αρρώστια, η [arosteea] illness, sickness.

άρρωστος [arostos] ill, sick, unwell.

αρσενικός [arseneekos] male || (γραμμ) masculine.

άρση, η [arsee] removal, lifting || (μεταφ) raising, abrogation.

αρτηρία, η [arteereea] artery || (οδός) thoroughfare.

άρτιος [arteeos] whole, entire || (αριθμός) even.

αρτοποιείο, το [artopieeo] bakery, baker's shop.

αρτοπωλείο, το [artopoleeo] baker's shop.

άρτος, ο [artos] bread.

άρτυμα, το [arteema] seasoning, sauce.

αρχαιοκαπηλία, η [arheokapeeleea] illicit trade in antiquities.

αρχαιολόγος, ο [arheologos] archeologist.

αρχαιολογία, η [arheoloyeea] archeology.

αρχαίος [arheos] ancient || antiquated.

αρχαιότης, η [arheotees] antiquity || (στα γραφεία) seniority.

αρχάριος [arhareeos] beginner, novice, apprentice.

αρχείο, το [arheeo] archives, records.

αρχέτυπο, το [arheteepo] archetype, original.

αρχή, η [arhee] beginning, start || (φιλοσ) principle || (διοίκ) authority || **κατ' αρχήν** in principle.

αρχηγείο, το [arheeyeeo] headquarters.

αρχηγία, η [arheeyeea] command, leadership.

αρχηγός, ο [arheegos] commander, leader, chief || (οικογενείας) head.

αρχιεπίσκοπος, ο [arhiepeeskopos] archbishop.

αρχιερέας, ο [arhiereas] prelate, high priest.

αρχίζω [arheezo] begin, start, commence.

αρχικός [arheekos] initial, first, original.

αρχιστράτηγος, ο [arheestrateegos] commander-in-chief, generalissimo.

αρχισυντάκτης, ο [arheeseentaktees] editor-in-chief.

αρχιτέκτων, ο [arheetekton] architect.

άρχοντας, ο [arhontas] lord, master, elder.

αρχοντιά, η [arhontia] distinction, nobility || wealth.

αρχοντικός [arhonteekos] fine, of distinction, lordly.

αρωγή, η [aroyee] help, assistance, aid.

άρωμα, το [aroma] aroma, perfume, odour || **αρωματικός** scented.

ας [as] let, may || ~ **είναι** so be it, let it be.

ασανσέρ, το [asanser] lift, elevator.

ασαφής [asafees] obscure, vague.

ασβέστης, ο [asvestees] lime.

ασβεστώνω [asvestono] whitewash.

ασέβεια, η [aseveea] disrespect || impiety.

ασεβής [asevees] disrespectful || impious.

ασέλγεια, η [aselya] lewdness, debauchery.

άσεμνος [asemnos] indecent, obscene, immodest.

ασήκωτος [aseekotos] unraised || (βαρύς) impossible to lift.

ασήμαντος [aseemantos] insignificant, unimportant.

ασημένιος [aseemeneeos] silver(y).

ασήμι, το [aseemee] silver || ασημικά πλ silverware.

άσημος [aseemos] obscure, insignificant, unimportant.

ασθένεια, η [astheneea] sickness, illness.

ασθενής [asthenees] ill, weak || (ο άρρωστος) patient.

ασθενικός [astheneekos] sickly.

ασθενώ [astheno] be ill, fall sick, get sick.

άσθμα, το [asthma] asthma.

αοιτία, η [aseeteea] undernourishment.

άσκηση, η [askeesee] exercise, practice || drill.

ασκητής, ο [askeetees] hermit.

άσκοπος [askopos] pointless, aimless, purposeless.

ασκός, ο [askos] (skin) bag || wineskin.

ασκούμαι [askoume] exercise, practise.

ασκώ [asko] exercise, practise.

ασπάζομαι [aspazome] kiss, embrace || (μεταφ) adopt, espouse.

ασπασμός, ο [aspasmos] embrace, kiss || greeting.

άσπαστος [aspastos] unbroken || unbreakable.

άσπιλος [aspeelos] immaculate, spotless.

ασπιρίνη, η [aspeereenee] aspirin.

ασπίδα, η [aspeeða] shield.

άσπλαγχνος [asplanghnos] hardhearted, pitiless, unmerciful.

άσπονδος [aspoνðos] irreconcilable, relentless.

ασπούδαστος [aspouðastos] uneducated, ignorant.

ασπράδι, το [aspraðee] white spot || (ματιού, αυγού) white.

ασπρειδερός [aspreeðeros] whitish.

ασπρίζω [aspreezo] whiten, bleach || (γίνομαι άσπρος) turn white.

ασπρομάλλης [aspromalees] whitehaired.

ασπροπρόσωπος [asproprosopos] uncorrupted || successful.

ασπρόρουχα, τα [asprorouha] πλ underclothes, linen.

άσπρος [aspros] white.

άσσος, ο [assos] ace.

αστάθεια, η [astatheea] instability, inconstancy, fickleness.

άσταθής [astathees] unsteady, fickle, unstable.

αστακός, ο [astakos] lobster.

άστατος [astatos] fickle, unstable.

άστεγος [astegos] homeless || roofless.

αστειεύομαι [astievome] joke, jest.

αστείο, το [asteeo] joke, pleasantry.

αστείος [asteeos] humorous, funny.

αστείρευτος [asteerevtos] inexhaustible, limitless.

αστέρι, το [asteree] star.

αστερισμός, ο [astereesmos] constellation.

αστεροσκοπείο, το [asteroskopeeo] observatory.

αστήρικτος [asteereektos] unsupported || (μεταφ) untenable.

αστιγματισμός, ο [asteegmateesmos] astigmatism.

αστικός [asteekos] urban || civic || ~ κώδικας civil code.

αστοιχείωτος [asteeheeotos] unlearned, ignorant.

αστόχαστος [astohastos] thoughtless, imprudent.

αστοχία, η [astoheea] failure || carelessness.

αστοχώ [astoho] miss the mark, fail || (λησμονώ) forget.

αστράγαλος, ο [astragalos] anklebone.

αστραπή, η [astrapee] lightning.

αστραπιαίος [astrapieos] lightning, quick.

αστράπτω [astrapto] lighten || flash, glitter.

αστρικός [astreekos] stellar, astral.

άστριφτος [astreeftos] not twisted.

άστρο, το [astro] star.

αστρολογία, η [astroloyeea] astrology.

αστρολόγος, ο [astrologos] astrologer.

αστροναύτης, ο [astronaftees] astronaut.

αστρονομία, η [astronomeea] astronomy.

αστρονόμος, ο [astronomos] astronomer.

αστροπελέκι, το [astropelekee] thunderbolt.

αστροφεγγιά, η [astrofengia] starlight.

άστρωτος [astrotos] (κρεββάτι) unmade || (τραπέζι) unlaid || (πάτωμα) bare || (δρόμος) unpaved.

άστυ, το [astee] city.

αστυνομία, η [asteenomeea] police.

αστυνομικός [asteenomeekos] policeman, of the police.

αστυνόμος, ο [asteenomos] police officer.

αστυφύλακας, ο [asteefeelakas] police constable.

ασυγκίνητος [aseengkeeneetos] unmoved, unfeeling.

ασυγκράτητος [aseengkrateetos] unsuppressible.

ασύγκριτος [aseengkreetos] incomparable.

ασυγύριστος [aseeyeereestos] untidy, disarranged.

ασυγχώρητος [aseenghoreetos] inexcusable, unforgivable.

ασυζήτητος [aseezeeteetos] unquestionable, incontrovertible.

ασυλία, η [aseeleea] asylum, immunity, inviolability.

ασύλληπτος [aseeleeptos] elusive, not caught || (μεταφ) inconceivable.

ασυλλόγιστος [aseeloyeestos] rash, thoughtless.

άσυλο, το [aseelo] shelter, refuge, asylum.

ασυμβίβαστος [aseemveevastos] irreconcilable, incompatible.

ασύμμετρος [aseemetros] disproportionate.

ασυμπλήρωτος [aseembleerotos] uncompleted, incomplete.

ασύμφορος [aseemforos] disadvantageous, not profitable.

ασυναγώνιστος [aseenagoneestos] unbeatable, unrivalled.

ασυναίσθητος [aseenestheetos] unconscious, inconsiderate.

ασυναρτησία, η [aseenarteeseea] incoherence || inconsistency.

ασυνάρτητος [aseenarteetos] incoherent || inconsistent.

ασυνείδητος [aseeneedeetos] unscrupulous, unconscionable.

ασυνέπεια, η [aseenepeea] inconsequence, inconsistency.

ασυνεπής [aseenepees] inconsistent.

ασυνήθιστος [aseeneetheestos] unusual, uncommon.

ασυρματιστής, ο [aseermateestees] wireless operator.

ασύρματος, ο [aseermatos] wireless || **σταθμός ασυρμάτου** wireless station.

ασύστολος [aseestolos] impudent, brazen.

άσφαιρος [asferos] blank.

ασφάλεια, η [asfaleea] security, safety || (ζωής κτλ) insurance || (αστυνομία) police || (πλεκτ) fuse || (όπλου) safety catch.

ασφαλής [asfalees] safe, secure, sure.

ασφαλίζω [asfaleezo] secure, assure || (ζωήκτλ) insure.

ασφαλιστήριο, το [asfaleesteereeo] insurance policy.

ασφάλιστρο, το [asfaleestro] insurance premium.

άσφαλτος, η [asfaltos] asphalt || (δρόμος) tarred road.

ασφαλώς [asfalos] surely, certainly || safely.

ασφυκτικός [asfeekteekos] suffocating.

ασφυξία, η [asfeekseea] suffocation, asphyxia.

άσχετος [ashetos] irrelevant, unrelated, unconnected.

ασχήμια, η [asheemeea] ugliness, deformity.

άσχημος [asheemos] ugly || unsightly || bad.

ασχολία, η [asholeea] occupation, business, job.

ασχολούμαι [asholoume] be occupied with, keep busy.

άσωτος [asotos] dissolute || prodigal, wasteful.

αταίριαστος [atereeastos] incompatible || dissimilar.

άτακτος [ataktos] irregular || disorderly || (παιδί) naughty, unruly.

αταξία, η [atakseea] confusion, disorder || unruliness.

ατάραχος [atarahos] calm, composed, quiet.

αταραξία, η [atarakseea] composure, calmness, serenity.

άταφος [atafos] unburied.

άτεκνος [ateknos] childless.

ατέλεια, η [ateleea] defect || (δασμού) exemption || (χαρακτήρος) imperfection.

ατελείωτος [ateleeotos] endless || unfinished, incomplete.

ατελής [atelees] incomplete || defective || (φόρου) tax-free.

ατελώνιστος [ateloneestos] duty-free || not cleared through customs.

ατενίζω [ateneezo] gaze, stare at, look fixedly at.

ατζαμής [adzamees] unskilled || awkward, clumsy.

ατίθασος [ateethasos] stubborn || (άλογο) difficult to tame.

ατιμάζω [ateemazo] dishonour, disgrace || (βιάζω) rape, ravish.

ατιμία, η [ateemeea] dishonour, disgrace, infamy.

άτιμος [ateemos] dishonest, infamous, disreputable || (συμπεριφορά) disgraceful.

ατιμώρητος [ateemoreetos] unpunished.

ατμάκατος, η [atmakatos] small steamboat.

ατμάμαξα, η [atmamaksa] locomotive.

ατμοκίνητος [atmokeeneetos] steam-driven.

ατμομηχανή, η [atmomeehanee] steam engine, locomotive.

ατμοπλοΐα, η [atmoploeea] steam navigation.

ατμόπλοιο, το [atmopleeo] steamship.

ατμός, ο [atmos] steam, vapour || (κρασίον) fume.

ατμόσφαιρα, η [atmosfera] atmosphere.

άτοκος [atokos] without interest.

άτολμος [atolmos] timid, fainthearted.

ατομικιστής [atomeekeestees] egoist.

ατομικός [atomeekos] personal || (ενέργεια κτλ) atomic.

ατομικότητα, η [atomeekoteeta] individuality.

άτομο, το [atomo] (θυσική) atom || (άνθρωπος) individual, person.

ατονία, η [atoneea] langour, weakness, dejection.

άτονος [atonos] languid, dull || (γραμμ) unaccented.

ατού, το [atoo] trump.

ατόφυος [atofeeos] solid, massive.

άτριφτος [atreeftos] not rubbed, not grated.

ατρόμητος [atromeetos] bold, dauntless, daring.

ατροφία, η [atrofeea] atrophy.

ατροφικός [atrofeekos] atrophied, emaciated.

ατρύγητος [atreeyeetos] ungathered, unharvested.

άτρωτος [atrotos] unwounded, unhurt || invulnerable.

ατσαλένιος [atsaleneeos] of steel, steely.

ατσάλι, το [atsalee] steel.

άτσαλος [atsalos] untidy, disorderly, unkempt || (ζωή) riotous, lawless.

ατσίδα, η [atseeða] alert person, wideawake person.

ατύχημα, το [ateeheema] mishap, accident, misfortune, injury.

ατυχής [ateehees], **άτυχος** [ateehos] unfortunate, unlucky, wretched.

ατυχία, η [ateeheea] misfortune, bad luck.

ατυχώ [ateeho] fail, have bad luck, meet with misfortune.

αυγερινός, ο [avgereenos] morning star.

αυγή, η [avyee] dawn, daybreak.

αυγό, το [avgo] egg.

αυγολέμονο, το [avgolemono] lemon and egg sauce or soup.

αυγοτάραχο, το [avgotaraho] botargo.

αυγουλιέρα, η [avgouliera] eggcup.

Αύγουστος, ο [avgoustos] August.

αυθάδεια, η [avthaðeea] audacity, insolence.

αυθάδης [avthaðees] impertinent, saucy.

αυθαιρεσία, η [avthereseea] highhanded act.

αυθαίρετος [avtheretos] arbitrary, high-handed.

αυθεντία, η [avthenteea] authority, authenticity.

αυθεντικός [avthenteekos] authentic, authoritative.

αυθημερόν [avtheemeron] on the very same day.

αυθόρμητος [avthormeetos] spontaneous.

αυθυποβολή, η [avtheepovolee] auto-suggestion.

αυλαία, η [avlea] curtain.

αυλάκι, το [avlakee] channel, ditch, trench || (ξύλου κτλ) groove.

αυλακωτός [avlakotos] grooved, furrowed, scored.

αυλή, η [avlee] yard, courtyard || (βασιλέως) court.

αυλόγυρος, ο [avloyeeros] enclosure, surrounding wall.

αυλός, ο [avlos] pipe, flute, reed.

άυλος [aeelos] immaterial, incorporeal.

αυξάνω [avksano] increase, augment || (ταχύτητα) accelerate.

αύξηση, η [avkseesee] increase || (γραμμ) augment.

αυξομείωση, η [avksomeeosee] fluctuation, variation.

αύξων [avkson] increasing || ~ **αριθμός** serial number.

αϋπνία, η [aeepneea] sleeplessness, insomnia.

άυπνος [aeepnos] sleepless, wakeful.

αύρα, η [avra] breeze.

αυριανός [avreeanos] of tomorrow.

αύριο [avreeo] tomorrow.

αυστηρός [avsteeros] severe, rigorous, austere.

αυστηρότητα, η [avsteeroteeta] severity, strictness, austerity.

Αυστραλία, η [avstraleea] Australia.

αυστραλιακός [avstraleeakos] Australian.

Αυστραλός, ο [avstralos] Australian.

Αυστρία, η [avstreea] Austria.

Αυστριακός, ο [avstreeakos] Austrian.

αυταπάρνηση, η [avtaparneesee] self-abnegation.

αυταπάτη, η [avtapatee] selfdelusion, self-deception.

αυταρέσκεια, η [avtareskeea] complacency.

αυτάρκεια, η [avtarkeea] contentment.

αυτάρκης [avtarkees] self-sufficient, satisfied.

αυταρχικός [avtarheekos] authoritative, dictatorial.

αυτί, το [avtee] ear.

αυτοβιογραφία, η
[avtoveeografeea] autobiography.

αυτόγραφο, το [avtografo]
autograph.

αυτοδημιούργητος
[avtoðeemeeouryeetos] self-made.

αυτοδιάθεση, η [avtoðeeathesee]
self-determination.

αυτοδικαίως [avtoðeekeos] of right,
de jure.

αυτοδιοίκηση, η [avtoðieekeesee]
self-government.

αυτοθυσία, η [avtotheeseea] self-
sacrifice.

αυτοκέφαλος [avtokefalos]
independent || (εκκλ) autocephalous.

αυτοκινητιστής, ο
[avtokeeneeteestees] motorist.

αυτοκίνητο, το [avtokeeneeto] car,
automobile (US).

αυτοκινητόδρομος, ο
[avtokeeneetoðromos] motorway,
highway.

αυτοκρατορία, η [avtokratoreea]
empire.

αυτοκράτωρας, ο [avtokratoras]
emperor.

αυτοκτονία, η [avtoktoneea] suicide.

αυτοκτονώ [avtoktono] commit
suicide.

αυτόματος [avtomatos] automatic.

αυτονόητος [avtonoeetos] self-
explanatory, obvious.

αυτοπεποίθηση, η
[avtopepeetheesee] self-confidence,
self-reliance.

αυτοπροσώπως [avtoprosopos]
personally.

αυτόπτης, ο [avtoptees] eyewitness.

αυτός [avtos] he || **ο ~** the same.

αυτοσυντήρηση
[avtoseenteereesee] self-preservation.

αυτοσυντήρητος
[avtoseenteereetos] self-supporting.

αυτοσχεδιάζω [avtosheðeeazo]
improvise, extemporize.

αυτοσχέδιος [avtosheðeeos]
improvised, impromptu, makeshift.

αυτοτελής [avtotelees] self-sufficient
|| independent.

αυτού [avtou] there.

αυτουργός, ο [avtourgos]
perpetrator.

αυτοφυής [avtofiees] indigenous,
natural.

αυτόφωρος [avtoforos] in the very
act, red-handed.

αυτόχειρας, ο [avtoheeras] suicide.

αυτόχθων, ο [avtohthon] indigenous,
aboriginal, native.

αυτοψία, η [avtopseea] (ιατρ) autopsy
|| (νομ) local inspection.

αυχένας, ο [avhenas] nape of the
neck || cervix || (μεταφ) neck.

αφάγωτος [afagotos] uneaten || not
having eaten || untouched.

αφαίμαξη, η [afemaksee]
bloodletting.

αφαίρεση, η [aferesee] deduction,
subtraction || (φιλοσ) abstraction.

αφαιρούμαι [aferoume] be absent-
minded.

αφαιρώ [afero] deduct, subtract ||
(κλέβω) steal, rob.

αφαλός, ο [afalos] navel.

αφάνεια, η [afaneea] obscurity,
oblivion.

αφανής [afanees] obscure, unknown ||
invisible.

αφανίζω [afaneezo] ruin, destroy.

αφάνταστος [afantastos]
unimaginable.

άφαντος [afantos] invisible, unseen.

αφασία, η [afaseea] muteness,
aphasia.

αφειδής [afeeðees] lavish,
extravagant.

αφελής [afelees] simple, ingenuous,
guileless.

αφέντης, ο [afentees] master, boss ||
owner.

αφεντικό, το [afenteeko] governor,
boss, employer.

αφερέγγυος [aferengeeos] insolvent.

άφεση, η [afesee] remission ||
discharge.

αφετηρία, η [afeteereea] starting
point || beginning.

αφή, η [afee] sense of touch || (αίσθηση)
feeling.

αφήγηση, η [afeeyeesee] narration,
account.

αφηγούμαι [afeegoume] narrate,
relate, tell.

αφηνιάζω [afeeneeazo] bolt || (για
ανθρώπους) run amok.

αφήνω [afeeno] let, permit || (μόνος)
let alone || (ελευθερώνω) let go of ||
(εγκαταλείπω) abandon.

αφηρημάδα, η [afeereemaða]
absentmindedness.

αφηρημένος [afeereemenos]
absentminded || (φίλος) abstract.

αφθαρσία, η [aftharseea]
indestructibility, incorruptibility.

άφθαρτος [afthartos] incorruptible,
indestructible.

άφθαστος [afthastos] unsurpassed,
incomparable, unexcelled.

αφθονία, η [afthoneea] abundance,
profusion.

άφθονος [afthonos] abundant,
plentiful, profuse.

αφθονώ [afthono] abound with, teem
with, be plentiful in.

αφιέρωμα, το [afieroma] offering,
dedication.

αφιερώνω [afierono] dedicate, devote
|| (βιβλίο κτλ) inscribe.

αφιέρωση, η [afierosee] dedication, devotion.

αφιλοκερδής [afeelokerðees] disinterested, selfless.

αφιλότιμος [afeeloteemos] wanting in self-respect, mean.

αφίνω [afeeno] βλ **αφήνω.**

άφιξη, η [afeeksee] arrival, coming.

αφιόνι, το [afonee] poppy || opium.

άφλεκτος [aflektos] nonflammable.

άφοβος [afovos] intrepid, fearless, bold.

αφομοιώνω [afomeeono] assimilate.

αφομοίωση, η [afomeeosee] assimilation.

αφοπλίζω [afopleezo] disarm || (φρούριο κτλ) dismantle.

αφοπλισμός, ο [afopleesmos] disarmament.

αφόρετος [aforetos] unworn, new.

αφόρητος [aforeetos] intolerable, insufferable.

αφορίζω [aforeezo] excommunicate.

αφορισμός, ο [aforeesmos] excommunication.

αφορμή, η [aformee] motive, pretext, cause.

αφορολόγητος [aforoloyeetos] untaxed, free from taxation.

αφορώ [aforo] concern || regard || **όσον αφορά** as regards.

αφοσιώνομαι [afoseeonome] devote o.s., be attached to.

αφοσίωση, η [afoseeosee] devotion, attachment, affection.

αφότου [afotou] since, as long as.

αφού [afou] since, after.

άφρακτος [afraktos] unfenced, unwalled.

αφράτος [afratos] light and crisp || frothy, foamy || (δέρμα) soft.

αφρίζω [afreezo] foam || (μεταφ) be furious.

αφρικανικός [afreekaneekos] African.

Αφρικανός, ο [afreekanos] African.

Αφρική, η [afreekee] Africa.

αφροδισιολόγος, ο [afroðeeseeologos] venereal disease specialist.

αφροδίσιος [afroðeeseeos] venereal.

αφρόντιστος [afronteestos] neglected, uncared for.

αφρός, ο [afros] foam || (κοινωνίας) cream || (σαπουνιού) lather.

αφρώδης [afroðees] frothy, foamy.

άφρων [afron] foolish, thoughtless, rash.

αφυδάτωση, η [afeeðatosee] dehydration.

αφύπνιση, η [afeepneesee] awakening || (μεταφ) dawning.

αφύσικος [afeeseekos] unnatural || (προσποιητός) affected.

άφωνος [afonos] mute, speechless, silent.

αφώτιστος [afoteestos] dark || (άνθρωπος) unenlightened.

αχ [ah] (επιφ) ah!, oh!, alas!

αχαΐρευτος [ahaeerevtos] scoundrel.

αχανής [ahanees] immense, enormous, vast.

αχαρακτήριστος [aharakteereestos] unprincipled, indescribable.

αχαριστία, η [ahareesteea] ingratitude.

αχάριστος [ahareestos] ungrateful.

άχαρος [aharos] ungraceful, awkward, unsightly || unpleasant.

αχηβάδα, η [aheevaða] cockle, sea shell, shellfish.

αχθοφόρος, ο [ahthoforos] porter.

αχινός, ο [aheenos] sea urchin.

αχλάδι, το [ahlaðee] pear.

άχνα, η [ahna] βλ **αχνός.**

αχνάρι, το [ahnaree] footprint || (μεταφ) pattern.

άχνη, η [ahnee] mist, evaporation || (xημ) corrosive sublimate.

αχνίζω [ahneezo] evaporate || steam.

αχνός, ο [ahnos] vapour, steam || (χρώμα) pale, colourless.

αχόρταγος [ahortagos] insatiable, greedy || (ζώο) voracious.

αχούρι, το [ahouree] stable, stall || (μεταφ) untidy place, pigsty.

αχρείαστος [ahreeastos] unnecessary, needless.

αχρείος [ahreeos] wicked, vile.

αχρησιμοποίητος [ahreeseemopieetos] unused.

αχρηστεύω [ahreestevo] make useless.

αχρηστία, η [ahreesteea] obsoleteness, uselessness.

άχρηστος [ahreestos] useless, worthless.

αχρονολόγητος [ahronoloyeetos] undated.

αχρωμάτιστος [ahromateestos] unpainted, uncoloured, plain.

άχρωμος [ahromos] colourless, uncoloured.

άχτι, το [ahtee] yearning, longing.

αχτίδα, η [ahteeða] ray, beam.

αχτένιστος [ahteneestos] uncombed, unkempt || (λόγος κτλ) unpolished.

άχυρο, το [aheero] straw, hay.

αχυρώνας, ο [aheeronas] barn, hayloft.

αχώνευτος [ahonevtos] undigested || indigestible.

αχώριστος [ahoreestos] inseparable.

άψητος [apseetos] not cooked, underdone.

αψηφώ [apseefo] disregard, disdain, scorn.

αψιμαχία, η [apseemaheea] skirmish.

αψίδα, η [apseeða] arch, vault || apse.

άψογος [apsogos] faultless, irreproachable.

αψυχολόγητος [apseeholoyeetos] ill-considered, impolitic.

άψυχος [apseehos] lifeless || (δειλός) cowardly, timid.

άωτον, το [aoton]: άκρον ~ acme, height of.

Β, β

βαγόνι, το [vagonee] carriage || (εμπορικό) wagon, truck || (βαγκόν-λι) sleeping car.

βάδην [vadheen] at a walking pace.

βαδίζω [vadheezo] walk || (στρατ) march || (πηγαίνω) go.

βάδισμα, το [vadheesma] step, walk, gait.

βαζελίνη, η [vazeleenee] vaseline.

βάζο, το [vazo] vase.

βάζω [vazo] put, set, place || (φορώ) put on || (φόρους κτλ) impose, lay || ~ εμπρός start, begin || ~ χέρι lay hands on || ~ τα δυνατά μου do my best.

βαθαίνω [vatheno] deepen || βλ και βαθύνω.

βαθειά [vatheea] deep(ly), profoundly.

βαθμηδόν [vathmeedon] by degrees, gradually.

βαθμιαίος [vathmieos] gradual, progressive.

βαθμίδα, η [vathmeeda] step, stair || (μεταφ) rank.

βαθμολογία, η [vathmologeea] (οργάνου) graduation || (μαθήματος) grades, marks.

βαθμός, ο [vathmos] degree || (στρατ) grade, rank || (μαθήματος) mark.

βάθος, το [vathos] depth, bottom || (φόντο) back, background.

βαθούλωμα, το [vathouloma] hollow, depression.

βαθουλώνω [vathoulono] hollow out || become hollow.

βάθρο, το [vathro] (βάση) basis, foundation || (αγάλματος κτλ) pedestal || (γεφύρας) pillar.

βαθύνω [vatheeno] deepen, hollow out, become deeper.

βαθύπλουτος [vatheeploutos] opulent.

βαθύς [vathees] deep || (σκότος κτλ) heavy, deep || (ύπνος) sound || (αίσθημα) profound || (πνεύμα) penetrating, sagacious.

βαθύτητα, η [vatheeteeta] depth, profundity, deepness.

βαθύφωνος [vatheefonos] bass, deep-voiced.

βάιο, το [vaeeo] palm branch.

βακαλάος, ο [vakalaos] cod.

βάκιλλος, ο [vakeelos] bacillus.

βακτηρίδιο, το [vakteereedeeo] bacillus.

βαλανίδι, το [valaneedee] acorn || βαλανιδιά oak tree.

βάλανος, ο [valanos] acorn.

βαλβίδα, η [valveedha] valve.

βαλές, ο [vales] knave (in cards).

βαλίτσα, η [valeetsa] suitcase, (hand)bag.

βαλκάνια, τα [valkaneea] πλ the Balkans.

βαλς, το [vals] waltz.

βάλσαμο, το [valsamo] balsam, balm || (μεταφ) consolation.

βαλσαμώνω [valsamono] embalm || (μεταφ) console, comfort.

βάλσιμο, το [valseemo] placing, setting, laying.

βάλτος, ο [valtos] marsh, fen, bog.

βαλτός [valtos] instigated, planted.

βαμβακερός [vamvakeros] of cotton.

βαμβάκι, το [vamvakee] cotton.

βάμμα, το [vamma] tincture, dye.

βαμμένος [vamenos] dyed, painted.

βάναυσος [vanavsos] rough, coarse, rude.

βάνδαλος, ο [vandalos] vandal.

βανίλ(λ)ια, η [vaneeleea] vanilla.

βαπόρι, το [vaporee] steamship.

βαπτίζω [vapteezo] baptize, christen || dip, plunge.

βάπτιση, η [vapteesee] βλ βάπτισμα.

βάπτισμα, το [vapteesma] baptism, christening.

βαπτιστικός [vapteesteekos] baptismal || (ουσ) godchild.

βάπτω [vapto] (χάλυψ) temper || (μπογιά) paint || (παπούτσια) polish.

βάραθρο, το [varathro] abyss, gulf, chasm.

βαραίνω [vareno] weigh down, make heavier || (κουράζω) weary || (αισθάνομαι βάρος) feel heavy || (μεταφ) carry weight.

βαράω [varao] βλ βαρώ.

βαρβαρικός [varvareekos] barbaric.

βάρβαρος [varvaros] barbarous, brutal, savage.

βάρδια, η [vardheea] watch, duty, shift.

βαρέλι, το [varelee] barrel, cask.

βαρετός [varetos] annoying, boring, tedious.

βαρήκοος [vareekoos] hard of hearing.

βαριά, η [varia] (σφυρί) hammer || (επιρ) seriously.

βαρίδι, το [vareedee] (counter)weight.

βαριέμαι [varieme] be bored, be tired (of) || (δε θέλω) not want (to) || δε βαριέσαι never mind!, don't bother!

βάρκα, η [varka] small boat, rowing boat, dinghy.

βαρκάρης, ο [varkarees] boatman.

βαρόμετρο, το [varometro] barometer.

βάρος, το [varos] weight, load, burden || σε ~ του at his expense.

βαρύθυμος [vareetheemos] sad, depressed.

βαρύνω [vareeno] weigh down, lie heavy || βλ και **βαραίνω.**

βαρύς [varees] heavy || (ποινή) severe, harsh || (σφάλμα) serious || (ύπνος) deep, heavy || (ζυγός) oppressive || (ευθύνη) grave || (άνθρωπος) slow, dull-witted.

βαρυσήμαντος [vareeseemantos] significant, grave, momentous.

βαρύτιμος [vareeteemos] precious, costly, valuable.

βαρύτονος [vareetonos] baritone || (γραμμ) with a grave accent.

βαρύφωνος [vareefonos] deep-voiced, bass.

βαρώ [varo] beat, hit, shoot || (σάλπιγγα) sound || (καμπάνα) toll.

βασανίζω [vasaneezo] torture, torment || (ένα θέμα κτλ) examine thoroughly, go into || (το μυαλό) rack.

βασανιστήριο, το [vasaneesteereeo] rack, torture chamber.

βάσανο, το [vasano] pain, trial, ordeal || (μεταφ) nuisance.

βασίζω [vaseezo] base.

βασικός [vaseekos] primary, basic, fundamental.

βασιλεία, η [vaseeleea] kingdom || reign.

βασίλειο, το [vaseeleeo] kingdom.

βασιλέας, ο [vaseeleas] king.

βασιλεύω [vaseeleuo] reign, rule.

βασιλιάς, ο [vaseelias] βλ **βασιλέας.**

βασιλική, η [vaseeleekee] basilica.

βασιλικός [vaseeleekos] royal, royalist || (ούσ) basil.

βασίλισσα, η [vaseeleesa] queen.

βασιλομήτωρ, η [vaseelomeetor] queen mother.

βασιλόπιττα, η [vaseelopeeta] New Year's cake.

βασιλόφρων [vaseelofron] royalist.

βάσιμος [vaseemos] sound, trustworthy.

βάση, η [vasee] base, foundation || (βαθμών) pass mark.

βασκανία, η [vaskaneea] evil eye.

βαστώ [vasto] (φέρω) bear, hold, support || (συγκρατώ) hold, control || (ύφασμα κτλ) keep, wear || (κρατώ) carry, hold.

βατ(τ), το [vat] watt.

βατόμουρο, το [vatomouro] blackberry.

βατός [vatos] (δρόμος) passable || (ποτάμι) fordable || (ύψωμα) accessible.

βάτραχος, ο [vatrahos] frog, toad.

βαυκαλίζω βαφή, η [vafee] dyeing || shoe polish || dye.

βάφομαι [vafome] make-up.

βαφτίσια, τα [vafteeseea] πλ christening.

βαφτισιμιός, ο [vafteeseemios] godson.

βάφω [vafo] βλ **βάπτω.**

βάψιμο, το [vapseemo] painting, make-up.

βγάζω [vgazo] take off, raise, draw out || (εξαλείφω) get out, wash out || (λάδι, χυμό κτλ) press, squeeze || (νόδι, χέρι) dislocate || (καπνό κτλ) give off || (παράγω) produce || (χρήματα) make, earn || (βουλευτή κτλ) elect || (διακρίνω) make out, read || (δίδω όνομα) name, call || (αποδεικνύω) prove || (αφαιρώ) take from || (εφημερίδα κτλ) publish || (περίπατο) take for a walk.

βγαίνω [vgeno] go out, come out, get out || (ανατέλλω) rise || (κυκλοφορώ) be out || (εκλέγομαι) be elected || (εξαλείφομαι) fade, come out.

βγαλμένος [vgalmenos] taken off, removed.

βγάλσιμο, το [vgalseemo] extraction, removal || (κοκκάλου) dislocation.

βδέλλα, η [vδella] leech.

βέβαιος [veveos] certain, sure, convinced.

βεβαιώνω [veveono] confirm, affirm, assure || certify.

βεβαίως [veveos] certainly, surely.

βεβαίωση, η [veveosee] confirmation || (χαρτί) certificate.

βεβαρημένος [vevareemenos] marked || (συνείδηση) heavy.

βέβηλος [veveelos] profane, sacrilegious, impious.

βεβιασμένος [veveeasmenos] forced.

βελάζω [velazo] bleat.

βελανίδι, το [velaneeδee] acorn.

βελγικός [velyeekos] Belgian.

Βέλγιο, το [velyo] Belgium.

Βέλγος ο [velgos] Belgian.

βέλο, το [velo] veil.

βελόνα, η [velona] needle.

βελονιά, η [velonia] stitch.

βέλος, το [velos] arrow, dart.

βελούδο, το [velouδo] velvet.

βελτιώνω [velteeono] improve, better.

βελτίωση, η [velteeosee] improvement.

βενζινάκατος, η [venzeenakatos] small motorboat.

βενζίνη, η [venzeenee] petrol.

βεντάλια, η [ventaleea] fan.

βεντέττα, η [venteta] vendetta || (ηθοποιός) star.

βέρα, η [vera] wedding ring.

βεράντα, η [veranta] veranda, porch.

βέργα, η [verga] stick, rod, switch, twig.

βερεσέ [verese] on credit, on trust.

βερίκοκκο, το [vereekoko] apricot.

βερνίκι, το [verneekee] varnish, polish || (μεταφ) veneer.

βέρος [veros] genuine, true, real.

βέτο, το [veto] veto.

βήμα, το [veema] step, pace || (βίδας) pitch, thread || (έλικος) twist || (έδρα) rostrum.

βηματίζω [veemateezo] step, pace, walk.

βήτα, το [veeta] the letter B.

βήχας, ο [veehas] cough.

βήχω [veeho] cough.

βία, η [veea] force, violence || hurry || (μετά βίας) with difficulty.

βιάζομαι [veeazome] be in a hurry, be rushed.

βιάζω [veeazo] force, compel || (παραβιάζω) break open || (παραβαίνω) violate || (ασελγώ) rape, ravish.

βίαιος [vieos] violent, forcible || fiery, passionate.

βιαιότητες, οι [vieoteetes] πλ acts of violence.

βιαίως [vieos] violently, forcibly.

βιασμός, ο [veeasmos] rape, violation.

βιαστής, ο [veeastees] ravisher, rapist.

βιαστικός [veeasteekos] urgent, pressing, hurried.

βιασύνη, η [veeaseenee] haste, urgency.

βιβλιάριο, το [veevleeareeo] booklet, card, bank book.

βιβλικός [veevleekos] biblical.

βιβλιογραφία, η [veevleeografeea] bibliography.

βιβλιοθηκάριος, ο [veevleeotheekareeos] librarian.

βιβλιοθήκη, η [veevleeotheekee] bookcase || library.

βιβλίο, το [veevleeo] book.

βιβλιοπώλης, ο [veevleeopolees] bookseller.

βίβλος, η [veevlos] Bible.

βίδα, η [veeδa] screw || (μεταφ) whim, caprice.

βιδώνω [veeδono] screw.

βίζα, η [veeza] visa.

βίζιτα, η [veezeeta] visit, call || visitor.

βίλλα, η [veela] villa.

βιογραφία, η [veeografeea] biography.

βιολέττα, η [veeoleta] violet.

βιολί, το [veeolee] violin, fiddle || αλλάζω ~ change one's tune.

βιολόγος, ο [veeologos] biologist.

βιομηχανία, η [veeomeehaneea] industry || manufacture.

βιομηχανικός [veeomeehaneekos] industrial.

βιοπαλαιστής, ο [veeopalestees] breadwinner.

βιοπάλη, η [veeopalee] working hard to make a living.

βίος, ο [veeos] life.

βιός, το [veeos] wealth, property.

βιοτεχνία, η [veeotehneea] handicraft.

βιοχημεία, η [veeoheemeea] biochemistry.

βιταμίνη, η [veetameenee] vitamin.

βιτρίνα, η [veetreena] shop window, showcase.

βίτσιο, το [veetseeo] bad habit.

βιώσιμος [veeoseemos] viable, feasible.

βλαβερός [vlaveros] harmful || (έντομο) noxious.

βλάβη, η [vlavee] harm, damage || (μηχανής) motor trouble, breakdown.

βλάκας, ο [vlakas] blockhead, fool, idiot.

βλακεία, η [vlakeea] nonsense, silliness.

βλακώδης [vlakoδees] stupid, silly.

βλάπτω [vlapto] harm, injure, damage.

βλαστάρι, το [vlastaree] sprout, bud || (οικογενείας) scion.

βλάστηση, η [vlasteesee] sprouting || (φυτεία) vegetation.

βλαστός, ο [vlastos] shoot, sprout || (μεταφ) scion, offspring.

βλασφημία, η [vlasfeemeea] blasphemy, curse.

βλασφημώ [vlasfeemo] curse, revile.

βλάχος, ο [vlahos] (μεταφ) bumpkin, boor.

βλέμμα, το [vlemma] look, glance, eye.

βλεννόρροια, η [vlenoreea] gonorrhoea.

βλέπω [vlepo] see, look at.

βλεφαρίδα, η [vlefareeδa] eyelash.

βλέφαρο, το [vlefaro] eyelid.

βλήμα, το [vleema] projectile.

βλογιά, η [vloya] smallpox.

βλοσυρός [vloseeros] fierce, stern, grim.

βόας, ο [voas] boa.

βογγητό, το [vongeeto] groan, moan.

βογγώ [vongo] moan, groan || roar.

βόδι, το [voδee] ox.

βοδινό, το [voδeeno] beef.

βοή, η [voee] shout, cry, humming, roaring || (όχλου) clamour.

βοήθεια, η [voeetheea] help, aid, assistance.

βοήθημα, το [voeetheema] help, assistance, relief.

βοηθητικός [voeetheeteekos] auxiliary || (άνεμος) favourable, fair.

βοηθός, ο [voeethos] assistant, helper, collaborator.

βοηθώ [voeetho] help, aid, give a hand, relieve.

βόθρος, ο [vothros] cesspool, ditch.

βολάν [volan] steering wheel, driving wheel.

βολβός, ο [volvos] bulb, kind of onion || (ματιού) eyeball.

βολεύομαι [volevome] get
comfortable || get fixed up.
βολεύω [volevo] accommodate, fit in,
suit || τα ~ get along, do well.
βολή, η [volee] throw, blow, stroke,
shot || (απόσταση) range.
βόλι, το [volee] ball, bullet.
βολιδοσκοπώ [voleeðoskopo] sound.
βολικός [voleekos] convenient, handy,
easy.
βολίδα, η [voleeða] sounding lead ||
(αστρο) meteor || (σφαίρα) bullet, ball.
βόλτα, η [volta] walk || (στροφή)
revolution || (κοχλίου) thread || κόβω
βόλτες I stroll about.
βόμβα, η [vomva] bomb.
βομβαρδίζω [vomvarðeezo] bomb,
bombard || (μεταφ) assail.
βομβαρδισμός, ο [vomvarðeesmos]
bombing.
βομβαρδιστικό, το
[vomvarðeesteeko] (αερο) bomber.
βόμβος, ο [vomvos] hum, buzz,
buzzing.
βορειοανατολικός
[voreeoanatoleekos] north-east(ern).
βορειοδυτικός [voreeoðeeteekos]
northwest(ern).
βόρειος [voreeos] north(ern).
βορείως [voreeos] northwards, to the
north, north.
βοριάς, ο [vorias] north wind.
βορράς, ο [vorras] north.
βοσκή, η [voskee] pasture.
βοσκός, ο [voskos] shepherd.
βοσκοτόπι, το [voskotopee] pasture
land.
βόσκω [vosko] graze || (μεταφ) drift.
βοτάνι, το [votanee] plant, herb.
βοτανικός [votaneekos] botanic(al).
βότανο, το [votano] herb, plant.
βοτανολόγος, ο [votanologos]
botanist.
βότρυς, ο [votrees] bunch of grapes.
βότσαλο, το [votsalo] pebble.
βουβάλι, το [vouvalee] buffalo.
βουβός [vouvos] dumb, mute.
βουδδιστής, ο [vouðeestees]
Buddhist.
βουή [vouee] βλ βοή.
βουίζω [voueezo] buzz, hum.
Βουλγαρία, η [voulgareea] Bulgaria.
Βουλγαρικός [voulgareekos]
Bulgarian.
Βουλγαρός, ο [voulgaros] Bulgarian.
βούλευμα, το [voulevma] decision,
ordinance, decree.
βουλευτής, ο [voulevtees] member
of parliament, deputy.
βουλή, η [voulee] parliament,
chamber || (θέληση) will, volition.
βούλησση, η [vouleesee] desire, will ||
κατά ~ at will.
βούλιαγμα, το [vouleeagma] sinking,
submergence || collapse.

βουλιάζω [vouleeazo] sink || (μεταφ)
ruin, be ruined.
βουλιμία, η [vouleemeea] insatiable
appetite.
βουλλοκέρι, το [voulokeree] sealing
wax.
βούλλωμα, το [vouloma] sealing,
stamping || (το αντικείμενο) cork,
stopper.
βουλλώνω [voulono] seal || (πωματίζω)
stop, choke up, fill.
βουνήσιος [vouneeseeos]
mountainous || (ουο) highlander.
βουνό, το [vouno] mountain.
βούρδουλας, ο [vourðoulas] whip,
lash.
βούρκος, ο [vourkos] mud, mire ||
(μεταφ) mire, gutter.
βουρκώνω [vourkono] fill with tears.
βούρλο, το [vourlo] (bul)rush.
βούρτσα, η [vourtsa] (hair)brush ||
(ρούχων) clothes brush || (δοντιών)
toothbrush.
βουρτσίζω [vourtseezo] brush, brush
down.
βουστάσιο, το [voustaseeo] ox stall,
cowshed.
βούτηγμα, το [vouteegma] plunging,
dipping || (μεταφ) plundering, stealing.
βούτημα, το [vouteema] hard biscuit.
βουτηχτής, ο [vouteehtees] diver ||
(μεταφ) thief.
βουτιά, η [voutia] dive || (μεταφ)
snatching, stealing.
βούτυρο, το [vouteero] butter.
βουτώ [vouto] plunge, dip || (κλέβω)
steal, snatch.
βραβείο, το [vraveeo] prize.
βραβεύω [vravevo] award, reward.
βράγχια, τα [vrangheea] πλ gills ||
(ιατρ) branchiae.
βραδιά, η [vraðia] evening.
βραδιάζω [vraðeeazo]: βραδιάζει it's
getting dark.
βραδινός [vraðeenos] evening.
βράδυ, το [vraðee] evening.
βραδύνω [vraðeeno] be late, be slow.
βραδύς [vraðees] slow, sluggish, tardy.
βραδύτης, η [vraðeetees] slowness,
tardiness.
βράζω [vrazo] boil, ferment, seethe.
βρακί, το [vrakee] trousers ||
underpants.
βράσιμο, το [vraseemo] boiling,
fermentation.
βράση, η [vrasee] boiling || (μούστου
κτλ) fermentation.
βρασμός, ο [vrasmos] boiling ||
(μεταφ) agitation, excitement.
βραστός [vrastos] boiled || boiling, hot.
βραχιόλι, το [vraheeolee] bracelet.
βραχίονας, ο [vraheeonas] arm,
forearm || branch.
βραχνιάζω [vrahneeazo] become
hoarse.

βραχνός [vrahnos] hoarse.

βράχος, ο [vrahos] rock.

βραχυκύκλωμα, το [vraheekeekloma] short circuit.

βραχυπρόθεσμος [vraheeprothesmos] short-dated || short-term.

βραχύτητα, η [vraheeteeta] shortness, brevity, conciseness.

βραχώδης [vrahoδees] rocky.

βρε [vre] (επιφ) you there!, hey, you!

βρεγμένος [vregmenos] wet, moist.

βρέξιμο, το [vrekseemo] wetting, watering, moistening.

βρεφοκομείο, το [vrefokomeeo] foundling hospital, public nursery.

βρέφος, το [vrefos] baby, infant.

βρέχω [vreho] water, wet, dampen, rain.

βρίζω [vreezo] abuse, swear at, insult || outrage.

βρισιά, η [vreesia] abuse, insult, outrage.

βρισίδι, το [vreeseeδee] stream of abuse.

βρίσκομαι [vreeskome] be, find o.s.

βρίσκω [vreesko] find || (τυχαίως) come across, discover || (σκέπτομαι) think, deem || (παίρνω) get, procure || (μαντεύω) guess.

βρογχίτιδα, η [vrongheeteeδa] bronchitis.

βροντερός [vronteros] thundering, noisy.

βροντή, η [vrontee] thunder.

βρόντος, ο [vrontos] noise, roar || heavy fall || στο βρόντο in vain.

βροντώ [vronto] (μεταφ) knock, make a noise.

βροχερός [vroheros] wet, rainy.

βροχή, η [vrohee] rain || ~ ψιλή drizzle.

βρυκόλακας, ο [vreekolakas] vampire, ghost.

βρύο, το [vreeo] moss || seaweed.

βρύση, η [vreesee] fountain, spring || (μεταλλική) tap.

βρυχώμαι [vreehome] roar, bellow.

βρώμα, η [vroma] filth, stink || (για πρόσωπο) hussy, bitch, slut.

βρωμερός [vromeros] stinking, smelly || (υπόθεση) nasty, odious, vile || (άτομο) stinking, dirty, slovenly.

βρώμη, η [vromee] oats.

βρωμιά, η [vromia] filth, dirt || (μεταφ) nasty business, corruption.

βρωμίζω [vromeezo] stink, dirty, sully.

βρώμικος [vromeekos] dirty, grubby || (μεταφ) nasty, odious, vile.

βρωμώ [vromo] give off a stench, smell badly, stink.

βυζαίνω [veezeno] suckle || (μεταφ) suck.

βυζαντινός [veezanteenos] Byzantine.

βυζί, το [veezee] breast.

βυθίζω [veetheezo] sink, plunge, dip.

βύθιση, η [veetheesee] sinking, submersion.

βύθισμα, το [veetheesma] (ναυτ) draught || sinking.

βυθοκόρος, η [veethokoros] dredger, dredge.

βυθός, ο [veethos] bottom of the sea.

βυρσοδεψείο, το [veersoδepseeo] tannery.

βύσσινο, το [veeseeno] sour cherry.

βυτίο, το [veeteeo] cask, barrel.

βωβός [vovos] dumb, mute, silent.

βώλος, ο [volos] clod || βώλοι πλ marbles.

βωμολοχία, η [vomoloheea] obscenity, scurrility.

βωμός, ο [vomos] altar.

Γ, γ

γαβάθα, η [gavatha] earthenware vessel || wooden bowl.

γάγγλιο, το [gangleeo] ganglion.

γάγγραινα, η [gangrena] gangrene || (μεταφ) canker.

γάδος, ό [gaδos] cod(fish).

γάζα, η [gaza] gauze.

γαζί, το [gazee] stitch || (της χειρός) handstitch || (της μηχανής) machine-stitch.

γάζωμα, το [gazoma] stitching.

γάιδαρος, ο [gaeeδaros] ass, donkey || (μεταφ) boor, ass.

γαϊδουράγκαθο, το [gaeeδourangatho] thistle.

γαϊδουριά, η [gaeeδouria] rudeness.

γαιοκτήμονας, η [geokteemonas] landowner.

γάλα, το [gala] milk.

γαλάζιος [galazeeos] azure, blue.

γαλαζοαίματος [galazoematos] blue-blooded.

γαλαζόπετρα, η [galazopetra] turquoise.

γαλακτερός [galakteros] milky, of milk.

γαλακτικός [galakteekos] lactic.

γαλακτοκομείο, το [galaktokomeeo] dairy farm.

γαλακτοπωλείο, το [galaktopoleeo] dairy.

γαλάκτωμα, το [galaktoma] emulsion.

γαλανόλευκος, η [galanolevkos] the Greek flag.

γαλανομμάτης [galanomatees] blue-eyed.

γαλανός [galanos] blue.

Γαλαξίας, ο [galakseeas] Milky Way.

γαλαρία, η [galareea] gallery.

γαλατάς, ο [galatas] milkman.

γαλβανίζω [galvaneezo] galvanize || (μεταφ) electrify, rouse, stimulate.

γαλέρα, η [galera] galley.

γαλέττα, η [galeta] hard tack.

γαλπνεύω [galeenevo] calm, quieten down.

γαλήνη, η [galeenee] calm, peace, serenity.

γαλήνιος [galeeneeos] calm, composed, serene.

Γαλλία, η [galea] France.

γαλλικός [galeekos] French.

Γάλλος, ο [galos] Frenchman.

γαλόνι, το [galonee] (μέτρο) gallon || (στρατ) stripe, pip.

γαλοπούλα, η [galopoula] turkey hen.

γάμα, το [gama] the letter G.

γαμήλιος [gameeleeos] nuptial, bridal || **γαμήλιο ταξίδι** honeymoon.

γάμπα, η [gamba] calf, leg.

γαμπρός, ο [gambros] bridegroom || son-in-law || brother-in-law.

γαμψός [gampsos] hooked, crooked.

γάντζος, ο [ganðzos] hook, grapple.

γαντζώνω [ganðzono] hook.

γάντι, το [gantee] glove.

γαργαλίζω [gargaleezo] tickle || (μεταφ) tempt, allure.

γαργάρα, η [gargara] gargle.

γαρδένια, η [garðeneea] gardenia.

γαρίδα, η [gareeða] shrimp, prawn.

γαρνίρισμα, το [garneereesma] adornment, garnishing, decoration.

γαρνίρω [garneero] garnish, trim.

γαρνιτούρα, η [garneetoura] garniture, trimming.

γαρυφαλιά, η [gareefalia] carnation || (μπαχαρικού) clove tree.

γαρύφαλλο, το [gareefalo] carnation || (μπαχαρικό) clove.

γαστραλγία, η [gastralyeea] stomachache.

γαστρικός [gastreekos] gastric.

γαστρίτιδα, η [gastreeteeða] gastritis.

γαστρονομία, η [gastronomeea] gastronomy.

γάτα, η [gata] cat.

γαυγίζω [gavyeezo] bark.

γαύγισμα, το [gavyeesma] barking, baying.

γδάρσιμο, το [gðarseemo] (πράξη) flaying || (αποτέλεσμα) scratch.

γδέρνω [gðerno] flay, skin || (μεταφ) fleece.

γδύνομαι [gðeenome] get undressed, strip.

γδύνω [gðeeno] undress || (μεταφ) rob.

γεγονός, το [yegonos] event, fact.

γειά, η [ya] health || ~ **σας** hello || so long, goodbye.

γείσο, το [yeeso] (αρχιτεκ) eaves || cornice || (κασκέτου) peak.

γειτονεύω [yeetonevo] be close to, be adjoining.

γειτονιά, η [yeetonia] neighbourhood, vicinity.

γελαστός [yelastos] smiling, pleasant, cheerful.

γελάω [yelao] βλ **γελώ**.

γελιέμαι [yelieme] be deceived, be mistaken.

γέλιο, το [yeleeo] laugh, laughter.

γελοιογραφία, η [yeleeografeea] caricature, cartoon.

γελοιοποίηση, η [yeleeopieesee] ridicule, derision.

γελοιοποιούμαι [yeleeopeeoume] make o.s. ridiculous.

γελοιοποιώ [yeleeopeeo] make ridiculous, ridicule.

γελοίος [yeleeos] ludicrous, ridiculous.

γελώ [yelo] laugh || (μάτια κτλ) smile, twinkle || (εξαπατώ) deceive, take in.

γεμάτος [yematos] full || (δρόμος κτλ) crowded, swarming || (όπλο, δένδρο κτλ) loaded || (δωμάτιο κτλ) packed, crammed || (παχύς) stout, plump.

γεμίζω [yemeezo] fill up || (πλοίο) load || (μαξιλάρι κτλ) stuff || (συμπληρώνω) fill out.

γέμισμα, το [yemeesma] filling || (στρώματος) stuffing || (φεγγαριού) waxing || (όπλου) charging, loading.

γεμιστός [yemeestos] stuffed.

Γενάρης [yenarees] January.

γενεά, η [yenea] race, generation, breed.

γενεαλογία, η [yenealoyeea] genealogy, lineage, pedigree.

γενέθλια, τα [yenethleea] πλ birthday, anniversary.

γενειάς, η [yenias] beard.

γενειοφόρος, ο [yeneeoforos] bearded.

γένεση, η [yenesee] origin, birth || (εκκλ) Genesis.

γενέτειρα, η [yeneteera] native country, birthplace.

γενετή, η [yenetee] **εκ γενετής** from birth.

γενετήσιος [yeneteeseeos] productive, generative, sexual.

γενίκευση, η [yeneekevsee] generalization.

γενικεύω [yeneekevo] generalize.

γενική [yeneekee] general, universal, wide || (γραμμ) genitive (case) || βλ και **γενικός**.

γενικός [yeneekos] general || βλ και **γενική**.

γενικότητα, η [yeneekoteeta] generality.

γέννα, η [yena] birth, childbirth || (μεταφ) breed.

γενναιοδωρία, η [yeneoðoreea] generosity.

γενναιόδωρος [yeneoðoros] generous, magnanimous.

γενναίος [yeneos] courageous, brave.

γενναιότητα, η [yeneoteeta] courage, bravery.

γενναιοφροσύνη, η [yeneofroseenee] generosity, liberality.

γενναιόφρων, ο [yeneofron] magnanimous, liberal.

γενναιόψυχος [yeneopseehos] generous, brave.

γέννημα, το [yeneema] offspring, product || (μωρό) progeny.

γέννηση, η [yeneesee] birth.

γεννητικός [yeneeteekos] genital, sexual.

γεννήτρια, η [yeneetreea] generator.

γεννώ [yeno] (για γυναίκα) give birth to, bring forth || (για άλογα) drop a foal || (για κουνέλια, γουρούνια) litter || (για πτηνά) lay || (μεταφ) create, breed, cause.

γεννώμαι [yenome] be born.

γένος, το [yenos] race, family, line || **το ανθρώπινο ~** mankind || (ζώων, φυτών) kind, species || (γραμμ) gender.

γερά [yera] strongly, hard, vigorously.

γεράκι, το [yerakee] hawk.

γεράματα, τα [yeramata] πλ old age.

γεράνι, το [yeranee] geranium.

γερανός, ο [yeranos] (πτηνό) crane || (μηχάνημα) crane, winch.

γερατειά [yeratia] βλ **γεράματα.**

Γερμανία, η [yermaneea] Germany.

γερμανικός [yermaneekos] German.

Γερμανός, ο [yermanos] German.

γέρνω [yerno] lean, bend || (για βάρκα κτλ) lean, tilt || (για ήλιο κτλ) go down, sink.

γερνώ [yerno] age, grow old.

γεροντικός [yeronteekos] senile.

γεροντοκόρη, η [yerontokoree] old maid, spinster.

γεροντοπαλήκαρο, το [yerontopaleekaro] old bachelor.

γέρος, ο [yeros] old man.

γερός [yeros] (άνθρωπος) vigorous, sturdy || (κράση) sound, healthy || (τροφή) solid, substantial, hearty || (ξύλο) sound || (πάτωμα) solid, firm || (τοίχος) strong || (επιχείρημα) strong, valid.

γερουσία, η [yerouseea] senate.

γερουσιαστής, ο [yerouseeastees] senator.

γεύμα, το [yevma] meal, dinner.

γεύομαι [yevome] taste, try.

γεύση, η [yevsee] taste, flavour.

γέφυρα, η [yefeera] bridge.

γεφυρώνω [yefeerono] bridge || build a bridge.

γεωγραφία, η [yeografeea] geography.

γεωγράφος, ο [yeografos] geographer.

γεώδης [yeoðees] earthy.

γεωλογία, η [yeoloyeea] geology.

γεωλόγος, ο [yeologos] geologist.

γεωμετρία, η [yeometreea] geometry.

γεωμετρικός [yeometreekos] geometric(al).

γεωπονία, η [yeoponeea] agriculture.

γεωργία, η [yeoryeea] agriculture, farming.

γεωργικός [yeoryeekos] agricultural.

γεωργός, ο [yeorgos] farmer.

γεώτρηση, η [yeotreesee] drilling.

γεωτρύπανο, το [yeotreepano] drill.

γη, η [yee] earth, land, ground.

γηγενής [yeegenees] native, indigenous.

γήινος [yeeinos] earthly, terrestrial.

γήπεδο, το [yeepeðo] ground, sportsground.

γήρας, το [yeeras] old age.

για [ya] for, because of, on behalf of || **γι' αυτό** therefore || **~ καλά** for certain, for good || **~ την ώρα** for the time being || **~ πού** whither? || **~ το Θεο** for God's sake || (επίρ) as, for || (συνδ) **~ να** in order to || **~ φαντάσου!** fancy that! || **~ πες μου** tell me.

γιαγιά, η [yayia] grandmother.

γιακάς, ο [yakas] collar.

γιαλός, ο [yalos] seashore.

γιαούρτι, το [yaourtee] yoghurt.

γιασεμί, το [yasemee] jasmine.

γιατί [yatee] why? || (συνδ) because.

γιατρεύω [yatrevo] cure, heal, treat.

γιατρός, ο [yatros] doctor.

γιγάντιος [yeeganteeos] gigantic.

γιγαντόσωμος [yeegandosomos] huge (in size).

γίγας, ο [yeegas] giant.

γίδα, η [yeeða] goat.

γιδοβοσκός, ο [yeeðovoskos] goatherd.

γιλέκο, το [yeeleko] waistcoat.

γίνομαι [yeenome] be done, become || (μεγαλώνω) grow || (στρέφω) turn || (γεγονός κτλ) happen, occur || (ωριμάζω) ripen || **~ καλά** recover || **τι γίνεσαι**; how are you?

γινόμενο, το [yeenomenon] product.

Γιουγκοσλαβία, η [yougoslaveea] Yugoslavia.

γιουγκοσλαβικός [yougoslaveekos] Yugoslavian.

Γιουγκοσλάβος, ο [yougoslavos] Yugoslav.

γιουχαΐζω [youhaeezo] hoot, jeer.

γιρλάντα, η [yeerlanta] garland, wreath.

γιώτ, το [yot] yacht.

γκαβός [gavos] cross-eyed || (κατ επέκτασιν) blind.

γκάζι, το [gazee] gas || πατώ ~ step on the gas.

γκαζιέρα, η [gaziera] cooking stove, primus stove.

γκαζόζα, η [gazoza] lemonade.

γκαρίζω [gareezo] bray.

γκαρσόνι, το [garsonee] waiter.

γκαρσονιέρα, η [garsoniera] bachelor flat.

γκάφα, η [gafa] blunder.

γκέμι, το [gemee] bridle, reins.

γκίνια, η [geeneea] bad luck.

γκιώνης, ο [geeonees] (scops) owl.

γκουβερνάντα, η [gouvernanta] governess.

γκρεμίζω [gremeezo] demolish, pull down, wreck.

γκρεμίζομαι [gremeezvome] fall, crumble, collapse.

γκρεμνός [gremnos] sheer drop, crag.

γκρίζος [greezos] grey.

γκρίνια, η [greeneea] grumble, nag, murmur.

γκρινιάζω [greeneeazo] complain, nag, grumble.

γλάρος, ο [glaros] seagull.

γλάστρα, η [glastra] flowerpot.

γλαύκωμα, το [glavkoma] glaucoma.

γλαφυρός [glafeeros] elegant, graceful.

γλείφω [gleefo] lick.

γλεντζές, ο [glenðzes] fun-loving person, reveller.

γλέντι, το [glenðee] party, feast.

γλεντώ [glenðo] amuse || (απολαμβάνω) enjoy || (επί χρημάτων) squander.

γλεύκος, το [glevkos] must.

γλιστερός [gleesteros] slippery.

γλίστρημα, το [gleestreema] slide, slip || (μεταφ) blunder, mistake.

γλιστρώ [gleestro] slide, slip || (μεταφ) slip away.

γλοιώδης [gleeoðes] slimy, sticky || (πρόσωπο) slippery.

γλόμπος, ο [glombos] globe.

γλουτός, ο [gloutos] buttock, rump.

γλύκα, η [gleeka] sweetness.

γλυκά, τα [gleeka] πλ pastries, confectionery.

γλυκαίνω [gleekeno] sweeten, make mild, soften.

γλυκάνισο, το [gleekaneeso] anise.

γλύκισμα, το [gleekeesma] cake, pastry.

γλυκομίλητος [gleekomeeleetos] soft-spoken, affable.

γλυκομιλώ [gleekomeelo] speak tenderly, speak kindly.

γλυκό, το [gleeko] jam, sweetmeat.

γλυκόξινος [gleekokseenos] bittersweet.

γλυκοχάραγμα, το [gleekoharagma] daybreak, twilight.

γλυκός [gleeko] affable, sweet ||

(καιρός) mild || (φως) subdued, mellow || (χρώμα) delicate || (ήχος) soft, sweet || (κρασί) sweet || (όνειρα) pleasant.

γλύπτης, ο [gleeptees] sculptor.

γλυπτική, η [gleepteekee] sculpture.

γλυπτός [gleeptos] sculptured, carved.

γλυτώνω [gleetono] save, deliver || (αμεταβ) escape.

γλύφω [gleefo] βλ γλείφω.

γλώσσα, η [glossa] tongue, language || (ψάρι) sole.

γλωσσάς, ο [glossas] chatterbox, gossip.

γλωσσικός [glosseekos] linguistic.

γλωσσολογία, η [glossologeea] linguistics.

γλωσσολόγος, ο [glossologos] linguist.

γλωσσομαθής [glossomathees] polyglot, linguist.

γνάθος, ο [gnathos] jaw.

γνέθω [gnetho] spin.

γνήσιος [gneeseeos] genuine, real || (παιδί) legitimate.

γνησίως [gneeseeos] genuinely, authentically.

γνωμάτευση, η [gnomatevsee] opinion, adjudication.

γνώμη, η [gnomee] opinion, view.

γνωμικό, το [gnomeeko] maxim, saying, adage.

γνωμοδότης, ο [gnomoðotees] adviser, councillor.

γνωμοδοτώ [gnomoðoto] give one's opinion, judge.

γνώμων, ο [gnomon] set square, level || (μεταφ) criterion, model.

γνωρίζω [gnoreezo] let it be known, inform || (έχω γνώση) know, be aware of || (αναγνωρίζω) discern, distinguish || (έχω σχέσεις) know, be acquainted with || (παρουσιάζω κάποιο) introduce.

γνωριμία, η [gnoreemeea] acquaintance, familiarity.

γνώριμος [gnoreemos] known, intimate.

γνώρισμα, το [gnoreesma] sign, mark, indication.

γνώση, η [gnosee] knowledge, notion || γνώσεις πλ knowledge, learning.

γνώστης, ο [gnostees] expert, connoisseur, specialist.

γνωστικός [gnosteekos] prudent.

γνωστοποίηση, η [gnostopieesee] notification, announcement.

γνωστοποιώ [gnostopeeo] notify, inform, advise.

γνωστός [gnostos] known || (φίλος) acquaintance.

γογγύλη, η [gongeelee] turnip.

γοερός [goeros] plaintive, woeful.

γόης, ο [goees] charmer.

γοητεία, η [goeeteea] charm || attractiveness.

γοπτευτικός [goeetevteekos] charming, captivating.

γοπτεύω [goeetevo] charm, attract.

γόπτρο, το [goeetro] prestige, reputation.

γομάρι, το [gomaree] load || (μεταφ) simpleton, beast.

γόμμα, η [gomma] gum || (σβυσήματος) india rubber, eraser.

γόμωση, η [gomosee] stuffing || (όπλο) charge.

γονατίζω [gonateezo] (make to) kneel || (μεταφ) humble || (αμεταβ) kneel down || (μεταφ) give way, yield.

γονατιστά [gonateesta] on one's knees, kneeling.

γόνατο, το [gonato] knee.

γονεάς, ο [goneas] father || **γονεις** πλ parents.

γονιμοποίηση, η [goneemopieesee] fertilization, impregnation.

γονιμοποιώ [goneemopeeo] fecundate, fertilize.

γόνιμος [goneemos] fertile, prolific || (μεταφ) inventive.

γονιμότητα, η [goneemoteeta] fecundity, fertility.

γόνος, ο [gonos] child, offspring || (σπέρμα) sperm, seed.

γόπα, η [gopa] bogue (fish) || (τσιγαρου) cigarette butt.

γοργός [gorgos] rapid, quick.

γορίλλας, ο [goreelas] gorilla.

γούβα, η [gouva] cavity, hole.

γουδί, το [goudee] mortar.

γουδοχέρι, το [goudoheree] pestle.

γουλί, το [goulee] stalk, stump || (μεταφ) bald.

γουλιά, η [goulia] sip.

γούνα, η [gouna] fur.

γουργουρητό, το [gourgoureeto] rumbling, rumble.

γούρι, το [gouree] good luck.

γουρλώνω [gourlono] open (eyes) wide, goggle.

γουρούνι, το [gourounee] pig, hog.

γουρσούζης, ο [goursouzees] luckless person, unlucky person.

γουρσουζιά, η [goursoozia] bad luck.

γουστάρω [goustaro] desire, feel like || (ευχαριστούμαι) delight in, enjoy.

γούστο, το [gousto] taste || (φιλοκαλία) good taste || **για** ~ for the hell of it.

γοφός, ο [gofos] haunch, hip.

Γραικός, ο [grekos] Greek.

γράμμα, το [gramma] letter, character.

γραμμάριο, το [grammareeo] gram(me).

γραμματεία, η [grammateea] secretariat, secretary's office.

γραμματέας, ο [grammateas] secretary.

γραμματική, η [grammateekee] grammar.

γραμμάτιο, το [grammateeo] bill of exchange || (χρεωστικό) promissory note.

γραμματοκιβώτιο, το [grammatokeevoteeo] letterbox, postbox.

γραμματόσημο, το [grammatoseemo] (postage) stamp.

γραμμένος [grammenos] written || (μεταφ) destined.

γραμμή, η [grammee] line, row || (επιρ) straight, in a row || **πρώτης** ~**ς** first-class.

γραμμικός [grameekos] linear.

γραμμόφωνο, το [grammofono] gramophone.

γρανίτης, ο [graneetees] granite.

γραπτός [graptos] written.

γραπτώς [graptos] in writing.

γραπώνω [grapono] seize, snatch.

γρασίδι, το [graseedee] grass.

γρατσουνίζω [gratsouneezo] scratch.

γρατσούνισμα, το [gratsouneesma] scratch.

γραφειοκράτης, ο [grafeeokratees] bureaucrat.

γραφειοκρατία, η [grafeeokrateea] bureaucracy.

γραφείο, το [grafeeo] desk, bureau || (δωμάτιο) study || (ίδρυμα) office, bureau.

γραφικός [grafeekos] of writing, clerical || (μεταφ) picturesque, colourful.

γραφικότης, η [grafeekotees] picturesqueness, vividness.

γραφίτης, ο [grafeetees] graphite.

γραφομηχανή, η [grafomeehanee] typewriter.

γράφω [grafo] write, record, compose || enrol.

γράψιμο, το [grapseemo] writing.

γρήγορα [greegora] quickly, promptly.

γρηγορώ [greegoro] watch, be alert || be awake.

γριά, η [greea] old woman.

γρίλλια, η [greeleea] grille.

γρίππη, η [greepee] influenza.

γρίφος, ο [greefos] riddle, puzzle, enigma.

γριφώδης [greefodees] enigmatic(al), obscure.

γροθιά [grothia] fist || punch.

γρονθοκόπημα, το [gronthokopeema] boxing, punch.

γρονθοκοπώ [gronthokopo] punch, pound.

γρουσούζης [groosoozees] βλ **γρουσούζης**.

γρυλισμός, ο [greeleesmos] grunting, snorting.

γρυλλίζω [greeleezo] grunt, squeal.

γρύλλος, ο [greelos] piglet || (έντομο) cricket || (μηχάνημα) jack.

γυάλα, n [yeeala] glass, jar || (ψαριών) bowl.

γυαλάδα, n [yeealaδa] brilliance, shine, gloss.

γυαλάδικο, το [yeealaδeeko] glassware || glass works.

γυαλένιος [yeealeneeos] glass.

γυαλί, το [yeealee] glass || πλ spectacles, glasses.

γυαλίζω [yeealeezo] polish, shine.

γυάλισμα, το [yeealeesma] polishing, glazing.

γυαλιστερός [yeealeesteros] polished, glossy.

γυαλόχαρτο, το [yeealoharto] glasspaper, sandpaper.

γυιός, ο [yos] son.

γυμνάζομαι [yeemnazome] train o.s., exercise, practise.

γυμνάζω [yeemnazo] exercise, train, drill.

γυμνασιάρχης, ο [yeemnaseearhees] secondary school headmaster.

γυμνάσια, τα [yeemnaseea] πλ manoeuvres.

γυμνάσιο, το [yeemnaseeo] secondary school, high school.

γυμναστήριο, το [yeemnasteereeo] gymnasium.

γυμναστής, ο [yeemnastees] P.T. instructor.

γυμναστική, n [yeemnasteekee] πλ gymnastics || exercise.

γύμνια, n [yeemneea] nudity, nakedness || poverty.

γυμνιστής, n [yeemneestees] nudist.

γυμνός [yeemnos] naked, bare, nude.

γυμνώνω [yeemnono] bare, expose || (μεταφ) strip.

γύμνωση, n [yeemnosee] disrobing || denudation || fleecing.

γυναίκα, n [yeeneka] woman || (σύζυγος) wife.

γυναικάς, ο [yeenekas] woman-chaser, rake.

γυναικείος [yeenekeeos] womanly, feminine.

γυναικολογία, n [yeenekologeea] gynaecology.

γυναικολόγος, ο [yeenekologos] gynaecologist.

γυναικόπαιδα, τα [yeenekopeδa] πλ women and children.

γυναικοπρεπής [yeenekoprepees] womanly, effeminate, womanish.

γυναικωνίτης, ο [yeenekoneetees] harem.

γυνή [yeenee] βλ γυναίκα.

γύπος, ο [yeepas] vulture.

γυρεύω [yeerevo] ask for, call for || (ελεημοσύνη) beg for || (να βρω κάτι) look for, seek || (αποζημίωση κτλ) claim || (διαζύγιο) apply for || (βοήθεια) request.

γυρίζω [yeereezo] turn, rotate, revolve || (σβούρα) spin || (στρέφω) turn || (αναστρέφω) turn || (επιστρέφω) return || (αμεταβ) turn, rotate || (ταινία) shoot.

γύρισμα, το [yeereesma] turn, revolution || (δρόμου, ποταμού) turn, twist, winding.

γυρισμός, ο [yeereesmos] return, coming back.

γυριστός [yeereestos] curved, turned up, crooked.

γυρνάω [yeernao] βλ γυρίζω.

γυρολόγος, ο [yeerologos] hawker, pedlar.

γύρος, ο [yeeros] circle, circumference || (φορέματος) hem || (περιστροφή) turn, revolution || (περπάτημα) walk || (βαρελιού) hoop.

γυρτός [yeertos] bent, inclined, curved.

γύρω [yeero] round, around, about, round about.

γυφτιά, n [yeeftia] stinginess, avarice, shabbiness.

γύφτος, ο [yeeftos] gipsy.

γύψινος [yeepseenos] plaster.

γύψος, ο [yeepsos] plaster of Paris.

γυψώνω [yeepsono] plaster.

γωνία, n [goneea] angle, corner || (εργαλείο) square, set square || (απόμερος τόπος) nook, den || (ψωμιού) crust of bread.

γωνιακός [goneeakos] angular || (της γωνίας) corner.

γωνιόλιθος, ο [goneeoleethos] cornerstone.

γωνιώδης [goneeoδees] angular.

Δ, δ

δα [δa] (indeclinable particle) όχι ~ certainly not! || τόσος ~ only so tall, so small.

δάγκωμα, το [δangoma] bite.

δαγκώνω [δangono] bite.

δαδί, το [δaδee] pinewood, firewood.

δαίδαλος [δeδalos] labyrinthine, intricate, complicated.

δαιμονίζω [δemoneezo] enrage, infuriate.

δαιμονισμένος [δemoneesmenos] (μεταφ) mischievous || possessed.

δαιμόνιο, το [δemoneeo] genius || (διάβολος) demon, fiend.

δαιμόνιος [δemoneeos] very clever, marvellous, divine.

δαίμων, ο [δemon] demon, devil, fiend.

δάκρυ, το [δakree] tear.

δακρύζω [δakreezo] shed tears, weep || (επί φυτών) sweat.

δακτυλήθρα, n [δakteeleethra] thimble.

δακτυλίδι, το [δakteeleeδee] ring.

δακτυλικός [δakteeleekos] digital, dactylic.

δάκτυλο, το [ðakteelo] βλ
δάκτυλος.

δακτυλογράφος, ο, η
[ðakteelografos] typist.

δάκτυλος, ο [ðakteelos] finger ||
(ποδιού) toe || (μονάς μήκους) inch.

δαμάζω [ðamazo] tame, subdue.

δαμαλισμός, ο [ðamaleesmos]
vaccination.

δαμάσκηνο, το [ðamaskeeno] plum ||
(ξηρό) prune.

δανείζομαι [ðaneezome] borrow.

δανείζω [ðaneezo] lend, loan.

δάνειο [ðaneeo] loan.

δανειστής, ο [ðaneestees] lender,
creditor.

Δανία, η [ðaneea] Denmark.

δανικός [ðaneekos] Danish.

Δανός, ο [ðanos] Dane.

δαντέλλα, η [ðantella] lace.

δαπάνη, η [ðapanee] expenditure,
expense, cost.

δαπανηρός [ðapaneeros] costly,
expensive.

δαπανώ [ðapano] spend, consume.

δάπεδο, το [ðapeðo] floor || ground.

δαρμός, ο [ðarmos] βλ **δάρσιμο.**

δάρσιμο, το [ðarseemo] beating ||
(γάλακτος) churning.

δασκάλα, η [ðaskala] teacher,
schoolmistress.

δασκαλεύω [ðaskalevo] coach, teach.

δάσκαλος, ο [ðaskalos] teacher,
schoolmaster.

δασμολόγιο, το [ðasmoloyeeo] tariff.

δασμός, ο [ðasmos] tax, (customs)
duty.

δάσος, το [ðasos] forest, woodland.

δασύς, ο [ðasees] thick, bushy, hairy.

δασώδης [ðasoðees] wooded, woody.

δαυλί, το [ðavlee] torch, firebrand.

δάφνη, η [ðafnee] laurel, bay tree,
bay.

δε [ðe] and || but || on the other hand || **ο
μεν... ο ~** the one... the other.

δεδομένα, τα [ðeðomena] πλ data,
facts.

δεδουλευμένος [ðeðoulemenos]: ~
τόκος accrued interest.

δέηση, η [ðeesee] prayer, supplication.

δείγμα, το [ðeegma] sample,
specimen || (ένδειξη) token, sign.

δειγματολόγιο, το
[ðeegmatologeeo] sample, collection.

δεικνύω [ðeekneeo] show, point out ||
(επί οργάνων) mark, indicate.

δείκτης, ο [ðeektees] indicator ||
(χειρός) forefinger || (ωρολογίου) hand ||
(ζυγού) index, cock || (πυξίδος) needle.

δεικτικός [ðeekteekos] indicative ||
(γραμμ) demonstrative.

δειλά [ðeela] timidly, faint-heartedly.

δείλι, το [ðeelee] (late) afternoon.

δειλία, η [ðeeleea] timidity, cowardice.

δειλιάζω [ðeeleeazo] lose courage, be
afraid.

δειλινό, το [ðeeleeno] (late)
afternoon.

δειλός [ðeelos] timid || cowardly,
fainthearted.

δεινός [ðeenos] horrid || (ικανός) able,
clever, expert.

δεισιδαιμονία, η [ðeeseeðemoneea]
superstition.

δεισιδαίμων [ðeeseeðemon]
superstitious.

δείχνω [ðeehno] βλ **δεικνύω.**

δέκα [ðeka] ten.

δεκάδα, η [ðekaða] set of ten.

δεκαδικός [ðekaðeekos] decimal.

δεκαετηρίδα, η [ðekaeteereeða]
decade || (εορτή) tenth anniversary.

δεκαετής, ο, η [ðekaetees] ten-year-
old.

δεκαετία, η [ðekaeteea] ten years,
decade.

δεκάζω [ðekazo] corrupt, bribe.

δεκάλογος, ο [ðekalogos] Decalogue,
Ten Commandments.

δεκανέας, ο [ðekaneas] corporal.

δεκανίκι, το [ðekaneekee] crutch.

δεκαπενθήμερο, το
[ðekapentheemero] fortnight.

δεκαπλάσιος [ðekaplaseeos] tenfold.

δεκάρα, η [ðekara] one tenth of a
drachma.

δεκάρι, το [ðekaree] ten-drachma
piece || (στα χαρτιά) ten.

δεκασμός, ο [ðekasmos] bribery,
corruption.

δέκατος [ðekatos] tenth.

Δεκέμβριος, ο [ðekemvreeos]
December.

δέκτης, ο [ðektees] receiver.

δεκτικός [ðekteekos] capable of,
susceptible to, receptive to.

δεκτός [ðektos] accepted || (γνώμη)
admissible.

δελεάζω [ðeleazo] tempt, entice, bait.

δελεαστικός [ðeleasteekos] tempting,
attractive.

δέλτα, το [ðelta] (γράμμα) delta ||
(ποταμού) delta.

δελτίο, το [ðelteeo] bulletin || (υγείας)
report || (ψηφοδέλτιο) ballot.

δελφίνι, το [ðelfeenee] dolphin.

δέμα, το [ðema] (πάκο) bale, bundle ||
(ταχυδρομικό) parcel.

δεμάτι, το [ðematee] bundle ||
(καρότων κτλ) bunch || (φρυγάνων)
faggot.

δε(ν) [ðe(n)] (negative particle) no, not.

δενδρολίβανο, το [ðenðroleevano]
rosemary.

δένδρο, το [ðenðro] tree.

δενδρόφυτος [ðenðrofeetos] full of
trees, wooded.

δένω [ðeno] bind, tie || (με αλυσίδα)
chain, link || (γραβάτα κτλ) tie || (βιβλίο)

bind || (προσδένω) fasten, fix || (καράβι) moor, berth || (γλυκό κτλ) thicken || (μεταφ) bind.

δεξαμενή, η [δeksamenee] tank, reservoir || (ναυτ) dock, basin.

δεξιά, η [δeksia] right hand || (πολιτ) right wing || (επίρ) to the right.

δεξιός [δekseeos] right || right-handed || (πολιτ) right-wing || (επιτήδειος) clever.

δεξιότητα, η [δekseeoteeta] skilfulness, cleverness.

δεξιόχειρας, ο [δekseeoheeras] right-handed (person).

δεξιώνομαι [δekseeonome] receive, welcome.

δεξίωση, η [δekseeosee] reception.

δέον, το [δeon] what is necessary.

δεόντως [δeondos] suitably, fitly, properly.

δέος, το [δeos] awe, fear, fright.

δέρας, το [δeras]: **το χρυσόμαλλον** ~ the golden fleece.

δέρμα, το [δerma] skin, pelt || leather.

δερμάτινος [δermateenos] of leather.

δερματίτιδα, η [δermateeδa] dermatitis.

δέρνω [δerno] beat, flog || (γάλα) churn.

δέσιμο, το [δeseemo] tying, binding || bandage.

δεσμά, τα [δesma] πλ chains, fetters, bonds.

δέσμευση, η [δesmevsee] tying, binding.

δεσμεύω [δesmevo] bind by a promise, pledge.

δέσμη, η [δesmee] bunch || (φύλλων) bundle.

δέσμιος, ο [δesmeeos] prisoner, captive.

δεσμός, ο [δesmos] tie, bond.

δεσμοφύλακας, ο [δesmofeelakas] prison warder.

δεσπόζω [δespozo] dominate, rule || (υπέρκειμαι) tower above, overlook || (μεταφ) rise above.

δεσποινίς, η [δespeenees] young lady || Miss.

δεσπότης, ο [δespotees] ruler, master || (εκκλ) (arch)bishop.

δεσποτικός [δespoteekos] despotic.

δετός [δetos] tied, bound.

Δευτέρα, η [δevtera] Monday.

δευτερεύων [δevterevon] secondary || subordinate.

δευτεροβάθμιος [δevterovathmeeos] second-degree.

δευτερόλεπτο, το [δevterolepto] second.

δεύτερος [δevteros] second || (σε ποιότητα) inferior.

δευτερότοκος [δevterotokos] second-born.

δέχομαι [δehome] accept, receive || (παραδέχομαι) approve || (δεξιούμαι)

welcome, greet || (υφίσταμαι) receive || (ανέχομαι) tolerate.

δήθεν [δeethen] apparently, as if, so-called.

δηκτικός [δeekteekos] biting, scathing.

δηλαδή [δeelaδee] that is to say, namely, viz.

δηλητηριάζω [δeeleeteereeazo] poison || (μεταφ) corrupt, taint.

δηλητηρίαση [δeeleeteereeasee] poisoning || (μεταφ) corruption.

δηλητήριο, το [δeeleeteereeo] poison, venom.

δηλώνω [δeelono] declare, state || (γέννηση κτλ) register, give notice || (εμπόρευμα) enter (good⬭).

δήλωση, η [δeelosee] declaration, statement || (γέννηση κτλ) register.

δημαγωγία, η [δeemagoyeea] demagogy.

δημαρχείο, το [δeemarheeo] town hall || city hall (US).

δήμαρχος, ο [δeemarhos] mayor.

δήμευση, η [δeemevsee] confiscation.

δημεύω [δeemevo] confiscate, seize.

δημητριακός [δeemeetreeakos]: **τα δημητριακά** cereals, crops.

δήμιος, ο [δeemeeos] executioner, hangman.

δημιουργία, η [δeemeeouryeea] creation.

δημιουργικός [δeemeeouryeekos] creative.

δημιουργός, ο [δeemeeourgos] creator.

δημιουργώ [δeemeeourgo] create || establish.

δημοδιδάσκαλος, ο [δeemoδeeδaskalos] primary schoolteacher.

δημοκράτης, ο [δeemokratees] democrat.

δημοκρατία, η [δeemokrateea] democracy || republic.

δημοκρατικός [δeemokrateekos] democratic, republican.

δημοπρασία, η [δeemopraseea] auction.

δήμος, ο [δeemos] municipality.

δημοσία [δeemoseea] (επιρ) publicly.

δημοσίευμα, το [δeemosievma] newspaper article, publication.

δημοσίευση, η [δeemosievsee] publication.

δημοσιεύω [δeemosievo] publish, make known.

δημοσιογράφος, ο [δeemoseeografos] journalist, reporter.

δημόσιο, το [δeemoseeo] the state, the public.

δημόσιος [δeemoseeos] public || (κρατικός) national.

δημοσιότητα, η [δeemoseeoteeta] publicity.

δημότης, ο [ðeemotees] citizen.

δημοτική, η [ðeemoteekee] demotic (Greek).

δημοτικός [ðeemoteekos] municipal || (δημοφιλής) popular.

δημοτικότητα, η [ðeemoteekoteeta] popularity.

δημοφιλής [ðeemofeelees] popular, well-liked.

δημοψήφισμα, το [ðeemopseefeesma] plebiscite.

δημώδης [ðeemoðees] popular, folk.

διά [ðia] for, by, with, about || (μετά γενικής) through, across, by means of || ~ **παντός** forever || ~ **μιας** at one go || ~ **θαλάσσης** by sea.

διαβάζω [ðeeavazo] read, study || (μετά προσοχής) peruse.

διαβάθμιση, η [ðeeavathmeesee] grading, graduation.

διαβάλλω [ðeeavalo] slander, defame, calumniate.

διάβαση, η [ðeeavasee] crossing, passage || (στενό) pass, ford.

διάβασμα, το [ðeeavasma] reading, lecture || studying.

διαβασμένος [ðeevasmenos] learned, prepared (for examination).

διαβατήριο, το [ðeevateereeo] passport.

διαβάτης, ο [ðeeavatees] passer-by.

διαβατός [ðeeavatos] passable || (ποταμός) fordable.

διαβεβαιώνω [ðeeaveveono] assure, assert, affirm.

διαβεβαίωση, η [ðeeaveveosee] assurance, affirmation.

διάβημα, το [ðeeaveema] step, measure, move.

διαβήτης, ο [ðeeaveetees] pair of compasses || (ιατρ) diabetes.

διαβιβάζω [ðeeaveevazo] transmit, forward, convey.

διαβίβαση, η [ðeeaveevasee] transmission, forwarding.

διαβιβρώσκω [ðeeaveevrosko] corrode || (σκουλίκι) eat into || (θάλασσα κτλ) erode.

διαβίωση, η [ðeeaveeosee] living.

διαβλέπω [ðeeavlepo] discern, penetrate, foresee.

διαβόητος [ðeeavoeetos] notorious.

διαβολεμένος [ðeeavolemenos] shrewd, cunning || (μεταφ) devilish.

διαβολή, η [ðeeavolee] slander, calumny.

διαβολικός [ðeeavoleekos] satanic, diabolical.

διάβολος, ο [ðeeavolos] devil, satan || (φασαρίας) noisy, boisterous.

διαβουλεύομαι [ðeeavoulevome] deliberate, confer || (μηχανορραφώ) plot.

διαβρέχω [ðeeavreho] wet, soak, steep.

διάβρωση, η [ðeeavrosee] corrosion.

διαγγέλλω [ðeeangelo] announce, notify.

διάγνωση, η [ðeeagnosee] diagnosis.

διάγραμμα, το [ðeeagrama] diagram, drawing, plan.

διαγραφή, η [ðeeagrafee] cancellation.

διαγράφω [ðeeagrafo] trace out || (σβήνω) efface, cancel.

διάγω [ðeeago] live, pass one's time.

διαγωγή, η [ðeeagoyee] behaviour, conduct, deportment.

διαγωνίζομαι [ðeeagoneezome] compete, contend.

διαγώνιος [ðeeagoneeos] diagonal.

διαγωνισμός, ο [ðeeagoneesmos] competition || (εξετάσεις) examination.

διαδέχομαι [ðeeaðehome] succeed, follow.

διάδηλος [ðeeaðeelos] manifest, evident.

διαδήλωση, η [ðeeaðeelosee] demonstration, manifestation.

διάδημα, το [ðeeaðeema] crown, diadem.

διαδίδω [ðeeaðeeðo] spread, circulate, propagate.

διαδικασία, η [ðeeaðeekaseea] procedure, legal inquiry.

διάδικος, ο, η [ðeeaðeekos] litigant.

διάδοση, η [ðeeaðosee] spreading || rumour.

διαδοχή, η [ðeeaðohee] succession.

διάδοχος, ο, η [ðeeaðohos] successor, crown prince.

διαδραματίζω [ðeeaðramateezo] play (a role), act.

διαδρομή, η [ðeeaðromee] course, distance || (εμβόλου) stroke.

διάδρομος, ο [ðeeaðromos] passage, corridor, hall.

διαζευκτικός [ðeeazevkteekos] (γραμμ) disjunctive.

διάζευξη, η [ðeeazevksee] separation, severance.

διαζύγιο, το [ðeeazeegeeo] divorce.

διάζωμα, το [ðeeazoma] frieze.

διαθέσιμος [ðeeatheseemos] available, free.

διάθεση, η [ðeeathesee] arrangement, disposal || (κέφι) mood, humour.

διαθέτω [ðeeatheto] dispose, arrange || (χρησιμοποιώ) employ, use, make available || (διανέμω) allot.

διαθήκη, η [ðeeatheekee] will, testament.

διάθλαση, η [ðeeathlasee] refraction.

διαίρεση, η [ðeeeresee] division, separation || (μεταφ) discord, difference.

διαιρέτης, ο [ðieretees] divisor, divider.

διαιρώ [ðiero] divide, separate.

διαισθάνομαι [ðiesthanome] feel, have a presentiment.

διαίσθηση, n [ðiestheesee] presentiment.

δίαιτα, n [ðieta] diet.

διαιτησία, n [ðieteeseea] arbitration.

διαιτητής, ο [ðieteetees] arbiter || (ποδοσφαίρου) referee || umpire.

διαιωνίζω [ðieoneezo] perpetuate || protract.

διαιώνιση, n [ðieoneesee] perpetuation.

διακαής [ðeeakaees] ardent, fervent, eager.

διακανονίζω [ðeeakanoneezo] regulate, adjust, settle.

διακατέχω [ðeeakateho] possess.

διάκειμαι [ðeeakeeme] be disposed, be inclined.

διακεκριμένος [ðeeakekreemenos] distinguished, eminent.

διάκενος [ðeeakenos] empty, hollow, vacant || **το διάκενο** void, vacuum.

διακήρυξη, n [ðeeakeereeksee] declaration, proclamation.

διακηρύττω [ðeeakeereeto] declare, proclaim, announce.

διακινδυνεύω [ðeeakeenðeenevo] risk, endanger, hazard.

διακλάδωση, n [ðeeaklaðosee] fork || (δρόμου κτλ) branch.

διακομίζω [ðeeakomeezo] transport, carry.

διάκονος, ο [ðeeakonos] deacon.

διακοπή, n [ðeeakopee] suspension, interruption, recess || (ρεύματος) cut.

διακόπτης, ο [ðeeakoptees] switch, stopcock.

διακόπτω [ðeeakopto] suspend, cut off, interrupt, discontinue.

διάκος, ο [ðeeakos] deacon.

διακόσμηση, n [ðeeakosmeesee] decoration, embellishment.

διακοσμητής, ο [ðeeakosmeetees] decorator.

διάκοσμος, ο [ðeeakosmos] ornamentation, decoration.

διακοσμώ [ðeeakosmo] decorate, adorn.

διακρίνω [ðeeakreeno] discern, discriminate.

διάκριση, n [ðeeakreesee] distinction || (κρίση) discretion.

διακύμανση, n [ðeeakeemansee] fluctuation, undulation.

διακωμωδώ [ðeeakomoðo] ridicule, satirize.

διαλαλώ [ðeealalo] proclaim, cry out, broadcast.

διαλεγμένος [ðeealegmenos] selected, chosen.

διαλέγω [ðeealego] choose, select, pick out.

διάλειμμα, το [ðeealeema] interval, recess || intermission.

διάλειψη, n [ðeealeepsee] irregularity.

διαλεκτική, n [ðeealekteekee] dialectics.

διαλεκτός [ðeealektos] chosen, select.

διάλεκτος, n [ðeealektos] dialect, idiom.

διάλεξη [ðeealeksee] lecture || conversation.

διαλεύκανση, n [ðeealevkansee] elucidation.

διαλλακτικός [ðeealakteekos] conciliatory.

διαλογή, n [ðeealoyee] sorting.

διαλογίζομαι [ðeealoyeezome] meditate, consider.

διαλογισμός, ο [ðeealoyeesmos] reflection, thought.

διάλογος, ο [ðeealogos] dialogue, conversation.

διάλυμα, το [ðeealeema] solution.

διάλυση, n [ðeealeesee] dissolution, decomposition || (εντός υγρού) solution || (εταιρείας κτλ) liquidation || (στρατ) disbanding.

διαλυτός [ðeealeetos] soluble, dissolvable.

διαλύω [ðeealeeo] dissolve || (εταιρεία) liquidate || (συμβόλαιο κτλ) annul, cancel || (εχθρό) disband, defeat, scatter || (αμφιβολία κτλ) dispel.

διαμάντι, το [ðeeamantee] diamond || **διαμαντικά** πλ jewellery, gems.

διαμαρτυρόμενος [ðeeamarteeromenos] Protestant.

διαμαρτυρώ [ðeeamarteero] protest.

διαμάχη, n [ðeeamahee] dispute, fight.

διαμελίζω [ðeeameleezo] dismember.

διαμένω [ðeeameno] reside, live, stay.

διαμέρισμα, το [ðeeamereesma] region, constituency, district || (οικία) apartment, flat.

διάμεσος [ðeeamesos] intermediary, intermediate.

διαμέτρημα, το [ðeeametreema] bore, calibre.

διάμετρος, n [ðeeametros] diameter || gauge.

διαμοιράζω [ðeeameerazo] distribute, share.

διαμονή, n [ðeeamonee] stay, residence, sojourn.

διαμορφώνω [ðeeamorfono] model, shape, form.

διανέμω [ðeeanemo] distribute || divide.

διανόηση, n [ðeeanoeesee] thought || intelligence.

διανοητικώς [ðeeanoeeteekos] intellectually.

διάνοια, n [ðeeaneea] intellect, mind.

διανοίγω [ðeeaneego] open (up).

διανομέας, ο [ðeeanomeas] distributor || (ταχυδρομικός) postman.

διανομή, η [δeeanomee] distribution.

διανοούμενοι, οι [δeeanooumenee] πλ intellectuals.

διανυκτερεύω [δeeaneekterevo] spend the night || stay open all night.

διανύω [δeeaneeo] go through, cover, terminate.

διαξιφισμός, ο [δeeakseefeesmos] sword-thrust || fencing.

διαπασών, η, το [δeeapason] tuning fork || (μουσ) octave.

διαπεραστικός [δeeaperasteekos] piercing, sharp || (βροχή) drenching.

διαπερνώ [δeeaperno] pierce, penetrate, pass through.

διαπιστευτήρια, τα [δeeapeestevteereea] credentials.

διαπιστώνω [δeeapeestono] ascertain, find out, confirm.

διαπίστωση, η [δeeapeestosee] ascertainment.

διάπλαση, η [δeeaplasee] (con)formation || moulding.

διαπλάσσω [δeeaplaso] form, shape || (μεταφ) educate, train.

διάπλατα [δeeaplata] wide-open.

διαπλάτυνση, η [δeeaplateensee] widening.

διαπλέω [δeeapleo] cross over, sail through.

διαπληκτισμός, ο [δeeapleekteesmos] dispute, quarrel.

διαπνοή, η [δeeapnoee] respiration.

διαποτίζω [δeeapoteezo] soak, saturate.

διαπραγματεύομαι [δeeapragmatevome] negotiate || discuss.

διαπραγμάτευση, η [δeeapragmatevsee] negotiation.

διαπράττω [δeeaprato] perpetrate, commit.

διαπρεπής [δeeaprepees] eminent, distinguished.

διαπρέπω [δeeaprepo] excel.

διάπυρος [δeeapeeros] red-hot || (μεταφ) fervent, eager.

διάρθρωση, η [δeearthrosee] articulation, joint, structure.

διάρκεια, η [δeearkeea] duration.

διαρκώ [δeearko] last, endure || continue.

διαρκώς [δeearkos] continually, constantly, always.

διαρρέω [δeeareo] traverse || (δοχείο) leak || (υγρού, νέα κτλ) leak out || (χρόνος) elapse, pass.

διαρρηγνύω [δeeareegneeo] tear, burst open, break.

διάρρηξη, η [δeeareeksee] breaking, rupture || (κλοπή) burglary.

διαρροή, η [δeearoee] flow || (σωλήνος) leakage.

διάρροια, η [δeeareea] diarrhoea.

διαρρυθμίζω [δeeareethmeezo] arrange, regulate.

διαρρύθμιση, η [δeeareethmeesee] arrangement, regulation.

διασαφηνίζω [δeeasafeeneezo] clarify, elucidate.

διασαφήνιση, η [δeeasafeeneesee] clarification, elucidation.

διασάφηση, η [δeeasafeesee] βλ **διασαφήνιση.**

διάσειση, η [δeeaseesee] concussion, shock.

διάσελο, το [δeeaselo] pass.

διάσημος [δeeaseemos] famous, celebrated, renowned.

διασκεδάζω [δeeaskeδazo] scatter, dispel || (ψυχαγωγώ) divert, amuse || (αμεταβ) amuse o.s.

διασκέδαση, η [δeeaskeδasee] dispersion || (ψυχαγωγία) entertainment.

διασκεδαστικός [δeeaskeδasteekos] diverting, entertaining.

διασκευάζω [δeeaskevazo] arrange, modify, alter.

διασκευή, η [δeeaskevee] arrangement, adaptation, modification.

διάσκεψη, η [δeeaskepsee] deliberation || conference.

διασκορπίζω [δeeaskorpeezo] scatter, disperse || (χρήμα) waste.

διάσπαση, η [δeeaspasee] distraction || (ατόμου) splitting.

διασπείρω [δeeaspeero] disseminate, disperse, scatter || (μεταφ) circulate.

διασπορά, η [δeeaspora] dispersion, scattering.

διασπώ [δeeaspo] sever, rupture.

διασταλτικός [δeeastalteekos] dilating, dilative.

διάσταση, η [δeeastasee] separation, disagreement || (μέτρο) dimension.

διασταυρώνω [δeeastavrono] cross || meet.

διασταύρωση, η [δeeastavrosee] crossing || (δρόμων) intersection.

διαστέλλω [δeeastelo] distinguish || (διανοίγω) distend, expand.

διάστημα, το [δeeasteema] space, interval, period || **κατά διαστήματα** from time to time || at intervals.

διαστολή, η [δeeastolee] distinction || (καρδιάς) diastole || (γραμμ) comma.

διαστρεβλώνω [δeeastrevlono] twist, bend || (μεταφ) alter, distort.

διαστρέφω [δeeastrefo] twist, bend || (μεταφ) pervert, corrupt.

διαστροφή, η [δeeastrofee] perversion, distortion.

διασύρω [δeeaseero] (μεταφ) defame, slander, backbite.

διασχίζω [δeeasheezo] tear || (μεταφ) cross, travel through.

διασώζω [δeeasozo] preserve, rescue, deliver.

διάσωση, η [δeeasosee] deliverance, rescue, preservation.

διαταγή, η [δeeatayee] order, command, instruction.

διάταγμα, το [δeeatagma] order, decree, edict.

διάταξη, η [δeeataksee] arrangement || (νόμου κτλ) provision.

διατάραξη, η [δeeataraksee] disturbance, upheaval.

διαταράσσω [δeeataraso] disturb, agitate.

διατάσσω [δeeataso] arrange || order, command.

διατείνομαι [δeeateenome] maintain, declare.

διατελώ [δeeatelo] be, stand.

διατέμνω [δeeatemno] intersect, split.

διατήρηση [δeeateereesee] maintenance, preservation, conservation.

διατηρώ [δeeateero] hold, maintain || preserve, conserve || (ψυχραιμία) keep.

διατίμηση, η [δeeateemeesee] tariff, rate, price list.

διατιμώ [δeeateemo] fix the price of, regulate the sale of.

διατομή [δeeatomee] cross-cut, cut.

διατρέφω [δeeatrefo] keep, feed, support.

διατρέχω [δeeatreho] run through || (απόσταση) cover, traverse.

διάτρηση, η [δeeatreesee] perforation, drilling, cutting.

διάτρητος [δeeatreetos] perforated, drilled.

διατριβή, η [δeeatreevee] stay || (μελέτη) study, thesis || (ασχολία) pastime.

διατροφή, η [δeeatrofee] food, board || (επί διαζυγίου) alimony.

διατρυπώ [δeeatreepo] pierce, bore through.

διάττων, ο [δeeaton] shooting star.

διατυμπανίζω [δeeateembaneezo] divulge, let out, give away.

διατυπώνω [δeeateepono] formulate, state.

διαύγεια, η [δeeavyeea] clearness, transparency.

διαφαίνομαι [δeeafenome] show through, appear, come in sight.

διαφανής [δeeafanees] clear, transparent.

διαφέρω [δeeafero] be different from, differ.

διαφεύγω [δeeafevgo] escape, get away, evade.

διαφημίζω [δeeafeemeezo] advertise.

διαφήμιση, η [δeeafeemeesee] advertisement, advertising.

διαφθείρω [δeeaftheero] spoil, damage || (μεταφ) corrupt.

διαφθορά, η [δeeafthora] corruption, depravity.

διαφορά, η [δeeafora] difference || dissension, contention.

διαφορετικός [δeeaforeteekos] different, dissimilar.

διαφορικό, το [δeeaforeeko] differential.

διαφορικός [δeeaforeekos] differential.

διάφορο, το [δeeaforo] profit, interest, gain.

διαφοροποίηση, η [δeeaforopieesee] differentiation.

διάφορος [δeeaforos] different, various, mixed || τα διάφορα miscellaneous.

διάφραγμα, το [δeeafragma] partition || (ανατ) diaphragm.

διαφυγή η [δeeafeeyee] escape, evasion || (υγρού κτλ) leak, leakage.

διαφύλαξη, η [δeeafeelaksee] preservation, protection.

διαφυλάσσω [δeeafeelaso] preserve, protect, keep.

διαφωνία, η [δeeafoneea] discord, disagreement.

διαφωνώ [δeeafono] disagree, differ.

διαφωτίζω [δeeafoteezo] clear up || enlighten.

διαφώτιση, η [δeeafoteesee] enlightenment.

διαχειρίζομαι [δeeaheereezome] administer, manage, handle.

διαχείριση, η [δeeaheereesee] management, handling, administration.

διαχειριστής, ο [δeeaheereestees] administrator || (στρατ) pay corps officer.

διαχέω [δeeaheo] diffuse, give out.

διάχυση, η [δeeaheesee] diffusion || (μεταφ) effusiveness, gaiety.

διαχυτικός [δeeaheeteekos] effusive, gushing, demonstrative.

διάχυτος [δeeaheetos] diffuse.

διαχωρίζω [δeeahoreezo] separate, divide.

διαχώριση, η [δeeahoreesee] separation.

διαψεύδομαι [δeeapsevδome] contradict o.s., fail.

διαψεύδω [δeeapsevδo] deny, give the lie to || disappoint.

διάψευση, η [δeeapsevsee] denial, contradiction || disappointment.

διγαμία, η [δeegameea] bigamy.

δίγαμος, ο [δeegamos] bigamist.

δίγλωσσος [δeeglosos] bilingual.

δίδαγμα, το [δeeδagma] teaching, moral || (εκκλ) lesson.

διδακτικός [δeeδakteekos] instructive, didactic.

διδακτορική, η [δeeδaktoreekee] (διατριβή) doctorate.

δίδακτρα, τα [δeeδaktra] πλ tuition fees.

διδάκτωρ, ο [δeeδaktor] doctor.

διδασκαλία, η [ðeeðaskeleea]
teaching, instruction.
διδάσκω [ðeeðasko] teach, instruct.
δίδυμος [ðeeðeemos] twin.
διεγείρω [ðieyeero] excite, rouse,
incite.
διέγερση, η [ðieyersees] excitation,
stimulation.
διεζευγμένος [ðiezevgmenos]
divorced.
διεθνής [ðiethnees] international.
διείσδυση, η [ðieesðeesee]
penetration, piercing.
διεισδύω [ðieesðeeo] penetrate, enter,
advance.
διεκδίκηση, η [ðiekðeekeesee] claim,
vindication.
διεκδικώ [ðiekðeeko] claim, contest.
διεκπεραιώνω [ðiekpereono] bring to
a conclusion || (στέλλω) forward.
διεκπεραίωση, η [ðiekpereosee]
forwarding, consignment.
διεκφεύγω [ðiekfevgo] slip away,
escape.
διέλευση, η [ðielevsee] crossing,
passing.
διένεξη, η [ðieneksee] dispute,
quarrel.
διενεργώ [ðienergo] operate, effect,
hold.
διεξάγω [ðieksago] conduct,
accomplish, carry out.
διεξέρχομαι [ðiekserhome] traverse,
travel through || (μεταφ) look into.
διεξοδικός [ðieksoðeekos] lengthy,
extensive, detailed.
διέξοδος, η [ðieksoðos] issue, outlet ||
(μεταφ) way out, alternative.
διέπω [ðiepo] govern, rule.
διερεύνηση, η [ðierevneesee]
investigation, research.
διερευνητικός [ðierevneeteekos]
searching, exploratory.
διερευνώ [ðierevno] search, explore,
examine.
διερμηνέας, ο [ðiermeeneas]
interpreter, translator.
διερμηνεύω [ðiermeenevo] interpret,
translate.
διέρχομαι [ðierhome] pass by, cross.
διερωτώμαι [ðierotome] ask o.s.,
wonder.
διεσπαρμένος [ðiesparmenos]
dispersed.
διεστραμμένος [ðiestramenos]
perverse, wicked.
διετής [ðietees] lasting two years || (επί
φυτών) biennial.
διετία, η [ðieteea] (space of) two
years.
διευθέτηση, η [ðievtheteesee]
arrangement, settlement.
διευθετώ [ðievtheto] arrange, settle ||
adjust.

διεύθυνση, η [ðievtheensee] address
|| direction || (εταιρείας) management.
διευθυντής, ο [ðievtheentees]
director || (σχολής) principal || (μουσ)
conductor || (θεάτρου) manager ||
(εφημερίδος) editor || (φυλακών)
governor, warden || (σωματείου)
president || (προσωπικού) personnel
manager.
διευθύνω [ðievtheeno] direct, guide ||
(επιχείρηση) manage || (εφημερίδα) edit ||
(βιομηχανία) handle, manage, direct ||
(έργα) superintend, oversee ||
(ορχήστρα) lead, conduct.
διευκόλυνση, η [ðievkoleensee]
easing, help.
διευκολύνω [ðievkoleeno] facilitate,
help forward.
διευκρινίζω [ðievkreeneezo] clear up,
explain.
διευκρίνιση, η [ðievkreeneesee]
elucidation, explanation.
διεύρυνση, η [ðievreensee] widening,
broadening, enlargement.
διεφθαρμένος [ðieftharmenos]
corrupt, immoral, dissolute.
δίζυγο, το [ðeezeego] parallel bars.
διήγημα, το [ðieegeema] story, tale.
διήγηση, η [ðieegeesee] narration.
διηγούμαι [ðieegoume] narrate,
relate, tell.
διήθηση, η [ðieetheesee] filtration,
percolation.
διηρημένος [ðieereemenos] divided,
separated.
διίσταμαι [ðieestame] (μεταφ) stand
apart || (μεταφ) disagree.
διισχυρίζομαι [ðieesheereezome]
maintain.
δικάζω [ðeekazo] try, judge.
δικαιόγραφο, το [ðeekeografo] title
deed.
δικαιοδοσία, η [ðeekeoðoseea]
jurisdiction, province.
δικαιολόγηση, η [ðeekeoloyeesee]
justification, excuse.
δικαιολογητικά, τα
[ðeekeoloyeeteeka] πλ documentary
proof.
δικαιολογία, η [ðeekeoloyeea]
justification, excuse.
δικαιολογώ [ðeekeologo] justify,
excuse, vindicate.
δίκαιο, το [ðeekeo] justice, right || law.
δίκαιος [ðeekeos] fair, just, righteous.
δικαιοσύνη, η [ðeekeoseenee]
justice, fairness.
δικαιούχος, ο [ðeekeouhos]
beneficiary.
δικαιώνω [ðeekeono] side with ||
justify, vindicate.
δικαίωμα, το [ðeekeoma] right, claim.
δικαίωση, η [ðeekeosee] justification,
vindication.

δίκανο, το [ðeekano] double-barrelled shotgun.

δικάσιμος, η [ðeekaseemos] day of trial.

δικαστήριο, το [ðeekasteereeo] law court, court of justice, tribunal.

δικαστής, ο [ðeekastees] judge, justice, magistrate.

δικαστικός [ðeekasteekos] judicial, judiciary.

δικέφαλος [ðeekefalos] two-headed.

δίκη, η [ðeekee] trial, suit, lawsuit, case.

δικηγόρος, ο, [ðeekeegoros] lawyer, barrister, attorney.

δικηγορώ [ðeekeegoro] practise as a lawyer, plead.

δικογραφία, η [ðeekografeea] file of proceedings || (δικηγόρου) brief.

δικονομία, η [ðeekonomeea] procedure.

δίκταμο, το [ðeektamo] dittany.

δικτατορία, η [ðeektatoreea] dictatorship.

δικτατορικός [ðeektatoreekos] dictatorial.

δίκτυο, το [ðeekteeo] net, network || (μεταφ) snare, trap.

δικτυωτό, το [ðeekteeoto] wire netting, lattice, grille, trellis.

δίλημμα, το [ðeeleema] dilemma.

διμερής [ðeemerees] bipartite.

διμοιρία, η [ðeemeereea] platoon, section.

δίνη, η [ðeenee] whirlpool, whirlwind.

δίνω [ðeeno] give, grant || (τιμή) offer || (παράγω) produce, yield || (μάχη) give battle || (γροθιά) deal a blow to.

διογκώνω [ðeeongono] swell, inflate.

διόγκωση, η [ðeeongosee] swelling, inflation.

διόδια, τα [ðeeoðeea] πλ toll || (ναυτ) port toll.

δίοδος, η [ðeeoðos] passage, pass, defile.

διοίκηση, η [ðieekeesee] administration, command.

διοικητήριο, το [ðieekeeteereeo] prefecture, commissioner's office.

διοικητής, ο [ðieekeetees] governor, commissioner, commandant.

διοικητικός [ðieekeeteekos] administrative.

διοικώ [ðieeko] administer, govern, rule, command.

διόλου [ðeeolou] (επιρ) not at all || όλως ~ entirely, quite.

διοξείδιο, το [ðeeokseeðeeo] dioxide.

διοπτεύω [ðeeopteevo] observe with binoculars || (ναυτ) take bearings of.

διόπτρα, η [ðeeoptra] binoculars.

διόραση, η [ðeeorasee] perspicuity.

διορατικός [ðeeorateekos] clear-sighted || (πνεύμα) shrewd, keen.

διορατικότητα, η [ðeeorateekoteeta] perspicacity.

διοργανώνω [ðeeorganono] organize, form, arrange.

διοργάνωση, η [ðeeorganosee] organization, arrangement.

διορθώνω [ðeeorthono] correct, put straight || (πανταλόνι) patch, mend || (μεταφ) remedy, make good.

διόρθωση, η [ðeeorthosee] correction, putting right.

διορθωτής, ο [ðeeorthotees] (τυπογρ) proofreader.

διορία, η [ðeeoreea] time limit, term, delay.

διορίζω [ðeeoreezo] appoint || order, fix.

διορισμένος [ðeeoreesmenos] appointed.

διορισμός, ο [ðeeoreesmos] appointment.

διόροφος [ðeeorofos] two-storeyed.

διόρυξη, η [ðeeoreeksee] digging, excavation.

διότι [ðeeotee] because.

διουρητικός [ðeeoureeteekos] diuretic.

διοχέτευση, η [ðeeohetevsee] (ηλεκ) conduct || (ύδατος) conveyance.

διοχετεύω [ðeeohetevo] conduct, convey || (μεταφ) transmit, divert.

δίπατος [ðeepatos] two-storeyed.

δίπλα, η [ðeepla] fold, pleat, wrinkle.

δίπλα [ðeepla] (επιρ) by, near, next door, close.

διπλά [ðeepla] twice as much.

διπλανός [ðeeplanos] nearby, next-door, adjacent.

διπλαρώνω [ðeeplarono] accost || (ναυτ) come alongside.

διπλασιάζω [ðeeplaseeazo] double.

διπλασιασμός, ο [ðeeplaseeasmos] reduplication.

διπλάσιος [ðeeplaseeos] double, twice as much.

διπλός [ðeeplos] double.

διπλότυπο, το [ðeeploteepo] duplicate, stub, counterfoil.

δίπλωμα, το [ðeeploma] diploma, degree || (τύλιγμα) folding, wrapping.

διπλωμάτης, ο [ðeeplomatees] diplomat.

διπλωματία, η [ðeeplomateea] diplomacy.

διπλωματικός [ðeeplomateekos] diplomatic.

διπλωματούχος [ðeeplomatouhos] having a diploma, holding a degree.

διπλώνω [ðeeplono] fold.

δίπλωση, η [ðeeplosee] folding, wrapping.

δίποδος [ðeepoðos] two-legged, two-footed.

διπρόσωπος [ðeeprosopos] two-faced, deceitful.

δίς [δees] twice.

διόκκι, το [δeesakee] saddlebag, travelling bag.

δισέγγονο, το [δeesengono] great-grandchild.

δισεκατομμύριο, το [δeesekatomeereeo] billion.

δίσεκτο, το [δeesekto]: ~ έτος leap year.

δισκίο, το [δeeskeeo] (ιατρ) tablet.

δισκοβόλος, ο [δeeskovolos] discus thrower.

δίσκος, ο [δeeskos] tray || (ζυγού) pan, scale || (αθλητ) discus || (πλίου κτλ) disk || (εκκλ) collection plate || (γραμμοφώνου) record.

δισταγμός, ο [δeestagmos] hesitation, doubt.

διστάζω [δeestazo] hesitate, doubt.

διστακτικός [δeestaktikos] hesitant, irresolute.

δίστηλος [δeesteelos] two-columned.

δίστιχο, το [δeesteeho] distich, couplet.

δισύλλαβος [δeeseelavos] of two syllables.

δίτροχος [δeetrohos] two-wheeled.

διυλίζω [δieeleezo] filter, distil, strain.

διύλιση η [δieeleesee] filtering, straining.

διυλιστήριο, το [δieeleesteereeo] filter, strainer || (πετρελαίου) refinery.

διφθερίτιδα, η [δeefthereeteeδa] diphtheria.

δίφθογγος, η [δeefthongos] diphthong.

διφορούμενος [δeeforoumenos] ambiguous.

δίφραγκο, το [δeefrango] two-drachma piece.

δίφυλλος [δeefeelos] two-leaved.

διχάζομαι [δeehazome] (μεταφ) become disunited, disagree.

διχάζω [δeehazo] divide, split || (μεταφ) estrange, disunite.

διχάλη, η [δeehalee] pitchfork.

διχαλωτός [δeehalotos] forked, cloven.

διχασμός, ο [δeehasmos] division || disagreement.

διχόνοια, η [δeehoneea] dissension, discord.

διχοτόμος [δeehotomos] bisector.

διχοτομώ [δeehotomo] bisect.

δίχρονος [δeehronos] (μηχανή) two-stroke (engine).

δίχως [δeehos] without || ~ άλλο without fail.

δίψα, η [δeepsa] thirst.

διψασμένος [δeepsasmenos] thirsty, eager (for).

διψώ [δeepso] feel thirsty || thirst for, be eager for.

διωγμός, ο [δeeogmos] persecution.

διώκω [δeeoko] pursue, chase, expel, persecute || (μεταφ) banish, dispel.

δίωξη, η [δeeoksee] persecution, hunting.

διώρυγα, η [δeeoreega] canal.

διώχνω [δeeohno] βλ διώκω.

δόγμα, το [δogma] dogma, creed, doctrine.

δογματικός [δogmateekos] dogmatic(al).

δόκανο, το [δokano] trap || (μεταφ) lure, snare.

δοκάρι, το [δokaree] beam, rafter, girder.

δοκιμάζω [δokeemazo] taste, try out || (αυτοκίνητο) test, try || (ρούχα) fit || (υποφέρω) undergo, suffer.

δοκιμασία, η [δokeemaseea] suffering.

δοκιμαστικός [δokeemasteekos] trial, test || ~ σωλήνας test tube.

δοκιμή, η [δokeemee] trial, test, testing || (θέατρο) rehearsal || (ρούχα) fitting.

δοκίμιο, το [δokeemeeo] treatise || (τυπογρ) printer's proof.

δόκιμος [δokeemos] esteemed, first-rate || ο ~ cadet.

δοκός, η [δokos] girder, beam.

δόλιος [δoleeos] fraudulent, crafty.

δόλιος [δoleeos] wretched, unlucky, poor.

δολιότης, η [δoleeotees] deceit, fraudulence, fraud.

δολοπλόκος [δoloplokos] treacherous, artful.

δόλος, ο [δolos] fraud, deceit, guile.

δολοφονία, η [δolofoneea] murder.

δολοφονικός [δolofoneekos] murderous.

δολοφόνος, ο, η [δolofonos] assassin, murderer.

δολοφονώ [δolofono] murder, assassinate.

δόλωμα, το [δoloma] bait, decoy.

δόνηση, η [δoneesee] vibration || (σεισμός) tremor, shock.

δόντι, το [δontee] tooth || (ελέφαντος) tusk || (μηχαν) cog.

δονώ [δono] vibrate, shake.

δόξα, η [δoksa] glory.

δοξάζω [δoksazo] glorify, celebrate, extol.

δοξάρι, το [δoksaree] (μους) bow.

δοξολογία, η [δoksoloyeea] doxology, Te Deum.

δόρυ, το [δoree] spear.

δορυφόρος, ο [δoreeforos] satellite.

δοσίλογος [δoseelogos] quisling.

δόση, η [δosee] portion || dose || (πληρωμή) instalment.

δοσοληψία, η [δosoleepseea] transaction.

δοτική, η [δoteekee] (γραμμ) dative (case).

δούκας, ο [ðoukas] duke.
δούκισσα, η [ðoukeesa] duchess.
δουλεία, η [ðouleea] slavery,
servitude.
δουλειά, η [ðoulia] work, affair,
business.
δούλεμα, το [ðoulema] teasing.
δουλευτής, ο [ðoulevtees] hard
worker, industrious worker.
δουλεύω [ðoulevo] work, operate ||
(έχω δουλειά) have a job || (ρολόι κτλ)
work, operate || (περιπαίζω) tease.
δούλη, η [ðoulee] slave.
δουλικός [ðouleekos] servile, slavish.
δουλοπρεπής [ðouloprepees] servile,
mean.
δούλος, ο [ðoulos] slave || servant.
δουλώνω [ðoulono] enslave, subjugate.
δούπος, ο [ðoupos] thump, bump.
δοχείο, το [ðoheeo] receptacle,
vessel, pot.
δρακόντειος [ðrakonteeos] (μεταφ)
severe, harsh.
δράκος, ο [ðrakos] ogre, dragon.
δράμα, το [ðrama] drama || (μεταφ)
trouble.
δραματική, η [ðramateekee] πλ
dramatics.
δραματικός [ðramateekos] dramatic,
tragic.
δράμι, το [ðrameeo] dram || (μεταφ)
tiny amount.
δραπετεύω [ðrapetevo] escape.
δραπέτης ο [ðrapetees] fugitive.
δράση, η [ðrasee] activity, action ||
άμεσος ~ flying squad.
δραστήριος [ðrasteereeos] active,
energetic, vigorous.
δραστηριότητα, η
[ðrasteereeoteeta] activity, energy,
effectiveness.
δράστης, ο, η [ðrastees] perpetrator,
culprit.
δραστικός [ðrasteekos] efficacious,
drastic, effective.
δραχμή, η [ðrahmee] drachma.
δρεπάνι, το [ðrepanee] sickle.
δριμύς [ðreemees] sharp, bitter,
severe, keen.
δρομάς, η [ðromas] dromedary.
δρομεάς, ο [ðromeas] runner.
δρομολόγιο, το [ðromoloyeeo]
itinerary || timetable.
δρόμος, ο [ðromos] road, street ||
(αθλητ) race || (απόσταση) distance.
δροσερός [ðroseros] cool, fresh.
δροσιά, η [ðrosia] freshness || dew.
δροσίζομαι [ðroseezome] refresh o.s.,
cool down.
δροσίζω [ðroseezo] cool, refresh || get
cool.
δροσιστικός [ðroseesteekos]
refreshing.
δρυμός, ο [ðreemos] forest, wood.

δρυοκολάπτης, ο [ðreeokolaptees]
woodpecker.
δρύς, η [ðrees] oak.
δρω [ðro] act, do, take effect.
δυάδα, η [ðeeaða] couple, pair.
δυαδικός [ðeeaðeekos] binary || dual.
δυΐκός [ðieekos] (γραμμ) dual
(number).
δύναμαι [ðeename] can, may || be able
to.
δυναμική, η [ðeenameekee]
dynamics.
δυναμικός [ðeenameekos] energetic,
dynamic.
δύναμη, η [ðeenamee] strength,
might, power, force.
δυναμίτιδα, η [ðeenameeteeða]
dynamite.
δυναμό, το [ðeenamo] dynamo.
δυνάμωμα, το [ðeenamoma]
intensification, strengthening.
δυναμώνω [ðeenamono] strengthen,
make stronger || (υγεία) become
stronger.
δυναμωτικός [ðeenamoteekos]
fortifying, strengthening || (ιατρ) tonic.
δυναστεία, η [ðeenastea] dynasty,
regime, rule.
δυνάστης, ο [ðeenastees] ruler,
potentate || (μεταφ) oppressor, despot.
δυνατά [ðeenata] strongly, hard ||
loudly.
δυνατός [ðeenatos] strong, powerful ||
(κυβέρνηση) powerful || (φωνή) loud ||
(άνοδος) possible || δυνατό! possibly!,
maybe!
δυνατότητα, η [ðeenatoteeta]
possibility.
δύο [ðeeo] two.
δυόσμος, ο [ðeeosmos] mint,
spearmint.
δυσανάγνωστος [ðeesanagnostos]
illegible.
δυσανάλογος [ðeesanalogos]
disproportionate.
δυσανασχετώ [ðeesanasheto] be
anxious, be indignant, get angry.
δυσαρέσκεια, η [ðeesareskeea]
displeasure, discontent.
δυσάρεστος [ðeesarestos]
unpleasant, disagreeable.
δυσαρεστημένος
[ðeeasaresteemenos] displeased,
dissatisfied.
δυσαρεστώ [ðeesaresto] displease,
dissatisfy.
δυσβάστακτος [ðeesvastaktos]
unbearable, heavy, overwhelming.
δύσβατος [ðeesvatos] inaccessible,
rough.
δυσειδής [ðeeseeðees] ugly, unsightly.
δυσεντερία, η [ðeesentereea]
dysentery.
δισεπίλυτος [ðeesepeeleetos] difficult
to solve.

δισεύρετος [δeesevretos] difficult to find.

δυσθυμία, η [δeestheemeea] sadness, depression.

δύσθυμος [δeestheemos] depressed, sad.

δύση, η [δeesee] west || (ηλίου) setting || (μεταφ) decline.

δύσκαμπτος [δeeskambtos] rigid, stiff, inflexible.

δυσκινησία, η [δeeskeeneeseea] sluggishness.

δυσκοιλιότητα, η [δeeskeeleeoteeta] constipation.

δυσκολεύομαι [δeeskolevome] find difficult, find hard, be hard put (to).

δυσκολεύω [δeeskolevo] make difficult, make hard.

δυσκολία, η [δeeskoleea] difficulty.

δυσκολο- [δeeskolo] (first component) difficult, hard.

δύσκολος [δeeskolos] difficult || (άνθρωπος) hard to please.

δυσμένεια, η [δeesmeneea] disfavour, disgrace.

δυσμενής [δeesmenees] adverse, unfavourable.

δύσμορφος [δeesmorfos] deformed, ugly.

δυσνόητος [δeesnoeetos] difficult to understand.

δυσοίωνος [δeeseeonos] inauspicious, ill-omened.

δυσοσμία, η [δeesosmeea] bad smell, stench, offensive odour.

δύσπεπτος [δeespeptos] indigestible.

δυσπιστία, η [δeespeesteea] mistrust, incredulity.

δύσπιστος [δeespeestos] incredulous, distrustful, unbelieving.

δυσπιστώ [δeespeesto] distrust, mistrust.

δύσπνοια, η [δeespneea] difficult breathing.

δυσπρόσιτος [δeesproseetos] inaccessible.

δυστοκία, η [δeestokeea] difficult birth || (μεταφ) indecision.

δύστροπος [δeestropos] perverse, peevish.

δυστροπώ [δeestropo] behave peevishly.

δυστύχημα, το [δeesteeheema] accident, stroke of bad luck.

δυστυχής [δeesteehees] unhappy, unfortunate.

δυστυχία, η [δeesteeheea] unhappiness, adversity, poverty.

δυστυχισμένος [δeesteeheesmenos] βλ δυστυχής.

δυστυχώ [δeesteeho] be unhappy, be unfortunate, be poor.

δυσφημίζω [δeesfeemeezo] defame, slander.

δυσφήμιση, η [δeesfeemeesee] calumny, slander.

δυσφόρητος [δeesforeetos] hard to endure.

δυσφορώ [δeesforo] be displeased || (με κάτι) be discontented.

δυσχεραίνω [δeeshereno] impede, make difficult.

δυσχέρεια, η [δeeshereea] difficulty || hardship.

δυσχερής [δeesherees] difficult.

δύσχρηστος [δeeshreestos] unwieldy, inconvenient, awkward.

δυσωδία, η [δeesoδeea] stench, stink.

δύτης, ο [δeetees] diver.

δυτικός [δeeteekos] west(ern).

δύω [δeeo] set || (μεταφ) decline, wane.

δώδεκα [δοδeka] twelve.

δωδεκάγωνο, το [δοδekagono] dodecagon.

δωδεκαδάκτυλο, το [δοδekaδakteelo] duodenum.

δωδεκάδα, η [δοδekaδa] dozen.

δωδεκαετής [δοδekaetees] twelve years old.

δωδεκαπλάσιος [δοδekaplaseeos] twelve-fold.

δωδέκατος [δοδekatos] twelfth.

δώμα, το [δoma] flat roof, terrace || apartment.

δωμάτιο, το [δomateeo] room || (ύπνου) bedroom.

δωρεά, η [δorea] bequest, present, gift || ~v (επιρ) gratis, free, for nothing.

δωροδοκία, η [δoroδokeea] bribery, corruption.

δωροδοκώ [δoroδoko] bribe, corrupt.

δώρο, το [δoro] gift, present.

δωσίλογος [δoseealogos] responsible, answerable.

Ε, ε

έ [e] (επιφ) well!, hey!, hallo!

εάν [ean] βλ αν.

έαρ, το [ear] spring.

εαυτός [eaftos] oneself || καθ' εαυτού really, exactly, precisely.

εβδομάδα, η [evδomaδa] week.

εβδομαδιαίος [evδomaδieos] weekly.

έβδομος [evδomos] seventh.

εβραϊκός [evraeekos] Jewish.

Εβραίος, ο [evreos] Hebrew, Jew.

έγγαμος [engamos] married.

εγγίζω [engeezo] draw near || (μεταφ) touch.

εγγλέζικος [englezeekos] English.

Εγγλέζος, ο [englezos] Englishman.

εγγόνι, το [engonee] grandchild.

εγγονός, ο [engonos] grandson.

εγγραφή, η [engrafee] registration, record, entry.

έγγραφο, το [engrafo] document.

εγγράφω [engrafo] register, enrol || (μάθημ) inscribe.

εγγύηση, η [engieesee] security, guarantee, bail.

εγγύς [engees] near, at hand.

εγγυώμαι [engeeome] guarantee, vouch for.

εγείρω [eyeero] raise, build.

έγερση, η [eyersee] raising, building || (από ύπνο) awakening.

εγκαθίσταμαι [engkatheestame] settle, put up, settle o.s.

εγκαθιστώ [engkatheesto] set up, settle, establish.

εγκαίνια, τα [engkeneea] πλ inauguration, opening.

έγκαιρος [engkeros] timely, opportune.

εγκάρδιος [engkarðeeos] cordial, affectionate.

εγκάρσιος [engkarseeos] transverse, slanting, oblique.

εγκαταλείπω [engkataleepo] abandon, desert.

εγκατάσταση, η [engkatastasee] installation, establishing.

έγκαυμα, το [engkavma] burn.

έγκειται [engkeete]: σε σας ~ it rests with you.

εγκέφαλος, ο [engkefalos] brain.

εγκλείω [engkleeo] enclose || confine || lock up.

έγκλημα, το [engkleema] crime || sin || ~τίας, ο criminal || ~τικός criminal || ~τικότης, η delinquency, wrongdoing, crime.

εγκοπή, η [engkopee] incision, notch, groove.

εγκόσμιος [engkosmeeos] mundane, worldly || social.

εγκράτεια, η [engkrateea] sobriety, moderation, temperance.

εγκρίνω [engkreeno] approve, ratify.

έγκριση, η [engkreesee] approval, sanction.

εγκύκλιος, η [engkeekleeos] circular letter.

εγκυκλοπαίδεια, η [engkeeklopeðeea] encyclopaedia.

έγκυος [engkeeos] pregnant.

έγκυρος [engkeeros] valid, sound, well-grounded.

εγκώμιο, το [engkomeeo] praise.

έννοια, η [egneea] care, anxiety, concern.

εγχείρηση, η [engheereesee] operation.

εγχειρίδιο, το [engheereeðeeo] manual.

έγχρωμος [enghromos] coloured.

εγχώριος [enghoreeos] local, native, domestic.

εγώ [ego] I || (ουσ) το ~ ego ||

εγωισμός, ο [egoeesmos] pride, conceit, selfishness.

έδαφος, το [eðafos] ground, earth, soil.

έδρα, η [eðra] seat, chair || (ανατ) bottom || (εκκλ) see.

εδραιώνω [eðreono] establish, strengthen, make firm.

εδρεύω [eðrevo] reside, have one's seat.

εδώ [eðo] here || ~ και τρία χρόνια three years ago.

εδώλιο, το [eðoleeo] bench, seat.

εθελοντής, ο [ethelontees] volunteer.

εθελουσίως [ethelouseeos] voluntarily.

έθιμο, το [etheemo] custom, tradition || habit.

εθιμοτυπία, η [etheemoteepeea] formality, etiquette.

εθνάρχης, ο [ethnarhees] national leader.

εθνικός [ethneekos] national.

εθνικότητα, η [ethneekoteeta] nationality.

εθνικόφρων [ethneekofron] patriotic, nationalistic.

έθνος, το [ethnos] nation.

ειδάλλως [eeðalos] if not, otherwise.

ειδεμή [eeðemee] otherwise.

ειδήμων [eeðeemon] expert, skilled, well-informed.

ειδήσεις, οι [eeðeesees] πλ news.

ειδικός [eeðeekos] special, particular || (άνθρωπος) specialist.

ειδοποίηση, η [eeðopieesee] notification, notice.

ειδοποιώ [eeðopeeo] notify, inform, advise.

είδος, το [eeðos] sort, kind, type || (βοτ) species || τα είδη goods, wares || kinds.

ειδύλλιο, το [eeðeeleeo] love affair || idyll.

ειδωλολάτρης, ο [eeðololatrees] pagan, heathen.

είδωλο, το [eeðolo] idol || image.

είθισται [eetheeste] it is the custom.

εικασία, η [eekaseea] conjecture, guess.

εικαστικός [eekasteekos] conjectural || εικαστικαί τέχναι fine arts.

εικόνα [eekona] image, picture || (εκκλ) icon.

εικονίζω [eekoneezo] portray, depict, represent.

εικονικός [eekoneekos] figurative || (επίθεση) sham || (πράξη) bogus || (τιμή) conventional.

εικόνισμα, το [eekoneesma] portrait || (αγιογραφία) icon.

εικονογραφία, η [eekonografeea] illustration || (εκκλ) iconography.

εικονοστάσι(ο), το [eekonostasee(o)] (εκκλ) shrine, screen.

είκοσι [eekosee] twenty.

εικοστός [eekostos] twentieth.

ειλικρίνεια, η [eeleekreeneea] sincerity, frankness.

ειλικρινής [eeleekreenees] sincere, candid.

είμαι [eeme] I am, I'm.

είναι [eene] be, is, it is || **το** ~ being.

ειρήνη, η [eereenee] peace.

ειρηνικός [eereeneekos] peaceful.

ειρηνοδικείο, το [eereenoδeekeeo] magistrate's court.

ειρμός, ο [eermos] train of thought, continuity.

ειρωνεύομαι [eeronevome] speak derisively, speak ironically.

ειρωνεία, η [eeroneea] irony, mockery.

εις [ees] in, among, at || (χρόνος) within || to, into, on.

εισαγγελέας, ο [eesangeleas] public prosecutor || district attorney (US).

εισάγω [eesago] import || (νομοσχέδιο) introduce || (φέρω πρώτα) introduce for the first time || (παρουσιάζω) present ||
εισαγωγέας, ο importer ||
εισαγωγή, η importation || (παρονσίαση) introduction ||
εισαγωγικά, τα inverted commas.

εισβάλλω [eesvalo] invade || (ποταμός) flow into.

εισβολή, η [eesvolee] invasion.

εισέρχομαι [eeserhome] come in, enter, go in.

εισήγηση, η [eeseeyeesee] report || suggestion.

εισηγούμαι [eeseegoume] propose, move || introduce.

εισιτήριο, το [eeseeteereeo] ticket.

εισόδημα, το [eesoδeema] income, revenue.

είσοδος, η [eesoδos] entry, entrance || admission.

εισπνέω [eespneo] inhale, breathe in.

εισπράκτορας, ο [eespraktoras] conductor || collector.

είσπραξη, η [eespraksee] collection || receipt.

εισπράττω [eesprato] collect.

εισφορά, η [eesfora] contribution.

εισχωρώ [eeshoro] penetrate, intrude, get in.

είτε [eete]: ~ ... ~ either ... or, whether ... or.

εκ [ek] from, out of, by, of || **εξ ανάγκης** of necessity || ~ **νέου** again || **εξ ίσου** equally.

εκ-, εξ- [ek, eks] out, off || completely, wholly.

έκαστος, ο [ekastos] each, every one || **καθ' εκάστην** every day || **τα καθ'έκαστα** the details.

εκάστοτε [ekastote] each time.

εκατέρωθεν [ekaterothen] on both sides, mutually.

εκατό [ekato] hundred || **τά** ~ per cent.

εκατομμύριο, το [ekatomeereeo] million.

εκατομμυριούχος, ο [ekatomeereeouhos] millionaire.

εκατονταετηρίδα, η [ekatontaeteereeδa] century || centenary.

εκατονταπλάσιος [ekatontaplaseeos] hundredfold.

εκατοστάρι, το [ekatostaree] hundred-drachma note.

εκατοστόμετρο, το [ekatostometro] centimetre.

εκατοστός [ekatostos] hundredth.

εκβάλλω [ekvalo] take out, extract || (απομακρύνω) repudiate || (εχθρό) drive out || (επί ποταμών) flow into.

έκβαση, η [ekvasee] issue, outcome, result.

εκβιάζω [ekveeazo] (κάποιο) force, compel || blackmail || (διάβαση κτλ) force.

εκβολή η [ekvolee] ejection || (ποταμού) mouth, estuary.

έκδηλος [ekδeelos] manifest, evident, obvious.

εκδηλώνω [ekδeelono] show, reveal.

εκδίδω [ekδeeδo] issue, publish || (απόφαση) pronounce || (συναλλαγματική) draw || (εγκληματία κτλ) extradite.

εκδίκηση, η [ekδeekeesee] vengeance, revenge.

εκδικητικός [ekδeekeeteekos] revengeful, vindictive.

εκδικούμαι [ekδeekoume] take revenge on, get even with.

εκδιώκω [ekδeeoko] expel, oust || (στρατ) dislodge, drive out.

εκδορά, η [ekδora] abrasion || skinning.

έκδοση, η [ekδosee] publication, edition || (χαρτονομίσματος) issue || (παραλλαγή) version, story || (εγκληματία κτλ) extradition.

εκδότης, ο [ekδotees] publisher, editor.

εκδοτικός [ekδoteekos] publishing || ~ **οίκος** publishing house.

εκδοχή, η [ekδohee] interpretation, version.

εκδρομή η [ekδromee] excursion, outing, trip.

εκεί [ekee] there || ~ **που** instead of, while, whereas.

εκείνος [ekeenos] he, that one there.

εκεχειρία, η [ekeheereea] truce, armistice.

έκθαμβος [ekthamvos] dazzled, astounded.

έκθεμα, το [ekthema] exhibit.

έκθεση, n [ekthesee] (στο ύπαιθρο) exposure || (ανθέων κτλ) exhibition || (εμπορευμάτων) display, exposition || (γραπτή) composition.

εκθέτης, ο [ekthetees] exhibitor || (μαθημ) exponent.

έκθετος [ekthetos] exposed.

εκθέτω [ektheto] expose, display, exhibit || (την ζωή) expose, imperil || (τέκνο) abandon || (σχέδια) state, disclose || (μεταφ) lay bare, expose.

εκθρονίζω [ekthroneezo] dethrone.

εκκαθαρίζω [ekathareezo] clear out, clean || (λογαριασμό) liquidate, settle.

εκκεντρικός [ekentreekos] eccentric.

εκκενώ [ekeno] empty (out), vacate || (ποτήρι κτλ) drain || (όπλο) fire || (οικία) leave.

εκκένωση, n [ekenosee] evacuation, emptying || (ηλεκ) discharge.

εκκίνηση, n [ekeeneesee] departure, starting off.

εκκλησία, n [ekleeseea] church || **εκκλησιαστικός** ecclesiastic(al).

έκκληση, n [ekleesee] appeal.

εκκρεμής [ekremees] unsettled, pending.

εκκωφαντικός [ekofanteekos] deafening.

εκλέγω [eklego] choose, pick out || elect.

έκλειψη, n [ekleepsee] eclipse || (μεταφ) disappearance.

εκλεκτικός [eklekteekos] choosy, selective.

εκλεκτός [eklektos] choice, select, picked || **ΟΙ ΕΚΛΕΚΤΟΙ** élite.

εκλιπαρώ [ekleeparo] entreat, implore.

εκλογέας, ο [eklogeas] elector, voter.

εκλογή, n [ekloyee] choice, selection || election.

εκλογές, οι [ekloges] ηλ elections.

εκλογικός [ekloyeekos] electoral.

εκμαγείο, το [ekmayeeo] (plaster) cast.

εκμαιεύω [ekmeyevo] extract, elicit.

εκμεταλλεύομαι [ekmetalevome] exploit.

εκμηδενίζω [ekmeedeneezo] annihilate.

εκμίσθωση, n [ekmeesthosee] leasing, lease.

εκμισθωτής, ο [ekmeesthotees] lessor, hirer.

εκμυστηρεύομαι [ekmeesteerevome] confide a secret, confess.

εκνευρίζω [eknevreezo] annoy, exasperate.

εκούσιος [ekouseeos] voluntary || willing.

εκπαίδευση, n [ekpeδevsee] education, training.

εκπαιδευτήριο, το [ekpeδevteereeo] school, institute.

εκπαιδευτικός [ekpeδevteekos] educational || (δάσκαλος) schoolteacher.

εκπαιδεύω [ekpeδevo] educate, train, instruct.

εκπατρίζω [ekpatreezo] expatriate.

εκπέμπω [ekpembo] send forth, emit || (από ραδιοφώνου) broadcast.

εκπίπτω [ekpeepto] decline, fall || (μεταφ) deduct, reduce, lower.

εκπληκτικός [ekpleekteekos] astonishing, surprising.

έκπληξη, n [ekpleeksee] surprise, astonishment.

εκπληρώ [ekpleero] fulfil, perform.

εκπλήσσω [ekpleeso] surprise, astonish.

εκπνέω [ekpneo] exhale || (πεθαίνω) die || (μεταφ) expire, terminate.

εκποιώ [ekpeeo] sell, dispose of.

εκπομπή, n [ekpombee] emission || (ραδιοφώνου) broadcast.

εκπρόθεσμος [ekprothesmos] overdue.

εκπρόσωπος, ο [ekprosopos] representative.

εκπροσωπώ [ekprosopo] represent.

έκπτωση, n [ekptosee] decline, fall || (δικαιωμάτων) loss || (τιμής κτλ) reduction, rebate, discount, deduction.

εκρήγνυμαι [ekreegneeme] explode, erupt, burst.

εκρηκτικός [ekreekteekos] explosive.

έκρηξη, n [ekreeksee] explosion, eruption, outburst.

εκσκαφή, n [ekskafee] excavation, cutting.

έκσταση, n [ekstasee] ecstasy, rapture.

εκστρατεία, n [ekstrateea] expedition, campaign.

εκσφενδονίζω [eksfenδoneezo] fling, throw, hurl.

έκτακτος [ektaktos] temporary, emergency || (ειδικός) special, exceptional, excellent.

εκτάκτως [ektaktos] temporarily || extraordinarily, unusually.

έκταση, n [ektasee] extent, stretch.

εκτεθειμένος [ektetheemenos] exposed || compromised.

εκτείνω [ekteeno] stretch, extend, prolong.

εκτέλεση, n [ektelesee] execution || performance, fulfilment.

εκτελεστικός [ektelesteekos] executive.

εκτελώ [ektelo] execute || perform, carry out.

εκτενής [ektenees] extensive, lengthy.

εκτεταμένος [ektetamenos] extensive, long.

εκτίθεμαι [ekteetheme] be embarrassed || display.

εκτίμηση, η [ekteemeesee] esteem, estimation, appreciation.

εκτιμώ [ekteemo] esteem, value, appreciate, estimate.

εκτοξεύω [ektoksevo] shoot, cast, hurl.

εκτοπίζω [ektopeezo] displace, dislodge || (εξορίζω) exile.

εκτόπισμα, το [ektopeesma] displacement.

έκτος [ektos] sixth.

εκτός [ektos] outside, save (for) || ~ της πόλεως outside the city || ~ από apart from, besides, except for || ~ αν unless || ~κινδύνου out of danger.

έκτοτε [ektote] ever since, since then.

εκτρέπομαι [ektrepome] deviate from || (μεταφ) go astray.

εκτρέπω [ektrepo] deflect, turn aside, divert.

εκτροχιάζομαι [ektroheeazome] become derailed || (μεταφ) go astray.

έκτρωμα, το [ektroma] monster, freak.

έκτρωση, η [ektrosee] abortion, miscarriage.

εκτυλίσσομαι [ekteeleesome] develop, evolve.

εκτυπώνω [ekteepono] print || emboss.

εκτυφλωτικός [ekteefloteekos] blinding.

εκφέρω [ekfero] express.

εκφοβίζω [ekfoveezo] intimidate, frighten.

εκφορά, η [ekfora] funeral, burial.

εκφορτωτής, ο [ekfortotees] unloader, docker.

εκφράζω [ekfrazo] express, reveal.

έκφραση, η [ekfrasee] expression.

εκφραστικός [ekfrasteekos] expressive.

εκφυλισμός, ο [ekfeeleesmos] degeneration.

εκφωνώ [ekfono] deliver a speech || read aloud.

εκχύλισμα, το [ekheeleesma] extract.

εκχωρώ [ekhoro] transfer, assign, cede || (θέση) make way.

έλα [ela] (επιφ) come, come now.

ελαιογραφία, η [eleografeea] oil painting.

ελαιόλαδο, το [eleolaðo] olive oil.

έλαιο, το [eleo] olive oil, oil.

ελαιοτριβείο, το [eleotreeveeo] olive press.

ελαιόχρωμα, το [eleohroma] oil paint.

ελαιώνας, ο [eleonas] olive grove.

έλασμα, το [elasma] metal plate, sheet iron.

ελαστικό, το [elasteeko] tyre || rubber, elastic.

ελαστικός [elasteekos] flexible, elastic.

ελατήριο, το [elateereeo] spring || (μεταφ) incentive, motive.

έλατο, το [elato] fir, fir tree.

ελάττωμα, το [elatoma] defect, fault.

ελαττώνω [elatono] diminish, lessen, decrease.

ελάττωση, η [elatosee] decrease, curtailment.

ελάφι, το [elafee] deer.

ελαφρόπετρα, η [elafropetra] pumice stone.

ελαφρός [elafros] light, slight || (καφές κτλ) mild, thin, weak.

ελαφρώνω [elafrono] reduce, lighten || feel relieved.

ελάχιστα [elaheesta] very little.

ελάχιστος [elaheestos] least, very little || του' λάχιστο(ν) at least.

Ελβετία, η [elveteea] Switzerland.

Ελβετίδα, η [elveteeða] Swiss woman.

ελβετικός [elveteekos] Swiss.

Ελβετός, ο [elvetos] Swiss man.

ελεγκτής, ο [elengtees] inspector, auditor.

έλεγχος, ο [elenghos] inspection, examination || (λογαρισσμού) verification, control, auditing || (μηχανής) testing, overhauling || (μεταφ) censure, check, reproach.

ελέγχω [elengho] check, control, test.

ελεεινός [eleyeenos] pitiful, wretched, vile.

ελεημοσύνη, η [eleyeemoseenee] alms, charity.

έλεος, το [eleos] mercy, pity.

ελευθερία, η [eleftereea] liberty, freedom.

ελεύθερος [eleftheros] free || (εργένης) unmarried.

ελευθερώνω [eleftherono] redeem, set free, release, rid.

ελεφαντόδοντο, το [elefantoðonto] tusk || ivory.

ελέφας, ο [elefas] elephant.

ελεώ [eleo] give alms to, commiserate with || **Κύριε ελέησον** (επιφ) Lord have mercy!, for Heaven's sake!

ελιά, η [elia] olive, olive tree || (προσώπου κτλ) mole.

ελιγμός, ο [eleegmos] twisting, winding || (στρατ) manoeuvre, movement.

έλικα(ς), η, ο [eleeka(s)] coil, spiral || (προπέλλα) screw, propeller || (βοτ) tendril.

ελικόπτερο, το [eleekoptero] helicopter.

ελίσσομαι [eleesome] wind, coil, twist || (στρατ) manoeuvre.

έλκηθρο, το [elkeethro] sledge, sled.

ελκυστικός [elkeesteekos] attractive, winsome.

ελκύω [elkeeo] charm, attract || draw, pull.

έλκω [elko] draw, pull, haul.

Ελλάδα, η [elaða] Greece.

Ελλάς, η [elas] Greece.

έλλειμμα, το [eleema] deficit, shortage.

έλλειψη, η [eleepsee] lack, want, deficiency || (μαθημ) ellipse.

Έλλην(ας), ο [eleen(as)] Greek (person).

Ελληνίδα, η [eleeneeða] Greek woman.

ελληνικά, τα [eleeneeka] πλ Greek (language).

ελληνικός [eleeneekos] Greek.

ελληνισμός, ο [eleeneesmos] the Greek people.

ελληνιστί [eleeneestee] in Greek.

ελλιπής [eleepees] defective, wanting.

έλξη, η [elksee] pulling, traction, drawing, attraction.

ελονοσία, η [elonoseea] malaria.

έλος, το [elos] marsh, swamp, morass.

ελπίδα, η [elpeeða] hope, expectation || **παρ'** ~ contrary to expectation.

ελώδης [eloðees] marshy, swampy.

εμβαδό, το [emvaðo] area.

εμβαθύνω [emvatheeno] (μεταφ) examine thoroughly, probe deeply.

έμβασμα, το [emvasma] remittance (of money).

εμβατήριο, το [emvateereeo] march.

έμβλημα, το [emvleema] emblem, crest, symbol.

εμβολιάζω [emvoleeazo] (φυτό) graft || (άνθρωπο) vaccinate, inoculate.

εμβόλιο, το [emvoleeo] vaccine || (φυτό) graft.

έμβολο, το [emvolo] piston, rod || (πλοίου) ram.

εμβρόντητος [emvronteetos] thunderstruck, stupefied.

έμβρυο, το [emvreeo] embryo, foetus.

εμένα [emena] me.

εμείς [emees] we.

εμετικός [emeteekos] emetic.

εμετός, ο [emetos] vomiting.

εμμένω [emeno] adhere to || persist, insist.

έμμεσος [emesos] indirect.

έμμηνα, τα [emeena] πλ menstruation.

έμμισθος [emeesthos] salaried, paid.

έμμονος [emonos] persistent, obstinate, persevering.

εμπάθεια, η [empatheea] animosity, ill feeling.

εμπαίζω [empezo] tease, mock, deceive.

εμπειρία, η [embeereea] experience, skill.

εμπειρογνώμων, ο, η [embeerognomon] expert, specialist.

έμπειρος [embeeros] experienced, skilled (in), able.

εμπιστεύομαι [embeestevome] (en)trust, confide.

εμπιστευτικός [embeestevteekos] confidential.

έμπιστος [embeestos] trustworthy, reliable, faithful || **εμπιστοσύνη, η** trust, confidence.

εμπλοκή, η [emblokee] (στρατ) engagement || (μηχανής) jamming || gear of car.

εμπλουτίζω [emblouteezo] enrich.

εμπνέομαι [embneome] feel inspired.

έμπνευση, η [embnevsee] inspiration.

εμπνέω [embneo] inspire.

εμποδίζω [emboðeezo] hinder, obstruct, prevent || hold back, impede.

εμπόδιο, το [emboðeeo] obstacle, impediment, obstruction.

εμπόρευμα, το [emborevma] merchandise.

εμπορεύομαι [emborevome] engage in commerce || deal in, trade in.

εμπορικός [emboreekos] commercial, mercantile.

εμπόριο, το [emboreeo] trade, commerce.

έμπορος, ο [emboros] merchant, trader, vendor.

εμποροϋπάλληλος, ο, η [emboroeepaleelos] shop assistant || clerk (US).

εμπρησμός, ο [embreesmos] arson.

εμπρηστικός [embreesteekos] incendiary || (μεταφ) fiery.

εμπρόθεσμος [embrothesmos] within the time limit.

εμπρός [embros] forward(s), before, in front of || ~ **σε** compared with || **πηγαίνω** ~ to succeed || ~ **από** in front of || **το ρολόι πάει** ~ the clock is fast || ~ **μου** in front of me || ~! hallo, come in || **βάζω** ~ to start.

εμφανής [emfanees] apparent, obvious, clear.

εμφανίζομαι [emfaneezome] appear, present o.s., make an appearance.

εμφανίζω [emfaneezo] exhibit, reveal || (φωτογρ) develop.

εμφάνιση, η [emfaneesee] appearance, presentation || (φωτογρ) development.

έμφαση, η [emfasee] stress, emphasis.

εμφύλιος [emfeeleeos]: ~ **πόλεμος** civil war.

έμφυτος [emfeetos] innate, inherent, intuitive.

εμψυχώνω [empseehono] encourage, stimulate.

εν [en] in, at, within || ~ **τούτοις**

however, nevertheless || ~ **τάξει** all right.

έν(α), το [en(a)] one || a, an.

εναγόμενος [enagomenos] defendant.

ενάγω [enago] sue, bring action against.

εναγωνίως [enagoneeos] anxiously, with anguish.

εναέριος [enaereeos] aerial, overhead || airy.

εναλλαγή, η [enalayee] permutation, exchange, interchange.

εναλλάξ [enalaks] alternately, in turn.

εναλλάσσω [enalaso] alternate, exchange.

έναντι [enantee] towards, against || βλ και **απέναντι.**

ενάντια [enanteea] adversely, contrarily || ~ **σε** against.

εναντίο(ν) [enanteeo(n)] against || contrary to.

εναντίο(ν), το [enanteeo(n)] the contrary.

ενάντιος [enanteeos] adverse, contrary, opposite || **απ' εναντίας** on the contrary.

εναπόκειται [enapokeete]: **σε σένα ~** it's up to you.

ενάρετος [enaretos] virtuous, upright.

έναρθρος [enarthros] articulate, jointed.

εναρκτήριος [enarkteereeos] inaugural.

εναρμονίζω [enarmoneezo] harmonize.

έναρξη, η [enarksee] opening, beginning, inauguration.

ένας, ο [enas] one || a, an || ~ ~ one by one || ~ **κι** ~ especially good, very bad || **ο** ~ **τον άλλο** one another.

ενασχόληση, η [enasholeesee] occupation, employment.

ένατος [enatos] ninth.

ένδεια, η [enδeea] deficiency || poverty.

ενδεικνύομαι [enδeekneeome] be called for, be necessary.

ενδεικνύω [enδeekneeo] indicate.

ενδεικτικό, το [enδeekteeko] certificate.

ενδεικτικός [enδeekteekos] indicative.

ένδειξη, η [enδeeksee] indication, sign.

ένδεκα [enδeka] eleven.

ενδέχεται [enδehete] it is possible, it is likely.

ενδεχόμενο, το [enδehomeno] eventuality, possibility.

ενδιάμεσος [enδeeamesos] intermediate, in-between.

ενδιαφέρομαι [enδeeaferome] be interested in.

ενδιαφέρον, το [enδeeaferon] interest, concern.

ενδιαφέρω [enδeeafero] concern, interest || ~**ν** interesting.

ενδίδω [enδeeδo] give way to || give way, bend.

ένδικος [enδeekos] legal, judicial.

ενδοιάζω [enδeeazo] hesitate, waver.

ένδο- [enδo] (combining form) within, in.

ένδοξος [enδoksos] celebrated, glorious, illustrious.

ενδότερος [enδoteros] inner, interior.

ενδοχώρα, η [enδohora] hinterland.

ένδυμα, το [enδeema] dress, garment, clothes || ~**σία, η** suit, dress, garb.

ενέδρα, η [eneδra] ambush.

ένεκα [eneka] on account of, because of.

ενενήντα [eneneenta] ninety.

ενέργεια, η [enerya] energy, action || (φαρμάκου) efficacy.

ενεργητικός [eneryeeteekos] energetic, active || (φάρμακο) effective.

ενεργός [energos] active || effective.

ενεργούμαι [energoume] move the bowels || take place.

ενεργώ [energo] act, take steps || (φάρμακο κτλ) take effect, work || (καθαρτικό) purge.

ένεση, η [enesee] injection.

ενεστώς, ο [enestos] (γραμμ) present tense.

ενετικός [eneteekos] Venetian.

ενεχυροδανειστής, ο [eneheeroδaneestees] pawnbroker.

ενήλικας [eneeleekas] of age, adult.

ενηλικιούμαι [eneeleekeeoume] come of age, reach majority.

ενήμερος [eneemeros] aware, informed.

ενημερώνω [eneemerono] inform, bring up to date.

ενθάρρυνση, η [entharreensee] encouragement, cheering up.

ενθαρρύνω [enthareeno] encourage, cheer up, hearten.

ένθερμος [enthermos] ardent, warm, hearty.

ενθουσιάζομαι [enthouseeazome] be enthusiastic about.

ενθουσιασμός, ο [enthouseeasmos] enthusiasm.

ενθύμιο, το [entheemeeo] keepsake, souvenir, memento.

ενθυμούμαι [entheemoume] recall, remember, recollect.

ενιαίος [enieos] single, uniform.

ενικός [eneekos] (γραμμ) singular (number).

ενίσχυση, η [eneesheesee] reinforcement, strengthening || (ηλεκ) amplification.

ενισχύω [eneesheeo] support, reinforce, assist.

εννέα [ennea] nine || ~ **κόσιοι** nine hundred.

εννιά [ennia] nine.

έννοια, η [enneea] sense, concept, meaning, interpretation.

έννοια, η [enyeea] concern, worry || (σκοτούρα) anxiety || ~ **σου** (επιφ) take care!, don't worry!

έννομος [ennomos] lawful, legal, legitimate.

εννοείται [ennoeete] it is understood, certainly.

εννοώ [ennoo] understand, mean, intend.

'ενοικιάζεται' [eneekeeazete] 'to let', 'for rent'.

ενοικιάζω [eneekeeazo] rent, let, hire.

ενοικιαστής, ο [eneekeeastees] tenant || (νομ) lessee.

ενοίκιο, το [eneekeeo] rent.

ένοικος, ο [eneekos] tenant, lodger.

ένοπλος [enoplos] armed, in arms.

ενορία, η [enoreea] parish.

ενόρκως [enorkos] under oath, on oath.

ενόσω [enoso] as long as.

ενότητα, η [enoteeta] unity, concord.

ενοχή, η [enohee] guilt, culpability.

ενόχληση, η [enohleesee] trouble, annoyance, inconvenience.

ενοχλητικός [enohleeteekos] troublesome, inconvenient, annoying.

ενοχλώ [enohlo] trouble, annoy, pester, inconvenience.

ενσάρκωση, η [ensarkosee] incarnation, embodiment.

ένσημο, το [enseemo] stamp.

ενσκήπτω [enskeepto] happen suddenly, break out || break into.

ένσταση, η [enstasee] objection.

ένστικτο, το [ensteekto] instinct.

ένταλμα, το [entalma] warrant, writ.

ένταση, η [entasee] strain, tension || intensity, intensification.

εντατικός [entateekos] intensive.

ενταύθα [entavtha] here || (ένδειξη επιστολής) in town, local.

εντείνω [enteeno] stretch || (τις προσπάθειες) intensify || (τις σχέσεις) overstrain.

έντεκα [enteka] eleven.

εντέλεια, η [enteleea] perfection.

εντελώς [entelos] completely, entirely, totally.

εντερικός [entereekos] intestinal.

έντερο, το [entero] intestine.

εντεταλμένος [entetalmenos] responsible for, charged with || (ουσ) delegate.

έντεχνος [entehnos] skilful, artistic, ingenious.

έντιμος [enteemos] honest || (οικογένεια κτλ) respectable, honourable.

έντοκος [entokos] with interest.

εντολή, η [entolee] order, mandate || authorization, commission.

εντομοκτόνο, το [entomoktono] insecticide.

έντομο, το [entomo] insect.

έντονος [entonos] (προσπάθεια) strenuous, intense || (φως) strong || (χρώμα) bright, deep.

εντοπίζω [entopeezo] localize || (πυρκαϊά) restrict, confine.

εντόπιος [entopeeos] local, native, indigenous.

εντός [entos] within, inside, in, into || ~ **ολίγου** soon.

εντόσθια, τα [entostheea] πλ entrails, intestines.

εντριβή, η [entreevee] massage || (μηχανική) friction.

έντυπο, το [enteepo] printed matter.

έντυπος [enteepos] printed.

εντυπωσιακός [enteeposeeakos] impressive, striking.

εντύπωση, η [enteeposee] impression, sensation, feeling.

ενώ [eno] while, whereas, since.

ενώνω [enono] unite, join, connect.

ενώπιο [enopeeo] in the presence of, in front of.

ένωση, η [enosee] union || (πλεκτ) short circuit.

εξ [eks] βλ **εκ.**

εξαγοράζω [eksagorazo] buy off, redeem, ransom, obtain by bribery.

εξαγριώνω [eksagreeono] infuriate, enrage.

εξάγω [eksago] take out, extract || (εμπόριο) export || (φιλοσ) deduce.

εξαγωγή, η [eksagoyee] export || (οδόντος) extraction.

εξάδελφος, ο [eksadelfos] cousin.

εξαερίζω [eksaereezo] ventilate, air.

εξαεριστήρας, ο [eksaereesteeras] ventilator.

εξαίρεση, η [ekseresee] exception, exemption (from), immunity (from).

εξαιρετικός [eksereteekos] exceptional, unusual, excellent, remarkable.

εξαίρετος [ekseretos] excellent, remarkable.

εξαιρώ [eksero] except, exempt.

εξαίσιος [ekseseeos] excellent, splendid.

εξακολουθώ [eksakoloutho] continue.

εξακόσιοι [eksakosiee] six hundred.

εξακριβώνω [eksakreevono] verify, ascertain, establish, clear up.

εξαλείφω [eksaleefo] efface, rub out, remove, obliterate.

έξαλλος [eksalos] beside o.s., frenzied.

εξάμβλωμα, το [eksamvloma] monstrosity.

εξαναγκάζω [eksanangazo] compel, force, coerce.

εξάνθημα, το [eksantheema] rash, pimples.

εξανίσταμαι [eksaneestame] rebel, protest.

εξαντλώ [eksantlo] exhaust.

εξαπατώ [eksapato] cheat, deceive, delude || be unfaithful to.

εξάπλωση, η [eksaplosee] spreading out, extension.

εξαπολύω [eksapoleeo] let loose, hurl.

εξάπτω [eksapto] excite, provoke || (περιέργεια κτλ) rouse, stir.

εξαργυρώνω [eksargeerono] cash, turn into money.

εξάρθρωση, η [eksarthrosee] dislocation.

έξαρση, η [eksarsee] (μεταφ) elevation, exaltation.

εξαρτήματα, τα [eksarteemata] πλ gear, tackle, rigging, accessories.

εξάρτηση, η [eksarteesee] dependence.

εξαρτώμαι [eksartome] depend on, turn on.

εξασθένηση, η [eksastheneesee] weakening, enfeeblement.

εξάσκηση, η [eksaskeesee] exercise, practice, training.

εξασκώ [eksasko] exercise, practise || (πίεση) exert.

εξασφαλίζω [eksasfaleezo] assure || (θέση) book, reserve.

εξατμίζω [eksatmeezo] evaporate || (μεταφ) vanish, melt away.

εξάτμιση, η [eksatmeesee] evaporation || (αυτοκινήτου) exhaust.

εξαφανίζομαι [eksafaneezome] disappear, vanish.

εξαφανίζω [eksafaneezo] eliminate, wipe out, destroy.

έξαφνα [eksafna] all of a sudden.

έξαψη, η [eksapsee] fit of anger || excitement, elation.

εξεγείρομαι [ekseyeerome] rise, rebel.

εξέδρα, η [ekseδra] platform, stand || (λιμανιού) pier.

εξελιγμένος [ekseleegmenos] developed, evolved.

εξέλιξη, η [ekseleeksee] evolution, development.

εξελίσσομαι [ekseleesome] unfold, evolve, develop.

εξερευνητής, ο [ekserevneetees] explorer.

εξερευνώ [ekserevno] investigate, explore.

εξέρχομαι [ekserhome] go out, leave || βλ και βγαίνω.

εξετάζω [eksetazo] examine, interrogate, investigate.

εξέταση, η [eksetasee] examination, inspection.

εξεύρεση, η [eksevresee] discovery, finding out, invention.

εξευτελίζω [eksevteleezo] cheapen, lower, humiliate.

εξέχω [ekseho] stand out, project || excel.

έξη, η [eksee] habit, custom, use.

εξήγηση, η [ekseeyeesee] explanation, interpretation.

εξηγούμαι [ekseegoume] explain, make clear, give an explanation.

εξηγώ [ekseego] explain || interpret.

εξή(κο)ντα [eksee(ko)nta] sixty.

εξημερώνω [ekseemerono] tame.

εξηντλημένος [ekseentleemenos] exhausted, used up.

εξής [eksees]: ως ~ as follows || τα ~ the following || στο ~ henceforth || και ούτω καθ'~ and so on.

εξιλεώνω [ekseeleono] appease, pacify || atone for.

εξίσταμαι [ekseestame] be astonished, wonder at.

εξίσωση, η [ekseesosee] balancing, equalizing || (μαθημ) equation.

εξόγκωμα, το [eksongoma] swelling, tumour, bulge.

εξογκώνω [eksongono] swell || (μεταφ) exaggerate.

έξοδο, το [eksoδo] expense.

έξοδος, η [eksoδos] opening, emergence || (πόρτα) exit || (στρατ) sortie || (έκκλ) exodus.

εξοικειώνω [ekseekeeono] familiarize, accustom.

εξολοθρεύω [eksolothrevo] exterminate, destroy.

εξομαλύνω [eksomaleeno] smooth down || level.

εξομοιώνω [eksomeeono] assimilate to, liken to, rank together.

εξομολόγηση, η [eksomoloyeesee] confession, acknowledgement.

εξομολογώ [eksomologo] confess.

εξοντόνω [eksontono] annihilate, exterminate.

εξοπλίζω [eksopleezo] arm, equip.

εξοργίζω [eksoryeezo] enrage, make angry.

εξορία, η [eksoreea] banishment, exile.

εξορίζω [eksoreezo] exile, banish.

εξορκίζω [eksorkeezo] conjure, exorcise.

εξουδετερώνω [eksouδeterono] neutralize.

εξουσία, η [eksouseea] power, authority, government.

εξουσιοδοτώ [eksouseeoδoto] give authority to, authorise, empower.

εξοφλώ [eksoflo] (λογαριασμό) pay off, liquidate || (μεταφ) fulfil.

εξοχή, η [eksohee] countryside || (εδαφική) eminence, protrusion || κατ' ~ preeminently, par excellence.

εξοχικός [eksoheekos] country, rural, rustic.

έξοχος [eksohos] excellent, eminent, notable.

εξοχότης, η [eksohotees] excellence || **η αυτού ~** His Excellency.

εξύβριση, η [ekseevreesee] abuse, insult, offence.

εξυμνώ [ekseemno] praise, celebrate.

εξυπακούεται [ekseepakouete] it is understood, it follows.

εξυπηρέτηση, η [ekseepeereteesee] assistance, service, attendance.

εξυπηρετικός [ekseepeereteekos] helpful, useful.

εξυπηρετώ [ekseepeereto] serve, assist, attend upon.

εξυπνάδα, η [ekseepnaδa] cleverness, shrewdness.

έξυπνος [ekseepnos] clever, intelligent, smart, witty.

εξυψώνω [ekseepsono] elevate, raise || (μεταφ) exalt, extol, glorify.

έξω [ekso] out, outside, without, abroad || **απ'** ~ from outside || (μάθημα) by heart || **από** outside, except for || **μια και** ~ at one go.

εξώγαμος [eksogamos] illegitimate, bastard.

εξώθυρα, η [eksotheera] outside door, gateway.

εξωθώ [eksotho] drive, push, force.

εξωκκλήσι, το [eksokleesee] chapel, (country) church.

εξώπορτα, η [eksoporta] βλ **εξώθυρα.**

εξωραΐζω [eksoraeezo] beautify, decorate, embellish.

έξωση, η [eksosee] eviction, expulsion.

εξώστης, ο [eksostees] balcony.

εξωτερικό, το [eksotereeko] exterior || foreign country, abroad.

εξωτερικός [eksotereekos] external || foreign.

εξωτικό, το [eksoteeko] spook, spectre, wraith.

εξωτικός [eksoteekos] exotic || outlandish.

εξωφρενικός [eksofreneekos] crazy || maddening || unreasonable, absurd.

εξώφυλλο, το [eksofeelo] cover, flyleaf || (παραθύρου) shutter.

εορτάζω [eortazo] celebrate.

εορτή, η [eortee] holiday || name day || festival.

επάγγελμα, το [epangelma] profession, vocation ||

επαγγελματίας, ο [epangelmateeas] craftsman, businessman.

έπαθλο, το [epathlo] prize, trophy.

έπαινος, ο [epenos] praise.

επαινώ [epeno] praise, speak highly of.

επακόλουθα, τα [epakoloutha] πλ consequences.

επακολουθώ [epakoloutho] follow, come after.

έπακρο, το [epakro]: **στο** ~ extremely, to the extreme.

επαλείφω [epaleefo] smear (with), anoint (with).

επαληθεύω [epaleethevo] establish, verify.

επάλληλος [epaleelos] successive, one after another.

επανάγω [epanago] bring back (again).

επανακτώ [epanakto] recover.

επαναλαμβάνω [epanalamvano] repeat, resume.

επανάληψη, η [epanaleepsee] resumption, repetition.

επανάσταση, η [epanastasee] revolution.

επαναστάτης, ο [epanastatees] revolutionary, rebel.

επαναστατικός [epanastateekos] revolutionary.

επαναστατώ [epanastato] revolt, rebel.

επαναφέρω [epanafero] restore, bring back.

επανειλημμένος [epaneeleemenos] repeatedly.

επανέρχομαι [epanerhome] return.

επάνοδος, η [epanoδos] return.

επανόρθωση, η [epanorthosee] reparation, restoration.

επαξίως [epakseeos] deservedly, worthily.

επάρατος [eparatos] (μεταφ) hateful, abominable.

επάρκεια, η [eparkeea] sufficiency, adequacy.

έπαρση, η [eparsee] conceit, haughtiness.

επαρχία, η [eparheea] province, district.

επαρχιώτης, ο [eparheeotees] provincial.

έπαυλη, η [epavlee] villa || country house.

επαφή, η [epafee] contact, touch.

επείγομαι [epeegome] be in a hurry, make haste.

επειγόντως [epeegontos] urgently.

επείγων [epeegon] urgent, pressing.

επειδή [epeeδee] because, as, for, since.

επεισόδιο, το [epeesoδeeo] episode, incident || (καυγάς) quarrel, dispute.

έπειτα [epeeta] next, then, afterwards || moreover || ~ **από** after.

επέκταση, η [epektasee] extension.

επεκτείνω [epekteeno] extend, prolong.

επεμβαίνω [epemveno] interfere, intervene.

επέμβαση, η [epemvasee] intervention, interference || (ιατρ) operation.

επένδυση, η [ependeesee] lining, covering || (οικον) investment.

επεξεργασία, η [epeksergaseea] processing, elaboration.

επεξήγηση, η [epekseeyeesee] explanation, elucidation.

επέρχομαι [eperhome] come suddenly, occur, happen.

επέτειος, η [epeteeos] anniversary.

επευφημώ [epefeemo] cheer, applaud.

επηρεάζω [epeereazo] influence, affect.

επί [epee] on, upon, over, above || (διάρκεια) for || ~ **πλέον** furthermore || ~ **τέλους** at last.

επιβάλλομαι [epeevalome] assert o.s. || be indispensable.

επιβάλλω [epeevalo] impose, inflict.

επιβαρύνω [epeevareeno] burden.

επιβατηγό, το [epeevateego] passenger ship.

επιβάτης, ο [epeevatees] passenger.

επιβατικό, το [epeevateeko] passenger vehicle, passenger ship.

επιβεβαιώνω [epeeveveono] confirm, corroborate.

επιβιβάζομαι [epeeveevazome] embark, go on board.

επιβιβάζω [epeeveevazo] put aboard.

επιβλαβής [epeevlavees] harmful.

επιβλέπω [epeevlepo] supervise.

επιβλητικός [epeevleeteekos] imposing.

επιβολή, η [epeevolee] imposition, infliction.

επιβουλεύομαι [epeevoulevome] plot against.

επιβραδύνω [epeevradeeno] retard, delay.

επίγειος [epeeyeeos] earthly, worldly.

επίγνωση, η [epeegnosee] knowledge, understanding.

επίγραμμα, το [epeegrama] epigram.

επιγραφή, η [epeegrafee] inscription || (βιβλίου) title.

επιδεικνύομαι [epeedeekneeome] show off, be pompous.

επιδεικνύω [epeedeekneeo] display || show off.

επιδεικτικός [epeedeekteekos] showy.

επιδείνωση, η [epeedeenosee] aggravation.

επίδειξη, η [epeedeeksee] display || showing off.

επιδέξιος [epeedekseeos] skilful.

επιδερμίδα, η [epeedermeeda] complexion || epidermis.

επίδεσμος, ο [epeedesmos] bandage.

επιδέχομαι [epeedehome] allow, be susceptible to, tolerate.

επιδημία, η [epeedeemeea] epidemic.

επιδιόρθωση, η [epeedeeorthosee] repair, mending.

επιδιώκω [epeedeeoko] aim at, pursue, seek.

επιδοκιμάζω [epeedokeemazo] approve.

επίδομα, το [epeedoma] allowance, extra pay.

επίδοση, η [epeedosee] presentation, delivery || (νομ) deposit || (μεταφ) progress, development || (αθλητ) record.

επίδραση, η [epeedrasee] effect, influence.

επιδρομή, η [epeedromee] invasion, raid.

επιδρώ [epeedro] influence, act upon.

επιεικής [epieekees] lenient, indulgent.

επιζήμιος [epeezeemeeos] harmful, injurious.

επιζώ [epeezo] survive, outlive.

επίθεση, η [epeethesee] attack || application.

επιθετικός [epeetheteekos] aggressive.

επίθετο, το [epeetheto] adjective || surname.

επιθεώρηση, η [epeetheoreesee] inspection || (περιοδικό) review || (θέατρο) revue.

επιθυμία, η [epeetheemeea] desire, wish.

επιθυμώ [epeetheemo] wish for, desire.

επίκαιρος [epeekeros] timely, opportune || topical.

επικαλούμαι [epeekaloume] invoke.

επίκειμαι [epeekeeme] be imminent || impend.

επικερδής [epeekerdees] profitable.

επικεφαλίδα, η [epeekefaleeda] headline || title.

επικίνδυνος [epeekeendeenos] dangerous, hazardous.

επικοινωνία, η [epeekeenoneea] contact, communication.

επικοινωνώ [epeekeenono] communicate.

επικός [epeekos] epic.

επικράτεια, η [epeekrateea] state, dominion.

επικρατώ [epeekrato] prevail, predominate.

επικρίνω [epeekreeno] criticize, censure.

επικροτώ [epeekroto] approve.

επικυρώνω [epeekeerono] ratify, confirm, sanction.

επιλαχών, ο [epeelahon] runner-up.

επιληψία, η [epeeleepseea] epilepsy.

επιλογή, η [epeeloyee] selection, choice.

επίλογος, ο [epeelogos] epilogue || conclusion.

επιλοχίας, ο [epeeloheeas] sergeant-major.

επίμαχος [epeemahos] disputed || controversial.

επιμελής [epeemelees] diligent, industrious, careful.

επιμελητήριο, το [epeemeleeteereeo] (εμπορικό) chamber of commerce.

επιμελητής, ο [epeemeleetees] superintendent || (university) tutor.

επιμελούμαι [epeemeloume] take care of.

επιμένω [epeemeno] insist, persist.

επιμήκης [epeemeekees] oblong, elongated.

επιμονή, η [epeemonee] insistence, perseverance.

επίμονος [epeemonos] persistent, stubborn, obstinate.

επινοώ [epeenoo] invent, contrive, devise.

επίπεδο, το [epeepeδo] level || (βιοτικό) standard of living.

επίπεδος [epeepeδos] plane, level, flat || even.

επιπίπτω [epeepeepto] fall upon.

έπιπλα, τα [epeepla] πλ furniture.

επιπλέω [epeepleo] float || (μεταφ) keep afloat.

επίπληξη, η [epeepleeksee] reproach, rebuke.

επιπλήττω [epeepleeto] reproach, chide.

επιπλοκή, η [epeeplokee] complication.

επιπλώνω [epeeplono] furnish.

επίπλωση, η [epeeplosee] furnishing.

επιπόλαιος [epeepoleos] superficial || frivolous.

επίπονος [epeeponos] laborious, toilsome.

επίρρημα, το [epeereema] adverb.

επιρροή, η [epeeroee] influence.

επίσημος [epeeseemos] official, formal.

επίσης [epeesees] likewise, also, too.

επισιτισμός, ο [epeeseeteesmos] provisioning, provisions.

επισκεπτήριο, το [epeeskepteereeo] visiting card || visiting hour.

επισκέπτης, ο [epeeskeptees] visitor.

επισκέπτομαι [epeeskeptome] visit, call upon.

επισκευάζω [epeeskevazo] repair, mend.

επισκευή, η [epeeskevee] repairing, mending.

επίσκεψη, η [epeeskepsee] visit, call.

επίσκοπος, ο [epeeskopos] bishop.

επισπεύδω [epeespevδo] hasten, rush.

επιστάτης, ο [epeestatees] supervisor || overseer || attendant.

επιστήθιος [epeesteetheeos]: ~ φίλος bosom friend.

επιστήμη, η [epeesteemee] science.

επιστημονικός [epeesteemoneekos] scientific.

επιστήμων, ο, η [epeesteemon] scientist, professional (person) || expert.

επιστολή, η [epeestolee] letter.

επιστράτευση, η [epeestratevsee] mobilization, call-up.

επιστρέφω [epeestrefo] return.

επιστροφή, η [epeestrofee] return.

επίστρωμα, το [epeestroma] covering.

επισυνάπτω [epeeseenapto] annex, attach.

επισύρω [epeeseero] attract, draw, catch one's eye.

επισφαλής [epeesfalees] precarious, risky || unstable.

επιταγή, η [epeetayee] order || cheque.

επιτακτικός [epeetakteekos] imperative.

επίταξη, η [epeetaksee] requisition.

επιτάφιος, ο [epeetafeeos] Good Friday procession.

επιταχύνω [epeetaheeno] accelerate, speed up.

επιτελείο, το [epeeteleeo] (general) staff.

επιτετραμμένος, ο [epeetetramenos] chargé d'affaires.

επίτευγμα, το [epeetevgma] achievement.

επίτευξη, η [epeetevksee] attainment || obtaining.

επιτήδειος [epeeteeδeeos] suitable for || clever, skilful.

επίτηδες [epeeteeδes] on purpose, purposely.

επιτηδευμένος [epeeteeδevmenos] affected.

επιτηρώ [epeeteero] supervise, oversee, watch.

επιτίθεμαι [epeeteetheme] attack, assail, assault.

επίτιμος [epeeteemos] honorary.

επιτόκιο, το [epeetokeeo] compound interest.

επίτομος [epeetomos] abridged, shortened, condensed.

επί τόπου [epeetopou] on the spot.

επιτρέπω [epeetrepo] allow, permit.

επιτροπή, η [epeetropee] committee, commission.

επίτροπος, ο [epeetropos] guardian, trustee || commissioner.

επιτυγχάνω [epeeteenghano] attain, get || get right || (κατά τύχην) meet, find || (στη δουλειά) succeed.

επιτυχής [epeeteehees] successful.

επιτυχία, η [epeeteeheea] success.

επιφάνεια [epeefaneea] surface.

επιφανής [epeefanees] eminent, prominent.

Επιφάνια, τα [epeefaneea] πλ Epiphany.

επιφέρω [epeefero] bring about, cause.

επιφυλακή, η [epeefeelakee]: σε ~ at the ready, on the alert.

επιφύλαξη, η [epeefeelaksee] circumspection || reservation.

επιφυλάσσομαι [epeefeelasome] reserve, intend.

επιφώνημα, το [epeefoneema] (γραμμ) interjection.

επιχείρημα, το [epeeheereema] argument || attempt.

επιχειρηματίας, ο [epeeheereemateeas] businessman.

επιχείρηση, η [epeeheereesee] undertaking || (οικον) enterprise, business || (στρατ) operation.

επιχρυσώνω [epeehreesono] gild.

εποικοδομητικός [epeekoδomeeteekos] constructive, edifying.

επόμενος [epomenos] next, following.

επομένως [epomenos] consequently, therefore.

επονομάζω [eponomazo] surname, name.

εποπτεύω [epoptevo] supervise, oversee, inspect.

επουλώνω [epoulono] heal.

εποχή, η [epohee] epoch, era || (του έτους) season.

επτά [epta] seven.

επτακόσιοι [eptakosiee] seven hundred.

επώδυνος [epoδeenos] painful.

επωμίδα, η [epomeeδa] epaulette.

επωμίζομαι [epomeezome] shoulder (a burden).

επωνυμία, η [eponeemeea] (nick)name || surname || (εταιρείας) title.

επώνυμο, το [eponeemo] surname, family name.

επωφελής [epofelees] profitable, beneficial, useful.

επωφελούμαι [epofeloume] take advantage, avail o.s., profit.

έρανος, ο [eranos] fund, collection.

ερασιτέχνης, ο [eraseetehnees] amateur.

εραστής, ο [erastees] lover.

εργάζομαι [ergazome] work || function.

εργαλείο, το [ergaleeo] tool, implement.

εργασία, η [ergaseea] work, job, business || (επιδεξιότητα) workmanship.

εργαστήριο, το [ergasteereeo] laboratory || studio || workshop.

εργάτης, ο [ergatees] labourer, worker || (ναυτ) windlass.

εργατιά, η [ergateea] working class.

εργατικός [ergateekos] industrious, of the working class.

εργένης, ο [ergenees] bachelor.

εργοδηγός, ο [ergoδeegos] foreman.

εργοδότης, ο [ergoδotees] employer.

εργολάβος, ο [ergolavos] contractor.

έργο, το [ergo] work || act, deed || (βιβλίο) book || (σινεμά) film.

εργοστάσιο, το [ergostaseeo] factory || works.

εργόχειρο, το [ergoheero] handiwork || (κέντημα) embroidery.

ερεθίζω [eretheezo] irritate, excite.

ερεθισμός, ο [eretheesmos] irritation.

ερείπιο, το [ereepeeo] ruin, wreck.

έρευνα, η [erevna] (re)search, investigation.

ερευνητής, ο [erevneetees] researcher || explorer.

ερευνώ [erevno] search, investigate.

ερημιά, η [ereemeea] solitude || wilderness.

έρημος, η [ereemos] desert || (επιθ) desolate, deserted.

ερημώνω [ereemono] lay waste, devastate.

έριδα, η [ereeδa] dispute, quarrel.

ερίφι, το [ereefee] kid.

έρμαιο, το [ermeo] prey || victim.

ερμηνεία, η [ermeeneea] interpretation.

ερμηνεύω [ermeenevo] interpret.

ερμητικός [ermeeteekos] hermetic.

ερπετό, το [erpeto] reptile.

έρπω [erpo] crawl, creep.

ερυθρόδερμος, ο [ereethroδermos] redskin.

ερυθρός [ereethros] red.

έρχομαι [erhome] come.

ερχόμενος [erhomenos] coming, next.

ερχομός, ο [erhomos] coming, arrival.

ερωμένη, η [eromenee] mistress.

ερωμένος, ο [eromenos] lover.

έρωτας, ο [erotas] love, passion.

ερωτευμένος [erotevmenos] in love.

ερωτεύομαι [erotevome] fall in love.

ερώτημα, το [eroteema] question, problem.

ερωτηματικό, το [eroteemateeko] question mark.

ερωτηματολόγιο, το [eroteematoloyeeo] questionnaire.

ερώτηση, η [eroteesee] question, query.

ερωτικός [eroteekos] erotic || amatory.

ερωτύλος [eroteelos] amorous.

ερωτώ [eroto] ask, inquire || question.

εσκεμμένος [eskemenos] premeditated || deliberately.

εσοδεία, η [esoδeea] crop, harvest.

έσοδο, το [esoðo] income, revenue, receipt.

εσοχή, η [esohee] recess, indentation.

εσπεριδοειδή, τα [espereeðoeeðee] πλ citrus fruits.

εσπερινός, ο [espereenos] vespers.

εσπευσμένος [espevsmenos] hasty, hurried.

εστία, η [esteea] hearth, fireplace || (οπίτι) home || (λίκνος) cradle || (σόμπας) burner.

εστιατόριο, το [esteeatoreeo] restaurant.

έστω [esto] so be it || ~ **και** even, if.

εσύ [esee] you.

εσχάρα, η [eshara] grill, gridiron, grid.

έσχατος [eshatos] extreme, utmost, last.

έσω [eso] within, inside.

εσωκλείω [esokleeo] enclose.

εσώρρουχα, τα [esorouha] πλ underclothes, underwear.

εσωτερικός [esotereekos] interior, inner, internal || domestic.

εταιρεία, η [etereea] company, society, firm, partnership.

ετερογενής [eterogenees] heterogeneous.

έτερος [eteros] (an)other || **αφ' ετέρου** on the other hand.

ετήσιος [eteeseeos] annual, yearly.

ετικέττα, η [eteeketa] label, price tag.

ετοιμάζομαι [eteemazome] get ready, prepare.

ετοιμάζω [eteemazo] prepare, make ready.

ετοιμασία, η [eteemaseea] preparation.

έτοιμος [eteemos] ready.

έτος, το [etos] year.

έτσι [etsee] thus, so, like this, like that, in this way || ~ **κι** ~ middling || in any case, || ~ **κι αλλοιώς** in any case, either way.

ετυμηγορία, η [eteemeegoreea] verdict.

ετυμολογία, η [eteemoloyeea] etymology.

ευ- [ev] well, easily.

ευαγγέλιο, το [evangeleeo] gospel.

Ευαγγελισμός, ο [evangeleesmos] Annunciation.

ευάερος [evaeros] well-ventilated, airy.

ευαισθησία, η [evestheeseea] sensitivity.

ευαίσθητος [evestheetos] sensitive.

ευανάγνωστος [evanagnostos] legible.

εύγε [evye] (επιφ) bravo!, good show!

ευγένεια, η [evgeneea] courtesy, politeness.

ευγενικός [evyeneekos], **ευγενής** [evyenees] polite, courteous.

εύγευστος [evyevstos] palatable, tasty.

ευγλωττία, η [evgloteea] eloquence.

ευγνωμοσύνη, η [evgnomoseenee] gratitude.

ευγνώμων [evgnomon] grateful, thankful.

ευδαιμονία, η [evðemoneea] prosperity || happiness.

ευδιάθετος [evðeeathetos] in good humour.

ευδιάκριτος [evðeeakreetos] discernible, distinct.

ευδοκιμώ [evðokeemo] succeed || thrive || prosper.

ευδοκώ [evðoko] be pleased to, deign, consent.

ευέξαπτος [eveksaptos] irritable, excitable.

ευεργέτης, ο [everyetees] benefactor.

ευεργετικός [everyeteekos] beneficial, beneficent, charitable.

εύζωνας, ο [evzonas] evzone.

ευήλιος [eveeleeos] sunny.

ευημερώ [eveemero] prosper.

ευθεία, η [evtheea] straight line || **κατ'** ~ direct, straight.

εύθετος [evthetos] suitable, proper, convenient.

εύθικτος [evtheektos] touchy, sensitive.

εύθραυστος [evthravstos] fragile, brittle.

ευθύγραμμος [evtheegramos] straight, rectilinear.

ευθυμία, η [evtheemeea] gaiety, cheerfulness.

εύθυμος [evtheemos] merry, gay, cheerful.

ευθύνη, η [evtheenee] responsibility.

ευθύνομαι [evtheenome] be responsible, be accountable.

ευθύς [evthees] (επιρ) immediately, at once.

ευθύς [evthees] straight, upright || (τίμιος) honest, straightforward.

ευκαιρία, η [evkereea] opportunity, chance || (εμπόριο) bargain.

εύκαιρος [evkeros] opportune || (ελεύθερος) available, free.

ευκάλυπτος [evkaleeptos] eucalyptus.

εύκαμπτος, ο [evkambtos] flexible, pliable.

ευκατάστατος [evkatastatos] well-to-do, well-off.

ευκίνητος [evkeeneetos] agile, nimble.

ευκοιλιότητα, η [evkeeleeoteeta] diarrhoea.

ευκολία, η [evkoleea] ease, convenience || (χάρη) favour.

εύκολος [evkolos] easy || convenient.

ευκολύνω [evkoleeno] facilitate.

ευκρατής [evkratees] temperate, mild.

ευλαβής [evlavees] devout, pious.

ευλογία, η [evloyeea] blessing, benediction.

ευλογιά, η [evloya] smallpox.

ευλογώ [evlogo] bless.

ευλύγιστος [evleeyeestos] flexible, supple, pliant.

ευμενής [evmenees] benevolent, kind, well-disposed.

ευμετάβλητος [evmetavleetos] changeable, inconstant.

ευνόητος [evnoeetos] easily understood || intelligible.

εύνοια, η [evneea] favour, goodwill.

ευνοϊκός [evnoeekos] propitious, favourable.

ευνοούμενος [evnooumenos] favourite.

ευνοώ [evnoo] favour.

ευπαθής [evpathees] sensitive, delicate.

ευπαρουσίαστος [evparouseea- stos] presentable, imposing.

εύπιστος [evpeestos] credulous, gullible.

εύπορος [evporos] well-off, prosperous.

ευπρέπεια, η [evprepeea] propriety || decency.

ευπρεπίζω [evprepeezo] put in order || adorn, embellish.

ευπρόσδεκτος [evprosδektos] welcome, acceptable.

ευπρόσιτος [evproseetos] accessible, approachable.

ευρετήριο, το [evreteereeo] index, catalogue.

ευρέως [evreos] widely, largely.

εύρημα, το [evreema] find, discovery.

ευρίσκω [evreesko] βλ **βρίσκω**.

ευρύς [evrees] wide, extended, broad.

ευρύχωρος [evreehoros] spacious, roomy.

ευρωπαϊκός [evropaeekos] European.

Ευρώπη, η [evropee] Europe.

ευσέβεια, η [evseveea] piety, devoutness.

ευσεβής [evsevees] pious, devout.

ευσπλαχνία, η [evsplanghneea] compassion, pity.

ευστάθεια, η [evstatheea] stability, firmness.

εύστοχος [evstohos] well-aimed, proper.

εύστροφος [evstrofos] agile, nimble, versatile.

ευσυνείδητος [evseeneeδeetos] conscientious || scrupulous.

εύσωμος [evsomos] well-built, stout, sturdy.

ευτέλεια, η [evteleea] meanness, baseness, cheapness.

ευτελής [evtelees] cheap, mean, worthless.

ευτύχημα, το [evteeheema] good luck, lucky thing.

ευτυχής [evteehees] lucky, fortunate, happy.

ευτυχία, η [evteeheea] happiness, good fortune.

ευτυχισμένος [evteeheesmenos] βλ **ευτυχής**.

ευτυχώς [evteehos] luckily, happily, fortunately.

ευυπόληπτος [eveepoleeptos] reputable, esteemed.

εύφλεκτος [evflektos] inflammable.

ευφορία, η [evforeea] fruitfulness, fertility.

ευφράδεια, η [evfraδeea] eloquence.

ευφυής [evfiees] intelligent, witty, clever.

ευφυΐα, η [evfieea] intelligence, wit, ingenuity.

ευχαρίστηση, η [evhareesteesee] satisfaction, pleasure.

ευχαριστίες, οι [evhareesties] πλ thanks.

ευχάριστος [evhareestos] pleasant, agreeable.

ευχαρίστως [evhareestos] gladly, with pleasure.

ευχαριστώ [evhareesto] thank || please, gratify || thank you.

ευχέρεια, η [evhereea] ease, facility.

ευχή, η [evhee] prayer || wish || blessing.

εύχομαι [evhome] wish, hope.

εύχρηστος [evhreestos] useful, handy || in general use.

εφ [ef] βλ **επί**.

εφάμιλλος [efameelos] equal to, on a par with, a match for.

εφάπαξ [efapaks] in a lump sum, once only.

εφαπτόμενη, η [efaptomenee] tangent.

εφαρμογή, η [efarmoyee] application, fitting.

εφαρμόζω [efarmozo] fit || apply || enforce.

έφεδρος, ο [efeδros] reservist.

εφεξής [efeksees] henceforth, hereafter.

έφεση, η [efesee] (νομ) appeal.

εφετείο, το [efeteeo] court of appeal.

εφέτος [efetos] this year.

εφεύρεση, η [efevresee] invention.

εφευρετικός [efevreteekos] inventive, ingenious.

έφηβος, ο [efeevos] youth, adolescent.

εφηβικός [efeeveekos] of youth, of puberty || **εφηβική ηλικία** adolescence.

εφημερεύω [efeemerevo] be on duty.

εφημερίδα, η [efeemereeða] newspaper, journal, gazette.

εφιάλτης, ο [efeeealtees] nightmare.

εφικτός [efeektos] possible, attainable, feasible.

εφιστώ [efeesto]: ~ **την προσοχή** draw attention to.

εφόδια, τα [efoðeea] πλ supplies, equipment || **εφοδιάζω** supply, equip, furnish.

έφοδος [efoðos] charge, assault, attack.

εφοπλιστής, ο [efopleestees] shipowner.

εφορεία, η [eforeea] tax office, revenue department.

έφορος, ο [eforos] inspector, director, keeper, curator.

εφτά [efta] βλ **επτά**.

εφτακόσιοι [eftakosiee] βλ **επτακόσιοι**.

εχεμύθεια, η [ehemeetheea] secrecy, discretion || **υπό** ~**ν** under pledge of secrecy.

εχθές [ehthes] yesterday.

έχθρα, η [ehthra] enmity, hostility.

εχθρεύομαι [ehthrevome] hate, dislike.

εχθρικός [ehthreekos] hostile, (of the) enemy, inimical.

εχθρικότητα, η [ehthreekoteeta] hostility.

εχθροπραξίες, οι [ehthropraksies] πλ hostilities.

εχθρός, ο [ehthros] enemy, foe.

εχίδνα, η [eheeðna] viper, adder.

έχω [eho] have, keep || consider || cost, be worth || ~ **δίκιο** I am right || **τι έχεις;** what's wrong?, what's the matter?

εψιλο, το [epseelo] the letter E.

έως [eos] till, until, to || as far as.

Z, ζ

ζαβολιά, η [zavolia] cheating, trickery.

ζαβός [zavos] crooked, perverse || clumsy.

ζακέτα, η [zaketa] jacket.

ζαλάδα, η [zalaða] giddiness, dizziness || headache.

ζάλη, η [zalee] dizziness.

ζαλίζομαι [zaleezome] become dizzy, become confused.

ζαλίζω [zaleezo] make dizzy, confuse, daze, stun.

ζαμπό, το [zambo] ham.

ζάπλουτος [zaploutos] very rich, opulent.

ζάρα, η [zara] crease, wrinkle.

ζάρια, τα [zareea] πλ dice.

ζαρκάδι, το [zarkaðee] roe(buck).

ζάρωμα, το [zaroma] creasing, wrinkling || crease, wrinkle.

ζαρώνω [zarono] crease, wrinkle || shrink.

ζαφείρι, το [zafeeree] sapphire.

ζαχαρένιος [zahareneeos] sugary || (μεταφ) honeyed.

ζάχαρη, η [zaharee] sugar.

ζαχαροκάλαμο, το [zaharokalamo] sugar cane.

ζαχαροπλαστείο, το [zaharoplasteeo] confectioner's (shop), cake shop.

ζαχαρωτά, τα [zaharota] πλ sweets.

ζεματίζω [zemateezo] scald || be very hot.

ζεματιστός [zemateestos] scalding, boiling.

ζενίθ, το [zeneeth] zenith.

ζερβός [zervos] left-handed || left.

ζέση, η [zesee] boiling || (μεταφ) warmth, fervour.

ζεσταίνομαι [zestenome] get warm, feel hot.

ζεσταίνω [zesteno] heat up, warm.

ζεστασιά, η [zestasia] warmth, heat.

ζέστη, η [zestee] heat, warmth || **κάνει** ~ it's hot, it's warm.

ζεστός [zestos] hot, warm.

ζευγαράκι, το [zevgarakee] pair (of lovers).

ζευγάρι, το [zevgaree] pair, couple || (βοδιών) yoke.

ζευγνύω [zevgneeo] yoke, harness, link.

ζεύγος, το [zevgos] pair, couple.

ζεύξη, η [zevksee] yoking || bridging, junction.

ζέφυρος, ο [zefeeros] light breeze.

ζήλεια, η [zeeleea] envy, jealousy.

ζηλευτός [zeelevtos] enviable, desirable || much desired.

ζηλεύω [zeelevo] envy, be jealous of.

ζηλιάρης [zeeleearees] envious, jealous.

ζήλος, ο [zeelos] zeal, ardour, eagerness.

ζηλότυπος [zeeloteepos] βλ **ζηλιάρης**.

ζημία, η [zeemeea] damage, loss, injury || harm.

ζημιώνω [zeemeeono] damage, cause a loss, injure.

ζήτα, το [zeeta] the letter Z.

ζήτημα, το [zeeteema] question, subject, matter || **είναι** ~ it's doubtful (whether).

ζήτηση, η [zeeteesee] demand || search, pursuit.

ζητιανεύω [zeeteeanevo] beg, ask for alms.

ζητιάνος, ο [zeeteeanos] beggar.

ζήτω [zeeto] long live!, up with!

ζητώ [zeeto] seek, ask for, look for, demand || beg.

ζητωκραυγή, η [zeetokravgee] cheer.

ζιζάνιο, το [zeezaneeo] (μεταφ) naughty person || (βοτ) weed.

ζόρι, το [zoree] force, violence || difficulty || **με το ~** against one's will.

ζορίζω [zoreezo] force, exert pressure on.

ζόρικος [zoreekos] hard, difficult || (επι ανθρωπος) hard to please, irksome.

ζούγκλα η [zoungla] jungle.

ζουζούνι, το [zouzounee] insect.

ζούλισμα, το [zouleesma] squeezing, crushing.

ζουμερός [zoumeros] juicy, succulent.

ζουμί, το [zoumee] juice || broth || (ψητού) gravy.

ζουμπούλι, το [zoumboulee] hyacinth.

ζούρλα, η [zourla] lunacy, folly.

ζουρλομανδύας, ο [zourlomanδeeas] strait jacket.

ζοφερός [zoferos] dark, gloomy.

ζοχάδα, η [zohaδa] peevishness, sourness, sullenness.

ζυγαριά, η [zeegaria] pair of scales, balance.

ζυγίζομαι [zeeyeezome] hover over.

ζυγίζω [zeeyeezo] weigh.

ζυγός, ο [zeegos] yoke || (παλάντζας) scale, beam.

ζυγός [zeegos] even (number) || **μονά ζυγά** odd or even.

ζυγώνω [zeegono] draw near.

ζύθος, ο [zeethos] beer, ale.

ζυμάρι, το [zeemaree] dough || **ζυμαρικά** pastry, pies, cakes.

ζύμη, η [zeemee] leaven, dough.

ζύμωμα, το [zeemoma] kneading.

ζυμώνομαι [zeemonome] ferment.

ζυμώνω [zeemono] knead || ferment.

ζύμωση, η [zeemosee] fermentation.

ζω [zo] live, experience || lead a life.

ζωγραφιά, η [zografia] painting, drawing.

ζωγραφική, η [zografeekee] painting.

ζωγραφιστός [zografeestos] painted.

ζωγράφος, ο [zografos] painter, artist.

ζώδιο, το [zoδeeo] sign of the zodiac.

ζωέμπορος, ο [zoemboros] cattle dealer.

ζωή, η [zoee] life, living || lifetime.

ζωπρεύω [zoerevo] become lively || brighten up.

ζωπρός [zoeros] lively, vivid || (θερμός) warm, animated || (χρώματος) bright || (εύθυμος) gay, full of life.

ζωπρότητα, η [zoeroteeta] heat, warmth || (κινήσεως) quickness, promptness || (βλέμματος) vivacity, brightness.

ζωικός [zoeekos] animal || vital, necessary.

ζωμός, ο [zomos] broth, soup.

ζωνάρι, το [zonaree] belt, sash, girdle, waistband.

ζώνη, η [zonee] zone || βλ και **ζωνάρι.**

ζωντανεύω [zontanevo] revive, return to life.

ζωντάνια, η [zontaneea] liveliness, alertness.

ζωντανός [zontanos] living, live, vivid || lively.

ζωντοχήρα, η [zontoheera] divorced woman, divorcée.

ζωντοχήρος, ο [zontoheeros] divorced man, divorcé.

ζωογονώ [zoogono] animate || (μεταφ) stimulate, excite.

ζωοκλοπή, η [zooklopee] cattle rustling, sheep stealing.

ζωολογία, η [zooloyeea] zoology.

ζώο, το [zoo] animal || (μεταφ) fool, ass.

ζωοτροφές, οι [zootrofes] πλ animal fodder, food stuffs.

ζωόφιλος [zoofeelos] fond of animals.

ζωπυρώ [zopeero] rekindle, revive.

ζωτικός [zoteekos] vital.

ζωτικότητα, η [zoteekoteeta] vitality || (μεταφ) vital importance.

ζωύφιο, το [zoeefeeo] insect, louse || πλ vermin.

Η, η

η [ee] the.

ή [ee] or || ~ ... ~ either ... or || (συγκριτικός) than.

ήβη, η [eevee] puberty.

ηγεμόνας, ο [eeyemonas] prince, sovereign || governor.

ηγεσία, η [eeyeseea] leadership.

ηγέτης, ο [eeyetees] leader, chief.

ηγούμαι [eegoume] lead, command.

ηγούμενος, ο [eegoumenos] abbot.

ήδη [eeδee] already, even now.

ηδονή, η [eeδonee] delight, sensual pleasure, lust.

ηδονικός [eeδoneekos] delightful || sensual.

ηθική, η [eetheekee] ethics || morality.

ηθικό, το [eetheeko] morale || morality, morals.

ηθικός [eetheekos] ethical, moral || virtuous, modest.

ηθογραφία, η [eethografeea] folk customs, folklore.

ηθοποιία, η [eethopieea] acting.

ηθοποιός, ο, η [eethopeeos] actor, actress.

ήθη, τα [eethee] πλ manners, habits, customs.

ήθος, το [eethos] character, nature, manner.

ηλεκτρίζω [eelektreezo] electrify.

ηλεκτρικό, το [eelektreeko] electricity.

ηλεκτρικός [eelektreekos] electric.

ηλεκτρισμός, ο [eelektreesmos] electricity.

ηλεκτρολόγος, ο [eelektrologos] electrician.

ηλεκτρονική, η [eelektroneekee] ηλ electronics.

ηλεκτρόνιο, το [eelektroneeo] electron.

ηλεκτροπληξία, η [eelektropleekseea] electric shock.

ηλιακός [eeleeakos] of the sun, solar.

ηλίαση, η [eeleeasee] sunstroke.

ηλίθιος [eeleetheeos] idiotic, stupid, silly.

ηλικία, η [eeleekeea] age.

ηλικιωμένος [eeleekeeomenos] aged, advanced in years.

ηλιοβασίλεμα, το [eeleeovaseelema] sunset.

ηλιοθεραπεία, η [eeleeotherapeea] sunbathing.

ηλιοκαμένος [eeleeokamenos] sunburnt, tanned.

ήλιος, ο [eeleeos] sun || (φυτό) sunflower.

ημέρα, η [eemera] day || της ~ς fresh, today's.

ημερεύω [eemerevo] tame, domesticate || calm down, appease.

ημερήσιος [eemereeseeos] daily, everyday.

ημερολόγιο, το [eemeroloyo] calendar, almanac || (πλοίου) logbook || (ατόμου) diary.

ημερομηνία, η [eemeromeeneea] date.

ημερομίσθιο, το [eemeromeestheeo] daily wage.

ήμερος [eemeros] domesticated || tame, gentle.

ημερώνω [eemerono] tame || calm down, pacify.

ημιαργία, η [eemeearyeea] half-day (holiday).

ημιεπίσημος [eemiepeeseemos] semi-official.

ημιθανής [eemeethanees] half-dead.

ημίθεος, ο [eemeetheos] demigod.

ημικύκλιο, το [eemeekeekleeo] semicircle.

ημιμαθής [eemeemathees] half-learned (person), having a smattering of learning.

ημίμετρα, τα [eemeemetra] ηλ half-measures.

ημιπληγία, η [eemeepleeyeea] stroke, paralysis.

ημισέληνος, η [eemeeseleenos] crescent.

ήμισυ, το [eemeesee] half.

ημισφαίριο, το [eemeesfereeo] hemisphere.

ημιτελής [eemeetelees] half-finished.

ημίφως, το [eemeefos] twilight || dim light.

ημίχρονο, το [eemeehrono] (αθλητ) half-time.

ημίωρο, το [eemeeoro] half-hour.

ηνίο, το [eeneeo] rein, bridle.

ηνωμένος [eenomenos] united, joint || Ηνωμένο Βασίλειο United Kingdom || Ηνωμένες Πολιτείες (Αμερικής) United States (of America).

ήπαρ, το [eepar] liver.

ήπειρος, η [eepeeros] continent || mainland, land.

ηπειρωτικός [eepeeroteekos] continental.

ήπιος [eepeeos] mild, indulgent || (ασθένεια) benign.

ηρεμία, η [eeremeea] quietness, tranquility, serenity.

ήρεμος [eeremos] calm, tranquil, peaceful, still.

ηρεμώ [eeremo] be calm || keep quiet, keep still.

ηρωικός [eeroeekos] heroic.

ηρωίνη, η [eeroeenee] heroin.

ήρωας, ο [eeroas] hero.

ηρωίδα, η [eeroeeða] heroine.

ηρωισμός, ο [eeroeesmos] heroism.

ησυχάζω [eeseehazo] grow quiet, rest, calm down.

ησυχία, η [eeseeheea] quietness, peace, serenity.

ήσυχος [eeseehos] quiet, peaceful, composed.

ήτα, το [eeta] the letter Η.

ήττα, η [eeta] defeat, beating.

ηττοπάθεια, η [eetopatheea] defeatism.

ήττον, το [eeton] less.

ηττώμαι [eetome] be defeated, succumb.

ηφαίστειο, το [eefesteeo] volcano.

ηχηρός [eeheeros] loud, ringing, resonant.

ηχητικός [eeheeteekos] producing sound, resounding.

ήχος, ο [eehos] sound.

ηχώ, η [eeho] echo, sound || (μεταφ) repercussion.

ηχώ [eeho] ring, sound, strike, reverberate.

Θ, θ

θα [tha] shall, will, should, would.

θάβω [thavo] bury, inter || (μεταφ) hide.

θαλαμηγός, η [thalameegos] yacht.

θάλαμος, ο [thalamos] room || (νοσοκομείου) ward || (πολιάτου κτλ) inner tube || (όπλου) chamber.

θάλασσα η [thalassa] sea || τα κάνω ~ mess up, fail.

θαλασσινά, τα [thalaseena] πλ shellfish.

θαλασσοδέρνω [thalassoðerno] buffet || (μεταφ) struggle against (adversity).

θαλασσόλυκος, ο [thalasoleekos] sea dog, mariner.

θαλασσοπόρος, ο [thalasoporos] navigator, seafarer.

θαλασσώνω [thalasono]: τα ~ turn things topsy-turvy, mess it up.

θαλερός [thaleros] green, in bloom || (μεταφ) fresh, vigorous.

θάμβος, το [thamvos] astonishment, wonder.

θάμνος, ο [thamnos] bush, shrub, scrub.

θαμπός [thambos] (χρώμα) lifeless, without lustre || dim, cloudy.

θάμπωμα, το [thamboma] dazzle || astonishment || (ματιού) dimness || (μυαλού) confusion.

θαμπώνω [thambono] dazzle || tarnish, blur, dim || grow dim.

θαμώνας, ο [thamonas] habitué, regular customer, frequent visitor.

θανάσιμος [thanaseemos] deadly, fatal.

θανατηφόρος [thanateeforos] deadly, murderous.

θανατικός [thanateekos] capital, of death.

θάνατος, ο [thanatos] death.

θανατώνω [thanatono] execute.

θανή, η [thanee] death || funeral.

θαρραλέος [tharaleos] plucky, daring, bold.

θαρρετός [tharetos] βλ θαρραλέος.

θαρρεύω [tharevo] venture, dare, hazard.

θάρρος, το [tharos] daring, courage, spunk, mettle.

θαρρώ [tharo] believe, think.

θαύμα, το [thavma] miracle, wonder.

θαυμάζω [thavmazo] wonder at, admire, be amazed at.

θαυμάσιος [thavmaseeos] admirable, marvellous, superb.

θαυμασμός, ο [thavmasmos] wonder, admiration, astonishment.

θαυμαστής, ο [thavmastees] admirer, fan.

θαυμαστικό, το [thavmasteeko] exclamation mark.

θαυμαστικός [thavmasteekos] admiring.

θαυμαστός [thavmastos] admirable, astonishing.

θαυματουργός [thavmatourgos] wondrous, miracle-making, miraculous.

θάψιμο, το [thapseemo] burial.

θεά, η [thea] goddess.

θέα, η [thea] view, sight, aspect.

θέαμα, το [theama] spectacle, show || θεαματικός spectacular, wonderful.

θεατής, ο [theatees] spectator, onlooker.

θεατός [theatos] visible, perceptible.

θεατρικός [theatreekos] theatrical || (μεταφ) pompous, showy.

θεατρίνος, ο [theatreenos] actor.

θέατρο, το [theatro] theatre, stage.

θεία, η [theea] aunt.

θειάφι, το [theeafee] sulphur.

θεϊκός [theyeekos] divine.

θείος, ο [theeos] uncle.

θείος [theeos] divine, holy, sacred.

θέλγητρο, το [thelyeetro] charm, enchantment, attraction.

θέλγω [thelgo] charm, enchant, fascinate.

θέλημα, το [theleema] will, wish, desire || θελημdτικός voluntary || willing.

θέληση, η [theleesee] will, volition, will power.

θελκτικός [thelkteekos] seductive, attractive, captivating.

θέλω [thelo] wish, want, require, need || be willing || ~ να πω I mean to say || θέλει δεν θέλει whether he likes it or not.

θέμα, το [thema] subject, point, topic || (γραμμ) stem, theme.

θεμέλιο, το [themeleeo] foundation || (μεταφ) basis, groundwork.

θεμιτός [themeetos] lawful, legal || permissible.

θεόγυμνος [theoyeemnos] stark naked.

θεοκρατία, η [theokrateea] theocracy.

θεολογία, η [theoloyeea] theology.

θεολογικός [theoloyeekos] theological.

θεολόγος, ο [theologos] theologian.

θεομηνία, η [theomeeneea] natural disaster, calamity.

θεοποιώ [theopeeo] (μεταφ) idolize, praise, laud.

θεόρατος [theoratos] enormous, colossal.

θεός, ο [theos] god.

θεοσεβής [theosevees] pious, devout.

θεότητα, η [theoteeta] deity.

Θεοτόκος, η [theotokos] the Virgin Mary.

θεοφάνεια, τα [theofaneea] πλ the Epiphany.

θεοφοβούμενος [theofovoumenos] godly, pious.

θεραπεία, η [therapeea] cure, treatment || recovery.

θεραπευτήριο, το [therapevteereeo] hospital, clinic || (σχολής) infirmary.

θεραπευτικός [therapevteekos] curative.

θεραπεύω [therapevo] cure, treat || (μεταφ) satisfy.

θεράπων, ο [therapon] servant || attendant.

θέρετρο, το [theretro] resort || country house.

θερίζω [thereezo] mow, cut || reap || (μεταφ) annihilate.

θερινός [thereenos] summer, summery.

θεριό, το [therio] beast.

θερισμός, ο [thereesmos] reaping, mowing, cutting.

θεριστής, ο [thereestees] reaper, mower.

θεριστικός [thereesteekos] of reaping, for mowing || sweeping.

θερμαίνομαι [thermenome] be feverish.

θερμαίνω [thermeno] heat up, warm up || (μεταφ) revive.

θέρμανση, η [thermansee] heating, warming.

θερμαστής, ο [thermastees] stoker.

θερμάστρα, η [thermastra] (heating) stove, furnace.

θέρμες, οι [therme] πλ hot springs.

θέρμη, η [thermee] fever || (μεταφ) ardour, zeal.

θερμίδα, η [thermeeδa] calorie.

θερμόαιμος [thermoemos] hot-blooded, irritable, touchy.

θερμοκήπιο, το [thermokeepeeo] hot house, greenhouse.

θερμοκρασία, η [thermokraseea] temperature.

θερμόμετρο, το [thermometro] thermometer.

θερμός [thermos] warm || (μεταφ) passionate, fervent, heated.

θερμοσίφωνας, ο [thermoseefonas] water heater.

θερμοστάτης, ο [thermostatees] thermostat.

θερμότητα, η [thermoteeta] heat, warmth || (μεταφ) zeal, earnestness.

θερμοφόρος, η [thermoforos] hot-water bottle.

θέρος, ο [theros] harvest.

θέρος, το [theros] summer.

θέση, η [thesee] place, seat || position || (στρατ) emplacement, location || (εργασίας) employment, job, office || (χώρος) room, space || (κατηγορία) class.

θεσμός, ο [thesmos] institution, law, decree.

θεσπίζω [thespeezo] decree, legislate, enact (laws).

θετικός [theteekos] positive, real, actual || (πληροφορία) definite.

θετός [thetos] adopted || foster.

θέτω [theto] put, set || impose.

θεωρείο, το [theoreeo] (θεάτρου) box || (τύπου κτλ) gallery.

θεώρημα, το [theoreema] theorem.

θεώρηση, η [theoreesee] visa || (εγγράφου) certification.

θεωρητικός [theoreeteekos] theoretical || imposing.

θεωρία, η [theoreea] theory.

θεωρώ [theoro] consider, regard, look at || certify, visa.

θήκη, η [theekee] box, case || (εργαλείων) toolbag.

θηλάζω [theelazo] suckle, nurse.

θηλαστικό, το [theelasteeko] mammal.

θηλειά, η [theelia] noose, loop, slipknot || buttonhole.

θηλή, η [theelee] nipple, teat.

θηλυκό, το [theeleeko] female.

θηλυκός [theeleekos] female || (γραμμ) feminine.

θηλυκότητα, η [theeleekoteeta] femininity.

θηλυπρεπής [theeleeprepees] effeminate, womanish.

θημωνιά, η [theemonia] stack, pile || (σανού) haystack.

θήρα, η [theera] chase, hunt || (κυνήγι) game, quarry.

θήραμα, το [theerama] game, prey.

θηρίο, το [theereeo] wild beast, brute || (μεταφ) monster, fiend.

θηριώδης [theereeoδees] fierce, savage, brutal, bestial.

θησαυρίζω [theesavreezo] hoard up, accumulate || become wealthy.

θησαυρός, ο [theesavros] treasure || (μεταφ) storehouse, thesaurus.

θησαυροφυλάκιο, το [theesavrofeelakeeo] treasury.

θήτα, το [theeta] the letter Θ.

θητεία, η [theeteea] military service || term of office.

θιασάρχης, ο [theeasarhees] manager, impresario.

θίασος, ο [theeasos] cast, troupe.

θίγω [theego] touch (upon) || (μεταφ) offend, insult.

θλάση, η [thlasee] breaking || (ιατρ) fracture, bruise.

θλιβερός [thleeveros] sad || (γεγονότα) deplorable, painful.

θλίβω [thleevo] press, crush || (μεταφ) afflict, distress.

θλιμμένος [thleemenos] distressed, afflicted || in mourning.

θλίψη, η [thleepsee] crushing || (μεταφ) grief, sorrow.

θνησιμότητα, η [thneeseemoteeta] death rate, mortality.

θνητός [thneetos] mortal.

θόλος [tholos] (αρχιτεκ) vault, dome || (ουρανίσκου) roof.

θολός [tholos] dull, blurred || (κρασί) turbid || (κατάσταση) confused.

θολώνω [tholono] make dull || (το μυαλό) confuse, disturb || (νερό κτλ) muddy || (ουρανός) get overcast.

θολωτός [tholotos] vaulted.
θόρυβος, ο [thoreevos] noise, turmoil, clamour.
θορυβούμαι [thoreevoume] worry, be uneasy.
θορυβώ [thoreevo] create a disturbance || disturb.
θορυβώδης [thoreevoδees] noisy, boisterous.
θρανίο, το [thraneeo] (school) desk, bench, seat.
θράσος, το [thrasos] impudence, insolence.
θρασύς [thrasees] impudent, brazen, saucy, bold.
θραύση, η [thravsee] fracture || destruction, ruin.
θραύσμα, το [thravsma] fragment || (λίθου) splinter.
θραύω [thravo] break, smash, crack.
θρεμμένος [thremenos] well-fed.
θρεπτικός [threpteekos] nourishing, nutritious.
θρέφω [threfo] βλ **τρέφω.**
θρέψη, η [threpsee] feeding, nourishing.
θρήνος, ο [threenos] lamentation, wailing.
θρηνώ [threeno] lament, mourn || complain.
θρησκεία, η [threeskeea] religion.
θρησκευτικός [threeskevteekos] religious || (ακρίβεια) scrupulous.
θρησκόληπτος [threeskoleeptos] fanatically religious.
θρήσκος [threeskos] religious.
θριαμβευτικός [threeamvefteekos] triumphant, triumphal.
θριαμβεύω [threeamvevo] triumph || (μεταφ) excel, prevail.
θρίαμβος, ο [threeamvos] triumph, victory.
θρόϊσμα, το [throeesma] rustle.
θρόμβωση, η [thromvosee] thrombosis.
θρόνος, ο [thronos] throne.
θρούμπα, το [throumba] ripe olive.
θρυλικός [threeleekos] legendary.
θρύλος, ο [threelos] legend || rumour.
θρύμμα, το [threema] fragment, scrap || **θρυμματίζω** break to pieces, shatter.
θυγατέρα, η [theegatera] daughter.
θυγατρικός [theegatreekos]: ~ **ή εταιρεία** subsidiary.
θύελλα, η [thiela] storm.
θυελλώδης [thieloδees] stormy.
θύλακας, ο [theelakas] satchel, pouch.
θύμα, το [theema] victim.
θυμάμαι [theemame] βλ **θυμούμαι.**
θυμάρι, το [theemaree] thyme.
θύμηση, η [theemeesee] memory, remembrance.

θυμητικό, το [theemeeteeko] memory.
θυμίαμα, το [theemeeama] incense.
θυμιατό, το [theemeeato] censer.
θυμίζω [theemeezo] remind, recall.
θυμός, ο [theemos] anger, rage.
θυμούμαι [theemoume] remember, recall.
θυμώνω [theemono] make angry, infuriate || get angry, flare up.
θύρα, η [theera] door, gate, doorway.
θυρίδα, η [theereδa] small window || (θεάτρου) box office || (τραπέζης) counter.
θυρωρός, ο [theeroros] hall porter, concierge.
θύσανος, ο [theesanos] crest, tuft || tassel.
θυσία, η [theeseea] sacrifice || **θυσιάζω** sacrifice.
θωπεία, η [thopeea] petting, patting, stroking, caress(ing).
θωρακίζω [thorakeezo] plate with steel.
θώρακας, ο [thorakas] cuirass, breastplate || thorax.
θωρηκτό, το [thoreekto] battleship.
θωριά, η [thoria] air, appearance || colour, complexion.
θωρώ [thoro] see, look.

Ι, ι

ιαματικός [yamateekos] curative, medicinal.
ίαμβος, ο [eeamvos] iambus.
Ιανουάριος, ο [yanouareeos] January.
Ιάπωνας, ο [yaponas] Japanese (man).
ιαπωνέζικος [yaponezeekos] Japanese.
Ιαπωνία, η [yaponeea] Japan.
ιάσιμος [yaseemos] curable.
ίαση, η [eeasee] cure, healing, recovery.
ιατρείο, το [yatreeo] doctor's surgery, clinic || infirmary.
ιατρική, η [yatreekee] medicine.
ιατρικός [yatreekos] medical.
ιατρός, ο, η [yatros] doctor, physician.
ιβίσκος, ό [eeveeskos] hibiscus.
ιδανικό, το [eeδaneeko] ideal.
ιδανικός [eeδaneekos] ideal.
ιδέα, η [eeδea] idea || notion, thought.
ιδεαλιστής, ο [eeδealeestees] idealist.
ιδεολογία, η [eeδeoloyeea] ideology.
ιδεολόγος, ο, η [eeδeologos] idealist.
ιδεώδης [eeδeoδees] ideal.
ιδιάζων [eeδeeazon] typical, singular.
ιδιαίτερος [eeδieteros] special,

characteristic || **o ~** private secretary || **τα ιδιαίτερα** private affairs.

ιδιαιτέρως [eeδieteros] in particular || privately.

ιδιοκτησία, η [eeδeeokteeseea] ownership || property, estate.

ιδιοκτήτης, ο [eeδeeokteetees] owner, proprietor || landlord.

ιδιόκτητος [eeδeeokteetos] privately owned.

ιδιοποιούμαι [eeδeeopeeoume] appropriate, usurp.

ιδιόρρυθμος [eeδeeoreethmos] peculiar, original, eccentric.

ίδιος [eeδeeos] same || own, oneself || particular || **~ με** same as || **εγώ ο ~** I myself.

ιδιοσυγκρασία, η [eeδeeoseengkraseea] temperament, idiosyncrasy.

ιδιοτελής [eeδeeotelees] selfish, self-centred.

ιδιότητα, η [eeδeeoteeta] property, quality, characteristic.

ιδιότροπος [eeδeeotropos] peculiar, eccentric || singular.

ιδιοφυής [eeδeeofiees] talented, gifted.

ιδίωμα, το [eeδeeoma] idiom, dialect || property, characteristic || **ιδιωματικός** idiomatic.

ιδιωματισμός, ο [eeδeeomateesmos] idiom.

ιδίως [eeδeeos] specially, particularly.

ιδιωτικός [eeδeeoteekos] private, particular.

ιδιώτης, ο [eeδeeotees] individual, layman.

ιδού [eeδou] (επιφ) look!, behold!, here it is!

ίδρυμα, το [eeδreema] institution, foundation || establishment.

ίδρυση, η [eeδreesee] establishment, founding.

ιδρυτής, ο [eeδreetees] founder.

ιδρύω [eeδreeo] found, establish.

ιδρώνω [eeδrono] perspire, sweat.

ιδρώτας, ο [eeδrotas] sweat.

ιεραπόστολος, ο [ierapostolos] missionary.

ιερέας, ο [iereas] priest.

ιεροκήρυκας, ο [ierokeereekas] preacher, missionary.

ιερό, το [iero] sanctuary, holy of holies.

ιερός [ieros] holy, sacred.

ιεροσυλία, η [ieroseeleea] sacrilege.

ίζημα, το [eezeema] sediment.

ιθαγένεια, η [eethageneea] nationality, citizenship.

ιθαγενής [eethagenees] native, indigenous.

ικανοποίηση, η [eekanopieesee] satisfaction, contentment.

ικανοποιητικός [eekanopieeteekos] satisfactory, sastisfying.

ικανοποιώ [eekanopeeo] satisfy, please || (τα πάθη) satiate || (πείνα) appease.

ικανός [eekanos] capable, able || sufficient || (εργάτης) skilful.

ικανότητα, η [eekanoteeta] capacity, competence, skill.

ικετεύω [eeketevo] implore, beg.

ίκτερος, ο [eekteros] jaundice.

ιλαρά, η [eelara] measles.

ιλιγγιώδης [eeleengeeoδees] giddy, dizzy.

ίλιγγος, ο [eeleengos] giddiness, dizziness.

ιμάντας, ο [eemandas] strap || (μηχανής) belt, band.

ιματιοθήκη, η [eemateeotheekee] wardrobe || cloakroom.

ίνα, η [eena] fibre, filament.

ίνδαλμα, το [eenδalma] ideal || illusion, fancy.

Ινδία, η [eenδeea] India.

Ινδιάνος, ο [eenδeeanos] (Red) Indian || **Ι ~** turkey.

ινδικός [eenδeekos] Indian.

**Ινδονησία, [eenδoneeseea] Indonesia.

ινδονησιακός [eenδoneeseeakos] Indonesian.

Ινδονήσιος, ο [eenδoneeseeos] Indonesian.

Ινδός, ο [eenδos] Indian.

ινστιτούτο, το [eensteetouto] institute || **~ καλλονής** beauty salon.

ίντσα, η [eentsa] inch.

ινώδης [eenoδees] fibrous || (κρέας) stringy.

ιξώδης [eeksoδees] glutinous, sticky, gummy.

ιός, ο [yos] venom || (ιατρ) virus || (μεταφ) malice, spite.

Ιούλιος, ο [youleeos] July.

Ιούνιος, ο [youneeos] June.

ιππασία, η [eepaseea] horsemanship || riding.

ιππέας, ο [eepeas] rider, horseman || (σκακιού) knight.

ιππικό, το [eepeeko] cavalry.

ιπποδρομίες, οι [eepoδromies] πλ races.

ιππόδρομος, ο [eepoδromos] racecourse || hippodrome.

ιπποδύναμη, η [eepoδeenamee] horsepower.

ιπποπόταμος, ο [eepopotamos] hippopotamus.

ίππος, ο [eepos] horse.

ιππότης, ο [eepotees] knight, chevalier.

ίπταμαι [eeptame] fly, soar.

ιπταμένη, η [eeptamenee] air hostess.

ιπτάμενος, ο [eeptamenos] flyer.

Ιράν, το [eeran] Iran.

ίριδα, η [eereeδa] rainbow || (ματιού) iris.

ιριδισμός, ο [eereeδeesmos] iridescence.

Ιρλανδία, η [eerlanδeea] Ireland.

ιρλανδικός [eeerlanδeekos] Irish.

Ιρλανδός, ο [eerlanδos] Irishman.

ίσα [eesa] equally, as far as || straight, directly || ~ ~ exactly, precisely || ~ **με** up to, until.

ίσαμε [eesame] βλ **ίσα με**.

ισάξιος [eesakseeos] equivalent (to).

ισάριθμος [eesareethmos] equal in number.

ισημερία, η [eeseemereea] equinox.

ισημερινός, ο [eeseemereenos] equinoctial || (ουσ) equator.

ισθμός, ο [eesthmos] isthmus.

ίσια [eeseea] βλ **ίσα**.

ίσιος [eeseeos] straight, erect || honest || equal to.

ισ(ι)ώνω [ees(ee)ono] straighten || make even, smooth.

ίσκιος, ο [eeskeeos] shade, shadow.

ισόβιος [eesoveeos] for life, lifelong.

ισόγειο, το [eesoyo] ground floor.

ισοδύναμος [eesoδeenamos] equivalent || equal in force.

ισοδυναμώ [eesoδeenamo] be equivalent to.

ισοζύγιο, το [eesozeeyo] balancing, balance || ~ **πληρωμών** balance of payments.

ισολογισμός, ο [eesoloyeesmos] balance sheet.

ισόπαλος [eesopalos] evenly matched, of equal strength.

ισοπεδώνω [eesopeδono] level up, level down, smooth.

ισόπλευρος [eesoplevros] equilateral.

ισορροπημένος [eesoropeemenos] well-balanced.

ισορροπία, η [eesoropeea] balance, equilibrium.

ισορροπώ [eesoropo] balance.

ίσος [eesos] equal to, the same as || **εξίσου** likewise.

ισότητα, η [eesoteeta] equality.

ισότιμος [eesoteemos] equal in rank || equal in value.

ισοφαρίζω [eesofareezo] equal, make equal || be equal to.

Ισπανία, η [eespaneea] Spain.

ισπανικός [eespaneekos] Spanish.

Ισπανός, ο [eespanos] Spaniard.

Ισραήλ, το [eesraeel] Israel.

ισραηλινός [eesraeeleenos] Israeli.

Ισραηλίτη, ο [eesraeeleetee] Israeli.

ιστιοπλοΐα, η [eesteeoploeea] sailing.

ιστιοφόρο, το [eesteeoforo] sailing ship.

ιστορία, η [eestoreea] history || story, tale.

ιστορίες, οι [eestories] πλ trouble, scene, quarrel.

ιστορικός [eestoreekos] historic(al) || (ουσ) historian.

ιστός, ο [eestos] mast, pole || (βιολ) tissue.

ισχιαλγία, η [eesheealyeea] sciatica.

ισχίο, το [eesheeo] hip.

ισχνός [eeshnos] lean, thin || (βλάστηση) scanty, sparse.

ισχυρίζομαι [eesheereezome] assert, maintain, declare.

ισχυρισμός, ο [eesheereesmos] assertion, contention, allegation.

ισχυρογνώμων [eesheerognomon] stubborn, headstrong, obstinate.

ισχυρός [eesheeros] strong, sturdy || (φωνή) loud || (άνεμος) stiff, strong.

ισχύς, η [eeshees] strength, power, force || (νόμου κτλ) validity.

ισχύω [eesheeo] have validity || be in force.

ισώνω [eesono] βλ **ισ(ι)ώνω**.

ίσως [eesos] perhaps, probably, maybe.

Ιταλία, η [eetaleea] Italy.

ιταλικός [eetaleekos] Italian.

Ιταλός, ο [eetalos] Italian (person).

ιτιά, η [eetia] willow tree.

ιχθυοπωλείο, το [eehtheeopoleeo] fishmonger's shop.

ιχθύς, ο [eehthees] fish.

ιχνογραφία, η [eehnografeea] sketching, drawing.

ίχνος, το [eehnos] footprint, track || trace, vestige || (μεταφ) mark, sign.

ιώδιο, το [yoδeeo] iodine.

ιωνικός [yoneekos] Ionic, Ionian.

ιώτα, το [yota] the letter I.

Κ, κ

κάβα, η [kava] wine cellar.

καβαλιέρος, ο [kavalieros] escort, partner.

καβάλλα, η [kavala] riding || (επιρ) on horseback || (σε τοίχο κτλ) astride.

καβαλλάρης, ο [kavalarees] rider, horseman || (εγχόρδου) bridge.

καβαλλέτο, το [kavaleto] easel.

καβαλλικεύω [kavaleekevo] mount a horse || (μεταφ) dominate.

καβαλλώ [kavalo] βλ **καβαλλικεύω**.

καβγαδίζω [kavgaδeezo] quarrel, wrangle, squabble.

καβγάς, ο [kavgas] row, quarrel.

καβγατζής, ο [kavgatzees] grouch, wrangler.

κάβος, ο [kavos] cape, headland || (ναυτ) cable.

καβούκι, το [kavoukee] shell.

κάβουρας, ο [kavouras] crab || crawfish.

καβουρδίζω [kavourδeezo] roast, brown || scorch.

καβούρι, το [kavouree] βλ **κάβουρας.**

καγκελάριος, ο [kangelareeos] chancellor.

κάγκελο, το [kangelo] (παραθύρου κτλ) bar || (σκάλας) balustrade || (κήπου) railings || (δικτυωτό) grille.

καγκάζω [kanghazo] guffaw.

κάδος, ο [kaðos] bucket, vat, tub, small barrel.

κάδρο, το [kaðro] (πλαίσιο) frame || (πίνακα) frame || (χάρτου) border || (φωτογραφία) framed picture.

καπμένος [kaeemenos] (μεταφ) miserable, wretched.

καπμός, ο [kaeemos] longing, yearning.

καθαίρεση, η [katheresee] dismissal, degradation.

καθαιρώ [kathero] dismiss, discharge || (ιερέα) unfrock.

καθαρεύουσα, η [katharevousa] formal Greek (language).

καθαρίζω [kathareezo] clean, clear || (κουκιά, φρούτα) peel, pare, shell || (μεταλλικά είδη) burnish || (νοτήρια) polish || (εξηγώ) explain, clarify || (λογαριασμούς) settle, clear up.

καθαριότητα, η [kathareeoteeta] cleanness, cleanliness || brightness.

καθάρισμα, το [kathareesma] cleaning || peeling || polishing.

καθαριστήριο, το [kathareesteereeo] dry cleaner's.

καθαρίστρια, η [kathareestria] charwoman, cleaning lady.

κάθαρμα, το [katharma] (μεταφ) rogue, rascal, scamp.

καθαρόαιμος [katharoemos] thoroughbred.

καθαρός [katharos] (πρόσωπο κτλ) neat, tidy || (φωνή) clear, distinct || (χρυσός) pure || (ουρανός) clear || (απάντηση) plain, straightforward || (ιδέα) clear, distinct || (κέρδος) clear, net || (έννοια) obvious, manifest, evident.

καθαρότητα, η [katharoteeta] cleanness, purity || clearness.

κάθαρση, η [katharsee] cleansing, refining || catharsis || quarantine.

καθαυτό [kathavto] exactly, precisely || really.

κάθε [kathe] each, every || ~ **άλλο** far from it || **το ~ τι** everything.

κάθειρξη, η [katheerksee] βλ **φυλάκιση.**

καθέκαστα, τα [kathekasta] πλ details, particulars.

καθελκύω [kathelkeeo] (ναυτ) launch.

καθένας [kathenas] everyone, each one, everybody.

καθεξής [katheksees] so forth, so on.

καθεστώς, το [kathestos]: **το ~** regime, status quo.

κάθετος [kathetos] vertical, perpendicular, upright.

καθηγητής, ο [katheeyeetees] professor, teacher.

καθήκι, το [katheekee] chamberpot || (μεταφ) rogue, vicious person.

καθήκον, το [katheekon] duty, task || **καθήκοτα** πλ functions, duties.

καθηλώνω [katheelono] pin down, fix || immobilize.

καθημερινός [katheemereenos] daily, everyday.

καθημερινώς [katheemereenos] daily.

καθησυχάζω [katheeseehazo] (ένα φόβο) calm, reassure, pacify || become calm.

καθιερώνω [kathierono] consecrate, dedicate || establish, validate.

καθίζηση, η [katheezeesee] subsidence, landslide.

καθίζω [katheezo] seat, place || (πλοίο) run aground.

καθισιό, το [katheesio] idleness, unemployment, inactivity.

κάθισμα, το [katheesma] chair, seat || (πλοίο) stranding.

καθίσταμαι [katheestame] become, get, grow.

καθιστός [katheestos] sitting (down).

καθιστώ [katheesto] (εγκαθιστώ) establish, install || (κάποιο) make, render || (διορίζω) appoint.

καθοδηγώ [kathoðeego] instruct, guide, lead.

κάθοδος, η [kathoðos] descent || alighting.

καθολικός [katholeekos] catholic || (γνώμη) unanimous || universal.

καθόλου [katholou] generally || (διόλου) not at all, no way.

κάθομαι [kathome] be seated, sit down, sit.

καθομιλουμένη, η [kathomeeloumenee] the spoken language.

καθορίζω [kathoreezo] determine, define, fix, decide.

καθορισμός, ο [kathoreesmos] defining, fixing, determination.

καθόσο [kathoso] as || according to what || being.

καθρέφτης, ο [kathreftees] mirror, looking-glass.

καθρεφτίζω [kathrefteezo] reflect, mirror.

καθυστερημένος [katheestereemenos] backward || late.

καθυστέρηση, η [katheestereesee] delay, lateness.

καθυστερούμενα, τα [katheesteroumena] πλ arrears.

καθώς [kathos] as well as, like, as || ~ **πρέπει** proper.

K

και [ke] and, also, too || ~ ... ~ both ... and || ~ **να** even if.

καΐκι, το [kaeekee] caique, sailing boat.

καϊμάκι, το [kaeemakee] cream || (του καφέ) froth.

καινοτομία, η [kenotomeea] innovation.

καινούργιος [kenouryos] new, fresh.

καιρικός [kereekos] of the weather.

καίριος [kereeos] timely || (πλήγμα) deadly, mortal || (σημείο) vital, important.

καιρός, ο [keros] time, period || weather || **με τον καιρό** in course of time.

καιροσκοπώ [keroskopo] wait for an opportunity, be an opportunist.

καισαρικός [kesareekos] Caesarean.

καίτοι [ketee] though, although.

καίομαι [keome] be on fire.

καίω [keo] burn.

κακά [kaka] badly, ill || bad things.

κακάο, το [kakao] cocoa.

κακαρίζω [kakareezo] cluck, gobble.

κακεντρέχεια, η [kakentreheea] malevolence, spite.

κακία, η [kakeea] wickedness, malice.

κακίζω [kakeezo] reproach, blame, reprimand.

κακοβαλμένος [kakovalmenos] untidy || badly placed.

κακόβουλος [kakovoulos] malicious.

κακογλωσσιά, η [kakogloseea] slander, calumny || gossip.

κακοήθης [kakoeethees] dishonest, vile || (ιατρ) malignant, serious.

κακόηχος [kakoeehos] dissonant, unpleasant to hear.

κακοκαιρία, η [kakokereea] bad weather.

κακοκεφιά, η [kakokefia] depression, bad mood.

κακομαθαίνω [kakomatheno] (μωρό κτλ) spoil || acquire bad habits.

κακομαθημένος [kakomatheemenos] ill-bred, spoilt, rude.

κακομεταχειρίζομαι [kakometaheereezome] maltreat, abuse.

κακομοίρης [kakomeerees] hapless, wretched.

κακό, το [kako] evil, harm, wrong, bad, mischief.

κακοπέραση, η [kakoperasee] privation, hardship.

κακοπιστία, η [kakopeesteea] perfidy, faithlessness.

κακοποιός [kakopeeos] criminal, ill-doer.

κακοποιώ [kakopeeo] maltreat || rape.

κακός [kakos] bad, wicked || (παιδί) mischievous || nasty, serious.

κακοσμία, η [kakosmeea] stench, stink.

κακοσυνηθίζω [kakoseeneetheezo] πλ **κακομαθαίνω.**

κακοτυχία, η [kakoteeheea] misfortune, bad luck.

κακούργημα, το [kakouryeema] crime, villainy, felony.

κακουργιοδικείο, το [kakouryoδeekeeo] criminal court.

κακούργος, ο [kakourgos] criminal || (μεταφ) villain, rogue.

κακουχία, η [kakouheea] hardship, privation.

κακοφαίνεται [kakofenete]: **μου** ~ it displeases me, it offends me.

κακοφτιαγμένος [kakofteeagmenos] badly made, badly wrought.

κακόφωνος [kakofonos] discordant, dissonant.

κάκτος, ο [kaktos] cactus.

κακώς [kakos] badly, wrongly.

κάκωση, η [kakosee] ill treatment || (αποτέλεσμα) suffering, hardship.

καλά [kala] well, all right || properly, thoroughly.

καλάθι, το [kalathee] basket || ~ **αχρήστων** wastepaper bin.

καλαισθησία, η [kalestheeseea] good taste, elegance.

καλαμάρι, το [kalamaree] inkstand, inkpot || (ψάρι) cuttlefish, squid.

καλαματιανός [kalamateeanos] (dance) of Kalamata.

καλάμι, το [kalamee] reed, cane || (ψαρέματος) fishing rod || (ανατ) shinbone.

καλαμοζάχαρο, το [kalamozakharo] cane sugar.

καλαμπόκι, το [kalambokee] maize, corn.

καλαμπούρι, το [kalambouree] joke, pun.

κάλαντα, τα [kalanta] πλ carols.

καλαπόδι, το [kalapoδee] (shoemaker's) last, shoe last.

καλαφατίζω [kalafateezo] caulk.

κάλεσμα, το [kalesma] invitation.

καλεσμένος [kalesmenos] invited || (ουσ) guest.

καλημαύκι, το [kaleemavkee] priest's high hat.

καλημέρα [kaleemera] (επιφ) good morning.

καληνύχτα [kaleeneehta] (επιφ) good night.

καληνυχτίζω [kaleeneehteezo] bid good night.

καλησπέρα [kaleespera] (επιφ) good afternoon || good evening.

κάλι, το [kalee] potash.

καλιακούδα, η [kaleeakouδa] crow.

καλλιέργεια, η [kalierya] cultivation, tilling || (μεταφ) cultivation.

καλλιεργώ [kaliergo] cultivate, till, grow.

καλλικάντζαρος, ο
[kaleekandzaros] sprite, spook, goblin.

καλλιστεία, τα [kaleesteea] πλ beauty competition.

καλλιτέχνης, ο [kaleetehnees] artist.

καλλιτεχνικός [kaleetehneekos] of art, of artists, artistic.

καλλονή, η [kalonee] beauty.

κάλλος, το [kalos] beauty, charm.

καλλυντικά, τα [kaleenteeka] πλ cosmetics, make-up.

καλλωπίζω [kalopeezo] beautify, decorate, adorn.

καλμάρω [kalmaro] become calm, relax.

καλντερίμι, το [kalntereemee] cobbled street, paving stone.

καλό, το [kalo] good, benefit || favour || blessing || **στο ~**! so long!

καλοαναθρεμμένος
[kaloanathremenos] well brought up.

καλοβαλμένος [kalovalmenos] well turned out, well-groomed, tidy.

καλόβολος [kalovolos] accommodating, easy-going, complaisant.

καλόγερος, ο [kaloyeros] monk || (σπυρί) boil, carbuncle || (παιχνίδι) hopscotch.

καλόγρια, η [kalogreea] nun.

καλοζώ [kalozo] live well || support comfortably.

καλοήθης [kaloeethees] moral, virtuous || (ιατρ) benign.

καλοθρεμμένος [kalothremenos] well-nourished || well-bred.

καλοκάγαθος [kalokagathos] kind-natured, good.

καλοκαίρι, το [kalokeree] summer || **καλοκαιρία** fine weather || **καλοκαιρινός** summer, summery.

καλοκαμωμένος [kalokamomenos] well-made || handsome.

καλοκάρδος [kalokarδos] good-hearted, cheerful.

καλοκοιτάζω [kalokeetazo] look closely at || look after well || ogle.

καλομαθαίνω [kalomatheno] spoil, pamper, pet || develop good habits.

καλομαθημένος [kalomatheemenos] pampered.

καλοντυμένος [kalonteemenos] well-dressed.

καλοπέραση, η [kaloperasee] comfort, happy life, good life.

καλοπερνώ [kaloperno] lead a pleasant life || be well treated.

καλοπιάνω [kalopeeano] coax, treat gently.

καλοπροαίρετος [kaloproeretos] well-disposed, obliging.

καλοριφέρ, το [kaloreefer] central heating || radiator, heater.

καλορρίζικος [kaloreezeekos] lucky.

κάλος, ο [kalos] corn.

καλός [kalos] (άνθρωπος) kind, good || (εργάτης) skilful || (υπάλληλος) able, efficient || (νέα) good, favourable || (τροφή) wholesome || (καρδιά) kind.

καλοσυνηθίζω [kaloseeneetheezo] βλ **καλομαθαίνω**.

καλούπι, το [kaloupee] form, mould.

καλούτσικος [kaloutseekos] not bad, passable, adequate.

καλπάζω [kalpazo] gallop || walk fast, run.

κάλπη, η [kalpee] ballot box.

κάλπικος [kalpeekos] counterfeit, false || (μεταφ) worthless.

κάλτσα, η [kaltsa] sock, stocking.

καλύβι, το [kaleevee] hut, cabin, hovel.

κάλυμμα, το [kaleema] wrapper, cover || (κρεββατιού) blanket, coverlet || (κεφαλής) cap, headdress || (τραπεζιτικό) margin, cover.

κάλυκας, ο [kaleekas] (βοτ) calyx || (στρατ) cartridge || (ανατ) calix.

καλύπτω [kaleepto] cover, veil, hide || (προθέσεις) cloak, mask, conceal.

καλύτερα [kaleetera] better.

καλυτερεύω [kaleeterevo] improve || get better.

καλύτερος [kaleeteros] better.

κάλυψη, η [kaleepsee] covering.

καλώ [kalo] call, beckon, name || (σε δείπνο) invite || (νομ) summon.

καλώδιο, το [kaloδeeo] rope || cable.

καλώς [kalos] well || rightly, properly || **έχει ~** good, agreed || **~ ωρίσατε** (επιφ) welcome!

καλωσορίζω [kalosoreezo] welcome.

καλωσύνη, η [kaloseenee] goodness, kindness || (καιρός) fine weather.

καμάκι, το [kamakee] harpoon, fish spear.

κάμαρα, η [kamara] room.

καμάρα, η [kamara] arch, archway, arcade || (θόλου) vault.

καμάρι, το [kamaree] pride, boast.

καμαριέρα, η [kamariera] chambermaid, parlourmaid.

καμαρότος, ο [kamarotos] steward, cabin boy.

καμαρώνω [kamarono] take pride in, glory in.

καμαρωτός [kamarotos] (αρχιτεκ) arched, vaulted || (υπερηφάνεια) proud, haughty.

καμέλια, η [kameleea] camellia.

καμήλα, η [kameela] camel.

καμηλοπάρδαλη, η
[kameeloparδalee] giraffe.

καμινάδα, η [kameenaδa] chimney, smokestack || funnel.

καμινέτο, το [kameeneto] spirit lamp.

καμίνι, το [kameenee] furnace, kiln.

καμιόνι, το [kameeonee] lorry, truck.

καμμιά [kamia] βλ **κανένας**.

καμουτσίκι, το [kamoutseekee] whip.

καμουφλάζ, το [kamouflaz] camouflage, disguise.

καμουφλάρω [kamouflaro] camouflage, disguise.

καμπάνα, η [kambana] bell.

καμπαναριό, το [kambanario] belfry, steeple.

καμπαρντίνα, η [kambarndeena] gabardine.

καμπή, η [kambee] bend, turn || (σωλήνα κτλ) elbow, knee.

κάμπια, η [kambeea] caterpillar.

καμπίνα, η [kambeena] cabin.

καμπινές, ο [kambeenes] toilet, rest room, W.C.

κάμπος, ο [kambos] plain, flat country.

κάμποσος [kambosos] considerable, some.

καμπούρα, η [kamboura] hump, hunch.

καμπούρης, ο [kambourees] hunchback.

καμπουριάζω [kamboureeazo] hunch || stoop.

κάμπτομαι [kambtome] bow || yield, sag || (τιμές) go down.

κάμπτω [kambto] bend, turn, curve.

καμπύλη, η [kambeelee] curve, bend.

καμπύλος [kambeelos] curved, rounded || crooked.

καμφορά, η [kamfora] camphor.

κάμψη, η [kampsee] bending, flexion || (τιμών) fall, drop.

καμώματα, τα [kamomata] πλ affected manners, antics.

καμώνομαι [kamonome] pretend, feign.

καν [kan] at least, even || **ούτε** ~ not even || ~ ... ~ either ... or.

Καναδάς, ο [kanaδas] Canada.

καναδικός [kanaδeekos] Canadian.

Καναδός, ο [kanaδos] Canadian.

κανακάρης [kanakarees] petted, spoilt || (ουσ) only child.

κανάλι, το [kanalee] channel, canal.

κανανές, ο [kanapes] sofa.

καναρίνι, το [kanareenee] canary.

κανάτα, η [kanata] jug, pitcher.

κανείς [kanees] someone, anyone || no one, nobody.

κανέλλα, η [kanela] cinnamon.

κανένας [kanenas] anyone, one, some || no, no one.

κανναβάτσο, το [kanvatso] canvas, pack cloth.

καννάβι, το [kanavee] hemp.

κάννη, η [kanee] barrel of a gun.

καννίβαλος, ο [kaneevalos] cannibal.

κανόνας, ο [kanonas] rule || (εκκλ) canon.

κανόνι, το [kanonee] cannon.

κανονίζω [kanoneezo] regulate || (υποθέσεις) settle, arrange || (λογαριασμούς) settle, close, pay off.

κανονικός [kanoneekos] regular, usual, ordinary || (εκκλ) canonical.

κανονισμός, ο [kanoneesmos] regulation, rule(s), by-laws.

κάνουλα, η [kanoula] tap || faucet (US).

καντάδα, η [kantaδa] serenade.

καντήλι, το [kanteelee] small olive-oil light, nightlight.

καντίνα, η [kanteena] canteen.

κάνω [kano] do, make, create, build || (υποκρίνομαι) play, sham || **τα** ~ **θάλασσα** (η **σαλάτα**) to make a mess of it || ~ **παιδί** to have a child || ~ **νερά** to leak || (μεταφ) to hedge || ~ **πως** to pretend that || **τι κάνετε;** how are you?

κάπα, η [kapa] peasant's cloak.

καπάκι, το [kapakee] lid, cover.

καπάρο, το [kaparo] deposit.

καπαρώνω [kaparono] give a deposit || book, engage.

καπέλλο, το [kapelo] hat.

καπετάνιος, ο [kapetaneeos] captain, skipper, chief.

καπηλεία, η [kapeeleea] (μεταφ) huckstering, exploiting.

καπηλειό, το [kapeelio] wine shop, taverna.

καπίστρι, το [kapeestree] bridle, halter.

καπλαμάς, ο [kaplamas] veneer.

καπνέμπορος, ο [kapnemboros] tobacco dealer, tobacconist.

καπνιά, η [kapnia] soot, lampblack.

καπνίζω [kapneezo] smoke || cure.

κάπνισμα, το [kapneesma] smoking.

καπνιστής, ο [kapneestees] smoker || (κρέατος) curer.

καπνιστός [kapneestos] smoked, smoke-cured.

καπνοδόχος, η [kapnoδohos] chimney || (πλοίου) funnel.

καπνοπώλης, ο [kapnopolees] tobacconist.

καπνός, ο [kapnos] smoke || tobacco || (μεταφ) **έγινε** ~ he vanished (into thin air).

κάποιος [kapeeos] someone || a certain.

κάπότα, η [kapota] shepherd's cloak.

κάποτε [kapote] from time to time, now and again, sometimes || once.

κάπου [kapou] somewhere || ~ ~ once in a while || ~ **δέκα** about ten.

κάππα, το [kappa] the letter K.

κάππαρη, η [kaparee] caper.

καπρίτσιο, το [kapreetseeo] caprice, whim, fancy.

κάπως [kapos] somehow, somewhat.

καραβάνα, η [karavana] mess tin || platter.

καραβάνι, το [karavanee] caravan.

καράβι, το [karavee] ship, boat, vessel.

καραβίδα, η [karaveeδa] crawfish.

καραβοκύρης, ο [karavokeerees] owner of a vessel || captain.

καραγκιόζης, ο [karangeeozees] (μεταφ) comical person, comedian.

καραδοκώ [karoδoko] watch for, look out for || waylay.

καρακάξα, η [karakaksa] magpie.

καραμέλα, η [karamela] sweet || caramel.

καραμούζα, η [karamouza] toy flute || (αυτοκινήτου) horn.

καραμπίνα, η [karambeena] carbine.

καραντίνα, η [karanteena] quarantine.

καράτι, το [karatee] carat.

καρατομώ [karatomo] behead, decapitate.

καράφα, η [karafa] carafe || (κρασιού) decanter.

καράφλα, η [karafla] baldness.

καρβέλι, το [karvelee] (round) loaf.

καρβουνιάρης, ο [karvouneearees] coal merchant || coalman.

κάρβουνο, το [karvouno] coal, charcoal.

κάργα [karga] quite full || tightly, closely.

κάρδαμο, το [karδamo] cress.

καρδιά, η [karδia] heart || (φρούτου) core, centre.

καρδιακός [karδiakos] affected with heart disease.

καρδιολόγος, ο [karδiologos] heart specialist.

καρδιοχτύπι, το [karδiohteepee] heartbeat || (μεταφ) anxiety.

καρέκλα, η [karekla] chair, seat.

καρίνα, η [kareena] keel.

καρκίνος, η [karkeenos] cancer || crab.

καρκίνωμα, το [karkeenoma] carcinoma.

καρμανιόλα, η [karmaneeola] guillotine || (στα χαρτιά) dishonest card game.

καρμπό, το [karbo] carbon paper.

καρναβάλι, το [karnavalee] carnival.

καρότο, το [karoto] carrot.

καρούλι, το [karoulee] reel, spool || pulley.

καρούμπαλο, το [karoumbalo] bump (on the head).

καρπαζιά, η [karpazia] clout on the head.

καρπός, ο [karpos] fruit || (ανατ) wrist.

καρπούζι, το [karpouzee] watermelon.

καρπούμαι [karpoume] reap the fruits of || (μεταφ) benefit by.

καρποφόρος [karpoforos] fruitful || effective || lucrative.

καρποφορώ [karpoforo] produce fruit || (μεταφ) succeed.

καρρέ, το [karre] (στα χαρτιά) foursome || (φουστανιού) open neck of dress.

καρρό, το [karo] (στα χαρτιά) diamond || (σχεδίου) check.

κάρρο, το [karo] cart, wagon.

καρροτσάκι, το [karotsakee] handcart, barrow || (μωρού) pram.

κάρτα, η [karta] postcard || visiting card.

καρτέρι, το [karteree] βλ **ενέδρα**.

καρτερώ [kartero] persevere, persist || wait for, expect.

καρύδι, το [kareeδee] walnut || Adam's apple || **καρυδιά, η** walnut tree, walnut (wood).

καρύκευμα, το [kareekevma] seasoning || (το μπαχαρικό) condiment, spice.

καρυοθραύστης, ο [kareeothravstees] nutcracker.

καρυοφύλλι, το [kareeofeelee] clove || (όπλου) flintlock.

καρφί, το [karfee] nail.

καρφίτσα, η [karfeetsa] pin || (κόσμημα) brooch.

καρφώνω [karfono] nail, pin || (μεταφ) fix.

καρχαρίας, ο [karhareeas] shark.

κασετίνα, η [kaseteena] (σχολική) pencil box || (κοσμημάτων) jewellery box.

κάσ(σ)α, η [kasa] case, box || (χρηματοκιβώτιο) safe || (μεταφ) coffin, bier.

κασέλα, η [kasela] wooden chest, trunk.

κασκέτο, το [kasketo] cap.

κασμήρι, το [kasmeeree] cashmere.

κασόνι, το [kasonee] packing case.

κασσίτερος, ο [kaseeteros] tin.

καστανιά, η [kastania] chestnut tree.

κάστανο, το [kastano] chestnut.

καστανός [kastanos] chestnut-coloured, maroon.

καστόρι, το [kastoree] beaver || felt.

κάστρο, το [kastro] castle, fortress.

κατά [kata] against, upon, during, according to, by, about || ~ **τύχη** by chance || ~ **βάθος** at bottom || **καθ' εκάστην** every day || ~ **διαβόλου** to the devil, to hell.

καταβαίνω [kataveno] βλ **κατεβαίνω**.

καταβάλλω [katavalo] overthrow, overcome, exhaust || (προσπάθειες) strive, endeavour || (χρήματα) pay, put down.

κατάβαση, η [katavasee] descent, alighting, getting off.

καταβιβάζω [kataveevazo] let down, take down || (ύψος) lower, reduce.

καταβολή, η [katavolee] (χρημάτων) paying in, deposit.

καταβρέχω [katavreho] sprinkle, soak, water.

καταβροχθίζω [katavrohtheezo] devour, eat ravenously, gulp down.

καταγγελία, η [katangeleea] denunciation || annulment, revocation.

καταγής [katayees] on the ground, on the floor.

καταγίνομαι [katayeenome] busy o.s. with, see to.

κάταγμα, το [katagma] fracture.

κατάγομαι [katagome] be descended from, come from.

καταγωγή, η [katagoyee] descent, origin, lineage.

καταγώγιο, το [katagoyo] hovel, hideout, den of vice.

καταδέχομαι [kataðehome] deign, condescend.

κατάδηλος [kataðeelos] evident, clear.

καταδίδω [kataðeeðo] denounce, betray.

καταδικάζω [kataðeekazo] condemn, sentence || (μεταφ) doom, proscribe.

καταδίκη, η [kataðeekee] sentence, conviction || censure, blame.

κατάδικος, ο, η [kataðeekos] prisoner, condemned person.

καταδιωκτικό, το [kataðeeokteeko] fighter (plane).

καταδιώκω [kataðeeoko] pursue, chase || (πολιτικώς) persecute, oppress.

κατάδοση, η [kataðosee] betrayal, denunciation.

καταδρομή, η [kataðromee] pursuit.

καταδρομικό, το [kataðromeeko] cruiser.

καταδυναστεύω [kataðeenastevo] oppress.

καταδύομαι [kataðeeome] dive, plunge.

καταζητώ [katazeeto] pursue, chase.

καταθέτω [katatheto] deposit, lay down || (σαν μάρτυρας) give evidence || (όπλα) lay down || (σχέδιο) introduce.

καταθλιπτικός [katathleepteekos] crushing, overwhelming.

καταιγίδα, η [kateyeeða] tempest, storm, hurricane.

καταίφι, το [kateeefee] kind of oriental cake.

κατακάθι, το [katakathee] residue, sediment, dregs.

κατάκειμαι [katakeeme] lie flat, lie down.

κατάκαρδα [katakarða] deeply, seriously, profoundly, to heart.

κατακέφαλα [katakefala] headlong, on the head.

κατακλύζω [katakleezo] flood, inundate || (μεταφ) invade, overrun.

κατακλυσμός, ο [katakleesmos] flood.

κατάκοιτος [katakeetos] bedridden.

κατάκοπος [katakopos] exhausted, deadbeat, dog-tired.

κατακόβω [katakovo] cut to pieces, cut up, lacerate.

κατακόρυφο, το [katakoreefo] zenith || (μεταφ) acme.

κατακόρυφος [katakoreefos] vertical, perpendicular.

κατακρατώ [katakrato] withhold, keep illegally.

κατακραυγή, η [katakravyee] outcry || protestation.

κατακρεουργώ [katakreourgo] butcher, massacre.

κατακρημνίζω [katakreemneezo] demolish, pull down.

κατακρίνω [katakreeno] blame, criticize, condemn.

κατάκτηση, η [katakteesee] conquest, subjugation.

κατακτώ [katakto] conquer, subjugate.

καταλαβαίνω [katalaveno] understand.

καταλαμβάνω [katalamvano] take, lay hold of, seize || (χώρο) take up.

καταλήγω [kataleego] end in, come to, result in, come to an end.

κατάληξη, η [kataleeksee] termination, ending.

καταληπτός [kataleeptos] comprehensible, intelligible, clear.

κατάληψη, η [kataleepsee] occupation, capture || (ιδέας) understanding, comprehension.

κατάλληλος [kataleelos] suitable, appropriate, fit, proper.

καταλογίζω [kataloyeezo] attribute, impute, ascribe.

κατάλογος, ο [katalogos] catalogue, list || (φαγητών) menu || (τιμών) inventory, register, roll.

κατάλοιπα, τα [kataleepa] waste || **ραδιενεργά** ~ radioactive waste.

κατάλυμα, το [kataleema] lodging, housing || (στρατ) barracks, billeting.

κατάλυση, η [kataleesee] abolition || (χημ) catalysis.

καταλύω [kataleeo] abolish, do away with || take up lodging.

καταμερίζω [katamereezo] share out, distribute, apportion.

καταμεσής [katamesees] in the very middle.

κατάμεστος [katamestos] quite full, crowded.

καταμετρώ [katametro] measure, survey, gauge.

κατάμουτρα [katamoutra] point-blank.

καταναλίσκω [katanaleesko] consume, spend, use up || (ποτά) drink.

κατανάλωση, n [katanalosee] consumption.

καταναλωτής, ο [katanalotees] consumer, customer.

κατανέμω [katanemo] distribute || (ευθύνες) allot, assign, share.

κατανόηση, n [katanoeesee] understanding, comprehension.

κατανοώ [katanoo] understand, comprehend.

κατάντημα, το [katanteema] wretched state.

καταντώ [katanto] be reduced to, bring to, end up as.

κατάνυξη, n [kataneeksee] compunction, piety.

καταπακτή, n [katapaktee] trap, pitfall.

καταπατώ [katapato] violate, encroach upon.

κατάπαυση, n [katapavsee] cessation, stopping, halting.

καταπέλτης, ο [katapeltees] catapult.

καταπέτασμα, το [katapetasma]: **τρώω το ~** to eat to bursting point.

καταπιάνομαι [katapeeanome] undertake, enter upon, engage upon.

καταπιέζω [katapiezo] oppress, crush, harass.

καταπίνω [katapeeno] swallow, gobble up || (για κύματα) engulf.

καταπίπτω [katapeepto] fall down, come down || collapse || (λιγοστεύω) diminish.

καταπλακώνω [kataplakono] flatten, crush.

κατάπλασμα, το [kataplasma] poultice.

καταπλέω [katapleo] sail in, sail down.

καταπληκτικός [katapleekteekos] amazing, wonderful, marvellous, astonishing.

κατάπληκτος [katapleektos] stupefied, amazed.

κατάπληξη, n [katapleeksee] surprise, astonishment.

καταπλήσσω [katapleeso] astonish, surprise, amaze, stupefy.

καταπνίγω [katapneego] strangle, throttle, suffocate || (εξέγερση) suppress, put down.

καταποντίζομαι [kataponteezome] go down, sink.

καταπραΰνω [katapraeeno] pacify, mollify, appease, calm, assuage.

κατάπτυστος [katapteestos] despicable, abject, low, villainous.

κατάπτωση, n [kataptosee] downfall || (εδάφους) landslide || (μεταφ) prostration, exhaustion || dejection, depression.

κατάρα, n [katara] curse, imprecation || (μεταφ) hell, woe, damnation.

καταραμένος [kataramenos] cursed, damned.

καταργώ [katargo] abolish, annul, cancel.

καταριέμαι [katarieme] curse, damn, call down curses on.

καταρράκτης, ο [kataraktees] cascade, waterfall || (τεχν) sluice.

καταρρέω [katareo] collapse, fall down || (μεταφ) give out.

καταρρίπτω [katareepto] (κάποιο) knock down || (τοίχο) pull down, demolish || (επιχείρημα) prove to be wrong || (ρεκόρ) beat, break || (αερο) shoot down.

καταρροή, n [kataroee] catarrh, head cold.

κατάρτι, το [katartee] mast.

καταρτίζω [katarteezo] organize, establish, form, prepare, construct.

καταρώμαι [katarome] βλ **καταριέμαι.**

κατάσβεση, n [katasvesee] extinction, blowing out || (μεταφ) suppression || (δίψας) slaking, quenching.

κατασκευάζω [kataskevazo] construct, make, erect, build || (ιστορία κτλ) invent, concoct, fabricate || (έργο τέχνης) fashion, model.

κατασκεύασμα, το [kataskevasma] fabrication, concoction || construction, creation.

κατασκευή, n [kataskevee] making, construction || (έργο) structure, edifice, building || (εφεύρεση) invention, fabrication.

κατασκήνωση, n [kataskeenosee] camp, encampment || camping.

κατάσκοπος, ο [kataskopos] spy, secret agent.

κάτασπρος [kataspros] pure white, white as a sheet.

κατασταλάζω [katastalazo] (μεταφ) end in, conclude, settle on.

κατάσταση, n [katastasee] situation, condition, state || (περιουσία) wealth, property || (ονομαστική) register, list.

καταστατικό, το [katastateeko] (εταιρείας) statute.

καταστέλλω [katastelo] suppress, overcome || curb, control, contain.

κατάστημα, το [katasteema] establishment, institution || shop, store || **καταστηματάρχης** shopkeeper.

κατάστιχο, το [katasteeho] accounts book || register.

καταστολή, n [katastolee] suppression || checking, bridling, controlling.

καταστρεπτικός [katastrepteekos] destructive, devastating, ruinous.

καταστρέφω [katastrefo] destroy, ruin, devastate || spoil, damage.

καταστροφή, η [katastrofee] destruction, ruin, disaster, catastrophe.

κατάστρωμα, το [katastroma] deck.

καταστρώνω [katastrono] draw up, make up, frame || lay down.

κατάσχεση, η [katashesee] seizure, confiscation || (λόγω χρέους) attachment.

κατάταξη, η [katataksee] classification, sorting, grading || (στρατ) induction.

κατατάσσομαι [katatasome] enlist.

κατατομή, η [katatomee] profile || vertical section, cutoff.

κατατόπια, τα [katatopeea] πλ locality, every nook and cranny.

κατατοπίζομαι [katatopeezome] find one's bearings.

κατατοπίζω [katatopeezo] direct, explain, inform.

κατατρέχω [katatreho] persecute, harass.

καταφανής [katafanees] obvious, evident, manifest.

καταφατικός [katafateekos] affirmative, positive.

καταφέρνω [kataferno] persuade, convince, manage, accomplish, succeed || **τα ~** succeed, manage.

καταφέρω [katafero] deal, strike || βλ και **καταφέρνω**.

καταφθάνω [katafthano] arrive || overtake, catch up, overhaul.

κατάφορτος [katafortos] overloaded.

καταφρονώ [katafrono] scorn, despise.

καταφύγιο, το [katafeeyo] refuge, hiding place.

κατάφυτος [katafeetos] covered with vegetation.

κατάφωτος [katafotos] profusely illuminated.

κατάχαμα [katahama] on the ground, on the floor.

καταχθόνιος [katahthoneeos] infernal, fiendish, devilish.

καταχραστής, ο [katahrastees] embezzler, defaulter.

καταχρεωμένος [katahreomenos] deep in debt.

κατάχρηση, η [katahreesee] abuse, misuse, breach of trust.

καταχρώμαι [katahrome] abuse, take advantage of, presume upon.

καταχωρώ [katahoro] enter in a register, insert, register, record.

καταψηφίζω [katapseefeezo] vote against, oppose.

κατάψυξη, η [katapseeksee] refrigeration.

κατεβάζω [katevazo] let down || (αποσκευές) take or bring down || (θερμοκρασία κτλ) lower, reduce || (κόστος) lessen, decrease || (αυλαία) drop.

κατεβαίνω [kateveno] come down, go down, descend.

κατέβασμα, το [katevasma] descent, lowering, taking down.

κατεβασμένος [katevasmenos] (τιμή) reduced || (κατηφής) depressed.

κατεδαφίζω [katedafeezo] demolish, pull down, raze.

κατειλημμένος [kateeleemenos] occupied, reserved.

κατεργάζομαι [katergazome] elaborate, work out, shape, fashion.

κατεργάρης, ο [katergarees] rascal, rogue || (επιθ) cunning, tricky.

κατέρχομαι [katerhome] βλ **κατεβαίνω**.

κατεύθυνση, η [kateftheensee] direction, line, course.

κατευθύνομαι [kateftheenome] turn, head (for).

κατευθύνω [kateftheeno] direct, guide, aim, turn.

κατευνάζω [katevnazo] calm, pacify, appease, mollify.

κατέχω [kateho] possess, own, have, hold || (θέση) occupy || (γνωρίζω) know.

κατεψυγμένος [katepseegmenos] frozen, icy, frigid, polar.

κατηγορηματικός [kateegoreemateekos] categorical, explicit.

κατηγορητήριο, το [kateegoreeteereeo] indictment.

κατηγορία, η [kateegoreea] accusation, charge || category, class, division.

κατήγορος, ο [kateegoros] plaintiff, accuser || **δημόσιος ~** public prosecutor.

κατηγορούμενο, το [kateegoroumeno] (γραμμ) complement || attribute.

κατηγορούμενος [kateegoroumenos] the accused || defendant.

κατηγορώ [kateegoro] accuse, charge || blame, criticize.

κατηφής [kateefees] gloomy, depressed.

κατήφορος, ο [kateeforos] descent, slope.

κατηχώ [kateeho] (εκκλ) catechize || (σε οργάνωση) initiate.

κάτι [katee] something || some.

κατοικία, η [kateekeea] dwelling, residence, home.

κατοικίδιος [kateekeeδeeos] domesticated.

κατοικώ [kateeko] live in, dwell in, inhabit, reside.

κατολίσθηση, η [katoleestheesee] landslide.

κατόπι(ι) [katop(i)ee] after, close after || then || behind || **~ν από** after.

κατοπτρίζω [katoptreezo] reflect, mirror || (μεταφ) represent.

κατόρθωμα, το [katorthoma] achievement, feat.

κατορθώνω [katorthono] succeed in, perform well.

κατορθωτός [katorthotos] feasible, possible, practicable.

κατουρλιό, το [katourlio] urine, piss (col).

κατουρώ [katouro] piss (col), urinate.

κατοχή, η [katohee] possession || (στρατ) occupation || (νομ) detention.

κάτοχος, ο [katohos] possessor, occupier || experienced person.

κατοχυρώνω [katoheerono] fortify || (μεταφ) secure, safeguard.

κατρακυλώ [katrakeelo] bring down, tumble down, come down.

κατράμι, το [katramee] tar, asphalt.

κατσαβίδι, το [katsaveeðee] screwdriver.

κατσάδα, η [katsaða] scolding, dressing-down, reprimand.

κατσαρίδα, η [katsareeða] cockroach.

κατσαρόλα, η [katsarola] saucepan.

κατσαρός [katsaros] curly, curled, fuzzy.

κατσίκα, η [katseeka] goat.

κατσικήσιος [katseekeeseeos] of a goat.

κατσίκι, το [katseekee] kid.

κατσουφιάζω [katsoufeeazo] look sour, look sullen, frown.

κάτω [kato] down, under, underneath, below || on the ground || στο ~ ~ after all || **απάνω** ~ approximately, about || **άνω** ~ upset, in a turmoil.

κατώτατος [katotatos] lowest, least, undermost.

κατώτερος [katoteros] lower || poorer (quality), inferior.

κατώφλι, το [katoflee] threshold, doorstep || (μεταφ) eve.

καυγάς, ο [kavgas] quarrel, wrangle, squabble, argument.

καύκαλο, το [kavkalo] skull || shell, carapace.

καύσιμα, τα [kavseema] πλ fuel.

καύσιμος [kavseemos] combustible, inflammable.

καύση, η [kavsee] burning || (χημ) combustion.

καυστικός [kavsteekos] caustic.

καύσωνας, ο [kavsonas] heatwave.

καυτερός [kavteros] hot || (υγρό) scalding || (μεταφ) caustic, biting.

καυτηριάζω [kavteereeazo] cauterize || (ζώα) brand || (μεταφ) stigmatize.

καυτός [kavtos] scalding, boiling, hot.

καύχημα, το [kavheema] boast, pride, glory.

καυχιέμαι [kavhieme] boast of, be proud of.

καφάσι, το [kafasee] trellis, lattice || (για φρούτα) crate.

καφενείο, το [kafeneeo] coffee house.

καφές, ο [kafes] coffee.

καφετζής, ο [kafetsees] coffee-house keeper.

καφετιέρα, η [kafetiera] coffee pot.

καχεκτικός [kahekteekos] sickly (person), weakly (person).

καχύποπτος [kaheepoptos] suspicious, distrustful.

κάψα, η [kapsa] excessive heat.

καψαλίζω [kapsaleezo] singe, broil || toast.

κάψιμο, το [kapseemo] burning || scald.

καψούλι, το [kapsoulee] (ιατρ) capsule.

κέδρος, ο [keðros] cedar tree, cedar (wood).

κείμενο, το [keemeno] text.

κειμήλιο, το [keemeeleeo] heirloom, treasure.

κελαϊδώ [kelaeeðo] sing, warble, chirp.

κελεπούρι, το [kelepouree] bargain || windfall, godsend.

κελευστής, ο [kelevstees] petty officer.

κελλάρι, το [kelaree] cellar || larder.

κελλί, το [kelee] cell || honeycomb.

κέλυφος, το [keleefos] shell, husk, bark.

κενό, το [keno] void, empty space, vacuum || (μεταφ) gap.

κενός [kenos] empty || (οικία) unoccupied, vacant.

κέντημα, το [kenteema] sting, bite || embroidery || (μεταφ) exhortation.

κεντρί, το [kentree] sting || thorn.

κεντρίζω [kentreezo] (βόδι) prick, goad || (άλογο) spur || (δένδρο) graft || (μεταφ) rouse, stir up.

κεντρικός [kentreekos] central, middle || principal.

κεντρομόλος [kentromolos] centripetal.

κέντρο, το [kentro] (πόλης) centre || (γεωμ) centre || (διασκέδασης) (night) club, taverna || **τηλεφωνικό** ~ telephone exchange.

κεντρόφυγος [kentrofeegos] centrifugal.

κεντώ [kento] embroider || (μεταφ) incite, rouse, awaken, stir up.

κενώνω [kenono] empty || (δρόμο) drain || (συρτάρι) clean out || (σπίτι) evacuate.

κένωση, η [kenosee] emptying, clearing out || bowel movement.

κεραία, η [kerea] antenna, feeler || (ασυρμάτου) aerial.

κεραμίδι, το [kerameeðee] tile, slate || **κεραμίδα** roof.

κεραμική, η [kerameekee] ceramics.

κεράσι, το [kerasee] cherry ||
κερασιά, η cherry tree.
κέρασμα, το [kerasma] treat.
κερατάς, ο [keratas] cuckold.
κέρατο, το [kerato] horn || (για
άνθρωπο) obstinate, perverse.
κεραυνοβόλος [keravnovolos] like
lightning.
κεραυνός, ο [keravnos] thunderbolt.
κερδίζω [kerðeezo] win, earn || get,
gain || profit by.
κέρδος, το [kerðos] earnings,
winnings || advantage.
κερδοσκοπώ [kerðoskopo] speculate.
κερένιος [kereneeos] wax, waxen.
κερί, το [keree] wax || taper, wax
candle.
κερκίδα, η [kerkeeða] tier of seats.
κέρμα, το [kerma] fragment || coin ||
(για μηχάνημα) token.
κερνώ [kerno] treat || stand or buy a
drink.
κετσές, ο [ketses] felt.
κεφαλαιοκρατία, η [kefaleokrateea]
capitalism.
κεφάλαια, τα [kefalea] πλ funds,
capital.
κεφάλαιο, το [kefaleo] capital, funds
|| (βιβλίου) chapter.
κεφαλαίο, το [kefaleo] capital
(letter).
κεφαλαιώδης [kefaleoðees] essential,
fundamental.
κεφαλή, η [kefalee] head || leader,
chief.
κεφάλι, το [kefalee] head || (μεταφ)
brains.
κεφάτος [kefatos] well-disposed,
merry, jovial.
κέφι, το [kefee] good humour, gaiety ||
στο ~ merry, mellow.
κεφτές, ο [keftes] meatball, rissole.
κεχρί, το [kehree] millet.
κεχριμπάρι, το [kehreembaree]
amber.
κηδεία, η [keeðeea] funeral
(procession).
κηδεμώνας, ο [keeðemonas]
guardian || curator.
κήλη, η [keelee] hernia, rupture.
κηλιδώνω [keeleeðono] stain, dirty ||
(μεταφ) sully, tarnish.
κηλίδα, η [keeleeða] spot, stain ||
(μεταφ) slur, blemish.
κήπος, ο [keepos] garden.
κηπουρική, η [keepoureekee]
gardening, horticulture.
κηπουρός, ο [keepouros] gardener.
κηρήθρα, η [keereethra] honeycomb.
κηροπήγιο, το [keeropeeyo]
candlestick, taper-stand.
κήρυγμα, το [keereegma]
proclamation || (εκκλ) sermon,
preaching.

κήρυκας, ο [keereekas] herald ||
(εκκλ) preacher.
κηρύσσω [keereeso] proclaim,
announce || (εκκλ) preach.
κήτος, το [keetos] cetacean, whale.
κηφήνας, ο [keefeenas] drone ||
(μεταφ) idler, loafer.
κιάλια, τα [kialeea] πλ binoculars,
opera glasses.
κίβδηλος [keevðeelos] adulterated,
counterfeit || (μεταφ) fraudulent.
κιβώτιο, το [keevoteeo] chest, box ||
~ ταχύτητων gearbox.
κιγκλίδωμα, το [keengleeðoma]
(φράκτης) barrier, fence || (σιδερένιο)
grating || (ξύλινο) lattice work ||
(παραθύρου) bar.
κιθάρα, η [keethara] guitar.
κιλό, το [keelo] kilogram.
κιμάς, ο [keemas] minced meat.
κιμωλία, η [keemoleea] chalk.
Κίνα, η [keena] China.
κινδυνεύω [keenðeenevo] endanger ||
be in danger, risk, venture.
κίνδυνος, ο [keenðeenos] danger,
peril, hazard, jeopardy.
κινέζικα, τα [keenezeeka] πλ Chinese
language.
κινέζικος [keenezeekos] Chinese.
Κινέζος, ο [keenezos] Chinese,
Chinaman || **οι Κινέζοι** the Chinese.
κίνημα, το [keeneema] movement ||
(μεταφ) rebellion, revolt.
κινηματογράφος, ο
[keeneematografos] cinema.
κίνηση, η [keeneesee] movement ||
(κυκλοφορίας) flow of traffic || (αξιών)
transactions.
κινητήρας, ο [keeneeteeras] motor.
κινητός [keeneetos] movable.
κίνητρο, το [keeneetro] motive.
κινίνη, η [keeneenee] quinine.
κινούμαι [keenoume] move.
κινώ [keeno] set in motion, move,
rouse, make go, set going.
κιόλα(ς) [keeola(s)] already, also,
even.
κιονοστοιχία, η [keeonosteeheea]
colonnade.
κιόσκι, το [keeoskee] kiosk.
κίσσα, η [keesa] magpie.
κισσός, ο [keesos] ivy.
κιτρινίζω [keetreeneezo] go yellow,
make yellow, pale.
κίτρινος [keetreenos] yellow || sallow,
pale.
κίτρο, το [keetro] citron.
κλαδευτήρι, το [klaðevteeree]
pruning hook, pruning scissors.
κλαδεύω [klaðevo] prune, trim.
κλάδος, ο [klaðos] branch, sector.
κλαίγομαι [klegome] complain, gripe.
κλαίω [kleo] cry, weep || feel sorry for,
weep for.

κλάμα, το [klama] crying, wailing, weeping.

κλάνω [klano] break wind, fart (col).

κλαρί, το [klaree] small branch.

κλάση, η [klasee] class, age group, category.

κλάσμα, το [klasma] fraction || fragment.

κλασσικός [klaseekos] classic(al) || (μεταφ) standard, standing.

κλαψιάρης [klapseearees] given to complaining || tearful, plaintive.

κλάψιμο, το [klapseemo] crying, grumbling.

κλέβω [klevo] βλ **κλέπτω.**

κλειδαριά, η [kleeδaria] lock || (ασφαλείας) safety lock || (κρεμαστή) padlock.

κλειδαρότρυπα, η [kleeδarotreepa] keyhole.

κλειδί, το [kieeδee] key.

κλειδώνω [kleeδono] lock up || (περιορίζω) confine, coop up.

κλείδωση, η [kleeδosee] joint.

κλείνω [kleeno] close, shut, shut up, seal || (με σύρτη) bolt || (βρύση) turn off || ~ **το μάτι** wink || ~ **τα εξήντα** I'm nearing sixty.

κλείσιμο, το [kleeseemo] closing, locking up || (μεταφ) conclusion.

κλεισούρα, η [kleesoura] pass || mustiness.

κλειστός [kleestos] shut, closed.

κλέπτης, ο [kleptees] thief, burglar || (πορτοφολιών) pickpocket.

κλέπτω [klepto] (κάτι) steal || (κάποιο) rob || (με απάτη) cheat, swindle.

κλεφτά [klefta] furtively, stealthily || hurriedly.

κλέφτης, ο [kleftees] thief || klepht.

κλεφτοπόλεμος, ο [kleftopolemos] guerrilla warfare.

κλεφτός [kleftos] stolen || furtive, stealthy.

κλεψιά, η [klepseea] βλ **κλοπή.**

κλέψιμο, το [klepseemo] theft, robbery, burglary.

κλεψύδρα, η [klepseeδra] water clock, sandglass.

κλήμα, το [kleema] vine || **κληματαριά, η** vine arbour, climbing vine || bower || **κληματόφυλλο, το** vine leaf.

κληρικός [kleereekos] clerical, of the clergy.

κληροδότημα, το [kleeroδoteema] legacy, bequest.

κληρονομιά, η [kleeronomeea] inheritance || heritage, legacy.

κληρονομικός [kleeronomeekos] hereditary.

κληρονόμος, ο, η [kleeronomos] heir, heiress.

κληρονομώ [kleeronomo] inherit, come into an estate.

κλήρος, ο [kleeros] lot, fate || (εκκλ) clergy || (μεταφ) lot, fortune.

κλήρωση, η [kleerosee] drawing of lottery, prize drawing.

κλήση, η [kleesee] call, calling || writ of summons.

κλητήρας, ο [kleeteeras] clerk || (δικαστικός) bailiff.

κλίβανος, ο [kleevanos] oven, kiln, furnace.

κλίμα, το [kleema] climate || (μεταφ) atmosphere.

κλίμακα, η [kleemaka] staircase, stairs, ladder || scale || (μουσ) gamut, scale.

κλιμακωτός [kleemakotos] graduated.

κλιματισμός, ο [kleemateesmos] air conditioning.

κλινήρης [kleeneerees] bedridden.

κλινική, η [kleeneekee] clinic, (private) hospital.

κλίνω [kleeno] lean, bend || (έχω τάση προς) tend || (γραμμ) decline, conjugate.

κλίση, η [kleesee] inclination, slope || proneness, tendency || (γραμμής) slope || (γραμμ) declension, conjugation || (στέγης) slant.

κλονίζομαι [kloneezome] stagger || (μεταφ) hesitate, falter, waver.

κλονίζω [kloneezo] shake, unsettle || (υγεία) damage, ruin.

κλονισμός, ο [kloneesmos] shaking, concussion || (μεταφ) hesitation, wavering.

κλοπή, η [klopee] theft, robbery, burglary.

κλοπιμαίος [klopeemeos] stolen || furtive, stealthy.

κλουβί, το [klouvee] cage.

κλούβιος [klouveos] bad, rotten || (μεταφ) empty-headed, stupid.

κλύσμα, το [kleesma] enema.

κλώθω [klotho] spin.

κλωνάρι, το [klonaree] branch (of tree) || shoot.

κλώσιμο, το [kloseemo] spinning.

κλώσσα, η [klosa] (brooding) hen.

κλωστή, η [klostee] thread, string.

κλωτσιά, η [klotsia] kick.

κλωτσώ [klotso] kick.

κνήμη, η [kneemee] shin || leg.

κόβομαι [kovome] cut o.s.

κόβω [kovo] (ψωμί) cut, slice || (μαλλιά) cut, trim || (νύχια) pare || (κρέας) carve || (νομίσματα) coin, mint || (νερό) turn off || (καφέ, σιτάρι) grind, mill || (κεφάλι) behead || (εφόδια) cut off || ~ **μονέδα** make money || ~ **εισιτήριο** buy a ticket || ~ **δεξιά** turn right.

κόγχη, η [konghee] marine shell || (ματιού) eye socket || (αρχιτεκ) niche.

κοιλάδα, η [keelaδa] valley, vale.

κοιλιά, η [keelia] belly, abdomen || (τοίχου) bulge.

κοίλος [keelos] hollow, sunken.
κοιλότητα, η [keeloteeta] hollowness || concavity.
κοιμάμαι [keemame] sleep, be asleep.
κοίμηση, η [keemeesee] (εκκλ) Assumption || sleeping.
κομητήριο, το [keemeeteereeo] cemetery, graveyard.
κοιμίζω [keemeezo] put to sleep || quiet, lull, beguile.
κοιμισμένος [keemeesmenos] (μεταφ) sluggish, stupid, dull.
κοιμούμαι [keemoume] βλ **κοιμάμαι.**
κοινοβουλευτικός [keenovoulevteekos] parliamentary, parliamentarian.
κοινοβούλιο, το [keenovouleeo] parliament || (στην Αγγλία) Houses of Parliament.
κοινό, το [keeno] the public.
κοινοποιώ [keenopeeo] notify, inform, announce || serve (a notice).
κοινοπολιτεία, η [keenopoleeteea] commonwealth.
κοινός [keenos] common || ordinary, vulgar || (εργασία κτλ) collective || (γραμμ) common (noun) || **κοινή γνώμη** public opinion || **από κοινού** in common, together.
κοινότητα, η [keenoteeta] community || parish || **Βουλή των Κοινοτήτων** House of Commons.
κοινοτοπία, η [keenotopeea] commonplace || banality.
κοινωνία, η [keenoneea] society, community, association || (εκκλ) Holy Communion.
κοινωνικός [keenoneekos] social, sociable || **κοινωνικός λειτουργός** social worker.
κοινωνώ [keenono] receive Holy Communion || administer Holy Communion.
κοιτάζω [keetazo] look at, pay attention to || consider, see || attend.
κοίτασμα, το [keetasma] layer, deposit, stratum.
κοιτίδα, η [keeteeδa] cradle || (μεταφ) origin, birthplace.
κοιτώνας, ο [keetonas] bedroom || dormitory.
κοκεταρία, η [koketareea] smartness, coquetry, stylishness.
κόκκαλο, το [kokalo] bone || (παπουτσιού) shoehorn || **έμεινε ~** he was astounded.
κοκκινέλι, το [kokeenelee] red wine.
κοκκινίζω [kokeeneezo] redden, blush, turn red.
κοκκινογούλι, το [kokeenogoulee] beetroot, beet.
κοκκινομάλλης [kokeenomalees] red-haired.

κόκκινος [kokeenos] red, scarlet || (μάγουλα) ruddy, rosy.
κόκκος, ο [kokos] grain || (καφέ) bean || (οκόνης) speck.
κοκκύτης, ο [kokeetees] whooping cough.
κόκορας, ο [kokoras] cock, rooster.
κοκορέτσι, το [kokoretsee] sheep's entrails.
κολάζω [kolazo] punish, chastise.
κολακεία, η [kolakeea] flattery, softsoaping.
κολακευτικός [kolakevteekos] complimentary.
κολακεύω [kolakevo] flatter, fawn upon.
κόλακας, ο [kolakas] flatterer, wheedler.
κόλαση, η [kolasee] hell.
κολατσιό, το [kolatsio] snack.
κολικός, ο [koleekos] colic.
κολιός, ο [kolios] kind of mackerel.
κόλλα, η [kola] glue, gum, paste || (κολλαρίσματος) starch || (χαρτιού) sheet of paper.
κολλάρο, το [kolaro] collar.
κολλέγιο, το [koleyo] college.
κόλλημα, το [koleema] glueing, sticking || soldering.
κολλητικός [koleeteekos] contagious, infectious.
κολλητός [koleetos] soldered || close-fitting || (εφαπτόμενος) contiguous.
κολλιέ, το [kolie] necklace.
κόλλυβα, τα [koleeva] πλ boiled wheat (given after funerals).
κολλώ [kolo] glue, stick, paste || solder, fuse || (αρρώστεια) get, catch || (σε κάποιο) stick to, attach to.
κολοκύθι, το [kolokeethee] vegetable marrow, pumpkin.
κολόνα, η [kolona] βλ **κολώνα.**
κολόνια, η [koloneea] eau de Cologne.
κολοσσιαίος [kolosieos] colossal, enormous.
κολοσσός, ο [kolosos] colossus, giant.
κόλπο, το [kolpo] trick, artifice, deceit.
κόλπος, ο [kolpos] breast, bosom || (γεωγραφικός) gulf, bay.
κολυμβήθρα, η [koleemveethra] font.
κολυμβητής, ο [koleemveetees] swimmer.
κολύμπι, το [koleembee] swimming.
κολυμπώ [koleembo] swim.
κολώνα, η [kolona] pillar, column.
κόμβος, ο [komvos] knot || junction.
κόμης, ο [komees] count, earl.
κομπτεία, η [kometeea] county, shire.
κομήτης, ο [kometees] comet.
κομιστής, ο [komeestees] carrier, bearer.

κόμιστρα, τα [komeestra] πλ carriage fees.

κόμμα, το [koma] (πολιτικό) party || (γραμμ) comma || (μαθημ) decimal point.

κομματάρχης, ο [komatarhees] party leader.

κομμάτι, το [komatee] piece || (ψωμί) slice || (ζάχαρη) lump || fragment, chip || (επιρ) a bit.

κομματιάζω [komateeazo] cut up, parcel out, tear, break.

κομμένος [komenos] sliced, cut || (κουρασμένος) exhausted.

κομ(μ)οδίνο, το [komodeeno] bedside table.

κομμουνιστής, ο [komouneestees] communist.

κόμμωση, η [komosee] hairdressing, hair style.

κομμωτήριο, το [komoteereeo] hairdressing salon.

κομπιάζω [kombeeazo] (μεταφ) hesitate.

κομπίνα, η [kombeena] racket (col).

κομπιναιζό, το [kombeenezo] slip, petticoat.

κομπόδεμα, το [kombodema] hoard of money, savings.

κομπολό(γ)ι, το [kombolo(y)ee] string of beads, worry beads.

κόμπος, ο [kombos] βλ **κόμβος**.

κομπόστα, η [kombosta] compote.

κομπρέσσα, η [kombresa] compress.

κομφόρ, τα [komfor] πλ home comforts, necessities.

κομψός [kompsos] fashionable, stylish, smart.

κονδύλιο, το [kondeeleeo] item, entry.

κονιάκ, το [koneeak] cognac, brandy.

κονίαμα, το [koneeama] mortar || plaster.

κονσέρβα, η [konserva] tinned food, canned food, preserve(s).

κονσέρτο, το [konserto] concert.

κοντά [konta] close to, close by, near || almost, nearly || ~ σε near, next to || ~ στα άλλα moreover.

κονταίνω [konteno] shorten, curtail || get shorter.

κοντάρι, το [kontaree] pole || (σημαίας) staff || (ναυτ) mast.

κοντεύω [kontevo] be about to, be nearly finished, be on the verge (of) || (πλησιάζω) approach, come near, draw near.

κόντημα, το [konteema] shortening, shrinking.

κοντινός [konteenos] neighbouring, near(by) || (δρόμος) short, quick.

κοντός [kontos] short || (ουσ) pole, post, stake.

κοντοστέκω [kontosteko] pause || hesitate, waver.

κόντρα [kontra] against, opposite.

κοπάδι, το [kopadee] flock || herd, drove || (λύκων) pack || (ανθρώπων) crowd, throng.

κοπάζω [kopazo] calm down, grow quiet, subside.

κοπανίζω [kopaneezo] beat, pound, grind.

κόπανος, ο [kopanos] pestle, crusher || (μεταφ) fool, idiot.

κοπέλλα, η [kopela] girl || (υπηρεσίας) servant, maid.

κοπή, η [kopee] cutting || stoppage.

κόπια, η [kopeea] copy, transcript.

κοπιάζω [kopeeazo] labour, toil || take the trouble (to).

κοπιαστικός [kopeeasteekos] wearisome, hard, fatiguing, troublesome.

κοπίδι, το [kopeedee] chisel.

κόπος, ο [kopos] fatigue, toil, labour, trouble, effort.

κόπρανα, τα [koprana] πλ excrement.

κοπριά, η [kopreea] dung, manure.

κοπρόσκυλο, το [koproskeelo] (μεταφ) worthless person, scoundrel.

κοπτήρας, ο [kopteeras] incisor || (χαρτοκοπτήρας) cutter.

κοπτική, η [kopteekee] cutting, tailoring.

κόπτω [kopto] βλ **κόβω**.

κόπωση, η [koposee] fatigue, weariness, toil.

κόρακας, ο [korakas] crow, raven.

κοράλλι, το [koralee] coral.

κορδέλλα, η [kordela] ribbon, band, tape || (μεταφ) zigzag, twist and turn.

κορδόνι, το [kordonee] cord, string.

κορδώνομαι [kordonome] strut, swagger, put on airs.

κορδώνω [kordono] tighten, stretch, extend.

κορεσμός, ο [koresmos] satisfaction, satiety.

κόρη, η [koree] girl || (παρθένα) virgin || (παιδί) daughter || (οφθαλμού) pupil.

κοριός, ο [korios] bedbug.

κοριτσάκι, το [koreetsakee] little girl.

κορίτσι, το [koreetsee] girl || virgin.

κορμί, το [kormee] body || trunk.

κορμός, ο [kormos] trunk.

κορμοστασιά, η [kormostasia] stature, bearing, figure.

κορνάρω [kornaro] sound one's horn, hoot.

κορνίζα, η [korneeza] frame || cornice.

κοροϊδεύω [koroeedevo] scoff at, laugh at, ridicule || deceive.

κορόιδο, το [koroeedo] laughing stock, butt, scapegoat.

κορσές, ο [korses] corset.

κορτάρω [kortaro] flirt, court.

κορυδαλλός, ο [koreeðalos] skylark, lark.

κορυφαίος, ο [koreefeos] leader, chief.

κορυφή, η [koreefee], **κορφή, η** [korfee] top || (όρους) top, peak || (γωνίας) vertex || (μεταφ) leading person, outstanding person.

κόρφος, ο [korfos] bosom.

κορώνα, η [korona] crown, coronet || ~ γράμματα heads or tails.

κοσκινίζω [koskeeneezo] sift, screen || (μεταφ) sift carefully.

κόσκινο, το [koskeeno] sieve, sifter.

κοσμάκης, ο [kosmakees] the man in the street.

κόσμημα, το [kosmeema] decoration, jewel || **κόσμηματα** πλ jewellery.

κοσμήτορας, ο [kosmeetoras] dean (of university).

κοσμικός [kosmeekos] lay || mundane || (γεγονός) social.

κόσμιος [kosmeeos] decent, modest, proper.

κόσμος, ο [kosmos] universe, world || (άνθρωποι) people || (στόλισμα) embellishment.

κοσμώ [kosmo] adorn, embellish.

κοστίζω [kosteezo] cost, be expensive.

κόστος, το [kostos] cost, price.

κοστούμι, το [kostoumee] suit.

κότερο, το [kotero] sailboat, yacht || (ναυτ) cutter.

κοτέτσι, το [kotetsee] hen coop.

κοτόπουλο, το [kotopoulo] chicken.

κοτρώνι, το [kotronee] large stone, boulder.

κοτσάνι, το [kotsanee] stem, stalk.

κότσι, το [kotsee] anklebone.

κότσια, τα [kotseea] πλ guts, strength.

κοτσίδα, η [kotseeða] tress, braid, pigtail.

κότσυφας, ο [kotseefas] blackbird.

κότ(τ)α, η [kota] hen || fowl.

κουβαλώ [kouvalo] carry, bring, transport.

κουβάρι, το [kouvaree] ball.

κουβαριάζω [kouvareeazo] wind into a ball || crumple || (μεταφ) cheat.

κουβαρίστρα, η [kouvareestra] bobbin, spool.

κουβάς, ο [kouvas] bucket, pail.

κουβέντα, η [kouventa] conversation, chat.

κουβεντιάζω [kouventeeazo] converse, discuss, chat.

κουβέρ, το [kouver] service charge, cover charge.

κουβέρτα, η [kouverta] blanket, coverlet || (ναυτ) deck.

κουδούνι, το [kouðounee] bell || (εισόδου) doorbell.

κουδουνίζω [kouðouneezo] ring, tinkle, jingle.

κουδουνίστρα, η [kouðouneestra] rattle.

κουζίνα, η [kouzeena] kitchen || (για μαγείρεμα) stove.

κουκέτα, η [kouketa] berth.

κουκί, το [koukee] broad bean || grain.

κούκλα, η [koukla] doll || (ράφτη) dummy || (καλαμποκιού) corn cob || (μεταφ) lovely child || pretty woman.

κούκος, ο [koukos] cuckoo || bonnet, cap.

κουκουβάγια, η [koukouvaya] owl.

κουκούλα, η [koukoula] cowl, hood || (τσαγιού) tea cosy.

κουκούλι, το [koukoulee] cocoon.

κουκουλώνω [koukoulono] keep secret || bury || wrap warmly.

κουκουνάρι, το [koukounaree] pine cone || seed of pine cone.

κουκούτσι, το [koukoutsee] stone, kernel, pip || (μεταφ) morsel, scrap.

κουλούρα, η [kouloura] roll, French roll || (ναυτ) lifebuoy.

κουλούρι, το [koulouree] ring-shaped biscuit.

κουλουριάζω [kouloureeazo] coil, roll up, fold.

κουμάντο, το [koumanto] order, control.

κουμπάρα, η [koumbara] godmother || matron of honour.

κουμπαράς, ο [koumbaras] moneybox, piggy bank.

κουμπάρος, ο [koumbaros] godfather || (σε γάμο) best man.

κουμπί, το [koumbee] button, stud || (φώτων) switch.

κουμπότρυπα, η [koumbotreepa] buttonhole.

κουμπώνω [koumbono] button up, fasten.

κουνάβι, το [kounavee] marten, ferret.

κουνέλι, το [kounelee] rabbit.

κούνημα, το [kouneema] shaking, swinging, wagging || (μεταφ) swaying.

κούνια, η [kouneea] cradle, cot, crib || (κήπου) swing.

κουνιάδα, η [kouneeaða] sister-in-law.

κουνιάδος, ο [kouneeaðos] brother-in-law.

κουνιστός [kouneestos] rocking || (μεταφ) swaying.

κουνούπι, το [kounoupee] mosquito.

κουνουπίδι, το [kounoupeeðee] cauliflower.

κουνιέμαι [kounieme] move, shake || get moving.

κουνώ [kouno] move, shake || (μαντήλι) wave || (ουρά) wag || (μωρό) rock || (κεφάλι) shake.

κούπα, η [koupa] cup, bowl, glass || (σε χαρτιά) heart.

κουπί, το [koupee] oar || **τραβώ ~ to** row.

κούρα, η [koura] cure || medical attendance.

κουράγιο, το [kourayo] bravery, fearlessness.

κουράζομαι [kourazome] get tired, tire o.s.

κουράζω [kourazo] tire, weary || bore || (όραση) strain.

κούραση, η [kourasee] weariness, fatigue || (μηχανής) wear and tear.

κουρασμένος [kourasmenos] tired, weary || (πρόσωπο) drawn.

κουραστικός [kourasteekos] tiresome, trying, troublesome.

κουραφέξαλα, τα [kourafeksala] πλ bullshit (col), balls (col).

κουρδίζω [kourðeezo] wind up || (βιολί) tune || (μεταφ) stir up, incite.

κουρέας, ο [koureas] barber.

κουρείο, το [koureeo] barber's shop.

κουρέλι, το [kourelee] rag, tatter, shred.

κούρεμα, το [kourema] haircut || shearing, clipping.

κουρεύω [kourevo] cut the hair of, trim, clip || (πρόβατο) shear || (χλόη) mow.

κουρκούτι, το [kourkoutee] batter || pap.

κούρσα, η [koursa] race || (διαδρομή) ride || (αμάξι) car.

κουρσάρος, ο [koursaros] pirate.

κουρσεύω [koursevo] plunder, raid.

κουρτίνα, η [kourteena] curtain.

κουσούρι, το [kousouree] defect, fault.

κουτάβι, το [koutavee] puppy.

κουτάλι, το [koutalee] spoon.

κουταμάρα, η [koutamara] foolishness, nonsense.

κούτελο, το [koutelo] forehead.

κουτί, το [koutee] box, case || (σπίρτων) matchbox || (κονσέρβας) tin.

κουτός [koutos] silly, foolish, slow-witted.

κουτουλώ [koutoulo] nod drowsily || butt.

κουτουρού [koutourou]: **στα ~** heedlessly, haphazardly, by chance.

κουτρουβάλα, η [koutrouvala] somersault.

κουτσαίνω [koutseno] limp || cripple.

κουτσομπολεύω [koutsombolevo] gossip, spread reports, tittle-tattle.

κουτσομπολιό, το [koutsombolio] gossip, tittle-tattle.

κουτσός [koutsos] crippled, limping.

κούτσουρο, το [koutsouro] log, stump.

κουφαίνομαι [koufenome] go deaf.

κουφαίνω [koufeno] deafen, make deaf.

κουφαμάρα, η [koufamara] deafness.

κουφάρι, το [koufaree] body || corpse.

κουφέτο, το [koufeto] sugared almond.

κούφιος [koufeeos] hollow, empty || (δόντι) decayed || (ήχος) muffled || (άνθρωπος) not serious, frivolous.

κουφόβραση, η [koufovrasee] sweltering heat.

κουφός [koufos] hard of hearing.

κούφωμα, το [koufoma] hollow, cavity || opening.

κοφίνι, το [kofeenee] basket, hamper, pannier.

κοφτά [kofta]: **ορθά ~** frankly, categorically.

κοφτερός [kofteros] sharp, cutting.

κόφτω [kofto] βλ **κόβω.**

κόχη, η [kohee] βλ **κώχη.**

κοχλάζω [kohlazo] boil, bubble || (μεταφ) seethe.

κοχλίας, ο [kohleeas] snail || (ήλος) screw.

κοχύλι, το [koheelee] sea shell.

κόψη, η [kopsee] cutting, slicing, clipping || edge.

κόψιμο, το [kopseemo] cut, gash || cutting || (ασθένια) bellyache (col).

κραγιόν, το [krayon] crayon || lipstick.

κραδαίνω [kraðeno] flourish, wave, vibrate.

κράζω [krazo] croak, caw || cry out || call.

κραιπάλη, η [krepalee] riot, orgy || drunkenness.

κράμα, το [krama] mixture, blend || alloy, amalgam.

κρανίο, το [kraneeo] cranium || skull.

κράνος, το [kranos] helmet.

κράξιμο, το [krakseemo] crowing, cawing.

κρασί, το [krasee] wine.

κράση, η [krasee] (σώματος) temperament, make-up.

κράσπεδο, το [kraspeðo] (λόφου) foot || (πεζοδρομίου) kerb || curb (US).

κρατήρας, ο [krateeras] crater.

κράτηση, η [krateesee] confinement, arrest || (μισθού) deduction(s).

κρατιέμαι [kratieme] hold one's own, be well preserved.

κρατικοποίηση, η [krateekopieesee] nationalization.

κρατικός [krateekos] national.

κράτος, το [kratos] influence, power, authority || the state.

κρατώ [krato] last, keep || (επιβάλλομαι) hold in check, rule || (κατάγομαι) be descended from || (βαστώ) have, hold || (υποβαστώ) support.

κραυγάζω [kravgazo] cry, howl, shout, scream.

κραυγή, η [kravyee] shout, cry, outcry.

κρέας, το [kreas] meat, flesh.

κρεββάτι, το [krevatee] bed.

κρεββατοκάμαρα, η [krevatokamara] bedroom.

κρεββατώνω [krevatono] confine to bed, lay up.

κρέμα, η [krema] cream.

κρεμάζω [kremazo] hang, suspend.

κρεμάλα, η [kremala] gallows, gibbet.

κρέμασμα, το [kremasma] suspension, hooking on || hanging.

κρεμαστός [kremastos] suspended.

κρεμάστρα, η [kremastra] hanger || hat rack || portmanteau.

κρεμιέμαι [kremieme] hang, be suspended.

κρεμμύδι, το [kremeeδee] onion.

κρεμ(ν)ώ [krem(n)o] hang, hook up, suspend.

κρεοπώλης, ο [kreopolees] butcher.

κρεουργώ [kreourgo] butcher || massacre.

κρεπ, το [krep] crêpe rubber || crape.

κρημνίζομαι [kreemneezome] fall, crumble, collapse.

κρημνίζω [kreemneezo] hurl down, pull down, wreck.

κρήνη, η [kreenee] fountain.

κρηπίδωμα, το [kreepeeδoma] foundation, base, groundwork || (ναυτ) breakwater || (σταθμού) railway platform.

κρησφύγετο, το [kreesfeeyeto] hideaway, retreat.

κριάρι, το [kreearee] ram.

κριθαράκι, το [kreetharakee] barley-shaped noodle || (ματιού) stye.

κριθάρι, το [kreetharee] barley.

κρίκος, ο [kreekos] link, buckle, ring || (ανυψώσεως) jack.

κρίμα, το [kreema] sin, guilt || pity, misfortune || τι ~! what a pity!, what a shame!

κρίνος, ο [kreenos] lily.

κρίνω [kreeno] judge, consider || (αποφασίζω) decide.

κριός, ο [krios] ram.

κρίσιμος [kreeseemos] critical, grave, momentous || trying.

κρίση, η [kreesee] judgment, view || (οικονομική) crisis, depression || (έλλειψη) deficiency, shortage || (πνεύματος) judgment.

κριτήριο, το [kreeteereeo] criterion, test.

κριτής, ο [kreetees] judge.

κριτική, η [kreeteekee] criticism, review.

κριτικός [kreeteekos] discerning, critical || (ουσ) critic.

κροκόδειλος, ο [krokoδeelos] crocodile.

κρόκος, ο [krokos] crocus || (αυγού) yolk.

κρόσσι, το [krosee] fringe.

κρόταφος, ο [krotafos] (ανατ) temple.

κρότος, ο [krotos] crash, bang, noise || (μεταφ) sensation.

κρουαζιέρα, η [krouaziera] cruise.

κρούση, η [krousee] striking, sounding || (στρατ) encounter.

κρούσμα, το [krousma] (ιατρ, νομ) case.

κρούστα, η [krousta] crust, rind || scab.

κρούω [krouo] strike, sound || knock on || (κουδούνι) ring.

κρυάδα, η [kreeaδa] cold, chill.

κρύβομαι [kreevome] go into hiding.

κρύβω [kreevo] βλ **κρύπτω**.

κρυμμένος [kreemenos] concealed.

κρύο, το [kreeo] cold.

κρυολόγημα, το [kreeoloyeema] (ιατρ) cold.

κρυοπάγημα, το [kreeopayeema] frostbite.

κρύος [kreeos] cold || indifferent, phlegmatic, cool.

κρύπτω [kreepto] hide, conceal || cover, screen || (μεταφ) withhold, hold back.

κρυστάλλινος [kreestaleenos] like crystal, very clear.

κρύσταλλο, το [kreestalo] crystal (glass).

κρυφά [kreefa] secretly, clandestinely, stealthily.

κρυφός [kreefos] private, secluded || (χαρά) secret, inner || (άνθρωπος) discreet, reticent.

κρύψιμο, το [kreepseemo] concealing, hiding.

κρυψίνους [kreepseenous] deceitful, underhand, sneaky.

κρυψώνας, ο [kreepsonas] hideout, lurking place.

κρυώνω [kreeono] grow cold, feel cold || cool down, chill.

κτένι, το [ktenee] comb || (τσουγκράνα) rake || **κτενίζω** to comb || (μεταφ) brush up, finish in detail || ~σμα combing || hair-dressing.

κτήμα, το [kteema] estate, land || **κτηματίας, ο** landowner, proprietor.

κτηνίατρος, ο [kteeneeatros] veterinary surgeon.

κτήνος, το [kteenos] brute, beast, animal || **κτήνη** cattle.

κτηνοτροφία, η [kteenotrofeea] stockbreeding.

κτηνώδης [kteenoδees] beastly, bestial || (όρεξη) hoggish.

κτήση, η [kteesee] acquisition, occupation, occupancy.

κτητικός [kteeteekos] (γραμμ) possessive || acquisitive.

κτίζω [kteezo] construct, erect, build.

κτίριο, το [kteereeo] building, edifice.

κτίσιμο, το [kteeseemo] building, erection.

κτίστης, ο [kteestees] builder, mason.

κτυπώ [kteepo] beat, strike, flog, thrash.

κυάνιο, το [keeaneeo] cyanide.

κυβέρνηση, η [keeverneesee] government, management.

κυβερνήτης, ο [keeverneetees] governor || (ναυτ) commander.

κυβερνητικός [keeverneeteekos] governmental.

κυβερνώ [keeverno] govern || (πλοίο) steer || (σπίτι) manage, direct.

κύβος, ο [keevos] cube || die.

κυδώνι, το [keedonee] quince || (όστρακο) kind of shellfish.

κύηση, η [kieesee] pregnancy || gestation.

κυκλάμινο, το [keeklameeno] cyclamen.

κυκλικός [keekleekos] circular.

κύκλος, ο [keeklos] circle || (ηλιακός κτλ) cycle, period || (προσώπων) set.

κυκλοφορία, η [keekloforeea] circulation || (αυτοκινήτων) traffic flow.

κυκλοφορώ [keekloforo] put into circulation, spread || go about.

κύκλωμα, το [keekloma] electric circuit || encirclement.

κυκλώνας, ο [keeklonas] cyclone.

κυκλώνω [keeklono] surround, encircle, envelop.

κύκνος, ο [keeknos] swan.

κυλάω [keelao] roll.

κυλιέμαι [keelieme] roll over || (χοίρος) wallow.

κυλικείο, το [keeleekeeo] buffet, sideboard || refreshment room.

κύλινδρος, ο [keeleenδros] cylinder || roller, barrel.

κυλότα, η [keelota] panties.

κύμα, το [keema] wave.

κυμαίνομαι [keemenome] undulate, wave, ripple || (μεταφ) fluctuate, waver, hesitate.

κυματίζω [keemateezo] wave, flutter || ripple.

κυματοθραύστης, ο [keematothravstees] breakwater.

κύμινο, το [keemeeno] cumin.

κυνήγι, το [keeneeyee] hunting, shooting, chase || game.

κυνηγός, ο [keeneegos] hunter, shooter.

κυνηγώ [keeneego] hunt, chase, run after || go shooting.

κυνικός [keeneekos] cynic(al).

κυοφορώ [keeoforo] be pregnant.

κυπαρίσσι, το [keepareesee] cypress tree.

κύπελλο, το [keepelo] cup, goblet, tumbler.

κυπριακός [keepreeakos] Cypriot.

Κύπριος, ο [keepreeos] Cypriot.

Κύπρος, η [keepros] Cyprus.

κύπτω [keepto] bend, bow || slant || (μεταφ) give way.

κυρά, η [keera] missus (col).

κυρία, η [keereea] lady, mistress || Mrs.

Κυριακή, η [keereeakee] Sunday.

κυριαρχία, η [keereearheea] sovereignty, dominion.

κυριαρχώ [keereearho] dominate, exercise authority || be sovereign.

κυριεύω [keerievo] subjugate, capture, dominate || (πάθος) seize, possess.

κυριολεκτικώς [keereeolekteekos] exactly, precisely, to the letter.

κύριος, ο [keereeos] master, sir, gentleman || Mr.

κύριος [keereeos] essential, vital || main, chief, leading.

κυριότητα, η [keereeoteeta] ownership.

κυρίως [keereeos] principally, chiefly, mainly, especially.

κύρος, το [keeros] authority, power || validity, weight.

κυρτός [keertos] bent, crooked || convex, bulging.

κυρώνω [keerono] confirm || (νόμο) sanction, approve || (απόφαση) ratify, validate.

κύρωση, η [keerosee] confirmation, sanction || penalty.

κύστη, η [keestee] bladder, cyst.

κύτος, το [keetos] (ναυτ) hold.

κυττάζω [keetazo] βλ κοιτάζω.

κύτταρο, το [keetaro] cell.

κυψέλη, η [keepselee] swarm (of bees) || beehive || (αυτιού) earwax.

κώδικας, ο [koδeekas] code || codex.

κωδωνοκρουσία, η [koδonokrouseea] chiming, ringing, pealing.

κωδωνοστάσιο, το [koδonostaseeo] belfry, church steeple.

κώκ, το [kok] coke.

κώλος, ο [kolos] arse (col), bottom, backside (col) || ~ και βρακί intimate.

κωλοφωτιά, η [kolofotia] glow-worm.

κώλυμα, το [koleema] obstacle, impediment.

κωλυσιεργώ [koleesiergo] obstruct, hinder.

κωλύω [koleeo] stop, prevent, hinder.

κώμα, το [koma] coma.

κωματώδης [komatoδees] comatose, lethargic.

κωμικός [komeekos] comic(al), funny || (ουσ) comedian.

κωμόπολη, η [komopolee] market town.

κωμωδία, η [komoδeea] comedy.

κώνος, ο [konos] cone.

κωπηλασία, η [kopeelaseea] rowing.
κωπηλάτης, ο [kopeelatees] rower.
κωφάλαλος [kofalalos] deaf-and-dumb.
κώχη, η [kohee] corner, nook, recess || (πανταλονιού) crease.

Λ, λ

λάβα, η [lava] lava.
λαβαίνω [laveno] βλ **λαμβάνω.**
λάβαρο, το [lavaro] banner, standard.
λαβείν, το [laveen] credit || **δούναι και** ~ debit and credit.
λαβή, η [lavee] handle, grip || pretext, excuse, reason.
λαβίδα, η [laveeδa] grip, nippers, hold || (χειρουργική) forceps.
λάβρα, η [lavra] excessive heat, suffocating heat.
λαβράκι, το [lavrakee] bass fish.
λαβύρινθος, ο [laveereenthos] labyrinth.
λαβωματιά, η [lavomatia] wound.
λαβώνω [lavono] wound.
λαγάνα, η [lagana] unleavened bread.
λαγκάδι, το [langaδee] ravine, narrow valley, defile.
λάγνος [lagnos] lewd, lascivious, wanton.
λαγός, ο [lagos] hare.
λαγωνικό, το [lagoneeko] hunting dog || greyhound, pointer.
λαδερός [laδeros] oily, greasy || cooked with oil.
λάδι, το [laδee] olive oil.
λαδομπογιά, η [laδomboya] oil paint.
λαδόχαρτο, το [laδoharto] greaseproof paper.
λαδώνω [laδono] apply oil || lubricate || (μεταφ) bribe.
λαδωτήρι, το [laδoteeree] cruet stand.
λάθος, το [lathos] error, mistake, slip, fault || **κατά** ~ by mistake.
λαθραίος [lathreos] furtive, clandestine, secret.
λαθραίως [lathreos] secretly, furtively, stealthily.
λαθρεμπόριο, το [lathremboreeo] smuggling || contraband.
λαθρέμπορος, ο [lathremboros] smuggler, contrabandist.
λαθρεπιβάτης, ο [lathrepeevatees] stowaway.
λαΐδη, η [leδee] (τίτλος) lady.
λαϊκός [laeekos] popular, familiar, vulgar || current, common || lay.
λαίμαργος [lemargos] gluttonous, greedy || (ουσ) gourmand.
λαιμός, ο [lemos] neck, throat, gullet || (μεταφ βουνών) gorge, pass.
λακέρδα, η [lakerδa] salted tunny fish.

λακές, ο [lakes] lackey, flunkey.
λακκάκι, το [lakakee] dimple.
λάκκος, ο [lakos], **λακκούβα, η** [lakouva] hole, pit || grave.
λακτίζω [lakteezo] kick, boot, lash out.
λακωνικός [lakoneekos] laconic, terse, brief.
λαλιά, η [lalia] voice || speech || (για πουλιά) singing, warbling.
λαλώ [lalo] speak, talk || crow || sing.
λάμα, η [lama] sheet, thin plate || (μαχαιριού) blade.
λαμαρίνα, η [lamareena] sheet iron, iron plate.
λαμβάνω [lamvano] take hold of, take || receive, obtain || ~ **την τιμή** I have the honour || ~ **χώρα** to take place, occur.
λάμδα, το [lamδa] the letter Λ.
λάμπα, η [lamba] lamp || (ηλεκτρική) electric lamp, bulb.
λαμπάδα, η [lambaδa] torch || candle, taper.
λαμποκοπώ [lambokopo] shine, gleam.
Λαμπρή, η [lambree] Easter.
λαμπρός [lambros] brillant, splendid, excellent, superb.
λαμπρώς [lambros] (επιφ) splendid!, excellent! || (επίρ) brilliantly.
λαμπτήρας, ο [lambteeras] βλ **λάμπα.**
λάμπω [lambo] shine, glitter, gleam || (μεταφ) excel.
λάμψη, η [lampsee] brightness, brilliance || glaze.
λανθάνω [lanthano] be latent || escape notice.
λανθασμένος [lanthasmenos] mistaken, wrong.
λανσάρω [lansaro] launch, advertise, present.
λαξεύω [laksevo] hew, chisel, carve.
λαογραφία, η [laografeea] folklore.
λαός, ο [laos] people, multitude, masses.
λαούτο, το [laouto] lute.
λαπάς, ο [lapas] pap, boiled rice || poultice || (μεταφ) indolent person.
λαρδί, το [larδee] lard, fat.
λαρύγγι, το [lareengee] throat, larynx, windpipe, gullet.
λαρυγγίτιδα, η [lareengeeteeδa] laryngitis.
λαρυγγολόγος, ο [lareengologos] throat specialist.
λασκάρω [laskaro] slacken, loosen || (ναυτ) cast off.
λάσπη, η [laspee] mud, mire || mortar || **έκοψε** ~ he escaped || he disappeared.
λασπώνω [laspono] cover with mud, dirty, soil.
λαστιχένιος [lasteeheneeos] rubber || elastic.

λάστιχο, το [lasteeho] rubber || elastic || rubber band || (αυτοκινήτου) tyre || (παιδιού) catapult, sling.

λατέρνα, η [laterna] barrel organ.

λατινικά, τα [lateeneeka] πλ Latin.

λατινικός [lateeneekos] Latin.

λατομείο, το [latomeeo] quarry.

λατρεία, η [latreea] adoration, worship || (αγάπη) fervent love.

λατρευτός [latrevtos] adorable, adored.

λάτρης, ο [latrees] worshipper || fan.

λάφυρο, το [lafeero] booty, spoils, loot.

λαχαίνω [laheno] meet, come across || (συμβαίνω) happen, occur || (στον κλήρο) fall to, win.

λαχαναγορά, η [lahanagora] vegetable market.

λαχανιάζω [lahaneeazo] pant, gasp.

λαχανικό, το [lahaneeko] vegetable, green.

λάχανο, το [lahano] cabbage.

λαχείο, το [laheeo] lottery, raffle.

λαχνός, ο [lahnos] lot, chance || prize, share.

λαχτάρα, η [lahtara] anxiety || (επιθυμία) yearning || (φόβος) dread, fright.

λαχταρώ [lahtaro] be impatient || (επιθυμώ) yearn, desire || (φοβάμαι) be frightened.

λέαινα, η [layena] lioness.

λεβάντα, η [levanta] lavender.

λεβέντης, ο [leventees] fine man, gentleman || brave man.

λεβεντιά, η [leventia] manliness.

λέβητας, ο [leveetas] cauldron || boiler.

λεβιές, ο [levies] lever.

λεγάμενος [legamenos]: **ο ~** you know who || the so-called.

λεγεώνα, η [leyeona] legion || great number.

λέγω [lego] say, tell, speak || (πιστεύω) think || (εννοώ) mean || **δεν σου ~** I do not deny it, but || **τι λες** (επιφ) you don't say!, fancy that! || **που λες** well! || **λες και** as if.

λεηλασία, η [leyeelaseea] plundering, looting, pillage.

λεηλατώ [leyeelato] plunder, loot.

λεία, η [leea] prey || booty, loot.

λειαίνω [lieno] smooth, level, plane, polish.

λείος [leeos] smooth, even, level.

λείπω [leepo] be absent, be missing, want, lack || **μου λείπει** I am missing, I lack || **μας έλειψες** we missed you || **λίγο έλειψε να** he nearly, he almost.

λειρί, το [leeree] cockscomb, crest.

λειτουργία, η [leetouryeea] function, operation || (εκκλ) mass, liturgy.

λειτουργός, ο, η [leetourgos] officer, official, civil servant.

λειτουργώ [leetourgo] function, work || (εκκλ) celebrate mass.

λείψανα, τα [leepsana] πλ remnants, remains || (εκκλ) relics.

λειψός [leepsos] deficient, defective.

λειώνω [leeono] melt, liquefy || (συνθλίβω) crush, smash || (διαλύω) dissolve || (παθαίνω φθορά) wear out, spoil.

λεκάνη, η [lekanee] basin, washbowl || pan.

λεκές, ο [lekes] stain, splash, spot || (μελάνης) blot.

λεκιάζω [lekeeazo] stain, soil, spot.

λελέκι, το [lelekee] stork || (μεταφ) tall person.

λεμβοδρομία, η [lemvoδromeea] regatta, boat race.

λέμβος, η [lemvos] rowboat || launch.

λεμονάδα, η [lemonaδa] lemonade.

λεμόνι, το [lemonee] lemon || **λεμονιά** lemon tree.

λεξικογραφία, η [lekseekografeea] lexicography.

λεξικό, το [lekseeko] lexicon, dictionary.

λεξιλόγιο, το [lekseeloyo] vocabulary || glossary.

λέξη, η [leksee] word.

λεοντάρι, το [leontaree] lion.

λεοπάρδαλη, η [leoparδalee] leopard.

λέπι, το [lepee] (ψαριού) scale (of fish).

λεπίδα, η [lepeeδa] blade.

λέπρα, η [lepra] leprosy.

λεπρός [lepros] leprous.

λεπτά, τα [lepta] πλ money.

λεπταίνω [lepteno] thin, make slender || refine.

λεπτοκαμωμένος [leptokamomenos] delicate, frail || thin, slim.

λεπτολογώ [leptologo] scrutinize, examine carefully, sift.

λεπτομέρεια [leptomereea] detail, particular || **λεπτομερειακός** detailed, of detail.

λεπτομερώς [leptomeros] minutely, closely, in detail.

λεπτό, το [lepto] (της ώρας) minute || (νόμισμα) lepton (one hundredth of a drachma).

λεπτός [leptos] thin, fine, slight, slim || (στη σκέψη) subtle || (ρουχιασμός) light || (των αισθήσεων) keen.

λεπτότητα, η [leptoteeta] delicacy, weakness || tactfulness, tact || subtlety.

λέρα, η [lera] dirt, filth || (άνθρωπος) rogue, rascal.

Λ

λερωμένος [leromenos] dirty, filthy, grubby, grimy.

λερώνομαι [leronome] get dirty.

λερώνω [lerono] dirty, soil, stain || (μεταφ) tarnish, taint.

λέσχη, η [leshee] club || casino.

λεύκα, η [levka] poplar.

λευκαίνω [levkeno] whiten || bleach || (τοίχο) whitewash.

λευκός [levkos] white, clean || blank.

λευκοσίδηρος [levkoseeδeeros] tin.

λευκόχρυσος, ο [levkohreesos] platinum.

λεύκωμα, το [levkoma] album || (ιατρ) albumin.

λευτεριά, η [levteria] freedom, liberty.

λευχαιμία, η [levhemeea] leukaemia.

λεφτά [lefta] βλ **λεπτά**.

λεφτό [lefto] βλ **λεπτό**.

λεχώνα, η [lehona] woman who has just given birth.

λέω [leo] βλ **λέγω**.

λεωφορείο, το [leoforeeo] bus, omnibus, coach.

λεωφόρος, η [leoforos] avenue, boulevard.

λήγω [leego] come to an end, terminate || (οίκο) mature, fall due.

λήθαργος, ο [leethargos] lethargy, drowsiness, stupor.

λήθη, η [leethee] forgetfulness, forgetting, oversight.

λημέρι, το [leemeree] retreat, hiding place, hideout, den.

ληξιαρχείο, το [leekseearheeo] registry office, parish register.

λήξη, η [leeksee] termination, conclusion || expiration date.

λησμονώ [leesmono] forget, neglect, omit.

ληστεία, η [leesteea] holdup, robbery.

ληστεύω [leestevo] rob, hold up.

ληστής, ο [leestees] brigand, bandit, robber.

λήψη, η [leepsee] receipt, receiving.

λιάζομαι [leeazome] sunbathe, lie in the sun.

λιακάδα, η [leeakaδa] sunshine.

λίαν [leean] much, very much, too.

λιανίζω [leeaneezo] cut to pieces, mince.

λιανικός [leeaneekos] retail.

λιανός [leeanos] thin, slender.

λιβάδι, το [leevaδee] βλ **λειβάδι**.

λιβανέζικος [leevanezeekos] Lebanese.

Λιβανέζος, ο [leevanezos] Lebanese.

λιβάνι, το [leevanee] incense, frankincense.

λιβανίζω [leevaneezo] burn incense || (μεταφ) flatter basely.

Λίβανο, το [leevano] Lebanon.

λίβρα, η [leevra] pound.

Λιβύη, η [leeviee] Libya.

λιβυκός [leeveekos] Libyan.

Λίβυος, ο [leeveeos] Libyan.

λιγάκι [leegakee] a little, a bit.

λίγδα, η [leegδa] fat, grease || dirt, stain.

λιγνίτης, ο [leegneetees] lignite.

λιγνός [leegnos] skinny, thin, slim.

λίγο [leego] a little, a bit || ~ **πολύ** more or less.

λίγος [leegos] a little, a bit || **παρά λίγο** nearly, almost.

λιγοστεύω [leegostevo] lessen, decrease.

λιγοστός [leegostos] very little, hardly enough.

λιγότερος [leegoteros] less.

λιγούρα, η [leegoura] nausea || faintness from hunger.

λιγοψυχία, η [leegopseeheea] faintheartedness || faintness.

λιγώνομαι [leegonome] long for, be impatient || be faint from desire.

λιγώνω [leegono] nauseate || make faint.

λιθάρι, το [leetharee] stone.

λίθινος [leetheenos] of stone.

λιθοβολώ [leethovolo] pelt with stones, stone.

λιθογραφία, η [leethografeea] lithography.

λιθόκτιστος [leethokteestos] built in stone.

λίθος, ο, η [leethos] stone || (ιατρ) calculus.

λιθόστρωτο, το [leethostroto] pavement, paved way.

λιθόστρωτος [leethostrotos] paved with stones.

λικέρ, το [leeker] liqueur.

λικνίζω [leekneezo] rock, lull to sleep || swing.

λίκνο, το [leekno] cradle, cot, crib.

λίμα, η [leema] (εργαλείο) file.

λιμάνι, το [leemanee] port, harbour.

λιμάρω [leemaro] file || chatter, gossip.

λιμενάρχης, ο [leemenarhees] harbour master.

λιμενικός [leemeneekos] of the port, of the harbour.

λιμήν, ο [leemeen] βλ **λιμάνι**.

λίμνη, η [leemnee] lake.

λιμνοθάλασσα, η [leemnothalasa] lagoon.

λιμοκτονώ [leemoktono] starve, famish.

λινάρι, το [leenaree] flax.

λινάτσα, η [leenatsa] sacking.

λινέλαιο, το [leeneleo] linseed oil.

λινός [leenos] linen.

λιοντάρι, το [leeontaree] lion.

λιπαίνω [leepeno] lubricate, grease || (με λίπασμα) manure, fertilize.

λιπαρός [leeparos] greasy, fatty ||
(γόνιμος) fat, rich.
λίπασμα, το [leepasma] fertilizer,
manure.
λιποθυμία, η [leepotheemeea]
faint(ing), swooning.
λιποθυμώ [leepotheemo] faint, lose
consciousness.
λίπος, το [leepos] fat, lard || grease.
λιποτάκτης, ο [leepotaktees]
deserter.
λίρα, η [leera] pound, sovereign.
λιρέττα, η [leereta] Italian lira.
λίστα, η [leesta] list, catalogue.
λιτανεία, η [leetaneea] religious
procession.
λιτός [leetos] temperate, frugal || plain.
λιτότητα, η [leetoteeta] temperance,
moderation || (οικον) austerity.
λίτρα, η [leetra] (βάρος) pound || litre.
λίτρο, το [leetro] βλ **λίτρα**.
λιχουδιά, η [leehouδia] titbit ||
appetizer.
λοβός, ο [lovos] lobe || husk || (αρχιτεκ)
foil.
λογαριάζω [logareeazo] count,
measure, compute || rely on, look to ||
(λαμβάνω υπόψη) consider || (πρόθεση
να) count on, aim to, mean to.
λογαριασμός, ο [logareeasmos]
count, calculation, computation || bill ||
accounts.
λογάριθμος, ο [logareethmos]
logarithm.
λογάς, ο [logas] gossip, babbler,
longwinded talker.
λόγγος, ο [longos] thicket.
λόγια, τα [loya] πλ words.
λογιάζω [loyazo] take into
consideration.
λογική, η [loyeekee] logic.
λογικός [loyeekos] rational, logical,
sensible || right, fair.
λόγιος, ο [loyos] scholar, man of
letters.
λογισμός, ο [loyeesmos] reasoning,
thought || reckoning || (μαθημ) calculus.
λογιστήριο, το [loyeesteereeo]
bursar's office || bursary.
λογιστής, ο [loyeestees] accountant,
bookkeeper || (ναυτ) purser.
λογιστική, η [loyeesteekee]
accountancy.
λογοδιάρροια, η [logoδeeareea]
unrestrained talkativeness, chattering.
λογοδοτώ [logoδoto] give an account,
account for.
λογοκρισία, η [logokreeseea]
censorship.
λογομαχία, η [logomaheea] dispute,
wrangle, controversy.
λογοπαίγνιο, το [logopegneeo] pun.
λόγος, ο [logos] (ομιλία) speech ||
(φράση κτλ) word, saying || (μνεία)
mention || rumour || (αίτιο) cause,

reason, purpose || (παράδειγμα)
instance, supposition || (αγόρευση)
speech, discourse || (λογοδοσία)
explanation, account || (υπόσχεση)
promise || (αναλογία) ratio, proportion.
λογοτέχνης, ο [logotehnees] author,
writer.
λογοτεχνία, η [logotehneea]
literature.
λόγχη, η [longhee] bayonet || spear,
lance.
λοιμός, ο [leemos] pestilence, pest,
plague.
λοιμώδης [leemoδees] contagious.
λοιπόν [leepon] then, thus, and so ||
well!, what then!
λοιπός [leepos] left, remaining || **και
τα λοιπά** and so forth, and so on.
λόξα, η [loksa] whim, mania, fancy.
λοξά [loksa] on the slant, obliquely || in
an underhand way.
λοξοδρομώ [loksoδromo] shift course,
deviate || (ναυτ) tack || (μεταφ) go
astray.
λοξός [loksos] oblique, slanting,
inclined.
λόξυγγας, ο [lokseengas] hiccup.
λόρδος, ο [lorδos] lord.
λοσιόν, η [losion] lotion.
λοστός, ο [lostos] crowbar, iron bar.
λοστρόμος, ο [lostromos] boatswain.
λούζομαι [louzome] wash one's hair.
λούζω [louzo] wash, bathe || (μεταφ)
reproach severely.
λουκάνικο, το [loukaneeko] sausage,
hot dog, frankfurter.
λουκέτο, το [louketo] padlock.
λούκι, το [loukee] pipe, conduit ||
gutter.
λουκούμι, το [loukoumee] Turkish
delight || (μεταφ) delicious (attr).
λουλάκι, το [loulakee] indigo.
λουλούδι, το [loulouδee] flower,
blossom.
λουξ [louks] luxurious, posh.
Λουξεμβούργο, το
[louksemvourgo] Luxembourg.
λουρί, το [louree] strap || (μηχανής)
belt, band.
λουρίδα, η [loureeδa] strip, belt, band.
λούσιμο, το [louseemo] washing
one's hair || (μεταφ) reprimanding.
λούσο, το [louso] smart clothes ||
sumptuousness, luxury.
λουστράρω [loustraro] gloss, glaze ||
(παπούτσια) polish.
λουστρίνια, τα [loustreeneea] πλ
patent leather shoes.
λούστρος, ο [loustros] shoeblack,
boot black.
λουτρά, τα [loutra] πλ baths, hot
springs.
λουτρό, το [loutro] bath || (δωμάτιο)
bathroom.

λουτρόπολη, η [loutropolee] bathing resort, spa.

λουφάζω [loufazo] remain silent || cringe with fear.

λοφίο, το [lofeeo] plume || (πτηνού) tuft, crest || (στρατ) pompom.

λόφος, ο [lofos] hill, height.

λοχαγός, ο [lohagos] captain.

λοχίας, ο [loheeas] sergeant.

λόχος, ο [lohos] company.

λυγερός [leeyeros] slim, lithe, graceful.

λυγίζω [leeyeezo] bend, curve || yield.

λυγμός, ο [leegmos] sob, sobbing.

λύκειο, το [leekeeo] private secondary school, lyceum.

λύκος, ο [leekos] wolf.

λυκόφως, το [leekofos] evening twilight, dusk.

λυμαίνομαι [leemenome] ravage, devastate, lay waste.

λυντσάρω [leentsaro] lynch.

λύνω [leeno] βλ **λύω**.

λύομαι [leeome] come undone.

λυπάμαι [leepame] be sorry, regret || pity.

λύπη, η [leepee] grief, chagrin, sorrow || pity, commiseration.

λυπημένος [leepeemenos] sad, grieved, distressed.

λυπούμαι [leepoume] βλ **λυπάμαι**.

λύσιμο, το [leeseemo] undoing, loosening || solution, solving || taking to pieces.

λύση, η [leesee] answer, solution || untying || dismantling.

λύσσα, η [leesa] rabies || (μεταφ) rage, fury, wrath.

λυσσά(ζ)ω [leesa(z)o] rage, go mad.

λυσσώ [leeso] (μεταφ) be furious.

λυτός [leetos] loose, untied, unfastened.

λύτρα, τα [leetra] πλ ransom money.

λυτρώνω [leetrono] deliver, free, set free.

λυτρωτής, ο [leetrotees] liberator, redeemer, rescuer.

λύω [leeo] unloose || (δεσμό κτλ) untie, unfasten || (διαλύω) dismantle || (βρίσκω λύση) resolve || (ναύω) close, discharge || (καταργώ) annul, break off.

λυώνω [leeono] βλ **λειώνω**.

λωλαίνω [loleno] drive mad, bewilder.

λωλός [lolos] foolish, crazy, mad.

λωποδύτης, ο [lopoδeetees] thief, blackleg.

λωρίδα, η [loreeδa] strip, band, belt.

Μ, μ

...{ma] but || by || ~ **το Θεό** by God!, be witness!

... **το** [magazee] shop, store.

μαγγάνι, το [manganee] (εργαλείο) tool, vice || (πηγαδιού) wheel || winch.

μαγγάνιο, το [manganeeo] manganese.

μαγγανοπήγαδο, το [manganopeegaδo] wheel well (for water).

μαγγώνω [mangono] grip, squeeze, clip.

μαγεία, η [mayeea] sorcery, witchcraft, magic || charm, fascination.

μάγειρας, ο [mayeeras] cook.

μαγειρεύω [mayeerevo] cook || (μεταφ) plot, manipulate.

μαγειρική, η [mayeereekee] cooking, cookery.

μαγευτικός [mayevteekos] charming, enchanting, delightful.

μαγεύω [mayevo] charm, fascinate, delight, attract.

μάγια, τα [maya] πλ witchcraft, spell, charm.

μαγιά, η [maya] yeast, leaven.

μαγικός [mayeekos] magic(al), fascinating, bewitching.

μαγιό, το [mayo] bathing suit, swimsuit.

μαγιονέζα, η [mayoneza] mayonnaise.

μάγισσα, η [mayeesa] witch, enchantress.

μαγκάλι, το [mangalee] brazier, firepan.

μάγκας, ο [mangas] urchin, rascal, bum.

μαγκούρα, η [mangoura] crook, heavy stick.

μαγνήσιο, το [magneeseeo] magnesium.

μαγνήτης, ο [magneetees] magnet.

μαγνητίζω [magneeteezo] magnetize || attract, captivate.

μαγνητικός [magneeteekos] magnetic || attractive.

μαγνητισμός, ο [magneeteesmos] magnetism.

μαγνητόφωνο, το [magneetofono] tape recorder.

μάγος, ο [magos] magician, wizard.

μαγουλάδες, οι [magoulaδes] mumps.

μάγουλο, το [magoulo] cheek (of face).

μάδημα, το [maδeema] plucking, depilation || (μεταφ) fleecing.

μαδώ [maδo] pluck, pluck off, remove the hair || (μεταφ) fleece.

μαέστρος, ο [maestros] conductor || (μεταφ) authority.

μάζα, η [maza] paste || lump || (ανθρώπων) mass, crowd.

μάζεμα, το [mazema] collecting, gathering || (υφάσματος) shrinking.

μαζεύομαι [mazevome] collect || nestle || settle down.

μαζεύω [mazevo] gather, collect || (μαλλί) wind || (για ρούχα) shrink.

μαζί [mazee] together, with, in one lot, jointly.

μαζικός [mazeekos] of the mass, collective.

Μάης, ο [maees] May.

μαθαίνω [matheno] learn || teach, train || (νέα) hear || learn.

μάθημα, το [matheema] lesson.

μαθηματικά, τα [matheemateeka] πλ mathematics.

μαθηματικός [matheemateekos] mathematical || (ουσ) mathematician.

μαθημένος [matheemenos] used to.

μάθηση, η [matheesee] learning, education.

μαθητευόμενος [matheetevomenos] apprentice, novice.

μαθητής, ο [matheetees] student, pupil || (φιλοσόφου) disciple.

μαία, η [mea] midwife.

μαίανδρος, ο [meanδros] meander, in-and-out.

μαιευτήρας, ο [mayevteeras] obstetrician.

μαιευτήριο, το [mayevteereeo] maternity hospital.

μαιευτική, η [mayevteekee] obstetrics.

μαϊμού, η [maeemou] monkey, ape.

μαίνομαι [menome] rage, be furious.

μαϊντανός, ο [maeentanos] parsley.

Μάιος, ο [maeeos] May.

μακάβριος [makavreeos] macabre, gruesome, ghastly.

μακάρι [makaree] (επιφ) would to God!.

μακαρίζω [makareezo] regard as fortunate, envy.

μακάριος [makareeos] happy, fortunate, blessed || calm, serene.

μακαρίτης [makareetees] late, deceased.

μακαρόνια, τα [makaroneea] πλ macaroni.

μακελειό, το [makelio] (μεταφ) slaughter, massacre.

μακέτα, η [maketa] model, drawing, plan.

μακραίνω [makreno] make longer || grow taller.

μακριά [makria] (a)far, far off, at a distance.

μακρινός [makreenos] far distant, far off || (ταξίδι) long.

μακρόβιος [makroveeos] long-lived.

μάκρος, το [makros] length || duration.

μακρύνω [makreno] βλ μακραίνω.

μακρύς [makrees] long, lengthy, extensive.

μαλάζω [malazo] massage, knead || soften, mollify, pacify || (πόνο) alleviate.

μαλάκιο, το [malakeeo] mollusc.

μαλακός [malakos] soft || mild, gentle || (κλίμα) genial.

μαλάκυνση, η [malakeensee] softening, enervation.

μαλακώνω [malakono] soften, get milder || assuage || become calmer.

μάλαμα, το [malama] gold.

μαλάσσω [malaso] βλ μαλάζω.

μαλθακός [malthakos] soft, effeminate, delicate.

μάλιστα [maleesta] more especially, particularly || yes, indeed || even.

μαλλί, το [malee] wool, fleece || hair.

μαλλιά, τα [malia] πλ hair (of the head) || ~ κουβάρια upside down.

μαλλιαρός [maleearos] hairy, long-haired || woolly.

μάλλινος [maleenos] woollen.

μάλλον [malon] more, better, rather.

μαλώνω [malono] argue || chide, reprimand, rebuke.

μαμά, η [mama] mother, mummy.

μάμμη, η [mamee] grandmother.

μαμμή, η [mamee] midwife.

μαμμούνι, το [mamounee] small insect, grub.

μανδύας, ο [manδeeas] mantle, cloak || (στρατ) greatcoat.

μάνι μάνι [maneemanee] quickly, in a jiffy.

μανία, η [maneea] fury, passion, mania || whim, fancy || έχω ~ με to be crazy about.

μανιακός [maneeakos] raving, frenzied || (παίκτης) inveterate.

μανιβέλλα, η [maneevela] starting handle || lever, bar.

μανικέτι, το [maneeketee] cuff.

μανίκι, το [maneekee] sleeve.

μανιτάρι, το [maneetaree] mushroom.

μανιώδης [maneeoδees] passionate, inveterate || furious, raging.

μάνα, η [mana] mother, mamma.

μανούλα, η [manoula] mummy || mom (US).

μανουάλιο, το [manoualeeo] candelabrum.

μανούβρα, η [manouvra] manoeuvre.

μανούρι, το [manouree] kind of white cheese.

μανταλάκι, το [mantalakee] clothes peg.

μάνταλο, το [mantalo] latch, bolt, bar.

μανταλώνω [mantalono] latch, lock up, bolt.

μανταρίνι, το [mantareenee] tangerine.

μαντάρισμα, το [mantareesma] darning || (υφάσματος) mending.

μαντάρω [mantaro] darn, mend.

μαντάτο, το [mantato] information, news.

M

μαντείο, το [manteeo] oracle.
μαντεύω [mantevo] foretell || guess || find out, fathom.
μαντήλι, το [manteelee] handkerchief.
μάντης, ο [mantees] wizard, prophet.
μαντινάδα, η [manteenaða] rhyming couplet.
μάντρα, η [mantra] pen, fold, sty || (περίφραγμα) enclosure, wall || yard.
μαντράχαλος, ο [mantrahalos] lanky fellow.
μαξιλάρι, το [makseelaree] pillow, cushion.
μάπας, ο [mapas] stupid fellow, imbecile.
μαραγκός, ο [marangos] carpenter || joiner.
μαράζι, το [marazee] pining, depression, languor.
μάραθ(ρ)ο, το [marath(r)o] fennel.
μαραίνομαι [marenome] fade, wither away, shrivel || (μεταφ) waste away.
μαραίνω [mareno] wither, dry up, fade.
μαρασμός, ο [marasmos] withering, fading away || (μεταφ) decay.
μαργαρίνη, η [margareenee] margarine.
μαργαρίτα, η [margareeta] daisy.
μαργαριτάρι, το [margareetaree] pearl.
μαρίδα, η [mareeða] whitebait, small fry.
μάρκα, η [marka] (εμπορ) make || (αυτοκινήτου) model || (νόμισμα) mark || (μεταφ) cunning fellow.
μαρμαρένιος [marmareneeos] of marble.
μάρμαρο, το [marmaro] marble.
μαρμελάδα, η [marmelaða] marmalade.
Μαροκινός, ο [marokeenos] Moroccan || μ~ (επιθ) Moroccan.
Μαρόκο, το [maroko] Morocco.
μαρούλι, το [maroulee] lettuce.
Μάρτης, ο [martees] March.
μαρτυρία, η [marteereea] deposition, giving of evidence || proof, token.
μαρτυρικός [marteereekos] insufferable, unbearable.
μαρτύριο, το [marteereeo] torment, suffering.
μαρτυρώ [marteero] give evidence, testify || (προδίδω) betray, inform against || (ενδεικνύω) show, indicate || (γίνομαι μάρτυς) suffer martyrdom (for Christ).
μάρτυς, ο [martees] witness || (εκκλ) martyr.
μας [mas] us || our.
μασέλα, η [masela] false teeth.
μασιά, η [masia] πλ tongs, fire-tongs || pincers.
μάσκα, η [maska] mask ||

μασκαράς, ο masquerader || (μεταφ) impostor, rascal, scoundrel.
μασόνος, ο [masonos] freemason.
μασουλώ [masoulo] chew, munch.
μασούρι, το [masouree] spool, bobbin || tube.
μάστιγα, η [masteega] whip || (μεταφ) curse, plague.
μαστίγιο, το [masteeyo] whip || switch.
μαστιγώνω [masteegono] whip, lash, flog.
μαστίζω [masteezo] infest, devastate, desolate.
μαστίχα, η [masteeha] mastic || (ποτό) mastic brandy.
μάστορας, ο [mastoras] artisan, workman || (μεταφ) expert, skilful person.
μαστορεύω [mastorevo] work || mend, repair.
μαστός, ο [mastos] breast || (μεταφ) hillock.
μαστροπός, ο, η [mastropos] procurer, procuress, pimp.
μασχάλη, η [mashalee] armpit.
μασώ [maso] chew, masticate || (τα λόγια) stammer.
ματαιόδοξος [mateoðoksos] vain, self-conceited.
μάταιος [mateos] vain, useless, unavailing || conceited.
ματαιώνω [mateono] frustrate, foil, cancel, stop.
μάτι, το [matee] eye || (φύλλου κτλ) bud || αυγό ~ fried egg (sunny-side up) || βάζω στο ~ to set one's heart on || έχω στο ~ to covet || κλείνω το ~ to wink || μάτια μου! my darling!
ματιά, η [matia] glance, gaze, eye, look || ~ζω cast an evil eye on, bewitch.
ματόκλαδο, το [matoklaðo] eyelash, lash.
ματόφυλλο, το [matofeelo] eyelid.
μάτσο, το [matso] truss, bunch, bundle || (ξύλων) faggot.
ματσούκα, η [matsouka] club, cudgel.
ματώνω [matono] bleed.
μαυραγορίτης, ο [mavragoreetees] black marketeer.
μαυρειδερός [mavreeðeros] blackish || brown.
μαυρίζω [mavreezo] blacken, darken || (από ήλιο) get tanned || (μεταφ) blackball, vote against.
μαυρίλα, η [mavreela] blackness, darkness, gloominess.
μαυροδάφνη, η [mavroðafnee] kind of sweet wine.
μαυροπίνακας, ο [mavropeenakas] blackboard || blacklist.
μαύρος [mavros] black || brown || (νέγρος) negro || (μεταφ) miserable, luckless.

μαχαίρι, το [maheree] knife || στα ~α at loggerheads.

μαχαιριά, η [maheria] stab.

μαχαιροβγάλτης, ο [maherovgaltees] cut-throat || bully.

μαχαιροπήρουνα, τα [maheropeerouna] πλ cutlery.

μαχαιρώνω [maherono] stab.

μαχαλάς, ο [mahalas] quarter, district, neighbourhood.

μάχη, η [mahee] battle, combat || struggle, fight.

μαχητής, ο [maheetees] combatant, fighter, soldier.

μαχητικός [maheeteekos] warlike, martial || combative, ready to fight.

μάχομαι [mahome] fight, combat, struggle || hate, abhor.

με [me] with, by, through, by means of, on, of || ~ τα πόδια on foot || ~ το καλό God willing || ~ το μήνα by the month || δύο ~ τρία two by three (feet etc) || ~ τον καιρό eventually, in the course of time || δύο ~ τρεις between two and three o'clock || έχω μανία ~ το to be mad on, be crazy about || γελώ ~ to laugh at || ~ τη σειρά in turn || ανάλογα ~ according to whether.

μεγάθυμος [megatheemos] generous, magnanimous.

μεγαλείο, το [megaleeo] splendour, grandeur || (μεταφ) splendid.

μεγαλειότητα, η [megaleeoteeta] majesty, grandeur || η Αυτού ~ His Majesty.

μεγαλειώδης [megaleeoδees] magnificent, superb, majestic.

μεγαλέμπορος, ο [megalemboros] wholesaler.

μεγαλεπήβολος [megalepeevolos] grandiose, imposing.

μεγαλοποιώ [megalopeeo] magnify, exaggerate, overdo.

μεγαλοπρεπής [megaloprepees] majestic, stately, splendid, magnificent.

μεγάλος [megalos] great, large, big, long.

μεγαλουργώ [megalourgo] achieve great things.

μεγαλόφρονας [megalofronas] generous, magnanimous || boastful, arrogant.

μεγαλοφυής [megalofiees] gifted, ingenious.

μεγαλόψυχος [megalopseehos] magnanimous, generous.

μεγαλύνω [megaleeno] magnify, exalt.

μεγαλώνω [megalono] increase, enlarge || (ανατρέφω) bring up, raise || (μεγαλοποιώ) magnify, exaggerate || grow up.

μέγαρο, το [megaro] mansion, palace, imposing building.

μέγας [megas] βλ μεγάλος.

μεγάφωνο, το [megafono] (ραδιοφώνου) loudspeaker || megaphone.

μέγγενη, η [mengenee] (εργαλείο) vice.

μέγεθος, το [meyethos] size, greatness, height, magnitude, extent, length.

μεγέθυνση, η [meyetheensee] enlargement, increase, extension.

μεγιστάνας, ο [meyeestanas] magnate, seigneur.

μέγιστος [meyeestos] greatest, largest || enormous, colossal.

μεδούλι, το [meδoulee] marrow.

μέδουσα, η [meδousa] kind of jellyfish.

μεζές, ο [mezes] titbit, snack.

μεζούρα, η [mezoura] tape measure.

μεθαύριο [methavreeo] the day after tomorrow.

μέθη, η [methee] intoxication, drunkenness || (μεταφ) enthusiasm.

μεθοδικός [methoδeekos] systematic, methodical.

μέθοδος, η [methoδos] method, system, process.

μεθόριος, η [methoreeos] boundary, frontier.

μεθύσι, το [metheesee] βλ μέθη.

μεθυσμένος [metheesmenos] drunk.

μεθώ [metho] make drunk, intoxicate || get drunk.

μειδίαμα, το [meeδeeama] smile.

μείζων [meezon] larger, greater || (μουσ) major.

μειοδοτώ [meeoδoto] bid the lowest price.

μείον [meeon] less, minus.

μειονέκτημα, το [meeonekteema] disadvantage, inconvenience.

μειονότητα, η [meeonoteeta] minority.

μειοψηφία, η [meeopseefeea] minority of votes.

μειώνω [meeono] lessen, diminish, reduce, decrease.

μείωση, η [meeosee] decrease, reduction || (μεταφ) humiliation.

μελαγχολία, η [melangholeea] melancholy, dejection, gloominess.

μελαγχολικός [melangholeekos] sad, depressed, gloomy.

μελαγχολώ [melangholo] become sad.

μελάνη, η [melanee] ink.

μελανιά, η [melania] inkstain || bruise || ~ζω bruise || turn blue with cold.

μελανοδοχείο, το [melanoδoheeo] inkstand, inkpot.

μελάτος [melatos] (αυγό) soft-boiled.

μελαχροινός [melahreenos] dark, brown, swarthy.

μελαψός [melapsos] dark-skinned, swarthy.

μέλει [melee]: **δεν με** ~ I don't care, I'm not interested.

μελέτη, η [meletee] (πραγματεία) treatise || study || (κτιρίου) plan, design || mediation, contemplation.

μελετηρός [meleteeros] studious.

μελετώ [meleto] study || (ερευνώ) search, investigate || (σκοπεύω) have in mind, intend || (πιάνο) practise.

μέλημα, το [meleema] concern, care, solicitude, duty.

μέλι, το [melee] honey.

μελίγγι, το [meleengee] (ανατ) temple.

μέλισσα, η [meleesa] bee.

μελίσσι, το [meleesee] beehive || swarm.

μελισσοκομία, η [meleesokomeea] beekeeping.

μελιτζάνα, η [meleedzana] eggplant.

μέλλον, το [melon] future || outlook.

μελλόνυμφος, ο, η [meloneemfos] husband-/wife-to-be.

μέλλω [melo] intend, be about to.

μέλλων [melon] future || **ο** ~ (γραμμ) future tense.

μέλος, το [melos] member || (μουσ) melody, air || (του σώματος) member, limb.

μελτέμι, το [meltemee] north wind, trade wind.

μελωδία, η [meloδeea] melody, tune.

μελωδικός [meloδikos] melodious, tuneful.

μεμβράνη, η [memvranee] membrane || (χαρτί) parchment.

μεμονωμένος [memonomenos] isolated, lonely, alone.

μεν [men] on the one hand || **οι** ~ ... **οι δε** some ... others.

μενεξές, ο [menekses] violet.

μένος, το [menos] fervour, zeal, eagerness || wrath, anger, fury.

μέντα, η [menta] mint, peppermint.

μένω [meno] remain, stop, stay || (απομένω) be left, survive || (διαμένω) reside, live || ~ **από** run out of, be short of.

μέρα, η [mera] βλ **ημέρα**.

μεράκι, το [merakee] ardent desire, yearning || (λύπη) regret, sorrow.

μεραρχία, η [merarheea] division.

μεριά, η [meria] place || side.

μερίδα, η [mereeδa] ration, portion, helping.

μερίδιο, το [mereeδeeo] share, portion.

μερικός [mereekos] partial, some, a few || **μερικά** πλ some, certain, a few.

μέριμνα, η [mereemna] care, anxiety, solicitude, concern.

μεριμνώ [mereemno] look after, care for, be anxious about.

μέρισμα, το [mereesma] dividend || allotment, part.

μερμήγκι, το [mermeengee] ant.

μεροκάματο, το [merokamato] day's wages.

μεροληπτώ [meroleepto] take sides, be partial, be one-sided.

μέρος, το [meros] part, party || (μερίδα) portion, share || (τόπος) place, spot || (πλευρά) side || (ρόλος) role || (γραμμ) part of speech || (αποχωρητήριο) W.C. || **κατά** ~ aside, apart.

μέσα [mesa] in(to) || inside || within || among || (πολιτ) means || ~ **σε** inside, within || in, into.

μεσάζω [mesazo] mediate, intercede.

μεσαίος [meseos] middle.

μεσαίωνας, ο [meseonas] Middle Ages || **μεσαιωνικός** medieval.

μεσάνυχτα, τα [mesaneehta] πλ midnight.

μέση, η [mesee] middle || (σώματος) waist || **αφήνω στη** ~ to leave incomplete, leave undone.

μεσήλικας [meseeleekas] middle-aged.

μεσημβρινός [meseemvreenos] of noon || (νότιος) southern || (ουσ) meridian.

μεσημέρι, το [meseemeree] noon || **μέρα** ~ in broad daylight || **μεσημεριανός** midday || **μεσημεριανός ύπνος** siesta.

μεσίστιος [meseesteeos] half-mast.

μεσιτεύω [meseetevo] intercede, intervene || be a broker.

μεσίτης, ο [meseetees] mediator || agent, broker.

μεσιτικό [meseeteeko]: ~ **γραφείο** house agency.

μεσογειακός [mesoyakos] Mediterranean.

Μεσόγειος, η [mesoyos] the Mediterranean.

μεσόκοπος [mesokopos] βλ **μεσήλικας**.

μεσολαβώ [mesolavo] intercede, intervene || (σε χρόνο) come between.

μέσο, το [meso] middle, midst || (τρόπος) method, means, way || **μέσα** πλ influence, pull, power.

μέσος [mesos] middle || medium || (όρος) mean, average.

μεσοφόρι, το [mesoforee] petticoat, underskirt.

μεστός [mestos] full, replete, crammed with || (ώριμος) ripe.

μεστώνω [mestono] mature, ripen, mellow.

μέσω [meso] through, via.

μετά [meta] with || after, in || (επίρ) afterwards.

μεταβαίνω [metaveno] go, proceed.

μεταβάλλω [metavalo] change, convert, transform.

μετάβαση, n [metavasee] going, passage, transference.

μεταβατικός [metavateekos] transitional, provisory || (γραμμ) transitive (verb).

μεταβιβάζω [metaveevazo] (διαταγή) transmit, hand on || (μεταφέρω) transport || (ιδιοκτησία) transfer, hand over.

μεταβλητός [metavleetos] variable, unsettled, changeable.

μεταβολή, n [metavolee] alteration, change || (στρατ) about-turn, half-turn.

μετάγγιση, n [metangeesee] transfusion, drawing off || (κρασιού κτλ) decanting.

μεταγενέστερος [metayenesteros] posterior, subsequent, later.

μεταγραφή, n [metagrafee] transfer.

μεταγωγικό, το [metagoyeeko] (ναυτ) transport ship.

μεταδίδω [metaðeeðo] impart, transmit || (ραδιοφωνία) broadcast || (αρρώστια) infect.

μετάδοση, n [metaðosee] transmission || (αρρώστιας) contagion, spreading || **αγία** ~ Holy Communion.

μεταδοτικός [metaðoteekos] contagious, infectious.

μετάθεση, n [metathesee] transfer, removal.

μεταθέτω [metatheto] transpose, transfer, remove, move.

μετακινώ [metakeeno] move, shift, displace.

μετακομίζω [metakomeezo] transport, transfer, remove || (σπίτι) move, change residence, move out.

μεταλλείο, το [metaleeo] mine.

μετάλλευμα, το [metalevma] ore.

μεταλλικός [metaleekos] metallic || mineral.

μετάλλινος [metaleenos] of metal.

μετάλλιο, το [metaleeo] medal.

μέταλλο, το [metalo] metal.

μεταμέλεια, n [metameleea] repentance, regrets.

μεταμόρφωση, n [metamorfosee] transformation, reformation || (εκκλ) transfiguration.

μεταμόσχευση, n [metamoshevsee] transplantation.

μεταμφίεση, n [metamfiesee] disguise, masquerade.

μεταμφιεσμένος [meemfiesmenos] disguised.

μετανάστευση, n [metanastevsee] emigration, (im)migration.

μεταναστεύω [metanastevo] (e)migrate, immigrate.

μετανάστης, ο [metanastees] (e)migrant, immigrant.

μετάνοια, n [metaneea] repentance, regret || (εκκλ) penance || (γονυκλισιά) genuflexion.

μετανοώ [metanoo] repent, regret, be sorry (for).

μετάξι, το [metaksee] silk.

μεταξοσκώληκας, ο [metaksoskoleekas] silkworm.

μεταξύ [metaksee] between, among, amongst, amid(st) || ~ **μας** between ourselves, between you and me || **εν τω** ~ meanwhile.

μεταξωτό, το [metaksoto] silk material, silk stuff.

μεταπείθω [metapeetho] dissuade, prevail upon.

μεταποιώ [metapeeo] transform, alter, convert.

μεταπολεμικός [metapolemeekos] postwar.

μετάπτωση, n [metaptosee] change, relapse.

μεταπωλώ [metapolo] resell, sell again.

μεταρρυθμίζω [metareethmeezo] reform, rearrange.

μετασχηματιστής, ο [metasheemateestees] transformer.

μετατοπίζω [metatopeezo] shift, displace.

μετατόπιση, n [metatopeesee] shifting || displacement.

μετατρέπω [metatrepo] transform, turn, change, alter || (για ποινή) commute.

μεταφέρω [metafero] transport, carry, convey || (οικον) transfer, carry over.

μεταφορά, n [metafora] transportation, conveyance || (γραμμ) metaphor.

μεταφορικά, τα [metaforeeka] πλ carriage fees.

μεταφράζω [metafrazo] translate.

μετάφραση, n [metafrasee] translation.

μεταφραστής, ο [metafrastees] translator.

μεταφυτεύω [metafeetevo] transplant.

μεταχειρίζομαι [metaheereezome] use, employ || treat, behave towards.

μεταχειρισμένος [metaheereesmenos] worn, used || (δεύτερο χέρι) secondhand.

μετεκπαίδευση, n [metekpeðevsee] postgraduate study.

μετέπειτα [metepeeta] after, afterwards, subsequently || **οι** ~ posterity, the descendants.

μετέχω [meteho] take part, participate || partake.

μετέωρο, το [meteoro] meteor, shooting star.

μετέωρος [meteoros] dangling, in the air || (μεταφ) hesitant, undecided || in suspense.

μετοικώ [meteeko] emigrate || (σπίτι) move house.

μετόπισθεν [metopeesthen]: **τα ~** the rear.

μετοχή, η [metohee] (οικον) stock, share || (γραμμ) participle.

μετοχικός [metoheekos] (οικον) of a share, of joint stock || (γραμμ) participial.

μέτοχος, ο [metohos] participant, sharer || (οικον) shareholder.

μέτρα, τα [metra] πλ measurements || proceedings, steps || **λαμβάνω ~** to take measures.

μέτρημα, το [metreema] measuring, mensuration || counting, numbering.

μετρημένος [metreemenos] measured, limited || (άνθρωπος) temperate, discreet, moderate.

μετρητά, τα [metreeta] πλ: **τα ~** cash, money || **τοις μετρητοίς** in cash, (for) ready money.

μετρητής, ο [metreetees] meter, counter, gauge.

μετρητός [metreetos] measurable, calculable.

μετριάζω [metreeazo] moderate, diminish, slacken, lessen.

μετρικός [metreekos] metric(al).

μετριοπάθεια, η [metreeopatheea] moderation, temperance.

μετριοπαθής [metreeopathees] moderate, sober, temperate.

μέτριος [metreeos] ordinary, moderate || mediocre || (καφές) semi-sweetened.

μετριόφρονας [metreeofronas] modest, unassuming, decent, retiring.

μετριοφροσύνη, η [metreeofroseenee] modesty, decency.

μέτρο, το [metro] measure, metre || (μεταφ) measure, step || (μουσ) bar, measure || (ποιητικό) metre, foot.

μετρώ [metro] measure, count, number, gauge.

μέτωπο, το [metopo] forehead, brow || (πρόσοψη) face, front, facade || (μάχη) front, battlefront.

μέχρι(ς) [mehree(s)] till, until, down to, up to || as far as || ~ **ενός** to the last man || ~ **τούδε** until now.

μη [mee] don't || not, no || lest.

μηδαμινός [meeδameenos] worthless, of no account, insignificant, trivial.

μηδέν, το [meeδen] nothing || zero || cipher.

μηδενίζω [meeδeneezo] nullify || mark with a zero.

μηδενικό, το [meeδeneeko] zero || cipher.

μηδενιστής, ο [meeδeneestees] nihilist.

μήκος, το [meekos] length || (γεωγραφικό) longitude || **κατά ~** in length, lengthwise.

μπλίγγι, το [meeleengee] (ανατ) temple.

μήλο, το [meelo] apple || (πρόσωπο) cheekbone || **μηλίτης** cider.

μηλόπηττα, η [meelopeeta] apple pie.

μην, ο [meen], **μήνας, ο** [meenas] month.

μηνιαίος [meenieos] monthly || month's.

μηνιάτικο, το [meeniateeko] month's wages || month's rent.

μηνίγγι, το [meeneengee] βλ **μπλίγγι.**

μηνιγγίτιδα, η [meeneengeeteeδa] meningitis.

μήνις, η [meenees] rage, anger, fury, wrath.

μήνυμα, το [meeneema] message, notice, announcement.

μήνυση, η [meeneesee] summons, charge.

μηνυτής, ο [meeneetees] plaintiff, complainant.

μηνύω [meeneeo] give notice || bring a charge against.

μήπως [meepos] lest in any way, in case || I wonder if.

μηρός, ο [meeros] thigh, leg.

μηρυκάζω [meereekazo] chew the cud, ruminate.

μήτε [meete] βλ **ούτε.**

μητέρα, η [meetera] mother.

μήτρα, η [meetra] uterus, womb || (χυτηρίου) mould, matrix, form.

μητρική [meetreekee]: ~ **γλώσσα** mother tongue, native language.

μητρόπολη, η [meetropolee] metropolis, capital || (εκκλ) cathedral.

μητροπολιτικός [meetropoleeteekos] metropolitan.

μητροπολίτης, ο [meetropoleetees] metropolitan bishop.

μητρότητα, η [meetroteeta] motherhood.

μητρυιά, η [meetria] stepmother.

μητρυιός, ο [meetrios] stepfather.

μητρώο, το [meetroo] register, roll, official list of names.

μηχανεύομαι [meehanevome] contrive, engineer, plot, bring about.

μηχανή, η [meehanee] machine, engine, works || (μεταφ) typewriter || camera.

μηχάνημα, το [meehaneema] machine, apparatus, contrivance.

μηχανική, η [meehaneekee] engineering, mechanics.

μηχανικός [meehaneekos] mechanical || (ουσ) engineer || mechanic || architect.

μηχανισμός, ο [meehaneesmos] mechanism, machinery.

μηχανοκίνητος [meehanokeeneetos]

[meehanokeeneetos] motorized || machine-operated.

μηχανοποιώ [meehanopeeo] mechanize.

μηχανορραφία, η [meehanorafeea] machination || intrigue.

μία, μια [meea, mia] one || a, an || ~ **και** since, seeing that || ~ **που** as, since.

μίασμα, το [meeasma] miasma, infection.

μιγάδας, ο [meegaðas] half-caste, mulatto || hybrid.

μίγμα, το [meegma] mixture, blend.

μίζα, η [meeza] (μηχανής) self-starter || (στα χαρτιά) stake.

μιζέρια, η [meezereea] misery, wretchedness || (τσιγγουνιά) meanness.

μικραίνω [meekreno] curtail, lessen || shorten, grow smaller.

μικρόβιο, το [meekroveeo] microbe.

μικρογραφία, η [meekrografeea] miniature.

μικροπρά(γ)ματα, τα [meekropra(g)mata] πλ trifles.

μικροπρεπής [meekroprepees] mean, base.

μικρός [meekros] small, little || short || young || (διαφορά) trivial.

μικροσκοπικός [meekroskopeekos] minute.

μικροσκόπιο, το [meekroskopeeo] microscope.

μικρόφωνο, το [meekrofono] microphone.

μικρόψυχος [meekropseehos] faint-hearted.

μικρύνω [meekreeno] βλ **μικραίνω**.

μικτό [meekto]: ~ **βάρος** gross weight.

μικτός [meektos] mixed, composite || (σχολείο) coeducational.

μιλιά, η [meelia] speech, word.

μίλι, το [meelee] mile.

μιλώ [meelo] speak.

μίμηση, η [meemeesee] imitation.

μιμητής, ο [meemeetees] imitator.

μιμητικός [meemeeteekos] imitative.

μιμόζα, η [meemoza] mimosa.

μίμος, ο [meemos] mimic, jester.

μιμούμαι [meemoume] imitate, copy, mimic.

μινιατούρα, η [meeneeatoura] miniature.

μίξη, η [meeksee] mixing, mixture, blend.

μισαλλόδοξος [meesaloðoksos] intolerant.

μισάνθρωπος, ο [meesanthropos] misanthrope.

μισητός [meeseetos] hated, hateful, odious.

μισθοδοτώ [meesthoðoto] pay a salary to, hire.

μισθολόγιο, το [meestholoyo] payroll || rate of pay.

μισθός, ο [meesthos] salary, wages, pay.

μισθοφόρος, ο [meesthoforos] mercenary, hired man.

μισθώνω [meesthono] hire, rent || let out, hire out.

μισθωτής, ο [meesthotees] tenant || hirer.

μισθωτός [meesthotos] salaried, paid.

μισό, το [meeso] half || **στα μισά** halfway, in the middle.

μισογύνης, ο [meesoyeenees] woman-hater, misogynist.

μίσος, το [meesos] hatred, aversion.

μισός [meesos] half.

μισοφέγγαρο, το [meesofengaro] halfmoon, crescent.

μίσχος, ο [meeshos] stalk (of leaf).

μισώ [meeso] hate, detest, loathe.

μίτρα, η [meetra] mitre.

μνεία, η [mnea] mention.

μνήμα, το [mneema] grave, tomb, sepulchre.

μνημείο, το [mneemeeo] monument, cenotaph.

μνήμη, η [mneemee] memory, mind, recollection.

μνημονεύω [mneemonevo] celebrate, commemorate || quote, mention || learn by heart.

μνημονικό, το [mneemoneeko] βλ **μνήμη**.

μνημόσυνο, το [mneemoseeno] requiem.

μνησίκακος [mneeseekakos] spiteful, vindictive.

μνηστεύομαι [mneestevome] get engaged.

μνηστή, η [mneestee] fiancée.

μνηστήρας, ο [mneesteeras] fiancé || (μεταφ) claimant.

μόδα, η [moða] fashion, custom, habit, way || **της** ~ **ς** fashionable.

μοδίστρα, η [moðeestra] dressmaker, seamstress.

μοιάζω [meeazo] look like.

μοίρα, η [meera] fate, destiny, fortune || (αερο) squadron || (γεωμ) degree.

μοιράζομαι [meerazome] share with.

μοιράζω [meerazo] share out, divide, distribute || (ρόλους) allot, assign || (διανέμω) deliver || (χαρτιά) deal || ~ **τη διαφορά** to split the difference.

μοιραίος [meereos] unavoidable || fatal, deadly.

μοιραίως [meereos] inevitably, fatally.

μοίραρχος, ο [meerarhos] captain of the gendarmerie.

μοιρολατρία, η [meerolatreea] fatalism.

μοιρολόγι, το [meeroloyee] dirge, lamentation.

μοιρολογώ [meerologo] lament, mourn.

μοιχεία, η [meeheea] adultery.

μολαταύτα [molatavta] nevertheless, yet, still.

μόλη [molee] barely, hardly, scarcely || as soon as.

μολονότι [molonotee] although, though.

μόλυβδος, ο [moleevδos] lead.

μολύβι, το [moleevee] lead || pencil.

μόλυνση, η [moleensee] contamination, infection, pollution.

μολύνω [moleeno] infect, contaminate, pollute.

μόλυσμα, το [moleesma] infection, contagion.

μομφή, η [momfee] blame, reproach, reprimand.

μονάδα, η [monaδa] unit.

μοναδικός [monaδeekos] unique, singular, only.

μοναξιά, η [monaksia] solitude, isolation, loneliness.

μονάρχης, ο [monarhees] monarch, sovereign.

μοναρχία, η [monarheea] monarchy.

μοναρχικός, ο [monarheekos] monarchist.

μοναστήρι, το [monasteeree] monastery.

μονάχα [monaha] only.

μοναχή, η [monahee] nun.

μοναχικός [monaheekos] monastic || (ερημικός) isolated, solitary, lonely.

μοναχοπαίδι, το [monahopeδee] only child.

μονάχος [monahos] alone, single, only, sole || real, authentic.

μοναχός, ο [monahos] monk.

μονή, η [monee] βλ **μοναστήρι**.

μόνιμος [moneemos] permanent, lasting, durable, fixed.

μονογαμία, η [monogameea] monogamy.

μονογενής [monoyenees] one and only.

μονόγραμμα, το [monograma] monogram, initials.

μονογραφή, η [monografee] initials.

μονόδρομος, ο [monoδromos] one-way street.

μονοιάζω [moneeazo] agree with, get on well with || reconcile.

μονοκατοικία, η [monokateekeea] one-family house.

μονοκόμματος [monokomatos] in one piece || stiff || forthright || massive.

μονομαχία, η [monomaheea] duel.

μονομερής [monomerees] one-sided, partial.

μονομιάς [monomias] all at once.

μόνο [mono] only, alone, solely, merely, nothing but || ~ που except that || ~ να provided that.

μονοπάτι, το [monopatee] footpath, pathway.

μονόπλευρος [monoplevros] one-sided, partial.

μονοπώλιο, το [monopoleeo] monopoly.

μονοπωλώ [monopolo] monopolize.

μόνος [monos] alone, single, by o.s., apart || ~ **μου** of my own accord, by myself.

μονός [monos] single || simple || (αριθμός) odd.

μονότονος [monotonos] monotonous, unvaried || (μεταφ) wearisome.

μονόφθαλμος [monofthalmos] one-eyed.

μοντέλο, το [montelo] model.

μοντέρνος [monternos] modern, up-to-date.

μονώνω [monono] set apart, cut off || insulate.

μόνωση, η [monosee] insulation || solitude, isolation.

μονωτικός [monoteekos] insulating.

μόριο, το [moreeo] particle || molecule.

μόρτης, ο [mortees] hooligan, blackguard.

μορφάζω [morfazo] grimace, make faces || (από πόνο) wince.

μορφασμός, ο [morfasmos] grimace || wince.

μορφή, η [morfee] shape, form || look, face, aspect || phase.

μορφίνη, η [morfeenee] morphine.

μορφολογία, η [morfoloyeea] morphology.

μορφώνω [morfono] shape, form || (εκπαιδεύω) train, educate, teach.

μόρφωση, η [morfosee] education, learning.

μορφωτικός [morfoteekos] cultural || instructive.

μόστρα, η [mostra] shop window, display || specimen, sample.

μοσχάρι, το [mosharee] calf || veal.

μοσχοβολώ [moshovolo] smell sweetly, be fragrant.

μοσχοκάρυδο, το [moshokareeδo] nutmeg.

μοσχολίβανο, το [mosholeevano] frankincense.

μοτοσυκλέτα, η [motoseekleta] motorbike, motorcycle.

μου [mou] me || my.

μουγγός [moungos] dumb, mute.

μουγγρίζω [moungreezo] roar, bellow || (άνεμος) howl, wail || (από πόνο) moan, groan.

μουδιάζω [mouδeeazo] become numb.

μουλάρι, το [moularee] mule.

μούμια, η [moumeea] mummy || shrivelled person.

μουντζούρα, η [mountzoura] smudge, stain, smear || (μεταφ) blemish.

μουντός [mountos] dull, dim.

μούρη, η [mouree] face || snout.

μούρλια, η [mourleea] madness ||
είναι ~ it's perfect!, it's a dream!

μουρλός [mourlos] mad, insane ||
bewildered.

μουρμουρητό, το [mourmoureeto]
murmuring || grumbling.

μουρμουρίζω [mourmoureezo]
mutter, murmur || (μεταφ) whisper ||
babble.

μούρο, το [mouro] mulberry ||
μουριά, η mulberry tree.

μουρούνα, η [mourouna] codfish.

μούσα, η [mousa] muse.

μουσακάς, ο [mousakas] moussaka,
minced meat with vegetables.

μουσαμάς, ο [mousamas] oilcloth,
linoleum || mackintosh.

μουσαφίρης, ο [mousafeerees]
guest, visitor.

μουσείο, το [mouseeo] museum.

μούσι, το [mousee] beard, goatee.

μουσική, η [mouseekee] music.

μουσικός [mouseekos] musical || (ουσ)
musician.

μούσκεμα, το [mouskema] wetting,
soaking || **τα κάνω** ~ to make a mess
of.

μουσκεύω [mouskevo] soak, wet,
damp || get wet.

μούσμουλο, το [mousmoulo] loquat.

μουσουργός, ο, η [mousourgos]
composer.

μουστάκι, το [moustakee]
moustache.

μουστάρδα, η [moustarδa] mustard.

μούστος, ο [moustos] must.

μούτρα, τα [moutra] πλ: **έχω** ~ **να** I
dare to || **πέφτω με τα** ~ to apply
o.s. enthusiastically || to tuck in.

μούτρο [moutro]: **είναι** ~ he's a thief,
he's deceitful.

μούτσος, ο [moutsos] cabin boy.

μούχλα, η [mouhla] mould, mildew.

μουχλιάζω [mouhleeazo] make
mouldy || become mouldy.

μοχθηρός [mohtheeros] wicked,
mischievous, malicious.

μόχθος, ο [mohthos] pains, fatigue,
trouble.

μοχλός, ο [mohlos] lever, (crow)bar ||
(μεταφ) promoter, instigator.

μπαγιάτικος [bayateekos] (ψωμί)
stale || rancid.

μπάγκος, ο [bangos] bench || counter.

μπάζα, τα [baza] πλ debris, rubble.

μπάζω [bazo] usher in, thrust in
(συμμαζεύομαι) shrink.

μπαίνω [beno] go into, get in, enter ||
(υφάσματ) shrink || (μεταφ) catch on,
understand || ~ **μέσα** to fall into debt ||
~ **σε μια σειρά** to settle down, fall
into line.

μπακάλης, ο [bakalees] grocer.

μπακάλικο, το [bakaleeko] grocer's
shop || grocery (US).

μπακαλιάρος, ο [bakaleearos] salted
codfish.

μπακίρι, το [bakeeree] copper.

μπακλαβάς, ο [baklavas] pastry of
almonds and honey.

μπαλαντέρ, ο [balanδer] (στα χαρτιά)
joker.

μπαλκόνι, το [balkonee] balcony.

μπάλα, η [bala] ball || bullet.

μπαλέτο, το [baleto] ballet.

μπαλόνι, το [balonee] balloon.

μπαλντάς, ο [balntas] axe, hatchet.

μπάλωμα, το [baloma] mending,
patching, repairing.

μπαλώνω [balono] patch, mend, repair
|| **τα** ~ to make excuses || to make up.

μπάμιες, οι [bamies] πλ okra, gumbo,
lady's fingers.

μπαμπάκι, το [bambakee] cotton.

μπαμπάς, ο [bambas] daddy, papa.

μπάμπουρας, ο [bambouras] hornet.

μπανάνα, η [banana] banana.

μπανιέρα, η [baniera] bathtub.

μπάνιο, το [baneeo] bath || bathing,
swimming || (λεκάνη) tub || (δωμάτιο)
bathroom.

μπάντα, η [banta] (ήσυχη γωνιά)
corner || (πλευρά) side || (μους) band ||
(συμμορία) gang, band || **βάζω στη** ~
to save || **κάνε στη** ~ make room,
stand aside.

μπαντιέρα, η [bantiera] banner,
standard.

μπαξές, ο [bakses] garden.

μπαούλο, το [baoulo] trunk, chest.

μπαρκάρω [barkaro] go on board ||
ship.

μπάρμπας, ο [barbas] old man ||
uncle.

μπαρμπούνι, το [barbounee] red
mullet.

μπαρούτι, το [baroutee] gunpowder ||
έγινε ~ he got furious.

μπάρρα, η [bara] bar, crowbar.

μπασμένος [basmenos] aware ||
knowledgeable || (ρούχα) shrunk.

μπάσταρδος, ο [bastarδos] bastard.

μπαστούνι, το [bastounee] walking
stick, cane || (χαρτιά) club.

μπαταρία, η [batareea] battery.

μπατζανάκης, ο [batzanakees]
brother-in-law.

μπάτσος, ο [batsos] slap, smack || (sl)
policeman.

μπαχαρικό, το [bahareeko] spice.

μπεζ [bez] beige.

μπεκάτσα, η [bekatsa] woodcock.

μπεκρής, ο [bekrees] drunkard,
tippler, boozer.

μπελάς, ο [belas] trouble,
embarrassment, annoyance.

μπέμπης, ο [bembees] baby.

μπενζίνα, η [benzeena] petrol || (πλοιάριο) motorboat.

μπέρδεμα, το [berdema] tangle, entanglement, confusion, disorder.

μπερδεύομαι [berdevome] get implicated in, become entangled || be confused.

μπερδεύω [berdevo] involve || confuse, make a muddle of || entangle.

μπερμπάντης, ο [bermbantees] rascal, scoundrel.

μπετό, το [beto] concrete.

μπετούγια, η [betouya] latch, catch.

μπήζω [beezo] drive in, hammer in || (βελόνα) stick in, thrust in.

μπιζέλι, το [beezelee] pea.

μπίρα, η [beera] beer.

μπισκότο, το [beeskoto] biscuit.

μπίτ(ι) [beet(ee)] entirely || not in the least.

μπιφτέκι, το [beeftekee] hamburger, steak.

μπλάστρι, το [blastree] plaster.

μπλε [ble] blue.

μπλέκω [bleko] complicate, perplex || get implicated.

μπλέξιμο, το [blekseemo] entanglement, involvement, complication.

μπλοκάρω [blokaro] blockade || block.

μπλούζα, η [blouza] blouse.

μπλόφα, η [blofa] bluff, deception.

μπογιά, η [boya] paint, dye || (παπουτσιών) boot polish.

μπόγιας, ο [boyas] dog-catcher || hangman.

μπογιατζής, ο [boyadzees] painter || polisher.

μπογιατίζω [boyateezo] paint, colour, coat || polish.

μπόι, το [boee] height, size.

μπόλι, το [bolee] graft || μπολιάζω vaccinate, inoculate || graft.

μπόλικος [boleekos] plentiful, abundant, numerous.

μπόμπα, η [bomba] bomb.

μπόρα, η [bora] rain squall, shower, storm.

μπορώ [boro] can, be able, may.

μπόσικος [boseekos] loose, slack || (μεταφ) trifling || unreliable.

μποστάνι, το [bostanee] melon field.

μποτίλια, η [boteeleea] bottle || μποτιλιάρω bottle || (μεταφ) block up, jam.

μπότα, η [bota] boot.

μπουγάδα, η [bougaδa] family wash, washing.

μπουζί, το [bouzee] spark plug.

μπουζούκι, το [bouzoukee] kind of mandolin, bouzouki.

μπούκα, η [bouka] hole, mouth, entrance || muzzle.

μπουκάλα, η [boukala] big bottle || έμεινε ~ he was left in the lurch.

μπουκάλι, το [boukalee] bottle.

μπουκιά, η [boukia] mouthful.

μπουκώνω [boukono] fill the mouth || (μεταφ) bribe.

μπουλούκι, το [bouloukee] crowd || band, troop.

μπουμπούκι, το [boumboukee] bud, sprout.

μπουμπουνητό, το [boumbouneeto] thundering, roll of thunder, rumble.

μπουνάτσα, η [bounatsa] fine weather || calm sea.

μπουνιά, η [bounia] punch, blow with the fist.

μπούρδα, η [bourδa] rubbish, hot air.

μπουρμπουλήθρα, η [bourmbouleethra] bubble.

μπουσουλώ [bousoulo] crawl.

μπούστος, ο [boustos] bust.

μπούτι, το [boutee] thigh || (αρνήσιο) leg of lamb.

μπουφές, ο [boufes] sideboard || buffet.

μπούφος, ο [boufos] horned owl || (μεταφ) booby.

μπουχτίζω [bouhteezo] have enough of || eat one's fill.

μπόχα, η [boha] stink, foul smell.

μπράβο [bravo] (επιφ) good show!, bravo!, good for you!

μπράτσο, το [bratso] arm.

μπριζόλα, η [breezola] chop, cutlet.

μπρίκι, το [breekee] coffee pot.

μπρος [bros] forward(s), in front of || βλ και εμπρός.

μπροστινός [brosteenos] in front || former.

μπρούμυτα [broumeeta] flat on one's face.

μπρούντζος, ο [broundzos] bronze, brass.

μπύρα, η [beera] βλ μπίρα.

μυ, το [mee] the letter M.

μυαλό, το [meealo] brain(s) || (γνώση) mind, intellect.

μυαλωμένος [meealomenos] learned, wise.

μύγα, η [meega] fly.

μύδι, το [meeδee] mussel.

μυελός, ο [mielos] marrow (of bone).

μυζήθρα, η [meezeethra] kind of white soft cheese.

μύηση, η [mieesee] initiation.

μυθικός [meetheekos] mythical, legendary || incredible.

μυθιστόρημα, το [meetheestoreema] novel, romance, story.

μυθιστοριογράφος, ο [meetheestoreeografos] novelist.

μυθολογία, η [meetholoyeea] mythology.

μύθος, ο [meethos] fable || myth || legend.

μυθώδης [meethoðees] fabled, legendary || untrue || incredible.

μυϊκός [mieekos] muscular.

μυκηθμός, ο [meekeethmos] bellowing, howling || lowing.

μύκητας, ο [meekeetas] fungus, mushroom.

μύλος, ο [meelos] mill || (ανεμόμυλος) windmill.

μυλωνάς, ο [meelonas] miller.

μύξα, η [meeksa] snot || mucus.

μυρίζω [meereezo] smell.

μύριοι [meeriee] ten thousand || (μεταφ) numberless.

μυρμήγκι, το [meermeengee] ant.

μυρτιά, η [meertia] myrtle.

μυρωδάτος [meeroðatos] aromatic, fragrant.

μυρωδιά, η [meeroðia] smell, scent, odour || (αρωματικό) fragrance, perfume || παίρνω ~ to get wind of.

μυς, ο [mees] muscle.

μυσαρός [meesaros] abominable, detestable, odious.

μυσταγωγία, η [meestagoyeea] initiation || holy ceremony.

μυστήριο, το [meesteereeo] mystery, secret.

μυστήριος [meesteereeos] mysterious, inexplicable.

μυστηριώδης [meesteereeoðees] mysterious, dark.

μυστικιστής, ο [meesteekeestees] mystic.

μυστικό, το [meesteeko] secret.

μυστικός [meesteekos] secret(ive) || reticent, discreet || (αστυνομικός) undercover man || ~ δείπνος Last Supper.

μυστικότητα, η [meesteekoteeta] secrecy, discretion.

μυστρί, το [meestree] trowel.

μυτερός [meeteros] pointed.

μύτη, η [meetee] nose || (άκρη) tip || (παπουτσιού) toe || (πένας) nib || (βελόνας) point.

μυώ [meeo] initiate into, admit into.

μυώδης [meeoðees] muscular, brawny, powerful.

μύωπας [meeopas] near-sighted, short-sighted.

μωαμεθανός, ο [moamethanos] Mohammedan.

μωβ [mov] mauve.

μώλος, ο [molos] mole, jetty, pier.

μωλωπίζω [molopeezo] bruise, contuse.

μώλωπας, ο [molopas] bruise, contusion.

μωρέ [more] (επιφ) hey you!, you!, I say!

μωρία, η [moreea] stupidity, foolishness.

μωρό, το [moro] baby, infant.

μωσαϊκό, το [mosaeeko] mosaic.

N, ν

να [na] that, to, in order to, so as to || here it is!

ναι [ne] yes, indeed, certainly.

νάιλον, το [naeelon] nylon.

νάνος, ο [nanos] dwarf.

νανουρίζω [nanoureezo] lull to sleep || (στην κούνια) rock || (στην αγκαλιά) nurse.

νανούρισμα, το [nanoureesma] lullaby || rocking to sleep.

ναός, ο [naos] church || temple.

ναργιλές, ο [naryeeless] hubble-bubble, hookah.

νάρθηκας, ο [nartheekas] (εκκλ) nave, narthex || (βοτ) fennel.

ναρκαλιευτικό, το [narkalievteeko] minesweeper.

νάρκη, η [narkee] numbness, torpor || (ναυτ) mine || (πνεύματος) sluggishness.

νάρκισσος, ο [narkeesos] narcissus.

ναρκώνω [narkono] numb || (μεταφ) dull, stupefy.

νάρκωση, η [narkosee] numbness || torpidity, sluggishness.

ναρκωτικά, τα [narkoteeka] πλ drugs, narcotics.

νάτριο, το [natreeo] sodium.

ναυάγιο, το [navayo] shipwreck || (μεταφ) wreck.

ναυαγός, ο [navagos] shipwrecked person.

ναυαρχείο, το [navarheeo] admiralty.

ναύαρχος, ο [navarhos] admiral.

ναύκληρος, ο [navkleeros] boatswain.

ναύλα, τα [navla] πλ fare, passage money.

ναυλώνω [navlono] charter, freight.

ναυμαχία, η [navmaheea] sea battle, naval action.

ναυπηγείο, το [navpeeyeeo] shipyard, dockyard.

ναυσιπλοΐα, η [navseeploeea] sailing, shipping || navigation.

ναύσταθμος, ο [navstathmos] dockyard, naval arsenal.

ναύτης, ο [navtees] sailor, seaman, mariner.

ναυτία, η [navteea] seasickness || nausea.

ναυτικό, το [navteeko] navy.

ναυτικός [navteekos] maritime || nautical || (άνδρας) seafarer.

ναυτιλία, η [navteeleea] navigation || shipping || ναυτιλιακός marine, naval, nautical.

ναυτολογώ [navtologo] enlist a crew, muster seamen.

νέα, η [nea] girl.

νέα, τα [nea] πλ news.

νεανικός [neaneekos] youthful, juvenile.

νεαρός [nearos] young || youthful, juvenile.

νέγρος, ο [negros] negro.

νέκρα, η [nekra] dead silence, stagnation.

νεκρικός [nekreekos] of death, funereal || gloomy.

νεκροθάπτης, ο [nekrothaptees] gravedigger.

νεκροκεφαλή, η [nekrokefalee] skull.

νεκρολογία, η [nekroloyeea] obituary.

νεκρός [nekros] dead, lifeless || (ουσ) ο ~ dead person.

νεκροταφείο, το [nekrotafeeo] cemetery, graveyard.

νεκροτομείο, το [nekrotomeeo] mortuary, morgue.

νεκροφόρα, η [nekrofora] hearse.

νεκροψία, η [nekropseea] autopsy, post-mortem.

νεκρώνω [nekrono] deaden || (τα πάθη) subdue.

νεκρώσιμος [nekroseemos] funeral.

νέκταρ, το [nektar] nectar.

νέμω [nemo] distribute, share.

νέο, το [neo] piece of news.

νεογέννητος [neoyeneetos] newborn.

νεογνό, το [neogno] newborn animal || newborn baby.

νεοελληνικά, τα [neoeleeneeka] πλ modern Greek (language).

νεοελληνικός [neoeleeneekos] of modern Greece.

νεόκτιστος [neokteestos] newly constructed.

νεολαία, η [neolea] youth.

νεόνυμφος, ο, η [neoneemfos] recently married man or woman.

νεόπλουτος [neoploutos] nouveau riche, parvenu.

νέος [neos] young || (καινούργιο) new, fresh || (επιπρόσθετο) further, additional || (σύγχρονος) modern || (ουσ) a young man.

νεοσσός, ο [neosos] nestling, chick.

νεοσύλλεκτος, ο [neoseelektos] recruit.

νεοσύστατος [neoseestatos] newly-established, newly-founded.

νεότητα, η [neoteeta] βλ **νεολαία**.

νεράιδα, η [neraeeda] fairy, Nereid.

νεράντζι, το [nerandzee] bitter orange.

νερό, το [nero] water || urine.

νερόβραστος [nerovrastos] boiled in water || (μεταφ) insipid, tasteless.

νερομπογιά, η [neromboya] watercolour.

νεροποντή, η [neropontee] shower of rain, downpour.

νερουλός [neroulos] watery, thin.

νεροχύτης, ο [neroheetees] kitchen sink.

νερώνω [nerono] mix with water.

νέτα σκέτα [netasketa] frankly, flatly.

νέτος [netos] net || (μεταφ) done, finished, completed.

νεύμα, το [nevma] sign, nod, wink, beckoning.

νευραλγία, η [nevralyeea] neuralgia.

νευραλγικός [nevralyeekos]: **νευραλγικό σημείο** weak spot.

νευριάζω [nevreeazo] make angry, irritate, vex || become angry.

νευρικός [nevreekos] nervous || excitable, highly strung.

νεύρο, το [nevro] nerve || muscle || vigour.

νευρόσπαστος, ο [nevrospastos] (μεταφ) nervous person.

νευρώδης [nevroðees] sinewy || nervous || (μεταφ) strong, spirited.

νευρωτικός [nevroteekos] neurotic.

νεύω [nevo] nod, make a sign, beckon, wink.

νεφελώδης [nefeloðees] cloudy, nebulous || (μεταφ) vague, hazy.

νέφος, το [nefos] cloud || (μεταφ) gloom, shadow.

νεφοσκεπής [nefoskepees] cloudy, overcast.

νεφρό, το [nefro] kidney.

νέφτι, το [neftee] turpentine, turps.

νεώριο, το [neoreeo] dry dock, dockyard.

νεωτερισμός, ο [neotereesmos] innovation || novelty, fashion.

νεώτερα, τα [neotera] πλ latest news.

νεώτερος [neoteros] younger || (γεγονός) recent, later || (νέα) fresh.

νήμα, το [neema] thread || (βαμβακερό) cotton thread || (μάλλινο) yarn.

νηνεμία, η [neenemeea] calmness, stillness.

νηολόγιο, το [neeoloyo] register of merchant shipping.

νηοπομπή, η [neeopombee] convoy, escort of ships.

νηπιαγωγείο, το [neepeeagoyeeo] kindergarten.

νήπιο, το [neepeeo] infant, baby, newborn child.

νησί, το [neesee] island.

νησιώτης, ο [neeseeotees] islander.

νήσος, η [neesos] βλ **νησί**.

νηστεία, η [neesteea] fast, fasting.

νηστεύω [neestevo] fast.

νηστικός [neesteekos] hungry.

νηφάλιος [neefaleeos] sober || (μεταφ) calm, cool, composed.

νιαουρίζω [neeaoureezo] miaow, mew.

νιάτα, τα [neeata] πλ youth.

νικέλιο, το [neekeleeo] nickel.

νίκη, η [neekee] victory, triumph.

νικητής, ο [neekeetees] victor || (σε παιχνίδι) winner.

νικηφόρος [neekeeforos] victorious, triumphant.

νικώ [neeko] (τον εχθρό) defeat, vanquish || (ανταγωνιστή) beat, surpass || (εμπόδια κτλ) surmount, overcome.

νίλα, η [neela] practical joke || calamity, ruin.

νιπτήρας, ο [neepteeras] washbasin, washstand.

νίπτω [neepto] wash || (μεταφ) wash out.

νισάφι, το [neesafee] mercy, compassion, pity.

νιφάδα, η [neefaða] snowflake.

Νοέμβρης, ο [noemvrees],
Νοέμβριος, ο [noemvreeos] November.

νοερός [noeros] mental, intellectual.

νόημα, το [noeema] reflection, thought || (έννοια) sense, meaning || (νεύμα) sign, wink.

νοημοσύνη, η [noeemoseenee] intelligence, intellect.

νοήμων [noeemon] intelligent, smart.

νόηση, η [noeesee] understanding, intellect || mind, wit.

νοητός [noeetos] comprehensible, conceivable.

νοθεία, η [notheea] falsification, adulteration.

νόθευση, η [nothevsee] adulteration, forgery.

νοθεύω [nothevo] falsify, forge, adulterate.

νόθος [nothos] bastard || (για ζώα κτλ) hybrid || (μεταφ) unstable.

νοιάζει [neeazee]: **με ~** I care, I am anxious about.

νοιάζομαι [neeazome] care about, look after || be anxious about.

νοίκι, το [neekee] rent || **νοικιάζω** rent, hire, let out || **νοικάρης, ο** tenant.

νοικοκυρά, η [neekokeera] housewife, mistress of the house || landlady.

νοικοκύρης, ο [neekokeerees] landlord || owner || (αυτεξούσιος) independent || wise.

νοικοκυριό, το [neekokeerio] housekeeping.

νοιώθω [neeotho] understand || feel, perceive || know.

νομαδικός [nomaðeekos] nomadic, roving.

νομαρχείο, το [nomarheeo] prefecture.

νομάρχης, ο [nomarhees] prefect, governor.

νομίζω [nomeezo] believe, think || suppose, presume.

νομικά, τα [nomeeka] πλ law studies, jurisprudence.

νομική, η [nomeekee] law.

νομικός [nomeekos] of the law, legal, lawful.

νομιμοποιώ [nomeemopeeo] legitimize, legalize, validate.

νόμιμος [nomeemos] legal, lawful, rightful.

νομιμότητα, η [nomeemoteeta] legitimacy, legality.

νομιμόφρονας [nomeemofronas] law-abiding, obedient, loyal.

νόμισμα, το [nomeesma] money, coin, currency.

νομοθεσία, η [nomotheseea] legislation, law-making.

νομοθέτης, ο [nomothetees] legislator, lawgiver.

νομομαθής, ο [nomomathees] jurist, legist.

νομός, ο [nomos] prefecture, province.

νόμος, ο [nomos] law, act (of Parliament), enactment.

νομοσχέδιο, το [nomosheðeeo] bill, draft of a law.

νομοταγής [nomotayees] law-abiding, loyal.

νονός, ο [nonos] godfather, sponsor.

νοοτροπία, η [nootropeea] mentality, mental character.

Νορβηγία, η [norveeyeea] Norway.

νορβηγικός [norveeyeekos] Norwegian.

Νορβηγός, ο [norveegos] Norwegian.

νοσηλεία, η [noseeleea] nursing, treatment, care of the sick.

νοσηλεύω [noseelevo] treat, tend, nurse.

νοσηρός [noseeros] unhealthy, sickly, weakly || (περιέργεια) morbid.

νοσοκομείο, το [nosokomeeo] hospital, infirmary.

νοσοκόμος, ο, η [nosokomos] nurse || (στρατ) hospital orderly.

νόσος, η [nosos] illness, disease, sickness.

νοσταλγία, η [nostalyeea] nostalgia || homesickness.

νοσταλγικός, [nostalyeekos] nostalgic || homesick.

νοσταλγώ [nostalgo] feel nostalgic for || crave for || be homesick.

νοστιμάδα, η [nosteemaða] tastiness || prettiness || piquancy.

νοστιμεύω [nosteemevo] flavour, make tasty || make attractive.

νόστιμος [nosteemos] tasty || attractive, charming.

νότα, η [nota] (διπλωματική) note || (μουσ) note.

νοτιά, η [notia] south || south wind.

νοτίζω [noteezo] moisten, dampen || become damp.

νοτιοανατολικός [noteeoanatoleekos] south-eastern.

νοτιοδυτικός [noteeoδeeteekos] south-western.

νότιος [noteeos] southern.

νότος, ο [notos] south.

νουθεσία, η [noutheseea] admonition, advice, counsel.

νουθετώ [noutheto] admonish, advise, give advice to.

νούμερο, το [noumero] number || (θεάτρου) act || odd character.

νουνός, ο [nounos] godfather, sponsor.

νους, ο [nous] mind, wit, intelligence, sense.

νούφαρο, το [noufaro] water lily.

νοώ [noo] comprehend, understand || think, reflect.

ντάης, ο [daees] bully, ruffian.

ντάμα, η [dama] lady || partner || (στα χαρτιά) queen || (παιχνίδι) game of draughts.

νταμιτζάνα, η [dameedzana] demijohn.

νταμπλάς, ο [damblas] apoplexy || (μεταφ) amazement, stupefaction.

νταντά, η [danda] child's nurse, nanny.

νταντέλα, η [dantela] lace.

νταούλι, το [daoulee] drum.

νταραβέρι, το [daraveree] relation, dealing || (φασαρία) fuss, trouble.

ντε [de]: **έλα ~** (επιφ) come on!, hurry up!

ντεπόζιτο, το [depozeeto] cistern || tank.

ντέρτι, το [dertee] regret, pain, sorrow || longing, yearning.

ντιβάνι, το [deevanee] divan.

ντολμάς, ο [dolmas] stuffed vine or cabbage leaves.

ντομάτα, η [domata] tomato.

ντόμπρος [dombros] sincere, candid, frank, honest.

ντόπιος [dopeeos] local, native.

ντόρος, ο [doros] trouble, din || (μεταφ) sensation.

ντουβάρι, το [douvaree] wall || (μεταφ) fool.

ντουέτο, το [doueto] duet.

ντουζίνα, η [douzeena] dozen.

ντουλάπα, η [doulapa] wardrobe.

ντουλάπι, το [doulapee] cupboard.

ντουνιάς, ο [dounias] people, mankind, humanity.

ντους, το [dous] shower bath.

ντρέπομαι [drepome] be bashful || be ashamed.

ντροπαλός [dropalos] shy, modest, timid.

ντροπή, η [dropee] shame || modesty, bashfulness.

ντροπιάζω [dropeeazo] shame.

ντυμένος [deemenos] dressed.

ντύνομαι [deenome] get dressed.

ντύνω [deeno] dress || (έπιπλα) upholster.

ντύσιμο, το [deeseemo] dressing || attire, outfit, dress.

νυ, το [nee] the letter N.

νυκτερινός [neektereenos] of night, nocturnal.

νυκτόβιος [neektoveeos] living by night.

νυκτοφύλακας, ο [neektofeelakas] night watchman.

νυμφεύω [neemfevo] marry, wed.

νύμφη, η [neemfee] bride || (μυθολογία) nymph || (ζωολ) larva.

νύξη, η [neeksee] hint, allusion.

νύστα, η [neesta] sleepiness, drowsiness.

νυστάζω [neestazo] be sleepy, feel sleepy.

νυσταλέος [neestaleos] sleepy || (μεταφ) dull, sluggish.

νύφη, η [neefee] βλ **νύμφη.**

νυφικός [neefeekos] bridal, nuptial.

νυφίτσα, η [neefeetsa] weasel.

νυχθημερόν [neehtheemeron] day and night.

νύχι, το [neehee] nail || (ποδιών) toenail || (ζώου) claw, talon || **νύχια** πλ clutches.

νύχτα, η [neehta] night, darkness || (επιρ) at night, by night.

νυχτερίδα, η [neehtereeδa] bat.

νυχτικό, το [neehteeko] nightgown.

νυχτώνω [neehtono]: **νυχτώνει** night falls.

νωθρός [nothros] sluggish, lazy, slothful.

νωπός [nopos] fresh, new, recent || (για ρούχα) still damp.

νωρίς [norees] early.

νώτα, τα [nota] πλ back || (στρατ) rear.

νωχελής [nohelees] indolent, idle, slothful.

Ξ, ξ

ξαγρυπνώ [ksagreepno] stay awake || watch over || burn the midnight oil.

ξαδέρφη, η [ksaδerfee] cousin.

ξάδερφος, ο [ksaδerfos] cousin.

ξακουστός [ksakoustos] renowned, celebrated, famous.

ξαλαφρώνω [ksalafrono] lighten the load of, help || (μεταφ) relieve || relieve one's mind.

ξανά [ksana] again, afresh, anew.

ξαναβάζω [ksanavazo] put back again, replace.

ξανάβω [ksanavo] irritate || become annoyed, get furious.

ξαναγυρίζω [ksanayeereezo] return, send back || turn again.

ξανακάνω [ksanakano] redo, remake, repeat.

ξαναλέω [ksanaleo] repeat, reiterate.

ξανανιώνω [ksananeeono] rejuvenate || become young again.

ξαναπαθαίνω [ksanapatheno] be taken in again || suffer again.

ξαναπαίρνω [ksanaperno] take again || (θάρρος) pluck up again || (υπάλληλος) take on again, rehire || (θέση) go back to.

ξαναπαντρεύομαι [ksanapanðrevome] remarry.

ξανασαίνω [ksanaseno] recover, refresh o.s., relax.

ξαναφορτώνω [ksanafortono] reload.

ξανθίζω [ksantheezo] become fairer.

ξανθομάλλης [ksanthomalees] fair-haired.

ξανθός [ksanthos] blond, fair, light || (στάχυ) yellow, golden.

ξάνοιγμα, το [ksaneegma] clearing up, brightening || launching out.

ξανοίγομαι [ksaneegome] confide one's secrets || spend freely.

ξανοίγω [ksaneego] (μεταφ) look, see || clear up.

ξάπλα, η [ksapla] sprawling around || lying down.

ξάπλωμα, το [ksaploma] lying down || stretching out, spreading.

ξαπλώνομαι [ksaplonome] spread || lie down.

ξαπλώνω [ksaplono] spread out || lie down.

ξαποσταίνω [ksaposteno] rest, relax.

ξαποστέλνω [ksapostelno] send off, forward || dismiss.

ξασπρίζω [ksaspreezo] whiten || blanch, pale, fade.

ξάστερα [ksastera] frankly, flatly, categorically.

ξάστερος [ksasteros] cloudless, bright || (μεταφ) lucid, clear.

ξαφνιάζομαι [ksafneeazome] be taken by surprise, be frightened.

ξαφνιάζω [ksafneeazo] startle, surprise, frighten, scare.

ξαφνικά [ksafneeka] all of a sudden.

ξαφνικό, το [ksafneeko] surprise || accident, mishap.

ξαφρίζω [ksafreezo] skim || (μεταφ) steal.

ξάφρισμα, το [ksafreesma] skimming || frothing.

ξεβάφω [ksevafo] fade || lose colour, discolour.

ξεβγάζω [ksevgazo] wash out || (προπέμπω) show out, get rid of.

ξεβράκωτος [ksevrakotos] trouserless || (μεταφ) penniless.

ξεγελώ [kseyelo] cheat, dupe, deceive.

ξεγεννώ [kseyeno] deliver a child || be delivered of.

ξεγνοιάζω [ksegneeazo] be free from care.

ξεγράφω [ksegrafo] efface, strike out || (μεταφ) wipe out || write off.

ξεδιαλέγω [kseðeealego] select, choose, sort.

ξεδιαλύνω [kseðeealeeno] get to the bottom of, unravel.

ξεδιάντροπος [kseðeeantropos] immodest, brazen.

ξεδιπλώνω [kseðeeplono] unfurl, open out, spread.

ξεδιψώ [kseðeepso] quench one's thirst || refresh.

ξεθαρρεύω [ksetharevo] become too bold.

ξεθεώνω [ksetheono] wear out, exhaust, harass, worry.

ξεθυμαίνω [ksetheemeno] escape, leak out || (μεταφ) calm down, abate.

ξεθωριάζω [ksethoreeazo] fade || lose colour, discolour.

ξεκαθαρίζω [ksekathareezo] liquidate, settle accounts || elucidate || kill off.

ξεκάνω [ksekano] sell off || kill, exterminate.

ξεκαρδίζομαι [ksekarðeezome] burst out laughing.

ξεκάρφωτος [ksekarfotos] (μεταφ) unconnected, irrelevant.

ξεκινώ [ksekeeno] set off, start, depart || drive off.

ξεκλείδωτος [ksekleeðotos] unlocked.

ξεκοκκαλίζω [ksekokaleezo] eat to the bone || (μεταφ) spend foolishly.

ξεκομμένα [ksekomena] to the point, frankly.

ξεκουμπώνω [ksekoumbono] unbutton, unfasten.

ξεκουράζομαι [ksekourazome] relax, rest.

ξεκουράζω [ksekourazo] rest, relieve, refresh, repose.

ξεκουφαίνω [ksekoufeno] deafen, stun.

ξελιγωμένος [kseleegomenos] be hungry for, hunger for.

ξελιγώνω [kseleegono] (μεταφ) wear o.s. out, tire.

ξελογιάζω [kseloyazo] seduce, lead astray, fascinate.

ξεμαλλιασμένος [ksemaleeasmenos] dishevelled.

ξεμοναχιάζω [ksemonaheeazo] take aside.

ξεμπαρκάρω [ksembarkaro] land || unload.

ξεμπερδεύω [ksemberðevo] unravel, disentangle || get clear of, get rid of.

ξεμπλέκω [ksembleko] free o.s. || ~ από get free of.

ξεμυαλίζω [ksemeealeezo] infatuate, turn the head of, lead astray.

ξένα, τα [ksena] nλ foreign parts.

ξεναγός, ο, η [ksenagos] tourist guide.

ξενητειά, η [kseneetia] foreign parts, foreign country.

ξενητεύομαι [kseneetevome] live abroad.

ξενίζω [kseneezo] surprise, astonish.

ξενικός [kseneekos] foreign, alien, outlandish.

ξενοιάζω [kseneeazo] be free from cares.

ξενοδοχείο, το [ksenoδoheeo] hotel.

ξενοδόχος, ο [ksenoδohos] hotelier, innkeeper.

ξενοικιάζομαι [kseneekeeazome] become vacant.

ξένος [ksenos] foreign, strange, unfamiliar || (ουσ) ~ foreigner, stranger || visitor.

ξενοφοβία, η [ksenofoveea] xenophobia.

ξενόφωνος [ksenofonos] foreign-speaking.

ξεντύνω [ksenteeno] undress, disrobe.

ξενυχτώ [kseneehto] stay up late, stay out all night.

ξενώνας, ο [ksenonas] spare room, guest room.

ξεπαγιάζω [ksepayazo] freeze || get frozen.

ξεπαστρεύω [ksepastrevo] exterminate, wipe out.

ξεπερασμένος [kseperasmenos] out-of-date, old-fashioned.

ξεπερνώ [kseperno] surpass, overtake || (σε δρόμο) outrun || (σε ύψος) be taller.

ξεπεσμός, ο [ksepesmos] decay, decline || (τιμών) fall || (νομίσματος) depreciation.

ξεπετιέμαι [ksepetieme] jump up suddenly, shoot up.

ξεπέφτω [ksepefto] reduce, abate || (τιμών) fall || (μεταφ) fall into disrepute.

ξεπλένω [ksepleno] rinse.

ξεπληρώνω [ksepleerono] pay off, discharge (a debt).

ξεπούλημα, το [ksepouleema] sale, sellout, liquidation || fire sale (US).

ξεπουλώ [ksepoulo] sell off || sell out, liquidate.

ξεπροβοδίζω [kseprovoδeezo] escort off, say goodbye to.

ξέρα, η [ksera] (θάλασσας) rock, reef || (καιρού) drought, dryness.

ξεραΐλα, η [kseraeela] aridity, dryness, drought.

ξεραίνομαι [kserenome] dry up, wither, get parched.

ξεραίνω [ksereno] dry up || parch, bake || (φυτά) wither.

ξερνώ [kserno] vomit, bring up || belch out.

ξερόβηχας, ο [kseroveehas] dry cough.

ξεροκαταπίνω [kserokatapeeno] swallow with embarrassment.

ξεροκέφαλος [kserokefalos] thickheaded || obstinate, stubborn.

ξερονήσι, το [kseroneesee] barren island, desert island.

ξερός [kseros] arid, dry, barren || (γλώσσα) parched || (ύφος) curt, snappish || ΕΜΕΙΝΕ ~ he was stumped || he dropped dead || ΕΠΕΣΕ ~ ΣΤΟΝ ΥΠΝΟ he dropped off to sleep.

ξεριζώνω [ksereezono] pull up, uproot || root out, wipe out.

ξέρω [ksero] know how to, understand, be aware of.

ξεσηκώνω [kseseekono] rouse, excite || (σχέδιο) transfer, copy.

ξεσκάζω [kseskazo] refresh o.s., relax.

ξεσκεπάζω [kseskepazo] unveil, uncover || reveal, disclose, let out.

ξεσκίζω [kseskeezo] rip up.

ξεσκονίζω [kseskoneezo] dust, give a dusting to.

ξεσκονόπανο, το [kseskonopano] duster, dust rag.

ξεσπάζω [ksespazo] (μεταφ) burst into, burst out.

ξεσπαθώνω [ksespathono] unsheathe one's sword || (μεταφ) speak out.

ξεστομίζω [ksestomeezo] utter, launch, hurl.

ξεστραβώνω [ksestravono] straighten out || become straight.

ξεστρώνω [ksestrono] take up, remove || (τραπέζι) clear away.

ξεσχίζω [ksesheezo] tear to pieces, lacerate.

ξετινάζω [kseteenazo] toss, shake, beat || (μεταφ) reduce to poverty.

ξετρελαίνω [ksetreleno] drive mad, bewilder || (από έρωτα) bewitch.

ξετρυπώνω [ksetreepono] appear suddenly, crop up.

ξετσίπωτος [ksetseepotos] shameless.

ξεύρω [ksevro] βλ ξέρω.

ξεφαντώνω [ksefantono] live fast, feast, revel.

ξεφεύγω [ksefevgo] elude || slip out.

ξεφλουδίζω [kseflouδeezo] peel || pare || shell || (το δέρμα) lose the skin.

ξεφορτώνομαι [ksefortonome] get rid of, shake off.

ξεφορτώνω [ksefortono] unload || (μεταφ) get rid of.

ξεφτέρι, το [ksefteree] sharp person, witty person.

ξεφτίζω [ksefteezo] fray out || (νήμα) pull out, unweave.

ξεφυλλίζω [ksefeeleezo] skim over, run through || strip the leaves, pluck.

ξεφυτρώνω [ksefeetrono] sprout, shoot up || appear suddenly.

ξεφωνητό, το [ksefoneeto] yell, shout, outcry, scream.

ξεφωνίζω [ksefoneezo] shout, bawl, yell, scream.

ξεχαρβαλωμένος [kseharvalomenos] shaky, loose, falling apart.

ξεχασμένος [ksehasmenos] forgotten.

ξεχειλίζω [kseheeleezo] overflow, run over.

ξεχειμωνιάζω [kseheemoneeazo] pass the winter, winter.

ξεχνώ [ksehno] forget, leave out, neglect.

ξεχρεώνω [ksehreono] pay up, discharge || settle, fulfil.

ξεχύνομαι [kseheenome] overflow.

ξεχύνω [kseheeno] pour out, overflow.

ξέχωρα [ksehora] apart, separately || ~ **από** apart from.

ξεχωρίζω [ksehoreezo] separate || single out || distinguish, discern || make one's mark.

ξεχωριστά [ksehoreesta] separately.

ξεχωριστός [ksehoreestos] separate || distinct, peculiar || distinguished, exceptional.

ξεψυχώ [ksepseeho] die, expire, give up the ghost.

ξηλώνω [kseelono] take apart, unstitch.

ξημερώματα [kseemeromata] πλ daybreak, dawn.

ξημερώνομαι [kseemeronome] stay awake till morning.

ξηρά, η [kseera] dry land, mainland.

ξηραίνω [kseereno] dry, drain.

ξηραντήριο, το [kseeranteereeo] drier.

ξηρασία, η [kseeraseea] aridity || drought.

ξηροί [kseeree]: ~ **καρποί** πλ dried fruit and nuts.

ξι, το [ksee] the letter Ξ.

ξινίζω [kseeneezo] turn sour, get sour.

ξινίλα, η [kseeneela] bitterness, acidity, tartness, sharpness.

ξινός [kseenos] sour, acid, sharp || (για φρούτα) unripe, green.

ξιπασμένος [kseepasmenos] vain, conceited.

ξιφασκία, η [kseefaskia] fencing, swordplay.

ξιφίας, ο [kseefeeas] swordfish.

ξιφολόγχη, η [kseefolonghee] bayonet.

ξιφομαχώ [kseefomaho] fence.

ξίφος, το [kseefos] sword.

ξοδεύομαι [ksoδevome] spend, incur expenses.

ξοδεύω [ksoδevo] spend, use up, consume, expend.

ξόρκι, το [ksorkee] exorcism || entreaty.

ξύγκι, το [kseengee] fat, lard, grease, tallow.

ξυδάτος [kseeδatos] pickled.

ξύδι, το [kseeδee] vinegar.

ξυλάνθρακας, ο [kseelanthrakas] charcoal.

ξυλεία, η [kseeleea] timber, lumber.

ξύλινος [kseeleenos] wooden, wood.

ξύλο, το [kseelo] wood || **τρώω** ~ to receive a beating || **έπεσε** ~ there was a fight.

ξυλοκάρβουνο, το [kseelokarvouno] charcoal.

ξυλοκόπος, ο [kseelokopos] woodcutter, lumberjack.

ξυλοκοπώ [kseelokopo] thrash, beat soundly.

ξυλοπόδαρο, το [kseelopoδaro] stilt.

ξυλουργική, η [kseelouryeekee] joinery, carpentry.

ξυλουργός, ο [kseelourgos] joiner, carpenter.

ξυλοφορτώνω [kseelofortono] thrash, leather, lick.

ξύνομαι [kseenome] scratch (o.s.).

ξύνω [kseeno] scratch, scrape || (μολύβι) sharpen || scrape off.

ξύπνημα, το [kseepneema] awakening, waking up.

ξυπνητήρι, το [kseepneeteeree] alarm clock.

ξύπνιος [kseepneeos] wakeful, awake || (μεταφ) alert, clever, intelligent.

ξυπνώ [kseepno] wake up, rouse.

ξυπόλυτος [kseepoleetos] barefooted, shoeless.

ξυράφι, το [kseerafee] razor.

ξυραφάκι, το [kseerafakee] razor blade.

ξυρίζομαι [kseereezome] shave, get shaved, have a shave.

ξυρίζω [kseereezo] shave.

ξύρισμα, το [kseereesma] shave, shaving.

ξυριστική [kseereesteekee]: ~ **μηχανή** safety razor.

ξύσιμο, το [kseeseemo] scratching, scraping || rubbing, erasing || sharpening.

ξυστός [kseestos] grated, scratched.

ξύστρα, η [kseestra] grater, scraper, rasp || pencil sharpener.

ξωκκλήσι, το [ksokleesee] country chapel.

ξωτικό, το [ksoteeko] ghost, spirit, goblin.

ξώφυλλο, το [ksofeelo] book cover || (παραθύρου) outside shutter.

O

Ο, ο

ο [o] the.

όαση, η [oasee] oasis.

οβελίας, ο [oveleeas] lamb on the spit.

οβίδα, η [oveeδa] explosive shell.

οβολός, ο [ovolos] mite, contribution.

ογδόντα [ogδonda] eighty.

ογδονκοστός [ogδoeekostos] eightieth.

ογδοντάρης, ο [ogδontarees] octogenarian.

όγδοος [ogδoos] eighth.

ογκόλιθος, ο [ongoleethos] block of stone.

όγκος, ο [ongos] volume, mass, bulk, lump || (ιατρ) tumour.

ογκούμαι [ongoume] swell, grow fatter || (μεταφ) increase, swell.

ογκώδης [ongoδees] voluminous, massive || (άτομο) stout, portly.

οδεύω [oδevo] walk, tramp, trudge || accompany || (προς) proceed, advance.

οδηγητής, ο [oδeeyeetees] guide.

οδηγία, η [oδeeyeea] direction, guidance || instruction, directions, orders.

οδηγός, ο [oδeegos] guide, conductor || (αυτοκινήτου) driver, chauffeur.

οδηγώ [oδeego] guide, lead || (αυτοκίνητο κτλ) drive || show how to, instruct.

οδοιπορία, η [oδeeporeea] walk, journey || march.

οδοιπορικά, τα [oδeeporeeka] πλ: ~ έξοδα travelling expenses.

οδοιπόρος, ο, η [oδeeporos] traveller, voyager.

οδοιπορώ [oδeeporo] walk, tramp || march || travel.

οδοκαθαριστής, ο [oδokathareestees] street sweeper.

οδοντιατρείο, το [oδonteeatreeo] dentist's surgery, dental clinic.

οδοντιατρική, η [oδonteeatreekee] dentistry.

οδοντίατρος, ο, η [oδonteeatros] dentist.

οδοντόβουρτσα, η [oδontovourtsa] toothbrush.

οδοντογλυφίδα, η [oδontogleefeeδa] toothpick.

οδοντόπαστα, η [oδontopasta] dentifrice, toothpaste.

οδοντοστοιχία, η [oδontosteeheea] (set of) false teeth.

οδοντωτός [oδontotos] toothed, jagged, cogged || ~ σιδηρόδρομος funicular railway.

οδοποιία, η [oδopieea] road construction, roadmaking.

οδός, η [oδos] street || (ευρεία) main street, thoroughfare || (εθνική) state highway || (εμπορική) trade route || **καθ' οδόν** on the way, along the road.

οδόστρωμα, το [oδostroma] road surface.

οδοστρωτήρας, ο [oδostroteeras] steamroller.

οδόφραγμα, το [oδofragma] barricade, roadblock, barrier.

οδύνη, η [oδeenee] pain, suffering || (ηθική) grief || affliction.

οδυνηρός [oδeeneeros] (πληγή) painful || (μέρος) sore || (θέαμα) harrowing.

οδυρμός, ο [oδeermos] lamentation, wailing.

οδύρομαι [oδeerome] lament, complain, moan.

όζον, το [ozon] ozone.

όζος, ο [ozos] knot || (των δακτύλων) knuckles.

οζώδης [ozoδees] knotty, gnarled.

οθόνη, η [othonee] screen.

Οθωμανός, ο [othomanos] Ottoman.

οίδημα, το [eeδeema] swelling.

οικειοθελώς [eekeeothelos] (υπακούω) voluntarily || (κάνω κάτι) purposely, wilfully.

οικειοποίηση, η [eekeeopieesee] appropriation.

οικειοποιούμαι [eekeeopeeoume] appropriate to o.s., usurp.

οικείος [eekeeos] intimate, familiar || sociable, affable || **οι οικείοι** relatives, close relations.

οικειότητα, η [eekeeoteeta] familiarity, closeness.

οίκημα, το [eekeema] dwelling, lodging, habitation.

οικία, η [eekeea] house, home.

οικιακός [eekeeakos] domestic, home || (ζώο) domesticated.

οικίζω [eekeezo] inhabit, colonize, settle.

οικισμός, ο [eekeesmos] settling, colonizing.

οικογένεια, η [eekoyeneea] family.

οικογενειακός [eekoyeneeakos] of the family.

οικογενειακώς [eekoyeneeakos] with the entire family.

οικοδέσποινα, η [eekoδespeena] lady of the house, hostess.

οικοδεσπότης, ο [eekoδespotees] master of the house, host.

οικοδομή, η [eekoδomee] construction, act of building || building under construction.

οικοδόμημα, το [eekoδomeema] building, structure.

οικοδόμηση, η [eekoδomeesee] construction, building, erection.

οικοδομική, η [eekoδomeekee] building.

οικοδομικός [eekoδomeekos] constructive.

οικοδομώ [eekoδomo] build, construct, raise.

οικοκυρά [eekokeera] βλ **νοικοκυρά.**

οικοκύρης [eekokeerees] βλ **νοικοκύρης.**

οίκον [eekon]: **κατ'** ~ at home.

οικονομία, η [eekonomeea] economy, husbandry, thrift || saving.

οικονομικά, τα [eekonomeeka] πλ finances || (επιρ) reasonably, cheaply.

οικονομικός [eekonomeekos] economic, financial || (φθηνά) reasonable, cheap.

οικονόμος, ο, η [eekonomos] steward, stewardess || (μεταφ) thrifty person.

οικονομώ [eekonomo] save, economize || find, get hold of || **τα** ~ make ends meet, make money.

οικόπεδο, το [eekopeðo] building site, plot.

οίκος, ο [eekos] house || business house.

οικοτροφείο, το [eekotrofeeo] boarding school.

οικότροφος, ο, η [eekotrofos] boarder.

οικουμένη, η [eekoumenee] world, universe.

οικουμενικός [eekoumeneekos] ecumenical.

οικτείρω [eekteero] feel compassion for, pity || despise, scorn.

οίκτος, ο [eektos] compassion, pity || contempt, scorn.

οικτρός [eektros] deplorable || wretched, miserable.

οινόπνευμα, το [eenopnevma] alcohol || **οινοπνευματώδης** alcoholic.

οίνος, ο [eenos] wine.

οιοσδήποτε [eeosðeepote] any(body) || any kind of, whoever, whichever.

οισοφάγος, ο [eesofagos] oesophagus.

οίστρος, ο [eestros] gadfly || (μεταφ) inspiration, goading.

οιωνός, ο [eeonos] omen, presage, portent.

οκνηρός [okneeros] lazy, idle, sluggish.

οκνός [oknos] nonchalant, languid, slack.

οκρίβαντας, ο [okreevantas] easel.

οκτάγωνος [oktagonos] octagonal.

οκτακόσιοι [oktakosiee] eight hundred.

οκταπόδι, το [oktapoðee] octopus.

οκτώ [octo] eight.

Οκτώβριος, ο [oktovreeos] October.

όλα, τα [ola] πλ everything || ~ **κι** ~ anything else but.

ολάκερος [olakeros] whole, entire, total, complete.

ολέθριος [olethreeos] ominous, disastrous, destructive.

όλεθρος, ο [olethros] calamity, destruction, ruin.

ολημερίς [oleemerees] all day long.

ολιγάριθμος [oleegareethmos] few in number, a few.

ολιγαρκής [oleegarkees] temperate, frugal, moderate.

ολιγαρχία, η [oleegarheea] oligarchy.

ολιγόλογος [oleegologos] concise, succinct || taciturn.

ολίγο [oleego] (a) little.

ολίγος [oleegos] short, a little, a few || **ολίγον κατ' ολίγον** gradually || **παρ' ολίγο να** nearly, almost.

ολιγοστεύω [oleegostevo] diminish, decrease, lessen.

ολιγοστός [oleegostos] scarcely enough, scanty, inconsiderable.

ολιγοψυχία, η [oleegopseeheea] timidity.

ολιγωρία, η [oleegoreea] negligence, neglect, indifference.

ολικός [oleekos] total, whole, complete.

ολικώς [oleekos] totally, utterly.

ολισθαίνω [oleestheno] slip, slide || (μεταφ) lapse into, slip into.

ολίσθημα, το [oleestheema] slip(ping), slide || mistake, fault.

ολισθηρός [oleestheeros] slippery, greasy.

ολκή, η [olkee] attraction, pull, weight || calibre, bore.

Ολλανδέζος, ο [olanðezos] Dutchman.

Ολλανδία, η [olanðeea] Holland.

ολλανδικός [olanðeekos] Dutch.

όλμος, ο [olmos] mortar.

όλο [olo] all || ~ **και περισσότερο** more and more, always.

ολογράφως [olografos] written in full.

ολόγυρα [oloyeera] all round, in a circle.

ολοένα [oloena] incessantly, constantly.

ολοήμερος [oloeemeros] lasting a whole day.

ολοίδιος [oloeeðeeos] the spitting image.

ολοίσιος [oloeeseeos] direct, straight || upright.

ολοκαύτωμα, το [olokavtoma] holocaust || sacrifice.

ολόκληρος [olokleeros] entire, whole, full, complete.

ολοκληρώνω [olokleerono] complete, finish || (μαθημ) integrate.

ολοκληρωτικός [olokleeroteekos] full, entire, complete || totalitarian || (μαθημ) integral.

ολόμαλλος [olomalos] all wool, pure wool.

ολομέλεια, η [olomeleea] total membership, all members present.

ολομερής [olomerees] entire, whole, complete.

ολομόναχος [olomonahos] quite alone.

ολονυχτίς [oloneehtees] the whole night long.

ολόρθος [olorthos] straight, upright, standing.

όλος [olos] all, whole || όλοι everyone, everybody || όλοι μας all of us, altogether || όλα όλα altogether, the total.

ολοσχερής [olosherees] utter, complete, full, entire.

ολοταχώς [olotahos] at full speed, at top speed.

ολότελα [olotela] entirely, altogether, completely.

ολοφάνερος [olofaneros] obvious, plain, clear.

ολόχαρος [oloharos] joyful, happy.

ολόχρυσος [olohreesos] all gold, solid gold.

ολόψυχος [olopseehos] wholeheartedly.

Ολυμπιακός [oleembeeakos] Olympic.

όλως [olos] wholly, altogether, totally || ~ διόλου completely, wholly || ~ υμέτερος yours truly.

ομάδα, η [omaδa] group, company, band, gang || (αθλητική) team.

ομαδικός [omaδeekos] collective.

ομαδικώς [omaδeekos] in a body, collectively.

ομαλός [omalos] even || level || smooth, regular || (βίος) uneventful || flat.

ομαλότητα, η [omaloteeta] regularity, smoothness, evenness.

ομελέτα, η [omeleta] omelette.

ομήγυρη, η [omeeyeeree] party, meeting, assembly, circle.

όμηρος, ο [omeeros] hostage.

όμικρο, το [omeekro] the letter O.

ομιλητής, ο [omeeleetees] speaker, lecturer.

ομιλητικός [omeeleeteekos] sociable, affable.

ομιλία, η [omeeleea] talk, conversation || speech, lecture.

όμιλος, ο [omeelos] company, group, club.

ομιλώ [omeelo] speak, talk.

ομίχλη, η [omeehlee] fog, mist.

ομιχλώδης [omeehloδees] foggy, misty.

ομοβροντία, η [omovronteea] salvo, volley.

ομογένεια, η [omoyeneea] homogeneity || fellow Greeks.

ομογενής [omoyenees] similar || of the same race || expatriate Greek.

ομοεθνής [omoethnees] of the same nation, fellow (countryman).

ομοειδής [omoeeδees] of the same kind || uniform, similar.

ομόθρησκος [omothreeskos] of the same religion.

ομόθυμος [omotheemos] unanimous.

ομοιάζω [omeeazo] resemble, look like || be like.

ομοιογενής [omeeoyenees] homogeneous || uniform.

ομοιοκαταληξία, η [omeeokataleekseea] rhyme, rime.

ομοιόμορφος [omeeomorfos] uniform, unvarying.

ομοιοπαθής [omeeopathees] fellow (sufferer), in the same boat.

όμοιος [omeeos] similar, (a)like, same, in conformity with.

ομοιότητα, η [omeeoteeta] resemblance, similarity, likeness.

ομοίωμα, το [omeeoma] likeness, image || effigy.

ομοιωματικά, τα [omeeomateeka] πλ ditto marks.

ομόκεντρος [omokentros] concentric.

ομολογία, η [omoloyeea] confession, avowal, acknowledgement, admission || (οικον) bond, share.

ομόλογο, το [omologo] bond, promissory note, obligation.

ομολογουμένως [omologoumenos] avowedly, admittedly.

ομολογώ [omologo] acknowledge, confess, admit.

ομόνοια, η [omoneea] concord, agreement, accord, peace.

ομόρρυθμος [omoreethmos]: ~ εταιρεία partnership (in business).

ομορφαίνω [omorfeno] beautify || become beautiful.

ομορφιά, η [omorfia] beauty, handsomeness.

όμορφος [omorfos] handsome, beautiful, nice.

ομοσπονδία, η [omospondeea] federation, confederacy.

ομότιμος [omoteemos]: ~ καθηγητής professor emeritus.

ομόφρονας [omofronas] having the same ideas, thinking alike.

ομοφυλοφιλία, η [omofeelofeeleea] homosexuality.

ομοφωνία, η [omofoneea] unanimity.

ομόφωνος [omofonos] unanimous.

ομπρέλλα, η [ombrella] umbrella.

ομφαλός, ο [omfalos] navel || (μεταφ) centre.

ομώνυμος [omoneemos] having the same name.

όμως [omos] yet, nevertheless, but, however.

ον, το [on] creature, being.

ονειρεύομαι [oneerevome] dream, have visions.

ονειροκρίτης, ο [oneerokreetees] dream interpreter.

όνειρο, το [oneero] dream || vision, imagination.

ονειροπολώ [oneeropolo] daydream || dream (of), build castles in the air.

ονειρώδης [oneeroδees] dreamlike, fantastic || grand.

όνομα, το [onoma] name || (γραμμ) noun || fame, reputation || **βγάζω ~** gain renown, become famous || **~ και πράμα** in every sense || **ονόματι** by name of.

ονομάζω [onomazo] name, call || appoint.

ονομασία, η [onomaseea] name, appellation || designation, appointment.

ονομαστική, η [onomasteekee] (γραμμ) nominative (case) || **~ εορτή** name day.

ονομαστικός [onomasteekos] nominal.

ονομαστός [onomastos] famous, famed, celebrated.

ονοματεπώνυμο, το [onomateponeemo] name and surname.

ονοματολογία, η [onomatoloyeea] nomenclature, terminology.

οντότητα, η [ontoteeta] entity, being || personality.

όντως [ontos] really, truly, in truth.

οξεία, η [okseea] (γραμμ) acute accent.

οξείδιο, το [okseeδeo] oxide.

οξείδωση, η [okseeδosee] oxidation || corrosion, rusting.

οξικός [okseekos] acetic.

όξινος [okseenos] sour, bitter, acid.

οξύ, το [oksee] acid.

οξυά, η [oksia] beech tree || beech.

οξυγονοκόλληση, η [okseegonokoleesee] oxyacetylene welding.

οξυγόνο, το [okseegono] oxygen.

οξυδέρκεια, η [okseeδerkeea] perspicacity, acumen || (μεταφ) discernment.

οξύθυμος [okseetheemos] irritable, touchy.

οξύνους [okseenous] sagacious, acute, keen, clever.

οξύνω [okseeno] sharpen, whet || (το νου) sharpen || (αισθήματα) stir up, arouse, provoke.

οξύς [oksees] sharp, pointed || piercing, shrill || (γεύση) sour, strong.

οξύτητα, η [okseeteeta] sharpness || keenness, acuteness.

οξύφωνος, ο [okseefonos] (μουσ) tenor.

όξω [okso] βλ **έξω.**

οπαδός, ο, η [opaδos] adherent, partisan, supporter.

όπερα, η [opera] opera.

οπή, η [opee] opening, aperture, hole, gap.

όπιο, το [opeeo] opium.

όπισθεν [opeesthen] behind, in the rear || **κάνω ~** go backwards, put in reverse.

οπίσθιος [opeestheeos] hind, posterior, back.

οπισθογραφώ [opeesthografo] endorse (a cheque).

οπισθοδρομικός [opeesthoδromeekos] retrogressive || (στις απόψεις) reactionary.

οπισθοφυλακή, η [opeesthofeelakee] rearguard.

οπισθοχώρηση, η [opeesthohoreesee] retreat, withdrawal.

οπίσω [opeeso] behind, back || again.

όπλα, τα [opla] βλ arms.

οπλή, η [oplee] hoof.

οπλίζω [opleezo] arm || (μεταφ) reinforce, strengthen.

οπλισμός, ο [opleesmos] armament, equipment || (καλωδίου) sheathing.

οπλιταγωγό, το [opleetagogo] troopship.

οπλίτης, ο [opleetees] soldier.

όπλο, το [oplo] arm, weapon || rifle || (αμύνης) branch of army.

οπλοπολυβόλο, το [oplopoleevolo] light machine gun.

οπλοστάσιο, το [oplostaseeo] arsenal, armoury.

οπλοφορία, η [oploforeea] carrying of arms.

όποιος [opeeos] whoever, whichever || **~ κι'** whosoever, anybody.

οποίος [opeeos] of what kind || **ο ~** who, which.

οποιοσδήποτε [opeeosδeepote] whoever, whatsoever.

οπόταν [opotan] whenever, when.

όποτε [opote] whenever, at any time.

οπότε [opote] at which time, when.

όπου [opou] where, wherever.

οπουδήποτε [opouδeepote] wheresoever, wherever.

οπτασία, η [optaseea] vision, apparition.

οπτική, η [opteekee] optics.

οπτικός [opteekos] optic(al) || (ουσ) optician.

οπωρικά, τα [oporeeka] πλ fruit.

οπωροπωλείο, το [oporopoleeo] fruit market.

οπωροφόρος [oporoforos] bearing fruit, fruit-producing.

όπως [opos] as, like || **~ ~** somehow or other, after a fashion || (συνδ) in order that, so as.

οπωσδήποτε [oposδeepote] howsoever, anyway, without fail || definitely.

όραμα, το [orama] vision ||

οραματίζομαι have visions, visualize.

όραση, n [orasee] sense of sight, vision.

ορατός [oratos] visible, perceptible.

ορατότητα, n [oratoteeta] visibility.

οργανικός [organeekos] organic.

οργανισμός, ο [organeesmos] organism || organization.

όργανο, το [organo] organ || (μουσ) instrument || implement, tool || (κατασκοπείας) agent.

οργανώνω [organono] organize, constitute, form.

οργάνωση, n [organosee] organization, arranging.

οργασμός, ο [orgasmos] orgasm, heat || (μεταφ) feverish activity.

οργή, n [oryee] anger, rage || **να πάρει n** ~ damn it!, damnation!

όργια, τα [orya] πλ orgies || (μεταφ) corrupt practices || **οργιάζω** revel, debauch.

οργίζω [oryeezo] anger, enrage, irritate.

οργυιά, n [orya] fathom.

όργωμα, το [orgoma] ploughing, tilling, tillage.

οργώνω [orgono] plough, till, furrow.

ορδή, n [orðee] horde, host, rabble.

ορειβασία, n [oreevaseea] mountain climbing.

ορειβάτης, ο [oreevatees] mountain climber.

ορειβατικός [oreevateekos] of climbing, of mountaineering.

ορεινός [oreenos] mountainous, hilly || of the mountains.

ορείχαλκος, ο [oreehalkos] brass, bronze.

ορεκτικό, το [orekteeko] appetizer, titbit || drink.

ορεκτικός [orekteekos] appetizing, savoury || tempting.

όρεξη, n [oreksee] appetite || desire, liking.

ορθά [ortha] right, rightly || upright || ~ **κοφτά** flatly, frankly.

ορθάνοιχτος [orthaneehtos] wide open.

όρθιος [ortheeos] on end, upright, erect, standing.

ορθογραφία, n [orthografeea] spelling, orthography || dictation.

ορθογώνιο, το [orthogoneeo] rectangle.

ορθογώνιος [orthogoneeos] right-angled || rectangular.

ορθοδοξία, n [orthoðokseea] orthodoxy.

ορθόδοξος [orthoðoksos] orthodox.

ορθολογισμός, ο [ortholoyeesmos] rationalism.

ορθοπεδική, n [orthopeðekee] orthopaedics.

ορθοποδώ [orthopoðo] walk straight || stand on sure ground, thrive.

ορθός [orthos] light || correct || proper || upright, erect, standing.

ορθοστασία, n [orthostaseea] standing.

ορθότητα, n [orthoteeta] accuracy || soundness || aptness.

όρθρος, ο [orthros] (εκκλ) matins || dawn, daybreak.

ορθώνομαι [orthonome] rise, get up || (άλογο) rear up.

ορθώνω [orthono] raise, pull up, lift up || redress.

ορθώς [orthos] βλ **ορθά.**

οριζόντιος [oreezonteeos] horizontal, level.

ορίζω [oreezo] mark, bound, delimit || fix, settle, define || rule, control, govern.

ορίζων, ο [oreezon] horizon.

όριο, το [oreeo] boundary, limit, border || (μεταφ) scope, boundary.

ορισμένος [oreesmenos] defined, fixed || certain, special.

ορισμός, ο [oreesmos] designation, fixing || definition || order, instruction.

ορίστε [oreeste] I beg your pardon? || come in, take a seat || may I help you? || **καλώς ορίσατε** (επιφ) welcome!

οριστική, n [oreesteekee] (γραμμ) indicative (mood).

οριστικός [oreesteekos] definitive, final.

ορκίζομαι [orkeezome] swear, take the oath.

ορκίζω [orkeezo] put on oath, swear in.

όρκος, ο [orkos] oath || vow.

ορκωμοσία, n [orkomoseea] swearing (in).

ορκωτός [orkotos] sworn || **οι ορκωτοί** the jury.

ορμή, n [ormee] vehemence || impulse, impetus || passion.

ορμητήριο, το [ormeeteereeo] starting place || motive.

ορμητικός [ormeeteekos] impetuous, hot-tempered, fiery.

ορμόνη, n [ormonee] hormone.

όρμος, ο [ormos] bay, inlet.

ορμώ [ormo] dash, rush || ~ **μαι** be urged || come from.

όρνεο, το [orneo] bird of prey.

όρνιθα, n [orneetha] hen, chicken, fowl.

ορνιθοσκαλίσματα, τα [orneethoskaleesmata] πλ scrawl, scribble.

ορνιθοτροφείο, το [orneethotrofeeo] poultry farm.

ορνιθώνας, ο [orneethonas] chicken coop, henhouse, hen roost.

όρνιο, το [orneeo] bird of prey || (μεταφ) dullard, dolt.

οροθεσία, η [orotheseea] fixing of boundaries.

ορολογία, η [oroloyeea] terminology.

οροπέδιο, το [oropedeeo] plateau, tableland.

όρος, το [oros] mountain.

όρος, ο [oros] term, condition, stipulation, proviso || limit, end || (επιστημονικός) term, definition.

ορρός, ο [oros] serum.

οροσειρά, η [oroseera] mountain range, mountain chain.

ορόσημο, το [oroseemo] boundary mark, boundary stone.

οροφή, η [orofee] ceiling, roof.

όροφος, ο [orofos] floor, storey.

ορτύκι, το [orteekee] quail.

όρυζα, η [oreeza] rice.

ορυκτέλαιο, το [oreekteleo] petroleum || lubricant.

ορυκτολογία, η [oreektoloyeea] mineralogy.

ορυκτό, το [oreekto] mineral, ore.

ορυκτός [oreektos] mineral, dug-up.

ορύσσω [oreeso] dig, excavate || **(πηγάδι)** bore, sink.

ορυχείο, το [oreeheeo] mine.

ορφανός [orfanos] orphan.

ορφανοτροφείο, το [orfanotrofeeo] orphanage.

όρχης [orhees] testicle || (λουλούδι) orchid.

ορχήστρα, η [orheestra] orchestra.

όσιος [oseeos] holy, blessed || saint.

οσμή, η [osmee] odour, smell, scent.

όσο [oso] as, as far as, as long as || ~ **για** as for || ~ **αφορά** as regards, with regard to || **εφ** ~ as long as, inasmuch as || ~ **νάρθει** until he comes || ~ **νάναι** nevertheless.

όσος [osos] as much as, as many as, all.

όσπριο, το [ospreeo] pulse, legume.

οστούν, το [ostoun] bone.

οστρακιά, η [ostrakia] scarlet fever.

όστρακο, το [ostrako] shell || (αρχαιολογία) potsherd.

οσφραίνομαι [osfrenome] smell, scent || (μεταφ) feel.

όσφρηση, η [osfreesee] sense of smell.

οσφύς, η [osfees] waist, loins, haunches.

όταν [otan] when, at the time when, whenever.

ότι [otee] (συνδ) that || (επιρ) as soon as || just (now).

ό, τι [otee] what(ever).

οτιδήποτε [oteedeepote] whatsoever || anything at all.

ότου [otou]: **έως** ~ until || **μέχρις** ~ until || **αφ** ~ since.

Ουγγαρία, η [oungareea] Hungary.

ουγγιά, η [oungia] ounce.

ουγγρικός [oungreekos] Hungarian.

Ούγγρος, ο [oungros] Hungarian.

ουδέ [oude] βλ **ούτε**.

ουδείς [oudees] no(body), no one, none.

ουδέποτε [oudepote] never.

ουδέτερος [oudeteros] neither || (επίθ) neutral || (γραμμ) neuter.

ουδόλως [oudolos] by no means, no wise, by no manner of means.

ούζο, το [ouzo] ouzo.

ουλή [oulee] scar.

ούλο, το [oulo] (ανατ) gum.

ούρα, τα [oura] πλ urine, piss (col).

ουρά, η [oura] tail || train of dress || queue || (φάλαγγας) rear || **λεφτά με** ~ loads of money.

ουραγός, ο [ouragos] person bringing up the rear, the last one.

ουρανής [ouranees] sky-blue.

ουράνιο, το [ouraneeo] uranium.

ουράνιο [ouraneeo]: ~ **τόξο** rainbow.

ουράνιος [ouraneeos] heavenly, celestial.

ουρανίσκος, ο [ouraneeskos] palate.

ουρανοκατέβατος [ouranokatevatos] heaven-sent || (μεταφ) unexpected.

ουρανοξύστης, ο [ouranokseestees] skyscraper.

ουρανός, ο [ouranos] sky, heaven || canopy.

ουρητήριο, το [oureeteereeo] urinal, john (col).

ουρικός [oureekos] uric, urinary.

ούριος [oureeos] (άνεμος) tail, favourable, fair.

ουρλιάζω [ourleeazo] howl, roar || (από πόνο) yell, scream || (από θυμό) bellow.

ούρλιασμα, το [ourleeasma] howl(ing), bellowing, yelling.

ουρώ [ouro] urinate.

ους, το [ous] ear.

ουσία, η [ouseea] matter, substance || essence || (μεταφ) gist, main point.

ουσιαστικό, το [ouseeasteeko] (γραμμ) substantive, noun.

ουσιαστικός [ouseeasteekos] substantial, essential.

ουσιώδης [ouseeodees] essential, vital, indispensable, capital.

ούτε [oute] not even || ~ ... ~ neither ... nor.

ουτοπία, η [outopeea] Utopia.

ούτω(ς) [outo(s)] so, such, thus || ~ **ώστε** so that, in order that.

ουχί [ouhee] βλ **όχι**.

οφειλέτης, ο [ofeeletees] debtor.

οφειλή, η [ofeelee] debt, sum due || (μεταφ) obligation, duty.

οφείλομαι [ofeelome] be due.

οφείλω [ofeelo] owe || be obliged to || ~ **να πάω** I should go.

όφελος, το [ofelos] profit, advantage, benefit.

οφθαλμαπάτη, η [ofthalmapatee] optical illusion.

οφθαλμίατρος, ο, η [ofthalmeeatros] eye specialist, oculist.

οφθαλμός, ο [ofthalmos] eye || (βιολ) bud.

οφθαλμοφανής [ofthalmofanees] obvious, manifest, evident.

όφις, ο [ofees] snake, serpent.

όχεντρα, η [ohentra] βλ **οχιά.**

οχέτευση, η [ohetevsee] drainage.

οχετός, ο [ohetos] drain, sewer || conduit, pipe.

όχημα, το [oheema] vehicle, carriage, coach.

όχθη, η [ohthee] (ποταμού) bank || (λίμνης) shore.

όχι [ohee] no || not.

οχιά, η [ohia] viper.

οχλαγωγία, η [ohlagoyeea] disturbance, riot, tumult.

οχληρός [ohleeros] tiresome, unpleasant, burdensome.

οχλοβοή, η [ohlovoee] uproar, din, hubbub.

οχλοκρατία, η [ohlokrateea] mob rule.

όχλος, ο [ohlos] populace, mob, crowd, rabble.

οχυρό, το [oheero] strong point, fort, stronghold.

οχυρώνομαι [oheeronome] (μεταφ) find an excuse, justify.

οχυρώνω [oheerono] fortify, entrench.

όψη, η [opsee] aspect, appearance, look || view, sight || countenance || face || **λαμβάνω υπ** ~ take into account || **εξ όψεως** by sight || **εν όψει** in view of || in view.

οψιγενής [opseeyenees] posthumous || late, belated.

όψιμος [opseemos] tardy, late, of a late season.

Π, π

παγανισμός, ο [paganeesmos] paganism.

παγερός [payeros] icy cold, freezing || (μεταφ) chilly, frigid.

παγετός, ο [payetos] frost.

παγετώδης [payetoδees] icy, icy cold, freezing.

παγετώνας, ο [payetonas] glacier.

παγίδα, η [payeeδa] trap, snare || (τάφρος) pitfall.

παγίδευμα, το [payeeδevma] ensnaring, trapping.

παγιδεύω [payeeδevo] snare, catch, entice.

πάγιος [payos] fixed, stable, firm || (καθεστώς) secure, durable || (δάνειο) consolidated loan || (πρόσοδος) steady income.

παγιώνω [payono] consolidate, make secure.

παγίως [payeeos] firmly, securely.

πάγκος, ο [pangkos] bench, seat.

παγκόσμιος [pangkosmeeos] universal,world-wide.

πάγκρεας, το [pangkreas] pancreas.

παγόβουνο, το [pagovouno] iceberg.

παγόδα, η [pagoδa] pagoda.

παγοδρομία, η [pagoδromeea] skating.

παγοθραύστης, ο [pagothravstees] icebreaker.

παγοπέδιλο, το [pagopeδeelo] iceskate.

πάγος, ο [pagos] ice, frost.

παγούρι, το [pagouree] can, tin, flask || (στρατ) canteen.

παγωμένος [pagomenos] frozen, frostbitten.

παγώνι, το [pagonee] peacock.

παγωνιά, η [pagonia] frost.

παγώνω [pagono] freeze, congeal, frost.

παγωτό, το [pagoto] ice cream.

παζαρεύω [pazarevo] haggle over, bargain for.

παζάρι, το [pazaree] market, bazaar || bargaining, haggling.

παθαίνω [patheno] undergo, suffer, be injured.

πάθημα, το [patheema] mishap, accident.

πάθηση, η [patheesee] complaint, sickness, affliction.

παθητικός [patheeteekos] passive, submissive || (γραμμ) passive (voice) || charged with passion || (οικ) debit.

παθολογία, η [patholoyeea] pathology.

παθολογικός [patholoyeekos] pathological.

παθολόγος, ο [pathologos] general practitioner.

πάθος, το [pathos] illness, passion || suffering || (έχθρα) animosity.

παιδαγωγείο, το [peδagoyeeo] children's school.

παιδαγωγία, η [peδagoyeea] education, pedagogy.

παιδαγωγικός [peδagoyeekos] educational, pedagogical.

παιδαγωγός, ο, η [peδagogos] tutor, preceptor, pedagogue.

παιδαγωγώ [peδagogo] educate, instruct, teach.

παιδάκι, το [peδakee] little child.

παιδαριώδης [peδareeoδees] puerile, childish || (εύκολο) quite simple, trivial.

παιδεία, η [peδeea] education, learning, instruction, culture.

παίδεμα, το [peδema] torture, trial, ordeal.

παιδεύομαι [peδevome] try hard, struggle.

παιδεύω [peðevo] pester, torture, torment.

παιδί, το [peðee] child, boy || chap.

παιδιαρίζω [peðeeareezo] act like a child.

παιδίατρος, ο, η [peðeeatros] paediatrician, child specialist.

παιδικός [peðeekos] child's, of children || childish || ~ **σταθμός** day nursery.

παίζω [pezo] play || (παιχνίδι) speculate, gamble || (μεταφ) swing, sway.

παίκτης, ο [pektees] player || gambler, gamester.

παινεύω [penevo] βλ **επαινώ**.

παίξιμο, το [pekseemo] playing || (με κάτι) toying with || (θεάτρου) performance || (παιχνίδι) gaming, gambling.

παίρνω [perno] receive, take hold of, get, contain || (πόλη κτλ) capture || (διά της βίας) wrench from || (υπηρέτη) hire, take on || (καφέ κτλ) take, have || (κρύο κτλ) catch, get || (σαν παράδειγμα) take, draw || (σημείωση) take (a note) || (κάτι για κάτι) take for, consider (as) || (με κάποια έννοια) understand, interpret || (χρήματα) be paid, draw, receive || (για γυναίκα) marry, wed || **τον** ~ **fall asleep** || ~ **από πίσω** follow closely.

παιχνίδι, το [pehneeðee] play, game, sport || (για παιδιά) toy, plaything.

παιχνιδιάρης [pehneeðeearees] playful, gay, mirthful.

πακετάρω [paketaro] pack, box.

πακέτο, το [paketo] pack, packet, parcel, box, bundle.

παλαβομάρα, η [palavomara] madness, lunacy, foolish act.

παλαβός [palavos] mad, insane, stupid || (παράτολμος) foolhardy.

παλαίμαχος [palemahos] veteran.

παλαιογραφία, η [paleografeea] pal(a)eography.

παλαιοπωλείο, το [paleopoleeo] secondhand shop, antique shop.

παλαιοπώλης, ο [paleopolees] secondhand dealer.

παλαιός [paleos] old || (μνημείο κτλ) ancient, old || (άλλοτε) former.

παλαιστής, ο [palestees] wrestler.

παλαίστρα, η [palestra] arena, ring.

παλαιώνω [paleono] wear out, become antiquated.

παλαμάκια, τα [palamakeea] πλ clapping, applause.

παλαμάρι, το [palamaree] (ναυτ) cable, mooring line.

παλάμη, η [palamee] palm || (μέτρο) span.

παλάτι, το [palatee] palace || mansion.

παλεύω [palevo] wrestle, struggle, fight.

πάλη, η [palee] wrestling || (μεταφ) struggle, strife, contest.

παλιανθρωπιά, η [palianthropia] villainy, meanness, roguery.

παλιάνθρωπος, ο [palianthropos] rogue, rascal, scamp.

παλιάτσος, ο [paliatsos] clown, buffoon.

πάλι [palee] again, once more, over again.

παλινδρομικός [paleenðromeekos] alternating, reciprocating, recoiling.

παλινόρθωση, η [paleenorthosee] restoration, re-establishment.

παλιόπαιδο, το [paliopeðo] bad boy, young scamp.

παλίρροια, η [paleereea] tide, floodtide.

παλληκαράς, ο [paleekaras] bully.

παλληκάρι, το [paleekaree] young man, brave person || (εργένης) bachelor.

παλληκαρίσια [paleekareeseea] boldly, bravely.

πάλλω [palo] throb, beat, palpitate || (ηλεκτ) vibrate.

παλμός, ο [palmos] oscillation, vibration || palpitation, throbbing || (ενθουσιασμού) feeling, eagerness.

παλούκι, το [paloukee] stake, pole || (μεταφ) difficulty.

παλτό, το [palto] overcoat.

παμπάλαιος [pampaleos] ancient || out-of-date.

πάμπλουτος [pamploutos] extremely wealthy.

παμπόνηρος [pamponeeros] very cunning, very sly.

πάμπτωχος [pamptohos] very poor, very needy.

πάμφθηνος [pamftheenos] very cheap, extremely cheap.

παμψηφεί [pampseefee] unanimously.

παν, το [pan] the whole world || (το κεφαλαιώδες) essentials, everything.

πανάγαθος [panagathos] merciful || extremely virtuous.

Παναγία, η [panayeea] the Virgin Mary.

πανάδα, η [panaða] brown patch, freckle.

πανάθλιος [panathleeos] wretched, miserable.

πανάκεια, η [panakeea] panacea.

πανάρχαιος [panarheos] very ancient.

πανδαιμόνιο, το [panðemoneeo] pandemonium.

πάνδεινος [panðeenos] disastrous, most terrible.

πανδοχείο, το [panðoheeo] inn.

πανδρειά, η [panðria] marriage, matrimony.

πανδρεύω [panðrevo] marry.

πανελλήνιος [paneleeneeos] panhellenic.

πανεπιστημιακός

Π

[panepeesteemeeakos] of the university.

πανεπιστήμιο, το [panepeesteemeeo] university.

πανέρι, το [paneree] wide basket.

πανευτυχής [panefteehees] very happy.

πανηγυρίζω [paneeyeereezo] celebrate, fête.

πανηγυρικός [paneeyeereekos] festive || (ουο) oration, panegyric.

πανηγύρι, το [paneeyeeree] festival, festivity || (εμπορικό) fair.

πανηγυρισμός, ο [paneeyeereesmos] celebration.

πάνθηρας, ο [pantheeras] panther.

πανί, το [panee] cloth, linen || (ναυτ) sail.

πανίδα, η [paneeδa] fauna.

πανικόβλητος [paneekovleetos] panic-stricken.

πανικός, ο [paneekos] panic.

πανίσχυρος [paneesheeros] all-powerful.

πάνινος [paneenos] of cloth, of linen, of cotton.

πανόμοιος [panomeeos] similar, alike.

πανομοιότυπο, το [panomeeoteepo] facsimile.

πανοπλία, η [panopleea] arms, armour.

πανόραμα, το [panorama] panorama.

πανούκλα, η [panoukla] plague, pestilence.

πανουργία, η [panouryeea] ruse, trick, cunning.

πανούργος [panourgos] malicious, tricky, wily, cunning.

πανσέληνος, η [panseleenos] full moon.

πανσές, ο [panses] pansy.

πάντα [panta] forever, always || anyway, in any case.

πανταλόνι, το [pantalonee] trousers || pants, knickers.

πανταχού [pantahoo] everywhere.

παντελής [pantelees] complete, absolute, entire.

παντελώς [pantelos] utterly, absolutely, totally.

παντζάρι, το [pandzaree] beetroot.

παντιέρα, η [pantiera] banner, flag.

παντοδύναμος [pantoδeenamos] omnipotent, all-powerful.

παντοειδώς [pantoeeδos] in every way.

παντοιοτρόπως [panteeotropos] in every way, by every means.

Παντοκράτορας, ο [pantokratoras] the Almighty.

παντομίμα, η [pantomeema] pantomime.

παντοπωλείο, το [pantopoleeo] grocer's shop || grocery (US).

παντοπώλης, ο [pantopolees] grocer.

πάντοτε [pantote] always, at all times, forever.

παντοτεινά [pantoteena] perpetually, everlastingly.

παντού [pantou] everywhere.

παντούφλα, η [pantoufla] slipper.

παντρειά, η [pantria] βλ **πανδρειά.**

παντρεύω [pantrevo] βλ **πανδρεύω.**

πάντως [pantos] anyhow, in any case, at any rate.

πανωλεθρία, η [panolethreea] heavy loss, total ruin.

πανώλη, η [panolee] plague, pestilence.

πανωφόρι, το [panoforee] overcoat.

παξιμάδι, το [pakseemaδee] rusk || (για βίδα) nut (of screw).

παπαδιά, η [papaδia] priest's wife.

παπάκι, το [papakee] duckling.

παπαρούνα, η [paparouna] poppy.

Πάπας, ο [papas] Pope.

παπάς, ο [papas] priest.

παπί, το [papee] young duck || **γίνομαι ~** get wet to the skin.

πάπια, η [papeea] duck || bedpan || **κάνω την ~** to act the innocent.

πάπλωμα, το [paploma] cotton quilt.

παπουτσάδικο, το [papoutsaδeeko] shoemaker's shop.

παπουτσής, ο [papoutsees] shoemaker, bootmaker.

παπούτσι, το [papoutsee] shoe.

παππούς, το [papoos] grandfather.

παρά [para] than || but || (προθ) near, close, by || (προσθήκη) in spite of, against my will || (αντίθεση) against, contrary to || (αφαίρεση) by, almost, nearly.

παραβαίνω [paraveno] break, violate, infringe.

παραβάλλω [paravalo] compare.

παραβάν, το [paravan] (folding) screen.

παραβαρύνω [paravareeno] overload, overburden || become very heavy.

παράβαση, η [paravasee] violation, transgression, breach.

παραβάτης, ο [paravatees] violator, transgressor.

παραβιάζω [paraveeazo] (πόρτα κτλ) force entry, break open || (νόμο) violate, infringe.

παραβλέπω [paravlepo] neglect, omit || turn a blind eye (to), ignore.

παραβολή, η [paravolee] comparison, collation || (εκκλ) parable || (μαθημ) parabola.

παράβολο, το [paravolo] fee, deposit.

παραγάδι, το [paragaδee] large fishing net.

παραγγελία, η [parangeleea]

command, commission, order ||
(μήνυμα) message || επί ~ made to
order.

παραγγέλω [parangelo] order,
command || inform.

παραγεμίζω [parayemeezo] fill up ||
become too full || (μαγειρική) stuff ||
cram.

παραγίνομαι [parayeenome] grow
too much || go too far || get overripe || ~
χοντρός grow too fat.

παράγκα, η [paranga] wooden hut,
shack.

παραγκωνίζω [parangoneezo] elbow,
thrust aside.

παραγνωρίζω [paragnoreezo] ignore
|| misinterpret || mistake identity of.

παράγομαι [paragome] be derived
from.

παράγοντας, ο [paragontas] βλ
παράγων.

παράγραφος, ο [paragrafos]
paragraph.

παράγω [parago] produce, bear ||
derive.

παραγωγή, η [paragoyee] production
|| output, generation || (γραμμ)
derivation.

παραγωγικός [paragoyeekos]
productive.

παραγωγός, ο [paragogos] producer,
grower.

παράγων, ο [paragon] agent, factor ||
(μαθημ) factor.

παράδειγμα, το [paraδeegma]
example || **παραδείγματος χάρη**
for example, for instance.

παραδειγματίζω [paraδeegmateezo]
set an example, exemplify.

παράδεισος, ο [paraδeesos] paradise.

παραδεκτός [paraδektos] admitted,
accepted || acceptable, admissible.

παραδέχομαι [paraδehome] admit,
acknowledge, confess, allow.

παραδίδομαι [paraδeeδome]
surrender, submit, yield.

παραδίδω [paraδeeδo] hand over ||
surrender || (μάθημα) teach, give
lessons.

παράδοξος [paraδoksos] peculiar,
odd, singular || unusual.

παραδόπιστος [paraδopeestos]
greedy, extremely fond of money.

παράδοση, η [paraδosee] delivery,
surrender || (της χώρας) tradition ||
(μαθήματος) teaching.

παραδουλεύτρα, η [paraδoulevtra]
charwoman.

παραδρομή, η [paraδromee]
carelessness, oversight.

παραείμαι [paraeeme] be beyond
measure, be too much.

παραζάλη, η [parazalee] confusion,
agitation, turmoil.

παραθαλάσσιος [parathalaseeos] by
the sea, coastal.

παραθερίζω [parathereezo] spend the
summer.

παραθεριστής, ο [parathereestees]
summer holidaymaker.

παραθέτω [paratheto] contrast,
compare || (αναφέρω) cite, quote.

παράθυρο, το [paratheero] window.

παραθυρόφυλλο, το
[paratheerofeelo] shutter.

παραίσθηση, η [parestheesee]
hallucination, illusion.

παραίτηση, η [pareteesee]
resignation, renunciation || abdication.

παραιτούμαι [paretoume] resign, give
up || (αποφεύγω) avoid.

παραιτώ [pareto] give up, leave,
desert.

παράκαιρος [parakeros]
unseasonable, inopportune, untimely.

παρακάλια, τα [parakaleea] πλ
supplications, pleading.

παρακαλώ [parakalo] ask, beg,
entreat || ~! don't mention it!, please!, a
pleasure!

παρακάμπτω [parakampto] get
round, surpass || (ένα θέμα) evade.

παρακάνω [parakano] exaggerate, go
too far.

παρακαταθήκη, η
[parakatatheekee] consignment,
deposit || stock || provisions ||
(παράδοση) heritage.

παρακάτω [parakato] lower down || at
a lower price.

παρακείμενος [parakeemenos]
adjoining, adjacent || ο ~ (γραμμ)
perfect tense.

παρακινώ [parakeeno] exhort, urge ||
instigate.

παρακλάδι, το [paraklaδee] shoot,
bough || (ποταμού) branch.

παράκληση, η [parakleesee] request,
plea || (εκκλ) prayer.

παρακμή, η [parakmee] decay,
decline.

παρακοή, η [parakoee] disobedience,
insubordination.

παρακολουθώ [parakoloutho] follow,
come behind || watch || go after || (την
έννοια) understand.

παρακούω [parakouo] hear wrongly ||
(απειθαρχώ) disobey.

παρακρατώ [parakrato] retain || keep
back || (για χρόνο) last too long.

παράκτιος [parakteeos] coastal,
inshore.

παραλαβή, η [paralavee] receipt,
receiving, delivery.

παραλαμβάνω [paralamvano]
receive, take delivery of || take
possession of.

παραλείπω [paraleepo] leave out,
miss, neglect, omit.

παράλειψη, η [paraleepsee] omission, neglect(ing).

παραλέω [paraleo] exaggerate, overcolour.

παραλήπτης, ο [paraleeptees] payee, addressee, consignee.

παραλήρημα, το [paraleereema] delirium, frenzy.

παραλία, η [paraleea] seashore, shore, coast, beach || **παραλιακός** of the seashore, of the coast.

παραλλαγή, η [paralayee] change, variation || (αστρον) deviation.

παράλληλος [paraleelos] parallel.

παραλογίζομαι [paraloyeezome] talk irrationally, rave.

παράλογος [paralogos] illogical, absurd, foolish.

παράλυση, η [paraleesee] paralysis || helplessness.

παράλυτος [paraleetos] paralytic, stiff, crippled || (ιατρ) paralyzed.

παραλύω [paraleeo] make loose, make shaky || slacken, relax || (ιατρ) paralyze.

παραμάνα, η [paramana] nurse, nanny || (καρφίτσα) safety pin.

παραμελώ [paramelo] neglect, leave undone, disregard.

παραμένω [parameno] stay by || remain, continue to exist || sojourn.

παράμερα [paramera] out of the way, apart.

παραμερίζω [paramereezo] set aside || get out of the way || fend off.

παραμιλώ [parameelo] speak too much || rave.

παραμονεύω [paramonevo] watch for, waylay.

παραμονή, η [paramonee] stay || eve.

παραμορφώνω [paramorfono] deform, disfigure, twist.

παραμύθι, το [parameethee] fable, story, fairy tale.

παρανόηση, η [paranoeesee] misunderstanding.

παρανομία, η [paranomeea] illegality || breach of the law.

παράνομος [paranomos] illegal, unlawful.

παρανομώ [paranomo] transgress a law.

παρανοώ [paranoo] misunderstand.

παράνυμφος, η [paraneemfos] bridesmaid.

παρανυχίδα, η [paraneeheeða] hangnail.

παράξενα [paraksena] oddly, strangely.

παραξενεύομαι [paraksenevome] be astonished, be amazed (at).

παραξενιά, η [paraksenia] caprice, fancy, whim.

παράξενος [paraksenos] peculiar, singular, odd.

παραξηλώνω [parakseelono] unsew, unstitch || **το** ~ I go too far, I exaggerate.

παραπανήσιος [parapaneeseeos] superfluous, to spare || (τιμή) excess, overly much.

παραπάνω [parapano] higher up || (επιπρόσθετα) in addition || **με το** ~ enough and to spare || ~ **από** over, more than, greater than.

παραπάτημα, το [parapateema] false step || (μεταφ) misconduct.

παραπατώ [parapato] slip, stumble || stagger.

παραπέμπω [parapembo] refer to || send, hand over.

παραπέρα [parapera] further on, over there.

παραπεταμένος [parapetamenos] thrown away || (μεταφ) disdained, scorned.

παραπέτασμα, το [parapetasma] curtain || (πολιτ) Iron Curtain.

παραπέτο, το [parapeto] parapet, breastwork.

παράπηγμα, το [parapeegma] wooden hut, shack, shanty.

παραπλανώ [paraplano] seduce, mislead, lead astray.

παραπλεύρως [paraplevros] next door || next to, beside.

παραπλήσιος [parapleeseeos] next to, nearby || (όμοιος) very like, similar.

παραποιώ [parapeeo] counterfeit || forge, tamper with.

παραπομπή, η [parapombee] referring || (σε βιβλίο) reference, footnote.

παραπονετικός [paraponeteekos] doleful, whining.

παραπονιάρης [paraponeearees] grumbling, grousing.

παραπονιέμαι [paraponieme] complain, grumble.

παράπονο, το [parapono] complaint, grievance.

παράπτωμα, το [paraptoma] fault, mistake || breach.

παράρτημα, το [pararteema] annexe, supplement || outbuilding || (τράπεζας) branch || (εφημερίδας) special edition, extra.

παράς, ο [paras] money, cash.

παράσημο, το [paraseemo] decoration, medal, order, insignia.

παρασημοφορώ [paraseemoforo] decorate, invest with an order.

παράσιτα, τα [paraseeta] πλ atmospherics || parasites.

παράσιτος, ο [paraseetos] sponger, hanger-on, parasite.

παρασιωπώ [paraseeopo] pass over in silence.

παρασκευάζω [paraskevazo] prepare, get ready, arrange.

παρασκεύασμα, το [paraskevasma] substance prepared, preparation.

παρασκευή, η [paraskevee] preparation || (ημέρα) Friday.

παρασκήνια, τα [paraskeeneea] πλ (θέατρο)wings || **παρασκηνιακός** behind the scenes.

παράσταση, η [parastasee] representation, portrayal || (παρουσία) presence, demeanour || (θεάτρου) show, performance || (νομ) appearance.

παραστατικός [parastateekos] expressive, descriptive, vivid.

παραστέκω [parasteko] assist, help, support.

παράστημα, το [parasteema] carriage, bearing, figure.

παραστράτημα, το [parastrateema] straying, misconduct.

παρασύνθημα, το [paraseentheema] password.

παρασύρω [paraseero] drag along, sweep away || run over || (σε σφάλμα) lead astray, carry away.

παράταξη, η [parataksee] array, parade, order || pomp, ceremony || (πολιτ) political party.

παράταση, η [paratasee] extension, protraction || renewal.

παρατάσσω [parataso] arrange, set in order, line up.

παρατατικός, ο [paratateekos] (γραμμ) imperfect tense.

παρατείνω [parateeno] prolong, lengthen || extend, defer.

παρατήρηση, η [parateereesee] observation, remark || (κουβέντα) comment || reproach, reprimand.

παρατηρητής, ο [parateereetees] observer, watcher, spotter.

παρατηρητικός [parateereeteekos] observing, keen || reproachful.

παρατηρώ [parateero] observe, perceive, notice || (επιτιμώ) reproach, blame.

παράτολμος [paratolmos] reckless, audacious, bold.

παρατραβώ [paratravo] draw out, prolong || last too long || (μεταφ) go too far.

παρατράγουδο, το [paratragoudo] untoward incident.

παρατσούκλι, το [paratsouklee] nickname.

παρατυπία, η [parateepeea] breach of formalities || irregularity.

πάραυτα [paravta] immediately, at once, forthwith.

παραφέρνω [paraferno] carry more than necessary || resemble.

παραφέρομαι [paraferome] flare up, lose one's temper.

παραφθορά, η [parafthora] alteration, corruption, change.

παραφορά, η [parafora] frenzy, outburst || rage.

παράφορος [paraforos] hotheaded, hasty, furious.

παραφορτώνω [parafortono] overload, overburden || (μεταφ) drive too hard.

παράφραση, η [parafrasee] paraphrase, free translation.

παραφρονώ [parafrono] become insane, go mad.

παραφροσύνη, η [parafroseenee] madness, insanity, foolish act.

παραφυάδα, η [parafiaδa] sprout, shoot.

παραφυλάω [parafeelao] lie in wait for || be on the watch for.

παραφωνία, η [parafoneea] dissonance || (μεταφ) discord, disagreement.

παραχαράκτης, ο [paraharaktees] forger, counterfeiter.

παραχωρώ [parahoro] grant, yield, concede || (παραδίδω) surrender, resign.

παρδαλός [parδalos] spotted || multicoloured, gaudy.

παρέα, η [parea] company, set, party || **κάνω ~ με** keep company with.

παρειά, η [paria] cheek || (μεταφ) wall.

παρείσακτος [pareesaktos] intrusive, intruding.

παρέκβαση, η [parekvasee] digression.

παρέκει [parekee] further on, a little further.

παρεκκλήσι, το [parekleesee] chapel.

παρεκκλίνω [parekleeno] deviate from, turn aside from || diverge.

παρεκτείνω [parekteeno] prolong, extend.

παρεκτός [parektos] except, save, besides.

παρεκτροπή, η [parektropee] aberration, deviation || (ηθική) misconduct, dissoluteness.

παρέλαση, η [parelasee] parade, march-past, procession.

παρελαύνω [parelavno] march past, parade.

παρέλευση, η [parelevsee] passage of time, passing.

παρελθόν, το [parelthon] the past.

παρεμβαίνω [paremveno] interfere, intervene, meddle with.

παρεμβάλλω [paremvalo] insert, interpose.

παρέμβαση, η [paremvasee] intervention, mediation.

παρεμβολή, η [paremvolee] insertion.

παρεμπιπτόντως [parempeeptontos] by the way.

παρεμφερής [paremferees] similar, of the same nature, resembling.

παρενέργεια, η [parenerya] side effect.

παρένθεση, η [parenthesee] insertion || (γραμμ) parenthesis.

παρενοχλώ [parenohlo] inconvenience, trouble, harass.

παρεξήγηση, η [parekseeyeesee] misunderstanding.

παρεξηγώ [parekseego] misunderstand, misinterpret, misconstrue.

παρεπόμενα, τα [parepomena] πλ consequences, issues.

παρερμηνεία, η [parermeeneea] misinterpretation.

παρέρχομαι [parerhome] elapse, pass || (τελειώνω) come to an end || (πηδώ) pass over || omit.

παρευρίσκομαι [parevreeskome] be present at, attend.

παρεφθαρμένος [pareftharmenos] defective (linguistically).

παρέχω [pareho] procure || give, supply || (ευκαιρία) occasion, bring about.

παρηγοριά, η [pareegoreea] consolation, comfort, solace.

παρηγορώ [pareegoro] console, comfort.

παρθενία, η [partheneea] virginity, maidenhood || chastity.

παρθενικός [partheneekos] virginal || (μεταφ) pure || maiden.

παρθένος, η [parthenos] virgin, maiden.

Παρθενώνας, ο [parthenonas] Parthenon.

παρίσταμαι [pareestame] be present at, assist (at) || arise.

παριστάνω [pareestano] represent, portray, depict || (ρόλο) perform || pretend to be.

πάρκο, το [parko] park.

παρμπρίζ, το [parbreez] (αυτοκινήτου) windscreen.

παρντόν [parnton] pardon me!

παροδικός [paroðeekos] passing, fleeting, momentary.

πάροδος, η [paroðos] side street || (χρόνου κτλ) passing, course.

παροικία, η [pareekeea] colony, quarter.

παροιμία, η [pareemeea] proverb, adage, saying.

παροιμιώδης [pareemeeoðees] proverbial || famous, renowned.

παρομοιάζω [paromeeazo] compare, liken || resemble, be similar.

παρόμοιος [paromeeos] similar, alike.

παρόν, το [paron] the present.

παρονομαστής, ο [paronomastees] (μαθημ) denominator.

παροξυσμός, ο [parokseesmos] fit, attack || incitement.

παρόρμηση, η [parormeesee] prompting, instigation || stimulation, exhortation.

παροτρύνω [parotreeno] βλ **παρακινώ.**

παρουσία, η [parouseea] presence, attendance || **δευτέρα** ~ second coming, doomsday.

παρουσιάζομαι [parouseeazome] appear || introduce o.s.

παρουσιάζω [parouseeazo] present, show, introduce.

παρουσιαστικό, το [parouseeasteeko] presence, demeanour, bearing.

παροχή, η [parohee] furnishing || contribution, donation || granting.

παρρησία, η [pareeseea] frankness, candour.

πάρσιμο, το [parseemo] capture, taking || (ελάττωση) trimming, lessening.

παρτέρι, το [parteree] flower bed.

παρτίδα, η [parteeða] part, portion || (παιγνιδιού) game (of cards).

παρωδία, η [paroðeea] parody, farce, travesty.

παρών [paron] present, actual.

παρωνυμία, η [paroneemeea] nickname || surname.

παρωπίδα, η [paropeeða] blinker, blind.

παρωχημένος [paroheemenos] past, gone by.

πας [pas] any, all, every || (οι πάντες) everybody, everyone.

πασαλείβομαι [pasaleevome] be smeared || get a smattering of knowledge.

πασαλείβω [pasaleevo] smear, daub || smudge.

πασάς, ο [pasas] pasha.

πασίγνωστος [paseegnostos] well-known, notorious.

πασιέντζα, η [pasiendza] patience, solitaire (card game).

πασπαλίζω [paspaleezo] sprinkle, powder (with).

πασπατεύω [paspatevo] pry about, feel, finger.

πάσσαλος, ο [passalos] stake, post, pole.

πάσσο, το [passo] stride, step || **πάω** ~ (στα χαρτιά) pass (at cards).

πάστα, η [pasta] dough, paste || (γλυκό) pastry, cake || (χαρακτήρας) character, sort.

παστέλι, το [pastelee] concoction of honey and sesame.

παστίτσιο, το [pasteetseeo] baked macaroni.

παστός [pastos] salted.

παστουρμάς, ο [pastourmas] seasoned cured meat.

παστρεύω [pastrevo] clean, cleanse || (μεταφ) destroy, exterminate.

παστρικός [pastreekos] clean, neat || (μεταφ) dishonest, depraved.

Πάσχα, το [pasha] Easter.

πασχαλιά, η [pashalia] lilac.

πασχίζω [pasheezo] try hard to, strive, endeavour.

πάσχω [pasho] be ill, suffer || ο πάσχων the patient, the sufferer.

πάταγος, ο [patagos] din, noise, bang || (μεταφ) sensation, stir.

παταγώδης [patagoδees] uproarious, noisy, loud.

πατάρι, το [pataree] loft, attic.

πατάτα, η [patata] potato.

πατέρας, ο [pateras] father.

πατερίτσα, η [patereetsa] crook, crutch || bishop's staff.

πατικώνω [pateekono] press down, crush, compress.

πάτημα, το [pateema] step, footstep || (ίχνος) footprint || (σταφυλιών) treading, pressing || excuse.

πατημασιά, η [pateemasia] footprint, trace, track.

πατινάρω [pateenaro] skate.

πάτος, ο [patos] bottom.

πατούσα, η [patousa] (ανατ) sole.

πατριάρχης, ο [patreearhees] patriarch.

πατριαρχείο, το [patreearheeo] patriarchate.

πατρίδα, η [patreeδa] native country, birthplace.

πατρικός [patreekos] paternal || fatherly.

πάτριος [patreeos] paternal, ancestral || native.

πατριώτης, ο [patreeotees] compatriot || patriot.

πατριωτικός [patreeoteekos] patriotic.

πατριωτισμός, ο [patreeoteesmos] patriotism.

πατρόν, το [patron] pattern (in dressmaking).

πατροπαράδοτος [patroparaδotos] usual, customary, traditional || hereditary.

πατρυιός, ο [patreeos] stepfather.

πατσαβούρα, η [patsavoura] dish cloth, rag || (μεταφ) rag (newspaper).

πατσάς, ο [patsas] (soup of) tripe.

πάτσι [patsee] even, quits.

πατώ [pato] step on || (κουδούνι κτλ) press || press down || (μεταφ) violate || run over || ~ πόδι I put my foot down.

πάτωμα, το [patoma] floor, ground || storey.

πατώνω [patono] lay a floor || touch bottom, reach bottom.

παύλα, η [pavla] dash (punctuation).

παύση, η [pavsee] stoppage, cessation, discharge || (μουσ) rest, pause.

παύω [pavo] cease, stop || cause to cease || (απολύω) dismiss || (σταματώ) stop, finish, give up.

παφλασμός, ο [paflasmos] splashing, gushing || bubbling up.

παχαίνω [paheno] βλ παχύνω.

παχιά [pahia] πλ: ~ λόγια empty words, empty promises.

πάχνη, η [pahnee] hoarfrost, rime.

παχνί, το [pahnee] manger, crib.

πάχος, το [pahos] plumpness || thickness || (λίπος) fat, grease || (στρώματος) depth.

παχουλός [pahoulos] plump, chubby.

παχύδερμος [paheeδermos] (μεταφ) insensitive.

παχύνω [paheeno] fatten || grow fat.

παχύς [pahees] trick || fleshy, fat || (σε λίπος) rich in fat || (λειβάδι) rich.

παχύσαρκος [paheesarkos] fat, stout, obese.

πάω [pao] go || take || carry || τα ~ καλά I get along well with || ~ περίπατο it's a washout || I go for a walk || ~ να σκάσω I'm ready to burst.

πεδιάδα, η [peδeeaδa] plain, flat country.

πέδιλο, το [peδeelo] sandal.

πεδινός [peδeenos] flat, level || (έδαφος) even, smooth.

πεδίο, το [peδeeo] plain, flat country, ground || (μάχης) field of battle || (οπτικό) field.

πεζεύω [pezevo] dismount.

πεζή [pezee] on foot.

πεζικό, το [pezeeko] infantry.

πεζογραφία, η [pezografeea] prose.

πεζογράφος, ο, η [pezografos] prose writer, novelist.

πεζοδρόμιο, το [pezoδromeeo] pavement || sidewalk (US).

πεζοναύτης, ο [pezonavtees] marine.

πεζοπορία, η [pezoporeea] walking, walk || (στρατ) march.

πεζός [pezos] pedestrian || (της πρόζας) in prose || (μεταφ) banal, trivial, common.

πεζούλι, το [pezoulee] parapet || bench || (σε λόφω) terrace.

πεθαίνω [petheno] die || (μεταφ) perish || be fond of, be mad about.

πεθερά, η [pethera] mother-in-law.

πεθερικά, τα [pethereeka] πλ in-laws.

πεθερός, ο [petheros] father-in-law.

πειθαρχία, η [peetharheea] discipline.

πειθαρχικός [peetharheekos] disciplinary || (υπάκουος) obedient, docile, submissive.

πειθαρχώ [peetharho] be obedient, obey one's superiors.

πειθήνιος [peetheeneeos] docile, obedient, submissive.

πείθω [peetho] convince, persuade.

πειθώ, η [peetho] persuasion, conviction.

πείνα, η [peena] hunger, famine, starvation || **πειναλέος** starving, famished, ravenous || **πεινασμένος** hungry, famished.

πεινώ [peeno] be hungry, be starving.

πείρα, η [peera] experience, background.

πείραγμα, το [peeragma] teasing || annoyance || (ασθένεια) malady.

πειραγμένος [peeragmenos] hurt, offended || (κρέας) tainted, spoilt.

πειράζει [peerazee]: ~; is it all right?, is it important?

πειράζω [peerazo] trouble, anger, annoy || tease || (την υγεία) upset, be bad for || (ενοχλώ) disturb.

πειρακτικός [peerakteekos] irritating, offensive, cutting.

πείραμα, το [peerama] experiment || trial, test || **πειραματικός** experimental.

πειρασμός, ο [peerasmos] temptation.

πειρατής, ο [peeratees] pirate, corsair || pirate taxi.

πείσμα, το [peesma] obstinacy, stubbornness || **πεισματάρης** obstinate, stubborn || **πεισματώδης** headstrong, stubborn ||
πεισματώνομαι be unyielding || **πεισματώνω** make obstinate, irritate || become obdurate.

πειστήριο, το [peesteereeo] proof.

πειστικός [peesteekos] convincing, persuasive.

πέλαγος, το [pelagos] open sea.

πελαγώνω [pelagono] (μεταφ) lose one's way, be at a loss, feel at sea.

πελαργός [pelargos] stork.

πελατεία, η [pelateea] clientèle, customers, patronage.

πελάτης, ο [pelatees] customer, patron, client || (ξενοδοχείου) guest.

πελεκάνος, ο [pelekanos] pelican.

πελεκούδι, το [pelekoudee] chip, paring, shaving.

πελεκώ [peleko] axe, hew, cut into shape, carve || (μεταφ) thrash.

πέλμα, το [pelma] (ανατ) sole || (τεχνική) shoe, flange.

Πελοπόννησος, η [peloponeesos] the Peloponnese.

πελτές, ο [peltes] tomato purée || (φρούτων) jelly.

πελώριος [peloreeos] enormous, mammoth || (σφάλμα) gross.

Πέμπτη, η [pemptee] Thursday.

πέμπτος [pemptos] fifth.

πενήντα [peneenta] fifty.

πενηνταριά, η [peneeentaria]: καμιά ~ about fifty.

πενθήμερος [pentheemeros] of five days.

πένθυμος [pentheemos] sorrowful, mournful, dismal || in mourning.

πένθος, το [penthos] bereavement || mourning.

πενθώ [pentho] lament, mourn || be in mourning.

πενία, η [peneea] poverty, want.

πενιχρός [peneehros] poor, mean || (γεύμα) poor, scant || paltry.

πέννα, η [pena] pen || (μουσ) plectrum || (νόμισμα) penny.

πένσα, η [pensa] tweezers, forceps || (ραπτικής) dart.

πεντάγραμμο, το [pentagramo] (μουσ) stave, staff.

πεντακόσιοι [pentakosiee] five hundred.

πεντάμορφος [pentamorfos] extremely beautiful.

πεντάρα, η [pentara] (μεταφ) farthing || nickel (US).

πεντάρι, το [pentaree] figure 5 || (στα χαρτιά) five (at cards).

πέντε [pente] five.

Πεντηκοστή, η [penteekostee] Whit Sunday.

πέος, το [peos] penis.

πεπειραμένος [pepeeramenos] experienced, versed in.

πεπεισμένος [pepeesmenos] convinced, certain, sure.

πέπλο, το [peplo] veil.

πεποίθηση, η [pepeetheesee] conviction, certainty, assurance.

πεπόνι, το [peponee] melon.

πεπτικός [pepteekos] digestive, peptic.

πέρα [pera] beyond, over, on the other side, over there || **εκεί** ~ yonder || ~ **για** ~ through and through || **εδώ** ~ here || ~ **από** beyond, across || **τα βγάζω** ~ manage, make out.

περαιτέρω [peretero] further || moreover.

πέραμα, το [perama] passage, ford || ferry.

πέρας, το [peras] end, extremity || completion, close.

πέρασμα, το [perasma] crossing, passage || (βελόνας) threading || (ασθενείας) passing || (τόπος) much-visited spot.

περασμένος [perasmenos] past, gone, last, by.

περαστικά [perasteeka]: ~! get well soon!

περαστικός [perasteekos] passing by || transient, transitory || (δρόμος) frequented, busy.

περατώνω [peratono] finish, bring to an end, complete.

περβάζι, το [pervazee] doorframe, frame, cornice.

περγαμηνή, η [pergameenee] parchment.

πέρδικα, η [perðeeka] partridge.

πέρδομαι [perðome] fart (col), break wind.

περηφάνεια, η [pereefaneea] βλ **υπερηφάνεια.**

περηφανεύομαι [pereefanevome] βλ **υπερηφανεύομαι.**

περήφανος [pereefanos] βλ **υπερήφανος.**

περί [peree] about, concerning, regarding, of || (με αιτ) round, near || round about, approximately || ~ **τίνος πρόκειται;** what's it all about?

περιαυτολογία, η [pereeavtoloyeea] boasting, bragging.

περιαυτολογώ [pereeavtologo] boast.

περιβάλλον, το [pereevalon] environment, surroundings.

περιβάλλω [pereevalo] encircle, surround || (ρούχα) clothe, dress.

περίβλημα, το [pereevleema] wrapper || (καρπού) shell, husk || casing.

περιβόητος [pereevoeetos] famous, renowned, infamous.

περιβολάρης, ο [pereevolarees] gardener.

περιβολή, η [pereevolee] garment, dress || surrounding.

περιβόλι, το [pereevolee] garden, orchard.

περίβολος, ο [pereevolos] enclosure, yard || (τοίχος) surrounding wall || park.

περιβρέχω [pereevreho] bathe, wash.

περίγελος, ο [pereeyelos] laughing stock.

περιγελώ [pereeyelo] mock, ridicule, derive || dupe, trick.

περιγιάλι, το [pereeyalee] seashore, coast.

περιγραφή, η [pereegrafee] description, account.

περιγράφω [pereegrafo] describe, portray.

περίδοξος [pereeðoksos] illustrious, famous.

περιεκτικός [periekteekos] capacious || (τροφή) substantial || (λόγος) comprehensive, concise, succinct.

περιεργάζομαι [periergazome] examine carefully.

περιέργεια, η [perierya] curiosity.

περίεργος [periergos] curious, strange, inquiring.

περιεχόμενο, το [periehomeno] contents || (σημασία) meaning.

περιέχω [perieho] contain, hold.

περιζήτητος [pereezeeteetos] in great demand, greatly prized.

περιηγητής, ο [perieeyeetees] tourist, traveller.

περιθάλπω [pereethalpo] attend, look after, treat.

περίθαλψη, η [pereethalpsee] attendance, care, relief.

περιθώριο, το [pereethoreeo] margin, room.

περικάλυμμα, το [pereekaleema] wrapper, covering, shell.

περικεφαλαία, η [pereekefalea] helmet.

περικλείω [pereekleeo] enclose, include.

περικοκλάδα, η [pereekoklaða] climbing plant || convolvulus.

περικοπή, η [pereekopee] cutting off, deduction || (από βιβλίο) extract, passage.

περικυκλώνω [pereekeeklono] surround.

περιλαίμιο, το [pereelemeeo] animal's collar || necklace.

περιλάλητος [pereelaleetos] celebrated, famous, renowned.

περιλαμβάνω [pereelamvano] contain, have, hold || (περιέχω) include, comprise.

περιληπτικός [pereeleepteekos] comprehensive || concise, succinct.

περίληψη, η [pereeleepsee] summary, précis, résumé.

περίλυπος [pereeleepos] sad, sorrowful || (έκφραση) gloomy, doleful.

περιμαζεύω [pereemazevo] gather up || (από τον δρόμο) rescue, harbour || (περιορίζω) check, control.

περιμένω [pereemeno] wait || wait for, expect.

περίμετρος, η [pereemetros] circumference, perimeter.

πέριξ [pereeks] about, round || **τα ~** the environs, suburb.

περιοδεία, η [pereeoðeea] tour, travelling, trip.

περιοδικό, το [pereeoðeeko] magazine, periodical.

περιοδικός [pereeoðeekos] periodic(al).

περίοδος, η [pereeoðos] period, era, age || season || (γυναικών) (menstrual) period.

περίοπτος [pereeoptos] overlooking, rising, conspicuous || noticeable.

περιορίζω [pereeoreezo] limit, restrict || (ελέγχω) control || (ελαττώνω) reduce, cut down, curtail.

περιορισμός, ο [pereeoreesmos] limitation || detention, restriction || (ελάττωση) reduction.

περιουσία, η [pereeouseea] property, estate || (πλούτη) fortune, wealth.

περιοχή, η [pereeohee] area, region, district || extent, expanse.

περιπαίζω [pereepezo] ridicule, mock || dupe, trick, take in.

περίπατο [pereepato]: **πάω ~** go for a stroll || (μεταφ) be a failure.

περίπατος, ο [pereepatos] walk, ride, drive, spin.

περιπέτεια, η [pereepeteea]

adventure || (μεταφ) misadventure, incident.

περιπετειώδης [pereepeteeoodees] full of adventures || (ιστορία) of adventure.

περιπλανώ [pereeplano] send long way round || ~ **μαι** wander, rove, lose one's way.

περιπλέκω [pereepleko] interlace, entangle || complicate, confuse, muddle.

περιπλέω [pereepleo] circumnavigate.

περιπλοκή, η [pereeplokee] complication, complexity, intricacy.

περίπλοκος [pereeplokos] complex, involved.

περιποίηση, η [pereepieesee] care, attendance, looking after.

περιποιητικός [pereepieeteekos] considerate, obliging.

περιποιούμαι [pereepeeoume] take care of || (ασθενή) nurse.

περίπολος, η [pereepolos] patrol.

περίπου [pereepou] about, nearly, almost.

περίπτερο, το [pereeptero] pavilion, kiosk.

περιπτώσει [pereeptosee]: **εν πάσει** ~ in any case, anyway.

περίπτωση, η [pereeptosee] case, condition, circumstance.

περίσκεψη, η [pereeskepsee] prudence, caution, discretion.

περισπασμός, ο [pereespasmos] diversion, distraction.

περίσσεια, η [pereeseea] excess, superabundance.

περίσσευμα, το [pereesevma] surplus, excess.

περισσεύω [pereesevo] be in excess, be left over.

περίσσιος [pereeseeos] (άφθονος) abundant || (περιττός) unnecessary.

περισσότερο [pereesotero] more.

περισσότερος [pereesoteros] more || **ο** ~ most.

περίσταση, η [pereestasee] circumstance, event, fact, occasion, situation.

περιστατικό, το [pereestateeko] incident, event.

περιστέλλω [pereestelo] repress, check, restrain, reduce.

περιστέρι, το [pereesteree] pigeon, dove.

περιστοιχίζω [pereesteeheezo] surround, encircle.

περιστολή, η [pereestolee] limitation, decrease, restriction, checking.

περιστρέφομαι [pereestrefome] revolve, spin, turn.

περιστρέφω [pereestrefo] (ρόδα κτλ) turn, rotate || (κλειδί) turn, twist.

περιστροφή, η [pereestrofee] revolution, turn, rotation.

περίστροφο, το [pereestrofo] revolver.

περισυλλέγω [pereeseelego] collect, gather.

περιτειχίζω [pereeteeheezo] build a wall round.

περιτομή, η [pereetomee] circumcision.

περίτρανος [pereetranos] obvious, clear, evident.

περιτριγυρίζω [pereetreeyeereezo] surround, encircle, border.

περίτρομος [pereetromos] terrified, frightened.

περιτροπή, η [pereetropee]: **εκ περιτροπής** by turns, in turn.

περιττός [pereetos] (προσπάθεια) useless, unavailing || superfluous, unnecessary, needless || ~ **αριθμός** odd number.

περιτύλιγμα, το [pereeteeleegma] wrapper, wrapping.

περιτυλίσσω [pereeteeleeso] wrap up || roll up.

περιφέρεια, η [pereefereea] (δένδρου) girth || (γεωμ) circumference || (χώρος) district, region.

περιφέρομαι [pereeferome] stroll, walk up and down, hang about || (η γη κτλ) turn round, rotate.

περιφέρω [pereefero] turn, revolve, rotate.

περίφημος [pereefeemos] famous, admirable, celebrated.

περίφραγμα, το [pereefragma] enclosure, hedge, fencing.

περίφραξη, η [pereefraksee] enclosing, fencing.

περιφραστικός [pereefrasteekos] periphrastic(al).

περιφρόνηση, η [pereefroneesee] contempt, scorn.

περιφρονητικός [pereefroneeteekos] disdainful, contemptuous, haughty.

περιφρονώ [pereefrono] hold in contempt, despise, spurn.

περιχαρής [pereeharees] cheerful, merry, joyful, gay.

περίχωρα, τα [pereehora] πλ neighbourhood, environs || (πόλη) suburb, outskirts.

περιωπή, η [pereeopee] eminence || (μεταφ) importance.

περνώ [perno] (ποτάμι, γέφυρα κτλ) pass, cross, go over || (κάτι σε κάποιο) pass, hand over || (κάτι μέσα σε κάτι) pass through || (τον καιρό) spend || (βελόνα) thread (a needle) || (υγρό από φίλτρο) filter, strain || (νόμο) get voted, pass || (στο δρόμο) pass, leave behind || ~ **για** mistake for || ~ **από** call at, go via.

περονιάζω [peroneeazo] pierce, go through.

περονόσπορος, ο [peronosporos] mildew.

περούκα, η [perouka] wig.

περπάτημα, το [perpateema] walking || gait.

περπατώ [perpato] walk || go across || (σκύλο κτλ) take for a walk.

Πέρσης, ο [persees] Iranian.

Περσία, η [perseea] Iran.

περσικός [perseekos] Iranian.

πέρ(υ)σι [per(ee)see] last year || **περ(υ)σινός** of last year.

πέσιμο, το [peseemo] falling, fall.

πεσμένος [pesmenos] fallen || impaired, worsened.

πέστροφα, η [pestrofa] trout.

πέταγμα, το [petagma] flying, flight || throwing away, casting.

πετάγομαι [petagome] fly up || rush || butt in.

πετάλι, το [petalee] pedal.

πεταλίδα, η [petaleeða] limpet.

πέταλο, το [petalo] petal || (αλόγου) horseshoe.

πεταλούδα, η [petalouða] butterfly || (λαιμοδέτου) bow, bow tie.

πεταλώνω [petalono] shoe (a horse).

πέταμα, το [petama] βλ **πέταγμα**.

πεταχτά [petahta]: **στα ~** hastily, hurriedly, quickly.

πεταχτός [petahtos] nimble || sticking out.

πετεινός, ο [peteenos] cock || (έπιπλου) hammer.

πετ(ι)μέζι, το [pet(ee)mezee] must turned into syrup || (επίθ, μεταφ) very sweet.

πέτο, το [peto] lapel.

πετονιά, η [petonia] fishing line.

πέτρα, η [petra] stone, rock || precious stone.

πετράδι, το [petraðee] pebble || precious stone.

πετρέλαιο, το [petreleo] petroleum, oil || (ακάθαρτο) crude oil.

πετρελαιοπηγή, η [petreleopeeyee] oil well.

πετρελαιοφόρο, το [petreleoforo] oil tanker.

πέτρινος [petreenos] made of stone.

πετροβολώ [petrovolo] pelt with stones.

πέτσα, η [petsa] skin || (γάλακτος) cream.

πετσέτα, η [petseta] table napkin || towel.

πετσί, το [petsee] skin, pelt, hide || leather, dressed skin.

πέτσινος [petseenos] leather.

πετσοκόβω [petsokovo] cut up, carve || cut badly, butcher.

πετυχαίνω [peteeheno] βλ **επιτυγχάνω**.

πετώ [peto] fly || (από χαρά) jump for joy || (στα σκουπίδια) throw away || **~ έξω** throw out || kick out (col).

πεύκο, το [pefko] pine.

πέφτει [peftee]: **δε σου ~ λόγος** you've got no say in the matter.

πέφτω [pefto] tumble, fall || drop, come down, subside || come off || occur || **~ στο κρεββάτι** I go to bed || **~ έξω** make a mistake || (ναυτ) run aground || **~ δίπλα** make up to || **~ με τα μούτρα** apply o.s., take up eagerly.

πέψη, η [pepsee] digestion.

πηγάδι, το [peegaðee] well.

πηγάζω [peegazo] spring from, originate, emanate.

πηγαινοέρχομαι [peeyenoerhome] go to and fro.

πηγαίνω [peeyeno] go || escort, take || βλ και **πάω**.

πηγή, η [peeyee] spring, source || (μεταφ) origin, cause.

πηγούνι, το [peegounee] chin.

πηδάλιο, το [peeðaleeo] rudder || helm || wheel.

πηδαλιούχος, ο [peeðaleeouhos] helmsman.

πήδημα, το [peeðeema] jump(ing), spring || sudden rise.

πηδώ [peeðo] leap, jump, vault || jump over || (παραλείπω) skip, leave out.

πήζω [peezo] coagulate, thicken, curdle.

πηκτός [peektos] coagulated, thick, curdled.

πηλάλα, η [peelala] quick running || (επίρ) at full speed.

πηλίκο, το [peeleeko] quotient.

πήλινος [peeleenos] earthen, of clay.

πηλός, η [peelos] clay || mud, slime, sludge.

πηνίο, το [peeneeo] bobbin, spool || (ηλεκ) coil.

πήξη, η [peeksee] coagulation, congealing || sticking in.

πηρούνι, το [peerounee] fork.

πήχη, η [peehee] measure of length (0.46 m).

πηχτός [peehtos] coagulated, jellied || thick.

πήχυς, ο [peehees] cubit || ell.

πι, το [pee] the letter Π || **στο ~ και φι** in two shakes of a lamb's tail.

πια [pia] not any longer || now, finally, at last, at long last.

πιάνο, το [peeano] piano.

πιάνομαι [peeanome] be caught at, be paralyzed || (τσακώνομαι) quarrel with.

πιάνω [peeano] take hold of, catch || occupy || (συζήτηση) engage || (περιέχω) contain, hold || (λιμάνι) land || **~ σπίτι** rent a house || **~ τόπο** come in useful || **~ κουβέντα** get into conversation || **~ δουλειά** start a job, find a job.

πιάσιμο, το [peeaseemo] hold, grasp ||

catching || (αφή) feeling, touch || (φυτού κτλ) taking root || (σώματος) stiffness, paralysis.

πιασμένος [peeasmenos] occupied, taken || (στο σώμα) cramped, (feeling) stiff.

πιατέλα, η [peeatela] large dish, flat dish.

πιατικά, τα [peeateeka] πλ crockery, earthenware.

πιάτσα, η [peeatsa] market || (ταξί) taxi rank.

πιέζω [piezo] press, squeeze, compress || oppress, force.

πίεση, η [piesee] pressure, oppression || (αίματος) blood pressure.

πιεστήριο, το [piesteereeo] press || (ελιών) oil press.

πιεστικός [piesteekos] pressing, oppressive || urgent.

πιέτα, η [pieta] pleat.

πιθαμή, η [peethamee] span of hand.

πιθανός [peethanos] probable, likely.

πιθανότητα, η [peethanoteeta] likelihood, probability.

πιθανώς [peethanos] probably, likely, in all likelihood.

πίθηκος, ο [peetheekos] ape.

πιθάρι, το [peetharee] jar.

πίκα, η [peeka] umbrage, pique || (στα χαρτιά) spade.

πικάντικος [peekanteekos] piquant, spicy.

πίκρα, η [peekra] grief, bitterness, affliction.

πικραίνομαι [peekrenome] be grieved, be embittered.

πικραίνω [peekreno] render bitter || grieve, distress.

πικροδάφνη, η [peekroδafnee] oleander.

πικρός [peekros] bitter || biting, harsh.

πικρόχολος [peekroholos] (μεταφ) touchy, irritable, snappy.

πιλάφι, το [peelafee] pilaf, rice dish.

πιλότος, ο [peelotos] pilot.

πίνακας, ο [peenakas] list, table || (του τείχου) notice board || (σχολείου) blackboard || (περιεχομένων) table of contents.

πινακίδα, η [peenakeeδa] nameplate || (αυτοκινήτου) licence plate, number plate.

πινακοθήκη, η [peenakotheekee] picture gallery, art gallery.

πινέζα, η [peeneza] drawing pin.

πινέλο, το [peenelo] artist's paintbrush.

πίνω [peeno] drink, take in || (τσιγάρο) smoke.

πιο [pio] more, greater.

πιοτό, το [pioto] drinking || liquor.

πίπα, η [peepa] pipe || cigarette holder.

πιπεράτος [peeperatos] peppery || biting, caustic, piquant.

πιπέρι, το [peeperee] pepper.

πιπεριά, η [peeperia] pepper || (δένδρο) pepper tree.

πιπιλίζω [peepeeleezo] suck, sip.

πισίνα, η [peeseena] swimming pool.

πισινός [peeseenos] back, posterior || ο ~ backside (col), arse (col), bum (col).

πίσσα, η [peesa] pitch, tar, asphalt.

πισσώνω [peesono] tar, pitch.

πίστα, η [peesta] ring || racetrack || (χορού) dance floor.

πιστευτός [peestevtos] trustworthy || credible.

πιστεύω [peestevo] believe, have faith in || suppose, fancy, think.

πίστη, η [peestee] faith, confidence, trust || fidelity || (οικον) credit, trustworthiness.

πιστόλι, το [peestolee] pistol.

πιστοποιητικό, το [peestopieeteeko] certificate.

πιστοποιώ [peestopieeo] certify, guarantee, vouch for.

πιστός [peestos] faithful, loyal, devoted || accurate.

πιστώνω [peestono] (οικον) credit with, give credit.

πίστωση, η [peestosee] credit, trust.

πιστωτής, ο [peestotees] creditor.

πίσω [peeso] behind || back || over again || πάει ~ το ρολόι the clock is slow || κάνω ~ move back || ~ μου behind me || ~ από behind, following.

πίτα, η [peeta] kind of cake, pie.

πίτουρο, το [peetouro] bran.

πιτσιλίζω [peetseeleezo] splash, sprinkle, dash (with).

πιτσιρίκος, ό [peetseereekos] small boy || kid (col).

πιτυρίδα, η [peeteereeδa] scurf, dandruff.

πιωμένος [piomenos] drunk, tipsy.

πλά(γ)ι, το [pla(y)ee] side || στο πλάι close by, near, beside.

πλαγιά, η [playa] slope of hill, hillside.

πλαγιάζω [playazo] go to bed || lie down || put to bed.

πλαγιαστός [playiastos] lying down, reclining.

πλάγιος [playeos] oblique || indirect || crooked, dishonest.

πλαγίως [playeeos] indirectly || next door.

πλαδαρός [plaδaros] flabby, soft || (προσπάθεια) feeble, ineffective.

πλάζ, η [plaz] bathing beach.

πλάθω [platho] mould, create, fashion.

πλάι [plaee] alongside, next door || ~ ~ side by side || ~ σε next to, along with.

πλαϊνός [plaeenos] adjoining, next door.

πλαίσιο, το [pleseeo] frame, framework || chassis || (μεταφ) scope, range.

πλαισιώνω [pleseeono] border, surround, frame, encircle.

πλάκα, η [plaka] slab, plate, paving stone || plaque || (σχολική) slate || (σαπούνι) cake || (γραμμοφώνου) record || (φωτογραφική) plate || σπάσαμε ~ we had a lot of fun || έχει ~ it's funny, it's hilarious.

πλακάκι, το [plakakee] floor tile, wall tile.

πλακόστρωτος [plakostrotos] paved, laid with tiles.

πλάκωμα, το [plakoma] pressure, crush || unexpected arrival.

πλακώνω [plakono] crush, press down || happen unexpectedly || come suddenly.

πλάνη, η [planee] mistake, delusion || (εργαλείο) plane.

πλανήτης, ο [planeetees] planet.

πλανίζω [planeezo] plane, smooth down.

πλανόδιος [planoδeeos] travelling || ~ έμπορος pedlar, hawker.

πλαντάζω [plantazo] be furious, fume, be enraged.

πλανώμαι [planome] ramble, wander || (κάνω λάθος) be mistaken, delude o.s.

πλασιέ, ο [plasie] commercial traveller, salesman.

πλάση, η [plasee] foundation, creation || moulding, formation.

πλάσμα, το [plasma] creature, being || invention, fiction || beauty.

πλάστιγγα, η [plasteenga] weighing machine, balance.

πλαστικός [plasteekos] plastic || comely.

πλαστογραφώ [plastografo] counterfeit || falsify.

πλαστός [plastos] false, forged || artificial, fictitious.

πλαταίνω [plateno] βλ πλατύνω.

πλάτανος, ο [platanos] plane tree.

πλατεία, η [plateea] town square || (θεάτρου) pit.

πλάτη, η [platee] back || shoulder blade.

πλατιά [platia] widely.

πλάτος, το [platos] width, broadness, breadth || (γεωγραφικό) latitude.

πλατύνω [plateeno] make wider, stretch, let out || become wider, broaden.

πλατύς [platees] wide, broad, large, ample || (μεταφ) far-reaching.

πλέγμα, το [plegma] network.

πλειοδοτώ [pleeoδoto] make highest offer or bid.

πλειονότητα, η [pleeonoteeta] majority.

πλειοψηφία, η [pleeopseefeea] majority (of votes).

πλειστηριασμός, ο [pleesteereeasmos] auction.

πλεκτός [plektos] knitted, plaited, woven.

πλέκω [pleko] plait, weave || (κάλτσες) knit.

πλεμόνι, το [plemonee] lung.

πλένω [pleno] βλ πλύνω.

πλέξιμο, το [plekseemo] knitting || braiding || (σε υπόθεση) involvement.

πλεξούδα, η [pleksouδa] plait, braid, tress.

πλέον [pleon] more || επί ~ in addition || not any longer || moreover || now.

πλεονάζω [pleonazo] abound, be plentiful || exceed, be superfluous.

πλεόνασμα, το [pleonasma] surplus, excess || (βάρους) overweight.

πλεονέκτημα, το [pleonekteema] advantage, benefit || gift, quality, merit.

πλεονέκτης, ο [pleonektees] greedy person, covetous person.

πλεονεκτώ [pleonekto] have the advantage || be greedy.

πλεονεξία, η [pleonekseea] cupidity, greed, avidity.

πλευρά, η [plevra] side || rib || (όρους) slope, declivity || (μεταφ) point of view.

πλευρίζω [plevreezo] (ναυτ) come alongside.

πλευρίτιδα, η [plevreeteeδa] pleurisy.

πλευρό, το [plevro] side || rib || (στρατ) flank.

πλεχτό, το [plehto] pullover || knitted article.

πλέω [pleo] navigate, sail || float || (μεταφ) wade, wallow.

πληγή, η [pleeyee] wound, injury, sore || (μεταφ) plague, evil, sore.

πλήγμα, το [pleegma] blow || wound.

πληγώνω [pleegono] wound, injure || offend, hurt.

πλήθη, τα [pleethee] πλ the masses.

πλήθος, το [pleethos] crowd || mass || great number.

πληθυντικός, ο [pleetheenteekos] (γραμμ) plural.

πληθύνω [pleetheeno] multiply, increase || augment.

πληθυσμός, ο [pleetheesmos] population.

πληθώρα, η [pleethora] abundance, excess, plenitude.

πληθωρισμός, ο [pleethoreesmos] inflation || plenitude.

πληκτικός [pleekteekos] boring, tiresome, irksome, dull, trying.

πλήκτρο, το [pleektro] (πιάνο κτλ) key || plectrum || drumstick.

πλημμέλημα, το [pleemeleema] misdemeanour, offence.

πλημμύρα, η [pleemeera] flood, inundation || (μεταφ) plenitude.

πλημμυρίζω [pleemeereezo] inundate, overflow || (μεταφ) swarm.

πλην [pleen] except, save || (επίρ) unless, except that || (συνδ) but || (μαθημ) minus || ~ **τούτου** besides, moreover.

πλήξη, η [pleeksee] tedium, weariness, boredom.

πληρεξούσιο, το [pleereksouseeo] power of attorney.

πληρεξούσιος, ο, η [pleereksouseeos] representative, proxy || plenipotentiary, deputy.

πλήρης [pleerees] full, complete, whole || swarming, teeming, packed.

πληροφορία, η [pleeroforeea] information, report.

πληροφορίες, οι [pleerofories] πλ information.

πληροφορική, η [pleeroforeekee] informatics, computer science.

πληροφορούμαι [pleeroforoume] learn, discover.

πληροφορώ [pleeroforo] inform, notify.

πληρώ [pleero] fill || fulfil, perform.

πλήρωμα, το [pleeroma] crew || fullness || filling, completion.

πληρωμή, η [pleeromee] payment, reward || salary, wages.

πληρώνω [pleerono] pay, settle || (μεταφ) pay up, discharge.

πληρωτής [pleerotees] payer.

πλησιάζω [pleeseeazo] approach, go near, put near, draw near.

πλησιέστερος [pleesiesteros] closer || **ο** ~ the nearest.

πλησίον [pleeseeon] near, close by || ~ neighbour.

πλήττω [pleeto] strike, hit, wound, afflict || (παθαίνω πλήξη) be bored, be weary.

πλινθόκτιστος [pleenthokteestos] built of bricks.

πλίνθος, η [pleenthos] brick, firebrick.

πλοηγός, ο [ploeegos] (ναυτ) pilot.

πλοιάριο, το [pleeareeo] small boat, launch.

πλοίαρχος, ο [pleearhos] (ναυτ) captain || (εμπορικού) master, skipper.

πλοίο, το [pleeo] ship, vessel, boat.

πλοκάμι, το [plokamee] tress, braid, plait || (χταποδιού) tentacle.

πλοκή, η [plokee] plot (of play).

πλους, ο [plous] sailing, passage || navigating.

πλουσιοπάροχος [plouseeoparohos] copious, generous, abundant.

πλούσιος [plouseeos] rich, wealthy || splendid, magnificent.

πλουτίζω [plouteezo] make rich || get rich.

πλούτη, τα [ploutee] πλ riches, wealth.

πλούτος, ο [ploutos] opulence, wealth || richness || (εδάφους) fertility.

πλυντήριο, το [pleenteereeo] laundry room || washing machine.

πλύνω [pleeno] wash, clean || brush || scrub.

πλύσιμο, το [pleeseemo] wash(ing).

πλυσταριό, το [pleestario] laundry room.

πλύστρα, η [pleestra] washerwoman || wash-board.

πλώρη, η [ploree] prow || **βάζω** ~ set sail (for).

πλωτάρχης, ο [plotarhees] lieutenant-commander.

πλωτός [plotos] navigable || floating || (γέφυρα) pontoon bridge.

πνεύμα, το [pnevma] ghost, soul, breath of life || mind || genius, spirit || (γραμμ) breathing || **Άγιο** ~ Holy Ghost.

πνευματικός [pnevmateekos] spiritual || intellectual, mental || pneumatic.

πνευμονία, η [pnevmoneea] pneumonia.

πνεύμονας, ο [pnevmonas] lung.

πνευστός [pnevstos] blown, wind (instrument).

πνέω [pneo] blow || ~ **τα λοίσθια** I breathe my last.

πνιγηρός [pneeyeeros] stifling, suffocating, choking.

πνιγμός, ο [pneegmos] suffocation, choking || drowning || throttling.

πνίγω [pneego] drown || stifle, suffocate || choke, throttle.

πνίξιμο, το [pneekseemo] drowning || strangulation.

πνοή, η [pnoee] breath(ing) || (μεταφ) inspiration.

ποδήλατο, το [podeelato] bicycle.

ποδηλατώ [podeelato] cycle, pedal.

πόδι, το [podee] foot, leg || (μέτρο) foot || (ποτηριού) stem || **στο** ~ standing || on the go || **σηκώνω στο** ~ cause a commotion.

ποδιά, η [podia] apron, overall || (παραθύρου) windowsill.

ποδόγυρος, ο [podoyeeros] border, hem.

ποδοπατώ [podopato] tread on, trample on, trample underfoot.

ποδοσφαιριστής, ο [podosfereestees] football player.

ποδόσφαιρο, το [podosfero] game of football.

πόζα, η [poza] pose, affectation.

ποζάρω [pozaro] pose, sit for || put on.

πόθος, ο [pothos] desire, wish, yearning.

ποθώ [potho] desire, long for, wish, be eager for.

ποίημα, το [pieema] poem.

ποίηση, η [pieese] poetry.

ποιητής, ο [pieetees] poet || creator, maker.

ποιητικός [pieeteekos] poetic.

ποικιλία, η [peekeeleea] variety, diversity, assortment.

ποικίλλω [peekeelo] embellish, adorn || vary, change.

ποικίλος [peekeelos] varied, diverse, different || miscellaneous.

ποιμένας, ο [peemenas] shepherd, herdsman.

ποίμνιο, το [peemneeo] flock, herd, drove || (εκκλ) flock.

ποινή, η [peenee] penalty, punishment, pain.

ποινικός [peeneekos] penal, criminal, felonious.

ποιόν, το [peeon] quality, property, attribute, nature.

ποιος [peeos] who?, which?, what?

ποιότητα, η [peeoteeta] quality, property.

πολεμικό, το [polemeeko] warship.

πολεμικός [polemeekos] warlike, bellicose || of war, martial.

πολέμιος [polemeeos] unfriendly, hostile || ο ~ enemy, adversary.

πολεμιστής, ο [polemeestees] fighter, warrior, combatant.

πόλεμος, ο [polemos] war, warfare.

πολεμοφόδια, τα [polemofodeea] πλ munitions, ammunition.

πολεμώ [polemo] fight, make war against || contend, strive (to).

πολεοδομία, η [poleodomeea] town planning.

πόλη, η [polee] city, town.

πολικός [poleekos] polar.

πολιορκία, η [poleeorkeea] siege, blockade.

πολιορκώ [poleeorko] besiege, surround || invest.

πολιτεία, η [poleeteea] state, government || country, nation || town.

πολίτευμα, το [poleetevma] system of government, regime.

πολιτεύομαι [poleetevome] go into politics, meddle in politics.

πολιτευτής, ο [poleetevtees] politician, statesman.

πολιτικά, τα [poleeteeka] πλ politics.

πολίτης, ο [poleetees] citizen || civilian.

πολιτική, η [poleeteekee] politics || policy.

πολιτικός [poleeteekos] civic, civilian || political || (ουσ) politician.

πολιτισμένος [poleeteesmenos] civilized, cultured.

πολιτισμός, ο [poleeteesmos] civilization, culture.

πολιτογραφώ [poleetografo] naturalize (as citizen).

πολιτοφυλακή, η [poleetofeelakee] militia, civil guard || national guard (US).

πολλαπλασιάζω [polaplaseeazo] multiply || propagate, increase.

πολλαπλασιασμός, ο [polaplaseeasmos] multiplication || increase.

πολλαπλάσιο, το [polaplaseeo] multiple.

πολλοί [polee] πλ many.

πόλο, το [polo] polo.

πόλος, ο [polos] pole.

πολτός, ο [poltos] pap || purée || rag pulp.

πολύ [polee] much || numerous, several || great, a lot || το ~ at the most.

πολυάνθρωπος [poleeanthropos] populous, crowded.

πολυάριθμος [poleeareethmos] numerous.

πολυάσχολος [poleeasholos] very busy, very occupied.

πολυβόλο, το [poleevolo] machine gun.

πολυγαμία, η [poleegameea] polygamy.

πολύγλωσσος [poleeglosos] polyglot.

πολυγράφος, ο [poleegrafos] duplicator.

πολυέλαιος, ο [polieleos] chandelier.

πολυζήτητος [poleezeeteetos] much sought-after.

πολυθρόνα, η [poleethrona] armchair.

πολυκατοικία, η [poleekateekeea] block of flats, apartment building.

πολυκοσμία, η [poleekosmeea] crowds of people.

πολύκροτος [poleekrotos] causing a commotion.

πολυλογάς, ο [poleelogas] chatterbox, babbler, gossip.

πολυλογία, η [poleeloyeea] loquacity, garrulity, babble.

πολυμελής [poleemelees] having many members, numerous.

πολυμερής [poleemerees] varied, diversified.

πολυμήχανος [poleemeehanos] very ingenious || cunning, crafty.

πολυπληθής [poleepleethees] very numerous, crowded.

πολύπλοκος [poleeplokos] intricate, complicated, very involved.

πολύπους, ο [poleepous] polyp || (ιατρ) polypus.

πολύπτυχος [poleepteehos] with many folds, many-pleated.

πολύς [polees] much, numerous, many, great || (χρόνος) long.

πολυσύνθετος [poleeseenthetos] very complex || compound.

πολυτέλεια, η [poleeteleea] luxury.

πολυτελής [poleetelees] sumptuous, splendid, rich.

πολυτεχνείο, το [poleetehneeo]

Polytechnic, National Technical School.

πολύτιμος [poleeteemos] valuable, precious, priceless.

πολυφαγία, η [poleefayeea] gluttony, voracity, greediness.

πολύχρωμος [poleehromos] multicoloured, variegated.

πολύωρος [poleeoros] lasting many hours, long-drawn-out.

Πολωνία, η [poloneea] Poland.

πολωνικός [poloneekos] Polish.

πόμολο, το [pomolo] door knob, handle.

πομπή, η [pompee] procession, parade || shame, stigma.

πομπός, ο [pompos] transmitter.

πομπώδης [pompoδees] pompous, bombastic.

πονεμένος [ponemenos] in distress || sad, hurt.

πονηρεύομαι [poneerevome] employ cunning, use wiles || become suspicious.

πονηρεύω [poneerevo] rouse suspicions of || make suspicious || become cunning.

πονηρία, η [poneereea] ruse, trick, guile || suspicion, slyness.

πονηρός [poneeros] cunning, wily, crafty || suspicious, distrustful || diabolical.

πονόδοντος, ο [ponoδontos] toothache.

πονοκέφαλος, ο [ponokefalos] headache.

πονόλαιμος, ο [ponolemos] sore throat.

πόνος, ο [ponos] suffering, pain || (τοκετού) labour || compassion, pity, sympathy.

ποντάρω [pontaro] punt || back, bet on.

ποντικός, ο [ponteekos] mouse, rat || (ανατ) muscle.

πόντος, ο [pontos] sea || (παιχνιδιού) point || (μέτρο) centimetre || (πλέξιμο) stitch || **Εύξεινος ~** Black Sea.

πονώ [pono] feel compassion for, sympathize with || hurt, pain || (αμετ) feel pain, suffer.

πορδή, η [porδee] fart (col).

πορεία, η [poreea] march, route || course, run.

πορεύομαι [porevome] proceed, go, walk, march.

πορθμείο, το [porthmeeo] ferry (boat).

πορθμός, ο [porthmos] strait, sound, channel.

πόρισμα, το [poreesma] deduction, inference, conclusion || finding || (μαθημ) corollary.

πορνείο, το [porneeo] brothel || whorehouse (US).

πόρνη, η [pornee] prostitute, whore.

πόρος, ο [poros] passage, ford || (του σώματος) pore || πλ means, income, resources.

πόρπη, η [porpee] buckle, clasp, brooch.

πορσελάνη, η [porselanee] china, porcelain.

πόρτα, η [porta] door, gate, doorway, gateway.

Πορτογαλία, η [portogaleea] Portugal.

πορτογαλικός [portogaleekos] Portuguese.

Πορτογάλος, ο [portogalos] Portuguese man.

πορτοκαλάδα, η [portokalaδa] orangeade.

πορτοκάλι, το [portokalee] orange.

πορτοκαλιά, η [portokalia] orange tree.

πορτοφολάς, ο [portofolas] pickpocket.

πορτοφόλι, το [portofolee] wallet.

πορτραίτο, το [portreto] portrait.

πορφύρα, η [porfeera] purple.

πορώδης [poroδees] porous.

πόσιμο [poseemo]: **~ νερό** drinking water.

πόσιμος [poseemos] drinkable.

ποσό, το [poso] quantity, amount || (χρήματος) sum.

πόσο [poso] how much.

πόσος [posos] how much?, how many?, how large?, how great?

ποσοστό, το [pososto] percentage, share, quota.

ποσότητα, η [posoteeta] quantity, amount.

πόστο, το [posto] strategic position.

ποσώς [posos] not at all, in no way, by no means.

ποτάμι, το [potamee], **ποταμός, ο** [potamos] river.

πότε [pote] when? || **~ ~** sometimes, from time to time || **~ ... ~** sometimes... sometimes.

ποτέ [pote] once, formerly || ever || (μετά από αρνητ) never || **~ πλέον** never again.

ποτήρι, το [poteeree] drinking glass.

πότης, ο [potees] heavy drinker, boozer.

ποτίζω [poteezo] water, irrigate || become damp, become saturated.

πότισμα, το [poteesma] watering, irrigation.

ποτιστήρι, το [poteesteeree] watering can.

ποτό, το [poto] drink, beverage.

πού [pou] where?, whither? || **για ~;** where are you going? || **~ να ξέρω;** how should I know? || **~ και ~** once in a while, now and then.

που [pou] who, whom, which, that ||

when || (συνδ) that || (επίρ) somewhere, where.

πουγγί, το [poungee] purse, bag || money.

πούδρα, η [pouðra] powder.

πουθενά [pouthena] not anywhere || nowhere.

πουκάμισο, το [poukameeso] shirt.

πουλάκι, το [poulakee] little bird || ~ **μου** my darling, my pet.

πουλάρι, το [poularee] foal, colt.

πουλερικά, τα [poulereeka] πλ poultry.

πούλημα, το [pouleema] βλ **πώληση.**

πουλί, το [poulee] bird.

πούλμαν, το [poulman] (motor) coach.

πουλώ [poulo] βλ **πωλώ.**

πούντα, η [pounda] cold, pleurisy.

πουντιάζω [pounteeazo] cool, chill || feel very cold.

πούπουλο, το [poupoulo] down, plume, feather.

πουρές, ο [poures] purée.

πουρμπουάρ, το [pourbouar] gratuity, tip.

πουρνάρι, το [pournaree] evergreen oak.

πούρο, το [pouro] cigar.

πούσι, το [pousee] mist, fog.

πούστης, ο [poustees] bugger, queen (col), queer (col).

πουτάνα, η [poutana] whore.

πράγμα, το [pragma] thing, object || matter, business, affair || (προϊόντα) goods || (ύφασμα) cloth.

πράγματι [pragmatee] in fact, actually.

πραγματεύομαι [pragmatevome] deal with, treat, handle || negotiate.

πραγματικός [pragmateekos] real, actual, substantial, authentic.

πραγματικότητα, η [pragmateekoteeta] reality, fact, truth.

πραγματογνώμονας, ο [pragmatognomonas] assessor, valuer || expert.

πραγματοποιώ [pragmatopeeo] carry out, realize, fulfil, work out.

πρακτικά, τα [prakteeka] πλ records, minutes, proceedings.

πρακτικός [prakteekos] useful, practical || vocational.

πρακτορείο, το [praktoreeo] agency, travel agency.

πράκτορας, ο [praktoras] agent || **μυστικός** ~ secret agent.

πραμάτεια, η [pramatea] goods, commodities.

πράξη, η [praksee] action, act || practice, experience || (γεννήσεως κτλ) certificate, registration || (οικον) deal, transaction || (μαθημ) operation.

πραξικόπημα, το [prakseekopeema] coup d'état.

πράος [praos] affable, gentle, kind.

πρασιά, η [prasia] flower bed or lawn round house.

πρασινάδα, η [praseenaða] verdure, greenery || green colour.

πράσινος [praseenos] green, verdant || unripe.

πράσο, το [praso] leek.

πρατήριο, το [prateereeo] specialist shop || ~ **βενζίνης** petrol station.

πράττω [prato] perform, act || do.

πραΰνω [praeeno] appease, calm, soothe, pacify.

πρέζα, η [preza] pinch.

πρέπει [prepee] it is necessary, it is proper that || ~ **να παω** I must go || **καθώς** ~ decent, honourable, a gentleman.

πρέπων [prepon] suitable, fitting, proper || decent, correct.

πρεσβεία, η [presveea] embassy, legation || delegation.

πρεσβευτής, ο [presvevtees] ambassador, minister || representative.

πρεσβεύω [presvevo] profess, avow, affirm, represent.

πρεσβυωπία, η [presveeopeea] long-sightedness.

πρέφα, η [prefa] card game || **το πήρε** ~ he smelt a rat.

πρήζομαι [preezome] become swollen, swell.

πρήζω [preezo] (μεταφ) infuriate.

πρήξιμο, το [preekseemo] swelling, tumour.

πρίγκηπας, ο [preengkeepas] prince.

πρίζα, η [preeza] plug, socket.

πριν [preen] before, previously, prior to || ~ **από μένα** ahead of me, in front of me || ~ **τον πόλεμο** before the war.

πριόνι, το [preeonee] saw, handsaw, hacksaw.

πριονίζω [preeoneezo] saw.

πρίσμα, το [preesma] prism.

προ [pro] before, in front of, ahead of, in the face of || ~ **ημερών** a few days ago || ~ **παντός** especially, above all.

προαγγέλλω [proangelo] predict, prophesy.

προάγω [proago] put forward, promote, advance || speed up, further || **η προαγωγή** (ουσ) advancement, promotion || **ο προαγωγός** (ουσ) pimp, pander.

προαίρεση, η [proeresee] intention, purpose || bent, bias.

προαιρετικός [proereteekos] optional || voluntary.

προαίσθηση, η [proestheesee] presentiment, foreboding.

προάλλες [proales] **τις** ~ just the other day, recently.

προαναφερθείς [proanafertrees] above-mentioned.

προασπίζω [proaspeezo] defend, protect, guard.

προάστειο, το [proasteeo] suburb.

προαύλιο, το [proavleeo] forecourt, courtyard.

πρόβα, η [prova] fitting of clothes || trial, rehearsal.

προβάδισμα, το [provaðeesma] precedence, priority.

προβαίνω [proveno] advance, move forward || proceed, make || ~ σε carry out, make.

προβάλλω [provalo] project, further || (σκιά) cast || (φιλμ) project, show || (αντίσταση) offer resistance || (αντίρρηση) raise || (δικαιολογία) put forward an excuse || (αμετ) appear suddenly in view.

προβάρω [provaro] try on, go for a fitting.

προβατίνα, η [provateena] ewe, lamb.

πρόβατο, το [provato] sheep.

προβιά, η [provia] animal's skin.

προβιβάζω [proveevazo] promote, push forward.

πρόβιος [proveeos] of a sheep.

προβλέπω [provlepo] foresee, forecast || prepare for, provide.

πρόβλεψη, η [provlepsee] forecast, anticipation.

πρόβλημα, το [provleema] problem || (μεταφ) riddle, puzzle.

προβλήτα, η [provleeta] jetty, mole.

προβολέας, ο [provoleas] searchlight, headlight || (σινεμά) projector.

προβολή, η [provolee] projection || (προϊόντος) promotion.

προβοσκίδα, η [provoskeeða] trunk || (εντόμου) proboscis.

προγενέστερος [proyenesteros] anterior, previous, former || (ουσ) precursor.

πρόγευμα, το [proyevma] breakfast.

προγνωστικό, το [prognosteeko] prediction, forecast || tip.

πρόγονος, ο [progonos] ancestor, forefather, forebear.

πρόγονος, ο, η [progonos] stepson, stepdaughter.

πρόγραμμα, το [programa] programme, plan, schedule.

προγράφω [prografo] proscribe, outlaw.

προγυμνάζω [proyeemnazo] exercise, train || tutor.

προδιαγράφω [proðeeagrafo] prearrange.

προδιάθεση, η [proðeeatesee] predisposition, liability (to), prejudice (against).

προδιαθέτω [proðeeatheto]

predispose, forewarn, influence, prejudice.

προδίδω [proðeeðo] reveal, betray || denounce, inform.

προδοσία, η [proðoseea] betrayal || treachery.

προδότης, ο [proðotees] traitor, informer.

πρόδρομος, ο [proðromos] forerunner, precursor || herald.

προεδρεία, η [proeðreea] presidency, chairmanship.

προεδρεύω [proeðrevo] preside, chair.

πρόεδρος, ο, η [proeðros] president, chairman || presiding judge.

προειδοποίηση, η [proeeðopieesee] previous warning, premonition.

προειδοποιώ [proeeðopeeo] let know || warn.

προεισαγωγή, η [proeesagoyee] introduction, preface.

προεκλογικός [proekloyeekos] pre-election.

προέκταση, η [proektasee] extension, prolongation.

προέλαση, η [proelasee] advance, forward movement.

προελαύνω [proelavno] advance, move forward.

προέλευση, η [proelevsee] provenance, place of origin.

προεξέχω [proekseho] jut out, project, protrude.

προεξοφλώ [proeksoflo] (χρέος) pay off in advance || receive in advance || take for granted, rely on.

προεξοχή, η [proeksohee] projection, protrusion, prominence.

προεργασία, η [proergaseea] preliminary work.

προέρχομαι [proerhome] originate, come from, issue from.

προετοιμάζω [proeteemazo] prepare, fit for, train for.

προετοιμασία, η [proeteemaseea] preparation.

προέχω [proeho] jut out || surpass || predominate.

πρόζα, η [proza] prose.

προηγούμαι [proeegoume] surpass, be ahead || precede, come before.

προηγούμενο, το [proeegoumeno] precedent.

προηγούμενος [proeegoumenos] preceding, previous, earlier.

προηγουμένως [proeegoumenos] previously, beforehand.

προθάλαμος, ο [prothalamos] anteroom, antechamber, waiting room.

πρόθεση, η [prothesee] purpose, design, intention || (γραμμ) preposition, prefix.

προθεσμία, η [prothesmeea] time limit, delay, term, option.

προθήκη, n [protheekee] shop window || showcase.

προθυμία, n [protheemeea] eagerness, readiness, alacrity.

πρόθυμος [protheemos] eager, willing, ready || obliging.

πρόθυρα, τα [protheera] πλ gates, approach || (μεταφ) verge, eve, threshold.

προίκα, n [preeka] dowry, marriage portion.

προικίζω [preekeezo] dower || endow (with), equip (with).

προικοθήρας, ο [preekotheeras] fortune hunter, dowry hunter.

προικοσύμφωνο, το [preekoseemfono] marriage contract.

προϊόν, το [proeeon] πλ product, production || proceeds.

προϊόντα, τα [proeeonta] πλ produce, articles, products.

προΐσταμαι [proeestame] direct, manage, supervise.

προϊστάμενος, ο [proeestamenos] superior, chief, supervisor.

πρόκα, n [proka] nail, tack.

προκαλώ [prokalo] challenge || provoke, incite.

προκαταβολή, n [prokatavolee] prepayment, advance payment || deposit.

προκαταβολικώς [prokatavoleekos] in advance, beforehand.

προκαταλαμβάνω [prokatalamvano] forestall, occupy beforehand.

προκατάληψη, n [prokataleepsee] bias, prejudice.

προκαταρκτικός [prokatarkteekos] preliminary, preparatory.

προκατειλημμένος [prokateeleemenos] biased, prejudiced.

προκάτοχος, ο [prokatohos] predecessor || previous holder, previous occupant.

πρόκειται [prokeete] it's a matter of || it's a question of || **περί τίνος ~;** what's it all about? || **~ να έλθω** I am due to come.

προκήρυξη, n [prokeereeksee] proclamation, announcement || manifesto.

πρόκληση, n [prokleesee] affront, challenge || provocation, instigation.

προκλητικός [prokleeteekos] provocative, provoking || seductive.

προκόβω [prokovo] progress, succeed, prosper, make good.

προκομμένος [prokomenos] hard-working, diligent.

προκοπή, n [prokopee] progress || industry || success.

προκρίνω [prokreeno] prefer, choose || predetermine.

προκυμαία, n [prokeemea] quay, pier, jetty.

προκύπτω [prokeepto] arise || result, ensue.

προλαβαίνω [prolaveno] get a start on, forestall || catch, overtake || (σε χρόνο) be on time, manage || have enough time for.

προλεγόμενα, τα [prolegomena] πλ preface, foreword.

προλέγω [prolego] forecast, predict || say previously.

προλετάριος [proletareeos] proletarian.

προληπτικός [proleepteekos] precautionary, preventive || superstitious.

πρόληψη, n [proleepsee] prevention || superstition.

πρόλογος, ο [prologos] prologue, preface, preamble.

προμαντεύω [promantevo] prophesy, foretell, predict.

πρόμαχος, ο [promahos] champion, defender, protector.

προμελέτη, n [promeletee] preliminary study || premeditation || **εκ προμελέτης** deliberately || premeditated.

προμεσημβρία, n [promeseemvreea] forenoon, morning.

προμήθεια, n [promeetheea] supply, provision, supplying, victualling || (ποσοστό) commission, brokerage.

προμηθευτής, ο [promeethevtees] provider, purveyor, supplier.

προμηθεύομαι [promeethevome] get, supply o.s. with.

προμηθεύω [promeethevo] supply, provide, furnish.

προμηνύω [promeeneeo] portend, presage, foretell.

προνοητικός [pronoeeteekos] having foresight, provident, careful.

πρόνοια, n [proneea] care, concern, precaution || providence, welfare.

προνόμιο, το [pronomeeo] privilege, advantage || gift, talent.

προνομιούχος [pronomeeouhos] privileged, favoured.

προνοώ [pronoo] foresee, forecast || provide for, think of.

προξενείο, το [prokseneeo] consulate.

προξενητής, ο [prokseneetees] intermediary, matchmaker.

προξενιά, n [proksenia] matchmaking.

πρόξενος, ο [proksenos] (διπλωμάτης) consul.

προξενώ [prokseno] cause, occasion, inflict, bring about.

προοδευτικός [prooodevteekos] progressive, forward || gradual.

προοδεύω [proodevo] progress, make headway || develop.

πρόοδος, n [proodos] advance,

progress || development, improvement || (μάθημ) progression.

προοίμιο, το [proeemeeo] preface, prelude, preamble.

προοπτική, η [proopteekee] perspective || prospect in view.

προορίζω [prooreezo] destine, intend, foreordain.

προορισμός, ο [prooreesmos] end, intention || destination.

προπαγάνδα, η [propaganδa] propaganda.

προπαρασκευή, η [proparaskevee] preparation || coaching.

προπέλα, η [propela] propeller.

πρόπερσι [propersee] two years ago.

προπέτασμα, το [propetasma] screen || ~ **καπνού** smoke screen.

προπληρώνω [propleerono] pay in advance.

πρόποδες, οι [propoδes] πλ foot of mountain.

προπολεμικός [propolemeekos] prewar.

προπόνηση, η [proponeesee] training, coaching.

πρόποση, η [proposee] toast (*drink*).

προπύλαια, τα [propeelea] πλ propylaea.

προπύργιο, το [propeeryo] rampart, bulwark, bastion.

προς [pros] towards || (για) for || at || in || ~ **όφελός μου** to my advantage, to my good || ~ **τιμή του** in his honour, for his sake || ~ **το παρόν** for the present || **ένα ~ ένα** one by one || **ως ~ εμέ** as far as I am concerned || ~ **Θεού!** for God's sake! || ~ **τούτοις** moreover || ~ **δε** in addition, furthermore.

προσάγω [prosago] put forward, exhibit, produce.

προσάναμα, το [prosanama] tinder, firewood || fuel.

προσανατολίζομαι [prosanatoleezome] find one's bearings.

προσανατολίζω [prosanatoleezo] orientate || direct, guide.

προσαράσσω [prosaraso] run aground, be stranded.

προσαρμογή, η [prosarmoyee] adaptation, accommodation || adjustment.

προσαρμόζω [prosarmozo] fit to || adapt, adjust, apply.

προσάρτημα, το [prosarteema] accessory, annexe, addition.

προσάρτηση, η [prosarteesee] annexation.

προσαρτώ [prosarto] append, attach || annex.

προσβάλλω [prosvalo] assail, attack || (υγεία) harm, injure || (δυσαρεστώ) hurt, offend || (διαθήκη) challenge.

προσβλητικός [prosvleeteekos] offensive, abusive, insolent.

προσβολή, η [prosvolee] onset, attack || (υγείας) fit, stroke || offence, insult.

προσγειώνομαι [prosyonome] land.

προσγείωση, η [prosyeeosee] landing, alighting.

προσδίδω [prosδeeδo] lend, add to, give.

προσδιορίζω [prosδeeoreezo] determine, define, fix || allocate, assign.

προσδοκώ [prosδoko] hope, expect, anticipate.

προσεγγίζω [prosengeezo] put near || approach, come near || (κατά προσέγγιση) approximate || (ναυτ) put in at, land at.

προσεκτικός [prosekteekos] attentive, heedful, mindful || careful.

προσέλευση, η [proselevsee] arrival, approach.

προσελκύω [proselkeeo] (προσοχή) attract, win, draw, catch || (υποστηρικτές) gain, win over.

προσέρχομαι [proserhome] attend, present o.s. || apply for.

προσευχή, η [prosevhee] prayer.

προσεύχομαι [prosevhome] pray, say one's prayers.

προσεχής [prosehees] next || forthcoming.

προσέχω [proseho] pay attention to, notice || be attentive, be mindful || (κάποιο) take care of.

προσεχώς [prosehos] shortly, soon, in a short time.

προσηλυτίζω [proseeleeteezo] convert, proselytize.

προσηλωμένος [proseelomenos] attached to, devoted to, absorbed in.

προσηλώνω [proseelono] nail, fix || (μεταφ) look fixedly (at).

πρόσθεση, η [prostheesees] addition, increase.

πρόσθετος [prosthetos] additional, extra.

προσθέτω [prostheto] add, sum up || mix with.

προσθήκη, η [prostheekee] addition, increase.

πρόσθιος [prostheeos] front, fore.

προσιτός [proseetos] attainable, accessible || (τιμή) reasonable, within one's means.

πρόσκαιρος [proskeros] transitory, passing, momentary.

προσκαλώ [proskalo] call, send for || (νομ) summon, subpoena || (σε γεύμα κτλ) invite.

προσκεκλημένος [proskekleemenos] invited.

προσκέφαλο, το [proskefalo] pillow, cushion.

πρόσκληση, η [proskleesee] call,

summons || (σε δεξίωση κτλ) invitation || (στρατ) calling up || (εισιτήριο δωρεάν) complimentary ticket.

προσκλητήριο, το [proskleeteereeo] invitation (card) || (στρατ) call, roll call || (ναυτ) muster roll.

προσκόλληση, η [proskoleesee] adherence, attaching || fidelity.

προσκολλώ [proskolo] stick, attach, paste on || second, attach.

προσκομίζω [proskomeezo] bring forward, bring || offer.

πρόσκοπος, ο [proskopos] scout || boy scout.

προσκρούω [proskrouo] crash || strike (against) || be opposed to.

προσκύνημα, το [proskeeneema] adoration || submission || place of pilgrimage.

προσκυνητής, ο [proskeeneetees] pilgrim.

προσκυνώ [proskeeno] adore, worship || pay homage to, yield.

προσλαμβάνω [proslamvano] take on, engage, employ.

προσμένω [prosmeno] wait for, hope for.

πρόσμειξη, η [prosmeeksee] blending, mixing.

πρόσοδος, η [prosoδos] income, revenue || (εμπόριο) profit || yield.

προσοδοφόρος [prosoδoforos] productive, profitable, lucrative.

προσόν, το [prason] aptitude, fitness, qualification || advantage.

προσοχή, η [prosohee] attention, notice || caution, precaution, care.

πρόσοψη, η [prosopsee] façade, front(age).

προσόψι, το [prosopsee] towel.

προσπάθεια, η [prospatheea] endeavour, effort, attempt, labour.

προσπαθώ [prospatho] try, attempt.

προσπερνώ [prosperno] overtake || (μεταφ) surpass.

προσποίηση, η [prospieesee] pretence, sham.

προσποιητός [prospieetos] affected, assumed, feigned.

προσποιούμαι [prospeeoume] affect, put on || pretend.

προσταγή, η [prostayee] order, ordering, command.

προστάζω [prostazo] order, direct, command.

προστακτική, η [prostakteekee] (γραμμ) imperative (mood).

προστασία, η [prostaseea] protection, defence.

προστατευόμενος, ο [prostatevomenos] protégé.

προστατευτικός [prostatevteekos] protecting || condescending.

προστατεύω [prostatevo] defend, protect || extend patronage to.

προστάτης, ο [prostatees] protector, patron || (ανατ) prostate.

προστίθεμαι [prosteetheme] be added, be mixed (with).

πρόστιμο, το [prosteemo] fine, penalty.

προστρέχω [prostreho] rush up, run up || resort to, turn to.

προστριβή, η [prostreevee] friction, rubbing || (μεταφ) dispute.

προστυχιά, η [prosteehia] vulgarity, rudeness, contemptible act.

πρόστυχος [prosteehos] vile, rude, ill-mannered || of bad quality.

προσύμφωνο, το [proseemfono] preliminary agreement, draft agreement.

πρόσφατος [prosfatos] recent, new || (μόδα) modern.

προσφέρομαι [prosferome] offer || be appropriate, be fitting.

προσφέρω [prosfero] offer, present, give.

προσφεύγω [prosfevgo] have recourse to, turn to.

προσφιλής [prosfeelees] dear, loved, precious.

προσφορά, η [prosfora] offer, offering, proposal, bid || thing offered.

πρόσφορος [prosforos] convenient, opportune, suitable.

πρόσφυγας, ο [prosfeegas] refugee.

προσφυγή, η [prosfeeyee] recourse, resort || (νομ) legal redress, appeal.

προσφυής [prosfiees] suitable, well-adapted, fitting.

πρόσχαρος [prosharos] cheerful, lively, merry, gay.

προσχέδιο, το [prosheδeeo] rough draft, sketch.

πρόσχημα, το [prosheema] pretext, excuse.

προσχωρώ [proshoro] join, go over (to) || cleave (to), adhere (to).

προσωδία, η [prosoδeea] prosody.

προσωνυμία, η [prosoneemeea] nickname, name.

προσωπάρχης, ο [prosoparhees] personnel officer, staff manager.

προσωπείο, το [prosopeeo] mask.

προσωπικό, το [prosopeeko] personnel, staff || (σπιτιού) servants.

προσωπικός [prosopeekos] personal.

προσωπικότητα, η [prosopeekoteeta] personality, individuality.

προσωπικώς [prosopeekos] personally.

προσωπίδα, η [prosopeeδa] mask.

πρόσωπο, το [prosopo] face, visage || person || (θεάτρου) role, character, part.

προσωπογραφία, η

[prosopografeea] portrait painting, portrait.

προσωποποίηση, η [prosopopieesee] personification || impersonation.

προσωρινός [prosoreenos] provisional, passing, fleeting.

πρόταση, η [protasee] proposal, suggestion, offer, motion || (γραμμ) sentence || clause.

προτείνω [proteeno] extend, stretch out, put forward || propose, suggest.

προτελευταίος [protelevteos] last but one.

προτεραιότητα, η [protereoteeta] priority, primacy.

προτέρημα, το [protereema] gift, faculty, advantage, talent.

πρότερος [proteros] earlier, previous to, prior (to).

προτέρων [proteron]: **εκ των ~** beforehand.

προτεσταντισμός, ο [protestanteesmos] Protestantism.

προτίθεμαι [proteetheme] intend, propose, mean, think.

προτίμηση, η [proteemeesee] preference, predilection.

προτιμότερος [proteemoteros] preferable to.

προτιμώ [proteemo] prefer, like better.

προτομή, η [protomee] bust.

προτού [protou] before || previously.

προτρέπω [protrepo] exhort, instigate, incite.

προτροπή, η [protropee] exhortation, prompting.

πρότυπο, το [proteepo] original, pattern, model, example || mould.

πρότυπος [proteepos] model.

προϋπαντώ [proeepanto] go to meet.

προϋπάρχω [proeeparho] pre-exist || (σε χρόνο) come before.

προϋπόθεση, η [proeepothesee] assumption, presumption.

προϋποθέτω [proeepotheto] presuppose, presume.

προϋπολογίζω [proeepoloyeezo] estimate, compute beforehand.

προϋπολογισμός, ο [proeepoloyeesmos] estimate || budget.

προφανής [profanees] obvious, evident, plain, clear.

προφανώς [profanos] obviously, evidently, manifestly.

πρόφαση, η [profasee] pretext, excuse, pretence.

προφέρ(ν)ω [profer(n)o] pronounce, utter, articulate.

προφητεία, η [profeeteea] prophecy, prophetic utterance.

προφητεύω [profeetevo] prophesy, predict.

προφήτης, ο [profeetees] prophet.

προφητικός [profeeteekos] prophetic.

προφθάνω [profthano] anticipate, forestall || catch, overtake, overhaul || (σε χρόνο) be in time for, have the time to.

προφορά, η [profora] pronunciation, accent.

προφτάνω [proftano] βλ **προφθάνω.**

προφυλακή, η [profeelakee] vanguard, outpost.

προφυλακίζω [profeelakeezo] hold in custody, detain.

προφυλακτήρας, ο [profeelakteeras] bumper (AUT).

προφυλακτικός [profeelakteekos] wary, careful || precautionary, preventive.

προφύλαξη, η [profeelaksee] precaution, cautiousness.

προφυλάσσομαι [profeelasome] take precautions, protect o.s.

προφυλάσσω [profeelaso] protect, preserve (from), defend.

πρόχειρος [proheeros] ready, handy || impromptu.

προχθές [prohthes] the day before yesterday.

προχωρώ [prohoro] go forward, advance || progress, gain ground.

προωθώ [proootho] impel || push forward, urge on.

πρόωρος [prooros] premature, untimely, hasty.

πρύμ(ν)η, η [preem(n)ee] stern, poop.

πρύτανης, ο [preetanees] head of university, dean.

πρώην [proeen] former, ex-.

πρωθυπουργός, ο [protheepourgos] prime minister, premier.

πρωί [proee] in the morning || (ουσ) morning.

πρώιμος [proeemos] untimely, premature || (για φυτά) precocious, early.

πρωινός [proeenos] morning || rising early.

πρωινό, το [proeeno] morning || (πρόγευμα) breakfast.

πρωκτός, ο [proktos] anus.

πρώρα, η [prora] prow, bows.

πρώτα [prota] first, at first || before, formerly, once.

πρωταγωνιστής, ο [protagoneestees] protagonist, hero.

πρωτάθλημα, το [protathleema] championship.

πρωτάκουστος [protakoustos] unheard-of, unprecedented.

πρωταρχικός [protarheekos] most important.

πρωτεία, τα [proteea] πλ first place, primacy, precedence.

πρωτεργάτης, ο [protergatees] perpetrator, pioneer, cause.

πρωτεύουσα, η [protevousa] capital, metropolis.

πρωτεύω [protevo] be first, lead, surpass, triumph (over).

πρωτοβάθμιος [protovathmeeos] of the first degree.

πρωτοβουλία, η [protovouleea] initiative.

πρωτοβρόχια, τα [protovroheea] πλ first rains in autumn.

πρωτόγονος [protogonos] primitive || (ήθη) rough, rude, unpolished.

πρωτοδικείο, το [protoδeekeeo] court of first instance.

πρωτοετής [protoetees] first-year.

πρωτόκολλο, το [protokolo] register, record || protocol, etiquette.

Πρωτομαγιά, η [protomaya] May Day.

πρωτομηνιά, η [protomeenia] first day of month.

πρώτο [proto] first, firstly, in the first place, to start with.

πρωτοπορεία, η [protoporeea] vanguard.

πρωτοπόρος, ο [protoporos] pioneer, forerunner, innovator.

πρώτος [protos] first, foremost || best, top || initial, elementary || (αριθμός) prime.

πρωτοστατώ [protostato] lead.

πρωτότοκος [prototokos] first-born, oldest.

πρωτοτυπία, η [prototeepeea] originality || eccentricity.

πρωτότυπο, το [prototeepo] original, pattern, model.

πρωτότυπος [prototeepos] original, novel, singular.

πρωτοφανής [protofanees] new, fresh || astonishing.

Πρωτοχρονιά, η [protohronia] New Year's Day.

πρωτύτερα [proteetera] earlier on, at first, before.

πταισματοδικείο, το [ptesmatoδeekeeo] police court.

πτέρυγα, η [ptereega] wing.

πτερύγιο, το [ptereeyo] fin || aileron, wing flap.

πτερωτός [pterotos] winged.

πτηνό, το [pteeno] bird, fowl.

πτηνοτροφία, η [pteenotrofeea] poultry farming.

πτήση, η [pteesee] flight, flying.

πτοώ [ptoo] intimidate, frighten, browbeat.

πτυχή, η [pteehee] fold, pleat || wrinkle || (πανταλονιού) crease.

πτυχίο, το [pteeheeo] diploma, certificate.

πτυχιούχος [pteeheeouhos] graduate, holding a diploma.

πτώμα, το [ptoma] corpse, dead body || (ζώου) carcass.

πτώση, η [ptosee] fall, tumble || collapse || drop || (γραμμ) case.

πτώχευση, η [ptohevsee] bankruptcy, failure, insolvency.

πτωχεύω [ptohevo] go bankrupt || become poor.

πτωχοκομείο, το [ptohokomeeo] poorhouse.

πτωχός [ptohos] poor, needy.

πυγμαχία, η [peegmaheea] boxing, pugilism.

πυγμή, η [peegmee] fist || (μεταφ) vigour, determination.

πυγολαμπίδα, η [peegolampeeδa] glow-worm, firefly.

πυθμένας, ο [peethmenas] bottom.

πυκνά [peekna] closely, densely, thickly.

πυκνός [peeknos] thick, dense, closely-packed, close || (γένεια) bushy.

πυκνότητα, η [peeknoteeta] density, compactness, thickness || (κυμάτων) frequency.

πυκνώνω [peeknono] thicken, condense, grow thick || make more frequent.

πυκνωτής, ο [peeknotees] (ηλεκ) condenser.

πύλη, η [peelee] gate, gateway.

πυξίδα, η [peekseeδa] (mariner's) compass || box.

πύο, το [peeo] pus, matter.

πυρ, το [peer] fire, firing.

πυρά, η [peera] fire || (μεταφ) sensation of burning.

πυρακτώνω [peeraktono] make red-hot, glow.

πυραμίδα, η [peerameeδa] pyramid.

πύραυλος, ο [peeravlos] rocket.

πύργος, ο [peergos] tower || castle, palace || (ναυτ) bridge house.

πυρετός, ο [peeretos] high temperature, fever || (μεταφ) activity, energy.

πυρετώδης [peeretoδees] feverish || (μεταφ) restless, feverish.

πυρήνας, ο [peereenas] stone, pip || centre, core || nucleus.

πυρηνέλαιο, το [peereeneleo] oil from stones || seed oil.

πυρηνικός [peereeneekos] nuclear.

πύρινος [peereenos] burning, fiery, red-hot || (μεταφ) ardent, fervent.

πυρίτης, ο [peereetees] pyrites, flint.

πυρίτιδα, η [peereeteeδa] gunpowder, powder.

πυρκαϊά, η [peerkaeea] fire, burning, conflagration.

πυροβολητής, ο [peerovoleetees] gunner.

πυροβολικό, το [peerovoleeko] artillery.

πυροβολισμός, ο [peerovoleesmos] firing, shot.

πυροβολώ [peerovolo] fire || shoot at || shell.

πυρομαχικά, τα [peeromaheeka] πλ munitions || ammunition.

πυροσβέστης, ο [peerosvestees] fireman.

πυροσβεστική [peerosvesteekee]: ~ υπηρεσία fire brigade.

πυροτέχνημα, το [peerotehneema] firework, cracker.

πυρπολικό, το [peerpoleeko] fire ship.

πυρπολώ [peerpolo] set on fire, burn down, consume by fire.

πυρσός, ο [peersos] torch, brand || beacon.

πυρώνω [peerono] get red-hot, heat.

πυτζάμα, η [peedzama] pyjamas.

πυώδης [peeodees] full of pus.

πωλείται [poleete]: ' ~ ' 'for sale'.

πώληση, η [poleesee] sale, selling.

πωλητής, ο [poleetees] seller || salesman || shop assistant.

πωλήτρια, η [poleetreea] seller || saleswoman.

πωλώ [polo] sell || (μεταφ) sell, betray.

πώμα, το [poma] stopper, plug || (μποτίλιας) cork || lid, cover.

πωρόλιθος, ο [poroleethos] porous stone.

πώρωση, η [porosee] hardening || (μεταφ) insensibility, callousness.

πώς [pos] how?, what? || ~ όχι; and why not? || ~! yes, certainly.

πως [pos] that.

πως [pos] somewhat, somehow, in any way.

P, ρ

ραββίνος, ο [raveenos] rabbi.

ραβδί, το [ravδee] cane, stick.

ραβδίζω [ravδeezo] flog, thrash, cane.

ράβδος, η [ravδos] stick, staff || (μαγική) wand || (εκκλ) pastoral staff || (σιδηροδρομική) rail.

ράβδωση, η [ravδosee] stripe || (αρχιτεκτονική) fluting || groove.

ραβδωτός [ravδotos] striped || fluted || lined, ruled.

ράβω [ravo] sew up, sew on || stitch || (κοστούμι) have a suit made.

ραγάδα, η [ragaδa] crack, fissure, chink.

ραγδαίος [ragδeos] violent, turbulent || (πτώση) rapid, headlong || (πρόοδος) rapid, speedy.

ραγδαίως [ragδeos] violently, impetuously, swiftly.

ραγίζω [rayeezo] crack, split.

ράγισμα, το [rayeesma] crack, fissure, split.

ραδιενέργεια, η [raδienerya] radioactivity.

ραδιενεργός [raδienergos] radioactive.

ραδίκι, το [raδeekee] chicory, dandelion.

ραδιογραφία, η [raδeeografeea] X-ray photography.

ραδιοθεραπεία, η [raδeeotherapeea] X-ray treatment.

ραδιολογία, η [raδeeoloyeea] radiology.

ράδιο, το [raδeo] radium.

ραδιοτηλεγράφημα, το [raδeeoteelegrafeema] radiotelegram.

ραδιοτηλεγραφία, η [raδeeoteelegrafeea] radiotelegraphy.

ραδιοτηλεφωνία, η [raδeeoteelefoneea] radiotelephony.

ραδιουργία, η [raδiouryeea] intrigue, machination.

ραδιούργος [raδiourgos] scheming, intriguing, plotting.

ραδιόφωνο, το [raδeeofono] radio.

ράθυμος [ratheemos] languid, listless, lazy.

ραίνω [reno] sprinkle, scatter, spread.

ράϊσμα [raeesma] βλ ράγισμα.

ρακένδυτος [rakenδeetos] in rags, tattered.

ρακί, το [rakee] kind of spirit.

ράκος, το [rakos] rag, tatters || (μεταφ) physical wreck.

ράμμα, το [rama] stitch, thread.

ραμμένος [ramenos] sewn.

ραμολής, ο [ramolees] imbecile, half-wit.

ραμφίζω [ramfeezo] peck at, pick up.

ράμφος, το [ramfos] (μεγάλων πουλιών) bill, beak || (μεταφ) burner, jet.

ρανίδα, η [raneeδa] drop, blob.

ραντεβού, το [rantevou] meeting, engagement, rendezvous.

ραντίζω [ranteezo] sprinkle, spray, water.

ράντισμα, το [ranteesma] sprinkling, watering.

ραντιστήρι, το [ranteesteeree] watering can || (εκκλ) sprinkler.

ράντσο, το [rantso] campbed.

ραπάνι, το [rapanee] radish.

ραπίζω [rapeezo] slap or smack in the face.

ράπισμα, το [rapeesma] clout, slap.

ραπτάδικο, το [raptaδeeko] βλ ραφτάδικο.

ράπτης, ο [raptees] tailor.

ραπτικά, τα [rapteeka] πλ fees for tailoring, fees for sewing.

ραπτική, η [rapteekee] βλ ραφτική.

ραπτομηχανή, η [raptomeehanee] sewing machine.

ράπτρια, η [raptreea] dressmaker.

ράπτω [rapto] βλ ράβω.

ράσο, το [raso] frock, cassock.

ρασοφόρος, ο [rasoforos] priest, monk.

ράτσα, η [ratsa] race, generation, breed || **από** ~ thoroughbred.

ραφείο, το [rafeeo] tailor's shop.

ραφή, η [rafee] dressmaking || stitching, seam.

ράφι, το [rafee] shelf || (τοίχου) bracket || **μένω στο** ~ be left on the shelf, be an old maid.

ραφινάρισμα, το [rafeenareesma] refinement.

ραφινάρω [rafeenaro] refine || purify, polish.

ραφτάδικο, το [raftaδeeko] tailor's shop.

ράφτης, ο [raftees] βλ **ράπτης**.

ραφτικά, τα [rafteeka] βλ **ραπτικά**.

ραφτική, η [rafteekee] dressmaking, sewing, tailoring.

ραχάτι, το [rahatee] lazing about, idling, leisure.

ράχη, η [rahee] back, backbone || (βιβλίου) spine || (βουνού) crest, ridge.

ραχιτικός [raheeteekos] suffering from rickets.

ραχοκοκκαλιά, η [rahokokalia] backbone, spine.

ράψιμο, το [rapseemo] sewing, stitching || tailoring, dressmaking.

ραψωδία, η [rapsoδeea] rhapsody.

ρεαλισμός, ο [realeesmos] realism.

ρεαλιστής, ο [realeestees] realist.

ρεβεγιόν, το [reveyion] midnight supper.

ρεβίθι, το [reveethee] chickpea.

ρέγγα, η [renga] herring.

ρέγουλα, η [regoula] order, regular arrangement || moderation, measure.

ρεζέρβα, η [rezerva] stock || (λάστιχου κτλ) spare wheel.

ρεζιλεύω [rezeelevo] ridicule, make a fool of || humiliate.

ρεζίλι, το [rezeelee] shame, derision, object of ridicule || **γίνομαι** ~ become a laughing stock.

ρεζιλίκι [rezeeleekee] βλ **ρεζίλι**.

ρείθρο, το [reethro] watercourse, rivulet || ditch, gutter (of street).

ρεκλάμα, η [reklama] advertisement || show, display.

ρεκλαμάρω [reklamaro] advertise.

ρεκόρ, το [rekor] record.

ρεμάλι, το [remalee] worthless person.

ρεματιά, η [rematia] ravine, torrent, riverbed.

ρεμβάζω [remvazo] muse, daydream, be in a reverie.

ρεμβασμός, ο [remvasmos] musing, reverie.

ρέμπελος [rembelos] lazy, sluggish || disorderly.

ρεπάνι, το [repanee] radish.

ρεπερτόριο, το [repertoreeo] repertoire.

ρεπό, το [repo] time off, break, rest period, rest.

ρέπω [repo] lean, incline, slope || (μεταφ) tend towards.

ρεσιτάλ, το [reseetal] recital.

ρέστα, τα [resta] πλ change.

ρετάλι, το [retalee] remnant.

ρετσίνα, η [retseena] resinated wine.

ρετσινόλαδο, το [retseenolaδo] castor oil.

ρεύμα, το [revma] current, stream, flow || (αέρος) draught.

ρευματισμός, ο [revmateesmos] rheumatism.

ρεύομαι [revome] belch.

ρεύση, η [revsee] outflow, flowing || emission.

ρευστοποιώ [revstopeeo] liquefy.

ρευστός [revstos] fluid, liquid || (μεταφ) fickle, inconstant, changeable.

ρευστότητα, η [revstoteeta] fluidity || (μεταφ) inconstancy.

ρεφενές, ο [refenes] share, quota.

ρεφορμιστής, ο [reformeestees] reformist.

ρέψιμο, το [repseemo] belching || decay.

ρέω [reo] flow, stream || (σταγόνες) trickle || (δάκρυα) fall.

ρήγας, ο [reegas] (χαρτιά) king.

ρήγμα, το [reegma] crack, breach, fissure, hole || (μεταφ) rupture.

ρήμα, το [reema] word, saying || (γραμμ) verb.

ρημάδι, το [reemaδee] ruin || wreckage, derelict || **κλείσ' το** ~ shut the blooming thing!

ρημάζω [reemazo] ruin, destroy || fall into ruins.

ρήξη, η [reeksee] rupture, breach || conflict, quarrel, dispute.

ρητίνη, η [reeteenee] resin.

ρητό, το [reeto] maxim, saying, motto.

ρητορεύω [reetorevo] make speeches, harangue.

ρητορική, η [reetoreekee] oratory.

ρητός [reetos] formal, explicit, flat, positive.

ρήτρα, η [reetra] clause, proviso, provision.

ρήτορας, ο [reetoras] orator.

ρητώς [reetos] explicitly, expressly, flatly.

ρηχά, τα [reeha] πλ shallows.

ρίγα, η [reega] ruler, measuring rule || line, stripe.

ρίγανη, η [reeganee] origanum.

ριγέ [reeye] striped.

ρίγος, το [reegos] shiver || thrill.

ριγώ [reego] shiver, tremble, thrill.

ριγωτός [reegotos] (χάρτης) lined, ruled || (ύφασμα) striped.

ρίζα, n [reeza] root || (βουνού) foot, base || (μεταφ) origin, source, cause.

ριζικό, το [reezeeko] destiny, fortune, lot, fate.

ριζικός [reezeekos] radical, fundamental.

ριζόγαλο, το [reezogalo] rice pudding.

ριζόνερο, το [reezonero] rice water.

ριζοσπάστης, ο [reezospastees] radical.

ριζοσπαστικός [reezospasteekos] radical.

ριζώνω [reezono] become established, become fixed, take root, grow.

ρίμα, n [reema] rhyme.

ρινικός [reeneekos] nasal.

ρινίσματα, τα [reeneesmata] πλ filings.

ρινόκερος, ο [reenokeros] rhinoceros.

ριξιά, n [reeksia] throw, cast(ing) || (όπλου) charge || shot, firing.

ρίξιμο, το [reekseemo] casting, throwing || dropping || (όπλου) firing, shooting.

ριπή, n [reepee] burst of firing, throwing || (ανέμου) gust, blast.

ρίπτω [reepto] βλ **ρίχνω**.

ρίχνομαι [reehnome] fling o.s., rush || (στο νερό) plunge.

ρίχνω [reehno] throw, fling, cast || (βόμβα) drop || (όπλο) shoot, fire || (ανατρέπω) overthrow, defeat || (τοίχο) pull down, demolish || (δένδρο) hew, fell || **ρίχνει βροχή** it's raining.

ριψοκινδυνεύω [reepsokeendeenevo] risk, endanger || take risks.

ρόγχος, ο [ronghos] rattle, blowing || death rattle.

ρόδα, n [roða] wheel.

ροδάκινο, το [roðakeeno] peach.

ροδαλός [roðalos] rosy, light pink.

ροδέλα, n [roðela] washer.

ρόδι, το [roðee] pomegranate.

ρόδινος [roðeenos] rosy || (μεταφ) rose-coloured, bright.

ροδίτης, ο [roðeetees] kind of pink grape.

ροδοδάφνη, n [roðoðafnee] oleander.

ροδοκόκκινος [roðokokeenos] ruddy, rose-red.

ρόδο, το [roðo] rose.

ροζ [roz] pink.

ροζιάρικος [rozeeareekos] gnarled.

ρόζος, ο [rozos] knot, node || (δακτύλων) knuckle.

ροή, n [roee] flow, flood || (ρύου) discharge, running.

ρόκα, n [roka] distaff || (χόρτο) rocket.

ροκάνα, n [rokana] (παιχνίδι) rattle.

ροκάνι, το [rokanee] plane.

ροκανίδι, το [rokaneeðee] chip, shaving.

ροκανίζω [rokaneezo] plane || (μεταφ) gnaw, crunch.

ροκέτα, n [roketa] rocket.

ρολό, το [rolo] cylindrical roll || shutter.

ρολογάς, ο [rologas] watchmaker, clockmaker.

ρολόι, το [roloee] (τοίχου) clock || (χεριού) watch || (μετρητής) meter || **πάει** ~ it's going smoothly.

ρόλος, ο [rolos] roll || (θεατρικός) part, role || (μεταφ) part || **δεν παίζει ρόλο** it's not important.

ρομάντζο, το [romantzo] romance.

ρομαντικός [romanteekos] romantic.

ρομαντικότητα, n [romanteekoteeta] romanticism.

ρόμβος, ο [romvos] rhombus.

ρόμπα, n [romba] dressing gown.

ρόπαλο, το [ropalo] club.

ροπή, n [ropee] inclination, propensity || (μηχανής) momentum.

ρουζ, το [rouz] rouge.

ρουθούνι, το [routhounee] nostril.

ρουθουνίζω [routhouneezo] snort, sniff, snuffle.

ρουκέτα [rouketa] βλ **ροκέτα**.

ρουλεμάν, το [rouleman] ball bearings, roller bearings.

ρουλέτα, n [rouleta] roulette.

Ρουμανία, n [roumaneea] Rumania.

ρουμανικός [roumaneekos] Rumanian.

Ρουμάνος, ο [roumanos] Rumanian.

ρούμι, το [roumee] rum.

ρουμπίνι, το [roumbeenee] ruby.

ρούπι, το [roupee] measure of length (.08 m) || **δεν το κουνάω** ~ I refuse to move.

ρους, ο [rous] βλ **ροή**.

ρουσφέτι, το [rousfetee] favour, string pulling, political favour.

ρουτίνα, n [routeena] routine.

ρούφη(γ)μα, το [roufee(g)ma] noisy sipping, gulp, sucking in.

ρουφηξιά, n [roufeeksia] mouthful, sip || (πίπας κτλ) puff.

ρουφήχτρα, n [roufeehtra] whirlpool.

ρουφιάνος, ο [roufeeanos] pimp || schemer.

ρουφώ [roufo] draw in, suck up, absorb, sip.

ρουχικά, τα [rouheeka] πλ clothing, garments.

ρούχο, το [rouho] cloth, stuff, material || (φόρεμα) dress, attire.

ρόφημα, το [rofeema] hot drink.

ροχαλητό, το [rohaleeto] snore, snoring.

ροχαλίζω [rohaleezo] snore.

ρόχαλο, το [rohalo] phlegm, spit.

ρυάκι, το [reeakee] stream, brook, rivulet.

ρύγχος, το [reenghos] muzzle, nose, snout || nozzle.

ρύζι, το [reezee] rice.

ρυζόγαλο, το [reezogalo] rice pudding.

ρυθμίζω [reethmeezo] (ρολόι) regulate, set right || (τα του σπιτιού) manage || (υποθέσεις) settle || (λογαριασμούς) close, make up.

ρυθμικός [reethmeekos] rhythmical.

ρύθμιση, η [reethmeesee] regulating, adjusting.

ρυθμιστής, ο [reethmeestees] regulator.

ρυθμός, ο [reethmos] rhythm, rate || (μουσ) cadence || (αρχιτεκτονική) order, style.

ρυμοτομία, η [reemotomeea] street plan, roadmaking.

ρυμούλκα, η [reemoulka] trailer.

ρυμούλκηση, η [reemoulkeesee] towing, dragging.

ρυμουλκό, το [reemoulko] tugboat, steam tug || (τρακτέρ) tractor.

ρυμουλκώ [reemoulko] tow, tug, drag, pull || (μεταφ) drag by the nose.

ρυπαίνω [reepeno] make dirty, soil || (μεταφ) defile, tarnish.

ρύπανση, η [reepansee] dirtying, blemishing, defiling || pollution.

ρύπος, ο [reepos] filth, dirt || (μεταφ) disgrace, shame.

ρυτίδα, η [reeteeða] wrinkle, seam, line || (της θάλασσας) ripple.

ρυτιδώνω [reeteeðono] wrinkle, line || get wrinkled.

ρω, το [ro] the letter P.

ρώγα, η [roga] nipple.

ρωγμή, η [rogmee] crack, split, cleft, crevice.

ρωμαίικα, τα [romeika] Modern Greek, Demotic Greek || **μίλα ~!** come to the point!

ρωμαϊκός [romaeekos] Roman.

Ρωμαίος, ο [romeos] Roman.

ρωμαλέος [romaleos] robust, strong, vigorous, sturdy.

ρώμη, η [romee] vigour, strength, force, robustness.

Ρώμη, η [romee] Rome.

Ρωμιός, ο [romios] modern Greek.

Ρωμιοσύνη, η [romioseenee] the modern Greek people.

Ρωσία, η [roseea] Russia.

Ρώσος, ο [rosos] Russian (person).

ρωτώ [roto] βλ **ερωτώ**.

Σ, σ

σα [sa] βλ **σαν**.

σάβανο, το [savano] winding sheet, shroud.

σάββατο, το [savato] Saturday.

σαββατοκύριακο, το [savatokeereeako] weekend.

σαβούρα, η [savoura] rubbish, junk, trash || ballast.

σαγανάκι, το [saganakee] frying pan || (φαγητό) dish of fried cheese.

σαγή, η [sayee] harness.

σαγηνεύω [sayeenevo] seduce, charm, attract.

σαγήνη, η [sayeenee] fascination, enchantment.

σαγόνι, το [sagonee] chin.

σαδισμός, ο [saðeesmos] sadism.

σαδιστής, ο [saðeestees] sadist.

σαθρός [sathros] rotted, decayed, rotten || (μεταφ) groundless.

σαιζόν, η [sezon] season.

σαΐτα, η [saeeta] arrow, dart || weaver's shuttle.

σάκα, η [saka] (μαθητική) satchel || (κυνηγού) game pouch, gamebag || briefcase.

σακάκι, το [sakakee] jacket, coat.

σακαράκα, η [sakaraka] (μεταφ) tin lizzie (col), old motorcar, old bike.

σακατεύω [sakatevo] cripple, mutilate, maim || (μεταφ) wear out, exhaust.

σακάτης, ο [sakatees] cripple, maimed person.

σακί, το [sakee] sack, bag.

σακίδιο, το [sakeeðeeo] haversack, satchel, small bag.

σακοράφα, η [sakorafa] sack needle, packing needle.

σάκος, ο [sakos] sack, bag, sackful || (ταχυδρομικός) mailbag || kitbag.

σακούλα, η [sakoula] sack, bag || paper bag.

σακούλι, το [sakoulee] sack, small bag.

σακουλιάζω [sakouleeazo] put into a bag, put into a sack, pocket || (για ρούχα) be loose-fitting, not fit well.

σαλάμι, το [salamee] sausage, salami.

σαλαμούρα, η [salamoura] brine.

σαλάτα, η [salata] salad || **τα κάνω ~** make a muddle of it, foul up the works.

σάλεμα, το [salema] moving, stirring, shaking.

σαλεύω [salevo] move, stir, shake || budge.

σάλι, το [salee] shawl.

σάλιαγκας, ο [saleeangas] snail.

σαλιάζω [saleeazo] salivate.

σαλιάρα, η [saleeara] baby's bib.

σαλιαρίζω [saleeareezo] chatter, prattle.

σαλιγκάρι [saleengaree] βλ **σάλιαγκας**.

σάλιο, το [saleeo] saliva, spittle.

σαλιώνω [saleeono] lick, moisten, dampen, wet.

Σ

σαλόνι, το [salonee] drawing room || (πλοίου) saloon.

σάλος, ο [salos] swell, surge || (πλοίου) rolling || (μεταφ) disturbance || tumult.

σαλπάρω [salparo] weigh anchor.

σάλπιγκα, η [salpeenga] trumpet, bugle || (ανατ) tube.

σαλπίζω [salpeezo] sound the trumpet.

σάλπισμα, το [salpeesma] trumpet call.

σαλτάρω [saltaro] jump, leap.

σαλτιμπάγκος, ο [salteembangos] fairground acrobat || (μεταφ) charlatan, buffoon.

σάλτος, ο [saltos] jump, leap, bound.

σάλτσα, η [saltsa] gravy, sauce.

σαμάρι, το [samaree] packsaddle.

σαμαρώνω [samarono] saddle, pack.

σαματάς, ο [samatas] (φασαρία) noise, din, roar || fight.

σάματι(ς) [samatee(s)] as though.

σαμπάνια, η [sampaneea] champagne.

σαμποτάζ, το [sampotaz] sabotage.

σαμποτάρω [sampotaro] sabotage.

σαμπρέλα, η [sambrela] inner tube.

σάμπως [sambos] as though || it appears that.

σαν [san] when, as soon as, if || like, as if || ~ σήμερα πέρσυ about a year ago today || ~ τι; like what? || ~ να as though.

σανατόριο, το [sanatoreeo] sanatorium.

σανδάλι, το [sanðalee] sandal.

σανίδα, η [saneeða] board, beam, plank || (σιδερώματος) ironing board.

σανιδώνω [saneeðono] floor, plank, cover with board.

σανός, ο [sanos] hay, fodder.

σαντιγύ, το [santeeyee] chantilly.

σάντουιτς, το [santoueets] sandwich.

σαντούρι, το [santouree] kind of string instrument.

σαπίζω [sapeezo] rot, spoil, decompose, decay.

σαπίλα, η [sapeela] decay, putridity || (μεταφ) corruption, dishonesty.

σάπιος [sapeeos] decomposed, rotten || corrupt, depraved, wicked.

σαπουνάδα, η [sapounaða] soapsuds, lather.

σαπούνι, το [sapounee] soap || (ξυρίσματος) shaving soap.

σαπουνίζω [sapouneezo] soap || lather.

σαπουνόφουσκα, η [sapounofouska] soap bubble.

σαπωνοποιός, ο [saponopeeos] soap manufacturer.

σάρα, η [sara]: η ~ και η μάρα rabble.

σαράβαλο, το [saravalo] ruin, wreck || sickly person.

σαράκι, το [sarakee] woodworm || (μεταφ) remorse, prick of conscience.

σαρακοστή, η [sarakostee] Lent.

σαράντα [saranta] forty.

σαρανταποδαρούσα, η [sarantapoðarousa] centipede.

σαρανταριά, η [sarantaria] forty.

σαραντίζω [saranteezo] become forty || be forty days since.

σαράφης, ο [sarafees] moneychanger.

σαρδέλα, η [sarðela] anchovy || sardine.

σαρδόνιος [sarðoneeos] sardonic, sarcastic.

σαρίκι, το [sareekee] turban.

σάρκα, η [sarka] flesh.

σαρκασμός, ο [sarkasmos] derision, raillery, sarcasm.

σαρκαστικός [sarkasteekos] sarcastic, jeering, mocking.

σαρκικός [sarkeekos] carnal, fleshy, sensual.

σαρκοβόρος [sarkovoros], σαρκοφάγος [sarkofagos] carnivorous, flesh-eating || η σαρκοφάγος sarcophagus.

σαρκώδης [sarkoðees] fleshy || (φρούτο) pulpy.

σάρκωμα, το [sarkoma] sarcoma, fleshy growth.

σάρπα, η [sarpa] scarf.

σάρωμα, το [saroma] sweeping.

σαρώνω [sarono] (δωμάτιο) sweep || (δρόμο) scavenge || (μεταφ) rake.

σας [sas] you || your.

σασ(σ)ί, το [sasee] chassis.

σαστίζω [sasteezo] disconcert, embarrass, confuse || get disconcerted.

σατανάς, ο [satanas] Satan || (μεταφ) devilish person.

σατανικός [sataneekos] devilish, satanical, fiendish.

σατέν, το [saten] satin.

σατράπης, ο [satrapees] satrap || (μεταφ) tyrant.

σάτυρα, η [sateera] satire, skit, lampoon.

σατυρίζω [sateereezo] satirize, ridicule.

σατιρικός [sateereekos] satirical.

σάτυρος, ο [sateeros] satyr || (μεταφ) debauchee.

σαύρα, η [savra] lizard.

σαφήνεια, η [safeeneea] clearness, distinctness, lucidity.

σαφηνίζω [safeeneezo] clarify, elucidate, explain.

σαφής [safees] clear, obvious, plain.

σαφώς [safos] clearly, obviously.

σαχλαμάρα, η [sahlamara] nonsense, rubbish.

σαχλός [sahlos] flat, flabby || stupid.

σβάρνα, η [svarna] harrow.

σβέλτος [sveltos] nimble || slim, slender.

σβέρκος, ο [sverkos] nape of neck, scruff.

σβήνω [sveeno] extinguish, quench, put out || (γράμματα) erase || (διά τριβής) rub out || (με πένα κτλ) strike out || (φωτιά) die out || (χρώμα) fade || (ενθουσιασμός) subside, die down.

σβήσιμο, το [sveeseemo] extinction || erasure, rubbing out.

σβηστός [sveestos] put out, extinguished, switched off.

σβούρα, η [svoura] spinning top.

σβύνω [sveeno] βλ σβήνω.

σβώλος, ο [svolos] lump (of earth) || ball, clod.

σγουραίνω [sgoureno] curl || become curly.

σγουρός [sgouros] curly, fuzzy, curled || curly-haired.

σε [se] you || to, at, in.

σέβας, το [sevas], σεβασμός, ο [sevasmos] regard, reverence, deference.

σεβάσμιος [sevasmeeos] venerable, respectable, reverend.

σεβαστός [sevastos] respected || respectable, considerable.

σέβη, τα [sevee] πλ respects.

σεβντάς, ο [sevntas] love, yearning.

σέβομαι [sevome] respect, venerate, admire, esteem.

σειρά, η [seera] series, succession || row, line, rank || (στην τάξη) turn || sequence, order || με τη ~ in turn, in order || μπαίνω σε ~ settle down.

σειρήνα, η [seereena] siren, enchantress || hooter, buzzer, alarm.

σειρήτι, το [seereetee] stripe, ribbon, braid.

σεισμικός [seesmeekos] seismic.

σεισμογράφος, ο [seesmografos] seismograph.

σεισμόπληκτος [seesmopleektos] struck by earthquake.

σεισμός, ο [seesmos] earthquake.

σείω [seeo] move, shake, wave.

σέλα, η [sela] saddle.

σέλας, το [selas] brightness, brilliance, radiance || βόρειο ~ northern lights, aurora borealis.

σελάχι, το [selahee] gun belt || (ψάρι) ray.

σελήνη, η [seleenee] moon.

σεληνιασμός, ο [seleeneeasmos] epilepsy.

σελνόφως, το [seleenofos] moonlight.

σελίδα, η [seleeδa] page (of book).

σελίνι, το [seleenee] shilling.

σέλινο, το [seleeno] celery.

σελώνω [selono] saddle.

σεμινάριο, το [semeenareeo] seminary.

σεμνός [semnos] decent, unassuming, modest || (ενδυμασία) simple, plain.

σεμνότητα, η [semnoteeta] dignity, modesty, decency.

σεμνότυφος [semnoteefos] prudish, demure, priggish.

σένα [sena] you.

σεντόνι, το [sentonee] sheet.

σεντούκι, το [sentoukee] linen closet || box, chest.

σέξ, το [seks] sex.

σεξουαλικότητα, η [seksoualeekoteeta] sexual instinct, sexuality.

Σεπτέμβρης, ο [septemvrees], Σεπτέμβριος, ο [septemvreeos] September.

σέρα, η [sera] greenhouse, glasshouse.

σερβίρισμα, το [serveereesma] waiting on, serving.

σερβίρω [serveero] wait at table, serve.

σερβιτόρα, η [serveetora] waitress.

σερβιτόρος, ο [serveetoros] waiter.

σερβίτσιο, το [serveetseeo] dinner service || place setting.

σεργιάνι, το [seryanee] walk, promenade.

σερμπέτι, το [sermbetee] sherbet, syrup.

σέρνομαι [sernome] creep, crawl, drag || drag o.s. along.

σέρνω [serno] draw, pull, drag || (βαρύ πράγμα) haul || (χορό) lead || ~ φωνή scream, shriek, cry out.

σεσημασμένος [seseesmasmenos] criminal.

σεφτές, ο [seftes] first sale (of a day).

σήκωμα, το [seekoma] raising, lifting || getting out of bed.

σηκωμός, ο [seekomos] rising, rebellion.

σηκώνομαι [seekonome] rise, stand up, get up || (επαναστατώ) rebel.

σηκώνω [seekono] raise, hoist, pick up, lift up || (μεταφέρω) carry || (αφυπνίζω) get up || (ανέχομαι) bear, tolerate || ~ το τραπέζι clear the table || ~ στο πόδι incite, rouse, disturb || ~ κεφάλι become arrogant, rebel.

σηκώτι, το [seekotee] liver.

σήμα, το [seema] signal, sign, mark, badge || ~ κατατεθέν trademark, registration mark.

σημαδεμένος [seemaδemenos] marked || maimed, scarred.

σημαδεύω [seemaδevo] mark || aim at, take aim at.

σημάδι, το [seemaδee] trace, scar, spot || (ένδειξη) sign, mark, indication.

σημαδούρα, η [seemaδoura] buoy.

σημαία, η [seemea] flag, ensign, colours, standard.

σημαίνω [seemeno] mean, be a sign

of, signify || (καμπάνα κτλ) ring, strike, sound, signal || (έχων σημασία) matter, be of consequence.

σημαιοφόρος, ο [seemeoforos] standard bearer || (ναυτ) ensign, sub-lieutenant || (μεταφ) leader.

σήμανση, η [seemansee] marking, stamping || noting of details.

σημαντικός [seemanteekos] important, significant || (πρόσωπο) remarkable, considerable || momentous.

σήμαντρο, το [seemantro] stamp, seal || (εκκλ) special monastery bell.

σημασία, η [seemasea] sense, meaning || importance, gravity, significance.

σημείο, το [seemeeo] sign, mark, proof, indication || (θέση, βαθμός) stage, point || (μαθημ) symbol, sign || ~ **του ορίζοντος** point of the compass.

σημείωμα, το [seemeeoma] written note, memorandum, record.

σημειωματάριο, το [seemeeomatareeo] notebook, agenda, diary.

σημείωση, η [seemeeosee] written note || remark, comment.

σημειωτέος [seemeeoteos] to be noted || noticeable, noteworthy.

σήμερα [seemera] today || ~ **το απόγευμα** this evening, this afternoon.

σήπομαι [seepome] rot, decay, decompose.

σηπτικός [seepteekos] septic.

σήραγγα, η [seeranga] tunnel.

σηψαιμία, η [seepsemeea] septicaemia, blood poisoning.

σήψη, η [seepsee] decay, putrefaction || (ιατρ) sepsis.

σθεναρός [sthenaros] sturdy, strong, vigorous, powerful, robust.

σθένος, το [sthenos] vigour, strength, energy || courage, pluck.

σιαγώνα, η [seeagona] jaw || (ανατ) jawbone.

σιάζω [seeazo] arrange, set in order, straighten, tidy || (επισκευάζω) repair, mend, patch.

σίαλος, ο [seealos] saliva, spittle.

σιάξιμο, το [seeakseemo] tidying.

σιγά [seega] softly, lightly, gently, slowly || ~ ~ carefully, by degrees.

σιγαλός [seegalos] silent, quiet, gentle, still || (επίρ) slowly.

σιγανός [seeganos] βλ **σιγαλός**.

σιγαρέτο, το [seegareto] cigarette.

σιγή, η [seeyee] silence, hush.

σίγμα, το [seegma] the letter Σ.

σιγοβράζω [seegovrazo] simmer.

σίγουρα [seegoura] for certain, for sure.

σίγουρος [seegouros] certain, assured, sure || (φάρμακο) infallible.

σιγώ [seego] keep quiet, remain silent || die down.

σίδερα, τα [seedera] πλ ironwork || (γραμμές) railway lines || (φυλακή) irons, fetters.

σιδεράς, ο [seederas] blacksmith, ironmonger.

σιδερένιος [seedereneos] of iron.

σιδερικά, τα [seedereeka] πλ scrap iron || ironware.

σίδερο, το [seedero] iron || (σιδερώματος) flatiron || (μαλλιών) curling tongs.

σιδέρωμα, το [seederoma] ironing, pressing.

σιδερώνω [seederono] iron.

σιδηροδρομικός [seedeerodromeekos] of railways.

σιδηροδρομικώς [seedeerodromeekos] by rail, by train.

σιδηρόδρομος, ο [seedeerodromos] railway, railroad.

σιδηροπυρίτης, ο [seedeeropeereetees] pyrites.

σίδηρος, ο [seedeeros] iron.

σιδηροτροχιά, η [seedeerotrohia] railway track.

σιδηρουργείο, το [seedeerouryeeo] forge, smithy.

σιδηρουργός, ο [seedeerourgos] blacksmith.

σιδηρωρυχείο, το [seedeeroreeheeo] iron mine.

σίελος, ο [sielos] βλ **σίαλος**.

σικ [seek] chic, stylishness || (επίθ) smart, stylish.

σίκαλη, η [seekalee] rye.

σιλό, το [seelo] silo.

σιλουέτα, η [seeloueta] silhouette, figure.

σιμά [seema] near, close by.

σιμιγδάλι, το [seemeegdalee] semolina.

σιμώνω [seemono] approach, draw near.

σινάπι, το [seenapee] mustard, mustard seed.

σινιάλο, το [seeneealo] βλ **σήμα**.

σινικός [seeneekos]: **σινική μελάνη** India ink.

σιντριβάνι, το [seentreevanee] fountain.

σιρόκος, ο [seerokos] south-east wind.

σιρόπι, το [seeropee] syrup.

σιταρένιος [seetareneos] wheaten, of wheat.

σιτάρι, το [seetaree] wheat, grain.

σιτεύω [seetevo] fatten || (το κρέας) hang, make tender.

σιτηρά, τα [seeteera] πλ cereals.

σιτίζω [seeteezo] feed, nurture, nourish.

σιτοβολόνας, ο [seetovolonas] granary, barn.

σίτος, ο [seetos] βλ **σιτάρι**.

σιφόνι, το [seefonee] siphon.

σιφονιέρα, η [seefoniera] chest of drawers.

σίφουνας, ο [seefounas] waterspout, whirlwind.

σιχαίνομαι [seehenome] loathe, detest, feel disgust for.

σιχαμένος [seehamenos] loathsome, sickening.

σιχαμερός [seehameros] disgusting, repulsive.

σιωπή η [seeopee] silence.

σιωπηλός [seeopeelos] silent, quiet, noiseless.

σιωπηρός [seeopeeros] tacit.

σιωπώ [seeopo] remain silent || hold one's tongue.

σκάβω [skavo] βλ **σκάπτω.**

σκάγι, το [skayee] small shot, pellet.

σκάζω [skazo] burst, open, split, crack || (ξύλο κτλ) split, splinter || (οβίδα) burst, explode || be exasperated, be infuriated (by) || **το ~** make off || **σκάσε!** shut up!

σκαθάρι, το [skatharee] scarab(ee).

σκάκι, το [skakee] chess.

σκάλα, η [skala] stairs, staircase, flight, ladder || (υπηρεσίας) backstairs || (αποβάθρα) wharf, landing stage || (λιμάνι) port || (μουσ) scale || (μαλλιών) wave.

σκαλί, το [skalee] step, flight, rung || grade.

σκαλίζω [skaleezo] hoe, weed, dig || (μέταλλο) chisel || (πέτρα κτλ) sculpture || (ξύλο) carve || (φωτιά) stir, poke || (βιβλιοθήκη κτλ) rummage, seek, search.

σκάλιωμα, το [skaleesma] weeding, hoeing || searching || carving, sculpting.

σκαλιστήρι, το [skaleesteeree] hoe, weeding fork.

σκαλιστής, ο [skaleestees] carver, engraver, chiseller.

σκαλιστός, [skaleestos] engraved, carved, chiselled, sculptured.

σκαλοπάτι, το [skalopatee] step, rung.

σκάλωμα, το [skaloma] scaling || (μεταφ) hitch, impediment.

σκαλώνω [skalono] climb, mount || (μεταφ) get held up, meet with an obstacle.

σκαλωσιά, η [skalosia] scaffolding.

σκαμνί, το [skamnee] stool || chair.

σκαμπίλι, το [skambeelee] slap, smack.

σκαμπιλίζω [skambeeleezo] slap.

σκανδάλη, η [skanðalee] trigger.

σκανδαλιάρης, ο [skanðaliarees] unruly or muddled or mischievous person.

σκανδαλίζομαι [skanðaleezome] be tempted || be shocked.

σκανδαλίζω [skanðaleezo] intrigue, allure || scandalize, shock, offend.

σκάνδαλο, το [skanðalo] scandal || intrigue.

σκανδαλώδης [skanðaloðees] scandalous, disgraceful.

σκαντζόχοιρος, ο [skandzoheeros] hedgehog.

σκαπάνη, η [skapanee] mattock, pickaxe, pick.

σκαπουλάρω [skapoularo] escape from, elude.

σκάπτω [skapto] dig up, scoop out || (τάφρο) excavate || (χαράσσω) engrave, carve, chisel.

σκάρα [skara] βλ **εσχάρα.**

σκαρί, το [skaree] slipway || (μεταφ) character, make-up, idiosyncrasy.

σκαρλατίνα, η [skarlateena] scarlet fever.

σκαρπίνι, το [skarpeenee] lace-up shoe.

σκάρτος [skartos] defective, useless, unserviceable.

σκαρφάλωμα, το [skarfaloma] climbing up, scrambling up.

σκαρφαλώνω [skarfalono] climb, clamber up, scramble up.

σκάρωμα, το [skaroma] (μεταφ) fabrication, invention.

σκαρώνω [skarono] (μεταφ) fabricate, invent.

σκασίλα, η [skaseela] chagrin, spite, vexation, distress || **σκασίλα μου!** I couldn't care less!

σκάσιμο, το [skaseemo] fissure, cracking || (δέρματος) chap || (διαφυγή) desertion, escape || (μαθήματος) playing truant.

σκασμός, ο [skasmos] suffocation || resentment || **~!** shut up!, hold your tongue!

σκαστός [skastos] noisy || loud || (στρατ) AWOL || (μαθητής) playing truant.

σκατά, τα [skata] πλ shit (col).

σκάφανδρο, το [skafanðro] diving suit.

σκάφη, η [skafee] trough, tub.

σκαφή, η [skafee] digging.

σκάφος, το [skafos] hull || ship, vessel, boat.

σκάψιμο, το [skapseemo] digging, ploughing || carving.

σκάω [skao] βλ **σκάζω.**

σκεβρός [skevros] crooked, warped, deformed.

σκεβρώνω [skevrono] warp, twist || get warped.

σκέλεθρο, το [skelethro], **σκελετός, ο** [skeletos] skeleton || framework, shape || (αυτοκινήτου) chassis.

σκελετώδης [skeletoðees] bony, emaciated.

σκελίδα, η [skeleeða] clove of garlic.

σκέλος, το [skelos] leg || side.

σκεπάζω [skepazo] cover || protect || hide.

σκεπάρνι, το [skeparnee] adze.

σκέπασμα, το [skepasma] roofing, covering || blanket || lid.

σκεπαστά [skepasta] secretly, on the quiet.

σκεπαστός [skepastos] covered in, veiled, roofed || (μεταφ) secret.

σκέπη, η [skepee] shelter, cover || (μεταφ) protection.

σκεπή, η [skepee] roof.

σκεπτικιστής, ο [skepteekeestees] sceptic, doubtful person.

σκεπτικός [skepteekos] sceptical || pensive, engrossed.

σκέπτομαι [skeptome] think, reflect || contemplate (doing).

σκέρτσα, τα [skertsa] πλ flirtatious ways.

σκέρτσο, το [skertso] charm || jesting, playfulness.

σκέτος [sketos] plain, simple || (καφές) without sugar.

σκεύος, το [skevos] utensil, implement || (εκκλ) vessel.

σκευοφόρος, ο [skevoforos] luggage van, baggage cart.

σκευωρία, η [skevoreea] scheme, machination, intrigue.

σκέψη, η [skepsee] thought, consideration || concern.

σκηνή, η [skeenee] scene, trouble, quarrel || (θεάτρου) action, stage || (τέντα) tent.

σκηνικά, τα [skeeneeka] πλ (stage) scenery.

σκηνικός [skeeneekos] of the stage, theatrical.

σκηνογραφία, η [skeenografeea] stage designing.

σκηνοθεσία, η [skeenotheseea] stage production || (μεταφ) fabrication.

σκηνοθέτης, ο [skeenothetees] stage manager.

σκήπτρο, το [skeeptro] sceptre || (μεταφ) superiority, prevalence.

σκήτη, η [skeetee] small monastery, cloister.

σκιά, η [skia] shade, shadow || phantom.

σκιαγραφώ [skeeagrafo] sketch, line.

σκιάδι, το [skeeaðee] straw hat || sunshade.

σκιάζομαι [skeeazome] be scared, take fright (at).

σκιάζω [skeeazo] shade || conceal the sun || veil, hide || (φοβίζω) frighten || (μεταφ) overshadow.

σκιάχτρο, το [skeeahtro] scarecrow || bogey.

σκιερός [skieros] shady, shadowy.

σκίζομαι [skeezome] struggle.

σκίζω [skeezo] split, cleave, tear, rip || ~ τα ρούχα μου I swear I'm innocent.

σκίουρος, ο [skeeouros] squirrel.

σκιρτώ [skeerto] bound, leap, bounce, hop.

σκίσιμο, το [skeeseemo] tear, rent, laceration || crack.

σκίτσο, το [skeetso] sketch, cartoon.

σκιώδης [skeeoðees] βλ σκιερός.

σκλαβιά, η [sklavia] servitude, slavery || (μεταφ) obligation, drudgery.

σκλάβος, ο [sklavos] slave || captive.

σκλαβώνω [sklavono] subjugate, enslave || (μεταφ) put under obligation.

σκληραγωγώ [skleeragogo] accustom to hardship, season, toughen.

σκληραίνω [skleereno] harden, make hard || become callous.

σκληρός [skleeros] hard, tough || cruel, heartless.

σκληροτράχηλος [skleerotraheelos] opinionated, headstrong, obstinate.

σκληρύνω [skleereeno] βλ σκληραίνω.

σκνίπα, η [skneepa] gnat, midge || (μεταφ) drunk as a lord.

σκοινί, το [skeenee] βλ σχοινί.

σκόλη, η [skolee] holiday, feast day.

σκολίωση, η [skoleeosee] scoliosis.

σκολνώ [skolno] repose || get off (work), leave.

σκόνη, η [skonee] dust, powder || (για δόντια) tooth powder.

σκονίζω [skoneezo] coat with dust.

σκοντάφτω [skontafto] knock against, stumble || come up against an obstacle.

σκόντο, το [skonto] discount, deduction.

σκόπελος, ο [skopelos] reef, rock, shoal || (μεταφ) stumbling block, danger.

σκοπευτήριο, το [skopevteereeo] shooting gallery, shooting range.

σκοπεύω [skopevo] take aim at || (με όπλο) take aim || (έχω σκοπό) intend, propose, plan.

σκοπιά, η [skopia] lookout || sentry box || (σιδηροδρομική) signal box.

σκόπιμος [skopeemos] opportune, convenient, expedient || intentional, deliberate.

σκοπίμως [skopeemos] intentionally, deliberately.

σκοποβολή, η [skopovolee] target practice, shooting.

σκοπός, ο [skopos] purpose, intent, intention || aim, goal || (φρουρός) sentinel || (στόχος) mark, target || (ήχος) tune, air.

σκορβούτο, το [skorvouto] scurvy.

σκορδαλιά, η [skorðalia] garlic sauce.

σκόρδο, το [skorðo] garlic.

σκόρος, ο [skoros] moth.
σκοροφαγωμένος
[skorofagomenos] moth-eaten.
σκορπίζω [skorpeezo] scatter,
disperse || (περιουσία) dissipate, waste ||
(φως) shed, spread || disintegrate, melt
away.
σκόρπιος [skorpeeos] dispersed.
σκορπιός, ο [skorpios] scorpion.
σκορπώ [skorpo] βλ σκορπίζω.
σκοτάδι, το [skotaðee] darkness,
obscurity || gloom.
σκοτεινιάζω [skoteeneeazo] darken,
become overcast || cloud over.
σκοτεινός [skoteenos] dark, dismal,
gloomy || (ουρανός) overcast || (νύχτα)
murky || (χαρακτήρας) sombre,
melancholy || (προθέσεις) underhand,
sinister || (λόγια) obscure, abstruse.
σκοτίζομαι [skoteezome] worry,
trouble o.s. || care for.
σκοτίζω [skoteezo] darken, obscure ||
worry, annoy, vex.
σκοτοδίνη, η [skotoðeenee] dizziness,
vertigo.
σκότος, το [skotos] darkness,
obscurity, gloom.
σκοτούρα, η [skotoura] (μεταφ) care,
nuisance || dizziness.
σκοτωμός, ο [skotomos] massacre,
killing || (μεταφ) hustle, jostle.
σκοτώνομαι [skotonome] hurt o.s.
seriously || (μεταφ) work o.s. to death.
σκοτώνω [skotono] kill || while away
(the time), kill time.
σκούζω [skouzo] howl, yell, scream.
σκουλαρίκι, το [skoulareekee]
earring.
σκουλήκι, το [skouleekee] worm ||
maggot, mite.
σκουντουφλώ [skountouflo] stumble,
bump against.
σκουντώ [skounto] push, jostle, shove.
σκούπα, η [skoupa] broom.
σκουπιδαριό, το [skoupeeðario]
rubbish dump.
σκουπίδι, το [skoupeeðee] rubbish,
garbage, refuse.
σκουπιδιάρης, ο [skoupeeðeearees]
dustman, garbage collector.
σκουπίζω [skoupeezo] sweep, wipe,
mop, dust, clean.
σκούρα, η [skoura]: τα βρήκα ~ I
found things difficult.
σκουριά, η [skouria] rust || ~ζω rust,
corrode.
σκούρος [skouros] dark-coloured,
brown.
σκουφία, η [skoufeea] cap, baby's
bonnet.
σκούφος, ο [skoufos] cap, beret,
bonnet.
σκύβαλα, τα [skeevala] πλ (μεταφ)
grain siftings || refuse.

σκύβω [skeevo] bend, lean, bow,
incline.
σκυθρωπός [skeethropos] sullen,
sulky, surly || (ύφος) morose.
σκύλα, η [skeela] bitch || (μεταφ) cruel
woman.
σκυλί, το [skeelee] dog || έγινε ~ he
got furious.
σκυλιάζω [skeeleeazo] infuriate ||
become enraged.
σκυλοβρίζω [skeelovreezo] berate
rudely.
σκυλολόι, το [skeeloloee] rabble,
mob, riffraff.
σκύλος, ο [skeelos] βλ σκυλί.
σκυλόψαρο, το [skeelopsaro]
dogfish || shark.
σκυταλοδρομία, η
[skeetaloðromeea] relay race.
σκυφτός [skeeftos] bending, stooping.
σκωληκοειδίτιδα, η
[skoleekoeeðeeteeða] appendicitis.
σμάλτο, το [smalto] enamel.
σμαράγδι, το [smaragðee] emerald.
σμέουρο, το [smeouro] raspberry.
σμηναγός, ο [smeenagos] (αερο)
flight lieutenant.
σμήναρχος, ο [smeenarhos] group
captain || colonel (US).
σμηνίας, ο [smeeneeas] sergeant.
σμηνίτης, ο [smeeneetees] airman.
σμήνος, το [smeenos] swarm || (αερο)
flight, squadron || crowd.
σμίγω [smeego] mingle, mix || meet,
come face to face with || join.
σμίκρυνση, η [smeekreensee]
reduction, diminution, decrease.
σμίλη, η [smeelee] chisel.
σμίξιμο, το [smeekseemo] mixing,
meeting, mating, joining.
σμόκιν, το [smokeen] dinner jacket.
σμπαράλια, τα [smbaraleea] πλ tiny
pieces.
σμπάρο, το [smbaro] shot.
σμύρη, η [smeeree] emery.
ονομπαρία, η [snombareea]
snobbishness.
σοβαρεύομαι [sovarevome] look
serious, speak seriously.
σοβαρό [sovaro]: ~ ποσό a
substantial sum.
σοβαρός [sovaros] serious, grave,
solemn.
σοβάς, ο [sovas] wall plaster.
σοβατίζω [sovateezo] plaster.
σόδα, η [soða] soda water ||
bicarbonate of soda.
σοδειά, η [soðia] βλ εσοδεία.
σόι [soee] lineage, breed || sort, kind ||
από ~ from a good family.
σοκάκι, το [sokakee] narrow street,
lane, alley.
σοκάρω [sokaro] shock, upset.
σόκιν [sokeen] shocking, suggestive.
σοκολάτα, η [sokolata] chocolate.

σόλα, η [sola] sole (of shoe).

σόλοικος [soleekos] incorrect, ungrammatical || (μεταφ) improper.

σολομός, ο [solomos] salmon.

σόμπα, η [somba] heater, heating stove.

σορός, ο [soros] bier, coffin || the dead (person).

σοσιαλιστής, ο [soseealeestees] socialist.

σου [sou] your.

σούβλα, η [souvla] skewer.

σουβλάκια, τα [souvlakeea] πλ meat on a skewer.

σουβλερός [souvleros] sharp, pointed.

σουβλί, το [souvlee] awl || spit.

σουβλιά, η [souvlia] injury from a pointed object || (πόνος) acute pain.

σουβλίζω [souvleezo] run through, pierce || (ψήνω) skewer || (πονώ) cause pain.

σουγιάς, ο [souyas] penknife.

σούζα [souza]: στέκομαι ~ obey blindly || (μεταφ) fawn.

Σουηδία, η [soueedeea] Sweden.

σουηδικός [soueedeekos] Swedish.

Σουηδός, ο [soueedos] Swede.

σουλατσάρω [soulatsaro] wander about, loaf.

σουλούπι, το [souloupee] outline, cut, contour.

σουλτανίνα, η [soultaneena] sort of seedless grape, sultana.

σουλτάνος, ο [soultanos] sultan.

σουμιές, ο [soumies] spring mattress.

σούπα, η [soupa] soup.

σουπιά, η [soupia] cuttlefish || (μεταφ) sneaky person.

σούρα, η [soura] fold, wrinkle, crease, pleat.

σουραύλι, το [souravlee] pipe, reed, flute.

σούρουπο, το [souroupo] dusk, nightfall.

σουρτούκης, ο [sourtoukees] gadabout.

σουρωμένος [souromenos] intoxicated.

σουρώνω [sourono] strain, filter || fold, pleat, crease || (αδυνατίζω) lose weight, grow thin || get drunk.

σουρωτήρι, το [souroteeree] strainer.

σουσάμι, το [sousamee] sesame.

σούσουρο, το [sousouro] noise, din || rustle || (μεταφ) scandal.

σούστα, η [sousta] spring (of seat) || (όχημα) cart || clasp, clip.

σούτ! [sout] (επιφ) hush!, shut up!

σουτζουκάκια, τα [soutzoukakeea] πλ meatballs.

σουτιέν, το [soutien] bra(ssiere).

σούφρα, η [soufra] pleat, crease, fold || (μεταφ) theft.

σουφρώνω [soufrono] fold, pleat, crease || (μεταφ) pinch, steal.

σοφία, η [sofeea] wisdom, learning || erudition.

σοφίζομαι [sofeezome] devise.

σοφίτα, η [sofeeta] attic, garret.

σοφός [sofos] wise || learned, lettered.

σπαγγοραμένος [spangoramenos] mean, tight-fisted.

σπάγγος, ο [spangos] twine, string || (μεταφ) mean person.

σπάζω [spazo] break, shatter, smash || ~ το κεφάλι μου think hard || ~ στο ξύλο beat.

σπαθί, το [spathee] sabre, sword || (στα χαρτιά) spade.

σπαθιά, η [spathia] sword stroke.

σπανάκι, το [spanakee] spinach.

σπάνη, η [spanee] rarity, shortage.

σπανίζω [spaneezo] become rare, be exceptional, be scarce.

σπάνιος [spaneeos] few and far between, uncommon.

σπανιότητα, η [spaneeoteeta] rarity, rareness, scarcity.

σπανίως [spaneeos] rarely.

σπανός [spanos] smooth-faced, beardless || raw, very young.

σπαράγγι, το [sparangee] asparagus.

σπαραγμός, ο [sparagmos] tearing || heartbreak, anguish.

σπαρακτικός [sparakteekos] heartbreaking, agonizing || (θέαμα) harrowing.

σπάραχνα, το [sparahna] πλ gills.

σπάργανα, τα [spargana] πλ swaddling clothes.

σπαρμένος [sparmenos] spread || strewn, sown.

σπαρτά, τα [sparta] πλ crops.

σπαρταριστός [spartareestos] (ψάρι) fresh || (κορίτσι) beautiful || vivid, very descriptive.

σπαρταρώ [spartaro] throb, palpitate, jump.

σπαρτός [spartos] βλ σπαρμένος.

σπάσιμο, το [spaseemo] break, fracture.

σπασμός, ο [spasmos] convulsion, twitching.

σπασμωδικός [spasmoδeekos] spasmodic || hasty.

σπατάλη, η [spatalee] lavishness, extravagance, waste.

σπάταλος [spatalos] wasteful, extravagant.

σπαταλώ [spatalo] waste, lavish, squander.

σπάτουλα, η [spatoula] spatula.

σπείρα, η [speera] coil, spiral || (ομάδα) band, gang, clique.

σπείρω [speero] sow || propagate.

σπεκουλάρω [spekoularo] speculate.

σπέρμα, το [sperma] seed, germ ||

semen, sperm || (μεταφ) offspring || cause, motive.

σπερμολογία, η [spermologeea] spreading of rumours.

σπέρνω [sperno] βλ **σπείρω.**

σπεύδω [spevδo] hurry, make haste.

σπήλαιο, το [speeleo], **σπηλιά, η** [speelia] cave, cavern, lair.

σπίθα, η [speetha] spark, flash.

σπιθαμή, η [speethamee] span.

σπιθοβολώ [speethovolo] sparkle, spark || gleam, glitter.

σπιθούρι, το [speethouree] pimple.

σπινθήρας, ο [speentheeras] (αυτοκινήτου) ignition spark.

σπιούνος, ο [speeounos] spy || stool pigeon.

σπιρούνι, το [speerounee] spur.

σπιρτάδα, η [speertaδa] pungency || (μεταφ) wit, intelligence.

σπίρτο, το [speerto] match || alcohol.

σπιρτόζος [speertozos] witty, clever, ingenious.

σπιτήσιος [speeteeseeos] home-made, domestic.

σπίτι, το [speetee], **σπιτικό, το** [speeteeko] house, home || (μεταφ) family || **από ~** wellborn.

σπιτικός [speeteekos] βλ **σπιτήσιος.**

σπιτονοικοκύρης, ο [speetoneekokeerees] householder, landlord.

σπιτώνω [speetono] lodge, house || (μεταφ) keep (a woman).

σπλάχνα, τα [splahna] nλ entrails, innards || (μεταφ) feelings || offspring.

σπλαχνικός [splahneekos] merciful, sympathetic.

σπλάχνο, το [splahno] offspring, child.

σπλήνα, η [spleena] spleen.

σπογγαλιεία, η [spongalieea] sponge fishing.

σπογγίζω [spongeezo] sponge up || mop up, wipe away.

σπόγγος, ο [spongos] sponge.

σπογγώδης [spongoδees] spongy.

σπονδή, η [sponδee] libation.

σπονδυλική [sponδeeleekee]: **~ στήλη** spine, backbone.

σπονδυλικός [sponδeeleekos] vertebral.

σπόνδυλος, ο [sponδeelos] vertebra || (κίονος) drum.

σπονδυλωτός [sponδeelotos] vertebrate.

σπορ, το [spor] sport, games, pastime.

σπορά, η [spora] sowing || seed time || (μεταφ) generation.

σποραδικός [sporaδeekos] dispersed, scanty.

σπορέλαιο, το [sporeleo] seed oil.

σπόρια, τα [sporeea] nλ seeds.

σπόρος, ο [sporos] seed, germ || semen.

σπουδάζω [spouδazo] study, attend school.

σπουδαίος [spouδeos] serious, important || exceptional.

σπουδασμένος [spouδasmenos] learned, educated.

σπουδαστής, ο [spouδastees] student.

σπουδή, η [spouδee] haste, keenness || (μελέτη) study.

σπουργίτης, ο [spouryeetees] sparrow.

σπρωξιά, η [sproksia] push, hustle, jostle, shoving.

σπρώξιμο, το [sprokseemo] pushing || encouraging.

σπρώχνω [sprohno] push, thrust, shove || encourage, incite.

σπυρί, το [speeree] grain || (εξάνθημα) pimple || boil.

σπυρωτός [speerotos] granular, granulated.

στάβλος, ο [stavlos] stable || cowshed.

σταγόνα, η [stagona] drop, dash.

σταγονόμετρο, το [stagonometro] dropper || **με το ~** in small doses, little by little.

σταδιοδρομία, η [staδeeoδromeea] career, course.

στάδιο, το [staδeo] stadium, athletic ground || (μεταφ) career, vocation.

στάζω [stazo] trickle, dribble, drip, leak.

σταθεροποίηση, η [statheropieesee] stabilization, steadying down.

σταθερός [statheros] stable, firm, steadfast, secure.

σταθμά, τα [stathma] nλ weights.

σταθμάρχης, ο [stathmarhees] station master.

στάθμευση, η [stathmevsee] stopping, waiting, parking || stationing.

σταθμεύω [stathmevo] stop, wait, stand, camp, park.

στάθμη, η [stathmee] level, plumbline || (νερού) water level.

σταθμίζω [stathmeezo] weigh, level || (μεταφ) appreciate, calculate.

σταθμός, ο [stathmos] station, halting place || (αυτοκινήτου) garage || parking lot (US) || (ταξί) taxi rank || stop, stay, wait || (στην ιστορία) landmark, stage.

στάκτη, η [staktee] ash, ashes, cinders.

σταλα(γ)ματιά, η [stala(g)matia] drop, dash.

σταλάζω [stalazo] drip, dribble, trickle.

σταλακτίτης, ο [stalakteetees] stalactite.

σταμάτημα, το [stamateema] stop, halting, checking || pause || block.

σταματώ [stamato] stop (working), check.

στάμνα, η [stamna] pitcher, jug.

στάμπα, η [stampa] stamp, seal || impression.

στάνη, η [stanee] sheepfold, pen.

στανιό, το [stanio]: με το ~ against one's will, involuntarily.

στάξιμο, το [stakseemo] dripping, trickling.

στάση, η [stasee] halt, stop, bus stop, station || (εργασίας) suspension, stoppage || (τρόπος) posture, position || (ιατρ) retention || (εξέγερση) revolt, rebellion || (μεταφ) behaviour, attitude.

στασιάζω [staseeazo] mutiny, rebel.

στασίδι, το [staseeδee] pew, stall.

στάσιμος [staseemos] motionless, stationary || (νερό) stagnant.

στατήρας, ο [stateeras] hundredweight.

στατική, η [stateekee] statics.

στατικός [stateekos] static(al).

στατιστική, η [stateesteekee] statistics.

σταυλάρχης, ο [stavlarhees] stable master.

σταύλος, ο [stavlos] stable || cowshed || (χοίρων) pig sty.

σταυροδρόμι, το [stavroδromee] crossroads || crossing.

σταυροειδής [stavroeeδees] cruciform, crosslike.

σταυροκοπιέμαι [stavrokopieme] cross o.s. over and over again.

σταυρόλεξο, το [stavrolekso] crossword puzzle.

σταυροπόδι [stavropoδee] cross-legged.

σταυρός, ο [stavros] cross, crucifix || stake, pale.

σταυροφορία, η [stavroforeea] crusade.

σταυρώνω [stavrono] crucify || (τα χέρια) cross || (διασταυρούμαι) cross, meet and pass, cut across.

σταυρωτός [stavrotos] crossways, crosswise || (σακάκι) double-breasted.

σταφίδα, η [stafeeδa] raisin || (σμυρναϊκή) sultana || **κορινθιακή** ~ currant || **γίνομαι** ~ get intoxicated.

σταφυλή, η [stafeelee] grapes || (ανατ) uvula.

σταφύλι, το [stafeelee] grape.

σταφυλόκοκκος, ο [stafeelokokos] staphylococcus.

στάχι, το [stahee] ear of corn, ear of wheat.

στάχτη, η [stahtee] βλ **στάκτη**.

σταχτής [stahtees] ashen, pale.

σταχτόνερο, το [stahtonero] lye.

στεγάζω [stegazo] roof || cover, house, shelter.

στεγανός [steyanos] airtight, hermetical, waterproof.

στέγαση, η [stegasee] housing, sheltering.

στέγασμα, το [steyasma] roof || cover, shelter.

στέγη, η [steyee] roof || (μεταφ) house, dwelling.

στεγνός [stegnos] dry || (μεταφ) skinny, spare.

στεγνώνω [stegnono] dry, become dry.

στείρος [steeros] barren, unproductive || (προσπάθεια) vain.

στέκα, η [steka] billiard cue || (μεταφ) woman as thin as a rake.

στέκει [stekee]: ~ **καλά** he is well-off || he is fit and well.

στέκομαι [stekome] stand up || come to a standstill, stop || (μεταφ) prove to be || happen.

στέκω [steko] stand, stand still, come to a stop.

στελέχη, τα [stelehee] πλ cadres, management staff.

στέλεχος, το [stelehos] stalk, stem || shank, rod || (τσεκ) counterfoil || (χερούλι) handle.

στέλλω [stelo], στέλνω [stelno] send, direct, dispatch, forward.

στέμμα, το [stema] crown, diadem.

στεναγμός, ο [stenagmos] sigh, sighing || moan, groan.

στενάζω [stenazo] sigh, heave a sigh || (μεταφ) moan.

στενεύω [stenevo] narrow down, take in, tighten || shrink, get narrow.

στενογραφία, η [stenografeea] shorthand, stenography.

στενοκέφαλος [stenokefalos] narrow-minded, strait-laced.

στενόμακρος [stenomakros] long and narrow, oblong.

στενό, το [steno] strait || (οροσειράς) pass, gorge.

στενός [stenos] narrow || tight-fitting || (μεταφ) close, intimate || (φίλος) dear.

στενότητα, η [stenoteeta] tightness, closeness || narrowness || ~ **χρήματος** lack of money.

στενοχωρημένος [stenohoreemenos] upset, sad || hard-up || ill at ease.

στενοχώρια, η [stenohoreea] lack of room || (δυσκολία) difficulty, inconvenience, discomfort.

στενόχωρος [stenohoros] narrow, limited, tight || troublesome.

στενοχωρώ [stenohoro] worry, embarrass, annoy.

στενωπός, η [stenopos] narrow street, back street || defile, pass.

στερεά, η [sterea] mainland || ~ **Ελλάδα** central Greece.

στερεοποιώ [stereopeeo] solidify.

στερεός [stereos] firm, compact, well-built || solid, substantial || (χρώμα) fast.

στερεότυπος [stereoteepos] stereotyped, invariable.

στερεύω [sterevo] dry up || stop, cease.

στερέωμα, το [stereoma] consolidation || support, fastening || (ουρανός) firmament.

στερεώνω [stereono] consolidate || make secure || ~ σε μια δουλειά settle down to one job.

στερήσεις, οι [steresees] πλ privation, want, loss.

στέρηση, η [stereesee] deprivation || shortage, absence.

στεριά, η [steria] terra firma.

στερλίνα, η [sterleena] pound sterling.

στέρνα, η [sterna] cistern, tank.

στέρνο, το [sterno] breastbone, chest.

στερνός [sternos] later, last.

στερούμαι [steroume] go without, lack || (φτώχεια) be needy.

στερώ [stero] deprive of, take away.

στέφανα, τα [stefana] πλ marriage wreaths.

στεφάνη, η [stefanee] crown || (αγγείου) brim || (βαρελιού) hoop || (άνθους) corolla || ring, band || (τροχού) tyre.

στεφάνι, το [stefanee] garland, wreath || (βαρελιού) hoop, band.

στεφανώνομαι [stefanonome] marry, get married.

στεφανώνω [stefanono] crown || be the best man at a wedding.

στέψη, η [stepsee] coronation || wedding ceremony.

στηθόδεσμος, ο [steethodesmos] βλ σουτιέν.

στήθος, το [steethos] chest, breast || (γυναικός) bosom.

στηθοσκοπώ [steethoskopo] examine with a stethoscope.

στήλη, η [steelee] staff, pillar, column || (μπαταρία) electric battery || (εφημερίδας) column.

στηλώνω [steelono] prop up, support || bolster up.

στημόνι, το [steemonee] warp.

στήνω [steeno] raise, hold up, erect, put up || ~ παγίδα lay a trap.

στήριγμα, το [steereegma] prop, support, stay.

στηρίζομαι [steereezome] lean on, rely on || be based on.

στηρίζω [steereezo] support || prop || base on, reckon on.

στητός [steetos] standing, upright.

στιβαρός [steevaros] strong, robust, steady, firm.

στιβάδα, η [steevaδa] pile, heap, mass.

στίβος, ο [steevos] track, ring, racetrack.

στίγμα, το [steegma] spot, brand, stain, stigma || disgrace || position, fix.

στιγμή, η [steegmee] instant, moment

|| (τυπογραφικό) dot, point || τελεία ~ full stop || άνω ~ colon.

στιγμιαίος [steegmieos] instantaneous || momentary, temporary.

στιγμιότυπο, το [steegmeeoteepo] snapshot, snap.

στίλβω [steelvo] shine, glitter, sparkle.

στιλβώνω [steelvono] polish, varnish, burnish.

στιλβωτήριο, το [steelvoteereeo] shoe shine parlour.

στιλέτο, το [steeleto] stiletto, dagger.

στιλπνός [steelpnos] brilliant, polished, bright.

στίξη, η [steeksee] punctuation || dot, spot, speckle.

στιφάδο, το [steefaδo] meat stew with onions.

στίφος, το [steefos] crowd, horde, throng || rabble, gang.

στιχομυθία, η [steehomeetheea] vivid dialogue.

στίχος, ο [steehos] line, row, file || verse.

στιχουργός, ο [steehourgos] rhymester, versifier.

στοά, η [stoa] colonnade, portico, arcade || passage || (ορυχείου) gallery || (μασωνική) (masonic) lodge.

στοίβα, η [steeva] pile, stack, mass.

στοιβάζω [steevazo] stack, pile up || crowd, squeeze.

στοιχεία, τα [steeheea] πλ elements, rudiments || (τυπογραφείου) printing types.

στοιχειό, το [steehio] ghost, phantom.

στοιχείο, το [steeheeo] component, element || (νομ) piece of evidence || (αλφαβήτου) letter || (ηλεκτ) cell || (μεταφ) factor.

στοιχειοθεσία, η [steeheeotheseea] typesetting.

στοιχειώδης [steeheeoδees] elementary, rudimentary || essential, capital.

στοιχειωμένος [steeheeomenos] haunted.

στοιχειώνω [steeheeono] become haunted, haunt.

στοίχημα, το [steeheema] bet, wager || stake || βάζω ~ lay a bet, wager.

στοιχηματίζω [steeheemateezo] bet, wager.

στοιχίζω [steeheezo] cost || (μεταφ) pain, grieve.

στοίχος, το [steehos] row, line, rank.

στόκος, ο [stokos] putty, stucco.

στολή, η [stolee] uniform || costume.

στολίδι, το [stoleeδee] jewellery || (στόλισμα) adornment, decoration.

στολίζω [stoleezo] adorn, decorate, deck, trim, embellish.

στολισμός, ο [stoleesmos] ornamenting, decoration, embellishing.

στόλος, ο [stolos] navy, fleet.

στόμα, το [stoma] mouth || lips.

στομάχι, το [stomahee] stomach.

στομαχιάζω [stomaheeazo] suffer from indigestion.

στόμιο, το [stomeeo] mouth, opening, aperture, entrance || muzzle.

στόμφος, ο [stomfos] boast, declamation.

στομώνω [stomono] blunt || temper, harden.

στορ, το [stor], στόρι, το [storee] blind, roller blind.

στοργή, η [storyee] affection, tenderness, love.

στουμπώνω [stoumbono] stuff, pad, plug || become stuffed.

στουπί, το [stoupee] oakum, wad, tow || (μεταφ) drunk as a lord.

στουπόχαρτο, το [stoupoharto] blotting paper.

στουρνάρι, το [stournaree] flint, gun flint.

στοχάζομαι [stohazome] think, meditate (on) || consider.

στοχασμός, ο [stohasmos] thought, meditation.

στοχαστικός [stohasteekos] thoughtful || discreet, wise.

στόχαστρο, το [stohastro] front sight (of gun).

στόχος, ο [stohos] mark, target, objective || aim, end.

στραβά [strava] obliquely, crookedly || wrongly, amiss || τόβαλε ~ he doesn't give a damn.

στραβισμός, ο [straveesmos] squinting.

στραβοκάνης [stravokanees] bandy-legged.

στραβομάρα, η [stravomara] blindness || (κακοτυχία) bad luck, mischance || (μεταφ) blunder, gross mistake, howler.

στραβόξυλο, το [stravokseelo] obstinate person, contrary fellow.

στραβοπάτημα, το [stravopateema] staggering || false step.

στραβός [stravos] crooked, awry, twisted || (λοξός) slanting || (ελαττωματικός) faulty || (τυφλός) blind.

στραβώνομαι [stravonome] go blind.

στραβώνω [stravono] bend, distort || make a mess of || spoil || (τυφλώνω) blind || (λυγίζω) become twisted.

στραγάλια, τα [stragaleea] πλ roasted chickpeas.

στραγγαλίζω [strangaleezo] strangle, throttle || stifle.

στραγγαλιστής, ο [strangaleestees] strangler.

στραγγίζω [strangeezo] drain, filter, press out, wring out || (κουράζομαι) get exhausted.

στραγγιστήρι, το [strangeesteeree] strainer, filter, colander.

στραμπουλίζω [strambouleezo] sprain, twist.

στραπατσάρω [strapatsaro] harm, damage || ruffle || (ταπεινώνω) humiliate.

στραπάτσο, το [strapatso] maltreatment || humiliation.

στράτα, η [strata] way, street, road.

στρατάρχης, ο [stratarhees] (field) marshal.

στράτευμα, το [stratevma] army, troops, forces.

στρατεύματα, τα [stratevmata] πλ troops.

στρατεύομαι [stratevome] serve in the army.

στρατεύσιμος [stratevseemos] subject to conscription.

στρατηγείο, το [strateeyeeo] headquarters.

στρατήγημα το [strateeyeema] stratagem || trick, ruse.

στρατηγία, η [strateeyeea] generalship.

στρατηγική, η [strateeyeekee] strategy.

στρατηγικός [strateeyeekos] strategic.

στρατηγός, ο [strateegos] general.

στρατί, το [stratee] βλ στράτα.

στρατιά, η [stratia] army, force.

στρατιώτης, ο [strateeotees] soldier, private || warrior.

στρατιωτικό, το [strateeoteeko] military service.

στρατιωτικός [strateeoteekos] military || ~ νόμος martial law.

στρατοδικείο, το [stratoðeekeeo] court-martial.

στρατοκρατία, η [stratokrateea] militarism, military government.

στρατολογία, η [stratoloyeea] conscription, call-up.

στρατόπεδο, το [stratopeðo] camp, encampment || side, party.

στρατός, ο [stratos] army, troops, forces.

στρατόσφαιρα, η [stratosfera] stratosphere.

στρατώνας, ο [stratonas] barracks.

στρεβλός [strevlos] crooked, deformed, twisted || (μεταφ) rough, difficult.

στρείδι, το [streeðee] oyster.

στρέμμα, το [strema] (approx) quarter of an acre.

στρέφομαι [strefome] turn, rotate || revolve.

στρέφω [strefo] turn, turn about || rotate, revolve.

στρεψοδικία, η [strepsoðeekeea] chicanery, quibbling, pettifoggery.

στρίβω [streevo] twist, rotate, turn || το ~ slip away, slip off.

στρίγ(γ)λα, η [stree(n)gla] witch, sorceress, shrew.

στριγ(γ)λιά, η [stree(n)glia] wickedness, shrewishness || (κραυγή) shrill cry, shriek.

στριμμένος [streemenos] twisted || ill-humoured, wicked, malicious.

στριφογυρίζω [streefoyeereezo] move round, turn round || whirl, spin.

στρίφωμα, το [streefoma] hemming.

στρίψιμο, το [streepseemo] twisting, turning.

στροβιλίζω [stroveeleezo] whirl, turn round, twirl.

στρόβιλος, ο [stroveelos] spinning top, peg top || (άνεμος) whirlwind || (χιόνι) eddying, swirling || (μηχανή) turbine || (σκόνης) whirling cloud.

στρογγυλεύω [strongeelevo] make round || grow plump, get stout.

στρογγυλός [strongeelos] round(ed) || (πρόσωπο) full || (αριθμός) round, even.

στρουθοκάμηλος, η [strouthokameelos] ostrich.

στρουμπουλός [stroumboulos] plump.

στρόφαλος, ο [strofalos] crank, handle || (αυτοκινήτου) starting handle.

στροφή, η [strofee] turn, revolution || (οδού) twist, bend || (κατευθύνσεως) detour, change of direction || (ποίηση) stanza || (μουσ) ritornello.

στρόφιγγα, η [strofeenga] hinge, pivot || tap.

στρυμώ(x)νω [streemo(h)no] squeeze, crowd, cram || press hard, oppress, annoy.

στρυφνός [streefnos] harsh || peevish || (χαρακτήρας) crabbed || (ύφος κτλ) obscure, difficult || (γεύση) sharp, biting.

στρώμα, το [stroma] couch, bed, mattress || (γεωλογίας) bed, layer, stratum || **στο ~** ill in bed.

στρώνομαι [stronome] apply o.s. || install o.s.

στρώνω [strono] spread, lay || (κρεβάτι) make || (δρόμο) pave || (μεταφ) be well under way || **~ το κρεβάτι** make the bed.

στρώση, η [strosee] layer || strewing || paving, flooring.

στρωσίδι, το [stroseedee] carpet || bedding.

στρωτός [strotos] strewn || paved || (ζωή) even, normal, regular.

στύβω [steevo] squeeze, wring, press || (μεταφ) rack one's brains || (στειρεύω) dry up, run dry.

στυγερός [steeyeros] abominable, heinous, horrible.

στυγνός [steegnos] doleful, despondent, gloomy.

στυλό, το [steelo] fountain pen.

στυλοβάτης, ο [steelovatees] pedestal, base || (μεταφ) pillar, founder.

στύλος, ο [steelos] pillar, column, pole || (μεταφ) prop, mainstay, breadwinner.

στυλώνω [steelono] support, prop up || fix.

στυπτικός [steepteekos] binding, styptic.

στυφός [steefos] sour, acrid, bitter.

στύψη, η [steepsee] alum.

στύψιμο, το [steepseemo] squeezing, pressing, wringing.

στωικός [stoeekos] stoic(al).

συ [see] you.

σύγγαμβρος, ο [seengamvros] brother-in-law.

συγγένεια, η [seengeneea] relationship, kinship || affinity, relation, connection.

συγγενής [seengenees] connected, related || (ουσ) relation, kinsman.

συγγενολό(γ)ι, το [seengenolo(y)ee] relations, relatives, kindred.

συγγνώμη, η [seengnomee] pardon, excuse || forgiveness.

σύγγραμμα, το [seengrama] work (of writing), treatise.

συγγραφέας, ο [seengrafeas] author, writer.

συγγράφω [seengrafo] write a work, compose.

συγκαίομαι [seengkeome] be chafed, be galled.

σύγκαλα, τα [seengkala] πλ: **στα ~ μου** normal, in good health.

συγκαλύπτω [seengkaleepto] hide, cloak, hush up, cover.

συγκαλώ [seengkalo] convene, convoke || (πρόσωπα) assemble, call together.

συγκαταβατικός [seengkatavateekos] accommodating || (τιμή) moderate, reasonable.

συγκατάθεση, η [seengkatathesee] assent, consent, acquiescence.

συγκαταλέγω [seengkatalego] include, number among || consider, regard.

συγκατανεύω [seengkatanevo] consent, assent, adhere to.

συγκατοικώ [seengkateeko] cohabit, live together.

συγκεκριμένος [seengkekreemenos] concrete, positive, clear, specific.

συγκεκριμένως [seengkekreemenos] plainly, concretely, actually.

συγκεντρώνομαι [seengkentronome] concentrate.

συγκεντρώνω [seengkentrono] collect, bring togther, concentrate || centralize.

συγκέντρωση, η [seengkentrosee] crowd, gathering, assembly || concentration || centralization.

συγκερασμός, ο [seengkerasmos] mixing, mingling || compromise.

συγκεχυμένος [seengkeheemenos] confused, jumbled || (ήχος) indistinct || (ρήμες) vague || (ιδέες) hazy, dim || (λόγοι) imprecise, obscure.

συγκίνηση, η [seengkeeneesee] emotion, sensation.

συγκινητικός [seengkeeneeteekos] moving, touching, stirring.

συγκινούμαι [seengkeenoume] be excited || be touched.

συγκινώ [seengkeeno] move, affect, touch || excite.

σύγκληση, η [seengkleesee] convocation, calling together.

σύγκλητος, η [seengkleetos] senate.

συγκλίνω [seengkleeno] converge, concentrate.

συγκλονίζω [seengkloneezo] shake, excite, stir up, shock.

συγκοινωνία, η [seengkeenoneea] communications || means of transport.

συγκοινωνώ [seengkeenono] communicate, be connected.

συγκολλώ [seengkolo] glue, join together || (μέταλλα) weld, solder || ~ **σαμπρέλα** mend a puncture.

συγκομιδή, η [seengkomeeδee] harvest, crop.

συγκοπή, η [seengkopee] syncopation || (ιατρ) heart failure || (γραμμ) contraction.

συγκράτηση, η [seengkrateesee] containing, bridling, restraining.

συγκρατούμαι [seengkratoume] control o.s., contain o.s.

συγκρατώ [seengkrato] check || (πάθη) govern || (θυμό) contain, control, suppress || (τα πλήθη) restrain.

συγκρίνω [seengkreeno] compare (with), liken (to).

σύγκριση, η [seengkreesee] comparison, parallel.

συγκριτικός [seengkreeteekos] comparative, compared (to).

συγκρότημα, το [seengkroteema] group, cluster || (κτίρια) complex || (μουσ) group, band.

συγκροτώ [seengkroto] form, compose || convoke, convene.

συγκρούομαι [seengkrouome] bump into, collide || clash, come to blows.

σύγκρουση, η [seengkrousee] collision, clash, fight, engagement.

σύγκρυο, το [seengkreeo] shivering, trembling.

συγκυρία, η [seengkeereea] coincidence, occurrence, chance || (οικον) conjuncture.

συγυρίζω [seeyeereezo] tidy up, arrange || (μεταφ) ill-treat.

συγχαίρω [seenghero] congratulate, compliment.

συγχαρητήρια, τα [seenghareeteereea] πλ congratulations.

συγχέω [seengheo] confound, confuse, perplex.

συγχορδία, η [seenghorδeea] harmony of sounds, accord.

συγχρονίζω [seenghroneezo] modernize, bring up to date.

σύγχρονος [seenghronos] contemporary || simultaneous || contemporaneous.

συγχύζω [seengheezo] get mixed up || worry, confound, harass.

σύγχυση, η [seengheesee] confusion, disorder || chaos, commotion.

συγχωνεύω [seenghonevo] amalgamate, blend, merge.

συγχώρηση, η [seenghoreesee] remission, pardon.

συγχωρητέος [seenghoreeteos] pardonable, excusable.

συ(γ)χωρείτε [see(ng)horeete]: **με ~** excuse me, I beg your pardon.

συγχωρώ [seenghoro] pardon, forgive, excuse || tolerate, permit.

συζήτηση, η [seezeeteesee] discussion, debate || **ούτε ~** it's out of the question.

συζητώ [seezeeto] discuss, argue, debate.

συζυγικός [seezeeyeekos] conjugal, marital.

σύζυγος, ο, η [seezeegos] consort, spouse, husband, wife.

συζώ [seezo] live together, cohabit.

συκιά, η [seekia] fig tree.

σύκο, το [seeko] fig.

συκοφάντης, ο [seekofantees] slanderer.

συκοφαντώ [seekofanto] slander.

συκώτι, το [seekotee] liver.

σύληση, η [seeleesee] spoliation, sacking.

συλλαβή, η [seelavee] syllable.

συλλαλητήριο, το [seelaleeteereeo] mass meeting, demonstration.

συλλαμβάνω [seelamvano] catch, lay hold of, capture, seize, arrest || (ιδέες) conceive.

συλλέγω [seelego] collect, gather.

συλλέκτης, ο [seelektees] collector.

σύλληψη, η [seeleepsee] capture, arrest, seizure || (ιδέας) conception.

συλλογή, η [seeloyee] set, assortment, collection || (σκέψη) thought, concern.

συλλογίζομαι [seeloyeezome] think out, reflect about, consider, reason (out).

συλλογικός [seeloyeekos] collective.

συλλογισμένος [seeloyeesmenos] pensive, thoughtful, absorbed (in).

συλλογισμός, ο [seeloyeesmos] thought, reflection || reasoning, syllogism.

σύλλογος, ο [seelogos] society, club, association.

συλλυπητήρια, τα [seeleepeeteereea] πλ condolences, sympathy.

συλλυπούμαι [seeleepoume] offer condolence || feel sorry for.

συμβαδίζω [seemvaδeezo] keep up with || go together, coexist.

συμβαίνω [seemveno] happen, take place, come about.

συμβάλλομαι [seemvalome] contract, enter into an agreement.

συμβάλλω [seemvalo] contribute to, pay one's share || (ποτάμι) meet, join, unite.

συμβάν, το [seemvan] event, accident, occurrence.

σύμβαση, η [seemvasee] agreement, contract, treaty, pact.

συμβία, η [seemveea] wife, consort.

συμβιβάζομαι [seemveevazome] compromise, agree with || be compatible with.

συμβιβάζω [seemveevazo] reconcile, arrange, adjust.

συμβιβασμός, ο [seemveevasmos] compromise, accommodation, adjustment, settlement.

συμβίωση, η [seemveeosee] living together, cohabitation.

συμβόλαιο, το [seemvoleo] contract, agreement.

συμβολαιογράφος, ο [seemvoleografos] notary public.

συμβολή, η [seemvolee] contribution || (ποταμών) confluence, junction.

συμβολίζω [seemvoleezo] symbolize, represent.

σύμβολο, το [seemvolo] symbol, mark, sign, emblem, token.

συμβουλεύομαι [seemvoulevome] consult, refer to, take advice.

συμβουλεύω [seemvoulevo] advise, recommend.

συμβουλή, η [seemvoulee] advice, counsel.

συμβούλιο, το [seemvouleeo] council, board, committee.

σύμβουλος, ο [seemvoulos] adviser, counsellor || councillor.

συμμαζεύω [seemazevo] tidy up, collect, assemble, gather together || (ελέγχω) restrain, check, hold.

συμμαχία, η [seemaheea] alliance, coalition.

σύμμαχος [seemahos] allied || (ουσ) ally.

συμμερίζομαι [seemereezome] share, have a part (in).

συμμετέχω [seemeteho] participate in, take part in, be a party to.

συμμετοχή, η [seemetohee] participation || sharing.

συμμετρία, η [seemetreea] symmetry, proportion.

συμμετρικός [seemetreekos] symmetrical || well-proportioned.

συμμορία, η [seemoreea] gang, band, body.

συμμορφώνομαι [seemorfonome] comply, conform, agree with, adapt to.

συμμορφώνω [seemorfono] adapt, conform || bring to heel.

συμπαγής [seembayees] solid, firm, compact, close.

συμπάθεια, η [seempatheea] compassion, sympathy || weakness (for) || favourite.

συμπαθής [seempathees] likeable, lovable.

συμπαθητικός [seempatheeteekos] likeable, lovable || sympathetic.

συμπάθιο, το [seempatheeo]: **με το ~** begging your pardon.

συμπαθώ [seempatho] feel compassion for || have a liking for.

σύμπαν, το [seempan] universe || everything, all, everybody.

συμπατριώτης, ο [seempatreeotees] compatriot, fellow countryman.

συμπεθεριά, η [seempetheria] relationship by marriage.

συμπέθεροι, οι [seempetheree] πλ fathers-in-law || relations by marriage.

συμπεραίνω [seempereno] conclude, presume, infer, surmise.

συμπέρασμα, το [seemperasma] conclusion, inference, end.

συμπεριλαμβάνω [seempereelamvano] include, contain, comprise.

συμπεριφέρομαι [seempereeferome] behave, conduct o.s.

συμπεριφορά, η [seempereefora] behaviour, conduct.

συμπίεση, η [seempiesee] compression, squeezing.

συμπίπτω [seempeepto] coincide, concur, converge || happen, change.

σύμπλεγμα, το [seemplegma] tangle || cluster || network.

συμπλέκομαι [seemplekome] come to blows, quarrel || fight.

συμπλέκτης, ο [seemblektees] (μηχαν) clutch.

συμπλήρωμα, το [seempleeroma] complement || supplement, addition.

συμπληρωματικός [seempleeromateekos] complementary, further || supplementary.

συμπληρώνω [seempleerono] complete, complement, finish || (θέση) fill || (φόρμα) fill in.

συμπλήρωση, η [seempleerosee] completion, filling, achievement.

συμπλοκή, η [seemplokee] fight, engagement, clash, brawl.

σύμπνοια, η [seempneea] harmony, agreement, understanding.

συμπολιτεία, η [seempoleeteea] confederation, confederacy.

συμπολίτης, ο [seempoleetees] fellow citizen, fellow countryman.

συμπονώ [seempono] feel compassion for, sympathize with.

συμπόσιο, το [seemposeeo] banquet, feast.

συμποσούμαι [seemposoume] come to, run (to).

σύμπραξη, η [seempraksee] cooperation, contribution.

συμπτύσσομαι [seempteesome] fall back, shorten.

συμπτύσσω [seempteeso] shorten, abridge, abbreviate, cut short.

σύμπτωμα, το [seemptoma] symptom || sign, indication.

σύμπτωση, η [seemptosee] coincidence, accident, chance.

συμπυκνώνω [seempeeknono] condense, compress.

συμπυκνωτής, ο [seempeeknotees] condenser.

συμφέρει [seemferee] it's worth it, it's to one's advantage.

συμφέρον, το [seemferon] advantage, interest, profit, benefit.

συμφεροντολογία, η [seemferontoloyeea] self-interest.

συμφιλιώνω [seemfeeleeono] reconcile, restore friendship, make up.

συμφορά, η [seemfora] calamity, disaster, misfortune.

συμφόρηση, η [seemforeesee] traffic jam, congestion || (ιατρ) stroke.

σύμφορος [seemforos] advantageous, profitable, useful.

συμφύρω [seemfeero] confuse, mingle, mix, jumble.

σύμφωνα [seemfona]: ~ με according to, in conformity with.

συμφωνητικό, το [seemfoneeteeko] agreement, deed of contract.

συμφωνία, η [seemfoneea] agreement, convention || accord, consent || (μουσ) symphony.

σύμφωνο, το [seemfono] (γράμμα) consonant || compact, agreement, pact.

σύμφωνος [seemfonos] in accord, in conformity with.

συμφωνώ [seemfono] concur, agree || match, go well together.

συμψηφίζω [seempseefeezo] counterbalance, make up for.

συν [seen] together, with || (μαθημ) plus || ~ τω χρόνω in time, gradually, eventually || ~ τοις άλλοις moreover, in addition.

συναγερμός, ο [seenayermos] alarm, call to arms, alert || (πολιτικός) rally, mass meeting.

συναγρίδα, η [seenagreeδa] kind of sea bream.

συνάγω [seenago] assemble, collect, bring together || (συμπεραίνω) infer, conclude, deduce.

συναγωγή, η [seenagoyee] collection, gathering, assembly || (εβραίων) synagogue.

συναγωνίζομαι [seenagoneezome] rival, compete || fight together.

συναγωνιστής, ο [seenagoneestees] rival, competitor || (συμπολεμιστής) brother in arms || (ανταγωνιστής) rival.

συνάδελφος, ο [seenaδelfos] colleague, fellow member.

συναινώ [seeneno] consent to, agree to, acquiesce.

συναίρεση, η [seeneresee] (γραμμ) contraction.

συναισθάνομαι [seenesthanome] become aware of, be conscious of, feel.

συναίσθημα, το [seenestheema] sentiment, feeling, sensation.

συναισθήματα, τα [seenestheemata] πλ emotions, feelings.

συναισθηματικός [seenestheemateekos] emotional, sentimental.

συναίσθηση, η [seenestheesee] feeling, sense, appreciation, consciousness.

συναλλαγή, η [seenalayee] exchange, dealings, trade || ελεύθερη ~ free trade.

συνάλλαγμα, το [seenalagma] foreign currency || draft, bill || τιμή συναλλάγματος rate of exchange.

συναλλαγματική, η [seenalagmateekee] bill of exchange.

συναλλάσσομαι [seenalasome] deal, trade, traffic || (συναναστρέφομαι) associate with.

συνάμα [seenama] together, in one lot, at the same time, at once.

συναναστρέφομαι [seenanastrefome] consort with, mix with.

συναναστροφή, η [seenanastrofee] association, company || party, reception.

συνάντηση, η [seenanteesee] falling in with, meeting || encounter.

συναντώ [seenanto] meet, happen (upon), run across.

συναντώμαι [seenantome] meet, come together.

σύναξη, η [seenaksee] concentration, meeting || collecting, receipts.

συναπτός [seenaptos] consecutive, successive || annexed, tied, appended.

συνάπτω [seenapto] annex, attach || (συμμαχία) contract, form || (δάνειο) incur || (ειρήνη) conclude || (μάχη) join, give battle || ~ σχέσεις make friends.

συναρμολογώ [seenarmologo] fit

together || join || make up, piece together.

συναρπάζω [seenarpazo] carry away, enrapture, entrance.

συνάρτηση, η [seenarteesee] attachment, connection || cohesion.

συνασπισμός, ο [seenaspeesmos] coalition, alliance, league.

συναυλία, η [seenavleea] concert.

συνάφεια, η [seenafeea] connection, link, reference.

συναφής [seenafees] adjacent (to) || linked, connected || like.

συνάχι, το [seenahee] cold (in the head), catarrh.

σύναψη, η [seenapsee] conclusion, arrangement || contraction || joining.

συνδεδεμένος [seenðeðemenos] closely associated with, having ties with.

σύνδεση, η [seenðesee] joining, binding together.

σύνδεσμος, ο [seenðesmos] bond, union || (στρατ) liaison || relationship, affinity || (γραμμ) conjunction.

συνδετήρας, ο [seenðeteeras] clip, paper clip.

συνδετικός [seenðeteekos] joining, connective || (γραμμ) copulative.

συνδέω [seenðeo] bind together, unite || (μεταφ) join, link, bind.

συνδιαλέγομαι [seenðealegome] converse (with), talk (to).

συνδιάσκεψη, η [seenðeeaskepsee] deliberation || conference.

συνδικάτο, το [seenðeekato] syndicate || (εργατών) trade union.

συνδράμω [seenðramo] support, help || contribute to.

συνδρομή, η [seenðromee] coincidence, conjunction || (βοήθεια) help, assistance || subscription, contribution.

συνδρομητής, ο [seenðromeetees] subscriber.

σύνδρομο, το [seenðromo] syndrome.

συνδυάζομαι [seenðeeazome] harmonize, go together, match.

συνδυάζω [seenðeeazo] unite, combine || match, pair || arrange.

συνδυασμός, ο [seenðeeasmos] combination, arrangement || matching.

συνεδριάζω [seeneðreeazo] meet, be in session.

συνέδριο, το [seeneðreeo] congress, convention, council.

σύνεδρος, ο [seeneðros] delegate || councillor || (δικαστηρίου) judge.

συνείδηση, η [seeneeðeesee] conscience.

συνειδητός [seeneeðeetos] conscious, wilful.

συνειρμός, ο [seeneermos] coherence, order, sequence.

συνεισφέρω [seeneesfero] contribute, subscribe.

συνεκτικός [seenekteekos] cohesive, binding, tenacious.

συνέλευση, η [seenelevsee] meeting, assembly.

συνεννόηση, η [seenenoeesee] understanding, concert, concord, agreement || exchange of views.

συνεννοούμαι [seenenooume] agree, come to an agreement || exchange views.

συνενοχή, η [seenenohee] complicity, abetment, connivance.

συνέντευξη, η [seenentevksee] interview, appointment, rendezvous.

συνενώ [seeneno] unite, join together.

συνεπάγομαι [seenepagome] lead to, involve, have as consequence, call for.

συνεπαίρνω [seeneperno] transport, carry away.

συνέπεια, η [seenepeea] result, outcome, consequence || consistency || κατά ~ consequently.

συνεπής [seenepees] true, in keeping with, consistent || punctual.

συνεπώς [seenepos] consequently, accordingly.

συνεπτυγμένος [seenepteegmenos] compact, succinct, brief.

συνεργάζομαι [seenergazome] cooperate, collaborate || contribute.

συνεργάτης, ο [seenergatees] collaborator || contributor.

συνεργείο, το [seeneryeeo] workroom, workshop || gang, shift, team of workers || repair shop.

συνεργία, η [seeneryeea] complicity, abetment, confederacy.

σύνεργο, το [seenergo] implement, tool, instrument.

συνεργός, ο [seenergos] accessary, accomplice, abettor, party (to).

συνερίζομαι [seenereezome] heed, take into account, keep up rivalry with.

συνέρχομαι [seenerhome] get over, recover || come together, meet, assemble.

σύνεση, η [seenesee] caution, good sense, prudence, judgment.

συνεσταλμένος [seenestalmenos] shy, modest, timid, circumspect.

συνεταιρισμός, ο [seenetereesmos] cooperative, association.

συνέταιρος, ο [seeneteros] partner, associate, colleague, co-partner.

συνετός [seenetos] wise, discreet, prudent, sensible, cautious.

συνεφέρνω [seeneferno] revive, bring round || come to.

συνέχεια, η [seeneheea] continuity || continuation, outcome || (επίρ) continuously, successively.

συνεχής [seenehees] continuous,

incessant, unceasing, continual || successive || adjacent.

συνεχίζω [seeneeheezo] continue, keep on, go on.

συνεχώς [seenehos] continually, endlessly.

συνήγορος, ο [seeneegoros] advocate, defender, counsel.

συνήθεια, η [seeneetheea] habit, custom, practice, use.

συνήθης [seeneethees] habitual, customary, usual, common, ordinary.

συνηθίζεται [seeneetheezete] it is usual, it is the fashion.

συνηθίζω [seeneetheezo] accustom to || get accustomed to || be in the habit of.

συνηθισμένος [seeneetheesmenos] accustomed, familiar || habitual, customary.

συνημμένος [seeneemenos] attached, connected, annexed, enclosed.

σύνθεση, η [seenthesee] mixture, composition || collocation || structure, synthesis.

συνθέτης, ο [seenthetees] composer || compositor.

συνθετικό, το [seentheteeko] component, constituent.

συνθετικός [seentheteekos] constituent, component || artificial, synthetic.

σύνθετος [seenthetos] compound, composite || intricate.

συνθέτω [seentheto] compose, make up.

συνθήκες, οι [seentheekes] πλ conditions, circumstances, situation.

συνθήκη, η [seentheekee] treaty, agreement, pact || convention.

συνθηκολογώ [seentheekologo] surrender, capitulate || negotiate a treaty.

σύνθημα, το [seentheema] signal, sign, password, watchword.

συνθηματικός [seentheemateekos] symbolic || in code.

συνθλίβω [seenthleevo] squeeze, compress, crush.

συνίσταμαι [seeneestame] consist of, be composed of.

συνιστώ [seeneesto] advise, recommend || (επιτροπή) establish, set up, form || (γνωρίζω) introduce.

συννεφιά, η [seenefia] cloudy weather || ~**ζω** become cloudy || (μεταφ) look sullen.

σύννεφο, το [seenefo] cloud.

συννυφάδα, η [seeneefaδa] wife of one's brother-in-law.

συνοδ(ε)ία η [seenoδeea] escort, retinue, suite, convoy, procession || (μουσ) accompaniment.

συνοδεύω [seenoδevo] accompany, go with, escort || (ναυτ) convoy.

συνοδοιπόρος, ο, η [seenoδeeporos] fellow traveller.

σύνοδος, η [seenoδos] congress, sitting, assembly || (εκκλ) synod.

συνοδός, ο, η [seenoδos] steward, escort || **ιπτάμενη** ~ air hostess.

συνοικέσιο, το [seeneekeseeo] arranged marriage, match.

συνοικία, η [seeneekeea] quarter, neighbourhood, ward.

συνοικιακός [seeneekeeakos] local, suburban.

συνοικισμός, ο [seeneekeesmos] settlement || colonization || quarter.

συνολικός [seenoleekos] total, whole.

σύνολο, το [seenolo] total, entirety.

συνομήλικος [seenomeeleekos] of the same age.

συνομιλητής, ο [seenomeeleetees] interlocutor.

συνομιλία, η [seenomeeleea] conversation, chat, talk || interview.

συνομοταξία, η [seenomotakseea] branch, group, class.

συνονόματος [seenonomatos] namesake, having the same name.

συνοπτικός [seenopteekos] summary, brief, synoptic, concise.

σύνορα, τα [seenora] πλ frontier, boundaries.

συνορεύω [seenorevo] have a common frontier, border on.

σύνορο, το [seenoro] boundary, border, frontier.

συνουσία, η [seenouseea] coition, intercourse, copulation.

συνοφρυόνομαι [seenofreeonome] frown, scowl || look sullen.

συνοχή, η [seenohee] coherence, cohesion || (ιδεών) sequence, chain.

σύνοψη, η [seenopsee] summary, compendium, synopsis || (εκκλ) prayer book, breviary.

συνταγή, η [seentayee] formula, prescription || recipe.

σύνταγμα, το [seentagma] constitution, charter || (στρατ) regiment.

συνταγματάρχης, ο [seentagmatarhees] colonel.

συνταγματικός [seentagmateekos] constitutional.

συντάκτης, ο [seentaktees] author, writer || (εφημερίδας) editor || (συνθήκης) drafter, framer.

συντακτικός [seentakteekos] component, constituent || (εφημερίδας) editorial || (γραμμ) syntactic(al).

σύνταξη, η [seentaksee] compilation || wording, writing || organization || (εφημερίδας) editing, editorial staff || pension || (γραμμ) construction, syntax.

συνταξιούχος, ο, η [seentaksiouhos] pensioner || retired officer.

συνταράσσω [seentaraso] agitate, shake, disturb, trouble || (μεταφ) disconcert.

συντάσσω [seentaso] arrange, compile || write, draft, draw up || (γραμμ) construe || constitute, form, organize || (νόμο) frame || (εφημερίδα) edit.

συνταυτίζω [seentavteezo] identify, regard as the same.

συντείνω [seenteeno] contribute to, concur.

συντέλεια, n [seenteleea]: ~ του κόσμου end of the world.

συντελεστής, ο [seentelestees] factor, component, contributor || (μαθημ) coefficient.

συντελώ [seentelo] finish, complete || contribute to, conduce to.

συντεταγμένη, n [seentetagmenee] coordinate.

συντετριμμένος [seentetreemenos] deeply afflicted, crushed.

συντεχνία, n [seentehneea] guild, fellowship, confraternity || trade union.

συντήρηση, n [seenteereesee] preservation, conservation || (μηχανής) maintenance.

συντηρητικός [seenteereeteekos] conservative, preserving.

συντηρώ [seenteero] preserve, conserve || keep up, maintain || (διατρέφω) maintain, support.

σύντομα [seentoma] in short, briefly || soon, at once, immediately.

συντομεύω [seentomevo] shorten, curtail, abridge.

συντομία, n [seentomeea] shortness, brevity || terseness.

σύντομος [seentomos] short, succinct, brief.

συντονίζω [seentoneezo] coordinate, harmonize, tune together.

συντρέχω [seentreho] help || meet, converge || contribute.

συντριβή, n [seentreevee] ruin || crushing, smashing.

συντρίβω [seentreevo] shatter, break, crush, smash || ruin, wear out.

συντρίμια, τα [seentreemeea] πλ debris, fragments, wreckage.

συντριπτικός [seentreepteekos] (μεταφ) crushing, overwhelming.

συντροφιά, n [seentrofia] companionship, company || gathering, society || (επίρ) together.

σύντροφος, ο, n [seentrofos] companion, mate, comrade || (εμπορ) associate, partner.

συνύπαρξη, n [seeneeparksee] coexistence.

συνυπάρχω [seeneeparho] coexist.

συνυπεύθυνος [seeneepevtheenos] jointly liable.

συνυφαίνω [seeneefeno] entwine || (μεταφ) conspire, intrigue.

συνωμοσία, n [seenomoseea] conspiracy, plot.

συνωμοτώ [seenomoto] conspire, plot.

συνώνυμο, το [seenoneemo] synonym.

συνωστισμός, ο [seenosteesmos] jostle, crush, scramble.

σύξυλος [seekseelos] with crew and cargo || έμεινε ~ he was amazed, he was speechless.

Συρία, n [seereea] Syria.

συριακός [seereeakos] Syrian.

σύριγγα, n [seereenga] pan pipes || syringe, tube.

Σύριος, ο [seereeos] Syrian.

σύρμα, το [seerma] wire.

συρματόπλεγμα, το [seermatoplegma] barbed wire || wire netting.

σύρραξη, n [seeraksee] clash, collision, shock, conflict.

συρρέω [seereo] crowd, throng, flock || flow into.

σύρριζα [seereeza] by the root, root and branch || very closely.

συρροή, n [seerooee] crowd, throng || inflow, influx || abundance, profusion.

συρτάρι, το [seertaree] drawer.

σύρτης, ο [seertees] bolt, bar.

συρτός [seertos] dragged || listless, drawling || (πόρτα) sliding || (ουο) kind of circular dance.

συρφετός, ο [seerfetos] mob, populace, common people.

σύρω [seero] βλ **σέρνω**.

συσκέπτομαι [seeskeptome] confer, deliberate, take counsel.

συσκευάζω [seeskevazo] pack, box, wrap, parcel.

συσκευασία, n [seeskevaseea] wrapping up, packing || (φαρμακευτική) preparation.

συσκευή, n [seeskevee] apparatus, contrivance.

σύσκεψη, n [seeskepsee] discussion, deliberation || conference, consultation.

συσκοτίζω [seeskoteezo] obscure, darken, black out || (μεταφ) confuse.

συσκότιση, n [seeskoteesee] blackout || confusion.

σύσπαση, n [seespasee] contraction, writhing, shrinking.

συσπειρούμαι [seespeeroume] roll into a ball, coil || (μεταφ) snuggle.

συσσίτιο, το [seeseeteeo] mess, common meal || soup kitchen.

σύσσωμος [seesomos] all together, entire, united, in a body.

συσσωρευτής, ο [seesorevtees] accumulator.

συσσωρεύω [seesorevo] accumulate, collect, pile up || amass.

συσταίνω [seesteno] βλ συνιστώ.

συστάδα, η [seestaδa] clump of trees, cluster, grove.

συστάσεις, οι [seestasees] πλ references, advice || recommendation, introductions.

σύσταση, η [seestasee] address.

σύσταση, η [seestasee] composition, structure || (πάχος) consistency || (σχηματισμός) formation, creation, setting up || (πρόταση) recommendation, recommending || (συμβουλή) advice, counsel.

συστατικά, τα [seestateeka] πλ component parts, ingredients || references, recommendations.

συστατική [seestateekee]: ~ επιστολή letter of introduction, letter of reference.

συστατικός [seestateekos] component, essential, constituent.

συστέλλομαι [seestelome] shrink, contract || feel shy, be timid.

συστέλλω [seestelo] contract, shrink, shrivel.

σύστημα, το [seesteema] method, system, plan || custom, habitude.

συστηματικός [seesteemateekos] systematic, methodical.

συστημένο [seesteemeno]: ~ γράμμα registered letter.

συστήνω [seesteeno] βλ συνιστώ.

συστολή, η [seestolee] shrinking, contraction || modesty, shame, bashfulness.

συσφίγγω [seesfeengo] tighten, constrict, draw tighter, grasp.

συσχετίζω [seesheteezo] compare, relate, put together.

σύφιλη, η [seefeelee] syphilis.

συχνά [seehna] often, frequently.

συχνάζω [seehnazo] frequent, haunt, resort.

συχνός [seehnos] frequent, repeated.

συχνότητα, η [seehnoteeta] frequency.

συχωράω [seehorao] forgive, tolerate.

σφαγείο, το [sfayeeo] slaughterhouse || butchery, slaughter.

σφαγή, η [sfayee] slaughter, carnage, massacre.

σφάγιο, το [sfayo] victim, animal for slaughter.

σφαδάζω [sfaδazo] writhe, jerk, squirm.

σφάζω [sfazo] slaughter, kill, massacre, murder.

σφαίρα, η [sfera] globe, sphere || ball || (όπλου) bullet || (μεταφ) sphere, field.

σφαλιάρα, η [sfaleeara] slap in the face || smack.

σφαλίζω [sfaleezo] enclose, shut in || (κλείνω) close, lock, bolt.

σφάλλω [sfalo] be wrong, make a mistake || misfire.

σφάλμα, το [sfalma] wrong act, fault || error, blunder, slip.

σφάχτης, ο [sfahtees] twinge, sharp pain.

σφενδόνη, η [sfenδonee] sling.

σφετερίζομαι [sfetereezome] purloin, embezzle || appropriate, usurp.

σφήκα, η [sfeeka] wasp.

σφην, η [sfeen)], σφήνα, η [sfeena] wedge.

σφηνώνω [sfeenono] push in, thrust in between || wedge.

σφίγγα, η [sfeenga] sphinx || (μεταφ) enigmatic.

σφίγγομαι [sfeengome] squeeze together || endeavour, try hard.

σφίγγω [sfeengo] squeeze, press || tighten, pull tighter || (σκληρύνω) become tight, stick.

σφίξη, η [sfeeksee] urgency, necessity.

σφίξιμο, το [sfeekseemo] pressing, tightening, squeezing || pressure, squeeze.

σφιχτός [sfeehtos] tight, hard, thick || stingy, tight-fisted.

σφοδρός [sfoδros] violent, wild, strong, severe, sharp.

σφοδρότητα, η [sfoδroteeta] violence, vehemence, wildness.

σφουγγάρι, το [sfoungaree] sponge.

σφουγγαρόπανο, το [sfoungaropano] mop, floorcloth.

σφραγίζω [sfrayeezo] set one's seal to, stamp || (μπουκάλι) cork || (δόντι) fill.

σφραγίδα, η [sfrayeeδa] seal, signet, stamp || (μεταφ) impression.

σφρίγος, το [sfreegos] youthful exuberance, vigour, pep.

σφυγμός, ο [sfeegmos] pulse || (μεταφ) caprice, whim.

σφύζω [sfeezo] throb, beat violently, pulsate.

σφύξη, η [sfeeksee] pulsation, throbbing, throb.

σφυρηλατώ [sfeereelato] hammer, batter, forge, pound away || trump up.

σφυρί, το [sfeeree] hammer.

σφύριγμα, το [sfeereegma] whistling, hissing.

σφυρίζω [sfeereezo] whistle, hiss, boo.

σφυρίχτρα, η [sfeereehtra] whistle || (ναυτ) pipe.

σφυροκοπώ [sfeerokopo] hammer || pound away.

σχεδία, η [sheδeea] raft, float.

σχεδιάγραμμα, το [sheδeeagrama] sketch, outline, draft.

σχεδιάζω [sheδeeazo] sketch, outline, design, draw || plan, intend, mean.

σχεδιαστής, ο [sheδeeastees] draughtsman, designer.

σχέδιο, το [sheδeeo] plan, design || sketch, outline || scheme || ~ πόλεως town planning.

σχεδόν [sheðon] almost, nearly, all but || not much, scarcely.

σχέση, η [shesee] relation, connection, reference || intercourse, relations.

σχετίζομαι [sheteezome] be intimate with, get acquainted with, make friends with.

σχετίζω [sheteezo] put side by side, connect, compare.

σχετικά [sheteeka] relative to, relatively || ~ **με** with reference to, regarding, referring to.

σχετικός [sheteekos] relative, pertinent.

σχετικότητα, η [sheteekoteeta] relativity.

σχήμα, το [sheema] form, shape || (μέγεθος) format, size || (ιερατικό) cloth || gesture || ~ **λόγου** figure of speech.

σχηματίζω [sheemateezo] form, model, shape || create, produce || constitute.

σχηματισμός, ο [sheemateesmos] forming, formation, fashioning, construction.

σχίζομαι [sheezome] crack, tear || fork.

σχίζω [sheezo] split, cleave || tear, rend, fissure.

σχίσμα, το [sheesma] crack || schism, dissension, breach.

σχισμάδα, η [sheesmaða] crack, split, fissure.

σχισμή, η [sheesmee] crack, fissure, split.

σχιστόλιθος, ο [sheestoleethos] schist, slate.

σχιστός [sheestos] split, slit, torn, open.

σχοινί, το [sheenee] rope, cord || clothes line.

σχοινοβάτης, ο [sheenovatees] acrobat, rope dancer.

σχολάω [sholao] stop work || rest, be on vacation || (από σχολείο) let out || (από εργασία) dismiss, discharge.

σχολαστικός [sholasteekos] pedantic, scholastic.

σχολείο, το [sholeeo] school.

σχολή, η [sholee] school, academy || free time, leisure.

σχολιάζω [sholeeazo] comment on, pass remarks (on), criticize || annotate, edit.

σχολιαστής, ο [sholeeastees] commentator || editor, annotator, scholiast.

σχολικός [sholeekos] of school, scholastic, educational.

σχόλιο, το [sholeeo] comment, commentary, annotation.

σώβρακο, το [sovrako] pants, drawers.

σώζομαι [sozome] escape || remain in existence.

σώζω [sozo] save, rescue || preserve, keep.

σωθικά, τα [sotheeka] πλ entrails, bowels, intestines, innards.

σωλήνας, ο [soleenas] pipe, tube, conduit || hose.

σωληνάριο, το [soleenareeo] small tube.

σώμα, το [soma] body, corpse || corps || ~ **στρατού** army corps, armed force, army.

σωματείο, το [somateeo] guild, association.

σωματέμπορος, ο [somatemboros] white slaver || pimp.

σωματικός [somateekos] of the body, physical.

σωματοφυλακή, η [somatofeelakee] bodyguard.

σωματώδης [somatoðees] corpulent, stout, portly.

σώνει [sonee]: ~ **και καλά** with stubborn insistence.

σώνω [sono] save, rescue, preserve || use up, consume || attain, reach || be enough, be sufficient.

σώος [soos] safe, entire, whole, unharmed || intact || ~ **κι αβλαβής** safe and sound.

σωπαίνω [sopeno] keep silent, say nothing.

σωριάζομαι [soreeazome] collapse, fall in.

σωρός, ο [soros] heap, mass, pile || a lot of, a stack of.

σωσίας, ο [soseeas] living image, double || stand-in.

σωσίβιο, το [soseeveeo] lifebelt, life jacket.

σώσιμο, το [soseemo] saving || finishing up, eating.

σωστά [sosta]: **με τα** ~ **του** in his right mind, in earnest.

σωστά [sosta] correctly, precisely, rightly, exactly, absolutely.

σωστός [sostos] correct, just, right || whole, entire || absolute.

σωτήρας, ο [soteeras] saviour, liberator, rescuer.

σωτηρία, η [soteereea] safety, security || salvation, deliverance, saving.

σωφέρ, ο [sofer] chauffeur, driver.

σώφρονας [sofronas] wise, sensible, prudent || moderate, sober, temperate.

σωφρονίζω [sofroneezo] reform, chastise, correct, bring to reason, render wise.

σωφροσύνη, η [sofroseenee] wisdom, prudence, sense, judgment || moderation, composure.

T, τ

τα [ta] πλ the || them.

ταβάνι, το [tavanee] ceiling.

ταβέρνα, η [taverna] tavern, inn, eating house.

τάβλα, η [tavla] board, plank || table || ~ στο μεθύσι dead drunk.

τάβλι, το [tavlee] backgammon.

ταγάρι, το [tagaree] bag, sack, wallet.

ταγγός [tangos] rancid, rank.

ταγή, η [tayee] fodder.

ταγιέρ, το [tayier] woman's suit.

τάγμα, το [tagma] order || (στρατ) battalion.

ταγματάρχης, ο [tagmatarhees] major.

τάδε [taðe] as follows, the following, this, that || **ο** ~ Mr so and so || such.

τάζω [tazo] promise, dedicate, vow.

ταΐζω [taeezo] feed || (μωρό) nurse.

ταινία, η [teneea] band, stretch, strip, ribbon || (κινηματογράφου) strip, film || (μηχανής) tape, ribbon || (ιατρ) tapeworm || (μετρήσεως) tape measure.

ταίρι, το [teree] helpmate, partner, mate || one of two || match, equal.

ταιριάζει [tereeazee]: **δεν** ~ it's not fitting, it's not proper.

ταιριάζω [tereeazo] match, pair, suit, harmonize.

ταιριαστός [tereeastos] well-suited, matched.

τάκος, ο [takos] wooden fixing block, stump.

τακούνι, το [takounee] heel.

τακτ, το [takt] tact.

τακτικά [takteeka] regularly, frequently.

τακτική, η [takteekee] tactics, strategy || method, regularity.

τακτικός [takteekos] regular || orderly, settled, quiet || fixed || (αριθμός) ordinal.

τακτοποίηση, η [taktopieesee] arrangement, accommodation || compromise.

τακτοποιώ [taktopeeo] arrange, set in order || settle, fix up.

τακτός [taktos] fixed, appointed, settled.

ταλαιπωρία, η [taleporeea] torment, hardship, pain, adversity.

ταλαίπωρος [taleporos] miserable, wretched, unfortunate.

ταλαιπωρούμαι [taleporoume] suffer, toil, labour.

ταλαιπωρώ [taleporo] harass, pester, torment.

ταλαντεύομαι [talantevome] swing, sway, rock || waver, hesitate.

ταλέντο, το [talento] talent, gift, faculty.

τάλιρο, το [taleero] coin of five drachmas.

τάμα, το [tama] βλ **τάξιμο**.

ταμείο, το [tameeo] cashier's office, booking office, cash desk || treasury, pension fund.

ταμίας, ο [tameeas] cashier, teller, treasurer.

ταμιευτήριο, το [tamievteereeo] savings bank.

ταμπακιέρα, η [tambakiera] cigarette case || snuff box.

ταμπέλα, η [tambela] nameplate, bill || registration plate.

ταμπλό, το [tamblo] painting, picture || (αυτοκινήτου) dashboard || switchboard || instrument panel.

ταμπούρλο, το [tambourlo] drum || (παιδικό) side drum.

τανάλια, τα [tanaleea] πλ pliers, tongs, tweezers.

τανκ, το [tank] (στρατ) tank.

τάξη, η [taksee] order, succession, regularity || class, rank, grade || (σχολείου) form || **εντάξει** O.K., all right || **τάξεις** πλ ranks || **πρώτης τάξεως** first-rate, first-class.

ταξί, το [taksee] taxi (cab).

ταξίαρχης, ο [takseearhees] brigadier || (εκκλ) archangel.

ταξιαρχία η [takseearheea] brigade.

ταξιδεύω [takseeðevo] travel, journey.

ταξίδι, το [takseeðee] trip, journey, travel, voyage.

ταξιδιώτης, ο [takseeðeeotees] traveller.

ταξιθέτρια, η [takseethetreea] theatre attendant, usher.

ταξικός [takseekos] class.

ταξίμετρο, το [takseemetro] taximeter.

τάξιμο, το [takseemo] vow, promise.

ταξινομώ [takseenomo] classify, class, arrange || grade.

τάπα, η [tapa] plug, cork, stopper || ~ στο μεθύσι dead drunk.

ταπεινός [tapeenos] modest, humble || abject, vile, base.

ταπεινοφροσύνη, η [tapeenofroseenee] humility, modesty.

ταπεινώνομαι [tapeenonome] be humiliated || lower o.s.

ταπεινώνω [tapeenono] humble, humiliate, mortify, embarrass.

ταπέτο, το [tapeto] carpet, rug.

ταπετσαρία, η [tapetsareea] tapestry, wall covering || upholstery.

ταπητουργία, η [tapeetouryeea] carpet-making.

τάραγμα, το [taragma] agitation, shaking.

ταράζω [tarazo] shake || disturb, upset.

ταραμάς, ο [taramas] preserved roe.

ταραξίας, ο [tarakseeas] rowdy person, agitator, noisy person.

ταράτσα, η [taratsa] flat roof, terrace.

ταραχή, η [tarahee] agitation, disturbance || upset.

ταραχοποιός, ο [tarahopeeos] βλ **ταραξίας.**

ταρίφα, η [tareefa] scale of charges, price list, rates.

ταριχεύω [tareehevo] embalm || preserve, cure, smoke.

ταρσανάς, ο [tarsanas] boatbuilder's yard.

τάρταρα, τα [tartara] πλ bowels of the earth.

τασάκι, το [tasakee] saucer || ashtray.

τάση, η [tasee] tension, strain || (ηλεκτ) voltage || (μεταφ) inclination, proclivity, tendency.

τάσι, το [tasee] shallow bowl, goblet.

τάσσομαι [tasome] place o.s. || (μεταφ) support.

τάσσω [taso] place, put || post, set || marshal || assign, fix.

ταυ, το [tav] the letter T.

ταυρομαχία, η [tavromaheea] bullfight.

ταύρος, ο [tavros] bull.

ταύτα [tavta] πλ these || **μετά ~** afterwards.

ταυτίζω [tavteezo] identify, regard as same.

ταυτόσημος [tavtoseemos] equivalent, synonymous.

ταυτότητα, η [tavtoteeta] identity, sameness || identity card.

ταυτόχρονος [tavtohronos] simultaneous.

ταφή, η [tafee] burial, interment.

τάφος, ο [tafos] grave, tomb, vault.

τάφρος, η [tafros] ditch, trench, drain || (οχυρού) moat.

τάχα(τες) [taha(tes)] perhaps, apparently, supposedly || as if.

ταχεία, η [taheea] express train.

ταχίνι, το [taheenee] ground sesame.

ταχυδακτυλουργία, η [taheeδakteelouryeea] conjuring trick, juggling.

ταχυδρομείο, το [taheeδromeeo] post, mail || post office.

ταχυδρομικώς [taheeδromeekos] by post, by mail.

ταχυδρόμος, ο [taheeδromos] postman.

ταχυδρομώ [taheeδromo] mail, post.

ταχύνω [taheeno] quicken, speed up, accelerate || hasten, push forward.

ταχυπαλμία, η [taheepalmeea] palpitation.

ταχύς [tahees] quick, brisk, rapid, fleet, swift, fast || prompt, speedy.

ταχύτητα, η [taheeteeta] swiftness, speed, rapidity || promptness || velocity, rate.

ταψί, το [tapsee] large shallow baking pan.

τέζα [teza] stretched, spread, tight ||

έμεινε ~ he kicked the bucket (col) || **~ στο μεθύσι** dead drunk.

τεθλασμένη, η [tethlasmenee] zigzag line, broken line.

τεθλασμένος [tethlasmenos] broken.

τεθλιμμένος [tethleemenos] grief-stricken, heartbroken.

τείνω [teeno] tighten, stretch out || strain || tend (to), lead (to), be inclined (to).

τείχος, το [teehos] wall, high wall.

τεκμήριο, το [tekmeereeo] sign, token, mark, clue, indication.

τεκτονισμός, ο [tektoneesmos] freemasonry.

τελάρο, το [telaro] embroidery frame || (θύρας) doorframe || (πίνακα) frame.

τελεία, η [teleea] full stop || **άνω ~** semicolon.

τελειοποιώ [teleeopeeo] perfect, improve, make better.

τέλειος [teleeos] perfect, faultless || ideal || accomplished.

τελειότητα, η [teleeoteeta] perfection, faultlessness.

τελειόφοιτος [teleeofeetos] final-year (student) || graduate.

τελειωμός, ο [teleeomos] end, finish || **τελειωμό δεν έχει** it is interminable, it is inexhaustible.

τελειώνω [teleeono] exhaust, finish up || end, conclude, finish || (μεταφ) die, be exhausted.

τελείως [teleeos] faultlessly, perfectly || completely, fully, entirely, utterly.

τελειωτικός [teleeoteekos] definitive, decisive, final, conclusive.

τελεσίγραφο, το [teleseegrafo] ultimatum.

τελεσίδικος [teleseeδeekos] final, irrevocable, decisive.

τέλεση, η [telesee] ceremony || perpetration || completion.

τελετάρχης, ο [teletarhees] master of ceremonies.

τελετή, η [teletee] celebration, rite || feast, festival.

τελευταίος [televteos] last || most recent.

τελευταίως [televteos] of late, recently.

τέλι, το [telee] thin wire.

τελικά [teleeka] in the end, finally.

τέλμα, το [telma] swamp, marsh, bog.

τέλος, το [telos] end || (φόρος) tax, duty || expiration, close || **~ πάντων** after all, at all events, finally || **επί τέλους** at last, at long last || **στο ~** at the end, finally || **εν τέλει** in the end, finally.

τελούμαι [teloume] happen, take place.

τελωνείο, το [teloneeo] customs house.

τελώνης, ο [telonees] customs officer.

T

τεμαχίζω [temaheezo] cut into pieces, separate, break up.

τεμάχιο, το [temaheeon] piece, parcel, bit, fragment, chunk.

τέμενος, το [temenos] temple, shrine, mosque, house of worship.

τέμνω [temno] cut, divide, open.

τεμπέλης [tembelees] lazy, indolent, idle.

τεμπελιάζω [tembeleeazo] loaf, get lazy, idle.

τέμπλο, το [templo] iconostasis, reredos.

τενεκεδένιος [tenekeðeneeos] made of tin.

τενεκές, ο [tenekes] tin || large can || (μεταφ) good-for-nothing.

τένις, το [tenees] tennis.

τένοντας, ο [tenontas] tendon.

τενόρος, ο [tenoros] tenor.

τέντα, η [tenta] tent || marquee.

τέντζερες, ο [tendzeres] cooking pot, kettle, casserole.

τεντώνω [tentono] stretch, tighten, bend || (μεταφ) strain.

τέρας, το [teras] monster, abortion, freak || (μεταφ) terror.

τεράστιος [terasteeos] prodigious, enormous, huge, vast.

τερατούργημα, το [teratouryeema] monstrosity || atrocious deed.

τερατώδης [teratoðees] prodigious, monstrous || ugly, frightful.

τέρμα, το [terma] extremity, terminus, end || (αθλητ) goal.

τερματίζω [termateezo] finish, put an end to, terminate, end.

τερματικό, το [termateeko] computer terminal.

τερματοφύλακας, ο [termatofeelakas] goalkeeper.

τερπνός [terpnos] delightful, agreeable, pleasing.

τερτίπι, το [terteepee] trick.

τέρψη, η [terpsee] delight, pleasure, amusement.

τέσσαρα [tessara] four || με τα ~ on all fours.

τέσσερις [tesseres] four.

τεταμένος [tetamenos] stretched, extended, strained.

τέτανος, ο [tetanos] tetanus.

Τετάρτη, η [tetartee] Wednesday.

τέταρτο, το [tetarto] quarter of an hour || quarto.

τέταρτος [tetartos] fourth.

τετελεσμένος [tetelesmenos] accomplished, achieved, done || τετελεσμένο γεγονός fait accompli || ~ μέλλων (γραμμ) future perfect tense.

τέτοιος [teteeos] similar, alike, such || ο ~ what's-his-name.

τετραγωνικός [tetragoneekos] square, quadrangular.

τετράγωνο, το [tetragono] (γεωμ) square, quadrangle || (πόλης) block.

τετράγωνος [tetragonos] square || (μεταφ) well-grounded, reasonable.

τετράδιο, το [tetraðeeo] exercise book, copybook.

τετρακόσιοι [tetrakosiee] four hundred.

τετράπαχος [tetrapahos] very stout, very fat, corpulent.

τετραπέρατος [tetraperatos] very clever, shrewd.

τετραπλάσιος [tetraplaseeos] four times as much.

τετράποδο, το [tetrapoðo] quadruped || (μεταφ) beast, brute.

τετράδα, η [tetraða] set of four.

τετράτροχος [tetratrohos] four-wheeled.

τετριμμένος [tetreemenos] worn-out || (μεταφ) hackneyed.

τεύτλο, το [tevtlo] beetroot, beet.

τεύχος, το [tevhos] issue (of a publication).

τέφρα, η [tefra] ashes, cinders.

τεφτέρι, το [tefteree] notebook || account book.

τέχνες, οι [tehnes] πλ: καλές ~ fine arts.

τέχνασμα, το [tehnasma] ruse, artifice, trick, device.

τέχνη, η [tehnee] art || profession || dexterity || (πολεμική) stratagem.

τεχνητός [tehneetos] sham, false, artificial || simulated, affected.

τεχνική, η [tehneekee] technique, means.

τεχνικός [tehneekos] technical, professional || (ουσ) technician.

τεχνίτης, ο [tehneetees] professional, craftsman || technician, mechanic || (μεταφ) specialist, expert.

τεχνολογία, η [tehnoloyeea] technology || (γραμμ) grammatical analysis.

τεχνοτροπία, η [tehnotropeea] artistic style.

τέως [teos] formerly, former, late || ο ~ πρόεδρος the ex-president.

τζάκι, το [dzakee] fireplace || heating range.

τζάμι, το [dzamee] window pane, pane of glass.

τζαμί, το [dzamee] mosque.

τζάμπα [dzamba] free, gratis, for nothing || to no purpose, wantonly.

τζαναμπέτης, ο [dzanambetees] peevish person || wicked person.

τζελατίνα, η [dzelateena] gelatine || celluloid holder.

τζίρος, ο [dzeeros] business turnover.

τζίτζικας, ο [dzeedzeekas] cicada.

τζίφρα, η [dzeefra] cipher || initial, monogram.

τζόγος, ο [dzogos] gambling.

τζόκεϋ, ο [dzokey] jockey.

τήβεννος, η [teevenos] toga || gown, robe.

τηγανητός [teeganeetos] fried.

τηγάνι, το [teeganee] frying pan.

τηγανίζω [teeganeezo] fry.

τήκομαι [teekome] thaw, melt || wither, pine, languish.

τήκω [teeko] melt, thaw.

τηλεβόας, ο [teelevoas] loudhailer, loudspeaker.

τηλεβόλο, το [teelevolo] cannon.

τηλεγράφημα, το [teelegrafeema] telegram, cable.

τηλέγραφος, ο [teelegrafos] telegraph.

τηλεγραφώ [teelegrafo] telegraph, wire.

τηλεόραση, η [teeleorasee] television.

τηλεπάθεια, η [teelepatheea] telepathy.

τηλεπικοινωνία, η [teelepeekeenoneea] telecommunications.

τηλεσκόπιο, το [teeleskopeeo] telescope.

τηλεφώνημα, το [teelefoneema] telephone call.

τηλεφωνητής, ο [teelefoneetees] telephone operator.

τηλέφωνο, το [teelefono] telephone, phone.

τηλεφωνώ [teelefono] telephone, call up.

τήξη, η [teeksee] melting, thawing || casting.

τήρηση, η [teereesee] observance || maintenance, keeping.

τηρώ [teero] keep, observe, follow, maintain.

τι [tee] what || what, how.

τι [tee] something || a bit.

τίγρη, η [teegree] tiger, tigress.

τιθασεύω [teethasevo] tame, domesticate.

τίθεμαι [teetheme] be arranged, be placed, be imposed.

τίλιο, το [teeleeo] infusion of lime flowers.

τιμαλφή, τα [teemalfee] πλ jewellery, jewels.

τιμάριθμος, ο [teemareethmos] cost of living.

τιμή, η [teemee] respect, honour || rate, price || value, worth.

τίμημα, το [teemeema] cost, price || value.

τιμητικός [teemeeteekos] honorary || honouring.

τίμιος [teemeeos] honest, upright || precious, valuable.

τιμιότητα, η [teemeeoteeta] honesty.

τιμοκατάλογος, ο [teemokatalogos] price list, tariff.

τιμολόγιο, το [teemoloyo] invoice, bill.

τιμόνι, το [teemonee] helm, rudder || tiller, wheel || (αυτοκινήτου) steering wheel || (ποδηλάτου) handlebars.

τιμονιέρης, ο [teemonierees] steersman, helmsman.

τιμώ [teemo] honour, respect, venerate, do honour to.

τιμώμαι [teemome] cost, be worth || be honoured.

τιμωρία, η [teemoreea] punishment, chastisement, penalty.

τιμωρώ [teemoro] punish, chastise || fine.

τινάζομαι [teenazome] leap, spring, start || brush one's clothes.

τινάζω [teenazo] shake off, shake || (πετώ) hurl, toss || (φτερουγίζω) flap || ~ **στον αέρα** blow up.

τίποτα [teepota] any, anything || nothing || ~! don't mention it!, forget it!

τιποτένιος [teepoteneeos] mean, trivial, trifling, worthless.

τιράντες, οι [teerantes] πλ pair of braces.

τιρμπουσόν, το [teermbouson] corkscrew.

τίτλος, ο [teetlos] title, right, claim || certificate.

τιτλοφορώ [teetloforo] entitle, confer a title.

τμήμα, το [tmeema] part, segment, section || (υπουργείου) branch, department || (αστυνομίας) police station.

τμηματάρχης, ο [tmeematarhees] chief of a department.

το [to] the || it.

τοιούτος [teeoutos] such || (μεταφ) homosexual.

τοιχογραφία, η [teehografeea] fresco, wall painting.

τοιχοκόλληση, η [teehokoleesee] bill posting, bill sticking.

τοίχος, ο [teehos] wall.

τοίχωμα, το [teehoma] inner wall, partition wall || inner surface.

τοκετός, ο [toketos] childbirth, confinement.

τοκίζω [tokeezo] lend at interest, invest.

τοκογλύφος, ο [tokogleefos] usurer.

τοκομερίδιο, το [tokomereedeeo] dividend coupon.

τόκος, ο [tokos] interest, rate.

τόλμη, η [tolmee] daring, audacity.

τολμηρός [tolmeeros] bold, courageous, daring, venturesome.

τολμώ [tolmo] dare, risk, hazard.

τομάρι, το [tomaree] hide, skin, leather.

τομέας, ο [tomeas] sector || incisor, chisel.

τομή, η [tomee] cut, gash, incision || (διαγράμματος) section.

τόμος, ο [tomos] volume, tome.

τονίζω [toneezo] accent || accentuate, stress, lay emphasis on || tone up.

τονισμός, ο [toneesmos] accentuation || emphasizing.

τόνος, ο [tonos] ton || (ψάρι) tuna fish || accent, tone || (γραμμ) accent || (μουσ) key || **μιλώ με τόνο** raise one's voice || **δίνω ~ σε** brighten up.

τονώνω [tonono] fortify, invigorate, brace up.

τονωτικός [tonoteekos] bracing, invigorating, tonic.

τοξικομανής, ο, η [tokseekomanees] drug addict.

τοξικός [tokseekos] toxic || poisonous.

τοξοειδής [toksoeeδees] bowed, arched, curved, bow-shaped.

τόξο, το [tokso] bow || (κτιρίου) arch || (γεωμ) arc, curve.

τοπίο, το [topeeo] landscape || site, locality.

τόπι, το [topee] ball || (υφάσματος) roll of cloth || (κανονιού) cannonball.

τοπικός [topeekos] local.

τοπογραφία, η [topografeea] topography.

τοποθεσία, η [topotheseea] location, site, position, place.

τοποθέτηση, η [topotheteesee] putting, placing || (οικον) investment, investing.

τοποθετώ [topotheto] place, set, put || (οικον) invest.

τόπος, ο [topos] place, position, site || (χώρα) country || (χώρος) space, room || (μαθημ) locus || **πιάνω τόπο** have effect, be of use || **έμεινε στον τόπο** he died suddenly.

τοπωνυμία, η [toponeemeea] place name.

τορνευτός [tornevtos] well-turned, turned.

τορνεύω [tornevo] turn a lathe, work a lathe || (μεταφ) give fine shape to.

τόρνος, ο [tornos] lathe.

τορπίλη, η [torpeelee] torpedo.

τορπιλίζω [torpeeleezo] torpedo.

τόσο [toso] so much || ~ ... **όσο** as much ... as, both ... and || **όχι και** ~ not so much.

τόσος [tosos] so big, so large, so great || so much, so many || ~ **δα** very little, very small, only so small || **άλλοι τόσοι** as many again || **κάθε τόσο** every now and again || **εκατόν τόσα** a hundred odd.

τότε [tote] then, at that time || in that case, therefore, thereupon || ~ **που** when.

τουαλέτα, η [toualeta] toilet || (γυναίκας) dress || (αίθουσα) dressing room || (τραπέζι) dressing table || (αποχωρητήριο) lavatory.

τούβλο, το [touvlo] brick || (μεταφ) simpleton.

τουλάχιστον [toulaheeston] at least, at all events.

τούλι, το [toulee] tulle.

τουλίπα, η [touleepa] tulip.

τουλούμι, το [touloumee] goatskin bottle || **βρέχει με το** ~ it's raining cats and dogs.

τούμπα, η [toumba] somersault, fall || mound || **κάνω τούμπες κωτσω** fall head over heels.

τούμπανο, το [toumbano] drum.

τουμπάρω [toumbaro] overturn, upset || (μεταφ) persuade || reverse.

τουναντίο(ν) [tounanteeo(n)] on the contrary.

τουπέ, το [toupe] cheek, audacity, nerve.

τουρισμός, ο [toureesmos] tourism, touring.

τουρίστας, ο [toureestas] tourist.

Τουρκία, η [tourkeea] Turkey.

τουρκικός [tourkeekos] Turkish.

τουρκοκρατία, η [tourkokrateea] Turkish domination of Greece.

Τούρκος, ο [tourkos] Turk || **γίνομαι** ~ get angry.

τουρλώνω [tourlono] pile up || swell out, become round.

τουρλωτός [tourlotos] piled up || rounded, bulging.

τουρνέ, η [tourne] theatrical tour.

τουρσί, το [toursee] pickle, brine.

τούρτα, η [tourta] gateau, layer cake, tart.

τουρτουρίζω [tourtoureezo] shiver, tremble, shudder.

τούτος [toutos] this one.

τούφα, η [toufa] tuft, bunch, cluster.

τουφέκι, το [toufekee] rifle, musket, gun.

τουφεκιά, η [toufekia] gunshot, rifle shot.

τουφεκίζω [toufekeezo] shoot, fire || execute.

τράβηγμα, το [traveegma] pulling, dragging, tug || (υγρού) drawing off.

τραβώ [travo] pull, drag, heave, haul || ~ **το δρόμο μου** go my own way || (όπλο, χρήματα κτλ) draw || **το τραβάει** he imbibes || (απορροφάω) absorb || (τουφεκιά) fire, shoot || (ταχύτητα) reach distance of || (προσελκύω) entice, attract || **δε με τραβάει** it doesn't attract me || (ζητώ) ask for, want || **ο καιρός τραβάει πανωφόρι** the weather calls for a coat || **η καρδιά μου** ~ **τσιγάρο** I need a smoke || (υποφέρω) undergo, endure, bear || (αμετ) make towards, head for || move on || (συνεχίζω) last, go on || (τσιμπούκι κτλ) suck, draw ||

τραβιέμαι (αμετ) draw back, leave || (εμπόριο) be in demand || (δεν υποφέρεται) it's unbearable.

τραγανίζω [traganeezo] crunch, munch, grind.

τραγανό, το [tragano] cartilage, grist.

τραγανός [traganos] crisp, brittle.

τραγί, το [trayee] kid.

τραγικός [trayeekos] calamitous, tragic || (ποιητής) tragic poet.

τράγος, ο [tragos] goat.

τραγούδι, το [tragouδee] song, air, tune.

τραγουδιστής, ο [tragouδeestees] singer, vocalist.

τραγουδιστός [tragouδeestos] sung || (φωνή) tuneful.

τραγουδώ [tragouδo] sing, chant || (σιγά) hum.

τραγωδία, η [tragoδeea] tragedy.

τραγωδός, ο, η [tragoδos] tragic actor, tragedian, tragic actress.

τραίνο, το [treno] railway train || (επιβατικό) passenger train.

τρακ, το [trak] stage fright.

τρακάρισμα, το [trakareesma] crash, collision || unexpected meeting.

τρακάρω [trakaro] knock against, collide with || meet by accident || (μεταφ) touch for a loan.

τρακατρούκα, η [trakatrouka] firecracker.

τράκο, το [trako], **τράκος, ο** [trakos] collision || (μεταφ) attack, assault.

τρακτέρ, το [trakter] farm tractor.

τραμ, το [tram] tram, tramcar, tramway.

τραμπούκος, ο [tramboukos] out-and-out rascal, scoundrel, rotter.

τρανός [tranos] powerful || large, grand || important, weighty.

τράνταγμα, το [trantagma] jolting, shake, shaking || jolt, jerk.

τραντάζω [trantazo] jolt, shake up and down.

τράπεζα, η [trapeza] table || (εμπορ) bank || **αγία** ~ altar.

τραπεζαρία, η [trapezareea] dining room.

τραπέζι, το [trapezee] table || dinner || **στρώνω** ~ set the table || **τους είχαμε** ~ we invited them to dinner.

τραπεζίτης, ο [trapezeetees] banker || (δόντι) molar.

τραπεζιτικός [trapezeeteekos] banking || (υπάλληλος) bank employee.

τραπεζομάντηλο, το [trapezomanteelo] tablecloth.

τράπουλα, η [trapoula] pack of cards.

τράτα, η [trata] seine || fishing boat.

τρατάρω [trataro] regale || pay for, offer.

τραυλίζω [travleezo] stammer, stutter, lisp.

τραυλός [travlos] stammering, stuttering.

τραύμα, το [travma] wound, hurt, injury || (μεταφ) wound, sore.

τραυματίας, ο [travmateeas] casualty, wounded person.

τραυματίζω [travmateezo] wound, hurt, injure.

τραχεία, η [traheea] trachea, windpipe.

τραχηλιά, η [traheelia] collar, collarette || bib.

τράχηλος, ο [traheelos] neck.

τραχύνω [traheeno] make harsh, make rough || irritate.

τραχύς [trahees] harsh, rough || (στη γεύση) tart, sharp || (στην ακοήο) harsh, grating || (χαρακτήρας) sour, crabbed.

τρεις [trees] three.

τρέλα, η [trela] madness, insanity || folly || (ιατρ) mania || (μεταφ) anything pleasing.

τρελαίνομαι [trelenome] go insane || be driven mad || be mad about.

τρελαίνω [treleno] drive mad, bewilder.

τρελοκομείο, το [trelokomeeo] madhouse.

τρελός [trelos] insane, mad || (ουσ) madman || (μωρό) mischievous.

τρεμοσβήνω [tremosveeno] flicker, sparkle.

τρεμούλα, η [tremoula] shivering, trembling || (φωνής) quiver || (από κρύο) shivering || scare.

τρέμω [tremo] tremble || (από κρύο) shiver || (από φόβο) shake || (το φως) flicker, waver || (φωνή) quiver.

τρέξιμο, το [trekseemo] running || (υγρού) flowing || (αίματος) flow, gush.

τρέπω [trepo] change, convert || turn, translate || ~ **δε φυγή** put to flight.

τρέφω [trefo] nourish, nurture || (ελπίδα) cherish, foster || (γένια) grow || support, keep.

τρεχάλα, η [trehala] running || (σαν επίρ) at full speed.

τρεχάματα, τα [trehamata] πλ running about || (μεταφ) cares.

τρεχάμενος [trehamenos] running.

τρεχαντήρι, το [trehanteeree] small sailing boat.

τρεχάτος [trehatos] running, hasty.

τρέχω [treho] run, race, hurry || (για υγρά) flow || leak || **τι τρέχει;** what's happening?, what's the matter?

τρεχούμενος [trehoumenos] current || (λογαριασμός) current.

τρία [treea] three.

τριάδα, η [treeaδa] trinity || trio.

τρίαινα, η [treena] trident.

τριακόσιοι [treeakosiee] three hundred.

τριανδρία, n [treeanδreea] triumvirate.

τριάντα [treeanta] thirty.

τριαντάφυλλο, το [treeantafeelo] rose.

τριάρι, το [treearee] figure 3 || three at cards || (διαμέρισμα) three-room apartment.

τριάδα, n [treeaδa] trinity || trio.

τριβή, n [treevee] friction, chafing, rubbing || wear and tear || (μεταφ) practice, use, experience.

τρίβομαι [treevome] wear out || disintegrate || (μεταφ) get experienced, get practice in.

τρίβω [treevo] rub || polish up || grate || (το σώμα) massage.

τριγμός, ο [treegmos] crackling, creaking || (δοντιών) grinding, gnashing.

τριγυρίζω [treeyeereezo], **τριγυρνώ** [treeyeerno] encircle || roam, hang about.

τριγωνικός [treegoneekos] triangular.

τριγωνομετρία, n [treegonometreea] trigonometry.

τρίγωνο, το [treegono] triangle.

τρίδυμα, τα [treeδeema] πλ triplets.

τριετής [trietees] of three years || (ηλικία) three years old || (φοιτητής) third-year.

τρίζω [treezo] crackle, crack, creak, squeak || (δόντια) grind, gnash, grit.

τριήρης, n [trieerees] trireme.

τρικαντό, το [treekanto] three-cornered hat, cocked hat.

τρικλίζω [treekleezo] stagger, totter, wobble, reel.

τρίκλωνος [treeklonos] three-stranded.

τρικούβερτος [treekouvertos] (μεταφ) splendid, terrific, wonderful.

τρικυμία, n [treekeemeea] storm, tempest, hurricane.

τρικυμιώδης [treekeemeeoδees] stormy, tempestuous, rough.

τρίλια, n [treeleea] trill.

τριμελής [treemelees] of three members.

τριμερής [treemerees] tripartite.

τριμηνία, n [treemeeneea] quarter of a year || quarter's rent.

τριμηνιαίος [treemeenieos] of three months, quarterly.

τρίμηνο, το [treemeeno] βλ **τριμηνία**.

τρίμηνος [treemeenos] βλ **τριμηνιαίος**.

τρίμμα, το [treema] fragment, morse, chip, particle.

τριμμένος [treemenos] showing signs of wear and tear || ground.

τρίξιμο, το [treekseemo] gnashing, grinding.

τρίπατος [treepatos] three-storeyed.

τριπλασιάζω [treeplaseeazo] treble, triple, triplicate.

τριπλάσιος [treeplaseeos] threefold, triple, treble.

τριποδίζω [treepoδeezo] trot.

τρίποδο, το [treepoδo] tripod || easel || three-legged support.

τρίπτυχο, το [treepteeho] triptych.

τρισδιάστατος [treesδeeastatos] three-dimensional.

τρισέγγονο, το [treesengono] great-great-grandchild.

τρισκατάρατος [treeskataratos] thrice-cursed || abominable.

Τρίτη, n [treetee] Tuesday.

τρίτο, το [treeto] third || (επίρ) thirdly.

τρίτος [treetos] third || third-party.

τρίφτης, ο [treeftees] grater, rasp.

τριφύλλι, το [treefeelee] clover, trefoil.

τρίχα, n [treeha] hair || bristle || fur || **στην ~** spruced up || **παρά ~** nearly.

τρίχες, οι [treehes] πλ nonsense, rubbish.

τριχιά, n [treehia] rope.

τριχοειδής [treehoeeδees] capillary.

τρίχωμα, το [treehoma] fur || (σώματος) hair.

τριχωτός [treehotos] hairy, shaggy.

τρίψιμο, το [treepseemo] massage, rubbing, friction || (στίλβωμα) polishing || grating, grinding, crushing.

τρίωρος [treeoros] of three hours.

τρόλλεϋ, το [troley] trolley bus.

τρόμαγμα, το [tromagma] fright, scare.

τρομάζω [tromazo] terrify, frighten || get scared.

τρομακτικός [tromakteekos] fearful, awful, frightening || (μεταφ) terrific.

τρομάρα, n [tromara] dread, fright, fear.

τρομερός [tromeros] terrible, dreadful, frightful || (μεταφ) terrific, astonishing.

τρομοκρατία, n [tromokrateea] terrorism || terror.

τρομοκρατώ [tromokrato] terrorize.

τρόμος, ο [tromos] trembling, shaking || dread, fright.

τρόμπα, n [tromba] pump.

τρομπέτα, n [trompeta] trumpet.

τρομπόνι, το [tromponee] trombone.

τρόπαιο, το [tropeo] trophy || triumph.

τροπάριο, το [tropareo] (εκκλ) hymn || (μεταφ) same old refrain.

τροπή, n [tropee] change || turn || (μαθημ) conversion.

τροπικός [tropeekos] tropical || (γραμμ) of manner.

τροπολογία, n [tropoloyeea] amendment, alteration, change, modification.

τροποποίηση, η [tropopieesee] modification, alteration, change.

τρόποι, οι [tropee] πλ manners, behaviour.

τρόπος, ο [tropos] way, manner, method || behaviour, conduct || (μουσ) mode || ~ του λέγειν so to speak.

τρούλλος, ο [troulos] dome, cupola.

τρουλλωτός [troulotos] domed, dome-shaped.

τροφή, η [trofee] food, nutrition || (ζώων) pasture, fodder || sustenance.

τρόφιμα, τα [trofeema] πλ provisions, food, victuals.

τρόφιμος, ο, η [trofeemos] lodger, boarder || paying guest || inmate || (μεταφ) nursling.

τροφοδοσία, η [trofoδoseea] provisioning, supplying || supply.

τροφοδότης, ο [trofoδotees] caterer, purveyor, provider, supplier.

τροφοδοτώ [trofoδoto] feed, provision, keep supplied, supply, serve.

τροχάδην [trohaδeen] hurriedly, hastily, at full speed || (μεταφ) fluently.

τροχαία, η [trohea]: ~ κίνηση traffic || η ~ traffic police.

τροχαίο [troheo]: ~ υλικό rolling stock.

τροχαίος, ο [troheos] trochee || (επίθ) wheeled, rolling.

τροχαλία, η [trohaleea] pulley, block.

τροχιά, η [trohia] track, groove, rut || (σιδηροδρόμου) track, rail || (δορυφόρου κτλ) orbit, trajectory.

τροχίζω [troheezo] sharpen, whet, grind || (μεταφ) train, exercise.

τρόχισμα, το [troheesma] sharpening, whetting, grinding || (μεταφ) exercising.

τροχονόμος, ο [trohonomos] traffic policeman.

τροχοπέδη, η [trohopeδee] brake, skid, wheel brake.

τροχός, ο [trohos] wheel || grindstone, whetstone.

τροχοφόρο, το [trohoforo] vehicle.

τρυγητής, ο [treeyeetees] grape harvester, vintager.

τρυγητός, ο [treeyeetos] grape harvest, vintage.

τρυγόνι, το [treegonee] turtledove.

τρύγος, ο [treegos] βλ **τρυγητός**.

τρυγώ [treego] gather grapes || (μεταφ) loot, fleece.

τρύπα, η [treepa] hole || (βελόνας) eye || (μεταφ) den, lair.

τρυπάνι, το [treepanee] drill, drilling machine.

τρύπημα, το [treepeema] perforating, boring, piercing || prick, punch.

τρυπητήρι, το [treepeeteeree] awl, punch, drill.

τρυπητό, το [treepeeto] strainer, colander.

τρύπιος [treepeeos] with holes, perforated, holed, riddled.

τρυπητός [treepeetos] perforated, holed, riddled.

τρυπώ [treepo] bore, make a hole, pierce || prick, punch.

τρυπώνω [treepono] hide, conceal || squeeze in || take refuge.

τρυφερός [treeferos] tender, soft || affectionate, affable, mild.

τρυφερότητα, η [treeferoteeta] tenderness, softness || affection, kindness.

τρώγλη, η [troglee] hole, lair, den || hovel, shack.

τρώγομαι [trogome] be edible || (μεταφ) be tolerable || **τρώγονται** they are quarrelling.

τρώγω [trogo] eat, bite || **με τρώει** it itches || ~ **ξύλο** get a beating || ~ **το κόσμο** look everywhere.

τρωκτικό, το [trokteeko] rodent.

τρωτός [trotos] vulnerable.

τρώω [troo] βλ **τρώγω**.

τσαγιέρα, η [tsayera] teapot.

τσαγκάρης, ο [tsangarees] shoemaker.

τσάι, το [tsaee] tea.

τσακάλι, το [tsakalee] jackal.

τσακίζομαι [tsakeezome] strive, struggle || (διπλώνω) fold.

τσακίζω [tsakeezo] break, shatter, smash || (μεταφ) weaken, wear out, enfeeble.

τσάκιση, η [tsakeesee] crease, pleat.

τσάκισμα, το [tsakeesma] breaking, shattering, smashing.

τσακμάκι, το [tsakmakee] tinderbox || cigarette lighter.

τσάκωμα, το [tsakoma] seizing, catching || quarrelling, dispute.

τσακώνομαι [tsakonome] quarrel.

τσακώνω [tsakono] catch in the act.

τσαλαβουτώ [tsalavouto] flounder, wallow, splash about || (μεταφ) do a sloppy job.

τσαλακώνω [tsalakono] crease, crumple, wrinkle.

τσαλαπατώ [tsalapato] trample underfoot, tread over.

τσαμπί, το [tsambee] bunch (of grapes), cluster.

τσάντα, η [tsanta] pouch || handbag || briefcase || (φωνίσματος) shopping bag || (ταχυδρόμου) satchel.

τσάπα, η [tsapa] hoe, pickaxe.

τσαπατσούλης [tsapatsoulees] untidy in one's work.

τσαπί, το [tsapee] βλ **τσάπα**.

τσάρκα, η [tsarka] walk, promenade, stroll.

τσαρούχι, το [tsarouhee] rustic shoe with pompom.

τσατσάρα, η [tsatsara] comb.

τσαχπινιά, η [tsahpeenia] coquetry, roguery, trickery.

τσεκ, το [tsek] cheque || check (US).

τσεκούρι, το [tsekouree] axe, hatchet.

τσέλιγκας, ο [tseleengas] chief shepherd.

τσεμπέρι, το [tsemberee] kerchief, veil.

τσέπη, η [tsepee] pocket || pocketful.

τσεπώνω [tsepono] pocket || (μεταφ) filch, swipe.

τσευδίζω [tsevðeezo] lisp, stammer, falter.

τσευδός [tsevðos] lisping, stammering.

τσεχικός [tseheekos] Czech.

Τσέχος, ο [tsehos] Czech.

Τσεχοσλοβακία, η [tsehoslovakeea] Czechoslovakia.

τσιγαρίζω [tseegareezo] fry lightly, brown, roast brown.

τσιγάρο, το [tseegaro] cigarette.

τσιγαροθήκη, η [tseegarotheekee] cigarette case.

τσιγαρόχαρτο, το [tseegaroharto] tissue paper.

τσιγγάνος, ο [tseenganos] gipsy.

τσιγγούνης [tseengounees] miserly, stingy || (ουσ) miser.

τσιγκέλι, το [tseengelee] meat hook.

τσιγκλώ [tseenglo] goad, prick, spur.

τσίγκος, ο [tseengos] zinc.

τσίκνα, η [tseekna] smell of burning meat.

τσικνίζω [tseekneezo] scorch, burn || have a burnt smell.

τσικουδιά, η [tseekouðia] terebinth || (ποτό) kind of spirit.

τσίμα [tseema]: ~ ~ scarcely || on the brink of.

τσιμέντο, το [tseemento] cement.

τσιμουδιά, η [tseemouðia]: **δεν έβγαλε** ~ he remained speechless || ~! not a word!, mum's the word!

τσίμπημα, το [tseembeema] prick, sting, pinch || bite, peck.

τσιμπιά, η [tseembia] pinch.

τσιμπίδα, η [tseembeeða] nippers, tongs, forceps, pincers.

τσιμπιδάκι, το [tseembeeðakee] tweezers || hairclip.

τσίμπλα, η [tseembla] mucus of eyes.

τσιμπούκι, το [tseemboukee] tobacco pipe.

τσιμπούρι, το [tseembouree] (έντομο) tick || (μεταφ) troublesome or bothersome person, pest.

τσιμπούσι, το [tseembousee] spread, repast, regalement, feast.

τσιμπώ [tseembo] prick, pinch, sting || (δαγκώνω) bite, peck || (φαγητό) nibble || (μεταφ) cadge || (συλλαμβάνω) seize, collar.

τσίνορο, το [tseenoro] eyelash.

τσίπα, η [tseepa] thin skin, crust || (μεταφ) shame.

τσιπούρα, η [tseepoura] gilthead.

τσίπουρο, το [tseepouro] kind of spirit.

τσιρίζω [tseereezo] screech, shriek, scream.

τσίρκο, το [tseerko] circus.

τσίρλα, η [tseerla] diarrhoea.

τσίρος, ο [tseeros] dried mackerel || (μεταφ) skinny person.

τσιρότο, το [tseeroto] sticking plaster.

τσίτα [tseeta] very tight || ~ ~ scarcely.

τσιτσίδι [tseetseeðee] stark naked.

τσιτσιρίζω [tseetseereezo] sizzle.

τσιτώνω [tseetono] stretch, tighten, strain.

τσιφλίκι, το [tseefleekee] large country estate, farm, ranch.

τσίχλα, η [tseehla] thrush || (αδύνατος) skinny person.

τσόκαρο, το [tsokaro] wooden shoe.

τσολιάς, ο [tsolias] evzone, kilted soldier.

τσο(μ)πάνης, ο [tso(m)panees] shepherd.

τσοντάρω [tsontaro] join on.

τσουβάλι, το [tsouvalee] sackful || sack.

τσουγκράνα, η [tsoungrana] rake.

τσουγκρανίζω [tsoungraneezo] scratch, rake.

τσουγκρίζω [tsoungreezo] strike against || clink glasses, touch glasses.

τσούζω [tsouzo] smart, sting, hurt.

τσουκάλι, το [tsoukalee] jug, pot || chamberpot.

τσουκνίδα, η [tsoukneeða] nettle.

τσούλα, η [tsoula] loose-living woman, whore.

τσουλάω [tsoulao] slip along, slide along || (όχημα) push.

τσουλούφι, το [tsouloufee] lock of hair.

τσουρέκι, το [tsourekee] bun, brioche.

τσούρμο, το [tsourmo] throng || band, troop.

τσουρουφλίζω [tsouroufleezo] grill brown, scorch.

τσουχτερός [tsouhteros] keen, smart, sharp || (κρύο) biting || harsh.

τσούχτρα, η [tsouhtra] jellyfish.

τσόφλι, το [tsoflee] shell || rind.

τσόχα, η [tsoha] felt.

τυγχάνω [teenghano] happen to be || obtain, attain.

τύλιγμα, το [teeleegma] winding, rolling, coiling, wrapping.

τυλίγω [teeleego] roll up, wind, coil || wrap up, fold round, twist.

τυλώνω [teelono] fill up.

τύμβος, ο [teemvos] grave, tomb.

τύμπανο, το [teembano] drum, tambour || (αυτιού) || eardrum || tympanum.

Τυνησία, η [teeneeseea] Tunisia.

τυνησιακός [teeneeseeakos] Tunisian.

Τυνήσιος, ο [teeneeseeos] Tunisian.

τυπικός [teepeekos] usual, conventional || typical.

τυπικότητα, η [teepeekoteeta] formality.

τυπογραφείο, το [teepografeeo] printing press, printer's.

τυπογραφία, η [teepografeea] printing.

τυπογράφος, ο [teepografos] printer.

τύποι, οι [teepee] πλ conventions, form.

τυποποίηση, η [teepopieesee] standardization.

τύπος, ο [teepos] print, imprint, stamp || (καλούπι) mould, matrix, form || (υπόδειγμα) model, type || (συμπεριφοράς) formality, rule of procedure || (οικίας) type, kind of || (μαθημ) formula || (εφημερίδες) the press || (για άνθρωπο) figure, character.

τυπώνω [teepono] print, stamp.

τυραννία, η [teeraneea] tyranny, oppression || torment, torture.

τύραννος, ο [teeranos] oppressor, tyrant.

τυραννώ [teerano] oppress || torture, harass.

τυρί, το [teeree] cheese.

τυροκομία, η [teerokomeea] cheese-making.

τυρόπιτα, η [teeropeeta] cheese pie || cheesecake.

τύρφη, η [teerfee] peat.

τύφλα, η [teefla] blindness || ~ στο μεθύσι dead drunk.

τυφλοπόντικας, ο [teefloponteekas] mole.

τυφλός [teeflos] blind.

τυφλώνομαι [teeflonome] grow blind, blind o.s.

τυφλώνω [teeflono] blind || (φως) dazzle || (μεταφ) deceive, hoodwink.

τύφος, ο [teefos]: **εξανθηματικός** ~ typhus || **κοιλιακός** ~ typhoid fever.

τυφώνας, ο [teefonas] typhoon, hurricane, cyclone.

τυχαίνω [teeheno] βλ **τυγχάνω.**

τυχαίος [teeheos] casual, fortuitous, chance.

τυχαίως [teeheos] by chance, by accident.

τυχερά [teehera] πλ casual profits, tips, perks.

τυχερό, το [teehero] fortune, destiny.

τυχερός [teeheros] fortunate, lucky.

τύχη, η [teehee] destiny, chance, fortune, lot, fate || (καλή) good luck || **στην** ~ haphazard, at random.

τυχοδιώκτης, ο [teehoδeeooktees] adventurer, opportunist.

τυχόν [teehon] by chance || **τα** ~ **έξοδα** incidental expenses.

τυχών [teehon]: **ο** ~ the first comer, anyone.

τύψη, η [teepsee] remorse, prick of conscience.

τώρα [tora] nowadays, at present, now || this minute || at once.

τωρινός [toreenos] present-day, contemporary, of today.

Υ, υ

ύαινα, η [iena] hyena.

υάκινθος, ο [yakeenthos] hyacinth.

ύαλος, η [eealos] glass.

υαλουργία, η [yalouryeea] glassmaking.

υαλουργός, ο [yalourgos] glassmaker.

υάρδα, η [yarδa] yard.

ύβος, ο [eevos] hump.

υβρεολόγιο, το [eevreoloyo] volley of abuse, tirade.

υβρίζω [eevreezo] insult, abuse, swear at.

ύβρη, η [eevree] insult, injury || oath.

υβριστικός [eevreesteekos] insulting, rude.

υγεία, η [eeyeea] health.

υγειονομικός [eeyonomeekos] sanitary.

υγιαίνω [eeyeno] be healthy.

υγιεινός [eeyeenos] healthy || wholesome.

υγιής [eeyees] healthy || (μεταφ) sound.

υγραίνω [eegreno] moisten, dampen, wet.

υγρασία, η [eegraseea] moisture, moistness, humidity.

υγροποιώ [eegropeeo] liquefy.

υγρός [eegros] fluid, liquid || humid, damp || watery.

υδαταγωγός, ο [eeδatagogos] water pipe.

υδατάνθρακας, ο [eeδatanthrakas] carbohydrate.

υδατοστεγής [eeδatosteyees] watertight, waterproof.

υδατοφράκτης, ο [eeδatofraktees] dam, weir.

υδραγωγείο, το [eeδragoyeeo] aqueduct.

υδραντλία, η [eeδrantleea] water pump.

υδράργυρος, ο [eeδraryeeros] mercury, quicksilver.

υδρατμός, ο [eeδratmos] vapour, steam.

υδραυλική, η [eeðravleekee] hydraulics.

υδραυλικός [eeðravleekos] hydraulic || (ουσ) plumber.

ύδρευση, η [eeðrevsee] water supply, drawing of water.

υδρόβιος [eeðroveeos] aquatic.

υδρόγειος, η [eeðroyos] earth.

υδρογόνο, το [eeðrogono] hydrogen.

υδρογραφία, η [eeðrografeea] hydrography.

υδροηλεκτρικός [eeðroeelektreekos] hydroelectric.

υδροκέφαλος [eeðrokefalos] hydrocephalous.

υδροκίνητος [eeðrokeeneetos] waterpowered.

υδροκυάνιο, το [eeðrokeeaneeo] prussic acid.

υδρόμυλος, ο [eeðromeelos] water mill.

υδροπλάνο, το [eeðroplano] seaplane.

υδρορρόη, η [eeðroroee] (στη στέγη) gutter.

υδροστάθμη, η [eeðrostathmee] water level.

υδροστατικός [eeðrostateekos] hydrostatic.

υδροστρόβιλος, ο [eeðrostroveelos] water turbine || whirlpool.

υδροφοβία, η [eeðrofoveea] rabies, hydrophobia.

υδροφόρος [eeðroforos] water-carrying || (ουσ) water carrier.

υδροχαρής [eeðroharees] water-loving.

υδροχλωρικός [eeðrohloreekos] hydrochloric.

υδρόχρωμα, το [eeðrohroma] whitewash.

υδρόψυκτος [eeðropseektos] water-cooled.

υδρωπικία, η [eeðropeekeea] dropsy.

ύδωρ, το [eeðor] water.

υιοθεσία, η [yotheseea] adoption.

υιοθετώ [yotheto] adopt, accept, support.

υιός, ο [yos] son.

ύλη, η [eelee] material, matter, stuff.

υλικό, το [eeleeko] material, stuff || element, ingredient.

υλικός [eeleekos] material, real.

υλισμός, ο [eeleesmos] materialism.

υλιστής, ο [eeleestees] materialist.

υλοτομία, η [eelotomeea] woodcutting, timber-felling.

υμένας, ο [eemenas] membrane || tissue, hymen.

ύμνος, ο [eemnos] hymn || anthem.

υμνώ [eemno] celebrate, praise, eulogize.

υνί, το [eenee] ploughshare.

υπάγομαι [eepagome] belong, be dependent || be answerable.

υπαγόρευση, η [eepagorevsee] dictation || (μεταφ) suggestion.

υπαγορεύω [eepagorevo] dictate || (μεταφ) inspire, suggest.

υπάγω [eepago] go || go under, rank.

υπαίθριος [eepethreeos] outdoor, in the open air || field.

ύπαιθρο, το [eepethro] open air, open country.

ύπαιθρος, η [eepethros] (χώρα) countryside.

υπαινιγμός, ο [eepeneegmos] hint, allusion, intimation.

υπαινίσσομαι [eepeneesome] hint at, allude to.

υπαίτιος [eepeteeos] responsible, culpable.

υπακοή, η [eepakoee] obedience || submission.

υπάκουος [eepakouos] obedient || submissive.

υπακούω [eepakouo] obey.

υπάλληλος, ο, η [eepaleelos] employee, clerk || (υπουργείου) official, functionary || **δημόσιος** ~ civil servant, government employee.

υπαξιωματικός, ο [eepakseeomateekos] non-commissioned officer.

υπαρκτός [eeparktos] existent || subsisting || real.

ύπαρξη, η [eeparksee] existence || being, life.

υπαρχηγός, ο [eeparheegos] deputy commander.

υπάρχω [eeparho] exist, be || live || **υπάρχει** there is || **τα υπαρχοντά μου** my possessions, my things.

υπασπιστής, ο [eepaspeestees] aide-de-camp || (στρατ) adjutant.

ύπατος, ο [eepatos] consul || (επίθ) highest, supreme.

υπέδαφος, το [eepeðafos] subsoil.

υπεισέρχομαι [eepeeserhome] enter secretly || glide into.

υπεκφεύγω [eepekfevgo] escape, avoid || slip away.

υπεκφυγή, η [eepekfeeyee] escape, subterfuge || evasion.

υπενθυμίζω [eepentheemeezo] remind of, call to mind || allude to.

υπενοικιάζω [eepeneekeeazo] sublet, rent from a tenant.

υπεξαίρεση, η [eepekseresee] pilfering, taking away.

υπέρ [eeper] over, upwards, above || (για) for, on behalf of || **τα ~ και τα κατά** pros and cons, for and against.

υπεραιμία, η [eeperemeea] excess of blood.

υπεραμύνομαι [eeperameenome] defend, support.

υπεράνθρωπος [eeperanthropos] superhuman || (ουσ) superman.

υπεράνω [eeperano] above, beyond, over.

υπερασπίζομαι [eeperaspeezome] defend o.s.

υπερασπίζω [eeperaspeezo] defend, protect || maintain.

υπεράσπιση, η [eeperaspeesee] defence || protection || the defendants.

υπεραστικός [eeperasteekos] long-distance.

υπερβαίνω [eeperveno] cross, surmount || exceed, go beyond, overdo.

υπερβάλλω [eepervalo] surpass, outdo, exceed || exaggerate, overdo, magnify.

υπέρβαση, η [eepervasee] exceeding || (traffic) violation || trespass.

υπερβολή, η [eepervolee] exaggeration || (γεωμ) hyperbola.

υπερβολικός [eepervoleekos] excessive || exaggerated, exaggerating.

υπέργηρος [eeperyeeros] extremely old, very old.

υπερδιέγερση, η [eeperδieyersee] over-excitement.

υπερένταση, η [eeperentasee] overstrain, overstress.

υπερευαίσθητος [eeperevestheetos] over-sensitive, hypersensitive.

υπερέχω [eepereho] excel, surpass, exceed.

υπερήλικος/κη [eepereeleekas] elderly person, very old person.

υπερηφάνεια, η [eepereefaneea] pride || haughtiness.

υπερηφανεύομαι [eepereefanevome] pride o.s. || be proud.

υπερήφανος [eepereefanos] proud || haughty.

υπερθεματίζω [eeperthemateezo] make higher bid || (μεταφ) outdo.

υπερθετικός [eepertheteekos] superlative.

υπερίπταμαι [eepereeptame] fly over, fly above.

υπερισχύω [eepereesheeo] predominate, prevail over || overcome, triumph.

υπεριώδης [eepereeoδees] ultraviolet.

υπερκόπωση, η [eeperkoposee] overwork, breakdown.

υπέρμαχος, ο, η [eepermahos] champion, defender.

υπέρμετρος [eepermetros] excessive, huge.

υπερνικώ [eeperneeko] overcome || subdue, master.

υπέρογκος [eeperongos] colossal, enormous || outrageous.

υπεροπτικός [eeperopteekos] haughty, presumptuous, arrogant.

υπεροχή, η [eeperohee] superiority, predominance.

υπέροχος [eeperohos] superior, excellent, eminent.

υπεροψία, η [eeperopseea] arrogance, disdain, haughtiness.

υπερπέραν, το [eeperperan] the beyond, afterlife.

υπερπηδώ [eeperpeeδo] surmount || jump over.

υπερπόντιος [eeperponteeos] overseas || transmarine.

υπέρταση, η [eepertasee] high blood pressure.

υπέρτατος [eepertatos] highest, greatest, supreme.

υπερτερώ [eepertero] excel, exceed, surpass || outnumber.

υπερτίμηση, η [eeperteemeesee] overestimation || (οικ) rise in price, increase in value.

υπερτιμώ [eeperteemo] overvalue, overestimate || (οικ) raise price of.

υπερτροφία, η [eepertrofeea] (ιατρ) hypertrophy.

υπέρυθροι [eepereethree] πλ: ~ ακτίνες infrared rays.

υπέρυθρος [eepereethros] reddish.

υπερύψηλος [eepereepseelos] very high, exceedingly high.

υπερυψώνω [eepereepsono] raise up || exalt.

υπερφυσικός [eeperfeeseekos] supernatural || (μεταφ) extraordinary, prodigious.

υπερωκεάνειο, το [eeperokeaneeo] liner.

υπερωρία, η [eeperoreea] overtime.

υπεύθυνος [eepevtheenos] responsible, answerable.

υπήκοος [eepeekoos] submissive, obedient || (ουσ) subject of state.

υπηκοότητα, η [eepeekooteeta] nationality, citizenship.

υπηρεσία, η [eepeereseea] service, attendance || duty, employ || (οικίας) domestic servant.

υπηρεσιακή [eepeereseeakee]: ~ κυβέρνηση caretaker government.

υπηρεσιακός [eepeereseeakos] of service.

υπηρέτης, ο [eepeeretees] servant.

υπηρέτρια, η [eepeeretreea] maid.

υπηρετώ [eepeereto] serve || do one's military service.

υπναλέος [eepnaleos] drowsy, sleepy.

υπναράς, ο [eepnaras] person who enjoys sleeping.

υπνοβάτης, ο [eepnovatees] sleepwalker.

ύπνος, ο [eepnos] sleep.

ύπνωση, η [eepnosee] hypnosis.

υπνωτίζω [eepnoteezo] hypnotize.

υπνωτικό, το [eepnoteeko] soporific drug, sleeping pill.

υπνωτισμός, ο [eepnoteesmos] hypnotism.

υπό [eepo] below, beneath || (μέσο) by, with.

υπόβαθρο, το [eepovathro] base, pedestal, stand.

υποβάλλω [eepovalo] submit, hand in || (υποτάσσω) subject || suggest, propose.

υποβαστάζω [eepovastazo] support, prop up, bear.

υποβιβάζω [eepoveevazo] lower || reduce, diminish || demote.

υποβλέπω [eepovlepo] suspect || cast glances at, leer.

υποβλητικός [eepovleeteekos] evocative.

υποβοηθώ [eepovoeetho] assist, back up, support.

υποβολέας, ο [eepovoleas] prompter || instigator.

υποβολή, η [eepovolee] submission, presentation || prompting, instigation.

υποβόσκω [eepovosko] smoulder || lie hidden.

υποβρύχιο, το [eepovreeheeo] submarine || (μεταφ) kind of sweet.

υπόγειο, το [eepoyo] basement, cellar.

υπόγειος [eepoyos] underground.

υπογραμμίζω [eepogrameezo] underline, emphasize.

υπογραφή, η [eepografee] signature.

υπογράφω [eepografo] sign || (μεταφ) approve, subscribe.

υποδαυλίζω [eepoδavleezo] fan the flame || (μεταφ) foment, excite.

υποδεέστερος [eepoδeesteros] inferior, lower.

υπόδειγμα, το [eepoδeegma] model, example, specimen || sample.

υποδειγματικός [eepoδeegmateekos] exemplary, representative.

υποδεικνύω [eepoδeekneeo] indicate || suggest, propose.

υπόδειξη, η [eepoδeeksee] indication || recommendation.

υποδέχομαι [eepoδehome] receive, welcome, greet.

υποδηλώ [eepoδeelo] convey, indicate, hint at.

υποδηματοποιείο, το [eepoδeematopieeo] shoemaker's shop.

υποδιαίρεση, η [eepoδieresee] subdivision.

υποδιαιρώ [eepoδiero] subdivide.

υποδιαστολή, η [eepoδeeastolee] decimal point || (γραμμ) comma.

υποδιευθυντής, ο [eepoδieftheendees] assistant director, vice-principal, deputy manager.

υπόδικος, ο [eepoδeekos] the accused.

υπόδουλος [eepoδoulos] enslaved.

υποδουλώνω [eepoδoulono] subjugate, enslave, subdue.

υποδοχή, η [eepoδohee] reception.

υποδύομαι [eepoδeeome] play the part, assume a role.

υποζύγιο, το [eepozeeyo] beast of burden.

υποθάλπω [eepothalpo] foment || protect, maintain || entertain, harbour.

υπόθεση, η [eepothesee] conjecture, supposition || matter, affair, business || (δικαστηρίου) case, action || (θεατρικού έργου κτλ) subject, plot, matter, theme.

υποθετικός [eepotheteekos] hypothetical, speculative || imaginary || (γραμμ) conditional.

υπόθετο, το [eepotheto] suppository.

υποθέτω [eepotheto] suppose, assume.

υποθηκεύω [eepotheekevo] mortgage.

υποθήκη, η [eepotheekee] mortgage.

υποκαθιστώ [eepokatheesto] replace, substitute.

υποκατάσταση, η [eepokatastasee] replacement, substitution.

υποκατάστημα, το [eepokatasteema] branch office || chain store (US).

υπόκειμαι [eepokeeme] be subject, be liable || lie under.

υποκειμενικός [eepokeemeneekos] subjective.

υποκείμενο, το [eepokeemeno] subject || individual || scamp.

υποκινώ [eepokeeno] stir up, excite, incite.

υποκλέπτω [eepoklepto] purloin, pilfer.

υποκλίνομαι [eepokleenome] bow, bend || yield.

υπόκλιση, η [eepokleesee] bow, curtsy.

υποκοριστικό, το [eepokoreesteeko] diminutive.

υπόκοσμος, ο [eepokosmos] underworld.

υποκρίνομαι [eepokreenome] act, play the part of, impersonate || dissemble.

υπόκριση, η [eepokreesee] pretending, acting || dissembling.

υποκρισία, η [eepokreeseea] hypocrisy.

υποκριτής, ο [eepokreetees] actor || hypocrite.

υποκριτικός [eepokreeteekos] feigned, insincere.

υπόκρουση, η [eepokrousee] accompaniment.

υποκύπτω [eepokeepto] bend, submit, succumb || yield.

υπόκωφος [eepokofos] hollow, deep || smothered.

υπόλειμμα, το [eepoleema] residue, remnant, rest.

υπολείπομαι [eepoleepome] be left || be inferior to.

υπόληψη, n [eepoleepsee] esteem || credit, reputation.
υπολογίζω [eepoloyeezo] estimate, calculate || consider.
υπολογισμός, ο [eepoloyeesmos] calculation, estimate || account.
υπολογιστής, ο [eepoloyeestees] : **(ηλεκτρονικός)** ~ computer.
υπόλογος [eepologos] responsible, accountable, liable.
υπόλοιπο, το [eepoleepo] remainder, balance.
υπόλοιπος [eepoleepos] remaining, rest of.
υπολοχαγός, ο [eepolohagos] lieutenant.
υπομένω [eepomeno] endure, tolerate.
υπόμνημα, το [eepomneema] memorandum.
υπόμνηση, n [eepomneesee] reminder || suggestion.
υπομονεύω [eepomonevo] be patient || endure.
υπομονή, n [eepomonee] patience, endurance.
υπομονητικός [eepomoneeteekos] patient, enduring.
υπόνοια, n [eeponeea] suspicion || surmise.
υπονομεύω [eeponomevo] undermine, sabotage.
υπόνομος, ο, n [eeponomos] sewer || **(στρατ)** mine.
υπονοώ [eeponoo] infer, mean.
υποπίπτω [eepopeepto] commit, fall into || come to the notice of.
υποπροϊόν, το [eepoproeeon] by-product.
υποπρόξενος, ο [eepoproksenos] vice-consul.
υποπτεύομαι [eepoptevome] suspect, have an idea.
ύποπτος [eepoptos] suspect, suspicious, suspected.
υποσημείωση, n [eeposeemeeosee] footnote, annotation.
υποσιτισμός, ο [eeposeeteesmos] undernourishment, malnutrition.
υποσκάπτω [eeposkapto] undermine, sabotage.
υποσκελίζω [eeposkeleezo] upset || supplant.
υποστάθμη, n [eepostathmee] dregs, sediment, residue.
υπόσταση, n [eepostasee] existence || foundation, basis || **(ιατρ)** hypostasis.
υπόστεγο, το [eepostego] shed, hangar || shelter.
υποστέλλω [eepostelo] strike, lower || slow down, reduce.
υποστήριγμα, το [eeposteereegma] support, prop.
υποστηρίζω [eeposteereezo] prop up, support || second, back || maintain.

υποστήριξη, n [eeposteereeksee] prop, support || backing.
υπόστρωμα, το [eepostroma] substratum || saddlecloth.
υποσυνείδητο, το [eeposeeneedeeto] subconscious.
υπόσχεση, n [eeposhesee] promise, pledge, engagement.
υπόσχομαι [eeposhome] promise, pledge.
υποταγή, n [eepotayee] obedience, subjection, submission.
υποτακτική, n [eepotakteekee] subjective.
υποτακτικός [eepotakteekos] obedient, submissive.
υπόταση, n [eepotasee] low blood pressure.
υποτάσσομαι [eepotasome] submit, give in.
υποτάσσω [eepotaso] subjugate, subdue.
υποτείνουσα, n [eepoteenousa] hypotenuse.
υποτελής [eepotelees] subordinate, tributary, vassal.
υποτίθεμαι [eepoteetheme] be supposed || suppose, consider.
υποτίμηση, n [eepoteemeesee] reduction in price, depreciation || underestimation.
υποτιμώ [eepoteemo] underestimate || lower the price of, depreciate.
υποτροπή, n [eepotropee] relapse, deterioration.
υποτροφία, n [eepotrofeea] scholarship.
υποτυπώδης [eepoteepoðees] sketchy, imperfectly formed.
ύπουλος [eepoulos] shifty, underhand, cunning.
υπουργείο, το [eepouryeeo] ministry.
υπουργικός [eepouryeekos] ministerial.
υπουργός, ο [eepourgos] minister || secretary (US).
υποφαινόμενος [eepofenomenos]: **ο** ~ the undersigned.
υποφερτός [eepofertos] tolerable || passable.
υποφέρω [eepofero] bear, support, endure || feel pain, suffer.
υποχθόνιος [eepohthoneeos] infernal, subterranean.
υποχονδρία, n [eepohonðreea] hypochondria || obsession.
υπόχρεος [eepohreos] obliged.
υποχρεώνω [eepohreono] oblige || compel.
υποχρέωση, n [eepohreosee] obligation, duty.
υποχρεωτικός [eepohreoteekos] obligatory || compulsory.

υποχώρηση, η [eepohoreesee] withdrawal, yielding || subsidence.

υποχωρώ [eepohoro] withdraw, give way || fall in, cave in.

υποψήφιος, ο [eepopseefeeos] candidate, applicant.

υποψηφιότητα, η [eepopseefeeoteeta] candidature, application.

υποψία, η [eepopseea] suspicion, misgiving.

υποψιάζομαι [eepopseeazome] suspect, have suspicions.

ύπτιος [eepteeos] lying on one's back.

ύστατος [eestatos] last, final.

ύστερα [eestera] afterwards, then, later || furthermore || ~ **από** after, following (this).

υστέρημα, το [eestereema] shortage, deficiency || small savings.

υστερία, η [eestereea] hysteria.

υστερικός [eestereekos] hysterical.

υστερισμός, ο [eestereesmos] hysteria, hysterics.

υστεροβουλία, η [eesterovouleea] afterthought || deceit.

υστερόγραφο, το [eesterografo] postscript.

ύστερος [eesteros] later || inferior || **εκ των υστέρων** on second thoughts, looking back.

υστερώ [eestero] come after || be inferior || deprive.

υφαίνω [eefeno] weave, spin || (μεταφ) plot.

ύφαλα, τα [eefala] πλ beam || part below waterline.

υφαλοκρηπίδα, η [eefalokreepeeða] continental shelf.

ύφαλος, η [eefalos] reef, shoal.

ύφανση, η [eefansee] weaving || weave.

υφαντός [eefandos] woven.

υφαντουργία, η [eefandouryeea] textile industry, weaving industry.

υφαρπάζω [eefarpazo] obtain by fraud.

ύφασμα, το [eefasma] cloth, fabric, stuff, material || **υφάσματα** textiles.

ύφεση, η [eefesee] decrease, abatement || (βαρομέτρου) depression || (μουσ) flat (note).

υφή, η [eefee] texture, web, weave.

υφηγητής, ο [eefeeyeetees] lecturer || assistant professor (US).

υφήλιος, η [eefeeleeos] earth, world, globe.

υφίσταμαι [eefeestame] bear, undergo, sustain || (είμαι) exist, be in force.

υφιστάμενος, το [eefeestamenos] subordinate, inferior.

ύφος, το [eefos] style || air, look, tone.

υφυπουργός, ο [eefeepourgos] undersecretary of state.

υψηλός [eepseelos] high, towering, tall || (μεταφ) lofty, great.

υψηλότητα, η [eepseeloteeta] Highness || **η Αυτού** ~ His Royal Highness.

υψηλόφρονας [eepseelofronas] generous || highminded, haughty.

υψικάμινος, η [eepseekameenos] blast furnace.

ύψιλον, το [eepseelon] the letter Y.

υψίπεδο, το [eepseepeðo] plateau.

ύψιστος [eepseestos] highest || (ουσ) God.

υψίφωνος, ο, η [eepseefonos] tenor || soprano.

υψόμετρο, το [eepsometro] altitude.

ύψος, το [eepsos] height, altitude || (μουσ) pitch.

ύψωμα, το [eepsoma] height, elevation || hillock.

υψώνω [eepsono] raise, elevate || increase || hoist.

ύψωση, η [eepsosee] raising, lifting, elevation || rise in price.

Φ, φ

φάβα, η [fava] yellow pea || pea purée.

φαγάς, ο [fagas] glutton, gourmand.

φαγγρί, το [fangree] sea bream.

φαγητό, το [fayeeto] meal, dish, food || dinner.

φαγκότο, το [fangoto] bassoon.

φαγοπότι, το [fagopotee] revel, eating and drinking.

φαγούρα, η [fagoura] itching, irritation.

φάγωμα, το [fagoma] corrosion, disintegration || (τσακωμός) quarrel, dispute, wrangling.

φαγωμάρα, η [fagomara] itch, irritation || (τσακωμός) arguing, dispute.

φαγωμένος [fagomenos] eaten || **είμαι** ~ I've eaten.

φαγώσιμα, τα [fagoseema] πλ provisions, victuals.

φαγώσιμος [fagoseemos] eatable, edible.

φαεινή [faeenee] ~ **ιδέα** brainwave, bright idea.

φαΐ, το [faee] food, meal.

φαιδρός [feðros] merry, cheerful || (μεταφ) ridiculous.

φαίνομαι [fenome] appear, come in sight || seem, look || show o.s. to be.

φαινόμενα, τα [fenomena] πλ: **κατά τα** ~ judging by appearances.

φαινομενικώς [fenomeneekos] apparently, outwardly.

φαινόμενο, το [fenomeno] wonder, prodigy || phenomenon.

φάκα, η [faka] mousetrap || snare.

φάκελος, ο [fakelos] envelope || file, cover, dossier, record.

φακή, η [fakee] lentils.
φακίδα, η [fakeeδa] freckle.
φακός, ο [fakos] lens || magnifying glass, magnifier.
φάλαγγα, η [falanga] phalanx || (στρατ) column || (στοίχος) row.
φάλαινα, η [falena] whale.
φαλάκρα, η [falakra] baldness || bald head.
φαλακραίνω [falakreno] go bald.
φαλακρός [falakros] bald(-headed) || bare.
φαλλός, ο [falos] phallus.
φάλτσο, το [faltso] wrong note, dissonance || (μεταφ) mistake, fault, error.
φαμίλια, η [fameeleea] family.
φάμπρικα, η [fambreeka] factory || fabrication, device, artifice.
φανάρι, το [fanaree] lamp, light, lantern || (αυτοκινήτου) headlamp || (φάρου) lighthouse.
φαναρτζής, ο [fanardzees] tinsmith || lampmaker.
φανατίζω [fanateezo] make fanatical, fanaticize.
φανατικός [fanateekos] overzealous, fanatical || (ουσ) fanatic, zealot.
φανατισμός, ο [fanateesmos] fanaticism.
φανέλα, η [fanela] flannel || vest || woollen cloth.
φανερός [faneros] clear, plain, evident, certain.
φανερώνω [fanerono] reveal, make plain.
φαντάζομαι [fandazome] imagine, fancy, think || (πιστεύω) believe.
φαντάζω [fandazo] make an impression, stand out || look glamorous.
φαντάρος, ο [fandaros] infantryman.
φαντασία, η [fandaseea] imagination || illusion || (υπερηφάνεια) vanity, pride || (μουσ) fantasia.
φαντασιοπληξία, η [fandaseeopleekseea] extravagant notion || caprice, whim.
φάντασμα, το [fandasma] phantom, ghost, spirit.
φαντασμαγορία, η [fandasmagoreea] phantasmagoria.
φαντασμένος [fandasmenos] presumptuous, vain.
φανταστικός [fandasteekos] illusory, imaginary || fantastic, extravagant.
φανταχτερός [fandahteros] showy, bright || gaudy, glaring.
φάντης, ο [fandees] (στα χαρτιά) knave.
φανφαρόνος, ο [fanfaronos] braggart, boaster, blusterer.
φάπα, η [fapa] slap, box on the ear, smack.
φάρα, η [fara] race, progeny, breed || crew.

φαράγγι, το [farangee] gorge, gully, precipice, ravine.
φαράσι, το [farasee] dustpan.
φαρδαίνω [farδeno] widen, broaden, become wider || stretch, extend.
φάρδος, το [farδos] width, breadth.
φαρδύς [farδees] wide, large, broad, ample.
φαρέτρα, η [faretra] quiver.
φαρμακείο, το [farmakeeo] chemist shop.
φαρμακερός [farmakeros] venomous || spiteful, bitter.
φαρμάκι, το [farmakee] poison || (μεταφ) anything bitter.
φάρμακο, το [farmako] drug, medicine, remedy.
φαρμακοποιός, ο [farmakopeeos] pharmacist, chemist || druggist (US).
φαρμακώνω [farmakono] poison || (μεταφ) cause grief || mortify.
φάρος, ο [faros] lighthouse, beacon.
φάρσα, η [farsa] trick, farce || practical joke.
φάρυγγας, ο [fareengas] pharynx, windpipe.
φασαρία, η [fasaree] disturbance || fuss, noise, bustle.
φασιανός, ο [faseeanos] pheasant.
φάση, η [fasee] phase || change, turn || aspect.
φασισμός, ο [faseesmos] fascism.
φασιστικός [faseesteekos] fascist.
φασκιά, η [faskia] swaddling band, swaddling clothes.
φασκόμπλο, το [faskomeelo] sage || sage tea.
φάσκω [fasko]: ~ και αντιφάσκω contradict o.s.
φάσμα, το [fasma] ghost, spirit || (φυσική) spectrum.
φασματοσκόπιο, το [fasmatoskopeeo] spectroscope.
φασόλι, το [fasolee] haricot bean, kidney bean.
φασο(υ)λάδα, η [faso(u)laδa] bean soup.
φασο(υ)λάκια, τα [faso(u)lakeea] πλ green beans.
φάτνη, η [fatnee] manger, crib, stall.
φατρία, η [fatreea] faction, clique, gang.
φατριάζω [fatreeazo] form factions, be factious.
φάτσα, η [fatsa] face || front || (επίρ) opposite.
φαυλοκρατία, η [favlokrateea] political corruption.
φαύλος [favlos] wicked, depraved || ~ κύκλος vicious circle.
φαφλατάς, ο [faflatas] chatterer, mumbler.
Φεβρουάριος, ο [fevrouareeos] February.
φεγγάρι, το [fengaree] moon.

Φ

φεγγίτης, ο [fengeetees] skylight, fanlight, garret window.

φεγγοβολώ [fengovolo] shine brightly.

φέγγω [fengo] shine, give light.

φείδομαι [feeδome] save, spare || be sparing of, be stingy.

φειδωλός [feeδolos] sparing, thrifty || stingy, mean, niggardly.

φελλός, ο [felos] cork.

φεουδαρχικός [feouδarheekos] feudal.

φέουδο, το [feouδo] fief.

φερέγγυος [ferengeeos] solvent, trustworthy.

φερέλπις [ferelpees] full of promise || hopeful.

φερετζές, ο [feredzes] veil (of a Moslem woman).

φέρετρο, το [feretro] coffin, bier.

φερμένος [fermenos] arrived, brought, imported.

φερμουάρ, το [fermouar] zip fastener.

φέρνω [ferno] βλ **φέρω.**

φέρομαι [ferome] conduct, behave || be reputed, be held as.

φέρσιμο, το [ferseemo] behaviour, conduct.

φέρω [fero] bring, carry, support || (στέλλω) fetch || (έχω πάνω μου) carry, have || (προξενώ) cause || (παράγω) bear, bring forth, bring in, yield || (φορώ) wear || (κατευθύνω) lead, conduct || ~ αντιρρήσεις protest || **φερ' ειπείν** for example.

φέσι, το [fesee] fez || **γίνομαι** ~ get dead drunk.

φέτα, η [feta] slice || (τυρί) kind of white cheese.

φετινός [feteenos] of this year.

φέτος [fetos] this year.

φευγάλα, η [fevgala] flight, escape, stampede.

φευγαλέος [fevgaleos] fleeting.

φευγατίζω [fevgateezo] help to escape.

φευγάτος [fevgatos] gone, fled, run away, left.

φεύγω [fevgo] leave, depart, get away || escape, flee || run away from, shun.

φήμη, η [feemee] report, rumour || reputation || renown, repute || fame.

φημίζομαι [feemeezome] be well-known.

φθάνω [fthano] catch, overtake, attain || (μεταφ) equal, be equal to || arrive, reach || draw near || ~ σε reach the point of, be reduced to || **φθάνει να** provided that.

φθαρτός [thartos] perishable, destructible, liable to decay.

φθείρομαι [ftheerome] decay, wash away || (μεταφ) lose importance.

φθείρω [ftheero] damage, spoil || corrupt, pervert, taint.

φθινόπωρο, το [ftheenoporo] autumn.

φθίνω [ftheeno] pine away || decay || decline, fail.

φθισικός [ftheeseekos] consumptive, tubercular.

φθίση, η [ftheesee] consumption || decline.

φθόγγος, ο [fthongos] voice, sound || (μους) note.

φθονερός [fthoneros] envious, jealous.

φθόνος, ο [fthonos] malicious envy, jealousy.

φθονώ [fthono] be envious of, begrudge.

φθορά, η [fthora] deterioration, damage, destruction || decay || loss.

φθορισμός, ο [fthoreesmos] fluorescence.

φι, το [fee] the letter Φ.

φιάλη, η [feealee] bottle, flagon, flask.

φιγούρα, η [feegoura] figure, image || (μεταφ) expression, air || **κάνω** ~ cut a fine figure.

φιγουράρω [feegouraro] show off, appear.

φίδι, το [feeδee] snake, serpent.

φιδωτός [feeδotos] winding, twisting.

φίλαθλος, ο, η [feelathlos] sports fan.

φιλαλήθης [feelaleethees] truthful.

φιλάνθρωπος, ο, η [feelanthropos] philanthropist, charitable person.

φιλαράκος, ο [feelarakos] beau || chum, pal || scoundrel, rascal.

φιλάργυρος [feelaryeeros] niggardly, miserly || (ουσ) miser.

φιλάρεσκος [feelareskos] coquettish, spruce.

φιλαρμονική, η [feelarmoneekee] (musical) band.

φιλαρχία, η [feelarheea] love of authority.

φιλάσθενος [feelasthenos] sickly, weakly, puny.

φιλελευθερισμός, ο [feelelevthereesmos] liberalism.

φιλελεύθερος, ο [feelelevtheros] liberal.

φιλέλληνας, ο, η [feeleleenas] philhellene.

φιλενάδα, η [feelenaδa] girlfriend || (μεταφ) mistress.

φιλές, ο [feeles] hairnet.

φιλέτο, το [feeleto] fillet of meat.

φιλεύω [feelevo] make a present || entertain.

φίλη, η [feelee] friend.

φιλήδονος [feeleeδonos] sensual, voluptuous.

φίλημα, το [feeleema] kiss.

φιλήσυχος [feeleeseehos] peace-loving, calm, quiet, serene.

φιλί, το [feelee] βλ **φίλημα**.

φιλία, η [feeleea] friendship.

φιλικός [feeleekos] friendly || of a friend.

φίλιππος, ο, η [feeleepos] horse lover || racegoer.

φιλιστρίνι, το [feeleestreenee] porthole.

φιλμ, το [feelm] film.

φίλντισι, το [feelnteesee] mother-of-pearl || ivory.

φιλόδοξος [feeloδoksos] ambitious || pretentious, showy.

φιλοδοξώ [feeloδokso] be ambitious || aspire to, desire strongly.

φιλοδώρημα, το [feeloδoreema] tip || gratuity.

φιλοκερδής [feelokerδees] greedy, covetous, eager for gain.

φιλολογία, η [feeloloyeea] literature || philology.

φιλόλογος, ο [feelologos] man of letters, philologist || scholar.

φιλομαθής [feelomathees] fond of learning.

φιλόμουσος [feelomousos] lover of music || fond of learning.

φιλονικία, η [feeloneekeea] dispute, wrangle.

φιλονικώ [feeloneeko] quarrel,wrangle.

φινοξενία, η [feelokseneea] hospitality.

φιλόξενος [feeloksenos] hospitable.

φιλοξενώ [feelokseno] entertain, give hospitality, receive.

φιλοπατρία, η [feelopatreea] patriotism.

φιλοπόλεμος [feelopolemos] warlike, martial.

φιλόπονος [feeloponos] assiduous, diligent, industrious.

φιλοπονώ [feelopono] prepare assiduously.

φίλος, ο [feelos] friend || (επιθ) dear, friendly.

φιλοσοφία, η [feelosofeea] philosophy.

φιλοσοφικός [feelosofeekos] philosophical.

φιλόσοφος, ο, η [feelosofos] philosopher.

φιλόστοργος [feelostorgos] loving, affectionate.

φιλοτελισμός, ο [feeloteleesmos] philately.

φιλοτέχνημα, το [feelotehneema] work of art.

φιλότεχνος [feelotehnos] art lover || artistic, skilful.

φιλοτιμία, η [feeloteemeea], **φιλότιμο, το** [feeloteemo] sense of honour, pride, self-respect, dignity.

φιλότιμος [feeloteemos] eager to excel || obliging || having a sense of pride and honour || generous.

φιλοτιμούμαι [feeloteemoume] make it a point of honour.

φιλοτιμώ [feeloteemo] put s.o. on his dignity.

φιλοφρόνηση, η [feelofroneesee] compliment, courtesy.

φίλτατος [feeltatos] dearest, most beloved.

φίλτρο, το [feeltro] filter || philtre.

φιλύποπτος [feeleepoptos] distrustful, suspicious.

φιλώ [feelo] kiss, embrace.

φιμώνω [feemono] muzzle, gag || (μεταφ) silence, hush.

φίμωτρο, το [feemotro] muzzle, gag.

Φινλανδία, η [feenlanδeea] Finland.

φινλανδικός [feenlanδeekos] Finnish.

Φινλανδός, ο [feenlanδos] Finn.

φίνος [feenos] fine.

φιόγκος, ο [feeongos] knot, bow.

φίρμα, η [feerma] firm || trade name.

φίσα, η [feesa] filing slip || gambling chip.

φίσκα [feeska] brimming over.

φιστίκι, το [feesteekee] pistachio nut || ~ **αράπικο** monkey nut, peanut.

φιτίλι, το [feeteelee] wick || (δυναμίτιδας) fuse.

φλάμπουρο, το [flambouro] pennon, standard.

φλάουτο, το [flaouto] flute.

φλέβα, η [fleva] vein || (μεταλλεύματος) lode || (μεταφ) talent.

Φλεβάρης, ο [flevarees] February.

φλέγμα, το [flegma] phlegm, mucus || (μεταφ) coolness, unconcern.

φλεγματικός [flegmateekos] phlegmatic || stolid.

φλεγμονή, η [flegmonee] inflammation, soreness.

φλέγομαι [flegome] burn, ignite || (μεταφ) flare up.

φλέγον [flegon]: ~ **ζήτημα** topical problem.

φλερτάρω [flertaro] flirt with.

φλυναφώ [fleenafo] prate, babble, prattle.

φλιτζάνι, το [fleedzanee] cup.

φλόγα, η [floga] flame, blaze || (μεταφ) passion, ardour.

φλογέρα, η [floyera] shepherd's pipe, reed.

φλογερός [floyeros] burning, flaming || (μεταφ) ardent, fervent.

φλογίζω [floyeezo] inflame, kindle.

φλόγωση, η [flogosee] inflammation, soreness.

φλοιός, ο [fleeos] peel, rind || (φυστικιού) shell || (δένδρου) bark || (γης) crust.

φλοίσβος, ο [fleesvos] rippling of waves || babbling.

φλοκάτη, η [flokatee] thick blanket, peasant's cape.

φλόκος, ο [flokos] jib.

φλομώνω [flomono] stun || grow wan.

φλούδα, η [flouða] βλ **φλοιός.**

φλουρί, το [flouree] gold coin.

φλυαρία, η [fleeareea] gossiping, chatter, prattle.

φλύαρος [fleearos] talkative.

φλυαρώ [fleearo] chatter, tattle, prattle.

φλυτζάνι, το [fleedzanee] cup.

φοβάμαι [fovame] be afraid.

φοβέρα, η [fovera] threat, menace, intimidation.

φοβερίζω [fovereezo] threaten, menace, intimidate.

φοβερός [foveros] terrible, frightful || amazing, formidable.

φόβητρο, το [foveetro] scarecrow || bogey || fright.

φοβητσιάρης [foveetseearees] fearful, timid, timorous.

φοβία, η [foveea] fear, phobia.

φοβίζω [foveezo] frighten || menace, threaten, intimidate.

φόβος, ο [fovos] fear, dread, fright.

φόδρα, η [foðra] lining.

φοίνικας, ο [feeneekas] palm tree || (καρπός) date || phoenix.

φοίτηση, η [feeteesee] attendance (at school).

φοιτητής, ο [feeteetees] student.

φοιτώ [feeto] be a student, attend a course of studies.

φόλα, η [fola] dog poison.

φονεύω [fonevo] murder, kill.

φονιάς, ο [fonias] murderer.

φονικό, το [foneeko] murder, homicide, carnage.

φόνος, ο [fonos] murder, homicide.

φόντο, το [fonto] bottom, base, back || (ζωγραφιάς) background || (κεφάλαιο) capital.

φόρα, η [fora] impulse, impetus || force || **βγάζω στη** ~ bring into the open, uncover.

φορά, η [fora] force || course, run, impetus || (κατεύθυνση) direction || (ευκαιρία) time || **άλλη** ~ another time || **άλλη μια** ~ once again || **μια** ~ once, only once.

φοράδα, η [foraða] mare.

φορατζής, ο [foradzees] tax collector.

φορβή, η [forvee] fodder, forage.

φορείο, το [foreeo] stretcher, litter.

φόρεμα, το [forema] dress, garment.

φορεσιά, η [foresia] dress, suit of clothes || attire.

φορέας, ο [foreas] carrier, porter || (οικον) agent, body.

φορητός [foreetos] portable, easy to carry.

φόρμα, η [forma] form, shape ||

mould, matrix || (εργάτη) overall || (ντοκουμέντο) form, document || **σε** ~ in good form, in tiptop shape.

φοροδιαφυγή, η [foroðeeafeeyee] tax evasion.

φορολογία, η [foroloyeea] taxation || tax, rate.

φορολογούμενος, ο [forologoumenos] taxpayer, ratepayer.

φορολογώ [forologo] tax, put a tax on.

φόρος, ο [foros] tax, rate, duty.

φορτηγό, το [forteego] lorry || truck (US) || (ναυτ) cargo vessel.

φορτίζω [forteezo] charge with electricity.

φορτικός [forteekos] intrusive, importunate || troublesome.

φορτίο, το [forteeo] cargo, load || burden, charge, weight.

φορτοεκφορτωτής, ο [fortoekfortotees] stevedore.

φόρτος, ο [fortos] burden, heavy load.

φορτσάρω [fortsaro] force || intensify || (ανέμου) increase, strengthen.

φόρτωμα, το [fortoma] loading || (μεταφ) burden, care.

φορτώνομαι [fortonome] pester, annoy, bother.

φορτώνω [fortono] load, pile (on) || take on cargo.

φορτωτική, η [fortoteekee] bill of lading.

φορώ [foro] wear || put on, get into || carry.

φουγάρο, το [fougaro] funnel, flue, tall chimney, smokestack.

φουκαράς, ο [foukaras] poor devil || unfortunate fellow.

φουμάρω [foumaro] smoke.

φούμος, ο [foumos] soot || lampblack.

φούντα, η [founta] tassel || tuft, crest.

φουντάρω [fountaro] (ναυτ) sink || cast anchor.

φουντούκι, το [fountoukee] hazelnut.

φουντώνω [fountono] become bushy || stretch out, spread || expand.

φουντωτός [fountotos] bushy, thick.

φούρια, η [foureea] haste.

φούρκα, η [fourka] rage, anger || (κρεμάλα) gallows, gibbet.

φουρκέτα, η [fourketa] hairpin.

φουρκίζω [fourkeezo] vex, harass.

φούρναρης, ο [fournarees] baker.

φουρνέλο, το [fournelo] grid || blasting charge.

φουρνιά, η [fournia] ovenful || (μεταφ) batch.

φούρνος, ο [fournos] oven || bakery || kiln, furnace.

φουρτούνα, η [fourtouna] tempest, storm || rough sea || (μεταφ) calamity, misfortune.

φούσκα, η [fouska] bladder || (παιχνίδι) balloon || blister || soap bubble.

φουσκάλα, η [fouskala] blister || bubble.

φουσκοθαλασσιά, η [fouskothalasia] surge of sea.

φούσκωμα, το [fouskoma] inflation, swelling || swaggering.

φουσκωμένος [fouskomenos] swollen, inflated, puffed up.

φουσκώνω [fouskono] swell, inflate, blow up || (λάστιχο) pump || (μεταφ) exaggerate || (ενοχλώ) irritate || (ζύμη) rise || (αναπνοή) puff, pant || (μεταφ) puff o.s. up.

φουσκωτός [fouskotos] puffed, inflated || curved.

φούστα, η [fousta] skirt.

φουστανέλα, η [foustanela] kind of kilt worn as part of the Greek national costume.

φουστάνι, το [foustanee] gown, dress, frock.

φούχτα, η [fouhta] handful || hollow of hand.

φράγκο, το [frango] franc || drachma.

φραγκοστάφυλο, το [frangostafeelo] redcurrant.

φραγκόσυκο, το [frangoseeko] prickly pear.

φράγμα, το [fragma] enclosure, fence || barrage, dam || barrier.

φραγμός, ο [fragmos] fence, barrier || (στρατ) barrage.

φράζω [frazo] surround, hedge || bar, block up, stop, obstruct.

φράκο, το [frako] dress coat, tails.

φράκτης, ο [fraktees] fence, enclosure, fencing.

φραμπαλάς, ο [frambalas] furbelow.

φράντζα, η [frandza] fringe.

φραντζόλα, η [frandzola] long loaf.

φράξιμο, το [frakseemo] enclosing, fencing || stopping up, blockage.

φράουλα, η [fraoula] strawberry.

φράπα, η [frapa] kind of large citrus fruit, grapefruit.

φρασεολογία, η [fraseoloyeea] phraseology.

φράση, η [frasee] phrase || period.

φράσσω [fraso] βλ **φράζω.**

φράχτης, ο [frahtees] fence, enclosure, fencing, hedge.

φρέαρ, το [frear] well || (μεταλλείο) pit, shaft.

φρεάτιο, το [freateeo] small well.

φρεγάδα, η [fregaδa] frigate.

φρένα, τα [frena] πλ reason, senses || brakes.

φρενάρισμα, το [frenareesma] braking.

φρενάρω [frenaro] brake || (μεταφ) check.

φρένες, οι [frenes] πλ mind, reason, wits || **έξω φρενών** off one's head, enraged || unbelievable.

φρενιάζω [freneeazo] get furious, fret and fume.

φρένο, το [freno] brake.

φρενοβλαβής [frenovlavees] mentally disturbed.

φρενοκομείο, το [frenokomeeo] madhouse, lunatic asylum.

φρενολογία, η [frenoloyeea] phrenology.

φρεσκάδα, η [freskaδa] freshness || coolness, chilliness.

φρεσκάρω [freskaro] freshen, cool || (ο καιρός) become worse.

φρέσκο, το [fresko] fresco || coolness, freshness, chilliness || **στο ~** in prison.

φρέσκος [freskos] fresh, new, recent || cool.

φρικαλέος [freekaleos] horrible, hideous, ghastly.

φρίκη, η [freekee] terror, horror || (επιφ) frightful.

φρικιάζω [freekeeazo] shiver, shudder || be disgusted.

φρικτός [freektos], **φρικώδης** [freekoδees] (θέαμα) horrible, ghastly || (εμφάνιση) hideous || (καιρός) horrid, vile || awful.

φρόκαλο, το [frokalo] sweepings, rubbish || broom.

φρόνημα, το [froneema] opinion, sentiment, morale || **φρονήματα** political convictions.

φρονηματίζω [froneemateezo] inspire self-confidence, render self-confident.

φρόνηση, η [froneesee] prudence, wariness, circumspection.

φρόνιμα [froneema] (επιφ) behave yourself.

φρονιμάδα, η [froneemaδa] wisdom, prudence || moderation || (παιδιού) quietness, good behaviour || (γυναίκας) modesty, chastity.

φρονιμεύω [froneemevo] become prudent, grow wise, be well-behaved.

φρονιμίτης, ο [froneemeetees] wisdom tooth.

φρόνιμος [froneemos] reasonable, sound, well-behaved || virtuous, wise.

φροντίζω [fronteezo] look after, care for || see to.

φροντίδα, η [fronteeδa] concern, care, anxiety.

φροντίδες, οι [fronteeδes] πλ things to do, cares.

φροντιστήριο, το [fronteesteereeo] coaching school || prep school.

φρονώ [frono] think, suppose, believe, consider.

φρουρά, η [froura] lookout, guard || garrison.

φρούριο, το [froureeo] fortress, stronghold.

φρουρός, ο [frouros] guard, sentinel, sentry || (μεταφ) guardian.

φρουρώ [frouro] guard, keep watch, stand sentry.

φρούτο, το [frouto] fruit, dessert.

φρυγανιά η [freegania] toast.

φρύδι, το [freeðee] eyebrow.

φταίξιμο, το [fteekseemo] fault, error, mistake, blame.

φταίχτης, ο [ftehtees] person responsible, culprit.

φταίω [fteo] be responsible, be to blame || make a mistake.

φτάνω [ftano] βλ **φθάνω.**

φτέρη, η [fteree] fern.

φτέρνα, η [fterna] heel.

φτερνίζομαι [fterneezome] sneeze.

φτέρνισμα, το [fterneesma] sneeze, sneezing.

φτερό, το [ftero] feather, plume || wing || (ξεσκονίσματος) feather duster || (αυτοκινήτου) mudguard || fender (US).

φτερούγα, η [fterouga] wing.

φτερουγίζω [fterouyeezo] flutter, flap.

φτηναίνω [fteeneno] cheapen, become cheaper, go down.

φτήνεια, η [fteeneea] cheapness, low price.

φτηνός [fteenos] cheap.

φτιά(χ)νομαι [fteea(h)nome] make up one's face || look better.

φτιά(χ)νω [fteea(h)no] arrange, tidy up, correct || (κατασκευάζω) make || have made || do.

φτιαχτός [fteeahtos] fabricated, affected.

φτυάρι, το [fteearee] shovel, spade, scoop.

φτύνω [fteeno] spit, expectorate || spit out.

φτύσιμο, το [fteeseemo] spitting.

φτυστός [fteestos]: ~ **ο πατέρας του** the spitting image of his father.

φτωχαίνω [ftoheno] impoverish, make poor || become poor.

φτώχεια, η [ftoheea] poverty, destitution.

φτωχεύω [ftohevo] become poor || go bankrupt.

φτωχικό, το [ftoheeko] humble abode.

φτωχικός [ftoheekos] poor, mean, scant || shabby.

φτωχός [ftohos] poor, needy, penniless.

φυγαδεύω [feegaðevo] help to escape.

φυγάδας, ο [feegaðas] runaway, deserter, fugitive, renegade.

φυγή, η [feeyee] escape, fleeing, flight.

φυγοδικία, η [feegoðeekeea] default.

φυγόδικος/κη [feegoðeekos] defaulter.

φυγόκεντρος [feegokentros] centrifugal.

φυγόπονος [feegoponos] lazy || (ουσ) slacker, shirker.

φύκια, τα [feekeea] πλ seaweed.

φυλάγομαι [feelagome] take precautions, take care.

φυλάγω [feelago] guard, protect || mind, tend || (αντικείμενο) keep, lay aside || lie in wait for.

φύλακας, ο [feelakas] keeper, guardian, watchman, guard, caretaker.

φυλακή, η [feelakee] prison, jail.

φυλακίζω [feelakeezo] incarcerate, imprison.

φυλάκιο, το [feelakeeo] guardhouse, post.

φυλάκιση, η [feelakeesee] imprisonment.

φυλακισμένος, ο [feelakeesmenos] prisoner.

φυλαχτό, το [feelahto] talisman, amulet, charm.

φυλετικός [feeleeteekos] tribal, racial.

φυλή, η [feelee] race, tribe, line.

φυλλάδα, η [feelaða] booklet, pamphlet, brochure.

φυλλάδιο, το [feelaðeeo] pamphlet || instalment, issue, part.

φυλλοκάρδια, τα [feelokarðeea] πλ bottom of one's heart.

φυλλομετρώ [feelometro] turn pages of, skim over, run through.

φύλλο, το [feelo] leaf || (λουλουδιού) petal || (χαρτιού κτλ) sheet || (σελίδα) page || (πόρτας κτλ) shutter, leaf || (χαρτοπαιξίας) (playing) card || (εφημερίδα) newspaper || ~ **πορείας** marching orders.

φυλλοξήρα, η [feelokseera] phylloxera.

φύλλωμα, το [feeloma] foliage.

φύλο, το [feelo] sex || race.

φυματικός [feemateekos] consumptive, tubercular.

φυματίωση, η [feemateeosee] tuberculosis, consumption.

φύομαι [feeome] grow, bud, sprout.

φύρα, η [feera] loss of weight, waste.

φυραίνω [feereno] shorten, shrink || lose weight, lose volume.

φύραμα, το [feerama] paste, dough || blend || (μεταφ) character, sort.

φύρδην [feerðeen]: ~ **μίγδην** pell-mell, helter-skelter.

φυσαλίδα, η [feesaleeða] bubble || blister.

φυσαρμόνικα, η [feesarmoneeka] accordion || mouth organ.

φυσέκι, το [feesekee] cartridge.

φυσερό, το [feesero] bellows.

φύση, η [feesee] nature.

φύσημα, το [feeseema] breath || puff || breathing.

φυσίγγιο, το [feeseengeeo] cartridge.

φυσικά, τα [feeseeka] πλ physics.

φυσικά [feeseeka] naturally, as a matter of fact.

φυσική, η [feeseekee] physics, natural philosophy.

φυσικό, το [feeseeko] custom, habit.

φυσικός [feeseekos] natural || physical || (ουσ) physicist.

φυσικότητα, η [feeseekoteeta] naturalness, artlessness.

φυσιογνωμία, η [feeseeognomeea] cast of features || countenance || well-known person.

φυσιολάτρης, ο [feeseeolatrees] lover of nature.

φυσιολογία, η [feeseeoloyeea] physiology.

φυσιολογικός [feeseeoloyeekos] physiological || (μεταφ) normal.

φύση, η [feesee] nature || character, temper || **φύσει** by nature.

φυσομανώ [feesomano] rage.

φυσώ [feeso] blow up || puff, blow out || pant || **φυσάει** it's windy.

φυτεία, η [feeteea] plantation || vegetation, bed of vegetables.

φύτεμα, το [feetema] planting.

φυτεύω [feetevo] plant, lay out || (μεταφ) lodge, stick.

φυτικός [feeteekos] vegetable.

φυτοζωώ [feetozoo] live in poverty, scrape through.

φυτοκομία, η [feetokomeea] horticulture.

φυτολογία, η [feetoloyeea] botany.

φυτό, το [feeto] plant, vegetable.

φύτρα, η [feetra] germ, embryo || (μεταφ) lineage, origin.

φυτρώνω [feetrono] grow, germinate, sprout.

φυτώριο, το [feetoreeo] nursery, plantation, seedbed.

φώκια, η [fokeea] seal.

φωλιά, η [foleea] nest, den, lair, hole || (μεταφ) hovel.

φωλιάζω [foleeazo] nestle, nest.

φωνάζω [fonazo] shout, call, summon || cry, scream, shriek.

φωνακλάς, ο [fonaklas] loud talker, noisy talker.

φωνή, η [fonee] sound || voice || cry, shout, scream.

φωνήεν, το [fonien] vowel.

φωνητική, η [foneeteekee] phonetics.

φωνητικός [foneeteekos] vocal || phonetic, phonic.

φως, το [fos] light || (μεταφ) sight || knowledge, illumination.

φωστήρ(ας), το [fosteer(as)] luminary || (μεταφ) learned, erudite person.

φωσφόρος, ο [fosforos] phosphorus.

φώτα, τα [fota] πλ lights || (μεταφ) knowledge, learning || (εκκλ) Epiphany.

φωταγωγός, ο [fotagogos] light well, skylight.

φωταγωγώ [fotagogo] illuminate.

φωταέριο, το [fotaereeo] gas (lighting).

φωταψία, η [fotapseea] illumination.

φωτεινός [foteenos] luminous, light, bright || clear, lucid.

φωτιά, η [fotia] fire || (καπνιστού) light || (μεταφ) great heat || fury || (σε τιμή) costliness.

φωτίζω [foteezo] illuminate, light up, light || enlighten, inform.

φώτιση, η [foteesee] enlightenment || inspiration.

φωτισμός, ο [foteesmos] lighting, illumination.

φωτοβολίδα, η [fotovoleeða] flare.

φωτογενής [fotogenees] photogenic.

φωτογραφείο, το [fotografeeo] photographic studio.

φωτογραφία, η [fotografeea] photograph || photography.

φωτογραφική, η [fotografeekee] photography || ~ **μηχανή** camera.

φωτογράφος, ο [fotografos] photographer.

φωτόμετρο, το [fotometro] light meter.

φωτοσκίαση, η [fotoskeeasee] shading, light and shade.

φωτοστέφανος, ο [fotostefanos] halo || (μεταφ) glory, prestige.

φωτοτυπία, η [fototeepeea] photocopy.

φωτοχυσία, η [fotoheeseea] illumination.

Χ, χ

χαβάς, ο [havas] tune, air, melody.

χαβιάρι, το [haviaree] caviar.

χαβούζα, η [havouza] cistern, reservoir.

χαγιάτι, το [hayiatee] upper gallery round courtyard.

χάδια, τα [haðeea] πλ petting, cajolery.

χαζεύω [hazevo] gape || idle about, loiter.

χάζι, το [hazee] pleasure, delight || **το κάνω ~** it entertains me.

χαζός [hazos] stupid, silly, foolish.

χαϊβάνι, το [haeevanee] beast || (μεταφ) jackass.

χάϊδεμα, το [haeeðema] caressing, pat, stroke || (μεταφ) cajolery.

χαϊδευτικός [haeeðevteekos] caressing, affectionate || (άνεμος) soft.

χαϊδεμένος [haeeðemenos] spoilt.

χαϊδεύομαι [haeeðevome] nuzzle, cuddle || seek attention.

χαϊδεύω [haeeðevo] caress, fondle, pat || pet, spoil || fawn upon.

χαιρέκακος [herekakos] malicious, mischievous.

χαίρετε [herete] (επιφ) hello, good day || be seeing you.

χαιρετίζω [hereteezo] hail, greet || salute.

χαιρέτισμα, το [hereteesma] salute, greeting, salutation, bow.

χαιρετισμός, ο [hereteesmos] βλ **χαιρέτισμα**.

χαιρετώ [hereto] βλ **χαιρετίζω**.

χαίρομαι [herome] be happy || enjoy.

χαίρω [hero] be pleased || ~ **άκρας υγείας** be in tiptop shape.

χαίτη, η [hetee] mane, shock of hair.

χακί, το [hakee] khaki.

χαλάζι, το [halazee] hail.

χαλάλι [halalee]: ~ **σου** you merit it, you can have it.

χαλαρός [halaros] relaxed, slack, loose.

χαλαρώνω [halarono] unbend || (σχοινί) loosen, slacken || (μεταφ) relax || (προσπάθεια) abate, ease up || (ζήλο) cool.

χάλασμα, το [halasma] ruin, demolition || (μηχανής) putting out of order || ruin.

χαλασμένος [halasmenos] rotten, turned bad || broken, not working || damaged, demolished.

χαλασμός, ο [halasmos] demolition, destruction || (μεταφ) disturbance, storm, excitement || catastrophe.

χαλάστρα, η [halastra]: **μου κάνουν** ~ they foiled my plans, they cramped my style.

χαλβάς, ο [halvas] halva || (μεταφ) indolent person, silly fellow.

χαλί, το [halee] carpet, rug.

χάλια, τα [haleea] πλ bad condition, sad plight.

χαλίκι, το [haleekee] pebble, small stone, gravel.

χαλιναγωγώ [haleenagogo] lead by the bridle || (μεταφ) check, curb || (πάθη) control, curb.

χαλινάρι, το [haleenaree] bridle, bit, rein || (μεταφ) curbing, holding back.

χαλκάς, ο [halkas] ring, link.

χάλκινος [halkeenos] of copper.

χαλκογραφία, η [halkografeea] copperplate engraving, art of copperplating.

χαλκομανία, η [halkomaneea] transfer design.

χαλκός, ο [halkos] copper, brass, bronze.

χαλνώ [halno] βλ **χαλώ**.

χάλυβας, ο [haleevas] steel.

χαλύβδινος [haleevδeenos] made of steel.

χαλώ [halo] demolish, break, ruin, spoil || (φθείρω) wear out || (νεύρα) fret || (υγεία) break down || (δαπανώ) spend, consume || (διαφθείρω) corrupt, pervert || (νόμισμα) change || (δόντι) decay ||

(κρέας) taint, go bad || ~ **τον κόσμο** move heaven and earth, make a fuss.

χαμαιλέοντας, ο [hameleondas] chameleon || (βοτ) thistle.

χαμάλης, ο [hamalees] porter || (μεταφ) vulgar fellow, scoundrel.

χαμάμι, το [hamamee] Turkish bath.

χαμένα [hamena]: **τα έχω** ~ be mixed up, be bewildered.

χαμένος [hamenos] lost, disappeared || (ουσ: στα χαρτιά) loser || (μεταφ) scoundrel, rascal || scatterbrain.

χαμηλός [hameelos] low || (φωνή) gentle, soft, subdued.

χαμηλόφωνα [hameelofona] in an undertone, softly.

χαμηλώνω [hameelono] lower, reduce, bring down || subside.

χαμίνι, το [hameenee] street urchin, mischievous youngster.

χαμόγελο, το [hamoyelo] smile.

χαμογελώ [hamoyelo] smile.

χαμόκλαδο, το [hamoklaδo] shrub.

χαμομήλι, το [hamomeelee] camomile.

χαμός, ο [hamos] loss, destruction, ruin || death.

χάμουρα, τα [hamoura] πλ harness, trappings.

χαμπάρι, το [hambaree] piece of news || **παίρνω** ~ become aware, perceive.

χάμω [hamo] down, on the ground.

χάνι, το [hanee] country inn, lodging house.

χανούμισσα, η [hanoumeesa] Turkish lady.

χαντάκι, το [hantakee] ditch, drain, trench || (οχυρού) moat.

χαντακώνω [hantakono] (μεταφ) destroy, ruin.

χάντρα, η [hantra] bead.

χάνομαι [hanome] lose o.s., get lost || **να χαθείς!** go to hell! || **χάσου** get out of my sight!

χάνω [hano] lose, go astray || (ευκαιρία) let slip || (καιρό) waste time || (τραίνο) lose, miss || become disconcerted, get confused.

χάος, το [haos] chaos, wild disorder || bottomless pit.

χάπι, το [hapee] pill.

χαρά, η [hara] joy || (υπερβολική) delight, glee || pleasure, enjoyment || ~ **θεού** delight || **μια** ~ very well, splendidly || **γεια** ~ so long!, goodbye! || hello! || ~ **στο πράμα** wonderful!, it's nothing! (ironic).

χάραγμα, το [haragma] tracing, engraving || incision, cut.

χαράδρα, η [haraδra] ravine, gorge, gully.

χαράζω [harazo] cut, engrave || rule lines || trace || (δρόμο κτλ) mark out, lay out.

χάρακας, ο [harakas] straight edge, ruler.

χαρακιά, η [harakia] scratch, incision, mark || groove || (γραμμή) line, stroke.

χαρακτήρας, ο [harakteeras] character, letter || temper, nature.

χαρακτηρίζω [harakteereezo] define, qualify || characterize.

χαρακτηριστικά, τα [harakteereesteeka] πλ person's features.

χαρακτηριστικός [harakteereesteekos] typical, distinctive, characteristic.

χαράκτης, ο [haraktees] engraver, carver.

χαρακτική, η [harakteekee] art of engraving.

χαράκωμα, το [harakoma] trench || (γραμμών) ruling.

χαραμάδα, η [haramaδa] fissure, crack, crevice.

χαράματα, τα [haramata] πλ dawn, daybreak.

χαραματιά, η [haramatia] incision, crack || (επιφάνειας) scratch, trace, engraving.

χαραμίζω [harameezo] waste, spend uselessly.

χάραξη, η [haraksee] engraving, tracing, incision || (δρόμου) laying out.

χαράσσω [harasso] engrave, carve || (γραμμές) rule || map out, trace || (δρόμο) lay out.

χαράτσι, το [haratsee] (μεταφ) oppressive tax.

χαρατσώνω [haratsono] exact money from || tax oppressively.

χαραυγή, η [haravyee] daybreak, dawn.

χαρέμι, το [haremee] harem.

χάρη, η [haree] grace, charm || good point || favour || gratitude || (ποινής) remittance, pardon || ~ **σε σένα** thanks to you || **λόγου** ~ for instance || **χάριν του** for, on behalf of || **παραδείγματος** ~ for example, for instance || **για** ~ **σου** for your sake, on your behalf.

χαριεντίζομαι [harienteezome] be in a teasing mood, jest || become very charming.

χαρίζω [hareezo] give, donate, present || (χρέος κτλ) remit.

χάρισμα, το [hareesma] talent, gift || accomplishment || (επιρ) free, gratis, for nothing.

χαριστικός [hareesteekos]: ~ **βολή** coup de grace.

χαριστικός [hareesteekos] prejudiced, partial.

χαριτολογώ [hareetologo] jest, speak wittily, speak amusingly.

χαριτωμένος [hareetomenos] charming, enchanting.

χάρμα, το [harma] delight, source of joy.

χαρμάνι, το [harmanee] mixture, blend.

χαρμόσυνος [harmoseenos] cheerful, glad.

χαροκόπος, ο [harokopos] pleasure-loving person, rake.

χάρος, ο [haros] death.

χαρούμενος [haroumenos] cheerful, joyful, happy.

χαρούπι, το [haroupee] carob.

χαρταετός, ο [hartaetos] kite.

χαρτζιλίκι, το [hardzeeleekee] pocket money.

χάρτης, ο [hartees] paper || (γεωγραφικός) map || (συνταγματικός) charter.

χαρτί, το [hartee] paper || (χαρτοπαιξίας) playing card || ~ **υγείας** toilet paper.

χάρτινος [harteenos] of paper.

χαρτοκόπτης, ο [hartokoptees] paper knife.

χαρτόνι, το [hartonee] cardboard, pasteboard.

χαρτονόμισμα, το [hartonomeesma] banknote || bill (US) || paper money.

χαρτοπαίκτης, ο [hartopektees] gambler, card player.

χαρτοπαιξία, η [hartopekseea] gambling, card playing.

χαρτοπόλεμος, ο [hartopolemos] confetti throwing.

χαρτοπώλης, ο [hartopolees] stationer, paper merchant.

χαρτόσημο, το [hartoseemo] stamp tax.

χαρτοφύλακας, ο [hartofeelakas] briefcase || (εκκλ) archivist.

χαρτοφυλάκιο, το [hartofeelakeeo] letter-case, briefcase || (μεταφ) portfolio.

χαρωπός [haropos] cheerful, happy.

χασάπης, ο [hasapees] butcher.

χασάπικο, το [hasapeeko] butcher's shop.

χάση, η [hasee]: **στη** ~ **και στη φέξη** once in a blue moon.

χάσιμο, το [haseemo] loss.

χασίσι, το [haseesee] hashish.

χάσκω [hasko] yawn, gape || stand ajar.

χάσμα, το [hasma] abyss, pit || lacuna, gap.

χασμουρητό, το [hasmoureeto] yawning, yawn.

χασμουριέμαι [hasmourieme] yawn.

χασμωδία, η [hasmoδeea] hiatus || disorder, confusion.

χασομερώ [hasomero] be idle || hang around, linger.

χασούρα, η [hasoura] loss.

χαστούκι, το [hastoukee] slap, smack, clout.

χατίρι, το [hateeree] favour, good turn || **για το ~ σου** for your sake.

χαυλιόδοντας, ο [havleeoðondas] tusk.

χαύνος [havnos] slack, indolent || faint-hearted.

χαφιές, ο [hafies] stool, nark, agent, informer.

χάφτω [hafto] swallow, gobble down || (μεταφ) take in.

χαχανίζω [hahaneezo] burst into laughter, laugh loudly.

χάχας, ο [hahas] moron, idiot.

χαψιά, η [hapsia] mouthful.

χαώδης [haoðees] chaotic, confused.

χέζομαι [hezome] be in a fright, be scared || **χέστηκα** I don't give a damn.

χέζω [hezo] defecate || (μεταφ) send to the devil.

χείλι, το [heelee], **χείλος, το** [heelos] lip || (μεταφ) brink, verge || (ποτηριού) brim, rim.

χείμαρρος, ο [heemaros] torrent, torrent bed.

χειμερινός [heemereenos] winter, wintry.

χειμώνας, ο [heemonas] winter.

χειμωνιάτικος [heemoneeateekos] βλ **χειμερινός**.

χειραφετώ [heerafeto] liberate, emancipate || manumit.

χειραψία, η [heerapseea] shake of the hand.

χειρίζομαι [heereezome] handle, manipulate, manage || (μηχανή) drive.

χειρισμός, ο [heereesmos] manipulation, working, driving || (υποθέσεως) handling, management.

χειριστήρια, τα [heereesteereea] πλ controls of a machine.

χειριστής, ο [heereestees] operator || pilot.

χειροβομβίδα, η [heerovomveeða] grenade.

χειρόγραφο, το [heerografo] manuscript.

χειροκίνητος [heerokeeneetos] hand-operated.

χειροκρότημα, το [heerokroteema] clapping, applause.

χειροκροτώ [heerokroto] applaud, cheer, clap.

χειρομαντεία, η [heeromandeea] palm reading.

χειρονομία, η [heeronomeea] flourish, gesture || gesticulation.

χειροπέδες, οι [heeropeðes] πλ pair of handcuffs.

χειροπιαστός [heeropeeastos] tangible.

χειροπόδαρα [heeropoðara] hand and foot.

χειροποίητος [heeropeeetos] handmade.

χειρότερα [heerotera] worse.

χειροτερεύω [heeroterevo] worsen, deteriorate.

χειρότερος [heeroteros] worse || **ο ~** the worst.

χειροτεχνία, η [heerotehneea] handicraft.

χειροτονία, η [heerotoneea] ordination, consecration.

χειρουργείο, το [heerouryeeo] operating theatre.

χειρουργική, η [heerouryeekee] surgery.

χειρουργικός [heerouryeekos] surgical.

χειρουργός, ο [heerourgos] surgeon.

χειροφίλημα, το [heerofeeleema] kissing of the hand.

χειρωνακτικός [heeronakteekos] manual.

χέλι, το [helee] eel.

χελιδόνι, το [heleeðonee] (ζωολ) swallow.

χελώνα, η [helona] tortoise, turtle.

χεράκι, το [herakee] tiny hand.

χέρι, το [heree] hand || arm || (χειρολαβή) handle || (μπογιάς) coat || (στο πλύσιμο) treatment, going-over || **~ ~** hand-in-hand || **~ με ~** quickly, directly || **βάζω ένα ~** give a hand || **βάζω ~** lay hands on, fondle || **από πρώτο ~** at first hand.

χερούλι, το [heroulee] handle, haft || (στάμνας) ear.

χερσαίος [herseos] terrestrial || (κλίμα) continental.

χερσόνησος, η [hersoneesos] peninsula.

χέρσος [hersos] uncultivated, fallow, waste.

χέσιμο, το [heseemo] defecation || (μεταφ) fright, terror || volley of abuse.

χημεία, η [heemeea] chemistry.

χημικός [heemeekos] chemical || (ουσ) chemist.

χήνα, η [heena] goose.

χήρα, η [heera] widow.

χηρεύω [heerevo] become widowed || (θέση) be unoccupied, be vacant.

χήρος, ο [heeros] widower.

χθές [hthes] yesterday.

χθεσινός [htheseenos] of yesterday || (πρόσφατος) latest, recent.

χι, το [hee] the letter X.

χιαστί [heeastee] crossways, crosswise, diagonally.

χίλια [heeleea]: **~ δυο** a thousand and two.

χιλιάδα, η [heeleeaða] thousand.

χιλιάρικο, το [heeleeareeko] thousand-drachma note.

χιλιετηρίδα, η [heelieteereeða], **χιλιετία, η** [heelieteea] millenium.

χιλιόγραμμο, το [heeliogramo] kilogramme.

χίλιοι [heeliee] thousand.

χιλιόμετρο, το [heeleeometro] kilometre.

χιλιοστό, το [heeleeosto] millimetre || thousandth part.

χιλιοστός [heeleeostos] thousandth.

χίμαιρα, η [heemera] chimera || (μεταφ) illusion.

χιμπαντζής, ο [heempandzees] chimpanzee.

χιονάνθρωπος, ο [heeonanthropos] snowman.

χιονάτος [heeonatos] snow-white, snowy.

χιόνι, το [heeonee] snow.

χιονιά, η [heeonia] snowy weather || snowball.

χιονίζει [heeoneezee] it is snowing.

χιονίστρα, η [heeoneestra] chilblain.

χιονοδρομία, η [heeonoðromeea] skiing.

χιονοθύελλα, η [heeonothiela] snowstorm, blizzard.

χιονόνερο, το [heeononero] sleet, melted snow.

χιονοστιβάδα, η [heeonosteevaða] avalanche, snowdrift.

χιούμορ, το [heeoumor] wit, humour || χιουμοριστικός humorous, humoristic.

χιτώνας, ο [heetonas] robe, tunic || (ματιού) cornea.

χλαίνη, η [hlenee] greatcoat || (ναυτ) duffel coat || cloak, capote.

χλαμύδα, η [hlameeða] mantle.

χλευάζω [hlevazo] mock, scoff at, make fun of.

χλευαστικός [hlevasteekos] mocking, sarcastic, derisive.

χλιαρός [hleearos] tepid, lukewarm || (άνεμος) mild || (μεταφ) weak, lax.

χλιδή, η [hleeðee] luxury, voluptuousness.

χλιμιντρίζω [hleemeendreezo] neigh, whinny.

χλοερός [hloeros] green, fresh, verdant.

χλόη, η [hloee] grass, turf, lawn || greenness, verdure.

χλωμιάζω [hlomeeazo] (go) pale || blanch.

χλωμός [hlomos] pale, pallid, wan.

χλώριο, το [hloreeo] chlorine, chloride.

χλωρίδα, η [hloreeða] flora.

χλωρός [hloros] green, unseasoned || fresh.

χλωροφόρμιο, το [hloroformeeo] chloroform.

χλωροφύλλη, η [hlorofeelee] chlorophyll.

χνάρι, το [hnaree] pattern, model || track.

χνούδι, το [hnouðee] down, fuzz, fluff.

χνουδωτός [hnouðotos] downy, fluffy.

χνώτο, το [hnoto] breath.

χόβολη, η [hovolee] embers, burning charcoal.

χοιρινό, το [heereeno] pork.

χοιρομέρι, το [heeromeree] ham, bacon.

χοίρος, ο [heeros] pig, hog, swine.

χολέρα, η [holera] cholera.

χολή, η [holee] bile || (ζώου) gall || (μεταφ) rancour, bitterness.

χολιάζω [holeeazo] get irritated || irritate || lose one's temper.

χολοσκάω [holoskao] afflict, grieve, exasperate || get riled.

χονδρικός [honðreekos] wholesale.

χονδροειδής [honðroeeðees] rough, clumsy, coarse || (ψεύδος) flagrant || vulgar.

χόνδρος, το [honðros] cartilage || grit.

χονδρός [honðros] big, fat, stout, thick || (σε τρόπους) vulgar, unpolished || (αστείο) coarse.

χοντραίνω [hondreno] become fat, make thicker, put on weight.

χοντροκέφαλος [hondrokefalos] stupid, thickheaded || obstinate, headstrong.

χοντροκοπιά, η [hondrokopia] clumsy job of work.

χοντρός [hondros] βλ χονδρός.

χορδή, η [horðee] chord, string || (ανατ) cord.

χορευτής, ο [horevtees] dancer || partner.

χορευτικός [horevteekos] for dancing, of dancing.

χορεύω [horevo] dance || dance with.

χορήγηση, η [horeeyeesee] granting, giving, supplying.

χορηγώ [horeego] provide, allocate, supply, grant.

χορογραφία, η [horografeea] choreography.

χοροδιδάσκαλος, ο [horoðeeðaskalos] dancing master.

χοροπηδώ [horopeeðo] leap about, gambol, caper.

χορός, ο [horos] dancing, dance || chorus, choir.

χοροστατώ [horostato] conduct divine service.

χόρτα, τα [horta] πλ green vegetables, wild greens.

χορταίνω [horteno] have enough, satiate || satisfy || (βαριέμαι) get bored with.

χορτάρι, το [hortaree] grass.

χορταρικά, τα [hortareeka] πλ vegetables, greens.

χορτασμός, ο [hortasmos] satisfaction, satiety.

χορταστικός [hortasteekos] satisfying, substantial, filling || abundant.

χορτάτος [hortatos] satisfied, satiated.

χόρτο, το [horto] grass, herb || (άγριο) weed.

χορτοφάγος [hortofagos] vegetarian || (ζώο) herbivorous.

χορωδία, n [horoδeea] choir, chorus.

χουζούρι, το [houzouree] rest, idleness, leisure.

χουρμάς, ο [hourmas] (βοτ) date.

χούφτα, n [houfta] handful || hollow of hand.

χουφτιά, n [houftia] handful.

χρειάζομαι [hreeazome] lack, want, require || be necessary, be useful.

χρεόγραφο, το [hreografo] security, debenture, bond.

χρέος, το [hreos] debt || obligation.

χρεωκοπία, n [hreokopeea] bankruptcy, failure.

χρεωκοπώ [hreokopo] go bankrupt, break.

χρεωλυσία, n [hreoleeseea] amortization, sinking fund.

χρεώνομαι [hreonome] get into debt.

χρεώνω [hreono] debit, charge.

χρεωστάσιο, το [hreostaseeo] moratorium.

χρεώστης, ο [hreostees] debtor.

χρεωστώ [hreosto] be in debt, owe, be indebted (to) || be obliged.

χρήμα, το [hreema] money.

χρηματίζομαι [hreemateezome] take bribes || hoard up money.

χρηματίζω [hreemateezo] serve as, be.

χρηματικός [hreemateekos] of money, monetary.

χρηματιστήριο, το [hreemateesteereeo] stock exchange.

χρηματιστής, ο [hreemateestees] stockbroker.

χρηματοδοτώ [hreematoδoto] finance, invest.

χρηματοκιβώτιο, το [hreematokeevoteeo] safe, strong-box, cash box.

χρήση, n [hreesee] use, usage, employment || enjoyment || application || (οικον) financial year || προς ~ for the use || εν χρήσει in use, used.

χρησιμεύω [hreeseemevo] be useful || be good for, serve.

χρησιμοποίηση, n [hreeseemopieesee] employment, utilization.

χρησιμοποιώ [hreeseemopieeo] use, utilize, make use of.

χρήσιμος [hreeseemos] useful, handy.

χρησιμότητα, n [hreeseemoteeta] usefulness, utility, benefit.

χρησμός, ο [hreesmos] oracle, divination.

χρηστός [hreestos] honourable, upright, virtuous.

χρίζω [hreezo] βλ χρίω.

χρίσμα, το [hreesma] chrism, unction || anointing.

χριστιανικός [hreesteeaneekos] Christian.

χριστιανισμός, ο [hreesteeaneesmos] Christianity.

χριστιανός, ο [hreesteeanos] Christian.

χριστιανοσύνη, n [hreesteeanoseenee] Christendom.

Χριστός, ο [hreestos] Christ.

Χριστούγεννα, τα [hreestouyena] πλ Christmas.

χρίω [hreeo] anoint || plaster.

χροιά, n [hreea] complexion, colour || shade, tone, nuance.

χρονιά, n [hroneea] year.

χρονικά, τα [hroneeka] πλ annals.

χρονικογράφος, ο [hroneekografos] chronicler.

χρονικό, το [hroneeko] chronicle.

χρονικός [hroneekos] of time, temporal.

χρόνιος [hroneeos] chronic, enduring, lasting.

χρονογράφημα, το [hronografeema] newspaper leader article.

χρονογράφος, ο [hronografos] leader writer.

χρονολογία, n [hronoloyeea] date || chronology.

χρονολογούμαι [hronologoume] date from, be dated.

χρονόμετρο, το [hronometro] chronometer.

χρόνος, ο [hronos] time, duration || age, period || (γραμμ) tense, quantity || ο ~ year || προ χρόνων some years ago || του χρόνου next year || χρόνια πολλά! happy name day!, happy birthday!, many happy returns!

χρονοτριβώ [hronotreevo] linger, loiter.

χρυσαλλίδα, n [hreesaleeδa] chrysalis.

χρυσάνθεμο, το [hreesanthemo] chrysanthemum.

χρυσάφι, το [hreesafee] gold.

χρυσαφικά, τα [hreesafeeka] πλ jewellery.

χρυσή, n [hreesee] jaundice.

χρυσικός, ο [hreeseekos] goldsmith || jeweller.

χρυσόδετος [hreesoδetos] mounted in gold.

χρυσοθήρας, ο [hreesotheeras] gold-digger, prospector.

χρυσόμαλλο [hreesomalo]: ~ δέρας golden fleece.

χρυσός, ο [hreesos] gold || (επίθ) golden || (μεταφ) kind-hearted, adorable.

χρυσοχοείο, το [hreesohoeeo] jeweller's shop, goldsmith's shop.

χρυσοχόος, ο [hreesohoos] goldsmith || jeweller.

χρυσόψαρο, το [hreesopsaro] goldfish.

χρυσώνω [hreesono] gild, gold-plate.

χρυσωρυχείο, το [hreesoreeheeo] gold mine.

χρώμα, το [hroma] colour, tint, hue || (μπογιά) paint, dye || complexion.

χρωματίζω [hromateezo] colour, paint, dye, tint.

χρωματικός [hromateekos] chromatic || of colour.

χρωματισμός, ο [hromateesmos] colouring, painting.

χρωματιστός [hromateestos] coloured.

χρώμιο, το [hromeeo] chromium, chrome.

χρωστικός [hrosteekos] colouring.

χρωστώ [hrosto] βλ **χρεωστώ**.

χταπόδι, το [htapodee] octopus.

χτένα, η [htena] βλ **χτένι**.

χτένι, το [htenee] comb.

χτενίζω [hteneezo] comb || (ομιλία κτλ) polish up.

χτένισμα, το [hteneesma] combing || hairstyle.

χτες [htes] βλ **χθές**.

χτεσινός [hteseenos] βλ **χθεσινός**.

χτήμα, το [hteema] βλ **κτήμα**.

χτίζω [hteezo] βλ **κτίζω**.

χτικιό, το [hteekio] tuberculosis || (μεταφ) torture, anguish.

χτίστης, ο [hteestees] bricklayer, builder.

χτυπάω [hteepao] βλ **χτυπώ**.

χτύπημα, το [hteepeema] blow, punch, kick, hit, knock || bruise, wound.

χτυπητός [hteepeetos] beaten || tawdry, garish, loud, striking.

χτυποκάρδι, το [hteepokardee] rapid beating of the heart.

χτύπος, ο [hteepos] blow, stroke || (καρδιάς) throb, beat || (ρολογιού) tick(ing).

χτυπώ [hteepo] knock, thrash, hit, beat, strike || hurt o.s. || (χέρια) clap || (πόδια) stamp || (χρόνο) beat || (αυγά κτλ) whisk || (ρολογιού κτλ) peal, strike, sound || **χτυπάει άσχημα** it jars, it looks bad || **μου χτυπάει στα νεύρα** it gets on my nerves || **χτυπιέμαι** come to blows || feel sorry, repent.

χυδαίος [heedeos] vulgar, trivial, crude, rude, coarse.

χυδαιότητα, η [heedeoteeta] vulgarity, coarseness, foul language.

χυλόπιτα, ο [heepoleeta] kind of macaroni || (μεταφ) failure in love.

χυλός, ο [heelos] pap, liquid paste.

χύμα [heema] confusedly, pell-mell || loose, unpacked, unbottled.

χυμός, ο [heemos] sap, juice.

χυμώ [heemo] rush upon, charge.

χυμώδης [heemodees] juicy, sappy.

χύνομαι [heenome] overflow, pour out || flow out || (μεταφ) charge against, rush upon.

χύνω [heeno] spill, tip over, pour out || (δάκρυα) shed || (μέταλλο) cast.

χύσιμο, το [heeseemo] discharge, pouring out, spilling || casting, moulding.

χυτήριο, το [heeteereeo] foundry, smelting works.

χυτός [heetos] moulded, cast || (σκορπισμένος) dispersed, scattered || (μαλλιά) flowing, loose || (ρούχα) tight-fitting.

χυτοσίδηρος, ο [heetoseedeeros] cast iron.

χύτρα, η [heetra] cooking pot, pot, porridge pot.

χωλ, το [hol] hall.

χωλαίνω [holeno] limp, be lame || (μεταφ) halt, hobble, move slowly.

χώμα, το [homa] soil, dust, earth || ground.

χωματένιος [homateneeos] earthen.

χώνευση, η [honevsee] digestion || (μετάλλων) casting, founding.

χωνευτήριο, το [honevteereeo] crucible, melting pot.

χωνευτικός [honevteekos] digestible, digestive.

χωνεύω [honevo] digest || (μέταλλο) cast, smelt || (μεταφ) tolerate, endure.

χωνί, το [honee] funnel, horn || (παγωτού) cone.

χώνομαι [honome] squeeze in || hide || (μεταφ) interfere.

χώνω [hono] thrust, force || bury || (κρύβω) hide.

χώρα, η [hora] country, place || chief town || (ανατ) region || **λαμβάνω ~** happen.

χωρατεύω [horatevo] joke.

χωρατό, το [horato] joke, jest, witticism.

χωράφι, το [horafee] field, land.

χωράω [horao] βλ **χωρώ**.

χωρητικότητα, η [horeeteekoteeta] volume, capacity || (ναυτ) tonnage.

χώρια [horeea] βλ **χωριστά**.

χωριανός, ο [horeeanos] fellow villager, countryman.

χωριάτης, ο [horeeatees] peasant, villager, countryman || (μεταφ) ill-mannered person, unpolished person.

χωριάτικος [horeeateekos] peasant, of the village || rustic.

χωρίζομαι [horeezome] leave, part from.

χωρίζω [horeezo] separate, disconnect, part, split || (δρόμοι) branch off ||

(ζεύγος) get a divorce || ~ με break up with, part from.

χωρικός [horeekos] village, rural, country || (ουσ) peasant, villager.

χωριό, το [horio] village, hamlet || (μεταφ) hometown.

χωρίς [horees] without, apart from || not including || ~ άλλο without fail || με ~ without.

χώρισμα, το [horeesma] sorting, separation || (δωματίου) wall, partition || compartment.

χωρισμένος [horeesmenos] divided || separated, divorced.

χωρισμός, ο [horeesmos] separation || partition || separating || divorce.

χωριστά [horeesta] apart, individually || (προθ) not counting, apart from, not including.

χωριστός [horeestos] separate, different, distinct, isolated.

χωρίστρα, η [horeestra] parting of hair.

χώρος, ο [horos] space, area, room || interval, distance.

χωροφύλακας, ο [horofeelakas] gendarme.

χωροφυλακή, η [horofeelakee] gendarmerie.

χωρώ [horo] fit into, have room || (περιέχω) hold, contain || δε χωράει αμφιβολία there's no doubt, undoubtedly.

χώσιμο, το [hoseemo] driving in, burying || hiding.

Ψ, ψ

ψάθα, η [psatha] straw, cane || (χαλί) rush mat || (καπέλο) straw hat || στη ~ penniless.

ψάθινος [psatheenos] made of straw.

ψαλίδα, η [psaleeδa] shears || centipede.

ψαλίδι, το [psaleeδee] scissors, pruning scissors || curling tongs.

ψαλιδίζω [psaleeδeezo] cut, trim || (μεταφ) reduce, cut down.

ψάλλω [psalo] sing, chant || extol, celebrate.

ψαλμός, ο [psalmos] psalm, chant.

ψαλμωδία, η [psalmoδeea] chanting of psalms || monotonous delivery.

ψάλτης, ο [psaltees] chorister, singer, chanter.

ψάξιμο, το [psakseemo] searching, quest, search.

ψαράδικο, το [psaraδeeko] fishing boat || fishmonger's shop.

ψαράδικος [psaraδeekos] of a fisherman.

ψαράς, ο [psaras] fisherman || fishmonger.

ψάρεμα, το [psarema] fishing, angling, netting.

ψαρεύω [psarevo] fish || sound, fish for information.

ψάρι, το [psaree] fish.

ψαρόβαρκα, η [psarovarka] fishing boat.

ψαροκόκαλο, το [psarokokalo] fish bone || (σχέδιο) herringbone.

ψαρόκολλα, η [psarokola] fish glue.

ψαρομάλλης, ο [psaromalees] grey-haired person.

ψαρονέφρι, το [psaronefree] fillet of meat.

ψαρός [psaros] grey, grizzled.

ψαύση, η [psavsee] touching, feeling, light touch.

ψαχνό, το [psahno] lean meat.

ψάχνομαι [psahnome] look through one's pockets.

ψάχνω [psahno] search for, look for || seek, rummage.

ψαχουλεύω [psahoulevo] search for, grope for, fumble around for.

ψεγάδι, το [psegaδee] fault, failing, shortcoming.

ψέγω [psego] blame, reprove, censure.

ψείρα, η [pseera] louse || vermin.

ψειριάζω [pseereeazo] get lousy.

ψειρίζω [pseereezo] delouse || (μεταφ) examine in great detail.

ψεκάζω [psekazo] spray.

ψεκαστήρας, ο [psekasteeras] spray, vapourizer || scent sprayer.

ψελλίζω [pseleezo] stammer, stutter.

ψέλνω [pselno] βλ ψάλλω.

ψέμα, το [psema] lie, falsehood, fib.

ψες [pses] last night.

ψευδαίσθηση, η [psevδestheesee] delusion, hallucination.

ψευδάργυρος, ο [psevδaryeeros] zinc.

ψευδής [psevδees] untrue, false || artificial, sham, fictitious || deceptive.

ψευδίζω [psevδeezo] βλ ψελλίζω.

ψευδολογώ [psevδologo] tell lies, tell stories, fib.

ψεύδομαι [psevδome] lie, fib.

ψευδομάρτυρας, ο, η [psevδomarteeras] false witness, perjurer.

ψευδομαρτυρώ [psevδomarteero] give false witness, commit perjury.

ψευδορκία, η [psevδorkeea] perjury.

ψευδορκώ [psevδorko] commit perjury, perjure.

ψευδός [psevδos] lisping, stammering, stuttering.

ψευδώνυμο, το [psevδoneemo] pseudonym, assumed name.

ψεύτης, ο [psevtees] liar, fibber || cheat, impostor.

ψευτιά, η [psevtia] untruth, lie.

ψευτίζω [psevteezo] adulterate || become adulterated.

ψεύτικος [psevteekos] false, untrue || artificial || (σε ποιότητα) inferior.

ψήγμα, το [pseegma] filings, shavings, chips.

ψηλά [pseela] high up, aloft.

ψηλαφώ [pseelafo] feel, touch, finger || (ψάχνω) feel one's way, grope.

ψηλομύτης [pseelomeetees] haughty, overbearing.

ψηλός [pseelos] high, tall, lofty, great.

ψήλωμα, το [pseeloma] eminence, elevation || making taller, growing.

ψηλώνω [pseelono] make taller, make higher || grow taller.

ψήνομαι [pseenome] become very hot || (στη δουλειά) become broken in.

ψήνω [pseeno] bake, roast, cook || (μεταφ) torture, worry, pester.

ψήσιμο, το [pseeseemo] baking, broiling, roasting, cooking, frying.

ψησταριά, η [pseestaria] barbecue apparatus.

ψητό, το [pseeto] roast meat, grilled meat || (μεταφ) the main point.

ψητός [pseetos] roast, baked, roasted.

ψηφιδωτό, το [pseefeeδoto] mosaic.

ψηφίζω [pseefeezo] vote || (νόμο) pass, carry.

ψηφίο, το [pseefeeo] cipher, figure || (αλφαβήτου) letter, character.

ψήφισμα, το [pseefeesma] decree, enactment, edict.

ψηφοδέλτιο, το [pseefoδelteeo] ballot paper.

ψηφοδόχος, η [pseefoδohos] ballot box.

ψηφοθηρώ [pseefotheero] solicit votes, canvass for votes.

ψήφος, ο, η [pseefos] vote, voting, suffrage.

ψηφοφορία, η [pseefoforeea] voting, ballot(ting).

ψι, το [psee] the letter Ψ.

ψιθυρίζω [pseetheereezo] mutter, murmur, whisper.

ψιθύρισμα, το [pseetheereesma] whisper(ing), muttering, murmuring.

ψίθυρος, ο [pseetheeros] murmur, whisper, mutter, growl.

ψιλά, τα [pseela] πλ small change || (μεταφ) cash, money.

ψιλικά, τα [pseeleeka] πλ haberdashery || small wares.

ψιλικαντζήδικο, το [pseeleekandzeeδeeko] haberdashery.

ψιλολογώ [pseelologo] examine carefully, sift.

ψιλός [pseelos] fine, slender, thin || shrill.

ψιλοτραγουδώ [pseelotragouδo] hum.

ψίχα, η [pseeha] kernel, crumb || (καρυδιού) edible part of nut || (μεταφ) bit, scrap.

ψιχάλα, η [pseehala] drizzle.

ψιχαλίζει [pseehaleezee] it's drizzling.

ψίχουλο, το [pseehoulo] crumb.

ψόγος, ο [psogos] blame, reproach.

ψοφίμι, το [psofeemee] carcass, carrion.

ψόφιος [psofeeos] (για ζώα) dead || (μεταφ) worn-out || ~ στην κούραση dead tired.

ψόφος, ο [psofos] noise, tumult || (θάνατος) death || (μεταφ) freezing cold.

ψοφώ [psofo] die || (μεταφ) ~ για yearn for, be mad on.

ψυγείο, το [pseeyeeo] refrigerator, icebox || (αυτοκινήτου) radiator.

ψυκτικός [pseekteekos] cooling.

ψύλλος, ο [pseelos] flea || (μεταφ) trifle.

ψύξη, η [pseeksee] refrigeration || chill, chilling.

ψυχαγωγία, η [pseehagoyeea] recreation, amusement, diversion, entertainment.

ψυχαγωγικός [pseehagoyeekos] recreational, entertaining.

ψυχανάλυση, η [pseehanaleesee] psychoanalysis.

ψυχή, η [pseehee] soul, ghost || heart, core || (θάρρος) energy, spirit.

ψυχιατρείο, το [pseeheeatreeo] mental hospital, asylum.

ψυχιατρική, η [pseeheeatreekee] psychiatry.

ψυχίατρος, ο [pseeheeatros] psychiatrist.

ψυχικό, το [pseeheeko] act of charity || alms, charity.

ψυχικός [pseeheekos] psychical || ψυχική διάθεση humour, mood, disposition || ψυχική οδύνη mental stress.

ψυχογιός, ο [pseehoyos] adopted son.

ψυχολογία, η [pseeholoyeea] psychology.

ψυχολογικός [pseeholoyeekos] psychological.

ψυχολόγος, ο [pseehologos] psychologist.

ψυχολογώ [pseehologo] read mind of || psychoanalyse.

ψυχομαχώ [pseehomaho] be at the last gasp.

ψυχοπαθής [pseehopathees] psychopath(ic).

ψυχοπαίδι, το [pseehopeδee] adopted child.

ψυχοπόνια, η [pseehoponeea] commiseration, pity.

ψυχορραγώ [pseehorago] βλ ψυχομαχώ.

ψύχος, το [pseehos] cold, chilliness.

ψυχοσύνθεση, η [pseehoseenthesee] person's psychological make-up.

ψύχρα, η [pseehra] chilly weather, cold.

ψυχραιμία, η [pseehremeea] self-control, sangfroid, coolness.

ψύχραιμος [pseehremos] cool, cool-headed.

ψυχραίνομαι [pseehrenome] be on bad terms with.

ψυχραίνω [pseehreno] cool, chill, make cold || (μεταφ) cool off.

ψυχρολουσία, η [pseehrolouseea] (μεταφ) telling off, rebuke.

ψυχρός [pseehros] cold || (μεταφ) indifferent, apathetic.

ψυχρότητα, η [pseehroteeta] coldness || indifference.

ψύχω [pseeho] freeze, chill, make cold.

ψύχωση, η [pseehosee] psychosis || craze, complex.

ψωμάκι, το [psomakee] roll, piece of bread.

ψωμάς, ο [psomas] baker.

ψωμί, το [psomee] bread || loaf || (μεταφ) living.

ψωμοζώ [psomozo] eke out one's living, live scantily.

ψωμοτύρι, το [psomoteeree] bread and cheese.

ψώνια, τα [psoneea] πλ provisions, shopping, purchases.

ψωνίζω [psoneezo] buy, purchase || go shopping || την ~ become queer, go mad.

ψώνιο, το [psoneeo] purchase || (μεταφ) mania.

ψώρα, η [psora] scabies, itch, mange || (μεταφ) pest.

ψωριάζω [psoreeazo] become itchy, be mangy.

ψωριάρης [psoreearees] mangy || (μεταφ) beggar, ragamuffin.

ψωρίαση, η [psoreeasee] psoriasis, itch(ing).

ψωροκώσταινα, η [psorokostena] poverty-stricken Greece, poor Greece.

ψωροπερηφάνεια, η [psoropereefaneea] pretensions, stupid pride.

Ω, ω

ω [o] (επιφ) oh!, ah!, aha!

ωάριο, το [oareeo] ovum.

ωδείο, το [odeeo] conservatory.

ωδή, η [odee] ode, song.

ωδική, η [odeekee] singing lesson || art of singing.

ωδικός [odeekos] singing, melodious.

ωδίνες, οι [odeenes] πλ childbirth pains || (μεταφ) difficulties.

ώθηση, η [otheesee] push, pushing, thrust, impulsion.

ωθώ [otho] push, thrust, impel || incite, urge.

ωκεανός, ο [okeanos] ocean.

ωλένη, η [olenee] forearm.

ωμέγα, το [omega] the letter Ω.

ωμοπλάτη, η [omoplatee] shoulder blade.

ώμος, ο [omos] shoulder.

ωμός [omos] uncooked, raw || hard, cruel, unrelenting.

ωμότητα, η [omoteeta] cruelty, ferocity.

ωμότητες, οι [omoteetes] πλ outrages, atrocities.

ωοειδής [ooeedees] oval, egg-shaped.

ωοθήκη, η [ootheekee] ovary || egg cup.

ωοτόκος [ootokos] oviparous, egg-laying.

ώρα, η [ora] hour, time || με την ~ on the hour || ~ με την ~ any minute || με τις ώρες for hours || στην ~ at the right time, on the dot, on time || της ώρας fresh, cooked to order.

ωραία [orea] beautiful || very well, perfectly, good.

ωραίος [oreos] handsome, comely, lovely || fine, good.

ωραιότητα, η [oreoteeta] beauty, good looks.

ωράριο, το [orareeo] working hours, timetable.

ωριαίος [orieos] hourly || lasting an hour.

ωριμάζω [oreemazo] become ripe, mature, mellow.

ωρίμανση, η [oreemansee] ripening, maturity.

ώριμος [oreemos] ripe, mature, mellow.

ωριμότητα, η [oreemoteeta] ripeness, maturity, full growth.

ωροδείκτης, ο [orodeektees] hour hand.

ωροσκόπιο, το [oroskopeeo] horoscope.

ωρύομαι [oreeome] howl, roar || yell, scream.

ως [os] until, till, down to, up to, as far as || (επίρ) about || ~ ότου να until.

ως [os] as, for, like, just as, such as || (συνδ) as, while, as soon as || βλ και ως.

ωσότου [osotou] until, by the time.

ώσπου [ospou] until.

ώστε [oste] thus, and so, so, accordingly, therefore || that || ούτως ~ thereby.

ωστόσο [ostoso] nevertheless || meanwhile.

ωτακουστής, ο [otakoustees] eavesdropper.

ωτομοτρίς, η [otomotrees] railcar.

ωτορινολαρυγγολόγος, ο [otoreenolareengologos] ear, nose and throat doctor.

ωφέλεια, η [ofeleea] benefit, utility, usefulness, profit, advantage || είδα ~ I benefited.

ωφέλημα, το [ofeleema] benefit, gain, particular profit, advantage.

ωφέλιμος [ofeleemos] beneficial, useful, of use, advantageous.

ωφελούμαι [ofeloume] benefit, profit from, turn to good account.

ωφελώ [ofelo] do good to, be useful to, benefit, aid.

ώχρα, η [ohra] ochre.

ωχριώ [ohreeo] become pale, make wan.

ωχρός [ohros] pallid, pale || (μεταφ) indistinct, dim.

ωχρότητα, η [ohroteeta] pallor, paleness.

Ω

A

a, an [ei,æn] *indefinite article* ένας, μια, ένα.

A.A. *n. abbr of Automobile Association; abbr of Alcoholics Anonymous.*

aback [ɔ'bæk] *ad:* **to be taken ~** ξαφνιάζομαι, σαστίζω.

abandon [ɔ'bændɔn] *vt* εγκαταλείπω, αφήνω.

abash [ɔ'bæʃ] *vt* ξεφτελίζω, ντροπιάζω.

abate [ɔ'beit] *vi* μειώνομαι, κοπάζω, καταργούμαι.

abbey ['æbi] *n* μονή, μοναστήρι.

abbot ['æbɔt] *n* ηγούμενος, αββάς.

abbreviate [ɔ'bri:vieit] *vt* συντομεύω.

abbreviation [ɔbri:vi'eiʃɔn] *n* σύντμηση, συντετμημένη λέξη.

abdicate ['æbdikeit] *vi* παραιτούμαι, εγκαταλείπω.

abdication [æbdi'keiʃɔn] *n* παραίτηση.

abdomen ['æbdɔmɔn] *n* κοιλιά.

abduction [æb'dʌkʃɔn] *n* απαγωγή.

aberration [æbɔ'reiʃɔn] *n* παρέκκλιση, παρεκτροπή.

abet [ɔ'bɛt] *vt* υποκινώ, παρακινώ.

abeyance [ɔ'beiɔns] *n:* **in ~** εκκρεμώ, αχρηστεύομαι.

abhor [ɔb'hɔ:*] *vt* απεχθάνομαι, σιχαίνομαι || **~rent** *a* απεχθής.

abide [ɔ'baid] *(irreg v) vt* ανέχομαι, αντέχω ♦ *vi* εμμένω, τηρώ || **to ~ by** τηρώ, συμμορφούμαι.

ability [ɔ'biliti] *n* ικανότητα, επιδεξιότητα, δύναμη.

ablaze [ɔ'bleiz] *a* φλεγόμενος, λάμπων.

able ['eibl] *a* ικανός, επιτήδειος.

ably ['eibli] *ad* επιδέξια, προκομμένα.

abnormal [æb'nɔ:mɔl] *a* ανώμαλος || **~ity** *n* ανωμαλία || (BIOL) τερατωδία, δυσμορφία.

aboard [ɔ'bɔ:d] *ad:* **to go ~** επιβιβάζομαι || **to be ~** ευρίσκομαι επί.

abode [ɔ'bɔud] *n* διαμονή, κατοικία.

abolish [ɔ'bɔliʃ] *vt* καταργώ.

abolition [æbɔ'liʃɔn] *n* κατάργηση.

abominable [ɔ'bɔminɔbl] *a* αποτρόπαιος, απαίσιος.

abominably [ɔ'bɔminɔbli] *ad* απαίσια.

aborigines [æbɔ'ridʒini:z] *npl* ιθαγενείς.

abort [ɔ'bɔ:t] *vt* αποβάλλω, διακόπτω ♦ *vi* αποβάλλομαι, ματαιούμαι.

abortion [ɔ'bɔ:ʃɔn] *n* έκτρωση, αποβολή.

abortive [ɔ'bɔ:tiv] *a* αποτυχημένος, πρόωρος, ανεπιτυχής.

abound [ɔ'baund] *vi* αφθονώ, βρίθω.

about [ɔ'baut] *prep* περί, γύρω από, κοντά ♦ *ad* (τρι)γύρω, κοντά || *(estimate)* περίπου || **to be ~ to** μόλις πρόκειται να.

above [ɔ'bʌv] *prep* πάνω από, πέρα από || *(in rank)* ανώτερος από, μεγαλύτερος από ♦ *ad* επάνω, στους ουρανούς || **~board** *a* τίμια και ειλικρινή, άψογα || **~ ground** επιφανειακός.

abrasion [ɔ'breiʒɔn] *n* φθορά, (εκ)τριβή, γδάρσιμο.

abrasive [ɔ'breiziv] *a* αποξεστικός || **~ material** μέσον λείανσεως.

abreast [ɔ'brest] *ad* παραπλεύρως, μαζί.

abridge [ɔ'bridʒ] *vt* συντομεύω, συντέμνω.

abroad [ɔ'brɔ:d] *ad* στο εξωτερικό, στα ξένα.

abrupt [ɔ'brʌpt] *a* απότομος, ξαφνικός, αγενής.

abscess ['æbsis] *n* απόστημα *nt*.

abscond [ɔb'skɔnd] *vi* φυγοδικώ, δραπετεύω, φεύγω κρυφά.

absence ['æbsɔns] *n* απουσία || *(lack of)* έλλειψη, ανυπαρξία || *(of mind)* αφηρημάδα.

absent ['æbsɔnt] *a* απών, απουσιάζων ♦ [æb'sɛnt] *vt:* **he ~ed himself** απουσίαζε || **~ee** *n* απών *m*, απουσιάζων *m* || **~eeism** *n* απουσία || **~-minded** *a* αφηρημένος.

absolute ['æbsɔlu:t] *a* απόλυτος, τέλειος, απεριόριστος || **~ly** *ad* τελείως.

absolve [ɔb'zɔlv] *vt* απαλλάσω, αθωώνω.

absorb [ɔb'zɔ:b] *vt* απορροφώ.

absorbent [ɔb'zɔ:bɔnt] *a, n* απορροφητικός || **~ cotton** *(US) n* απορροφητικό βαμβάκι.

absorbing [ɔb'zɔ:biŋ] *a* ενδιαφέρων.

abstain [ɔb'stein] *vi* απέχω, συγκρατούμαι || **to ~ from** αποφεύγω.

abstinence ['æbstinɔns] *n* αποχή, εγκράτεια.

abstract ['æbstrækt] *a* αφηρημένος ♦ *n* το αφηρημένο || *(summary)* περίληψη || *(excerpt)* απόσπασμα *nt* ♦ [æb'strækt] *vt (remove)* αφαιρώ.

abstruse [æb'stru:s] *a* ασαφής, δυσνόητος.

absurd [ɔb'sɔ:d] *a* γελοίος, παράλογος || **~ity** *n* παραλογισμός.

abundance [ɔ'bʌndɔns] *n* αφθονία, περίσσευμα *nt*.

abundant [ɔ'bʌndɔnt] *a* άφθονος, πλούσιος.

abuse [ɔ'bju:z] *vt (misuse)* κακομεταχειρίζομαι, καταχρώμαι || *(speak harshly)* βρίζω ♦ [ɔ'bju:s] *n*

κακομεταχείριση, κατάχρηση ||
(swearing) βρισιές fpl.
abusive [ə'bjuːsɪv] a υβριστικός.
abut [ə'bʌt] vi συνορεύω με.
abysmal [ə'bɪzml] a φοβερός,
απερίγραπτος.
abyss [ə'bɪs] n άβυσσος.
academic [ækə'dɛmɪk] n, a
ακαδημαϊκός.
academy [ə'kædəmɪ] n ακαδημία.
accede [æk'siːd] vi (agree) συμφωνώ,
προσχωρώ || (to throne) ανέρχομαι.
accelerate [æk'sɛləreɪt] vt επιταχύνω,
επισπεύδω ♦ vi επιταχύνομαι.
acceleration [æksɛlə'reɪʃən] n
επιτάχυνση.
accelerator [ək'sɛləreɪtə*] n (AUT)
γκάζι.
accent ['æksɛnt] n τόνος || (of speech)
προφορά ♦ [æk'sɛnt] vt τονίζω || ~uate
vt τονίζω.
accept [ək'sɛpt] vt (gift etc) δέχομαι ||
(agree) παραδέχομαι || ~able a
(απο)δεκτός, ευπρόσδεκτος,
παραδεκτός || ~ance n αποδοχή,
παραδοχή.
access ['æksɛs] n (entrance) είσοδος f ||
(COMPUT) πρόσβαση || ~ time (COMPUT)
χρόνος προσπέλασης || ~ible a
προσιτός, ευπρόσιτος.
accessories [æk'sɛsəriz] npl
εξαρτήματα ntpl, συμπληρώματα ntpl ||
(toilet) είδη ntpl τουαλέτας.
accessory [æk'sɛsəri] a
συμπληρωματικός ♦ n (to a crime etc)
συνένοχος || (part) εξάρτημα nt.
accident ['æksɪdənt] n (mishap)
δυστύχημα nt, ατύχημα nt || (chance) τύχη
|| by ~ κατά τύχη || ~ally ad τυχαία.
acclaim [ə'kleɪm] vt επευφημώ,
ζητωκραυγάζω, αναφωνώ ♦ n
ζητωκραυγή.
acclimatize [ə'klaɪmətaɪz] vt: to
become ~d to εγκλιματίζομαι.
accommodate [ə'kɒmədeɪt] vt (be
suitable for) εξοικονομώ, διευθετώ,
προσαρμόζω || (lodge) στεγάζω, παρέχω
κατάλυμα || (supply etc) εξοικονομώ,
εφοδιάζω.
accommodating [ə'kɒmədeɪtɪŋ] a
εξυπηρετικός, πρόθυμος.
accommodation [əkɒmə'deɪʃən] n
(lodging) κατάλυμα nt, στέγαση || (loan)
δάνειο || (adjustment) προσαρμογή.
accompaniment [ə'kʌmpənɪmənt] n
συνοδεία || (MUS) ακομπανιαμέντο.
accompany [ə'kʌmpəni] vt συνοδεύω,
συντροφεύω.
accomplice [ə'kʌmplɪs] n συνένοχος,
συνεργός.
accomplish [ə'kʌmplɪʃ] vt περατώνω,
συμπληρώνω || ~ed a (skilled) τέλειος ||
~ment n (ability) ικανότητα, προσόντα
ntpl || (completion) εκπλήρωση.
accord [ə'kɔːd] n συμφωνία, ομοφωνία
|| of my own ~ αυθόρμητα ♦ vt (grant)
παρέχω, χορηγώ || (agree with) συμφωνώ

|| ~ance n συμφωνία || in ~ance with
σύμφωνα με || ~ing to prep σύμφωνα
με, κατά τον || ~ingly ad επομένως.
accordion [ə'kɔːdiən] n ακορντεόν nt
inv.
accost [ə'kɒst] vt πλησιάζω, πλευρίζω.
account [ə'kaunt] n (bill) λογαριασμός,
υπολογισμός || (credit) λογαριασμός ||
(story) αφήγηση, περιγραφή || (financial
report) ανάλυση, έκθεση || on no ~ για
κανένα λόγο || on ~ of εξαιτίας || to ~
for vt ειξηγώ || to take into ~ λαμβάνω
υπόψη || ~able a υπόλογος, υπεύθυνος
|| (explicable) ευεξήγητος.
accountant [ə'kauntənt] n λογιστής.
accumulate [ə'kjuːmjuleɪt] vt
συσσωρεύω, μαζεύω ♦ vi
συσσωρεύομαι.
accumulation [əkjuːmju'leɪʃən] n
συσσώρευση, μάζεμα nt.
accuracy ['ækjurəsi] n ακρίβεια.
accurate ['ækjurɪt] a ακριβής, ορθός ||
~ly ad με ακρίβεια, σωστά.
accusation [ækjuː'zeɪʃən] n κατηγορία.
accuse [ə'kjuːz] vt κατηγορώ || ~d n
κατηγορούμενος || ~r n ενάγων m,
μηνυτής, κατήγορος.
accustom [ə'kʌstəm] vt συνηθίζω,
εθίζω || ~ed a συνηθισμένος.
ace [eɪs] n άσσος.
ache [eɪk] vi πονώ.
achieve [ə'tʃiːv] vt κατορθώνω,
επιτυγχάνω, φθάνω || ~ment n
κατόρθωμα, επίτευξη.
acid ['æsɪd] a οξύς, ξινός ♦ n (CHEM) οξύ
nt || ~ test n αποφασιστική δοκιμασία,
τελικό κριτήριο || ~ity n (CHEM) οξύτητα,
ξινίλα.
acknowledge [ək'nɒlɪdʒ] vt (admit)
αναγνωρίζω, παραδέχομαι || (thank) είμαι
ευγνώμων, απαντώ || ~ment n
αναγνώριση, παραδοχή || (of letter etc)
βεβαίωση.
acne ['ækni] n ακμή, σπυράκια ntpl.
acorn ['eɪkɔːn] n βαλανίδι.
acoustic [ə'kuːstɪk] a ακουστικός || ~s
npl ακουστική.
acquaint [ə'kweɪnt] vt γνωρίζω,
πληροφορώ || ~ance n (person)
γνωριμία, γνωστός/ή m/f || (knowledge)
γνώση, εξοικείωση.
acquiesce [ækwɪ'ɛs] vi συναινώ,
συγκατατίθεμαι, δέχομαι.
acquire [ə'kwaɪə*] vt αποκτώ.
acquisition [ækwɪ'zɪʃən] n απόκτημα nt,
απόκτηση.
acquisitive [ə'kwɪzɪtɪv] a πλεονέκτης,
αρπακτικός.
acquit [ə'kwɪt] vt (free from accusation)
απαλλάσσω, αθωώνω || (conduct o.s.)
εκπληρώ, καταφέρνω || ~tal n αθώωση,
απαλλαγή.
acre ['eɪkə*] n 4 στρέμματα ntpl.
acrobat ['ækrəbæt] n ακροβάτης.
across [ə'krɒs] prep (through) δια μέσου
♦ ad (crosswise) εγκάρσια, λοξά,

σταυρωτά || (distance) πλάτος, μήκος || ~
the road (στο δρόμο) απέναντι.

act [ækt] n (deed) πράξη, ενέργεια || (law
or decree) νόμος, νομοθέτημα nt || (of
play) πράξη (έργου) ♦ vti (take action)
ενεργώ, δρω, πράττω || (part) παίζω,
παριστάνω, κάνω || (pretend)
προσποιούμαι, υποκρίνομαι, υποδύομαι
|| ~ing n (THEAT) ηθοποιία, παίξιμο ♦ a
αναπληρωματικός.

action ['ækʃən] n (deed) πράξη || (motion)
λειτουργία, ενέργεια || (battle) μάχη || to
bring an ~ against κάνω αγωγή κατά ||
naval ~ ναυμαχία || to take ~ ενεργώ.

active ['æktiv] a (lively) ενεργητικός,
ζωηρός || (working) δραστήριος, ενεργός
|| (GRAM) ενεργητικός || on ~ service εν
ενεργεία.

activity [æk'tiviti] n δραστηριότητα,
δράση.

actor ['æktə*] n ηθοποιός.

actress ['æktris] n ηθοποιός f,
θεατρίνα.

actual ['æktjuəl] a πραγματικός,
αληθινός || ~ly ad πράγματι.

acumen ['ækjumɛn] n οξύνοια, ευφυΐα.

acute [ə'kju:t] a οξύς, διαπεραστικός ||
~ly ad έντονα || ~ accent n οξεία.

ad [æd] abbr of advertisement.

A.D. ad (abbr of Anno Domini) μ.Χ.

Adam ['ædəm] n Αδάμ || ~'s apple n
καρύδι του λαιμού.

adamant ['ædəmənt] a αμετάπειστος,
άκαμπτος.

adapt [ə'dæpt] vt προσαρμόζω,
εναρμόζω ♦ vi: to ~ to προσαρμόζομαι
|| ~able a προσαρμόσιμος, ευάρμοστος
|| ~ation n προσαρμογή || (of play etc)
διασκευή || ~er n (ELEC) προσαρμοστής.

add [æd] vt προσθέτω, αθροίζω || to ~
up vt προσθέτω.

adder ['ædə*] n (snake) οχιά, όχεντρα.

addict ['ædikt] n: drug ~ ναρκομανής
♦ [ə'dikt] vt αφοσιώνω, παραδίδω || ~ed
to επιρρεπής σε || ~ion n ροπή προς,
εθισμός.

adding machine ['ædiŋməʃi:n] n
αθροιστική μηχανή.

addition [ə'diʃən] n πρόσθεση,
προσθήκη || in ~ επί πλέον,
επιπροσθέτως || ~al a πρόσθετος.

address [ə'drɛs] n διεύθυνση || (speech)
προσφώνηση, λόγος || (manners)
συμπεριφορά || (COMPUT) διεύθυνση || vt
απευθύνω || (speak) προσφωνώ ||
(envelope) γράφω διεύθυνση.

addressee [ædrɛ'si:] n παραλήπτης.

adenoids ['ædinɔidz] npl κρεατάκια.

adept ['ædɛpt] a: ~ at έμπειρος σε,
ικανός σε.

adequate ['ædikwit] a επαρκής, ικανός.

adhere [əd'hiə*] vi (stick to)
προσκολλώμαι || (support) εμμένω,
προσχωρώ || to ~ to προσχωρώ,
εμμένω.

adhesive [əd'hi:ziv] a συγκολλητικός,

κολλώδης ♦ n κολλητική ουσία || ~
tape n λευκοπλάστης.

adjacent [ə'dʒeisənt] a παρακείμενος,
γειτονικός, συνορεύων.

adjective ['ædʒɛktiv] n επίθετο.

adjoin [ə'dʒɔin] vi γειτονεύω, συνορεύω
με, συνάπτω || ~ing a συνεχόμενος,
παρακείμενος.

adjourn [ə'dʒɜːn] vt (postpone)
αναβάλλω ♦ vi αναβάλλομαι,
διακόπτομαι.

adjudicator [ə'dʒu:dikeitə*] n
διαιτητής, δικαστής.

adjust [ə'dʒʌst] vt (put right) ρυθμίζω,
κανονίζω || (to fit) προσαρμόζω,
εφαρμόζω || ~able a ρυθμιζόμενος,
ρυθμιστός || ~ment n ρύθμιση,
τακτοποίηση.

adjutant ['ædʒətənt] n υπασπιστής.

ad lib [æd'lib] ad κατά βούληση ♦ ad-lib
vi αυτοσχεδιάζω.

administer [əd'ministə*] vt (manage)
διευθύνω, διαχειρίζομαι, διοικώ ||
(dispense) απονέμω || (medicine) παρέχω,
δίνω.

administration [ədminis'treiʃən] n
διοίκηση, διαχείριση, διεύθυνση || ~ of
justice απονομή δικαιοσύνης.

administrative [əd'ministrətiv] a
διοικητικός.

administrator [əd'ministreitə*] n
διευθυντής, διοικητής || (of will)
εκτελεστής.

admirable ['ædmərəbl] a θαυμαστός,
θαυμάσιος.

admiral ['ædmərəl] n ναύαρχος.

Admiralty ['ædmərəlti] n ναυαρχείο.

admiration [ædmə'reiʃən] n
θαυμασμός, κατάπληξη.

admire [əd'maiə*] vt θαυμάζω || ~r n
θαυμαστής.

admission [əd'miʃən] n (entrance)
είσοδος f, εισαγωγή || (fee) τιμή
εισιτηρίου || (confession) παραδοχή,
αναγνώριση.

admit [əd'mit] vt (let in) επιτρέπω την
είσοδο, εισέρχομαι || (confess)
παραδέχομαι, αναγνωρίζω || (receive as
true) (επι)δέχομαι || ~tance n εισδοχή,
είσοδος f || ~tedly ad ομολογουμένως.

ado [ə'du:] n: without more ~ χωρίς
περισσότερη φασαρία.

adolescence [ædəu'lɛsns] n εφηβική
ηλικία.

adolescent [ædəu'lɛsnt] a, n έφηβος.

adopt [ə'dɔpt] vt υιοθετώ || (accept)
παραδέχομαι, αποδέχομαι || ~ed son n
θετός || ~ion n υιοθεσία || (of idea etc)
αποδοχή, έγκριση.

adore [ə'dɔ:*] vt λατρεύω, υπεραγαπώ.

adorn [ə'dɔːn] vt κοσμώ, στολίζω,
καλλωπίζω.

adrenalin [ə'drɛnəlin] n αδρεναλίνη.

Adriatic [eidri'ætik] n Αδριατική.

adrift [ə'drift] ad έρμαιο || (col) τα έχω
χαμένα.

adult ['ædʌlt] a, n ενήλικος, έφηβος || (LAW) ενήλικος.

adulterate [ə'dʌltəreit] vt νοθεύω, αλλοιώνω, νερώνω.

adultery [ə'dʌltəri] n μοιχεία.

advance [əd'vɑːns] n πρόοδος f, προχώρηση || (money) προκαταβολή, πίστωση || (in prices) αύξηση, ύψωση ♦ vi προχωρώ || (MIL) προελαύνω || (price) ανατιμώμαι, ανεβαίνω || ~d a προχωρημένος || (ideas) προοδευτικός || (study etc) ανώτερος || ~d ignition n προανάφλεξη || in ~ προκαταβολικά || in ~ of πριν από, (ε)νωρίτερα || ~ booking n: to make an ~ booking κλείνω θέση.

advantage [əd'vɑːntidʒ] n πλεονέκτημα nt, προτέρημα nt || to take ~ of (profit by) επωφελούμαι από, εκμεταλλεύομαι || (misuse) καταχρώμαι || ~ over υπεροχή.

advantageous [ædvən'teidʒəs] a επωφελής, λυσιτελής.

advent ['ædvənt] n έλευση, εμφάνιση || (REL) σαραντάμερο || the Second A~ n Δευτέρα Παρουσία.

adventure [əd'ventʃə*] n περιπέτεια || (bold undertaking) τόλμημα nt || ~r n τολμηρός || (in bad sense) τυχοδιώκτης.

adventurous [əd'ventʃərəs] a ριψοκίνδυνος, τυχοδιωκτικός.

adverb ['ædvɜːb] n επίρρημα nt.

adversary ['ædvəsəri] n αντίπαλος, ανταγωνιστής.

adverse ['ædvɜːs] a αντίθετος, ενάντιος, δυσμενής.

adversity [əd'vɜːsiti] n ατυχία, αναποδιά.

advertise ['ædvətaiz] vt διαφημίζω, ρεκλαμάρω.

advertisement [əd'vɜːtismənt] n διαφήμιση, ρεκλάμα || (poster) αφίσα.

advertiser ['ædvətaizə*] n διαφημιστής.

advertising ['ædvətaiziŋ] n διαφήμιση, ρεκλάμα || ~ agency n διαφημιστικό γραφείο.

advice [əd'vais] n συμβουλή || (information) πληροφορία, είδηση.

advisable [əd'vaizəbl] a φρόνιμος, σκόπιμος.

advise [əd'vaiz] vt συμβουλεύω, συνιστώ || (apprise) ειδοποιώ || ~r n σύμβουλος.

advisory [əd'vaizəri] a συμβουλευτικός.

advocate ['ædvəkit] n (LAW) δικηγόρος, συνήγορος || (supporter) υποστηρικτής ♦ ['ædvəkeit] vt υποστηρίζω, συνιστώ || (LAW) συνηγορώ.

aerial ['ɛəriəl] a εναέριος ♦ n κεραία || ~ photograph n εναέριος φωτογραφία.

aeroplane ['ɛərəplein] n αεροπλάνο.

aerosol ['ɛərəsɒl] n αεροζόλ nt inv.

aesthetic [iːs'θetik] a αισθητικός || (artistic) καλαίσθητος.

afar [ə'fɑː*] ad: from ~ από μακριά.

affable ['æfəbl] a προσηνής, γλυκομίλητος, κατάδεκτικός.

affair [ə'fɛə*] n υπόθεση, δουλειά || (matter) πράγμα nt.

affect [ə'fekt] vt (influence) θίγω, επηρεάζω || (feign) προσποιούμαι, κάνω τον || ~ation n προσποίηση || ~ed a προσποιητός || (moved) συγκινημένος || (MED) προσβλημένος.

affection [ə'fekʃən] n αγάπη, στοργή || ~ate a φιλόστοργος.

affiliate [ə'filieit] vt εισάγω, συνεργάζομαι.

affinity [ə'finiti] n συγγένεια.

affirmation [æfə'meiʃən] n (δια)βεβαίωση || (assent) κατάφαση.

affirmative [ə'fɜːmətiv] a καταφατικός, βεβαιωτικός ♦ n κατάφαση || in the ~ καταφατικά.

affix [ə'fiks] vt επισυνάπτω, προσαρτώ, θέτω.

afflict [ə'flikt] vt θλίβω, πικραίνω || (MED) προσβάλλω || ~ion n θλίψη, λύπη || (misfortune) ατύχημα nt, συμφορά.

affluence ['æfluəns] n (abundance) αφθονία || (wealth) πλούτος.

affluent ['æfluənt] a πλούσιος.

afford [ə'fɔːd] vt (have the means) δύναμαι, έχω τα μέσα || (provide) παρέχω, προσφέρω.

affront [ə'frʌnt] vt προσβάλλω, ντροπιάζω ♦ n προσβολή.

Afghanistan [æf'gænistæn] n Αφγανιστάν nt.

afield [ə'fiːld] ad: far ~ μακριά.

afloat [ə'fləut] ad: I am ~ επιπλέω.

afraid [ə'freid] a έμφοβος, φοβισμένος || to be ~ of φοβούμαι || to be ~ to δεν τολμώ || ~ that φοβούμαι ότι.

afresh [ə'freʃ] ad από την αρχή, πάλι.

Africa ['æfrikə] n Αφρική || ~n n Αφρικανός/n m/f ♦ a αφρικάνικος.

aft [ɑːft] ad προς την πρύμνη, προς τα πίσω.

after ['ɑːftə*] prep μετά, ύστερα από || (according to) κατά ♦ ad έπειτα, ύστερα ♦ a επόμενος || cj αφού || some time ~ λίγο αργότερα || what is he ~? τι ζητά || τι ψάχνει; || ~ all τέλος πάντων, επί τέλους || ~ five (o'clock) περασμένες πέντε || ~ you, sir! παρακαλώ!, περάστε!

after- ['ɑːftə*] (in compds) a μετά, μέλλων.

aftermath ['ɑːftəmæθ] n συνέπεια, επακόλουθο.

afternoon ['ɑːftə'nuːn] n απόγευμα nt || good ~! χαίρετε!

afterthought ['ɑːftəθɔːt] n μεταγενεστέρα σκέψη.

afterwards ['ɑːftəwədz] ad αργότερα, στη συνέχεια.

again [ə'gen] ad πάλι, ξανά || ~ and ~ επανειλημμένως, πάλι και πάλι.

against [ə'genst] prep κατά, εναντίον.

age [eidʒ] n ηλικία || (generation) γενεά || (period) εποχή || (century) αιώνας m ♦ vti γερνώ || (wine etc) ωριμάζω || ~ of ~ ενηλικιωμένος, ενήλικος || ~d a

ηλικιωμένος, γέρος || ~d 20 (years)
ηλικίας 20 ετών || ~less a αγέραστος,
αιώνιος.

agency ['eɪdʒənsɪ] n, a (επί)δράση,
ενέργεια || (factor) παράγοντας, αίτιο ||
(intervention) υπηρεσία, οργανισμός ||
(office) πρακτορείο, αντιπροσωπεία.

agenda [ə'dʒɛndə] n ημερησία διάταξη ||
(notebook) ατζέντα, σημειωματάριο.

agent ['eɪdʒənt] n πράκτορας,
αντιπρόσωπος || (cause) παράγοντας,
συντελεστής.

aggravate ['ægrəveɪt] vt επιδεινώνω,
χειροτερεύω || (provoke) εντείνω,
ερεθίζω.

aggregate ['ægrɪgɪt] n άθροισμα nt,
σύνολο ♦ a συνολικός.

aggression [ə'greʃən] n επίθεση,
επιδρομή.

aggressive [ə'gresɪv] a επιθετικός ||
(vigorous) δραστήριος.

aggrieved [ə'griːvd] a θλιμμένος,
πικραμένος.

aghast [ə'gɑːst] a κατάπληκτος,
εμβρόντητος.

agile ['ædʒaɪl] a ευκίνητος, ελαφρός.

agitate ['ædʒɪteɪt] vt (set in motion)
(ανα)ταράσσω || (excite) ταράσσω,
ανησυχώ || (POL) κινούμαι, κάνω κίνηση ||
to ~ for δημιουργώ κίνηση για.

agitation [ædʒɪ'teɪʃən] n αναταραχή.

agitator ['ædʒɪteɪtə*] n υποκινητής,
ταραχοποιός.

agnostic [æg'nɒstɪk] a, n αγνωστικός.

ago [ə'gəʊ] ad περασμένος, πριν, από
πριν || long ~ προ πολλού || some time
~ προ καιρού.

agog [ə'gɒg] a ανυπόμονος.

agonizing ['ægənaɪzɪŋ] a σπαρακτικός,
φρικτός.

agony ['ægənɪ] n αγωνία, βάσανο.

agree [ə'griː] vti (consent)
συγκατατίθεμαι, αποδέχομαι || (have
same opinion) συμφωνώ, είμαι σύμφωνος
|| (of climate etc) ταιριάζω, ωφελώ || (come
to an agreement) συμβιβάζομαι || it does
not ~ with me με πειράζει, με ενοχλεί,
δεν μου ταιριάζει || ~d a (of persons)
είμαι σύμφωνος || (of things) εγκρίνεται!,
σύμφωνοι! || ~ment n συμφωνία ||
(formal) σύμβαση, συνθήκη.

agricultural [ægrɪ'kʌltʃərəl] a
γεωργικός.

agriculture ['ægrɪkʌltʃə*] n γεωργία.

aground [ə'graʊnd] ad (NAUT) στη
στεριά || to run ~ προσαράσσω,
καθίζω, εξοκέλλω.

ahead [ə'hed] ad εμπρός, προ || to get
~ προχωρώ, προηγούμαι || ~ of μπρος
από.

A.I. n (abbr of artificial intelligence) T.N.

aid [eɪd] n βοήθεια, συνδρομή || (assistant)
βοηθός ♦ vt βοηθώ, συντρέχω.

ailment ['eɪlmənt] n αδιαθεσία,
αρρώστια.

aim [eɪm] n (point) σκόπευση || (target)
στόχος || (purpose) σκοπός, αντικείμενο

♦ vti (throw) ρίχνω, κτυπώ || (point)
σκοπεύω || (intend) επιδιώκω || ~less a
άσκοπος, ασυνάρτητος.

air [ɛə*] n αέρας m || (tune) μέλος nt,
σκοπός, ήχος || (appearance)
παρουσιαστικό, αέρας, ύφος ♦ vt αερίζω
|| (question) εκθέτω, ανακινώ || (opinions)
επιδεικνύω, αποκαλύπτω || ~borne a
αεροφερόμενος || ~ conditioning n
κλιματισμός || ~craft n αεροσκάφος nt,
αεροπλάνο || ~craft carrier n
αεροπλανοφόρο || ~force n (πολεμική)
αεροπορία || ~gun n αεροβόλο || ~
hostess n αεροσυνοδός || ~line n
αεροπορική γραμμή || ~liner n
επιβατικό αεροπλάνο || ~mail n: by
~mail αεροπορικώς || ~plane n (US)
αεροπλάνο || ~ pocket n κενόν nt
αέρος || ~port n αεροΛιμήν m || ~ raid
n αεροπορική επιδρομή || ~tight a
αεροστεγής, ερμητικός.

aisle [aɪl] n διάδρομος || (of church)
πτέρυγα.

ajar [ə'dʒɑː*] ad μισοανοιγμένος.

akin [ə'kɪn] a συγγενεύων.

à la carte [ælæ'kɑːt] ad α-λα-κάρτ.

alarm [ə'lɑːm] n (of danger) συναγερμός,
κραυγή κινδύνου || (device) σύστημα
ειδοποίησης || (fright) φόβος, αναταραχή
♦ vt τρομάζω, φοβίζω, ταράσσω || ~
clock n ξυπνητήρι.

Albania [æl'beɪnɪə] n Αλβανία || ~n n
Αλβανός/ίδα m/f ♦ a αλβανικός.

album ['ælbəm] n λεύκωμα nt, άλμπουμ
nt inv.

alcohol ['ælkəhɒl] n αλκοόλ nt inv,
οινόπνευμα nt || ~ic a, n αλκοολικός.

alcove ['ælkəʊv] n παστάς, αλκόβα || (of
wall) σηκός, αχιβάδα.

alderman ['ɔːldəmən] n δημοτικός
σύμβουλος.

ale [eɪl] n μπύρα.

alert [ə'lɜːt] a άγρυπνος, προσεκτικός ||
(nimble) ευκίνητος, σβέλτος ♦ n
επιφυλακή, συναγερμός.

algebra ['ældʒɪbrə] n άλγεβρα.

Algeria [æl'dʒɪərɪə] n Αλγερία ||
Algerian a αλγερίνικος ♦ n
Αλγερινός/ή m/f.

alias ['eɪlɪæs] ad άλλως ♦ n ψευδώνυμο,
πλαστό όνομα nt.

alibi ['ælɪbaɪ] n άλλοθι || (col) δικαιολογία.

alien ['eɪlɪən] n, a ξένος, αλλοδαπός ||
~ate vt (turn away) αποσπώ, αποξενώ ||
~ation n αποξένωση.

alight [ə'laɪt] a αναμμένος, φλεγόμενος
♦ vi κατέρχομαι, κατεβαίνω || (of birds)
κάθομαι.

align [ə'laɪn] vt ευθυγραμμίζω || ~ment
n ευθυγράμμιση.

alike [ə'laɪk] a όμοιος, παρόμοιος, ίδιος
♦ ad ομοίως, ίδια.

alive [ə'laɪv] a ζωντανός || (lively) ζωηρός
|| (teeming) βρίθων, γεμάτος.

alkali ['ælkəlaɪ] n άλκαλι.

all [ɔːl] a, pron πας, όλος, όλοι, πάντες ♦ n
όλο, σύνολο, ολότητα ♦ ad εντελώς,

τελείως, όλο || **after** ~ στο κατω-κάτω || ~ **in** ~ στο σύνολο || **above** ~ προπαντός.

all- [ɔːl] (in compds) a ολο-, παν-, παντο-, τελείως.

allay [əˈleɪ] vt καταπραϋνω, γλυκαίνω || (lessen) καθησυχάζω, ανακουφίζω.

allegation [ælɪˈgeɪʃən] n ισχυρισμός, υπαινιγμός.

allege [əˈledʒ] vt ισχυρίζομαι, επικαλούμαι || ~**dly** ad δήθεν.

allegiance [əˈliːdʒəns] n πίστη, υπακοή.

allegory [ˈælɪgɔrɪ] n αλληγορία.

allergic [əˈlɜːdʒɪk] a αλλεργικός.

allergy [ˈælədʒɪ] n αλλεργία.

alleviate [əˈliːvɪeɪt] vt ελαφρώνω, ανακουφίζω.

alley [ˈælɪ] n δρομίσκος, πάροδος f, δρομάκος.

alliance [əˈlaɪəns] n συμμαχία || (marriage) επιγαμία, συμπεθεριά.

allied [ˈælaɪd] a: ~ **to** συγγενεύω με.

alligator [ˈælɪgeɪtə*] n αλλιγάτορας.

all-in [ˈɔːlɪn] a (exhausted) εξαντλημένος.

alliteration [əlɪtəˈreɪʃən] n παρήχηση.

all-night [ˈɔːlˈnaɪt] a (café etc) ολονύκτιος, διανυκτερεύων.

allocate [ˈæləkeɪt] vt διαθέτω, παραχωρώ || (for special purpose) κατανέμω, αναθέτω.

allocation [æləˈkeɪʃən] n εκχώρηση, απονομή.

allot [əˈlɒt] vt παραχωρώ, διαθέτω, κατανέμω || ~**ment** n (share) μερίδιο, τμήμα nt.

all-out [ˈɔːlˈaʊt] ad με όλες τις δυνάμεις.

allow [əˈlaʊ] vt επιτρέπω || (grant) παρέχω, δίδω || (acknowledge) αναγνωρίζω, (παρα)δέχομαι || **to** ~ **for** αφήνω περιθώριο για || ~**ance** n επίδομα nt, εισόδημα nt.

alloy [ˈælɔɪ] n κράμα nt ♦ vt αναμιγνύω, συντήκω || (fig) νοθεύω.

all-round [ˈɔːlˈraʊnd] a τελειότατος, αρτιότατος.

all-time [ˈɔːlˈtaɪm] a παντοτινός.

allude [əˈluːd] vi: **to** ~ υπονοώ, υπαινίσσομαι.

alluring [əˈljʊərɪŋ] a δελεαστικός, γοητευτικός.

allusion [əˈluːʒən] n υπαινιγμός, νύξη.

ally [ˈælaɪ] n σύμμαχος ♦ [əˈlaɪ] vt συνδέω, ενώνω ♦ vi συμμαχώ, συνδέομαι.

almighty [ɔːlˈmaɪtɪ] a: **the A**~ ο Παντοδύναμος.

almond [ˈɑːmənd] n αμύγδαλο || (tree) αμυγδαλιά.

almost [ˈɔːlməʊst] ad σχεδόν, περίπου.

alms [ɑːmz] npl ελεημοσύνη, ψυχικό.

alone [əˈləʊn] a μόνος, μονάχος, μοναχός ♦ ad μόνο.

along [əˈlɒŋ] ad: **move** ~ προχωρώ, βηματίζω || εμπρός!, έλα λοιπόν! ♦ prep κατά μήκος || ~**side** ad, prep πλευρισμένος, πλάι-πλάι || **all** ~ από καιρό, απ' την αρχή.

aloof [əˈluːf] a, ad μακριά, σε απόσταση.

aloud [əˈlaʊd] ad μεγαλοφώνως, φωναχτά, δυνατά.

alphabet [ˈælfəbet] n αλφάβητο || ~**ical** a αλφαβητικός.

alpine [ˈælpaɪn] a αλπικός.

Alps [ælps] npl: **the** ~ οι Άλπεις.

already [ɔːlˈredɪ] ad ήδη, κιόλας.

alright [ɔːlˈraɪt] = **all right** || see **right**.

also [ˈɔːlsəʊ] ad επίσης, ακόμη και.

altar [ˈɒltə*] n βωμός, θυσιαστήριο || (church) Αγία Τράπεζα.

alter [ˈɒltə*] vt μεταβάλλω, τροποποιώ, μεταποιώ ♦ vi μεταβάλλομαι || ~**ation** n μεταβολή, αλλαγή, αλλοίωση.

alternate [ɒlˈtɜːnɪt] a εναλλάσσων, εναλλασσόμενος ♦ [ˈɒltɜːneɪt] vt εναλλάσσω, χρησιμοποιώ εναλλάξ ♦ vi εναλλάσσομαι (with με) || ~**ly** ad εναλλάξ, αλληλοδιαδόχως.

alternative [ɒlˈtɜːnətɪv] n εκλογή, λύση || ~**ly** ad εναλλάξ.

alternator [ˈɒltɜːneɪtə*] n (ELEC) εναλλάκτης.

although [ɔːlˈðəʊ] cj αν και, μολονότι, καίτοι.

altitude [ˈæltɪtjuːd] n ύψος, υψόμετρο.

alto [ˈæltəʊ] n (male) οξύφωνος || (female) κοντράλτο.

altogether [ɔːltəˈgeðə*] ad τελείως, ολοσχερώς, εντελώς.

aluminium [æljuˈmɪnɪəm], (US) **aluminum** [əˈluːmɪnəm] n αλουμίνιο, αργίλιο.

always [ˈɔːlweɪz] ad πάντα, πάντοτε, διαρκώς.

am [æm] see **be**.

a.m. ad (abbr of ante meridiem) π.μ.

amass [əˈmæs] vt συσσωρεύω, μαζεύω.

amateur [ˈæmətə*] n ερασιτέχνης ♦ a ερασιτεχνικός.

amaze [əˈmeɪz] vt εκπλήσσω, καταπλήσσω, θαμπώνω || ~**ment** n κατάληξη, έκπληξη, ξάφνιασμα nt.

amazing [əˈmeɪzɪŋ] a καταπληκτικός, απίστευτος.

ambassador [æmˈbæsədə*] n πρεσβευτής, πρέσβυς m.

ambiguity [æmbɪˈgjuɪtɪ] n αμφιλογία, ασάφεια, διφορούμενο.

ambiguous [æmˈbɪgjuəs] a αμφίλογος, αβέβαιος, ασαφής.

ambition [æmˈbɪʃən] n φιλοδοξία.

ambitious [æmˈbɪʃəs] a φιλόδοξος.

amble [ˈæmbl] vi βαδίζω ήρεμα.

ambulance [ˈæmbjuləns] n ασθενοφόρο αυτοκίνητο.

ambush [ˈæmbuʃ] n ενέδρα, καρτέρι ♦ vt παρασύρω σε ενέδρα.

amenable [əˈmiːnəbl] a υπάκουος, πρόθυμος.

amend [əˈmend] vt διορθώνω, τροποποιώ ♦ vi διορθώνομαι ♦ n: **to make** ~**s** επανορθώνω, αποζημιώνω || ~**ment** n τροποποίηση, διόρθωση.

amenity [ɔ'mi:nɪtɪ] n χάρη, ομορφιά, άνεση.

America [ɔ'mɛrɪkɔ] n Αμερική.

American [ɔ'mɛrɪkɔn] a αμερικανικός ♦ n Αμερικανός/ίδα m/f.

amiable ['eɪmɪɔbl] a ευγενικός, φιλόφρων.

amicable ['æmɪkɔbl] a φιλικός || ~ **settlement** n συμβιβασμός.

amid(st) [ɔ'mɪd(st)] prep ανάμεσα, αναμεταξύ.

amiss ['mɪs] a, ad εσφαλμένα, κακά, στραβά || **to take** ~ παίρνω στραβά, παρεξηγώ.

ammunition [æmju'nɪʃɔn] n πολεμοφόδια ntpl, πυρομαχικά ntpl.

amnesia [æm'ni:zɪɔ] n αμνησία.

amnesty ['æmnɪstɪ] a αμνηστία.

amok [ɔ'mɒk] ad = **amuck.**

among(st) [ɔ'mʌŋ(st)] prep μεταξύ, μέσα, ανάμεσα.

amoral [æ'mɒrɔl] a άσχετος με την ηθική.

amorous ['æmɔrɔs] a ερωτόληπτος, ερωτιάρης.

amount [ɔ'maunt] n ποσό, σύνολο, ποσότητα ♦ vi ανέρχομαι, ισοδυναμώ || **to** ~ **to** ανέρχομαι.

ampere ['æmpɛɔ*] n αμπέρ nt inv.

amphibious [æm'fɪbɪɔs] a αμφίβιος.

amphitheatre ['æmfɪθɪɔtɔ*] n αμφιθέατρο.

ample ['æmpl] a (enough) αρκετός, πλήρης || (big) ευρύς, πλατύς || (abundant) άφθονα, πλούσια.

amplifier ['æmplɪfaɪɔ*] n ενισχυτής.

amputate ['æmpjuteɪt] vt αποκόπτω, ακρωτηριάζω.

amuck [ɔ'mʌk] ad: **to run** ~ παθαίνω αμόκ, παραφέρομαι.

amuse [ɔ'mju:z] vt διασκεδάζω, ξεκουράζω || ~**ment** n διασκέδαση, θέαμα nt, αναψυχή.

amusing [ɔ'mju:zɪŋ] a διασκεδαστικός, ξεκαρδιστικός.

an [æn] see **a.**

anaemia [ɔ'ni:mɪɔ] n αναιμία.

anaemic [ɔ'ni:mɪk] a αναιμικός.

anaesthetic [ænɪs'θɛtɪk] n αναισθητικό.

analgesic [ænæl'dʒi:sɪk] a, n αναληπτικός.

analogy [ɔ'nælɔdʒɪ] n αναλογία.

analyse ['ænɔlaɪz] vt αναλύω.

analysis [ɔ'nælɪsɪs] n ανάλυση.

anarchist ['ænɔkɪst] n αναρχικός.

anarchy ['ænɔkɪ] n αναρχία.

anatomy [ɔ'nætɔmɪ] n ανατομία.

ancestor ['ænsɪstɔ*] n πρόγονος, προπάτορας.

ancestry ['ænsɪstrɪ] n καταγωγή.

anchor ['æŋkɔ*] n άγκυρα ♦ vi αγκυροβολώ, ρίχνω άγκυρα, αράζω.

anchovy ['æntʃɔvɪ] n αντσούγια, χαμψί.

ancient ['eɪnʃɔnt] a αρχαίος, παλαιός.

and [ænd, ɔnd] cj και.

anecdote ['ænɪkdɔut] n ανέκδοτο.

anew [ɔ'nju:] ad πάλι, ξανά.

angel ['eɪndʒɔl] n άγγελος, αγγελούδι.

anger ['æŋgɔ*] n οργή, θυμός, παραφορά ♦ vt εξοργίζω, θυμώνω.

angle ['æŋgl] n γωνία || (viewpoint) άποψη ♦ vt ψαρεύω || ~r n ψαράς (με καλάμι).

Anglican ['æŋglɪkɔn] n Αγγλικανός.

angling ['æŋglɪŋ] n ψάρεμα nt.

Anglo- ['æŋglɔu] prefix αγγλο-.

angrily ['æŋgrɪlɪ] ad οργισμένα, θυμωμένα.

angry ['æŋgrɪ] a οργισμένος, θυμωμένος.

anguish ['æŋgwɪʃ] n αγωνία, αδημονία, πόνος.

angular ['æŋgjulɔ*] a γωνιακός, γωνιώδης.

animal ['ænɪmɔl] n ζώο ♦ a ζωικός.

animate ['ænɪmɪt] a έμψυχος, ζωντανός ♦ ['ænɪmeɪt] vt ζωογονώ, δίδω κίνηση || ~d a ζωντανός, ζωηρός.

animosity [ænɪ'mɒsɪtɪ] n εχθρότητα, έχθρα.

aniseed ['ænɪsi:d] n γλυκάνισο.

ankle ['æŋkl] n αστράγαλος.

annex ['ænɛks] n (also: **annexe**) παράρτημα nt ♦ [ɔ'nɛks] vt προσαρτώ.

annihilate [ɔ'naɪɔleɪt] vt εκμηδενίζω, εξαφανίζω.

anniversary [ænɪ'vɜːsɔrɪ] n επέτειος f.

annotate ['ænɔuteɪt] vt σχολιάζω.

announce [ɔ'nauns] vt (αν)αγγέλλω, ανακοινώ || ~**ment** n αναγγελία, ανακοίνωση || ~r n εκφωνητής.

annoy [ɔ'nɔɪ] vt ενοχλώ, πειράζω || ~**ance** n ενόχληση, μπελάς || ~**ing** a ενοχλητικός, οχληρός.

annual ['ænjuɔl] a ετήσιος, χρονιάρικος ♦ n (book) επετηρίδα, ημερολόγιο || ~**ly** ad ετησίως.

annuity [ɔ'njuːɪtɪ] n πρόσοδος f, επίδομα nt.

annul [ɔ'nʌl] vt ακυρώνω, διαλύω, καταργέλλω || ~**ment** n ακύρωση, κατάργηση.

annum ['ænɔm] see **per.**

anoint [ɔ'nɔɪnt] vt χρίω, αλείφω.

anomaly [ɔ'nɒmɔlɪ] n ανωμαλία.

anonymous [ɔ'nɒnɪmɔs] a ανώνυμος.

another [ɔ'nʌðɔ*] a, pron άλλος (ένας), ακόμη (ένας) || **one** ~ ο ένας τον άλλο.

answer ['ɑːnsɔ*] n απάντηση || (solution) λύση ♦ vt απαντώ || (suit) ανταποκρίνομαι || **to** ~ **for** vt εγγυούμαι για || ~**able** a υπεύθυνος, υπόλογος.

ant [ænt] n μυρμήγκι.

antagonist [æn'tægɔnɪst] n ανταγωνιστής, αντίπαλος || ~**ic** a εχθρικός, ανταγωνιστικός.

antagonize [æn'tægɔnaɪz] vt προκαλώ ανταγωνισμό, προκαλώ εχθρότητα.

Antarctic [ænt'ɑːktɪk] a ανταρκτικός.

antelope ['æntɪlɔup] n αντιλόπη.

antenatal ['æntɪ'neɪtl] a πριν τη γέννηση.

antenna [æn'tɛnɔ] n κεραία.

anthem ['ænθɔm] n ύμνος.

anthology [æn'θɒlədʒɪ] n ανθολογία.

anthropologist [ænθrə'pɒlədʒɪst] n ανθρωπολόγος.

anthropology [ænθrə'pɒlədʒɪ] n ανθρωπολογία.

anti-aircraft ['æntɪ'ɛəkrɑːft] a αντιαεροπορικός.

antibiotic ['æntɪbaɪ'ɒtɪk] n αντιβιοτικό.

anticipate [æn'tɪsɪpeɪt] vt προλαμβάνω || (foresee) προβλέπω, προσδοκώ.

anticipation [æntɪsɪ'peɪʃən] n πρόληψη, πρόβλεψη || (expectation) προσδοκία.

anticlimax ['æntɪ'klaɪmæks] n αντικλίμακα, κατάπτωση, παρακμή.

anticlockwise ['æntɪ'klɒkwaɪz] ad αριστερόστροφα.

antics ['æntɪks] npl κόλπα ntpl, αστεία ntpl.

anticyclone ['æntɪ'saɪkləʊn] n αντικυκλώνας.

antidote ['æntɪdəʊt] n αντίδοτο.

antifreeze ['æntɪ'friːz] n αντιψυκτικό, αντιπηκτικό.

antiquarian [æntɪ'kwɛərɪən] n αρχαιοδίφης, αρχαιόφιλος.

antiquated ['æntɪkweɪtɪd] a αρχαϊκός, απηρχαιωμένος, πεπαλαιωμένος.

antique [æn'tiːk] n αρχαίο, παλιό, αντίκα || ~s npl αρχαιότητες, αντίκες.

antiquity [æn'tɪkwɪtɪ] n αρχαιότητα.

antiseptic [æntɪ'septɪk] a, n αντισηπτικό.

antisocial ['æntɪ'səʊʃəl] a αντικοινωνικός.

antlers ['æntləz] npl κέρατα (ελαφιού).

anus ['eɪnəs] n δακτύλιος, έδρα.

anvil ['ænvɪl] n άκμονας, αμόνι.

anxiety [æŋ'zaɪətɪ] n ανησυχία, φόβος.

anxious ['æŋkʃəs] a ανήσυχος, στενοχωρημένος || (impatient) ανυπόμονος || ~ly ad ανήσυχα, ανυπόμονα.

any ['ɛnɪ] pron, a κανείς, καμμιά, κανένα || (whosoever) οποιοσδήποτε, κάθε ♦ ad καθόλου, πια || ~body pron κανείς, καμμιά, οποιοσδήποτε, καθένας || ~how ad οποιοσδήποτε, όπως κι αν είναι || ~one pron οποιοσδήποτε, καθένας, όλοι || ~thing pron τίποτε, κάτι, οτιδήποτε || ~way ad οπωσδήποτε ♦ cj οπωσδήποτε, εν πάση περιπτώσει || ~where ad οπουδήποτε, πουθενά.

apart [ə'pɑːt] ad χωριστά, κατά μέρος || ~ from εκτός του ότι.

apartheid [ə'pɑːteɪt] n φυλετική διάκριση.

apartment [ə'pɑːtmənt] n (flat) διαμέρισμα nt.

apathetic [æpə'θetɪk] a απαθής, αδιάφορος.

apathy ['æpəθɪ] n απάθεια, αδιαφορία.

ape [eɪp] n πίθηκος, μαϊμού f ♦ vt μιμούμαι.

aperitif [ə'perɪtɪv] n ορεκτικό.

aperture ['æpətjʊə*] n άνοιγμα nt, οπή, σχισμή.

apex ['eɪpɛks] n κορυφή.

apologetic [əpɒlə'dʒetɪk] a απολογητικός.

apologize [ə'pɒlədʒaɪz] vi ζητώ συγγνώμη.

apology [ə'pɒlədʒɪ] n απολογία, συγγνώμη.

apostle [ə'pɒsl] n απόστολος.

apostrophe [ə'pɒstrəfɪ] n απόστροφος.

appal [ə'pɔːl] vt τρομάζω, προκαλώ φρίκη || ~ling a τρομερός, φρικτός.

apparatus [æpə'reɪtəs] n συσκευή, μηχάνημα nt.

apparent [ə'pærənt] a φαινόμενος, εμφανής, φανερός || ~ly ad προφανώς, όπως φαίνεται.

apparition [æpə'rɪʃən] n φάντασμα nt.

appeal [ə'piːl] n έκκληση, κλήση προσφυγή || (LAW) κλήση, έφεση || (charm) γοητευτική, ελκυστική ♦ vi προσφεύγω, απευθύνομαι || ~ing a συγκινητικός, συμπαθητικός.

appear [ə'pɪə*] vi φαίνομαι, εμφανίζομαι || ~ance n εμφάνιση, παρουσία, παρουσιαστικό || to put in or make an ~ance εμφανίζομαι, παρουσιάζομαι.

appease [ə'piːz] vt κατευνάζω, ικανοποιώ.

appendicitis [əpendɪ'saɪtɪs] n σκωληκοειδίτιδα.

appendix [ə'pendɪks] n παράρτημα nt, εξάρτημα nt || (ANAT) σκωληκοειδής απόφυση.

appetite ['æpɪtaɪt] n όρεξη || loss of ~ n ανορεξία.

appetizing ['æpɪtaɪzɪŋ] a ορεκτικός, ελκυστικός.

applaud [ə'plɔːd] vt χειροκροτώ, επευφημώ.

applause [ə'plɔːz] n χειροκροτήματα ntpl, επιδοκιμασία.

apple ['æpl] n μήλο || ~ pie n μηλόπιτα || ~ tree n μηλιά.

appliance [ə'plaɪəns] n όργανο, μηχάνημα nt, εργαλείο.

applicable [ə'plɪkəbl] a εφαρμόσιμος, κατάλληλος.

applicant ['æplɪkənt] n υποψήφιος, αιτητής.

application [æplɪ'keɪʃən] n (request) αίτηση || (hard work) επιμέλεια, προσοχή, προσήλωση || (putting into practice) εφαρμογή, χρήση.

apply [ə'plaɪ] vi εφαρμόζω || (place on) επιθέτω, βάζω || (for job etc) απευθύνομαι, υποβάλλω αίτηση || to ~ the brake πατώ φρένο, φρενάρω || to ~ o.s. προσηλούμαι, αφοσιώνομαι.

appoint [ə'pɔɪnt] vt (δι)ορίζω, ονομάζω || ~ment n συνάντηση, ραντεβού nt inv.

apportion [ə'pɔːʃən] vt κατανέμω, διανέμω, μοιράζω.

appreciable [ə'priːʃəbl] a υπολογίσιμος, αισθητός.

appreciate [ə'priːʃeɪt] vt εκτιμώ, υπολογίζω, αποδίδω σημασία ♦ vi (ECON) ανατιμούμαι, υπερτιμούμαι.

appreciation [əpriːʃiˈeiʃən] n εκτίμηση || (ECON) υπερτίμηση, ανατίμηση.

apprehend [æpriˈhend] vt συλλαμβάνω, αντιλαμβάνομαι.

apprehension [æpriˈhenʃən] n (fear) φόβος, ανησυχία || (understanding) αντίληψη, νόηση || (arrest) σύλληψη.

apprehensive [æpriˈhensiv] a (worried) ανήσυχος, φοβισμένος.

apprentice [əˈprentis] n μαθητευόμενος ♦ vt τοποθετώ σαν μαθητευόμενο || ~ship n μαθητεία, μαθήτευση.

approach [əˈprəutʃ] n προσέγγιση, πλησίασμα nt || (path) είσοδος f, οδός f || (GOLF) κτύπημα nt ♦ vti πλησιάζω, προσεγγίζω || ~able a ευπρόσιτος, προσηνής, προσιτός.

appropriate [əˈprəupriit] a κατάλληλος, αρμόδιος, ταιριαστός ♦ [əˈprəuprieit] vt οικειοποιούμαι, ιδιοποιούμαι, παίρνω.

approval [əˈpruːvəl] n έγκριση.

approve [əˈpruːv] vti εγκρίνω, επιδοκιμάζω, επικυρώνω || ~d a εγκριθείς, εγκεκριμένος.

approximate [əˈprɒksimit] a κατά προσέγγιση ♦ [əˈprɒksimeit] vt προσεγγίζω, πλησιάζω.

approximation [əprɒksiˈmeiʃən] n προσέγγιση, εγγύτητα.

apricot [ˈeiprikɒt] n βερύκκοκο.

April [ˈeiprəl] n Απρίλιος.

apron [ˈeiprən] n ποδιά.

apt [æpt] a (suitable) κατάλληλος, αρμόζων || (ready) υποκείμενος σε.

aptitude [ˈæptitjuːd] n ικανότητα.

aqualung [ˈækwəlʌŋ] n συσκευή καταδύσεως, ακουαλάνγκ nt inv.

aquarium [əˈkwɛəriəm] n ενυδρείο, ακουάριο.

aquatic [əˈkwætik] a υδρόβιος || ~ sports npl θαλάσσια σπόρ nt inv.

aqueduct [ˈækwidʌkt] n υδραγωγείο.

Arab [ˈæræb] a αραβικός.

Arabia [əˈreibiə] n Αραβία || ~n a άραβας, αραβικός ♦ n Άραβας, Αράπης/ίνα m/f.

Arabic [ˈærəbik] a αραβικός ♦ n αραβική γλώσσα.

arable [ˈærəbl] a καλλιεργήσιμος.

arbitrary [ˈɑːbitrəri] a αυθαίρετος.

arbitration [ɑːbiˈtreiʃən] n διαιτησία || ~ court n διαιτητικό δικαστήριο.

arbitrator [ˈɑːbitreitə*] n διαιτητής.

arc [ɑːk] n τόξο.

arcade [ɑːˈkeid] n στοά, καμάρα.

arch [ɑːtʃ] n αψίδα, καμάρα ♦ a (chief) αρχι- ♦ vt (bend) λυγίζω, καμπουριάζω.

archaeologist [ɑːkiˈɒlədʒist] n αρχαιολόγος.

archaeology [ɑːkiˈɒlədʒi] n αρχαιολογία.

archaic [ɑːˈkeiik] a αρχαϊκός.

archbishop [ˈɑːtʃˈbiʃəp] n αρχιεπίσκοπος.

archer [ˈɑːtʃə*] n τοξότης || ~y n τοξοβολία.

archetype [ˈɑːkitaip] n αρχέτυπο.

archipelago [ɑːkiˈpeligəu] n αρχιπέλαγος nt.

architect [ˈɑːkitekt] n αρχιτέκτονας || ~ural a αρχιτεκτονικός || ~ure n αρχιτεκτονική.

archives [ˈɑːkaivz] npl αρχεία ntpl, έγγραφα ntpl.

archway [ˈɑːtʃwei] n στοά, αψιδωτή είσοδος.

Arctic [ˈɑːktik] a αρκτικός.

ardent [ˈɑːdənt] a φλογερός, ζωηρός.

ardour [ˈɑːdə*] n ζέση, μανία, πόθος.

arduous [ˈɑːdjuəs] a τραχύς, δύσκολος, κοπιώδης.

are [ɑː*] see be.

area [ˈɛəriə] n περιοχή, έκταση, χώρος || (MATH) εμβαδό.

arena [əˈriːnə] n παλαίστρα, κονίστρα, αρένα.

aren't [ɑːnt] = are not || see be.

argue [ˈɑːgjuː] vti (discuss) συζητώ, πραγματεύομαι || (prove) (απο)δεικνύω || (reason) φέρω επιχειρήματα, παρατάσσω.

argument [ˈɑːgjumənt] n επιχείρημα nt, συζήτηση || (dispute) φιλονικία, λογομαχία || (of play) σύνοψη, περίληψη || ~ative a συζητητικός.

aria [ˈɑːriə] n σκοπός, άρια.

arid [ˈærid] a ξηρός, άνυδρος.

arise [əˈraiz] (irreg v) vi σηκώνομαι || (appear) εμφανίζομαι, απορρέω.

aristocracy [æriˈstɒkrəsi] n αριστοκρατία.

aristocrat [ˈæristəkræt] n αριστοκράτης.

arithmetic [əˈriθmətik] n αριθμητική.

arm [ɑːm] n βραχίονας, μπράτσο || (hand) χέρι || (weapon) όπλο ♦ vt (εξ)οπλίζω, αρματώνω || ~s npl όπλα ntpl || ~ed forces npl ένοπλες δυνάμεις.

armchair [ˈɑːmtʃɛə*] n πολυθρόνα.

armful [ˈɑːmful] n αγκαλιά.

armistice [ˈɑːmistis] n ανακωχή.

armour, (US) armor [ˈɑːmə*] n θωράκιον || (panoply) αρματωσιά || ~ed car n τεθωρακισμένο άρμα μάχης.

armoury [ˈɑːməri] n οπλοστάσιο, οπλαποθήκη.

armpit [ˈɑːmpit] n μασχάλη.

army [ˈɑːmi] n στρατός || (of people etc) πλήθος nt.

aroma [əˈrəumə] n άρωμα nt, μυρωδιά || ~tic a αρωματικός.

around [əˈraund] ad (τρι)γύρω, ολόγυρα || (about) περίπου ♦ prep περί, γύρω.

arouse [əˈrauz] vt διεγείρω, αφυπνίζω, ξυπνώ.

arrange [əˈreindʒ] vt τακτοποιώ, διαρρυθμίζω, διευθετώ, κανονίζω || ~ment n τακτοποίηση, ρύθμιση, διευθέτηση.

arrears [əˈriəz] npl καθυστερούμενα ntpl, εκπρόθεσμος || in ~ καθυστερούμενα.

arrest [ə'rɛst] *n (making prisoner)* σύλληψη, κράτηση || *(halt)* αναχαίτιση, σταμάτημα *nt* ♦ *vt* σταματώ, αναχαιτίζω || *(LAW)* συλλαμβάνω.

arrival [ə'raivl] *n* άφιξη, ερχομός || **new** ~ *n* νεοαφιχθείς/ίσα *m/f* || *(baby)* νεογέννητο.

arrive [ə'raiv] *vi* αφικνούμαι, φθάνω *(at* σε*)* || *(at a conclusion)* καταλήγω.

arrogance [ˈærəgəns] *n* αλαζονεία, έπαρση, αυθάδεια.

arrogant [ˈærəgənt] *a* αλαζόνας, υπερόπτης, αυθάδης.

arrow [ˈærəu] *n* βέλος *nt*, σαΐτα.

arsenal [ˈɑːsinl] *n* οπλοστάσιο.

arsenic [ˈɑːsnik] *n* αρσενικό.

arson [ˈɑːsn] *n* εμπρησμός.

art [ɑːt] *n* τέχνη || ~ **gallery** *n* πινακοθήκη.

artery [ˈɑːtəri] *n* αρτηρία.

artful [ˈɑːtful] *a (person)* επιδέξιος, εφευρετικός || *(crafty)* πονηρός, δόλιος.

arthritis [ɑːˈθraitis] *n* αρθρίτιδα.

artichoke [ˈɑːtitʃəuk] *n* αγκινάρα.

article [ˈɑːtikl] *n (of agreement etc)* άρθρο, όρος || *(GRAM)* άρθρο || *(newspaper etc)* άρθρο || *(items)* είδος *nt*, αντικείμενο.

articulate [ɑːˈtikjulit] *a* αρθρωτός, έναρθρος || *(in expression)* σαφής, ευκρινής || ~**d** *a* έναρθρος.

artificial [ɑːtiˈfiʃl] *a* τεχνητός, ψεύτικος || ~ **intelligence (A.I.)** *(COMPUT)* τεχνητή νοημοσύνη (T.N.) || ~ **respiration** *n* τεχνητή αναπνοή.

artillery [ɑːˈtiləri] *n* πυροβολικό.

artisan [ˈɑːtizæn] *n* τεχνίτης, βιοτέχνης, εργάτης.

artist [ˈɑːtist] *n* καλλιτέχνης/ιδα *m/f* || *(painter)* ζωγράφος || ~**ic** *a* καλλιτεχνικός.

artless [ˈɑːtlis] *a* άτεχνος || *(natural)* απέριττος, φυσικός || *(naive)* αφελής, απονήρευτος.

as [æz, əz] *ad (in main clause)* επίσης, εξίσου, τόσο ... όσο || ~ **regards** όσο για || *cj (in subject clause)* όσο, τόσο ... όσο, σαν || *(time)* ενώ, καθώς || *(because)* επειδή || *(manner)* do ~ **you like** κάμετε όπως σας αρέσει || ~ **is** όπως είναι.

asbestos [æzˈbɛstəs] *n* αμίαντος, άσβεστος.

ascend [əˈsɛnd] *vi* ανέρχομαι, ανεβαίνω.

ascension [əˈsɛnʃən] *n* ανάβαση, άνοδος *f*, ανάληψη || **A~ Day** *n* της Αναλήψεως.

ascent [əˈsɛnt] *n* άνοδος *f*, ανάβαση || *(incline)* ανήφορος, ανωφέρεια, κλίση.

ascertain [æsəˈtein] *vt* διαπιστώνω, εξακριβώνω.

ascetic [əˈsɛtik] *a* ασκητικός.

ash [æʃ] *n* τέφρα, στάχτη || *(tree)* μελία, φλαμούρι.

ashamed [əˈʃeimd] *a*: **to be** ~ είμαι ντροπιασμένος, ντρέπομαι.

ashen [ˈæʃən] *a* σταχτής || *(person)* ωχρός, κίτρινος.

ashore [əˈʃɔː*] *ad* στην ξηρά, προσαραγμένος.

ashtray [ˈæʃtrei] *n* στακτοδοχείο.

Asia [ˈeiʃə] *n* Ασία || ~**n** *a* ασιατικός || ~**tic** *a* ασιατικός || ~ **Minor** *n* Μικρά Ασία.

aside [əˈsaid] *ad* κατά μέρος, πλάι, παράμερα || ~ **from** εκτός, πέρα.

ask [ɑːsk] *vt* (ε)ρωτώ, ζητώ, προσκαλώ || **to** ~ **a question** υποβάλλω ερώτηση.

askance [əˈskɑːns] *ad*: **to look at s.o.** ~ κοιτάζω με δυσπιστία.

askew [əˈskjuː] *ad* λοξά, στραβά.

asleep [əˈsliːp] *a*, *ad* κοιμισμένος || *(foot)* μουδιασμένος || **to fall** ~ αποκοιμιέμαι.

asparagus [əsˈpærəgəs] *n* σπαράγγι.

aspect [ˈæspɛkt] *n* θέα, όψη, προσανατολισμός.

asphalt [ˈæsfælt] *n* άσφαλτος *f* || ~ **road** *n* ασφαλτοστρωμένος (δρόμος).

asphyxiate [æsˈfiksieit] *vt* πνίγω.

aspiration [æspəˈreiʃən] *n* φιλοδοξία, βλέψη || *(GRAM)* δασεία προφορά.

aspire [əsˈpaiə*] *vi*: **to** ~ **to** φιλοδοξώ, αποβλέπω.

aspirin [ˈæsprin] *n* ασπιρίνη.

ass [æs] *n* γάιδαρος.

assailant [əˈseilənt] *n* επιτιθέμενος.

assassin [əˈsæsin] *n* δολοφόνος || ~**ate** *vt* δολοφονώ || ~**ation** *n* δολοφονία.

assault [əˈsɔːlt] *n* έφοδος, επίθεση ♦ *vt* επιτίθεμαι, εξορμώ || *(person)* βιάζω.

assemble [əˈsɛmbl] *vt* συγκεντρώνω, συναθροίζω || *(machine etc)* ενώνω, συναρμολογώ ♦ *vi* συγκεντρούμαι, συγκεντρώνομαι.

assembly [əˈsɛmbli] *n* συνέλευση, συγκέντρωση || *(machines)* συναρμολόγηση, συγκρότημα *nt* || ~ **line** *n* τράπεζα συναρμολογήσεως, αλυσίδα.

assent [əˈsɛnt] *n* συγκατάθεση, έγκριση ♦ *vi* συγκατατίθεμαι, συναινώ, επικυρώ.

assert [əˈsɜːt] *vt* επιβάλλω, διεκδικώ || *(ascertain)* βεβαιώ, υποστηρίζω || ~**ion** *n* ισχυρισμός, υποστήριξη.

assess [əˈsɛs] *vt* καταλογίζω, υπολογίζω, επιβάλλω (φόρο) || *(property)* εκτιμώ, φορολογώ || ~**ment** *n* καταλογισμός, εκτίμηση || *(tax)* φόρος || ~**or** *n* ελεγκτής (εφοριακός).

asset [ˈæsɛt] *n* περιουσιακό στοιχείο || *(qualities)* προσόν *nt*, αξία, ατού *nt inv* || ~**s** *npl* περιουσία || *(ECON)* ενεργητικό.

assiduous [əˈsidjuəs] *a* επιμελής, προσεκτικός.

assign [əˈsain] *vt* προορίζω, παρέχω, παραχωρώ, δίδω || ~**ment** *n* ανατιθεμένη εργασία.

assimilate [əˈsimileit] *vt* εξομοιώνω || *(food)* αφομοιώνω.

assist [əˈsist] *vt* βοηθώ, συντρέχω, μετέχω || ~**ance** *n* βοήθεια, αρωγή || ~**ant** *n* βοηθός *m/f* ♦ *a* βοηθητικός, αναπληρωματικός.

assizes [əˈsaiziz] *npl*: **court of** ~ ορκωτό δικαστήριο.

associate [ə'səuʃıt] n εταίρος, συνέταιρος, συνεργάτης ♦ [ə'səuʃıeıt] vti: to ~ with συνδέω, συνεταιρίζω, συνεργάζομαι, συναναστρέφομαι.

association [əsəusı'eıʃən] n (club) εταιρεία, οργανισμός, σωματείο || (keeping company) συναναστροφή, σχέση || ~ **football** n ποδόσφαιρο.

assorted [ə'sɔːtıd] a ταιριασμένος.

assortment [ə'sɔːtmənt] n συλλογή || (arrangement) τακτοποίηση, ταξινόμηση.

assume [ə'sjuːm] vt (take for granted) υποθέτω, θεωρώ || (duty) αναλαμβάνω, αναδέχομαι || ~d name n ψευδώνυμο.

assumption [ə'sʌmpʃən] n (supposition) υπόθεση, εικασία.

assurance [ə'ʃuərəns] n (certainty) βεβαιότητα || (confidence) διαβεβαίωση, υπόσχεση || (insurance) ασφάλεια (ζωής).

assure [ə'ʃuə*] vt (δια)βεβαιώ, εξασφαλίζω || ~d a βέβαιος.

asterisk ['æstərısk] n αστερίσκος.

astern ['əstɜːn] ad πίσω, προς τα πίσω.

asthma ['æsmə] n άσθμα nt || ~tic a ασθματικός.

astonish [ə'stonıʃ] vt εκπλήσσω, καταπλήσσω || ~ment n έκπληξη, κατάπληξη.

astound [ə'staund] vt καταπλήσσω.

astray [ə'streı] ad: to go ~ περιπλανώμαι, παραστρατίζω, ξεστρατίζω.

astride [ə'straıd] a, prep καβάλλα, ασεβάλ.

astrologer [əs'trolədʒə*] n αστρολόγος.

astrology [əs'trolədʒı] n αστρολογία.

astronaut ['æstrənɔːt] n αστροναύτης.

astronomer [əs'tronəmə*] n αστρονόμος.

astronomy [əs'tronəmı] n αστρονομία.

astute [əs'tjuːt] a έξυπνος, τετραπέρατος || (crafty) πανούργος, πονηρός.

asunder [ə'sʌndə*] ad χωριστά, κομματιαστά.

asylum [ə'saıləm] n (refuge) άσυλο, καταφύγιο || (for insane) ψυχιατρείο.

at [æt] prep (of place) σε || (of time) σε, κατά, περί || ~ **six o'clock** στις έξι || ~ **first** στην αρχή || ~ **home** στο σπίτι || ~ **least** τουλάχιστο || ~ **last** επί τέλους || (of cause) για || ~ **all** καθόλου || **not** ~ **all** καθόλου.

ate [eıt] pt of **eat**.

atheist ['eıθııst] n άθεος, αθεϊστής.

athlete ['æθliːt] n αθλητής/τρια m/f.

athletic [æθ'letık] a αθλητικός || ~**s** n αθλητισμός, σπορ nt inv.

Atlantic [ət'læntık] n Ατλαντικός.

atlas ['ætləs] n άτλας.

atmosphere ['ætməsfıə*] n ατμόσφαιρα.

atmospheric [ætməs'ferık] a ατμοσφαιρικός.

atom ['ætəm] n άτομο || ~**ic bomb** n

ατομική βόμβα || ~**ic energy** n ατομική ενέργεια.

atonement [ə'təunmənt] n έκτιση, επανόρθωση.

atrocious [ə'trəuʃəs] a φρικτός, φρικαλέος.

atrocity [ə'trosıtı] n αγριότητα, φρίκη (εγκλήματος).

attach [ə'tætʃ] vt συνδέω, προσαρτώ, (επι)συνάπτω || **to** ~ **importance to** δίνω σημασία σε || ~**ed** a αποπασμένος, προσαρτημένος || ~**ment** n προσάρτηση, προσκόλληση || (devotion to) αφοσίωση, στοργή.

attaché [ə'tæʃeı] n ακόλουθος || ~ **case** n χαρτοφύλακας.

attack [ə'tæk] n επίθεση, προσβολή ♦ vt επιτίθεμαι, προσβάλλω || ~**er** n επιτιθέμενος.

attain [ə'teın] vt φθάνω, κατορθώνω || ~**ment** n επίτευξη, πραγματοποίηση || (learning) γνώση, προσόν nt.

attempt [ə'tempt] n απόπειρα, προσπάθεια, δοκιμή ♦ vt αποπειρώμαι, προσπαθώ.

attend [ə'tend] vt (be present) παρευρίσκομαι, (visit) επισκέπτομαι, συχνάζω || (wait on) υπηρετώ ♦ vi (listen) εισακούω || (look after) ασχολούμαι || **to** ~ **to** προσέχω, φροντίζω || ~**ance** n (presence) συμμετοχή, παρουσία || ~**ant** n ακόλουθος, υπηρέτης/τρια m/f ♦ a συνοδεύων.

attention [ə'tenʃən] n προσοχή || (care) περιποίηση, φροντίδα.

attentive [ə'tentıv] a προσεκτικός, περιποιητικός.

attest [ə'test] vt επικυρώ, βεβαιώ, καταθέτω σαν μάρτυρας.

attic ['ætık] n σοφίτα.

attitude ['ætıtjuːd] n στάση.

attorney [ə'tɜːnı] n δικηγόρος, πληρεξούσιος || **district** ~ n εισαγγελέας || **A~ general** n γενικός εισαγγελέας || **power of** ~ n πληρεξούσιο.

attract [ə'trækt] vt ελκύω, έλκω, τραβώ, γοητεύω || ~**ion** n (PHYS) έλξη || (of person) γοητεία || (THEAT) ατραξιόν f inv|| ~**ive** a ελκυστικός, γοητευτικός.

attribute ['ætrıbjuːt] n χαρακτηριστικό γνώρισμα nt || (GRAM) επίθετο ♦ [ə'trıbjuːt] vt: **to** ~ **to** αποδίδω (σε).

auburn ['ɔːbən] a πυρόξανθος.

auction ['ɔːkʃən] n πλειστηριασμός, δημοπρασία ♦ vt πλειστηριάζω, βγάζω στο σφυρί || ~**eer** n προϊστάμενος δημοπρασιών.

audacious [ɔː'deıʃəs] a τολμηρός, παράτολμος || (insolent) θρασύς, αναιδής.

audacity [ɔː'dæsıtı] n τόλμη, θάρρος nt || (insolence) αναίδεια.

audible ['ɔːdıbl] a ακουστός, ακουόμενος.

audience ['ɔːdıəns] n (formal interview)

ακρόαση || *(gathering)* ακροατήριο || *(THEAT)* θεατές *mpl.*
audit ['ɔːdɪt] *n* έλεγχος, επαλήθευση ♦ *vt* ελέγχω || ~**or** *n* ελεγκτής || *(student)* ακροατής.
audition [ɔː'dɪʃən] *n* ακρόαση *(τραγουδιστού κτλ).*
auditorium [ɔːdɪ'tɔːrɪəm] *n* αίθουσα, θέατρο.
augment [ɔːg'mɛnt] *vt* (επ)αυξάνω, μεγαλώνω.
augur ['ɔːgə*] *vi* προοιωνίζομαι, προβλέπω.
August ['ɔːgəst] *n* Αύγουστος.
aunt [ɑːnt] *n* θεία || ~**y**, ~**ie** *n* θείτσα.
aura ['ɔːrə] *n* ατμόσφαιρα, φωτοστέφανος.
auspices ['ɔːspɪsɪz] *npl* αιγίδα || *(omens)* οιωνοί || **under the** ~ **of** υπό την αιγίδα του.
auspicious [ɔːs'pɪʃəs] *a* ευνοϊκός, ευοίωνος.
austere [ɒs'tɪə*] *a* αυστηρός.
austerity [ɒs'tɛrɪtɪ] *n* αυστηρότητα || *(of habits etc)* λιτότητα.
Australia [ɒs'treɪlɪə] *n* Αυστραλία || ~**n** *n* Αυστραλός/ίδα *m/f* ♦ *a* αυστραλιακός.
Austria ['ɒstrɪə] *n* Αυστρία || ~**n** *n* Αυστριακός/ή *m/f* ♦ *a* αυστριακός.
authentic [ɔː'θɛntɪk] *a* αυθεντικός, γνήσιος.
author ['ɔːθə*] *n* συγγραφέας || *(cause)* δημιουργός, πρωταίτιος.
authoritarian [ɔːθɒrɪ'tɛərɪən] *a* απολυταρχικός.
authority [ɔː'θɒrɪtɪ] *n* εξουσία, άδεια, εντολή || *(specialist)* αυθεντία || *(POL)* υπηρεσία.
authorize ['ɔːθəraɪz] *vt* εξουσιοδοτώ, επιτρέπω.
auto ['ɔːtəʊ] *n (US)* = **automobile**.
autobiography [ɔːtəʊbaɪ'ɒgrəfɪ] *n* αυτοβιογραφία.
autograph ['ɔːtəgrɑːf] *n* αυτόγραφο.
automatic [ɔːtə'mætɪk] *a* αυτόματος.
automation [ɔːtə'meɪʃən] *n* αυτοματοποίηση.
automaton [ɔː'tɒmətən] *n* αυτόματο.
automobile ['ɔːtəməbiːl] *n (US)* αυτοκίνητο, αμάξι.
autonomous [ɔː'tɒnəməs] *a* αυτόνομος.
autopsy ['ɔːtɒpsɪ] *n* νεκροψία.
autumn ['ɔːtəm] *n* φθινόπωρο.
auxiliary [ɔːg'zɪlɪərɪ] *a* βοηθητικός, επικουρικός.
avail [ə'veɪl] *n* χρησιμότητα, ωφέλεια, όφελος ♦ *vti* ωφελώ, βοηθώ, εξυπηρετώ.
availability [əveɪlə'bɪlɪtɪ] *n* διαθεσιμότητα.
available [ə'veɪləbl] *a* διαθέσιμος, προσιτός.
avalanche ['ævəlɑːnʃ] *n* χιονοστιβάδα || *(fig)* συρροή, πλημμύρα.
avant-garde ['ævɑːŋ'gɑːd] *n* πρωφυλακή.
Ave. *abbr of* **Avenue.**

avenge [ə'vɛndʒ] *vt* εκδικούμαι.
avenue ['ævənjuː] *n* λεωφόρος *f.*
average ['ævərɪdʒ] *n* μέσο, μέσος όρος || *(NAUT)* αβαρία ♦ *a* μέσος, μέτριος ♦ *vti* εξάγω το μέσο όρο.
averse [ə'vɜːs] *a* αντίθετος εναντίος || **to be** ~ **to** εναντιούμαι σε.
aversion [ə'vɜːʃən] *n* αποστροφή, απέχθεια || *(col)* αντιπάθεια.
avert [ə'vɜːt] *vt* αποστρέφω || *(prevent)* αποτρέπω, απομακρύνω.
aviary ['eɪvɪərɪ] *n* πτηνοτροφείο.
aviation [eɪvɪ'eɪʃən] *n* αεροπορία.
avid ['ævɪd] *a:* ~ **for** άπληστος, αχόρταγος για || ~**ly** *ad* άπληστα.
avocado [ævə'kɑːdəʊ] *n* αβοκάντο.
avoid [ə'vɔɪd] *vt* αποφεύγω || ~**able** *a* αποφευκτός || ~**ance** *n* αποφυγή.
await [ə'weɪt] *vt* αναμένω, περιμένω.
awake [ə'weɪk] *(irreg v) vti* ξυπνώ, αφυπνίζω, εφυπνίζομαι ♦ *a* ξύπνιος, άγρυπνος.
awakening [ə'weɪknɪŋ] *n* αφύπνιση, ξύπνημα *nt.*
award [ə'wɔːd] *n* βραβείο || *(LAW)* διαιτησία ♦ *vt* επιδικάζω || *(reward)* απονέμω.
aware [ə'wɛə*] *a:* ~ **(of)** πληροφορημένος, γνώστης || ~**ness** *n* συνείδηση.
away [ə'weɪ] *ad* μακριά || *(absent)* απουσιάζω, λείπω.
awe [ɔː] *n* φόβος, τρόμος || *(deep respect)* σεβασμός ♦ *vt* τρομάζω || ~-**inspiring** *a* επιβλητικός.
awful ['ɔːfəl] *a (very bad)* τρομερός, φοβερός || ~**ly** *ad* τρομερά, τρομακτικά.
awhile [ə'waɪl] *ad* για λίγο, μια στιγμή.
awkward ['ɔːkwəd] *a* αδέξιος, ανεπιτήδειος.
awning ['ɔːnɪŋ] *n* σκηνή, τέντα.
awoke [ə'wəʊk] *pt, pp of* **awake.**
awry [ə'raɪ] *ad* λοξός, στραβός || **to go** ~ πηγαίνω στραβά.
ax [æks] *(US)* = **axe.**
axe [æks] *n* τσεκούρι ♦ *vt* περιορίζω || *(dismiss)* απολύω.
axiom ['æksɪəm] *n* αξίωμα *nt.*
axle ['æksl] *n* άξονας.
ay(e) [aɪ] *interj (yes)* ναι || **the** ~**es** *npl* τα ναι, τα υπέρ.

B

B.A. *see* **bachelor.**
babble ['bæbl] *n* μωρολογία, τραύλισμα *nt* ♦ *vi* τραυλίζω, φλυαρώ.
babe [beɪb] *n* μωρό, μπέμπης.
baboon [bə'buːn] *n* μπαμπουίνος.
baby ['beɪbɪ] *n* βρέφος *nt*, νήπιο, μωρό || ~ **carriage** *n (US)* καροτσάκι μωρού || ~**ish** *a* μωρουδίστικος || ~-**sit** *vi* μπέμπισιτ, φυλάω νήπιο, προσέχω μωρό || ~-**sitter** *n* φύλακας νηπίων, μπέμπισιτερ.
bachelor ['bætʃələ*] *n* άγαμος, εργένης

B

|| **B~ of Arts (B.A.)** *n* ≈ πτυχιούχος πανεπιστημίου (θεωρητικών επιστημών) || **B~ of Science (B.Sc.)** *n* ≈ πτυχιούχος πανεπιστημίου (θετικών επιστημών).

back [bæk] *n* (person, horse) ράχη, πλάτη, νώτα *ntpl* || (house etc) το πίσω μέρος || (SPORT) μπάκ *nt inv* ♦ *vt* (support) υποστηρίζω || (movement) κάνω πίσω || (SPORT) ποντάρω ♦ *vi* (go backwards) οπισθοχωρώ, κάνω πίσω ♦ *a* οπίσθιος, πισινός ♦ *ad* πίσω, προς τα πίσω || (again) πάλι || (in time) εδώ και λίγα χρόνια || **to ~ out** *vi* ανακαλώ, αποσύρομαι || (col) το σκάω || **to ~ up** *vt* (COMPUT) εξασφαλίζω || ~**biting** *n* κουτσομπολιό || ~**bone** *n* ραχοκοκκαλιά || (firmness) θάρρος *nt*, κουράγιο || ~**cloth** *n* φόντο || ~**er** *n* (SPORT) παίκτης || (COMM) χρηματοδότης || ~**fire** *n* πρόωρη έκρηξη || ~**ground** *n* (scene) βάθος *nt*, φόντο || (information) προϊστορία, το ιστορικό || (education etc) προσόντα *ntpl* || ~**hand** *n* (blow) ανάποδη καρπαζιά || ~**handed** *a* ύπουλος || ~**handed compliment** διφορούμενο κομπλιμέντο, διφορούμενη φιλοφρόνηση || ~**ing** *n* υποστήριξη || (movement) οπισθοδρόμηση || ~**number** *n* (newspaper etc) παληό φύλλο || ~ **pay** *n* καθυστερούμενος μισθός |||| ~**side** *n* (col) πισινός || ~**up disk** *n* (COMPUT) εφεδρικός δίσκος ~**ward** *a* οπίσθιος, προς τα πίσω || (child etc) καθυστερημένο || ~**wards** *ad* προς τα πίσω || (flow) αντίθετα || ~ **yard** *n* πίσω αυλή.

bacon ['beɪkən] *n* καπνιστό χοιρινό, μπέικον *nt inv*.

bacteria [bæk'tɪərɪə] *npl* μικρόβια *ntpl*.

bad [bæd] *a* κακός, άσχημος.

badge [bædʒ] *n* διακριτικό, σήμα *nt*, έμβλημα *nt*.

badger ['bædʒə*] *n* ασβός ♦ *vt* παρενοχλώ, βασανίζω.

badly ['bædlɪ] *ad* κακά, άσχημα || ~ **off** σε δύσκολη οικονομική κατάσταση φτωχός.

bad-tempered ['bæd'tɛmpəd] *a* δύστροπος, γκρινιάρης.

baffle ['bæfl] *vt* (puzzle) ματαιώνω, τα χάνω.

bag [bæg] *n* σάκκος, σακκούλα || (handbag) τσάντα ♦ *vt* σακκουλιάζω || (capture etc) σκοτώνω, πιάνω || ~**ful** *n* σακκουλιά.

baggage ['bægɪdʒ] *n* αποσκευές *fpl*, βαλίτσες *pl*.

bagpipes ['bægpaɪps] *npl* γκάιντα.

bail [beɪl] *n* εγγύηση *vt* (prisoner) ελευθερώνω με εγγύηση || **to ~ out** (boat) βγάζω τα νερά, αδειάζω || *see also* **bale**.

bailiff ['beɪlɪf] *n* δικαστικός κλητήρας.

bait [beɪt] *n* δόλωμα *nt* ♦ *vt* δελεάζω, δολώνω || (harass) βασανίζω.

bake [beɪk] *vt* ψήνω σε φούρνο ♦ *vi*

ψήνομαι || ~**r** *n* φούρναρης || ~**ry** *n* φουρνάρικο.

baking ['beɪkɪŋ] *n* ψήσιμο.

balance ['bæləns] *n* ζυγός, ζυγαριά || (equilibrium) ισορροπία || (of account) υπόλοιπο || (ECON) ισολογισμός ♦ *vt* ζυγίζω, σταθμίζω || (counterbalance) ισορροπώ, ισοζυγίζω || ~**d** *a* ισορροπημένος || (equal) ίσος, ισοδύναμος || ~ **sheet** *n* ισολογισμός.

balcony ['bælkənɪ] *n* εξώστης, μπαλκόνι.

bald [bɔːld] *a* φαλακρός || (plain) γυμνός, ξηρός.

bale [beɪl] *n* δέμα *nt*, μπάλα, κόλος || **to ~ or bail out** (AVIAT) πηδώ με αλεξίπτωτο.

Balkan ['bɔːlkən] *a* Βαλκανικός.

ball [bɔːl] *n* σφαίρα, μπάλα, τόπι || (dance) χοροεσπερίδα, χορός.

ballad ['bæləd] *n* μπαλάντα.

ballast ['bæləst] *n* έρμα, σαβούρα.

ball bearing ['bɔːl'bɛərɪŋ] *n* σφαιροτριβέας, ρουλεμάν *nt inv*.

ballerina [bælə'riːnə] *n* μπαλαρίνα.

ballet ['bæleɪ] *n* μπαλέτο.

balloon [bə'luːn] *n* αερόστατο, μπαλόνι.

ballot ['bælət] *n* ψηφοδέλτιο.

ballpoint (pen) ['bɔːlpɔɪnt (pɛn)] *n* στυλό, πένα διαρκείας.

ballroom ['bɔːlrʊm] *n* αίθουσα χορού.

balmy ['bɑːmɪ] *a* γλυκός, κατευναστικός || (col) παλαβός.

balustrade [bæləs'treɪd] *n* κιγκλίδωμα *nt*, κάγκελλα *ntpl*.

bamboo [bæm'buː] *n* μπαμπού *nt inv*, καλάμι.

ban [bæn] *n* απαγόρευση || (church) αφορισμός ♦ *vt* απαγορεύω.

banal [bə'nɑːl] *a* κοινός, χυδαίος.

banana [bə'nɑːnə] *n* μπανάνα.

band [bænd] *n* δεσμός, δέσιμο, στεφάνι || (group) ομάδα, συντροφιά || (MUS) ορχήστρα, μπάντα ♦ *vi* (+ together) συνασπίζομαι ♦ *vt* (tie) δένω.

bandage ['bændɪdʒ] *n* επίδεσμος, φασκιά.

bandit ['bændɪt] *n* ληστής.

bandy(-legged) ['bændɪ('lɛgd)] *a* στραβοπόδης, στραβοκάνης.

bang [bæŋ] *n* (blow) κτύπημα *nt* || (noise) θόρυβος ♦ *vti* κτυπάω, κρούω.

banish ['bænɪʃ] *vt* εξορίζω, εκτοπίζω.

banister(s) ['bænɪstə*(z)] *n(pl)* κιγκλίδωμα *nt*, κάγκελλα *ntpl*.

banjo ['bændʒəʊ] *n* μπάντζο.

bank [bæŋk] *n* τράπεζα || (ground) ανάχωμα *nt*, ύψωμα *nt* || (of river) όχθη ♦ *vt* (tilt) κλίνω, στρέφω || (pile up) σωριάζω || (money) καταθέτω, βάζω || ~ **account** *n* τραπεζιτικός λογαριασμός || ~**er** *n* τραπεζίτης || ~ **holiday** *n* αργία τραπεζών || ~**note** *n* τραπεζογραμμάτιο, μπανκανότα.

bankrupt ['bæŋkrʌpt] *n* πτωχεύσας, χρεωκοπημένος ♦ *vt* πτωχεύω || ~**cy** *n* πτώχευση, χρεωκοπία.

banner ['bænə*] *n* σημαία, μπαντιέρα.

banns [bænz] npl αγγελία γάμου.

banquet ['bæŋkwit] n συμπόσιο, γλέντι, τσιμπούσι.

baptism ['bæptɪzəm] n βάφτισμα nt.

baptize [bæp'taɪz] vt βαφτίζω.

bar [ba:*] n (rod) ράβδος f, κοντάρι || (of soap etc) κομμάτι, πλάκα || (pub) μπάρ nt inv, ποτοπωλείο || (obstacle) φραγμός, εμπόδιο || (in court) εδώλιο || (MUS) μπάρα ♦ vt (fasten) κλείνω, αμπαρώνω, κιγκλιδώνω || (hinder) φράσσω, εμποδίζω || (exclude) απαγορεύω, αποκλείω || the B~ δικηγορικό επάγγελμα nt.

barbaric [ba:'bærɪk] a βάρβαρος, αγροίκος.

barbarity [ba:'bærɪtɪ] n βαρβαρότητα, αγριότητα.

barbarous ['ba:bərəs] a βάρβαρος.

barbecue ['ba:bɪkju:] n σχάρα.

barbed wire ['ba:bd'waɪə*] n συρματόπλεγμα nt.

barber ['ba:bə*] n κουρέας, μπαρμπέρης.

barbiturate [ba:'bɪtjurɪt] n βαρβιτουρικό.

bare [bɛə*] a γυμνός || (living etc) λιγοστός ♦ vt γυμνώνω || (reveal) αποκαλύπτω || ~**back** ad χωρίς σέλλα || ~**faced** a ξεδιάντροπος, αναιδής || ~**foot** a ξυπόλητος || ~**ly** ad μόλις.

bargain ['ba:gɪn] n συναλλαγή, αγορά || (bought cheaply) ευκαιρία || **into the** ~ επί πλέον, από πάνω.

barge [ba:dʒ] n φορτηγίδα, μαούνα || **to** ~ **in** vi επεμβαίνω.

baritone ['bærɪtəʊn] n βαρύτονος.

bark [ba:k] n (tree) φλοιός, φλούδα || (dog) γαύγισμα nt ♦ vi (dog) γαυγίζω.

barley ['ba:lɪ] n κριθάρι.

barmaid ['ba:meɪd] n σερβιτόρα του μπαρ.

barman ['ba:mən] n μπάρμαν m inv.

barn [ba:n] n (σιτ)αποθήκη || (US) σταύλος.

barnacle ['ba:nəkl] n ανατίφη, στρειδόνι.

barometer [bə'rɒmɪtə*] n βαρόμετρο.

baron ['bærən] n βαρώνος || ~**ess** n βαρώνη.

barracks ['bærəks] npl στρατώνας, μπαράκα.

barrage ['bæra:ʒ] n (dam) φράγμα nt|| (MIL) πυρ nt φραγμού, μπαράζ nt inv.

barrel ['bærəl] n βυτίο, βαρέλι || (measure) βαρέλι || (gun) κάννη.

barren ['bærən] a στείρος, άγονος.

barricade [bærɪ'keɪd] n προπέτασμα nt φράγμα nt ♦ vt φράσσω.

barrier ['bærɪə*] n φραγμός || (obstruction) εμπόδιο.

barrister ['bærɪstə*] n δικηγόρος m/f.

barrow ['bærəʊ] n (cart) μονότροχο, χειράμαξα.

bartender ['ba:tɛndə*] n (US) = **barman.**

base [beɪs] n βάση ♦ vt βασίζω, στηρίζω ♦ a ταπεινός, πρόστυχος || (inferior)

φθηνός || ~**ball** n μπέιζ-μπώλ nt inv|| ~**ment** n υπόγειο.

bash [bæʃ] vt (col) κτυπώ, τσακίζω.

bashful ['bæʃful] a ντροπαλός.

basic ['beɪsɪk] a βασικός, θεμελιώδης || ~**ally** ad βασικά.

basilica [bə'zɪlɪkə] n βασιλική.

basin ['beɪsn] n λεκάνη || (NAUT) νεωδόχος f, δεξαμενή.

basis ['beɪsɪs] n βάση.

bask [ba:sk] vi λιάζομαι.

basket ['ba:skɪt] n καλάθι, πανέρι || ~**ball** n καλαθόσφαιρα, μπάσκετ nt inv.

bass [beɪs] n (MUS) βαθύφωνος, μπάσος.

bassoon [bə'su:n] n φαγκότο.

bastard ['ba:stəd] n νόθος/n m/f, μπάσταρδος.

baste [beɪst] vt (sewing) παρραράβω, ξυλίζω, ραβδίζω || (cooking) βουτυρώνω.

bastion ['bæstɪən] n (stronghold) προμαχώνας.

bat [bæt] n (SPORT) ρόπαλο, μαγγούρα || (ZOOL) νυκτερίδα ♦ vi κτυπώ με το ρόπαλο || **off one's own** ~ εξ ιδίας πρωτοβουλίας.

batch [bætʃ] n φουρνιά (ψωμί) || (set) σωρός, ομάδα.

bath [ba:θ] n λουτρό, μπάνιο || (tub) λουτήρας, μπανιέρα ♦ vt λούω, μπανιαρίζω || ~**s** npl δημόσια λουτρά ntpl, μπάνια ntpl, χαμάμ nt inv|| ~**chair** καροτσάκι (αναπήρων) αναπηρική καρέκλα.

bathe [beɪð] vi λούομαι, κάνω μπάνιο ♦ vt λούω, πλένω || ~**r** n κολυμβητής/ήτρια m/f, λουόμενος/n m/f.

bathing ['beɪðɪŋ] n κολύμπι || ~ **cap** n σκούφος του μπάνιου || ~ **costume** n μπανιερό, μαγιό nt inv.

bathmat ['ba:θmæt] n ψάθα του μπάνιου.

bathroom ['ba:θrum] n λουτρό.

bath towel ['ba:θtaʊəl] n πετσέτα του μπάνιου.

baton ['bætən] n ράβδος f|| (conductor's) μπαγκέτα || (truncheon) γκλώμπ nt inv.

battalion [bə'tælɪən] n τάγμα nt.

batter ['bætə*] n κουρκούτι ♦ vt κτυπώ, κοπανίζω.

battery ['bætərɪ] n (MIL) πυροβολαρχία || (cell) συστοιχία.

battle ['bætl] n μάχη ♦ vi μάχομαι, πολεμώ || ~**field** n πεδίο μάχης || ~**ments** npl επάλξεις fpl, παραπέτο, πολεμίστρες fpl|| ~**ship** n θωρηκτό.

bawdy ['bɔ:dɪ] a ασελγής, αισχρός.

bawl [bɔ:l] vi κραυγάζω, σκούζω.

bay [beɪ] n (of sea) κόλπος, κόρφος || (tree) δάφνη || **at** ~ σε δύσκολη θέση, στα στενά.

bayonet ['beɪənɪt] n ξιφολόγχη, μπαγιονέττα.

bay window ['beɪ'wɪndəʊ] n παράθυρο σε προεξοχή τοίχου.

bazaar [bə'za:*] n παζάρι || (for charity) φιλανθρωπική αγορά.

B.B.C. *abbr of British Broadcasting Corporation.*

B.C. *ad (abbr of before Christ)* π.X.

be [bi:] *(irreg v) vi (exist)* είμαι, υπάρχω || *(live)* είμαι, ζω, κατοικώ || *(stay)* είμαι, κάνω || *(cost)* είμαι, κοστίζω || *(location)* είμαι, ευρίσκομαι || *(visit)* είμαι, επισκέπτομαι || *(take place)* είμαι, γίνομαι.

beach [bi:tʃ] *n* παραλία, ακρογιαλιά ♦ *vt* προσγιαλώ, αράζω || *(run aground)* προσαράσσω.

beacon ['bi:kən] *n* φάρος, φανάρι.

bead [bi:d] *n* χάντρα, πέρλα || *(perspiration)* σταγονίδι.

beak [bi:k] *n* ράμφος *nt*, μύτη.

beaker ['bi:kə*] *n* γυάλινο ποτήρι.

beam [bi:m] *n* δοκός *f*, δοκάρι || *(of balance)* ζυγοστάτης, μπράτσο || *(of light)* αχτίδα, δέσμη || *(smile)* λάμψη, ακτινοβολία ♦ *vi* ακτινοβολώ, λάμπω.

bean [bi:n] *n (broad)* κουκί || *(kidney)* φασόλι || *(string)* φασολάκι.

bear [bɛə*] *(irreg v) n* αρκούδα ♦ *vt (carry)* φέρω, βαστώ, σηκώνω || *(support)* υποβαστάζω, στηρίζω || *(put up with)* υποφέρω, αντέχω, ανέχομαι || *(produce)* γεννώ, παράγω || ~**able** *a* υποφερτός, ανεκτός.

beard [biəd] *n* γένι, μούσι || ~**ed** *a* με γένεια.

bearing ['bɛəriŋ] *n (behaviour)* συμπεριφορά, ύφος *nt* || *(relation)* σχέση, έννοια || ~**s** *npl*: **I lose my** ~**s** χάνω τον προσανατολισμό.

beast [bi:st] *n* ζώο, κτήνος *nt*, θηρίο || *(person)* ζώο, παλιάνθρωπος || ~**ly** *a* κτηνώδης, βρώμικος.

beat [bi:t] *(irreg v) n (stroke)* κτύπημα *nt* || *(pulsation)* σφυγμός, παλμός || *(of policeman)* περιπολία || *(MUS)* χρόνος, μέτρο ♦ *vt* κτυπώ, δέρνω, ματσουκώνω || *(defeat)* υπερτερώ, νικώ || **to ~ about the bush** γυρίζω γύρω-γύρω από ένα θέμα || **to ~ time** κρατώ το χρόνο || **to ~ off** *vt* διώχνω, απωθώ || **to ~ up** *vt* σπάζω στο ξύλο || ~**en track** *n* πεπατημένη || ~**er** *n (for eggs, cream)* κτυπητήρι.

beautiful ['bju:tiful] *a* ωραίος, εξαίσιος, υπέροχος || ~**ly** *ad* θαυμάσια, υπέροχα.

beauty ['bju:ti] *n* ομορφιά || *(woman)* καλλονή.

beaver ['bi:və*] *n* κάστορι, κάστορας.

because [bi'kɒz] *cj* διότι, γιατί, επειδή || ~ **of** εξαιτίας (+ *genitive*).

beckon ['bɛkən] *vt* γνέφω, κάνω νόημα.

become [bi'kʌm] *vt (befit)* αρμόζω, ταιριάζω ♦ *vi* γίνομαι, καταντώ.

becoming [bi'kʌmiŋ] *a* αρμόζων || *(dress etc)* ταιριαστός, που πηγαίνει.

bed [bɛd] *n* κρεββάτι || *(of river)* κοίτη || *(foundation)* στρώμα *nt*, στρώση || *(garden)* πρασιά || ~ **and breakfast** *n* δωμάτιο με πρωινό || ~**clothes** *npl* σεντόνια *ntpl* και κουβέρτες *fpl* || ~**ding** *n* στρώματα *ntpl*.

bedlam ['bɛdləm] *n (uproar)* φασαρία, θόρυβος.

bedraggled [bi'drægld] *a* κουρελιασμένος.

bedridden ['bɛdridn] *a* κρεββατωμένος, κατάκοιτος.

bedroom ['bɛdrum] *n* υπνοδωμάτιο, κρεββατοκάμαρα.

bed-sitter ['bɛd'sitə*] *n* υπνοδωμάτιο.

bee [bi:] *n* μέλισσα.

beech [bi:tʃ] *n* οξυά.

beef [bi:f] *n* βωδινό.

beehive ['bi:haiv] *n* κυψέλη.

beeline ['bi:lain] *n:* **to make a** ~ **for** πηγαίνω κατ, ευθείαν.

been [bi:n] *pp of* **be.**

beer [biə*] *n* μπύρα.

beetle ['bi:tl] *n* σκαθάρι.

beetroot ['bi:tru:t] *n* πατζάρι, κοκκινογούλι.

befall [bi'fɔ:l] *vti* συμβαίνω, τυχαίνω.

before [bi'fɔ:*] *prep (in place)* προ, εμπρός, ενώπιον || *(of time)* πριν, προ ♦ *cj* προ, πριν, πριν να ♦ *ad (of place)* εμπρός, προ, μπροστά || *(of time)* πριν, πρωτύτερα, προτού.

befriend [bi'frɛnd] *vt* βοηθώ, προστατεύω.

beg [bɛg] *vti* ζητώ, παρακαλώ || *(for alms)* ζητιανεύω.

began [bi'gæn] *pt of* **begin.**

beggar ['bɛgə*] *n* ζητιάνος/α *m/f*, επαίτης.

begin [bi'gin] *(irreg v) vti* αρχίζω, αρχινώ || **to ~ with** πρώτα-πρώτα, πριν ν'αρχίσουμε || ~**ner** *n* αρχάριος/α *m/f*, πρωτάρης/α *m/f* || ~**ning** *n* αρχή.

begrudge [bi'grʌdʒ] *vt* δίνω με το ζόρι, λυπούμαι.

begun [bi'gʌn] *pp of* **begin.**

behalf [bi'hɑ:f] *n* εκ μέρους, υπέρ || **on ~ of** για λογαριασμό του, εκ μέρους.

behave [bi'heiv] *vi (συμπερι)*φέρομαι.

behaviour, *(US)* **behavior** [bi'heivjə*] *n* συμπεριφορά, φέρσιμο.

behind [bi'haind] *prep* πίσω από || *(time)* καθυστερημένος ♦ *ad* όπισθεν, πίσω από ♦ *n* πισινός.

behold [bi'həuld] *vt* βλέπω, αντικρύζω.

beige [beiʒ] *a* μπεζ.

being ['bi:iŋ] *n* ύπαρξη, γέννηση || *(person)* ον *nt*, είναι *nt inv.*

belch [bɛltʃ] *vi* ρεύομαι.

belfry ['bɛlfri] *n* καμπαναριό.

Belgian ['bɛldʒiən] *n* Βέλγοβ/Βελγίδα *m/f* ♦ *a* βελγικός.

Belgium ['bɛldʒəm] *n* Βέλγιο.

belie [bi'lai] *vt* διαψεύδω, ξεγελώ.

belief [bi'li:f] *n (trust)* πίστη || *(idea)* γνώμη, δοξασία.

believable [bi'li:vəbl] *a* πιστευτός.

believe [bi'li:v] *vt* πιστεύω, δέχομαι ♦ *vi* πιστεύω, έχω εμπιστοσύνη || ~**r** *n* πιστός/ή *m/f.*

belittle [bi'litl] *vt* υποτιμώ, περιφρονώ.

bell [bɛl] *n* καμπάνα || *(in house)* κουδούνι.

belligerent [bɪ'lɪdʒərənt] a *(fig)* καυγατζής.

bellow ['bɛləʊ] vti μουγγρίζω, μουγκαρίζω ♦ μουγκρητό.

bellows ['bɛləʊz] npl φυσερό.

belly ['bɛlɪ] n κοιλιά.

belong [bɪ'lɒŋ] vi ανήκω || it does not ~ here δεν ανήκει εδώ || to ~ to vt ανήκω, μετέχω σε || *(a place)* κατάγομαι από || ~ings npl περιουσία, υπάρχοντα ntpl.

beloved [bɪ'lʌvɪd] a πολυαγαπημένος ♦ n αγαπητός.

below [bɪ'ləʊ] prep υπό, κάτω από, κάτω θεν ♦ ad από κάτω.

belt [bɛlt] n ζώνη, ταινία || *(round waist)* ζωνάρι, λουρί ♦ vt ζώνω || *(beat)* δέρνω με λουρί.

bench [bɛntʃ] n κάθισμα nt, πάγκος || *(workshop)* τεζάκι, πάγκος || *(of judge)* έδρα.

bend [bɛnd] *(irreg v)* n καμπή, στροφή, γωνία ♦ vt κάμπτω, λυγίζω || *(NAUT)* δένω ♦ vi *(stoop)* σκύβω.

beneath [bɪ'niːθ] prep κάτωθεν, χαμηλότερα, υπό ♦ ad από κάτω.

benefactor ['bɛnɪfæktə*] n ευεργέτης, δωρητής.

beneficial [bɛnɪ'fɪʃəl] a ωφέλιμος, χρήσιμος.

benefit ['bɛnɪfɪt] n όφελος nt, ωφέλεια ♦ vt ωφελώ ♦ vi επωφελούμαι.

benevolent [bɪ'nɛvələnt] a αγαθοεργός, καλοπροαίρετος.

bent [bɛnt] n *(inclination)* κλίση, ροπή ♦ a: to be ~ on αποφασισμένος να ♦ pt, pp of bend.

bequeath [bɪ'kwiːð] vt κληροδοτώ, αφήνω.

bequest [bɪ'kwɛst] n κληροδότημα.

bereaved [bɪ'riːvd] n *(person)* τεθλιμμένος.

bereavement [bɪ'riːvmənt] n απώλεια, πένθος nt.

beret ['bɛreɪ] n μπερέ nt inv, σκούφος.

berry ['bɛrɪ] n ρόγα, μούρο.

berserk [bɜ'sɜːk] a: to go ~ γίνομαι έξω φρενών.

berth [bɜːθ] n *(anchoring)* όρμος || *(ship, train)* κλίνη, καμπίνα ♦ vt προσορμίζω, πλευρίζω ♦ vi αγκυροβολώ, πλευρίζω.

beseech [bɪ'siːtʃ] *(irreg v)* vt ικετεύω, εκλιπαρώ.

beset [bɪ'sɛt] vt κυκλώνω, περισφίγγω.

beside [bɪ'saɪd] prep πλάι, κοντά, δίπλα || to be ~ o.s. είμαι εκτός εαυτού.

besides [bɪ'saɪdz] prep εκτός από ♦ ad εκτός αυτού, ακόμη, άλλωστε.

besiege [bɪ'siːdʒ] vt πολιορκώ.

best [bɛst] a καλύτερος ♦ ad καλύτερα || at ~ το καλύτερο, ακόμα και || to make the ~ of it όσο μπορώ καλύτερα || ~ man n παράνυμφος, κουμπάρος.

bestow [bɪ'stəʊ] vt παρέχω, απονέμω.

bestseller ['bɛst'sɛlə*] n βιβλίο μεγάλης κυκλοφορίας.

bet [bɛt] *(irreg v)* n στοίχημα nt ♦ vt στοιχηματίζω, βάζω στοίχημα.

betray [bɪ'treɪ] vt προδίδω, αποκαλύπτω || *(be false)* εξαπατώ || ~al n προδοσία.

better ['bɛtə*] a καλύτερος ♦ ad καλύτερα ♦ vt καλυτερεύω, βελτιώνω ♦ n: to get the ~ of νικώ κάποιο, υπερέχω || he thought ~ of it άλλαξε γνώμη || ~ off a *(richer)* πιο εύπορος, πλουσιότερος.

betting ['bɛtɪŋ] n στοίχημα(τα) nt.

between [bɪ'twiːn] prep μεταξύ, ανάμεσα ♦ ad ανάμεσα.

beverage ['bɛvərɪdʒ] n ποτό.

beware [bɪ'wɛə*] vt προσέχω, φοβούμαι || '~ of the dog' 'προσοχή, σκύλος'.

bewildered [bɪ'wɪldəd] a ζαλισμένος, χαμένος.

bewitching [bɪ'wɪtʃɪŋ] a γοητευτικός, μαγευτικός.

beyond [bɪ'jɒnd] prep *(of place)* πέρα από || *(of time)* πέραν του || *(in addition)* εκτός, πέρα από ♦ ad πέρα από, εκεί κάτω.

bias ['baɪəs] n *(slant)* λοξότητα || *(prejudice)* προκατάληψη, συμπάθεια || ~(s)ed a προκατειλημμένος, επηρεασμένος.

bib [bɪb] n σαλιάρα, μπούστος.

Bible ['baɪbl] n Βίβλος f, Ευαγγέλιο.

bibliography [bɪblɪ'ɒɡrəfɪ] n βιβλιογραφία.

bicker ['bɪkə*] vi καυγαδίζω || ~ing n καυγάς.

bicycle ['baɪsɪkl] n ποδήλατο.

bid [bɪd] *(irreg v)* n προσφορά || *(CARDS)* δήλωση ♦ vt *(command)* διατάσσω, προστάζω || *(offer)* προσφέρω, πλειοδοτώ || *(greeting)* χαιρετώ || *(goodbye)* αποχαιρετώ || ~der n *(person)* πλειοδότης || ~ding n *(order)* εντολή, παραγγελία || *(offer)* πλειοδοσία.

bidet ['biːdeɪ] n μπιντέ nt inv.

big [bɪɡ] a μεγάλος, σπουδαίος.

bigamy ['bɪɡəmɪ] n διγαμία.

bigot ['bɪɡət] n στενοκέφαλος, φανατικός || ~ed a στενοκέφαλος || ~ry n μισαλλοδοξία.

bike [baɪk] n ποδήλατο.

bikini [bɪ'kiːnɪ] n μπικίνι nt inv.

bile [baɪl] n χολή.

bilingual [baɪ'lɪŋɡwəl] a δίγλωσσος.

bill [bɪl] n *(notice)* αγγελία, αφίσα || *(account)* λογαριασμός || *(law)* νομοσχέδιο || *(note)* γραμμάτιο || *(beak)* ράμφος nt, μύτη || *(US)* χαρτονόμισμα nt.

billet ['bɪlɪt] n *(MIL)* κατάλυμα nt || *(job)* θέση.

billfold ['bɪlfəʊld] n *(US)* πορτοφόλι.

billiards ['bɪlɪədz] n μπιλιάρδο.

billion ['bɪlɪən] n *(Brit)* τρισεκατομμύριο || *(US)* δισεκατομμύριο.

billy goat ['bɪlɪɡəʊt] n τράγος.

bin [bɪn] n κασέλα, κασόνι, κιβώτιο.

bind [baɪnd] *(irreg v)* vt *(tie)* δένω || *(together)* προσδένω || *(a book)* δένω ||

(oblige) δεσμεύω, δένω || ~**ing** *n* σύνδεση, δέση, δέσιμο || *(book)* βιβλιοδεσία.

binoculars [bɪ'nɒkjuːləz] *npl* κιάλια *ntpl*.

biochemistry ['baɪəʊ'kemɪstrɪ] *n* βιοχημεία.

biography [baɪ'ɒgrəfɪ] *n* βιογραφία.

biological [baɪə'lɒdʒɪkəl] *a* βιολογικός.

biology [baɪ'ɒlədʒɪ] *n* βιολογία.

birch [bɜːtʃ] *n (tree)* σημύδα || *(for whipping)* βέργα.

bird [bɜːd] *n* πουλί || ~'**s-eye view** *n* θέα από ψηλά.

birth [bɜːθ] *n* γέννα, τοκετός || *(beginning)* γέννηση || **of good** ~ καλής καταγωγής || ~ **certificate** *n* πιστοποιητικό γεννήσεως || ~ **control** *n* έλεγχος γεννήσεων || ~**day** *n* γενέθλια *ntpl* || ~**place** *n* τόπος γεννήσεως || ~ **rate** *n* γεννήσεις *fpl*.

biscuit ['bɪskɪt] *n* παξιμάδι, μπισκότο.

bisect [baɪ'sɛkt] *vt* διχοτομώ.

bishop ['bɪʃəp] *n* επίσκοπος, δεσπότης.

bit [bɪt] *n (piece)* κομμάτι || *(of tool)* τρυπάνι || *(of horse)* στομίδα, χαβιά, χαλινάρι || *(COMPUT)* bit *nt inv*.

bitch [bɪtʃ] *n (dog)* σκύλα || *(unpleasant woman)* παλιοθήλυκο.

bite [baɪt] *(irreg v)* *n* δάγκωμα *nt* || *(mouthful)* μπουκιά ♦ *vti* δαγκώνω || *(insect)* τσιμπώ || **a** ~ **to eat** μπουκιά, λίγο φαγητό.

biting ['baɪtɪŋ] *a* δηκτικός.

bitter ['bɪtə*] *a* πικρός || *(feeling)* φαρμακερός, δηκτικός, πικρός ♦ *n (beer)* πικρή μπύρα || **to the** ~ **end** μέχρι τέλους, μέχρι εσχάτων || ~**ness** *n* πικρία, πίκρα || ~**sweet** *a* γλυκόπικρος.

bizarre [bɪ'zɑː*] *a* παράξενος, αλλόκοτος.

blab [blæb] *vti* τα λέω όλα, προδίδω.

black [blæk] *a* μαύρος || *(without light)* σκοτεινός ♦ *vt (shoes)* βάφω, λουστράρω || *(eye)* μαυρίζω || ~ **and blue** γεμάτος σημάδια, καταμαυρισμένος || ~**berry** *n* βατόμουρο || ~**bird** *n* κότσυφας || ~**board** *n* πίνακας, μαυροπίνακας || ~**currant** *n* μαύρο φραγκοστάφυλλο || ~**en** *vt* μαυρίζω, λερώνω || ~**leg** *n* απεργοσπάστης || ~**list** *n* μαύρος πίνακας || ~**mail** *vt* εκβιάζω || ~**mailer** *n* εκβιαστής || ~ **market** *n* μαύρη αγορά || ~**out** *n (MIL)* συσκότιση || *(ELEC)* διακοπή ρεύματος || *(faint)* σκοτοδίνη, λιποθυμία || ~**smith** *n* σιδεράς.

bladder ['blædə*] *n* κύστη || *(of football etc)* σαμπρέλλα.

blade [bleɪd] *n (leaf etc)* φύλλο || *(of tool etc)* λεπίδα, λάμα || *(of oar etc)* πτερύγιο, φτερό.

blame [bleɪm] *n* μομφή, ψόγος, φταίξιμο ♦ *vt* κατηγορώ, ψέγω || ~**less** *a* άψογος, ανεύθυνος.

bland [blænd] *a* ήπιος, μειλίχιος.

blank [blæŋk] *a (page)* λευκός, άγραφος || *(vacant)* ανέκφραστος, χαμένα,

συγχισμένος ♦ *n* κενό || *(cartridge)* άσφαιρο φυσίγγι.

blanket ['blæŋkɪt] *n* κλινοσκέπασμα *nt*, κουβέρτα.

blare [blɛə*] *n* δυνατός ήχος, ούρλιασμα *nt* ♦ *vi* αντηχώ, διασαλπίζω.

blasphemy ['blæsfɪmɪ] *n* βλαστήμια.

blast [blɑːst] *n (gust)* φύσημα *nt*, ριπή || *(NAUT)* σφύριγμα *nt* || *(MINING)* φουρνέλο ♦ *vt* βάζω φουρνέλο || ~-**off** *n (SPACE)* εκτόξευση.

blatant ['bleɪtənt] *a* κραυγαλέος, ολοφάνερος.

blaze [bleɪz] *n (fire)* φλόγα, ανάφλεξη, φωτιά ♦ *vi* παίρνω φωτιά || *(person)* εξάπτομαι ♦ *vt*: **to** ~ **a trail** χαράσσω δρόμο.

blazer ['bleɪzə*] *n* σπορ σακάκι.

bleach [bliːtʃ] *n* άσπρισμα *nt*, μπουγάδα ♦ *vt* ασπρίζω, ξεβάφω || *(hair)* αποχρωματίζω.

bleak [bliːk] *a* ψυχρός, μελαγχολικός.

bleary-eyed ['blɪərɪ'aɪd] *a* με θολωμένα μάτια.

bleat [bliːt] *n* βέλασμα *nt* ♦ *vt* βελάζω.

bled [blɛd] *pt, pp* of **bleed**.

bleed [bliːd] *(irreg v)* *vi* χύνω αίμα, χάνω αίμα ♦ *vt* φλεβοτομώ, παίρνω αίμα.

bleeding ['bliːdɪŋ] *a* ματωμένος.

blemish ['blɛmɪʃ] *n* ελάττωμα *nt*, κηλίδα ♦ *vt* κηλιδώνω || *(reputation)* καταστρέφω.

blend [blɛnd] *n* χαρμάνι, μίγμα *nt* ♦ *vt* ανακατεύω, συγχωνεύω ♦ *vi (colours etc)* ταιριάζω.

bless [blɛs] *vt* ευλογώ, δοξάζω || ~**ing** *n* ευλογία, ευτύχημα *nt*.

blew [bluː] *pt* of **blow**.

blight [blaɪt] *n (disease)* ερυσίβη, συρίκι, συναπίδι || *(fig)* πληγή ♦ *vt* καταστρέφω.

blimey ['blaɪmɪ] *excl (col)* να με πάρει ο διάβολος.

blind [blaɪnd] *a* τυφλός, στραβός || *(alley etc)* αδιέξοδος ♦ *n* τέντα || *(excuse)* πρόσχημα *nt*, υποκρισία ♦ *vt* τυφλώνω, στραβώνω || ~**fold** *a* με δεμένα μάτια ♦ *vt* δένω τα μάτια || ~**ly** *ad* στα τυφλά, στα στραβά || ~**ness** *n* τυφλότητα, στραβομάρα.

blink [blɪŋk] *vti* ανοιγοκλείνω τα μάτια, μισοκλείνω τα μάτια || ~**ers** *npl* παρωπίδες *fpl*.

blinking ['blɪŋkɪŋ] *a (col)* = **bloody**.

bliss [blɪs] *n* μακαριότητα, ευδαιμονία.

blister ['blɪstə*] *n (on skin)* φυσαλίδα, φουσκάλα || *(on surfaces etc)* φουσκάλα ♦ *vti* φουσκαλιάζω, φλυκταινούμαι.

blithe [blaɪð] *a* χαρούμενος, εύθυμος.

blitz [blɪts] *n* μπλιτς *nt inv*, αιφνίδια επίθεση.

blizzard ['blɪzəd] *n* χιονοθύελλα.

bloated ['bləʊtɪd] *a* φουσκωμένος, πρησμένος.

bloc [blɒk] *n (POL)* συνασπισμός, μπλόκ *nt inv*.

block [blɒk] *n (piece)* τεμάχιο, μεγάλο κομμάτι || *(for chopping)* επικόπανο, πικόπι || *(traffic)* συνωστισμός, διακοπή || *(obstacle)* εμπόδιο || *(city)* τετράγωνο ♦ *vt* φράσσω, εμποδίζω || ~**ade** n αποκλεισμός, μπλόκο ♦ vt αποκλείω, μπλοκάρω || ~**age** n εμπλοκή, μπλοκάρισμα nt.

bloke [bləʊk] n (col) άνθρωπος.

blond(e) [blɒnd] a ξανθός, ξανθή ♦ n ξανθός, ξανθιά.

blood [blʌd] n αίμα nt || (kinship) συγγένεια || (descent) καταγωγή || ~**donor** n αιμοδότης/τρια m/f || ~**group** n ομάδα αίματος || ~ **pressure** n πίεση αίματος || ~**shed** n αιματοχυσία || ~**shot** a κόκκινος || ~**stained** a αιματοσταγής, ματωμένος || ~**stream** n κυκλοφοριακό σύστημα nt || ~**thirsty** a αιμοβόρος || ~ **transfusion** n μετάγγιση αίματος || ~**y** a (col) παλιο-, βρωμο- || (lit) αιματηρός || ~**y-minded** a τζαναμπέτης.

bloom [blu:m] n (flower) λουλούδι || (perfection) άνθηση, ακμή ♦ vi ανθίζω || in ~ στην άνθησή του.

blossom [ˈblɒsəm] n άνθος nt ♦ vi ανθίζω.

blot [blɒt] n λεκές m || (disgrace) κηλίδα ♦ vt (stain) λεκιάζω || (dry ink) στυπώνω, τραβώ || to ~ **out** vt εξαφανίζω, σβήνω.

blotchy [ˈblɒtʃɪ] a γεμάτος κοκκινίλες.

blotting paper [ˈblɒtɪŋpeɪpə*] n στυπόχαρτο.

blouse [blaʊz] n μπλούζα.

blow [bləʊ] (irreg v) n (with fist) κτύπημα nt, γροθιά || (with stick) ραβδισμός || (of air) φύσημα nt || (of fate) πλήγμα nt ♦ vt φυσάω || (a fuse) καίομαι || (col: squander) σπαταλάω || at a single ~ μ'ένα κτύπημα || to ~ one's top ξεσπάω || to ~ over vi περνώ, ξεθυμαίνω || to ~ up vi σκάω, ανατινάσσω ♦ vt (tyre) φουσκώνω || ~**lamp** n καμινευτήρι || ~**out** n (AUT) κλατάρισμα nt || ~**y** a ανεμώδης.

blubber [ˈblʌbə*] n λίπος nt φάλαινας.

blue [blu:] a γαλάζιος, γαλανός || (paint) μπλέ || (with cold etc) μελανιασμένος ♦ a: to have the ~s μελαγχολώ || ~**bell** n ζμπούλι || ~**bottle** n κρεατόμυγα || ~**print** n κυανοτυπία, σχέδιο.

bluff [blʌf] n (deception) μπλόφα, απάτη ♦ vt μπλοφάρω, εξαπατώ ♦ a ντόμπρος.

blunder [ˈblʌndə*] n μεγάλο λάθος nt, χοντροκοπιά ♦ vi κάνω γκάφα.

blunt [blʌnt] a αμβλύς, στομωμένος || (person) μονοκόμματος ♦ vt αμβλύνω, στομώνω || ~**ly** ad απότομα, ντόμπρα.

blur [blɜ:*] n θολούρα, θαμπάδα (stain) μουτζούρα ♦ vti θολώνω, θαμπώνω.

blurt [blɜ:t] to ~ **out** vt λέω κάτι απερίσκεπτα, αποκαλύπτω.

blush [blʌʃ] vi κοκκινίζω ♦ n κοκκίνισμα nt.

bluster [ˈblʌstə*] vi (of wind) φυσώ δυνατά || (of person) κάνω φασαρία, κομπάζω.

boar [bɔ:*] n γουρούνι αρσενικό, κάπρι.

board [bɔ:d] n (of wood) σανίδα, τάβλα || (notice) πινακίδα, ταμπλώ nt inv || (of paper) χαρτόνι || (meal) φαΐ || (of men) συμβούλιο, επιτροπή ♦ vt (feed) δίνω τροφή || (ship, train) επιβαίνω, μπαρκάρω || (with planks) σανιδώνω || ~ and lodging φαΐ και ύπνος || to ~ up vt (περι)φράσσω με σανίδες || ~**er** n οικότροφος || (lodger) ένοικος || ~**ing house** n πανσιόν f inv || ~**ing school** n σχολή με οικοτροφείο || ~**ing school pupil** n εσωτερικός.

boast [bəʊst] vi καυχώμαι, κομπορρημονώ ♦ n κομπασμός, καυχησιολογία || ~**ful** a καυχησιάρης, φανφαρόνος.

boat [bəʊt] n βάρκα, καΐκι || (ship) καράβι || ~**er** (hat) ναυτική ψάθα || ~**ing** n λεμβοδρομία με βάρκα || ~**swain** [ˈbəʊsən] n λοστρόμος.

bob [bɒb] vi ανεβοκατεβαίνω.

bobbin [ˈbɒbɪn] n πηνίο, κουβαρίστρα || (ELEC) μπομπίνα.

bobsleigh [ˈbɒbsleɪ] n μπομπσλέϊ nt inv, έλκηθρο.

bodice [ˈbɒdɪs] n στήθος nt φορέματος, μπούστος.

bodily [ˈbɒdɪlɪ] ad σωματικά || (together) συλλογικά, όλοί μαζί.

body [ˈbɒdɪ] n σώμα nt, κορμί || (legislative etc) σώμα, σωματείο || (collection) μεγάλο πλήθος nt, μάζα || (of car etc) σώμα, κύριο μέρος nt || ~**guard** n σωματοφύλακας || ~**work** n καρότσα.

bog [bɒg] n έλος nt ♦ vi: to get ~ged down βουλιάζω.

boggle [ˈbɒgl] vi διστάζω.

bogus [ˈbəʊgəs] a ψεύτικος.

boil [bɔɪl] vt (potatoes etc) βράζω ♦ vi βράζω, κοχλάζω ♦ n (MED) καλόγερος || to come to the ~ παίρνω βράση || ~**er** n λέβης, καζάνι || ~**ing point** n σημείο βρασμού.

boisterous [ˈbɔɪstərəs] a θορυβώδης, ταραχώδης.

bold [bəʊld] a τολμηρός, θαρραλέος || ~**ness** n τολμηρότητα, θάρρος nt.

bollard [ˈbɒləd] n δέστρα.

bolster [ˈbəʊlstə*] n μαξιλάρα || to ~ up vt (υπο)στηρίζω.

bolt [bəʊlt] n (of door etc) σύρτης, μάνταλο || (rush away) εξόρμηση, φυγή ♦ vt (a door etc) μανταλώνω, κλειδώνω || (food) καταβροχθίζω ♦ vi (rush away) φεύγω, εξορμώ || (escape) δραπετεύω.

bomb [bɒm] n βόμβα ♦ vt βομβαρδίζω || ~**ard** [bɒmˈbɑ:d] vt βομβαρδίζω, σφυροκοπώ || ~**ardment** n βομβαρδισμός || ~**er** n (person) βομβαρδιστής || (AVIAT) βομβαρδιστικό || ~**ing** βομβαρδισμός || ~**shell** n (fig) κατάπληξη, σαν βόμβα.

bona fide [ˈbəʊnəˈfaɪdɪ] a καλής πίστεως.

bond [bɒnd] n (link) δεσμός, συνάφεια || (promise) υπόσχεση, σύμβαση || (ECON) ομολογία.

bone [bəʊn] n κόκκαλο ♦ vt ξεκοκκαλίζω || ~**-dry** a εντελώς ξηρός, κατάξερος.

bonfire ['bɒnfaɪə*] n φωτιά.

bonnet ['bɒnɪt] n γυναικείο καπέλλο || (child's) σκουφίτσα || (cap) σκούφος, μπερές m || (Brit: of car) καπό.

bonus ['bəʊnəs] n επιμίσθιο, επίδομα nt.

bony ['bəʊnɪ] a κοκκαλιάρης.

boo [bu:] vt αποδοκιμάζω, γιουχαΐζω.

book [buk] n βιβλίο, κιτάπι ♦ vt (ticket etc) βγάζω εισιτήριο || (a room) κλείνω δωμάτιο || (person) πληρώνω, τιμωρούμαι || ~case n βιβλιοθήκη || ~ing office n πρακτορείο εισιτηρίων || ~-keeping n λογιστική || ~let n φυλλάδιο, βιβλιαράκι || ~maker n (RACING) μπουκμέικερ m inv || ~ seller n βιβλιοπώλης || ~shop n βιβλιοπωλείο || ~stall n πάγκος βιβλιοπώλου || ~store n = ~shop.

boom [bu:m] n (noise) κρότος, βόμβος || (NAUT) απόστης || (port) φράγμα nt || (busy period) μπούμ nt inv, κύμα nt ευημερίας, αιχμή ευημερίας ♦ vi ανέρχομαι, ανεβαίνω.

boon [bu:n] n (blessing) όφελος nt.

boorish ['bʊərɪʃ] a άξεστος, αγροίκος.

boost [bu:st] n προώθηση ♦ vt προωθώ, ενισχύω.

boot [bu:t] n μπότα || (Brit: of car) πορτμπαγκάζ nt inv ♦ vt (kick) λακτίζω, κλωτσάω || to ~ (in addition) επί πλέον.

booze [bu:z] n ποτό ♦ vi ξεφαντώνω, μεθοκοπώ.

border ['bɔ:də*] n (frontier) σύνορο, μεθόριος f || (edge) γύρος, σειρίτι, μπορντούρα || (page etc) πλαίσιο, βινιέτα || to ~ on vt συνορεύω με || ~line n (fig) εγγίζων τα όρια.

bore [bɔ:*] pt of bear || n (person or thing) πληκτικός, ενοχλητικός, αφόρητος || (of gun etc) διαμέτρημα nt ♦ vt τρυπώ, ανοίγω τρύπα || (weary) πλήττω, λιμάρω || ~dom n πλήξη, ανία.

boring ['bɔ:rɪŋ] a ανιαρός, βαρετός.

born [bɔ:n] pp: to be ~ γεννιέμαι.

borough ['bʌrə] n (διοικητική) περιφέρεια.

borrow ['bɒrəʊ] vt δανείζομαι.

bosom ['bʊzəm] n στήθος nt, κόρφος.

boss [bɒs] n κύφωμα nt, καμπούρα || (master) το αφεντικό ♦ vt διευθύνω, κάνω το διευθυντή || ~y a αυταρχικός.

bosun ['bəʊsn] n = boatswain || see boat.

botanical [bə'tænɪkəl] a βοτανικός.

botanist ['bɒtənɪst] n βοτανολόγος m/f.

botany ['bɒtənɪ] n βοτανική.

botch [bɒtʃ] vt φτιάνω σαπατσούλικα, κουτσουτσιάχνω || (patch) κουτσουμπαλώνω.

both [bəʊθ] a, pron αμφότεροι, και οι δύο ♦ ad και... και || ~ όχι μόνο... αλλά και....

bother ['bɒðə*] n ενόχληση, μπελάς ♦ vt ενοχλώ, πειράζω, σκοτίζω ♦ vi στενοχωριέμαι, νοιάζομαι.

bottle ['bɒtl] n φιάλη, μπουκάλι, μποτίλια ♦ vt εμφιαλώνω, μπουκαλάρω, μποτιλιάρω || ~neck n (production)

δυσχέρεια || (traffic) συνωστισμός || ~- opener n ανοιχτήρι για μπουκάλες.

bottom ['bɒtəm] n κάτω μέρος nt, βάθος nt || (of sea etc) πυθμένας, βυθός || (seat) πισινός, ποπός || (ship) πλοίο || κάτω μέρος nt, κάτω-κάτω || (lowest) κατώτατος || ~less a απύθμενος.

bough [baʊ] n κλάδος, κλαδί.

bought [bɔ:t] pt, pp of buy.

boulder ['bəʊldə*] n λίθος, λιθάρι, ογκόλιθος.

bounce [baʊns] n (rebound) αναπήδηση, γκελ nt inv ♦ vi κάνω γκελ, αναπηδώ || (col: person) μπαίνω-βγαίνω ξαφνικά ♦ vt κάνω μπάλα να κάνει γκελ.

bound [baʊnd] pt, pp of bind || n όριο, σύνορο || (restriction) όρια ntpl || (leap) πήδημα nt ♦ vi (spring, leap) πηδώ, σκιρτώ || (limit) περιορίζω ♦ a προορίζομενς , για, κατευθυνόμενος προς.

boundary ['baʊndərɪ] n όριο, σύνορο.

bouquet ['bʊkeɪ] n μπουκέτο.

bout [baʊt] n (contest) γύρος, αγώνας, συνάντηση || (of illness) προσβολή.

bow [bəʊ] n (curve) καμπή || (ribbon) φιόγκος || (weapon) τόξο, δοξάρι || (MUS) δοξάρι βιολιού.

bow [baʊ] vi υποκλίνομαι, σκύβω το κεφάλι ♦ vt κλίνω, κάμπτω || (submit) υποκύπτω, υποτάσσομαι ♦ n υπόκλιση, κλίση (της κεφαλής) || (of ship) πλώρη.

bowels [baʊəlz] npl έντερα ntpl, σπλάχνα ntpl || (fig) σπλάχνα ntpl.

bowl [bəʊl] n (basin) λεκάνη, γαβάθα || (of pipe) λουλάς || (wooden ball) σφαίρα ♦ vti παίζω μπάλα, ρίχνω μπάλα || ~s npl παιχνίδι της μπάλας.

bow-legged ['bəʊlɛgɪd] a στραβοπόδης, στραβοκάνης.

bowler ['bəʊlə*] n παίκτης της μπάλας || (hat) μελόν nt.

bowling ['bəʊlɪŋ] n (game) παιχνίδι της μπάλας, μπόλιγκ nt inv.

bow tie ['bəʊ'taɪ] n παπιγιόν nt inv, πεταλούδα.

box [bɒks] n κιβώτιο || (small) κουτί || (THEAT) θεωρείο || (s.o.'s ears) καρπαζώνω || (package) πακετάρω ♦ vi πυγμαχώ, παίζω μποξ || ~er n (person) πυγμάχος, μποξέρ m inv || (dog) μπόξερ m inv || ~ing n (SPORT) πυγμαχία, μποξ nt inv || ~ office n ταμείο (θεάτρου) || ~ room n αποθήκη οικίας.

boy [bɔɪ] n αγόρι, παιδί.

boycott ['bɔɪkɒt] n μπούκοτάρισμα ♦ vt αποκλείω, μπουκοτάρω.

boyfriend ['bɔɪfrɛnd] n φίλος, αγαπημένος.

boyish ['bɔɪɪʃ] a παιδιάστικος, αγορίστικος.

bra [bra:] n σουτιέν nt inv, στηθόδεσμος.

brace [breɪs] n (clamp) δεσμός || (pair) ζευγάρι || (support) στύλωμα nt || (tool) ματικάπι ♦ vt συνδέω, στερεώνω || (o.s.) τονώνω, δυναμώνω || ~s npl τιράντες fpl.

bracelet ['breɪslɪt] n βραχιόλι.

bracing ['breɪsɪŋ] a τονωτικός.

bracken ['brækən] n φτέρη.

bracket ['brækit] n (support) υποστήριγμα nt, ωτίδα, κρεμάθρα || (round) παρένθεση || (square) αγκύλη || (group) ομάδα ♦ vt βάζω σε παρένθεση || (associate) συνδέω.

brag [bræg] vi καυχώμαι.

braid [breid] n (of hair) πλεξίδα, πλεξούδα || (officer's etc) σειρήτι, κορδόνι.

Braille [breil] n Μπράϊλ nt inv.

brain [brein] n εγκέφαλος, μυαλό || (person) διάνοια || ~s npl μυαλά ntpl || ~washing n πλύση εγκεφάλου || ~wave n έμπνευση, επινόηση || ~y a ευφυής.

braise [breiz] vt ψήνω στην κατσαρόλα.

brake [breik] n (on vehicle) τροχοπέδη, φρένο ♦ vti φρενάρω, πατώ φρένο.

bramble ['bræmbl] n βάτος.

branch [brɑːntʃ] n (of tree) κλάδος, κλαδί || (division) κλάδος || (office) υποκατάστημα nt ♦ vi διακλαδούμαι, χωρίζομαι.

brand [brænd] n (trademark) μάρκα || (on cattle) σφράγιση με καυμένο σίδηρο.

brand-new ['brænd'njuː] a κατακαίνουργιος, ολοκαίνουργιος, του κουτιού.

brandy ['brændɪ] n κονιάκ nt inv.

brash [bræʃ] a αναιδής, αδιάντροπος.

brass [brɑːs] n μπρούτζος || ~ band n μπάντα, φανφάρα.

brat [bræt] n κουτσούβελο, διαβολάκι.

bravado [brəˈvɑːdəʊ] n παλληκαρισμός.

brave [breiv] a γενναίος || (show) περίφημος ♦ n ερυθρόδερμος πολεμιστής ♦ vt αψηφώ || ~ry n θάρρος nt, ανδρεία.

brawl [brɔːl] n καυγάς ♦ vi καυγαδίζω.

brawn [brɔːn] n μυϊκή δύναμη, δύναμη || (COOKING) πηχτή.

brazen ['breizn] a (metal) μπρούτζινος || (shameless) αναιδής, ξετσίπωτος ♦ vt : to ~ it out καυχώμαι ξεδιάντροπα.

brazier ['breiziə*] n μαγκάλι, φουφού f inv.

Brazil [brəˈzil] n Βραζιλία || ~ian a βραζιλιανός ♦ n Βραζιλιάνος/n m/f || ~nut n Βραζιλιανό καρύδι.

breach [briːtʃ] n (gap) ρήγμα nt, τρύπα || (of trust, duty) παραβίαση, παράβαση || (quarrel) ρήξη, τσάκωμα nt ♦ vt γκρεμίζω.

bread [brɛd] n ψωμί || (living) καθημερινό ψωμί || ~ and butter n μέσα συντηρήσεως || ~crumbs npl ψίχουλα ntpl || ~winner n στήριγμα nt της οικογενείας.

break [breik] (irreg v) vt (crush) συντρίβω, τσακίζω || (apart) σπάω || (promise) αθετώ || (silence etc) διακόπτω || (habit) κόβω || (the law) παραβιάζω ♦ vi θραύομαι, τσακίζομαι || (friendship etc) τα χαλώ || (dissolve) διαλύομαι ♦ n (gap) ρήξη, άνοιγμα nt, χάσμα nt || (rest) διακοπή, διάλειμμα nt || (chance) ευκαιρία, τύχη || (fracture) ρωγμή || to ~

free or **loose** vi δραπετεύω, απελευθερώνομαι || to ~ in vt (a horse etc) δαμάζω || (conversation) διακόπτω ♦ vi (burglar) κάνω διάρρηξη || to ~ out vi ξεσπώ || (of prison) δραπετεύω || to ~ up vi διαλύομαι ♦ vt χωρίζω, συντρίβω, τεμαχίζω || ~able a εύθραυστος || ~age n σπάσιμο, ράγισμα nt || ~down n (in discussions) διακοπή || (of health) κατάρρευση || (mental) χάσιμο του μυαλού || ~er n (NAUT) κύμα nt.

breakfast ['brɛkfəst] n πρωινό, κολατσιό.

breakthrough ['breikθruː] n δίοδος f, ρήγμα nt.

breakwater ['breikwɔːtə*] n κυματοθραύστης.

breast [brɛst] n (of woman) μαστός, βυζί || (of man, animal) στήθος nt || ~stroke n απλωτή.

breath [brɛθ] n πνοή, αναπνοή || out of ~ λαχανιασμένος.

breathe [briːð] vti αναπνέω || ~r n ανάσα.

breathless ['brɛθlɪs] a λαχανιασμένος.

bred [brɛd] pt, pp of **breed**.

breed [briːd] (irreg v) n γενεά, ράτσα ♦ vt γεννώ, φέρνω || (animals) τρέφω ♦ vi αναπαράγομαι || ~er n (person) αναπαραγωγός m/f, κτηνοτρόφος m/f || ~ing n ανατροφή.

breeze [briːz] n αύρα, αεράκι.

breezy ['briːzɪ] a εύαερος || (person) γεμάτος ζωή.

brevity ['brɛvitɪ] n βραχύτητα, συντομία.

brew [bruː] vt (drinks) παρασκευάζω (μπύρα) αποστάζω || (tea) βράζω || (plot) μηχανορραφώ ♦ vi βράζομαι || (storm etc) έρχεται || ~ery n ζυθοποιία, ποτοποιία.

bribe [braib] n δωροδοκία ♦ vt δωροδοκώ, λαδώνω || ~ry n δωροδοκία, μπούκωμα nt.

brick [brik] n πλίνθος, τούβλο || ~layer n τουβλάς || ~work n πλινθοδομή.

bridal ['braidl] a νυφικός, γαμήλιος.

bride [braid] n νύφη || ~groom n γαμπρός || ~smaid n παράνυφη.

bridge [bridʒ] n γεφύρι, γιοφύρι || (NAUT) γέφυρα || (CARDS) μπριτζ nt inv || (of nose) ράχη της μύτης ♦ vt γεφυρώνω.

bridle ['braidl] n χαλινάρι, γκέμι ♦ vt (a horse) χαλινώνω || (control) χαλιναγωγώ.

brief [briːf] a σύντομος, βραχύς ♦ n (LAW) δικογραφία, φάκελος ♦ vt δίδω οδηγίες, ενημερώνω || ~s npl κοντή κυλόττα || ~case n χαρτοφύλακας || ~ing n καταρτισμός, οδηγίες fpl.

brigade [briˈgeid] n (MIL) ταξιαρχία || see **fire**.

brigadier [brigəˈdiə*] n ταξίαρχος.

bright [brait] a (as light) φωτεινός, λαμπερός, γυαλιστερός || (weather) φωτεινός, καθαρός || (clever) έξυπνος, ευφυής || (colour) ζωηρός, λαμπρός ||

~ **en** vti ζωηρεύω, φωτίζομαι, αστράφτω.

brilliance ['brɪljəns] n λαμπρότητα, εξυπνάδα || (of surface etc) φωτεινότητα || (of style) ζωηρότητα.

brilliant ['brɪljənt] a φωτεινός, λαμπρός || (person) σπουδαίος, λαμπρός || (splendid) έξοχος.

brim [brɪm] n (of cup) χείλος nt || (of hat) γύρος, μπορ nt inv ♦ vi ξεχειλίζω || ~ful a ξέχειλος.

brine [braɪn] n σαλαμούρα, άρμη.

bring [brɪŋ] (irreg v) vt φέρω, φέρνω || to ~ about vt επιτυγχάνω, καταφέρνω || to ~ off vt φέρω σε πέρας || to ~ round or to vt επαναφέρω, συνεφέρω || to ~ up vt (raise) ανατρέφω, μεγαλώνω || (introduce) προβάλλω, θέτω.

brisk [brɪsk] a ζωηρός.

bristle ['brɪsl] n γουρουνότριχα ♦ vi ανατριχιάζω.

Britain ['brɪtən] n Βρεττανία.

British ['brɪtɪʃ] a Βρετανικός, αγγλικός || the ~ npl οι Άγγλοι mpl || ~ Isles npl Βρεττανικαί Νήσοι fpl.

Briton ['brɪtən] n Βρετανός/ίδα m/f.

brittle ['brɪtl] a εύθραυστος.

broach [brəʊtʃ] vt (subject) θίγω (ζήτημα).

broad [brɔːd] a ευρύς, φαρδύς, πλατύς || (daylight) το φως της ημέρας || (general) απλό, γενικό || (accent) χωριάτικη προφορά || ~cast n εκπομπή ♦ vti μεταδίδω ραδιοφωνικώς || ~casting n εκπομπή, μετάδοση || ~en vt ευρύνω, πλαταίνω ♦ vi ευρύνομαι, ανοίγω || ~ly ad ευρέως, πλατειά || ~-minded a με ανοικτό μυαλό, ανεκτικός, ευρείας αντιλήψεως.

broccoli ['brɒkəlɪ] n μπρόκολο.

brochure ['brəʊʃjʊə*] n φυλλάδιο, μπροσούρα.

broke [brəʊk] pt of break ♦ a απένταρος || ~n pp of break || ~n-hearted a με ραγισμένη καρδιά.

broker ['brəʊkə*] n μεσίτης, χρηματιστής.

bronchitis [brɒŋ'kaɪtɪs] n βρογχίτιδα.

bronze [brɒnz] n μπρούντζος || ~d a ηλιοψημένος, μαυρισμένος.

brooch [brəʊtʃ] n καρφίτσα.

brood [bruːd] n κλώσσισμα nt, γενιά ♦ vi κλωσσώ || (meditate) μελαγχολώ.

brook [brʊk] n (stream) ρυάκι, ρέμα nt.

broom [brʊm] n σκούπα || ~stick n σκουπόξυλο.

Bros. (abbr of Brothers) Αφοι (Αδελφοί mpl).

broth [brɒθ] n ζουμί κρέατος, σούπα.

brothel ['brɒθl] n μπορντέλο, οίκος ανοχής.

brother ['brʌðə*] n αδελφός || ~-in-law n γαμπρός, κουνιάδος.

brought [brɔːt] pt, pp of bring.

brow [braʊ] n (forehead) κούτελο, μέτωπο || (eyebrow) φρύδι || (of hill etc) χείλος nt, φρύδι.

brown [braʊn] a καστανός, καφετής ♦ n καφετής ♦ vti σκουραίνω, μαυρίζω || (cooking) καβουρδίζω || ~ie n (girl guide) προσκοπίνα.

browse [braʊz] vi (examine casually) ξεφυλλίζω, βόσκω, τριγυρίζω.

bruise [bruːz] n μώλωπας, κτύπημα nt ♦ vti κτυπώ, κτυπιέμαι.

brunette [bruː'net] n μελαχροινή.

brunt [brʌnt] n ορμή, φόρα.

brush [brʌʃ] n βούρτσα || (paint) πινέλο || (fight) σύγκρουση ♦ vt βουρτσίζω || (lightly) ξεσκονίζω || to ~ aside vt παραμερίζω || ~wood n θάμνοι mpl, χαμόκλαδα ntpl.

brusque [bruːsk] a απότομος, τραχύς.

Brussels sprout ['brʌslz'spraʊt] n (Βελγικό) λαχανάκι, πετί-σού.

brutal ['bruːtl] a κτηνώδης || ~ity n κτηνωδία.

brute [bruːt] n κτήνος nt, θηρίο.

B.Sc. abbr see **bachelor**.

bubble ['bʌbl] n μπουρμπουλήθρα, φουσκάλα ♦ vi κοχλάζω || (river, wine) αφρίζω || to ~ over (fig) ξεχειλίζω.

buck [bʌk] n ελάφι αρσενικό || (rabbit) κούνελος ♦ vt ενθαρρύνω, δίνω κουράγιο || to ~ up vt ενθαρρύνομαι, (ξανα) παίρνω κουράγιο.

bucket ['bʌkɪt] n κουβάς, κάδος.

buckle ['bʌkl] n πόρπη, φιούμπα ♦ vt κουμπώνω, θηλυκώνω || (bend) λυγίζω, στραβώνω.

bud [bʌd] n μπουμπούκι.

Buddhism ['bʊdɪzəm] n Βουδδισμός.

budding ['bʌdɪŋ] a που μπουμπουκιάζει.

buddy ['bʌdɪ] n φιλαράκος.

budge [bʌdʒ] vti κινούμαι, υποχωρώ.

budgerigar ['bʌdʒərɪgaː*] n παπαγαλάκι.

budget ['bʌdʒɪt] n προϋπολογισμός.

buff [bʌf] a (colour) σαμουά, κρεατί.

buffalo ['bʌfələʊ] n βουβάλι.

buffer ['bʌfə*] n αποσβεστήρας, αμορτισέρ nt inv.

buffet ['bʌfɪt] n πλήγμα nt, κτύπημα nt || ['bʊfeɪ] (bar) αναψυκτήριο || (food) μπουφές m inv ♦ vt πλήττω, κτυπώ.

buffoon [bə'fuːn] n παλιάτσος, καραγκιόζης.

bug [bʌg] n (insect) κοριός || (US) ζωύφιο || (spy device) κρυφό μικρόφωνο || (COMPUT) λάθος nt, σφάλμα nt.

bugle ['bjuːgl] n σάλπιγγα.

build [bɪld] (irreg v) vt οικοδομώ, χτίζω || ~er n οικοδόμος, κατασκευαστής || ~ing n κτίριο, οικοδομή || ~ing society n οικοδομικός συνεταιρισμός || ~-up n διαφήμιση.

built [bɪlt] pt, pp of build || well-~ a (person) γεροδεμένος || ~-in a (cupboard) εντοιχισμένος.

bulb [bʌlb] n (BOT) βολβός || (ELEC) λάμπα, γλόμπος.

Bulgaria [bʌl'gɛərɪə] n Βουλγαρία.

bulge [bʌldʒ] n διόγκωση, φούσκωμα nt ♦ vti προεξέχω, εξογκούμαι, φουσκώνω.

bulk [bʌlk] n μέγεθος nt, όγκος || (greater part) μεγαλύτερο μέρος nt|| ~**head** n διάφραγμα nt|| ~**y** a ογκώδης, χοντρός.

bull [bul] n ταύρος || (rubbish) ψέματα ntpl, αρλούμπες fpl|| ~**dog** n μπουλντόγκ m inv.

bulldozer ['buldəuzə*] n μπουλντόζα.

bullet ['bulit] n σφαίρα, βόλι.

bulletin ['bulitin] n δελτίο, ανακοινωθέν nt.

bullfight ['bulfait] n ταυρομαχία.

bullion ['buljən] n χρυσός (άργυρος) σε ράβδους.

bullock ['bulək] n βόδι, μοσχάρι.

bull's-eye ['bulzai] n κέντρο (στόχου).

bully ['buli] n τύραννος ♦ vt απειλώ, τρομοκρατώ.

bum [bʌm] n (col) πισινός || (tramp) αλήτης, ακαμάτης || **to ~ around** vi κοπροσκυλιάζω.

bump [bʌmp] n (blow) κτύπημα nt, τίναγμα nt|| (bruise) πρήξιμο, καρούλα, καρούμπαλο ♦ vti κτυπώ, σκοντάφτω || ~ **er** n (car) προφυλακτήρας ♦ a: ~ **er harvest** πλούσια (σοδειά).

bumpy ['bʌmpi] a ανώμαλος (δρόμος).

bun [bʌn] n σταφιδόψωμο, κουλουράκι.

bunch [bʌntʃ] n μάτσο, φούχτα, χούφτα, δέμα nt.

bundle ['bʌndl] n δέμα nt, μπόγος ♦ vt πακετάρω, δένω || (also: ~ **off**) ξεφορτώνομαι.

bung [bʌŋ] n πώμα nt, τάπα ♦ vt (throw) ρίχνω, χώνω.

bungalow ['bʌŋgələu] n μπάγκαλο, εξοχικό σπίτι.

bungle ['bʌŋgl] vt τα κάνω θάλασσα, είμαι αδέξιος.

bunion ['bʌnjən] n κάλος.

bunk [bʌŋk] n κλίνη, κουκέτα.

bunker ['bʌŋkə*] n αποθήκη καυσίμων, καρβουνιέρα.

bunny ['bʌni] n κουνελάκι.

bunting ['bʌntiŋ] n ύφασμα nt για σημαίες, σημαιοστολισμός.

buoy [bɔi] n (NAUT) σημαδούρα || (lifebuoy) σωσσίβιο || ~ **ant** a (of person) εύθυμος, κεφάτος || **to ~ up** vt ενισχύω, αναθαρρύνω, ενθαρρύνω.

burden ['bɜːdn] n φόρτωμα nt, βάρος nt, δυσβάστακτο βάρος ♦ vt (επι)βαρύνω, φορτώνω.

bureau [bjuə'rəu] n γραφείο που κλείνει || (for information etc) υπηρεσία πληροφοριών.

bureaucracy [bjuə'rɔkrəsi] n γραφειοκρατία.

burglar ['bɜːglə*] n διαρρήκτης/τρια m/f.: || ~ **alarm** n κουδούνι ασφαλείας || ~ **ize** vt (US) διαρρηγνύω || ~ **y** n διάρρηξη.

burgle ['bɜːgl] vt διαρρηγνύω.

burial ['beriəl] n ταφή || ~ **ground** n νεκροταφείο.

burlesque [bɜː'lesk] n επιθεώρηση, μπυρλέσκ nt inv.

burly ['bɜːli] a γεροδεμένος.

burn [bɜːn] (irreg v) n έγκαυμα nt ♦ vt καίω ♦ vi φλέγομαι || **to ~ one's fingers** (fig) βρίσκω το μπελά μου || ~ **ing question** n φλέγον ζήτημα nt.

burnt [bɜːnt] pt, pp of **burn** ♦ a καμένος, ψημένος.

burrow ['bʌrəu] n φωλιά, τρύπα, λαγούμι ♦ vti σκάβω λαγούμι, ανοίγω τρύπα.

burst [bɜːst] (irreg v) n έκρηξη, ριπή ♦ vt (explode) προκαλώ έκρηξη || (break) σπάζω || (break out) διαρρηγνύω, σπάω ♦ vi (tank etc) διαρρηγνύομαι, σπάζω || (flower) σκάζω, ανοίγω || (into pieces) γίνομαι κομμάτια.

bury ['beri] vt (inter) θάβω || (hide) κρύβομαι, χώνω, βυθίζομαι.

bus [bʌs] n λεωφορείο.

bush [buʃ] n θάμνος, χαμόκλαδο.

bushy ['buʃi] a δασύς, πυκνός.

busily ['bizili] ad δραστήρια.

business ['biznis] n επιχείρηση, δουλειά || (concern) δουλειά || ~ **man** n επιχειρηματίας.

bus stop ['bʌsstɔp] n στάση λεωφορείου.

bust [bʌst] n (statue) προτομή, μπούστος || (of woman) στήθος nt.

bustle ['bʌsl] n (θορυβώδης) κίνηση, πάταγος ♦ vi πηγαινοέρχομαι, βιάζομαι.

busy ['bizi] a απασχολημένος, πολυάσχολος ♦ vt ασχολούμαι, φροντίζω || ~ **body** n πολυπράγμονας, παπατρέχας.

but [bʌt] cj (still, yet, besides) αλλά, μα ♦ ad (only, except, as) μόνο, μόλις, δεν... παρά ♦ prep (except) εκτός, παρά.

butane ['bjuːtein] n βουτάνιο.

butcher ['butʃə*] n χασάπης || (savage) σφαγέας ♦ vt σφάζω.

butler ['bʌtlə*] n μπάτλερ m inv, αρχιυπηρέτης.

butt [bʌt] n (cask) βαρέλι, βουτσί || (target) στόχος || (of cigarette) αποτσίγαρο, γόπα || (thick end) χοντρό άκρο ♦ vt κτυπώ με το κεφάλι.

butter ['bʌtə*] n βούτυρο ♦ vt βουτυρώνω || **to ~ up** vt (fig) κολακεύω, ξεσκονίζω.

butterfly ['bʌtəflai] n πεταλούδα.

buttocks ['bʌtəks] npl γλουτοί mpl, τα οπίσθια ntpl.

button ['bʌtn] n κουμπί ♦ vti κουμπώνω || ~ **hole** n κουμπότρυπα.

buttress ['bʌtris] n αντέρεισμα nt.

buy [bai] (irreg v) vt αγοράζω || **to ~ up** vt αγοράζω χονδρικώς || ~ **er** n αγοραστής.

buzz [bʌz] n βούισμα nt ♦ vi βουίζω.

buzzard ['bʌzəd] n ικτίνος.

buzzer ['bʌzə*] n βομβητής, ψιθυριστής.

by [bai] prep (near, beside) παρά, πλάι, δίπλα, κοντά || (through) διά, από || (with) από, με || ~ **and large** κατά κανόνα || ~ **far** κατά πολύ || ~ **name** κατ' όνομα.

by-election ['baiilekʃn] n αναπληρωματικές εκλογές fpl.

bygone ['baɪgɒn] a περασμένος, παλιός ♦ n: let ~s be ~s περασμένα, ξεχασμένα.

bypass ['baɪpɑːs] n (MECH) βοηθητική δίοδος.

byproduct ['baɪprɒdʌkt] n υποπροϊόν.

bystander ['baɪstændə*] n παριστάμενος.

byte [baɪt] n (COMPUT) byte.

C

C. abbr of **centigrade**.

cab [kæb] n αμάξι, ταξί || (of train, truck) θέση οδηγού.

cabaret ['kæbəreɪ] n καμπαρέ nt inv.

cabbage ['kæbɪdʒ] n λάχανο.

cabin ['kæbɪn] n καλύβα || (NAUT) καμπίνα || ~ **cruiser** n θαλαμηγός f χωρίς κατάρτια.

cabinet ['kæbɪnɪt] n κομό || (POL) υπουργικό συμβούλιο || ~**maker** n επιπλοποιός.

cable ['keɪbl] n καλώδιο || (message) τηλεγράφημα nt ♦ vti τηλεγραφώ || ~ **railway** n κρεμαστός σιδηρόδρομος.

cackle ['kækl] n κακάρισμα nt ♦ vi κακαρίζω.

cactus ['kæktəs] n κάκτος.

caddie, caddy ['kædɪ] n κάντι.

cadet [kə'dɛt] n (NAUT) δόκιμος || (MIL) εύελπις || (AVIAT) ίκαρος.

cadge [kædʒ] vt ζητιανεύω, σελεμίζω.

Caesarean [siː'zɛərɪən] a: ~ (**section**) καισαρική (τομή).

café ['kæfeɪ] n καφενείο || (with food) κοφεστιατόριο || (bar) καφεμπάρ nt inv.

cafeteria [kæfɪ'tɪərɪə] n καφετηρία.

cage [keɪdʒ] n κλουβί ♦ vt εγκλουβίζω.

cagey ['keɪdʒɪ] a (col) πονηρός.

cajole [kə'dʒəʊl] vt καλοπιάνω.

cake [keɪk] n κέικ nt inv, γλύκισμα nt || (pie) πίτα || (of soap etc) πλάκα.

calamity [kə'læmɪtɪ] n συμφορά, καταστροφή.

calcium ['kælsɪəm] n ασβέστιο.

calculate ['kælkjuleɪt] vti υπολογίζω, λογαριάζω.

calculating ['kælkjuleɪtɪŋ] a υπολογιστικός, εσκεμμένος.

calculation [kælkju'leɪʃən] n υπολογισμός.

calculus ['kælkjuləs] n λογισμός.

calendar ['kæləndə*] n ημερολόγιο.

calf [kɑːf] n (cow) μοσχάρι || (skin) βιδέλο || (ANAT) κνήμη, γάμπα.

calibre, (US) caliber ['kælɪbə*] n διαμέτρημα nt || (fig) αξία ικανότητα.

call [kɔːl] vt καλώ, φωνάζω || (meeting) συγκαλώ || (TEL) κλήση, πρόσκληση ♦ vi (visit) επισκέπτομαι, έρχομαι ♦ n (shout) φωνή, κραυγή || (visit) επίσκεψη || ~**box** n τηλεφωνικός θάλαμος || ~ **er** n (visitor) επισκέπτης/τρια m/f || ~ **girl** n κοκότα || ~**ing** n (profession) επάγγελμα nt || to ~ **for** vt καλώ, έρχομαι || to ~ **off** vt

ακυρώνω, σταματώ, διακόπτω || to ~ **on** vt (visit) επισκέπτομαι || to ~ **up** vt (MIL) (επι)στρατεύω || (TEL) (προς)καλώ, τηλεφωνώ.

callous ['kæləs] a σκληρός, άκαρδος.

calm [kɑːm] n αταραξία ♦ vti καθησυχάζω ♦ a ήρεμος, ατάραχος || ~**ness** n ησυχία, κάλμα || to ~ **down** vi καταπραύνω, καλμάρω ♦ vt ηρεμώ, καθησυχάζω.

calorie ['kælərɪ] n θερμίδα.

camber ['kæmbə*] n καμπυλότητα, κυρτότητα.

came [keɪm] pt of **come**.

camel ['kæməl] n καμήλα.

cameo ['kæmɪəʊ] n καμέα.

camera ['kæmərə] n φωτογραφική μηχανή || ~**man** n οπερατέρ m inv.

camouflage ['kæməflɑːʒ] n καμουφλάρισμα nt ♦ vt καμουφλάρω.

camp [kæmp] n κατασκήνωση || (MIL) στρατόπεδο ♦ vi κατασκηνώνω || (MIL) στρατοπεδεύω.

campaign [kæm'peɪn] n εκστρατεία ♦ vi (also fig) εκστρατεύω, κάνω καμπάνια.

campbed ['kæmp'bɛd] n κρεββάτι εκστρατείας, ράντσο.

camper ['kæmpə*] n σκηνίτης, εκδρομέας.

camping ['kæmpɪŋ] n: to go ~ πηγαίνω σε κατασκήνωση.

campsite ['kæmpsaɪt] n τόπος κατασκηνώσεως.

can [kæn] auxiliary v (be able) δύναμαι, μπορώ || (be allowed) επιτρέπεται, μπορώ || (know how) γνωρίζω, ξέρω ♦ n τενεκές m, κουτί ♦ vt κονσερβοποιώ.

Canada ['kænədə] n Καναδάς.

Canadian [kə'neɪdɪən] a καναδικός ♦ n Καναδός/n m/f.

canal [kə'næl] n (waterway) διώρυγα, κανάλι || (ANAT) σωλήνας, πόρος.

canary [kə'nɛərɪ] n καναρίνι ♦ a καναρινί (χρώμα).

cancel ['kænsəl] vt (check etc) ακυρώνω || (strike out) διαγράφω || (MATH) εξαλείφω || ~**lation** n ακύρωση, ματαίωση.

cancer ['kænsə*] n καρκίνος.

candid ['kændɪd] a ειλικρινής.

candidate ['kændɪdeɪt] n υποψήφιος/α m/f.

candle ['kændl] n κερί || ~**stick** n κηροπήγιο.

candour ['kændə*] n ευθύτητα, ντομπροσύνη.

candy ['kændɪ] n καραμέλα.

cane [keɪn] n (bamboo etc) καλάμι || (stick) μπαστούνι ♦ vt (beat) ραβδίζω.

canine ['kænaɪn] a σκυλήσιος.

canister ['kænɪstə*] n τενεκεδάκι, κουτί.

cannabis ['kænəbɪs] n κάνναβη f.

canned ['kænd] a (food) κονσερβοποιημένο.

cannibal ['kænɪbəl] n καννίβαλος m/f, ανθρωποφάγος m/f || ~**ism** n ανθρωποφαγία.

cannon ['kænən] n (gun) πυροβόλο, κανόνι.

cannot ['kænɒt] = **can not** || see **can**.

canoe [kə'nuː] n μονόξυλο, κανό || ~**ing** n κανό.

canon ['kænən] n κανόνας || (criterion) κριτήριο || (clergyman) εφημέριος.

can opener ['kænəupnə*] n ανοιχτήρι.

canopy ['kænəpɪ] n σκιάδα, προστέγασμα nt.

can't [kænt] = **can not** || see **can**.

cantankerous [kæn'tæŋkərəs] a διεστραμμένος, καυγατζής.

canteen [kæn'tiːn] n (shop) καντίνα || (MIL) παγούρι.

canter ['kæntə*] n τριποδισμός ♦ vi καλπάζω ελαφρά.

canvas ['kænvəs] n κανναβάτσο || (NAUT) πανιά ntpl || (ART) μουσαμάς || **under** ~ σε σκηνές.

canvass ['kænvəs] vt (election) ψηφοθηρώ || (discuss) συζητώ, ερευνώ.

canyon ['kænjən] n φαράγγι, χαράδρα.

cap [kæp] n (hat) σκούφος, τραγιάσκα || (top) κάλυμμα nt ♦ vt στέφω, στεφανώνω || (bottle etc) πωματίζω, σφραγίζω || (outdo) υπερβάλλω.

capability [keɪpə'bɪlətɪ] n ικανότητα.

capable ['keɪpəbl] a ικανός || ~ **of** ικανός να.

capacity [kə'pæsɪtɪ] n (space) χωρητικότητα || (ability) ικανότητα || (position) ιδιότητα.

cape [keɪp] n (garment) κάπα, μπελερίνα || (GEOG) ακρωτήρι.

capital ['kæpɪtl] n (city) πρωτεύουσα || (ECON) κεφάλαιο || (letter) κεφαλαίο γράμμα || ~**ism** n καπιταλισμός, κεφαλαιοκρατία || ~**ist** a καπιταλιστής || ~ **punishment** n θανατική ποινή.

capitulate [kə'pɪtjuleɪt] vi συνθηκολογώ.

capitulation [kəpɪtju'leɪʃən] n συνθηκολόγηση.

capricious [kə'prɪʃəs] a ιδιότροπος, ασταθής.

capsize [kæp'saɪz] vti ανατρέπω, μπατάρω.

capstan ['kæpstən] n εργάτης.

capsule ['kæpsjuːl] n (ANAT) κάψα || (MED) καψούλα.

captain ['kæptɪn] n (leader) αρχηγός || (MIL) λοχαγός || (NAUT) πλοίαρχος ♦ vt οδηγώ, διευθύνω.

caption ['kæpʃən] n επικεφαλίδα || (of picture) λεζάντα.

captivate ['kæptɪveɪt] vt γοητεύω, σαγηνεύω, δελεάζω.

captive ['kæptɪv] n, a αιχμάλωτος.

captivity [kæp'tɪvɪtɪ] n αιχμαλωσία.

capture ['kæptʃə*] vt συλλαμβάνω, αιχμαλωτίζω || (fort etc) κυριεύω ♦ n σύλληψη || (objective) κατάληψη.

car [kɑː*] n (motor) αυτοκίνητο, αμάξι || (railway) βαγόνι.

carafe [kə'ræf] n καράφα.

caramel ['kærəməl] n καραμέλα.

carat ['kærət] n καράτι.

caravan ['kærəvæn] n καραβάνι || (house on wheels) τροχόσπιτο.

caraway ['kærəweɪ]: ~ **seed** n κύμινο.

carbon ['kɑːbən] n άνθρακας || (paper) καρμπόν nt inv || ~ **copy** n καρμπό nt inv || ~ **ribbon** n ταινία καρμπόν.

carburettor [kɑːbju'retə*] n καρμπυρατέρ nt inv.

carcass ['kɑːkəs] n πτώμα nt, κουφάρι, ψοφίμι.

card [kɑːd] n (playing) τραπουλόχαρτο || (visiting) επισκεπτήριο || (general) δελτάριο || ~**board** n χαρτόνι || ~ **game** n χαρτοπαιξία.

cardiac ['kɑːdɪæk] a καρδιακός.

cardigan ['kɑːdɪgən] n πλεκτή ζακέτα.

cardinal ['kɑːdɪnl] a: ~ **number** απόλυτος αριθμός.

care [kɛə*] n (worry, attention) φροντίδα, μέριμνα, προσοχή ♦ vi φροντίζω, με νοιάζει || ~ **of** (abbr c/o) φροντίδι του || **to** ~ **about** vt με ενδιαφέρει, με νοιάζει || **to take** ~ προσέχω || **to take** ~ **of** vt ενδιαφέρομαι για, φροντίζω για || **to** ~ **for** vt ενδιαφέρομαι || (love) αγαπώ, αρέσω.

career [kə'rɪə*] n σταδιοδρομία, καριέρα ♦ vi τρέχω, ορμώ.

carefree ['kɛəfriː] a αμέριμνος, ξένοιαστος.

careful ['kɛəful] a προσεκτικός, επιμελής || ~**ly** ad προσεχτικά.

careless ['kɛəlɪs] a απρόσεκτος, απερίσκεπτος || ~**ness** n απροσεξία, αμέλεια.

caress [kə'res] n θωπεία, χάδι ♦ vt θωπεύω, χαϊδεύω.

caretaker ['kɛəteɪkə*] n επιστάτης.

car-ferry ['kɑːferɪ] n πορθμείο οχημάτων, φέρρυ-μποτ nt inv.

cargo ['kɑːgəu] n φορτίο.

caricature ['kærɪkətjuə*] n γελοιογραφία, καρικατούρα.

carnation [kɑː'neɪʃən] n γαρύφαλλο.

carnival ['kɑːnɪvəl] n (public celebration) αποκρηές fpl, καρναβάλι.

carol ['kærəl] n (Christmas) κάλαντα ntpl.

carp [kɑːp] n (fish) κυπρίνος, σαζάνι || **to** ~ **at** vt επικρίνω, κατσαδιάζω, αντιλέγω.

car park ['kɑːpɑːk] n χώρος παρκαρίσματος.

carpenter ['kɑːpɪntə*] n μαραγκός.

carpentry ['kɑːpɪntrɪ] n ξυλουργική.

carpet ['kɑːpɪt] n τάπης, χαλί ♦ vt στρώνω με χαλί.

carriage ['kærɪdʒ] n (vehicle) άμαξα, όχημα nt || (carrying) μεταφορά || (fees) μεταφορικά ntpl || (bearing) συμπεριφορά, ύφος nt || ~ **return** επαναφορά κυλίνδρου || ~**way** n (part of road) αμαξιτή οδός.

carrier ['kærɪə*] n (μετα)φορέας, κομιστής || ~**-bag** n μεγάλη χαρτοσακκούλα.

carrot ['kærət] n καρότο.

carry ['kærɪ] vt (transport, hold)

(μετα)φέρω, βαστάζω, κουβαλώ || *(responsibility)* έχω ευθύνες || to be carried away *(fig)* παρασύρομαι || to ~ on *vti* συνεχίζω, επιμένω || to ~ out *vt (orders)* εκτελώ.

cart [kɑːt] *n* κάρο ♦ *vt* μεταφέρω με κάρο.

cartilage ['kɑːtılıdʒ] *n* χόνδρος, τραγανό.

carton ['kɑːtən] *n* κουτί από χαρτόνι.

cartoon [kɑː'tuːn] *n (PRESS)* γελοιογραφία, σκίτσο || *(CINE)* κινούμενες εικόνες, *fpl*, μίκυ-μάους *nt inv.*

cartridge ['kɑːtrɪdʒ] *n (for gun)* φυσίγγι, φυσέκι.

carve [kɑːv] *vti* σκαλίζω, χαράσσω, κόβω.

carving ['kɑːvɪŋ] *n (in wood etc)* γλυπτική, σκάλισμα *nt* || ~ knife *n* μαχαίρι για κόψιμο.

car wash ['kɑːwɒʃ] *n* πλύσιμο αυτοκινήτου.

cascade [kæs'keɪd] *n* καταρράκτης.

case [keɪs] *n (box)* θήκη, κιβώτιο, κασόνι || *(instance)* περίπτωση || *(state)* κατάσταση, ζήτημα *nt* || *(GRAM)* πτώση || *(LAW)* υπόθεση || in ~ σε περίπτωση που || in any ~ εν πάσει περιπτώσει.

cash [kæʃ] *n* μετρητά (χρήματα) *ntpl* ♦ *vt* εξαργυρώνω || ~desk *n* ταμείο.

cashier [kæ'ʃɪə] *n* ταμίας, κασιέρης.

cashmere [kæʃ'mɪə] *n* κασμήρι.

cash register ['kæʃ'redʒɪstə] *n* μηχανή ταμείου, ταμειακή μηχανή.

casing ['keɪsɪŋ] *n* περίβλημα *nt*, πλαίσιο, θήκη.

casino [kə'siːnəu] *n* καζίνο.

cask [kɑːsk] *n* βαρέλι.

casket ['kɑːskɪt] *n (box)* κουτί, κασετίνα || *(US)* φέρετρο.

casserole ['kæsərəul] *n (pot)* τσουκάλι, ντάμπζ || *(meal)* γιουβέτσι.

cassock ['kæsək] *n* ράσο.

cast [kɑːst] *(irreg v) vt (throw)* ρίχνω, πετώ || *(shed)* βγάζω, απορρίπτω || *(THEAT)* διανέμω ρόλους, αναθέτω ρόλο || *(metal)* χύνω, καλουπώνω ♦ *n (THEAT)* θίασος || to ~ off *vti* βγάζω || *(NAUT)* αποπλέω.

caste [kɑːst] *n* κοινωνική τάξη, κάστα.

cast iron ['kɑːst'aɪən] *n* χυτοσίδηρος.

castle ['kɑːsl] *n (fortress)* φρούριο || *(mansion)* πύργος.

castor ['kɑːstə] *n (wheel)* καρούλι, ρόδα || ~ oil *n* ρετσινόλαδο || ~ sugar *n* ψιλή ζάχαρη.

castrate [kæs'treɪt] *vt* μουνουχίζω.

casual ['kæʒjul] *a (occasional)* τυχαία || *(work, attitude)* τυχαίος, απερίσκεπτος || *(meeting)* τυχαίος || ~ly *ad* αδιάφορα.

casualty ['kæʒjultɪ] *n* τραυματίας.

cat [kæt] *n* γάτα.

catalogue, *(US)* catalog ['kætəlɒg] *n* κατάλογος ♦ *vt* εγγράφω σε κατάλογο.

catalyst ['kætəlɪst] *n* καταλύτης.

catapult ['kætəpʌlt] *n* καταπέλτης.

cataract ['kætərækt] *n (waterfall)* καταρράκτης || *(MED)* καταρράκτης.

catarrh [kə'tɑː*] *n* κατάρρους *m.*

catastrophe [kə'tæstrəfɪ] *n* καταστροφή, συμφορά.

catch [kætʃ] *(irreg v) n (for window etc)* δόντι, μπετούγια, ασφάλεια || *(SPORT, breath)* πιάσιμο || *(fish)* πιάνω (πολλά ψάρια) || *(HUNT)* θήραμα *nt* || *vt (seize)* πιάνω, αρπάζω || *(surprise)* συλλαμβάνω || *(in time)* (προ)φθάνω, πιάνω στα πράσα || to ~ a cold αρπάζω κρύο.

catching ['kætʃɪŋ] *a (MED)* μεταδοτικός, κολλητικός.

catch phrase ['kætʃfreɪz] *n* σύνθημα *nt.*

catchy ['kætʃɪ] *a (tune)* ελκυστικός.

categorical [kætɪ'gɒrɪkəl] *a* κατηγορηματικός.

category ['kætɪgərɪ] *n* κατηγορία, τάξη.

cater ['keɪtə*] *vi (food)* τροφοδοτώ, σερβίρω || ~ing *n* προμήθεια, τροφοδοσία || to ~ for *(fig)* φροντίζω, ικανοποιώ.

caterpillar ['kætəpɪlə*] *n* κάμπια.

cathedral [kə'θiːdrəl] *n* καθεδρικός ναός, μητρόπολη.

catholic ['kæθəlɪk] *a* καθολικός, παγκόσμιος, ευρύς || C~ *n* καθολικός/η *m/f* ♦ *a (REL)* καθολικός.

cattle ['kætl] *npl* κτήνη *ntpl*, ζώα *ntpl.*

catty ['kætɪ] *a* δηκτικός, πονηρός.

cauliflower ['kɒlɪflauə*] *n* κουνουπίδι.

cause [kɒːz] *n (reason)* αιτία, αφορμή, λόγος || *(object)* υπόθεση, χάρη ♦ *vt* προξενώ, κάνω να.

causeway ['kɒːzweɪ] *n* υψωμένος δρόμος.

caustic ['kɒːstɪk] *a (burning)* καυστικός || *(sarcastic)* σαρκαστικός.

caution ['kɒːʃən] *n (care)* προσοχή || *(warning)* προειδοποίηση ♦ *vt* προειδοποιώ.

cautious ['kɒːʃəs] *a* προσεκτικός.

cavalry ['kævəlrɪ] *npl* ιππικό.

cave [keɪv] *n* σπηλιά || ~man *n* τρωγλοδύτης ♦ to ~ in *vi* καταρρέω, σωριάζομαι.

cavern ['kævən] *n* σπηλιά.

caviar(e) ['kævɪɑː*] *n* χαβιάρι.

cavity ['kævɪtɪ] *n* κοίλωμα *nt*, τρύπα.

C.B.I. *abbr of* Confederation of British Industry Συνομοσπονδία Βρεττανικών Βιομηχάνων.

cc *abbr of* cubic centimetres; carbon copy.

cease [siːs] *vti* παύω, σταματώ, τελειώνω || ~fire *n* ανακωχή || ~less *a* ακατάπαυστος, αδιάκοπος.

cedar ['siːdə*] *n* κέδρος.

ceiling ['siːlɪŋ] *n* ταβάνι || *(fig)* ανώτατο ύψος.

celebrate ['selɪbreɪt] *vt* γιορτάζω || *(wedding etc)* τελώ || ~d *a* διάσημος.

celebration [selɪ'breɪʃən] *n* γιορτασμός, τελετή.

celebrity [sɪ'lebrɪtɪ] *n (person)* διασημότητα.

celery ['selərɪ] *n* σέλινο.

celestial [sɪ'lestɪəl] *a* ουράνιος.

cell [sel] *n (in monastery)* κελλί || *(in jail)*

φυλακή || *(ELEC)* στοιχείο || *(BIOL)* κύτταρο.

cellar ['sɛlə*] *n* υπόγειο, κελλάρι || *(wine)* κάβα.

cello ['tʃɛləu] *n* βιολοντσέλο.

cellophane ['sɛləfeɪn] *n* (R) σελοφάν *inv*.

cellular ['sɛljulə*] *a* κυτταρικός, κυψελοειδής.

cellulose ['sɛljuləus] *n* κελλουλόζη, κυτταρίνη.

cement [sə'mɛnt] *n* τσιμέντο ♦ *vt (lit)* συγκολλώ με τσιμέντο || *(fig)* στερεώνω, κατοχυρώνω.

cemetery ['sɛmɪtrɪ] *n* νεκροταφείο.

cenotaph ['sɛnəta:f] *n* κενοτάφιο.

censer ['sɛnsə*] *n* θυμιατήρι, λιβανιστήρι.

censor ['sɛnsə*] *n* λογοκριτής, ελεγκτής || ~**ship** *n* λογοκρισία.

censure ['sɛnʃə*] *vt* επικρίνω, ψέγω.

census ['sɛnsəs] *n* απογραφή.

cent [sɛnt] *n* σέντ || *(col)* πεντάρα.

centenary [sɛn'ti:nərɪ] *n* εκατονταετηρίδα.

center ['sɛntə*] *n (US)* = **centre**.

centigrade ['sɛntɪɡreɪd] *a* εκατονταβάθμιος.

centilitre, *(US)* **centiliter** ['sɛntɪliːtə*] *n* εκατοστόλιτρο.

centimetre, *(US)* **centimeter** ['sɛntɪmiːtə*] *n* εκατοστόμετρο.

centipede ['sɛntɪpiːd] *n* σαρανταποδαρούσα.

central ['sɛntrəl] *a* κεντρικός || ~ **heating** *n* κεντρική θέρμανση || ~**ize** *vt* συγκεντρώνω || ~ **processing unit (CPU)** *(COMPUT)* κεντρική μονάδα επεξεργασίας (KME).

centre ['sɛntə*] *n* κέντρο.

century ['sɛntjurɪ] *n* αιώνας.

ceramic [sɪ'ræmɪk] *a* κεραμικός.

cereal ['sɪərɪəl] *n (any grain)* δημητριακά *ntpl*, σιτηρά *ntpl*.

ceremony ['sɛrɪmənɪ] *n* εθιμοτυπία *(religious)* τελετή.

certain ['sɜːtən] *a (sure)* βέβαιος, σίγουρος, ασφαλής || *(some, one)* ωρισμένος, κάποιος || **for** ~ σίγουρα || ~**ly** *ad* ασφαλώς, σίγουρα || ~**ty** *n* βεβαιότητα, σιγουριά.

certificate [sə'tɪfɪkɪt] *n* πιστοποιητικό, βεβαίωση.

certify ['sɜːtɪfaɪ] *vti* πιστοποιώ, βεβαιώ, κυρώνω.

cf. *abbr* = compare.

chafe [tʃeɪf] *vti* τρίβω, ερεθίζομαι, φθείρομαι.

chaffinch ['tʃæfɪntʃ] *n* σπίνος.

chain [tʃeɪn] *n* αλυσίδα, καδένα || *(mountains)* σειρά ♦ *vt (also:* ~ **up)** δένω με αλυσίδα, δεσμεύω || ~ **reaction** *n* αλυσωτή αντίδραση || ~ **store** *n* υποκατάστημα *nt*.

chair [tʃɛə*] *n* καρέκλα || *(UNIV etc)* έδρα ♦ *vt (preside)* προεδρεύω || ~**man** *n* πρόεδρος || *(director)* διευθυντής.

chalet ['ʃæleɪ] *n* σαλέ *nt inv*.

chalice ['tʃælɪs] *n* δισκοπότηρο.

chalk [tʃɔːk] *n (GEOL)* ασβεστόλιθος || *(crayon)* κιμωλία.

challenge ['tʃælɪndʒ] *n* πρόκληση ♦ *vt* προκαλώ || *(dispute)* αμφισβητώ || ~**r** *n* διεκδικητής.

challenging ['tʃælɪndʒɪŋ] *a* προκλητικός.

chamber ['tʃeɪmbə*] *n (compartment)* δωμάτιο || *(of gun etc)* θαλάμη (όπλου) || ~ **of commerce** *n* Εμπορικό Επιμελητήριο || ~**maid** *n* καμαριέρα || ~ **music** *n* μουσική δωματίου.

chamois ['ʃæmwɑː] *n*: ~ **leather** *n* σαμουά *nt inv*.

champagne [ʃæm'peɪn] *n* σαμπάνια.

champion ['tʃæmpɪən] *n (SPORT)* πρωταθλητής/τρια *m/f* || *(of cause)* πρόμαχος || ~**ship** *n* πρωτάθλημα *nt*.

chance [tʃɑːns] *n (opportunity)* ευκαιρία || *(possibility)* ελπίδα, πιθανότητα ♦ *a* τυχαίος ♦ *vt*: **to** ~ **it** διακινδυνεύω, παίζω στην τύχη || **to take a** ~ δοκιμάζω.

chancel ['tʃɑːnsəl] *n* ιερό (ναού).

chancellor ['tʃɑːnsələ*] *n (UNIV)* πρύτανης *m* || **C**~ **of the Exchequer** *n* Υπουργός Οικονομικών.

chandelier [ʃændə'lɪə*] *n* πολύφωτο, πολυέλαιος.

change [tʃeɪndʒ] *vt* αλλάζω, τροποποιώ || *(exchange)* ανταλλάσσω || *(trains)* αλλάζω ♦ *vi* αλλάζω, μεταβάλλομαι ♦ *n (alteration)* αλλαγή, μεταβολή || *(coins)* ψιλά *ntpl* || *(balance)* ρέστα *ntpl* || ~**able** *a (weather)* άστατος || ~**over** *n (to new system)* αλλαγή συστήματος.

changing ['tʃeɪndʒɪŋ] *a* ευμετάβλητος, αλλάζων || ~**-room** *n (in shop)* βεστιάριο.

channel ['tʃænl] *n (of stream)* κοίτη || *(of bay etc)* δίαυλος, μπούκα || *(strait)* πορθμός, στενό || *(of communication)* οδός *f*, δρόμος || *(RAD etc)* ζώνη συχνοτήτων || *(TV)* κανάλι ♦ *vt* αυλακώνω || **the (English) C**~ *n* Μάγχη || **C**~ **Islands** *npl* νησιά της Μάγχης.

chant [tʃɑːnt] *n* τραγούδι || *(church)* ψαλμός ♦ *vt* τραγουδώ || *(church)* ψάλλω.

chaos ['keɪɒs] *n* χάος *nt*.

chap [tʃæp] *n* ρωγμή, σκάσιμο, τύπος ♦ *vt (skin)* σκάζω από το κρύο.

chapel ['tʃæpəl] *n* παρεκκλήσι.

chaperon ['ʃæpərəun] *n* συνοδός κοριτσιού ♦ *vt* συνοδεύω.

chaplain ['tʃæplɪn] *n* εφημέριος.

chapter ['tʃæptə*] *n (of book)* κεφάλαιο.

char [tʃɑː*] *vt (burn)* μαυρίζω με κάψιμο ♦ *n (cleaner)* παραδουλεύτρα.

character ['kærɪktə*] *n (qualities)* χαρακτήρας || *(LITER, THEAT etc)* πρόσωπο, χαρακτήρας || *(peculiar person)* τύπος, χαρακτήρας || *(letter, sign, COMPUT)* χαρακτήρας, στοιχείο, γράμμα || ~**s per second (c.p.s.)** χαρακτήρες *mpl* ανά δευτερόλεπτο (χ.α.δ.) || ~**istic** *a*

χαρακτηριστικός ♦ *n* χαρακτηριστικό γνώρισμα *nt*.
charade [ʃəˈrɑːd] *n* συλλαβόγριφος, φάρσα.
charcoal [ˈtʃɑːkəʊl] *n* ξυλοκάρβουνο.
charge [tʃɑːdʒ] *n* (*price*) τίμημα *nt*, τιμή || (*accusation*) κατηγορία || (*load for gun*) γόμωση || (*attack*) έφοδος *f*, προσβολή ♦ *vt* (*fill, load*) γεμίζω, φορτίζω || (*a price*) ζητώ (τιμή), χρεώνω || (*a battery*) επιφορτίζω || (*attack*) εφορμώ || (*accuse*) κατηγορώ ♦ *vi* επιπίπτω, προσβάλλω || in ~ of φροντίζω, που φροντίζει || to take ~ αναλαμβάνω, είμαι υπεύθυνος.
charitable [ˈtʃærɪtəbl] *a* φιλάνθρωπος, ελεήμονας.
charity [ˈtʃærɪtɪ] *n* (*institution*) φιλανθρωπικό ίδρυμα || αγαθοεργία.
charlady [ˈtʃɑːleɪdɪ] *n* παραδουλεύτρα.
charm [tʃɑːm] *n* (*attractiveness*) γοητεία || (*for luck*) φυλαχτό ♦ *vt* μαγεύω, γοητεύω || ~ing *a* γοητευτικός.
chart [tʃɑːt] *n* (*of information*) γραφική παράσταση, διάγραμμα *nt* || (*NAUT*) χάρτης.
charter [ˈtʃɑːtə*] *vt* ναυλώνω ♦ *n* καταστατικός χάρτης || ~ **flight** *n* ναυλωμένη πτήση || ~ed **accountant** *n* λογιστής.
charwoman [ˈtʃɑːwʊmən] *n* = **charlady**.
chase [tʃeɪs] *vt* (*run after*) κυνηγώ, (κατα)-διώκω ♦ *n* (*act of chasing*) κυνήγι, καταδίωξη.
chasm [ˈkæzəm] *n* χάσμα *nt*, κενό.
chassis [ˈʃæsɪ] *n* σασσί *nt inv*.
chastity [ˈtʃæstɪtɪ] *n* αγνότητα, παρθενία.
chat [tʃæt] *vi* κουβεντιάζω ♦ *n* (*friendly, casual talk*) φιλική κουβεντούλα.
chatter [ˈtʃætə*] *vi* φλυαρώ || (*of teeth*) τρέμω, κτυπώ ♦ *n* φλυαρία, τερετισμός || ~ **box** *n* (*esp child*) φλύαρος.
chatty [ˈtʃætɪ] *a* (*style*) ομιλητικός, πολυλογάς.
chauffeur [ˈʃəʊfə*] *n* οδηγός, σωφέρ *m inv*.
cheap [tʃiːp] *a* (*joke*) άνοστο (αστείο) || (*poor quality*) φτηνός, πρόστυχος, μικρής αξίας || ~ **en** *vt* (*person*) υποτιμώ, ξευτελίζω || ~ **ly** *ad* φτηνά.
cheat [tʃiːt] *vti* (εξ)απατώ, κοροϊδεύω ♦ *n* αγύρτης, κατεργάρης || ~ **ing** *n* (*at cards*) κλέψιμο || (*general*) παγαποντιά.
check [tʃek] *vt* (*examine*) ελέγχω || (*halt*) σταματώ, αναχαιτίζω ♦ *n* (*examination*) έλεγχος, επαλήθευση || (*restraint*) περιορισμός || (*restaurant bill*) λογαριασμός || (*pattern*) καρρώ *nt inv* || (*US*) = **cheque** || ~ **ers** *npl* (*US*) ντάμα || ~ **mate** *n* ματ *nt inv* || ~ **point** *n* σημείο ελέγχου || ~ **up** *n* (*MED*) γενική εξέταση.
cheek [tʃiːk] *n* παρειά, μάγουλο || (*impudence*) αναίδεια || ~ **bone** *n* μήλο (παρειάς) || ~ **y** *a* αναιδής.
cheer [tʃɪə*] *n* (*joy*) ευθυμία || (*shout*) ζητωκραυγή ♦ *vt* (*shout*) επευφημώ,

ζητωκραυγάζω || (*comfort*) χαροποιώ || (*encourage*) ενθαρρύνω ♦ *vi*: to ~ up κάνω κέφι || ~ **good** ~ *n* φαγητά *ntpl* || ~ **ful** *a* χαρωπός καλόκεφος || ~ **fulness** *n* ευθυμία || (*of fireplace etc*) ζεστασιά || ~ **ing** *n* ζητοκραυγές *fpl*, χειροκροτήματα *ntpl* ♦ *a* ενθαρρυντικός, προκαλών το κέφι || ~ **io** *interj* (*in departure*) γεια χαρά || (*greeting*) γεια σου || ~ **less** *a* μελαγχολικός, κακόκεφος.
cheese [tʃiːz] *n* τυρί.
chef [ʃef] *n* αρχιμάγειρας.
chemical [ˈkemɪkəl] *a* χημικός.
chemist [ˈkemɪst] *n* (*MED*) φαρμακοποιός *m/f* || (*scientist*) χημικός *m/f* || ~ **ry** *n* χημεία || ~ **'s** (*shop*) *n* φαρμακείο.
cheque [tʃek] *n* επιταγή || ~ **book** *n* βιβλιάριο επιταγών.
chequered [ˈtʃekəd] *a* (*fig*) περιπετειώδης.
cherish [ˈtʃerɪʃ] *vt* (*a hope*) τρέφω || (*love*) λατρεύω || (*look after*) περιποιούμαι.
cherry [ˈtʃerɪ] *n* (*tree*) κερασιά || (*fruit*) κεράσι.
chess [tʃes] *n* σκάκι || ~ **board** *n* σκακιέρα || ~ **man** *n* πιόνι, πεσσός.
chest [tʃest] *n* (*ANAT*) στήθος *nt* || (*box*) κιβώτιο, μπαούλο || to get sth off one's ~ ξελαφρώνω || ~ of **drawers** *n* σιφονιέρα, κομό.
chestnut [ˈtʃesnʌt] *n* κάστανο || ~ (**tree**) *n* καστανιά.
chew [tʃuː] *vti* μασώ || ~ **ing gum** *n* τσίχλα.
chic [ʃiːk] *a* κομψός, σικ.
chick [tʃɪk] *n* πουλάκι.
chicken [ˈtʃɪkɪn] *n* (*bird, food*) κοτόπουλο.
chickenpox [ˈtʃɪkɪnpɒks] *n* ανεμοβλογιά.
chicory [ˈtʃɪkərɪ] *n* κιχώρι, αντίδι.
chief [tʃiːf] *n* αρχηγός *m/f*, διευθυντής/διευθύντρια *m/f* ♦ *a* κύριος, πρωτεύων, πρώτος || ~ **ly** *ad* κυρίως, προπάντων.
chilblain [ˈtʃɪlbleɪn] *n* χιονίστρα.
child [tʃaɪld] *n* παιδί || ~ **birth** *n* τοκετός, γέννα || ~ **hood** *n* παιδικά χρόνια *ntpl* || ~ **ish** *a* παιδαριώδης, παιδιάστικος || ~ **like** *a* αφελής, παιδιάστικος || ~ **ren** [ˈtʃɪldrən] *npl of* **child** παιδιά, παιδάκια *ntpl*.
chill [tʃɪl] *n* (*coldness*) ψυχρότητα, κρυάδα || (*cold*) κρυολόγημα *nt* ♦ *a* ψυχρός κρύος || ~ **y** *a* ψυχρός, κρύος.
chime [tʃaɪm] *n* κωδωνοκρουσία ♦ *vi* ηχώ αρμονικά.
chimney [ˈtʃɪmnɪ] *n* καπνοδόχος *f*, καμινάδα.
chimpanzee [tʃɪmpænˈziː] *n* χιμπαντζής.
chin [tʃɪn] *n* πηγούνι.
china [ˈtʃaɪnə] *n* πορσελάνη || (*dishes, cups*) πιάτα *ntpl*.
China [ˈtʃaɪnə] *n* Κίνα.
Chinese [ˈtʃaɪˈniːz] *a* κινέζικος ♦ *n*

(person) Κινέζος/α m/f|| *(language)* κινεζική.

chink [tʃɪŋk] n *(opening)* ρωγμή, σκάσιμο || *(noise)* ήχος (μετάλλου κτλ).

chip [tʃip] n απόκομμα nt, θρύμμα nt ♦ vt θραύω, θρυμματίζω, αποκόπτω || to ~ in vi *(CARDS)* ποντάρω || *(interrupt)* παρεμβαίνω || συνεισφέρω.

chiropodist [kɪ'rɔpədɪst] n πεντικιουρίστας.

chirp [tʃɜːp] n τερετισμός, τιτίβισμα nt, κελάδημα nt ♦ vi τερετίζω, τιτιβίζω, κελαϊδώ.

chisel ['tʃɪzl] n σμίλη.

chit [tʃit] n σημείωμα nt, γραπτή άδεια.

chitchat ['tʃitʃæt] n κουβέντα.

chloride ['klɔːraɪd] n χλωρίδιο.

chlorine ['klɔːriːn] n χλώριο.

chloroform ['klɔrəfɔːm] n χλωροφόρμιο.

chock [tʃɔk] n μόρσος, τάκος.

chocolate ['tʃɔklit] n σοκολάτα.

choice [tʃɔis] n εκλογή, προτίμηση || *(variety)* ποικιλία ♦ a εκλεκτός.

choir ['kwaɪə*] n χορός || ~boy n παιδί χορωδίας.

choke [tʃəuk] vi *(be unable to breathe)* πνίγομαι ♦ vt *(stop breathing of)* ασφυκτιώ, στραγγαλίζω || *(block)* εμφράσσω ♦ n *(AUT)* διαχύτης, εμφράκτης.

cholera ['kɔlərə] n χολέρα.

choose [tʃuːz] *(irreg v)* vt διαλέγω, προτιμώ || *(decide)* αρέσω, προτιμώ.

chop [tʃɔp] vt *(cut with a blow)* κόβω, αποκόβω || *(into pieces)* κατακόβω, διαμελίζω, λιανίζω ♦ vi: to ~ and change πωλώ και αγοράζω ♦ n *(blow)* κτύπημα nt|| *(meat)* μπριζολάκι || ~py a ταραγμένος, κυματώδης || ~sticks npl ξυλαράκια ntpl (για το πιλάφι), κινέζικο πιρούνι.

choral ['kɔːrəl] a χορικός.

chord [kɔːd] n χορδή.

chore [tʃɔə*] n βαρετή δουλειά.

choreographer [kɔri'ɔɡrəfə*] n χορογράφος m/f.

chortle ['tʃɔːtl] vi καγχάζω, κακαρίζω.

chorus ['kɔːrəs] n *(choir etc)* χορός, χορωδία || *(many voices)* τραγούδι εν χορώ || ~ of praise n *(fig)* συναυλία επαίνων.

chose [tʃəuz] pt of choose.

chosen ['tʃəuzn] pp of choose.

Christ [kraist] n Χριστός.

christen ['krɪsn] vt βαφτίζω || ~ing n βάπτισμα nt.

Christian ['krɪstiən] n Χριστιανός/n m/f ♦ a χριστιανικό || ~ name n όνομα nt|| ~ity n χριστιανισμός.

Christmas ['krɪsməs] n Χριστούγεννα ntpl|| ~ card n χριστουγεννιάτικη κάρτα.

chrome [krəum] n επιχρωμίωση.

chromium ['krəumiəm] n χρώμιο.

chronic ['krɔnik] a *(MED)* χρόνιος.

chronicle ['krɔnɪkl] n χρονικό, χρονογράφημα nt.

chronological [krɔnə'lɔdʒɪkəl] a χρονολογικός.

chrysanthemum [krɪ'sænθəməm] n χρυσάνθεμο.

chubby ['tʃʌbi] a παχουλός, στρουμπουλός.

chuck [tʃʌk] vt πετώ, ρίχνω ♦ n σφιγκτήρας, τσόκ nt inv.

chuckle ['tʃʌkl] vi γελώ χαμηλόφωνα.

chum [tʃʌm] n στενός φίλος.

chunk [tʃʌŋk] n χοντρό κομμάτι.

church [tʃɜːtʃ] n *(building)* εκκλησία, ναός || ~yard n αυλόγυρος εκκλησίας, νεκροταφείο.

churlish ['tʃɜːliʃ] a άξεστος, δύστροπος.

churn [tʃɜːn] n *(for butter)* βουτίνα, καρδάρα, ντουρβάνι.

chute [ʃuːt] n τσουλήθρα.

chutney ['tʃʌtni] n τσάτνυ nt inv *(αρωματικό)*.

CID n *(abbr of Criminal Investigation Department)* ≈ Ανακριτικό Τμήμα.

cider ['saɪdə*] n μπλίτης *(οίνος)*.

cigar [sɪ'ɡɑː*] n πούρο.

cigarette [sɪɡə'rɛt] n τσιγάρο, σιγαρέττο || ~ case n τσιγαροθήκη, ταμπακιέρα || ~ end n γόπα, αποτσίγαρο || ~ holder n πίπα.

cinder ['sɪndə*] n ανθρακιά, θράκα, στάκτη.

cine ['sɪni]: ~-camera n κινηματογραφική μηχανή || ~-film n κινηματογραφική ταινία.

cinema ['sɪnəmə] n *(THEAT)* σινεμά nt inv || *(motion pictures)* κινηματογράφος.

cinnamon ['sɪnəmən] n κανέλα.

cipher ['saɪfə*] n *(zero)* μηδενικό || *(code)* κρυπτογράφηση || *(person)* μηδενικός.

circle ['sɜːkl] n *(ring, figure)* κύκλος, γύρος || *(of friends)* κύκλος, συντροφιά ♦ vi περιστρέφομαι, στριφογυρίζω ♦ vt *(surround)* περικυκλώνω ♦ vi *(move in a circle)* κάνω τον κύκλο, κάνω κύκλους.

circuit ['sɜːkit] n *(moving around)* κυκλικός δρόμος, περιστροφή || *(tour by judges)* περιοδεία (δικαστού) || *(ELEC)* κύκλωμα nt|| ~ous a κυκλικός, έμμεσος.

circular ['sɜːkjulə*] a κυκλικός || *(in a circle)* κυκλοτερής ♦ n εγκύκλιος, διαφημιστικό γράμμα.

circulate ['sɜːkjuleɪt] vi κυκλοφορώ ♦ vt θέτω σε κυκλοφορία.

circulation [sɜːkju'leɪʃən] n κυκλοφορία.

circumcise ['sɜːkəmsaɪz] vt περιτέμνω.

circumference [sə'kʌmfərəns] n περιφέρεια.

circumspect ['sɜːkəmspɛkt] a προσεκτικός, μετρημένος.

circumstances ['sɜːkəmstənsiz] npl *(facts connected with sth)* περιστάσεις fpl, συνθήκες fpl, συμβάντα ntpl|| *(financial condition)* οικονομική κατάσταση.

circus ['sɜːkəs] n τσίρκο.

cistern ['sistən] n δεξαμενή, ντεπόζιτο.

cite [saɪt] vt (mention, quote) αναφέρω, παραπέμπω.

citizen ['sɪtɪzn] n (city dweller) αστός/n m/f|| πολίτης/ισσα m/f|| ~**ship** n πολιτικά δικαιώματα ntpl.

citrus fruit ['sɪtrəs 'fru:t] n εσπεριδοειδή ntpl.

city ['sɪtɪ] n πόλη || **the C~** το εμπορικό κέντρο του Λονδίνου.

civic ['sɪvɪk] a αστικός, πολιτικός.

civil ['sɪvl] a πολιτικός || (polite) ευγενικός || ~ **engineer** n πολιτικός μηχανικός m/f || ~**ian** n πολίτης/ισσα m/f, ιδιώτης m/f ♦ a πολιτικός || ~ **law** n αστικόν δίκαιο || ~ **servant** n δημόσιος m/f υπάλληλος || C~ **Service** n Δημόσιες Υπηρεσίες fpl || ~ **war** n εμφύλιος πόλεμος.

civilization [sɪvɪlaɪ'zeɪʃən] n πολιτισμός.

civilized ['sɪvɪlaɪzd] a πολιτισμένος.

claim [kleɪm] vt απαιτώ, ζητώ, διεκδικώ ♦ n αίτηση, απαίτηση, αξίωση || ~**ant** n απαιτητής/τήτρια m/f|| (LAW) ενάγων/ουσα m/f, δικαιούχος/α m/f.

clam [klæm] n αχιβάδα.

clamber ['klæmbə*] vi σκαρφαλώνω.

clammy ['klæmɪ] a ιδρωμένος, κολλώδης.

clamp [klæmp] n σφιγκτήρας, σύνδεσμος ♦ vt (συσ)σφίγγω.

clang [klæŋ] n κλαγγή, κρότος ♦ vti αντηχώ, κροτώ.

clap [klæp] vti κτυπώ, χειροκροτώ || ~**ping** n χειροκρότημα nt.

claret ['klærət] n μαύρο κρασί, μπορντώ nt inv.

clarification [klærɪfɪ'keɪʃən] n (fig) διευκρίνιση.

clarify ['klærɪfaɪ] vt διευκρινίζω.

clarinet [klærɪ'net] n κλαρίνο.

clarity ['klærɪtɪ] n διαύγεια.

clash [klæʃ] n σύγκρουση, αντίθεση || (sound) δυνατό και πικρό κτύπημα ♦ vi συγκρούομαι.

clasp [klɑ:sp] n πόρπη, κόπιτσα ♦ vt αγκαλιάζω, σφίγγω.

class [klɑ:s] n (rank) τάξη || (sort) τάξη, είδος nt, κατηγορία || (SCH) τάξη ♦ vt ταξινομώ, βαθμολογώ.

classic ['klæsɪk] n κλασσικός ♦ a (traditional) κλασσικός || ~**al** a κλασσικός.

classification [klæsɪfɪ'keɪʃən] n ταξινόμηση, κατάταξη.

classify ['klæsɪfaɪ] vt ταξινομώ, κατατάσσω.

classroom ['klɑ:srum] n αίθουσα παραδόσεων, τάξη.

clatter ['klætə*] n θόρυβος, γδούπος ♦ vi κροτώ, θορυβώ.

clause [klɔ:z] n (of contract etc) όρος, άρθρο, διάταξη || (GRAM) πρόταση.

claustrophobia [klɔ:strə'fəubɪə] n κλειστοφοβία.

claw [klɔ:] n νύχι || (of quadrupeds) χηλή, οπλή ♦ vt νυχιάζω, γρατσουνίζω.

clay [kleɪ] n άργιλος, πηλός.

clean [kli:n] a (free from dirt) καθαρός,

παστρικός || (guiltless) καθαρός, τίμιος || (lines) καθαρές (γραμμές), σαφές περίγραμμα ♦ vt καθαρίζω, παστρεύω || ~**er** n (person) καθαριστής/ρια m/f|| ~**ing** n κάθαρση, καθάρισμα nt || ~**liness** n καθαριότητα, πάστρα || ~**-up** n καθαρισμός || **to** ~ **out** vt καθαρίζω || (col) ξεπεντζαρίζω || **to** ~ **up** vt κάνω καθαρισμό, σιάζω || (col) κερδίζω.

cleanse [klenz] vt αποκαθαίρω, καθαρίζω, πλένω.

clear [klɪə*] a (water etc) καθαρός, διαυγής || (sound) καθαρός (ήχος) || (meaning) σαφής, καθαρός || (certain) σαφής || (road) ανοικτός ♦ vt καθαρίζω, ξεκαθαρίζω ♦ vi (become clear) διευκρινίζεται || ~**ance** n (sale) εκποίηση, ξεπούλημα nt || (free space) απελευθέρωση, εκκένωση || (permission) άδεια || ~**-cut** a σαφής, συγκεκριμένος || ~**ing** n καθάρισμα nt || ~**ly** ad σαφώς, προφανώς, σαφαλώς || ~**way** n (Brit) εθνική οδός χωρίς στάθμευση || **to** ~ **up** vi διαλύω, ξεκαθαρίζω ♦ vt τακτοποιώ, σιάζω || ξεκαθαρίζω.

clench [klentʃ] vt (teeth etc) σφίγγω.

clergy ['klɜ:dʒɪ] n κλήρος, ιερατείο || ~**man** n κληρικός, ιερωμένος, παπάς.

clerical ['klerɪkəl] a κληρικός, ιερατικός || του γραφείο.

clerk [klɑ:k, (US) klɜ:rk] n (US) (salesman, woman) υπάλληλος m/f|| (in office) γραφέας m.

clever ['klevə*] a (with hands) επιδέξιος, καπάτσος || (in mind) ευφυής, σπιρτόζος || ~**ly** ad ευφυώς, έξυπνα.

cliché ['kli:ʃeɪ] n στερεότυπο, κλισέ nt inv.

click [klɪk] vi κτυπώ, κάνω τικ-τάκ ♦ n κλικ nt inv, ξηρός κρότος.

client ['klaɪənt] n πελάτης/ισσα m/f|| ~**ele** [kli:ɑ:n'tel] n πελατεία.

cliff [klɪf] n γκρεμός.

climate ['klaɪmɪt] n κλίμα nt.

climax ['klaɪmæks] n αποκορύφωμα nt.

climb [klaɪm] vti ανέρχομαι, ανεβαίνω, σκαρφαλώνω ♦ n ανέβασμα nt, ανηφορά || ~**er** n (of mountains) ορειβάτης m/f|| ~**ing** n: to go ~ ing κάνω ορειβασία.

clinch [klɪntʃ] vt (fig: decide) συνάπτω, κλείνω.

cling [klɪŋ] vi προσκολλιέμαι, πιάνομαι.

clinic ['klɪnɪk] n κλινική || ~**al** a κλινικός.

clink [klɪŋk] n κτύπημα nt (ποτηριών) ♦ vti κτυπώ, ηχώ.

clip [klɪp] n συνδετήρας, τσιμπιδάκι ♦ vt (papers) συνδέω || (hair) κουρεύω, ψαλιδίζω || (hedge) κόβω || ~**pers** npl (instrument) κουρευτική μηχανή.

clique [kli:k] n κλίκα.

cloak [kləuk] n πανωφόρι || (fig) κάλυμμα nt, πέπλο || ~**room** n (for coats etc) γκαρνταρόμπα || (W.C.) αποχωρητήριο, μέρος nt, καμπινέτο.

clock [klɒk] n ρολόι || ~**wise** ad

δεξιότροφος || ~ **work** n μηχανισμός ρολογιού.

clog [klɒg] n (shoe) τσόκαρο ♦ vti εμποδίζω, κωλύω, φράσσω.

close [kləʊs] a (near) κοντινός, εγγύς, διπλανός || (atmosphere etc) ασφυκτικός, πνιγηρός, στενός || (mean) σφιχτός || (weather) κλειστός, βαρύς ♦ ad (near) κοντά, από κοντά, σφιχτά || ~**ly** ad προσεκτικά, στενά, κατά πόδας.

close [kləʊz] vt (shut) κλείνω || (end) τελειώνω, τερματίζω ♦ vi κλείομαι || (end) τερματίζομαι ♦ n (end) τέλος nt || **to** ~ **down** vti κλείνω, διακόπτω || ~**d** a (road) απαγορεύεται η διάβαση || ~**d shop** n κλειστό κατάστημα nt.

closet [klɒzit] n μικρό δωμάτιο || (store-room) αποθήκη.

close-up [kləʊsʌp] n λεπτομέρεια.

closure [kləʊzə*] n κλείσιμο, τερματισμός.

clot [klɒt] n (esp blood) θρόμβος, σβώλος ♦ vi θρομβούμαι, πήζω.

cloth [klɒθ] n (material) ύφασμα nt, πανί || (for cleaning) πατσαβούρα.

clothe [kləʊð] vt ντύνω, καλύπτω || ~**s** npl ρούχα ntpl ~**s brush** n βούρτσα || ~**s line** n σχοινί απλώματος ρούχων || ~**s peg** n μανταλάκι.

clothing [kləʊðiŋ] n = **clothes** || see **clothe**.

cloud [klaʊd] n σύννεφο || (of dust etc) νέφος nt, σύννεφο || ~**burst** n μπόρα || ~**y** a συνεφιασμένος || (wine etc) θολωμένο.

clout [klaʊt] n κτύπημα nt ♦ vt κτυπώ, καρπαζώνω.

clove [kləʊv] n γαρύφαλο.

clover [kləʊvə*] n τριφύλλι || ~ **leaf** n τριφύλλι.

clown [klaʊn] n παλιάτσος, κλάουν nt inv ♦ vi κάνω τον παλιάτσο.

club [klʌb] n (stick) ρόπαλο, ματσούκα || (society) λέσχη || (golf) κλόμπ nt inv || (CARDS) σπαθί ♦ vt κτυπώ με ρόπαλο, με κλόμπ ♦ vi: **to** ~ **together** συνεισφέρω, βάζω ρεφενέ || ~**house** n λέσχη.

cluck [klʌk] vi κακαρίζω.

clue [kluː] n νύξη, ένδειξη || **he hasn't a** ~ δεν έχει ιδέα.

clump [klʌmp] n συστάδα (δένδρων), μεγάλο κομμάτι.

clumsy [klʌmzi] a (person) αδέξιος, ατζαμής || (object) βαρύς, άκομψος.

clung [klʌŋ] pt, pp of **cling**.

cluster [klʌstə*] n συστάδα, ομάδα || (of grapes) τσαμπί || (of stars) σύμπλεγμα nt ♦ vi συγκεντρώνομαι, μαζεύομαι.

clutch [klʌtʃ] n (grip, grasp) άρπαγμα nt, σφικτό πιάσιμο || (AUT) αμπραγιάζ nt inv, συμπλέκτης ♦ vt αρπάζω, πιάνω σφικτά.

clutter [klʌtə*] vt παραγεμίζω, κάνω ανωκάτω.

coach [kəʊtʃ] n (bus) λεωφορείο, πούλμαν nt inv || (teacher) φροντιστής || (RAIL) άμαξα, βαγόνι || (trainer)

προγυμναστής/άστρια m/f || vt προγυμνάζω.

coagulate [kəʊˈægjuleit] vti πήζω.

coal [kəʊl] n άνθρακας, κάρβουνο, γαιάνθρακας.

coalfield [kəʊlfiːld] n ανθρακοφόρος περιοχή.

coalition [kəʊəˈliʃən] n συνασπισμός.

coalmine [kəʊlmain] n ανθρακωρυχείο.

coarse [kɔːs] a (lit) τραχύς, ακατέργαστος || (fig) άξεστος, χυδαίος.

coast [kəʊst] n παραλία, ακτή || ~**al** a παράκτιος, παραλιακός || ~**er** n ακτοπλοϊκό || ~**guard** n ακτοφυλακή || ~**line** n ακτή, παραλία.

coat [kəʊt] n (garment) σακάκι || (of animal) προβιά || (layer etc) στρώμα nt, χέρι ♦ vt (with paint etc) επιχρίω || ~ **of arms** n οικόσημο || ~ **hanger** n κρεμαστάρι || ~**ing** n επίστρωμα nt, χέρι.

coax [kəʊks] vt καλοπιάνω, καταφέρνω.

cobbler [kɒblə*] n μπαλωματής.

cobble(stone)s [kɒbl(stəʊn)z] npl βότσαλα ntpl, καλντερίμι.

cobra [kəʊbrə] n κόμπρα.

cobweb [kɒbwɛb] n ιστός αράχνης, αραχνιά.

cocaine [kəˈkein] n (MED) κοκαΐνη.

cock [kɒk] n (poultry) κόκορας, πετεινός || (bird etc) αρσενικό πουλί || (tap, faucet etc) κρουνός, κάνουλα ♦ vt σηκώνω, βάζω στραβά (το καπέλο) || (a gun) σηκώνω το λύκο || ~**erel** n κοκοράκι.

cockle [kɒkl] n κοχύλι.

cockney [kɒkni] n Λονδρέζος κατωτέρας τάξης, κόκνυ inv.

cockpit [kɒkpit] n (AVIAT) θέση χειριστού.

cockroach [kɒkrəʊtʃ] n κατσαρίδα.

cocktail [kɒkteil] n (drink) κοκτέιλ nt inv || ~ **cabinet** n μπάρ nt inv || ~ **party** n πάρτυ κοκτέιλ nt inv.

cocoa [kəʊkəʊ] n κακάο.

coconut [kəʊkənʌt] n καρύδα.

cocoon [kəˈkuːn] n κουκούλι.

cod [kɒd] n μουρούνα.

code [kəʊd] n (of laws) κώδικας || (signals) σύστημα nt κρυπτογραφίας.

codify [kəʊdifai] vt κωδικοποιώ.

coerce [kəʊˈɜːs] vt πιέζω, αναγκάζω.

coercion [kəʊˈɜːʃən] n καταπίεση.

coexistence [kəʊigˈzistəns] n συνύπαρξη.

coffee [kɒfi] n καφές m.

coffin [kɒfin] n φέρετρο, κάσα.

cog [kɒg] n (of wheel etc) δόντι.

cognac [kɒnjæk] n κονιάκ nt inv.

coherent [kəʊˈhiərənt] a (consistent) συναφής, συνεπής.

coil [kɔil] n κουλούρα, σπείρωμα nt || (ELEC) πηνίο ♦ vt συσπειρώνω, τυλίγω, κουλουριάζω.

coin [kɔin] n νόμισμα nt, κέρμα nt || ~**age** n (system) νομισματικό σύστημα nt || νόμισμα nt.

coincide [kəʊinˈsaid] vi συμπίπτω,

συμφωνώ || ~nce [kəʊ'ɪnsɪdəns] n σύμπτωση.

coke [kəʊk] n κώκ nt inv.

colander ['kʌləndə*] n τρυπητό, σουρωτήρι.

cold [kəʊld] a ψυχρός, κρύος ♦ n ψύχος nt, κρύο || (illness) κρυολόγημα nt || to have ~ feet (γ)κιοτέβω || to give the ~ shoulder φέρομαι ψυχρά || ~ly ad ψυχρά, κρύα.

coleslaw ['kəʊlslɔ:] n λαχανοσαλάτα.

colic ['kɒlik] n κωλικόπονος.

collaborate [kə'læbəreit] vi συνεργάζομαι.

collaboration [kəlæbə'reiʃən] n συνεργασία.

collapse [kə'læps] vi καταρρέω ♦ n κατάρρευση.

collapsible [kə'læpsəbl] a πτυσσόμενος, διπλωτός.

collar ['kɒlə*] n (of coat, shirt) κολλάρο, γιακάς || ~bone n κλειδί του ώμου.

collate [kɒ'leit] vt (αντι)παραβάλλω.

colleague ['kɒli:g] n συνάδελφος m/f, συνεργάτης m/f.

collect [kə'lekt] vt συλλέγω, μαζεύω ♦ vi συναθροίζομαι || ~ion n συλλογή || (money) είσπραξη || ~ive a συλλογικός || (POL) κολλεκτίβο.

collector [kə'lektə*] n (of art etc) συλλέκτης/τρια m/f || (of money) εισπράκτορας.

college ['kɒlidʒ] n (non-specialized) κολλέγιο || (esp Oxford and Cambridge) πανεπιστήμιο.

collide [kə'laid] vi συγκρούομαι, τρακάρω.

collision [kə'liʒən] n σύγκρουση.

colloquial [kə'ləʊkwiəl] a της καθομιλουμένης.

colon ['kəʊlən] n (GRAM) διπλή στιγμή.

colonel ['kɜ:nl] n συνταγματάρχης.

colonial [kə'ləʊniəl] a αποικιακός.

colonize ['kɒlənaiz] vt αποικίζω.

colony ['kɒləni] n αποικία || (of immigrants etc) παροικία.

color ['kʌlə*] n (US) = colour.

colossal [kə'lɒsl] a κολοσσιαίος.

colour ['kʌlə*] n χρώμα nt|| (paints etc) βαφή, μπογιά || (of skin) χρώμα nt ♦ vt χρωματίζω, βάφω || (news) χρωματίζω, γαρνίρω || ~s npl χρώματα ntpl|| (NAUT) σημαία || ~-blind a δαλτωνικός || ~ed a χρωματιστός, έγχρωμος || (fig) εξοχκωμένος || ~ film n (for camera) έγχρωμο φίλμ || ~ful a ζωντανός || ~ television n έγχρωμη τηλεόραση.

colt [kəʊlt] n πώλος, πουλάρι.

column ['kɒləm] n (pillar) κίονας, στύλος, κολώνα || (of troops) φάλαγγα || (of page) στήλη || ~ist n αρθρογράφος m/f.

coma ['kəʊmə] n κώμα nt, λήθαργος.

comb [kəʊm] n (for hair) κτένι, χτένα || (of cock) λειρί || (honey) κηρήθρα ♦ vt (hair) κτενίζω || (search) ερευνώ, ψάχνω.

combat ['kɒmbæt] n πάλη, διαμάχη ♦ vt (κατα)πολεμώ.

combination [kɒmbi'neiʃən] n συνδυασμός, ένωση.

combine [kəm'bain] vti συνδυάζω, συνεργάζομαι, ενούμαι ♦ ['kɒmbain] n συνδυασμός, εταιρεία, συνδικάτο || ~ harvester n θεριστική και αλωνιστική μηχανή.

combustion [kəm'bʌstʃən] n καύση, ανάφλεξη.

come [kʌm] (irreg v) vi (approach) έρχομαι, φθάνω || (reach) τελειώνω, φθάνω, βρίσκομαι || (become) γίνομαι, συμβαίνω || (result) καταλήγω || to ~ about vi συμβαίνω, γίνομαι || to ~ across vt συναντώ || to ~ by (visit) περνώ || (find) βρίσκω, αποκτώ || to ~ in for vt έχω μερίδιο, μετέχω || to ~ into vt (enter) μπαίνω μέσα, εμφανίζομαι || (inherit) κληρονομώ || (fashion) γίνομαι της μόδας || to ~ out with vt βγαίνω, βγάζω || to ~ to vt (bill) φθάνω || (grief) μού συμβαίνει δυστύχημα || (nothing) αποτυγχάνω || (notice) αντιλαμβάνομαι || to ~ up to vt ανεβαίνω || (amount) φθάνω || to ~ up with vt προφταίνω || ~back n επάνοδος f.

comedian [kə'mi:diən] n κωμικός.

comedown ['kʌmdaʊn] n ξεπεσμός.

comedy ['kɒmidi] n κωμωδία.

comet ['kɒmit] n κομήτης.

comfort ['kʌmfət] n (of body) άνεση || (of mind) παρηγοριά ♦ vt παρηγορώ || ~able a αναπαυτικός, άνετος.

comic ['kɒmik] n (actor) κωμικός || (magazine) κόμικς ntpl inv ♦ a (also: ~al) κωμικός, αστείος.

comma ['kɒmə] n (GRAM) κόμμα nt.

command [kə'mɑ:nd] n (order) διαταγή || (control) εξουσία, κυριαρχία, διοίκηση || (COMPUT) εντολή ♦ vt (order) διατάζω || (be in charge) διοικώ, εξουσιάζω , ελέγχω || (be able to get) κατέχω, διαθέτω ♦ vi προστάζω || ~eer [kɒmən'diə*] vt επιτάσσω || ~er n (MIL) διοικητής || (NAUT) πλωτάρχης.

commandment [kə'mɑ:ndmənt] n εντολή.

commando [kə'mɑ:ndəʊ] n κομμάντο m inv, καταδρομέας.

commemorate [kə'meməreit] vt γιορτάζω.

commemoration [kəmemə'reiʃən] n: in ~ of εις μνήμην του.

commemorative [kə'memərətiv] a αναμνηστικός.

commence [kə'mens] vti αρχίζω.

commend [kə'mend] vt συνιστώ, επαινώ || ~ation [kɒmen'deiʃən] n έπαινος.

commensurate [kə'menʃərit] a ανάλογος.

comment ['kɒment] n σχόλιο, εξήγηση ♦ vi (+ on) σχολιάζω, επεξηγώ || ~ary n (SPORT) ρεπορτάζ nt inv || σχόλιο || ~ator n σχολιαστής/σχολιάστρια m/f.

commerce ['kɒmɜːs] n εμπόριο.

commercial [kə'mɜːʃəl] a εμπορικός ♦ n (TV) διαφήμιση || ~ize vt εμπορεύομαι.

commiserate [kə'mɪzəreɪt] vi: to ~ with συμπονώ, συλλυπούμαι.

commission [kə'mɪʃən] n (duty) εντολή, παραγγελία || (fee) προμήθεια || (MIL) βαθμός αξιωματικού || (reporting body) επιτροπή ♦ vt αναθέτω, επιφορτίζω || out of ~ εκτός ενεργείας, χαλασμένο || ~aire n θυρωρός || ~er n μέλος nt επιτροπής, αρμοστής.

commit [kə'mɪt] vt (a crime) διαπράττω (έγκλημα) || (to paper) καταγράφω || (to memory) απομνημονεύω || (entrust) εμπιστεύομαι, αναθέτω || ~ment n δέσμευση, υποχρέωση.

committee [kə'mɪtɪ] n επιτροπή.

commodity [kə'mɒdɪtɪ] n εμπόρευμα nt.

common ['kɒmən] a (shared) κοινός || (knowledge etc) κοινός, συνήθης || (ordinary, usual) συνήθης, συνηθισμένος || (mean, low) χυδαίος, πρόστυχος || (frequent) συνήθης ♦ n: in ~ από κοινού || ~ly ad συνήθως || C~ Market n Κοινή Αγορά || ~place a κοινοτοπία, πεζός || ~room n αίθουσα καθηγητών || ~sense n κοινός νούς || the C~wealth n Κοινοπολιτεία.

commotion [kə'məuʃən] ταραχή.

communal [kɒmju:nl] a κοινοτικός.

commune ['kɒmju:n] n (group of people living communally) κοινότητα ♦ [kə'mju:n] vi (+ with) συναναστρέφομαι.

communicate [kə'mju:nɪkeɪt] vt (transmit) ανακοινώνω, μεταδίδω ♦ vi (connect) συγκοινωνώ || (be in touch) (+ with)επικοινωνώ.

communication [kəmju:nɪ'keɪʃən] n ανακοίνωση, μετάδοση || συγκοινωνία, επικοινωνία || ~s npl (transport etc) συγκοινωνία || ~ cord n κώδων m κινδύνου.

communion [kə'mju:nɪən] n κοινότητα || (REL) θρησκευτική ομάδα || (Holy) C~ n (Αγία) Μετάληψη.

communiqué [kə'mju:nɪkeɪ] n ανακοινωθέν nt.

communism ['kɒmjunɪzəm] n κομμουνισμός.

communist ['kɒmjunɪst] n κομμουνιστής/ίστρια m/f ♦ a κομμουνιστικός.

community [kə'mju:nɪtɪ] n κοινότητα || (the public) κοινωνία, το κοινό || ~ centre n αίθουσα αναψυχής.

commutation ticket [kɒmju'teɪʃəntɪkɪt] n (US) εισιτήριο διαρκείας.

compact [kəm'pækt] a συμπαγής, σφιχτός ♦ ['kɒmpækt] n (agreement) σύμβαση, συμφωνία || (powder) πουδριέρα.

companion [kəm'pænɪən] n σύντροφος m/f, συνάδελφος m/f, ταίρι || ~ship n συντροφία.

company ['kʌmpənɪ] n (business)

εταιρεία || (of people) παρέα, συντροφιά || (MIL) λόχος || (guests) κόσμος || to keep s.o. ~ κάνω παρέα.

comparable ['kɒmpərəbl] a συγκρίσιμος, ανάλογος, παραβλητός.

comparative [kəm'pærətɪv] a συγκριτικός, σχετικός.

compare [kəm'pɛə*] vt συγκρίνω, παραβάλλω || (+ with) παρομοιάζω ♦ vi συγκρίνομαι.

comparison [kəm'pærɪsn] n σύγκριση || παρομοίωση || in ~ (with) συγκρινόμενος (με).

compartment [kəm'pɑ:tmənt] n (NAUT) διαμέρισμα nt || (RAIL) βαγκόν-λι nt inv.

compass ['kʌmpəs] n (instrument) πυξίδα || ~es npl διαβήτης.

compassion [kəm'pæʃən] n ευσπλαχνία, οίκτος || ~ate a φιλεύσπλαχνος.

compatible [kəm'pætɪbl] a συμβιβάσιμος, σύμφωνος.

compatibility [kəmpætɪ'bɪlɪtɪ] n (COMPUT) συμβατότητα.

compel [kəm'pɛl] vt αναγκάζω, υποχρεώνω.

compendium [kəm'pɛndɪəm] n σύνοψη, επιτομή.

compensate ['kɒmpɛnseɪt] vt αποζημιώνω ♦ vi: to ~ for αντισταθμίζω.

compensation [kɒmpɛn'seɪʃən] n (money) αποζημίωση || (satisfaction) ικανοποίηση.

compere ['kɒmpɛə*] n κομπέρ m/f inv.

compete [kəm'pi:t] vi συναγωνίζομαι, ανταγωνίζομαι || (for prize) διαγωνίζομαι.

competence ['kɒmpɪtəns] n ικανότητα, επιδεξιότητα.

competent ['kɒmpɪtənt] a ικανός, επιδέξιος || (office etc) αρμόδιος.

competition [kɒmpɪ'tɪʃən] n άμιλλα || (rivalry) ανταγωνισμός, συναγωνισμός.

competitive [kəm'pɛtɪtɪv] a ανταγωνιστικός, συναγωνιστικός.

competitor [kəm'pɛtɪtə*] n ανταγωνιστής/ίστρια m/f, αντίπαλος m/f.

compile [kəm'paɪl] vt συλλέγω, συναθροίζω.

complacency [kəm'pleɪsnsɪ] n αυτάρκεια.

complacent [kəm'pleɪsənt] a αυτάρκεσος, ευχαριστημένος.

complain [kəm'pleɪn] vi παραπονιέμαι, γκρινιάζω || ~t n παράπονο, γκρίνια || (illness) αρρώστια.

complement ['kɒmplɪmənt] n πληρότητα || (MATH) συμπλήρωμα nt || (esp ship's crew etc) πλήρες πλήρωμα nt || ~ary a συμπληρωματικός.

complete [kəm'pli:t] a πλήρης, συμπληρωμένος, τέλειος ♦ vt συμπληρώνω, αποτελειώνω || ~ly πλήρως, εντελώς.

completion [kəm'pli:ʃən] *n* συμπλήρωση, αποπεράτωση.

complex ['kɒmplɛks] *a* πολύπλοκος, πολυσύνθετος ♦ *n* (*mental*) σύμπλεγμα *nt*, κόμπλεξ *nt inv* || (*of buildings*) σύμπλεγμα *nt*.

complexion [kəm'plɛkʃən] *n* χρώμα *nt*, χροιά.

complexity [kəm'plɛksıtı] *n* περιπλοκή.

complicate ['kɒmplıkeıt] *vt* περιπλέκω || ~**d** *a* μπλεγμένος.

complication [kɒmplı'keıʃən] *n* περιπλοκή.

compliment ['kɒmplımənt] *n* φιλοφρόνηση, κομπλιμέντο ♦ ['kɒmplıment] *vt* κομπλιμεντάρω, συγχαίρω || ~**s** *npl* ευχές *fpl*, χαιρετισμοί *mpl* || ~**ary** *a* φιλοφρονητικός, κομπλιμεντόζος.

comply [kəm'plaı] *vi:* **to** ~ **with** συμμορφούμαι, ενδίδω, εκπληρώ.

component [kəm'pəʊnənt] *a* συνθετικός, συστατικός ♦ *n* συστατικό || (*PHYS*) συνιστώσα δύναμη.

compose [kəm'pəʊz] *vt* συντάσσω, γράφω || (*MUS*) μελοποιώ, συνθέτω || (*calm*) ηρεμώ || ~**d** *a* ατάραχος, ήρεμος || ~ **r** *n* (*MUS*) μουσουργός, συνθέτης.

composite ['kɒmpəzıt] *a* σύνθετος, μικτός.

composition [kɒmpə'zıʃən] *n* σύνθεση || (*structure*) σύσταση.

compost ['kɒmpɒst] *n* (*fertilizer*) φουσκί.

composure [kəm'pəʊʒə*] *n* ηρεμία αταραξία.

compound ['kɒmpaʊnd] *n* (*GRAM*) σύνθετος λέξη || (*enclosure*) κλειστός χώρος || (*CHEM*) ένωση ♦ *a* σύνθετος.

comprehend [kɒmprı'hɛnd] *vt* (*understand*) καταλαβαίνω || (*include*) συμπεριλαμβάνω.

comprehension [kɒmprı'hɛnʃən] *n* κατανόηση, αντίληψη.

comprehensive [kɒmprı'hɛnsıv] *a* περιεκτικός.

compress [kəm'prɛs] *vt* συμπιέζω ♦ ['kɒmprɛs] *n* (*MED*) επίθεμα *nt*, κομπρέσσα || ~**ion** *n* (συμ) πίεση, σύμπτυξη.

comprise [kəm'praız] *vi* αποτελούμαι από.

compromise ['kɒmprəmaız] *n* συμβιβασμός ♦ *vt* (*expose*) εκθέτω ♦ *vi* (*agree*) συμβιβάζομαι.

compulsion [kəm'pʌlʃən] *n* βία, καταναγκασμός.

compulsory [kəm'pʌlsərı] *a* (*obligatory*) υποχρεωτικός.

computer [kəm'pju:tə*] *n* υπολογιστής.

comrade ['kɒmrıd] *n* σύντροφος/φισσα *m/f*, συνάδελφος *m/f* || ~**ship** *n* καμαραντερί.

concave ['kɒn'keıv] *a* κοίλος, βαθουλός.

conceal [kən'si:l] *vt* (απο) κρύπτω.

concede [kən'si:d] *vt* (*admit*) παραδέχομαι ♦ *vi* (*yield*) παραχωρώ.

conceit [kən'si:t] *n* ματαιοδοξία, ξιπασιά || ~**ed** *a* φαντασμένος, ξιπασμένος.

conceivable [kən'si:vəbl] *a* διανοητός, δυνατός.

conceive [kən'si:v] *vt* (*imagine*) φαντάζομαι || (*child*) συλλαμβάνω.

concentrate ['kɒnsəntreıt] *vi* (+ *on*) συγκεντρώνομαι ♦ *vt* συγκεντρώνω.

concentration [kɒnsən'treıʃən] *n* συγκέντρωση || ~ **camp** *n* στρατόπεδο συγκεντρώσεως.

concept ['kɒnsɛpt] *n* ιδέα, έννοια.

conception [kən'sɛpʃən] *n* σύλληψη, αντίληψη.

concern [kən'sɜːn] *n* (*affair*) ενδιαφέρον, συμφέρον || (*business*) επιχείρηση || (*anxiety*) ανησυχία ♦ *vt* ενδιαφέρομαι, ενδιαφέρω || ~**ed** *a* (*anxious*) ανήσυχος || ~**ing** *prep* όσο αφορά.

concert ['kɒnsət] *n* συνεννόηση, συμφωνία || (*MUS*) συναυλία || **in** ~ από συμφώνου, μαζί || ~ **hall** *n* αίθουσα συναυλιών.

concertina [kɒnsə'ti:nə] *n* ακορντεό *nt inv*.

concerto [kən'tʃɛətəʊ] *n* κονσέρτο.

concession [kən'sɛʃən] *n* παραχώρηση, εκχώρηση.

conciliation [kənsılı'eıʃən] *n* συμφιλίωση.

concise [kən'saıs] *a* σύντομος, συνοπτικός.

conclude [kən'klu:d] *vt* (*end*) τελειώνω, περαίνω || (*settle*) συνάπτω, κλείνω || (*decide*) συμπεραίνω, καταλήγω ♦ *vi* τερματίζω.

conclusion [kən'klu:ʒən] *n* συμπέρασμα *nt*, τέλος *nt* || **in** ~ εν τέλει.

conclusive [kən'klu:sıv] *a* αποφασιστικός, πειστικός.

concoct [kən'kɒkt] *vt* (*drink etc*) κατασκευάζω || (*plan etc*) εφευρίσκω, καταστρώνω.

concrete ['kɒnkri:t] *n* σκυροκονίαμα *nt*, μπετό ♦ *a* συγκεκριμένος.

concur [kən'kɜː*] *vi* συμπίπτω, συμφωνώ.

concurrently [kən'kʌrəntlı] *ad* από κοινού.

concussion [kən'kʌʃən] *n* τράνταγμα *nt* || (*MED*) διάσειση.

condemn [kən'dɛm] *vt* καταδικάζω || ~**ation** *n* καταδίκη, μομφή.

condensation [kɒndɛn'seıʃən] *n* συμπύκνωση.

condense [kən'dɛns] *vi* συμπυκνούμαι ♦ *vt* συμπυκνώνω || ~**d milk** *n* συμπυκνωμένο γάλα.

condescend [kɒndı'sɛnd] *vi* καταδέχομαι || ~**ing** *a* καταδεκτικός, ευπροσήγορος.

condition [kən'dıʃən] *n* (*state*) κατάσταση, συνθήκη || (*term*) όρος ♦ *vt* ρυθμίζω, καθορίζω || on ~ that υπό τον όρο να || ~al a υπό όρους, προϋποθετικός.

condolences [kən'dəʊlənsiz] npl συλλυπητήρια ntpl.

condone [kən'dəʊn] vt συγχωρώ, παραβλέπω.

conducive [kən'djuːsiv] a συντελεστικός.

conduct ['kɒndʌkt] n (behaviour) διαγωγή || (management) διεξαγωγή ♦ [kən'dʌkt] vt (people) οδηγώ, φέρω || (affairs) διευθύνω, εκτελώ || (MUS) διευθύνω || ~ed tour n ξενάγηση || ~or n (orchestra) μαέστρος || (bus) εισπράκτορας || ~ress n (bus) εισπρακτόρισσα.

cone [kəʊn] n (MATH) κώνος || (ice cream) παγωτό χωνάκι || (pine) κουκουνάρι.

confectioner [kən'fɛkʃənə*] n ζαχαροπλάστης || ~'s (shop) n ζαχαροπλαστείο || ~y n ζαχαροπλαστείο.

confederation [kənfɛdə'reiʃən] n συνομοσπονδία.

confer [kən'fɜː*] vt (grant) απονέμω, παρέχω ♦ vi (consult) συζητώ, διασκέπτομαι || ~ence ['kɒnfərəns] n (συν)διάσκεψη, συμβούλιο.

confess [kən'fɛs] vti (admit) (εξ)ομολογώ || (REL) εξομολογούμαι || ~ion n ομολογία || (REL) εξομολόγηση.

confetti [kən'fɛti] n χαρτοπόλεμος, κονφετί nt inv.

confide [kən'faid] vi: to ~ in εμπιστεύομαι.

confidence ['kɒnfidəns] n (trust) εμπιστοσύνη || (secret) μυστικό || ~ trick n κόλπο, απάτη.

confident ['kɒnfidənt] a βέβαιος, σίγουρος || ~ial a (secret) εμπιστευτικός || (trusted) της εμπιστοσύνης.

confine [kən'fain] vt περιορίζω || (shut up) εγκλείω || ~d a (space) περιορισμένος || ~ment n (limiting) περιορισμός || (birth) λοχεία, τοκετός.

confirm [kən'fɜːm] vt (report) επιβεβαιώνω || (appointment) επικυρώνω || ~ation n (general) επιβεβαίωση || (REL) χρίσμα nt, μύρωση || ~ed a έμμονος, αμετάπειστος.

confiscate ['kɒnfiskeit] vt δημεύω.

confiscation [kɒnfis'keiʃən] n δήμευση.

conflict ['kɒnflikt] n σύγκρουση, διαμάχη, αντίθεση ♦ [kən'flikt] vi συγκρούομαι, διαφέρω, αντιμάχομαι || ~ing a αντιφατικός, συγκρουόμενος.

conform [kən'fɔːm] vi (+ to) συμμορφώνομαι, προσαρμόζομαι.

confront [kən'frʌnt] vt αντιμετωπίζω || ~ation n αντιμετώπιση.

confuse [kən'fjuːz] vt συγχύζω, ταράσσω.

confusing [kən'fjuːziŋ] a συγκεχυμένος.

confusion [kən'fjuːʒən] n (disorder) σύγχυση || (tumult) αναστάτωση,

αναμπουμπούλα || (embarrassment) σάστισμα nt.

congeal [kən'dʒiːl] vi πήζω.

congenial [kən'dʒiːniəl] a ταιριαστός, ευχάριστος.

congested [kən'dʒɛstid] a (overcrowded) συνωστισμένος.

congestion [kən'dʒɛstʃən] n (of traffic etc) συμφόρηση, συνωστισμός.

conglomeration [kənglɒmə'reiʃən] n σύμφυρμα nt, σύμπηγμα nt.

congratulate [kən'grætjuleit] vt (+ on) συγχαίρω.

congratulations [kəngrætju'leiʃənz] npl συγχαρητήρια ntpl.

congregate ['kɒŋgrigeit] vi συναθροίζομαι.

congregation [kɒŋgri'geiʃən] n συνάθροιση, εκκλησίασμα nt.

congress ['kɒŋgrɛs] n συνέλευση, συνέδριο || (US) Κογκρέσσο || ~man n (US) μέλος nt του Κογκρέσσου.

conical ['kɒnikəl] a κωνικός, κωνοειδής.

conifer ['kɒnifə*] n κωνοφόρο (δένδρο).

conjecture [kən'dʒɛktʃə*] n εικασία, συμπερασμός ♦ vti εικάζω, συμπεραίνω.

conjugal ['kɒndʒʊgəl] a συζυγικός.

conjunction [kən'dʒʌŋkʃən] n σύνδεσμος || in ~ with από κοινού με.

conjure ['kʌndʒə*] vti πλέκω, μηχανεύομαι || to ~ up vt επινοώ, επικαλούμαι || ~r n ταχυδακτυλουργός.

conjuring ['kʌndʒəriŋ] n: ~ trick n ταχυδακτυλουργία.

conk [kɒŋk]: to ~ out vi (col) σβήνω.

connect [kə'nɛkt] vti (train) συνδέω, συνδέομαι, συνδυάζω || ~ion n (joining) σύνδεση, συνάφεια || (relation) σχέση, συσχετισμός || in ~ ion with σχετικά με.

connexion [kə'nɛkʃən] n = connection || see connect.

connoisseur [kɒnə'sɜː*] n ειδήμονας, τεχνοκρίτης.

conquer ['kɒŋkə*] vt (overcome) υπερνικώ, υποτάσσω || (by war) κατακτώ, κυριεύω || ~or n κατακτητής/ήτρια m/f, νικητής/ήτρια m/f.

conquest ['kɒŋkwɛst] n κατάκτηση.

conscience ['kɒnʃəns] n συνείδηση.

conscientious [kɒnʃi'ɛnʃəs] a ευσυνείδητος.

conscious ['kɒnʃəs] a συνειδητός, συναισθανόμενος || ~ness n συναίσθηση.

conscript ['kɒnskript] n στρατεύσιμος, κληρωτός || ~ion [kən'skripʃən] n στρατολογία.

consecrate ['kɒnsikreit] vt εγκαινιάζω, χειροτονώ || (devote) αφιερώνω.

consecutive [kən'sɛkjutiv] a διαδοχικός.

consensus [kən'sɛnsəs] n κοινή συναίνεση, επικρατούσα γνώμη.

consent [kən'sɛnt] n συγκατάβαση, συναίνεση ♦ vi (+ to) συγκατατίθεμαι.

consequence ['kɒnsɪkwəns] n
(importance) σπουδαιότητα || (result,
effect) συνέπεια, επακόλουθο.
consequently ['kɒnsɪkwəntlɪ] ad
επομένως, συνεπώς.
conservation [kɒnsə'veɪʃən] n
συντήρηση, διατήρηση.
conservative [kən'sɜːvətɪv] a
συντηρητικός, μετριοπαθής || C~ a
(party) συντηρητικός || n Συντηρητικός/ή
m/f.
conservatory [kən'sɜːvətrɪ] n
(greenhouse) θερμοκήπιο, σέρρα || (MUS)
ωδείο.
conserve [kən'sɜːv] vt συντηρώ,
διατηρώ.
consider [kən'sɪdə*] vt (think over)
μελετώ || (take into account) λαμβάνω
υπόψη || (deem) θεωρώ.
considerable [kən'sɪdərəbl] a
σημαντικός, αξιόλογος.
considerate [kən'sɪdərɪt] a διακριτικός,
αβρός.
consideration [kənsɪdə'reɪʃən] n
(thoughtfulness) αβροφροσύνη,
διακριτικότητα || (serious thought) μελέτη,
σκέψη || (reason) λόγος || (reward) αμοιβή.
considering [kən'sɪdərɪŋ] prep
λαμβανομένου υπόψη.
consign [kən'saɪn] vt αποστέλλω,
παραδίδω || ~ment n αποστολή.
consist [kən'sɪst] vi (+ of) συνίσταμαι,
αποτελούμαι.
consistency [kən'sɪstənsɪ] n (firmness)
συνοχή, συνέπεια, σταθερότητα ||
(density) πυκνότητα, στερεότητα.
consistent [kən'sɪstənt] a σταθερός,
συνεπής, σύμφωνος.
consolation [kɒnsə'leɪʃən] n
παρηγοριά.
console [kən'səul] vt παρηγορώ ||
(COMPUT) πληκτρολόγιο.
consolidate [kən'sɒlɪdeɪt] vt
συγχωνεύω, παγιώνω.
consommé [kən'sɒmeɪ] n ζωμός
κρέατος, κονσομέ nt inv.
consonant ['kɒnsənənt] n (GRAM)
σύμφωνο.
consortium [kən'sɔːtɪəm] n
κοινοπραξία, κονσόρτιουμ nt inv.
conspicuous [kən'spɪkjuəs] a
καταφανής, περίβλεπτος || (prominent)
αξιοσημείωτος, σημαντικός.
conspiracy [kən'spɪrəsɪ] n συνωμοσία.
conspire [kən'spaɪə*] vi συνωμοτώ,
συνεργώ.
constable ['kʌnstəbl] n αστυφύλακας,
χωροφύλακας.
constabulary [kən'stæbjulərɪ] n
αστυνομία.
constant ['kɒnstənt] a σταθερός,
συνεχής || ~ly ad σταθερά, συνεχώς.
constellation [kɒnstə'leɪʃən] n
αστερισμός.
consternation [kɒnstə'neɪʃən] n
κατάπληξη.

constipated ['kɒnstɪpeɪtɪd] a
δυσκοίλιος.
constituency [kən'stɪtjuənsɪ] n
εκλογική περιφέρεια.
constituent [kən'stɪtjuənt] n (elector)
ψηφοφόρος m/f || (essential part)
συστατικό.
constitute ['kɒnstɪtjuːt] vt (amount to)
συνιστώ, αποτελώ.
constitution [kɒnstɪ'tjuːʃən] n (laws)
σύνταγμα nt || (health) κράση || ~al a
συνταγματικός.
constrain [kən'streɪn] vt εξαναγκάζω ||
~t n εξαναγκασμός || (feelings) ταραχή,
τράκ nt inv.
constrict [kən'strɪkt] vt συσφίγγω ||
~ion n σύσφιγξη, σφίξιμο.
construct [kən'strʌkt] vt κατασκευάζω,
οικοδομώ || ~ion n κατασκευή,
οικοδόμηση || (GRAM) σύνταξη, ερμηνεία
|| ~ive a εποικοδομητικός,
δημιουργικός.
construe [kən'struː] vt ερμηνεύω.
consul ['kɒnsəl] n πρόξενος || ~ate
['kɒnsjulɪt] n προξενείο.
consult [kən'sʌlt] vt συμβουλεύομαι ||
~ant n (MED) ειδικός γιατρός || (other
specialist) σύμβουλος m/f || ~ation n
συμβούλιο, συνδιάσκεψη || ~ing room
n ιατρείο.
consume [kən'sjum] vt καταναλίσκω ||
~r n καταναλωτής.
consumption [kən'sʌmpʃən] n
κατανάλωση || (MED) φθίση, φυματίωση.
contact ['kɒntækt] n επαφή ♦ vt
έρχομαι σε επαφή με || ~ lenses npl
φακοί mpl επαφής.
contagious [kən'teɪdʒəs] a
μεταδοτικός, κολλητικός.
contain [kən'teɪn] vt περιέχω || to ~
o.s. συγκρατούμαι || ~er n (small)
δοχείο || (TRANSPORT) (εμπορευματικό)
κιβώτιο.
contaminate [kən'tæmɪneɪt] vt
μολύνω, μιαίνω.
contamination [kəntæmɪ'neɪʃən] n
μόλυνση, μίανση.
contemplate ['kɒntəmpleɪt] vt (look at)
κυττάζω, παρατηρώ || (meditate) μελετώ,
αναπολώ || (intend) σκεδιάζω.
contemplation [kɒntəm'pleɪʃən] n
σκέψη, συλλογή.
contemporary [kən'tɛmpərərɪ] a
σύγχρονος ♦ n σύγχρονος/η m/f,
συνομήλικος/η m/f.
contempt [kən'tɛmpt] n περιφρόνηση ||
~ible a αξιοκαταφρόνητος || ~uous a
περιφρονητικός.
contend [kən'tɛnd] vt (strive)
(συν)αγωνίζομαι || (argue) ισχυρίζομαι ||
~er n (competitor) ανταγωνιστής/ίστρια
m/f.
content [kən'tɛnt] a ικανοποιημένος,
ευχαριστημένος ♦ vt ικανοποιώ ♦
['kɒntɛnt] n (of article etc) περιεχόμενο ||
~s npl (of room) περιεχόμενα ntpl || (of
book) (πίνακας) περιεχομένων || (of

barrel) περιεκτικότητα || ~**ed** *a* ικανοποιημένος.

contention [kən'tɛnʃən] *n (dispute)* αγώνας, διαμάχη || *(opinion)* ισχυρισμός.

contentment [kən'tɛntmənt] *n* ικανοποίηση.

contest ['kɔntɛst] *n* αγώνας, πάλη ♦ [kən'tɛst] *vt* διαμφισβητώ, διεκδικώ, αγωνίζομαι || ~**ant** *n* αγωνιζόμενος/η *m/f*, διεκδικητής/ήτρια *m/f*.

context ['kɔntɛkst] *n* συμφραζόμενα *ntpl*.

continent ['kɔntinənt] *n* ήπειρος *f*|| the C~ Ευρώπη || ~**al** *a* ηπειρωτικός.

contingency [kən'tindʒənsi] *n* ενδεχόμενο, σύμπτωση.

contingent [kən'tindʒənt] *n* ενδεχόμενος || *(MIL)* τμήμα στρατού ή ναυτικού ♦ *a* (+ *(up)on)* εξαρτώμενος από.

continual [kən'tinjuəl] *a (endless)* συνεχής, αδιάκοπος || *(often repeated)* συχνός || ~**ly** *ad* συνεχώς.

continuation [kəntinju'eiʃən] *n* συνέχεια, συνέχιση.

continue [kən'tinjuː] *vi* συνεχίζομαι || *(remain)* (παρα)μένω || συνεχίζω || *(resume)* εξακολουθώ.

continuity [kɔnti'njuːiti] *n* συνέχεια.

continuous [kən'tinjuəs] *a* συνεχής, αδιάκοπος.

contort [kən'tɔːt] *vt* συστρίβω, παραμορφώνω || ~**ion** *n* στρίψιμο || *(of face)* μορφασμός || ~**ionist** *n* ακροβάτης/ισσα *m/f*.

contour ['kɔntuə*] *n (shape)* περίγραμμα *nt* || *(of map)* ισούψείς καμπύλες *fpl*.

contraband ['kɔntrəbænd] *n* λαθρεμπόριο, κοντραμπάντο.

contraception [kɔntrə'sɛpʃən] *n* πρόληψη συλλήψεως.

contraceptive [kɔntrə'sɛptiv] *n* αντισυλληπτικό.

contract ['kɔntrækt] *n* συμβόλαιο, συμφωνία ♦ [kən'trækt] *vi (to do sth)* συμφωνώ, συμβάλλομαι || *(become smaller)* συστέλλομαι, στενεύω || ~**ion** *n* συστολή, μάζεμα *nt* || ~**or** *n* εργολάβος, προμηθευτής.

contradict [kɔntrə'dikt] *vt (say the opposite)* αντιλέγω || *(deny)* διαψεύδω || ~**ion** *n (in terms)* αντίφαση || *(denial)* διάψευση.

contralto [kən'træltəʊ] *n* μεσόφωνος, κοντράλτο.

contraption [kən'træpʃən] *n* μηχανή, μαραφέτι.

contrary ['kɔntrəri] *a (opposite)* ενάντιος, αντίθετος || *(unfavourable)* αντίθετος, δυσμενής || **on the** ~ τουναντίον.

contrast ['kɔntrɑːst] *n* σύγκριση, αντίθεση ♦ [kən'trɑːst] *vt* συγκρίνω, αντιπαραβάλλω.

contravene [kɔntrə'viːn] *vt (a rule etc)* παραβαίνω, καταπατώ || *(conflict with)* διαψεύδω, προσκρούω.

contribute [kən'tribjuːt] *vi (help)* συμβάλλω, βοηθώ || *(subscribe)* συνεισφέρω ♦ *vt* καταβάλλω.

contribution [kɔntri'bjuːʃən] *n* συνεισφορά, συνεργασία.

contributor [kən'tribjutə*] *n* συνεισφέρων/ουσα *m/f* συνεργάτης/ιδα *m/f*.

contrite ['kɔntrait] *a* συντριμμένος, μετανοών.

contrive [kən'traiv] *vt (bring about)* καταφέρνω.

control [kən'trəʊl] *vt (check)* συγκρατώ, χαλιναγωγώ || *(direct)* διευθύνω, εξουσιάζω ♦ *n (check)* έλεγχος, επίβλεψη || *(restraint)* χαλινός || ~**s** *npl* χειριστήριο, έλεγχος || ~ **key** *n (COMPUT)* πλήκτρο ελέγχου.

controversial [kɔntrə'vɜːʃəl] *a* συζητήσιμος.

controversy [kən'trɔvəsi] *n* συζήτηση, διαφωνία.

convalesce [kɔnvə'lɛs] *vi* αναρρωνύω || ~**nce** *n* ανάρρωση || ~**nt** *a*, *n* αναρρωνύων.

convene [kən'viːn] *vti* συγκαλώ, συνέρχομαι.

convenience [kən'viːniəns] *n (being convenient)* καταλληλότητα, συμφωνία || *(thing)* ευκολία, άνεση.

convenient [kən'viːniənt] *a* κατάλληλος, βολικός, χρήσιμος.

convent ['kɔnvənt] *n* μονή γυναικών.

convention [kən'vɛnʃən] *n (assembly)* συνέδριο, συνέλευση || *(custom)* έθιμο, συνήθεια || ~**al** *a (traditional)* εθιμοτυπικός, συνηθισμένος.

converge [kən'vɜːdʒ] *vi* συγκλίνω.

conversant [kən'vɜːsənt] *a* (+ *with)* οικείος, γνωστός.

conversation [kɔnvə'seiʃən] *n* συνδιάλεξη, συνομιλία, κουβέντα || ~**al** *a* ομιλητικός, καθομιλούμενος.

converse [kən'vɜːs] *vi* συνομιλώ, συνδιαλέγομαι ♦ ['kɔnvɜːs] *a* αντίθετος || ~**ly** *ad* αντίστροφα, αντιθέτως.

conversion [kən'vɜːʃən] *n* μετατροπή || *(esp REL)* προσηλύτιση || ~ **table** *n* πίνακας μετατροπών.

convert [kən'vɜːt] *vt (change)* μετατρέπω || *(esp REL)* προσηλυτίζω ♦ ['kɔnvɜːt] *n (AUT)* προσήλυτος || ~**ible** *n (AUT)* καμπριολέ *nt inv*.

convex ['kɔn'vɛks] *a* κυρτός.

convey [kən'vei] *vt (carry)* μεταφέρω || *(communicate)* μεταβιβάζω, μεταδίδω || ~**or belt** *n* μεταφορέας.

convict [kən'vikt] *vt* καταδικάζω ♦ ['kɔnvikt] *n* κατάδικος/η *m/f*|| ~**ion** *n (verdict)* καταδίκη || *(belief)* πεποίθηση.

convince [kən'vins] *vt* πείθω.

convincing [kən'vinsiŋ] *a* πειστικός.

convoy ['kɔnvɔi] *n* συνοδεία, νηοπομπή.

convulse [kən'vʌls] *vt (esp with laughter)* ξεραίνομαι στα γέλια.

convulsion [kən'vʌlʃən] *n* σπασμός.

coo [kuː] vi (dove) τερετίζω σαν περιστέρι.

cook [kuk] vt μαγειρεύω ♦ vi ψήνομαι ♦ n μάγειρας || ~book n βιβλίο μαγειρικής || ~er n συσκευή μαγειρέματος || ~ery n μαγειρική || ~ery book n = cookbook || ~ie n (US) μπισκότο || ~ing n μαγειρική.

cool [kuːl] a (fairly cold) δροσερός || (calm) ψύχραιμος || (unfriendly) ψυχρός, αδιάφορος || (impudent) αναιδής, θρασύς ♦ vti δροσίζω, κρυώνω || ~ness n ψύχρα, ψυχρότητα.

coop [kuːp] n κοτέτσι, κλούβα ♦ vt: to ~ up (fig) περιορίζω, κλείνω.

co-op ['kəʊ'ɒp] n = cooperative.

cooperate [kəʊ'ɒpəreit] vi συνεργάζομαι.

cooperation [kəʊɒpə'reiʃən] n συνεργασία.

cooperative [kəʊ'ɒpərətiv] a συνεργατικός ♦ n (farmers) συνεταιρισμός || ~ store n (retail) πρατήριο συνεταιρισμού.

coordinate [kəʊ'ɔːdineit] vt συνδυάζω, συντονίζω.

coordination [kəʊɔːdi'neiʃən] n συντονισμός.

coot [kuːt] n φαλαρίδα, λούφα.

cope [kəʊp] vi (+ with) αντιμετωπίζω, αντεπεξέρχομαι.

co-pilot ['kəʊ'pailət] n δεύτερος χειριστής.

copper ['kɒpə*] n χαλκός, μπακίρι || (coin) δεκάρα || (sl: policeman) αστυφύλακας.

coppice ['kɒpis] n, **copse** [kɒps] n δασύλλιο, λόχμη.

copulate ['kɒpjuleit] vi συνουσιάζομαι, γαμώ.

copy ['kɒpi] n (imitation) αντίγραφο, αντιγραφή || (of book) αντίτυπο ♦ vt αντιγράφω, απομιμούμαι || (COMPUT) αντιγράφω || ~cat n τετράδιο || ~ right n μιμητής/τρια m/f|| ~right n πνευματική ιδιοκτησία || ~right reserved απαγορεύεται η αναδημοσίευση.

coral ['kɒrəl] n κοράλλιο || ~ reef n κοραλλιογενές νησί.

cord [kɔːd] n σχοινί, χορδή || see vocal.

cordial ['kɔːdiəl] a εγκάρδιος || ~ly ad (invite) εγκάρδια, θερμά.

cordon ['kɔːdn] n (ornamental) κορδόνι || (of police etc) ζώνη.

corduroy ['kɔːdərɔi] n κοτλέ nt inv.

core [kɔː*] n πυρήνας, καρδιά ♦ vt αφαιρώ το πυρήνα.

cork [kɔːk] n φελλός || (of bottle) πώμα nt || ~screw n τιρμπουσόν nt inv.

cormorant ['kɔːmərənt] n φαλακροκόρακας, καλικατζού f inv.

corn [kɔːn] n σιτηρά ntpl, δημητριακά ntpl || (US: maize) καλαμπόκι || (on foot) κάλος.

cornea ['kɔːniə] n κερατοειδής.

corned ['kɔːnd]: ~ beef n βοδινό κρέας σε κονσέρβα.

corner ['kɔːnə*] n (of street) γωνία || (of room) γωνία, κώχη || (fig) δύσκολη θέση ♦ vt φέρω σε δύσκολη θέση, στριμώχνω || (ECON) μονοπωλώ ♦ vi (turn) παίρνω στροφή || ~ kick n κόρνερ nt inv || ~stone n ακρογωνιαίος λίθος, βάση.

cornet ['kɔːnit] n (MUS) κορνέττα || (ice cream) χωνάκι.

cornflour ['kɔːnflaʊə*] n καλαμποκάλευρο, κορνφλάουερ nt inv.

cornice ['kɔːnis] n κορνίζα.

cornstarch ['kɔːnstɑːtʃ] n (US) = cornflour.

corny ['kɔːni] a (joke) σαχλός.

coronary ['kɒrənəri] a στεφανιαίος ♦ n στεφανιαία || ~ thrombosis n θρόμβωση της στεφανιαίας.

coronation [kɒrə'neiʃən] n στέψη.

coroner ['kɒrənə*] n ιατροδικαστής m/f.

corporal ['kɔːpərəl] n (MIL) δεκανέας || (AVIAT) υποσμηνίας ♦ a σωματικός.

corporation [kɔːpə'reiʃən] n σωματείο || (esp business) εταιρεία.

corps [kɔː*] n (στρατιωτικό) σώμα nt.

corpse [kɔːps] n πτώμα nt, κουφάρι.

corpulent ['kɔːpjulənt] a παχύσαρκος.

corpuscle ['kɔːpʌsl] n σωματίδιο || (blood corpuscle) αιμοσφαίριο.

corral [kə'rɑːl] n μάντρα.

correct [kə'rekt] a (accurate) ακριβής, ορθός, διορθωμένος || (proper) άψογος, όπως πρέπει ♦ vt (papers etc) διορθώνω || (make right) επανορθώνω || ~ion n διόρθωση || ~ly ad ορθά, σωστά.

correlate ['kɒrileit] vt σχετίζομαι, συσχετίζω.

correlation [kɒri'leiʃən] n συσχετισμός, συσχέτιση.

correspond [kɒris'pɒnd] vi (agree with) ανταποκρίνομαι, ταιριάζω || (write) αλληλογραφώ || ~ence n (letters) αλληλογραφία || (similarity) αντιστοιχία, αντανάκριση || ~ence course n μάθημα nt αλληλογραφίας || ~ent n (reporter) ανταποκριτής/τρια m/f || ~ing a αντίστοιχος.

corridor ['kɒridɔː*] n διάδρομος.

corroborate [kə'rɒbəreit] vt επιβεβαιώνω, ενισχύω.

corroboration [kərɒbə'reiʃən] n επιβεβαίωση, επίρρωση.

corrode [kə'rəʊd] vti διαβρώνω, σκουριάζω.

corrosion [kə'rəʊʒən] n διάβρωση, σκωρίαση.

corrugated ['kɒrəgeitid] a κυματοειδής || ~ cardboard n κυματοειδές χαρτόνι || ~ iron n αυλακωτό έλασμα nt.

corrupt [kə'rʌpt] a διεφθαρμένος ♦ vt διαφθείρω || ~ion n διαφθορά, δεκασμός.

corset ['kɔːsit] n κορσές m.

cortège [kɔː'teiʒ] n νεκρώσιμος πομπή.

cortisone ['kɔːtizəʊn] n κορτιζόνη.

cosh [kɒʃ] n μαγκούρα, βούρδουλας ♦ vt κτυπώ με βούρδουλα.

cosiness ['kəuzinis] n άνεση.

cosmetic [kɒz'mɛtik] n καλλυντικό.

cosmic ['kɒzmik] a κοσμικός.

cosmonaut ['kɒzmənɔːt] n αστροναύτης, κοσμοναύτης.

cosmopolitan [kɒzmə'pɒlitən] a κοσμοπολιτικός.

cosmos ['kɒzmɒs] n κόσμος, σύμπαν nt.

cost [kɒst] (irreg v) n κόστος nt, τιμή, δαπάνη ♦ vt κοστίζω, || it ~s £5 στοιχίζει πέντε λίρες || it ~s too much στοιχίζει πολλά || it ~ him his life τού κόστισε τη ζωή || at all ~s πάση θυσία.

costly ['kɒstli] a (expensive) δαπανηρός || (jewellery etc) πολύτιμος.

cost price ['kɒstprais] n τιμή κόστους.

costume ['kɒstjuːm] n (style of dress) ένδυμα nt, φορεσιά, μόδα || (woman's outer clothes) ενδυμασία, κοστούμι || (for bathing) μπανιερό, μαγιό nt inv.

cosy ['kəuzi] a αναπαυτικός, ζεστός.

cot [kɒt] n (child's bed) κρεββατάκι.

cottage ['kɒtidʒ] n εξοχικό σπιτάκι || ~ cheese n άσπρο τυρί.

cotton ['kɒtn] n βαμβάκι, μπαμπάκι || ~ wool n ακατέργαστο βαμβάκι.

couch [kautʃ] n ντιβάνι, καναπές m ♦ vt εκφράζω, συγκαλύπτω.

cough [kɒf] vi βήχω ♦ n βήχας || ~ drop n παστίλια για το βήχα.

could [kud] pt of can || ~n't = could not || see can.

council ['kaunsl] n συμβούλιο || ~lor n σύμβουλος m/f.

counsel ['kaunsəl] n (LAW) δικηγόρος m/f|| (opinion) συμβουλή || ~lor n σύμβουλος.

count [kaunt] vt (add up) μετρώ, αριθμώ || (include) υπολογίζω, συμπεριλαμβάνω ♦ vi (be of importance) υπολογίζομαι, στηρίζομαι ♦ n (reckoning) αρίθμηση, μέτρηση, λογαριασμός || (nobleman) κόμης || to ~ on vt υπολογίζω, στηρίζομαι σε || to ~ up vt προσθέτω.

counter ['kauntə*] n θυρίδα, γκισέ nt inv || (machine that counts) μετρητής ♦ vt αντιτίθεμαι, αντιπαντώ || ad εναντίον, αντιθέτως || ~act vt αντιδρώ, εξουδετερώνω || ~-attack n αντεπίθεση || ~balance vt αντιστοθμίζω || ~-espionage n αντικατασκοπεία.

counterfeit ['kauntəfit] a πλαστός, κίβδηλος ♦ n παραποίηση, απάτη ♦ vt πλαστογραφώ.

counterfoil ['kauntəfɔil] n στέλεχος nt.

counterpart ['kauntəpaːt] n αντίστοιχο, ταίρι.

countess ['kauntis] n κόμισσα, κοντέσσα.

countless ['kauntlis] a αναρίθμητος, αμέτρητος.

country ['kʌntri] n (land) χώρα || (of birth) πατρίδα || (rural district) ύπαιθρος f, εξοχή, επαρχία || (region) περιοχή || ~ dancing n εθνικός χορός, λαϊκός χορός || ~ house n εξοχικό σπίτι || ~man n

(national) (συμ)πατριώτης || (rural) επαρχιώτης, χωριάτης || ~side n ύπαιθρος f.

county ['kaunti] n κομπτεία, επαρχία || ~ town n πρωτεύουσα κομπτείας.

coup [kuː] n (also: ~ d'état) πραξικόπημα nt.

coupé ['kuːpei] n κουπέ nt inv.

couple ['kʌpl] n ζευγάρι, δύο ♦ vt ενώνω, ζευγαρώνω.

couplet ['kʌplit] n δίστοιχο.

coupling ['kʌpliŋ] n σύζευξη.

coupon ['kuːpɒn] n κουπόνι, απόκομμα nt.

courage ['kʌridʒ] n θάρρος nt, γενναιότητα || ~ous a θαρραλέος.

courier ['kuriə*] n αγγελιοφόρος.

course [kɔːs] n (path, track) διαδρομή || (line of action) πορεία, δρόμος || (series, procedure) μάθημα nt, κουρ nt inv|| (career, journey) πορεία || (part of meal) φαγητό, πιάτο || of ~ φυσικά, και βέβαια || in the ~ of κατά τη διάρκεια του || in due ~ εν καιρώ δέοντι || see golf.

court [kɔːt] n (attendants of sovereign) αυλή || (residence of sovereign) (βασιλική) αυλή || (of justice) δικαστήριο ♦ vt κορτάρω, προσκαλώ, επιδιώκω || see tennis.

courteous ['kɔːtiəs] a ευγενής.

courtesy ['kɔːtisi] n ευγένεια.

courthouse ['kɔːthaus] n (US) δικαστικό μέγαρο.

courtier ['kɔːtiə*] n αυλικός.

court-martial ['kɔːt'maːʃəl] n στρατοδικείο.

court room ['kɔːtrum] n αίθουσα δικαστηρίου.

courtyard ['kɔːtjaːd] n αυλή.

cousin ['kʌzn] n ξάδελφος/η m/f.

cove [kəuv] n όρμος.

cover ['kʌvə*] vt (place over) καλύπτω, σκεπάζω || (shield, screen) καλύπτω, προστατεύω, κρύβω || (deal with) καλύπτω, περιλαμβάνω || (protect) προστατεύω ♦ n κάλυμμα nt, σκέπασμα nt|| ~age n (of news) ρεπορτάζ nt inv|| ~charge n κουβέρ nt inv|| ~ing n κάλυψη, σκέπασμα nt, επένδυση || ~ing letter n επιβεβαιωτική επιστολή.

covet ['kʌvit] vt εποφθαλμιώ.

cow [kau] n αγελάδα.

coward ['kauəd] n άνανδρος/n m/f, δειλός/n m/f|| ~ice n δειλία || ~ly a άνανδρος, δειλός.

cowboy ['kaubɔi] n καουμπόι nt inv.

cower ['kauə*] vi μαζεύομαι, τρέμω.

cowshed ['kauʃed] n βουστάσιο.

coxswain ['kɒksn] n (abbr: cox) πηδαλιούχος.

coy [kɔi] a ντροπαλός, σεμνός.

c.p.s. abbr see character.

CPU abbr see central.

crab [kræb] n κάβουρας || ~ apple n αγριόμηλο.

crack [kræk] n (sharp noise) κρότος, τριγμός || (of whip) στράκα || (split) ρωγμή, σκάσιμο ♦ vt (noise) κροτώ || (split) θραύω, ραγίζω ♦ a λαμπρός, εκλεκτός || ~er n (firework) βαρελότο, στράκα || (biscuit) παξιμαδάκι, μπισκότο || to ~ up vi κομματιάζω || (fig) καταρρέω.

crackling ['kræklɪŋ] n κροταλισμός, τρίξιμο || (of pig) πέσα ψημένου γουρουνιού.

cradle ['kreɪdl] n κοιτίδα, λίκνο, κούνια.

craft [krɑːft] n (skill) τέχνη, χειροτεχνία, επάγγελμα nt || (cunning) πανουργία, δόλος || (boat) σκάφος nt, βάρκα || ~sman n τεχνίτης || ~smanship n τέχνη || ~y a πανούργος, πονηρός, πολυμήχανος.

crag [kræg] n κατάβραχο, γκρεμός || ~gy a απόκρημνος, βραχώδης.

cram [kræm] vt μπάζω, χώνω.

cramp [kræmp] n (MED) σπασμός, κράμπα ♦ vt εμποδίζω, περιορίζω.

crane [kreɪn] n γερανός, κρένι.

crank [kræŋk] n (lever) (χειρο)στρόφαλος, μανιβέλα || (person) ιδιότυπος, εκκεντρικός ♦ vt βάζω μπρος με μανιβέλλα || ~shaft n στροφαλοφόρος (άξωνας).

cranny ['krænɪ] n σχισμή, ρωγμή.

crash [kræʃ] n κρότος, βρόντος || (AVIAT) συντριβή, πτώση || (AUT) σύγκρουση || (ECON) κραχ nt inv ♦ vti πέφτω, συντρίβομαι || ~ helmet n προστατευτικό κράνος || ~ landing n αναγκαστική προσγείωση.

crate [kreɪt] n κασόνι, κοφίνι, καφάσι.

crater ['kreɪtə*] n κρατήρας.

cravat(e) [krə'væt] n γραβάτα.

crave [kreɪv] vi (+ for) εκλιπαρώ, ποθώ.

craving ['kreɪvɪŋ] n πόθος, λαχτάρα.

crawl [krɔːl] vi έρπω, σέρνομαι ♦ n σύροιμο, βραδυπορία || (swimming) κρώουλ nt inv.

crayon ['kreɪən] n κραγιόνι, παστέλ nt inv.

craze [kreɪz] n μανία, λόξα.

crazy ['kreɪzɪ] a (foolish) ανόητος || (insane) παράφρονας, τρελλός, μουρλός.

creak [kriːk] n τριγμός ♦ vi τρίζω.

cream [kriːm] n καϊμάκι, κρέμα, σαντιγί f inv || (polish) αλοιφή || (cosmetic) κρέμα || (colour) ιβουάρ nt inv, κρεμ || ~ cake n πάστα, τούρτα || ~y a καϊμακλίδικος, βουτιράτο.

crease [kriːs] n πτυχή, τσάκισμα nt, τσαλάκωμα nt ♦ vti διπλώνω, ζαρώνω, τσαλακώνω.

create [kriː'eɪt] vt (bring into being) δημιουργώ || (cause) προξενώ || (COMPUT: file) δημιουργώ.

creation [kriː'eɪʃən] n δημιούργημα nt.

creative [kriː'eɪtɪv] a δημιουργικός.

creator [kriː'eɪtə*] n δημιουργός.

creature ['kriːtʃə*] n πλάσμα nt, ον nt.

credentials [krɪ'dɛnʃəlz] npl (papers) διαπιστευτήρια ntpl, πιστοποιητικά ntpl.

credibility [krɛdə'bɪlɪtɪ] n αξιοπιστία, (το) πιστευτό.

credible ['krɛdɪbl] a πιστευτός, αξιόπιτος.

credit ['krɛdɪt] n πίστη, πίστωση || (recognition) αναγνώριση ♦ vt πιστεύω || ~able a έντιμος, αξιέπαινος || ~ card n κάρτα πιστώσεως || ~or n πιστωτής.

creed [kriːd] n πίστη, θρήσκευμα nt.

creek [kriːk] n κολπίσκος || (US) ρέμα nt.

creep [kriːp] (irreg v) vi έρπω, σύρομαι || ~er n (animal) ερπετό || (plant) αναρριχητικό || ~y a (frightening) ανατριχιαστικός.

cremate [krɪ'meɪt] vt αποτεφρώνω, καίω.

cremation [krɪ'meɪʃən] n καύση (νεκρού).

crematorium [krɛmə'tɔːrɪəm] n κρεματόριο.

crêpe [kreɪp] n κρέπ(ι) nt inv.

crept [krɛpt] pt, pp of **creep.**

crescent ['krɛsnt] n ημισέληνος f || (esp street) ημικυκλικός δρόμος.

cress [krɛs] n κάρδαμο.

crest [krɛst] n (tuft) λοφίο, λειρί || (of wave) κορυφή || (badge) κορωνίδα, οικόσημο || ~fallen a κατηφής, αποθαρρημένος.

Crete [kriːt] n Κρήτη.

crevasse [krɪ'væs] n σχισμή.

crevice ['krɛvɪs] n ρωγμή, χαραμάδα.

crew [kruː] n πλήρωμα nt || ~-cut n πολύ κοντό μαλλί.

crib [krɪb] n (child's bed) παιδικό κρεβάτι || (copy) αντιγραφή.

crick [krɪk] n πιάσιμο.

cricket ['krɪkɪt] n (insect) γρύλλος, τριζόνι || (game) κρίκετ nt inv.

crime [kraɪm] n (wicked act) κακούργημα nt || (lawbreaking) έγκλημα nt.

criminal ['krɪmɪnl] n εγκληματίας, κακούργος ♦ a εγκληματικός, ποινικός.

crimson ['krɪmzn] n πορφυρό, βυσσινί ♦ a κατακόκκινος.

cringe [krɪndʒ] vi φέρομαι δουλοπρεπώς, σκύβω.

crinkle ['krɪŋkl] vt ζαρώνω, τσαλακώνω || (rustle) τρίβω.

cripple ['krɪpl] n ανάπηρος, χωλός ♦ vt τραυματίζω, σακατεύω, παραλύω.

crisis ['kraɪsɪs] n (time of danger etc) κρίση.

crisp [krɪsp] a τραγανός, αφράτος, φρέσκος ♦ n ξεροτηγανισμένη πατάτα.

criss-cross ['krɪskrɒs] a σταυρωτός, καφασιτός.

criterion [kraɪ'tɪərɪən] n κριτήριο.

critic ['krɪtɪk] n (THEAT etc) τεχνοκρίτης, κριτικός || επικριτής || ~al a (like a critic) κριτικός || (danger) κρίσιμος || (severe) αυστηρός || ~ally ad με κριτική διάθεση, κρίσιμος || ~ism ['krɪtɪsɪzəm] n (judgment) κριτική || (finding fault) επίκριση || ~ize ['krɪtɪsaɪz] vt (επι)κρίνω, κατακρίνω.

croak [krəʊk] vi (crow) κρώζω || (frog) κοάζω ♦ n (of crow) κρωγμός || (of frog) κοασμός.

crochet ['krəʊʃeɪ] n κροσέ nt.

crockery ['krɒkərɪ] n πήλινα σκεύη ntpl.

crocodile ['krɒkədaɪl] n κροκόδειλος.

crocus ['krəʊkəs] n κρόκος.

crook [krʊk] n (criminal) λωποδύτης, απατεώνας || (of shepherd) γκλίτσα || ~ed a αγκυλωτός.

crop [krɒp] n συγκομιδή, σοδιά || to ~ up vi (fig) παρουσιάζομαι, προκύπτω.

croquet ['krəʊkeɪ] n κροκέ nt.

croquette [krəʊ'ket] n κροκέτα, κεφτές m.

cross [krɒs] n (of Christ) σταυρός || (mark) σταυρός || (breed) διασταύρωση || (misfortune) εμπόδιο, δυσκολία ♦ vt (pass over) διασχίζω, περνώ || (make sign) σταυροκοπιέμαι || (place across) σταυρώνω || (mix breeds) διασταυρώνω || (cheque) διαγραμμίζω ♦ a θυμωμένος, κακόκεφος || ~-country (race) n ανώμαλος δρόμος || ~-examination n εξέταση κατ'αντιπαράσταση || ~-examine vt εξετάζω κατ'αντιπαράσταση || ~-eyed a αλλοίθωρος || ~ing n (road etc) διάβαση, πέρασμα nt || (sea passage) διάπλους m || (place for crossing) διάβαση || at ~-purposes παρεξηγημένοι, σε αντίθεση || ~-reference n παραπομπή || ~roads n σταυροδρόμι || ~section n εγκάρσια τομή || ~ wind n πλάγιος άνεμος || ~word (puzzle) n σταυρόλεξο.

crotch [krɒtʃ] n διακλάδωση δένδρου, καβάλος του πανταλονιού.

crotchet ['krɒtʃɪt] n ιδιοτροπία, βίδα.

crotchety ['krɒtʃɪtɪ] a (person) ιδιότροπος.

crouch [kraʊtʃ] vi σκύβω, μαζεύομαι.

crow [krəʊ] n κορώνη, κουρούνα ♦ vi κράζω, λαλώ || (fig) κομπάζω.

crowbar ['krəʊbɑ:*] n λοστός.

crowd [kraʊd] n πλήθος nt, όχλος, συρροή ♦ vt (fill) γεμίζω ♦ vi (flock together) συνωθούμαι, συνωστίζομαι || ~ed a γεμάτος.

crown [kraʊn] n (royal headdress) στέμμα nt, κορώνα || (of tooth) κορώνα || (top of head etc) κορυφή, κορφή || (of flowers) στεφάνι ♦ vt (put crown on) στεφανώνω || (be at top of) πάνω απ'όλα, αποκορυφώνω || ~ jewels npl κοσμήματα του Στέμματος ntpl || ~ prince n διάδοχος του θρόνου.

crucial ['kru:ʃəl] a αποφασιστικός, κρίσιμος.

crucifix ['kru:sɪfɪks] n εσταυρωμένος || ~ion n σταύρωση.

crucify ['kru:sɪfaɪ] vt σταυρώνω, βασανίζω.

crude [kru:d] a (unfinished) ακατέργαστος || (petroleum) αργό πετρέλαιο || (harsh) ωμός, άξεστος || (humour) χοντρό χιούμορ.

cruel ['kruəl] a (vicious) αιμοβόρος, αμείλικτος || (severe, distressing) σκληρός, ωμός || (hard-hearted) σκληρόκαρδος ||

~ty n σκληρότητα, ασπλαχνία || (to wife) κακοποίηση.

cruise [kru:z] n περίπλους m, κρουαζιέρα ♦ vi κάνω κρουαζιέρα, περιπλέω || ~r n καταδρομικό.

crumb [krʌm] n ψίχουλο || (fig) απομεινάρι.

crumble ['krʌmbl] vti καταρρέω, θρυμματίζομαι.

crumbly ['krʌmblɪ] a εύθρυπτος.

crumpet ['krʌmpɪt] n είδος τηγανίτας.

crumple ['krʌmpl] vt τσαλακώνω, ζαρώνω.

crunch [krʌntʃ] n τραγάνισμα nt || (sound) τρίξιμο ♦ vt μασώ, τραγανίζω || ~y a τραγανιστός.

crusade [kru:'seɪd] n σταυροφορία.

crush [krʌʃ] n σύνθλιψη, συνωστισμός ♦ vt συνθλίβω || (a rebellion) συντρίβω, καταβάλλω ♦ vi (material) τσαλακώνω || ~ing a συντριπτικός.

crust [krʌst] n (of bread) κόρα || (of cake etc) κρούστα || (of earth etc) φλοιός, κρούστα.

crutch [krʌtʃ] n δεκανίκι, πατερίτσα.

crux [krʌks] n ουσία, κεντρικό σημείο.

cry [kraɪ] vi (sell etc) διαλαλώ || (shout) φωνάζω, βάζω τις φωνές || (weep) κλαίω, θρηνώ ♦ n φωνή, κλάμα nt.

crypt [krɪpt] n κρύπτη.

cryptic ['krɪptɪk] a μυστικός, δυσνόητος.

crystal ['krɪstl] n (natural form) κρύσταλλος || (clear glass) κρύσταλλο || ~-clear a κρυστάλλινος || ~lize vti (lit) (απο)κρυσταλλώνω || (fig) (απο)κρυσταλλούμαι.

cu. abbr: ~ ft. = cubic feet; ~ in. = cubic inches.

cub [kʌb] n νεογνό ζώο.

cube [kju:b] n (figure) κύβος.

cubic ['kju:bɪk] a κυβικός.

cubicle ['kju:bɪkəl] n θαλαμίσκος.

cuckoo ['kuku:] n κούκος.

cucumber ['kju:kʌmbə*] n αγγούρι.

cuddle ['kʌdl] vti αγκαλιάζω, κουκουλώνομαι ♦ n αγκάλιασμα nt.

cue [kju:] n (hint) νύξη, υπαινιγμός || (in billiards) στέκα.

cuff [kʌf] n (of shirt, coat etc) μανικέτι || (US) = turn-up || ~link n μανικετόκουμπο ntpl.

cuisine [kwɪ'zi:n] n μαγειρική.

cul-de-sac ['kʌldə'sæk] n αδιέξοδο.

culinary ['kʌlɪnərɪ] a μαγειρικός.

culminate ['kʌlmɪneɪt] vi αποκορυφώνομαι, μεσουρανώ.

culmination [kʌlmɪ'neɪʃən] n μεσουράνημα nt, κολοφών m.

culprit ['kʌlprɪt] n ένοχος.

cult [kʌlt] n (religious) λατρεία || (mode) μόδα, λόξα.

cultivate ['kʌltɪveɪt] vt καλλιεργώ.

cultivation [kʌltɪ'veɪʃən] n καλλιέργεια.

cultural ['kʌltʃərəl] a πνευματικός, μορφωτικός.

culture ['kʌltʃə*] n (refinement)

καλλιέργεια || (intellectual development)
ανάπτυξη, κουλτούρα || ~d a
μορφωμένος, καλλιεργημένος.

cumbersome ['kʌmbəsəm] a
ενοχλητικός, βαρύς, δυσκίνητος.

cumulative ['kju:mjulətɪv] a
επισωρευτικός, αθροιστικός.

cunning ['kʌnɪŋ] n πανουργία,
καπατσοσύνη ♦ a πονηρός,
τετραπέρατος.

cup [kʌp] n κούπα, φλυτζάνι || (prize)
κύπελλο.

cupboard ['kʌbəd] n ντουλάπι, αρμάρι.

cupful ['kʌpfəl] n φλυτζανιά.

cupola ['kju:pələ] n θόλος, τρούλλος.

curable ['kjuərəbl] a ιάσιμος, που
γιατρεύεται.

curator [kjuə'reɪtə*] n έφορος
(μουσείου).

curb [kɜ:b] vt χαλιναγωγώ, ελέγχω ♦ n
χαλινός, φραγμός || see **kerb(stone)**.

curfew ['kɜ:fju:] n απαγόρευση της
κυκλοφορίας.

curiosity [kjuərɪ'ɒsɪtɪ] n περιέργεια ||
(strange object) περίεργο αντικείμενο.

curious ['kjuərɪəs] a (φιλο)περίεργος ||
(strange) περίεργος, παράξενος.

curl [kɜ:l] n βόστρυχος, μπούκλα || (of lips
etc) στρίψιμο ♦ vti (hair etc) σγουραίνω ||
(lips) στρίβω, στραβώνω || (wrap) τυλίγω ||
~ **er** n ρολό ntpl, μπικουτί nt inv.

curly ['kɜ:lɪ] a κατσαρός, σγουρός.

currant ['kʌrənt] n Κορινθιακή
σταφίδα.

currency ['kʌrənsɪ] n νόμισμα nt || (of
ideas) κυκλοφορία, πέραση.

current ['kʌrənt] n ρεύμα nt, ροή, ρέμα
nt ♦ a κυκλοφορών, εν χρήσει || ~
account n τρεχούμενος λογαριασμός ||
~ **affairs** npl επίκαιρα ntpl || ~**ly** ad
γενικώς, σήμερα.

curriculum [kə'rɪkjuləm] n κύκλος
μαθημάτων || ~ **vitae** n περίληψη
προσόντων.

curry ['kʌrɪ] n κάρρι nt || ~ **powder** n
σκόνη κάρρι.

curse [kɜ:s] vi βλαστημώ, υβρίζω ♦ vt
καταριέμαι, αναθεματίζω ♦ n κατάρα,
ανάθεμα nt || (bad language) βλαστήμια.

cursor ['kɜ:sə*] n (COMPUT) δείκτης
θέσεως.

cursory ['kɜ:sərɪ] a γρήγορος,
βιαστικός.

curt [kɜ:t] a απότομος, κοφτός.

curtail [kɜ:'teɪl] vt περικόπτω,
περιορίζω.

curtain ['kɜ:tn] n (esp at window)
κουρτίνα || (THEAT) αυλαία,
παραπέτασμα nt.

curtsy ['kɜ:tsɪ] n υπόκλιση ♦ vi κάνω
υπόκλιση.

curve [kɜ:v] n καμπή.

cushion ['kuʃən] n μαξιλαράκι.

custard ['kʌstəd] n ψημένη κρέμα.

custodian [kʌs'təudɪən] n φύλακας,
επιστάτης.

custody ['kʌstədɪ] n επιτήρηση,
κηδεμονία || (under arrest) κράτηση.

custom ['kʌstəm] n (fashion) έθιμο,
συνήθεια || (business) πελατεία || ~**ary**
a συνηθισμένος || ~-**made** a καμωμένο
επί παραγγελία.

customer ['kʌstəmə*] n πελάτης/τισσα
m/f.

customs ['kʌstəmz] n (taxes) δασμοί mpl
|| **C**~ (place) τελωνείο || **C**~ **officer** n
τελωνειακός υπάλληλος.

cut [kʌt] vt (irreg v) (divide) κόβω, χαράζω
|| (wound) πληγώνω || (reduce) κατεβάζω
(τιμές) ♦ n (sharp stroke) κόψη, κόψιμο ||
(wound) τομή, κόψιμο, πληγή || (reduction)
περικοπή, μείωση || (share) μερίδιο.

cute [kju:t] a χαριτωμένος.

cuticle ['kju:tɪkl] n (on nail) επιδερμίδα.

cutlery ['kʌtlərɪ] n μαχαιροπήρουνα
ntpl.

cutlet ['kʌtlɪt] n κοτολέττα.

cutout ['kʌtaut] n (ELEC) διακόπτης.

cutprice ['kʌtpraɪs] a τιμή ελαττωμένη.

cutting ['kʌtɪŋ] n αιχμή, κόψη.

cwt abbr of **hundredweight(s)**.

cyanide ['saɪənaɪd] n κυανίδη.

cycle ['saɪkl] n (bicycle) ποδήλατο ||
(series) κύκλος, περίοδος f || (of poems etc)
κύκλος ♦ vi πηγαίνω με ποδήλατο.

cycling ['saɪklɪŋ] n ποδηλατοδρομία,
ποδήλατο.

cyclist ['saɪklɪst] n ποδηλατιστής.

cyclone ['saɪkləun] n κυκλώνας.

cygnet ['sɪgnɪt] n μικρός κύκνος.

cylinder ['sɪlɪndə*] n κύλινδρος || (of gas
etc) φιάλη, μπουκάλα || ~ **block** n
συγκρότημα nt κυλίνδρου || ~ **capacity**
n όγκος κυλίνδρου || ~ **head** n κεφαλή
κυλίνδρου.

cymbals ['sɪmbəlz] npl κύμβαλα ntpl.

cynic ['sɪnɪk] n κυνικός || ~**al** a κυνικός,
δύσπιστος || ~**ism** ['sɪnɪsɪzəm] n
κυνισμός, χοτηροκουβέντα.

cypress ['saɪprɪs] n κυπαρίσσι.

Cyprus ['saɪprəs] n Κύπρος f.

cyst [sɪst] n κύστις.

czar [zɑ:] n τσάρος || ~**ina** n τσαρίνα.

Czech [tʃek] a τσεχικός || n Τσέχος/α
m/f.

Czechoslavakia ['tʃekəusləu'vækɪə] n
Τσεχοσλοβακία.

D

dab [dæb] vt επαλείφω ♦ n (tap) ελαφρό
κτύπημα nt || (smear) μικρή ποσότητα,
λίγο.

dad(dy) ['dæd(ɪ)] n μπαμπάς,
μπαμπάκας || **daddy-long-legs** n
τιπούλη, αλογατάκι.

daffodil ['dæfədɪl] n ασφόδελος.

daft [dɑ:ft] a ανόητος, τρελλός.

dagger ['dægə*] n εγχειρίδιο, στιλέττο.

dahlia ['deɪlɪə] n ντάλια.

daily ['deɪlɪ] a ημερήσιος ♦ n
καθημερινή (εφημερίδα).

dainty ['deɪntɪ] a κομψός, νόστιμος.

dairy ['dɛərɪ] n (shop) γαλακτοπωλείο, γαλατάδικο || (on farm) γαλακτοκομείο ♦ a γαλακτοκομικό.

daisy ['deɪzɪ] n μαργαρίτα || ~ wheel n (on printer) μαργαρίτα || ~ wheel printer n εκτυπωτής μαργαρίτας.

dam [dæm] n (for water) φράγμα nt, ανάχωμα nt ♦ vt φράσσω.

damage ['dæmɪdʒ] n βλάβη, ζημιά ♦ vt βλάπτω, ζημιώνω || ~s npl (LAW) αποζημίωση.

dame [deɪm] n κυρία, κυρά.

damn [dæm] vt καταδικάζω ♦ a (col) διάβολος || ~ it να πάρει ο διάβολος!, να πάρει η ευχή! || ~ing a καταδικαστικός, επιβαρυντικός.

damp [dæmp] a υγρός, νοτερός ♦ n υγρασία, υγρότητα ♦ vt (also: ~en) υγραίνω, μουσκεύω || (discourage) μειώνω, ελαττώνω, κόβω || ~ness n υγρασία, υγρότητα.

damson ['dæmzən] n δαμάσκηνο.

dance [dɑːns] n χορός || (party) χορευτική συγκέντρωση, πάρτυ nt inv ♦ vi χορεύω || ~ hall n χορευτικό κέντρο || ~r n χορευτής, χορεύτρια.

dancing ['dɑːnsɪŋ] n χορός.

dandelion ['dændɪlaɪən] n αγριοραδίκι.

dandruff ['dændrəf] n πιτυρίδα.

dandy ['dændɪ] n κομψευόμενος, δανδής.

Dane [deɪn] n Δανός/έζα m/f.

danger ['deɪndʒə*] n κίνδυνος || ~! (sign) προσοχή || in ~ διατρέχω κίνδυνο || ~ous a επικίνδυνος.

dangle ['dæŋgl] vti αιωρούμαι, ταλαντεύομαι, κρέμομαι.

Danish ['deɪnɪʃ] a δανικός ♦ n Δανική γλώσσα.

dare [dɛə*] vt τολμώ ♦ vi: to ~ (to) do sth τολμώ να κάνω κάτι || I ~ say ασφαλώς, πιθανώς.

daring ['dɛərɪŋ] a τολμηρός, άφοβος.

dark [dɑːk] a (dim) σκοτεινός, μαύρος || (gloomy) σκοτεινός, μελαγχολικός || (colour) μελαχροινός, μελαψός ♦ n σκοτάδι || (ignorance) σε άγνοια || after ~ αφού νυχτώσει || ~en vti σκοτεινιάζω || ~ness n σκότος nt, σκοτάδι || ~ room n σκοτεινός θάλαμος.

darling ['dɑːlɪŋ] n πολυαγαπημένος.

darn [dɑːn] n μαντάρισμα nt ♦ vt μπαλώνω, καρικώνω.

dart [dɑːt] n (quick move) ορμή || (weapon) βέλος nt, σαΐτα ♦ vi εξακοντίζω, ορμώ || ~s n σαΐτα || ~board n στόχος σαΐτας.

dash [dæʃ] n (rush) εξόρμηση || (waves) χτύπημα nt, σπάσιμο || (mark) παύλα ♦ vt (lit) ρίχνω, χτυπώ, κατασ τρέφω ♦ vi εφορμώ, πέφτω || ~board n ταμπλό nt inv || ~ing a (person) ορμητικός, ζωηρός.

data ['deɪtə] npl δεδομένα ntpl, στοιχεία ntpl || ~base n βάση δεδομένων || ~ processing n κατεργασία στοιχείων.

date [deɪt] n (point in time) χρονολογία, ημερομηνία || (with person) ραντεβού nt

inv || (fruit) χουρμάς ♦ vt (letter etc) βάζω ημερομηνία || (person) δίνω ραντεβού || ~d a με χρονολογία.

daub [dɔːb] vt (smear) πασαλείβω, αλείφω || (paint badly) μουντζουρώνω.

daughter ['dɔːtə*] n θυγατέρα, κόρη || ~-in-law n νύφη.

dawdle ['dɔːdl] vi χασομερώ, τεμπελιάζω.

dawn [dɔːn] n αυγή ♦ vi υποφώσκω, χαράζω || (become apparent) αποκαλύπτω.

day [deɪ] n ημέρα, μέρα || (24 hours) εικοσιτετράωρο || (date, time) ημερομηνία || (daylight) φως nt της ημέρας || ~ by ~ ημέρα με την ημέρα || ~break n αυγή, χάραμα nt || ~dream n ονειροπόλημα nt, ρεμβασμός ♦ vi ονειροπολώ, ρεμβάζω || ~light n φως nt της ημέρας || ~time n ημέρα.

daze [deɪz] vt θαμπώνω, ζαλίζω ♦ n θάμπωμα nt, ζάλη.

dazzle ['dæzl] vt θαμπώνω, τυφλώνω ♦ n θάμπωμα nt, τύφλωμα nt.

dead [dɛd] a νεκρός, πεθαμένος || (without feeling) αναίσθητος || (exact) πλήρης, ακριβής ♦ ad τελείως, ακριβώς, απολύτως || the ~ npl οι νεκροί mpl, οι πεθαμένοι mpl || ~en vt νεκρώνω, κατασιγάζω || ~ end n αδιέξοδο || ~ heat n ισοπαλία || ~line n (χρονικό) όριο || ~lock n αδιέξοδο || ~ly a θανατηφόρος, θανάσιμος || (fig) αδυσώπητος, αφόρητος || ~ pan a (πθοποιός) χωρίς έκφραση.

deaf [dɛf] a κουφός || ~-aid n ακουστικό κωφών || ~en vt (ξε)κουφαίνω || ~ening a εκκωφαντικός || ~-mute n κωφάλαλος/η m/f || ~ness n κουφαμάρα.

deal [diːl] (irreg v) n συμφωνία, δουλειά ♦ vti (CARDS) μοιράζω, δίνω || a great ~ of ποσότητα, πολύ || to ~ with vt αντιμετωπίζω, λαμβάνω μέτρα || ~er n έμπορος, αντιπρόσωπος || (CARDS) μοιραστής.

dear [dɪə*] a (beloved) αγαπητός, προσφιλής || (expensive) ακριβός, δαπανηρός ♦ n προσφιλής, αγαπημένος || ~ me Θεέ μου || D~ Sir αξιότιμε, αγαπητέ κύριε || D~ John αγαπητέ Γιάννη || ~ly ad (love) με αγάπη || (pay) ακριβά.

death [dɛθ] n θάνατος || ~bed n νεκροκρέββατο || ~ certificate n πιστοποιητικό θανάτου || ~ duties npl (Brit) φόρος κληρονομιάς || ~ly a νεκρικός, ωχρός || ~ penalty n ποινή θανάτου || ~ rate n θνησιμότητα.

debase [dɪ'beɪs] vt ξεφτελίζω, υποβιβάζω.

debate [dɪ'beɪt] n συζήτηση ♦ vt συζητώ || (consider) σκέφτομαι.

debauchery [dɪ'bɔːtʃərɪ] n ακολασία.

debit ['dɛbɪt] n δούναι, παθητικό ♦ vt χρεώνω.

debris ['dɛbriː] n συντρίμματα ntpl, μπάζα.

debt [dɛt] n χρέος nt, οφειλή || **to be in ~** χρωστώ || **~or** n οφειλέτης, χρεώστης.

debug [di:'bʌg] vt (COMPUT) αφαιρώ λάθη or σφάλματα.

début ['deibu:] n πρώτη εμφάνιση, ντεμπούτο.

decade ['dɛkeid] n δεκαετία.

decadence ['dɛkədəns] n παρακμή.

decay [di'kei] n παρακμή, φθορά, κατάπτωση ♦ vi παρακμάζω, μαραίνομαι.

decease [di'si:s] n θάνατος || **~d** n μακαρίτης/ισσα m/f.

deceit [di'si:t] n απάτη, δόλος || **~ful** a δόλιος, απατηλός.

deceive [di'si:v] vt εξαπατώ, κοροϊδεύω.

decelerate [di:'sɛləreit] vti επιβραδύνω, κόβω ταχύτητα.

December [di'sɛmbə*] n Δεκέμβρης, Δεκέμβριος.

decency ['di:sənsi] n (fit behaviour) ευπρέπεια, σεμνότητα || (respectability) κοσμιότητα.

decent ['di:sənt] a (respectable) ευπρεπής, συμμαζεμένος || (pleasant) αρκετά καλός.

deception [di'sɛpʃən] n εξαπάτηση, τέχνασμα nt.

deceptive [di'sɛptiv] a απατηλός.

decibel ['dɛsibɛl] n ντεσιμπέλ nt inv.

decide [di'said] vt (settle) κρίνω, αποφασίζω ♦ vi (determine) αποφασίζω, καταλήγω || **to ~ to do** αποφασίζω να κάνω || **~d** a αποφασισμένος, οριστικός || **~dly** ad αποφασιστικά, βεβαίως.

deciduous [di'sidjuəs] a φυλλοβόλος.

decimal ['dɛsiməl] a δεκαδικός ♦ n δεκαδικό || **~ point** n υποδιαστολή.

decimate ['dɛsimeit] vt αποδεκατίζω.

decipher [di'saifə*] vt ξεδιαλύνω, βγάζω.

decision [di'siʒən] n απόφαση.

decisive [di'saisiv] a αποφασιστικός.

deck [dɛk] n (NAUT) κατάστρωμα nt, κουβέρτα || (of bus) όροφος || (of cards) τράπουλα || **~chair** n σαιζ-λογκ f inv.

declaration [dɛklə'reiʃən] n δήλωση, διακήρυξη.

declare [di'klɛə*] vt (state) δηλώνω || (war) κηρύσσω || (in customs) δηλώνω.

decline [di'klain] n (decay) παρακμή, πτώση, πέσιμο || (lessening) πέσιμο, κατάπτωση ♦ vt (refuse) αρνούμαι || (GRAM) κλίνω ♦ vi φθίνω, εξασθενίζω, αδυνατίζω.

declutch ['di:'klʌtʃ] vi ντεμπραγιάρω.

decode ['di:'kəud] vt αποκρυπτογραφώ.

decompose [di:kəm'pəuz] vi (rot) αποσυντίθεμαι, σαπίζω.

decontaminate [di:kən'tæmineit] vt απολυμαίνω.

décor ['deikɔ:*] n διακόσμηση, ντεκόρ nt inv.

decorate ['dɛkəreit] vt (renew paint etc) χρωματίζω, βάφω || (adorn) (δια)κοσμώ, στολίζω || (give medal etc) παρασημοφορώ.

decoration [dɛkə'reiʃən] n (of house) διακόσμηση || (MIL) παράσημο.

decorator ['dɛkəreitə*] n διακοσμητής/τρια m/f.

decoy ['di:kɔi] n δέλεαρ nt inv, δόλωμα nt.

decrease [di:'kri:s] n μείωση, ελάττωση ♦ vti μειώνω, ελαττώνομαι.

decree [di'kri:] n διάταγμα nt, βούλευμα nt.

decrepit [di'krɛpit] a παραγηρασμένος || (furniture etc) ξεχαρβαλωμένος.

dedicate ['dɛdikeit] vt αφιερώνω.

dedication [dɛdi'keiʃən] n αφιέρωση.

deduce [di'dju:s] vt συμπεραίνω.

deduct [di'dʌkt] vt αφαιρώ || **~ion** n αφαίρεση, συμπέρασμα nt || (in price etc) έκπτωση.

deed [di:d] n πράξη, έργο || (LAW) έγγραφο.

deep [di:p] a (water) βαθύς || (breath) βαθειά || (voice) βαθειά, βαρειά || **in ~ water** σε μεγάλη δυσκολία || **~en** vt εμβαθύνω, βαθαίνω || **~freeze** n κατάψυξη || **~seated** a βαθειά ριζωμένος.

deer [diə*] n ελάφι.

deface [di'feis] vt παραμορφώνω.

defamation [dɛfə'meiʃən] n δυσφήμηση.

default [di'fɔ:lt] n παράλειψη, αθέτηση || (LAW) απουσία || (COMPUT) παράλειψη ♦ vi παραλείπω καθήκον, φυγοδικώ || **by ~** ερήμην || **~er** n φυγόδικος.

defeat [di'fi:t] n (overthrow) ανατροπή, ματαίωση || ήττα, συντριβή ♦ vt νικώ, ανατρέπω || **~ist** a ηττοπαθής.

defect ['di:fɛkt] n ατέλεια, ελάττωμα nt ♦ [di'fɛkt] vi λιποτακτώ || **~ive** a ελλιπής, ελαττωματικός.

defence [di'fɛns] n (MIL, SPORT) άμυνα, υπεράσπιση || δικαιολογία || **~less** a ανυπεράσπιστος.

defend [di'fɛnd] vt υπερασπίζω || **~ant** n εναγόμενος || **~er** n υπερασπιστής, υπέρμαχος.

defensive [di'fɛnsiv] a αμυντικός ♦ n άμυνα.

defer [di'fɜ:*] vt αναβάλλω.

deference ['dɛfərəns] n σεβασμός.

defiance [di'faiəns] n αψηφισιά, περιφρόνηση.

defiant [di'faiənt] a προκλητικός, αψηφών.

deficiency [di'fiʃənsi] n έλλειψη, ατέλεια.

deficient [di'fiʃənt] a ατελής, ελλιπής.

deficit ['dɛfisit] n έλλειμμα nt.

define [di'fain] vt (καθ)ορίζω || (explain) εξηγώ, καθορίζω.

definite ['dɛfinit] a (fixed) (καθ)ορισμένος || (clear) σαφής || (GRAM) οριστικό || **~ly** ad σαφώς.

definition [dɛfi'niʃən] n (καθ)ορισμός.

definitive [dɪˈfɪnɪtɪv] a οριστικός, τελικός.

deflate [diːˈfleɪt] vt ξεφουσκώνω || (currency) υποτιμώ.

deflation [diːˈfleɪʃən] n (FIN) υποτίμηση.

deflect [dɪˈflɛkt] vt εκτρέπω, παρεκκλίνω.

deform [dɪˈfɔːm] vt παραμορφώνω, ασχημίζω || ~ed a δύσμορφος παραμορφωμένος || ~ity n δυσμορφία, παραμόρφωση.

defraud [dɪˈfrɔːd] vt εξαπατώ, κλέβω.

defrost [diːˈfrɒst] vt (fridge) ξεπαγώνω.

deft [dɛft] a επιτήδειος, επιδέξιος.

defunct [dɪˈfʌŋkt] a μακαρίτης.

defy [dɪˈfaɪ] vt (challenge) προκαλώ || (ignore) αψηφώ.

degenerate [dɪˈdʒɛnəreɪt] vi εκφυλίζομαι ♦ [dɪˈdʒɛnərɪt] a εκφυλισμένος.

degradation [dɛgrəˈdeɪʃən] n ξεφτελισμός, υποβιβασμός.

degrading [dɪˈgreɪdɪŋ] a ξεφτελιστικός, ταπεινωτικός.

degree [dɪˈgriː] n (step, stage) βαθμός || (UNIV) πτυχίο || (measurement) μοίρα || by ~ s βαθμηδόν.

dehydrated [diːhaɪˈdreɪtɪd] a αφυδατωμένος.

de-ice [diːˈaɪs] vt (windscreen) ξεπαγώνω.

deign [deɪn] vi καταδέχομαι, ευαρεστούμαι.

deity [ˈdiːɪtɪ] n θεότητα.

dejected [dɪˈdʒɛktɪd] a κατηφής, άκεφος.

dejection [dɪˈdʒɛkʃən] n κατήφεια, ακεφιά.

delay [dɪˈleɪ] vt αναβάλλω, καθυστερώ ♦ vi βραδύνω, αργώ ♦ n αργοπορία, αναβολή, επιβράδυνση || without ~ χωρίς καθυστέρηση.

delegate [ˈdɛlɪgɪt] n αντιπρόσωπος, απεσταλμένος ♦ [ˈdɛlɪgeɪt] vt εντέλλομαι, εξουσιοδοτώ.

delegation [dɛlɪˈgeɪʃən] n αντιπροσωπεία.

delete [dɪˈliːt] vt αφαιρώ, σβήνω.

deliberate [dɪˈlɪbərɪt] a (intentional) εσκεμμένος || (slow) αργός, επιφυλακτικός ♦ [dɪˈlɪbəreɪt] vi διαλογίζομαι, συνδιασκέπτομαι || ~ly ad εσκεμμένα.

delicacy [ˈdɛlɪkəsɪ] n (daintiness) ευαισθησία, λεπτότητα || (refinement) λεπτότητα || (choice food) λιχουδιές fpl.

delicate [ˈdɛlɪkɪt] a (fine) λεπτός, απαλός || (fragile) λεπτός || (situation) λεπτός, δύσκολος || (MED) λεπτή, ευπαθής.

delicious [dɪˈlɪʃəs] a νόστιμος, ευχάριστος.

delight [dɪˈlaɪt] n ευχαρίστηση, τέρψη ♦ vt χαιροποιώ, τέρπω || ~ful a γοητευτικός, πολύ ευχάριστος.

delinquency [dɪˈlɪŋkwənsɪ] n εγκληματικότητα, αδίκημα nt.

delinquent [dɪˈlɪŋkwənt] n εγκληματίας,

παραπτωματίας ♦ a παραπτωματικός || (FCON) εκπρόθεσμος.

delirium [dɪˈlɪrɪəm] n παραλήρημα nt.

deliver [dɪˈlɪvə*] vt (distribute) (παρα)δίδω, διανέμω || (pronounce) εκφωνώ, μεταδίδω || (free) απαλλάσσω, ελευθερώνω, σώζω || ~ y n παράδοση, διανομή || (of speech) παράδοση, εκφώνηση.

delta [ˈdɛltə] n δέλτα nt.

delude [dɪˈluːd] vt εξαπατώ.

deluge [ˈdɛljuːdʒ] n κατακλυσμός.

delusion [dɪˈluːʒən] n (aut)απάτη.

de luxe [dɪˈlʌks] a ντε λουξ.

demand [dɪˈmɑːnd] vt απαιτώ, αξιώνω ♦ n αξίωση, απαίτηση || (call for a commodity) ζήτηση || in ~ ζητούμαι || on ~ επί τη εμφανίσει || ~ing a απαιτητικός, διεκδικητικός.

demarcation [diːmɑːˈkeɪʃən] n οροθεσία.

demented [dɪˈmɛntɪd] a παράφρονας, τρελλός.

demise [dɪˈmaɪz] n αποβίωση.

demobilization [ˈdiːməubɪlaɪˈzeɪʃən] n αποστράτευση.

democracy [dɪˈmɒkrəsɪ] n δημοκρατία.

democrat [ˈdɛməkræt] n δημοκράτης || ~ic a δημοκρατικός.

demolish [dɪˈmɒlɪʃ] vt (lit) κατεδαφίζω, κατακρημνίζω || (fig) συντρίβω.

demolition [dɛməˈlɪʃən] n κατεδάφιση.

demonstrate [ˈdɛmənstreɪt] vt αποδεικνύω || (protest) διαδηλώνω.

demonstration [dɛmənˈstreɪʃən] n απόδειξη, επίδειξη || (POL) διαδήλωση.

demonstrator [ˈdɛmənstreɪtə*] n (POL) διαδηλωτής.

demoralize [dɪˈmɒrəlaɪz] vt εξαχρειώνω, αποθαρρύνω.

demote [dɪˈməut] vt υποβιβάζω.

demure [dɪˈmjuə*] a σοβαρός, μετριόφρονας.

den [dɛn] n τρώγλη, φωλιά || (room) καμαρούλα.

denial [dɪˈnaɪəl] n άρνηση.

Denmark [ˈdɛnmɑːk] n Δανία.

denomination [dɪnɒmɪˈneɪʃən] n (name) ονομασία || (REL) δόγμα nt, θρήσκευμα nt.

denote [dɪˈnəut] vt δείχνω, εμφαίνω.

denounce [dɪˈnauns] vt καταγγέλω.

dense [dɛns] a πυκνός || (stupid) βλάκας, αμαθής.

density [ˈdɛnsɪtɪ] n πυκνότητα.

dent [dɛnt] n κοίλωμα nt, βαθούλωμα nt ♦ vt κοιλαίνω, βαθουλώνω.

dental [ˈdɛntl] a (GRAM) οδοντόφωνος || ~ surgeon n = dentist.

dentist [ˈdɛntɪst] n οδοντίατρος m/f || ~ry n οδοντιατρική.

denture [ˈdɛntʃə*] n οδοντοστοιχία, μασέλα.

deny [dɪˈnaɪ] vt (declare untrue) διαψεύδω, αρνούμαι || (disown) απαρνιέμαι, ανακαλώ || (refuse) αρνούμαι.

deodorant [di:'oudərənt] n αποσμητικό.

depart [di'pɑːt] vi αναχωρώ.

department [di'pɑːtmənt] n τμήμα nt, υπηρεσία, κλάδος || (UNIV, SCH) τμήμα nt || (POL) διεύθυνση, γραφείο || (US) υπουργείο || ~ **store** n μεγάλο εμπορικό κατάστημα nt.

departure [di'pɑːtʃə*] n αναχώρηση || **new** ~ n νέα τάση.

depend [di'pend] vi: **it** ~**s** εξαρτάται || **to** ~ **on** vti εξαρτώμαι από || ~**able** a αξιόπιστος || (car, machine etc) απολύτου ασφαλείας || ~**ent** n (person) προστατευόμενος ♦ a (+ on) εξαρτώμενος από || ~**ence** n εξάρτηση || (trust) εμπιστοσύνη.

depict [di'pikt] vt περιγράφω, απεικονίζω.

depleted [di'pliːtid] a εξηντλημένος.

deplorable [di'plɔːrəbl] a θλιβερός, αξιοθρήνητος.

deplore [di'plɔː*] vt αποδοκιμάζω, λυπούμαι πολύ.

deploy [di'plɔi] vt αναπτύσσω.

depopulation ['diːpɔpju'leiʃən] n ελάττωση πληθυσμού.

deport [di'pɔːt] vt εκτοπίζω, απελαύνω || ~**ation** n απέλαση, εκτοπισμός || ~**ment** n συμπεριφορά.

depose [di'pəuz] vt εκθρονίζω.

deposit [di'pɔzit] n κατάθεση || (down payment) προκαταβολή, καπάρο || (CHEM) ίζημα nt, κατακάθι ♦ vt (bank) (παρα)καταθέτω, αποταμιεύω || (place) τοποθετώ, βάζω || ~ **account** n λογαριασμός καταθέσεως || ~**or** n καταθέτης.

depot ['depəu] n αποθήκη || (MIL) βάση ανεφοδιασμού || (US: for buses etc) σταθμός.

depravity [di'præviti] n αχρειότητα, διαφθορά.

depreciate [di'priːʃieit] vt υποτιμώ ♦ vi υποτιμούμαι, πέφτω.

depreciation [dipriːʃi'eiʃən] n υποτίμηση, πέσιμο.

depress [di'pres] vt (make sad) συντρίβω, αποθαρρύνω || (press down) καταπιέζω, κατεβάζω || ~**ed** a (person) μελαγχολικός, αποκαρδιωμένος || (area) φτωχός, υπανάπτυκτος || ~**ing** a καταθλιπτικός, αποθαρρυντικός || ~**ion** n (ECON) ύφεση, κρίση || (hollow) κοιλότητα, λακούβα || (METEOROLOGY) βαρομετρική ύφεση.

deprivation [depri'veiʃən] n στέρηση.

deprive [di'praiv] vt (+ of) στερώ του || ~**d** a στερημένος.

depth [depθ] n βάθος nt, πυθμένας, βαθύτητα || **in the** ~**s of** στην καρδιά του.

deputation [depju'teiʃən] n αποστολή, επιτροπή.

deputize ['depjutaiz] vi (+ for) αναπληρώ, αντιπροσωπεύω.

deputy ['depjuti] a αναπληρωτικός,

βοηθητικός ♦ n αναπληρωτής, αντικαταστάτης.

derail [di'reil] vt εκτροχιάζω || ~**ment** n εκτροχίαση.

deranged [di'reindʒd] a παράφρονας, στριμμένος.

derelict ['derilikt] a εγκαταλελειμμένος.

deride [di'raid] vt χλευάζω, εμπαίζω.

derision [di'riʒən] n εμπαιγμός, χλευασμός.

derivative [di'rivətiv] a παράγωγος.

derive [di'raiv] vt παράγω, αποκομίζω ♦ vi κατάγομαι, παράγομαι.

dermatitis [dɜːmə'taitis] n δερματίτιδα.

derogatory [di'rɔgətəri] a ξεφτελιστικός, δυσφημιστικός, μειωτικός.

derrick ['derik] n γερανός || (of oil well) ικρίωμα nt γεωτρήσεως.

descend [di'send] vti κατεβαίνω || (rain etc) πέφτω ♦ vi: **to** ~ **from** κατάγομαι || ~**ant** n απόγονος.

descent [di'sent] n (coming down) κάθοδος f, κατέβασμα nt || (origin) καταγωγή.

describe [dis'kraib] vt περιγράφω.

description [dis'kripʃən] n περιγραφή || (kind, sort) είδος nt, τύπος.

descriptive [dis'kriptiv] a περιγραφικός.

desecrate ['desikreit] vt βεβηλώνω.

desert ['dezət] n έρημος f ♦ [di'zɜːt] vt εγκαταλείπω ♦ vi (MIL) λιποτακτώ || ~**er** n λιποτάκτης || ~**ion** n λιποταξία.

deserve [di'zɜːv] vt αξίζω.

deserving [di'zɜːviŋ] a άξιος, αξιόλογος.

design [di'zain] n (plan) σχέδιο, σκοπός, επιδίωξη || (drawing) σχέδιο, τύπος || (the art) σχέδιο ♦ vt (plan) σχεδιάζω || (purpose) προορίζω || **to have** ~**s on** έχω βλέψεις σε.

designate ['dezigneit] vt (προ)ορίζω, διορίζω ♦ ['dezignit] a εκλεγείς.

designation [dezig'neiʃən] n ορισμός, τίτλος.

designer [di'zainə*] n (TECH) μελετητής || (ART) σχεδιαστής.

desirable [di'zaiərəbl] a επιθυμητός.

desire [di'zaiə*] n επιθυμία, πόθος ♦ vt επιθυμώ, ποθώ || (ask for) ζητώ.

desk [desk] n γραφείο || (of student) θρανίο.

desolate ['desəlit] a (barren, dismal) έρημος.

desolation [desə'leiʃən] n ερήμωση, καταστροφή.

despair [dis'peə*] n απόγνωση, απελπισία ♦ vi (+ of) απελπίζομαι για.

despatch [dis'pætʃ] = **dispatch**.

desperate ['despərit] a (hopeless) απελπιστικός || (reckless) απεγνωσμένος, σκληρός.

desperation [despə'reiʃən] n απόγνωση.

despicable [dis'pikəbl] a αηδής, σιχαμερός, αξιοκατάφρόντος.

despise [dɪs'paɪz] vt περιφρονώ.

despite [dɪs'paɪt] prep παρά, σε πείσμα.

despondent [dɪs'pɒndənt] a απελπισμένος, συντριμμένος.

dessert [dɪ'zɜːt] n επιδόρπιο || **~spoon** n κουταλάκι του γλυκού.

destination [dɛstɪ'neɪʃən] n προορισμός.

destiny ['dɛstɪnɪ] n προορισμός || (fate) μοίρα.

destitute ['dɛstɪtjuːt] a άπορος.

destroy [dɪs'trɔɪ] vt καταστρέφω || **~er** n (NAUT) αντιτορπιλλικό.

destruction [dɪs'trʌkʃən] n καταστροφή.

destructive [dɪs'trʌktɪv] a καταστρεπτικός.

detach [dɪ'tætʃ] vt αποσπώ, αφαιρώ || **~able** a αφαιρούμενος, κινητός || **~ed** a (attitude) ανεπηρέαστος || **~ment** n (MIL) απόσπασμα nt || (fig) απόσπαση, αμεροληψία.

detail ['diːteɪl] n λεπτομέρεια || (MIL) απόσπασμα nt ♦ vt εκθέτω λεπτομερώς || (MIL) ορίζω, αποσπώ || **in ~** λεπτομερώς.

detain [dɪ'teɪn] vt κρατώ, εμποδίζω || (imprison) φυλακίζω, κρατώ.

detect [dɪ'tɛkt] vt ανακαλύπτω, διακρίνω || **~ion** [dɪ'tɛkʃən] n ανακάλυψη || **~ive** n μυστικός αστυνομικός, ντετέκτιβ m inv || **~ive story** n αστυνομικό μυθιστόρημα nt || **~or** n ανιχνευτής.

detention [dɪ'tɛnʃən] n κράτηση.

deter [dɪ'tɜː] vt αποτρέπω.

detergent [dɪ'tɜːdʒənt] n απορρυπαντικό, καθαρτικό.

deteriorate [dɪ'tɪərɪəreɪt] vi επιδεινούμαι, χειροτερεύω.

deterioration [dɪtɪərɪə'reɪʃən] n επιδείνωση.

determination [dɪtɜːmɪ'neɪʃən] n απόφαση, αποφασιστικότητα.

determine [dɪ'tɜːmɪn] vt (καθ)ορίζω, αποφασίζω || **~d** a αποφασιστικός, αποφασισμένος.

deterrent [dɪ'tɛrənt] n προληπτικό ♦ a αποτρεπτικός.

detest [dɪ'tɛst] vt απεχθάνομαι, αποστρέφομαι, σιχαίνομαι || **~able** a απεχθής, σιχαμένος.

detonate ['dɛtəneɪt] vti εκρηγνύω, εκπυροκροτώ.

detonator ['dɛtəneɪtə*] n επικρουστήρας, πυροκροτητής.

detour ['diːtuə*] n απόκλιση, στροφή, λοξοδρόμηση.

detract [dɪ'trækt] vi (+ from) δυσφημώ, μειώνω.

detriment ['dɛtrɪmənt] n: to the ~ of προς βλάβη του || **~al** a βλαβερός, επιζήμιος.

devaluation [dɪvælju'eɪʃən] n υποτίμηση.

devalue ['diː'væljuː] vt υποτιμώ.

devastate ['dɛvəsteɪt] vt ερημώνω, καταστρέφω.

devastating ['dɛvəsteɪtɪŋ] a εξολοθρευτικός.

develop [dɪ'vɛləp] vt (make grow) αναπτύσσω || (film) εμφανίζω ♦ vi (unfold) αναπτύσσομαι, εκδηλούμαι || (grow) αναπτύσσομαι || **~ing** a (country) αναπτυσσόμενη || **~ment** n ανάπτυξη.

deviate ['diːvɪeɪt] vi εκτρέπομαι, παρεκκλίνω.

deviation [diːvɪ'eɪʃən] n παρέκκλιση.

device [dɪ'vaɪs] n επινόημα nt, τέχνασμα nt.

devil ['dɛvl] n διά(β)ολος, δαίμονας || **~ish** a διαβολικός.

devious ['diːvɪəs] a (means) έμμεσος, παρεκκλίνων || (person) ύπουλος.

devise [dɪ'vaɪz] vt επινοώ, μηχανεύομαι.

devoid [dɪ'vɔɪd] a: ~ of στερημένος, χωρίς...

devote [dɪ'vəut] vt αφιερώνω || **~d** a αφοσιωμένος || **~e** n λάτρης, οπαδός.

devotion [dɪ'vəuʃən] n αφοσίωση, λατρεία.

devour [dɪ'vauə*] vt καταβροχθίζω.

devout [dɪ'vaut] a ευσεβής, θρήσκος.

dew [djuː] n δρόσος, δροσιά.

dexterity [dɛks'tɛrɪtɪ] n επιδεξιότητα.

diabetes [daɪə'biːtiːz] n διαβήτητα.

diabetic [daɪə'bɛtɪk] a, n διαβητικός.

diagnose ['daɪəgnəuz] vt κάνω διάγνωση.

diagnosis [daɪəg'nəusɪs] n διάγνωση.

diagonal [daɪ'ægənl] a, n διαγώνιος.

diagram ['daɪəgræm] n διάγραμμα nt, σχέδιο.

dial ['daɪəl] n (esp TEL) δίσκος επιλογής, καντράν nt inv ♦ vt καλώ, παίρνω || **~ling tone** n ένδειξη ελεύθερης γραμμής.

dialect ['daɪəlɛkt] n διάλεκτος f.

dialogue ['daɪəlɒg] n διάλογος.

diameter [daɪ'æmɪtə*] n διάμετρος f.

diamond ['daɪəmənd] n διαμάντι || (CARDS) καρρό.

diapers ['daɪəpəz] npl (US) πάνες fpl.

diaphragm ['daɪəfræm] n διάφραγμα nt.

diarrhoea [daɪə'riːə] n διάρροια.

diary ['daɪərɪ] n ημερολόγιο.

dice [daɪs] npl ζάρια ntpl ♦ vt (vegetables) κόβω σε κύβους.

Dictaphone ['dɪktəfəun] n (R) Dictaphone nt.

dictate [dɪk'teɪt] vt υπαγορεύω || (impose) επιβάλλω ♦ ['dɪkteɪt] n πρόσταγμα nt, διαταγή.

dictation [dɪk'teɪʃən] n υπαγόρευση.

dictator [dɪk'teɪtə*] n δικτάτορας.

dictatorship [dɪk'teɪtəʃɪp] n δικτατορία.

diction ['dɪkʃən] n ύφος λόγου, λεκτικό.

dictionary ['dɪkʃənrɪ] n λεξικό.

did [dɪd] pt of do || **~n't** = **did not** || see do.

die [daɪ] vi πεθαίνω, τα τινάζω || (end) σβήνω || to ~ away vi εξασθενίζω, σβήνω || to ~ down vi εξασθενίζω, πέφτω || to ~ out vi αποθνήσκω, σβήνω.

diesel ['diːzəl]: ~ **engine** n ντήζελ nt inv.

diet ['daɪət] n (food) (δια)τροφή || (special course) δίαιτα ♦ vi κάνω δίαιτα.

differ ['dɪfə*] vi διαφέρω, ξεχωρίζω || (disagree) διαφωνώ || ~**ence** n διαφορά || (disagreement) διαφωνία, διαφορά || ~**ent** a διάφορος, διαφορετικός || ~**ential** [dɪfə'renʃəl] n (AUT) διαφορικό || (wages) διαφορική || ~**entiate** vti διαφοροποιώ, ξεχωρίζω.

difficult ['dɪfɪkəlt] a δύσκολος || ~**y** n δυσκολία, δυσχέρεια.

diffidence ['dɪfɪdəns] n επιφυλακτικότητα, ντροπαλότητα.

diffident ['dɪfɪdənt] a διστακτικός, άτολμος.

diffuse [dɪ'fjuːs] a διάχυτος ♦ [dɪ'fjuːz] vt διαχέω, σκορπώ.

dig [dɪg] (irreg v) vt (hole, garden) σκάβω || (nails) χώνω || (delve into) ψάχνω, τρυπώ ♦ n (prod) κάρφωμα nt, πείραγμα nt || (ARCH) εσκαφή || **to** ~ **up** vt εσκάπτω, ξερριζώνω, ξεθάβω.

digest [daɪ'dʒɛst] vt χωνεύω || (work over) επεξεργάζομαι ♦ ['daɪdʒɛst] n περίληψη, σύνοψη || ~**ion** n χώνευση.

digit ['dɪdʒɪt] n (number) ψηφίο, αριθμός || (toe, finger) δάκτυλος.

dignified ['dɪgnɪfaɪd] a αξιοπρεπής.

dignity ['dɪgnɪtɪ] n αξιοπρέπεια.

digress [daɪ'grɛs] vi εκτρέπομαι, ξεφεύγω || ~**ion** n εκτροπή, παρέκβαση.

digs [dɪgz] npl (Brit col) δωμάτιον.

dilapidated [dɪ'læpɪdeɪtɪd] a σαραβαλιασμένος.

dilate [daɪ'leɪt] vti διαστέλλω, πλαταίνω, διαστέλλομαι.

dilemma [daɪ'lɛmə] n δίλημμα nt.

diligent ['dɪlɪdʒənt] a επιμελής.

dilute [daɪ'luːt] vt αραιώνω, νερώνω ♦ a αραιός.

dim [dɪm] a αμυδρός, μουντός, σκοτεινός || (stupid) κουτός ♦ vt χαμηλώνω, θολώνω.

dime [daɪm] n (US) δέκατο του δολλαρίου.

dimension [dɪ'mɛnʃən] n διάσταση, έκταση || ~**s** npl διαστάσεις fpl.

diminish [dɪ'mɪnɪʃ] vti ελαττώνω, ελαττώνομαι.

diminutive [dɪ'mɪnjutɪv] a υποκοριστικός ♦ n υποκοριστικό.

din [dɪn] n θόρυβος, πάταγος.

dine [daɪn] vi γευματίζω, τρώγω || ~**r** n τραπεζαρία τραίνου || (person) γευματίζων.

dinghy ['dɪŋgɪ] n μικρή βάρκα.

dingy ['dɪndʒɪ] a μαυρισμένος, βρώμικος.

dining car ['daɪnɪŋkɑː*] n βαγκόν-ρεστωράν nt inv.

dining room ['daɪnɪŋrʊm] n τραπεζαρία.

dinner ['dɪnə*] n γεύμα nt, φαΐ || (public) επίσημο γεύμα || ~ **jacket** n σμόκιν nt

inv || ~ **party** n τραπέζι || ~ **time** n ώρα φαγητού.

diocese ['daɪəsɪs] n επισκοπή.

dip [dɪp] n (slope) κλίση, πλαγιά || (bath) βουτιά ♦ vt εμβαπτίζω, βουτώ || (AUT) χαμηλώνω || (flag) κατεβάζω ♦ vi (slope) γέρνω, κατηφορίζω, χαμηλώνω.

diphtheria [dɪf'θɪərɪə] n διφθερίτιδα.

diphthong ['dɪfθɒŋ] n δίφθογγος f.

diploma [dɪ'pləʊmə] n δίπλωμα nt.

diplomacy [dɪ'pləʊməsɪ] n διπλωματία.

diplomat ['dɪpləmæt] n διπλωμάτης || ~**ic** a διπλωματικός.

dipstick ['dɪpstɪk] n βυθομετρική ράβδος f.

dire [daɪə*] a καταστρεπτικός, τρομερός, έσχατος.

direct [daɪ'rɛkt] a (straight) ευθύς, ίσιος || (immediate) άμεσος ♦ vt (manage) διευθύνω, διοικώ || (aim) κατευθύνω, δείχνω.

direction [dɪ'rɛkʃən] n (control) διεύθυνση, διαχείριση || (of traffic) ρύθμιση || (of movement) κατεύθυνση, φορά || ~**s** npl (for use) οδηγίες fpl || ~**al** a κατά διεύθυνση.

directly [dɪ'rɛktlɪ] ad (in straight line) κατευθείαν, ίσια || (at once) αμέσως.

director [dɪ'rɛktə*] n διευθυντής/ρια m/f, ο γενικός.

directory [dɪ'rɛktərɪ] n (esp TEL) (τηλεφωνικός) κατάλογος || (COMPUT) κατάλογος.

dirt [dɜːt] n ακαθαρσία, βρωμιά, ρύπος nt || ~ **road** n (US) χωματόδρομος || ~**y** a ρυπαρός λερωμένος, ακάθαρτος || (mean) βρώμικος, πρόστυχος ♦ vt λερώνω, μουντζουρώνω.

disability [dɪsə'bɪlɪtɪ] n ανικανότητα || (physical) αναπηρία.

disabled [dɪs'eɪbld] a ανίκανος, σακατεμένος, ανάπηρος.

disadvantage [dɪsəd'vɑːntɪdʒ] n μειονέκτημα nt, ελάττωμα nt || (sell at) ζημιά || ~**ous** [dɪsædvɑːn'teɪdʒəs] a ασύμφορος, δυσμενής.

disagree [dɪsə'griː] vi διαφωνώ || **to** ~ **with** vt δεν ταιριάζω, δεν πηγαίνω || (food) πειράζω || ~**able** a δυσάρεστος, αντιπαθητικός || ~**ment** n διαφωνία, διάσταση, ασυμφωνία.

disallow ['dɪsə'laʊ] vt αρνούμαι, απορρίπτω, απαγορεύω.

disappear [dɪsə'pɪə*] vi εξαφανίζομαι || ~**ance** n εξαφάνιση.

disappoint [dɪsə'pɔɪnt] vt απογοητεύω, χαλώ, στενοχωρούμαι || ~**ing** a απογοητευτικός || ~**ment** n απογοήτευση, λύπη.

disapproval [dɪsə'pruːvəl] n αποδοκιμασία.

disapprove [dɪsə'pruːv] vi (+ of) αποδοκιμάζω, επικρίνω.

disarm [dɪs'ɑːm] vt αφοπλίζω || ~**ament** n αφοπλισμός.

disaster [dɪ'zɑːstə*] n συμφορά, δυστύχημα nt.

disastrous [dɪˈzɑːstrəs] a ολέθριος, καταστρεπτικός.

disband [dɪsˈbænd] vt απολύω, διαλύω.

disbelief [ˈdɪsbəˈliːf] n δυσπιστία.

disc [dɪsk] n δίσκος.

discard [dɪsˈkɑːd] vt απορρίπτω, αφήνω.

discern [dɪˈsɜːn] vt διακρίνω, ξεχωρίζω || ~ing a οξυδερκής, διακριτικός.

discharge [dɪsˈtʃɑːdʒ] vt (unload ship etc) ξεφορτώνω || (fire a gun) πυροβολώ || (dismiss) απολύω || (MIL) αποστρατεύω || (perform duties) εκτελώ, εκπληρώ ♦ n (MED) απέκκριμα nt || (MIL) αποστράτευση || (flow) εκκένωση.

disciple [dɪˈsaɪpl] n μαθητής/ήτρια m/f, οπαδός.

discipline [ˈdɪsɪplɪn] n πειθαρχία ♦ vt πειθαρχώ, τιμωρώ.

disclaim [dɪsˈkleɪm] vt απαρνούμαι.

disclose [dɪsˈkləʊz] vt αποκαλύπτω.

disclosure [dɪsˈkləʊʒə*] n αποκάλυψη, εκδήλωση.

disco [ˈdɪskəʊ] n abbr of discothèque.

discoloured [dɪsˈkʌləd] a ξεβαμμένο, ξεθωριασμένο.

discomfort [dɪsˈkʌmfət] n (uneasiness) δυσφορία, στενοχώρια || (lack of comfort) έλλειψη ανέσεως, κακουχία.

disconcert [dɪskənˈsɜːt] vt ταράσσω, συγχύζω.

disconnect [ˈdɪskəˈnɛkt] vt διασπώ, αποσυνδέω.

discontent [ˈdɪskənˈtɛnt] n δυσαρέσκεια || ~ed a δυσαρεστημένος.

discontinue [ˈdɪskənˈtɪnjuː] vti διακόπτω, καταργώ.

discord [ˈdɪskɔːd] n (quarrelling) διαφωνία, διχόνοια || (MUS) παραφωνία || ~ant a ασύμφωνος, παράφωνος.

discothèque [ˈdɪskəʊtɛk] n δισκοθήκη.

discount [ˈdɪskaʊnt] n έκπτωση, σκόντο || (bank) προεξόφληση, υφαίρεση ♦ [dɪsˈkaʊnt] vt (disbelieve) περιφρονώ, δεν πιστεύω.

discourage [dɪsˈkʌrɪdʒ] vt (take away confidence) αποθαρρύνω || (disapprove) αποδοκιμάζω, αποτρέπω.

discouraging [dɪsˈkʌrɪdʒɪŋ] a αποθαρρυντικός.

discourteous [dɪsˈkɜːtɪəs] a αγενής.

discover [dɪsˈkʌvə*] vt ανακαλύπτω || ~y n ανακάλυψη.

discredit [dɪsˈkrɛdɪt] vt δυσπιστώ, υποτιμώ.

discreet [dɪsˈkriːt] a νουνεχής, διακριτικός.

discrepancy [dɪsˈkrɛpənsɪ] n διαφορά, ασυμφωνία.

discretion [dɪsˈkrɛʃən] n (prudence) φρόνηση, σύνεση || (right to decide) βούληση.

discriminate [dɪsˈkrɪmɪneɪt] vi κάνω διάκριση, ξεχωρίζω.

discriminating [dɪsˈkrɪmɪneɪtɪŋ] a διακριτικός, μεροληπτικός.

discrimination [dɪskrɪmɪˈneɪʃən] n διάκριση, ορθοφροσύνη.

discuss [dɪsˈkʌs] vt συζητώ || ~ion n συζήτηση.

disdain [dɪsˈdeɪn] vt περιφρονώ || n περιφρόνηση || ~ful a υπεροπτικός, περιφρονητικός.

disease [dɪˈziːz] n νόσημα nt, ασθένεια.

disembark [dɪsɪmˈbɑːk] vti αποβιβάζω, αποβιβάζομαι.

disengage [dɪsɪnˈgeɪdʒ] vt (AUT) αποσυμπλέκω.

disentangle [ˈdɪsɪnˈtæŋgl] vt διαχωρίζω, ξεμπλέκω.

disfigure [dɪsˈfɪgə*] vt παραμορφώνω.

disgrace [dɪsˈgreɪs] n (general) δυσμένεια || (thing) αίσχος nt, ντροπή ♦ vt ντροπιάζω, ξεφτελίζω || ~ful a επονείδιστος.

disgruntled [dɪsˈgrʌntld] a δυσαρεστημένος, κατσουφιασμένος.

disguise [dɪsˈgaɪz] vt (change appearance) μεταμφιέζω || (hide) αποκρύπτω ♦ n μεταμφίεση, απόκρυψη.

disgust [dɪsˈgʌst] n αηδία ♦ vt αηδιάζω || ~ing a αηδιαστικός, σιχαμερός.

dish [dɪʃ] n πιάτο || (meal) φαγητό || to ~ up vt παρουσιάζω, σερβίρω || ~ cloth n πιατόπανο.

dishearten [dɪsˈhɑːtn] vt αποθαρρύνω, απελπίζω.

dishevelled [dɪˈʃɛvəld] a ξεμαλλιασμένος, ανακατωμένος.

dishonest [dɪsˈɒnɪst] a ανέντιμος, κακοήθης || ~y n κακοήθεια, ατιμία.

dishonour [dɪsˈɒnə*] n αίσχος nt, ατιμία.

dishwasher [ˈdɪʃwɒʃə*] n πλυντήριο πιάτων.

disillusion [dɪsɪˈluːʒən] vt απογοητεύω.

disinfect [dɪsɪnˈfɛkt] vt απολυμαίνω || ~ant n απολυμαντικό.

disintegrate [dɪsˈɪntɪgreɪt] vi αποσυντίθεμαι, θρυμματίζομαι.

disinterested [dɪsˈɪntrɪstɪd] a αφιλοκερδής, αδιάφορος.

disjointed [dɪsˈdʒɔɪntɪd] a ασυνάρτητος, εξαρθρωμένος.

disk [dɪsk] n = disc.

diskette [dɪsˈkɛt] n (COMPUT) δισκέτα.

dislike [dɪsˈlaɪk] n αντιπάθεια, αποστροφή ♦ vt αντιπαθώ, απεχθάνομαι.

dislocate [ˈdɪsləʊkeɪt] vt (bone) εξαρθρώνω, στραμπουλίζω || ξεχαρβαλώνω, χαλώ.

dislodge [dɪsˈlɒdʒ] vt εκτοπίζω, εκδιώκω.

disloyal [dɪsˈlɔɪəl] a άπιστος.

dismal [ˈdɪzməl] a ζοφερός, μελαγχολικός.

dismantle [dɪsˈmæntl] vt παροπλίζω, λύω.

dismay [dɪsˈmeɪ] n κατάπληξη, φόβος ♦ vt (dishearten) πτοώ, φοβίζω, απογοητεύω.

dismiss [dɪsˈmɪs] vt (discharge) απολύω, παύω || (out of mind) διώχνω, βγάζω || (send away) απομακρύνω, διώχνω || (LAW)

απορρίπτω, απαλλάσσω || ~al n
απόλυση, παύση.
disobedience [dɪsə'biːdɪəns] n
ανυπακοή, παρακοή.
disobedient [dɪsə'biːdɪənt] a
ανυπάκουος, πεισματάρης.
disobey ['dɪsə'beɪ] vt παρακούω,
παραβαίνω.
disorder [dɪs'ɔːdə*] n (confusion)
ακαταστασία, αταξία || (commotion)
ταραχή, φασαρία || (MED) διαταραχή.
disorderly [dɪs'ɔːdəlɪ] a (untidy)
ακατάστατος || (unruly) άτακτος,
απείθαρχος.
disown [dɪs'əun] vt απαρνούμαι,
αποκηρύττω.
disparaging [dɪs'pærɪdʒɪŋ] a
δυσφημιστικό.
disparity [dɪs'pærɪtɪ] n ανισότητα,
διαφορά.
dispatch [dɪs'pætʃ] vt (goods) στέλνω,
διεκπεραιώνω ♦ n αποστολή,
διεκπεραίωση || (esp MIL) αναφορά,
μήνυμα nt.
dispel [dɪs'pel] vt διασκορπίζω.
dispensary [dɪs'pensərɪ] n φαρμακείο.
dispense [dɪs'pens] vt διανέμω, χορηγώ
|| to ~ with vt κάνω χωρίς.
disperse [dɪs'pɜːs] vt διασκορπίζω ♦ vi
διασκορπίζομαι.
displace [dɪs'pleɪs] vt εκτοπίζω || ~d
person n πρόσφυγας.
display [dɪs'pleɪ] n (of goods) έκθεση,
επίδειξη || (of feeling) εκδήλωση || (MIL)
επίδειξη ♦ vt επιδεικνύω, εκθέτω.
displease [dɪs'pliːz] vt δυσαρεστώ.
displeasure [dɪs'pleʒə*] n
δυσαρέσκεια.
disposal [dɪs'pəuzəl] n (of property)
διάθεση || at one's ~ στη διάθεση.
dispose [dɪs'pəuz]: to ~ of vt
απαλλάσσομαι, ξεφορτώνομαι.
disposed [dɪs'pəuzd] a διατεθειμένος.
disposition [dɪspə'zɪʃən] n (character)
προδιάθεση, χαρακτήρας.
disproportionate [dɪsprə'pɔːʃnɪt] a
δυσανάλογος.
disprove [dɪs'pruːv] vt αναιρώ,
ανασκευάζω.
dispute [dɪs'pjuːt] n αμφισβήτηση,
φιλονεικία ♦ vt αμφισβητώ, διεκδικώ.
disqualify [dɪs'kwɒlɪfaɪ] vt καθιστώ
ακατάλληλο || (SPORT) αποκλείω.
disregard ['dɪsrɪ'gɑːd] vt παραβλέπω,
αγνοώ, περιφρονώ.
disreputable [dɪs'repjutəbl] a
ανυπόληπτος, κακόφημος.
disrespectful [dɪsrɪ'spektful] a ασεβής.
disrupt [dɪs'rʌpt] vt διασπώ, διαλύω ||
~ion n διάσπαση.
dissatisfaction ['dɪssætɪs'fækʃən] n
δυσαρέσκεια.
dissatisfied ['dɪs'sætɪsfaɪd] a
δυσαρεστημένος.
dissect [dɪ'sekt] vt κατατέμνω,
διαμελίζω.

dissent [dɪ'sent] n διχογνωμία,
διαφωνία ♦ vi διαφωνώ.
dissident ['dɪsɪdənt] a διΐστάμενος,
διαφωνών.
dissipate ['dɪsɪpeɪt] vt (waste) σπαταλώ,
ασωτεύω || (disperse) (δια)σκορπίζω.
dissociate [dɪ'səuʃɪeɪt] vt αποσπώ,
διαχωρίζω, απομακρύνω.
dissolute ['dɪsəluːt] a άσωτος, έκλυτος.
dissolve [dɪ'zɒlv] vt διαλύω ♦ vi
διαλύομαι, λυώνω.
dissuade [dɪ'sweɪd] vt αποτρέπω,
μεταπείθω.
distance ['dɪstəns] n απόσταση,
διάστημα nt || in the ~ μακρυά.
distant ['dɪstənt] a (far away) μακρυά,
μακρυνός || απομεμακρυσμένος,
επιφυλακτικός.
distaste ['dɪs'teɪst] n αποστροφή,
απέχθεια || ~ful a δυσάρεστος,
απεχθής.
distil [dɪs'tɪl] vt αποστάζω, διϋλίζω ||
~lery n ποτοποιείο.
distinct [dɪs'tɪŋkt] a (different)
διαφορετικός || (clear) ευδιάκριτος,
σαφής || ~ion n (difference) διαφορά ||
(honour etc) διάκριση, τιμή || (medal etc)
παράσημο || ~ive a διακριτικός,
χαρακτηριστικός || ~ly ad ευδιάκριτα,
καθαρά.
distinguish [dɪs'tɪŋgwɪʃ] vt διακρίνω,
ξεχωρίζω, διαφοροποιώ || ~ed a
(eminent) διακεκριμένος || ~ing a
χαρακτηριστικός, διακριτικός.
distort [dɪs'tɔːt] vt (out of shape)
διαστρέφω, στραβώνω || (fig)
διαστρεβλώνω, παραποιώ || ~ion n
παραμόρφωση, διαστρέβλωση.
distract [dɪs'trækt] vt αποσπώ, περισπώ
|| (drive mad) περιπλέκω, τρελλαίνω ||
~ion n (inattention) περίσπαση,
αφηρημάδα || (distress) διατάραξη,
αναστάτωση || (diversion) διασκέδαση.
distraught [dɪs'trɔːt] a ταραγμένος,
συγχυσμένος.
distress [dɪs'tres] n (grief) απελπισία,
αγωνία, πίκρα || (suffering) αθλιότητα,
δυστυχία || (difficulty) κίνδυνος, σε
δύσκολη θέση ♦ vt θλίβω, στενοχωρώ ||
~ing a δυσάρεστος, οδυνηρός || ~
signal n σήμα nt κινδύνου.
distribute [dɪs'trɪbjuːt] vt (give out)
διανέμω, μοιράζω || (spread) εξαπλώνω.
distribution [dɪstrɪ'bjuːʃən] n διανομή,
κατανομή.
distributor [dɪs'trɪbjutə*] n (COMM)
διανομέας, αντιπρόσωπος || (AUT etc)
διανομέας.
district ['dɪstrɪkt] n (of country) περιοχή,
περιφέρεια || (of town) συνοικία || ~
attorney n (US) εισαγγελέας || ~ nurse
n (Brit) επισκέπτρια νοσοκόμος.
distrust [dɪs'trʌst] n δυσπιστία, υποψία
♦ vt δυσπιστώ προς, υποπτεύομαι.
disturb [dɪs'tɜːb] vt (upset) ταράσσω,
ενοχλώ || (agitate) ταράσσω, κλονίζω ||

~ance n διατάραξη, φασαρία || ~ing a ενοχλητικός, αντισυχπτικός.

disused ['dɪs'juːzd] a αχρηστευμένος, απηρχαιωμένος.

ditch [dɪtʃ] n τάφρος f, χαντάκι.

ditto ['dɪtəʊ] n ομοίως.

divan [dɪ'væn] n (bed) ντιβάνι.

dive [daɪv] n (into water) βουτιά || (AVIAT) βύθιση ♦ vi βυθίζομαι, βουτώ || ~r n (professional) δύτης.

diverge [daɪ'vɜːdʒ] vi διίσταμαι, αποκλίνω.

diverse [daɪ'vɜːs] a διάφορος, ποικίλος.

diversify [daɪ'vɜːsɪfaɪ] vt διαφοροποιώ, ποικίλλω.

diversion [daɪ'vɜːʃən] n απόκλιση, λοξοδρομία || (of traffic) διοχέτευση || (pastime) διασκέδαση.

diversity [daɪ'vɜːsɪtɪ] n ανομοιότητα, ποικιλία.

divert [daɪ'vɜːt] vt αποσπώ, εκτρέπω || (entertain) διασκεδάζω.

divide [dɪ'vaɪd] vt διανέμω, (δια)μοιράζω, χωρίζω ♦ vi διαιρώ, χωρίζω.

dividend ['dɪvɪdɛnd] n μέρισμα nt, τοκομερίδιο || (MATH) διαιρετέος.

divine [dɪ'vaɪn] a θείος, θεϊκός.

diving board ['daɪvɪŋbɔːd] n εξέδρα για βουτιές.

divinity [dɪ'vɪnɪtɪ] n θεότητα || (study) θεολογία.

division [dɪ'vɪʒən] a (dividing) διανομή, μοιρασιά || (MATH) διαίρεση || (MIL) μεραρχία || (part) τμήμα nt || (of opinion) διχόνοια, διαίρεση.

divorce [dɪ'vɔːs] n διαζύγιο, διάζευξη ♦ vt χωρίζω || ~d a χωρισμένος.

divulge [daɪ'vʌldʒ] vt αποκαλύπτω, φανερώνω.

dizziness ['dɪzɪnɪs] n ίλιγγος, ζάλη.

dizzy ['dɪzɪ] a ζαλισμένος.

do [duː] (irreg v) vt κάνω, εκτελώ, εκπληρώ, τελειώνω, ταιριάζω, αρκώ ♦ vi (act, proceed) κάνω || (be suitable) ταιριάζω, κάνω ♦ n (party) πάρτυ nt inv.

docile ['dəʊsaɪl] a πειθήνιος, υπάκουος.

dock [dɒk] n (NAUT) νεοδόχος, δεξαμενή || (court) εδώλιο ♦ vi (NAUT) δεξαμενίζομαι || ~er n φορτοεκφορτωτής, λιμενεργάτης.

docket ['dɒkɪt] n περιληπτική επιγραφή.

dockyard ['dɒkjaːd] n ναύσταθμος.

doctor ['dɒktə*] n (MED) γιατρός m/f|| (UNIV) διδάκτωρ m/f.

doctrine ['dɒktrɪn] n δόγμα nt, θεωρία.

document ['dɒkjʊmɛnt] n έγγραφο || ~ary [dɒkjʊ'mɛntərɪ] n (film) ντοκυμαντέρ nt inv.

dodge [dɒdʒ] n υπεκφυγή, τέχνασμα nt ♦ vt ξεφεύγω, αποφεύγω ♦ vi εκφεύγω, παραμερίζω, κάνω πλάι.

dog [dɒg] n σκυλί || (human) παλιάνθρωπος || ~ **biscuit** n μπισκότο για σκύλους || ~ **collar** n λαιμοδέτης (σκύλου) || (col) κολλάρο κληρικού.

dogged ['dɒgɪd] a ισχυρογνώμων, πεισματάρης.

dogma ['dɒgmə] n δόγμα nt || ~tic [dɒg'mætɪk] a (stubborn) κατηγορηματικός, δογματικός.

doings ['duːɪŋz] npl (activities) πράξεις fpl, έργα ntpl.

doldrums ['dɒldrəmz] npl: in the ~ άκεφος.

dole [dəʊl] n (Brit: for unemployed) επίδομα nt ανεργίας || to be on the ~ παίρνω επίδομα ανεργίας || to ~ out vt διανέμω, μοιράζω.

doleful ['dəʊlful] a λυπητερός, πένθιμος.

doll [dɒl] n κούκλα ♦ vt: to ~ o.s. up στολίζομαι.

dollar ['dɒlə*] n δολλάριο, τάληρο.

dolphin ['dɒlfɪn] n δελφίνι.

dome [dəʊm] n θόλος, τρούλλος.

domestic [də'mɛstɪk] a (of the house) οικιακός, του σπιτιού || (of the country) εσωτερικός, εγχώριος || (tame: of animal) οικιακός || ~ated a εξημερωμένος.

dominant ['dɒmɪnənt] a επικρατών, υπερισχύων.

dominate ['dɒmɪneɪt] vt δεσπόζω, κυριαρχώ.

domination [dɒmɪ'neɪʃən] n κυριαρχία.

domineering [dɒmɪ'nɪərɪŋ] a δεσποτικός, αυταρχικός.

dominion [də'mɪnɪən] n (rule) κυριαρχία, εξουσία || (land) κτήση (αποικία).

dominoes ['dɒmɪnəʊz] npl ντόμινο.

donate [dəʊ'neɪt] vt δωρίζω.

donation [dəʊ'neɪʃən] n δωρεά.

done [dʌn] pp of **do**.

donkey ['dɒŋkɪ] n γάιδαρος, γαϊδούρι.

donor ['dəʊnə*] n δωρητής.

don't [dəʊnt] = **do not** || see **do**.

doom [duːm] n (fate) μοίρα || (death) θάνατος, καταστροφή ♦ vt: to be ~ed είμαι καταδικασμένος.

door [dɔː*] n πόρτα || ~**bell** n κουδούνι (της πόρτας) || ~**handle** n πόμολο, (χειρο)λαβή || ~**man** n θυρωρός, πορτιέρης || ~**mat** n ψάθα εξώπορτας || ~**step** n σκαλοπάτι.

dope [dəʊp] n (drug) ναρκωτικό.

dopey ['dəʊpɪ] a (col) βλάκας || (doped) χασικλωμένος.

dormant ['dɔːmənt] a λανθάνων, κοιμώμενος.

dormitory ['dɔːmɪtrɪ] n υπνοθάλαμος.

dosage ['dəʊsɪdʒ] n δόση.

dose [dəʊs] n δόση ♦ vt δίνω φάρμακο.

dot [dɒt] n στιγμή || **on the** ~ στη στιγμή, στην ώρα.

dote [dəʊt]: **to** ~ **on** vt αγαπώ τρελλά.

double ['dʌbl] a διπλός, διπλάσιος ♦ ad διπλά, διπλάσια, δύο-δύο ♦ n (match) ωσίας, ταίρι ♦ vt διπλασιάζω || (fold in two) διπλώνω ♦ vi διπλασιάζομαι, διπλώνομαι || **at the** ~ τροχάδην || ~**s** npl (TENNIS) διπλός (αγώνας) || ~ **bass** n κοντραμπάσσο || ~ **bed** n διπλό κρεββάτι || ~-**breasted** a σταυρωτός || ~-**cross** n προδοσία ♦ vt προδίδω,

εξαπατώ || ~-**decker** n διόροφο
(λεωφορείο) || ~ **room** n δίκλινο.
doubly ['dʌblɪ] ad διπλάσια.
doubt [daut] n αμφιβολία ♦ vt
αμφιβάλλω, αμφιβωτώ || **without** ~
χωρίς καμμιά αμφιβολία || ~**ful** a
αμφίβολος || ~**less** ad αναμφιβόλως.
dough [dəυ] n ζυμάρι || ~**nut** n τηγανίτα,
λουκουμάς.
dove [dʌv] n περιστέρι.
dovetail ['dʌvteɪl] n ψαλιδωτή ένωση ♦
vt ταιριάζω.
dowdy ['daudɪ] a άκομψος,
κακοντυμένος.
down [daun] n (fluff) πούπουλο, χνούδι
♦ ad κάτω, χάμω ♦ prep πιο κάτω, προς
τα κάτω, χαμηλότερα ♦ vt κατεβάζω,
ρίχνω κάτω, νικώ || ~ **with X!** κάτω ο Χ
|| ~-**and-out** a κατεστραμμένος, στην
ψάθα || ~-**at-heel** a μπατίρης || ~**cast**
a κατηφής || ~**fall** n πτώση, παρακμή ||
~**hearted** a αποθαρρυμένος,
κακόκεφος || ~**hill** ad κατηφορικώς,
προς τα κάτω || ~**pour** n μπόρα ||
~**right** a ευθύς, ειλικρινής, απόλυτος ||
~**stairs** ad κάτω || a κάτω, στο κάτω
πάτωμα || ~**stream** ad με το ρεύμα ||
~**town** ad στην πόλη || ~**ward** a
κατηφορικός, κατερχόμενος || ~**wards**
ad προς τα κάτω, και κάτω.
dowry ['dauri] n προίκα.
doz. abbr of **dozen**.
doze [dəυz] vi λαγοκοιμάμαι ♦ n
υπνάκος.
dozen ['dʌzn] n δωδεκάδα.
Dr. abbr of **doctor** || abbr of **drive** (n).
drab [dræb] a (dull) μονότονος, ανιαρός.
drachma ['drækmə] n δραχμή.
draft [drɑːft] n (rough copy) (προ)σχέδιο ||
(ECON) γραμμάτιο, συναλλαγματική || (US
MIL) στρατολογία ♦ vt συντάσσω,
ετοιμάζω προσχέδιο || see **draught**.
drag [dræg] vt (pull) σέρνω || (NAUT)
βυθοκορώ ♦ vi βραδυπορώ, σέρνομαι ♦
n (bore) φορτικός άνθρωπος || **to** ~ **on**
vi συνεχίζω ανιαρά.
drain [dreɪn] n (lit) οχετός, αγωγός,
αυλάκι || (fig) ψυγή, διαρροή, εξάντληση
♦ vt (water) αποχετεύω || (fig) αδειάζω,
απομυζώ ♦ vi (of water) στάζω,
στραγγίζω || ~**age** n αποχέτευση,
αποστράγγιση || ~**pipe** n σωλήνας
αποχετεύσεως, υδρορρόη.
dram [dræm] n δράμι || (col) σταγόνα.
drama ['drɑːmə] n δράμα nt || ~**tic**
[drə'mætɪk] a δραματικός || ~**tist** n
δραματουργός, δραματουργός.
drank [dræŋk] pt of **drink**.
drape [dreɪp] vt κοσμώ με ύφασμα,
ντύνω || ~**s** npl (US) κουρτίνες fpl || ~**r** n
υφασματέμπορος.
drastic ['dræstɪk] a δραστικός,
αποφασιστικός.
draught [drɑːft] n (air) ρεύμα nt (αέρος)
|| (NAUT) βύθισμα nt || ~**s** n (game) ντάμα,
νταμιέρα || (beer) **on** ~ (μπύρα) του
βαρελιού || ~**board** n αβάκιον.

draughtsman ['drɑːftsmən] n
σχεδιαστής.
draughty ['drɑːftɪ] a με πολλά ρεύματα.
draw [drɔː] (irreg v) vt (pull) σέρνω,
τραβώ, σηκώνω || (attract) ελκύω, τραβώ ||
(a picture) χαράσσω, σχεδιάζω,
ζωγραφίζω || (take out) εξάγω, βγάζω,
τραβάω ♦ vi (SPORT) έρχομαι ισόπαλος ♦
n (SPORT) ισοφάριση || (lottery) κλήρωση ||
to ~ **to a close** πλησιάζω στο τέλος ||
to ~ **out** vi (train) ξεκινώ || (lengthen)
παρατείνω, τραβώ σε μάκρος ♦ vt (take
out) αποσύρω, τραβώ || **to** ~ **up** vi (stop)
φθάνω ♦ vt (document) συντάσσω,
καταστρώνω || ~**back** n μειονέκτημα nt,
ελάττωμα nt || ~**bridge** n κρεμαστή
γέφυρα.
drawer [drɔː*] n συρτάρι.
drawing ['drɔːɪŋ] n σχέδιο, σκίτσο || (art
of drawing) σχέδιο || ~ **pin** n πινέζα || ~
room n σαλόνι, σάλα.
drawl [drɔːl] n συρτή φωνή ♦ vi σέρνω
τη φωνή.
dread [drɛd] n τρόμος, φόβος, ανησυχία
♦ vt φοβούμαι, τρέμω || ~**ful** a φοβερός,
τρομερός.
dream [driːm] (irreg v) n όνειρο || (fancy)
ονειροπόληση ♦ vi ονειρεύομαι ♦ a
ονειρώδης || ~**er** n ονειροπόλος || ~**y** a
ονειροπόλος, φαντασιόπληκτος, θολός.
dreary ['drɪərɪ] a μονότονος, πληκτικός.
dredge [drɛdʒ] vt βυθοκορώ, εκβαθύνω
|| ~**r** n βυθοκόρος.
dregs [drɛgz] npl κατακάθι, μούργα.
drench [drɛntʃ] vt καταβρέχω,
μουσκεύω.
dress [drɛs] n ενδυμασία, ρούχα ntpl,
ντύσιμο || (esp woman's) φόρεμα nt,
φουστάνι ♦ vt ντύνω, στολίζω || (a wound)
επενδύω || (food) ετοιμάζω για μαγείρεμα
|| **to** ~ **up** vi ντύνομαι || ~ **circle** n
πρώτος εξώστης || ~**er** n (person) που
ντύνεται καλά || (US) κομψός || ~**ing** n
(MED) επίδεση || (for food) ετοιμασία,
σάλτσα || ~**ing gown** n ρόμπα || ~**ing
room** n (THEAT) καμαρίνι || ~**ing table** n
τουαλέττα (έπιπλο) || ~**maker** n
ράφτρα, μοδίστρα || ~**making** n
ραπτική || ~ **rehearsal** n τελευταία
πρόβα, γενική δοκιμή.
drew [druː] pt of **draw**.
dribble ['drɪbl] vi (trickle) στάζω ♦ vt
(SPORT) κάνω τρίπλες.
dried [draɪd] a ξηρός, απεξηραμένος,
στεγνός.
drift [drɪft] n (driven by tide etc)
κατεύθυνση, διεύθυνση, ταχύτητα ||
(mass of snow etc) χιονοστιβάδα,
συσσώρευση || (meaning) έννοια, νόημα
nt ♦ vi (off course) παρασύρομαι, ξεπέφτω
|| (aimlessly) περιφέρομαι άσκοπα ||
~**wood** n ξύλο που επιπλέει.
drill [drɪl] n (tool) τρυπάνι, δράπανο ||
(MIL) γυμνάσια ntpl, άσκηση ♦ vt (bore)
τρυπώ, ανοίγω || (exercise) εκπαιδεύω,
γυμνάζω || vi (+ for) κάνω γεώτρηση.
drink [drɪŋk] (irreg v) n (liquid) ποτό,

αναψυκτικό || (alcoholic) ποτό ♦ vti (swallow liquid) πίνω || ~ er n πότης || ~ing water n πόσιμο νερό.

drip [drɪp] n στάξιμο, σταλαγματιά ♦ vi στάζω, σταλάζω || ~ping n στάξιμο || (fat) λίπος ψητού || ~ping wet a μουσκεμένος.

drive [draɪv] (irreg v) n (trip in car) κούρσα, διαδρομή || (road) δρόμος πάρκου || (campaign) καμπάνια, έρανος || (energy) ενεργητικότητα, δραστηριότητα || (SPORT) κτύπημα nt || (COMPUT: also: disk ~) μονάδα δίσκου ♦ vt (car etc) οδηγώ, σωφάρω || (urge) διώχνω, σπρώχνω || (nail etc) καρφώνω, μπάζω || (operate) κινώ, βάζω μπρος || (force) αναγκάζω, παρακινώ ♦ vi (at controls) οδηγώ, χειρίζομαι || (travel) πηγαίνω, τρέχω.

driver ['draɪvə*] n οδηγός || ~'s license n (US) άδεια οδηγού.

driving ['draɪvɪŋ] a (rain) νεροποντή || ~ instructor n δάσκαλος οδηγήσεως || ~ lesson n μάθημα nt οδηγήσεως || ~ licence n (Brit) άδεια οδηγού || ~ school n σχολή οδηγών || ~ test n εξέταση για άδεια οδηγού.

drizzle ['drɪzl] n ψιχάλισμα nt ♦ vi ψιχαλίζω.

droll [drəʊl] a αστείος, κωμικός.

dromedary ['drɒmɪdərɪ] n κάμηλος f n δρομάς.

drone [drəʊn] n (bee) κηφήνας || (sound) βόμβος, βουητό ♦ vi σαλιαρίζω, μωρολογώ.

droop [druːp] vi νέφτω, γέρνω, σκύβω.

drop [drɒp] n (of liquid) σταγόνα, στάλα || (fall) πτώση, πέσιμο || (MED) σταγόνα ♦ vt (let fall) ρίχνω, αφήνω να πέσει || (lower) κατεβάζω, χαμηλώνω || (cease) εγκαταλείπω, παρατώ, αφήνω ♦ vi (fall) νέφτω || to ~ off vi (sleep) αποκοιμιέμαι || to ~ out vi (withdraw) αποσύρομαι.

dross [drɒs] n ακαθαρσίες fpl, απορρίμματα ntpl.

drought [draʊt] n ξηρασία.

drove [drəʊv] pt of drive ♦ n (crowd) πλήθος nt ανθρώπων, κοπάδι.

drown [draʊn] vt πνίγω || (flood) πλημμυρίζω ♦ vi πνίγομαι.

drowsy ['draʊzɪ] a νυσταλέος, νυσταγμένος.

drudgery ['drʌdʒərɪ] n μόχθος, αγγαρεία.

drug [drʌg] n (MED) φάρμακο || (narcotic) ναρκωτικό ♦ vt δίνω ναρκωτικό σε, ντοπάρω || ~ addict n τοξικομανής, πρεζάκιας || ~gist n (US) φαρμακοποιός m/f || ~store n (US) φαρμακείο.

drum [drʌm] n (MUS) τύμπανο, τούμπανο || (barrel) βαρέλι || ~mer n τυμπανιστής.

drunk [drʌŋk] pp of drink ♦ n μέθυσος, μπεκρής || ~ard n μεθύστακας || ~en a μεθυσμένος || ~enness n μέθη, μεθύσι.

dry [draɪ] a (not wet) ξηρός, ξερός || (of well) στερεμένος || (rainless) άνυδρος || (uninteresting) ξερός, κρύος || (wine) μπρούσκο ♦ vt ξηραίνω, στεγνώνω,

στίβω ♦ vi ξεραίνομαι, στεγνώνω || to ~ up vi ξεραίνομαι || (of well) στερεύω || ~-cleaner n καθαριστήριο || ~er n στεγνωτής, στεγνωτήριο || ~ rot n σαράκι.

dual ['djʊəl] a διπλός, δυϊκός || ~ nationality n διπλή υπηκοότητα || ~-purpose a διπλής χρήσεως.

dubbed [dʌbd] a (CINE) ντουμπλαρισμένο.

dubious ['djuːbɪəs] a αμφίβολος, αμφιβάλλων, αβέβαιος.

duchess ['dʌtʃɪs] n δούκισσα.

duck [dʌk] n πάπια ♦ vt βουτώ, σκύβω ♦ vi βουτώ || ~ling n παπάκι.

duct [dʌkt] n αγωγός, σωλήνας.

dud [dʌd] n μη εκραγείσα οβίδα ♦ a άχρηστος, τενεκές m, αποτυχημένος.

due [djuː] a (owing) οφειλόμενος, λήγων || (deserved) ανήκων, δίκαιος, σωστός || (expected) αναμενόμενος ♦ ad κατ'ευθείαν, ίσια προς || ~s npl (debt) τέλη ntpl, δασμός || (balance) οφειλόμενο, ανήκον || ~ to n το οφειλόμενο σε, λόγω.

duel ['djʊəl] n μονομαχία.

duet [djuː'et] n δυωδία, ντουέτο.

dug [dʌg] pt, pp of dig.

duke [djuːk] n δούκας.

dull [dʌl] a (person) βραδύνους, κουτός || (boring) πληκτικός, ανιαρός || (weather) βαρύς, σκοτεινός ♦ vt (soften, weaken) εξασθενίζω, ξεθωριάζω.

duly ['djuːlɪ] ad δεόντως, εγκαίρως.

dumb [dʌm] a (lit) βουβός, μουγγός || (stupid) ανόητος, κουτός, πλίθιος.

dummy ['dʌmɪ] n (model) κούκλα, ανδρείκελο || (substitute) ομοίωμα nt || (for baby) πιπιλίστρα ♦ a πλαστός, ψεύτικος, εικονικός.

dump [dʌmp] n σκουπιδότοπος || (storing place) αποθήκη ♦ vt ξεφορτώνω, απορρίπτω || ~ing n (COMM) πουλώ φτηνά || (rubbish) ανατροπή, εκφόρτιση.

dumpling ['dʌmplɪŋ] n κομμάτι ζύμης βρασμένο με κρέας || (pie) πίτα.

dunce [dʌns] n αμαθής, ντουμπάρι.

dune [djuːn] n αμμόλοφος.

dung [dʌŋ] n κοπριά.

dungarees [dʌŋgə'riːz] npl φόρμα εργάτη.

dungeon ['dʌndʒən] n μπουντρούμι, φυλακή.

dupe [djuːp] n θύμα nt, απάτη, κορόιδο ♦ vt εξαπατώ, κοροϊδεύω.

duplicate ['djuːplɪkɪt] a διπλός, διπλάσιος ♦ n διπλότυπο ♦ ['djuːplɪkeɪt] vt αντιγράφω || in ~ εις διπλούν.

durable ['djʊərəbl] a ανθεκτικός, διαρκής.

duration [djuə'reɪʃən] n διάρκεια.

during ['djʊərɪŋ] prep κατά τη διάρκεια.

dusk [dʌsk] n σούρουπο.

dust [dʌst] n σκόνη, κονιορτός, στάκτη ♦ vt ξεσκονίζω, πασπαλίζω || ~bin n (Brit) τενεκές nt σκουπιδιών || ~er n ξεσκονόπανο || (feather) φτερό || ~man

E

n (Brit) οδοκαθαριστής, σκουπιδιάρης || ~y a σκονισμένος.

Dutch [dʌtʃ] a ολλανδικός ♦ n (LING) Ολλανδικά || **the** ~ npl οι Ολλανδοί || ~**man** n Ολλανδέζος || ~**woman** n Ολλανδέζα.

duty ['dju:tɪ] n καθήκον nt || (job) καθήκον(τα), υποχρέωση || (MIL) υπηρεσία || (tax) δασμός, φόρος || **on** ~ εν υπηρεσία || ~**-free** a αφορολόγητος ♦ n αφορολόγητα ntpl.

dwarf [dwɔ:f] n νάνος.

dwell [dwɛl] (irreg v) vi διαμένω, κατοικώ || ~ **on** vt εμμένω σε, επιμένω || ~**ing** n κατοικία.

dwindle ['dwɪndl] vi ελαττώνομαι, μικραίνω.

dye [daɪ] n βαφή, χρωματισμός ♦ vt βάφω.

dying ['daɪɪŋ] a (man) ετοιμοθάνατος.

dynamic [daɪ'næmɪk] a δυναμικός || ~**s** n δυναμική.

dynamite ['daɪnəmaɪt] n δυναμίτιδα.

dynamo ['daɪnəməʊ] n γεννήτρια, δυναμό.

dynasty ['dɪnəstɪ] n δυναστεία.

dysentery ['dɪsntrɪ] n δυσεντερία.

E

each [i:tʃ] a καθένας, κάθε ♦ pron κάθε || ~ **other** ο ένας τον άλλο, αλλήλους.

eager ['i:gə*] a ένθερμος, ανυπόμονος, πρόθυμος.

eagle ['i:gl] n αετός.

ear [ɪə*] n αυτί || (for music) λεπτή ακοή || (of corn) στάχυ nt || ~**ache** n ωταλγία, αυτόπονος || ~**drum** n τύμπανο.

earl [ɜ:l] n κόμης, κόντες m.

early ['ɜ:lɪ] a (before the season) πρώιμος, πρώιμος || (in the morning) πρωινός ♦ ad (in the morning) πρωί || (in time) ενωρίς.

earn [ɜ:n] vt κερδίζω, βγάζω || (acquire) αποκτώ, κατακτώ.

earnest ['ɜ:nɪst] a σοβαρός || (ardent) διάπυρος, ένθερμος || **in** ~ ad στα σοβαρά.

earnings ['ɜ:nɪŋz] npl απολαβές fpl, αποδοχές fpl || (of a firm) κέρδη ntpl.

earphones ['ɪəfəʊnz] npl ακουστικά ntpl.

earring ['ɪərɪŋ] n σκουλαρίκι.

earth [ɜ:θ] n (planet) γη, κόσμος || (soil) γη, έδαφος, χώμα nt || (ELEC) γη, προσγείωση ♦ vt (ELEC) προσγειώνω || ~**enware** n πήλινα ntpl || ~**quake** n σεισμός.

earwig ['ɪəwɪg] n (insect) φορφικούλη, ψαλίδα.

ease [i:z] n (facility) ευχέρεια, ευκολία, άνεση || (comfort) ανάπαυση, άνεση, ξεκούραση ♦ vt (reduce pain etc) ανακουφίζω, καταπραΰνω || (remove pressure) καθησυχάζω, ξεφορτώνω || **at** ~! ανάπαυση! || **to** ~ **off** or **up** vi ελαττώνω, εργάζομαι αργότερα.

easily ['i:zɪlɪ] ad ήρεμα, εύκολα.

east [i:st] n (direction) ανατολή || (in direction) ανατολικά ntpl ♦ a ανατολικός ♦ ad προς ανατολάς, ανατολικά || **the** E~ Ανατολή.

Easter ['i:stə*] n Πάσχα nt, Λαμπρή.

eastern ['i:stən] a (from, of the east) ανατολικός.

eastward(s) ['i:stwəd(z)] ad προς ανατολάς.

easy ['i:zɪ] a (not difficult) ευχερής, εύκολος || (life) ξεκούραστος, άνετος || (manner) άνετος, αβίαστος || (yielding) καλόβολος ♦ ad εύκολα, ήρεμα, ήσυχα.

eat [i:t] (irreg v) vt (swallow) τρώγω || (one's words) καταπίνω || (consume) (κατα)τρώγω, υπονομεύω || **to** ~ **away** vt καταρρώγω, προσβάλλω || ~**able** a φαγώσιμος.

eavesdrop ['i:vzdrɒp] vi (+ **on**) κρυφακούω.

ebb [ɛb] n άμπωτη || (fig) παρακμή, πέσιμο ♦ vi κατεβαίνω, πέφτω.

ebony ['ɛbənɪ] n έβενος, αμπανός.

ebullient [ɪ'bʌlɪənt] a (enthusiastic) εκδηλωτικός, ενθουσιώδης.

eccentric [ɪk'sɛntrɪk] a (odd) εκκεντρικός, παράξενος ♦ n (person) ιδιότροπος.

ecclesiastical [ɪkli:zɪ'æstɪkl] a εκκλησιαστικός.

echo ['ɛkəʊ] n ηχώ f, αντήχηση, αντίλαλος ♦ vt αντηχώ || vi αντηχώ, απηχώ, αντιλαλώ.

eclipse [ɪ'klɪps] n έκλειψη ♦ vt προκαλώ έκλειψη || (fig) επισκιάζω.

economic [i:kə'nɒmɪk] a οικονομικός || ~**al** a οικονομικός || (of person) φειδωλός || ~**s** npl οικονομικά ntpl.

economist [ɪ'kɒnəmɪst] n οικονομολόγος m/f.

economize [ɪ'kɒnəmaɪz] vi (+ **on**) οικονομώ, κάνω οικονομία σε.

economy [ɪ'kɒnəmɪ] n οικονομία.

ecstasy ['ɛkstəsɪ] n έκσταση, μάγευμα nt.

ecstatic [ɛk'stætɪk] a εκστατικός.

ecumenical [i:kju'mɛnɪkl] a οικουμενικός.

eczema ['ɛksɪmə] n έκζεμα nt.

edge [ɛdʒ] n (boundary) όχθη, παρυφή, άκρη || (of garment) ούγια || (brink) ακμή, χείλος, άκρη || (of knife) κόψη, ακμή || **on** ~ = **edgy**.

edgy ['ɛdʒɪ] a εκνευρισμένος.

edible ['ɛdɪbl] a φαγώσιμος.

edict ['i:dɪkt] n διάταγμα nt.

edifice ['ɛdɪfɪs] n οικοδόμημα nt, κτίριο.

edit ['ɛdɪt] vt εκδίδω, διευθύνω || (COMPUT) συντά σσω επιμελούμαι || ~**ion** [ɪ'dɪʃən] n έκδοση || ~**or** n (of newspaper) (αρχι)συντάκτης || (of book) εκδότης, επιμελητής εκδόσεως || ~**orial** a εκδοτικός, συντακτικός ♦ n (κύριο) άρθρο.

educate ['ɛdjukeɪt] vt εκπαιδεύω, σπουδάζω, μαθαίνω.

education [ɛdju'keɪʃən] n (system)

εκπαίδευση || (schooling) σπουδές fpl,
εκπαίδευση, μόρφωση || ~al a
εκπαιδευτικός, μορφωτικός.
EEC n (abbr of European Economic
Community) Ε.Ο.Κ. f (ευρωπαϊκή
οικονομική Κοινότητα).
eel [i:l] n χέλι.
eerie ['ιərι] a μυστηριώδης, παράξενος,
τρομακτικός.
effect [ι'fεkt] n (result) ενέργεια,
επίδραση, επιρροή, αποτέλεσμα nt||
(impression) εντύπωση, αίσθηση ♦ vt
πραγματοποιώ, επιτυγχάνω || ~s npl
(sound, visual) σκηνικά ntpl εφφέ|| in ~
πράγματι, πραγματικά || ~ive a
αποτελεσματικός, ουσιαστικός.
effeminate [ι'fεminιt] a θηλυπρεπής,
γυναικωτός.
effervescent [εfə'vεsnt] a
(ανα)βράζων, αεριούχος || (person)
ζωηρός.
efficiency [ι'fιʃənsι] n
αποτελεσματικότητα, δραστικότητα || (of
machine) απόδοση.
efficient [ι'fιʃənt] a αποτελεσματικός ||
(person) ικανός, επιδέξιος.
effigy ['εfιdʒι] n ομοίωμα nt, εικόνα.
effort ['εfət] n προσπάθεια || ~less a
χωρίς προσπάθεια, εύκολος.
effrontery [ι'frʌntərι] n αυθάδεια,
αδιαντροπιά.
e.g. ad (abbr of exempli gratia)
παραδείγματος χάρη, π.χ.
egalitarian [ιgælι'tεərιən] a
ισοπεδωτικός.
egg [εg] n αυγό || to ~ on vt εξωθώ,
παρακινώ, σπρώχνω || ~cup n αυγοθήκη
|| ~plant n μελιτζανιά || ~shell n τσόφλι
αυγού.
ego ['i:gəu] n το εγώ.
egotist ['εgəutιst] n περιαυτολόγος.
Egypt ['i:dʒιpt] n Αίγυπτος || ~ian
[i:'dʒιpʃən] n Αιγύπτιος ♦ a αιγυπτιακός.
eiderdown ['aιdədaun] n (quilt)
πουπουλένιο πάπλωμα nt.
eight [eιt] num οκτώ, οχτώ || ~een num
δέκα οκτώ || **eighth** a όγδοος || ~y num
ογδόντα.
Eire ['εərə] n Ιρλανδία.
either ['aιðə*] a εκάτερος, έκαστος,
καθένας ♦ pron ο ο ένας ή ο άλλος,
έκαστος || cj ή ... ή, είτε...είτε ♦ ad
ούτε...ούτε.
eject [ι'dʒεkt] vt εκβάλλω, βγάζω ||
(throw out) διώχνω, βγάζω έξω || ~or
seat n εκτοξευόμενο κάθισμα nt.
elaborate [ι'læbərιt] a επιμελημένος,
εξονυχιστικός, περίπλοκος ♦ [ι'læbəreιt]
vt επεξεργάζομαι, δουλεύω,
επιμελούμαι.
elapse [ι'læps] vi παρέρχομαι, περνώ.
elastic [ι'læstιk] n ελαστικό, λάστιχο ♦ a
ελαστικός, εύκαμπτος || ~ band n
λαστιχάκι.
elated [ι'leιtιd] a συνεπαρμένος,
έξαλλος.
elation [ι'leιʃən] n έπαρση, χαρά, κέφι.

elbow ['εlbəu] n αγκώνας.
elder ['εldə*] a πρεσβύτερος,
μεγαλύτερος ♦ n μεγαλύτερος || (tree)
ακτή, σαμπούκος || ~ly a ηλικιωμένος.
elect [ι'lεkt] vt εκλέγω ♦ a εκλεκτός ||
~ion n εκλογή || ~ioneering n
ψηφοθηρία || ~or n ψηφοφόρος m/f||
~oral a εκλογικός || ~orate n οι
ψηφοφόροι mpl.
electric [ι'lεktrιk] a (appliance)
ηλεκτρικός || ~al a ηλεκτρικός || ~
blanket n θερμοφόρα κουβέρτα || ~
chair n (US) ηλεκτρική καρέκλα || ~
cooker n η. κουζίνα, μάτι || ~ current n
η. ρεύμα nt|| ~ fire n ηλεκτρική σόμπα.
electrician [ιlεk'trιʃən] n
ηλεκτρολόγος.
electricity [ιlεk'trιsιtι] n ηλεκτρισμός.
electrify [ι'lεktrιfaι] vt (εξ)ηλεκτρίζω.
electrocute [ι'lεktrəkju:t] vt θανατώνω
με ηλεκτρισμό, με ηλεκτροπληξία.
electron [ι'lεktrɔn] n ηλεκτρόνιο.
electronic [εlək'trɔnιk] a ηλεκτρονικός
|| ~s n ηλεκτρονική.
elegance ['εlιgəns] n κομψότητα.
elegant ['εlιgənt] a κομψός.
element ['εləmənt] n (all senses)
στοιχείο || ~ary [εlι'mεntərι] a
στοιχειώδης.
elephant ['εlιfənt] n ελέφαντας.
elevate ['εlιveιt] vt (αν)υψώνω.
elevation [εlι'veιʃən] n (height) ύψος,
ύψωμα nt.
elevator ['εlιveιtə*] n ανελκυστήρας,
ασανσέρ nt inv.
eleven [ι'lεvən] a έντεκα ♦ n (team)
ομάδα έντεκα παικτών || ~ses npl
κολατσό.
elf [εlf] n έλφα, αγερικό, ξωτικό.
elicit [ι'lιsιt] vt εξάγω, αποσπώ, βγάζω.
eligible ['εlιdʒιbl] a εκλέξιμος,
κατάλληλος.
eliminate [ι'lιmιneιt] vt αποβάλλω,
διαγράφω || (MATH) εξαλείφω.
elimination [ιlιmι'neιʃən] n
αποκλεισμός, διαγραφή.
elite [ι'li:t] n εκλεκτή τάξη, αφρόκρεμα.
elm [εlm] n φτελιά.
elocution [εlə'kju:ʃən] n ευγλωττία,
απαγγελία.
elongated ['i:lɔŋgeιtιd] a επιμήκης,
μακρύς.
elope [ι'ləup] vi απάγομαι, φεύγω
εκουσίως κλέβομαι || ~ment n εκουσία
απαγωγή.
eloquence ['εlɔkwəns] n ευφράδεια.
eloquent ['εlɔkwənt] a ευφραδής,
εύγλωττος.
else [εls] ad οποιοσδήποτε άλλος, επί
πλέον, αλλού || (otherwise) άλλως,
αλλοιώς || ~where ad αλλού.
elucidate [ι'lu:sιdeιt] vt διευκρινίζω, δι
ασαφηνίζω.
elude [ι'lu:d] vt ξεφεύγω, διαφεύγω.
elusive [ι'lu:sιv] a άπιαστος, απατηλός.
emaciated [ι'meιsιeιtιd] a
αδυνατισμένος, πετσί και κόκκαλο.

emanate ['ɛməneɪt] vi απορρέω, προέρχομαι, πηγάζω.

emancipate [ɪ'mænsɪpeɪt] vt απελευθερώνω.

emancipation [ɪmænsɪ'peɪʃən] n χειραφέτηση, απελευθέρωση.

embalm [ɪm'bɑːm] vt ταριχεύω, βαλσαμώνω.

embankment [ɪm'bæŋkmənt] n ανάχωμα nt.

embargo [ɪm'bɑːgəʊ] n απαγόρευση, περιορισμός.

embark [ɪm'bɑːk] vt επιβιβάζω ♦ vi επιβιβάζομαι || to ~ on vt αρχίζω || ~ation [ɛmbɑː'keɪʃən] n μπαρκάρισμα nt.

embarrass [ɪm'bærəs] vt φέρω σε αμηχανία, στενοχωρώ || ~ing a (humiliating) ενοχλητικός, ξεφτελιστικός || ~ment n στενοχώρια, αμηχανία, μπλέξιμο.

embassy ['ɛmbəsɪ] n πρεσβεία.

embed [ɪm'bɛd] vt κώνω, θάβω.

embellish [ɪm'bɛlɪʃ] vt καλλωπίζω, στολίζω.

embers ['ɛmbəz] npl θράκα.

embezzle [ɪm'bɛzl] vt καταχρώμαι || ~ment n κατάχρηση, σφετερισμός.

embitter [ɪm'bɪtə*] vt πικραίνω.

emblem ['ɛmbləm] n (symbol) σύμβολο || (badge etc) έμβλημα nt.

embodiment [ɪm'bɒdɪmənt] n ενσάρκωση, προσωποποίηση.

embody [ɪm'bɒdɪ] vt (ideas) ενσαρκώνω, πραγματοποιώ || (new features) ενσωματώνω, περιλαμβάνω.

emboss [ɪm'bɒs] vt αναγλύφω, χαράσσω αναγλύφως.

embrace [ɪm'breɪs] vt (clasp) εναγκαλίζομαι, αγκαλιάζω || (include) περιλαμβάνω, περικλείω ♦ n εναγκαλισμός, ασπασμός.

embroider [ɪm'brɔɪdə*] vt κεντώ, κάνω κέντημα || ~y n κέντημα nt.

embryo ['ɛmbrɪəʊ] n (fig) έμβρυο.

emerald ['ɛmərld] n σμαράγδι.

emerge [ɪ'mɜːdʒ] vi αναδύομαι, (ξε)βγαίνω, ξεπροβάλλω.

emergence [ɪ'mɜːdʒəns] n εμφάνιση.

emergency [ɪ'mɜːdʒənsɪ] n επείγουσα ανάγκη ♦ a (action) έκτακτος || ~ exit n έξοδος f κινδύνου.

emery ['ɛmərɪ] n: ~ board n γυαλόχαρτο || ~ paper n σμυριδόχαρτο.

emetic [ɪ'mɛtɪk] n εμετικό.

emigrant ['ɛmɪgrənt] n μετανάστης/ρια m/f ♦ a μεταναστευτικός.

emigrate ['ɛmɪgreɪt] vi μεταναστεύω.

emigration [ɛmɪ'greɪʃən] n μετανάστευση.

eminence ['ɛmɪnəns] n (distinction) ανωτερότητα, διασημότητα || (ECCL) εξοχότητα.

eminent ['ɛmɪnənt] a διακεκριμένος, έξοχος, διάσημος.

emission [ɪ'mɪʃən] n (of gases) εκπομπή, αποβολή.

emit [ɪ'mɪt] vt εκπέμπω, αναδίνω.

emotion [ɪ'məʊʃən] n συγκίνηση, (ψυχική) αναταραχή || ~al a (person) ευσυγκίνητος, ευαίσθητος || (scene) συγκινητικός || ~ally ad με συγκίνηση, συναισθηματικά.

emotive [ɪ'məʊtɪv] a συγκινητικός.

emperor ['ɛmpərə*] n αυτοκράτορας.

emphasis ['ɛmfəsɪs] n έμφαση.

emphasize ['ɛmfəsaɪz] vt τονίζω, υπογραμμίζω.

emphatic [ɪm'fætɪk] a εμφατικός.

empire ['ɛmpaɪə*] n αυτοκρατορία.

empirical [ɛm'pɪrɪkl] a εμπειρικός.

employ [ɛm'plɔɪ] vt (use) χρησιμοποιώ, εφαρμόζω || (hire) απασχολώ, έχω || ~ee n υπάλληλος m/f|| ~er n εργοδότης/ρια m/f|| ~ment n (job) απασχόληση, δουλειά, εργασία || (jobs collectively) χρήση, χρησιμοποίηση.

empress ['ɛmprɪs] n αυτοκράτειρα.

emptiness ['ɛmptɪnɪs] n κενό.

empty ['ɛmptɪ] a κενός, άδειος ♦ vt (contents) κενώνω, αδειάζω || (container) αδειάζω || ~-handed a με άδεια χέρια.

emulate ['ɛmjʊleɪt] vt αμιλλώμαι, μιμούμαι, ακολουθώ.

emulsion [ɛ'mʌlʃən] n γαλάκτωμα nt.

enable [ɪ'neɪbl] vt καθιστώ ικανό, διευκολύνω, επιτρέπω.

enamel [ɪ'næml] n βερνίκι, σμάλτο, λάκα || (of teeth) σμάλτο.

enamoured [ɪ'næməd] a (+ of) ερωτευμένος.

enchant [ɪn'tʃɑːnt] vt (bewitch) μαγεύω || (delight) γοητεύω || ~ing a (delightful) γοητευτικός.

encircle [ɪn'sɜːkl] vt (περι)κυκλώνω, (περι)σφίγγω.

enclose [ɪn'kləʊz] vt (shut in) περικλείω, (περι)μαντρώνω || (in a letter etc) εγκλείω, εσωκλείω.

enclosure [ɪn'kləʊʒə*] n (space) φράκτης, μαντρότοιχος || (in a letter) συνημμένο, εσώκλειστο.

encore ['ɒŋkɔː*] n πάλι, μπις.

encounter [ɪn'kaʊntə*] n συνάντηση || (battle) σύγκρουση ♦ vt (meet) συναντώ.

encourage [ɪn'kʌrɪdʒ] vt ενθαρρύνω, δίνω κουράγιο || ~ment n εμψύχωση, ενθάρρυνση.

encroach [ɪn'krəʊtʃ] vi (+ (up)on) καταπατώ.

encyclop(a)edia [ɛnsaɪkləʊ'piːdɪə] n εγκυκλοπαίδεια.

end [ɛnd] n (finish) τέρμα nt, τέλος nt || (of book, day, rope, street, queue) άκρη, τέλος nt, ουρά || (purpose) σκοπός, επιδίωξη ♦ a τελικός, ακραίος ♦ vt τερματίζω, τελειώνω ♦ vi τερματίζομαι, καταλήγω.

endanger [ɪn'deɪndʒə*] vt διακινδυνεύω, (εκ)θέτω σε κίνδυνο.

endeavour [ɛn'dɛvə*] n προσπάθεια ♦ vi προσπαθώ, πασχίζω.

ending ['ɛndɪŋ] n τέλος nt, κατάληξη.

endless ['ɛndlɪs] a ατελείωτος, απέραντος.

endorse [ɪn'dɔːs] vt (cheque etc) οπισθογραφώ, θεωρώ || (approve) υποστηρίζω, εγκρίνω || ~**ment** n οπισθογράφηση || (of action) έγκριση.

endow [ɛn'dau] vt προικίζω || (equip) διωρίζω.

end product ['ɛndprodʌkt] n τελικό προϊόν.

endurance [ɛn'djuərəns] n αντοχή.

endure [ɛn'djuə*] vt υπομένω, ανέχομαι ♦ vi διαρκώ, αντέχω.

enemy ['ɛnəmi] n εχθρός ♦ a εχθρικός.

energetic [ɛnə'dʒɛtik] a ενεργητικός, δραστήριος.

energy ['ɛnədʒi] n (of person) ενέργεια, δύναμη || (PHYS) ενέργεια.

enforce [ɛn'fɔːs] vt επιβάλλω, εκτελώ, εφαρμόζω.

engage [ɛn'geidʒ] vt (hire) προσλαμβάνω, παίρνω || (take part in) απασχολώ, επισύρω, τραβώ || (begin fight) επιτίθεμαι || (TECH) συνδέω, βάζω || ~**d** a (to marry) αρραβωνιασμένος || (TEL) κατειλημμένη, μιλάει || (in use) απησχολημένος, πιασμένος || (person) είμαι προσκεκλημένος, έχω κλείσει || ~**ment** n (appointment) δέσμευση, ραντεβού nt inv || (to marry) μνηστεία, αρραβώνιασμα nt || (MIL) συμπλοκή, σύγκρουση || ~**ment ring** n βέρα.

engaging [ɛn'geidʒiŋ] a θελκτικός, που τραβάει.

engender [ɛn'dʒɛndə*] vt γεννώ, προκαλώ.

engine ['ɛndʒin] n (AUT) μηχανή, κινητήρας, μοτέρ nt inv || (RAIL) ατμομηχανή, ωτομοτρίς || ~ **failure** or **trouble** n βλάβη μηχανής ή κινητήρα.

engineer [ɛndʒi'niə*] n μηχανικός || (US RAIL) μηχανοδηγός.

engineering [ɛndʒi'niəriŋ] n μηχανολογία.

England ['iŋglənd] n Αγγλία.

English ['iŋgliʃ] a αγγλικός ♦ n (LING) (τα) Αγγλικά || the ~ npl οι 'Αγγλοι mpl || the ~ **Channel** n n Μάγχη || ~**man** n 'Αγγλος, Εγγλέζος || ~**woman** n Αγγλίδα.

engrave [ɛn'greiv] vt χαράσσω.

engraving [ɛn'greiviŋ] n χαρακτική.

engrossed [ɛn'grəust] a απορροφημένος.

engulf [ɛn'gʌlf] vt καταβροχθίζω, καταποντίζω.

enhance [ɛn'haːns] vt εξαίρω, ανυψώ, ανεβάζω.

enigma [ɛ'nigmə] n a ινίγμα nt || ~**tic** [ɛnig'mætik] a αινιγματικός, μυστηριώδης.

enjoy [ɛn'dʒɔi] vt μου αρέσει, χαίρομαι (κάτι) || (privileges etc) απολαμβάνω, κατέχω || ~**able** a απολαυστικός, ευχάριστος || ~**ment** n απόλαυση.

enlarge [ɛn'laːdʒ] vt μεγεθύνω,

επεκτείνω || (PHOT) μεγεθύνω, μεγαλώνω || ~**ment** n μεγέθυνση.

enlighten [ɛn'laitn] vt διαφωτίζω || ~**ed** a φωτισμένος || ~**ment** n διαφώτιση.

enlist [ɛn'list] vt στρατολογώ, προσλαμβάνω ♦ vi στρατολογούμαι, κατατάσσομαι.

enmity ['ɛnmiti] n έχθρα, εχθρότητα.

enormity [ɪ'nɔːmiti] n μέγεθος nt, τερατωδία.

enormous [ɪ'nɔːməs] a τεράστιος, πελώριος, κολοσσιαίος || ~**ly** ad πάρα πολύ, καταπληκτικά.

enough [ɛ'nʌf] n αρκετός, επαρκής, ικανός ♦ a αρκετός || ad αρκετά.

enquire [ɛn'kwaiə*] = **inquire**.

enrich [ɛn'ritʃ] vt (εμ)πλουτίζω.

enrol [ɛn'rəul] vt (MIL) στρατολογώ ♦ vi εγγράφω, προσλαμβάνω, παίρνω || ~**ment** n στρατολογία || (SCH) αριθμός μαθητών.

ensign ['ɛnsain] n (flag) σημαία || (NAUT) σημαιοφόρος.

enslave [ɛn'sleiv] vt υποδουλώνω, σκλαβώνω.

ensue [ɛn'sjuː] vi έπομαι, επακολουθώ.

ensure [ɪn'ʃuə*] vt (make certain) (εξ)ασφαλίζω.

entail [ɛn'teil] vt συνεπάγομαι, επιφέρω.

enter ['ɛntə*] vt (go into) εισέρχομαι, μπαίνω || (join) εισέρχομαι, κατατάσσομαι, γίνομαι || (write in) εγγράφω, γράφω ♦ vi εισέρχομαι, μπαίνω || **to ~ for** vt εγγράφω || **to ~ into** vt (agreement) μπαίνω, συνάπτω, μετέχω || (argument) μπαίνω || **to ~ upon** vt αναλαμβάνω, αρχίζω.

enterprise ['ɛntəpraiz] n τόλμη, θάρρος nt || (COMM) επιχείρηση.

enterprising ['ɛntəpraiziŋ] a τολμηρός.

entertain [ɛntə'tein] vt (as guest) φιλοξενώ, περιποιούμαι || (amuse) διασκεδάζω || ~**er** n ντιζέρ m/f inv || ~**ing** a διασκεδαστικός || ~**ment** n (amusement) διασκέδαση || (show) θέαμα nt.

enthralled [in'θrɔːld] a γοητευμένος, κατακτημένος.

enthusiasm [in'θuːziæzəm] n ενθουσιασμός.

enthusiast [in'θuːziæst] n • θαυμαστής/ρια m/f, λάτρης m/f || ~**ic** [inθuːzi'æstik] a ενθουσιώδης, μανιώδης.

entice [ɛn'tais] vt (tempt) δελεάζω, ξεμυαλίζω.

entire [ɛn'taiə*] a ολόκληρος, ολόκαιρος, πλήρης || ad ακέραια, πλήρως || ~**ty** nː in its ~**ty** συνολικά.

entitle [ɛn'taitl] vt (allow) εξουσιοδοτώ, δίνω το δικαίωμα, επιτρέπω || (name) τιτλοφορώ.

entrance ['ɛntrəns] n είσοδος f, μπάσιμο ♦ [ɛn'traːns] vt γοητεύω, μαγεύω || ~ **examination** n εισαγωγικές εξετάσεις fpl || ~ **fee** n τιμή εισιτηρίου, τιμή εγγραφής.

entrant ['entrənt] *n* αρχάριος/α *m/f*, υποψήφιος/α *m/f*.

entrenched [in'trentʃt] *a* οχυρωμένος.

entrust [in'trʌst] *vt (confide)* εμπιστεύομαι || *(put in charge)* επιφορτίζω, αναθέτω.

entry ['entri] *n (place)* είσοδος *f* || *(act)* είσοδος *f*, εμφάνιση || *(in dictionary)* εγγραφή, καταχώριση || 'no ~' 'απαγορεύεται η είσοδος' || ~ **form** *n* αίτηση εγγραφής, δελτίο εγγραφής.

enunciate [i'nʌnsieit] *vt* προφέρω.

envelop [in'veləp] *vt* (περι)καλύπτω, τυλίγω, σκεπάζω.

envelope ['envələup] *n* φάκελλος.

envious ['enviəs] *a* ζηλόφθονος, φθονερός, ζηλιάρης.

environment [in'vaiərənmənt] *n* περιβάλλον || ~**al** *a* του περιβάλλοντος.

envoy ['envɔi] *n* απεσταλμένος.

envy ['envi] *n* φθόνος, ζήλεια || *(object of envy)* αντικείμενο ζήλειας ♦ *vt* φθονώ, ζηλεύω.

enzyme ['enzaim] *n* ένζυμο.

ephemeral [i'femərəl] *a* εφήμερος.

epic ['epik] *n* έπος, επικό ποίημα ♦ *a* επικός.

epidemic [epi'demik] *n* επιδημία.

epilepsy ['epilepsi] *n* επιληψία.

epileptic [epi'leptik] *a, n* επιληπτικός.

epilogue ['epilɔg] *n* επίλογος.

episode ['episəud] *n* επεισόδειο.

epistle [i'pisl] *n* επιστολή, γράμμα *nt*.

epitome [i'pitəmi] *n* επιτομή, περίληψη, σύνοψη.

epitomize [i'pitəmaiz] *vt* συνοψίζω, κάνω περίληψη.

epoch ['iːpɒk] *n* εποχή.

equable ['ekwəbl] *a* ομοιόμορφος, ίσος.

equal ['iːkwl] *a (same)* ίσος || *(qualified)* αντάξιος, ανταποκρίνομαι προς ♦ *n* ίσος, ομότιμος, όμοιος ♦ *vt* ισούμαι, είμαι ίσος || ~ **to** αντάξιος, ανταποκρινόμενος || **without** ~ ασυναγώνιστος || ~**ity** *n* ισότητα || ~**ize** *vt* εξισώνω, αντισταθμίζω || ~**izer** *n* εξισωτής, αντισταθμιστής || ~**ly** *ad* εξ ίσου, ομοίως || ~**(s) sign** *n* σημείο ισότητας.

equanimity [ekwə'nimiti] *n* γαλήνη, πρεμία.

equate [i'kweit] *vt* εξισώνω.

equation [i'kweiʒən] *n* εξίσωαση.

equator [i'kweitə*] *n* ισημερινός || ~**ial** [ekwə'tɔːriəl] *a* ισημερινός.

equilibrium [iːkwi'libriəm] *n* ισορροπία.

equinox ['iːkwinɒks] *n* ισημερία.

equip [i'kwip] *vt* εφοδιάζω, εξοπλίζω || ~**ment** *n* εφόδια *ntpl*, εφοδιασμός, υλικά *ntpl*.

equitable ['ekwitəbl] *a* δίκαιος.

equity ['ekwiti] *n* δίκαιο, τιμιότητα.

equivalent [i'kwivələnt] *a* ισότιμος || *(TECH)* ισοδύναμος ♦ *n* αντίστοιχο.

equivocal [i'kwivɒkl] *a (doubtful)*

διφορούμενος, αμφίβολος || *(suspicious)* ύποπτος.

era ['iərə] *n* εποχή.

eradicate [i'rædikeit] *vt* ξεριζώνω.

erase [i'reiz] *vt* εξαλείφω, σβήνω || *(COMPUT)* διαγράφω || ~**r** *n* γομολάστιχα, γόμα.

erect [i'rekt] *a* ορθός, όρθιος, στητός, σηκωμένος ♦ *vt* υψώνω, αναγείρω, κτίζω.

erection [i'rekʃən] *n* όρθωση, σήκωμα *nt*, ανέγρεση.

ermine ['əːmin] *n* ερμίνα.

erode [i'rəud] *vt* διαβρώνω, τρώγω.

erosion [i'rəuʒən] *n* διάβρωση.

erotic [i'rɒtik] *a* ερωτικός || ~**ism** [i'rɒtisizəm] *n* ερωτισμός.

err [əː*] *vi (make mistakes)* σφάλλω, σφάλλομαι || *(sin)* πλανώμαι, αμαρτάνω.

errand ['erənd] *n* παραγγελία, αποστολή || ~ **boy** *n* ο μικρός.

erratic [i'rætik] *a* άτακτος, ακανόνιστος, εκκεντρικός.

erroneous [e'rəuniəs] *a* εσφαλμένος, λανθασμένος.

error ['erə*] *n* σφάλμα *nt*, λάθος *nt*.

erudite ['erjudait] *a* πολυμαθής, διαβασμένος.

erupt [i'rʌpt] *vi* κάνω έκρηξη || ~**ion** *n* έκρηξη, ξέσπασμα *nt*.

escalate ['eskəleit] *vt* ανεβάζω ♦ *vi* ανεβαίνω.

escalator ['eskəleitə*] *n* κυλιόμενη κλίμακα.

escapade [eskə'peid] *n* ξέκασμα *nt*, περιπέτεια.

escape [is'keip] *n (getting away)* (δια)φυγή, δραπέτευση, σκάσιμο || *(leakage)* εκφυγή, διαρροή ♦ *vi (get free)* δραπετεύω, (δια)σώζομαι || *(unpunished)* ξεφεύγω, γλυτώνω || *(leak)* διαφεύγω, διαρρέω, τρέχω ♦ *vt (be forgotten)* διαφεύγω, είμαι απαρατήρητος.

escort ['eskɔːt] *n (MIL)* συνοδεία, φρουρά || *(of lady)* συνοδός, καβαλιέρος ♦ [is'kɔːt] *vt* συνοδεύω.

Eskimo ['eskiməu] *n* Εσκιμώος/α *m/f*.

especially [is'peʃəli] *ad* ειδικώς, ιδιαιτέρως, κυρίως.

espionage ['espiɔnɑːʒ] *n* κατασκοπεία.

esquire [es'kwaiə*] *n (abbr* Esq.*)*: J. Brown E~ Κύριο J. Brown.

essay ['esei] *n (SCH)* έκθεση || *(LITER)* δοκίμιο.

essence ['esns] *n (quality)* ουσία || *(perfume)* άρωμα *nt*, μυρουδιά.

essential [i'senʃl] *a (necessary)* ουσιώδης, ουσιαστικός || *(basic)* βασικός, απαραίτητος ♦ *n* ουσία, το απαραίτητο || ~**ly** *ad* ουσιαστικά, κυρίως.

establish [es'tæbliʃ] *vt (set up)* ιδρύω, θεμελιώνω, εγκαθιστώ || *(prove)* στηρίζω, στερεώνω, αποδεικνύω || ~**ment** *n (setting up)* ίδρυση, δημιουργία, επιβολή || *(house of business)* ίδρυμα *nt*, κατάστημα *nt*, οίκος || *(MIL)* σύνθεση (μονάδας) || **the** E~**ment** το Κατεστημένο.

estate [ɛs'teɪt] n (landed property) κτήμα nt, ακίνητο || (property left) κληρονομία || ~ **agent** n κτηματομεσίτης || ~ **car** n (Brit) στέισον-βάγκον nt inv.

esteem [ɛs'tiːm] n εκτίμηση.

estimate ['ɛstɪmɪt] n (opinion) εκτίμηση || (price quoted) (προ)υπολογισμός, τιμολόγιο ♦ ['ɛstɪmeɪt] vt εκτιμώ, υπολογίζω, λογαριάζω.

estimation [ɛstɪ'meɪʃən] n (judgment) κρίση, γνώμη || (esteem) εκτίμηση, υπόληψη.

estuary ['ɛstjʊərɪ] n εκβολή.

etching ['ɛtʃɪŋ] n χαλκογραφία.

eternal [ɪ'tɜːnl] a αιώνιος, ατελείωτος || ~ly ad αιωνίως.

eternity [ɪ'tɜːnɪtɪ] n αιωνιότητα.

ether ['iːθə*] n αιθέρας.

ethical ['ɛθɪkl] a ηθικός.

ethics ['ɛθɪks] npl ηθική.

ethnic ['ɛθnɪk] a εθνικός.

etiquette ['ɛtɪkɛt] n εθιμοτυπία, ετικέτα.

eulogy ['juːlədʒɪ] n εγκώμιο.

euphemism ['juːfəmɪzəm] n ευφημισμός.

euphoria [juː'fɔːrɪə] n ευφορία.

Europe ['jʊərəp] n Ευρώπη || ~**an** a ευρωπαϊκός.

euthanasia [juːθə'neɪzɪə] n ευθανασία.

evacuate [ɪ'vækjʊeɪt] vt εκκενώνω, μεταφέρω.

evacuation [ɪvækjʊ'eɪʃən] n εκκένωση, μεταφορά.

evade [ɪ'veɪd] vt αποφεύγω, ξεφεύγω, διαφεύγω.

evaluate [ɪ'væljʊeɪt] vt εκτιμώ, υπολογίζω.

evangelist [ɪ'vændʒəlɪst] n Ευαγγελιστής.

evaporate [ɪ'væpəreɪt] vi εξατμίζομαι, ξεθυμαίνω ♦ vt εξατμίζω || ~**d milk** n γάλα nt εβαπορέ.

evaporation [ɪvæpə'reɪʃən] n εξάτμιση.

evasion [ɪ'veɪʒən] n (avoiding question) υπεκφυγή, πρόφαση.

evasive [ɪ'veɪsɪv] a ασαφής, ακαθόριστος.

even ['iːvən] a ομαλός, επίπεδος, ίσιος || (score etc) ισόπαλος, πάτσι || (number) άρτιος, ζυγός ♦ vt σιάζω, ισώνω, εξισώνω ♦ ad ακόμη, και αν, ή ακόμη || (emphasis) και αν ακόμα || ~ **if** και αν || to ~ **out** or **up** vi πατσίζω, ανταποδίδω τα ίσα.

evening ['iːvnɪŋ] n (time) βράδυ nt || (event) εσπερίδα, βραδυνή συγκέντρωση || in the ~ το βράδυ || ~ **class** n βραδυνό μάθημα || ~ **dress** n (man's) φράκο || (woman's) βραδυνή τουαλέτα.

evenly ['iːvənlɪ] ad ομοιόμορφα, ομαλά, κανονικά.

event [ɪ'vɛnt] n (happening) γεγονός, περίπτωση, έκβαση || (SPORT) άθλημα nt, αγώνας, μάτς nt inv || in the ~ **of** σε περίπτωση || ~**ful** a γεμάτος γεγονότα, αλησμόνητος.

eventual [ɪ'vɛntjʊəl] a (final) οριστικός, αναπόφευκτος, τελικός || ~**ity** n πιθανότητα || ~**ly** ad (at last) τελικά || (given time) πιθανώς.

ever ['ɛvə*] ad ποτέ, καμμιά φορά || (always) πάντα, πάντοτε || ~ **so big** τόσος δα || ~ **so many** τόσοι και τόσοι || ~**green** a αειθαλής || ~**lasting** a αιώνιος, διαρκής, άφθαρτος.

every ['ɛvrɪ] a καθένας, κάθε || ~ **other day** μέρα παρά μέρα || ~**body** pron όλοι, όλος ο κόσμος, καθένας || ~**day** a (daily) κάθε μέρα, καθημερινός || (commonplace) συνηθισμένος, κοινός || ~**one** = ~**body** || ~**thing** pron τα πάντα, όλα, κάθε τι || ~**where** ad παντού.

evict [ɪ'vɪkt] vt εκδιώκω, εξώνω, διώχνω || ~**ion** n έξωση, εκβολή.

evidence ['ɛvɪdəns] n (sign) σημάδι, σημείο, ένδειξη || (proof) απόδειξη, μαρτυρία || in ~ (obvious) διακρίνομαι, ξεχωρίζω.

evident ['ɛvɪdənt] a προφανής, κατάδηλος, φανερός || ~**ly** ad προφανώς, ολοφάνερα.

evil ['iːvɪl] a κακός ♦ n το κακό || (sin) κακία, αμαρτία.

evocative [ɪ'vɔkətɪv] a επικλητικός.

evoke [ɪ'vəʊk] vt επικαλούμαι, ξαναφέρνω στο νου.

evolution [iːvə'luːʃən] n εξέλιξη, ανέλιξη.

evolve [ɪ'vɒlv] vt αναπτύσσω, συνάγω ♦ vi εξελίσσομαι, απορρέω.

ewe [juː] n προβατίνα.

ex- [ɛks] a (former) πρώην, τέως.

exact [ɛg'zækt] a ακριβής, σωστός ♦ vt (obedience etc) απαιτώ, ζητώ || (payment) αποσπώ, παίρνω || ~**ing** a απαιτητικός, κουραστικός || ~ **ly** ad ακριβώς, σωστά.

exaggerate [ɛg'zædʒəreɪt] vti υπερβάλλω, μεγαλοποιώ, (παρα)φουσκώνω.

exaggeration [ɛgzædʒə'reɪʃən] n υπερβολή, μεγαλοποίηση.

exalt [ɛg'zɔːlt] vt εξυμνώ, εκθειάζω, επαινώ.

exam [ɛg'zæm] n abbr of **examination**.

examination [ɛgzæmɪ'neɪʃən] n (SCH, UNIV) εξετάσεις fpl, διαγωνισμός || (MED) ιατρική εξέταση || (inquiry) ανάκριση, εξέταση || (CUSTOMS) έλεγχος, έρευνα.

examine [ɛg'zæmɪn] vt (MED, SCH) εξετάζω || (consider) εξετάζω, ερευνώ || (baggage) ερευνώ, ελέγχω || ~**r** n εξεταστής/ρια m/f, επιθεωρητής/ρια m/f.

example [ɪg'zɑːmpl] n δείγμα nt, παράδειγμα nt, υπόδειγμα nt || for ~ παραδείγματος χάριν, λόγου χάριν.

exasperate [ɛg'zɑːspəreɪt] vt εξάπτω, εξαγριώνω.

excavate ['ɛkskəveɪt] vt (hollow out) σκάπτω, ανοίγω, βαθαίνω || (unearth) ανασκάπτω, κάνω ανασκαφές.

excavation [ɛkskə'veɪʃən] n ανασκαφή.

excavator ['ekskəveitə*] n εκσκαφέας.

exceed [ek'si:d] vt (number) υπερβαίνω, (ξε)περνώ || (limit) υπερβαίνω || (powers) υπερβαίνω, εξέρχομαι || (hopes) υπερβάλλω || ~ingly ad υπερβολικά, πολύ.

excel [ek'sel] vi διακρίνομαι, διαπρέπω, ξεχωρίζω ♦ vt υπερέχω, υπερτερώ, ξεπερνώ.

excellence ['eksələns] n αξία, υπεροχή, αρετή.

Excellency ['eksələnsi] n: His ~ n Αυτού Εξοχότης.

excellent ['eksələnt] a εξαίρετος, θαυμάσιος, εξαίσιος.

except [ek'sept] prep (also: ~ for) εκτός, έξω από, εξαιρουμένου του ♦ vt εξαιρώ, αποκλείω || ~ing prep= **except** || ~ion n εξαίρεση || **to take** ~ion to προσβάλλομαι, αντιλέγω || ~ional a εξαιρετικός, έξοχος, ασύγκριτος.

excerpt ['eksə:pt] n απόσπασμα nt.

excess [ek'ses] n υπερβολή, πληθώρα ♦ a (fare, baggage) υπερβάλλων || ~ive a υπερβολικός.

exchange [eks'tʃeindʒ] n ανταλλαγή || (foreign money) συνάλλαγμα nt || (TEL) κέντρο ♦ vt (goods) ανταλλάσσω, αλλάζω || (greetings, blows) ανταλλάσσω || see **rate**.

exchequer [eks'tʃekə*] n δημόσιο ταμείο, θησαυροφυλάκιο.

excise ['eksaiz] n φόρος ♦ [ek'saiz] vt φορολογώ.

excitable [ek'saitəbl] a ευερέθιστος, ευέξαπτος.

excite [ek'sait] vt (εξ)ερεθίζω, εξεγείρω, κεντρίζω || ~d a συγκινημένος, εκνευρισμένος || **to get** ~d εξάπτομαι || ~ment n έξαψη, αναστάτωση.

exciting [ek'saitiŋ] a συναρπαστικός, συγκινητικός.

exclaim [eks'kleim] vi φωνάζω, αναφωνώ.

exclamation [eksklə'meiʃən] n αναφώνηση, κραυγή || ~ mark n θαυμαστικό.

exclude [iks'klu:d] vt αποκλείω.

exclusion [iks'klu:ʒən] n απόκλειση.

exclusive [iks'klu:siv] a (select) αποκλειστικός, περιορισμένος || (sole) αποκλειστικός, μοναδικός || (news etc) αποκλειστικός || ~ly ad αποκλειστικά, μόνο.

excommunicate [ekskə'mju:nikeit] vt αφορίζω, αναθεματίζω.

excrement ['ekskrimənt] n απόπατημα nt, σκατά ntpl.

excruciating [eks'kru:ʃieitiŋ] a φρικτός, ανυπόφορος.

excursion [eks'kə:ʃən] n εκδρομή.

excuse [eks'kju:s] n δικαιολογία, πρόφαση ♦ [eks'kju:z] vt (let off) απαλλάσσω, συγχωρώ || (overlook) δικαιολογώ || ~ **me!** συγγνώμη, με συγχωρείτε.

execute ['eksikju:t] vt (perform) εκτελώ,

εκπληρώ, ενεργώ || (put to death) εκτελώ, θανατώνω.

execution [eksi'kju:ʃən] n εκτέλεση || ~**er** n δήμιος, μπόγιας.

executive [eg'zekjutiv] n (COMM) διευθυντής/ρια m/f || (POL) εκτελεστική εξουσία ♦ a εκτελεστικός.

executor [eg'zekjutə*] n εκτελεστής.

exemplary [ig'zempləri] a υποδειγματικός.

exemplify [ig'zemplifai] vt παραδειγματίζω.

exempt [ig'zempt] a απαλλαγμένος, εξαιρεμένος ♦ vt εξαιρώ, απαλλάσσω || ~ion n απαλλαγή.

exercise ['eksəsaiz] n (of duties) άσκηση || (physical) γυμναστική || (SCH) σχολική άσκηση, γυμναστική || (MIL) άσκηση, γυμνάσια ntpl ♦ vt (muscle) εξασκώ, γυμνάζω || (power) εξασκώ || **to** ~ **patience** εξαντλώ υπομονή, κάνω υπομονή || ~ **book** n τετράδιο (μαθητού).

exhaust [ig'zɔ:st] n (fumes) εξάτμιση, καυσαέρια ntpl || (pipe) σωλήνας εξαγωγής ♦ vt (weary) εξαντλώ, κατακουράζω || (use up) εξαντλώ, στειρεύω || ~**ed** a εξαντλημένος || ~ing a εξαντλητικός, κουραστικός || ~ion n εξάντληση, αποκάμωμα nt, τσάκισμα nt || ~ive a εξαντλητικός, πλήρης.

exhibit [ig'zibit] n (ART) έκθεμα nt, έκθεση || (LAW) τεκμήριο ♦ vt εκθέτω, παρουσιάζω, επιδεικνύω || ~ion [eksi'biʃən] n (ART) έκθεση || (of temper etc) επίδειξη, γελοιοποίηση || ~ionist n επιδείξιας || ~or n εκθέτης/ρια m/f.

exhilarating [ig'ziləreitiŋ] a φαιδρυντικός, ευχάριστος.

exhort [eg'zɔ:t] vt προτρέπω, ενθαρρύνω.

exile ['eksail] n εξορία || (person) εξόριστος.

exist [eg'zist] vi υπάρχω, υφίσταμαι, είμαι, ζω || ~**ence** n (state of being) ύπαρξη || (way of life) ζωή.

exit ['eksit] n έξοδος f.

exotic [ig'zɔtik] a εξωτικός.

expand [iks'pænd] vt (spread) διαστέλλω, ευρύνω, απλώνω || (operations) επεκτείνω, αναπτύσσω ♦ vi διαστέλλομαι, φουσκώνω.

expanse [eks'pæns] n έκταση.

expansion [iks'pænʃən] n επέκταση, ανάπτυξη || (PHYS) διαστολή, εκτόνωση.

expatriate [eks'pætrieit] vt εκπατρίζω, εκπατρίζομαι.

expect [iks'pekt] vt (anticipate) αναμένω, προσδοκώ, περιμένω || (require) απαιτώ, αναμένω || (suppose) σκέπτομαι, φρονώ, πιστεύω || (baby) περιμένω ♦ vi: **to be** ~ing περιμένω παιδί || ~ant a (hopeful) περιμένων, αναμένων || (mother) επίτοκος || ~ation [ekspek'teiʃən] n (hope) προσδοκία, ελπίδα || ~ations npl ελπίδες fpl.

expedience [eks'pi:diəns] n,

expediency [εks'pi:dιǝnsι] n σκοπιμότητα, ωφελιμότητα.

expedient [εks'pi:dιǝnt] a σκόπιμος, πρόσφορος, κατάλληλος ♦ n μέσο, τρόπος, τέχνασμα nt.

expedite ['εkspιdaιt] vt επισπεύδω, επιταχύνω.

expedition [εkspι'dιʃǝn] n (journey) αποστολή, εκστρατεία.

expel [εks'pεl] vt διώχνω, βγάζω || (alien) απελαύνω.

expend [εks'pεnd] vt (time) αφιερώνω, διαθέτω || (money) δαπανώ, ξοδεύω || (effort) δαπανώ, εξαντλώ || ~able a αναλώσιμος || ~iture n δαπάνη, κατανάλωση, έξοδα ntpl.

expense [εks'pεns] n (cost) δαπάνη, έξοδα ntpl || (high cost) βάρος, ακρίβεια || ~s npl αποζημίωση, δαπάνες fpl || at the ~ of με τη θυσία του, εις βάρος του || ~ account n έξοδα ntpl παραστάσεις.

expensive [εks'pεnsιv] a πολυδάπανος, δαπανηρός, ακριβός.

experience [εks'pιǝrιǝns] n (happening) δοκιμασία, περιπέτεια || (knowledge) πείρα, εμπειρία ♦ vt δοκιμάζω, υφίσταμαι, αισθάνομαι || ~d a πεπειραμένος, έμπειρος.

expert ['εkspǝ:t] n ειδικός, εμπειρογνώμων, πραγματογνώμων ♦ a έμπειρος, ειδικός || ~ise n πραγματογνωμοσύνη.

expiration [εkspι'reιʃǝn] n εκπνοή.

expire [εks'paιǝ*] vi (end) εκπνέω, λήγω, τελειώνω || (die) αποθνήσκω, πεθαίνω || (ticket) λήγω.

expiry [εks'paιǝrι] n εκπνοή, λήξη.

explain [εks'pleιn] vt (make clear) εξηγώ, λύω, ερμηνεύω || (account for) εξηγούμαι, δικαιολογούμαι || to ~ away vt εξηγώ, δικαιολογώ.

explanation [εksplǝ'neιʃǝn] n εξήγηση.

explanatory [εks'plænǝtǝrι] a ερμηνευτικός, εξηγητικός.

explicit [εks'plιsιt] a ρητός, σαφής, καθαρός, κατηγορηματικός.

explode [εks'plǝud] vi σκάω, ανατινάζομαι.

exploit ['εksplɔιt] n κατόρθωμα nt, ανδραγάθημα nt ♦ [ιks'plɔιt] vt εκμεταλλεύομαι || ~ation n εκμετάλλευση.

exploration [εksplǝ'reιʃǝn] n εξερεύνηση, έρευνα.

exploratory [εks'plɔrǝtǝrι] a (fig) δοκιμαστικός.

explore [εks'plɔ:*] vt (for discovery) εξερευνώ || (examine) εξετάζω, (εξ)ερευνώ || ~r n εξερευνητής.

explosion [εks'plǝuʒǝn] n (lit) έκρηξη, εκτόνωση || (fig) ξεχείλισμα nt, ξέσπασμα nt.

explosive [εks'plǝuzιv] a εκρηκτικός ♦ n εκρηκτική ύλη.

exponent [εks'pǝunǝnt] n

ερμηνευτής/ρια m/f, υπέρμαχος || (MATH) εκθέτης.

export [εks'pɔ:t] vt εξάγω ♦ ['εkspɔ:t] n εξαγωγή ♦ a (trade) εξαγωγικός || ~ation n εξαγωγή || ~er n εξαγωγέας.

expose [εks'pǝuz] vt (uncover) εκθέτω, αποκαλύπτω, ξεσκεπάζω || (leave unprotected) αφήνω απροστάτευτο, εκθέτω || (plot) αποκαλύπτω.

exposed [εks'pǝuzd] a (position) εκτεθειμένος.

exposure [εks'pǝuʒǝ*] n τράβηγμα nt, πόζα, φωτογραφία || (MED) έκθεση || ~ meter n φωτόμετρο.

expound [εks'paund] vt αναπτύσσω, εκθέτω, εξηγώ.

express [εks'prεs] a (clearly stated) σαφής, ρητός || (speedy) ταχύς ♦ n (fast train) ταχεία, εξπρές nt inv ♦ ad (speedily) γρήγορα, χωρίς σταθμό ♦ vt (idea) εκφράζω, διατυπώνω || (feeling) εκφράζω, εκδηλώνω || to ~ o.s. εκφράζομαι || ~ion n (phrase) φράση, έκφραση, τρόπος εκφράσεως || (look on face) έκφραση || (showing) εκδήλωση || ~ive a εκφραστικός || ~ly ad ρητώς, επίτηδες.

expulsion [εks'pʌlʃǝn] n απέλαση, αποβολή.

exquisite [εks'kwιzιt] a άριστος, ευχάριστος, λεπτός.

extend [εks'tεnd] vt (visit) παρατείνω || (building) επεκτείνω, μεγαλώνω || (hand) τείνω, δίνω || to ~ a welcome εύχομαι, καλωσορίζω.

extension [εks'tεnʃǝn] n (general) έκταση, επέκταση, άπλωμα nt || (building) επέκταση, εύρυνση || (TEL) εσωτερική γραμμή.

extensive [εks'tεnsιv] a εκτεταμένος, εκτενής, μεγάλος || ~ly ad (travel) ευρέως || (use) εκτεταμένα.

extent [εks'tεnt] n έκταση, σημασία, μέγεθος nt.

exterior [εks'tιǝrιǝ*] a εξωτερικός ♦ n εξωτερικό, έξω.

exterminate [εks'tǝ:mιneιt] vt εξοντώνω, εξολοθρεύω.

extermination [εkstǝ:mι'neιʃǝn] n εξολόθρευση, εκρίζωση.

external [εks'tǝ:nl] a εξωτερικός.

extinct [εks'tιŋkt] a (animal etc) εξαλειμμένος, εξαφανισμένος || ~ion n εξαφάνιση, σβήσιμο.

extinguish [εks'tιŋgwιʃ] vt σβήνω || ~er n πυροσβεστήρας.

extort [ιks'tɔ:t] vt (+ from) αποσπώ || ~ion [ιks'tɔ:ʃǝn] n αναγκαστική είσπραξη, απόσπαση || ~ionate a υπερβολικός.

extra ['εkstrǝ] a πρόσθετος, έκτακτος, έξτρα ♦ ad πέρα από, εξαιρετικά, πολύ ♦ n συμπλήρωμα || (newspaper) έκτακτος έκδοση || (THEAT) κομπάρσος.

extract [εks'trækt] vt (distil) αποστάζω || (select) εξάγω, βγάζω, παίρνω ♦ ['εkstrækt] n (LITER) απόσπασμα nt,

εκλογή || (COOKING) εκκύλισμα nt|| ~ion n
εξαγωγή, βγάλσιμο || (origin) καταγωγή,
προέλευση.

extradite ['ɛkstrədaɪt] vt εκδίδω
(εγκληματία).

extradition [ɛkstrə'dɪʃən] n έκδοση
(εγκληματία).

extraneous [ɛks'treɪnɪəs] a ξένος,
άσχετος.

extraordinary [ɛks'trɔːdnrɪ] a
έκτακτος, εξαιρετικός || (strange)
παράξενος, αλλόκοτος.

extravagant [ɛks'trævəgənt] a (lavish)
υπερβολικός, παράλογος || (wasteful)
σπάταλος, άσωτος.

extreme [ɛks'triːm] a (last) ακραίος,
έσχατος, μακρυνός || (very great)
υπερβολικός, μέγιστος || (not moderate)
των άκρων, εξαιρετικός ♦ n άκρο, άκρη ||
~s npl άκρα ntpl|| ~ly ad υπερβολικά,
εις το έπακρο.

extremist [ɛks'triːmɪst] a αδιάλλακτος,
των άκρων ♦ n εξτρεμιστής/ρια m/f.

extremity [ɛks'trɛmɪtɪ] n (farthest end)
άκρο, άκρη || (necessity) εσχάτη ανάγκη ||
extremities npl (ANAT) τα άκρα ntpl.

extricate ['ɛkstrɪkeɪt] vt εξάγω, βγάζω,
ξεμπλέκω.

extrovert ['ɛkstrəʊvɜːt] a, n
εξωστρεφής.

exuberant [ɪg'zjuːbərənt] a διαχυτικός,
ζωηρός.

exude [ɪg'zjuːd] vt εξιδρώ, εκχύνω.

exult [ɪg'zʌlt] vi χαίρομαι, αγάλλομαι,
θριαμβεύω.

eye [aɪ] n (ANAT) οφθαλμός, μάτι || (of
needle) μάτι, τρύπα || (for perception) καλό
μάτι, μάτι ζωγράφου κτλ ♦ vt υποβλέπω,
εποφθαλμιώ, κοιτάζω || **to keep an** ~
on προσέχω, επιβλέπω, παρακολουθώ ||
in the ~s **of** ενώπιο, στα μάτια || (in the
public ~) διάσημος || **up to the** ~s **in**
πνιγμένος στο, φορτωμένος με || ~**ball**
n βολβός οφθαλμού || ~**brow** n φρύδι ||
~**lash** n βλεφαρίδα, ματοτσίνουρο ||
~**lid** n βλέφαρο || ~-**opener** n έκπληξη,
αποκάλυψη || ~**shadow** n σκιά ματιών ||
~**sight** n όραση || ~**sore** n ασχήμια ||
~**witness** n αυτόπτης μάρτυρας.

F

F. abbr of **Fahrenheit.**

fable ['feɪbl] n μύθος, παραμύθι.

fabric ['fæbrɪk] n (cloth) ύφασμα nt, πανί.

fabulous ['fæbjʊləs] a (imaginary)
μυθικός, μυθώδης || (wonderful) μυθικός ||
(unbelievable) υπερβολικός.

facade [fə'sɑːd] n πρόσοψη.

face [feɪs] n (ANAT) πρόσωπο, φάτσα,
μούρη || (appearance) φυσιογνωμία ||
(grimace) μορφασμός || (front) όψη,
εμφάνιση || (of clock) καντράν nt inv ♦ vt
(look towards) αντικρύζω, γυρίζω ||
(bravely) αντιμετωπίζω || **in the** ~ **of**
ενώπιο, μπρος από, σε || **to** ~ **up to** vt

αντιμετωπίζω || ~ **cream** n κρέμα (του
προσώπου).

facet ['fæsɪt] n (single part) μέρος,
πλευρά || (of gem) έδρα διαμαντιού.

facetious [fə'siːʃəs] a ευτράπελος,
αστείος, περιπαικτικός || ~**ly** ad
ευτράπελα, πειραχτά.

face to face ['feɪstuː'feɪs] ad πρόσωπο
με πρόσωπο, φάτσα με φάτσα.

face value ['feɪs'væljuː] n ονομαστική
αξία.

facial ['feɪʃəl] a του προσώπου,
καθάρισ, μάσκα.

facile ['fæsaɪl] a (US: easy) εύκολος.

facilitate [fə'sɪlɪteɪt] vt (δι)ευκολύνω.

facility [fə'sɪlɪtɪ] n (ease) ευχέρεια,
ευκολία || **facilities** npl ανέσεις fpl,
ευκολίες fpl.

facsimile [fæk'sɪmɪlɪ] n πανομοιότυπο ||
(also: ~ machine) τηλεαντιγραφικό.

fact [fækt] n γεγονός nt, πραγματικότητα
|| see **matter.**

faction ['fækʃən] n φατρία, κόμμα nt.

factor ['fæktə*] n παράγων,
συντελεστής.

factory ['fæktərɪ] n εργοστάσιο.

factual ['fæktjʊəl] a πραγματικός.

faculty ['fækəltɪ] n (ability) ικανότητα,
προσόν || (UNIV) σχολή || (US: teaching
staff) διδακτικό προσωπικό.

fade [feɪd] vt (cause to fade) ξεθωριάζω,
ξεβάφω ♦ vi (grow dim) εξασθενίζω,
αδυνατίζω, πέφτω || (lose colour)
ξασπρίζω ξεθωριάζω, ξεβάφω || (wither)
μαραίνομαι.

fag [fæg] n αγγαρεία, μόχθος || (col:
cigarette) τσιγάρο || ~**ged** a (exhausted)
εξαντλημένος.

Fahrenheit ['færənhaɪt] n Φαρενάιτ inv.

fail [feɪl] vt (exam) απορρίπτω,
αποτυχάνω ♦ vi (run short) λείπω || (lose
power) εγκαταλείπω, χάνω, εξασθενίζω ||
(light) εξασθενίζω, πέφτω, σβήνω ||
(remedy) αποτυγχάνω || **to** ~ **to do** sth
(neglect) παραλείπω κάνω κάτι || (be
unable) αποτυγχάνω || **without** ~ χωρίς
άλλο || ~**ing** n (shortcoming) ελάττωμα nt,
αδυναμία ♦ prep ελλείψει || ~**ure** n
(person) αποτυχημένος || (MECH) διακοπή,
βλάβη.

faint [feɪnt] a αδύνατος, ασθενής,
αμυδρός, δειλός ♦ n λιποθυμία,
αναισθησία ♦ vi λιποθυμώ || ~-**hearted**
a δειλός, μικρόψυχος, φοβιτσιάρης ||
~**ly** ad ντροπαλά, αδύνατα, άτονα, μόλις
|| ~**ness** n (of voice) αδυναμία || (of light)
αμυδρότητα.

fair [fɛə*] a (beautiful) ωραίος, όμορφος ||
(light) ξανθός, άσπρος || (weather) καλός
καιρός, καλοκαιριά || (just, honest)
δίκαιος, έντιμος, τίμιος || (tolerable)
υποφερτός || (conditions) έτσι και έτσι ||
(sizeable) αρκετός, μεγάλος ♦ ad (play)
τίμια, δίκαια, έντιμα ♦ n (COMM)
πανήγυρη, έκθεση || (fun fair) λούνα-παρκ
nt inv, πανηγύρι || ~**ly** ad έντιμα, δίκαια ||
(rather) αρκετά καλά, σχεδόν,

F

καλούτσικα || ~ness n τιμιότητα, εντιμότητα.

fairy ['fɛərɪ] n νεράιδα || ~ tale n παραμύθι.

faith [feɪθ] n (trust) εμπιστοσύνη, πίστη || (REL) πίστη, θρήσκευμα nt, θρησκεία || in good ~ με καλή πίστη || ~ful a πιστός || ~fully ad πιστά, έντιμα || (in letter) υμέτερος.

fake [feɪk] n (thing) ψεύτικο είδος nt, απομίμηση || (person) απατεώνας ♦ a ψεύτικο, πλαστό ♦ vt παραποιώ, πλαστογραφώ.

falcon ['fɔːlkən] n γεράκι.

fall [fɔːl] (irreg v) n πτώση, κατέβασμα nt || (drop) πτώση, πέσιμο || (of snow) πτώση || (US: autumn) φθινόπωρο ♦ vi πέφτω || ~s npl (waterfall) καταρράκτης || to ~ down vi (person) πέφτω χάμω || (building) καταρρέω, γκρεμίζομαι || (fail) αποτυγχάνω, πέφτω || to ~ flat vi πάω χαμένο, πέφτω στα κούφια, πέφτω || to ~ for vt (trick) πιάνομαι κορόιδο, πέφτω στην παγίδα || to ~ off vi (drop off) πέφτω || (diminish) πέφτω, φθίνω, μειούμαι, ολιγοστεύω || to ~ out vi τσακώνομαι, τα χαλώ || to ~ through vi αποτυγχάνω, γκρεμίζομαι || to ~ under vi υπάγομαι σε.

fallacy ['fæləsɪ] n σόφισμα nt, πλάνη.

fallen ['fɔːlən] pp of fall.

fallible ['fæləbl] a σφαλερός.

fallout ['fɔːlaʊt] n ραδιενεργός σκόνη.

fallow ['fæləʊ] a χέρσος, ακαλλιέργητος.

false [fɔːls] a (untrue) ψεύτικος, λαθεμένος || (sham) πλαστός, τεχνητός, κίβδηλος || under ~ pretences με απάτη || ~ alarm n αδικαιολόγητος φόβος || ~ly ad ψεύτικα, απατηλά || ~ teeth npl μασέλες fpl.

falter ['fɔːltə*] vi διστάζω, κοντοστέκω, κομπιάζω || (in speech) τραυλίζω, ψευδίζω || ~ing a διστακτικός, ασταθής.

fame [feɪm] n φήμη.

familiar [fə'mɪlɪə*] a (well-known) γνωστός, γνώριμος || (intimate) οικείος, στενός, φιλικός || to be ~ with ξέρω, γνωρίζω || ~ity n οικειότητα, εξοικείωση || ~ize vt εξοικειούμαι με, συνηθίζω.

family ['fæmɪlɪ] n οικογένεια, φαμίλια || ~ allowance n επίδομα nt οικογενείας || ~ business n οικογενειακή επιχείρηση || ~ doctor n οικογενειακός γιατρός || ~ life n οικογενειακή ζωή.

famine ['fæmɪn] n λιμός, πείνα.

famished ['fæmɪʃt] a πειναμένος.

famous ['feɪməs] a διάσημος, περίφημος, φημισμένος.

fan [fæn] n (folding) βεντάλια || (ELEC) ανεμιστήρας || (SPORT etc) φανατικός θαυμαστής/ρια m/f, λάτρης m/f ♦ vt αερίζω, ανεμίζω || to ~ out vi αναπτύσσω, απλώνω.

fanatic [fə'nætɪk] n φανατικός || ~al a φανατικός.

fan belt ['fænbɛlt] n ιμάντας, ταινία, λουρί.

fancied ['fænsɪd] a φανταστικός, φαντασιώδης.

fanciful ['fænsɪfʊl] a (odd) παράξενος, ιδιότροπος || (imaginative) φανταστικός.

fancy ['fænsɪ] n (liking) συμπάθεια, αγάπη, τσίμπημα nt || (imagination) φαντασία ♦ a φαντασιώδης, φανταχτερός, φανταζί ♦ vt (like) συμπαθώ, μου αρέσει || (imagine) φαντάζομαι, υποθέτω || (just) ~ (that)! για φαντάσου || ~ dress n μεταμφίεση || ~-dress ball n χορός μεταμφιεσμένων, μπαλ μασκέ nt inv.

fang [fæŋ] n δόντι || (of snake) φαρμακερό δόντι.

fantastic [fæn'tæstɪk] a παράξενος, φαντασιώδης, αλλόκοτος.

fantasy ['fæntəzɪ] n φαντασία, καπρίτσιο.

far [fɑː*] a μακρυνός, απώτερος ♦ ad μακρυά || (very much) κατά πολύ, τόσο πολύ || ~ away, ~ off πολύ μακρυά || by ~ ασυγκρίτως, κατά πολύ || so ~ ως εδώ, μέχρι εδώ || ~away a μακρυνός || the F~ East 'Απω Ανατολή.

farce [fɑːs] n κωμωδία, φάρσα.

farcical ['fɑːsɪkəl] a γελοίος, κωμικός, σαν φάρσα.

fare [fɛə*] n εισιτήριο, ναύλα ntpl || (food) φαΐ ♦ vi τα πάω, πηγαίνω || ~well n αποχαιρετισμός ♦ excl αντίο!, χαίρετε!, γειά σου! ♦ a αποχαιρετιστήριος.

far-fetched ['fɑːfɛtʃt] a εξεζητημένος, παρατραβηγμένος.

farm [fɑːm] n αγρόκτημα nt, φάρμα ♦ vt καλλιεργώ || ~er n γεωργός m/f, αγρότης/ισσα m/f, φαρμαδόρος || ~hand n αγροτικός εργάτης || ~house n αγροικία || ~ing n γεωργία, καλλιέργεια || ~land n αγροτική έκταση || ~yard n περίβολος αγροικίας.

far-reaching ['fɑː'riːtʃɪŋ] a μεγάλης εκτάσεως, μεγάλης σπμασίας.

far-sighted ['fɑː'saɪtɪd] a προνοητικός, διορατικός.

fart [fɑːt] (col) n πορδή ♦ vi πέρδομαι, κλάνω.

farther ['fɑːðə*] a μακρυνότερος, απώτερος ♦ ad μακρύτερα, περαιτέρω.

farthest ['fɑːðɪst] a απώτατος, μακρυνότερος ♦ ad μακρύτατα, πιο μακρυά.

fascinate ['fæsɪneɪt] vt γοητεύω, μαγεύω.

fascinating ['fæsɪneɪtɪŋ] a γοητευτικός, μαγευτικός.

fascination [fæsɪ'neɪʃən] n γοητεία, μάγεμα nt.

fascism ['fæʃɪzəm] n φασισμός.

fascist ['fæʃɪst] n φασιστής, φασίστας/ρια m/f ♦ a φασιστικός.

fashion ['fæʃən] n (custom) ράψιμο, μόδα || (manner) τρόπος, συνήθεια, μορφή ♦ vt σχηματίζω, διαμορφώνω, πλάθω || in ~ της μόδας || out of ~ ντεμοντέ || after a ~ όπως-όπως, έτσι κι έτσι || ~able a (clothes) της μόδας, μοντέρνος || (place) κοσμικός || ~ show n επίδειξη μόδας.

fast [faːst] a (swift) ταχύς, γρήγορος || (ahead of time) που τρέχει, που πάει εμπρός || (steady, firm) σταθερός, στερεός, σφικτός || (firmly fixed) στερεός, γερός ♦ ad (rapidly) γρήγορα || (firmly) στερεά, γερά ♦ n νηστεία ♦ vi νηστεύω.

fasten ['faːsn] vt (attach) στερεώνω, σφίγγω || (with rope) δένω || (coat) κουμπώνω ♦ vi δένομαι, κουμπώνομαι || ~er n, ~ing n (on box) συνδετήρας, ενδέτης || (on clothes) αγκράφα, φερμουάρ nt inv.

fastidious [fæs'tıdıəs] a δύσκολος, δύστροπος, στριφνός.

fat [fæt] a παχύς, χονδρός, εύσωμος ♦ n (of person) ξύγγι, πάχος nt || (on meat) λίπος nt, ξύγγι || (for cooking) λίπος nt.

fatal ['feıtl] a (ending in death) θανάσιμο || (disastrous) μοιραίος, καταστρεπτικός, ολέθριος || ~ism n μοιρολατρεία, φαταλισμός || ~ity n (road death etc) θάνατος, θύμα nt || ~ly ad μοιραία, αναπόφευκτα, θανάσιμα.

fate [feıt] n (destiny) μοίρα, πεπρωμένο, το γραφτό || (death) μοίρα, θάνατος || ~ful a (prophetic) προφητικός || (important) υψίστης σημασίας, αποφασιστικός.

father ['faːðə*] n (parent) πατέρας || (priest) πάτερ, πατήρ || (early leader) πατέρας, δημιουργός || ~-in-law n πεθερός || ~ly a πατρικός, σαν πατέρας.

fathom ['fæðəm] n οργυιά ♦ vt (sound) βυθομετρώ || (understand) βολιδοσκοπώ, καταλαβαίνω.

fatigue [fə'tiːg] n (weariness) κούραση, κόπωση, κάματος ♦ vt κουράζω, καταπονώ.

fatten ['fætn] vt παχαίνω, σιτεύω ♦ vi παχαίνω, χοντραίνω.

fatty ['fætı] a (food) παχύς, λιπαρός.

fatuous ['fætjʊəs] a ανόητος, ηλίθιος, χαζός.

faucet ['fɔːsıt] n (US) κάνουλα, βρύση.

fault [fɔːlt] n (offence) σφάλμα nt, λάθος nt || (defect) ελάττωμα nt || (blame) λάθος nt, φταίξιμο || (GEOL) ρήγμα nt, ρωγμή || at ~ σφάλλω, λαθεύω, είμαι φταίστης || ~less a άψογος, τέλειος || ~y a ελαττωματικός, λανθασμένος.

fauna ['fɔːnə] n πανίδα.

favour, (US) favor ['feıvə*] n (approval) εύνοια, συμπάθεια || (kindness) χάρη, χατήρι ♦ vt (plan) προτιμώ, υποστηρίζω, μεροληπτώ || (in race) παίζω το φαβορί || in ~ of υπέρ || ~able a ευνοϊκός || ~ably ad ευνοϊκά, συμπαθητικά || ~ite a ευνοούμενος, αγαπητός ♦ n ευνοούμενος, αγαπητό || ~itism n ευνοιοκρατία, ρουσφετολογία.

fawn [fɔːn] a, n (colour) πυρόξανθος.

fax [fæks] n (col) τηλεαντιγραφικό έντυπο || (machine) τηλεαντιγραφικό ♦ vt στέλλω με το τηλεαντιγραφικό.

fear [fıə*] n φόβος, τρόμος ♦ vt φοβούμαι, τρέμω, ανησυχώ || no ~! μη φοβάσαι!, δεν είναι πιθανό! || ~ful a (timid) δειλός, φοβιτσιάρης || (terrible) φοβερός, τρομερός || ~less a ατρόμητος, άφοβος.

feasibility [fiːzə'bılıtı] n (το) πραγματοποιήσιμο.

feasible ['fiːzəbl] a δυνατός, κατορθωτός.

feast [fiːst] n τραπέζι, φαγοπότι, γλέντι ♦ vi (+ on) απολαμβάνω, χορταίνω || ~ day n (REL) γιορτή.

feat [fiːt] n κατόρθωμα nt.

feather ['feðə*] n φτερό.

feature ['fiːtʃə*] n χαρακτηριστικό || (article) κύριο άρθρο || (film) κυρία ταινία ♦ vti χαρακτηρίζω, τονίζω, εμφανίζω || ~less a πλαδαρός, ασήμαντος.

February ['februərı] n Φεβρουάριος.

fed [fɛd] pt, pp of feed || to be ~ up vi βαριέμαι, μπουχτώνω, αηδιάζω.

federal ['fɛdərəl] a ομόσπονδος, ομοσπονδιακός.

federation [fɛdə'reıʃən] n ομοσπονδία, συνασπισμός.

fee [fiː] n (payment) αμοιβή || (for entrance) δίδακτρα ntpl, τέλος nt.

feeble ['fiːbl] a (person) φιλασθενής, αρρωστιάρης || (excuse) αδύνατος, αμφίβολος || ~-minded a διανοητικώς ανεπαρκής.

feed [fiːd] (irreg v) n τροφή, τάισμα nt, τροφοδότηση ♦ vt τρέφω, θρέφω || (machine etc) τροφοδοτώ || to ~ on vt τρέφω με, τρέφομαι με || ~back n ανάδραση.

feel [fiːl] (irreg v) n (touch) αφή, πιάσιμο || (feeling) αίσθηση, αίσθημα nt ♦ vt (touch) αγγίζω || (examine) ψηλαφώ, ψαύω, πιάνω || (be mentally aware of) αισθάνομαι, νοιώθω || (think, believe) νοιώθω || (give impression) αισθάνομαι, νοιώθω || ~er n βολιδοσκόπηση || ~ing n (sensation) αφή, αίσθηση nt || (emotion) ευαισθησία, συγκίνηση || (opinion) εντύπωση, γνώμη, αίσθημα nt.

feet [fiːt] npl of foot.

feign [feın] vt προσποιούμαι, υποκρίνομαι || ~ed a προσποιητός, ψεύτικος.

feint [feınt] n προσποίηση || (MIL) ψευδεπίθεση.

fell [fɛl] pt of fall ♦ vt (tree) κόβω, ρίχνω κάτω ♦ n (hill) βραχώδης λόφος.

fellow ['fɛləʊ] n (companion) σύντροφος, συνάδελφος || (member of society) εταίρος, μέλος || (man) άνθρωπος, φουκαράς, τύπος || ~ citizen n συμπολίτης/ρια m/f || ~ countryman n συμπατριώτης || ~ feeling n συναδελφοσύνη || ~ men npl συνάνθρωποι || ~ship n (group) (συν)αδελφότητα, εταιρεία || (friendliness) συντροφιά, συντροφικότητα.

felony ['fɛlənı] n κακούργημα nt.

felt [felt] pt, pp of **feel** ♦ n πίλημα nt, τσόχα.

female ['fiːmeɪl] n θηλυκό, γυναίκα ♦ a θηλυκός, γυναικείος.

feminine ['femɪnɪn] a (GRAM) θηλυκό || (qualities) θηλυκός, γυναικείος.

feminist ['femɪnɪst] n φεμινιστής, φεμινίστρια m/f.

fence [fens] n φράγμα nt, φράχτης ♦ vt (also ~ **in**, ~ **off**) περιφράσσω, (περι) μαντρώνω ♦ vi ξιφομαχώ.

fencing ['fensɪŋ] n (swordplay) ξιφασκία, ξιφομαχία || (fences) περίφραξη, φράκτης.

fend [fend] vi: **to ~ for o.s.** φροντίζω, συντηρούμαι, καταφέρνω.

fender ['fendə*] n κυγκλίδωμα, πυρομάχος || (US: wing, mudguard) προφυλακτήρας.

fennel ['fenl] n μάραθο.

ferment [fə'ment] vi ζημούμαι, βράζω ♦ ['fɜːment] n ζύμωση, αναβρασμός || ~ation n ζύμωση, βράσιμο.

fern [fɜːn] n φτέρη.

ferocious [fə'rəʊʃəs] a άγριος, θηριώδης.

ferry ['feri] n (small) πέραμα nt, πορθμείο || (large: also ~**boat**) φέρρυ-μποτ nt inv ♦ vt διεκπεραιώ, διαπορθμεύω, περνώ.

fertile ['fɜːtaɪl] a (AGR) εύφορος, γόνιμος || (BIOL) γονιμοποιός.

fertility [fə'tɪlɪtɪ] n ευφορία, γονιμότητα.

fertilize ['fɜːtɪlaɪz] vt γονιμοποιώ || ~**r** n λίπασμα nt.

fervent ['fɜːvənt] a θερμός, φλογερός.

festival ['festɪvəl] n (REL etc) γιορτή, πανηγύρι || (ART, MUS) φεστιβάλ nt inv.

festive ['festɪv] a γιορταστικός, γιορτάσιμος || (person) εύθυμος, κεφάτος || **the ~ season** (Christmas) εποχή γιορτών.

fetch [fetʃ] vt πηγαίνω να φέρω || (a price) αποφέρω, πιάνω.

fetching ['fetʃɪŋ] a γοητευτικός, ελκυστικός.

fête [feɪt] n γιορτή, πανηγύρι.

fetters ['fetəz] npl δεσμά ntpl, αλυσίδες fpl.

fetus ['fiːtəs] n (US) = **foetus**.

feud [fjuːd] n έχθρα, έριδα, βεντέτα ♦ vi είμαι στα χέρια με || ~**al** a φεουδαλικός, τιμαριωτικός || ~**alism** n φεουδαλισμός.

fever ['fiːvə*] n πυρετός, θέρμη || ~**ish** a (MED) πυρετώδης || ~**ishly** ad (fig) πυρετωδώς, με τα μούτρα.

few [fjuː] a λίγοι, μερικοί || **a ~** μερικοί, λίγοι || ~**er** a λιγότεροι, σπανιότεροι || ~**est** ελάχιστοι, λιγοστοί.

fiancé [fɪ'ɑːŋseɪ] n αρραβωνιαστικός, αρραβωνιαστής || ~**e** n αρραβωνιαστικιά.

fiasco [fɪ'æskəʊ] n φιάσκο, αποτυχία.

fib [fɪb] n ψεμματάκι, μπούρδα ♦ vi ψεύδομαι.

fibre, (US) **fiber** ['faɪbə*] n ίνα || ~**glass** n υαλοβάμβακας.

fickle ['fɪkl] a αλλοπρόσαλος, αλαφρομυαλός.

fiction ['fɪkʃən] n (invention) φαντασία || (novels) μυθιστορήματα ntpl || ~**al** a των μυθιστορημάτων.

fictitious [fɪk'tɪʃəs] a φανταστικός.

fiddle ['fɪdl] n (violin) βιολί || (swindle) κομπίνα ♦ vt (cheat) ξεγελώ ♦ vi παίζω, μαστορεύω, χάνω (το χρόνο) || **to ~ with** vt παίζω, μαστορεύω || ~**r** n βιολιστής/ρια m/f.

fidelity [fɪ'delɪtɪ] n πίστη, αφοσίωση, πιστότητα.

fidget ['fɪdʒɪt] vi κάνω νευρικές κινήσεις || ~**y** a ακίνητος, νευρικός, ανήσυχος.

field [fiːld] n (land) χωράφι, κάμπος, περιοχή || (SPORT: ground) γήπεδο || (SPORT: in race) τα άλογα ntpl || (range) έκταση, πεδίο || (battleground) πεδίο || (COMPUT) πεδίο || ~ **marshal** n στρατάρχης || ~**work** n (MIL) έργο εκστρατείας.

fiend [fiːnd] n δαίμονας, τέρας nt || ~**ish** a διαβολικός.

fierce [fɪəs] a θηριώδης, μανιασμένος.

fiery ['faɪərɪ] a (of fire) φλογερός, καφτερός, φλεγόμενος || (person) ζωηρός, ορμητικός, ζωντανός.

fifteen [fɪf'tiːn] num δέκα πέντε.

fifth [fɪfθ] a πέμπτος.

fiftieth ['fɪftɪɪθ] a πεντηκοστός.

fifty ['fɪftɪ] num πενήντα.

fig [fɪg] n σύκο || (tree) συκιά.

fight [faɪt] (irreg v) n (between people) καυγάς, πιάσιμο || (campaign) μάχη, αγώνας, πάλη ♦ vt πολεμώ, μάχομαι ♦ vi (struggle against) μάχομαι, αγωνίζομαι, παλεύω || ~**er** n πολεμιστής, μαχητής || (AVIAT) καταδιωκτικό || ~**ing** n μάχη, καυγάς || (SPORT) πυγμαχία.

figurative ['fɪgərətɪv] a μεταφορικός, παραστατικός.

figure ['fɪgə*] n (shape) μορφή, σχήμα nt || (of person) παράστημα nt, κορμοστασιά, σιλουέττα || (picture) εικόνα, απεικόνιση || (person) πρόσωπο, άνθρωπος || προσωπικότητα || (MATH) σχήμα nt || (cipher) αριθμός, ψηφίο, νούμερο ♦ vt (US: imagine) υπολογίζω, λογαριάζω ♦ vi (appear) εμφανίζομαι, φαντάζομαι || **to ~ out** vt υπολογίζω, λογαριάζω || ~**head** n (NAUT) ξόανο, γοργόνα || (fig) διακοσμητικό πρόσωπο.

filament ['fɪləmənt] n νήμα nt.

file [faɪl] n (tool) ρίνη, λίμα || (dossier) φάκελλος, αρχείο || (folder) φάκελλος, ντοσιέ nt inv || (row) στοίχος, γραμμή, αράδα || (COMPUT) αρχείο ♦ vt (wood) λιμάρω || (nails) λιμάρω || (papers) ταξινομώ, αρχειοθετώ || (claim) καταθέτω, υποβάλλω ♦ vi: **to ~ in/out** μπαίνω/βγαίνω ένας-ένας || **in single ~** σε μονή γραμμή.

filing ['faɪlɪŋ] n (of papers) ταξινόμηση, αρχειοθέτηση || ~**s** npl ρινίσματα ntpl, λιμαδούρα || ~ **cabinet** n δελτιοθήκη, αρχειοθήκη.

fill [fɪl] vt (make full) πληρώ, γεμίζω ||

(occupy completely) συμπληρώνω, γεμίζω || *(satisfy)* ικανοποιώ, χορταίνω || *(position etc)* κατέχω, γεμίζω ♦ *n* πληρομονή, κορεσμός, γέμισμα *nt* || **to ~ the bill** *(fig)* ανταποκρίνομαι || **to ~ in** *vt (hole)* γεμίζω, βουλώνω || *(form)* συμπληρώνω || **to ~ up** *vt (container)* γεμίζω τελείως || *(form)* συμπληρώνω.

fillet ['fɪlɪt] *n (food)* φιλέτο ♦ *vt* χωρίζω τα φιλέτα.

filling ['fɪlɪŋ] *n (for cakes, pies etc)* γέμισιν || *(for tooth)* σφράγισμα *nt*, βούλωμα *nt* || **~ station** *n* πρατήριο βενζίνης, βενζινάδικο.

fillip ['fɪlɪp] *n (reviver)* αναζωογόνηση, τόνωση.

film [fɪlm] *n (thin layer)* ελαφρό στρώμα *nt*, μεμβράνη || *(PHOT)* (φωτο)ταινία, φίλμ *nt inv*, πλάκα || *(moving picture)* ταινία, φίλμ *nt inv* ♦ *vt (scene)* γυρίζω ταινία, φιλμάρω || **~ star** *n* αστέρας του κινηματογράφου.

filter ['fɪltə*] *n* φίλτρο || *(PHOT)* φίλτρο ♦ *vt* διυλίζω, φιλτράρω, λαμπικάρω ♦ *vi (fig)* διεισδύω, εισχωρώ || **~ tip** *n* επιστόμιο φίλτρου.

filth [fɪlθ] *n (lit)* ακαθαρσίες *fpl*, σκουπίδια *ntpl*, βρώμα || *(fig)* ηθική φθορά, βρωμιά, αισχρολογία || **~y** *a* ακάθαρτος, ρυπαρός, βρώμικος.

fin [fɪn] *n (fish)* πτερύγιο, φτερό.

final ['faɪnl] *a* τελικός, τελευταίος, οριστικός ♦ *n (SPORT)* τελικός (αγώνας) || **~s** *npl (UNIV)* απολυτήριοι εξετάσεις *fpl* || **~e** [fɪ'nɑːlɪ] *n (THEAT)* φινάλε *nt inv* || *(MUS)* φινάλε *nt inv* || **~ist** *n (SPORT)* φιναλίστης || **~ize** *vt* οριστικοποιώ || **~ly** *ad (lastly)* τελικά || *(eventually)* στο τέλος || *(irrevocably)* οριστικά, τελικά.

finance [faɪ'næns] *n* οικονομία ♦ *vt* χρηματοδοτώ || **~s** *npl* οικονομικά *ntpl*.

financial [faɪ'nænʃəl] *a (policy)* οικονομική (πολιτική) || *(year)* οικονομικόν (έτος).

financier [faɪ'nænsɪə*] *n* κεφαλαιούχος, χρηματοδότης.

find [faɪnd] *(irreg v) vt (come across)* βρίσκω || *(discover, get)* ανακαλύπτω, βρίσκω || *(learn)* ανακαλύπτω, διαπιστώνω || *(declare)* αποφαίνομαι, κηρύσσω ♦ *n* ανακάλυψη, εύρημα *nt* || **to ~ out (about)** *vt* ανακαλύπτω, αναζητώ, πληροφορούμαι || **~ings** *npl (LAW)* απόφαση, ετυμηγορία || *(of report)* διαπίστωση, συμπέρασμα *nt*.

fine [faɪn] *a (thin, slender)* λεπτός, ψιλός, ψιλόλιγνος || *(delicate)* λεπτός, φίνος || *(handsome)* ωραίος, όμορφος || *(pure)* καθαρός || *(rainless)* ωραίος, καλός ♦ *ad (well)* θαυμάσια, περίφημα || *(small)* λεπτά, λεπτομερώς, ψιλά ♦ *n (LAW)* ποινική ρήτρα, πρόστιμο ♦ *vt (LAW)* επιβάλλω πρόστιμο || **~ arts** *n* καλές τέχνες *fpl*.

finery ['faɪnərɪ] *n* στολίδια *ntpl*, στόλισμα *nt*.

finesse [fɪ'nɛs] *n* τέχνασμα *nt*, πανουργία, φινέτσα.

finger ['fɪŋgə*] *n* δάκτυλος, δάχτυλο ♦ *vt* ψαύω, ψηλαφώ, πιάνω || **~nail** *n* νύχι || **~print** *n* δακτυλικό αποτύπωμα || **~tip** *n* άκρη του δακτύλου.

finicky ['fɪnɪkɪ] *a* μικρολόγος, λεπτολόγος.

finish ['fɪnɪʃ] *n (end)* τέλος *nt* || *(SPORT)* τερματισμός, τέλος, τέρμα *nt* || *(completion)* τελείωμα *nt*, αποπεράτωση, συμπλήρωμα *nt* ♦ *vt (also:* **~ off, ~ up)** τερματίζω, τελειώνω, αποτελειώνω ♦ *vi (general)* τελειώνω, τερματίζομαι, λήγω || *(SPORT)* τερματίζω || **~ing line** *n* τέρμα *nt* || **~ing school** *n* σχολείο γενικής μορφώσεως.

finite ['faɪnaɪt] *a* πεπερασμένος, περιωρισμένος.

Finland ['fɪnlənd] *n* Φινλανδία.

Finn [fɪn] *n* Φινλανδός/n *m/f* || **~ish** *a* φινλανδικός ♦ *n (LING)* φιννική.

fiord [fjɔːd] *n* φιόρδ *nt inv*.

fir [fəː*] *n* έλατο.

fire [faɪə*] *n (element)* πύρ *nt* || *(in grate)* φωτιά || *(damaging)* πυρκαγιά || *(MIL)* πύρ *nt*, βολή ♦ *vt (cause to burn)* ανάβω, βάζω φωτιά || *(gun etc)* πυροδοτώ, βάλλω, ρίχνω || *(fig: imagination)* ενθουσιάζω, εξάπτω || *(col: dismiss)* απολύω, παύω, διώχνω ♦ *vi (gun)* πυροβολώ || **on ~** καίομαι, πίρνω φωτιά || **~ alarm** *n* σειρήνα πυρκαγιάς || **~ arm** *n* (πυροβόλο) όπλο || **~ brigade** *n* πυροσβεστική (υππρεσία) || **~ engine** *n* πυροσβεστική αντλία || **~ escape** *n* σκάλα πυρκαγιάς || **~ extinguisher** *n* πυροσβεστήρος || **~man** *n* πυροσβέστης || *(RAIL)* θερμαστής || **~place** *n* τζάκι || **~side** *n* κοντά στο τζάκι || **~ station** *n* πυροσβεστικός σταθμός || **~wood** *n* καυσόξυλα *ntpl* || **~works** *npl (lit)* πυροτεχνήματα *ntpl*.

firing ['faɪərɪŋ] *n (MIL)* βολή, πυροβολισμός, πυρ *nt* || **~ squad** *n* εκτελεστικό απόσπασμα *nt*.

firm [fəːm] *a (solid)* στερεός, σφιχτός || *(determined)* αμετάκινητος, σταθερός ♦ *n* οίκος, εταιρεία, φίρμα || **~ly** *ad* σταθερά, στερεά, γερά.

first [fəːst] *a (time)* πρώτος || *(place)* πρώτος ♦ *ad (before others)* πρώτος || *(firstly = in the first place)* πρωτίστως, πρώτα-πρώτα || *(sooner = before then)* στην αρχή, μάλλο, πρώτα || *(person: in race)* πρώτος || *(UNIV)* λίαν καλώς, άριστα || *(AUT)* πρώτη (ταχύτητα) || **at ~** κατά πρώτο, στην αρχή || **~ of all** πρώτ απ'όλα, κατ'αρχή || **~-aid kit** *n* σακκίδιο πρώτων βοηθειών || **~-class** *a* πρώτης τάξης || **~-hand** *a* από πρώτο χέρι || **~ lady** *n (US)* πρώτη κυρία || **~ly** *ad* πρωτίστως, πρώτα-πρώτα || **~ name** *n* μικρό όνομα || **~ night** *n* πρώτη, πρεμιέρα || **~-rate** *a* πρώτης τάξεως.

fiscal ['fɪskəl] *a* οικονομικος.

fish [fɪʃ] *n* ψάρι ♦ *vt* ψαρεύω ♦ *vi* ψαρεύω

|| to go ~ing πάω για ψάρεμα ||
~erman n ψαράς || ~ery n αλιεία,
ψαρική || ~ing boat n ψαρόβαρκα ||
~ing line n αρμίδι, πετονιά || ~ing rod
n καλάμι || ~ market n ιχθυαγορά ||
~monger n ιχθυοπώλης || ~y a
(suspicious) ύποπτος, βρώμικος.

fission ['fɪʃn] n διάσπαση.

fissure ['fɪʃə*] n σχισμή, ρωγμή.

fist [fɪst] n πυγμή, γροθιά.

fit [fɪt] a (MED, SPORT) σε φόρμα, υγιής ||
(suitable) κατάλληλος, αρμόζων, καλός ||
(qualified, worthy) ικανός ♦ vt (suit)
συμφωνώ, ταιριάζω || (insert, attach)
πηγαίνω, μπαίνω ♦ vi (correspond)
εφαρμόζω, πιάνω || (of clothes) πηγαίνω,
έρχομαι ♦ n (of clothes) εφαρμογή,
ταίριασμα nt || (MED, of coughing)
παροξυσμός || (MED: serious, epilepsy)
προσβολή || (of anger) ξέσπασμα nt,
έκρηξη || (of laughter) ξέσπασμα nt || to ~
in vi συμφωνώ, ταιριάζω ♦ vt ενώνω,
συνδέω || to ~ out vt εξαρτίζω,
εφοδιάζω, ντύνω || to ~ up vt
εφαρμόζω, ταιριάζω, μοντάρω || ~fully,
by ~s and starts ακανόνιστα, άστατα ||
~ness n (suitability) ικανότητα,
καταλληλότητα || (MED) υγεία || ~ter n
εφαρμοστής || (of clothes) δοκιμαστής ||
~ting a κατάλληλος, πρέπων,
ταιριαστός ♦ n (of dress) πρόβα,
προβάρισμα nt || (piece of equipment)
εφαρμογή, μοντάρισμα nt || ~tings npl
επιπλώσεις fpl, εξαρτήματα ntpl, σύνεργα
ntpl.

five [faɪv] num πέντε || ~r n (Brit) πεντάρι
(λίρες).

fix [fɪks] vt (fasten) τοποθετώ, στερεώνω,
καρφώνω || (determine) καθορίζω,
(προσδι)ορίζω, ρυθμίζω || (repair)
επισκευάζω, επιδιορθώνω || (drink)
ετοιμάζω, φτιάχνω ♦ n: in a ~ σε
μπελάδες, σε μπλέξιμο, σε σκοτούρες ||
~ed a σταθερός, αμετάβλητος,
στερεωμένος || ~ture n
ακινητοποιημένο έπιπλο, εξάρτημα nt.

fizz [fɪz] n απίθισμα nt, άφρισμα ♦ vi
σπιθίζω.

fizzle ['fɪzl] vi αφρίζω, τσιρίζω || to ~
out vi σθήνω, αποτυχάνω.

fizzy ['fɪzɪ] a αεριούχος, αφρώδης.

fjord [fjɔːd] n = fiord.

flabbergasted ['flæbəgɑːstɪd] a
κατάπληκτος, εμβρόντητος.

flabby ['flæbɪ] a πλαδαρός, άτονος.

flag [flæg] n (banner) σημαία || (also:
~stone) πλάκα, πλακόλιθος ♦ vi
(strength) εξασθενίζω, χαλαρούμαι ||
(spirit) κάμπτομαι, πέφτω, σπάω || to ~
down vt σταματώ.

flagon ['flægən] n καράφα.

flagpole ['flægpəul] n κοντάρι.

flagrant ['fleigrənt] a κατάφωρος,
καταφανής.

flair [flɛə*] n φυσική κλίση, ικανότητα.

flake [fleik] n (of rust) λέπι, τρίμα nt,

φύλλο || (of snow) νιφάδα, στούπα ♦ vi
(also: ~ off) ξελεπίζω, ξεφλουδίζομαι.

flame [fleim] n φλόγα.

flamingo [flə'mingəu] n φλαμίγκος.

flange [flændʒ] n φλάντζα.

flank [flæŋk] n (side) λαγόνα, πλαγιά ||
(MIL) πλευρά ♦ vt ευρίσκομαι πλάι.

flannel ['flænl] n φανέλα || ~s npl
(trousers) φανελένιο πανταλόνι.

flap [flæp] n κάπάκι || (of pocket) καπάκι
(τσέπης) || (of envelope) κλείσιμο
(φακέλλου) ♦ vt (of birds) φτερουγίζω ♦
vi (sail, flag) ανεμίζομαι, κυματίζω.

flare [flɛə*] n φωτοβολίδα || (in skirt etc)
φάρδεμα nt || to ~ up vi (into flame)
αστράφτω, ανάβω || (in anger) ανάβω,
εξάπτομαι.

flash [flæʃ] n αναλαμπή, λάμψη || (news
flash) τελευταία είδηση || (PHOT) φλάς nt
inv ♦ vt (light) κάνω να λάμψει, ρίχνω ||
(torch) ρίχνω, ανάβω || (message)
μεταδίδω ♦ vi αστράφτω, γυαλίζω || in a
~ στη στιγμή || to ~ by or past vt
περνώ σαν αστραπή || ~back n
αναδρομή || ~ bulb n λάμπα φλάς || ~er n
(AUT) φανάρι του στόπ.

flashy ['flæʃɪ] a (pej) φανταχτερός,
χτυπητός.

flask [flɑːsk] n τσότρα, φλασκί || (CHEM)
φιάλη || (vacuum flask) θερμό.

flat [flæt] a (level) επίπεδος, ίσιος || (dull)
χωρίς προοπτικές, θαμπό || (below pitch)
σε ύφεση, μπεμόλ || (beer) ξεθυμασμένο
|| (tyre) ξεφουσκωμένο, πεσμένο ♦ n
(rooms) διαμέρισμα nt || (MUS) ύφεση ||
(AUT) ξεφουσκωμένο λάστιχο || ~ broke
a απένταρος, πατήρος || ~footed a με
πλατειά πόδια || ~ly ad σαφώς,
κατηγορηματικά || ~ten vt (also: ~ten
out) επιπεδώνω, ισώνω.

flatter ['flætə*] vt κολακεύω || ~er n
κόλακας || ~ing a κολακευτικός || ~y n
κολακεία.

flaunt [flɔːnt] vt επιδεικνύω, δείχνω.

flavour, (US) flavor ['fleivə*] n γεύση
♦ vt καρικεύω, αρωματίζω || ~ing n
καρίκευμα nt, άρωμα nt.

flaw [flɔː] n ελάττωμα nt || ~less a
άψογος, τέλειος.

flax [flæks] n λινάρι || ~en a κατάξανθος.

flea [fliː] n ψύλλος.

fled [fled] pt, pp of flee.

flee [fliː] (irreg v) vi (κατα)φεύγω ♦ vt
φεύγω.

fleece [fliːs] n δορά, δέρμα nt, τομάρι ♦
vt (rob) λποτεύω, ξεγυμνώνω, γδύνω.

fleet [fliːt] n (NAUT) στόλος || (of cars)
συνοδεία, πομπή.

fleeting ['fliːtiŋ] a φευγαλέος,
περαστικός.

Flemish ['flemiʃ] a Φλαμανδικός ♦ n
(LING) Φλαμανδική.

flesh [fleʃ] n σάρκα || (meat) κρέας nt || (of
fruit) σάρκα.

flew [fluː] pt of fly.

flex [fleks] n εύκαμπτο καλώδιο ♦ vt

κάμπτομαι || ~**ibility** n ευκαμψία ||
~**ible** a εύκαμπτος || (plans) ελαστικός.

flick [flɪk] vt κτυπώ ελαφρά.

flicker ['flɪkə*] n (of light) τρεμούλιασμα
nt, παίξιμο ♦ vi τρέμω, τρεμοσβύνω.

flier ['flaɪə*] n ιπτάμενος, αεροπόρος.

flight [flaɪt] n (flying) πτήση, πέταμα nt ||
(of squadron) σμήνος nt || (journey)
διαδρομή || (also: ~ **of steps**)
σκαλοπάτια ntpl, κλίμακα || **to take** ~
τρέπομαι σε φυγή || **to put to** ~ τρέπω
σε φυγή || ~ **deck** n κατάστρωμα nt
απογειώσεως.

flimsy ['flɪmzɪ] a σαθρός, λεπτός, μικρής
αντοχής || (weak) αδύνατος, ασθενής,
πρόχειρος.

flinch [flɪntʃ] vi υποχωρώ, δειλιάζω.

fling [flɪŋ] (irreg v) vt ρίχνω, πετώ.

flint [flɪnt] n (in lighter) τσακμακόπετρα.

flip [flɪp] vt δίνω ελαφρό κτύπημα.

flippant ['flɪpənt] a ελαφρύς, αφελής.

flirt [flɜːt] vi φλερτάρω ♦ (woman) n
φιλάρεσκη, κοκέτα || ~**ation** n φλέρτ nt
inv, φλερτάρισμα nt.

flit [flɪt] vi πηγαινοέρχομαι.

float [fləʊt] n πλωτήρας, φλοτέρ nt inv ||
(esp in procession) αποκριάτικο άρμα ♦ vi
(επι)πλέω || (swimming) κολυμπώ
ανάσκελα || (in air) πλέω ♦ vt (company)
ιδρύω || (loan) εκδίδω δάνειο || (rumour)
διαδίδω, κυκλοφορώ || ~**ing** a (lit)
επιπλέων || (fig: population) κινητός
πληθυσμός.

flock [flɒk] n ποίμνιο, κοπάδι || (of people)
πλήθος nt, κοπάδι.

flog [flɒg] vt μαστιγώνω, ραβδίζω.

flood [flʌd] n πλημμύρα, κατακλυσμός ♦
vt πλημμυρίζω, κατακλύζω || ~**ing** n
πλημμύρισμα nt, ξεχείλισμα || ~**light** n
προβολέας ♦ vt φωτίζω με προβολέα.

floor [flɔː*] n (of room) δάπεδο, πάτωμα
nt || (storey) όροφος, πάτωμα nt ♦ vt
(person) ρίχνω κάτω || **ground** ~ (Brit),
first ~ (US) ισόγειο || **first** ~ (Brit),
second ~ (US) πρώτο πάτωμα ||
~**board** n σανίδα || ~ **show** n νούμερα
ntpl.

flop [flɒp] vi (fail) αποτυγχάνω,
καταρρέω || (fall) κάνω πλάφ,
σωριάζομαι.

floppy ['flɒpɪ] a πλαδαρός || (COMPUT:
also: ~ **disk**) δισκέτα, εύκαμπτος
(δίσκος).

flora ['flɔːrə] npl χλωρίδα || ~**l** a ανθικός,
λουλουδένιος.

florid ['flɒrɪd] a ανθηρός, γεμάτος
στολίδια.

florist ['flɒrɪs] n ανθοπώλης || ~'**s**
(**shop**) n ανθοπωλείο.

flounce [flaʊns] n βολάν ♦ vi: **to** ~
in / out μπαίνω/βγαίνω απότομα.

flounder ['flaʊndə*] vi παραπατώ,
σπαρταρώ, τσαλαβουτώ.

flour ['flaʊə*] n αλεύρι.

flourish ['flʌrɪʃ] vi (thrive, prosper)
προοδεύω, ανθώ, προκόβω ♦ vt
κραδαίνω, κουνώ ♦ n (ornament)

στόλισμα nt, κόσμημα nt, τζίφρα ||
επίδειξις, φανφάρα || ~**ing** a (thriving)
ακμαίος.

flout [flaʊt] vt αψηφώ, περιφρονώ.

flow [fləʊ] n (movement) ροή, ρεύμα nt ||
(stream: lit, fig) ρους m, χύση, χείμαρρος ||
(of dress) χυτές γραμμές fpl, ντραπέ nt inv
♦ vi ρέω, χύνομαι || κυνώ || (traffic, supply)
κυκλοφορώ, κινούμαι || (robes, hair)
χύνομαι, πέφτω.

flower ['flaʊə*] n άνθος nt, λουλούδι ♦
vi ανθίζω || ~ **bed** n παρτέρι, βραγιά ||
~**pot** n γλάστρα || ~**y** a
πολυγαρνιρισμένος.

flowing ['fləʊɪŋ] a (movement) ρέων ||
(hair) χυτός || (style) ρέων, άνετος.

flown [fləʊn] pp of **fly**.

flu [fluː] n γρίππη.

fluctuate ['flʌktjueɪt] vi κυμαίνομαι.

fluctuation [flʌktjuˈeɪʃən] n
διακύμανση.

fluency ['fluːənsɪ] n ευγλωττία,
ευφράδεια.

fluent ['fluːənt] a ευφράδης, στρωτός ||
~**ly** ad ευχερώς, άνετα.

fluff [flʌf] n χνούδι || ~**y** a χνουδάτος.

fluid ['fluːɪd] n ρευστό, υγρό ♦ a (lit)
ρευστός, ρέων || (fig: plans) ρευστός,
ευμετάβλητος.

fluke [fluːk] n (col: lucky stroke) κατά τύχη.

flung [flʌŋ] pt, pp of **fling**.

fluorescent [fluəˈresnt] a φθορίζων.

fluoride ['fluəraɪd] n φθοριούχο.

flurry ['flʌrɪ] n (of activity) αναστάτωση,
ταραχή.

flush [flʌʃ] n (blush) κοκκίνισμα nt,
ερύθημα nt || (of excitement) ξέσπασμα nt
|| (CARDS) χρώμα nt, φλας nt inv ♦ vt
ποτίζω, καθαρίζω, τραβώ (το καζανάκι)
♦ vi (blush) κοκκινίζω ♦ a επίπεδος,
λείος, στην ίδια επιφάνεια || ~**ed** a
(blushing) κόκκινος, ξαναμμένος || (with
anger) κόκκινος.

fluster ['flʌstə*] n αναστάτωση || ~**ed** a
ταραγμένος.

flute [fluːt] n φλογέρα, φλάουτο.

fluted ['fluːtɪd] a αυλακωτός.

flutter ['flʌtə*] n (of wings) φτερούγισμα
nt || (of excitement) αναστάτωση,
συγκίνηση ♦ vi (of birds) φτερουγίζω ||
τρέμω, ταράσσομαι.

flux [flʌks] n: **in a state of** ~ σε ρευστή
κατάσταση.

fly [flaɪ] (irreg v) n (insect) μύγα || (on
trousers: also **flies**) μπροστινό άνοιγμα nt
♦ vt (plane) πετώ, πιλοτάρω || (passengers)
μεταφέρω αεροπορικώς ♦ vi (travel by
air) πετώ || (flee) φεύγω, τρέχω || (of flag)
κυματίζω || ~**er** n = **flier** || ~**ing** n
(activity) πτήση, αεροπορία ♦ a (rapid)
γρήγορος, πεταχτός, σύντομος,
βιαστικός || ~**ing saucer** n ιπτάμενος
δίσκος || ~**ing start** n καλή αρχή, ταχύ
ξεκίνημα nt || ~**over** n (Brit) εναέριος f
διάβαση || ~**past** n παρέλαση
αεροπλάνων || ~**wheel** n σφόνδυλος,
βολάν nt inv.

foal [fəul] *n* πουλάρι.

foam [fəum] *n* αφρός || (*plastic etc*) αφρολέξ *nt inv* ♦ *vi* αφρίζω.

fob [fɔb]: **to ~ off** *vt* πασσάρω, κοροϊδεύω.

focal ['fəukəl] *a* εστιακός.

focus ['fəukəs] *n* εστία ♦ *vt* συγκεντρώνω, ρυθμίζω || **in ~** ρυθμισμένος, ευκρινής || **out of ~** μη ρυθμισμένος, θαμπός.

fodder ['fɔdə*] *n* φορβή, χόρτο.

foe [fəu] *n* εχθρός, αντίπαλος.

foetus ['fiːtəs] *n* έμβρυο.

fog [fɔg] *n* ομίχλη ♦ *vt* (*issue*) θολώνω, περιπλέκω || **~gy** *a* ομιχλώδης.

foible ['fɔibl] *n* αδυναμία.

foil [fɔil] *vt* ανατρέπω, προλαμβάνω ♦ *n* (*of metal*) έλασμα *nt*, φύλλο || (*person*) αντίθεση || (*fencing*) ξίφος *nt*.

fold [fəuld] *n* (*bend, crease*) πτυχή, ζάρα, δίπλα ♦ *vt* διπλώνω, πτυχώνω || **to ~ up** *vi* (*map etc*) τυλίγω, διπλώνω || (*business*) κλείνω το μαγαζί, χρεωκοπώ || **~er** *n* (*pamphlet*) διαφημιστικό φυλλάδιο || (*portfolio*) φάκελλος, ντοσιέ *nt inv* || **~ing** *a* (*chair, bed etc*) πτυσσόμενος, τσακιστός.

foliage ['fəuliidʒ] *n* φυλλωσιά.

folio ['fəuliəu] *n* φύλλο.

folk [fəuk] *n* άνθρωποι *mpl* ♦ *a* λαϊκός || **~s** *npl* άνθρωποι *mpl*, συγγενείς *mpl*, δικοί μου *mpl* || **~lore** *n* λαογραφία || **~song** *n* δημοτικό τραγούδι.

follow ['fɔləu] *vt* (*come after*) (παρ)ακολουθώ || (*obey*) ακολουθώ || (*go along path*) ακολουθώ, παίρνω || (*profession*) ακολουθώ, ασκώ || (*understand*) καταλαβαίνω, παρακολουθώ ♦ *vi* (*after*) ακολουθώ, συνοδεύω || (*result*) έπομαι, προκύπτω || **to ~ up** *vt* συνεχίζω, εκμεταλλεύομαι || **~er** *n* οπαδός || **~ing** *a* ακολουθών, επόμενος ♦ *n* οπαδοί *mpl*, ακολουθία.

folly ['fɔli] *n* ανοησία, τρέλλα.

fond [fɔnd] *a*: **to be ~ of** (*person*) είμαι αφοσιωμένος, συμπαθώ, αγαπώ || (*thing*) μου αρέσει, τρελλαίνομαι για || **~ness** *n* (+ *for*) αφοσίωση, συμπάθεια *ατε* || αγάπη για τάση στο.

font [fɔnt] *n* κολυμβήθρα.

food [fuːd] *n* τροφή, τρόφιμα *ntpl*, φαΐ, φαγητό || **~ poisoning** *n* δηλητηρίαση || **~stuffs** *npl* είδη διατροφής.

fool [fuːl] *n* (*silly person*) ηλίθιος, βλάκας, κουτός, χαζός || (*clown*) παλιάτσος ♦ *vt* (*deceive*) εξαπατώ, ♦ *vi* (*act like a fool*) κάνω το βλάκα || **~hardy** *a* παράτολμος, απερίσκεπτος || **~ish** *a* παράλογος, γελοίος || **~proof** *a* (*plan etc*) αλάνθαστος.

foot [fut] *n* (*of person*) πόδι, ποδάρι || (*of animal*) πόδι || (*base*) πέλμα *nt*, πόδι, κάτω άκρο || (*measure*) αγγλικό πόδι (0.3μ) ♦ *vt* (*bill*) πληρώνω, κάνω τα έξοδα || **on ~** πεζή, με τα πόδια || **~ball** *n* (*ball*) μπάλα || (*game*) ποδόσφαιρο || **~baller** *n* ποδοσφαιριστής || **~brake** *n*

ποδόφρενο || **~bridge** *n* γέφυρα πεζών || **~hills** *npl* χαμηλοί λόφοι *mpl* || **~hold** *n* πάτημα *nt*, στήριγμα *nt* || **~ing** *n* (*lit*) σίγουρη θέση, πάτημα *nt* || (*fig*) θέση, κατάσταση || **~lights** *npl* ράμπα, προσκήνιο || **~man** *n* (*servant*) υπηρέτης, λακές *m* || **~-and-mouth** (**disease**) *n* αφθώδης πυρετός || **~note** *n* υποσημείωση || **~path** *n* μονοπάτι || **~sore** *a* με πονεμένα πόδια || **~step** *n* βήμα *nt*, πάτημα *nt* || (*trace*) ίχνος *m*, πατησιά || **~wear** *n* παπούτσι.

for [fɔː*] *prep* για || (*in spite of*) μόλο || *cj* διότι, γιατί || **what ~?** γιατί;, για ποιο λόγο;.

forage ['fɔridʒ] *n* βοσκή, χορτονομή, χόρτο || *vi* (*col*) ψάχνω για.

foray ['fɔrei] *n* επιδρομή, διαρπαγή.

forbearing [fɔː'bɛəriŋ] *a* υπομονετικός, ανεκτικός.

forbid [fə'bid] (*irreg v*) *vt* απαγορεύω || **~den** *a* απαγορευμένος || **~ding** *a* αποκρουστικός, δυσάρεστος.

force [fɔːs] *n* (*strength*) δύναμη, ισχύς *f* || (*compulsion*) εξαναγκασμός, ζόρι || (*body of men*) δύναμη ♦ *vt* (*compel*) εξαναγκάζω, εκβιάζω || (*break open*) παραβιάζω || **to ~ into** *vt* πιέζω, σπρώχνω, μπάζω || **be in ~** ισχύω || **the F~s** *npl* οι δυνάμεις *fpl* || **~d** *a* (*smile*) προσποιητός, ψεύτικος || (*landing*) αναγκαστικός || **~ful** *a* αποφασιστικός, δραστήριος.

forcibly ['fɔːsəbli] *ad* με το ζόρι, αποφασιστικά.

ford [fɔːd] *n* πέραμα ♦ *vt* περνώ.

fore [fɔː*] *a* πρόσθιος, μπροστινός ♦ *n*: **to the ~** στο προσκήνιο, διαπρέπων.

forearm ['fɔːrɑːm] *n* αντιβράχιο.

foreboding [fɔː'bəudiŋ] *n* κακό προαίσθημα *nt*, κακός οιωνός.

forecast ['fɔːkɑːst] *n* πρόβλεψη, πρόγνωση ♦ *vt* προβλέπω.

forecourt ['fɔːkɔːt] *n* προαύλιο.

forefathers ['fɔːfɑːðəz] *npl* πρόγονοι *mpl*.

forefinger ['fɔːfiŋgə*] *n* δείκτης.

forefront ['fɔːfrʌnt] *n* πρόσοψη || (*fig*) πρώτη σειρά.

forego [fɔː'gəu] *vt* προηγούμαι || **~ing** *a* προειρημένος || **~ne** ['fɔːgɔn] *a* (*conclusion*) προκαθορισμένος.

foreground ['fɔːgraund] *n* πρώτο πλάνο.

forehead ['fɔrid] *n* μέτωπο, κούτελο.

foreign ['fɔrin] *a* (*country*) ξένος, άσχετος || (*trade*) εξωτερικός || (*accent*) ξενικός || (*body*) ξένος || **~er** *n* ξένος, αλλοδαπός || **~ exchange** *n* συνάλλαγμα *nt* || **F~ Minister** *n* υπουργός εξωτερικών.

foreman ['fɔːmən] *n* προϊστάμενος, εργοδηγός.

foremost ['fɔːməust] *a* πρώτος, πρώτιστος, επί κεφαλής.

forensic [fə'rɛnsik] *a*: **~ medicine** *n* ιατροδικαστική.

forerunner ['fɔːrʌnə*] n πρόδρομος.

foresee [fɔːˈsiː] vt προβλέπω || ~able a δυνάμενος να προβλεφθεί.

foresight ['fɔːsait] n πρόβλεψη, πρόνοια.

forest ['fɒrist] n δάσος nt, ρουμάνι.

forestall [fɔːˈstɔːl] vt προλαμβάνω.

forestry ['fɒristri] n δασοκομία.

foretaste ['fɔːteist] n προαίσθηση.

foretell [fɔːˈtel] vt προλέγω, προμηνύω.

forever [fɔˈrevə*] ad παντοτεινά, για πάντα.

foreword ['fɔːwɜːd] n πρόλογος.

forfeit ['fɔːfit] n ποινική ρήτρα ♦ vt χάνω (δια κατασχέσεως), χάνω.

forge [fɔːdʒ] n καμίνι, σιδεράδικο ♦ vt (falsely) πλάθω, πλαστογραφώ || (shape) σφυρηλατώ || **to ~ ahead** vi προηγούμαι, προχωρώ || ~r n (criminal) πλαστογράφος, παραχαράκτης || ~ry n (activity) πλαστογράφηση || (article) πλαστός, κίβδηλο (αντικείμενο).

forget [fɔˈget] vti λησμονώ, ξεχνώ, παραλείπω || ~ful a ξεχασιάρης, απρόσεκτος || ~fulness n απερισκεψία, έλλειψη μνήμης.

forgive [fɔˈgiv] vt συγχωρώ || ~ness n συγχώρηση.

forgo [fɔˈgəu] vt παραιτούμαι, αποφεύγω, κάνω χωρίς.

fork [fɔːk] n (for food) πηρούνι || (farm tool) δικράνα, διχάλα || (branch) διακλάδωση ♦ vi (road) διχάζομαι, χωρίζομαι || **to ~ out** vti (col: pay) πληρώνω || ~ed a διχαλωτός.

form [fɔːm] n (structure) μορφή, σχήμα nt, φόρμα || (class) τάξη || (bench) μπάγκος || (document) έντυπο, τύπος || (also: mental, physical condition) κατάσταση, φόρμα ♦ vt (shape) διαμορφώνω, σχηματίζω, φτιάνω || (make part of) συγκροτώ, σχηματίζω.

formal ['fɔːməl] a (according to rule) επίσημος, εθιμοτυπικός || (stiff) τυπικός || (dress) επίσημος || ~ity n (of occasion) τύπος, τυπικότητα || ~ly ad (ceremoniously) τυπικά, με διατυπώσεις || (officially) επίσημα, τυπικά.

format ['fɔːmæt] n σχήμα nt ♦ vt (COMPUT) τρόπος παρουσιάσεως.

formation [fɔːˈmeiʃən] n διαμόρφωση, σχηματισμός || (forming) σχηματισμός, διάπλαση || (group) σχηματισμός, διάταξη, τάξη.

formative ['fɔːmətiv] a (years) διαπλαστικός, μορφωτικός.

former ['fɔːmə*] a παλαιότερος, προγενέστερος, πρώην, τέως || (opposite of latter) πρώτος || ~ly ad άλλοτε, παλαιότερα.

formidable ['fɔːmidəbl] a φοβερός, τρομερός.

formula ['fɔːmjulə] n τύπος || (fig) τύπος, στερεοτυπία, κλισέ nt inv || (MATH) τύπος || ~te ['fɔːmjuleit] vt διατυπώνω.

forsake [fɔˈseik] (irreg v) vt εγκαταλείπω, αφηνώ, αρνούμαι.

fort [fɔːt] n φρούριο.

forte ['fɔːti] n δύναμη, φόρτε nt inv.

forth [fɔːθ] ad προς τα εμπρός, προς τα έξω || (in space) εμπρός, μπροστά || (in time) από τώρα και εμπρός || ~coming a (επ)ερχόμενος, προσεχής.

fortieth ['fɔːtiiθ] a τεσσαρακοστός.

fortification [fɔːtifiˈkeiʃən] n (walls etc) οχύρωμα nt, οχύρωση.

fortify ['fɔːtifai] vt (strengthen) ενισχύω, δυναμώνω, τονώνω || (protect) οχυρώνω.

fortnight ['fɔːtnait] n δεκαπενθήμερο || ~ly a δεκαπενθήμερος ♦ ad κάθε δεκαπέντε.

fortress ['fɔːtris] n φρούριο, κάστρο.

fortunate ['fɔːtʃənit] a ευτυχής, τυχερός, ευμενής || ~ly ad ευτυχώς.

fortune ['fɔːtʃən] n (chance) τύχη, σύμπτωση, καλοτυχία || (wealth) πλούτος, περιουσία || ~teller n μάντης, χαρτορίχτρα.

forty ['fɔːti] num σαράντα.

forward ['fɔːwəd] a (lying ahead) πρόσθιος, μπροστινός || (movement) κίνηση προστά, προοδευτικός || (advanced) με πρώωρο ♦ ad (προς τα) εμπρός, μπρος || (SPORT) κυνηγός ♦ vt (mail etc) αποστέλλω, διεκπεραιώνω || (help) προωθώ, ευνοώ, προάγω || ~s ad από τώρα και στο εξής.

fossil ['fɒsl] n απολίθωμα nt.

foster ['fɒstə*] vt καλλιεργώ, τρέφω || ~ child n θετό παιδί || ~ mother n θετή μητέρα, ψυχομάνα.

fought [fɔːt] pt, pp of **fight**.

foul [faul] a ακάθαρτος, ρυπαρός, βρωμερός, μολυσμένος || (language) βρωμολόχος, πρόστυχος, αισχρός || (weather) κακοκαιρίας ♦ n (SPORT) φάουλ nt inv ♦ vt (mechanism) φράσσω, μπλέκω, πιάνω || (SPORT) κάνω φάουλ.

found [faund] pt, pp of **find** ♦ vt (establish) ιδρύω, θεμελιώνω, κτίζω || ~ation n (act) ίδρυση, θεμελίωση, θεμέλιο nt || (fig) ίδρυμα nt, κληροδότημα nt || ~ations npl (building) θεμέλια ntpl.

founder ['faundə*] n ιδρυτής ♦ vi (NAUT) βυθίζομαι, βουλιάζω.

foundry ['faundri] n χυτήριο.

fount [faunt] n (source) πηγή || ~ain n πηγή || (jet of water) συντριβάνι || ~ain pen n στυλογράφος, στυλό.

four [fɔː*] num τέσσερα || **on all ~s** με τα τέσσερα || ~**some** n διπλή παρτίδα || ~**teen** num δέκα τέσσερα || ~**teenth** a δέκατος τέταρτος || ~**th** a τέταρτος.

fowl [faul] n πουλί, πουλερικό.

fox [fɒks] n αλεπού f.

foyer ['fɔiei] n φουαγιέ nt inv.

fraction ['frækʃən] n (part) κομμάτι || (MATH) κλάσμα nt.

fracture ['fræktʃə*] n (of bone) κάταγμα nt ♦ vt θραύω, τσακίζω, προκαλώ κάταγμα.

fragile ['frædʒail] a εύθραυστος.

fragment ['frægmənt] n θραύσμα nt, θρύμμα nt, σύντριμμα nt || (part) κομμάτι, απόκομμα nt, απόσπασμα nt || ~ary a αποσπασματικός, τμηματικός.

fragrance ['freigrəns] n άρωμα nt, μυρωδιά.

fragrant ['freigrənt] a εύοσμος, μυρωδάτος.

frail [freil] a ευπαθής, ασθενικός.

frame [freim] n σκελετός, πλαίσιο || (border) πλαίσιο, κορνίζα ♦ vt (put into frame) πλαισιώνω, κορνιζάρω || (put together) καταστρώνω, διαμορφώνω, κατασκευάζω || (col: incriminate) μηχανορραφώ, σκηνοθετώ || ~ of mind n πνευματική κατάσταση, διάθεση || ~work n σκελετός, πλαίσιο.

France [frɑːns] n Γαλλία.

franchise ['fræntʃaiz] n προνόμιο.

frank [fræŋk] a ειλικρινής || ~ly ad ειλικρινά, ντόμπρα || ~ness n ειλικρίνεια.

frantic ['fræntik] a έξαλλος, μανιώδης || ~ally ad μανιασμένα, έξαλλα.

fraternal [frəˈtɜːnl] a αδελφικός.

fraternity [frəˈtɜːniti] n (club) οργάνωση || (spirit) αδελφότητα || (US SCH) φοιτητική οργάνωση.

fraternize ['frætənaiz] vi (with) συναδελφώνομαι με.

fraud [frɔːd] n (trickery) δόλος, απάτη || (trick) κόλπο, απάτη, παγίδα || (person) απατεώνας, κατεργάρης.

fraudulent ['frɔːdjulənt] a δόλιος, απατηλός.

fray [frei] n σύρραξη, καυγάς, σύγκρουση ♦ vt τρίβω, ταράζω, ξεφτίζω ♦ vi ξεφτίζομαι, τρίβομαι || ~ed a τριμμένος, φαγωμένος.

freak [friːk] n ιδιοτροπία, καπρίτσιο || (col) τέρας nt ♦ a περίεργο φαινόμενο.

freckle ['frekl] n πανάδα.

free [friː] a (at liberty) ανεξάρτητος, ελεύθερος || (loose) ελεύθερος || (not occupied) ελεύθερος || (gratis) δωρεάν, τζάμπα || (liberal) φιλελεύθερος, γενναιόφρων, ανοιχτός ♦ vt (set free) (απ)ελευθερώνω || (unblock) αποφράσσω, καθαρίζω || ~dom n ελευθερία, ανεξαρτησία || ~lance a ανεξάρτητος || ~ly ad ελεύθερα, αβίαστα || ~mason n μασώνος || ~trade n ελεύθερο εμπόριο || ~way n (US) αυτοκινητόδρομος || ~wheel vi πηγαίνω με ελεύθερο τροχό || ~ will n ελεύθερα θέληση.

freeze [friːz] (irreg v) vi (become ice) ψύχω, καταψύχω, παγώνω || (feel cold) κρυώνω ♦ vt (lit) (κατα)ψύχω, παγώνω || (fig) δεσμεύω, ακινητοποιώ ♦ n (lit) (κατά)ψυξη, παγωνιά || (fig, ECON) δέσμευση || ~r n καταψύκτης, ψυγείο καταψύξεως.

freezing ['friːziŋ] a: ~ cold a παγερό κρύο || ~ point n σημείο ψύξεως, πήξεως.

freight [freit] n (goods) φορτίο, εμπορεύματα ntpl || (money charged)

ναύλος || ~ car n (US) φορτηγό βαγόνι || ~er n (NAUT) φορτηγό.

French [frentʃ] a γαλλικός ♦ n (LING) (τα) Γαλλικά || the ~ npl οι Γάλλοι || ~ fried potatoes npl πατάτες τηγανιτές fpl || ~man n Γάλλος || ~ window n τζαμόπορτα || ~woman n Γαλλίδα.

frenzy ['frenzi] n φρενίτιδα, τρέλλα, παραλήρημα nt.

frequency ['friːkwənsi] n συχνότητα, πυκνότητα || (PHYS) συχνότητα.

frequent ['friːkwənt] a (happening often) συχνός, διαδεδομένος, συνηθισμένος || (numerous) άφθονος, πολυάριθμος ♦ [friːˈkwent] vt συχνάζω || ~ly ad συχνά.

fresco ['freskəu] n νωπογραφία, φρέσκο.

fresh [freʃ] a (new, additional) νέος, καινούριος, φρέσκος || (recent) νέος, πρωτότυπος || (not stale) νωπός, φρέσκος || (not tired) ρωμαλαίος, ξεκούραστος, φρέσκος || (cool) καθαρός, δροσερός || (cheeky) αναιδής, ζωηρός || ~ en (also: ~en up) vi φρεσκάρω, συνέρχομαι ♦ vt αναζωογονώ, φρεσκάρω || ~ly ad πρόσφατα, νεο-, φρεσκο- || ~ness n φρεσκάδα, δροσερότητα || ~water a του γλυκού νερού.

fret [fret] vi ταράσσομαι, ανησυχώ, στενοχωριέμαι.

friar ['fraiə*] n μοναχός, καλόγηρος.

friction ['frikʃən] n (resistance) τριβή, τρίψιμο || (disagreement) προστριβή, τσάκωμα nt.

Friday ['fraidi] n Παρασκευή || see good.

fridge [fridʒ] n ψυγείο.

fried [fraid] a τηγανισμένο.

friend [frend] n φίλος, γνωστός, γνώριμος || ~liness n φιλία || ~ly a (person) ευμενής, φιλικός || (attitude) φιλικός || ~ship n φιλία.

frieze [friːz] n (ARCHIT) διάζωμα nt, ζωφόρος.

frigate ['frigit] n φρεγάτα.

fright [frait] n τρόμος, φόβος || (ugly) άσχημος, σκιάχτρο || ~ en vt (κατα)τρομάζω, φοβίζω || ~ening a τρομακτικός, τρομερός || ~ful a (col) τρομερός, φρικτός || ~fully ad τρομερά, τρομακτικά.

frigid ['fridʒid] a ψυχρός, παγερός, κρύος.

frill [fril] n βολάν nt inv.

fringe [frindʒ] n (border) κροσσός, κρόσι || (fig) περιθώριο, παρυφή.

frisky ['friski] a παιχνιδιάρης, κεφάτος.

fritter ['fritə*] n τηγανίτα, σβίγγος || to ~ away vt σπαταλώ.

frivolity [friˈvɔliti] n επιπολαιότητα.

frivolous ['frivələs] a επιπόλαιος.

frizzy ['frizi] a σγουρός.

fro [frəu] see to.

frock [frɔk] n (of monk) ράσο || (of woman) φουστάνι.

frog [frɔg] n βάτραχος || ~man n βατραχάνθρωπος.

frolic ['frɒlɪk] n παιχνίδι, γλέντι ♦ vt διασκεδάζω, παιχνιδίζω.

from [frɒm] prep από.

front [frʌnt] n (of house) πρόσοψη, μπροστινό, φάτσα || (MIL) μέτωπο || (POL) μέτωπο || (meteorology) μέτωπο || (fig: appearances) όψη, μούτρα ntpl, αναίδεια ♦ a (forward) πρόσθιος, μπροστινός || (first) μπροστινός, πρώτος || (door) κυρία είσοδος f, μπροστινή πόρτα || ~al a μετωπικός || ~ier n σύνορο, μεθόριος f || ~-page a της πρώτης σελίδας || ~-wheel drive n κίνηση στους προσινούς τροχούς.

frost [frɒst] n παγετός, παγωνιά || ~bite n κρυοπάγημα ntl || ~ed a (glass) μάτ, αδιαφανής || ~y a παγερός, παγωμένος.

froth [frɒθ] n αφρός || (on beer) κολλάρο.

frown [fraun] n συνοφρύωση, κατσούφιασμα nt ♦ vi συνοφρυούμαι, σκυθρωπάζω || to ~ upon vt κάνω μούτρα σε.

froze [frəʊz] pt of **freeze** || ~n pp of **freeze** || (COMM) παγωμένος || ~n food n κατεψυγμένος.

frugal ['fruːgəl] a λιτός, οικονομικός.

fruit [fruːt] n φρούτο, καρπός || ~s npl καρποί mpl, κέρδη ntpl || ~ful a καρποφόρος, γόνιμος || ~ion [fruː'ɪʃən] n εκπλήρωση, απόλαυση.

frustrate [frʌs'treɪt] vt ματαιώνω, εξουδετερώνω, εμποδίζω || ~d a απογοητευμένος.

frustration [frʌs'treɪʃən] n ματαίωση, απογοήτευση.

fry [fraɪ] vt τηγανίζω || **small ~** npl οι ανθρωπάκοι mpl || ~ing pan n τηγάνι.

ft. abbr of **foot, feet.**

fuchsia ['fjuːʃə] n φούξια.

fudge [fʌdʒ] n ζαχαρωτό.

fuel [fjʊəl] n (oil) καύσιμη ύλη, πετρέλαιο || (petrol) καύσιμα ntpl, βενζίνη || (wood) καυσόξυλα ntpl || (coal) κάρβουνο || (gas) καύσιμο αέριο || ~ oil n (diesel fuel) ακάθαρτο πετρέλαιο || ~ tank n ντεπόζιτο βενζίνης.

fugitive ['fjuːdʒɪtɪv] n φυγάδας, δραπέτης.

fulfil [fʊl'fɪl] vt (accomplish) εκπληρώνω || (obey) εκτελώ, εισακούω || ~ment n εκπλήρωση, εκτέλεση.

full [fʊl] a (box, bottle) πλήρης, γεμάτος || (vehicle) πλήρης, γεμάτος || (person: satisfied) χορτάτος, μπουκωμένος || (session) ολομέλεια || (complete) ολόκληρος || (moon) πανσέληνος || (price) ολόκληρος || (speed) ολοταχώς || (skirt) φαρδύς, γεμάτος || in ~ χωρίς έκπτωση, ολογράφως, στο ακέραιο || ~back n οπισθοφύλακας || ~ stop n τελεία || ~-time a (work) με πλήρες ωράριο ♦ ad ακριβώς, τελείως || ~y ad πλήρως, τελείως, απολύτως.

fumble ['fʌmbl] vti ψαχουλεύω, χειρίζομαι αδέξια.

fume [fjuːm] vi (smoke) βγάζω καπνό, καπνίζω || (be furious) εξάπτομαι,

λυσσάζω || ~s npl ατμοί mpl, αναθυμιάσεις fpl, καπνιές fpl.

fumigate ['fjuːmɪgeɪt] vt απολυμαίνω.

fun [fʌn] n διασκέδαση, κέφι, αστείο, χωρατό || to make ~ of κοροϊδεύω, περιπαίζω.

function ['fʌŋkʃən] n (use) λειτουργία, έργο, λειτούργημα nt || (public occasion) τελετή, δεξίωση ♦ vi λειτουργώ || ~al a λειτουργικός || ~ key n (COMPUT) πλήκτρο λειτουργίας.

fund [fʌnd] n (capital) ταμείο, κεφάλαιο, παρακαταθήκη || (store) απόθεμα nt, πηγή.

fundamental [fʌndə'mɛntl] a θεμελιώδης || ~s npl στοιχεία ntpl, βασικές αρχές fpl || ~ly ad ουσιαστικά, βασικά.

funeral ['fjuːnərəl] n κηδεία ♦ a νεκρώσιμος, πένθιμος.

fun fair ['fʌnfɛə*] n λούνα-παρκ pl inv.

fungus ['fʌŋgəs] n μύκητας, μανιτάρι.

funnel ['fʌnl] n χωνί || (of ship) φουγάρο.

funny ['fʌnɪ] a (comical) αστείος, κωμικός || (strange) παράξενος, περίεργος.

fur [fɜː*] n γούνα, γουναρικό || ~ coat n γούνινο παλτό.

furious ['fjʊərɪəs] a μαινόμενος, λυσσαλέος, αγριεμένος || ~ly ad άγρια, με μανία.

furlong ['fɜːlɒŋ] n = 220 υάρδες (201 μέτρα).

furlough ['fɜːləʊ] n (US) άδεια.

furnace ['fɜːnɪs] n κλίβανος, κάμινος, φούρνος.

furnish ['fɜːnɪʃ] vt (with furniture) επιπλώνω || (supply) παρέχω, προμηθεύω, προσφέρω || ~ings npl έπιπλα ntpl, επίπλωση.

furniture ['fɜːnɪtʃə*] n έπιπλα ntpl.

furrow ['fʌrəʊ] n αυλακώνω.

furry ['fɜːrɪ] a γούνινος.

further ['fɜːðə*] comp of **far** || a (additional) νέος, πρόσθετος, μεταγενέστερος || (more distant) μακρινότερος ♦ ad (more) περαιτέρω, περισσότερο || (moreover) άλλωστε, επί πλέον ♦ vt προάγω, υποστηρίζω || ~more ad εκτός απ'αυτό, εξάλλου.

furthest ['fɜːðɪst] superl of **far**.

furtive ['fɜːtɪv] a λαθραίος, κρυμμένος, ύπουλος.

fury ['fjʊərɪ] n οργή, θυμός, μανία.

fuse [fjuːz] n (ELEC) ασφάλεια || (cord) φυτίλι ♦ vt τήκω, λειώνω ♦ vi (ELEC) τήκομαι, λυώνω || ~ box n κιβώτιο ασφαλειών.

fuselage ['fjuːzəlɑːʒ] n άτρακτος, σκελετός.

fusion ['fjuːʒən] n (union) συγχώνευση, σύμπραξη.

fuss [fʌs] n (dispute) φασαρία, θόρυβος, ταραχή || (bustle) φασαρία, αναστάτωση, || ~y λεπτολόγος, ιδιότροπος.

futile ['fjuːtaɪl] a (useless) φρούδος,

μάταιος || (unimportant) ασήμαντος, κούφιος.
futility [fju:'tılıtı] n ματαιότητα.
future ['fju:tʃə*] a μέλλων, μελλοντικός ♦ n μέλλον || in (the) ~ στο μέλλον.
futuristic [fju:tʃə'rıstık] a φουτουριστικός.
fuze [fju:z] (US) = **fuse**.
fuzzy ['fʌzı] a (indistinct) θαμπός || (from drink) σουρωμένος.

G

g. abbr of **gram(s)**.
gabble ['gæbl] vi φλυαρώ.
gable ['geıbl] n αέτωμα nt.
gadget ['gædʒıt] n μαραφέτι.
gag [gæg] n φίμωτρο || (funny phrase) αστείο, κασκαρίκα ♦ vt φιμώνω, αποστομώνω.
gaiety ['geıtı] n ευθυμία.
gaily ['geılı] ad εύθυμα, χαρούμενα.
gain [geın] vt (obtain) αποκτώ, κερδίζω || (win over) κερδίζω, παίρνω || (make progress) προχωρώ, προηγούμαι ♦ vi (improve) κερδίζω, κατακτώ || (clock etc) τρέχω μπρος ♦ n κέρδος nt, αύξηση || ~ful a επικερδής.
gal. abbr of **gallon**.
gala ['gɑːlə] n γιορτή.
galaxy ['gæləksı] n (stars) γαλαξίας.
gale [geıl] n θύελλα, φουρτούνα || ~ warning n αναγγελία θύελλας.
gallant ['gælənt] a (fine, brave) γενναίος, ηρωικός || (to women) γαλάντης, περιποιητικός || ~ry n γενναιότητα, λεβεντιά || (to women) περιποιητικότητα.
gall-bladder ['gɔːlblædə*] n χοληδόχος κύστη.
gallery ['gælərı] n (ART) πινακοθήκη || (THEAT) γαλαρία, εξώστης.
galley ['gælı] n (of ship) μαγειρείο || (vessel) γαλέρα.
gallon ['gælən] n γαλόνι (θ4.54 χλγρ.).
gallop ['gæləp] n καλπασμός, γκάλοπ nt inv ♦ vi καλπάζω.
gallows ['gæləuz] npl αγχόνη, κρεμάλα.
gallstone ['gɔːlstəun] n χολόλιθος.
gamble ['gæmbl] vi παίζω ♦ vt (risk) ριψοκινδυνεύω ♦ n (τυχερό) παιχνίδι || ~r n (χαρτο)παίκτης.
gambling ['gæmblıŋ] n παιχνίδι, παίξιμο.
game [geım] n (play) παιχνίδι, διασκέδαση || (animals) θήραμα nt, κυνήγι ♦ a θαρραλέος, τολμηρός || ~keeper n φύλακας κυνηγιού.
gammon ['gæmən] n οπίσθια μπούτια ntpl, χοιρομέρι.
gang [gæŋ] n συμμορία, σπείρα.
gangrene ['gæŋgriːn] n γάγγραινα.
gangster ['gæŋstə*] n γκάγκστερ m inv.
gangway ['gæŋweı] n (of ship) διαβάθρα, μαδέρι || (aisle) διάδρομος.
gaol [dʒeıl] n = **jail**.

gap [gæp] n (opening) τρύπα, ρήγμα nt|| (empty space) διάκενο.
gape [geıp] vi χάσκω, χασμουριέμαι.
gaping ['geıpıŋ] a χαίνων.
garage ['gærɑːʒ] n γκαράζ nt inv.
garbage ['gɑːbıdʒ] n σκουπίδια ntpl|| ~ can n (US) σκουπιδοτενεκές m.
garbled ['gɑːbld] a (story) παραμορφωμένος, αλλοιωμένος.
garden ['gɑːdn] n κήπος, μπαξές m ♦ vi ασχολούμαι με κηπουρική || ~er n κηπουρός, περιβολάρης || ~ing n κηπουρική.
gargle ['gɑːgl] vi γαργαρίζω ♦ n γαργάρα.
gargoyle ['gɑːgɔıl] n υδρορρόη.
garish ['gεərıʃ] a φανταχτερός, κακόγουστος.
garland ['gɑːlənd] n στέφανος, γιρλάντα.
garlic ['gɑːlık] n σκόρδο.
garment ['gɑːmənt] n φόρεμα nt.
garnish ['gɑːnıʃ] vt (food) γαρνίρω ♦ n γαρνιτούρα.
garret ['gærıt] n σοφίτα.
garrison ['gærısən] n φρουρά ♦ vt εγκαθιστώ φρουρά.
garrulous ['gærυləs] a φλύαρος, πολυλογάς.
garter ['gɑːtə*] n καλτσοδέτα.
gas [gæs] n αέριο || (coal gas) φωταέριο, γκάζ nt inv || (MED) αναισθητικό || (US: gasoline) βενζίνη ♦ vt δηλητηριάζω με αέριο || ~ cooker n κουζίνα || ~ cylinder n φιάλη αερίου || ~ fire n σόμπα του γκαζιού.
gash [gæʃ] n εγκοπή, μαχαιριά ♦ vt κόβω, πληγώνω.
gasket ['gæskıt] n (TECH) παρένθεμα nt.
gasmask ['gæsmɑːsk] n αντιασφυξιογόνα μάσκα.
gas meter ['gæsmiːtə*] n μετρητής του γκαζιού.
gasoline ['gæsəliːn] n (US) βενζίνη.
gasp [gɑːsp] vi ασθμαίνω, λαχανιάζω ♦ n κομμένη αναπνοή, ρόγχος.
gas ring ['gæsrıŋ] n μάτι του γκαζιού.
gas station ['gæssteıʃən] n (US) βενζινάδικο.
gas stove ['gæs'stəυv] n κουζίνα του γκαζιού.
gassy ['gæsı] a (drink) αεριούχος.
gastric ['gæstrık] a γαστρικός.
gastronomy [gæs'trɒnəmı] n γαστρονομία.
gate [geıt] n πύλη, πόρτα || (of estate etc) καγκελόπορτα, αυλόπορτα || ~crasher n (party) απρόσκλητος επισκέπτης, τζαμπατζής || ~way n πύλη, είσοδος f.
gather ['gæðə*] vt συλλέγω, μαζεύω || (gain) συμπεραίνω, συνάγω ♦ vi (assemble) συγκεντρώνομαι, μαζεύομαι || ~ing n συγκέντρωση, μάζεμα nt.
gauche [gəυʃ] a χωρίς τακτ.
gaudy ['gɔːdı] a επιδεικτικός, φανταχτερός.
gauge [geıdʒ] n (of metal) διάμετρος,

διαμέτρημα nt|| (RAIL) πλάτος, μετατρόχιο || (measure) μετρητής, (εν)δείκτης ♦ vt (δια)μετρώ, εκτιμώ.
gaunt [gɔːnt] a (lean) ισχνός, κοκκαλιάρης || (grim) άγριος, συντετριμμένος.
gauze [gɔːz] n γάζα.
gave [geɪv] pt of **give**.
gay [geɪ] a (merry) εύθυμος || (brightly coloured) λαμπρός, ζωηρός || (homosexual) ομοφυλόφιλος.
gaze [geɪz] n ατενές βλέμμα nt|| **to ~ at** vt ατενίζω, καρφώνω.
gazelle [gəˈzɛl] n γαζέλα.
G.B. abbr see **great**.
G.C.E. n abbr of **General Certificate of Education.**
gear [gɪə*] n (equipment) είδη ntpl|| (MECH) μηχανισμός, οδοντωτός τροχός || (AUT) γρανάζι || **in ~** κινούμενος, στην ταχύτητα || **out of ~** νεκρό σημείο, εκτός λειτουργίας || **~box** n κιβώτιο ταχυτήτων || **~-lever,** (US) **~shift** n μοχλός ταχυτήτων.
geese [giːs] npl of **goose.**
gelatin(e) [ˈdʒɛlətiːn] n ζελατίνη, πηκτή.
gelignite [ˈdʒɛlɪgnaɪt] n ζελινίτης.
gem [dʒɛm] n πολύτιμος λίθος, πέτρα.
gender [ˈdʒɛndə*] n γένος nt.
general [ˈdʒɛnərəl] n ~ στρατηγός ♦ a γενικός || **~ election** n γενικές εκλογές fpl|| **~ization** n γενίκευση || **~ize** vi γενικεύω, εκλαΐκεύω || **~ly** ad γενικά, κατά κανόνα || **~ practitioner (G.P.)** n ≈ γιατρός m/f παθολόγος.
generate [ˈdʒɛnəreɪt] vt παράγω, (επι)φέρω προκαλώ || (ELEC) παράγω.
generation [dʒɛnəˈreɪʃən] n (into being) γέννηση, γένεση || (descent in family) γενεά, γενιά || (of same period) (σημερινή) γενεά || (about 30 years) (μια) γενεά || **third / fourth ~** a (COMPUT) τρίτης/τέταρτης γενεάς.
generator [ˈdʒɛnəreɪtə*] n γεννήτρια.
generosity [dʒɛnəˈrɒsɪtɪ] n γενναιοδωρία, γενναιοψυχία.
generous [ˈdʒɛnərəs] a γενναιόδωρος, μεγαλόψυχος || (col) γενναίος, πλούσιος || **~ly** ad γενναιόδωρα, μεγαλόψυχα.
genetics [dʒɪˈnɛtɪks] npl γενετική.
genial [ˈdʒiːnɪəl] a εύκρατος, ήπιος, προσηνής.
genitals [ˈdʒɛnɪtlz] npl γεννητικά όργανα ntpl.
genitive [ˈdʒɛnɪtɪv] n γενική (πτώση).
genius [ˈdʒiːnɪəs] n (person) ιδιοφυΐα, μεγαλοφυΐα || (ability) πνεύμα nt.
genteel [dʒɛnˈtiːl] a ευγενής, κομψός.
gentile [ˈdʒɛntaɪl] n εθνικός, μη Ιουδαίος.
gentle [ˈdʒɛntl] a ήπιος, μαλακός, ευγενής.
gentleman [ˈdʒɛntlmən] n ευγενής, κύριος, τζέντλεμαν m inv.
gentleness [ˈdʒɛntlnɪs] n λεπτότητα.
gently [ˈdʒɛntlɪ] ad ήρεμα, μαλακά.
gentry [ˈdʒɛntrɪ] n αρχοντολόι.

gents [dʒɛnts] n άνδρες mpl, κύριοι mpl.
genuine [ˈdʒɛnjuɪn] a γνήσιος, αυθεντικός, αληθινός || **~ly** ad ειλικρινά, γνησίως.
geographical [dʒɪəˈgræfɪkəl] a γεωγραφικός.
geography [dʒɪˈɒgrəfɪ] n γεωγραφία.
geological [dʒɪəˈlɒdʒɪkəl] a γεωλογικός.
geologist [dʒɪˈɒlədʒɪst] n γεωλόγος.
geology [dʒɪˈɒlədʒɪ] n γεωλογία.
geometric(al) [dʒɪəˈmɛtrɪk(əl)] a γεωμετρικός.
geometry [dʒɪˈɒmɪtrɪ] n γεωμετρία.
geranium [dʒɪˈreɪnɪəm] n γεράνι.
germ [dʒɜːm] n (of disease) μικρόβιο || (bud or seed) σπέρμα nt|| (beginning) σπέρμα nt.
German [ˈdʒɜːmən] a γερμανικός ♦ n (person) Γερμανός || (LING) Γερμανικά.
Germany [ˈdʒɜːmənɪ] n Γερμανία.
germination [dʒɜːmɪˈneɪʃən] n βλάστηση, κύηση.
gesticulate [dʒɛsˈtɪkjuleɪt] vi χειρονομώ.
gesture [ˈdʒɛstʃə*] n χειρονομία, νεύμα nt.
get [gɛt] (irreg v) vt (fetch) πηγαίνω να φέρω || (become) γίνομαι || (persuade) πείθω, καταφέρνω || (catch) (συλ)λαμβάνω, πιάνω ♦ vi (reach) πηγαίνω, φθάνω, γίνομαι || **to ~ along** vi (of people) πηγαίνω καλά || (depart) προχωρώ, (ώρα) να φύγω || **to ~ at** vt (facts) φθάνω, βρίσκω, πλησιάζω || **to ~ away** vi (leave) αναχωρώ, αποχωρώ || (escape) φεύγω, το σκάω || **to ~ down** vt κατεβάζω, γράφω || **to ~ in** vi (train) μπαίνω, πιάνω φιλίες || **to ~ on** vi (well, badly etc) τα πάω καλά || **to ~ out** vi βγάζω, αφαιρώ, βγαίνω || **to ~ over** vt (illness) συνέρχομαι, τελειώνω || **to ~ up** vi (in morning) σηκώνομαι || **~away** n φυγή, δραπέτευση.
geyser [ˈgiːzə*] n θερμοπίδακας, γκάιζερ nt inv|| (heater) θερμοσίφωνας.
ghastly [ˈgɑːstlɪ] a φρικτός, τρομερός || (pale) ωχρός.
gherkin [ˈgɜːkɪn] n αγγουράκι.
ghetto [ˈgɛtəʊ] n γκέττο.
ghost [gəʊst] n φάντασμα nt|| **~ly** a σαν φάντασμα.
giant [ˈdʒaɪənt] n γίγαντας ♦ a γιγαντιαίος.
gibberish [ˈdʒɪbərɪʃ] n αλαμπουρνέζικα ntpl.
gibe [dʒaɪb] n σκώμμα nt, πείραγμα nt.
giblets [ˈdʒɪblɪts] npl εντόσθια ntpl (πουλερικών).
giddiness [ˈgɪdɪnɪs] n ίλιγγος, ζάλη.
giddy [ˈgɪdɪ] a (dizzy) ζαλισμένος || (frivolous) επιπόλαιος.
gift [gɪft] n δώρο || (talent) προσόν, ταλέντο || **~ed** a προικισμένος, με ταλέντο.
gigantic [dʒaɪˈgæntɪk] a γιγαντιαίος.
giggle [ˈgɪgl] vi χασκογελώ ♦ n νευρικό γέλιο.

G

gild [gɪld] *(irreg v) vt* (επι)χρυσώνω.

gill [dʒɪl] *n (measure = ¼ pint)* ⅛ του λίτρου ♦ [gɪl] *n (fish)* βράγχιο, σπάραχνο.

gilt [gɪlt] *pp of* gild ♦ *n* επιχρύσωση, χρύσωμα *nt* ♦ *a* (επι)χρυσωμένος.

gin [dʒɪn] *n (liquor)* τζίν *nt inv*.

ginger ['dʒɪndʒə*] *n* πιπερόριζα || ~ beer *n* τζιτζιμπύρα || ~bread *n* μελόψωμο || ~-haired *a* κοκκινοτρίχης.

gingerly ['dʒɪndʒəlɪ] *ad* προσεκτικά, μαλακά.

gipsy ['dʒɪpsɪ] *n* τσιγγάνος, γύφτος.

giraffe [dʒɪ'rɑːf] *n* καμηλοπάρδαλη.

girder ['gɜːdə*] *n* δοκός *f*.

girdle ['gɜːdl] *n* ζωνάρι ♦ *vt* (περι)ζώνω.

girl [gɜːl] *n (child)* κοριτσάκι, κορίται || *(young woman)* νέα, κοπέλα || ~friend *n (of girl)* φιλενάδα || *(of boy)* φιλενάδα, φίλη || ~ish *a* κοριτσίστικος.

girth [gɜːθ] *n (measurement)* περιφέρεια, περίμετρος || *(strap)* έπονο, ίγγλα.

gist [dʒɪst] *n* ουσία, έννοια.

give [gɪv] *(irreg v) vt (hand over)* δίνω, χαρίζω || *(supply)* παρέχω, απονέμω ♦ *vi (break)* υποχωρώ, λυγίζω || to ~ away *vt (give free)* χαρίζω || *(betray)* καταδίδω, προδίδω || to ~ back *vt* αποδίδω, ξαναδίδω, γυρίζω || to ~ in *vi (yield, agree)* υποχωρώ, υποκύπτω ♦ *vt (hand in)* παραδίδω || to ~ up *vi (surrender)* παραδίδομαι ♦ *vt (post, office)* παραιτούμαι, εγκαταλείπω || to ~ way *vi* θραύομαι, υποχωρώ, αντικαθίσταμαι || ~r *n* δωρητής, δότης.

glacier ['glæsɪə*] *n* παγετώνας.

glad [glæd] *a* ευχαριστημένος, ευχάριστος || ~den *vt* χαροποιώ.

gladly ['glædlɪ] *ad* ευχάριστα, με χαρά.

glamorous ['glæmərəs] *a* γοητευτικός, μαγευτικός.

glamour ['glæmə*] *n* γοητεία, μαγεία.

glance [glɑːns] *n* βλέμμα *nt*, ματιά ♦ *vi (+ at) (look)* ρίχνω ματιά || γλιστρώ πλαγίως.

glancing ['glɑːnsɪŋ] *a (blow)* πλάγιος.

gland [glænd] *n* αδένας || ~ular *a* αδενικός.

glare [glɛə*] *n (light)* εκτυφλωτική λάμψη || *(fierce stare)* άγριο βλέμμα *nt* ♦ *vi (angrily)* απαστράπτω, λάμπω || αγριοκοιτάζω.

glaring ['glɛərɪŋ] *a (mistake)* έκδηλος, ολοφάνερος.

glass [glɑːs] *n (substance)* γυαλί || *(vessel)* ποτήρι || *(mirror)* καθρέφτης || ~es *npl* γυαλιά *ntpl* || ~house *n (AGR)* θερμοκήπιο, σέρρα || ~ware *n* γυαλικά *ntpl* || ~y *a (eye)* σαν γυαλί, ανέκφραστος.

glaze [gleɪz] *vt (furnish with glass)* βάζω τζάμια || *(finish)* βερνικώνω, γυαλίζω ♦ *n* βερνίκι.

glazier ['gleɪzɪə*] *n* τζαμιτζής.

gleam [gliːm] *n* ακτίδα, λάμψη ♦ *vi* ακτινοβολώ, λάμπω || ~ing *a* αστραφτερός.

glee [gliː] *n* ευθυμία, χαρά || ~ful *a* εύθυμος, χαρούμενος.

glen [glɛn] *n* χαράδρα, δερβένι.

glib [glɪb] *a* εύγλωττος, επιπόλαιος || ~ly *ad* εύκολα, πονηρά.

glide [glaɪd] *vi* γλυστρώ, κυλώ ♦ *n* γλίστρημα || ~r *n (AVIAT)* ανεμόπτερο.

gliding ['glaɪdɪŋ] *n* ολίσθηση, ανεμοπορία.

glimmer ['glɪmə*] *n* αμυδρό φως *nt*.

glimpse [glɪmps] *n* γρήγορη ματιά ♦ *vt* βλέπω φευγαλέα.

glint [glɪnt] *n* λάμψη ♦ *vi* λάμπω, απαστράπτω.

glisten ['glɪsn] *vi* απαστράπτω, σπιθίζω.

glitter ['glɪtə*] *vi* λάμπω, σπινθηροβολώ ♦ *n* λαμποκόπημα *nt*, γυάλισμα *nt*.

gloat [gləut] : to ~ over *vt* κοιτάζω με χαιρεκακία.

global ['gləubl] *a* παγκόσμιος.

globe [gləub] *n (light)* γλόμπος, λάμπα || *(earth)* σφαίρα, υδρόγειος σφαίρα.

gloom [gluːm] *n (also: ~iness) (darkness)* σκότος *nt*, σκοτάδι || *(depression)* μελαγχολία, σκεψιά μελαγχολικά, σκυθρωπά || ~y *a* σκοτεινός, βαρύς, μελαγχολικός.

glorify ['glɔːrɪfaɪ] *vt* εκθειάζω, εξυμνώ, δοξάζω.

glorious ['glɔːrɪəs] *a* ένδοξος, δοξασμένος, λαμπρός.

glory ['glɔːrɪ] *n (splendour)* δόξα, μεγαλείο || *(fame)* τιμή, φήμη, δόξα.

gloss [glɒs] *n (shine)* στιλπνότητα, λούστρο, γυαλάδα.

glossary ['glɒsərɪ] *n* λεξιλόγιο, γλωσσάριο.

glossy ['glɒsɪ] *a (surface)* στιλπνός, γυαλιστερός.

glove [glʌv] *n* γάντι.

glow [gləu] *vi* πυρακτούμαι, κοκκινίζω || *(look hot)* ζεσταίνομαι, ανάβω || *(with emotion)* αστράπτω, λάμπω ♦ *n (heat)* πυράκτωση || *(colour)* ροδαλότητα, κοκκινάδα || *(feeling)* σφρίγος *nt*, φλόγα.

glower ['glauə*] *vi* στραβοκοιτάζω.

glucose ['gluːkəus] *n* γλυκόζη.

glue [gluː] *n* κόλλα ♦ *vt* κολλώ.

glum [glʌm] *a* σκυθρωπός, κατσούφης.

glut [glʌt] *n* υπεραφθονία ♦ *vt (ECON)* πλημμυρίζω.

glutton ['glʌtn] *n* λαίμαργος, φαγάς || ~ous *a* αδηφάγος || ~y *n* λαιμαργία.

glycerin(e) ['glɪsəriːn] *n* γλυκερίνη.

gm, gms *abbr of* gram(s).

gnarled [nɑːld] *a* ροζιάρικος.

gnat [næt] *n* σκνίπα.

gnaw [nɔː] *vt* ροκανίζω, τραγανίζω.

gnome [nəum] *n* νάνος.

go [gəu] *(irreg v) vi (travel)* πηγαίνω, πάω || *(progress)* κινούμαι, πάω || *(function)* πάω, τρέχω, λειτουργώ || *(depart)* αναχωρώ, φεύγω || *(disappear)* χάνομαι || *(be sold)* (+ for) πουλιέμαι για || *(fit, suit)* πηγαίνω, ταιριάζω || *(become)* γίνομαι || *(break etc)* σπάζω, κόβομαι, πωλούμαι ♦ *n (energy)* δραστηριότητα, διάθεση || *(attempt)* δοκιμή, προσπάθεια, απόπειρα || to ~ ahead *vi (proceed)* προχωρώ, προοδεύω

|| to ~ along with vt (agree to support) συμφωνώ, ταιριάζω || to ~ away vi (depart) φεύγω || to ~ back vi (return) επιστρέφω || to ~ back on vt (promise) παραβαίνω, αθετώ || to ~ by vi (years, time) περνώ || to ~ down vi (sun) κατεβαίνω, γέρνω, πέφτω || to ~ for vt (fetch) πάω για || (like) συμπαθώ || to ~ in vi (enter) εισέρχομαι, μπαίνω || (fit) μπαίνω || to ~ into vt (enter) μπαίνω || (study) εξετάζω, μελετώ || to ~ off vi (depart) εξέρχομαι, φεύγω || (milk) ξινίζω || (explode) εκπυροκροτώ ♦ vt (dislike) ξεθυμαίνω, αντιπαθώ || to ~ on vi (continue) συνεχίζω, εξακολουθώ || to ~ out vi (fire, light) σβήνω || (of house) βγαίνω || to ~ over vt (examine, check) εξετάζω, επαναλαμβάνω || to ~ up vi (price) ανεβαίνω || (explode) αναπινάσσομαι || to ~ without vt περνώ χωρίς.

goad [gəud] vt κεντρίζω, προκαλώ ♦ n βούκεντρο, κίνητρο.

go-ahead ['gəuəhεd] a δραστήριος.

goal [gəul] n (purpose) σκοπός || (on sports field) τέρμα nt || (score) γκωλ nt inv || ~keeper n τερματοφύλακας || ~-post n δοκός f.

goat [gəut] n κατοίκα, γίδα.

gobble ['gɔbl] vt καταβροχθίζω.

go-between ['gəubitwiːn] n μεσάζων, μεσολαβητής.

god [gɔd] n θεός || G~ Θεός || ~child n βαφτιστικός || ~dess n θεά || ~father n νουνός || ~forsaken a εγκαταλειμμένος, καταραμένος || ~mother n νουνά || ~send n θείο δώρο, κελεπούρι.

goggle ['gɔgl] vi γουρλώνω || ~s npl προστατευτικά γυαλιά ntpl.

going ['gəuiŋ] n (condition of ground) κατάσταση εδάφους ♦ a (rate) τρέχουσα (τιμή) || (concern) δραστήριος || ~s-on npl δραστήρια ntpl.

gold [gəuld] n χρυσός, χρυσάφι || ~en a χρυσός, χρυσαφένιος || ~fish n χρυσόψαρο || ~ mine n χρυσορυχείο.

golf [gɔlf] n γκόλφ nt inv || ~ club (society) λέσχη του γκόλφ || (stick) κλόμπ nt inv || ~ course n γήπεδο του γκόλφ || ~er n παίκτης του γκόλφ.

gondola ['gɔndələ] n γόνδολα.

gone [gɔn] pp of go.

gong [gɔŋ] n γκόγκ nt inv, κουδούνι.

good [gud] n (well-being) το καλό, όφελος || (goodness) αρετή, καλό ♦ a (well-behaved) καλός, έντιμος || (virtuous) τίμιος, αγαθός, καλός || (well-done) εξαιρετικός, καλός || (suitable) ταιριαστός, που πάει || (sound) σε καλή κατάσταση || ~s npl κινητά, αγαθά, είδη || a ~ deal, a ~ many αρκετός, πολύς || ~bye! αντίο! || γειά σου! || στο καλό! || G~ Friday n Μεγάλη Παρασκευή || ~-looking a όμορφος || ~ morning! καλημέρα! || ~ness n καλωσύνη, αρετή || ~will n καλή θέληση, κέφι.

goose [guːs] n χήνα.

gooseberry ['guzbəri] n φραγκοστάφυλο.

gooseflesh ['guːsflεʃ] n ανατριχίλα.

gore [gɔː*] vt κερατίζω ♦ n πηκτό αίμα nt.

gorge [gɔːdʒ] n στενό, φαράγγι ♦ vti παρατρώγω.

gorgeous ['gɔːdʒəs] a πολύχρωμος, εξαίσιος.

gorilla [gə'rilə] n γορίλλας.

gorse [gɔːs] n σπάρτο.

gory ['gɔːri] a (details) αιματοβαφής.

go-slow ['gəu'sləu] n απεργία κωλυσιεργίας.

gospel ['gɔspəl] n ευαγγέλιο.

gossip ['gɔsip] n (idle talk) κουβεντολόι || (person) κουτσομπόλης ♦ vi κουτσομπολεύω, φλυαρώ.

got [gɔt] pt, pp of get || ~ten (US) pp of get.

gout [gaut] n αρθρίτιδα, ποδάγρα.

govern ['gʌvən] vt (general) κυβερνώ, διοικώ, διευθύνω || (GRAM) συντάσσομαι με.

governess ['gʌvənis] n γκουβερνάντα, νταντά.

governing ['gʌvəniŋ] a διευθύνων, διοικών, κατευθυντήριος.

government ['gʌvnmənt] n κυβέρνηση || (management) διοίκηση || ~al a κυβερνητικός.

governor ['gʌvənə*] n κυβερνήτης, διοικητής.

Govt. abbr of **government**.

gown [gaun] n φόρεμα nt, φουστάνι || (of judge etc) τήβεννος.

G.P. n abbr see **general**.

grab [græb] vt αρπάζω, πιάνω ♦ n αρπαγή || (excavator) αρπάγη.

grace [greis] n (charm) χάρη || (favour, kindness) εύνοια, χατήρι || (God's blessing) θεία χάρη || (short prayer) προσευχή ♦ vt (honour) τιμώ || (adorn) στολίζω, ομορφαίνω || 5 days' ~ 5 μέρες προθεσμία || ~ful a χαριτωμένος, κομψός || ~fully ad χαριτωμένα.

gracious ['greiʃəs] a (kind, courteous) καλός, αγαθός, καλόβολος.

gradation [grə'deiʃən] n διαβάθμιση.

grade [greid] n (degree, rank) βαθμός, τάξη, βαθμίδα || (slope) κλίση ♦ vt (classify) διαβαθμίζω, ταξινομώ || ~ crossing n (US) ισόπεδος διάβαση.

gradient ['greidiənt] n κλίση.

gradual ['grædjuəl] a βαθμιαίος || ~ly ad βαθμηδόν.

graduate ['grædjuit] n πτυχιούχος ♦ ['grædjueit] vi αποφοιτώ.

graduation [grædju'eiʃən] n αποφοίτηση || (grade) διαβάθμιση.

graft [grɑːft] n (shoot) μπόλι, κεντρί || (on humans) μόσχευμα nt || (unfair means) δωροδοκία, ρεμούλα ♦ vt μπολιάζω || ~ing n μεταμόσχευση.

grain [grein] n (seed) κόκκος, σπυρί ||

(crop) δημητριακά *ntpl* || *(small particle)* ψήγμα *nt*, κόκκος || *(fibre)* κόκκος, υφή.

grammar ['græmə*] *n* γραμματική.

grammatical [grə'mætikəl] *a* γραμματικός.

gram(me) [græm] *n* γραμμάριο.

gramophone ['græməfəʊn] *n* γραμμόφωνο.

granary ['grænərɪ] *n* σιταποθήκη.

grand [grænd] *a (fine, splendid)* μεγάλος, μεγαλοπρεπής || *(final)* πλήρης, ολόκληρος || ~**daughter** *n* εγγονή || ~**eur** *n* μεγαλείο || ~**father** *n* παππούς *m* || ~**iose** *a (imposing)* μεγαλοπρεπής || *(pompous)* πομπώδης, φαντασμένος || ~**mother** *n* γιαγιά || ~ **piano** *n* πιάνο με ουρά || ~**son** *n* έγγονος || ~**stand** *n* εξέδρα.

granite ['grænɪt] *n* γρανίτης.

granny ['grænɪ] *n (col)* γιαγιά, γρηούλα.

grant [grɑ:nt] *vt (bestow)* απονέμω, δίνω || *(allow)* (απο)δέχομαι ♦ *n* δωρεά, επιχορήγηση.

granule ['grænju:l] *n* κοκκίδιο, κοκκίο.

grape [greɪp] *n* σταφύλι, ρώγα.

grapefruit ['greɪpfru:t] *n* φράπα, γκρέιπ-φρουτ *nt inv.*

graph [grɑ:f] *n* διάγραμμα *nt*, γραφική παράσταση || ~**ic** *a (vivid)* ζωηρός, εκφραστικός || *(drawing, writing)* γραφικός.

grapple ['græpl] *vi (+ with)* πιάνομαι, έρχομαι στα χέρια.

grasp [grɑ:sp] *vt* πιάνω, σφίγγω, αρπάζω || *(understand)* συλλαμβάνω, κατανοώ ♦ *n (handgrip)* λαβή, πιάσιμο, σφίξιμο || *(possession)* έλεγχος, εξουσία || *(understanding)* αντίληψη, γνώση || ~**ing** *a* άπληστος, πλεονέκτης.

grass [grɑ:s] *n* χορτάρι, γρασίδι || ~**hopper** *n* ακρίδα || ~**land** *n* λιβάδι || ~**snake** *n* νερόφιδο || ~**y** *a* χορταριασμένος, πράσινος.

grate [greɪt] *n* σχάρα, κάγκελο ♦ *vi (scrape)* ξύνω || *(make harsh sound)* τρίζω || *(irritate)* ενοχλώ ♦ *vt (into small pieces)* τρίβω.

grateful ['greɪtful] *a* ευγνώμονας, ευχάριστος || ~**ly** *ad* με ευγνωμοσύνη.

grater ['greɪtə*] *n* ξύστρα, τρίφτης.

gratify ['grætɪfaɪ] *vt* ευχαριστώ, ικανοποιώ.

gratifying ['grætɪfaɪɪŋ] *a* ευχάριστος.

grating ['greɪtɪŋ] *n (iron bars)* κιγκλίδωμα *nt*, κάγκελα *ntpl* ♦ *a (noise)* κακόηχος, στριγκός.

gratitude ['grætɪtju:d] *n* ευγνωμοσύνη.

gratuity [grə'tju:ɪtɪ] *n* φιλοδώρημα *nt.*

grave [greɪv] *n* τάφος ♦ *a* βαρύς, σοβαρός, δυσάρεστος || ~**digger** *n* νεκροθάφτης.

gravel ['grævəl] *n* χαλίκι.

gravestone ['greɪvstəʊn] *n* επιτάφιος πλάκα.

graveyard ['greɪvjɑ:d] *n* νεκροταφείο.

gravitate ['grævɪteɪt] *vi* έλκομαι, ρέπω προς.

gravity ['grævɪtɪ] *n* βαρύτητα, βάρος *nt* || *(seriousness)* σοβαρότητα.

gravy ['greɪvɪ] *n* είδος *nt* σάλτσας.

gray [greɪ] *a* = **grey**.

graze [greɪz] *vi (feed)* βόσκω ♦ *vt (touch)* ψαύω, εγγίζω || *(scrape)* ξύνω ♦ *n (MED)* ξέγδαρμα *nt.*

grease [gri:s] *n (fat)* λίπος *nt*, ξύγγι || *(lubricant)* γράσο, λάδι ♦ *vt* λαδώνω, γρασάρω || ~**proof** *a* μη διαπερατός από λάδι.

greasy ['gri:sɪ] *a* λιπαρός, λαδωμένος.

great [greɪt] *a (large)* μεγάλος || *(important)* σπουδαίος || *(distinguished)* μεγάλος || **G~ Britain** *(G.B.)* *n* Μεγάλη Βρεττανία || ~**-grandfather** *n* πρόπαππος || ~**-grandmother** *n* προμάμη || ~**ness** *n* μεγαλείο, μέγεθος *nt.*

Greece [gri:s] *n* Ελλάδα.

greed [gri:d] *n (also: ~iness)* απληστία, πλεονεξία || ~**ily** *ad* άπληστα || ~**y** *a* άπληστος, πλεονέκτης || *(gluttonous)* λαίμαργος, αδηφάγος.

Greek [gri:k] *n (person)* Έλληνας/νίδα *m/f* || *(LING)* Ελληνικά *ntpl* ♦ *a* ελληνικός.

green [gri:n] *a* πράσινος, άγουρος || *(inexperienced)* άπειρος || ~**grocer** *n* μανάβης || ~**house** *n* θερμοκήπιο.

greet [gri:t] *vt* χαιρετίζω || ~**ing** *n* χαιρετισμός || ~**ings!** χαιρετισμούς! *mpl.*

gregarious [grɪ'gɛərɪəs] *a* κοινωνικός.

grenade [grɪ'neɪd] *n* (χειρο)βομβίδα.

grew [gru:] *pt of* **grow**.

grey [greɪ] *a* σταχτής, γκρίζος, ψαρός || *(dismal)* σκοτεινός || ~**-haired** *a* γκριζομάλλης, ψαρομάλλης || ~**hound** *n* λαγωνικό.

grid [grɪd] *n (of bars)* σχάρα, πλέγμα *nt* || *(network)* πλέγμα, δίκτυο || *(of map)* δικτυωτό, τετραγωνισμός || ~**iron** *n* σχάρα.

grief [gri:f] *n* θλίψη, λύπη, ατύχημα *nt.*

grievance ['gri:vəns] *n* παράπονο.

grieve [gri:v] *vi* λυπούμαι, θλίβομαι ♦ *vt* λυπώ, πικραίνω.

grill [grɪl] *n (on cooker)* σχάρα || *(of food)* της σχάρας ♦ *vt* ψήνω στη σχάρα || *(interrogate)* ανακρίνω.

grille [grɪl] *n (on car etc)* γρίλλιες *fpl.*

grim [grɪm] *a* φρικαλέος, απειλητικός, σκληρός.

grimace [grɪ'meɪs] *n* γκριμάτσα ♦ *vi* μορφάζω.

grime [graɪm] *n* ακαθαρσία, λέρα, φούμο.

grimly ['grɪmlɪ] *ad* απαίσια, σκληρά, αυστηρά.

grimy ['graɪmɪ] *a* ακάθαρτος, βρώμικος.

grin [grɪn] *n* χαμόγελο, μειδίαμα *nt* ♦ *vi* χαμογελώ, μορφάζω.

grind [graɪnd] *(irreg v)* *vt (crush)* τρίβω, αλέθω, κοπανίζω || *(sharpen)* τροχίζω, τορνάρω, λειαίνω || *(teeth)* τρίζω ♦ *n (bore)* αγγαρεία, μαγγανοπήγαδο.

grip [grɪp] *n (firm hold)* σφίξιμο, πιάσιμο || *(handle)* λαβή || *(mastery)* πυγμή, γνώση, επιβολή || (suitcase) βαλιτσάκι ♦ vt πιάνω, σφίγγω.

gripes [graɪps] npl (bowel pains) κωλικόπονοι mpl.

gripping ['grɪpɪŋ] a (exciting) συγκινητικός, συναρπαστικός.

grisly ['grɪzlɪ] a φρικιαστικός, τρομακτικός.

gristle ['grɪsl] n χόνδρος, τραγανό.

grit [grɪt] n (sand) αμμόλιθος, ακαθαρσίες fpl || (courage) τόλμη, θάρρος nt ♦ vt (teeth) τρίζω.

groan [grəʊn] n αναστεναγμός ♦ vi (ανα)στενάζω.

grocer ['grəʊsə*] n μπακάλης || ~ies npl είδη μπακαλικής.

groggy ['grɒgɪ] a (dazed, staggering) κλονιζόμενος, σουρωμένος, ασταθής.

groin [grɔɪn] n βουβών m.

groom [gruːm] n ιπποκόμος || (bridegroom) γαμπρός ♦ vt (o.s.) ντύνομαι.

groove [gruːv] n αυλάκι, διάξυσμα nt || (rut) ρουτίνα.

grope [grəʊp] vi ψηλαφώ, ψάχνω.

gross [grəʊs] a (coarse) χονδροειδής, σωματώδης || (very bad) χοντρός, καταφανής || (total) ολικός, χονδρικός ♦ n γρόσσα, δώδεκα δωδεκάδες || ~ly ad χονδροειδώς, υπερβολικά.

grotesque [grəʊ'tɛsk] a αλλόκοτος, παράλογος.

grotto ['grɒtəʊ] n σπηλιά, κρύπτη.

ground [graʊnd] pt, pp of **grind** ♦ n (surface) έδαφος nt, γη, χώμα nt || (piece of land) οικόπεδο, γη || (reason) λόγος, αιτία, βάση || ~s npl (dregs) κατακάθι, ίζημα nt || (land) περιοχή, κήποι mpl, πάρκο ♦ vt (run ashore) προσαράσσω, εξοκέλλω || (compel to stay) καθηλώνω || (instruct) διδάσκω εντατικά ♦ vi εξοκέλλω || ~ing n (instruction) οι βάσεις fpl || ~sheet n μουσαμάς εδάφους || ~work n θεμέλιος ntpl, βάσις.

group [gruːp] n ομάδα, παρέα ♦ vt συνδυάζω, συνδέω, συγκεντρώνω.

grouse [graʊs] n (bird) χαμωτίδα, αγριόγαλος || (complaint) γκρίνια ♦ vi (complain) γκρινιάζω.

grove [grəʊv] n άλσος nt, ασύλιο.

grovel ['grɒvl] vi (in fear) σέρνομαι, κυλιέμαι || (abase o.s.) ταπεινώνομαι, πέφτω στα πόδια.

grow [grəʊ] (irreg v) vi (in size) μεγαλώνω, αναπτύσσομαι || (be produced) φύομαι || (become) καθίσταμαι, γίνομαι ♦ vt (raise crops etc) καλλιεργώ || **to ~ up** vi μεγαλώνω || ~**er** n καλλιεργητής || ~**ing** a αυξανόμενος, που μεγαλώνει.

growl [graʊl] vi μουγγρίζω ♦ n μούγγρισμα nt, βρυχηθμός.

grown-up ['grəʊn'ʌp] a ώριμος ♦ n ενήλικος.

growth [grəʊθ] n (development) ανάπτυξη || (increase) αύξηση, μεγάλωμα nt || (what has grown) καλλιέργεια || (MED) σάρκωμα nt.

grub [grʌb] n (larva) σκουλίκι || (col: food) φαγητό || ~**by** a ακάθαρτος, βρώμικος.

grudge [grʌdʒ] n (μνησι)κακία, έχθρα ♦ vt ζηλεύω για, δείχνω απροθυμία || **to bear a** ~ κρατώ κακία για.

grudging ['grʌdʒɪŋ] a απρόθυμος, φειδωλός.

gruelling ['grʊəlɪŋ] a εξαντλητικός.

gruesome ['gruːsəm] a φρικτός, απαίσιος.

gruff [grʌf] a τραχύς, απότομος.

grumble ['grʌmbl] vi γκρινιάζω, μουγγρίζω ♦ n μουγγρητό, γκρίνια.

grumpy ['grʌmpɪ] a κατσούφης, γκρινιάρης.

grunt [grʌnt] n γρύλλισμα nt ♦ vi γρυλλίζω.

guarantee [gærən'tiː] n (of goods) εγγύηση || (promise to pay) εγγύηση, ενέχυρο ♦ vt εγγυώμαι.

guard [gɑːd] n (defence) φρουρά, προφύλαξη || (sentry) σκοπός || (official) φύλακας ♦ vt φυλάσσω, προστατεύω, φρουρώ || ~**ed** a υπό φρούρησιν || (words etc) επιφυλακτικός || ~**ian** n (keeper) φύλακας, προστάτης || (of child) κηδεμόνας.

guerilla [gə'rɪlə] n αντάρτης || ~ **warfare** n ανταρτοπόλεμος.

guess [gɛs] vti μαντεύω || (US) νομίζω ♦ n εικασία, γνώμη.

guest [gɛst] n καλεσμένος, ξένος || (of hotel) πελάτης || ~ **house** n πανσιόν f inv || ~ **room** n (in private house, for friends) δωμάτιο των ξένων.

guffaw [gʌ'fɔː] n καγχασμός ♦ vi ξεσπώ στα γέλια.

guidance ['gaɪdəns] n (control) καθοδήγηση || (advice) συμβουλές fpl, οδηγίες fpl.

guide [gaɪd] n (person) οδηγός m/f, συνοδός m/f, ξεναγός m/f || (book etc) οδηγός ♦ vt (καθ)οδηγώ || **girl** ~ n προσκοπίνα || ~**book** n οδηγός || ~**d missile** n κατευθυνόμενο βλήμα nt || ~**lines** npl οδηγός.

guild [gɪld] n (old: company) συντεχνία || (society) ένωση, σωματείο || ~**hall** n (Brit: town hall) δημαρχείο.

guile [gaɪl] n τέχνασμα nt, δόλος || ~**less** a άδολος.

guillotine ['gɪlətiːn] n λαιμητόμος f, γκιλοτίνα.

guilt [gɪlt] n ενοχή || ~**y** a ένοχος.

guise [gaɪz] n (appearance) μορφή, εμφάνιση.

guitar [gɪ'tɑː*] n κιθάρα || ~**ist** n κιθαριστής.

gulf [gʌlf] n κόλπος, κόρφος || (abyss) χάσμα nt.

gull [gʌl] n γλάρος.

gullet ['gʌlɪt] n οισοφάγος.

gullible ['gʌlɪbl] a εύπιστος, αφελής.

gully ['gʌlɪ] n ρεματιά, στενό, υπόνομος.

gulp [gʌlp] vi (hastily) καταπίνω, καταβροχθίζω ♦ (choke) κομπιάζομαι, πνίγομαι ♦ n ρουφηξιά, γουλιά.

gum [gʌm] n (of teeth) ούλο || (for sticking) γόμα, γόμμι || (for chewing) τσίχλα, μαστίχα ♦ vt κολλώ, αλείφω με γόμα || ~**boots** npl μπότες από καουτσούκ.

gun [gʌn] n (cannon) πυροβόλο, κανόνι || (rifle) τουφέκι || (revolver) πιστόλι || ~**fire** n βολή, πυρ nt, κανονιοβολισμός || ~**man** n ληστής, κακοποιός || ~**ner** n πυροβολητής || ~**powder** n πυρίτιδα, μπαρούτι || ~**shot** n τουφεκιά, κανονιά.

gurgle ['gɜːgl] n παφλασμός, κελάρισμα nt.

gush [gʌʃ] n εκροή, διάχυση, ξέσπασμα nt ♦ vi (out) εκχύνομαι, αναπηδώ || (be moved) συγκινούμαι, αναλύομαι σε.

gusset ['gʌsɪt] n (MECH) επένθεμα nt.

gust [gʌst] n ανεμοριπή, μπουρίνι.

gut [gʌt] n (intestine) έντερο, σπλάχνο || (string) χορδή || ~**s** npl θάρρος nt.

gutter ['gʌtə*] n (channel) λούκι, σούγελο || (of street) ρείθρο, χαντάκι.

guttural ['gʌtərəl] a λαρυγγικός.

guy [gaɪ] n (NAUT) πρόδρομος, γκάγια f || (effigy) ανδρείκελο, σκιάχτρο || (man, fellow) τύπος, παιδί.

guzzle ['gʌzl] vi καταβροχθίζω, ρουφώ.

gym(nasium) [dʒɪm('neɪzɪəm)] n γυμναστήριο.

gymnast ['dʒɪmnæst] n γυμναστής || ~**ics** n γυμναστική.

gyn(a)ecologist [gaɪnɪ'kɔlədʒɪst] n γυναικολόγος.

gypsy ['dʒɪpsɪ] n = **gipsy.**

gyrate [dʒaɪ'reɪt] vi περιστρέφομαι.

H

habit ['hæbɪt] n συνήθεια, έθιμο || (dress) φόρεμα nt.

habitation [hæbɪ'teɪʃən] n κατοικία, διαμονή.

habitual [hə'bɪtjuəl] a συνήθης, συνηθισμένος || ~**ly** ad συνήθως.

hack [hæk] vt κατακόβω, πετσοκόβω ♦ n άλογο που νοικιάζεται.

hackneyed ['hæknɪd] a ξεφτελισμένος, φθαρμένος.

had [hæd] pt, pp of **have.**

haddock ['hædɔk] n βακαλάος.

haemorrhage, hemorrhage (US) ['hemərɪdʒ] n αιμορραγία.

haemorrhoids, hemorrhoids (US) ['hemərɔɪdz] npl αιμορροΐδες fpl.

haggard ['hægəd] a κάτωχρος, χαμένος.

haggle ['hægl] vi κάνω παζάρι.

hail [heɪl] n (meteorology) χαλάζι ♦ vt (greet) χαιρετώ ♦ vi (meteorology) ρίχνει χαλάζι || to ~ **from** vt προέρχομαι από || ~**stone** n κόκκος χαλάζης.

hair [hɛə*] n (general) τρίχα, μαλλιά ntpl || (one hair) τρίχα || ~**'s breadth** n παρά τρίχα || ~**brush** n βούρτσα μαλλιών || ~**cut** n κούρεμα nt || ~**do** n κτένισμα nt || ~**dresser** n κομμωτής/ώτρια m/f, κουρέας || ~**drier** n στεγνωτήρας || ~**net** n δίχτυ nt για τα μαλλιά || ~**oil** n

λάδι για τα μαλλιά || ~**pin** n (lit) φουρκέτα || (bend) απότομη στροφή || ~**raising** a τρομακτικός || ~**style** n κόμμωση, χτενισιά || ~**y** a τριχωτός, μαλλιαρός.

half [haːf] n μισό ♦ a μισός ♦ ad κατά το ήμισυ, μισό || ~**breed, ~caste** n μιγάδας || ~**hearted** a χλιαρός, με μισή καρδιά || ~**hour** n ημίωρο, μισή (ώρα) || ~**penny** n μισή πέννα || ~**price** μισή τιμή, μισό εισιτήριο || ~**way** ad στο ήμισυ της αποστάσεως, μισοστρατής.

halibut ['hælɪbət] n ιππόγλωσσος, είδος γλώσσας.

hall [hɔːl] n μεγάλη αίθουσα || (building, house) δημόσιο κτίριο || (dining) τραπεζαρία || (entrance) είσοδος f, χωλ nt inv.

hallo [hə'ləu] excl = **hello.**

hallucination [həluːsɪ'neɪʃən] n παραίσθηση, αυταπάτη.

halo ['heɪləu] n (of saint) φωτοστέφανος || (of sun, moon) άλως f, αλώνι.

halt [hɔːlt] n στάση, σταμάτημα nt ♦ vt σταματώ ♦ vi σταθμεύω, σταματώ.

halve [haːv] vt χωρίζω στα δύο, μοιράζω.

ham [hæm] n χοιρομέρι, ζαμπό nt inv.

hamburger ['hæmbɜːgə*] n μπιφτέκι από κιμά.

hamlet ['hæmlət] n χωριουδάκι.

hammer ['hæmə*] n σφυρί ♦ vt κτυπώ δυνατά, σφυρηλατώ.

hammock ['hæmək] n αμάκ nt inv, κούνια || (NAUT) αιώρα, μπράντα.

hamper ['hæmpə*] n καλάθι ♦ vt εμποδίζω, παρακωλύω.

hand [hænd] n χέρι || (of clock) δείκτης || (worker) εργάτης || (help) βοήθεια ♦ vt δίνω || βοηθώ || ~**s** npl (NAUT) πλήρωμα nt || to ~ **down** vt μεταβιβάζω || to ~ **over** vt παραδίδω || at ~ κοντά || in ~ στη διάθεσή μου || υπό τον έλεγχό μου || ~**s up** ψηλά τα χέρια || ~**bag** n τσάντα || ~**book** n εγχειρίδιο || (guide) οδηγός || ~**brake** n χειρόφρενο || ~**cuffs** npl χειροπέδες fpl || ~**ful** n φούχτα, φουχτιά.

handicap ['hændɪkæp] n εμπόδιο, μειονέκτημα nt || (SPORT) χάντικαπ nt inv ♦ vt παρεμποδίζω, δυσχεραίνω || (SPORT) βάζω χάντικαπ.

handicraft ['hændɪkrɑːft] n χειροτεχνία, τέχνη.

handkerchief ['hæŋkətʃɪf] n μαντήλι.

handle ['hændl] n (of door etc) πόμολο, (χειρο)λαβή || (of cup etc) χερούλι || (for winding) χειρολαβή, χερούλι ♦ vt (use, treat) μεταχειρίζομαι || (manipulate) χειρίζομαι || (touch) πιάνω, αγγίζω || (COMM) διεκπεραιώνω, διαχειρίζομαι.

hand-luggage ['hændlʌgɪdʒ] n αποσκευές fpl του χεριού.

handmade ['hændmeɪd] a χειροποίητος.

handsome ['hænsəm] a ωραίος,

όμορφος || (generous) σημαντικός, γενναιόδωρος.

handwriting ['hændraitiŋ] n γραφή, γράψιμο.

handy ['hændi] a επιδέξιος || (useful) βολικός, χρήσιμος.

handyman ['hændimən] n πολυτεχνίτης.

hang [hæŋ] (irreg v) vt αναρτώ, κρεμώ || (one's head) σκύβω || (wallpaper) κολλώ ♦ vi κρέμομαι || to ~ about vi περιφέρομαι, τριγυρίζω, τεμπελιάζω.

hangar ['hæŋə*] n υπόστεγο.

hanger ['hæŋə*] n κρεμάστρα.

hanger-on ['hæŋər'ɒn] n κολλιτσίδα.

hangover ['hæŋəuvə*] n (MED) πονοκέφαλος (από μεθύσι).

hanker ['hæŋkə*] vi: to ~ after ποθώ διακαώς, λαχταρώ.

haphazard [hæp'hæzəd] a στην τύχη, τυχαία.

happen ['hæpən] vi συμβαίνω, τυγχάνω || ~ing n συμβάν, γεγονός.

happily ['hæpili] ad ευτυχώς.

happiness ['hæpinis] n ευτυχία.

happy ['hæpi] a ευτυχισμένος, τυχερός, επιτυχημένος || ~-go-lucky a ξένοιαστος.

harass ['hærəs] vt παρενοχλώ, βασανίζω.

harbour, harbor (US) ['haːbə*] n λιμάνι, καταφύγιο ♦ vt στεγάζω, παρέχω άσυλο.

hard [haːd] a σκληρός, στερεός || (task) δύσκολος, δυσχερής || (person etc) αυστηρός, αλύπντος || (work) επίπονος, σκληρός ♦ ad δυνατά, σκληρά, δύσκολα || ~ by κοντά || ~-boiled a (egg) σφιχτό || (person) σκληρός || ~en vi σκληραίνω || ~-hearted a σκληρόκαρδος, αλύπντος.

hardly ['haːdli] ad μόλις.

hardship ['haːdʃip] n κακουχία, δοκιμασία, ταλαιπωρία.

hard-up [haːd'ʌp] a απένταρος.

hardware ['haːdwɛə*] n σιδηρικά ntpl, είδη ntpl, καγκελαρίας.

hardy ['haːdi] a σκληραγωγημένος || (brave) τολμηρός, θαρραλέος.

hare [hɛə*] n λαγός.

harem ['haːriːm] n χαρέμι.

harm [haːm] n κακό, βλάβη, ζημιά ♦ vt βλάπτω, θίγω || ~ful a επιβλαβής, βλαβερός || ~less a άκακος, αβλαβής, ακίνδυνος.

harmonica [haː'mɒnikə] n φυσαρμόνικα.

harmonious [haː'məuniəs] a αρμονικός || (MUS) μελωδικός.

harmonize ['haːmənaiz] vt εναρμονίζω || (agree) συμφωνώ ♦ vi εναρμονίζομαι, ταιριάζω.

harmony ['haːməni] n (MUS) αρμονία || (agreement) συμφωνία.

harness ['haːnis] n σαγή, χάμουρα ntpl, χαμούρωμα nt ♦ vt (horse) χαμουρώνω.

harp [haːp] n άρπα || ~ist n αρπιστής.

harpoon [haː'puːn] n καμάκι.

harrow ['hærəu] n βωλοκόπος, σβάρνα ♦ vt βωλοκοπώ.

harrowing ['hærəuiŋ] a θλιβερός, σπαρακτικός.

harsh [haːʃ] a σκληρός, τραχύς || ~ly ad σκληρά, απότομα || ~ness n τραχύτητα, σκληρότητα || (of taste) ξυνίλα.

harvest ['haːvist] n συγκομιδή, εσοδεία || (season) θέρος nt, εποχή θερισμού ♦ vt θερίζω, μαζεύω.

harvester ['haːvistə*] n θεριστική μηχανή.

has [hæz] see have.

hash [hæʃ] n κιμάς ♦ vt κατακόπτω, κάνω κιμά.

hashish ['hæʃiːʃ] n χασίς nt inv.

haste [heist] n βία, βιασύνη, γρηγοράδα || ~n vt σπεύδω, επιταχύνω ♦ vi βιάζομαι, κάνω γρήγορα.

hastily ['heistili] ad βιαστικά.

hasty ['heisti] a βιαστικός, οξύθυμος.

hat [hæt] n καπέλλο.

hatch [hætʃ] n καταπακτή, μπουκαπόρτα ♦ vi εκκολάπτομαι, βγαίνω, σκάω ♦ vt κλωσώ.

hatchet ['hætʃit] n τσεκούρι.

hate [heit] vt μισώ ♦ n μίσος nt || ~ful a μισητός.

hatred ['heitrid] n έχθρα, μίσος nt.

haughty ['hɔːti] a υπεροπτικός, αυθάδης.

haul [hɔːl] n τράβηγμα nt || (fish) δίχτυά ♦ vt έλκω, τραβώ, σύρω || ~age n μεταφορά εμπορευμάτων.

haunch [hɔːntʃ] n ισχίο, γοφός.

haunt [hɔːnt] n λημέρι, στέκι ♦ vt συχνάζω σε || (of ghosts) στοιχειώνω.

have [hæv] (irreg v) vt έχω, κατέχω || (be obliged) αναγκάζω, έχω να, πρέπει να || (meal) λαμβάνω, παίρνω || (obtain) παίρνω || (children etc) γεννώ, κάνω || to ~ on vt φορώ.

haven ['heivn] n λιμάνι || (refuge) καταφύγιο, άσυλο.

haversack ['hævəsæk] n σακκίδιο || (MIL) γυλιός.

havoc ['hævək] n πανωλεθρία, καταστροφή.

hawk [hɔːk] n γεράκι.

hay [hei] n σανός, άχυρο || ~ fever n αλλεργικό συνάχι || ~stack n θημωνιά.

haywire ['haiwaiə*] a (col) it's gone ~ δεν πάει καλά.

hazard ['hæzəd] n (chance) τύχη || (danger) κίνδυνος ♦ vt διακινδυνεύω, ριψοκινδυνεύω || ~ous a ριψοκίνδυνος.

haze [heiz] n καταχνιά.

hazelnut ['heizlnʌt] n φουντούκι.

hazy ['heizi] a (weather) καταχνιασμένος || (vague) αμυδρός, αόριστος.

he [hiː] pron αυτός, εκείνος || αρσενικός.

head [hɛd] n (ANAT) κεφάλι || (leader) αρχηγός, προϊστάμενος, διευθυντής || (top) άκρο ♦ a πρωτεύων, κύριος ♦ vt ηγούμαι, διευθύνω, διοικώ || to ~ for vt κινούμαι προς, κατευθύνομαι || ~ache n κεφαλόπονος, πονοκέφαλος || ~ing n

επικεφαλίδα, τίτλος || ~lamp n
προβολέας, φανάρι || ~land n ακρωτήρι
|| ~light = ~lamp || ~line n
επικεφαλίδα, τίτλος || ~long ad με το
κεφάλι, απερίσκεπτος || ~master n
διευθυντής σχολείου || ~mistress n
διευθύντρια (σχολείου) || ~-on a κατά
μέτωπο || ~quarters (H.Q.) npl
αρχηγείο, στρατηγείο || ~rest n
προσκέφαλο || ~strong a
ισχυρογνώμονας, ξεροκέφαλος || ~
waiter n αρχισερβιτόρος, μαίτρ m inv ||
~way n πρόοδος f || ~wind n
αντίθετος άνεμος, αέρας κόντρα || ~y a
ορμητικός, φουριόζος || (drink etc) που
ζαλίζει, βαράει στο κεφάλι.

heal [hi:l] vt θεραπεύω, γιατρεύω ♦ vi
επουλώνομαι, γιατρεύομαι.

health [helθ] n υγεία || (toast) πρόποση ||
~y a υγιής, εύρωστος, γερός.

heap [hi:p] n σωρός || πλήθος nt ♦ vt
γεμίζω, συσσωρεύω.

hear [hɪə*] (irreg v) vt ακούω || ακρόομαι
|| (learn) ακούω, μαθαίνω || ~ing n (sense)
ακοή || ακρόαση || (LAW) (ακροαματική)
εξέταση μαρτύρων || ~ing aid n
ακουστικά ntpl βαρυκοΐας || ~say n
φήμη, διάδοση.

hearse [hɜ:s] n νεκροφόρα.

heart [ha:t] n (ANAT) καρδιά || (centre)
καρδιά || (courage) θάρρος nt || (emotion)
ψυχή || (tenderness) καρδιά, ψυχή ||
(CARDS) κούπα || ~ attack n καρδιακή
προσβολή || ~beat n παλμός καρδιάς ||
~breaking a θλιβερός, λυπηπερός ||
~broken a περίλυπος, θλιμμένος ||
~burn n καρδιαλγία, καούρα
(στομάχου) || ~felt a εγκάρδιος,
γκαρδιακός.

hearth [ha:θ] n τζάκι || πυροστιά.

heartily ['ha:tɪlɪ] ad ειλικρινά, με όρεξη,
τελείως.

heartless ['ha:tlɪs] a άκαρδος.

hearty ['ha:tɪ] a εγκάρδιος || (healthy)
εύρωστος || (meal) πλούσιος, θρεπτικός.

heat [hi:t] n θερμότητα || (weather) ζέστη,
κάψα || (anger) έξαψη, οργή || (SPORT)
αγώνας δρόμου, κούρσα ♦ vt θερμαίνω,
ζεσταίνω || to ~ up vi ανάβω, (υπερι-)
θερμαίνομαι || ~ed a ζεστός,
θερμασμένος || ~er n θερμάστρα,
σόμπα.

heath [hi:θ] n (Brit) χέρσα γη, ρεικιά ||
ρείκη.

heathen ['hi:ðən] n ειδωλολάτρης,
εθνικός ♦ a ειδωλολατρικός.

heather ['hɛðə*] n (ε)ρείκι.

heating ['hi:tɪŋ] n θέρμανση.

heatstroke ['hi:tstrəʊk] n
θερμοπληξία.

heatwave ['hi:tweıv] n κύμα nt ζέστης,
καύσωνας.

heave [hi:v] (irreg v) vt σηκώνω,
ανυψώνω || (throw) ρίχνω ♦ vi ανυψώνομαι
|| (NAUT) βιράρω ♦ n ανύψωση, σήκωμα
nt || φούσκωμα nt.

heaven ['hɛvən] n ουρανός || for ~'s

sakel για όνομα του Θεού! || **good** ~s!
Θεέ μου! || ~ly a ουράνιος || (col)
περίφημος.

heavily ['hɛvɪlɪ] ad βαρειά, δυνατά.

heavy ['hɛvɪ] a βαρύς || (difficult)
δύσκολος, δύσβατος || (abundant)
άφθονος.

Hebrew ['hi:bru:] n (person) Εβραίος/α
m/f || (LING) Εβραϊκά ntpl ♦ a εβραϊκός.

heckle ['hɛkl] vt βομβαρδίζω με
ενοχλητικές ερωτήσεις.

hectic ['hɛktɪk] a πυρετώδης ||
ταραχώδης.

hedge [hɛdʒ] n φράχτης, φραγμός ♦ vt
(surround) περιφράσσω, φράσσω ♦ vi
υπεκφεύγω, μασώ τα λόγια μου.

hedgehog ['hɛdʒhɒg] n σκαντζόχοιρος.

heed [hi:d] vt προσέχω ♦ n προσοχή ||
~less a απρόσεκτος, αμέριμνος.

heel [hi:l] n φτέρνα || (of shoe) τακούνι ♦
vt (shoe) βάζω τακούνι σε.

hefty ['hɛftɪ] a δυνατός, ρωμαλέος.

heifer ['hɛfə*] n δαμάλι.

height [haıt] n (of person) ανάστημα nt,
μπόι || (of object) ύψος nt, ύψωμα nt ||
ακμή || (of mountain) κορυφή || ~en vt
υψώνω, αυξάνω.

heir [ɛə*] n κληρονόμος || ~ess n n
κληρονόμος || ~loom n οικογενειακό
κειμήλιο.

held [hɛld] pt, pp of hold.

helicopter ['hɛlɪkɒptə*] n ελικόπτερο.

hell [hɛl] n κόλαση.

he'll [hi:l] = he will, he shall || see
will, shall.

hellish ['hɛlɪʃ] a απαίσιος, καταχθόνιος.

hello [hə'ləʊ] excl (greeting) γεια σου! ||
(TEL) αλλό! || (surprise) μπα, μπα!

helm [hɛlm] n τιμόνι, δοιάκι.

helmet ['hɛlmɪt] n κράνος nt, κάσκα ||
περικεφαλαία.

helmsman ['hɛlmzmən] n
πηδαλιούχος.

help [hɛlp] n βοήθεια ♦ vt βοηθώ,
ενισχύω || (prevent) αποφεύγω, εμποδίζω
|| (serve food) σερβίρω || ~er n βοηθός
m/f || ~ful a χρήσιμος || ~ing n μερίδα ||
~less a αβοήθητος, σε αμηχανία.

hem [hɛm] n στρίφωμα nt || to ~ in vt
περικυκλώνω, στρυμώνω.

hemisphere ['hɛmɪsfɪə*] n ημισφαίριο.

hemp [hɛmp] n κάνναβη, καννάβι.

hen [hɛn] n κότα, θηλυκό πουλί || ~coop
n κοτέτσι.

hence [hɛns] ad απ'εδώ, από τώρα ||
(therefore) απ'αυτό.

henchman ['hɛntʃmən] n πιστός
οπαδός, μπράβος.

her [hɜ:*] pron αυτή ♦ a δικός της.

herald ['hɛrəld] n κήρυκας, πρόδρομος
♦ vt αναγγέλλω, προμηνύω,
προαγγέλλω.

heraldry ['hɛrəldrɪ] n οικοσημολογία.

herb [hɜ:b] n βότανο, χόρτο.

herd [hɜ:d] n (general) κοπάδι.

here [hɪə*] ad εδώ ♦ n εδώ || ~! να! ||
come ~! έλα (δω)! || ~after ad στο

εξής ♦ n μέλλουσα ζωή || ~by ad μ'αυτό, διά του παρόντος.

hereditary [hɪ'redɪtrɪ] a κληρονομικός.

heredity [hɪ'redɪtɪ] n κληρονομικότητα.

heresy ['herɪsɪ] n αίρεση.

heretic ['herətɪk] n αιρετικός || ~al [hɪ'retɪkəl] a αιρετικός.

herewith ['hɪə'wɪð] ad με το παρόν, μ'αυτό.

heritage ['herɪtɪdʒ] n κληρονομία.

hermit ['hɜːmɪt] n ερημίτης.

hernia ['hɜːnɪə] n κήλη.

hero ['hɪərəʊ] n ήρωας, παλικάρι || (of a story) πρωταγωνιστής || ~ic a ηρωικός.

heroin ['herəʊɪn] n ηρωίνη.

heroine ['herəʊɪn] n ηρωίδα, πρωταγωνίστρια.

heroism ['herəʊɪzm] n ηρωϊσμός.

heron ['herən] n ερωδιός, τσικνιάς.

herring ['herɪŋ] n ρέγγα.

hers [hɜːz] pron αυτής, δικός της.

herself [hɜː'self] pron η ίδια, τον εαυτό της.

he's [hiːz] = **he is, he has** || see be, have.

hesitant ['hezɪtənt] a διστακτικός.

hesitate ['hezɪteɪt] vi διστάζω.

hesitation [hezɪ'teɪʃən] n δισταγμός, ενδοιασμός.

het up ['het'ʌp] a θυμωμένος, στενοχωρημένος.

hew [hjuː] (irreg v) vt κατακόπτω, πελεκώ.

hexagon ['heksəgən] n εξάγωνο.

heyday ['heɪdeɪ] n ακμή, άνθος nt, καλές μέρες fpl.

hi [haɪ] excl ε!, συ! || (US) καλημέρα!, γεια σου!

hibernate ['haɪbəneɪt] vi διαχειμάζω.

hiccough, hiccup ['hɪkʌp] vi έχω λόξυγγα || ~s npl λόξυγγας.

hid [hɪd] pt of hide.

hidden ['hɪdn] pp of hide.

hide [haɪd] (irreg v) n δέρμα nt, πετσί, τομάρι ♦ vt (από) κρύβω ♦ vi κρύβομαι || ~-and-seek n κρυφτό.

hideous ['hɪdɪəs] a φρικτός, αποκρουστικός, άσχημος.

hiding ['haɪdɪŋ] n (beating) σπάσιμο στο ξύλο || in ~ (concealed) κρυμμένος || ~ place n κρυψώνας.

hierarchy ['haɪərɑːkɪ] n ιεραρχία.

high [haɪ] a (far up) ψηλός || (tall) ψηλός || (rank) ανώτερος, σπουδαίος || (class) ανώτερος || (price) μεγάλος, ψηλός || (pressure etc) ψηλός, μεγάλος || (opinion) μεγάλη εκτίμηση σε ♦ ad ψηλά, πλούσια || ~chair n ψηλό καρεκλάκι για μωρά || ~-handed a αυθαίρετα || ~-heeled a με ψηλά τακούνια || ~light n (fig) αποκορύφωμα nt, το μεγάλο νούμερο || ~ly ad εξαιρετικά, πάρα πολύ || ~ly strung a ευερέθιστος, νευρικός || H~ Mass n μεγάλη λειτουργία (των Καθολικών) || ~ness n (title) υψηλότητα || ~-pitched a (voice) διαπεραστικός, οξύς.

high school ['haɪskuːl] n γυμνάσιο.

highway ['haɪweɪ] n εθνική οδός f.

hijack ['haɪdʒæk] vt κάνω αεροπειρατία || ~er n (AVIAT) αεροπειρατής.

hike [haɪk] vi πεζοπορώ ♦ n πεζοπορία || ~r n πεζοπόρος.

hiking ['haɪkɪŋ] n πεζοπορία.

hilarious [hɪ'leərɪəs] a ιλαρός, εύθυμος.

hilarity [hɪ'lærɪtɪ] n ιλαρότητα, ευθυμία.

hill [hɪl] n λόφος || ~y a λοφώδης.

hilt [hɪlt] n λαβή (ξίφους) || up to the ~ τελείως.

him [hɪm] pron αυτόν, σ'αυτόν.

himself [hɪm'self] pron τον εαυτό του, (αυτός) ο ίδιος.

hind [haɪnd] a οπίσθιος ♦ n έλαφος f.

hinder ['hɪndə*] vt εμποδίζω, κωλύω.

hindrance ['hɪndrəns] n εμπόδιο.

Hindu ['hɪn'duː] n Ινδός/ή m/f.

hinge [hɪndʒ] n άρθρωση, μεντεσές m ♦ vt κρεμώ σε μεντεσέδες ♦ vi (fig) εξαρτώμαι.

hint [hɪnt] n νύξη, υπαινιγμός ♦ vi υπαινίσσομαι.

hip [hɪp] n ισχίο, γοφός.

hippopotamus [hɪpə'pɒtəməs] n ιπποπόταμος.

hire ['haɪə*] n μίσθωση, ενοικίαση ♦ vt (worker) μισθώνω, πληρώνω, προσλαμβάνω || (rent) ενοικιάζω || (car) νοικιάζω || 'for ~' 'ελεύθερον', 'ενοικιάζεται' || ~ purchase (H.P.) n με δόσεις.

his [hɪz] pron δικός του ♦ a αυτού, (δικός) του.

hiss [hɪs] n σφύριγμα nt ♦ vi αποδοκιμάζω, σφυρίζω.

historian [hɪs'tɔːrɪən] n ιστορικός.

historic(al) [hɪs'tɒrɪk(əl)] a ιστορικός.

history ['hɪstərɪ] n ιστορία.

hit [hɪt] (irreg v) n κτύπημα nt || (success) επιτυχία ♦ vt κτυπάω, πλήττω || (target) ευστοχώ.

hitch [hɪtʃ] n τίναγμα nt, τράβηγμα nt || (bend) θηλειά || (fig) εμπόδιο ♦ vt δένω, προσδένω || (jerk) τραντάζω.

hitch-hike ['hɪtʃhaɪk] vi κάνω ωτοστόπ || ~r n αυτός που κάνει ωτοστόπ.

hive [haɪv] n κυψέλη.

H.M.S. abbr of His (Her) Majesty's Ship.

hoard [hɔːd] n θησαυρός, σωρός ♦ vt συσσωρεύω, θησαυρίζω, αποκρύπτω.

hoarding ['hɔːdɪŋ] n αποθησαυρισμός, απόκρυψη.

hoarse [hɔːs] a βραχνιασμένος.

hoax [həʊks] n αστείο, τέχνασμα nt, φάρσα.

hobble ['hɒbl] vi χωλαίνω, κουτσαίνω.

hobby ['hɒbɪ] n μεράκι, χόμπυ nt inv.

hobo ['həʊbəʊ] n (US) αλήτης.

hock [hɒk] n (wine) άσπρο κρασί του Ρήνου.

hockey ['hɒkɪ] n χόκεϊ nt inv.

hoe [həʊ] n σκαλιστήρι ♦ vt σκαλίζω.

hog [hɒg] n γουρούνι.

hoist [hɔɪst] n ανελκυστήρας || τράβηγμα nt, σηρώξιμο nt ♦ vt ανυψώνω.

hold [həʊld] (irreg v) n λαβή, πιάσιμο || (influence) έχω επιρροή πάνω σε || (NAUT) αμπάρ ♦ vt (grasp) κρατώ || (keep) κρατώ, φέρω || (contain) περιέχω || (keep back) συγκρατώ, σταματώ || (meeting etc) συγκαλώ, κάνω || (title) κατέχω, έχω || to ~ back vt συγκρατώ || (secret) αποκρύβω || (control) αναχαιτίζω || to ~ down vt κρατώ || to ~ out vt εκτείνω || (resist) αντέχω || to ~ up vt (support) υποστηρίζω || (display) επιδεικνύω || (stop) σταματώ, καθυστερώ || (rob) ληστεύω ♦ vi (withstand pressure) αντέχω || ~er n κάτοχος m/f || (handle) λαβή, σφιγκτήρας || ~ing n (share) μετοχή || ~up n καθυστέρηση || (robbery) ληστεία.

hole [həʊl] n τρύπα ♦ vt τρυπώ, ανοίγω.

holiday ['hɒlɪdeɪ] n γιορτή, αργία || (annual) διακοπές fpl || ~-maker n παραθεριστής/ρια m/f.

holiness ['həʊlɪnɪs] n αγιότητα.

Holland ['hɒlənd] n Ολλανδία.

hollow ['hɒləʊ] a βαθουλός, κοίλος || (empty) κούφιος || (false) ψεύτικος ♦ n κοίλωμα nt, βαθούλωμα nt, γούβα || to ~ out vt βαθουλώνω, σκάβω.

holly ['hɒlɪ] n (tree) πουρνάρι.

holster ['həʊlstə*] n πιστολιοθήκη.

holy ['həʊlɪ] a άγιος, ιερός || (divine) θείος.

homage ['hɒmɪdʒ] n υποταγή.

home [həʊm] n σπίτι, κατοικία || (native country) πατρίδα || (institution) άσυλο ♦ a (country) πατρίδα || (local) εγχώριος, ντόπιος ♦ ad στο σπίτι, στην πατρίδα || at ~ στο σπίτι || (at ease) άνετα || ~coming n επάνοδος f, επαναπατρισμός || ~less a άστεγος || ~-made a σπιτίσιος, ντόπιος || ~sick a νοσταλγός || ~ward(s) ad προς το σπίτι || ~work n κατ'οίκον εργασία.

homicide ['hɒmɪsaɪd] n (US) ανθρωποκτονία.

homogeneous [hɒmə'dʒiːnɪəs] a ομοιογενής.

homosexual ['hɒməʊ'sɛksjʊəl] a ομοφυλόφιλος ♦ n ομοφυλόφιλος, ανώμαλος.

honest ['ɒnɪst] a τίμιος, έντιμος, ευθύς || ~ly ad τίμια || ~y n εντιμότητα.

honey ['hʌnɪ] n μέλι || ~comb n κερήθρα || ~moon n μήνας του μέλιτος.

honk [hɒŋk] n (AUT) κορνάρισμα nt ♦ vi κορνάρω.

honor ['ɒnə*] (US) = honour.

honorary ['ɒnərərɪ] a τιμητικός || (degree etc) επίτιμος.

honour ['ɒnə*] n τιμή, υπόληψη ♦ vt τιμώ || (bill) εξοφλώ, πληρώνω || ~s npl (UNIV) τίτλος, τιμητική διάκριση || ~able a έντιμος || (title) εντιμότατος.

hood [hʊd] n κουκούλα, σκούφος || (cover) κάλυμμα nt || (US AUT) καπό || ~wink vt εξαπατώ, κοροϊδεύω.

hoof [huːf] n οπλή, πέλμα nt, νύχι.

hook [hʊk] n αγκίστρι, γάντζος ♦ vt αγκιστρώνω, γαντζώνω.

hooligan ['huːlɪgən] n ταραχοποιός.

hoop [huːp] n στεφάνι, τσέρκι.

hoot [huːt] n (of owl) σκούξιμο || (AUT) κορνάρισμα n ♦ vi γιουχαΐζω, σφυρίζω || ~er n (NAUT) σειρήνα, σφυρίχτρα || (AUT) κλάξον nt inv, κόρνα.

hop [hɒp] n χοροπήδημα nt, πήδημα nt ♦ vi σκιρτώ, πηδώ, χοροπηδώ.

hope [həʊp] n ελπίδα ♦ vt ελπίζω || ~ful a γεμάτος ελπίδες, ελπιδοφόρος || ~less a (without hope) απελπισμένος || (useless) μάταιος.

hops [hɒps] npl λυκίσκος.

horde [hɔːd] n ορδή, στίφος.

horizon [hə'raɪzn] n ορίζοντας || ~tal [hɒrɪ'zɒntl] a οριζόντιος.

hormone ['hɔːməʊn] n ορμόνη.

horn [hɔːn] n κέρατο || (insect) κεραία || (MUS) κέρας nt, κόρνα || (AUT) κλάξον nt inv || ~ed a με κέρατα.

hornet ['hɔːnɪt] n σφήκα.

horny ['hɔːnɪ] a κεράτινος, σκληρός.

horoscope ['hɒrəskəʊp] n ωροσκόπιο.

horrible ['hɒrɪbl] a φρικτός, φρικώδης, απαίσιος.

horrid ['hɒrɪd] a φρικτός, αποτρόπαιος || (col) κακός.

horrify ['hɒrɪfaɪ] vt τρομάζω || (shock) σκανδαλίζω.

horror ['hɒrə*] n φρίκη, τρόμος.

hors d'oeuvres [ɔ'dɜːvr] npl ορεκτικά ntpl, μεζεδάκια ntpl, ορντέβρ nt inv.

horse [hɔːs] n άλογο || on ~back καβάλα || ~ chestnut n αγριοκάστανο || ~-drawn a ιπποκίνητο || ~power n (h.p.) ιπποδύναμη || ~-racing n ιπποδρομίες fpl || ~shoe n πέταλο.

horticulture ['hɔːtɪkʌltʃə] n κηπουρική.

hose [həʊz] n (water) σωλήνας ποτίσματος || ~pipe n μάνικα, σωλήνας.

hosiery ['həʊʒərɪ] n πλεκτά είδη και κάλτσες pl.

hospitable [hɒs'pɪtəbl] a φιλόξενος.

hospital ['hɒspɪtl] n νοσοκομείο.

hospitality [hɒspɪ'tælɪtɪ] n φιλοξενία.

host [həʊst] n οικοδεσπότης || (hotel) ξενοδόχος, χανιτζής || (large number) πλήθος nt, στρατιά.

hostage ['hɒstɪdʒ] n όμηρος.

hostel ['hɒstəl] n οικοτροφείο, χάνι.

hostess ['həʊstɛs] n οικοδέσποινα.

hostile ['hɒstaɪl] a εχθρικός.

hostility [hɒs'tɪlɪtɪ] n εχθρότητα || hostilities npl εχθροπραξίες fpl.

hot [hɒt] a θερμός, ζεστός || (fiery) οξύθυμος, αναμμένος || ~ dog n λουκάνικο || ~-water bottle n θερμοφόρα.

hotel [həʊ'tɛl] n ξενοδοχείο || (residential) πανσιόν f inv.

hound [haʊnd] n σκυλί, λαγωνικό ♦ vt καταδιώκω, παροτρύνω.

hour ['aʊə*] n ώρα || ~ly a, ad κάθε ώρα.

house [haʊs] n σπίτι, κατοικία || (PARL) βουλή || (THEAT) ακροατήριο ♦ [haʊz] vt στεγάζω || (store) αποθηκεύω || ~boat n πλωτό σπίτι || ~breaking n διάρρηξη

σπιτιού || ~hold n σπίτι || οικογένεια,
σπιτικό || ~keeper n οικονόμος m/f ||
~keeping n νοικοκυριό || ~wife n
νοικοκυρά || ~work n δουλειές του
νοικοκυριού.

housing ['hauzɪŋ] n στέγαση.

hovel ['hɒvl] n καλύβα.

hover ['hɒvə*] vi μετεωρίζομαι,
πλανώμαι || (between) διστάζω,
ταλαντεύομαι || ~craft n χόβερκραφτ nt
inv.

how [hau] ad πώς, με ποιο τρόπο ||
(extent) πόσο || and ~! (US) και βέβαια!,
ασφαλώς! || ~ever ad όπως κι αν ||
(much) οσοδήποτε, όσο κι αν || (yet)
ωστόσο, κι όμως.

howl [haul] n ούρλιασμα nt, ουρλιαχτό ♦
vi ουρλιάζω, σκούζω.

howler ['haulə*] n ωρύόμενος ||
(mistake) γκάφα, χοντροκοπιά.

h.p., H.P. see hire; horse.

H.Q. abbr of headquarters.

hub [hʌb] n (of wheel) αφαλός || (of
activity) κέντρο.

hubbub ['hʌbʌb] n φασαρία, θόρυβος,
οχλοβοή.

huddle ['hʌdl] n σωρός, κουβάρι || vi
συσσωρεύομαι, μαζεύομαι,
κουλουριάζομαι.

hue [hjuː] n χροιά, χρώμα, απόχρωση.

huff [hʌf] n παραφορά, θυμός.

hug [hʌg] n αγκάλιασμα nt ♦ vt
αγκαλιάζω, σφίγγω || (NAUT) to ~ the
shore παραπλέω, πλέω πλάι-πλάι στην
ακτή.

huge [hjuːdʒ] a πελώριος, θεόρατος,
τεράστιος.

hulk [hʌlk] n (NAUT) ξαρματωμένο πλοίο,
σαπιοκάραβο || (person) μπατάλης,
χοντράνθρωπος || ~ing a δυσκίνητος,
χοντρός, βαρύς.

hull [hʌl] n σκάφος nt, κουφάρι πλοίου.

hullo [hə'ləu] excl = hello.

hum [hʌm] n βόμβος, βουητό, ψίθυρος
♦ vi βουίζω, ψιθυρίζω || μουρμουρίζω.

human ['hjuːmən] a ανθρώπινος ♦ n
άνθρωπος.

humane [hjuː'meɪn] a ανθρωπιστικός,
φιλάνθρωπος.

humanity [hjuː'mænɪtɪ] n ανθρωπότητα
|| (kindness) φιλανθρωπία.

humble ['hʌmbl] a ταπεινός, απλός ||
(unimportant) ασήμαντος ♦ vt ταπεινώνω,
ξευτελίζω.

humbly ['hʌmblɪ] ad ταπεινά, απλά.

humdrum ['hʌmdrʌm] a μονότονος,
ανιαρός, πληκτικός.

humid ['hjuːmɪd] a υγρός, νοτερός ||
~ity n υγρασία, νότισμα nt.

humiliate [hjuː'mɪlɪeɪt] vt ταπεινώνω,
ξευτελίζω, κουρελιάζω.

humiliation [hjuːmɪlɪ'eɪʃən] n
ταπείνωση, κουρέλιασμα nt.

humility [hjuː'mɪlɪtɪ] n ταπεινότητα,
μετριοφροσύνη.

humor ['hjuːmə*] (US) = humour.

humorist ['hjuːmərɪst] n χιουμορίστας.

humorous ['hjuːmərəs] a γεμάτος
χιούμορ, εύθυμος.

humour ['hjuːmə*] n χιούμορ nt inv,
κέφι, διάθεση ♦ vt κάνω τα χατήρια,
κάνω τα κέφια.

hump [hʌmp] n καμπούρα.

hunch [hʌntʃ] n ύβος, καμπούρα ||
(suspicion) υποψία ♦ vt κυρτώνω,
καμπουριάζω || ~back n καμπούρης/α
m/f.

hundred ['hʌndrɪd] num, n εκατό ||
~weight n (weight = 112 pounds)
στατήρας.

hung [hʌŋ] pt, pp of hang.

Hungarian [hʌŋ'gɛərɪən] a ουγγρικός ♦
n (person) Ούγγρος/Ουγγαρέζα m/f ||
(LING) (τα) Ουγγρικά.

Hungary ['hʌŋgərɪ] n Ουγγαρία.

hunger ['hʌŋgə*] n πείνα || (desire)
σφοδρή επιθυμία ♦ vi πεινώ λαχταρώ.

hungrily ['hʌŋgrɪlɪ] ad άπληστα,
αχόρταγα, πεινασμένα.

hungry ['hʌŋgrɪ] a πεινασμένος.

hunt [hʌnt] n κυνήγι || (seeking)
αναζήτηση ♦ vt κυνηγώ || (search)
διώχνω ♦ vi κυνηγώ || (seek) ψάχνω ||
~er n κυνηγός || ~ing n κυνήγι.

hurdle ['hɜːdl] n (lit) φράκτης || (fig)
εμπόδιο.

hurl [hɜːl] vt εκσφενδονίζω, ρίχνω.

hurrah [hu'rɑː] n, **hurray** [hu'reɪ] n
ζητωκραυγή.

hurricane ['hʌrɪkən] n καταιγίδα,
λαίλαπας.

hurried ['hʌrɪd] a βιαστικός || ~ly ad
βιαστικά.

hurry ['hʌrɪ] n βία, βιασύνη ♦ vi
βιάζομαι, είμαι βιαστικός ♦ vt
επισπεύδω, βιάζω.

hurt [hɜːt] (irreg v) n κακό || (wound)
τραύμα nt, πληγή || (damage) βλάβη, ζημιά
♦ vt κτυπώ, τραυματίζω, πληγώνω ||
(insult) προσβάλλω, πειράζω ♦ vi πονώ,
θίγομαι || ~ful a βλαβερός.

hurtle ['hɜːtl] vt εκσφενδονίζω ♦ vi
(rush) εφορμώ, ρίχνομαι.

husband ['hʌzbənd] n άνδρας, σύζυγος.

hush [hʌʃ] n σιωπή, σιγή ♦ vt
(καθ)ησυχάζω ♦ vi σωπαίνω || ~!
σιωπή!, σούτ!

husk [hʌsk] n φλοιός, φλούδα, τσόφλι.

husky ['hʌskɪ] a (voice) βραχνός ||
γεροδεμένος ♦ n σκύλος ελκύθρου.

hustle ['hʌsl] n σπουδή, βιασύνη || (push)
σπρωξίδι ♦ vt (push) σπρώχνω ||
σκουντώ, βιάζω.

hut [hʌt] n καλύβα || (MIL) παράπηγμα nt.

hutch [hʌtʃ] n κλουβί.

hyacinth ['haɪəsɪnθ] n υάκινθος.

hybrid ['haɪbrɪd] n μιγάδας, μικτογενής,
νόθος ♦ a νόθος, μπασταρδεμένος.

hydrant ['haɪdrənt] n σωλήνας
πυρκαϊάς, στόμιο υδρολωψίας.

hydraulic [haɪ'drɔːlɪk] a υδραυλικός.

hydroelectric ['haɪdrəʊɪ'lektrɪk] a
υδροηλεκτρικός.

hydrogen ['haɪdrədʒən] n υδρογόνο.

hyena [haɪˈiːnə] n ύαινα.
hygiene [ˈhaɪdʒiːn] n υγιεινή.
hygienic [haɪˈdʒiːnɪk] a υγιεινός.
hymn [hɪm] n ύμνος, υμνωδία.
hyphen [ˈhaɪfən] n ενωτικό σημείο.
hypnosis [hɪpˈnəʊsɪs] n ύπνωση.
hypnotism [ˈhɪpnətɪzəm] n υπνωτισμός.
hypnotist [ˈhɪpnətɪst] n υπνωτιστής.
hypnotize [ˈhɪpnətaɪz] vt υπνωτίζω.
hypocrisy [hɪˈpɒkrɪsɪ] n υποκρισία.
hypocrite [ˈhɪpəkrɪt] n υποκριτής.
hypocritical [hɪpəˈkrɪtɪkl] a
υποκριτικός.
hypothesis [haɪˈpɒθɪsɪs] n υπόθεση.
hypothetic(al) [haɪpəˈθetɪk(əl)] a
υποθετικός.
hysteria [hɪsˈtɪərɪə] n υστερία.
hysterical [hɪsˈterɪkl] a υστερικός.
hysterics [hɪsˈterɪks] npl υστερία.

I

I [aɪ] pron εγώ.
ice [aɪs] n πάγος || (refreshment) παγωτό ♦
vt (cake) γκλασάρω ♦ vi (also ~ up)
παγώνω || ~ **axe** n πέλεκυς m πάγου ||
~**berg** n παγόβουνο || ~**box** n (US)
ψυγείο || ~ **cream** n παγωτό || ~-**cold** a
παγερός, παγωμένος || ~ **hockey** n
χόκεϋ στον πάγο.
icicle [ˈaɪsɪkl] n σταλακτίτης πάγου.
icing [ˈaɪsɪŋ] n κρούστα για κέικ,
γκλασάρισμα nt.
icon [ˈaɪkɒn] n εικόνα.
icy [ˈaɪsɪ] a (slippery) γλιστερός || (frozen)
παγετώδης, παγωμένος.
I'd [aɪd] = **I would**, **I had** || see
would, **have**.
idea [aɪˈdɪə] n ιδέα || (plan) σκοπός, ιδέα.
ideal [aɪˈdɪəl] n ιδανικό, ιδεώδες nt ♦ a
ιδανικός, ιδεώδης || ~**ist** n ιδεαλιστής.
identical [aɪˈdentɪkəl] a όμοιος, ίδιος,
απαράλλακτος.
identification [aɪdentɪfɪˈkeɪʃən] n
εξακρίβωση ταυτότητας, συνταύτιση.
identify [aɪˈdentɪfaɪ] vt (person)
διαπιστώνω, εξακριβώνω || (regard as
same) ταυτίζω.
identity [aɪˈdentɪtɪ] n ταυτότητα.
ideology [aɪdɪˈɒlədʒɪ] n ιδεολογία.
idiocy [ˈɪdɪəsɪ] n ηλιθιότητα.
idiom [ˈɪdɪəm] n ιδίωμα nt || (dialect)
διάλεκτος.
idiosyncrasy [ɪdɪəˈsɪŋkrəsɪ] n
ιδιοσυγκρασία.
idiot [ˈɪdɪət] n ηλίθιος, ανόητος || ~**ic**
[ɪdɪˈɒtɪk] a ηλίθιος.
idle [ˈaɪdl] a αργός || (lazy) οκνηρός,
τεμπέλης || (useless) μάταιος, ανωφελής ||
~**ness** n αργία, τεμπελιά || ~**r** n
αργόσχολος.
idol [ˈaɪdl] n είδωλο || ~**ize** vt λατρεύω,
θαυμάζω.
idyllic [ɪˈdɪlɪk] a ειδυλλιακός.
i.e. ad (abbr of id est) δηλ. (δηλαδή).

if [ɪf] cj (condition) εάν, αν, όταν || (whether)
αν.
ignite [ɪgˈnaɪt] vt αναφλέγω, ανάβω.
ignition [ɪgˈnɪʃən] n ανάφλεξη || ~ **key** n
(AUT) κλειδί (ξεκινήσεως).
ignorance [ˈɪgnərəns] n άγνοια.
ignorant [ˈɪgnərənt] a αμαθής, αγνοών.
ignore [ɪgˈnɔː*] vt αγνοώ, αψηφώ.
I'll [aɪl] = **I will**, **I shall** || see **will**,
shall.
ill [ɪl] a άρρωστος || (evil) κακός ♦ n κακό,
ατυχία || ~-**advised** a ασύνετος,
απερίσκεπτος || ~-**at-ease** a
στενοχωρημένος, ανήσυχος.
illegal [ɪˈliːgəl] a παράνομος || ~**ly** ad
παράνομα.
illegible [ɪˈledʒəbl] a δυσανάγνωστος.
illegitimate [ɪlɪˈdʒɪtɪmɪt] a νόθος.
ill-fated [ˈɪlˈfeɪtɪd] a κακότυχος.
ill-feeling [ˈɪlˈfiːlɪŋ] n κακία, έχθρα.
illicit [ɪˈlɪsɪt] a παράνομος, αθέμιτος.
illiterate [ɪˈlɪtərɪt] a αγράμματος.
ill-mannered [ˈɪlˈmænəd] a
κακότροπος, κακομαθημένος.
illness [ˈɪlnɪs] n ασθένεια, αρρώστεια.
illogical [ɪˈlɒdʒɪkəl] a παράλογος.
ill-treat [ˈɪlˈtriːt] vt
κακομεταχειρίζομαι.
illuminate [ɪˈluːmɪneɪt] vt φωτίζω,
φωταγωγώ.
illumination [ɪluːmɪˈneɪʃən] n φωτισμός,
φωταγώγηση.
illusion [ɪˈluːʒən] n αυταπάτη, πλάνη.
illusive [ɪˈluːsɪv] a, **illusory** [ɪˈluːsərɪ] a
απατηλός.
illustrate [ˈɪləstreɪt] vt εικονογραφώ.
illustration [ɪləsˈtreɪʃən] n
εικονογράφηση, εικόνα.
illustrious [ɪˈlʌstrɪəs] a ένδοξος,
επιφανής.
ill will [ˈɪlˈwɪl] n κακοβουλία, κακία.
I'm [aɪm] = **I am** || see **be**.
image [ˈɪmɪdʒ] n (statue) εικόνα, είδωλο ||
(likeness) ομοίωμα nt, αναπαράσταση ||
(reflection) είδωλο || ~**ry** n ρητορικά
σχήματα ntpl.
imaginable [ɪˈmædʒɪnəbl] a διανοητός.
imaginary [ɪˈmædʒɪnərɪ] a φανταστικός.
imagination [ɪmædʒɪˈneɪʃən] n
φαντασία.
imaginative [ɪˈmædʒɪnətɪv] a
ευφάνταστος, επινοητικός.
imagine [ɪˈmædʒɪn] vt φαντάζομαι,
διανοούμαι.
imbalance [ɪmˈbæləns] n ανισότητα,
ανισορροπία.
imbecile [ˈɪmbəsiːl] n βλάκας, ηλίθιος.
imbue [ɪmˈbjuː] vt (εμ)ποτίζω,
διαποτίζω.
imitate [ˈɪmɪteɪt] vt μιμούμαι,
αντιγράφω.
imitation [ɪmɪˈteɪʃən] n (απο)μίμηση.
imitator [ˈɪmɪteɪtə*] n μιμητής.
immaculate [ɪˈmækjʊlɪt] a άσπιλος,
άμωμος.
immaterial [ɪməˈtɪərɪəl] a ασήμαντος,
άυλος.

immature [ımə'tjuə*] a ανώριμος,
άγουρος.

immediate [ı'mi:dıət] a (near) άμεσος,
προσεχής || (present) επείγων, άμεσος ||
(not separated) πλησιέστερος || (instant)
άμεσος, στιγμιαίος || ~**ly** ad (at once)
αμέσως, στη στιγμή.

immense [ı'mens] a απέραντος,
άπειρος || ~**ly** ad με απέραντα.

immerse [ı'mɜːs] vt εμβαπτίζω, βυθίζω,
βουτώ.

immigrant ['ımıgrənt] n μετανάστης.

immigration [ımı'greıʃən] n
μετανάστευση.

imminent ['ımınənt] a επικείμενος,
άμεσος.

immobilize [ı'məubılaız] vt
ακινητοποιώ.

immoral [ı'mɒrəl] a ανήθικος,
κακοήθης || ~**ity** [ımə'rælıtı] n
ανηθικότητα.

immortal [ı'mɔːtl] a αθάνατος,
άφθαρτος ♦ n αθάνατος || ~**ize** vt
αποθανατίζω.

immune [ı'mjuːn] a απρόσβλητος.

immunize ['ımjunaız] vt ανοσοποιώ.

impact ['ımpækt] n (lit) σύγκρουση,
κτύπημα nt || (fig) επίδραση.

impair [ım'pεə*] vt βλάπτω, εξασθενίζω.

impale [ım'peıl] vt ανασκολοπίζω,
παλουκώνω.

impartial [ım'pɑːʃəl] a αμερόληπτος ||
~**ity** n αμεροληψία.

impassable [ım'pɑːsəbl] a αδιάβατος.

impatience [ım'peıʃəns] n
ανυπομονησία.

impatient [ım'peıʃənt] a ανυπόμονος ||
~**ly** ad ανυπόμονα, βιαστικά.

impeccable [ım'pεkəbl] a άψογος,
τέλειος.

impede [ım'piːd] vt εμποδίζω,
παρακωλύω.

impediment [ım'pεdımənt] n κώλυμα
nt, εμπόδιο.

impending [ım'pεndıŋ] a επικείμενος.

imperative [ım'pεrətıv] a επιτακτικός ♦
n (GRAM) προστακτική.

imperceptible [ımpə'sεptəbl] a
ανεπαίσθητος, αδιόρατος.

imperfect [ım'pɜːfıkt] a ελαττωματικός
|| (incomplete) ελλειπής || ~**ion** n ατέλεια,
ελάττωμα nt.

imperial [ım'pıərıəl] a αυτοκρατορικός ||
(majestic) μεγαλοπρεπής.

impersonal [ım'pɜːsnl] a απρόσωπος.

impersonate [ım'pɜːsəneıt] vt
προσωποποιώ, υποδύομαι, παριστάνω.

impersonation [ımpɜːsə'neıʃən] n
προσωποποίηση, ενσάρκωση, μίμηση.

impertinent [ım'pɜːtınənt] a αυθάδης,
άσχετος.

impervious [ım'pɜːvıəs] a
αδιαπέραστος, στεγανός,
ανεπηρέαστος.

impetuous [ım'pεtjuəs] a ορμητικός,
βίαιος.

impetus ['ımpıtəs] n ώθηση, ορμή.

impinge [ım'pındʒ]: **to** ~ **on** vt
συγκρούομαι, καταπατώ.

implausible [ım'plɔːzəbl] a απίθανος.

implement ['ımplımənt] n όργανο,
εργαλείο, σύνεργο ♦ ['ımplımənt] vt
εφαρμόζω.

implicate ['ımplıkeıt] vt εμπλέκω,
αναμιγνύω.

implication [ımplı'keıʃən] n
ενοχοποίηση, υπαινιγμός.

implicit [ım'plısıt] a υπονοούμενος,
σιωπηρός || (complete) απόλυτος,
αμέριστος.

implore [ım'plɔː*] vt ικετεύω, εκλιπαρώ.

imply [ım'plaı] vt υπονοώ, υπαινίσσομαι,
προϋποθέτω.

impolite [ımpə'laıt] a αγενής.

imponderable [ım'pɒndərəbl] a
ασταθμητος, ανεξιχνίαστος.

import [ım'pɔːt] vt εισάγω ♦ ['ımpɔːt] n
εισαγωγή || (meaning) σημασία.

importance [ım'pɔːtəns] n
σπουδαιότητα, σοβαρότητα || (value)
σημασία, αξία.

important [ım'pɔːtənt] a σημαντικός,
σπουδαίος.

importer [ım'pɔːtə*] n εισαγωγέας.

impose [ım'pəuz] vt επιβάλλω, επιτάσσω
|| (on s.o.) επωφελούμαι.

imposing [ım'pəuzıŋ] a επιβλητικός.

impossibility [ımpɒsə'bılıtı] n (το)
αδύνατο.

impossible [ım'pɒsəbl] a αδύνατος,
ακατόρθωτος, ανυπόφορος.

impostor [ım'pɒstə*] n αγύρτης,
απατεώνας.

impotence ['ımpətəns] n (esp sexual)
ανικανότητα.

impotent ['ımpətənt] a ανίκανος,
ανίσχυρος.

impound [ım'paund] vt κατάσχω.

impoverished [ım'pɒvərıʃt] a
πάμπτωχος, εξαντλημένος.

impracticable [ım'præktıkəbl] a
ακατόρθωτος, απραγματοποίητος.

impractical [ım'præktıkəl] a μη
πρακτικός.

impregnable [ım'prεgnəbl] a
απόρθητος.

impregnate ['ımprεgneıt] vt
γονιμοποιώ, εμποτίζω.

impress [ım'prεs] vt (influence) κάνω
εντύπωση || (imprint) εντυπώνω,
εγχαράσσω.

impression [ım'prεʃən] n (mark)
αποτύπωση, αποτύπωμα nt || (printed
copy) έκδοση || (effect) εντύπωση,
αίσθηση || (belief) ιδέα, εντύπωση, γνώμη
|| ~**able** a ευαίσθητος, ευσυγκίνητος ||
~**ist** n ιμπρεσσιονιστής.

impressive [ım'prεsıv] a
εντυπωσιακός, συγκινητικός.

imprison [ım'prızn] vt φυλακίζω ||
~**ment** n φυλάκιση.

improbable [ım'prɒbəbl] a απίθανος.

impromptu [ım'prɒmptjuː] a

αυτοσχέδιος, εκ του προχείρου ♦ *ad* εκ του προχείρου.

improper [ɪmˈprɒpə*] *a (wrong)* εσφαλμένος || *(unsuitable)* ανάρμοστος || *(indecent)* απρεπής.

impropriety [ɪmprəˈpraɪətɪ] *n* απρέπεια, ακαταλληλότητα.

improve [ɪmˈpruːv] *vt* βελτιώνω, κάνω καλύτερο ♦ *vi (become better)* βελτιούμαι, καλυτερεύω || ~**ment** *n* βελτίωση, πρόοδος *f*.

improvisation [ɪmprəvaɪˈzeɪʃən] *n* αυτοσχεδιασμός.

improvise [ˈɪmprəvaɪz] *vi* αυτοσχεδιάζω || *vt* κάνω εκ του προχείρου.

impudent [ˈɪmpjudənt] *a* αναιδής, αναίσχυντος.

impulse [ˈɪmpʌls] *n (sudden desire)* ορμή, ορμέμφυτο || ώθηση, αυθόρμητη διάθεση.

impulsive [ɪmˈpʌlsɪv] *a* αυθόρμητος, ορμέμφυτος.

impunity [ɪmˈpjuːnɪtɪ] *n* ατιμωρησία.

impure [ɪmˈpjuə*] *a* ακάθαρτος || *(bad)* μιαρός, αισχρός.

impurity [ɪmˈpjuərɪtɪ] *n* ακαθαρσία, ξένο σώμα *nt*.

in [ɪn] *prep* μέσα σε, εντός, σε || *(made of)* σε || *(expressed in)* σε, με || *(dressed in)* με ♦ *ad* εντός, μέσα || ~**s and outs** *npl* τα μέσα και τα έξω.

in., **ins** *abbr of* **inch(es)**.

inability [ɪnəˈbɪlɪtɪ] *n* ανικανότητα, αδυναμία.

inaccessible [ɪnækˈsɛsəbl] *a* απρόσιτος, απλησίαστος.

inaccuracy [ɪnˈækjʊrəsɪ] *n* ανακρίβεια.

inaccurate [ɪnˈækjʊrɪt] *a* ανακριβής, εσφαλμένος.

inactivity [ɪnækˈtɪvɪtɪ] *n* αδράνεια, αργία.

inadequacy [ɪnˈædɪkwəsɪ] *n* ανεπάρκεια, ατέλεια.

inadequate [ɪnˈædɪkwɪt] *a* ανεπαρκής, ατελής.

inadvertently [ɪnədˈvɜːtəntlɪ] *ad* απρόσεκτα, από αμέλεια.

inadvisable [ɪnədˈvaɪzəbl] *a* ασύμφορος.

inane [ɪˈneɪn] *a* κενός, ανόητος.

inanimate [ɪnˈænɪmɪt] *a* άψυχος.

inappropriate [ɪnəˈprəʊprɪɪt] *a* ακατάλληλος, ανάρμοστος.

inapt [ɪnˈæpt] *a* ανεπιτήδειος, αδέξιος || ~**itude** *n* ανικανότητα, αδεξιότητα.

inarticulate [ɪnɑːˈtɪkjʊlɪt] *a* άναρθρος, βουβός, ασύνδετος.

inasmuch [ɪnəzˈmʌtʃ]: ~ **as** *ad* επειδή, εφόσον.

inattention [ɪnəˈtɛnʃən] *n* απροσεξία, αφηρημάδα.

inattentive [ɪnəˈtɛntɪv] *a* απρόσεκτος, αμελής.

inaudible [ɪnˈɔːdəbl] *a* ανεπαίσθητος, ασθενής.

inaugural [ɪˈnɔːgjʊrəl] *a* εναρκτήριος.

inaugurate [ɪˈnɔːgjʊreɪt] *vt* εγκαινιάζω.

inauguration [ɪnɔːgjʊˈreɪʃən] *n* εγκαινιασμός, εγκαίνια *ntpl*.

inborn [ˈɪnˈbɔːn] *a* έμφυτος.

inbred [ˈɪnˈbrɛd] *a* έμφυτος, φυσικός.

Inc. *abbr see* **incorporated.**

incapability [ɪnkeɪpəˈbɪlɪtɪ] *n* ανικανότητα.

incapable [ɪnˈkeɪpəbl] *a* ανίκανος.

incapacitate [ɪnkəˈpæsɪteɪt] *vt* καθιστώ ανίκανο.

incarnate [ɪnˈkɑːnɪt] *a* ενσαρκωμένος.

incarnation [ɪnkɑːˈneɪʃən] *n* ενσάρκωση.

incendiary [ɪnˈsɛndɪərɪ] *a* εμπρηστικός ♦ *n* εμπρηστής.

incense [ˈɪnsɛns] *n* θυμίαμα *nt*, λιβάνι ♦ [ɪnˈsɛns] *vt* εξοργίζω, εξαγριώνω.

incentive [ɪnˈsɛntɪv] *n* κίνητρο, ελατήριο, τονωτικό.

incessant [ɪnˈsɛsnt] *a* αδιάκοπος || ~**ly** *ad* αδιάκοπα.

incest [ˈɪnsɛst] *n* αιμομιξία.

inch [ɪntʃ] *n* ίντσα *(.0254 μ.)*.

incidence [ˈɪnsɪdəns] *n* πρόσπτωση, περίπτωση.

incident [ˈɪnsɪdənt] *n* επεισόδιο, περιπέτεια || ~**al** *a* τυχαίος, συμπτωματικός || ~**ally** *ad* παρεπιπτόντως.

incinerator [ɪnˈsɪnəreɪtə*] *n* αποτεφρωτήρας.

incision [ɪnˈsɪʒən] *n* εντομή, χαραματιά.

incisive [ɪnˈsaɪsɪv] *a* κοφτερός || *(cutting)* δηκτικός.

incite [ɪnˈsaɪt] *vt* υποκινώ, παροτρύνω.

inclination [ɪnklɪˈneɪʃən] *n* κλίση, τάση, διάθεση.

incline [ˈɪnklaɪn] *n* κλίση ♦ [ɪnˈklaɪn] *vi* κλίνω, γέρνω || *(be disposed)* ρέπω, τείνω.

include [ɪnˈkluːd] *vt (συμ)περιλαμβάνω, περιέχω.

inclusion [ɪnˈkluːʒən] *n* συμπερίληψη.

inclusive [ɪnˈkluːsɪv] *a* συμπεριλαμβάνων, περιέχων.

incognito [ɪnˈkɒgnɪtəʊ] *ad* ινκόγνιτο.

incoherent [ɪnkəʊˈhɪərənt] *a* ασυνάρτητος.

income [ˈɪnkʌm] *n* εισόδημα *nt* || ~ **tax** *n* φόρος εισοδήματος.

incoming [ˈɪnkʌmɪŋ] *a (tide)* ανερχόμενος, εισερχόμενος.

incompatible [ɪnkəmˈpætəbl] *a* ασυμβίβαστος.

incompetence [ɪnˈkɒmpɪtəns] *n* αναρμοδιότητα, ανικανότητα.

incompetent [ɪnˈkɒmpɪtənt] *a* ανίκανος, αναρμόδιος.

incomplete [ɪnkəmˈpliːt] *a* ατελής.

incomprehensible [ɪnkɒmprɪˈhɛnsəbl] *a* ακατανόητος, ακατάληπτος.

inconclusive [ɪnkənˈkluːsɪv] *a* μη πειστικός.

incongruous [ɪnˈkɒŋgrʊəs] *a* ασύμφωνος, ανάρμοστος.

inconsequential [ɪnkɒnsɪˈkwɛnʃəl] *a* ανακόλουθος, ασήμαντος.

inconsiderate [ɪnkən'sɪdərɪt] a απερίσκεπτος, αδιάκριτος.

inconsistent [ɪnkən'sɪstənt] a ασυνεπής, αντιφατικός.

inconspicuous [ɪnkən'spɪkjuəs] a αφανής, απαρατήρητος.

inconstant [ɪn'kɒnstənt] a ευμετάβολος, ασταθής.

incontinent [ɪn'kɒntɪnənt] a ακρατής.

inconvenience [ɪnkən'viːnɪəns] n δυσχέρεια, ενόχληση, μπελάς.

inconvenient [ɪnkən'viːnɪənt] a στενόχωρος, ενοχλητικός, ακατάλληλος.

incorporate [ɪn'kɔːpəreɪt] vt ενσωματώνω, συγχωνεύω.

incorporated [ɪn'kɔːpəreɪtɪd] a ενσωματωμένος, συγχωνευμένος || ~ **company** (US, abbr Inc.) ανώνυμος (εταιρεία).

incorrect [ɪnkə'rɛkt] a εσφαλμένος, ανακριβής.

incorruptible [ɪnkə'rʌptəbl] a αδιάφθορος, ακέραιος, αδέκαστος.

increase ['ɪnkriːs] n αύξηση ♦ [ɪn'kriːs] vt αυξάνω, μεγαλώνω ♦ vi αυξάνομαι.

increasingly [ɪn'kriːsɪŋlɪ] ad διαρκώς περισσότερο.

incredible [ɪn'krɛdəbl] a απίστευτος.

incredulous [ɪn'krɛdjuləs] a δύσπιστος.

increment ['ɪnkrɪmənt] n αύξηση.

incriminate [ɪn'krɪmɪneɪt] vt ενοχοποιώ.

incubation [ɪnkju'beɪʃən] n επώαση, κλώσημα nt.

incubator ['ɪnkjubeɪtə*] n κλωσσομηχανή.

incur [ɪn'kɜː*] vt υφίσταμαι, διατρέχω, προκαλώ.

incurable [ɪn'kjuərəbl] a ανίατος, αγιάτρευτος.

incursion [ɪn'kɜːʃən] n επιδρομή.

indebted [ɪn'dɛtɪd] a υποχρεωμένος, υπόχρεος.

indecent [ɪn'diːsnt] a απρεπής, άσεμνος.

indecision [ɪndɪ'sɪʒən] n αναποφασιστικότητα, αοριστία.

indecisive [ɪndɪ'saɪsɪv] a μή αποφασιστικός.

indeed [ɪn'diːd] ad πράγματι, πραγματικά, αληθινά.

indefinable [ɪndɪ'faɪnəbl] a απροσδιόριστος.

indefinite [ɪn'dɛfɪnɪt] a αόριστος || ~ly ad επ'αόριστον.

indelible [ɪn'dɛləbl] a ανεξίτηλος.

indemnify [ɪn'dɛmnɪfaɪ] vt αποζημιώνω, εξασφαλίζω.

indentation [ɪndɛn'teɪʃən] n (typing) οδόντωση, χάραγμα nt.

independence [ɪndɪ'pɛndəns] n ανεξαρτησία.

independent [ɪndɪ'pɛndənt] a ανεξάρτητος.

indescribable [ɪndɪs'kraɪbəbl] a απερίγραπτος.

index ['ɪndɛks] n ευρετήριο || ~ **finger** n δείκτης.

India ['ɪndɪə] n Ινδία || ~n a n Ινδός/Ινδή m/f|| (of America) ερυθρόδερμος ♦ a ινδικός, ινδιάνικος.

indicate ['ɪndɪkeɪt] vt δεικνύω, εμφαίνω, έδηλω.

indication [ɪndɪ'keɪʃən] n ένδειξη, σημείο.

indicative [ɪn'dɪkətɪv] a (GRAM) οριστική (έγκλιση).

indicator ['ɪndɪkeɪtə*] n (sign) δείκτης.

indict [ɪn'daɪt] vt μηνύω, ενάγω, καταγγέλλω || ~**able** a ενακτέος || ~**ment** n μήνυση, κατηγορία.

indifference [ɪn'dɪfrəns] n αδιαφορία.

indifferent [ɪn'dɪfrənt] a (not caring) αδιάφορος || (unimportant) αδιάφορος || (neither good nor bad) συνηθισμένος, έτσι κι έτσι || (moderate) μέτριος, ουδέτερος || (impartial) αμερόληπτος.

indigenous [ɪn'dɪdʒɪnəs] a γηγενής, ιθαγενής, ντόπιος.

indigestible [ɪndɪ'dʒɛstəbl] a δυσκολοχώνευτος.

indigestion [ɪndɪ'dʒɛstʃən] n δυσπεψία.

indignant [ɪn'dɪgnənt] a αγανακτισμένος.

indignation [ɪndɪg'neɪʃən] n αγανάκτηση.

indignity [ɪn'dɪgnɪtɪ] n προσβολή, ταπείνωση.

indirect [ɪndɪ'rɛkt] a πλάγιος, έμμεσος || ~**ly** ad έμμεσα.

indiscreet [ɪndɪs'kriːt] a αδιάκριτος, απρόσεκτος.

indiscretion [ɪndɪs'krɛʃən] n αδιακρισία, ακριτομύθια.

indiscriminate [ɪndɪs'krɪmɪnɪt] a χωρίς διακρίσεις, τυφλός.

indispensable [ɪndɪs'pɛnsəbl] a απαραίτητος.

indisposed [ɪndɪs'pəuzd] a αδιάθετος, απρόθυμος.

indisputable [ɪndɪs'pjuːtəbl] a αναμφισβήτητος, αναμφίβολος.

indistinct [ɪndɪs'tɪŋkt] a αδιόρατος, συγκεχυμένος, αμυδρός.

individual [ɪndɪ'vɪdjuəl] n άτομο, πρόσωπο ♦ a ιδιαίτερος, ατομικός || ~**ist** n ατομικιστής || ~**ity** n ατομικότητα, προσωπικότητα.

indoctrinate [ɪn'dɒktrɪneɪt] vt διδάσκω, κατηχώ, εμποτίζω.

indoctrination [ɪndɒktrɪ'neɪʃən] n εμποτισμός, διδασκαλία.

indolent ['ɪndələnt] a νωθρός, τεμπέλης.

Indonesia [ɪndəu'niːzɪə] n Ινδουσία || ~n n Ινδουήσιος, ο ♦ a ινδουσιακός.

indoor ['ɪndɔː*] a του σπιτιού, εσωτερικός || ~s ad μέσα στο κτίριο.

indubitable [ɪn'djuːbɪtəbl] a αναμφίβολος, βέβαιος.

induce [ɪn'djuːs] vt πείθω, προτρέπω, προκαλώ || ~**ment** n προτροπή, κίνητρο.

indulge [ɪnˈdʌldʒ] vt ικανοποιώ || *(allow pleasure)* εντρυφώ, παραδίδομαι || ~**nce** n επιείκια, διασκέδαση, εντρύφηση || ~**nt** a επιεικής, συγκαταβατικός.

industrial [ɪnˈdʌstrɪəl] a βιομηχανικός || ~**ist** n βιομήχανος || ~**ize** vt εκβιομηχανίζω.

industrious [ɪnˈdʌstrɪəs] a φιλόπονος, επιμελής.

industry [ˈɪndəstrɪ] n βιομηχανία || *(diligence)* φιλοπονία.

inebriated [ɪˈniːbrɪeɪtɪd] a μεθυσμένος.

inedible [ɪnˈedɪbl] a μη φαγώσιμος.

ineffective [ɪnɪˈfektɪv] a, **ineffectual** [ɪnɪˈfektjʊəl] a ατελέσφορος, μάταιος.

inefficiency [ɪnɪˈfɪʃənsɪ] n ανικανότητα, ανεπάρκεια.

inefficient [ɪnɪˈfɪʃənt] a ανίκανος, ατελέσφορος.

inelegant [ɪnˈelɪgənt] a άκομψος, άγαρμπος.

ineligible [ɪnˈelɪdʒəbl] a μη εκλέξιμος, ακατάλληλος.

inept [ɪˈnept] a άτοπος, ανόητος.

inequality [ɪnɪˈkwɒlɪtɪ] n ανισότητα.

ineradicable [ɪnɪˈrædɪkəbl] a αξερρίζωτος.

inert [ɪˈnɜːt] a αδρανής.

inertia [ɪˈnɜːʃə] n αδράνεια.

inescapable [ɪnɪsˈkeɪpəbl] a αναπόφευκτος.

inessential [ˈɪnɪˈsenʃəl] a μη απαραίτητος.

inestimable [ɪnˈestɪməbl] a ανεκτίμητος.

inevitable [ɪnˈevɪtəbl] a αναπόφευκτος.

inexact [ɪnɪgˈzækt] a ανακριβής.

inexhaustible [ɪnɪgˈzɔːstəbl] a ανεξάντλητος.

inexorable [ɪnˈeksərəbl] a αδυσώπητος, αμείλικτος.

inexpensive [ɪnɪksˈpensɪv] a φθηνός, ανέξοδος.

inexperience [ɪnɪksˈpɪərɪəns] n απειρία || ~**d** a άπειρος.

inexplicable [ɪnɪksˈplɪkəbl] a ανεξήγητος.

inextricable [ɪnɪksˈtrɪkəbl] a αδιέξοδος, άλυτος.

infallibility [ɪnfæləˈbɪlɪtɪ] n (το) αλάνθαστο.

infallible [ɪnˈfæləbl] a αλάνθαστος, σίγουρος.

infamous [ˈɪnfəməs] a κακόφημος.

infamy [ˈɪnfəmɪ] n ατιμία, κακοήθεια.

infancy [ˈɪnfənsɪ] n νηπιακή ηλικία || *(early stages)* απαρχές fpl, πρώτη περίοδος.

infant [ˈɪnfənt] n νήπιο, βρέφος nt || ~**ile** a παιδικός, παιδιάστικος || ~ **school** n κατώτερο δημοτικό σχολείο.

infantry [ˈɪnfəntrɪ] n πεζικό || ~**man** n στρατιώτης, φαντάρος.

infatuated [ɪnˈfætjʊeɪtɪd] a ξεμυαλισμένος, συνεπαρμένος.

infatuation [ɪnfætjuˈeɪʃən] n ξεμυάλισμα nt, τρέλα.

infect [ɪnˈfekt] vt μολύνω, μιαίνω, βρωμίζω || *(influence)* επηρεάζω || ~**ion** n μόλυνση, επίδραση || ~**ious** a μολυσματικός, μεταδοτικός.

infer [ɪnˈfɜː*] vt συνάγω, συμπεραίνω, υπονοώ || ~**ence** [ˈɪnfərəns] n συμπέρασμα nt, πόρισμα nt.

inferior [ɪnˈfɪərɪə*] a κατώτερος, υποδεέστερος ♦ n κατώτερος, υφιστάμενος || ~**ity** n κατωτερότητα, μειονεκτικότητα || ~**ity complex** n (ψυ)πλέγμα nt κατωτερότητας.

infernal [ɪnˈfɜːnl] a καταχθόνιος, διαβολικός, απαίσιος.

inferno [ɪnˈfɜːnəʊ] n κόλαση.

infertile [ɪnˈfɜːtaɪl] a άγονος, άκαρπος.

infertility [ɪnfɜːˈtɪlɪtɪ] n (το) άγονο, στειρότητα.

infest [ɪnˈfest] vt λυμαίνομαι, κατακλύζω.

infidelity [ɪnfɪˈdelɪtɪ] n απιστία.

infiltrate [ˈɪnfɪltreɪt] vti (δι)εισδύω, εισχωρώ.

infinite [ˈɪnfɪnɪt] a άπειρος, απέραντος.

infinitive [ɪnˈfɪnɪtɪv] n απαρέμφατο.

infinity [ɪnˈfɪnɪtɪ] n άπειρο, απεραντοσύνη.

infirmary [ɪnˈfɜːmərɪ] n νοσοκομείο, θεραπευτήριο.

infirmity [ɪnˈfɜːmɪtɪ] n αδυναμία, αναπηρία.

inflame [ɪnˈfleɪm] vt *(excite)* εξάπτω, ερεθίζω.

inflammable [ɪnˈflæməbl] a εύφλεκτος.

inflammation [ɪnfləˈmeɪʃən] n φλόγωση, ερεθισμός.

inflate [ɪnˈfleɪt] vt φουσκώνω || *(ECON)* προκαλώ πληθωρισμό.

inflation [ɪnˈfleɪʃən] n πληθωρισμός.

inflexible [ɪnˈfleksəbl] a άκαμπτος, αλύγιστος.

inflict [ɪnˈflɪkt] vt καταφέρω, δίνω, επιβάλλω || ~**ion** n επιβολή, βάρος nt, τιμωρία.

inflow [ˈɪnfləʊ] n εισροή.

influence [ˈɪnfluəns] n επίδραση, επιρροή ♦ vt επηρεάζω, επιδρώ.

influential [ɪnfluˈenʃəl] a σημαίνων, με επιρροή.

influenza [ɪnfluˈenzə] n γρίππη.

influx [ˈɪnflʌks] n εισροή, διείσδυση.

inform [ɪnˈfɔːm] vt πληροφορώ, ειδοποιώ.

informal [ɪnˈfɔːml] a ανεπίσημος, παράτυπος || ~**ity** n ανεπισημότητα.

information [ɪnfəˈmeɪʃən] n πληροφορίες fpl, είδηση.

informative [ɪnˈfɔːmətɪv] a κατατοπιστικός, πληροφοριακός.

informer [ɪnˈfɔːmə*] n καταδότης, χαφιές m inv.

infra-red [ɪnfrəˈred] a υπέρυθρος.

infrequent [ɪnˈfriːkwənt] a σπάνιος.

infringe [ɪnˈfrɪndʒ] vt παραβαίνω, παραβιάζω ♦ vi καταπατώ || ~**ment** n παράβαση.

infuriating [ɪnˈfjʊərɪeɪtɪŋ] a εξοργιστικός.

ingenious [ɪnˈdʒiːnɪəs] a οξύνους, πολυμήχανος.

ingenuity [ɪndʒɪˈnjuːɪtɪ] n ευφυΐα, οξύνοια.

ingot [ˈɪŋɡət] n ράβδος f, χελώνα.

ingratiate [ɪnˈɡreɪʃɪeɪt] vt αποκτώ εύνοια.

ingratitude [ɪnˈɡrætɪtjuːd] n αγνωμοσύνη.

ingredient [ɪnˈɡriːdɪənt] n συστατικό.

inhabit [ɪnˈhæbɪt] vt κατοικώ, μένω || ~ant n κάτοικος m/f.

inhale [ɪnˈheɪl] vt εισπνέω, ρουφώ.

inherent [ɪnˈhɪərənt] a (+ in) συμφυής, έμφυτος.

inherit [ɪnˈhɛrɪt] vt κληρονομώ || ~ance n κληρονομία.

inhibit [ɪnˈhɪbɪt] vt εμποδίζω, αναχαιτίζω, απαγορεύω || ~ion n απαγόρευση, αναχαίτιση.

inhospitable [ɪnhɒsˈpɪtəbl] a αφιλόξενος.

inhuman [ɪnˈhjuːmən] a απάνθρωπος.

inimitable [ɪˈnɪmɪtəbl] a αμίμητος.

iniquity [ɪˈnɪkwɪtɪ] n αδικία, κακοήθεια.

initial [ɪˈnɪʃəl] a αρχικός, πρώτος ♦ n αρχικό ♦ vt μονογραφώ || ~ly ad αρχικά, κατ' αρχήν.

initiate [ɪˈnɪʃɪeɪt] vt αρχίζω, εισάγω || (in a society) μυώ.

initiation [ɪnɪʃɪˈeɪʃən] n μύηση.

initiative [ɪˈnɪʃɪətɪv] n πρωτοβουλία.

inject [ɪnˈdʒɛkt] vt εγχέω, εισάγω, κάνω ένεση || ~ion n έγχυση, ένεση.

injure [ˈɪndʒə*] vt βλάπτω, ζημιώνω, πληγώνω.

injury [ˈɪndʒərɪ] n βλάβη, τραύμα nt, ζημιά.

injustice [ɪnˈdʒʌstɪs] n αδικία.

ink [ɪŋk] n μελάνι.

inkling [ˈɪŋklɪŋ] n υποψία, υπόνοια.

inlaid [ˈɪnˈleɪd] a εμπαιστός.

inland [ˈɪnlænd] a εσωτερικός, μεσόγειος ♦ ad στο εσωτερικό, στα ενδότερα || ~ **revenue** n (Brit) Τμήμα Εσωτερικών Προσόδων.

in-laws [ˈɪnlɔːz] npl πεθερικά ntpl.

inlet [ˈɪnlɛt] n ορμίσκος, είσοδος f.

inmate [ˈɪnmeɪt] n ένοικος/n m/f.

inn [ɪn] n πανδοχείο, ξενοδοχείο.

innate [ɪˈneɪt] a έμφυτος.

inner [ˈɪnə*] a εσωτερικός.

innocence [ˈɪnəsns] n αθωότητα, αφέλεια.

innocent [ˈɪnəsnt] a αθώος, αγνός, αφελής.

innocuous [ɪˈnɒkjʊəs] a αβλαβής.

innovation [ɪnəʊˈveɪʃən] n καινοτομία, νεωτερισμός.

innuendo [ɪnjʊˈɛndəʊ] n υπαινιγμός.

innumerable [ɪˈnjuːmərəbl] a αναρίθμητος.

inoculation [ɪnɒkjʊˈleɪʃən] n μπόλιασμα nt.

inopportune [ɪnˈɒpətjuːn] a άκαιρος, άτοπος.

inordinately [ɪˈnɔːdɪnɪtlɪ] ad υπερβολικά.

inorganic [ɪnɔːˈɡænɪk] a ανόργανος.

in-patient [ˈɪnpeɪʃənt] n εσωτερικός (ασθενής).

input [ˈɪnpʊt] n εισαγωγή ♦ vt εισάγω, τροφοδοτώ.

inquest [ˈɪnkwɛst] n ανάκριση, έρευνα.

inquire [ɪnˈkwaɪə*] vi ρωτώ, ζητώ ♦ vt (price) ρωτώ την τιμή || to ~ into vt ερευνώ, εξετάζω.

inquiring [ɪnˈkwaɪərɪŋ] a (mind) ερευνητικός.

inquiry [ɪnˈkwaɪərɪ] n ερώτηση || (search) έρευνα, ανάκριση || ~ **office** n υπηρεσία πληροφοριών.

inquisitive [ɪnˈkwɪzɪtɪv] a περίεργος, αδιάκριτος.

inroad [ˈɪnrəʊd] n εισβολή, επιδρομή.

insane [ɪnˈseɪn] a παράφρονας, τρελός.

insanitary [ɪnˈsænɪtərɪ] a ανθυγιεινός.

insanity [ɪnˈsænɪtɪ] n παραφροσύνη, τρέλα.

insatiable [ɪnˈseɪʃəbl] a ακόρεστος, άπληστος.

inscription [ɪnˈskrɪpʃən] n επιγραφή, αφιέρωση.

inscrutable [ɪnˈskruːtəbl] a ανεξιχνίαστος, μυστηριώδης.

insect [ˈɪnsɛkt] n έντομο, ζουζούνι || ~**icide** n εντομοκτόνο.

insecure [ɪnsɪˈkjʊə*] a επισφαλής.

insecurity [ɪnsɪˈkjʊərɪtɪ] n ανασφάλεια, (το) επισφαλές nt.

insensible [ɪnˈsɛnsəbl] a αναπαίσθητος, αναίσθητος.

insensitive [ɪnˈsɛnsɪtɪv] a αναίσθητος, χωρίς ντροπή.

inseparable [ɪnˈsɛpərəbl] a αχώριστος, αναπόσπαστος.

insert [ɪnˈsɜːt] vt παρεμβάλλω, καταχωρώ, εισάγω ♦ [ˈɪnsɜːt] n παρεμβολή, ένθεμα nt || ~**ion** n παρεμβολή, καταχώρηση, βάλσιμο.

inshore [ˈɪnˈʃɔː*] a, ad κοντά στην ακτή.

inside [ˈɪnˈsaɪd] n (το) μέσα, εσωτερικό (μέρος) ♦ a εσωτερικός ♦ ad εσωτερικά, μέσα ♦ prep εντός, μέσα || ~-**forward** n (SPORT) μέσος κυνηγός || ~ **out** ad ανάποδα, το μέσα έξω || ~r n μεμυημένος, γνώστης.

insidious [ɪnˈsɪdɪəs] a ύπουλος, δόλιος.

insight [ˈɪnsaɪt] n διορατικότητα, οξύνοια.

insignificant [ɪnsɪɡˈnɪfɪkənt] a ασήμαντος, τιποτένιος.

insincere [ɪnsɪnˈsɪə*] a ανειλικρινής.

insinuate [ɪnˈsɪnjʊeɪt] vt αφήνω να εννοηθεί, υπαινίσσομαι.

insinuation [ɪnsɪnjʊˈeɪʃən] n υπαινιγμός.

insipid [ɪnˈsɪpɪd] a ανούσιος, σαχλός.

insist [ɪnˈsɪst] vi (+ on) επιμένω, εμμένω || ~ence n επιμονή || ~ent a επίμονος.

insolence [ˈɪnsələns] n αναίδεια, θρασύτητα.

insolent ['insələnt] a αναιδής, θρασύς.

insoluble [in'sɒljubl] a άλυτος, αδιάλυτος.

insolvent [in'sɒlvənt] a αφερέγγυος, αναξιόχρεος.

insomnia [in'sɒmniə] n αϋπνία.

inspect [in'spekt] vt επιθεωρώ, επιτηρώ, επιβλέπω || ~ion n επιθεώρηση, επιτήρηση || ~or n επιθεωρητής/τρια m/f|| (RAIL) επιστάτης/άτρια m/f, επόπτης/όπτρια m/f.

inspiration [inspə'reiʃən] n έμπνευση.

inspire [in'spaiə*] vt εμπνέω.

inspiring [in'spaiəriŋ] a εμπνέων.

instability [instə'biliti] n αστάθεια.

install [in'stɔːl] vt εγκαθιστώ, μοντάρω || (in office) εγκαθιστώ || ~ation n εγκατάσταση, τοποθέτηση.

instalment, installment (US) [in'stɔːlmənt] n δόση, παρτίδα.

instance ['instəns] n περίπτωση, παράδειγμα nt || for ~ παραδείγματος χάρη.

instant ['instənt] n στιγμή ♦ a άμεσος, επείγων || ~ **coffee** n στιγμιαίος καφές || ~**ly** ad αμέσως, στη στιγμή.

instead [in'sted] ad αντί γι' αυτό || ~ **of** αντί.

instigation [insti'geiʃən] n παρακίνηση, υποκίνηση.

instil [in'stil] vt εμποτίζω, βάζω.

instinct ['instiŋkt] n ένστικτο, ορμέμφυτο || ~**ive** a ενστικτώδης || ~**ively** ad ενστικτωδώς.

institute ['institjuːt] n ίδρυμα nt, ινστιτούτο ♦ vt θεσπίζω, ιδρύω, εγκαθιστώ.

institution [insti'tjuːʃən] n (custom) θεσμός, θέσμιο || (organization) ίδρυμα nt, οργάνωση || (beginning) ίδρυση, σύσταση.

instruct [in'strʌkt] vt (order) παραγγέλλω, διατάσσω || (teach) διδάσκω, μαθαίνω || ~ion n διδασκαλία || (direction) οδηγία || ~ions npl εντολές fpl, οδηγίες fpl || ~ive a διδακτικός, ενημερωτικός || ~or n δάσκαλος/άλα m/f, εκπαιδευτής/εύτρια m/f || (US) επιμελητής/ήτρια m/f.

instrument ['instrumənt] n (implement) εργαλείο, όργανο || (MUS) όργανο || ~al a ενόργανος || (helpful) συντελεστικός, συμβάλλων || ~alist n οργανοπαίκτης || ~ **panel** n ταμπλό nt inv.

insubordinate [insə'bɔːdənit] a ανυπότακτος, ανυπάκουος.

insubordination ['insəbɔːdi'neiʃən] n ανυπακοή, ανυποταξία.

insufferable [in'sʌfərəbl] a ανυπόφορος, αφόρητος.

insufficient [insə'fiʃənt] a ανεπαρκής, λειψός || ~**ly** ad ανεπαρκώς.

insular ['insjulə*] a (narrow-minded) με στενές αντιλήψεις.

insulate ['insjuleit] vt μονώνω || (set apart) απομονώνω.

insulating ['insjuleitiŋ]: ~ **tape** n μονωτική ταινία.

insulation [insju'leiʃən] n (ELEC) μόνωση.

insulin ['insjulin] n (for diabetic) ινσουλίνη.

insult ['insʌlt] n προσβολή, βρισιά ♦ [in'sʌlt] vt βρίζω, προσβάλλω || ~**ing** a προσβλητικός.

insuperable [in'suːpərəbl] a ανυπέρβλητος.

insurance [in'ʃuərəns] n ασφάλεια || ~ **agent** n πράκτορας ασφαλειών || ~ **policy** n ασφαλιστήριο.

insure [in'ʃuə*] vt (εξ)ασφαλίζω.

insurrection [insə'rekʃən] n επανάσταση, εξέγερση.

intact [in'tækt] a άθικτος, απείραχτος.

intake ['inteik] n (MECH) εισαγωγή.

intangible [in'tændʒəbl] a ακαθόριστος.

integral ['intigrəl] a (essential) αναπόσπαστος || (complete) ολοκληρωτικός.

integrate ['intigreit] vti ολοκληρώνω.

integration [inti'greiʃən] n ολοκλήρωση.

integrity [in'tegriti] n ακεραιότητα, εντιμότητα.

intellect ['intilekt] n διάνοια, νόηση, μυαλό || ~**ual** a διανοητικός, πνευματικός ♦ n διανοούμενος.

intelligence [in'telidʒəns] n νοημοσύνη || (information) πληροφορία.

intelligent [in'telidʒənt] a ευφυής, νοήμων, μυαλωμένος || ~**ly** ad ευφυώς, έξυπνα.

intelligible [in'telidʒəbl] a (κατα)νοητός, καταληπτός.

intemperate [in'tempərit] a ακρατής, μέθυσος.

intend [in'tend] vt (mean) προτίθεμαι || to ~ to do sth σκοπεύω να κάνω κάτι.

intense [in'tens] a έντονος, ισχυρός || ~**ly** ad υπερβολικά, έντονα.

intensify [in'tensifai] vt εντείνω, επιτείνω.

intensity [in'tensiti] n ένταση, σφοδρότητα, ορμή.

intensive [in'tensiv] a εντατικός.

intent [in'tent] n πρόθεση || **to all** ~**s and purposes** ουσιαστικά, πραγματικά.

intention [in'tenʃən] n πρόθεση || (plan) σκοπός || ~**al** a σκόπιμος, εσκεμμένος || ~**ally** ad εσκεμμένα, σκόπιμα.

intently [in'tentli] ad προσεκτικά, έντονα.

inter [in'tɜː*] vt ενταφιάζω, θάβω.

inter- ['intə*] prefix διά-, μεσο(ο)-, μεταξύ.

interact [intər'ækt] vi αλληλεπιδρώ || ~**ion** n αλληλεπίδραση.

intercede [intə'siːd] vi επεμβαίνω, μεσολαβώ, μεσιτεύω.

intercept [intə'sept] vt ανακόπτω, συλλαμβάνω, πιάνω || ~**ion** n σύλληψη, υποκλοπή.

interchange ['intə'tʃeindʒ] n (exchange) ανταλλαγή || (roads) μεταλλαγή ♦

[ɪntə'tʃeɪndʒ] vt ανταλλάσσω || ~able a ανταλλάξιμος, εναλλάξιμος.

intercom ['ɪntəkɒm] n σύστημα εσωτερικής επικοινωνίας.

interconnect [ɪntəkə'nɛkt] vi αλληλοσυνδέω.

intercontinental [ɪntəkɒntɪ'nɛntl] a διηπειρωτικός.

intercourse ['ɪntəkɔːs] n συναλλαγή, σχέσεις fpl || (sexual) συνουσία.

interest ['ɪntrɪst] n (curiosity) ενδιαφέρον nt || (advantage) συμφέρον nt || (money paid) τόκος || (COMM: stake) συμφέροντα ntpl, συμμετοχή ♦ vt ενδιαφέρω, προσελκύω || ~ed a ενδιαφερόμενος || (attentive) με ενδιαφέρον || to be ~ed in ενδιαφέρομαι για || ~ing a ενδιαφέρων.

interface ['ɪntəfeɪs] n (COMPUT) θύρα, υποδοχή.

interfere [ɪntə'fɪə*] vi επεμβαίνω || (+ with) συγκρούομαι με, ανακατεύομαι || ~nce n (general) επέμβαση, ανάμιξη || (TV) παράσιτα ntpl.

interim ['ɪntərɪm] a προσωρινός ♦ n: in the ~ στο μεταξύ.

interior [ɪn'tɪərɪə*] n εσωτερικό || (inland) ενδοχώρα ♦ a εσωτερικός.

interjection [ɪntə'dʒɛkʃən] n (GRAM) επιφώνημα nt.

interlock [ɪntə'lɒk] vi συνδέομαι ♦ vt συνδέω, συμπλέκω.

interloper ['ɪntələupə*] n παρείσακτος.

interlude ['ɪntəluːd] n διάλειμμα nt || (THEAT) ιντερμέτζο.

intermarry [ɪntə'mærɪ] vi επιμιγνύομαι.

intermediary [ɪntə'miːdɪərɪ] n μεσάζων/άζουσα m/f, μεσίτης/ίτρια m/f.

intermediate [ɪntə'miːdɪət] a μεσολαβών, ενδιάμεσος.

intermission [ɪntə'mɪʃən] n διάλειμμα nt, διακοπή.

intermittent [ɪntə'mɪtənt] a διαλείπων || ~ly ad διακεκομμένα.

intern [ɪn'tɜːn] vt περιορίζω ♦ ['ɪntɜːn] n (US) εσωτερικός γιατρός m/f.

internal [ɪn'tɜːnl] a εσωτερικός || ~ly ad (MED) εσωτερικά || ~ revenue n (US) Τμήμα Εσωτερικών Προσόδων.

international [ɪntə'næʃnəl] a διεθνής ♦ n (SPORT) διεθνής (παίκτης).

internment [ɪn'tɜːnmənt] n εγκάθειρξη, περιορισμός.

interplay ['ɪntəpleɪ] n αλληλεπίδραση.

interpret [ɪn'tɜːprɪt] vt εξηγώ || (translate) μεταφράζω || (THEAT) ερμηνεύω || ~ation n ερμηνεία, εξήγηση || ~er n διερμηνέας m/f.

interrelated [ɪntərɪ'leɪtɪd] a αλληλένδετος.

interrogate [ɪn'tɛrəgeɪt] vt ερωτώ, ανακρίνω.

interrogation [ɪntɛrə'geɪʃən] n ανάκριση, εξέταση.

interrogative [ɪntə'rɒgətɪv] a ερωτηματικός.

interrogator [ɪn'tɛrəgeɪtə*] n ανακριτής.

interrupt [ɪntə'rʌpt] vt διακόπτω, εμποδίζω || ~ion n διακοπή.

intersect [ɪntə'sɛkt] vt τέμνω, διακόπτω, κόβω ♦ vi (roads) διασταυρώνομαι || ~ion n (roads) διασταύρωση, σταυροδρόμι.

intersperse [ɪntə'spɜːs] vt διασπείρω, αναμιγνύω.

interval ['ɪntəvəl] n διάλειμμα nt, διάστημα nt || (MUS) διάστημα nt || at ~s κατά διαστήματα.

intervene [ɪntə'viːn] vi μεσολαβώ, παρεμβαίνω, επεμβαίνω.

intervention [ɪntə'vɛnʃən] n μεσολάβηση, παρέμβαση.

interview ['ɪntəvjuː] n (PRESS etc) συνέντευξη || (for job) συνάντηση, ραντεβού nt inv ♦ vt παίρνω συνέντευξη || ~er n εκείνος που παίρνει συνέντευξη.

intestate [ɪn'tɛstɪt] a χωρίς διαθήκη.

intestine [ɪn'tɛstɪn] n έντερο.

intimacy ['ɪntɪməsɪ] n οικειότητα || (sexual) συνουσία.

intimate ['ɪntɪmɪt] a ενδόμυχος, ιδιαίτερος || (familiar) οικείος, στενός ♦ ['ɪntɪmeɪt] vt υποδηλώ, εκδηλώνω, υπαινίσσομαι || ~ly ad στενά, κατά βάθος.

intimidate [ɪn'tɪmɪdeɪt] vt (εκ)φοβίζω, φοβερίζω.

intimidation [ɪntɪmɪ'deɪʃən] n εκφοβισμός.

into ['ɪntu] prep (movement) σε, εντός, μέσα || (change) σε.

intolerable [ɪn'tɒlərəbl] a ανυπόφορος, αφόρητος.

intolerance [ɪn'tɒlərəns] n μισαλλοδοξία.

intolerant [ɪn'tɒlərənt] a μισαλλόδοξος, αδιάλλακτος.

intonation [ɪntəu'neɪʃən] n διακύμανση της φωνής.

intoxicate [ɪn'tɒksɪkeɪt] vt μεθώ, ζαλίζω || ~d a μεθυσμένος.

intoxication [ɪntɒksɪ'keɪʃən] n μεθύσι, παραζάλη.

intractable [ɪn'træktəbl] a ανυπάκουος, ατίθασος.

intransigent [ɪn'trænsɪdʒənt] a αδιάλλακτος.

intransitive [ɪn'trænsɪtɪv] a αμετάβατος.

intravenous [ɪntrə'viːnəs] a ενδοφλέβιος.

intrepid [ɪn'trɛpɪd] a ατρόμητος, άφοβος.

intricacy ['ɪntrɪkəsɪ] n περιπλοκή, (το) περίπλοκο.

intricate ['ɪntrɪkɪt] a περίπλοκος || (of thoughts) συγκεχυμένος.

intrigue [ɪn'triːg] n μηχανορραφία ♦ vt (make curious) διεγείρω την περιέργεια.

intriguing [ɪn'triːgɪŋ] a (fascinating) περίεργος, μυστηριώδης.

intrinsic [ɪn'trɪnsɪk] a ουσιαστικός, πραγματικός.

introduce [ɪntrə'djuːs] vt (person) συνιστώ, συστήνω || (sth new) παρουσιάζω, μπάζω || (subject) εισάγω.

introduction [ɪntrə'dʌkʃən] n παρουσίαση, σύσταση || (book) εισαγωγή, πρόλογος.

introductory [ɪntrə'dʌktərɪ] a εισαγωγικός.

introspective [ɪntrəu'spɛktɪv] a ενδοσκοπικός.

introvert ['ɪntrəuvɜːt] a, n ενδόστροφος.

intrude [ɪn'truːd] vi (+ on) επιβάλλω, επεμβαίνω || ~ r n παρείσακτος.

intrusion [ɪn'truːʒən] n επέμβαση, διείσδυση.

intuition [ɪntju:'ɪʃən] n διαίσθηση, ενόραση.

intuitive [ɪn'tjuːɪtɪv] a διαισθητικός, ενστικτώδης.

inundate ['ɪnʌndeɪt] vt (fig) κατακλύζω, πλημμυρίζω.

invade [ɪn'veɪd] vt εισβάλλω, καταπατώ || ~ r n επιδρομέας, εισβολέας.

invalid ['ɪnvəlɪd] n ασθενής m/f, ανάπηρος/n m/f ◆ [ɪn'vælɪd] a (not valid) άκυρος || ~ate vt ακυρώνω, αναιρώ.

invaluable [ɪn'væljuəbl] a ανεκτίμητος.

invariable [ɪn'vɛərɪəbl] a αμετάβλητος.

invasion [ɪn'veɪʒən] n εισβολή, επιδρομή.

invective [ɪn'vɛktɪv] n βρισιά, λοιδωρία.

invent [ɪn'vɛnt] vt εφευρίσκω || (make up) πλάθω || ~ion n εφεύρεση || ~ive a εφευρετικός, δημιουργικός || ~or n εφευρέτης.

inventory ['ɪnvəntrɪ] n απογραφή, κατάλογος.

inverse ['ɪn'vɜːs] n αντίστροφος, ανάστροφος.

invert [ɪn'vɜːt] vt αντιστρέφω || ~ed commas npl εισαγωγικά ntpl.

invertebrate [ɪn'vɜːtɪbrɪt] n ασπόνδυλο.

invest [ɪn'vɛst] vt (ECON) επενδύω || (control) παρέχω, αναθέτω.

investigate [ɪn'vɛstɪgeɪt] vt ερευνώ, εξετάζω.

investigation [ɪnvɛstɪ'geɪʃən] n έρευνα, εξέταση.

investigator [ɪn'vɛstɪgeɪtə*] n ερευνητής/ήτρια m/f, αναζητητής/ήτρια m/f.

investiture [ɪn'vɛstɪtʃə*] n τελετή απονομής αξιώματος.

investment [ɪn'vɛstmənt] n επένδυση.

investor [ɪn'vɛstə*] n κεφαλαιούχος m/f, επενδύτης m/f.

inveterate [ɪn'vɛtərɪt] a (habitual) φανατικός, αδιόρθωτος.

invigorating [ɪn'vɪgəreɪtɪŋ] a αναζωογονητικός, τονωτικός.

invincible [ɪn'vɪnsəbl] a αήττητος.

inviolate [ɪn'vaɪəlɪt] a απαραβίαστος, απαράβατος.

invisible [ɪn'vɪzəbl] a (general) αόρατος, άδηλος || (ink) συμπαθητική μελάνη.

invitation [ɪnvɪ'teɪʃən] n πρόσκληση.

invite [ɪn'vaɪt] vt (προς)καλώ || (attract) ελκύω, προκαλώ.

inviting [ɪn'vaɪtɪŋ] a δελεαστικός, ελκυστικός.

invoice ['ɪnvɔɪs] n τιμολόγιο ◆ vt τιμολογώ.

invoke [ɪn'vəuk] vt επικαλούμαι, απαιτώ.

involuntarily [ɪn'vɒləntərɪlɪ] ad ακουσίως, αθέλητα.

involuntary [ɪn'vɒləntərɪ] a ακούσιος, αθέλητος.

involve [ɪn'vɒlv] vt (include) συνεπάγομαι || (entangle) (περι)πλέκω, ανακατώνω || ~d a πλεγμένος || ~ment n ανάμιξη, μπλέξιμο.

invulnerable [ɪn'vʌlnərəbl] a άτρωτος.

inward ['ɪnwəd] a εσωτερικός, προς τα μέσα || ~(s) ad προς τα μέσα || ~ly ad εσωτερικά, μέσα.

iodine ['aɪədiːn] n ιώδιο.

iota [aɪ'əutə] n (fig) γιώτα nt, τίποτε, ελάχιστη ποσότητα.

I O U n (abbr of I owe you) γραμμάτιο.

I.Q. n (abbr of intelligence quotient) δείκτης ευφυίας.

Iran [ɪ'rɑːn] n Ιράν nt inv, Περσία.

Iraq [ɪ'rɑːk] n Ιράκ nt inv.

irascible [ɪ'ræsɪbl] a ευέξαπτος, οξύθυμος.

irate [aɪ'reɪt] a θυμωμένος, εξαγριωμένος.

Ireland ['aɪələnd] n Ιρλανδία.

iris ['aɪərɪs] n (ANAT) ίριδα || (BOT) ίρδα, ρίδι.

Irish ['aɪərɪʃ] a ιρλανδικός || the ~ npl οι Ιρλανδοί || ~man n Ιρλανδός || ~woman n Ιρλανδή.

irk [ɜːk] vt ενοχλώ, στενοχωρώ.

iron ['aɪən] n σίδηρος || (flat iron) σίδερο || (golf club) ρόπαλο του γκόλφ ◆ a σιδερένιος ◆ vt σιδερώνω || ~s npl (chains) αλυσίδες fpl, δεσμά ntpl || to ~ out vt (crease) σιδερώνω || (difficulties) εξομαλύνω || ~ curtain n σιδηρούν παραπέτασμα nt.

ironic(al) [aɪ'rɒnɪk(əl)] a ειρωνικός || ~ally ad ειρωνικά.

ironing ['aɪənɪŋ] n σιδέρωμα nt || ~ board n σανίδα σιδερώματος.

ironmonger ['aɪənmʌŋgə*] n σιδηροπώλης || ~'s (shop) n σιδηροπωλείο.

iron ore ['aɪənɔː*] n σιδηρομετάλλευμα nt.

ironworks ['aɪənwɜːks] n σιδηρουργείο.

irony ['aɪərənɪ] n ειρωνεία.

irrational [ɪ'ræʃənl] a παράλογος.

irreconcilable [ɪrɛkən'saɪləbl] a αδιάλλακτος, ασυμβίβαστος.

irredeemable [ɪrɪ'diːməbl] a (COMM) ανεξαγόραστος.

irrefutable [ɪrɪ'fjuːtəbl] a ακαταμάχητος, αδιάψευστος.

irregular [ɪˈregjulə*] a *(not regular)* ακανόνιστος, άτακτος || *(not smooth)* ανώμαλος || *(against rule)* αντικανονικός, αντίθετος || ~**ity** n ανωμαλία.
irrelevance [ɪˈreləvəns] n (το) άσχετο.
irrelevant [ɪˈreləvənt] a άσχετος, ξεκάρφωτος.
irreparable [ɪˈrepərəbl] a ανεπανόρθωτος, αγιάτρευτος.
irreplaceable [ɪrɪˈpleɪsəbl] a αναντικατάστατος.
irrepressible [ɪrɪˈpresəbl] a ακατάσχετος, ακάθεκτος.
irreproachable [ɪrɪˈprəʊtʃəbl] a άμεμπτος, άψογος.
irresistible [ɪrɪˈzɪstəbl] a ασυγκράτητος, ακαταμάχητος.
irresolute [ɪˈrezəluːt] a αναποφάσιστος, διστακτικός.
irrespective [ɪrɪˈspektɪv]: ~ **of** prep ανεξάρτητα από.
irresponsible [ɪrɪsˈpɒnsəbl] a απερίσκεπτος, ελαφρόμυαλος.
irreverent [ɪˈrevərənt] a ασεβής, ανευλαβής.
irrevocable [ɪˈrevəkəbl] a αμετάκλητος, ανέκκλητος.
irrigate [ˈɪrɪgeɪt] vt αρδεύω, ποτίζω.
irrigation [ɪrɪˈgeɪʃən] n άρδευση, πότισμα nt.
irritable [ˈɪrɪtəbl] a οξύθυμος, ευέξαπτος.
irritate [ˈɪrɪteɪt] vt *(annoy)* (εξ)ερεθίζω, εκνευρίζω || *(skin etc)* ερεθίζω.
irritation [ɪrɪˈteɪʃən] n ερεθισμός, θυμός.
is [ɪz] see **be**.
Islam [ˈɪzlɑːm] n Ισλάμ nt inv.
island [ˈaɪlənd] n νησί || ~**er** νησιώτης/ιώτισσα m/f.
isle [aɪl] n νήσος f, νησάκι.
isn't [ˈɪznt] = **is not** || see **be**.
isolate [ˈaɪsəleɪt] vt (απο)μονώνω || ~**d** a απομονωμένος, απόμερος.
isolation [aɪsəˈleɪʃən] n απομόνωση.
isotope [ˈaɪsəʊtəʊp] n ισότοπο.
Israel [ˈɪzreɪl] n Ισραήλ m inv || ~**i** n Ισραηλινός/ή m/f ♦ adj ισραηλινός.
issue [ˈɪʃuː] n *(question)* υπόθεση, ζήτημα nt || *(giving out)* έκδοση, διανομή, χορήγηση || *(copy)* τεύχος, φύλλο || *(offspring)* απόγονοι mpl ♦ vt *(rations)* διανέμω || *(orders)* εκδίδω, δημοσιεύω || *(equipment)* διανέμω, εκδίδω || **at** ~ υπό συζήτηση.
isthmus [ˈɪsməs] n ισθμός.
it [ɪt] pron τον, την, το, αυτό.
Italian [ɪˈtæliən] a ιταλικός ♦ n *(person)* Ιταλός/ίδα m/f || *(LING)* Ιταλικά ntpl.
italic [ɪˈtælɪk] a κυρτός, πλάγιος || ~**s** npl πλάγια γραφή.
Italy [ˈɪtəlɪ] n Ιταλία.
itch [ɪtʃ] n *(fig)* πόθος, όρεξη || *(MED)* φαγούρα, ψώρα ♦ vi έχω φαγούρα || ~**ing** n φαγούρα.
it'd [ˈɪtd] = **it would, it had** || see **would, have**.

item [ˈaɪtəm] n *(on list)* είδος nt, κονδύλι, εγγραφή || *(in programme)* νούμερο || *(in agenda)* θέμα nt || *(in newspaper)* είδηση || ~**ize** vt αναλύω.
itinerant [ɪˈtɪnərənt] a περιοδεύων.
itinerary [aɪˈtɪnərəri] n δρομολόγιο.
it'll [ˈɪtl] = **it will, it shall** || see **will, shall**.
its [ɪts] poss a του || poss pron δικό του.
it's [ɪts] = **it is, it has** || see **be, have**.
itself [ɪtˈself] pron τον εαυτό του.
I.T.V. n *(abbr of Independent Television)* Ανεξάρτητο Τηλεοπτικό Κανάλι.
I've [aɪv] = **I have** || see **have**.
ivory [ˈaɪvərɪ] n ελεφαντοστούν nt || ~ **tower** n *(fig)* τόπος μονώσεως.
ivy [ˈaɪvɪ] n κισσός.

J

jab [dʒæb] vti κτυπώ, κεντώ, χώνω.
jabber [ˈdʒæbə*] vi φλυαρώ, τραυλίζω.
jack [dʒæk] n *(MECH)* γρύλλος || *(CARDS)* βαλές m, φάντης || **to** ~ **up** vt σηκώνω με γρύλλο.
jacket [ˈdʒækɪt] n ζακέτα, σακάκι || *(MECH)* χιτώνιο, πουκάμισο.
jack-knife [ˈdʒæknaɪf] n μεγάλος σουγιάς, κολοκοτρώνης.
jade [dʒeɪd] n *(stone)* νεφρίτης.
jaded [ˈdʒeɪdɪd] a κουρασμένος, τσακισμένος.
jagged [ˈdʒægɪd] a ανώμαλος, οδοντωτός, μυτερός.
jail [dʒeɪl] n φυλακή || ~**break** n δραπέτευση || ~**er** n δεσμοφύλακας.
jam [dʒæm] n *(fruit)* μαρμελάδα || *(stoppage)* εμπλοκή, φράξιμο nt, στρίμωγμα nt ♦ vt σφηνώνω, σφίγγω, στριμώχνω ♦ vi σφίγγομαι, φρακάρω, κολλώ.
jangle [ˈdʒæŋgl] vti ηχώ κακόηχα, κουδουνίζω.
janitor [ˈdʒænɪtə*] n *(caretaker)* θυρωρός m/f, επιστάτης/άτρια m/f.
January [ˈdʒænjuəri] n Ιανουάριος.
Japan [dʒəˈpæn] n Ιαπωνία || ~**ese** a ιαπωνικός ♦ n *(LING)* Ιαπωνικά ntpl.
jar [dʒɑː*] n *(glass)* βάζο, λαγήνι, στάμνα ♦ vi τραντάζω, συγκρούομαι.
jargon [ˈdʒɑːgən] n επαγγελματική φρασεολογία, αλαμπουρνέζικα ntpl.
jasmin(e) [ˈdʒæzmɪn] n γιασεμί.
jaundice [ˈdʒɔːndɪs] n ίκτερος, χρυσή || ~**d** a *(attitude)* κακόβουλος, φθονερός.
jaunt [dʒɔːnt] n βόλτα, περίπατος || ~**y** a ζωηρός, ξένοιαστος.
javelin [ˈdʒævlɪn] n ακόντιο, κοντάρι.
jaw [dʒɔː] n σαγόνι, μασέλα.
jazz [dʒæz] n τζαζ f inv || **to** ~ **up** vt ζωηρεύω, επιταχύνω || ~ **band** n τζάζ-μπαντ f inv.
jealous [ˈdʒeləs] a *(envious)* ζηλιάρης || *(watchful)* ζηλότυπος, προσεκτικός || ~**ly** ad ζηλότυπα, με επιμέλεια || ~**y** n ζήλεια.
jeans [dʒiːnz] npl ντρίλινο παντελόνι.

jeep [dʒi:p] n τζίπ nt inv.

jeer [dʒɪə*] vi (+ at) κοροϊδεύω, χλευάζω, γιουχαΐζω ♦ n εμπαιγμός, γιούχα.

jelly ['dʒɛlɪ] n ζελέ f || ~fish n μέδουσα, τσούχτρα.

jeopardize ['dʒepədaɪz] vt διακινδυνεύω.

jeopardy ['dʒepədɪ] n: in ~ σε κίνδυνο.

jerk [dʒɜːk] n τίναγμα nt, τράνταγμα nt || (US: idiot) χαζός ♦ vti τινάζω, τραντάζω.

jerkin ['dʒɜːkɪn] n πέτσινο σακκάκι.

jerky ['dʒɜːkɪ] a απότομος, κοφτός.

jersey ['dʒɜːzɪ] n φανέλα.

jest [dʒest] n χωρατό, αστείο ♦ vi κάνω αστεία, αστειεύομαι.

jet [dʒet] n (stream) πίδακας, αναπήδηση || (spout) στόμιο, μπεκ nt inv || (AVIAT) τζέτ nt inv || ~-black a κατάμαυρος || ~ engine n κινητήρας τζέτ.

jettison ['dʒetɪsn] vt απορρίπτω.

jetty ['dʒetɪ] n μώλος, αποβάθρα.

Jew [dʒuː] n Εβραίος.

jewel ['dʒuːəl] n κόσμημα nt || (fig) πολύτιμη, πέτρα || ~ler, (US) ~er n κοσμηματοπώλης || ~(l)er's (shop) n κοσμηματοπωλείο || ~(le)ry n κοσμήματα ntpl, διαμαντικά ntpl.

Jewess ['dʒuːɪs] n Εβραία.

Jewish ['dʒuːɪʃ] a εβραϊκός.

jib [dʒɪb] n (NAUT) αρτέμων inv, φλόκος ♦ vi αρνούμαι, κωλώνω, κλωτσώ.

jibe [dʒaɪb] n πείραγμα nt, αστείο.

jiffy ['dʒɪfɪ] n (col): in a ~ στη στιγμή, αμέσως.

jigsaw ['dʒɪgsɔː] n (also: ~ puzzle) (παιχνίδι) συναρμολόγησης.

jilt [dʒɪlt] vt διώχνω, στρίβω.

jingle ['dʒɪŋgl] n κουδούνισμα nt, ♦ vti κουδουνίζω.

jinx [dʒɪŋks] n (col) γρουσούζης.

jitters ['dʒɪtəz] npl (col): to get the ~ τρέμω, φοβάμαι.

job [dʒɔb] n έργο, εργασία || (position) θέση, δουλειά || (difficult task) αγγαρεία || ~less a άνεργος.

jockey ['dʒɔkɪ] n τζόκεϋ m inv ♦ vi ελίσσομαι, μανουβράρω.

jocular ['dʒɔkjulə*] a αστείος, εύθυμος.

jog [dʒɔg] vt σπρώχνω, σκουντώ ♦ vi (move jerkily) κλυδωνίζω, τραντάζω.

join [dʒɔɪn] vt (fasten) ενώνω, συνδέω, ματίζω || (club) εγγράφομαι, γίνομαι μέλος ♦ vi (the army) κατατάσσομαι ♦ n ένωση, ραφή.

joiner [dʒɔɪnə*] n μαραγκός || ~y n ξυλουργική.

joint [dʒɔɪnt] n (TECH) αρμός, άρθρωση || (of meat) κομμάτι κρέατος || (col: place) καταγώγιο, τρώγλη || ~ly ad μαζί.

joist [dʒɔɪst] n δοκάρι, πατερό.

joke [dʒəuk] n αστείο, χωρατό, καλαμπούρι ♦ vi αστειεύομαι || ~r n αστειολόγος || (CARDS) μπαλαντέρ m inv.

jolly ['dʒɔlɪ] a εύθυμος, χαρούμενος, κεφάτος ♦ ad (col) εξαιρετικά, πολύ.

jolt [dʒəult] n τίναγμα nt, τράνταγμα nt || (col) ξάφνιασμα ♦ vt τινάζω, κουνώ.

jostle ['dʒɔsl] vt σπρώχνω.

jot [dʒɔt] n: not one ~ ούτε ίχνος, ούτε κατά κεραία || to ~ down vt σημειώνω, γράφω || ~ter n σημειωματάριο.

journal ['dʒɜːnl] n εφημερίδα, περιοδικό || ~ese n δημοσιογραφικό ύφος || ~ism n δημοσιογραφία || ~ist n δημοσιογράφος m/f.

journey ['dʒɜːnɪ] n ταξίδι, διαδρομή.

joy [dʒɔɪ] n χαρά, ευθυμία || ~ful a περιχαρής, χαρμόσυνος || ~ous a εύθυμος || ~ride n περίπατος με αυτοκίνητο.

Jr., Jun., Junr. abbr of junior.

jubilant ['dʒuːbɪlənt] a χαρούμενος, πανηγυρίζων.

jubilation [dʒuːbɪ'leɪʃən] n αγαλλίαση, χαρά.

jubilee ['dʒuːbɪliː] n γιορτή.

judge [dʒʌdʒ] n (in court) δικαστής ♦ vt δικάζω, κρίνω ♦ vi (estimate) υπολογίζω, θεωρώ || judg(e)ment n (sentence) δικαστική απόφαση || (opinion) κρίση, γνώμη.

judicial [dʒuː'dɪʃəl] a (LAW) δικαστικός.

judicious [dʒuː'dɪʃəs] a συνετός, γνωστικός, φρόνιμος.

judo ['dʒuːdəu] n τζούντο nt inv.

jug [dʒʌg] n κανάτι, στάμνα.

juggle ['dʒʌgl] vi ταχυδακτυλουργώ, εξαπατώ || ~r n ταχυδακτυλουργός.

Jugoslav ['juːgəu'slɑːv] = Yugoslav.

juice [dʒuːs] n χυμός, ζουμί.

juicy ['dʒuːsɪ] a χυμώδης, ζουμερός.

jukebox ['dʒuːkbɒks] n τζουκ μποξ nt inv.

July [dʒuː'laɪ] n Ιούλιος.

jumble ['dʒʌmbl] n ανακάτεμα nt, κυκεώνας, μπέρδεμα nt ♦ vt (also: ~ up) ανακατεύω, μπερδεύω.

jumbo ['dʒʌmbəu] attr. ~ jet n τζάμπο τζέτ nt inv.

jump [dʒʌmp] vi πηδώ ♦ vt πηδώ πάνω από, υπερπηδώ ♦ n πήδημα nt, άλμα nt || ~ed-up a (col) νεόπλουτος.

jumper ['dʒʌmpə*] n μπλούζα, ριχτή ζακέτα.

jumpy ['dʒʌmpɪ] a νευρικός.

junction ['dʒʌŋkʃən] n (road) διασταύρωση || (RAIL) διακλάδωση.

juncture ['dʒʌŋktʃə*] n: at this ~ στο σημείο αυτό.

June [dʒuːn] n Ιούνιος.

jungle ['dʒʌŋgl] n (tropical) ζούγκλα.

junior ['dʒuːnɪə*] a (in age) νεότερος || (in rank) κατώτερος, υφιστάμενος ♦ n (US: school) πρωτελειόφοιτος/n m/f.

junk [dʒʌŋk] n (rubbish) σκουπίδια ntpl, παλιοπράγματα || (ship) τζόγκα || ~shop n παλιατζίδικο.

jurisdiction [dʒuərɪs'dɪkʃən] n δικαιοδοσία.

jurisprudence [dʒuərɪs'pruːdəns] n νομολογία, νομομάθεια.

juror ['dʒuərə*] n ένορκος m/f.

jury ['dʒuərɪ] n ένορκοι mpl || (of contest) κριτική επιτροπή || ~man n = juror.

just [dʒʌst] *a (fair, right)* δίκαιος, σωστός || *(exact)* ακριβής ♦ *ad (exactly)* ακριβώς || *(barely)* μόλις || ~ **as I arrived** μόλις έφθασα || **I have** ~ **arrived** μόλις ήλθα || ~ **a little** τόσο δα, λίγο || ~ **now** πριν λίγο, μόλις τώρα || ~ **you and me** εμεις μόνο συ κι εγώ.

justice ['dʒʌstɪs] *n (fairness)* δικαιοσύνη || *(magistrate)* δικαστικός, δικαστής.

justifiable [dʒʌstɪ'faɪəbl] *a* δικαιολογήσιμος, εύλογος.

justification [dʒʌstɪfɪ'keɪʃən] *n* δικαίωση, δικαιολογία.

justify ['dʒʌstɪfaɪ] *vt (prove right)* αιτιολογώ || *(defend etc)* δικαιώνω, δικαιολογώ.

justly ['dʒʌstlɪ] *ad* δίκαια, ορθά.

justness ['dʒʌstnɪs] *n* ορθότητα, το δίκαιο.

jut [dʒʌt] *vi (also:* ~ **out)** προεξέχω.

juvenile ['dʒuːvənaɪl] *a* νεανικός, παιδικός ♦ *n* νέος/α *m/f*.

juxtapose ['dʒʌkstəpəʊz] *vt* (αντι)παραθέτω.

K

K *(abbr of one thousand)* K.

kaleidoscope [kə'laɪdəskəʊp] *n* καλειδοσκόπιο.

kangaroo [kæŋgə'ruː] *n* καγκουρώ *f inv*.

keel [kiːl] *n* τρόπιδα, καρίνα.

keen [kiːn] *a* ζωηρός, επιμελής, θερμός || ~**ness** *n* ζήλος, ενθουσιασμός.

keep [kiːp] *(irreg v) vt (have)* έχω, κρατώ, συντηρώ || *(take care of)* φυλάω, συντηρώ, τρέφω || *(detain)* (κατα)κρατώ, καθυστερώ || *(be faithful)* τηρώ, σέβομαι, μένω πιστός σε ♦ *vi (continue)* συνεχίζω, εξακολουθώ || *(of food)* διατηρούμαι, κρατώ || *(remain: quiet etc)* μένω, στέκομαι ♦ *n* τροφή, συντήρηση, έξοδα *ntpl* συντηρήσεως || *(tower)* (ακρο) πύργος || **to** ~ **back** *vti* κρατώ, πίσω, απομακρύνομαι, κρύβω || **to** ~ **on** *vi* συνεχίζω, εξακολουθώ να φορώ || '~ **out**' 'απαγορεύεται η είσοδος' || **to** ~ **up** *vi (+ with)* διατηρώ, καλλιεργώ || ~**ing** *n (care)* φύλαξη, συντήρηση || **in** ~**ing with** σύμφωνα με, ανάλογα με.

keg [kɛg] *n* βαρελάκι.

kennel ['kɛnl] *n* σπιτάκι σκύλου.

kept [kɛpt] *pt, pp of* **keep**.

kerb(stone) ['kɜːb(stəʊn)] *n* κράσπεδο πεζοδρομίου.

kernel ['kɜːnl] *n* πυρήνας, κόκκος, ψύχα.

kerosene ['kɛrəsiːn] *n* φωτιστικό πετρέλαιο, παραφίνη.

ketchup ['kɛtʃəp] *n* κέτσαπ *nt inv*, σάλτσα τομάτας.

kettle ['kɛtl] *n* χύτρα.

key [kiː] *n* κλειδί || *(to problem)* κλείδα || *(set of answers)* κλείδα, λύση || *(lever)* πλήκτρο || *(MUS)* τόνος ♦ *a (position etc)* βασικός, καίριος || **to** ~ **in** *vt*

πληκτρολογώ || ~**board** *n* πλήκτρο, κλαβιέ *nt inv* || *(of computer, typewriter)* πληκτρολόγιο ♦ *vt (COMPUT)* πληκτρολογώ || ~**hole** *n* κλειδαρότρυπα || ~**note** *n* κυρία ιδέα || ~ **ring** *n* κρίκος κλειδιών.

khaki ['kɑːkɪ] *n, a* χακί.

kick [kɪk] *vt* λακτίζω, κλωτσώ ♦ *vi (col)* παραπονιέμαι, αντιρρώ ♦ *n* λάκτισμα *nt*, κλωτσιά || *(thrill)* συγκίνηση || **to** ~ **around** *vi (col)* σέρνομαι, χαζεύω || **to** ~ **off** *vi (SPORT)* δίνω την πρώτη κλωτσιά || ~**-off** *n (SPORT)* εναρκτήριο λάκτισμα.

kid [kɪd] *n (child)* πιτσιρίκος, παιδάκι || *(goat)* κατσικάκι, ρίφι || *(leather)* σεβρό.

kidnap ['kɪdnæp] *vt* απάγω, κλέβω || ~**per** *n* απαγωγέας || ~**ping** *n* απαγωγή.

kidney ['kɪdnɪ] *n* νεφρό.

kill [kɪl] *vt (murder)* φονεύω, σκοτώνω || *(destroy)* αφανίζω, αφανίζω ♦ *n* κυνήγι || ~**er** *n* φονιάς/φόνισσα *m/f*.

kiln [kɪln] *n* καμίνι, κλίβανος.

kilo ['kiːləʊ] *n* κιλό || ~**gramme**, ~**gram** *(US) n* χιλιόγραμμο || ~**metre**, ~**meter** *(US) n* χιλιόμετρο || ~**watt** *n* κιλοβάτ *nt inv*.

kilt [kɪlt] *n* φουστανέλα.

kimono [kɪ'məʊnəʊ] *n* κιμονό.

kin [kɪn] *n* συγγενείς *mpl*, συγγενολόι.

kind [kaɪnd] *a* καλός, καλοκάγαθος, καλόβολος ♦ *n* είδος *nt* || ~ **of** *a*ς το πούμε, κάποιος || **two of a** ~ του ιδίου φυράματος || **in** ~ *(merchandise)* σε είδος || *(same way)* με το ίδιο νόμισμα.

kindergarten ['kɪndəgɑːtn] *n* νηπιαγωγείο.

kindhearted ['kaɪnd'hɑːtɪd] *a* καλόκαρδος.

kindle ['kɪndl] *vt* ανάβω || *(rouse)* εξάπτω, προκαλώ.

kindly ['kaɪndlɪ] *a* καλός, ευγενικός ♦ *ad* ευγενικά, μαλακά, φιλικά.

kindness ['kaɪndnɪs] *n* αγαθότητα, καλωσύνη.

kindred ['kɪndrɪd] *a* συγγενής, συγγενικός.

king [kɪŋ] *n* βασιλιάς || *(CARDS)* ρήγας || ~**dom** *n* βασίλειο || ~**fisher** *n* ψαροφάγος, μπιρμπίλι.

kink [kɪŋk] *n* ζάρα, στράβωμα *nt* || ~**y** *a (fig)* ιδιότροπος || *(hair)* σγουρός.

kiosk ['kiːɒsk] *n (TEL)* θάλαμος || *(shop)* κιόσκι, περίπτερο.

kipper ['kɪpə*] *n* καπνιστή ρέγγα.

kiss [kɪs] *n* φιλί, φίλημα *nt* ♦ *vt* φιλώ *nt* ♦ *vi*: **they** ~**ed** φιλήθηκαν.

kit [kɪt] *n* σύνεργα *ntpl*, ατομικά είδη *ntpl* || ~**bag** *n* σάκκος.

kitchen ['kɪtʃɪn] *n* κουζίνα || ~ **garden** *n* λαχανόκηπος || ~ **sink** *n* νεροχύτης.

kite [kaɪt] *n (*χαρτ*)*αετός || *(bird)* τσίφτης.

kitten ['kɪtn] *n* γατάκι.

kitty ['kɪtɪ] *n (pool of money)* κοινό ταμείο.

kleptomaniac [kleptəʊ'meɪniæk] *n* κλεπτομανής *m/f*.

knack [næk] *n* επιδεξιότητα, κόλπο.

knapsack ['næpsæk] *n* δισάκκι, γυλιός.

K

knead [niːd] vt ζυμώνω.

knee [niː] n γόνατο || ~**cap** n επιγονατίδα.

kneel [niːl] (irreg v) vi γονατίζω.

knell [nɛl] n καμπάνισμα nt, κωδωνοκρουσία.

knelt [nɛlt] pt, pp of **kneel**.

knew [njuː] pt of **know**.

knickers ['nɪkəz] npl κιλότα.

knife [naɪf] n μαχαίρι ♦ vt μαχαιρώνω.

knight [naɪt] n ιππότης || (CHESS) άλογο || ~**hood** n ιπποτισμός, ο τίτλος του ιππότη.

knit [nɪt] vt πλέκω ♦ vi συγκολλώ || ~**ting** n πλέξιμο, πλεκτική || ~**ting machine** n πλεκτομηχανή || ~**ting needle** n βελόνα (του πλεξίματος) || ~**wear** n πλεκτό, τρικό.

knives [naɪvz] npl of **knife**.

knob [nɔb] n (of door) πόμολο || (butter etc) κομμάτι.

knock [nɔk] vt (criticize) βρίζω, κακολογώ ♦ vi προσκρούω, χτυπώ ♦ n κτύπημα nt|| **to ~ off** vi (finish) σταματώ || **to ~ out** vt βγάζω, τινάζω, || (SPORT) βγάζω νοκ-άουτ || ~**er** n (on door) κτυπητήρι || ~-**kneed** a στραβοπόδης, στραβοκάνης || ~**out** n (lit) νοκ-άουτ nt inv.

knot [nɔt] n (of rope etc) κόμπος, δεσμός || (of ribbon) κόμπος || (measure) κόμβος ♦ vt δένω κόμπο.

know [nəʊ] (irreg v) vti (be aware of) ξέρω || (recognize) γνωρίζω, διακρίνω, ξέρω || **to ~ how to do** ξέρω πώς || ~-**all** n παντογνώστης/τρια m/f|| ~-**how** n μέθοδος f, τέχνη || ~**ing** a έξυπνος, πονηρός || ~**ingly** ad σκόπιμας, πονηρά.

knowledge ['nɔlɪdʒ] n (what one knows) γνώση, μάθηση || (information) είδηση, πληροφορίες fpl|| ~**able** a καλά πληροφορημένος, μορφωμένος.

known [nəʊn] pp of **know**.

knuckle ['nʌkl] n φάλαγγα, κλείδωση.

K.O. n abbr of **knockout**.

koran [kɒˈrɑː] n κοράνιο.

L

l. abbr of **litre**.

lab [læb] n abbr of **laboratory**.

label ['leɪbl] n ετικέτα ♦ vt επιγράφω, κολλώ ετικέτα.

labor ['leɪbə*] n (US) = **labour**.

laboratory [ləˈbɔrətərɪ] n εργαστήριο.

laborious [ləˈbɔːrɪəs] a κοπιώδης, επίπονος.

labour ['leɪbə*] n εργασία, μόχθος || (workmen) εργάτες mpl|| ~**er** n εργάτης/τρια m/f|| L~ **Party** n εργατικό κόμμα.

lace [leɪs] n δαντέλα || (braid) σειρήτι || (cord) κορδόνι ♦ vt δένω, πλέκω, βάζω δαντέλες.

lack [læk] vti στερούμαι ♦ n έλλειψη || **for ~ of** λόγω ελλείψεως.

lackadaisical [lækəˈdeɪzɪkəl] a άτονος, νωθρός.

laconic [ləˈkɒnɪk] a λακωνικός.

lacquer ['lækə*] n βερνίκι, λάκα.

lad [læd] n (boy) αγόρι || (young man) παλληκάρι.

ladder ['lædə*] n (lit) σκάλα, ανεμόσκαλα || (fig) (κοινωνική) κλίμακα.

laden ['leɪdn] a φορτωμένος.

ladle ['leɪdl] n κουτάλα.

lady ['leɪdɪ] n κυρία || (title) λαίδη || '**Ladies**' (lavatory) 'Κυριών', 'Γυναικών' || ~**bird**, ~**bug** (US) n λαμπρίτσα, πασχαλίτσα || ~-**in-waiting** n Κυρία των Τιμών || ~**like** a αρχοντικός, ευγενικός.

lag [læg] n (delay) καθυστέρηση, επιβράδυνση ♦ vi (also: ~ **behind**) βραδυπορώ ♦ vt (pipes) επενδύω, φασκιώνω.

lager ['lɑːgə*] n ελαφρά μπύρα, λάγκερ f inv.

lagging ['lægɪŋ] n μονωτική επένδυση.

lagoon [ləˈguːn] n λιμνοθάλασσα.

laid [leɪd] pt, pp of **lay** || **to be ~ up** είμαι κρεβατωμένος.

lair [lɛə*] n φωλιά, άντρο.

lake [leɪk] n λίμνη.

lamb [læm] n αρνάκι || (meat) αρνί || ~**chop** n παϊδάκι.

lame [leɪm] a κουτσός || (excuse) μη πειστικός.

lament [ləˈment] n θρήνος ♦ vt θρηνώ, οδύρομαι || ~**able** a αξιοθρήνητος.

laminated ['læmɪneɪtɪd] a φυλλωτός.

lamp [læmp] n λύχνος, λυχνάρι || (globe) λάμπα || (in street) φανάρι || ~**post** n φανοστάτης || ~**shade** n αμπαζούρ nt inv.

lance [lɑːns] n λόγχη ♦ vt εγχειρίζω, ανοίγω || ~ **corporal** n υποδεκανέας.

lancet ['lɑːnsɪt] n νυστέρι.

land [lænd] n γη, στερεά || (ground) γη, έδαφος nt|| (country) χώρα || (estate) κτήμα nt ♦ vi (from ship) αποβιβάζομαι || (AVIAT) προσγειούμαι || (fig: arrive, fall) πέφτω ♦ vt (obtain) πιάνω, λαμβάνω || (passengers, goods) αποβιβάζω, ξεφορτώνω || ~**ing** n απόβαση || (AVIAT) προσγείωση || (platform) πλατύσκαλο || ~**ing craft** n αποβατικό σκάφος || ~**ing stage** n αποβάθρα || ~**ing strip** n λωρίδα προσγειώσεως || ~**lady** n σπιτονοικοκυρά || ~**locked** a μεσόγειος || ~**lord** n σπιτονοικοκύρης || (innkeeper) ξενοδόχος || ~**lubber** n στεριανός || ~**mark** n ορόσημο || ~**owner** n γαιοκτήμονας.

landscape ['lændskeɪp] n τοπίο || (painting) ζωγραφική τοπίων.

landslide ['lændslaɪd] n (GEOG) (κατ)ολίσθηση || (POL) εντυπωσιακή στροφή.

lane [leɪn] n δρομίσκος, μονοπάτι || (of road) λωρίδα, διάδρομος || (SPORT) ατομική πίστα, λωρίδα.

language ['læŋgwɪdʒ] n γλώσσα ||

(national) γλώσσα, διάλεκτος f|| *(style)* γλώσσα, ομιλία.

languid ['læŋgwid] *a* νωθρός, αδρανής.

languish ['læŋgwiʃ] *vi* λυώνω, μαραίνομαι.

lank [læŋk] *a* μακρυά και ίσια || ~y μακρύς και λεπτός.

lanolin ['lænəʊlin] *n* λανολίνη.

lantern ['læntən] *n* φανάρι.

lap [læp] *n* ποδιά, γόνατα *ntpl* || *(SPORT)* γύρος, βόλτα ♦ *vt* γλείφω ♦ *vi (of waves)* παφλάζω || ~**dog** *n* χαϊδεμένο σκυλάκι.

lapel [lə'pɛl] *n* πέτο.

lapse [læps] *n* σφάλμα *nt* || *(moral)* παράβαση || *(of time)* παρέλευση, εκπνοή.

larceny ['lɑːsənɪ] *n* κλοπή.

lard [lɑːd] *n* λαρδί.

larder ['lɑːdə*] *n* αποθήκη τροφίμων, κελλάρι.

large [lɑːdʒ] *a (broad)* ευρύχωρος, εκτενής || *(big, numerous)* μεγάλος || **at** ~ *(free)* ελεύθερος || *(extensively)* γενικά || ~**ly** *ad* σε μεγάλο βαθμό || ~-**scale** *a* σε μεγάλη κλίμακα, μεγάλος.

lark [lɑːk] *n (bird)* κορυδαλός || *(joke)* αστείο, φάρσα || **to** ~ **about** *vi (col)* αστιεύομαι, κάνω φάρσες.

larva ['lɑːvə] *n* νύμφη.

laryngitis [lærɪn'dʒaɪtɪs] *n* λαρυγγίτιδα.

larynx ['lærɪŋks] *n* λάρυγγι.

lash [læʃ] *n (stroke)* καμτσικιά ♦ *vt (beat against)* δέρνω, ξεσπώ, κτυπώ || *(whip)* μαστιγώνω || *(bind)* (προς)δένω || **to** ~ **out** *vi (with fists)* επιτίθεμαι, εφορμώ || *(spend money)* κάνω σπατάλες.

lass [læs] *n* κορίτσι, κοπέλα.

lasso [læ'suː] *n* λάσσο ♦ *vt* πιάνω με λάσσο.

last [lɑːst] *a* τελευταίος, τελικός ♦ *ad* τελευταία ♦ *n (person or thing)* τελευταίος, ύστατος || *(for shoe)* καλαπόδι ♦ *vi (continue, hold out)* διαρκώ, παραμένω || *(remain)* συντηρούμαι, διατηρούμαι || **at** ~ επί τέλους || ~ **night** χθες το βράδυ || ~ **week** την περασμένη βδομάδα || ~**ing** *a* διαρκείας, που κρατά || ~-**minute** *a* της τελευταίας στιγμής.

latch [lætʃ] *n* μάνταλο, σύρτης || *(yale lock)* λουκέτο || ~**key** *n* απλό κλειδί, αντικλείδι.

late [leɪt] *a* καθυστερημένος, αργοπορημένος || *(not early)* αργά || *(recent)* παλιός, πρώην, τέως || *(recently dead)* μακαρίτης ♦ *ad* καθυστερημένα, αργά || *(late hour)* αργά || **of** ~ πρόσφατα || ~ **in the day** αργά το βραδάκι || ~**comer** *n* αργοπορημένος || ~**ly** *ad* πρόσφατα, τελευταία || ~**ness** *n (of person)* αργοπορία || *(of hour)* προχωρημένη ώρα.

latent ['leɪtənt] *a* αφανής, κρυφός.

later ['leɪtə*] *comp a, comp ad* of **late**.

lateral ['lætərəl] *a* πλάγιος, πλευρικός.

latest ['leɪtɪst] *sup a, sup ad* of **late** || *n (news)* το νεώτερο || **at the** ~ το αργότερο.

lathe [leɪð] *n* τόρνος.

lather ['lɑːðə*] *n* σαπουνάδα ♦ *vt* σαπουνίζω ♦ *vi* κάνω αφρό.

Latin ['lætɪn] *n* Λατινική (γλώσσα) ♦ *a* λατινικός || ~-**America** *n* Λατινική Αμερική ~-**American** *a* λατινοαμερικανικός ♦ *n* Λατινοαμερικανός/ίδα *m/f*.

latitude ['lætɪtjuːd] *n* γεωγραφικό πλάτος *nt* || *(freedom)* ευρυχωρία, περιθώριο.

latrine [lə'triːn] *n* αποχωρητήριο, μέρος *nt*.

latter ['lætə*] *a (more recent)* ο δεύτερος, άλλος || *(later)* τελευταίος, πρόσφατος ♦ *n (opposite of former)* ο δεύτερος, άλλος || ~**ly** *ad* τώρα τελευταία, πρόσφατα.

lattice work ['lætɪswɜːk] *n* δικτυωτό, καφάσι.

laudible ['lɔːdəbl] *a* αξιέπαινος.

laugh [lɑːf] *n* γέλιο ♦ *vi* γελώ || **to** ~ **at** *vt* διασκεδάζω, περιγελώ, γελώ για || **to** ~ **off** *vt* γελοιοποιώ || ~**able** *a* γελοίος, αστείος, διασκεδαστικός || ~**ing stock** *n* περίγελως, κορόιδο || ~**ter** *n* γέλιο.

launch [lɔːntʃ] *n (of ship)* καθέλκυση || *(of rocket)* εκτόξευση || *(ship)* άκατος || *(motor)* βενζινάκατος *f* ♦ *vt (ship)* καθελκύω || προβάλλω, βάζω εμπρός || ~**ing** *n* καθέλκυση, εκτόξευση || ~**(ing) pad** *n* πλατφόρμα εκτόξευσης.

launder ['lɔːndə*] *vt* πλένω και σιδερώνω || ~**ette** *n* πλυντήριο αυτοεξυπηρέτησης.

laundry ['lɔːndrɪ] *n (place)* πλυντήριο || *(clothes)* ρούχα *ntpl* για πλύσιμο.

laureate ['lɔːrɪɪt] *a see* **poet**.

laurel ['lɒrəl] *n* δάφνη.

lava ['lɑːvə] *n* λάβα.

lavatory ['lævətrɪ] *n* αποχωρητήριο, τουαλέτα.

lavender ['lævɪndə*] *n* λεβάντα.

lavish ['lævɪʃ] *a* γενναιόδωρος, σπάταλος || *(abundant)* άφθονος, πλούσιος ♦ *vt* κατασπαταλώ, διασπαθίζω || ~**ly** *ad* άφθονα, σπάταλα.

law [lɔː] *n* νόμος, νομικά *ntpl* || *(system of laws)* δίκαιο || *(of game etc)* κανόνες *mpl* || ~-**abiding** *a* νομοταγής || ~**breaker** *n* παραβάτης του νόμου || ~ **court** *n* δικαστήριο || ~**ful** *a* νόμιμος || ~**less** *a* άνομος, παράνομος.

lawn [lɔːn] *n* πρασιά, γρασίδι || ~**mower** *n* χορτοκόπτης || ~ **tennis** *n* τέννις *nt inv*.

law school ['lɔːskuːl] *n* σχολή νομικής.

law student ['lɔːstjuːdənt] *n* φοιτητής/ήτρια *m/f* νομικής.

lawsuit ['lɔːsuːt] *n* δίκη.

lawyer ['lɔːjə*] *n* νομικός *m/f*, δικηγόρος *m/f*.

lax [læks] *a* χαλαρός || *(morals etc)* έκλυτος, άτακτος.

laxative ['læksətɪv] *n* καθάρσιο.

laxity ['læksɪtɪ] *n* χαλαρότητα.

lay [leɪ] *(irreg v) pt* of **lie** || *a* λαϊκός, μη

L

ειδικός ♦ vt (put down) τοποθετώ, θέτω, βάζω || (lay low) ξαπλώνω, σωριάζω || (prepare) βάζω, στρώνω || (eggs) γεννώ, κάνω || to ~ aside vt θέτω κατά μέρος, βάζω || to ~ by vt αποταμιεύω, οικονομώ || to ~ down vt παραδίδω || (plan) σχεδιάζω || to ~ off vt (workers) απολύω || to ~ on vt επιβάλλω, επιθέτω || to ~ out vt απλώνω || (spend) ξοδεύω || (plan) σχεδιάζω || to ~ up vt (store) αποθηκεύω || (ship) παροπλίζω || ~-by n βοηθητική λωρίδα στάθμευσης.

layer ['leɪə*] n στρώμα nt.

layette [leɪ'et] n τα μωρουδιακά ntpl.

layman ['leɪmən] n λαϊκός.

layout ['leɪaut] n σχέδιο.

laze [leɪz] vi τεμπελιάζω, χασομερώ ||

laziness ['leɪzɪnɪs] n τεμπελιά, χάζεμα nt || lazy ['leɪzɪ] a οκνηρός, τεμπέλης.

lb. abbr. of pound (weight).

lead [led] n μόλυβδος || (of pencil) μολύβι, γραφίτης.

lead [liːd] (irreg v) n (front position) πρώτη θέση, αρχηγία || (distance, time ahead) προπορεία || (example) καθοδήγηση, παράδειγμα nt || (clue) υπαινιγμός || (THEAT) πρωταγωνιστής/ίστρια m/f ♦ vt οδηγώ, καθοδηγώ || (group etc) ηγούμαι, διευθύνω ♦ vi άγω, καταλήγω, πηγαίνω || to ~ astray vt παραπλανώ || to ~ away vt (παρα)σύρω || to ~ back vt επαναφέρω || to ~ on vt προτρέπω κεντρίζω || to ~ to vt (street) οδηγώ σε, πηγαίνω σε || (result in) καταλήγω || to ~ up to vt οδηγώ σε || ~er n αρχηγός, ηγέτης || (newspaper) κύριο άρθρο || ~ership n ηγεσία, αρχηγία || ~ing a κύριος, ηγετικός, σημαίνων || ~ing lady n (THEAT) πρωταγωνίστρια || ~ing light n (person) ηγετική φυσιογνωμία.

leaf [liːf] n φύλλο || (thin sheet) φύλλο || (table) φύλλο (τραπεζιού).

leaflet ['liːflɪt] n φυλλάδιο.

league [liːg] n σύνδεσμος, ένωση, συμμαχία || (measure) λεύγα.

leak [liːk] n διαφυγή, διαρροή || (hole) τρύπα ♦ vt (liquid etc) διαρρέω (δια)φεύγω || (NAUT) κάνω νερά ♦ vi (of pipe etc) διαρρέω, τρέχω || to ~ out vi (liquid etc) διαρρέω || (information) διαδίδομαι.

lean [liːn] (irreg v) a (thin) λιγνός || (meat) άπαχος || (poor) ισχνός, φτωχός ♦ n άπαχο κρέας nt ♦ vi κλίνω, γέρνω ♦ vt ακουμπώ, στηρίζομαι || to ~ back vi γέρνω τα πίσω || to ~ forward vi γέρνω προς τα εμπρός || to ~ on vt στηρίζομαι, ακουμπώ || to ~ over vi κύπτω || ~ing n κλίση, τάση || ~t [lent] pt, pp of lean || ~-to n υπόστεγο.

leap [liːp] (irreg v) n πήδημα nt ♦ vi πηδώ || by ~s and bounds αλματωδώς, καλπάζων || to ~ frog n καβάλες fpl, βαρελάκια ntpl || ~t [lept] pt, pp of leap || ~ year n δίσεκτος χρόνος.

learn [lɜːn] (irreg v) vti μαθαίνω || ~ed a μορφωμένος, πολυμαθής || ~er n (also

AUT) μαθητευόμενος, αρχάριος || ~ing n (εκ)μάθηση, μόρφωση.

lease [liːs] n εκμίσθωση, ενοικίαση, συμβόλαιο ♦ vt εκμισθώνω, ενοικιάζω.

leash [liːʃ] n λουρί, αλυσίδα.

least [liːst] a ελάχιστος, μικρότατος, λιγώτερος ♦ n (το) λιγώτερο, (το) μικρότερο || at ~ τουλάχιστο || not in the ~ καθόλου, ποτέ.

leather ['leðə*] n δέρμα nt, πετσί ♦ a δερμάτινος, πέτσινος.

leave [liːv] (irreg v) vt (go away from) φεύγω, εγκαταλείπω || (go without taking) αφήνω || (let stay) αφήνω || (give by will) αφήνω ♦ vi (depart) φεύγω ♦ n άδεια || (MIL) άδεια || on ~ με άδεια || to take one's ~ of αποχαιρετώ, φεύγω || to ~ out vt παραλείπω.

leaves [liːvz] npl of leaf.

Lebanon ['lebənən]: the ~ ο Λίβανος.

lecherous ['letʃərəs] a λάγνος, ασελγής.

lecture ['lektʃə*] n διάλεξη, μάθημα nt ♦ vi κάνω διάλεξη, κάνω μάθημα || ~r n ομιλητής/ήτρια m/f, υφηγητής/ήτρια m/f.

led [led] pt, pp of lead.

ledge [ledʒ] n άκρο, χείλος nt, ράφι || (of rock) ύφαλος, ξέρα.

ledger ['ledʒə*] n καθολικό (κατάστιχο).

lee [liː] n (from wind) προκάλυμμα nt.

leek [liːk] n πράσο.

leer [lɪə*] vi στραβοκοιτάζω.

leeway ['liːweɪ] n (fig) χαμός χρόνου, περιθώριο.

left [left] pt, pp of leave ♦ a αριστερός ♦ n (το) αριστερό, n αριστερά || the L ~ (POL) n αριστερά || ~-handed a αριστερόχειρας || ~-luggage (office) n γραφείο καταθέσεως αποσκευών || ~-overs npl πλεονάσματα ntpl, υπολείμματα ntpl || ~-wing n (POL) αριστερός.

leg [leg] n πόδι, γάμπα || (of table etc) πόδι || (on trouser etc) γάμπα.

legacy ['legəsɪ] n κληροδότημα nt || (from ancestors) κληρονομία.

legal ['liːgəl] a νομικός || (allowed) νόμιμος || ~ize vt νομιμοποιώ || ~ly ad νόμιμα, νομικώς || ~ tender n νόμισμα nt (υποχρεωτικά δεκτό).

legend ['ledʒənd] n θρύλος, μύθος || ~ary a θρυλικός, μυθικός.

legible ['ledʒəbl] a ευανάγνωστος.

legion ['liːdʒən] n λεγεώνα ♦ a (countless) αναρίθμητος.

legislate ['ledʒɪsleɪt] vi νομοθετώ.

legislation [ledʒɪs'leɪʃən] n νομοθεσία.

legislative ['ledʒɪslətɪv] a νομοθετικός.

legislature ['ledʒɪslətʃə*] n νομοθετικό σώμα nt.

legitimacy [lɪ'dʒɪtɪməsɪ] n νομιμότητα, γνησιότητα.

legitimate [lɪ'dʒɪtɪmɪt] a νομικός, λογικός.

leisure ['leʒə*] n σχόλη, άνεση, ελεύθερες ώρες fpl ♦ a της σχόλης, της αργίας || at ~ ελεύθερος, έχων καιρό || ~ly a οβίαστος, αργός, άνετος.

lemon ['lemən] n λεμόνι || (colour) λεμονής || ~ade n λεμονάδα.

lend [lend] (irreg v) vt δανείζω || (dignity etc) (προς)δίδω || it ~s itself to προσφέρεται, κάνει για || ~er n δανειστής/ίσρια m/f || ~ing library n δανειστική βιβλιοθήκη.

length [leŋθ] n μήκος nt, μάκρος nt || (of road, pipe etc) μήκος nt || (of material) κομμάτι || at ~ (finally) επί τέλους || (time) για πολλή ώρα || (extent) εν εκτάσει || ~en vt μακραίνω, επιμηκύνω ♦ vi επεκτείνομαι, παρατείνομαι || ~ways ad κατά μήκος, στο μάκρος || ~y a μακροσκελής, εκτενής.

leniency ['li:nɪənsɪ] n ηπιότητα, επιείκεια.

lenient ['li:nɪənt] a ήπιος, επιεικής.

lens [lenz] n φακός.

lent [lent] pt, pp of **lend** || **L~** n Σαρακοστή.

lentil ['lentl] n φακή.

leopard ['lepəd] n λεοπάρδαλη.

leper ['lepə*] n λεπρός/n m/f.

leprosy ['leprəsɪ] n λέπρα.

lesbian ['lezbɪən] a λεσβιακός ♦ n λεσβία.

less [les] a comp of **little** || λιγότερος ♦ ad λιγότερο ♦ n λιγότερο.

lessen ['lesn] vi μειούμαι, μικραίνω, λιγοστεύω ♦ vt μειώνω, ελαττώνω, μικραίνω.

lesson ['lesn] n μάθημα nt.

lest [lest] cj μήπως, μη τυχόν.

let [let] (irreg v) vt (allow) αφήνω, επιτρέπω || (lease) ενοικιάζω, εκμισθώνω ♦ n: without ~ or hindrance χωρίς εμπόδιο, ελεύθερα || ~'s go ας πάμε || 'to ~' 'ενοικιάζεται' || to ~ down vt κατεβάζω || (disappoint) απογοητεύω, εγκαταλείπω || to ~ go vti ελευθερώνω, χαλαρώνω || to ~ off vt απαλλάσσω, αφήνω, συγχωρώ, απολύω || to ~ out vt αφήνω || (garment) ανοίγω || (scream) αφήνω || to ~ up vi μειούμαι, ελαττούμαι.

lethal ['li:θəl] a θανατηφόρος.

lethargic [le'θα:dʒɪk] a ληθαργικός, νυσταλέος.

lethargy ['leθədʒɪ] n λήθαργος, ατονία.

letter ['letə*] n (sign) γράμμα nt, στοιχείο || επιστολή, γράμμα || ~box n γραμματοκιβώτιο || ~ing n γράμματα ntpl, μαρκάρισμα nt.

lettuce ['letɪs] n μαρούλι.

let-up ['letʌp] n (col) μείωση, χαλάρωση.

leukaemia, leukemia (US) [lu:'ki:mɪə] n λευκαιμία.

level ['levl] a επίπεδος, οριζόντιος ♦ ad οριζοντίως ♦ n επίπεδο, επίπεδος επιφάνεια || (height) στάθμη ♦ vt ισοπεδώνω, οριζοντιώνω || on the ~ (lit) επίπεδο, στο αλφάδι || (fig: honest) τίμιος, εντάξει || to ~ off or out vi εξισώνω || ~ crossing n επίπεδος

diάβαση || ~-**headed** a ισορροπημένος, ψύχραιμος.

lever ['li:və*] n μοχλός ♦ vt κινώ μοχλό || ~age n ενέργεια μοχλού, μόχλευση.

levity ['levɪtɪ] n ελαφρότητα, έλλειψη σοβαρότητας.

levy ['levɪ] n (taxes) είσπραξη || (MIL) στρατολογία ♦ vt εισπράττω, επιβάλλω || (MIL) στρατολογώ.

lewd [lu:d] a λάγνος, ασελγής.

liability [laɪə'bɪlɪtɪ] n (being liable) ευθύνη, υποχρέωση || (debt) υποχρέωση, οφειλή || (disadvantage) προδιάθεση, τάση.

liable ['laɪəbl] a (responsible) υπεύθυνος || (likely) υποκείμενος.

liaison [li:'eɪzɒn] n (coordination) σύνδεσμος.

liar ['laɪə*] n ψεύτης.

libel ['laɪbəl] n λίβελλος, δυσφήμιση ♦ vt διασύρω, δυσφημώ.

liberal ['lɪbərəl] a (generous) γενναιόδωρος || (open-minded) φιλελεύθερος ♦ n φιλελεύθερος || **L~ Party** Φιλελεύθερο Κόμμα.

liberate ['lɪbəreɪt] vt απελευθερώνω.

liberation [lɪbə'reɪʃən] n απελευθέρωση.

liberty ['lɪbətɪ] n ελευθερία || at ~ ελεύθερος, εύκαιρος.

librarian [laɪ'breərɪən] n βιβλιοθηκάριος m/f.

library ['laɪbrərɪ] n βιβλιοθήκη.

libretto [lɪ'bretəʊ] n λιμπρέττο.

Libya ['lɪbɪə] n Λιβύη || ~n a λιβυκός ♦ n (person) Λίβυος/a m/f.

lice [laɪs] npl of **louse**.

licence, license (US) ['laɪsəns] n (permit) άδεια, έγκριση, προνόμιο || (lack of control) κατάχρηση || ~ plate n (US AUT) πινακίδα.

license ['laɪsəns] vt δίνω άδεια, παρέχω άδεια || ~d a (for alcohol: premises) με άδεια πωλήσεως ποτού || ~e n προνομιούχος.

licentious [laɪ'senʃəs] a ακόλαστος.

lichen ['laɪkən] n λειχήνα.

lick [lɪk] vt γλείφω || (of flames etc) παίζω με, εγγίζω, καταβροχθίζω ♦ n γλείψιμο || (small amount) μικρή ποσότητα.

licorice ['lɪkərɪs] n γλυκόρριζα.

lid [lɪd] n κάλυμμα nt, καπάκι.

lido ['li:dəʊ] n (for swimming) δημόσια πισίνα.

lie [laɪ] (irreg v) n ψέμα nt ♦ vi (speak) λέω ψέματα || (rest) είμαι ξαπλωμένος, μένω || (of object: be situated) κείμαι, ευρίσκομαι.

lieu [lu:] n: in ~ of αντί του, στη θέση του.

lieutenant [lef'tenənt] n (army) υπολοχαγός || [lu:'tenənt] (US) υποσμηναγός.

life [laɪf] n (being alive) ζωή || (way of living) τρόπος ζωής, ζωή || (time of life) ζωή, διάρκεια ζωής, βίος || (story) βίος, βιογραφία || (energy, vigour) ζωηρότητα, ζωή, κίνηση || ~ assurance n ασφάλεια ζωής || ~belt n σωσίβιο || ~boat n ναυαγοσωστική λέμβος f|| ~guard n ναυαγοσώστης|| ~ jacket n σωσίβιο || ~less a (dead) νεκρός || χωρίς ζωή, χωρίς κέφι || ~like a ρεαλιστικός, ζωντανός || ~line n (lit) σωσίβιο σχοινί || ~long a ισόβιος, ολόκληρης ζωής || ~-sized a φυσικού μεγέθους || ~ span n διάρκεια ζωής, μέσος όρος ζωής || ~ time n ζωή.

lift [lɪft] vt (αν)υψώνω, σηκώνω || (col: steal) κλέβω ♦ vi υψώνομαι, σηκώνομαι ♦ n ανύψωση, σήκωμα nt || (AVIAT) άνωση || (machine, elevator) ανελκυστήρας, ασανσέρ nt inv|| (free ride) παίρνω στο αυτοκίνητο.

ligament [ˈlɪɡəmənt] n σύνδεσμος.

light [laɪt] (irreg v) n φως nt || (giving light) φως nt, φωτισμός || (for cigarette) φωτιά || (lamp) φως nt, λάμπα || (brightness) λάμψη || (of dawn) λάμψη || (information) διαφώτιση || (aspect) φως nt, όψη, άποψη ♦ vt ανάβω || (set burning) ανάβω || (brighten) φωτίζω, φέγγω ♦ a (bright) φωτεινός || (colour) ανοιχτόχρωμος, ξανθός || (not heavy) ελαφρός || (easy to do) εύκολος || (delicate) ελαφρός, απαλός || (cheerful) εύθυμος || ~ up vi (lamps) ανάβω, φωτίζω || (face) αστράφτω, λάμπω ♦ vt (illuminate) (δια)φωτίζω || ~ bulb n λάμπα, λαμπτήρας || ~en vi (brighten) φωτίζομαι || (flash lightning) αστράφτω ♦ vt (give light to) φωτίζω || (make less heavy) ελαφρώνω || ~er n (cigarette lighter) αναπτήρας || (boat) φορτηγίδα || ~-headed a ζαλισμένος || (thoughtless) επιπόλαιος, απερίσκεπτος || ~-hearted a εύθυμος, χαρούμενος || ~house n φάρος || ~ing n (on road) φωτισμός || (in theatre) φωτισμός || ~ly ad ελαφρώς, ελαφρά || ~ meter n (PHOT) μετρητής φωτός || ~ness n ελαφρότητα.

lightning [ˈlaɪtnɪŋ] n αστραπή, κεραυνός || ~ conductor n αλεξικέραυνο.

light year [ˈlaɪtjɪə*] n έτος φωτός.

like [laɪk] vt μου αρέσει, συμπαθώ, προτιμώ ♦ prep σαν, όπως, ως ♦ a (similar) όμοιος, ίδιος || (equal) ίσος, παρόμοιος ♦ ad όπως, σαν ♦ n όμοιος || ~able a ευχάριστος, συμπαθητικός.

likelihood [ˈlaɪklɪhud] n πιθανότητα.

likely [ˈlaɪklɪ] a πιθανός, που μπορεί να ♦ ad πιθανό, ίσως.

like-minded [laɪkˈmaɪndɪd] a με την αυτή γνώμη.

liken [ˈlaɪkən] vt συγκρίνω, παρομοιάζω.

likewise [ˈlaɪkwaɪz] ad ομοίως, επίσης, επί πλέον.

liking [ˈlaɪkɪŋ] n κλίση, τάση, συμπάθεια, γούστο.

lilac [ˈlaɪlək] n πασχαλιά.

lily [ˈlɪlɪ] n κρίνο.

limb [lɪm] n μέλος nt, άκρο || (of tree) κλάδος.

limber [ˈlɪmbə*] : to ~ up vi γίνομαι ευλύγιστος.

limbo [ˈlɪmbəu] n: to be in ~ (fig) είμαι σε κατάσταση αβεβαιότητας.

lime [laɪm] n (tree) γλυκολεμονιά, κίτριο || φιλύρα || (fruit) γλυκολέμονο, κίτριο || (GEOL) ασβέστης.

limelight [ˈlaɪmlaɪt] n (fig) το προσκήνιο, δημοσιότητα.

limestone [ˈlaɪmstəun] n ασβεστόλιθος.

limit [ˈlɪmɪt] n όριο, σύνορο, πέρας nt ♦ vt περιορίζω || ~ation n περιορισμός, ανικανότητα || ~ed a περιωρισμένος, στενός || ~ed company (Ltd.) n εταιρεία περιωρισμένης ευθύνης.

limousine [ˈlɪməziːn] n λιμουζίνα.

limp [lɪmp] n χωλότητα ♦ vi χωλαίνω, κουτσαίνω ♦ a απαλός, πλαδαρός, μαλακός || (without energy) λυωμένος, τσακισμένος.

limpet [ˈlɪmpɪt] n πεταλίδα.

line [laɪn] n (cord, wire, string) σχοινί, γραμμή, σύρμα nt || (narrow mark) γραμμή || (row, series) σειρά, γραμμή || (course, direction) κατεύθυνση, τρόπος, πορεία || (class of goods) σειρά, συλλογή, είδος nt || (poetry etc) στίχος, γραμμή ♦ vt (coat etc) φοδράρω || (border) χαράσσω || in ~ with σύμφωνα με || to ~ up vi μπαίνω στη γραμμή || σχηματίζω ουρά ♦ vt παρατάσσω, βάζω στη γραμμή.

linear [ˈlɪnɪə*] a (of length) του μήκους, γραμμική.

linen [ˈlɪnɪn] n λινό ύφασμα nt || (articles) ασπρόρουχα ntpl.

liner [ˈlaɪnə*] n πλοίο γραμμής.

linesman [ˈlaɪnzmən] n (SPORT) λάινσμαν m inv.

line-up [ˈlaɪnʌp] n παράταξη.

linger [ˈlɪŋɡə*] vi (remain long) χρονοτριβώ, παρατείνομαι || (delay) αργοπορώ, βραδύνω.

lingerie [ˈlænʒəriː] n γυναικεία εσώρουχα ntpl.

lingering [ˈlɪŋɡərɪŋ] a παρατεταμένος, βραδύς, αργοπός.

lingo [ˈlɪŋɡəu] n (col) γλώσσα, διάλεκτος f.

linguist [ˈlɪŋɡwɪst] n γλωσσολόγος m/f, γλωσσομαθής m/f.

linguistic [lɪŋˈgwɪstɪk] a γλωσσολογικός || ~s n γλωσσολογία.

lining [ˈlaɪnɪŋ] n φόδρα.

link [lɪŋk] n (of chain) κρίκος || δεσμός σύνδεσμος ♦ vt συνδέω, ενώνω || ~s npl γήπεδο γκολφ|| ~-up n (communication) σύνδεση.

linoleum [lɪˈnəuliəm] n μουσαμάς, δαπέδου.

lion [ˈlaɪən] n λιοντάρι, || ~ess n λέαινα.

lip [lɪp] n χείλι, χείλος nt || to pay ~ service (+to) κάνω ψεύτικες υποσχέσεις || ~stick n κραγιόν nt inv.

liqueur [lɪˈkjuə*] n λικέρ nt inv.

liquid [ˈlɪkwɪd] n υγρό ♦ a (substance) υγρός, ρευστός || (asset) ρευστός, διαθέσιμος || ~ate vt διαλύω,

ξεκαθαρίζω, χρεωκοπώ|| ~ation n
διάλυση, εξόφληση, χρεωκόπηση..
liquor ['lɪkə*] n (strong drink)
οινοπνευματώδες ποτό.
lisp [lɪsp] n τραυλισμός, ψεύδισμα nt.
list [lɪst] n (of names etc) κατάλογος || (on
ship) κλίση, γέρσιμο ♦ vt (write down)
εγγράφω, καταγράφω ♦ vi (of ship)
κλίνω, γέρνω.
listen ['lɪsn] vi ακούω, προσέχω|| to ~
to vt ακούω || ~er n ακροατής/άτρια
m/f.
listless ['lɪstlɪs] a άτονος, νωθρός,
αδιάφορος.
lit [lɪt] pt, pp of **light**.
litany ['lɪtənɪ] n λιτανεία.
liter ['liːtə*] n (US) = **litre**.
literacy ['lɪtərəsɪ] n βαθμός μόρφωσης.
literal ['lɪtərəl] a (word for word) κατά
λέξη || (usual meaning) κατά κυριολεξία ||
~ly ad κυριολεκτικά.
literary ['lɪtərərɪ] a λογοτεχνικός,
φιλολογικός.
literate ['lɪtərɪt] a εγγράμματος.
literature ['lɪtərɪtʃə*] n φιλολογία,
λογοτεχνία.
litre ['liːtə*] n λίτρο.
litter ['lɪtə*] n (untidy bits) σκουπίδια ntpl
|| (young animals) γέννα, νεογνά ntpl ♦ vt
κάνω άνω-κάτω, βρωμίζω με σκουπίδια.
little ['lɪtl] a (small) μικρός, λίγος, κοντός
|| (unimportant) ασήμαντος ♦ ad ελάχιστα,
λίγο ♦ n λίγο.
liturgy ['lɪtədʒɪ] n λειτουργία.
live [lɪv] vi ζω || (pass one's life) ζω || (last)
ζω, διαρκώ || (dwell) κατοικώ, διαμένω,
ζω || to ~ down vt κάνω να ξεχαστεί,
υπερνικώ || to ~ on vt τρέφομαι με,
συντηρούμαι με || to ~ up to vt
εφαρμόζω, τιμώ, εκπληρώνω.
live [laɪv] a (a living) ζωντανός || (burning)
αναμμένος || (wire) ηλεκτρισμένος με
ρεύμα || (broadcast) ζωντανό πρόγραμμα.
livelihood ['laɪvlɪhud] n τα προς το ζην.
lively ['laɪvlɪ] a ζωηρός.
liver ['lɪvə*] n (ANAT) συκώτι.
livery ['lɪvərɪ] n στολή υπηρέτη.
lives [laɪvz] npl of **life**.
livestock ['laɪvstɒk] n ζώα ntpl, κτήνη
ntpl.
livid ['lɪvɪd] a (lit) πελιδνός, ωχρός ||
(furious) οργισμένος.
living ['lɪvɪŋ] n τα προς το ζην, βίος ♦ a
ζωντανός || (wage) βασικός μισθός || ~
room n σαλόνι.
lizard ['lɪzəd] n σαύρα.
load [ləud] n φορτίο, φόρτωμα nt ♦ vt
φορτώνω, γεμίζω.
loaf [ləuf] n καρβέλι ♦ vi χαζεύω,
τεμπελιάζω.
loan [ləun] n δάνειο, δανεισμός ♦ vt
δανείζω || on ~ απεσπασμένος.
loathe [ləuð] vt σιχαίνομαι.
loathing ['ləuðɪŋ] n σιχαμός, απδία.
loaves [ləuvz] npl of **loaf**.
lobby ['lɒbɪ] n προθάλαμος, είσοδος f ♦
vt επηρεάζω βουλευτές.

lobe [ləub] n λοβός.
lobster ['lɒbstə*] n αστακός.
local ['ləukəl] a τοπικός, επιτόπιος ♦ n
(pub) ταβέρνα || **the ~s** npl ντόπιοι mpl||
~ity n θέση, μέρος, τοποθεσία || ~ly ad
τοπικά, επιτόπια.
locate [ləu'keɪt] vt εντοπίζω || (establish)
τοποθετώ.
location [ləu'keɪʃən] n τοποθεσία.
loch [lɒx] n λίμνη.
lock [lɒk] n (of door) κλειδαριά || (of canal
etc) υδροφράκτης, φράγμα nt || (of hair)
βόστρυχος, μπούκλα ♦ vt κλειδώνω ||
σφίγγω, στερεώνω ♦ vi (door etc)
ασφαλίζομαι || (wheels) σφηνώνω,
μπλοκάρομαι.
locker ['lɒkə*] n αρμάρι, ντουλάπι,
αποθήκη.
locket ['lɒkɪt] n μενταγιόν nt inv.
locomotive [ləukə'məutɪv] n ατμάμαξα,
ατμομηχανή.
locust ['ləukəst] n ακρίδα.
lodge [lɒdʒ] n εξοχικό σπίτι || (at gate)
σπιτάκι του φύλακα || (meeting place)
στοά ♦ vi φιλοξενούμαι, διαμένω || (rent
a room) είμαι νοικάρης || (stick)
αφηνώνομαι, πιάνομαι ♦ vt καταθέτω,
υποβάλλω || ~r n ένοικος m/f.
lodgings ['lɒdʒɪŋz] npl δωμάτια ntpl.
loft [lɒft] n υπερώο, σοφίτα.
lofty ['lɒftɪ] a ψηλός || (proud)
υπεροπτικός, αγέρωχος.
log [lɒg] n (of wood) κούτσουρο || (of ship
etc) ημερολόγιο.
logarithm ['lɒgərɪθəm] n λογάριθμος.
logbook ['lɒgbuk] n ημερολόγιο
(πλοίου).
loggerheads ['lɒgəhedz] n: at ~
τσακωμένος, στα μαχαίρια.
logic ['lɒdʒɪk] n λογική || ~al a λογικός.
loin [lɔɪn] n πλευρό ntpl, λαγόνες mpl.
loiter ['lɔɪtə*] vi χρονοτριβώ, χαζεύω.
loll [lɒl] vi ξαπλώνω, χουζουρεύω.
lollipop ['lɒlɪpɒp] n γλειφιτζούρι.
London ['lʌndən] n Λονδίνο || ~er n
(person) Λονδρέζος/α m/f.
lone [ləun] a (solitary) μόνος, μοναχικός ||
~liness n μοναξιά, ερημιά || ~ly a (sad)
μελαγχολικός, έρημος, ακατοίκητος.
long [lɒŋ] a μακρύς, εκτενής || (length)
μάκρος ♦ ad (time) για πολλή ώρα ||
(during) όλη, σ όλη ♦ vi (+ for) ποθώ,
λαχταρώ || **before** ~ σύντομα || **as** ~ **as**
εφ' όσο || **in the** ~ **run** στο τέλος,
τελικά || ~-**distance** a (TEL)
υπεραστικός || (SPORT) μεγάλων
αποστάσεων || ~-**haired** a μακρυμάλλης
|| ~-**hand** n κανονική γραφή || ~-**ing** n
πόθος, λαχτάρα ♦ a γεμάτος λαχτάρα.
longitude ['lɒŋgɪtjuːd] n μήκος.
long: ~ **jump** n άλμα εις μήκος ||
~-**lost** a χαμένος προ πολλού || ~-
playing record (L.P.) n δίσκος μακράς
διαρκείας || ~-**range** a μεγάλης
διαρκείας, μεγάλης ακτίνας || ~-
sighted a πρεσβύωπας, οξυδερκής || ~-
standing a παλιός, μακροχρόνιος || ~-

suffering a υπομονητικός, μακρόθυμος || ~-**term** a μακροπρόθεσμος, μακροχρόνιος || ~ **wave** n μακρύ κύμα || ~-**winded** a ατελείωτος, φλύαρος.

loo [luː] n μέρος nt.

loofah ['luːfə] n (ελ)λύφι.

look [luk] vi (see) κοιτάζω, βλέπω || (seem) φαίνομαι || (face) βλέπω, αντικρύζω ♦ n βλέμμα nt, ματιά || ~**s** npl όψη, εμφάνιση || **to** ~ **after** vt φροντίζω για || **to** ~ **down on** vt (fig) περιφρονώ || **to** ~ **for** vt ψάχνω, ζητώ || (expect) προσδοκώ || **to** ~ **forward to** vt προσδοκώ || **to** ~ **out for** vt αναζητώ, ψάχνω, προσέχω || **to** ~ **to** vt φροντίζω για, βασίζομαι σε || **to** ~ **up** vt καλυτερεύω ♦ vt επισκέπτομαι, ψάχνω (σε βιβλίο) || **to** ~ **up to** vt σέβομαι || ~**out** n (watch) προσοχή || (view) θέα || (MIL) φρούρηση, φρουρός.

loom [luːm] n αργαλειός ♦ vi διαφαίνομαι, διακρίνομαι.

loop [luːp] n βρόχος, θηλιά ♦ vt κάνω θηλιά, δένω με θηλιά || ~**hole** n (for escape) υπεκφυγή, διέξοδος f.

loose [luːs] a χαλαρός || (free) ελεύθερος, λυμένος || (slack) απρόσεκτος, απαλός ♦ vt λύνω, λασκάρω, χαλαρώνω || **at a** ~ **end** χωρίς απασχόληση || ~**ly** ad χαλαρά, ασαφώς || ~**n** vt λύνω, λασκάρω.

loot [luːt] n λάφυρο, λεία, πλιάτσικο ♦ vt λαφυραγωγώ, λεηλατώ || ~**ing** n λεηλασία.

lop [lɔp] : **to** ~ **off** vt (απο)κόβω, κλαδεύω.

lop-sided ['lɔp'saidid] a ετεροβαρής, που γέρνει.

lord [lɔːd] n άρχοντας, αφέντης || (Brit) λόρδος || **the L** ~ ο Κύριος || ~**ly** a μεγαλοπρεπής, αγέρωχος || ~**ship** n (title) εξοχότητα.

lore [lɔː*] n ειδική γνώση, παραδόσεις fpl.

lorry ['lɔri] n φορτηγό (αυτοκίνητο), καμιόνι || ~ **driver** n οδηγός φορτηγού.

lose [luːz] (irreg v) vt (most senses) χάνω || (waste) σπαταλώ, χάνω || ♦ vi χάνω || ~**r** n νικημένος χαμένος.

loss [lɔs] n απώλεια, χάσιμο || (what is lost) απώλεια || (harm) ζημιά || **to be at a** ~ τα έχω χαμένα, βρίσκομαι σε αμηχανία.

lost [lɔst] pt, pp of **lose** ♦ a χαμένος || ~ **property** n (γραφείο) απολεσθέντων αντικειμένων.

lot [lɔt] n (large quantity) πολύ || (for prize) κλήρος || (group of objects) σύνολο, σε παρτίδες || **a** ~ **of** ένα σωρό, πολύ || ~**s of** πλήθος, ένα σωρό.

lotion ['ləuʃən] n λοσιόν f inv.

lottery ['lɔtəri] n λαχείο.

loud [laud] a βροντερός, θορυβώδης, μεγαλόφωνος || (showy) κτυπητός ♦ ad δυνατά, μεγαλόφωνα || ~**ly** ad δυνατά, μεγαλόφωνα || ~**speaker** n μεγάφωνο.

lounge [laundʒ] n μικρό σαλόνι, χωλ nt inv ξενοδοχείου ♦ vi περιφέρομαι

άσκοπα, χαζεύω || ~ **suit** n καθημερινό κοστούμι.

louse [laus] n ψείρα.

lousy ['lauzi] a (lit) ψειριάρης || (fig) βρωμερός, άθλιος.

lout [laut] n άξεστος, ντουβάρι.

lovable ['lʌvəbl] a αξιαγάπητος.

love [lʌv] n αγάπη, έρωτας, στοργή || (person loved) αγαπημένος, ερωμένος || (SPORT) μηδέν ♦ vt (person) αγαπώ || (activity) λατρεύω, αγαπώ || **to** ~ **to do** μου αρέσει να κάνω || **to make** ~ κάνω έρωτα, φλερτάρω || ~ **affair** n ερωτική υπόθεση || ~ **letter** n ερωτικό γράμμα nt || ~ **life** n ερωτική ζωή.

lovely ['lʌvli] a ωραίος, χαριτωμένος, ευχάριστος.

lovemaking ['lʌvmeikiŋ] n ερωτοτροπία, κόρτε nt inv.

lover ['lʌvə*] n (general) φιλο- || (man) εραστής, φίλος.

lovesong ['lʌvsɔŋ] n ερωτικό τραγούδι.

loving ['lʌviŋ] a τρυφερός, στοργικός.

low [ləu] a (not tall) χαμηλός || (rank) ταπεινός, κατώτερος || (common) χυδαίος, άξεστος || (not loud) αδύνατος, χαμηλός || (weak) κακόκεφος || (tide) άμπωτη ♦ ad χαμηλά || (not loudly) χαμηλόφωνα, χαμηλά ♦ n (low point) ναδίρ nt inv || (meteorology) βαρομετρικό χαμηλό || ~-**cut** a (dress) ντεκολτέ.

lower ['ləuə*] vt κατεβάζω, χαμηλώνω || (make less) ελαττώνω.

lowly ['ləuli] a ταπεινός, μετριόφρονας.

loyal ['lɔiəl] a πιστός, αφοσιωμένος || ~**ty** n πίστη, αφοσίωση.

lozenge ['lɔzindʒ] n παστίλια.

L.P. n abbr see long-playing record.

Ltd. abbr see limited.

lubricant ['luːbrikənt] n λιπαντικό, γράσο.

lubricate ['luːbrikeit] vt λιπαίνω, λαδώνω, γρασάρω.

lucid ['luːsid] a σαφής, διαυγής || ~**ity** n σαφήνεια, διαύγεια.

luck [lʌk] n τύχη || ~**ily** ad ευτυχώς || ~**y** a τυχερός.

lucrative ['luːkrətiv] a επικερδής.

ludicrous ['luːdikrəs] a αλλόκοτος, γελοίος, αστείος.

lug [lʌg] vt σέρνω με δυσκολία.

luggage ['lʌgidʒ] n αποσκευές fpl || ~ **rack** n (in train etc) δίχτυ nt για βαλίτσες.

lukewarm ['luːkwɔːm] a χλιαρός || (indifferent) αδιάφορος.

lull [lʌl] n ανάπαυλα, κόπαση ♦ vt νανουρίζω || (calm) καθησυχάζω, καταπραΰνω.

lullaby ['lʌləbai] n νανούρισμα nt.

lumbago [lʌm'beigəu] n οσφυαλγία.

lumber ['lʌmbə*] n (old articles) παλιατσούρες fpl || (wood) ξυλεία || ~**jack** n ξυλοκόπος.

luminous ['luːminəs] a φωτεινός, φωτισμένος.

lump [lʌmp] n (σ)βώλος, μεγάλο κομμάτι || (swelling) εξόγκωμα nt,

καρσύμπαλο || (of sugar) κομμάτι ♦ vt
σβωλιάζω, συσσωρεύω || a ~ sum
στρογγυλό ποσό, ολική τιμή || ~y a
σβωλιασμένος.
lunacy ['lu:nəsɪ] n παραφροσύνη.
lunar ['lu:nə*] a σεληνιακός.
lunatic ['lu:nətɪk] n παράφρονας ♦ a
παράφρονας, τρελός.
lunch [lʌntʃ] n (also: ~**eon**) γεύμα ||
~**time** n μεσημβρινή διακοπή.
lung [lʌŋ] n πνεύμονας || ~ **cancer** n
καρκίνος των πνευμόνων.
lunge [lʌndʒ] vi μπήγω, κτυπώ ξαφνικά,
εφορμώ.
lurch [lɜːtʃ] vi τρικλίζω, ταλαντεύομαι ♦
n τρίκλισμα nt, μπότζι.
lure [lɜːk*] n δελέασμα nt, δόλωμα nt,
έλξη ♦ vt δελεάζω, θέλγω.
lurid ['ljuərɪd] a (shocking) τρομερός.
lurk [lɜːk] vi παραμονεύω, κρύβομαι.
luscious ['lʌʃəs] a γευστικός, χυμώδης,
γλυκύτατος.
lush [lʌʃ] a γεμάτος χυμούς || (countryside)
πλούσιος σε βλάστηση.
lust [lʌst] n σαρκική επιθυμία ♦ vi (+
after) εποφθαλμιώ, ορέγομαι || ~**ful** a
λάγνος.
lustre, luster (US) ['lʌstə*] n λάμψη,
στιλπνότητα.
lusty ['lʌstɪ] a εύρωστος, σφριγηλός.
lute [luːt] n λαούτο.
Luxembourg ['lʌksəmbɜːg] n
Λουξεμβούργο.
luxuriant [lʌg'zjuərɪənt] a άφθονος,
πλούσιος.
luxurious [lʌg'zjuərɪəs] a πολυτελής,
πλούσιος.
luxury ['lʌkʃərɪ] n πολυτέλεια, λούσο.
lying ['laɪɪŋ] n κείμενος || (not truthful)
ψευδόμενος ♦ a ψεύτικος.
lynch [lɪntʃ] vt λυντσάρω.
lyre ['laɪə*] n λύρα.
lyric ['lɪrɪk] n λόγια ntpl τραγουδιού ♦ a
λυρικός || ~**al** a (fig) ενθουσιώδης,
λυρικός.

M

M. abbr of **metre, mile, million**.
M. A. abbr see **master**.
mac [mæk] n (raincoat) αδιάβροχο.
macaroni [mækə'rəʊnɪ] n μακαρόνια
ntpl.
mace [meɪs] n (spice) μοσχοκάρυδο.
machine [mə'ʃiːn] n (general) μηχανή,
μηχάνημα nt ♦ vt (dress etc)
επεξεργάζομαι, κατεργάζομαι || ~ **gun** n
πολυβόλο || ~**ry** n μηχανές fpl || (parts)
μηχανήματα ntpl || (of government)
μηχανισμός.
machinist [mə'ʃiːnɪst] n μηχανουργός.
mackerel ['mækrəl] n σκουμπρί.
mackintosh ['mækɪntɒʃ] n αδιάβροχο.
mad [mæd] a παράφρονας, τρελός ||
(foolish) παράλογος.
madam ['mædəm] n κυρία.

madden ['mædn] vt τρελαίνω.
made [meɪd] pt, pp of **make** || ~**-to-
measure** a κατά παραγγελία.
madly ['mædlɪ] ad τρελά, άγρια.
madman ['mædmən] n (maniac)
φρενοβλαβής, τρελός.
madness ['mædnɪs] n παραφροσύνη,
τρέλα.
Madonna [mə'dɒnə] n Παναγία.
magazine [mægə'ziːn] n περιοδικό.
maggot ['mægət] n σκουλίκι.
magic ['mædʒɪk] n μαγεία ♦ a μαγικός,
μαγεμένος || ~**al** a μαγικός || ~**ian** n
μάγος.
magistrate ['mædʒɪstreɪt] n
ειρηνοδίκης.
magnanimous [mæg'nænɪməs] a
μεγαλόψυχος.
magnate ['mægneɪt] n μεγιστάνας.
magnet ['mægnɪt] n μαγνήτης || ~**ic** a
μαγνητικός || ~**ism** n μαγνητισμός.
magnification [mægnɪfɪ'keɪʃən] n
μεγέθυνση.
magnificence [mæg'nɪfɪsəns] n
μεγαλοπρέπεια.
magnificent [mæg'nɪfɪsənt] a
μεγαλοπρεπής.
magnify ['mægnɪfaɪ] vt μεγεθύνω,
υπερβάλλω || ~**ing glass** n
μεγεθυντικός φακός.
magnitude ['mægnɪtjuːd] n μέγεθος nt,
σπουδαιότητα.
magnolia [mæg'nəʊlɪə] n μανόλια.
magpie ['mægpaɪ] n καρακάτσα.
mahogany [mə'hɒgənɪ] n μαόνι.
maid [meɪd] n (servant) υπηρέτρια.
maiden ['meɪdən] n κορίτσι, παρθένος f
♦ a (lady) άγαμος || ~ **name** n
οικογενειακό όνομα || ~ **speech** n
παρθενικός λόγος || ~ **voyage** n
παρθενικό ταξίδι.
mail [meɪl] n επιστολές fpl, ταχυδρομείο
|| (system) ταχυδρομείο ♦ vt (US)
ταχυδρομώ || ~**box** n γραμματοκιβώτιο
|| ~**-order** n ταχυδρομική εντολή.
maim [meɪm] vt ακρωτηριάζω,
σακατεύω.
main [meɪn] a κύριος, πρωτεύων ♦ n
(pipe) κεντρικός αγωγός || **in the** ~
γενικά, ως επί το πλείστο || ~**frame**
(computer) n Η/Υ μεγάλου μεγέθους ||
~**land** n στερεά, ηπειρωτική χώρα || ~
road n κεντρική οδός f || ~**stay** n (fig)
κύριο έρεισμα nt, στήριγμα nt.
maintain [meɪn'teɪn] vt (machine)
διατηρώ, συντηρώ || (support) συντηρώ,
τρέφω || (traditions) συντηρώ, συνεχίζω ||
(an opinion) υποστηρίζω.
maintenance ['meɪntɪnəns] n (TECH)
συντήρηση.
maisonette [meɪzə'net] n διαμέρισμα
nt, μονοκατοικία.
maize [meɪz] n αραποσίτι, καλαμπόκι.
majestic [mə'dʒestɪk] a μεγαλοπρεπής.
majesty ['mædʒɪstɪ] n μεγαλείο ||
His / Her M~ n Αυτού/Αυτή
Μεγαλειότης.

M

major ['meɪdʒə*] n (MIL) ταγματάρχης ♦ a (MUS) μείζων.

majority [mə'dʒɒrɪtɪ] n πλειοψηφία || (number) πλειονότητα.

make [meɪk] (irreg v) vt (build, shape, produce) κάνω, φτιάχνω, δημιουργώ || (appoint) κάνω, ορίζω || (cause to do) αναγκάζω, κάνω, υποχρεώνω || (reach) φθάνω || (earn) κάνω, αποκτώ, κερδίζω, βγάζω || (do, perform) κάνω || (amount to) κάνω || (prepare) φτιάχνω ♦ n (style) κατασκευή, τύπος || (kind) μάρκα || to ~ for vt (place) κατευθύνομαι, πηγαίνω || to ~ out vi επιτυγχάνω, καταφέρνω ♦ vt (write out) συντάσσω, βγάζω, ετοιμάζω || (understand) καταλήγω, καταλαβαίνω || (pretend) προσποιούμαι, παριστάνω || to ~ up vt (make) συντάσσω, φτιάχνω, πλάθω || (face) βάφομαι, μακιγιάρομαι, φτιάχνομαι || (settle) ρυθμίζω, συμφιλιώνω, διευθετώ || to ~ up for vt ανακτώ, αναπληρώνω || ~believe n προσποίηση, υπόκριση ♦ a προσποιητός, ψεύτικος || ~r n κατασκευαστής/άστρια m/f, δημιουργός m/f || ~shift a προσωρινή λύση || ~-up n (cosmetics) μακιγιάζ nt inv || σύσταση || (THEAT) μακιγιάζ nt inv, βάψιμο.

making ['meɪkɪŋ] n: in the ~ εν εξελίξει.

malaise [mæ'leɪz] n αδιαθεσία.

malaria [mə'leərɪə] n ελονοσία.

Malaysia [mə'leɪzɪə] n Μαλαισία.

male [meɪl] n άνδρας ♦ a αρσενικός.

malevolent [mə'levələnt] a κακόβουλος.

malfunction [mæl'fʌŋkʃən] vi λειτουργώ ελαττωματικά.

malice ['mælɪs] n κακεντρέχεια, έχθρα.

malicious [mə'lɪʃəs] a κακόβουλος, μοχθηρός.

malign [mə'laɪn] vt δυσφημίζω, κακολογώ.

malignant [mə'lɪgnənt] a (tumour) κακοήθης.

malleable ['mælɪəbl] a ελάσιμος, μαλακός.

mallet ['mælɪt] n ξύλινο σφυρί, κόπανος.

malnutrition [mælnju'trɪʃən] n υποσιτισμός.

malpractice [mæl'præktɪs] n αδίκημα nt, κατάχρηση.

malt [mɔːlt] n βύνη.

Malta ['mɔːltə] n Μάλτα.

maltreat [mæl'triːt] vt κακομεταχειρίζομαι.

mammal ['mæməl] n θηλαστικό, μαστοφόρο.

mammoth ['mæməθ] a γιγαντιαίος, πελώριος.

man [mæn] n άνθρωπος || (male) άνδρας || (race) ανθρωπότητα ♦ vt επανδρώνω.

manage ['mænɪdʒ] vi (succeed) καταφέρνω ♦ vt χειρίζομαι, διευθύνω, διοικώ || ~able a ευχείριστος || (person) εύκολος || ~ment n χειρισμός,

διαχείριση || (directors) διεύθυνση, διοίκηση || ~r n διευθυντής || ~ress n διευθύντρια || ~rial a διευθυντικός, τεχνοκρατικός.

managing ['mænɪdʒɪŋ] a: ~ director n γενικός διευθυντής.

mandarin ['mændərɪn] n (orange) μανταρίνι || (man) μανδαρίνος.

mandate ['mændeɪt] n (instruction) εντολή || (commission) εντολή.

mandatory ['mændətərɪ] a υποχρεωτικός.

mandolin(e) ['mændəlɪn] n μαντολίνο.

mane [meɪn] n χαίτη.

maneuver [mə'nuːvə*] (US) = **manoeuvre**.

manfully ['mænfəlɪ] ad παλληκαρίσια.

mangle ['mæŋgl] vt καταξεσκίζω, κατακόβω.

mango ['mæŋgəʊ] n μάγγο.

manhandle ['mænhændl] vt ξυλοφορτώνω, κακομεταχειρίζομαι.

manhole ['mænhəʊl] n ανθρωποθυρίδα, είσοδος f υπονόμου.

manhood ['mænhʊd] n ανδρικότητα, ανδρική ηλικία.

man-hour ['mæn'aʊə*] n ώρα εργασίας.

manhunt ['mænhʌnt] n ανθρωποκυνήγι.

mania ['meɪnɪə] n (craze) μανία, πάθος nt || (madness) τρέλα || ~c n μανιακός.

manicure ['mænɪkjʊə*] n μανικιούρ nt inv ♦ vt φτιάχνω τα νύχια || ~ set n κασετίνα του μανικιούρ.

manifest ['mænɪfest] vt επιδεικνύω, εκδηλώνω ♦ a έκδηλος, προφανής || ~ation n εκδήλωση.

manifesto [mænɪ'festəʊ] n διακήρυξη, μανιφέστο.

manipulate [mə'nɪpjuleɪt] vt χειρίζομαι, μανουβράρω.

mankind [mæn'kaɪnd] n ανθρωπότητα.

manly ['mænlɪ] a ανδρικός, ανδροπρεπής, αντρίκιος.

manner ['mænə*] n τρόπος || (custom) συμπεριφορά, είδος nt || ~s npl συμπεριφορά, τρόποι mpl || ~ism n (of person) ιδιορρυθμία, ιδιοτροπία.

manoeuvre [mə'nuːvə*] vti ελίσσομαι, μανουβράρω ♦ n (MIL) ελιγμός, άσκηση.

manor ['mænə*] n τιμάριο, κτήμα nt || ~ house n αρχοντικό σπίτι.

manpower ['mænpaʊə*] n το εργατικό δυναμικό.

manservant ['mænsɜːvənt] n υπηρέτης, καμαριέρης.

mansion ['mænʃən] n μέγαρο.

manslaughter ['mænslɔːtə*] n ανθρωποκτονία.

mantelpiece ['mæntlpiːs] n γείσωμα nt τζακιού.

mantle ['mæntl] n μανδύας.

manual ['mænjuəl] a χειρωνακτικός ♦ n εγχειρίδιο.

manufacture [mænju'fæktʃə*] vt κατασκευάζω, βιομηχανοποιώ ♦ n

κατασκευή, βιομηχανία || ~r n
βιομήχανος.
manure [mə'njuə*] n κοπριά, λίπασμα
nt.
manuscript ['mænjuskrɪpt] n
χειρόγραφο.
many ['mɛnɪ] a πολλοί, αρκετοί ♦ n
αρκετοί, πολλοί, όσοι.
map [mæp] n χάρτης ♦ vt χαρτογραφώ ||
to ~ out vt χαράσσω, καθορίζω,
κανονίζω.
maple ['meɪpl] n σφενδάμι.
mar [maː*] vt βλάφτω, χαλώ,
παραμορφώνω.
marathon ['mærəθən] n μαραθώνιος.
marauder [mə'rɔːdə*] n λεηλάτης,
ληστής.
marble ['maːbl] n μάρμαρο || ~s n
(game) βώλος, μπίλια.
March [maːtʃ] n Μάρτιος, Μάρτης.
march [maːtʃ] vi βαδίζω, βηματίζω,
οδηγώ ♦ n (tune) εμβατήριο || (walk)
πορεία, βάδισμα nt || ~-past n
παρέλαση.
mare [mɛə*] n φοράδα.
margarine [maːdʒə'riːn] n μαργαρίνη.
margin ['maːdʒɪn] n (page) περιθώριο ||
(extra amount) περιθώριο || ~al a
περιθωριακός.
marigold ['mærɪgəʊld] n κατιφές m.
marijuana [mærɪ'waːnə] n μαριχουάνα.
marina [mə'riːnə] n (for boats) μαρίνα.
marine [mə'riːn] a θαλάσσιος, ναυτικός
|| (MIL) πεζοναυτικός ♦ n (MIL)
πεζοναύτης.
marital ['mærɪtl] a συζυγικός.
maritime ['mærɪtaɪm] a θαλασσινός,
ναυτικός.
marjoram ['maːdʒərəm] n
μαντζουράνα.
mark [maːk] n (coin) μάρκα || (scar etc)
σημάδι, ίχνος, στίγμα nt || (sign) σημείο,
ένδειξη || (target) στόχος, σημάδι ||
(grade) βαθμός ♦ vt (make a mark)
μαρκάρω, σημαδεύω || (indicate) δεικνύω,
εκδηλώνω, δείχνω || (watch etc) προσέχω,
κοιτάζω || (exam) διορθώνω, βαθμολογώ
|| **to ~ time** κάνω βήμα σημειωτό ||
(make no progress) δεν προχωρώ || **to ~
out** vt σημαδεύω || ~**ed** a έντονος,
σαφής, φανερός, εμφανής || ~**er** n (sign)
δείκτης.
market ['maːkɪt] n αγορά || (overseas)
αγορά || (demand) ζήτηση ♦ vt (COMM: new
product) πουλώ || (project) προβάλλω || ~
day n ημέρα αγοράς || ~ **garden** n (Brit)
περιβόλι κηπουρικών || ~**ing** n αγορά,
πώληση || ~ **place** n αγορά, παζάρι.
marksman ['maːksmən] n σκοπευτής ||
~**ship** n σκοπευτική ικανότητα.
marmalade ['maːməleɪd] n μαρμελάδα.
maroon [mə'ruːn] vt (usually passive)
εγκαταλείπω σε έρημη ακτή ♦ a (colour)
ερυθρόφαιος.
marquee [maː'kiː] n μεγάλη τέντα.
marquess, marquis ['maːkwɪs] n
μαρκήσιος.

marriage ['mærɪdʒ] n (institution)
παντρειά || (wedding) γάμος.
married ['mærɪd] a (person, life)
έγγαμος.
marrow ['mærəʊ] n μυελός, μεδούλι ||
(vegetable) κολοκύθι.
marry ['mærɪ] vt νυμφεύω, παντρεύω ♦
vi (also: **get married**) νυμφεύομαι,
παντρεύομαι.
Mars [maːz] n Άρης.
marsh [maːʃ] n έλος nt, βάλτος.
marshal ['maːʃəl] n (US) σερίφης ♦ vt
παρατάσσω, συγκεντρώνω || see **field**.
marshy ['maːʃɪ] a ελώδης.
martial ['maːʃəl] a πολεμικός,
στρατιωτικός || ~ **law** n στρατιωτικός
νόμος.
martyr ['maːtə*] n μάρτυρας || (fig)
βασανιζόμενος || ~**dom** n μαρτύριο.
marvel ['maːvəl] n θαύμα nt ♦ vi (+ at)
εκπλήσσομαι, θαυμάζω || ~**lous**, (US)
~**ous** a θαυμάσιος, καταπληκτικός.
Marxism ['maːksɪzəm] n μαρξισμός.
Marxist ['maːksɪst] n μαρξιστής.
mascara [mæs'kaːrə] n μάσκαρα.
mascot ['mæskət] n μασκότ nt inv.
masculine ['mæskjulɪn] a αρσενικός ||
(manly) ανδροπρεπής, ρωμαλέος ||
(GRAM) αρσενικός ♦ n το αρσενικό.
masculinity [mæskju'lɪnɪtɪ] n
αρρενότητα, ανδρικό ύφος.
mashed [mæʃt] a: ~ **potatoes** npl
πατάτες fpl πουρέ.
mask [maːsk] n προσωπίδα, μάσκα ||
(pretence) προσωπείο ♦ vt καλύπτω,
αποκρύπτω.
masochist ['mæsəʊkɪst] n μαζοχιστής.
mason ['meɪsn] n (stonemason) κτίστης ||
(freemason) τέκτονας || ~**ic** [mə'sɒnɪk] a
τεκτονικός, μασονικός || ~**ry** ['meɪsnrɪ]
n λιθοδομή, χτίσιμο.
masquerade [mæskə'reɪd] n
μεταμφίεση ♦ vi μεταμφιέζομαι.
mass [mæs] n (PHYS) μάζα || (information,
people) όγκος, μάζα, πλήθος nt ||
(majority) το μεγαλύτερο μέρος, η
πλειοψηφία || (REL) λειτουργία ♦ vt
συγκεντρώνω, αθροίζω, μαζεύω ♦ vi
συγκεντρώνομαι, μαζεύομαι.
massacre ['mæsəkə*] n σφαγή,
μακελειό ♦ vt σφάζω.
massage ['mæsaːʒ] n μάλαξη, μασσάζ
nt inv ♦ vt μαλάσσω, κάνω μασσάζ.
masseur [mæ'sɜː*] n μασσέρ m inv.
masseuse [mæ'sɜːz] n μασέζ f inv.
massive ['mæsɪv] a ογκώδης, δυνατός.
mass media ['mæs'miːdɪə] npl μέσα
ntpl μαζικής επικοινωνίας.
mass production ['mæsprə'dʌkʃən] n
μαζική παραγωγή.
mast [maːst] n ιστός, κατάρτι || (pole)
στήλη, στύλος.
master ['maːstə*] n κύριος, αφεντικό ||
(teacher) δάσκαλος, καθηγητής || (head)
αρχηγός || (of ship) καπετάνιος || (artist)
μεγάλος καλλιτέχνης ♦ vt εξουσιάζω,
ελέγχω || (learn) μαθαίνω τέλεια || ~**ly** a

έντεχνος, αριστοτεχνικός || ~**mind** n
εγκέφαλος ♦ vt συλλαμβάνω,
πραγματοποιώ || **M~ of Arts (M.A.)** n
ανώτερος πτυχιούχος θετικών
επιστημών || ~**piece** n αριστούργημα nt
|| ~ **stroke** n αριστοτεχνικό κτύπημα nt
|| ~**y** n εξουσία, υπεροχή, μαεστρία.
masturbate ['mæstəbeɪt] vi
μαλακίζομαι.
masturbation [mæstə'beɪʃən] n
μαλακία.
mat [mæt] n ψάθα, χαλάκι || (material for
table) στρωσίδι τραπεζιού || (tangled mass)
μπλεγμένα νήματα ntpl κτλ ♦ vti μπλέκω,
μπερδεύω.
match [mætʃ] n (matchstick) σπίρτο ||
(game) αγώνας || (equal) ταίρι || (marriage)
συνοικέσιο ♦ vt (be like) εναρμονίζω,
ταιριάζω || (equal strength etc) εξισούμαι
με, φθάνω ♦ vi συμβιβάζομαι, συμφωνώ,
ταιριάζω || ~**box** n κουτί σπίρτα || ~**ing**
a προσαρμογή || ~**less** a απαράμιλλος.
mate [meɪt] n σύντροφος, συνάδελφος
|| (husband, wife) σύζυγος, ταίρι || (NAUT)
υπονλοίαρχος ♦ vi (chess) κάνω μάτ || (of
animal) ζευγαρώνομαι.
material [mə'tɪərɪəl] n ύλη, υλικό ♦ a
σημαντικός, ουσιώδης || (of matter)
υλικός || (opposite of spirit) υλικός || ~**s** npl
υλικά ntpl, εφόδια ntpl || ~**istic** a
υλιστικός || ~**ize** vi πραγματοποιούμαι,
γίνομαι.
maternal [mə'tɜːnl] a μητρικός ||
(relatives) από τη μητέρα.
maternity [mə'tɜːnɪtɪ] n μητρότητα || ~
dress φόρεμα nt εγγύου || ~ **hospital**
μαιευτήριο.
mathematical [mæθə'mætɪkəl] a
μαθηματικός.
mathematician [mæθəmə'tɪʃən] n
μαθηματικός m/f.
mathematics [mæθə'mætɪks] n,
maths [mæθs] n μαθηματικά ntpl.
matinée ['mætɪneɪ] n παράσταση
(απογευματινή).
mating ['meɪtɪŋ] n ζευγάρωμα nt,
βάτεμα nt.
matriarchal [meɪtrɪ'ɑːkl] a
μητριαρχικός.
matrimonial [mætrɪ'məunɪəl] a
γαμήλιος, συζυγικός.
matrimony ['mætrɪmənɪ] n γάμος,
έγγαμη ζωή.
matron ['meɪtrən] n (MED) προϊσταμένη
|| (SCH) επιμελήτρια, οικονόμος f || ~**ly** a
σεβάσμιος, ατάραχος.
matt [mæt] a (paint) μουντός, μάτ.
matter ['mætə*] n ουσία, ύλη || (affair)
υπόθεση, θέμα nt, πράγμα nt || (question,
issue etc) ζήτημα nt || (discharge) πύο,
έμπυο ♦ vi έχω σημασία, ενδιαφέρω ||
what is the ~ ? τι συμβαίνει; || **as a ~**
of fact στην πραγματικότητα || ~- **of-**
fact a πεζός, πρακτικός.
mattress ['mætrɪs] n στρώμα nt.
mature [mə'tjuə*] a ώριμος ♦ vi
ωριμάζω.

maturity [mə'tjuərɪtɪ] n ωριμότητα.
maul [mɔːl] vt κακοποιώ, κοπανίζω.
mauve [məuv] a (colour) μώβ.
max. abbr of **maximum.**
maxim ['mæksɪm] n απόφθεγμα nt,
γνωμικό.
maximum ['mæksɪməm] a ανώτατος,
μεγαλύτερος ♦ n ανώτατο όριο,
μάξιμουμ nt inv.
May [meɪ] n Μάιος.
may [meɪ] (irreg v) vi (be possible) ίσως να
|| (have permission) έχω την άδεια να,
μπορώ να.
maybe ['meɪbiː] ad ίσως, πιθανό.
May Day ['meɪdeɪ] n Πρωτομαγιά.
mayonnaise [meɪə'neɪz] n μαγιονέζα.
mayor [mεə*] n δήμαρχος || ~**ess** n
(wife) κυρία δημάρχου || (lady mayor) n
δήμαρχος.
maze [meɪz] n (network) λαβύρινθος,
κυκεώνας.
me [miː] pron (after prep) με, εμένα.
meadow ['medəu] n λειβάδι.
meagre, meager (US) ['miːgə*] a
ισχνός, πενιχρός.
meal [miːl] n φαγητό || (grain)
χοντράλευρο || ~**time** n ώρα φαγητού.
mean [miːn] (irreg v) a άθλιος, φτωχός,
ταπεινός || (stingy) φιλάργυρος,
τσιγκούνης || (average) μέσος, μεσαίος ♦
vt (signify) εννοώ, σημαίνω, θέλω να πω ||
(intend) προτίθεμαι, σκοπεύω || (be
resolved) προορίζω ♦ n (average) μέσος
όρος, μέσο || ~**s** npl μέσα ntpl, τρόποι
mpl || (wealth) πόροι mpl, μέσα ntpl,
περιουσία || **by ~s of** με τη βοήθεια
του/της || **by all ~s** οπωσδήποτε.
meander [mɪ'ændə*] vi ελίσσομαι,
σχηματίζω μαιάνδρους.
meaning ['miːnɪŋ] n (intention) λόγος,
σκοπός || (sense of word) έννοια, σημασία,
νόημα nt || ~**ful** a με σημασία, που λέει
πολλά || ~**less** a χωρίς νόημα.
meanness ['miːnnɪs] n μικρότητα,
μικροπρέπεια.
meant [ment] pt, pp of **mean.**
meantime ['miːntaɪm] ad,
meanwhile ['miːnwaɪl] ad εν τω
μεταξύ, στο μεταξύ.
measles ['miːzlz] n ιλαρά || **German ~**
n ερυθρά.
measly ['miːzlɪ] a (col) ασήμαντος,
ανάξιος, τιποτένιος.
measure ['meʒə*] vt (find size) μετρώ ||
(test) δοκιμάζω, αναμετρούμαι με || (be
certain size) είναι, έχει διαστάσεις ♦ n
(unit) μέτρο || (tape measure) μεζούρα,
μέτρο || (plan) μέτρο, ενέργεια, πράξη || (a
law) μέτρο || ~**d** a μετρημένος || ~**ment**
n (way of measuring) μέτρηση, μέτρημα nt
|| (amount measured) μέτρα ntpl,
διαστάσεις fpl.
meat [miːt] n (flesh) κρέας nt || ~ **pie** n
κρεατόπιτα || ~**y** a (lit) σαρκώδης || (fig)
ουσιαστικός, μεστός, ζουμερός.
mechanic [mɪ'kænɪk] n τεχνίτης,
μηχανικός || ~**s** n μηχανική || ~**al** a

μηχανικός || (automatically) μηχανικός, αυτόματος.

mechanism ['mɛkənɪzəm] n μηχανισμός.

mechanization [mɛkənaɪ'zeɪʃən] n μηχανοποίηση.

medal ['mɛdl] n μετάλλιο || ~**lion** [mɪ'dæliən] n μενταγιό || ~**list**, ~**ist** (US) n κάτοχος μεταλλίου.

meddle ['mɛdl] vi (+ with) ανακατεύομαι, επεμβαίνω.

media ['miːdiə] npl (of communication) μέσα ntpl.

mediate ['miːdieɪt] vi μεσολαβώ.

mediation [miːdɪ'eɪʃən] n μεσολάβηση.

mediator ['miːdieɪtə*] n μεσολαβητής.

medical ['mɛdɪkəl] a (science) ιατρικός || (student) (φοιτητής) ιατρικής.

medicated ['mɛdɪkeɪtɪd] a εμποτισμένος με φάρμακο.

medicinal [mɛ'dɪsɪnl] a φαρμακευτικός, ιατρικός, θεραπευτικός.

medicine ['mɛdsɪn] n ιατρική || (drugs) φάρμακο, γιατρικό || ~ **chest** n φαρμακείο.

medieval [mɛdɪ'iːvəl] a μεσαιωνικός.

mediocre [miːdɪ'əʊkə*] a μέτριος, της αράδας.

mediocrity [miːdɪ'ɒkrɪtɪ] n μετριότητα.

meditate ['mɛdɪteɪt] vi (+ on) μελετώ, σκέπτομαι, συλλογίζομαι.

meditation [mɛdɪ'teɪʃən] n συλλογισμός, διαλογισμός.

Mediterranean (Sea) [mɛdɪtə'reɪnɪən(siː)] n Μεσόγειος (θάλασσα).

medium ['miːdiəm] a μεσαίος, μέτριος ♦ n μέσο, μέσος όρος || (means) μέσο, όργανο.

medley ['mɛdlɪ] n σύμφυρμα nt, κυκεώνας, μίγμα nt.

meek [miːk] a πράος, ήρεμος, πειθήνιος.

meet [miːt] vt συναντώ, απαντώ, ανταμώνω || (come across) βρίσκω, απαντώ, διασταυρώνομαι || (go towards) προχωρώ, πηγαίνω || (pay, satisfy) εκπληρώνω, ανταποκρίνομαι, τιμώ ♦ vi (by arrangement) συναντώμαι, βλέπομαι || (fight) αντιμετωπίζω || (join) συναντώμαι, συναθροίζομαι, συνέρχομαι || to ~ with vt (problems) συναντώ, αντιμετωπίζω || (US: people) συναντώ, γνωρίζω || ~**ing** n συνάντηση, συνάθροιση, συνέλευση || ~ **ing place** n τόπος συναντήσεως.

megaphone ['mɛgəfəʊn] n μεγάφωνο.

melancholy ['mɛlənkəlɪ] n μελαγχολία, κατήφεια ♦ a μελαγχολικός.

mellow ['mɛləʊ] a ώριμος || (delicate) απαλός, γλυκός || (aged) απαλός ♦ vi ωριμάζω, απαλύνομαι.

melodious [mɪ'ləʊdɪəs] a μελωδικός.

melodrama ['mɛləʊdraːmə] n μελόδραμα nt.

melody ['mɛlədɪ] n μελωδία.

melon ['mɛlən] n πεπόνι.

melt [mɛlt] vi τήκομαι, λυώνω || (disappear) χάνομαι, διαλύομαι ♦ vt τήκω, λυώνω || to ~ **away** vi λυώνω, διαλύομαι || to ~ **down** vt λυώνω, τήκω || ~**ing point** n σημείο τήξεως || ~**ing pot** n (fig) χωνευτήριο, ρευστή κατάσταση.

member ['mɛmbə*] n μέλος nt || **M**~ **of Parliament (M.P.)** n βουλευτής/ίνα m/f || ~**ship** n μέλη ntpl, αριθμός μελών.

membrane ['mɛmbreɪn] n μεμβράνη.

memento [mə'mɛntəʊ] n ενθύμιο, ενθύμηση.

memo ['mɛməʊ] n (COMM) υπόμνημα nt, σημείωση.

memoirs ['mɛmwaːz] npl απομνημονεύματα ntpl.

memorable ['mɛmərəbl] a αξιομνημόνευτος, αξέχαστος.

memorandum [mɛmə'rændəm] n (COMM) υπόμνημα nt, σημείωση.

memorial [mɪ'mɔːrɪəl] n μνημείο ♦ a αναμνηστικός, επιμνημόσυνος.

memorize ['mɛməraɪz] vt αποστηθίζω, μαθαίνω απ' έξω.

memory ['mɛmərɪ] n μνήμη, μνημονικό, θυμητικό || (thing recalled) ανάμνηση, θύμηση || (COMPUT) μνήμη || in ~ of εις μνήμην του, εις ανάμνησιν του.

men [mɛn] npl of **man**.

menace ['mɛnɪs] n απειλή, φοβέρα ♦ vt απειλώ, φοβερίζω.

menacing ['mɛnɪsɪŋ] a απειλητικός.

menagerie [mɪ'nædʒərɪ] n θηριοτροφείο.

mend [mɛnd] vt (επι)διορθώνω, βελτιώνω ♦ vi αναρρώνω ♦ n επιδιόρθωση, επισκευή || to be on the ~ συνέρχομαι, πάω καλύτερα.

menial ['miːnɪəl] a ταπεινός, δουλοπρεπής.

meningitis [mɛnɪn'dʒaɪtɪs] n μηνιγγίτιδα.

menopause ['mɛnəʊpɔːz] n εμμηνόπαυση.

menstruation [mɛnstru'eɪʃən] n εμμηνόρροια, περίοδος f.

mental ['mɛntl] a διανοητικός, νοερός, πνευματικός || (col: abnormal) τρελός || ~**ity** n νοοτροπία.

mention ['mɛnʃən] n μνεία ♦ vt αναφέρω || **don't** ~ **it!** παρακαλώ!

menu ['mɛnjuː] n (also COMPUT) μενού nt inv.

mercantile ['mɜːkəntaɪl] a εμπορικός.

mercenary ['mɜːsɪnərɪ] a φιλοχρήματος, πλεονέκτης ♦ n μισθοφόρος.

merchandise ['mɜːtʃəndaɪz] n εμπορεύματα ntpl.

merchant ['mɜːtʃənt] n έμπορος ♦ a εμπορικός || ~ **navy** n εμπορικό ναυτικό.

merciful ['mɜːsɪfʊl] a εύσπλαχνος.

merciless ['mɜːsɪlɪs] a ανελέητος, άσπλαχνος.

mercury ['mɜːkjʊrɪ] n υδράργυρος.

mercy ['mɜːsɪ] n ευσπλαχνία, έλεος nt|| (blessing) ευλογία || at the ~ of στο έλεος τού.

mere [mɪə*] a απλός, τίποτε άλλο από || ~ly ad απλώς, μόνο.

merge [mɜːdʒ] vt απορροφώ, συγχωνεύω || (COMPUT) αναμιγνύω ♦ vi (become absorbed) απορροφούμαι, συγχωνεύομαι || ~r n (COMM) συγχώνευση.

meridian [mə'rɪdɪən] n μεσημβρινός.

meringue [mə'ræŋ] n μαρέγγα.

merit ['mɛrɪt] n αξία, προσόν ♦ vt αξίζω.

mermaid ['mɜːmeɪd] n γοργόνα.

merriment ['mɛrɪmənt] n ευθυμία, διασκέδαση.

merry ['mɛrɪ] a εύθυμος, φαιδρός, χαρωπός || (col: after drink) στο κέφι, πιωμένος.

mesh [mɛʃ] n θηλειά (δικτύου) ♦ vti (gears) εμπλέκω, εμπλέκομαι.

mesmerize ['mɛzməraɪz] vt μαγνητίζω, υπνωτίζω.

mess [mɛs] n σαλάτα, θάλασσα || (untidy state) ακαθαρσία, άνω-κάτω || (MIL) συσσίτιο, τραπέζι || (officers' mess) λέσχη αξιωματικών || to ~ about vi χασομερώ || to ~ about with vt νασπατεύω, σαχλαμαρίζω || to ~ up vt χαλώ, μπλέκω, περιπλέκω.

message ['mɛsɪdʒ] n μήνυμα nt, διάγγελμα nt, είδηση.

messenger ['mɛsɪndʒə*] n αγγελιαφόρος.

messy ['mɛsɪ] a ακάθαρτος, ακατάστατος.

met [mɛt] pt, pp of **meet**.

metabolism [mɛ'tæbəlɪzəm] n μεταβολισμός.

metal ['mɛtl] n μέταλλο || ~lic a μεταλλικός || ~lurgy n μεταλλουργία.

metaphor ['mɛtəfɔː*] n μεταφορά.

metaphysics [mɛtə'fɪzɪks] n μεταφυσική.

meteor ['miːtɪə*] n μετέωρο || ~ic a μετεωρικός, λαμπρός || ~ological a μετεωρολογικός || ~ology n μετεωρολογία.

meter ['miːtə*] n (instrument) μετρητής || (US) = **metre**.

method ['mɛθəd] n μέθοδος f || ~ical a μεθοδικός.

Methodist ['mɛθədɪst] a, n Μεθοδιστής.

methylated spirits ['mɛθɪleɪtɪd'spɪrɪts] n (also: **meths**) μεθυλικό οινόπνευμα nt.

meticulous [mɪ'tɪkjuləs] a λεπτολόγος, σχολαστικός.

metre ['miːtə*] n μέτρο.

metric ['mɛtrɪk] a μετρικός.

metronome ['mɛtrənəʊm] n μετρονόμος.

metropolis [mɪ'trɒpəlɪs] n μητρόπολη.

mews [mjuːz] n αδιέξοδο.

Mexican ['mɛksɪkən] a μεξικανικός ♦ n Μεξικανός/ίδα m/f.

Mexico ['mɛksɪkəʊ] n Μεξικό.

mezzanine ['mɛzəniːn] n ημιόροφος, μέτζο.

miaow [miː'aʊ] vi νιαουρίζω.

mice [maɪs] npl of **mouse**.

microbe ['maɪkrəʊb] n μικρόβιο.

microcomputer ['maɪkrəʊkəm'pjuːtə*] n μικροϋπολογιστής.

microfilm ['maɪkrəʊfɪlm] n μικροφίλμ nt inv.

microphone ['maɪkrəfəʊn] n μικρόφωνο.

microscope ['maɪkrəskəʊp] n μικροσκόπιο.

microscopic [maɪkrə'skɒpɪk] a μικροσκοπικός.

mid [mɪd] a μέσος, μεσαίος || in ~ course στο μέσο, στην ακμή.

midday ['mɪd'deɪ] n μεσημέρι.

middle ['mɪdl] n μέσο ♦ a μέσος, μεσαίος || ~-aged a μεσήλικας || the M~ Ages npl o Μεσαίωνας || ~ class n μεσαία τάξη, αστική τάξη || ~-class a αστικός || M~ East n Μέση Ανατολή || ~man n μεταπωλητής, μεσίτης || ~name n όνομα nt πατρός.

midge [mɪdʒ] n σκνίπα.

midget ['mɪdʒɪt] n νάνος, ανθρωπάκι ♦ a μικρός, μικροσκοπικός.

midnight ['mɪdnaɪt] n μεσάνυχτα ntpl.

midst [mɪdst] n: in the ~ of στο μέσο.

midsummer ['mɪd'sʌmə*] n μεσοκαλόκαιρο.

midway ['mɪd'weɪ] ad (+between) στο μέσο ♦ a μέσος.

midweek ['mɪd'wiːk] ad στα μέσα της εβδομάδος.

midwife ['mɪdwaɪf] n μαία, μαμμή || ~ry ['mɪdwɪfərɪ] n μαιευτική.

midwinter ['mɪd'wɪntə*] n στο μέσο του χειμώνα, μεσοχείμωνο.

might [maɪt] pt of **may** || n ισχύς, δύναμη || ~y a ισχυρός, δυνατός ♦ ad (col) πολύ, τρομερά.

migraine ['miːgreɪn] n ημικρανία.

migrant ['maɪgrənt] n μεταναστευτικός, περαστικός ♦ a αποδημητικός, μεταναστευτικός.

migrate [maɪ'greɪt] vi (birds) αποδημώ.

migration [maɪ'greɪʃən] n μετανάστευση.

mike [maɪk] n (microphone) μικρόφωνο.

mild [maɪld] a (rebuke) επιεικής, μαλακός || (warm) ήπιος, εύκρατος || (taste) ελαφρός || (slight) ελαφρός ♦ n (beer) ελαφριά μπύρα.

mildew ['mɪldjuː] n μούχλα, σείρηκας.

mildness ['maɪldnɪs] n ηπιότητα, γλύκα, επιείκεια.

mile [maɪl] n μίλι (1609 μ) || ~age n απόσταση σε μίλια || ~stone n μιλιοδείκτης || (fig) ιστορικός σταθμός.

militant ['mɪlɪtənt] n οπαδός της αμέσου δράσεως ♦ a μαχητικός.

military ['mɪlɪtərɪ] a στρατιωτικός ♦ n oι στρατιωτικοί mpl, στρατός.

militate ['mılıteıt] vi (+ against) αντιστρατεύομαι, αντιμάχομαι.

militia [mı'lıʃə] n εθνοφυλακή.

milk [mılk] n γάλα nt ♦ vt (cow) αρμέγω || (fig) εκμεταλλεύομαι, μαδώ || ~man n γαλατάς || **M~y Way** n Γαλαξίας.

mill [mıl] n μύλος || (building) μύλος || (factory) εργοστάσιο ♦ vt (grind) αλέθω ♦ vi (move around) στριφογυρίζω.

millenium [mı'lenıəm] n χιλιετηρίδα.

miller ['mılə*] n μυλωνάς.

millet ['mılıt] n κεχρί, σόργο.

milligram(me) ['mılıgræm] n χιλιοστόγραμμο.

millilitre, milliliter (US) ['mılıli:tə*] n χιλιοστόλιτρο.

millimetre, millimeter (US) ['mılımi:tə*] n χιλιοστόμετρο.

milliner ['mılınə*] n καπελλού f || ~y n γυναικεία καπέλλα ntpl.

million ['mıljən] n εκατομμύριο || ~aire n εκατομμυριούχος.

mime [maım] n μίμος, μιμόδραμα nt ♦ vti μιμούμαι, παίζω με μιμική.

mimic ['mımık] n μίμος, μιμητής/ήτρια m/f ♦ vti μιμούμαι, κοροϊδεύω, αντιγράφω || ~ry n μίμηση, μιμική.

min. abbr of **minute(s), minimum.**

mince [mıns] vt ψιλοκόβω, κάνω κιμά || (words) μασώ ♦ vi βαδίζω με προσποιητή χάρη ♦ n (meat) κιμάς || ~**meat** n μείγμα nt με φρούτα και σταφίδες || ~ **pie** n πίτα με φρούτα και σταφίδες, κρεατόπιτα || ~**r** n κρεατομηχανή.

mind [maınd] n νούς m, μυαλό || (intelligence) σκέψη, γνώμη, ιδέα || (memory) μνήμη, ανάμνηση, θύμηση ♦ vti φροντίζω, προσέχω || (be careful) προσέχω || (object to) έχω αντίρρηση, ενοχλούμαι, πειράζομαι || **on my ~** στη σκέψη μου, ανησυχώ || **to my ~** κατά τη γνώμη μου || **out of one's ~** τρελός || **never ~!** δεν πειράζει, άστο, μην αννησυχείς || **to bear** or **keep in ~** δεν ξεχνώ, λαμβάνω υπόψη || **to make up one's ~** αποφασίζω || **'~ the step'** 'πρόσεχε το σκαλοπάτι' || ~**ful** a προσεκτικός || ~**less** a απερίσκεπτος, αδιάφορος, απρόσεκτος.

mine [maın] poss pron δικός μου, δική μου, δικό μου ♦ n ορυχείο, μεταλλείο || (NAUT) νάρκη || (source) πηγή ♦ vt εξορύσσω || (NAUT) ναρκοθετώ ♦ vi εκμεταλλεύομαι || ~**field** n ναρκοπέδιο || ~**r** n μεταλλωρύχος, ανθρακωρύχος.

mineral ['mınərəl] a ορυκτός, μεταλλευτικός ♦ n ορυκτό, μετάλλευμα nt || ~ **water** n επιτραπέζιο νερό, μεταλλικό νερό.

minesweeper ['maınswi:pə*] n ναρκαλιευτικό.

mingle ['mıŋgl] vt αναμιγνύω ♦ vi (+ with) αναμιγνύομαι.

mingy ['mındʒı] a (col) στριμμένος, γύφτος, μίζερος.

miniature ['mınıtʃə*] n μικρογραφικός ♦ n μικρογραφία, μινιατούρα || (model) μακέτα || **in ~** μικρού σχήματος.

minibus ['mınıbʌs] n μικρό λεωφορείο.

minicab ['mınıkæb] n μικρό ταξί.

minicomputer ['mınıkəm'pju:tə:*] n μικρο-υπολογιστής.

minimal ['mınıml] a ελάχιστος.

minimize ['mınımaız] vt ελαττώνω, μικραίνω, περιορίζω.

minimum ['mınıməm] n ελάχιστο, κατώτατο όριο, μίνιμουμ nt inv ♦ a κατώτατος, ελάχιστος.

mining ['maınıŋ] n εξόρυξη || (NAUT) ναρκοθέτηση ♦ a μεταλλευτική, ορυκτική.

miniskirt ['mınıskз:t] n κοντή φούστα, μίνι.

minister ['mınıstə*] n υπουργός m/f || (ECCL) ιερέας || ~**ial** [mınıs'tıərıəl] a υπουργικός, κυβερνητικός.

ministry ['mınıstrı] n (government) υπουργείο, κυβέρνηση || (ECCL) το ιερατείο, κλήρος.

mink [mıŋk] n είδος νιφίτσας ♦ a: ~ **coat** n παλτό από μινκ.

minor ['maınə*] a μικρότερος, μικρός || (MUS) ελάσσων ♦ n (under 18: Brit) ανήλικος.

minority [maı'nɒrıtı] n μειοψηφία, μειονότητα.

minstrel ['mınstrəl] n ραψωδός, τραγουδιστής.

mint [mınt] n (plant) δυόσμος || (sweet) μέντα || (for coins) νομισματοκοπείο ♦ a (condition) καινούργιος, κατακαίνουργιος || ~ **sauce** n σάλτσα με δυόσμο.

minuet [mınju'εt] n μενουέτο.

minus ['maınəs] n σημείο του πλην ♦ prep πλην, μείον.

minute [maı'nju:t] a μικροσκοπικός, ελάχιστος || (detailed) λεπτομερής ♦ ['mınıt] n λεπτό (της ώρας) || (moment) στιγμή || ~**s** npl πρακτικά ntpl.

miracle ['mırəkl] n (esp REL) θαύμα nt.

miraculous [mı'rækjuləs] a θαυματουργός, υπερφυσικός, θαυμαστός.

mirage ['mıra:ʒ] n αντικατοπτρισμός, οπτική απάτη.

mirror ['mırə*] n καθρέφτης, κάτοπτρο ♦ vt αντικατοπτρίζω, αντανακλώ.

mirth [mз:θ] n ευθυμία, χαρά, κέφι.

misadventure [mısəd'ventʃə*] n κακοτυχία, ατύχημα nt.

misapprehension ['mısæprı'henʃən] n (misunderstanding) παρεξήγηση.

misbehave ['mısbı'heıv] vi φέρομαι άσχημα.

miscalculate ['mıs'kælkjuleıt] vt υπολογίζω λανθασμένα.

miscalculation ['mıskælkju'leıʃən] n λανθασμένος υπολογισμός.

miscarriage ['mıskærıdʒ] n αποτυχία || (of justice) δικαστικό λάθος || (MED) αποβολή.

miscellaneous [mɪsɪ'leɪnɪəs] a ποικίλος, ανάμικτος.

mischance [mɪs'tʃɑːns] n αποτυχία, ατύχημα nt.

mischievous ['mɪstʃɪvəs] a κατεργάρης, σκανταλιάρης.

misconception ['mɪskən'sepʃən] n εσφαλμένη αντίληψη.

misconduct [mɪs'kɒndʌkt] n παράπτωμα nt, κακή διαγωγή.

miscount ['mɪs'kaʊnt] vt μετρώ λανθασμένα.

misdemeanour, misdemeanor (US) [mɪsdɪ'miːnə*] n (less important offence) παράπτωμα, πλημμέλημα nt.

misdirect ['mɪsdɪ'rɛkt] vt (person, letter) δίνω λανθασμένες οδηγίες, διευθύνω άσχημα.

miser ['maɪzə*] n φιλάργυρος, τσιγκούνης.

miserable ['mɪzərəbl] a δυστυχισμένος, θλιβερός || (poor) άθλιος, ελεεινός, φτωχός.

miserly ['maɪzəlɪ] a τσιγκούνικος.

misery ['mɪzərɪ] n δυστυχία, βάσανο || (poverty) αθλιότητα, φτώχια.

misfire ['mɪs'faɪə*] vi ρετάρω, παθαίνω αφλογιστία || (plan) πέφτω στο κενό.

misfit ['mɪsfɪt] n (person) απροσάρμοστος.

misfortune [mɪs'fɔːtʃən] n ατυχία, ατύχημα nt.

misgiving [mɪs'gɪvɪŋ] n (often pl) ανησυχία, αμφιβολία, φόβος.

misguided ['mɪs'gaɪdɪd] a πλανόμενος, παραμορφωμένος.

mishandle ['mɪs'hændl] vt (manage badly) κακομεταχειρίζομαι.

mishap ['mɪshæp] n ατυχία, αναποδιά.

mishear ['mɪs'hɪə*] vt (hear wrongly) παρακούω.

misinform ['mɪsɪn'fɔːm] vt πληροφορώ κακώς.

misinterpret ['mɪsɪn'tɜːprɪt] vt παρερμηνεύω.

misjudge ['mɪs'dʒʌdʒ] vt κρίνω λανθασμένα.

mislay [mɪs'leɪ] vt (misplace, lose) παραπετώ, χάνω.

mislead [mɪs'liːd] vt (deceive) παραπλανώ, εξαπατώ || ~ing a παραπλανητικός.

misnomer ['mɪs'nəʊmə*] n λανθασμένη ονομασία.

misogynist [mɪ'sɒdʒɪnɪst] n μισογύνης.

misplace ['mɪs'pleɪs] vt (mislay) τοποθετώ κατά λάθος, χάνω.

misprint ['mɪsprɪnt] n τυπογραφικό λάθος.

misread ['mɪs'riːd] vt κακοδιαβάζω, παρερμηνεύω.

misrepresent ['mɪsrɛprɪ'zɛnt] vt διαστρέφω, παραμορφώνω.

miss [mɪs] vt αστοχώ, αποτυγχάνω || (not notice) δε βλέπω, χάνω || (train etc) χάνω || (omit) παραλείπω || (regret absence) μού

λείπει, αποζητώ ♦ vi αντιλαμβάνομαι ♦ n (fall short) αστοχία || (failure) αποτυχία.

Miss [mɪs] n: ~ X Δεσποινίδα X, Δεσποινίς X, Δις X || ~ Smith Δεσποινίδα Σμίθ, Δις Σμίθ.

misshapen ['mɪs'ʃeɪpən] a παραμορφωμένος.

missile ['mɪsaɪl] n (esp nuclear) βλήμα nt.

missing ['mɪsɪŋ] a (person) απών, αγνοούμενος || (thing) χαμένος.

mission ['mɪʃən] n αποστολή || (church) ιεραποστολή || ~ary n ιεραπόστολος.

misspent ['mɪs'spɛnt] a (youth) χαμένα (νειάτα).

mist [mɪst] n ομίχλη, καταχνιά ♦ vi (also: ~ over, ~ up) σκεπάζω με ομίχλη, θαμπώνω.

mistake [mɪs'teɪk] n σφάλμα nt, λάθος nt ♦ vt παρανοώ, παρερμηνεύω || (for another) παίρνω για άλλο, παραγνωρίζω || ~ n a (person) σφάλλω, κάνω λάθος || (identity) παραγνωρίζω.

mister ['mɪstə*] n (abbr Mr) κύριος (Κος) || see **Mr**.

mistletoe ['mɪsltəʊ] n ιξός, γκί.

mistreat [mɪs'triːt] vt κακομεταχειρίζομαι.

mistress ['mɪstrɪs] n (teacher) δασκάλα || (of house) κυρία, οικοδέσποινα || (lover) ερωμένη, μαιτρέσσα || see **Mrs**.

mistrust ['mɪs'trʌst] vt δυσπιστώ, υποπτεύομαι.

misty ['mɪstɪ] a ομιχλώδης, θαμπός, σκοτεινιασμένος.

misunderstand ['mɪsʌndə'stænd] vti παρανοώ, παρεξηγώ || ~ing n παρανόηση, παρεξήγηση.

misunderstood ['mɪsʌndə'stʊd] a (person) παρεξηγημένος.

misuse ['mɪs'juːs] n κακή χρήση ♦ ['mɪs'juːz] vt κάνω κατάχρηση, χρησιμοποιώ λανθασμένα.

miter ['maɪtə*] n (US) = **mitre**.

mitigate ['mɪtɪgeɪt] vt μετριάζω, καταπραΰνω.

mitre ['maɪtə*] n λοξή ένωση, ονυχωτή ένωση || (ECCL) μίτρα.

mitt(en) ['mɪt(n)] n είδος nt γαντιού.

mix [mɪks] vt αναμιγνύω, ανακατώνω ♦ vi αναμιγνύομαι, ταιριάζω ♦ n (mixture) μίξη, μίγμα nt || to ~ up vt ανακατεύω || (confuse) μπερδεύω || ~ed a (assorted) ανάμικτος || (school etc) μικτός || ~ed-up a (confused) συγχυσμένος, μπερδεμένος || ~r n (for food) μίξερ || (person) κοινωνικός || ~ture n (assortment) αμάλγαμα nt, ανακάτεμα nt || (MED) μίγμα nt || ~-up n (confusion) σύγχυση, ανακατωσούρα.

moan [məʊn] n (groan) γογγυσμός, βογγητό || (complaint) γκρίνια, μουρμουρητό ♦ vi στενάζω, βογγώ, γογγύζω.

moat [məʊt] n τάφρος f.

mob [mɒb] n όχλος, το πλήθος nt ♦ vt (star etc) πολιορκώ, κυκλώνω.

mobile ['məubaıl] a ευκίνητος, κινητός, ευμετάβολος.

mobility [məu'bılıtı] n ευκινησία, κινητικότητα.

mock [mɒk] vt εμπαίζω, κοροϊδεύω, περιπαίζω ♦ a ψεύτικος, φτιαστός || ~**ery** n (derision) εμπαιγμός, κοροϊδία || (object) περίγελος, κοροϊδο || ~**ing** a (tone) ειρωνικός, σαρκαστικός || ~**-up** n υπόδειγμα nt || (model) μακέτα.

model ['mɒdl] n ομοίωμα nt, μοντέλο || (example) πρότυπο, υπόδειγμα nt || (person) μοντέλο || (of clothes) μανεκέν nt inv ♦ vt (δια)πλάθω, διαμορφώνω, σχεδιάζω || (display clothes) κάνω επίδειξη (ρούχων) ♦ a (railway: toy) τραινάκι || (child) υπόδειγμα || ~**ling**, ~**ing** (US) n σχεδίασμα nt, πλάσιμο || (of styles) επίδειξη μόδας.

modem ['məudɛm] n (COMPUT) modem.

moderate ['mɒdərıt] a μέτριος, μέσος || (fairly good) μέτριος, της σειράς ♦ n (POL) μετριοπαθής ♦ ['mɒdəreıt] vi προϊσταμαι, προεδρεύω ♦ vt μετριάζω, περιορίζω || ~**ly** ad μετρημένα, συγκρατημένα, μέτρια.

moderation [mɒdə'reıʃən] n μετριασμός, μετριοπάθεια.

modern ['mɒdən] a σύγχρονος, μοντέρνος || ~**ization** n (εκ)συγχρονισμός || ~**ize** vt συγχρονίζω, ανανεώνω.

modest ['mɒdıst] a (attitude) μετριόφρων, σεμνός || (meal, home) ταπεινός, μέτριος || ~**y** n μετριοφροσύνη, σεμνότητα, ταπεινότητα.

modicum ['mɒdıkəm] n: with a ~ of με ελάχιστο, με λίγο.

modification [mɒdıfı'keıʃən] n τροποποίηση, μετριασμός.

modify ['mɒdıfaı] vt τροποποιώ, μετριάζω.

module ['mɒdjuːl] n (space) θαλαμίσκος.

mohair ['məuhɛə*] n μαλλί μοχαίρ nt inv.

moist [mɒıst] a υγρός, νοτισμένος || ~**en** vt υγραίνω, μουσκεύω || ~**ure** n υγρασία.

molar ['məulə*] n γομφίος, μυλίτης, τραπεζίτης.

mold [məuld] (US) = **mould**.

mole [məul] n (spot) κρεατοελιά || (animal) τυφλοπόντικας || (pier) κυματοθραύστης, μώλος.

molecule ['mɒlıkjuːl] n μόριο.

molest [məu'lɛst] vt (παρ)ενοχλώ, πειράζω.

molt [məult] (US) = **moult**.

molten ['məultən] a χυτός, λυωμένος.

moment ['məumənt] n στιγμή || (importance) βαρύτητα, σπουδαιότητα || ~**ary** a στιγμιαίος, προσωρινός || ~**ous** a βαρυσήμαντος, σημαντικός.

momentum [məu'mɛntəm] n ορμή, φόρα.

monarch ['mɒnək] n μονάρχης || ~**y** n μοναρχία.

monastery ['mɒnəstrı] n μοναστήρι.

monastic [mə'næstık] a μοναχικός, μοναστικός.

Monday ['mʌndı] n Δευτέρα.

monetary ['mʌnıtərı] a νομισματικός, χρηματικός.

money ['mʌnı] n χρήμα nt, νόμισμα nt, παράς || (wealth) χρήματα ntpl, πλούτη ntpl || ~**lender** n τοκιστής, τοκογλύφος || ~ **order** n ταχυδρομική επιταγή.

mongol ['mɒŋgəl] n (child) πάσχων εκ μογγολισμού ♦ a μογγολικός.

mongrel ['mʌŋgrəl] n μιγάδας ♦ a μιγαδικός, μιξιγενής.

monitor ['mɒnıtə*] n παρεναίτης, επιμελητής || (television monitor) ελεγκτής || (COMPUT) οθόνη ♦ vt (broadcasts) ελέγχω.

monk [mʌŋk] n καλόγηρος, μοναχός.

monkey ['mʌŋkı] n πίθηκος, μαϊμού f || ~ **nut** n αραπιφύστικο || ~ **wrench** n γαλλικό κλειδί.

mono- ['mɒnəu] prefix μον(ο).

monochrome ['mɒnəkrəum] a (TV) μονόχρωμος.

monocle ['mɒnəkl] n μονύελο, μονόκλ nt inv.

monogram ['mɒnəgræm] n μονόγραμμα nt, μονογραφη.

monolithic [mɒnəu'lıθık] a μονολιθικός.

monologue ['mɒnəlɒg] n μονόλογος.

monopoly [mə'nɒpəlı] n μονοπώλιο.

monorail ['mɒnəureıl] n μονόραβδος f.

monosyllabic ['mɒnəusı'læbık] a (person) μονοσυλλαβικός.

monotone ['mɒnətəun] n μονοτονία ήχου, μονότονη ομιλία.

monotonous [mə'nɒtənəs] a μονότονος.

monotony [mə'nɒtənı] n μονοτονία.

monsoon [mɒn'suːn] n θερινός μουσώνας.

monster ['mɒnstə*] n (huge animal) τέρας nt, τερατούργημα nt || (wicked person) τέρας.

monstrosity [mɒns'trɒsıtı] n τερατωδία, κτηνωδία.

monstrous ['mɒnstrəs] a τερατώδης, εκτρωματικός.

montage [mɒn'taːʒ] n (picture) μοντάζ nt inv, μοντάρισμα nt.

month [mʌnθ] n μήνας || ~**ly** a μηνιαίος, μηνιάτικος ♦ ad μηνιαίως, κάθε μήνα ♦ n (magazine) μηνιαίο περιοδικό.

monument ['mɒnjumənt] n μνημείο || ~**al** a μνημειακός || (work etc) μνημειώδης.

moo [muː] vi (cow) μηκώμαι, μουγκρίζω.

mood [muːd] n διάθεση, κέφι || (GRAM) έγκλιση || ~**y** a κακόκεφος, κατσούφης, σκυθρωπός, ιδιότροπος.

moon [muːn] n σελήνη, φεγγάρι || ~**light** n σεληνόφως nt, φεγγάρι || ~**lit** a φεγγαρόλουστος.

moor [muə*] n (Brit: heath) έλος nt, βάλτος, ρεικότοπος ♦ vt (ship)

πρυμνοδετώ, δένω (πλοίο) ♦ vi
πλευρίζω, πέρτω δίπλα.
moorings ['mʊərɪŋz] npl πρυμνήσια ntpl,
πρυμάτσες fpl, ναύδετα ntpl.
moorland ['mʊələnd] n έλος nt, βάλτος,
ρεικότοπος.
moose [muːs] n άλκη n Αμερικανική.
mop [mɒp] n πατσαβούρα || (duster)
ξεσκονιστήρι ♦ vt σφουγγαρίζω || ~ of
hair n ξεντένιστα μαλλιά ntpl.
mope [mɒup] vi μελαγχολώ, πλήττω.
moral ['mɒrəl] a ηθικός, ψυχικός ♦ n
επιμύθιο, ηθικό δίδαγμα nt || ~s npl ήθη
ntpl || ~e n ηθικό || ~ity n ηθικότητα,
ηθικό αίσθημα nt.
morass [mə'ræs] n έλος nt || (fig)
βόρβορος.
morbid ['mɔːbɪd] a νοσηρός,
αρρωστιάρικος.
more [mɔː] a περισσότερος ♦ ad
περισσότερο, πιο πολύ || ~ or less
σχεδόν, πάνω κάτω || ~ than ever
περισσότερο παρά ποτέ.
moreover [mɔː'rəʊvə] ad επί πλέον,
εκτός τούτου.
morgue [mɔːg] n νεκροτομείο.
moribund ['mɒrɪbʌnd] a
ετοιμοθάνατος.
morning ['mɔːnɪŋ] n πρωί ♦ a πρωινός ||
in the ~ το πρωί.
Moroccan [mə'rɒkən] a, n Μαροκινός.
Morocco [mə'rɒkəʊ] n Μαρόκο.
moron ['mɔːrɒn] n καθυστερημένος ||
(col) ηλίθιος, βλάκας || ~ic [mə'rɒnɪk] a
ηλίθιος, βλακώδης.
morose [mə'rəʊs] a κακότροπος,
σκυθρωπός.
morphine ['mɔːfiːn] n μορφίνη.
Morse [mɔːs]: ~ code n μορσικός
κώδικας.
morsel ['mɔːsl] n (of food) μπουκιά,
κομματάκι.
mortal ['mɔːtl] a θνητός || (deadly)
θανάσιμος, θανατηφόρος || (very great)
τρομερός ♦ n (human being) θνητός
(άνθρωπος) || ~ity n θνητότητα || (death
rate) θνησιμότητα.
mortar ['mɔːtə] n ασβεστοκονίαμα nt,
πηλός, λάσπη || (bowl) λάσπη || (weapon)
όλμος.
mortgage ['mɔːgɪdʒ] n υποθήκη.
mortuary ['mɔːtjuəri] n νεκροθάλαμος.
mosaic [məʊ'zeɪɪk] n μωσαϊκό,
ψηφιδωτό.
Moscow ['mɒskəʊ] n Μόσχα.
Moslem ['mɒzlɛm] n Μουσουλμάνος/α
m/f ♦ a μουσουλμανικός.
mosque [mɒsk] n τέμενος nt, τζαμί.
mosquito [mɒs'kiːtəʊ] n κουνούπι.
moss [mɒs] n βρύο || ~y a βρυώδης,
βρυόφυτος.
most [məʊst] a περισσότερος, πιο πολύς
♦ ad πιο, πιο πολύ ♦ n οι περισσότεροι ||
at the (very) ~ το πιο πολύ || to make
the ~ of επωφελούμαι || ~ly ad ως επί
το πλείστο, κυρίως, συνήθως.
M.O.T. n (abbr of Ministry of Transport):

the ~ (test) αναγκαστικός, ετήσιος
τεχνικός έλεγχος οχημάτων.
motel [məʊ'tɛl] n μοτέλ nt inv.
moth [mɒθ] n βότριδα, σκώρος || ~ball n
ναφθαλίνη (σε μπάλλες) || ~-eaten a
σκωροφαγωμένος.
mother ['mʌðə] n μπτέρα, μάνα ♦ vt
(spoil) χαϊδεύω, κανακεύω ♦ a (tongue,
country) μπτρική (γλώσσα) || ~hood n
μπτρότητα || ~-in-law n πεθερά || ~ly a
μπτρικά, σαν μάνα || ~-to-be n σε
ενδιαφέρουσα.
motif [məʊ'tiːf] n μοτίφ nt inv, θέμα nt,
μοτίβο.
motion ['məʊʃən] n κίνηση || (proposal)
πρόταση ♦ vi κάνω νόημα, νεύω || ~less
a ακίνητος || ~ picture n ταινία, φιλμ nt
inv.
motivated ['məʊtɪveɪtɪd] a
αιτιολογούμενος, κινητήριος.
motivation [məʊtɪ'veɪʃən] n κίνητρο,
ελατήριο.
motive ['məʊtɪv] n κίνητρο, αίτιο,
ελατήριο ♦ a κινητήριος.
motley ['mɒtlɪ] a (heterogeneous)
πολύχρωμος, ετερογενής.
motor ['məʊtə] n κινητήρας, μηχανή ||
(automobile) αυτοκίνητο ♦ vi ταξιδεύω με
αυτοκίνητο || ~bike n μοτοσυκλέτα ||
~boat n βενζινάκατος f || ~car n
αυτοκίνητο || ~cycle n ~ bike ||
~cyclist n μοτοσυκλετιστής || ~ing ♦ a
χρήση του αυτοκινήτου, οδήγηση ♦ a
του αυτοκινήτου, της οδηγήσεως || ~ist
n αυτοκινητιστής || ~ oil n λάδι
κινητήρων || ~ racing n
αυτοκινητοδρομία || ~ scooter n
σκούτερ nt inv, βέσπα || ~ vehicle n
αυτοκίνητο || ~way n (Brit)
αυτοκινητόδρομος.
mottled ['mɒtld] a διάστικτος,
ποικιλόχρωμος.
motto ['mɒtəʊ] n ρητό, μόττο, αρχή.
mould [məʊld] n τύπωμα, μήτρα, καλούπι ||
(shape) τύπωμα nt, πρότυπο || (mildew)
μούχλα ♦ vt χύνω σε τύπους || (fig)
διαπλάθω, διαμορφώνω || ~er vi (decay)
σαπίζω, φθείρομαι || ~ing n (in plaster)
τυποποιία, χυτό αντικείμενο || (in wood)
κορνίζα || ~y a (food etc) μουχλιασμένος.
moult [məʊlt] vi μαδώ.
mound [maʊnd] n ανάχωμα nt,
λοφίσκος, πρόχωμα nt.
mount [maʊnt] n (high hill) όρος nt,
βουνό || (horse) άλογο || (for jewel etc)
κορνίζα, υποστήριγμα nt, σκελετός ♦ vt
(get on horse) ανεβάζω, ανεβαίνω στο ||
(put in setting) μοντάρω, δένω, κορνιζάρω
|| (exhibition) ανεβάζω || (attack)
οργανώνω επίθεση ♦ vi (also: ~ up)
ανέρχομαι, ανεβαίνω.
mountain ['maʊntɪn] n όρος nt, βουνό ||
(pile) σωρός, πλήθος nt || ~eer n
(climber) ορειβάτης || ~eering n
ορειβασία || to go ~eering κάνω
ορειβασία || ~ous a ορεινός || ~ side n
πλευρά βουνού.

mourn [mɔːn] vt πενθώ, θρηνώ ♦ vi
(+ for) θρηνώ, κλαίω || ~**er** n πενθών,
πενθοφορών || ~**ful** a πένθιμος || ~**ing**
n πένθος nt || in ~**ing** (period etc) έχω
πένθος || (dress) πένθιμα ρούχα ntpl,
μαύρα ntpl.

mouse [maus] n ποντικός || (COMPUT)
ποντίκι || ~**trap** n ποντικοπαγίδα, φάκα.

moustache [məs'tɑːʃ] n μουστάκι.

mouth [mauθ] n (ANAT) στόμα nt ||
(opening) στόμιο || (entrance) εκβολή,
στόμιο ♦ [mauð] vt (words) ομιλώ με
στόμφο || ~**ful** n μπουκιά || ~ **organ** n
φυσαρμόνικα || ~**piece** n επιστόμιο ||
(speaker) όργανο, φερέφωνο,
εκπρόσωπος || ~**wash** n γαργάρα || ~-
watering a γαργαλιστικός.

movable ['muːvəbl] a κινητός.

move [muːv] n (movement) κίνηση || (in
game) κίνηση || (step) ενέργεια, βήμα nt ||
(from house) μετακόμιση ♦ vt (μετα)κινώ,
μετατοπίζω || (stir, rouse) συγκινώ,
γίνομαι (εξωφρενών κλ) ♦ vi (general)
κινούμαι, κουνιέμαι || (travel)
μετακινούμαι, φεύγω || (take action)
ενεργώ || (go elsewhere) μετακομίζω || to
get a ~ on σπεύδω, κάνω γρήγορα || to
~ **house** μετοικώ, μετακομίζω || to ~
about vi περιφέρομαι, τριγυρίζω || to ~
away vi απομακρύνομαι, φεύγω || to ~
back vi υποχωρώ, ξαναγυρίζω πίσω || to
~ **forward** vi προχωρώ ♦ vt κινώ προς
τα εμπρός || to ~ **in** vi (house)
μετακομίζω (στο νέο σπίτι),
εγκαθίσταμαι || to ~ **on** vi προχωρώ,
τραβώ το δρόμο μου ♦ vt κάνω να
κυκλοφορεί || to ~ **out** vi (house)
μετακομίζω (αλλού), αδειάζω || ~**ment**
n κίνηση, μετακίνηση || (social etc) κίνημα
nt, κίνηση || (MUS) μέρος nt.

movie ['muːvɪ] n (film) φιλμ nt inv || **the
~s** (cinema) σινεμά nt inv || ~ **camera** n
(amateur) κινηματογραφική μηχανή.

moving ['muːvɪŋ] a (lit) κινούμενος,
κινητός || (stirring) συνταρακτικός,
συγκινητικός || (touching) συγκινητικός.

mow [məʊ] (irreg v) vt θερίζω || to ~
down vt θερίζω || ~**er** n (machine)
θεριστική μηχανή.

M.P. abbr see **member**.

m.p.g. (abbr of miles per gallon) ≈ χ.α.λ.
(χιλιόμετρα ανά λίτρο).

m.p.h. (abbr of miles per hour) ≈ χ.α.ω.
(χιλιόμετρα ανά ώρα).

Mr ['mɪstə*] n: ~ **Smith** Κύριος Σμιθ,
Κος Σμιθ.

Mrs ['mɪsɪz] n: ~ **Smith** Κυρία Σμιθ, Κα
Σμιθ.

much [mʌtʃ] a πολύς ♦ ad πολύ, συχνά,
σχεδόν ♦ n πολλά, πολύ || **how ~ is it?**
πόσο κάνει; || **too ~** πάρα πολύ.

muck [mʌk] n (lit) κοπριά, βρωμιά || (fig)
σύγχυση, καταστροφή || to ~ **about** vi
(col) περιφέρομαι άσκοπα, χαζεύω ♦ vt
(col) λασπώνω, βρωμίζω || to ~ **up** vt
(col: ruin) χαλάω μια δουλειά || ~**y** a
(dirty) βρώμικος, βρωμερός.

mud [mʌd] n λάσπη.

muddle ['mʌdl] n ακαταστασία, σαλάτα,
μπέρδεμα nt ♦ vt (also: ~ **up**) μπερδεύω,
κάνω άνω-κάτω || to ~ **through** vi
καταφέρνω κουτσά-στραβά.

muddy ['mʌdɪ] a λασπώδης,
λασπωμένος.

mudguard ['mʌdɡɑːd] n φτερό
(αυτοκινήτου).

mudpack ['mʌdpæk] n μάσκα (από
πηλό).

mud-slinging ['mʌdslɪŋɪŋ] n
συκοφαντία, κακογλωσσιά.

muffle ['mʌfl] vt πνίγω (ήχο) || (wrap up)
κουκουλώνω, σκεπάζω || ~**d** a
υπόκουφος, πνιγμένος.

mug [mʌɡ] n (cup) μεγάλο φλυτζάνι,
φλυτζάνα || (col: face) μούτρο, φάτσα ||
(col: dupe) χαζός, κορόιδο ♦ vt (assault)
κτυπώ από πίσω || ~**ging** n (assault)
επίθεση με ληστεία.

muggy ['mʌɡɪ] a (weather) βαρύς
(καιρός), υγρός.

mule [mjuːl] n ημίονος, μουλάρι.

mull [mʌl]: to ~ **over** vt γυροφέρνω
στο μυαλό.

mulled [mʌld] a (wine) ζεστό κρασί με
κανέλλα.

multi ['mʌltɪ] prefix πολύ-.

multicoloured, multicolored (US)
['mʌltɪ'kʌləd] a πολύχρωμος.

multiple ['mʌltɪpl] n πολλαπλάσιο ♦ a
πολλαπλός || ~ **store** n κατάστημα nt με
πολλά υποκαταστήματα.

multiplication [mʌltɪplɪ'keɪʃən] n
πολλαπλασιασμός.

multiply ['mʌltɪplaɪ] vt πολλαπλασιάζω
♦ vi πολλαπλασιάζομαι.

multitude ['mʌltɪtjuːd] n πλήθος nt.

mum [mʌm] n (col) μαμά.

mumble ['mʌmbl] vti μουρμουρίζω,
μασώ ♦ n μπερδεμένα λόγια ntpl,
μουρμούρα.

mummy ['mʌmɪ] n μούμια || (col) μαμά.

mumps [mʌmps] n παρωτίτιδα
μαγουλάδες fpl.

munch [mʌntʃ] vti μασουλίζω,
τραγανίζω.

mundane ['mʌn'deɪn] a εγκόσμιος,
γήινος.

municipal [mjuː'nɪsɪpəl] a δημοτικός.

munitions [mjuː'nɪʃənz] npl
πολεμοφόδια ntpl.

mural ['mjʊərəl] n τοιχογραφία.

murder ['mɜːdə*] n φόνος, δολοφονία
|| (fig: col) φονικό ♦ vt φονεύω, σκοτώνω,
δολοφονώ || ~**er** n φονιάς, δολοφόνος
|| ~**erous** a (δολο)φονικός || ~**ess** n
φόνισσα.

murky ['mɜːkɪ] a σκοτεινός, ζοφερός.

murmur ['mɜːmə*] n ψίθυρος,
μουρμουρητό ♦ vi ψιθυρίζω,
μουρμουρίζω, παραπονούμαι.

muscle ['mʌsl] n μυς m.

muscular ['mʌskjʊlə*] a μυϊκός,
γεροδεμένος.

Muse [mjuːz] n Μούσα.

muse [mjuːz] *vi* ρεμβάζω, ονειροπολώ.
museum [mjuːˈzɪəm] *n* μουσείο.
mush [mʌʃ] *n* πολτός.
mushroom[ˈmʌʃrum] *n* μανιτάρι ♦ *vi* ξεφυτρώνω.
mushy [ˈmʌʃi] *a* πολτώδης, μαλακός.
music [ˈmjuːzɪk] *n* μουσική || **to face the ~** ακούω εξάψαλμο || **~al** *n* μουσική παράσταση ♦ *a* μουσικός, φιλόμουσος || **~ian** *n* μουσικός *m/f* || **~ stand** αναλόγιο μουσικου.
muslin [ˈmʌzlɪn] *n* μουσελίνα.
mussel [ˈmʌl] *n* μύδι.
must [mʌst] *auxiliary v (obligation)* **I ~ do it** πρέπει να το κάνω || **I ~ not do it** δεν πρέπει να το κάνω || *(probability)* **he ~ be there by now** πρέπει να είναι εκεί τώρα ♦ *n* η γλύκος, μούστος || **it is a ~** είναι αναγκαίο.
mustache [ˈmʌstæʃ] *n (US)* = **moustache.**
mustard [ˈmʌstəd] *n (condiment)* μουστάρδα.
mustn't [ˈmʌsnt] = **must not.**
musty [ˈmʌsti] *a* μουχλιασμένος || *(col)* παλιατσούρα, μαγιάτικος.
mute [mjuːt] *n* βουβός/ή *m/f*, μουγγός/ή *m/f*.
mutilate [ˈmjuːtɪleɪt] *vt* ακρωτηριάζω, σακατεύω.
mutilation [mjuːtɪˈleɪʃən] *n* ακρωτηριασμός, σακάτεμα *nt*.
mutinous [ˈmjuːtɪnəs] *a* στασιαστικός, ανταρτικός.
mutiny [ˈmjuːtɪni] *n* στάση, ανταρσία ♦ *vi* στασιάζω.
mutter [ˈmʌtə*] *vti* μουρμουρίζω.
mutton [ˈmʌtn] *n* αρνήσιο κρέας *nt*.
mutual [ˈmjuːtjuəl] *a* αμοιβαίος, κοινός || **~ly** *ad* αμοιβαίως.
muzzle [ˈmʌzl] *n (mouth and nose)* ρύγχος *nt*, μουσούδα || *(straps)* φίμωτρο || *(of gun)* στόμιο, στόμα *nt* ♦ *vt* φιμώνω.
my [maɪ] *poss a* δικός μου, μου.
myopic [maɪˈɒpɪk] *a* μυωπικός.
myself [maɪˈsɛlf] *pron* εγώ ο ίδιος, τον εαυτό μου.
mysterious [mɪsˈtɪərɪəs] *a* μυστηριώδης.
mystery [ˈmɪstəri] *n* μυστήριο.
mystic [ˈmɪstɪk] *n* μυστικός, μυστικιστής || **~al** *a* μυστικιστικός, μυστηριώδης.
mystification [mɪstɪfɪˈkeɪʃən] *n* αμηχανία, απάτη.
mystify [ˈmɪstɪfaɪ] *vt* προκαλώ έκπληξη.
myth [mɪθ] *n* μύθος || **~ical** *a* μυθικός || **~ological** *a* μυθολογικός || **~ology** *n* μυθολογία.

N

nab [næb] *vt* αρπάζω, συλλαμβάνω.
nag [næg] *n (horse)* μικρό άλογο *(ιπποασίας)* || *(person)* γκρινιάρης, καυγατζής ♦ *vti* γκρινιάζω, καυγαδίζω || **~ging** *n* καυγάς, φασαρία.

nail [neɪl] *n* νύχι || *(spike)* καρφί, πρόκα ♦ *vt* καρφώνω || **to ~ down** *vt (fig)* δεσμεύω || **~ brush** *n* βούρτσα των νυχιών || **~ file** *n* λίμα (για νύχια) || **~ polish** *n* βερνίκι των νυχιών, μανό || **~ scissors** *npl* ψαλιδάκι (για νύχια) || **~ varnish** *n* βερνίκι για τα νύχια.
naïve [naɪˈiːv] *a* αφελής.
naked [ˈneɪkɪd] *a* γυμνός || *(uncovered)* εκτεθειμένος, καθαρός || **~ness** *n* γυμνότητα.
name [neɪm] *nt || (reputation)* φήμη, υπόληψη ♦ *vt* ονομάζω || *(call by name)* αναφέρω, κατονομάζω || *(appoint)* ορίζω, διορίζω || **in the ~ of** εξ ονόματός του || *(authority of)* εν ονόματι || **~less** *a* άγνωστος, ανώνυμος || **~ly** *ad* δηλαδή || **~sake** *n* ομώνυμος, συνονόματος.
nanny [ˈnæni] *n (for child)* νταντά.
nap [næp] *n (sleep)* υπνάκος || **to have a ~** τον παίρνω λιγάκι.
nape [neɪp] *n* αυχένας, σβέρκος.
napkin [ˈnæpkɪn] *n* πετσέτα φαγητού || *(Brit)* χαρτοπετσέτα, πάνα (βρέφους).
nappy [ˈnæpi] *n (for baby)* πάνα.
narcissus [naːˈsɪsəs] *n* νάρκισσος.
narcotic [naːˈkɒtɪk] *n* ναρκωτικό *nt*.
nark [naːk] *vt (col: annoy)* εξερεθίζω, εξαγριώνω.
narration [nəˈreɪʃən] *n* διήγηση.
narrative [ˈnærətɪv] *n* διήγημα *nt*, αφήγηση ♦ *a* αφηγηματικός.
narrator [nəˈreɪtə*] *n* αφηγητής.
narrow [ˈnærəu] *a* στενός, στενόχωρος ♦ *vi* στενεύω || **to ~ down** *vt* περιορίζω || **~ly** *ad (miss)* μόλις, παρά λίγο || **~-minded** *a* στενοκέφαλος.
nasal [ˈneɪzəl] *a* ένρινος, ρινικός, της μύτης.
nastiness [ˈnaːstɪnɪs] *n* κακία, αχρειότητα, προστυχιά.
nasty [ˈnaːsti] *a (mess)* δυσάρεστος, βρώμικος || *(business)* δύσκολος, επικίνδυνος, φοβερός || *(person)* πρόστυχος, ρεμάλι, κακός.
nation [ˈneɪʃən] *n* έθνος *nt* || **~al** [ˈnæʃənl] *a* εθνικός ♦ *n* υπήκοος *m/f*, πολίτης/ίτισσα *m/f* || **~al anthem** *n* εθνικός ύμνος || **~alism** *n* εθνικισμός || **~alist** *a, n* εθνικιστής/ίστρια *m/f*, εθνικόφρων || **~ality** *n* εθνικότητα || **~alization** *n* εθνικοποίηση || **~alize** *vt* εθνικοποιώ || **~ally** *ad* από εθνικής άποψης || **~-wide** *a* πανεθνικό ♦ *ad* σ' ολόκληρη τη χώρα.
native [ˈneɪtɪv] *n* ντόπιος/ια *m/f* || *(non-European)* ιθαγενής *m/f* ♦ *a* εγχώριος || *(country etc)* γενέθλιος, μητρικός || *(inborn)* έμφυτος, φυσικός.
NATO [ˈneɪtəu] *n* NATO (Οργανισμός Βορειοατλαντικού Συμφώνου).
natter [ˈnætə*] *vi (col: chat)* κουβεντιάζω.
natural [ˈnætʃrəl] *a* φυσικός || *(inborn)* έμφυτος, φυσικός || **~ist** *n* φυσιοδίφης || **~ize** *vt* πολιτογραφώ || *(plant etc)*

εγκλιματίζω || ~ly ad φυσικά, βέβαια || ~ness n φυσικότητα.

nature ['neɪtʃə*] n φύση || (sort, kind) είδος nt, χαρακτήρας || by ~ εκ φύσης.

naughty ['nɔːtɪ] a (child) άτακτος, κακός.

nausea ['nɔːsɪə] n ναυτία, αναγούλα || (disgust) αηδία, αποστροφή || ~te vt αηδιάζω (κάτι), προ ξενώ ναυτία.

nauseating ['nɔːsɪeɪtɪŋ] a αηδιαστικός, σιχαμερός.

nautical ['nɔːtɪkəl] a ναυτικός.

naval ['neɪvl] a ναυτικός.

nave [neɪv] n κλίτος, νάρθηκας.

navel ['neɪvl] n ομφαλός, αφαλός.

navigable ['nævɪgəbl] a πλωτός.

navigate ['nævɪgeɪt] vt (ship etc) κυβερνώ, διευθύνω ♦ vi ναυσιπλοώ, πλέω, ταξιδεύω.

navigation [nævɪ'geɪʃən] n ναυτιλία, πλους m, διάπλους m.

navigator ['nævɪgeɪtə*] n ναυτίλος, πλοηγός || (explorer) θαλασσοπόρος || (AVIAT) αεροναυτίλος.

navy ['neɪvɪ] n ναυτικό || ~ **blue** n (colour) ακούρος μπλε, μπλε μαρίν.

nay [neɪ] ad (no) όχι || (also) τι λέω, ή καλύτερα.

Nazi ['nɑːtsɪ] n Ναζιστής.

neap tide ['niːp'taɪd] a άμπωτη.

near [nɪə*] a (close) εγγύς, κοντινός || (related) πλησίον, στενός ♦ ad (space) κοντά, πλησίον || (time) περί, εγγύς, κοντά ♦ prep (also: ~ to) κοντά σε, παρά, || (space) παρά, κοντά || (time) περί, κοντά ♦ vt πλησιάζω || ~by a κοντινός, πλαϊνός ♦ ad πολύ κοντά, εγγύτατα || N~ East n Εγγύς Ανατολή || ~ly ad σχεδόν, περίπου || ~ miss n λίγο έλειψε (να), παρά λίγο (να) || ~ness n εγγύτητα, στενότητα || ~side n (AUT) αριστερή πλευρά.

neat [niːt] a (tidy) καθαρός, καλοβαλμένος, κομψός || (clever) καλοβαλμένος, επιτυχής, κομψός || (pure) καθαρός, αγνός, χωρίς νερό.

nebulous ['nɛbjʊləs] a νεφελώδης.

necessarily ['nɛsɪsərɪlɪ] ad απαραιτήτως, κατ' ανάγκη.

necessary ['nɛsɪsərɪ] a αναγκαίος, απαραίτητος.

necessitate [nɪ'sɛsɪteɪt] vt κάνω αναγκαίο, υποχρεώνω.

necessity [nɪ'sɛsɪtɪ] n ανάγκη.

neck [nɛk] n λαιμός, αυχένας, τράχηλος, σβέρκος || (narrow part) λαιμός, στένωμα nt || ~ **and** ~ στα ίσια, ισόπαλος πλάι-πλάι.

necklace ['nɛklɪs] n περιδέραιο, κολιέ nt inv.

neckline n ['nɛklaɪn] λαιμός, ντεκολτέ nt inv.

necktie n ['nɛktaɪ] γραβάτα.

née [neɪ] a το γένος.

need [niːd] n ανάγκη, χρεία || (poverty) ένδεια, φτώχεια ♦ vt (of person) χρειάζομαι || (of thing) απαιτώ, ζητώ (κάτι) || **to** ~ **to do** έχω ανάγκη να κάνω.

needle ['niːdl] n βελόνι nt || (knitting) βελόνα f || (compass etc) βελόνη f.

needless ['niːdlɪs] a άχρηστος, περιττός.

needlework ['niːdlwɜːk] n εργόχειρο.

needy ['niːdɪ] a ενδεής, άπορος.

negation [nɪ'geɪʃən] n άρνηση.

negative ['nɛgətɪv] n (PHOT) αρνητικό ♦ a αρνητικός.

neglect [nɪ'glɛkt] vt παραμελώ ♦ n αμέλεια, παραμέληση.

negligée ['nɛglɪʒeɪ] n νυχτικό.

negligence ['nɛglɪdʒəns] n αμέλεια.

negligent ['nɛglɪdʒənt] a αμελής, απρόσεκτος || ~ly ad απρόσεκτα, αμελώς.

negligible ['nɛglɪdʒəbl] a αμελητέος.

negotiable [nɪ'gəʊʃɪəbl] a (cheque) εμπορεύσιμος, μετατρεπτός, μεταβιβάσιμος.

negotiate [nɪ'gəʊʃɪeɪt] vi διαπραγματεύομαι ♦ vt (treaty) διαπραγματεύομαι || (difficulty) διαβαίνω, ξεπερνώ.

negotiation [nɪgəʊʃɪ'eɪʃən] n διαπραγμάτευση.

negotiator [nɪ'gəʊʃɪeɪtə*] n διαπραγματευτής.

Negress ['niːgrɛs] n νέγρα, μαύρη.

Negro ['niːgrəʊ] n νέγρος, μαύρος.

neighbour, neighbor (US)['neɪbə*] n γείτονας/γειτόνισσα m/f || ~**hood** n γειτονιά, περιοχή || ~**ing** a γειτονικός || ~**ly** a καλός γείτονας, γειτονικός.

neither ['naɪðə*] a ούτε ο ένας ούτε ο άλλος, κανένας || cj ούτε ... ούτε, ούτε (και) ♦ pron κανένας.

neo- ['niːəʊ] prefix νεο-.

neon ['niːɒn] n νέο || ~ **light** n φως με νέο.

nephew ['nɛvjuː] n ανεψιός.

nerve [nɜːv] n νεύρο || (courage) σθένος nt, θάρρος nt || (impudence) θράσος nt || ~-**racking** a εκνευριστικός.

nervous ['nɜːvəs] a νευρικός || (timid) ντροπαλός, νευρικός, δειλός || ~ **breakdown** n νευρικός κλονισμός || ~**ly** ad δειλά, φοβισμένα || ~**ness** n νευρικότητα, δειλία.

nest [nɛst] n φωλιά.

nestle ['nɛsl] vi φωλιάζω, κουλουριάζομαι.

net [nɛt] n δίκτυο, δίχτυ nt || (hair) φιλές m, δίχτυ nt ♦ a καθαρός.

Netherlands ['nɛðələndz] npl Ολλανδία.

netting ['nɛtɪŋ] n δικτύωμα nt, πλέγμα nt.

network ['nɛtwɜːk] n δίκτυο.

neurotic [njʊə'rɒtɪk] a νευρωτικός ♦ n νευροπαθής.

neuter ['njuːtə*] a ουδέτερος ♦ n ουδέτερο.

neutral ['njuːtrəl] a ουδέτερος || ~**ity** n ουδετερότητα.

never ['nɛvə*] ad ποτέ || ~-**ending** a

ατελείωτος || ~theless ad εντούτοις, παρ' όλα αυτά.

new [nju:] a νέος, καινούργιος || (clothes etc) καινουργής, καινούριος || (modern) σύγχρονος, μοντέρνος || (at work etc) αρχάριος, άπειρος || ~born a νεογέννητος || ~comer n φρεσκοφερμένος/νη m/f, νεοφερμένος/νη m/f|| ~ly ad τελευταία, πρόσφατα || ~ moon n καινούργιο φεγγάρι || ~ness n νεότητα, φρεσκάδα.

news [nju:z] n νέα ntpl, ειδήσεις fpl|| ~agent n πράκτορας εφημερίδων || ~flash n έκτακτη είδηση || ~letter n δελτίο ειδήσεων || ~paper n εφημερίδα || ~reel n ταινία επικαίρων.

New Year [nju:'jiə*] n Νέο Έτος || ~'s Day n Πρωτοχρονιά || ~'s Eve n παραμονή της Πρωτοχρονιάς.

New Zealand [nju:'zi:lənd] n Νέα Ζηλανδία.

next [nɛkst] a πλησιέστερος, γειτονικός, πλαϊνός || (in time) προσεχής, επόμενος ♦ ad έπειτα, κατόπιν, μετά ♦ prep: ~ to κοντά σε, σχεδόν || the ~ day την άλλη μέρα, την επομένη || ~ year n επόμενο έτος nt, άλλος χρόνος, του χρόνου || ~ of kin n πλησιέστερος συγγενής.

N.H.S. abbr of National Health Service.

nibble ['nibl] vt δαγκώνω, μασουλίζω, τρώγω σιγά-σιγά.

nice [nais] a ευχάριστος, καλός, ωραίος || (exact) λεπτός, ευαίσθητος || ~-looking a ωραίος, όμορφος || ~ly ad ωραία, ευχάριστα.

nick [nik] n (cut) χαραγή, εγκοπή || in the ~ of time στην κατάλληλη στιγμή.

nickel ['nikl] n νικέλιο || (US) πεντάρα (5 σέντς).

nickname ['nikneim] n παρατσούκλι.

nicotine ['nikəti:n] n νικοτίνη.

niece [ni:s] n ανεψιά.

niggling ['niɡliŋ] a ασημαντολόγος.

night [nait] n νύχτα, βράδυ || good ~ καλή νύχτα || at or by ~ τη νύχτα || ~cap n (drink) νυκτερινό ρόφημα nt|| ~club n νυκτερινό κέντρο || ~dress n νυχτικό || ~fall n σούρουπο || ~life n νυχτερινή ζωή || ~ly a νυχτερινός, βραδινός ♦ ad κάθε νύχτα, κάθε βράδυ || ~mare n εφιάλτης || ~school n βραδυνή σχολή || ~-time n νύχτα || ~watchman n νυκτοφύλακας.

nightingale ['naitiŋɡeil] n αηδόνι.

nil [nil] n μηδέν, τίποτε.

nimble ['nimbl] a εύστροφος, ευκίνητος.

nine [nain] num εννέα, εννιά || ~teen num δεκαεννιά || ~ty num ενενήντα.

ninth [nainθ] a ένατος.

nip [nip] vt (pinch etc) τσιμπώ, δαγκώνω ♦ n τσίμπημα nt, δάγκωμα nt.

nipple ['nipl] n (ANAT) θηλή, ρώγα.

nitrogen ['naitrədʒən] n άζωτο.

no [nəu] a κανείς, καθόλου ♦ ad όχι, καθόλου, μη ♦ n άρνηση, αρνητική ψήφος f.

nobility [nəu'biliti] n (social class) ευγενείς mpl.

noble ['nəubl] a ευγενής, μεγαλοπρεπής ♦ n ευγενής, ευπατρίδης.

nobody ['nəubədi] pron κανείς, κανένας, ♦ n (unimportant person) μηδαμινότητα, τιποτένιος.

nod [nɒd] vi νεύω, νέφω, κάνω νόημα || (droop with sleep) νυστάζω, κουτουλώ ♦ n νεύμα nt, νόημα nt, κουτούλισμα nt.

noise [nɔiz] n κρότος, βοή || (unpleasant) θόρυβος.

noisily ['nɔizili] ad θορυβωδώς, με φασαρία.

noisy ['nɔizi] a θορυβώδης.

nomad ['nɒmæd] n: νομάδας || ~ic a νομαδικός.

nominal ['nɒminl] a ονομαστικός, εικονικός.

nominate ['nɒmineit] vt προτείνω, ονομάζω || (appoint) διορίζω.

nomination [nɒmi'neiʃən] n πρόταση, υποψηφιότητα, διορισμός.

nominee [nɒmi'ni:] n υποψήφιος/ήφια m/f.

non- [nɒn] prefix μη-, αντι-, αν-, α- || ~alcoholic a χωρίς οινόπνευμα.

nonchalant ['nɒnʃələnt] a ψύχραιμος, αδιάφορος.

nondescript ['nɒndiskript] a ακαθόριστος, αχαρακτήριστος.

none [nʌn] a κανένας ♦ pron κανένας, καμμιά, κανένα ♦ ad καθόλου.

nonentity [nɒ'nɛntiti] n μηδαμινότητα, ασήμαντος άνθρωπος.

nonplussed ['nɒn'plʌst] a (τα έχω) χαμένα, βρίσκομαι σε αμηχανία.

nonsense ['nɒnsəns] n ανοησία, παραλογισμός.

non-stop ['nɒn'stɒp] a χωρίς σταθμό.

noodles ['nu:dlz] npl φιδές m.

noon [nu:n] n μεσημέρι.

no one ['nəuwʌn] pron = nobody.

noose [nu:s] n βρόχος, θηλειά.

nor [nɔ:*] cj ούτε, μήτε.

norm [nɔ:m] n κανόνας, τύπος, μέτρο.

normal ['nɔ:məl] a κανονικός, συνηθισμένος, ομαλός || ~ly ad κανονικά.

north [nɔ:θ] n βορράς, βοριάς || (of country etc) τα βόρεια ♦ a βόρειος ♦ ad βορείως, προς βορρά || ~-east a βορειοανατολικός || ~ern a βόρειος, βορεινός || N~ Pole n Βόρειος Πόλος || N~ Sea n Βόρειος Θάλασσα || ~ward(s) ad προς βορρά || ~-west a βορειοδυτικός.

Norway ['nɔ:wei] n Νορβηγία.

Norwegian [nɔ:'wi:dʒən] a νορβηγικός ♦ n Νορβηγός/Νορβηγίδα m/f.

nose [nəuz] n μύτη || (smell) όσφρηση, μύτη || ~bleed n ρινορραγία, μάτωμα nt της μύτης || ~-dive n κάθετη εφόρμηση || ~y a περίεργος, αδιάκριτος.

nostalgia [nɒs'tældʒiə] n νοσταλγία.

nostalgic [nɒs'tældʒik] a νοσταλγικός.

nostril ['nɒstril] n ρουθούνι.

not [nɒt] ad δεν, μη, όχι.
notable [ˈnəutəbl] a αξιοσημείωτος, σημαντικός.
notch [nɒtʃ] n εγκοπή, χαραγή, οδόντωση.
note [nəut] n νότα, τόνος, πλήκτρο || (short letter) γραμματάκι, σημείωμα nt || (remark) σημείωση, υπόμνημα nt || (reputation) φήμη διάκριση ♦ vt σημειώνω, παρατηρώ || (write down) σημειώνω, (κατα)γράφω ~**book** n σημειωματάριο, καρνέ nt inv || ~-**case** n πορτοφόλι || ~**d** a σημαίνων, διακεκριμένος, διάσημος || ~**paper** n χαρτί αλληλογραφίας.
nothing [ˈnʌθiŋ] n μηδέν, τίποτε || **for** ~ (free) δωρεάν, τζάμπα.
notice [ˈnəutis] n (announcement) αγγελία, αναγγελία || (attention) προσοχή, παρατήρηση || (warning) ειδοποίηση, προειδοποίηση ♦ vt (observe) παρατηρώ, αντιλαμβάνομαι, προσέχω || ~**able** a αξιοσημείωτος, αξιοπρόσεκτος || ~ **board** n (Brit) ενοικιαστήριο, πίνακας ανακοινώσεων.
notification [nəutifiˈkeiʃən] n (αν)αγγελία, ανακοίνωση, δήλωση, γνωστοποίηση.
notify [ˈnəutifai] vt πληροφορώ, ειδοποιώ, γνωστοποιώ.
notion [ˈnəuʃən] n αντίληψη, ιδέα || (fancy) γνώμη, ιδέα, σκέψη.
notorious [nəuˈtɔːriəs] a περιβόητος, πασίγνωστος.
notwithstanding [nɒtwiθˈstændiŋ] ad παρ᾽, όλα αυτά, εντούτοις, όμως.
nougat [ˈnuːgɑː] n μαντολάτο.
nought [nɔːt] n (zero) μηδέν || τίποτε, μηδέν.
noun [naun] n όνομα, ουσιαστικό.
nourish [ˈnʌriʃ] vt (δια)τρέφω || ~**ing** a θρεπτικός.
novel [ˈnɒvəl] n μυθιστόρημα nt ♦ a νέος, πρωτότυπος || ~**ist** n μυθιστοριογράφος m/f || ~**ty** n νεωτερισμός.
November [nəuˈvɛmbə*] n Νοέμβριος.
novice [ˈnɒvis] n αρχάριος, μαθητευόμενος.
now [nau] ad τώρα, λοιπόν || **right** ~ αμέσως, στη στιγμή || ~ **and then** κάπου-κάπου, καμμιά φορά, || ~ **and again** κάθε τόσο, μερικές φορές, που και που || ~**adays** ad σήμερα.
nowhere [ˈnəuwɛə*] ad πουθενά.
nozzle [ˈnɒzl] n στόμιο (σωλήνα), προφύσιο, ακροφύσιο.
nuclear [ˈnjuːkliə*] a (energy etc) πυρηνικός.
nucleus [ˈnjuːkliəs] n πυρήνας.
nude [njuːd] a γυμνός, γδυτός ♦ n (ART) γυμνό.
nudge [nʌdʒ] vt αγκωνίζω, σκουντώ.
nudist [ˈnjuːdist] n γυμνιστής/γυμνίστρια m/f.
nudity [ˈnjuːditi] n γυμνότητα.

nuisance [ˈnjuːsns] n ενόχληση, μπελάς.
null [nʌl] a άκυρος.
numb [nʌm] a ναρκωμένος, μουδιασμένος ♦ vt ναρκώνω, μουδιάζω.
number [ˈnʌmbə*] n αριθμός, ψηφίο, νούμερο || (sum) αριθμός, σύνολο, άθροισμα nt || (quantity) πολλοί mpl, πλήθος nt || (GRAM) αριθμός || (issue) αριθμός (τεύχους) ♦ vt (αν)αριθμώ, μετρώ || (amount to) ανέρχομαι, φθάνω, αριθμώ || ~ **plate** n (Brit AUT) πινακίδα κυκλοφορίας αυτοκινήτου.
numeral [ˈnjuːmərəl] n αριθμός.
numerical [njuːˈmɛrikəl] a (order) αριθμητικός.
numerous [ˈnjuːmərəs] a πολυάριθμος.
nun [nʌn] n μοναχή, καλόγρια.
nurse [nɜːs] n νοσοκόμος/ νοσοκόμα m/f || (for children) παραμάνα, τροφός f ♦ vt (patient, invalid) περιποιούμαι, νοσηλεύω || (fig) φροντίζω, επιμελούμαι, συγκρατώ.
nursery [ˈnɜːsəri] n παιδικός σταθμός, βρεφοκομείο || (plants) φυτώριο || ~ **rhyme** n παιδικό τραγουδάκι || ~ **school** n νηπιαγωγείο.
nursing [ˈnɜːsiŋ] n (profession) επάγγελμα nt νοσοκόμου || ~ **home** n (ιδιωτική) κλινική.
nut [nʌt] n περικόχλιο, παξιμάδι || (fruit) καρύδι, ξηρός καρπός || ~**s** a (col: crazy) τρελός.
nutcracker [ˈnʌtkrækə*] n καρυοθραύστης.
nutmeg [ˈnʌtmɛg] n μοσχοκάρυδο.
nutrient [ˈnjuːtriənt] n θρεπτικό, τρόφιμο.
nutritious [njuːˈtriʃəs] a θρεπτικός.
nutshell [ˈnʌtʃɛl] n: **in a** ~ σύντομος, με λίγα λόγια.
nylon [ˈnailɒn] a, n νάυλον nt inv.

O

oaf [əuf] n αδέξιος, άξεστος.
oak [əuk] n δρύς, βαλανιδιά ♦ a δρύινος.
O.A.P. abbr see **old**.
oar [ɔː*] n κώπη, κουπί.
oasis [əuˈeisis] n όαση.
oath [əuθ] n όρκος || (swearword) βλαστήμια.
oats [əuts] npl βρώμη.
obedience [əˈbiːdiəns] n υπακοή, ευπείθεια.
obedient [əˈbiːdiənt] a υπάκουος.
obesity [əuˈbiːsiti] n παχυσαρκία.
obey [əˈbei] vti υπακούω.
obituary [əˈbitjuəri] n νεκρολογία.
object [ˈɒbdʒikt] n αντικείμενο || (target) στόχος, σκοπός, αντικείμενο || (GRAM) αντικείμενο ♦ [əbˈdʒɛkt] vi (+ to) (proposal) αντιτίθεμαι, αποδικιμάζω || (a noise etc) αποκρούω, επικρίνω || ~**ion** n αντίρρηση, αντιλογία || (obstacle) εμπόδιο, δυσκολία || ~**ionable** a

O

απαράδεκτος, ανεπιθύμητος || ~ive n αντικειμενικός σκοπός ♦ a (impartial) αντικειμενικός || ~or n αντιρρησίας, αντιλέγων.

obligation [ɒblɪˈgeɪʃən] n υποχρέωση.

obligatory [ɒˈblɪgətɔrɪ] a υποχρεωτικός.

oblige [ɔˈblaɪdʒ] vt υποχρεώνω, επιβάλλω || (do a favour) εξυπηρετώ, υποχρεώνω.

obliging [ɔˈblaɪdʒɪŋ] a υποχρεωτικός, εξυπηρετικός.

oblique [ɔˈbliːk] a λοξός, πλάγιος.

obliterate [ɔˈblɪtəreɪt] vt εξαλείφω, σβήνω, καταστρέφω.

oblivious [ɔˈblɪvɪəs] a (+ of) επιλήσμων, ξεχασιάρης.

oblong [ˈɒblɒŋ] n επίμηκες σχήμα nt, ορθογώνιο ♦ a επίμηκης, μακρουλός.

obnoxious [əbˈnɒkʃəs] a απεχθής, δυσάρεστος.

oboe [ˈəʊbəʊ] n όμποε nt.

obscene [əbˈsiːn] a αισχρός, πρόστυχος.

obscenity [əbˈsɛnɪtɪ] n αισχρότητα, αχρειότητα.

obscure [əbˈskjʊə*] a σκοτεινός, σκούρος || (unnoticed) άσημος, ταπεινός ♦ vt συσκοτίζω, σκεπάζω.

obscurity [əbˈskjʊərɪtɪ] n σκοτάδι, αφάνεια.

obsequious [əbˈsiːkwɪəs] a δουλοπρεπής.

observance [əbˈzɜːvəns] n τήρηση, τύπος.

observant [əbˈzɜːvənt] a παρατηρητικός, προσεκτικός.

observation [ɒbzəˈveɪʃən] n παρατήρηση, παρακολούθηση.

observatory [əbˈzɜːvətrɪ] n αστεροσκοπείο.

observe [əbˈzɜːv] vt (the law etc) τηρώ, κρατώ || (study) παρατηρώ, κοιτάζω || (understand) διακρίνω, αντιλαμβάνομαι || ~r n παρατηρητής, τηρητής.

obsess [əbˈsɛs] vt κατέχω, βασανίζω || ~ion n έμμονη ιδέα || ~ive a καταθλιπτικός, βασανιστικός.

obsolescence [ɒbsəˈlɛsns] n τάση προς αχρηστία, παλαίωμα nt.

obsolete [ˈɒbsəliːt] a απαρχαιωμένος.

obstacle [ˈɒbstəkl] n εμπόδιο, πρόσκομμα || ~ **race** n δρόμος μετ' εμποδίων.

obstetrics [ɒbˈstɛtrɪks] n μαιευτική.

obstinate [ˈɒbstɪnɪt] a επίμονος, πεισματάρης || ~ly ad επίμονα.

obstruct [əbˈstrʌkt] vt φράσσω, εμποδίζω || ~ion n κωλυσιεργία, εμπόδιο.

obtain [əbˈteɪn] vt παίρνω, αποκτώ, επιτυγχάνω || ~able a επιτευκτός, εφικτός.

obtrusive [əbˈtruːsɪv] a ενοχλητικός, φορτικός.

obvious [ˈɒbvɪəs] a προφανής, ευνόητος || ~ly ad προφανώς, φανερά.

occasion [əˈkeɪʒən] n (time) ευκαιρία,

φορά || (event) αφορμή, περίσταση || (reason) λόγος, αιτία ♦ vt προξενώ || ~al a σποραδικός, τυχαίος || (drink) που και που || ~ally ad κάπου-κάπου.

occult [ɒˈkʌlt] n: the ~ οι απόκρυφες επιστήμες.

occupant [ˈɒkjʊpənt] n κάτοχος m/f || (of house) ένοικος m/f.

occupation [ɒkjʊˈpeɪʃən] n απασχόληση, ασχολία, επάγγελμα nt || (of country) κατάληψη, κτήση || ~al a (hazard) επαγγελματικός.

occupier [ˈɒkjʊpaɪə*] n (of house) ένοικος/n m/f.

occupy [ˈɒkjʊpaɪ] vt (take possession) κατέχω, κατακτώ || (live in) κατοικώ || (hold) κατέχω || (employ) απασχολώ.

occur [əˈkɜː*] vi συμβαίνω, γίνομαι, λαμβάνω χώρα || (be found) συναντώμαι, εμφανίζομαι || (+ to) παρουσιάζεται στη σκέψη || it ~s to me μου έρχεται || ~rence n γεγονός nt, συμβάν nt.

ocean [ˈəʊʃən] n ωκεανός || ~-going a υπερωκεάνειος.

ochre [ˈəʊkə*] n ώχρα.

o'clock [əˈklɒk] ad: it is 5 ~ είναι πέντε n (ώρα).

octagonal [ɒkˈtægənl] a οκταγώνιος.

octane [ˈɒkteɪn] n οκτάνιο.

octave [ˈɒktɪv] n οχτάβα.

October [ɒkˈtəʊbə*] n Οκτώβριος.

octopus [ˈɒktəpəs] n χταπόδι.

odd [ɒd] a (number) περιττός, μονός || (not part of set) μονός, παράταιρος || (with some left over) αυτός που περισσεύει || (strange) περίεργος, παράξενος || (casual) τυχαίος || ~ity n παραδοξότητα || (person) παράξενος άνθρωπος || ~ly ad περίεργως, περίεργα || ~ments npl υπολείμματα ntpl || ~s npl ανισότητα, διαφορά || (advantage) πλεονέκτημα nt, πιθανότητες fpl || (chances) πιθανότητες fpl || (at racetrack) στοίχημα nt, ποντάρισμα nt || at ~s βρίσκομαι, είμαι τσακωμένος || ~s and ends npl απομεινάρια ntpl, μικροπράγματα ntpl.

ode [əʊd] n ωδή.

odious [ˈəʊdɪəs] a απεχθής, μισητός.

odour, odor (US) [ˈəʊdə*] n οσμή, μυρουδιά || ~less a άοσμος.

of [ɒv, əv] prep από, περί, παρά.

off [ɒf] ad (absent) μακριά || (of switch) κλειστό || (milk) όχι φρέσκος, χαλασμένος ♦ prep από, μακριά από, λιγώτερο από.

offal [ˈɒfəl] n εντόσθια ntpl.

off-colour, off-color (US) [ˈɒfˈkʌlə*] a (ill) χλωμός.

offence [əˈfɛns] n (crime) παράπτωμα nt, αδίκημα nt || (insult) προσβολή.

offend [əˈfɛnd] vt προσβάλλω || ~er n παραβάτης m/f || ~ing a προσβλητικός, πειρακτικός.

offense [əˈfɛns] n (US) = **offence**.

offensive [əˈfɛnsɪv] a προσβλητικός, δυσάρεστος || (weapon) επιθετικός.

offer [ˈɒfə*] n προσφορά ♦ vt

προσφέρω, προτείνω || ~**ing** n (esp REL) θυσία, προσφορά.

offhand ['ɒf'hænd] a αυθόρμητος, απότομος ♦ ad στη στιγμή, απότομα.

office ['ɒfɪs] n (position) γραφείο || ~r n (MIL) αξιωματικός, αξιωματούχος || ~ **work** n εργασία γραφείου.

official [ə'fɪʃəl] a (authorized) επίσημος, υπηρεσιακός ♦ n υπάλληλος m/f (δημόσιος) || ~**ly** ad επίσημα.

officious [ə'fɪʃəs] a αυταρχικός, ενοχλητικός.

offing ['ɒfɪŋ] n: **in the** ~ εν όψει, στα ανοιχτά.

off line [ɒf'laɪn] a (COMPUT) έμμεση σύνδεση και προπέλαση || (switched off) αποσυνδεδεμένος.

off-season ['ɒfsiːzn] a μη εποχιακός, εκτός εποχής, νεκρή εποχή.

offset ['ɒfset] vt αντισταθμίζω, αποζημιώνω.

offshore ['ɒf'ʃɔ:*] ad στα ανοιχτά ♦ a χερσαίος, στεριανός.

offside ['ɒf'saɪd] a (AUT) έξω πλευρά, δεξιά πλευρά ♦ n (SPORT) οφσάιντ.

offspring ['ɒfsprɪŋ] n απόγονος, βλαστός.

often ['ɒfən] ad συχνά, πολλές φορές.

oh [əʊ] excl ω!, αχ!

oil [ɔɪl] n πετρέλαιο, λάδι ♦ vt λαδώνω || ~**can** n λαδικό || ~**field** n πετρελαιοφόρος περιοχή || ~-**fired** a καίων πετρέλαιο || ~ **painting** n ελαιογραφία || ~ **refinery** n διυλιστήριο || ~**skins** npl μουσαμάς || ~ **tanker** n δεξαμενόπλοιο || ~ **well** n πετρελαιοπηγή || ~**y** a ελαιώδης, λαδερός.

ointment ['ɔɪntmənt] n αλοιφή.

O.K., okay ['əʊ'keɪ] excl πολύ καλά, εντάξει ♦ n έγκριση ♦ vt εγκρίνω.

old [əʊld] a γέροντας, γέρος, ηλικιωμένος || (of age) της ηλικίας, χρονών || (worn) παλιός || (former) παλιός, πρώην, τέως || (friend) παλιός (σύντροφος) || ~ **age** n (βαθειά) γεράματα ntpl || ~ **age pensioner** (O.A.P.) n συνταξιούχος m/f || ~**en** a (old) παλιό, του παλιού || ~-**fashioned** a οπαδός του παλιού καιρού || (out of date) απαρχαιωμένος, παλιάς μόδας || ~ **maid** n γεροντοκόρη.

olive ['ɒlɪv] n (fruit) ελιά, ελαία ♦ a (colour) λαδής, ελαιόχρους || ~ **oil** n ελαιόλαδο, λάδι.

Olympic [əʊ'lɪmpɪk] a Ολυμπιακός || ~ **Games** npl (also: ~s) Ολυμπιακοί αγώνες mpl.

omelet(te) ['ɒmlɪt] n ομελέτα.

omen ['əʊmen] n οιωνός, σημάδι.

ominous ['ɒmɪnəs] a δυσοίωνος, δυσμενής.

omission [əʊ'mɪʃən] n παράλειψη, παραδρομή.

omit [əʊ'mɪt] vt παραλείπω.

on [ɒn] prep πάνω σε, σε, κατά, περί ♦ ad εμπρός, προς τα εμπρός, σε λειτουργία || ~ **and off** κάπου-κάπου || ~ **the left** αριστερά, στ, αριστερά || ~ **Friday** την Παρασκευή.

once [wʌns] ad μια φορά, άλλοτε, κάποτε || cj μόλις, από τη στιγμή που, μια και || **at** ~ αμέσως, στη στιγμή || (same time) ταυτόχρονα, σύγχρονα || **all at** ~ (suddenly) εντελώς ξαφνικά || (speaking etc) όλοι μαζί || ~ **more** ακόμη μια φορά || **more than** ~ πολλές φορές || ~ **and for all** μια και καλή || ~ **upon a time** μια φορά (και ένα καιρό).

oncoming ['ɒnkʌmɪŋ] a (traffic) επερχόμενος, προσεγγίζων.

one [wʌn] a ένας, μία, ένα || (only) μόνος, μοναδικός ♦ n ένα, ένας, μια ♦ pron ένας, αυτός, κανείς, τέτοιος || **this** ~ αυτός εδώ || **that** ~ αυτός εκεί || ~ **by** ~ ένας-ένας || ~ **another** αλλήλους || ~-**man** a (business) (δουλειά) για έναν άνθρωπο || ~**self** pron εαυτό || ~-**way** a (street, traffic) μονής κατευθύνσεως.

onion ['ʌnjən] n κρεμμύδι.

on line [ɒn'laɪn] a (COMPUT) άμεση σύνδεση και προσπέλαση || (switched on) συνδεδεμένος.

onlooker ['ɒnlʊkə*] n θεατής.

only ['əʊnlɪ] ad μόνο ♦ a μόνος.

onset ['ɒnset] n (beginning) απαρχή.

onshore ['ɒnʃɔ:*] a, ad προς την ακτή.

onslaught ['ɒnslɔ:t] n εφόρμηση, επίθεση.

onto ['ɒntʊ] prep=**on to.**

onus ['əʊnəs] n βάρος nt, ευθύνη, καθήκον nt.

onwards ['ɒnwədz] ad (place) προς τα εμπρός, και πέρα || (time) και στο εξής.

ooze [u:z] vi (liquid) στάζω, εκρέω, διεισδύω.

opaque [əʊ'peɪk] a αδιαφανής, θαμπός.

open ['əʊpən] a ανοιχτός || (unlimited) ανοικτός, απεριόριστος || (without cover) ακάλυπτος, ξέσκεπος || (clear) φανερός, έκδηλος || (question) φανερός, έκδηλος || (free) ελεύθερος, ανοιχτός || (sincere) ειλικρινής, απροκάλυπτος ♦ vt ανοίγω || (letter) αποσφραγίζω, ανοίγω || (box) λύνω, ανοίγω ♦ vi αρχίζω, ανοίγω || (shop) ανοίγω || (play) αρχίζω || **to** ~ **out** vt ανοίγω, ξεδιπλώνω || **to** ~ **up** vt (route) ανοίγω, χαράσσω, διανοίγω || ~-**air** a υπαίθριος || ~**er** n (for cans) ανοικτήρι || ~**ing** n άνοιγμα nt, ρωγμή || (beginning) έναρξη || (good chance) ευκαιρία || ~**ly** ad φανερά, ειλικρινά, δημόσια || ~-**minded** a απροκάλυπτος με ανοιχτό μυαλό || ~-**necked** a ανοιχτό || (φόρεμα) ντεκολτέ.

opera ['ɒpərə] n μελόδραμα nt, όπερα || ~ **house** n λυρική σκηνή, όπερα.

operate ['ɒpəreɪt] vt (machine) ενεργώ, κινώ, διευθύνω ♦ vi λειτουργώ, δρώ, ενεργώ || (MED) (+ on) χειρουργώ, εγχειρίζω.

operation [ɒpə'reɪʃən] n λειτουργία, δράση || (MED) εγχείρηση || (MIL) επιχείρηση.

operative ['ɒpərətɪv] a ενεργός, ισχύων, χειρουργικός.

operator ['ɒpəreɪtə*] n (of machine) χειριστής, οπερατέρ m inv || (TEL) τηλεφωνήτρια.

operetta [ɒpə'retə] n οπερέττα.

opinion [ə'pɪnjən] n γνώμη, ιδέα, δοξασία.

opium ['əupɪəm] n όπιο.

opponent [ə'pəunənt] n αντίπαλος.

opportune ['ɒpətjuːn] a επίκαιρος, εύθετος, κατάλληλος.

opportunist [ɒpə'tjuːnɪst] n καιροσκόπος.

opportunity [ɒpə'tjuːnɪtɪ] n ευκαιρία.

oppose [ə'pəuz] vt αντιτάσσω, αντικρούω, καταπολεμώ || ~ d a (+ to) αντίθετος (προς), αντιτιθέμενος.

opposing [ə'pəuzɪŋ] a (side) αντίθετος, αντίπαλος.

opposite ['ɒpəzɪt] a αντίθετος, αντικρυνός || (direction) αντίθετος ♦ ad απέναντι, αντίκρυ ♦ prep απέναντι ♦ n αντίστοιχο, αντίθετο || ~ number n (person) αντίστοιχος.

opposition [ɒpə'zɪʃən] n αντίσταση, αντίθεση || (party) αντιπολίτευση.

oppress [ə'pres] vt καταπιέζω, καταδυναστεύω || (heat etc) καταθλίβω, βασανίζω || ~ion n καταπίεση, στενοχώρια || ~ive a καταθλιπτικός, πνιγηρός.

opt [ɒpt] vi: to ~ for διαλέγω, επιλέγω.

optical ['ɒptɪkəl] n οπτικός.

optician [ɒp'tɪʃən] n οπτικός.

optimism ['ɒptɪmɪzəm] n αισιοδοξία.

optimist ['ɒptɪmɪst] n αισιόδοξος || ~ic a αισιόδοξος.

optimum ['ɒptɪməm] a ευνοϊκός, άριστος.

option ['ɒpʃən] n εκλογή || (right to choose) δικαίωμα nt εκλογής || ~al a προαιρετικός.

opulent ['ɒpjulənt] a πλούσιος, άφθονος.

or [ɔː*] cj ή.

oracle ['ɒrəkl] n χρησμός, μαντείο.

oral ['ɔːrəl] a προφορικός ♦ n (exam) προφορικές (εξετάσεις) fpl.

orange ['ɒrɪndʒ] n πορτοκάλι || (colour) πορτοκαλλί.

oration [ɔː'reɪʃən] n λόγος.

orbit ['ɔːbɪt] n τροχιά ♦ vt (earth) περιστρέφομαι.

orchard ['ɔːtʃəd] n οπωρόκηπος, περιβόλι.

orchestra ['ɔːkɪstrə] n ορχήστρα || ~l [ɔː'kestrəl] a ορχηστρικός.

orchid ['ɔːkɪd] n ορχεοειδές φυτό.

ordain [ɔː'deɪn] vt (προ)ορίζω, θεσπίζω διορίζω || (ECCL) χειροτονώ.

ordeal [ɔː'diːl] n βασανιστήριο.

order ['ɔːdə*] n (arrangement) τάξη, σειρά, διαδοχή || (instruction) διαταγή, εντολή, διάταγμα nt || (rank, class) τάξη || (ECCL) βαθμός ιερωσύνης || (MIL) τάγμα nt || (decoration) παράσημο || (COMM)

επιταγή, παραγγελία ♦ vt διατάσσω || διευθετώ, ταξινομώ || (COMM) παραγγέλλω || ~ form n έντυπο εντολής || ~ly n αγγελιαφόρος, ορτινάντσα ♦ a φρόνιμος, τακτικός, ήσυχος || (tidy) συγυρισμένος, τακτικός.

ordinary ['ɔːdnrɪ] a συνήθης, συνηθισμένος || (commonplace) της αράδας, κοινός.

ore [ɔː*] n ορυκτό, μετάλλευμα nt.

organ ['ɔːgən] n (all senses) όργανο || ~ic [ɔː'gænɪk] a οργανικός, ενόργανος.

organism ['ɔːgənɪzəm] n οργανισμός.

organist ['ɔːgənɪst] n οργανοπαίκτης.

organization [ɔːgənaɪ'zeɪʃən] n οργάνωση, οργανισμός.

organize ['ɔːgənaɪz] vt οργανώνω || ~r n (δι)οργανωτής.

orgasm ['ɔːgæzəm] n οργασμός, παροξυσμός.

orgy ['ɔːdʒɪ] n όργιο.

Orient ['ɔːrɪənt] n: the ~ Ανατολή, Άπω Ανατολή.

oriental [ɔːrɪ'entəl] a ανατολικός, ασιατικός ♦ n Ασιάτης.

orientate ['ɔːrɪenteɪt] vt προσανατολίζω.

origin ['ɒrɪdʒɪn] n αρχή, γένεση, καταγωγή.

original [ə'rɪdʒɪnl] a (first) αρχικός || (new) πρωτότυπος || (individual) ιδιότυπος, πρωτότυπος ♦ n πρωτότυπο || ~ity [ərɪdʒɪ'nælɪt] n πρωτοτυπία || ~ly ad αρχικά, εξ αρχής.

originate [ə'rɪdʒɪneɪt] vi κατάγομαι, προέρχομαι ♦ vt γεννώ, δημιουργώ.

originator [ə'rɪdʒɪneɪtə*] n δημιουργός, εγκαινιαστής.

ornament ['ɔːnəmənt] n κόσμημα nt, στολίδι || ~al a (δια)κοσμητικός.

ornate [ɔː'neɪt] a διακοσμημένος, φανταχτερός.

ornithology [ɔːnɪ'θɒlədʒɪ] n ορνιθολογία.

orphan ['ɔːfən] n ορφανός/ή m/f ♦ vt ορφανεύω || ~age n ορφανοτροφείο.

orthodox ['ɔːθədɒks] a ορθόδοξος || (conventional) καθιερωμένος.

orthopaedic, orthopedic (US) [ɔːθəu'piːdɪk] a ορθοπεδικός.

ostensibly [ɒs'tensəblɪ] ad κατά τα φαινόμενα, δήθεν.

ostentatious [ɒsten'teɪʃəs] a επιδεικτικός, φιγουρατζής, φανταχτερός.

ostracize ['ɒstrəsaɪz] vt εξοστρακίζω.

ostrich ['ɒstrɪtʃ] n στρουθοκάμηλος f.

other ['ʌðə*] a άλλος || (additional) άλλος, επιπρόσθετος || (opposite) άλλος, απέναντι ♦ pron άλλος ♦ ad: ~ than διαφορετικά από, εκτός από || ~wise ad αλλιώς, αλλιώτικα || (in other ways) κατά τα άλλα || (or else) διαφορετικά, αλλιώς, ειδεμή.

otter ['ɒtə*] n ενυδρίδα.

ought [ɔːt] auxiliary v πρέπει, θα έπρεπε || **I** ~ **to do it** πρέπει να το κάνω || **you** ~

to go πρέπει να φύγεις || **he ~ to win** πρέπει να κερδίσει.

ounce [auns] n ουγγιά.

our [auə*] poss a δικός μας || **~s** poss pron δικός μας || **~selves** pron εμείς οι ίδιοι.

oust [aust] vt διώχνω, εκτοπίζω.

out [aut] ad έξω || (not indoors) εκτός || (not alight) αβησμένος || (open) που βγήκε, βγαλμένος || (made known) γνωστός, που απεκαλύφθη || (in reckoning) σε λάθος, έξω || **~ of** prep έξω από || (from among) από || (without) χωρίς || **made ~ of** wood καμωμένος από ξύλο || **~-of-bounds** a απαγορευμένος || **~-of-date** a ξεπερασμένος || **~ of doors** ad έξω, στο ύπαιθρο || **~ of order** a χαλασμένος || **~-of-the-way** a παράμερος, απόμερος || (unusual) ασυνήθης, ασυνήθιστος.

outboard (motor) ['autbɔːd('mɔutə*)] n εξωλέμβιος (κινητήρας).

outbreak ['autbreik] n έκρηξη, ξέσπασμα nt, έναρξη.

outburst ['autbɜːst] n έκρηξη, ξέσπασμα nt.

outcast ['autkaːst] n απόβλητος.

outcome ['autkʌm] n έκβαση, πέρας nt.

outcry ['autkrai] n (κατα)κραυγή.

outdated ['aut'deitid] a παλιωμένος, ξεπερασμένος.

outdo [aut'duː] vt υπερβαίνω, υπερέχω.

outdoor ['autdɔː*] a υπαίθριος, εξωτερικός.

outdoors ['aut'dɔːz] ad στο ύπαιθρο.

outer ['autə*] a εξωτερικός || **~ space** n διάστημα nt.

outfit ['autfit] n εξοπλισμός, εργαλεία ntpl, απαιτούμενα ntpl.

outgoings ['autgɔuiŋz] npl (expenses) έξοδα ntpl, πληρωμές fpl.

outgrow [aut'grəu] vt γίνομαι ψηλότερος από, ξεπερνώ.

outing ['autiŋ] n εκδρομή.

outlaw ['autlɔː] n λησταής, παράνομος ♦ vt βάζω εκτός νόμου.

outlay ['autlei] n δαπάνη, έξοδα ntpl.

outlet ['autlet] n διέξοδος f, άνοιγμα nt.

outline ['autlain] n περίμετρος f, περίγραμμα nt || (summary) περίληψη.

outlive [aut'liv] vt επιζώ.

outlook ['autluk] n (prospect) πρόβλεψη.

outlying ['autlaiiŋ] a απόκεντρος, απόμερος.

outmoded [aut'məudid] a ντεμοντέ.

outnumber [aut'nʌmbə*] vt υπερτερώ αριθμητικά.

outpatient ['autpeiʃənt] n εξωτερικός ασθενής m/f.

outpost ['autpəust] n (people, also place) προφυλακή, φυλάκιο.

output ['autput] n παραγωγή, απόδοση, προϊόν nt ♦ vt (COMPUT) εκτυπώνω.

outrage ['autreidʒ] n προσβολή, κατάφωρο αδίκημα nt ♦ vt προσβάλλω, πληγώνω, ταράζω || **~ous** a σκανδαλώδης, τερατώδης, αχρείος.

outright ['autrait] ad απερίφραστα,

ωμά, ξάστερα || (once and for all) τελείως, εντελώς ♦ a τέλειος, οριστικός.

outset ['autset] n αρχή, ξεκίνημα nt.

outside ['aut'said] n εξωτερικό ♦ a εξωτερικός, πιθανός ♦ ad απ' έξω, έξω ♦ prep έξω από, εκτός, από, πέραν του || **~r** n (in race etc) χωρίς πιθανότητες fpl || (independent) ξένος/n m/f, θεατής.

outsize ['autsaiz] a μεγάλων διαστάσεων.

outskirts ['autskɜːts] npl προάστια ntpl, περίχωρα ntpl.

outspoken [aut'spəukən] a ειλικρινής, ντόμπρος.

outstanding [aut'stændiŋ] a προέχων, κύριος, σημαντικός || (person) διακεκριμένος, σπουδαίος, διαπρεπής || (unsettled) εκκρεμής, απλήρωτος.

outstay [aut'stei] vt (welcome) μένω περισσότερο από.

outstretched ['autstretʃt] a (hand) απλωμένος, με ανοιχτές αγκάλες.

outward ['autwəd] a (sign) εξωτερικός || (journey) προς τα έξω, έξω || **~ly** ad εξωτερικά, φαινομενικά.

outwit [aut'wit] vt ξεγελώ.

oval ['əuvəl] a ωοειδής, ελλειψοειδής ♦ n ωοειδές σχήμα nt.

ovary ['əuvəri] n ωοθήκη.

ovation [əu'veiʃən] n επευφημία.

oven ['ʌvn] n κλίβανος, φούρνος.

over ['əuvə*] ad (above) από πάνω, πάνω από || (across) απέναντι, πέρα || (finished) περασμένος, τελειωμένος || (too much) πέραν του δέοντος, επί πλέον || (again) φορές (συνέχεια), πάλι ♦ prep (above) από πάνω, πάνω || (across) απέναντι || (in rank) υπεράνω, ανώτερος || (about) περί, για || **all ~** (everywhere) παντού, σ' όλο || (finished) τελειωμένος, περασμένος || **and ~** πολλές φορές, επανειλημμένα || **~ and above** πέρα από.

over- ['əuvə*] prefix υπέρ-, παρά-.

overall ['əuvərɔːl] n (Brit: for woman etc) ποδιά || **~s** npl (industrial etc) φόρμα.

overbalance [əuvə'bæləns] vi ανατρέπω, υπερέχω.

overbearing [əuvə'bɛəriŋ] a αυταρχικός, δεσποτικός, υπεροπτικός.

overboard [əuvə'bɔːd] ad στη θάλασσα (από πλοίο).

overcast ['əuvəkaːst] a συννεφιασμένος, σκοτεινιασμένος.

overcharge [əuvə'tʃaːdʒ] vt (price) παίρνω πολλά, πουλώ σε, υπερβολική τιμή.

overcoat ['əuvəkəut] n επανωφόρι, παλτό.

overcome [əuvə'kʌm] vt νικώ, καταβάλλω.

overcrowded [əuvə'kraudid] a υπερπλήρες, παραγεμισμένο.

overdo [əuvə'duː] vt (cook) παραψήνω || (exaggerate) υπερβάλλω, μεγαλοποιώ, παρακάνω.

overdose ['əuvədəus] n υπερβολική δόση.

overdraft ['əʊvədraːft] n ανάληψη χωρίς αντίκρισμα.

overdrawn [əʊvə'drɔːn] a (account) see **overdraft**.

overdrive ['əʊvədraɪv] n (AUT) οβερντράιβ.

overdue ['əʊvədjuː] a καθυστερημένος, εκπρόθεσμος.

overestimate ['əʊvər'estɪmeɪt] vt υπερεκτιμώ, υπερτιμώ.

overexcited ['əʊvərɪk'saɪtɪd] a υπερδιεγειρόμενος.

overexpose ['əʊvərɪks'pəʊz] vt (PHOT) υπερεκθέτω, υπερφωτίζω.

overflow [əʊvə'fləʊ] vi ξεχειλίζω ♦ ['əʊvəfləʊ] n υπερχείλιση, ξεχείλισμα nt.

overgrown ['əʊvə'grəʊn] a (garden) κατάφυτος, γεμάτος από, σκεπασμένος με.

overhaul [əʊvə'hɔːl] vt (repair) εξετάζω, επιθεωρώ, ελέγχω ♦ ['əʊvəhɔːl] n προσεκτική εξέταση, επιθεώρηση, επισκευή.

overhead ['əʊvəhed] a εναέριος, γενικός ♦ ['əʊvə'hed] ad επάνω, υπεράνω, ψηλά || ~s npl γενικά έξοδα ntpl.

overhear [əʊvə'hɪə*] vt ακούω τυχαία, κρυφακούω.

overjoyed [əʊvə'dʒɔɪd] a περιχαρής, γεμάτος χαρά.

overland ['əʊvəlænd] a χερσαίος, στεριανός ♦ [əʊvə'lænd] ad (journey) διά ξηράς.

overlap [əʊvə'læp] vi καβαλικεύω, σκεπάζω μερικώς ♦ ['əʊvəlæp] n επικάλυψη, καβαλίκεμα nt.

overleaf ['əʊvə'liːf] ad στο πίσω μέρος (της σελίδας).

overload [əʊvə'ləʊd] vt παραφορτώνω, υπερφορτίζω.

overlook [əʊvə'lʊk] vt κοιτάζω πάνω από, δεσπόζω || (not notice) παραβλέπω, παραμελώ || (pardon) παραβλέπω, συγχωρώ.

overnight ['əʊvə'naɪt] a ολονύκτιος, ξενυχτισμένος ♦ ad όλη τη νύκτα, ξενύχτι.

overpass ['əʊvəpaːs] n (road) ανυψωμένη διάβαση.

overpower [əʊvə'paʊə*] vt καταβάλλω, συντρίβω, καταπνίγω || ~ing a συντριπτικός, αποπνικτικός.

overrate ['əʊvə'reɪt] vt υπερτιμώ.

override [əʊvə'raɪd] vt (invalidate) υπερβαίνω, ανατρέπω.

overriding [əʊvə'raɪdɪŋ] a πρωταρχικός, δεσπόζων.

overrule [əʊvə'ruːl] vt ανατρέπω, αγνοώ, αναιρώ.

overseas ['əʊvə'siːz] ad στο εξωτερικό ♦ a (trade) εξωτερικός.

overshadow ['əʊvə'ʃædəʊ] vt επισκιάζω.

overshoot ['əʊvə'ʃuːt] vt (runway) προσγειώνομαι μακριά.

oversight ['əʊvəsaɪt] n παράβλεψη, παραδρομή.

oversleep ['əʊvə'sliːp] vi παρακοιμάμαι.

overstate ['əʊvə'steɪt] vt (case) μεγαλοποιώ, υπερβάλλω || ~ment n υπερβολή, μεγαλοποίηση.

overt [əʊ'vɜːt] a έκδηλος, καταφανής, φανερός.

overtake [əʊvə'teɪk] vt προσπερνώ, ξεπερνώ ♦ vi συμβαίνω σε, τυχαίνω σε.

overtaking [əʊvə'teɪkɪŋ] n ξεπέρασμα nt.

overthrow [əʊvə'θrəʊ] vt ανατρέπω || (vanquish) συντρίβω.

overtime ['əʊvətaɪm] n υπερωρία.

overture ['əʊvətjʊə*] n (MUS) εισαγωγή, ουβερτούρα.

overturn [əʊvə'tɜːn] vt ανατρέπω, αναποδογυρίζω ♦ vi ανατρέπομαι.

overweight ['əʊvə'weɪt] a με βάρος ανώτερο του κανονικού.

overwhelm [əʊvə'welm] vt συντρίβω, κατακλύζω, καταβάλλω || ~ing a συντριπτικός, ακαταμάχητος.

overwork ['əʊvə'wɜːk] n καταπόνηση, υπερκόπωση ♦ vt παραφορτώνω, παρακουράζω ♦ vi εργάζομαι υπερβολικά, παρακουράζομαι.

overwrought ['əʊvə'rɔːt] a σε υπερένταση, παρακουρασμένος.

owe [əʊ] vt οφείλω, χρωστώ.

owing to ['əʊɪŋtuː] prep λόγω, ένεκα, συνεπεία, εξ αιτίας.

owl [aʊl] n κουκουβάγια.

own [əʊn] vt (κατ)έχω, είμαι κύριος ♦ a δικός (μου) ♦ n δικός (μου), ιδιαίτερος || **all my** ~ μου ανήκει, όλο δικό μου || **on one's** ~ ανεξάρτητα, μόνος (μου) || **to** ~ **up** vi (confess) ομολογώ || ~**er** n ιδιοκτήτης/ήτρια m/f, κύριος/ία m/f || ~**ership** n κυριότητα, ιδιοκτησία.

ox [ɒks] n βόδι.

oxide ['ɒksaɪd] n οξείδιο.

oxygen ['ɒksɪdʒən] n οξυγόνο || ~ **mask** n μάσκα οξυγόνου || ~ **tent** n ασκός οξυγόνου.

oyster ['ɔɪstə*] n στρείδι.

oz. abbr of **ounce(s)**.

ozone ['əʊzəʊn] n όζον nt.

P

p [piː] abbr of **penny, pence**.

p.a. abbr of **per annum**.

pace [peɪs] n βήμα nt, βάδισμα nt || (speed) ταχύτητα ♦ vi βαδίζω, βηματίζω, περπατώ || **to keep** ~ **with** συμβαδίζω || ~**maker** n προπονητής || (MED) βηματοδότης.

Pacific (Ocean) [pə'sɪfɪk('əʊʃən)] n Ειρηνικός (Ωκεανός).

pacifist ['pæsɪfɪst] n ειρηνόφιλος/η m/f.

pacify ['pæsɪfaɪ] vt ειρηνεύω, καθησυχάζω.

pack [pæk] n (bundle) δέμα nt, πακέτο || (wolves) αγέλη, κοπάδι || (cards) δεσμίδα, τράπουλα || (gang) συμμορία ♦ vt (case) συσκευάζω, πακετάρω, κάνω δέμα || *(bags)* μαζεύω (τα ρούχα μου).

package ['pækɪdʒ] n δέμα nt.

packet ['pækɪt] n δεματάκι, πακέτο.

pack ice ['pækaɪs] n σωρός πάγων, ογκόπαγοι mpl.

packing ['pækɪŋ] n *(action)* πακετάρισμα nt || *(material)* συσκευασία || ~ **case** n κιβώτιο συσκευασίας, κασόνι.

pact [pækt] n συμφωνία, συνθήκη.

pad [pæd] n *(pillow)* μαξιλαράκι || *(notebook)* μπλόκ nt inv || *(for inking)* ταμπόν nt inv ♦ vt *(παρα)*γεμίζω.

paddle ['pædl] n *(oar)* κουπί, αναδευτήρας ♦ vt *(boat)* κωπηλατώ, τραβώ κουπί ♦ vi *(in sea)* κωπηλατώ ήρεμα, τσαλαβουτώ.

paddling pool ['pædlɪŋpuːl] n λιμνούλα (για παιδιά).

paddock ['pædək] n περίβολος, μάντρα (για άλογα).

paddy ['pædɪ] n: ~ **field** n οριζοφυτεία.

padlock ['pædlɒk] n λουκέτο.

padre ['pɑːdrɪ] n παπάς.

paediatrics [piːdɪ'ætrɪks] n παιδιατρική.

pagan ['peɪgən] a ειδωλολατρικός.

page [peɪdʒ] n *(of book)* σελίδα || *(boy servant)* νεαρός υπηρέτης, γκρούμ m inv || *(wedding)* ακόλουθος, παράνυμφος ♦ vt *(in hotel etc)* στέλνω μικρό να φωνάξει (κάποιον).

pageant ['pædʒənt] n φαντασμαγορικό θέαμα nt, επιβλητική πομπή.

paid [peɪd] pt, pp of **pay.**

pail [peɪl] n κάδος, κουβάς.

pain [peɪn] n πόνος || ~**s** npl *(efforts)* κόπος || ~**ed** a *(expression)* θλιμμένος, πικραμένος, πονεμένος || ~**ful** a οδυνηρός || *(physically)* που πονεί || *(difficult)* επίπονος || ~**killing drug** n ναυσίπονο || ~**less** a ανώδυνος || **painstaking** a φιλόπονος, προσεκτικός.

paint [peɪnt] n χρώμα nt, μπογιά ♦ vt ζωγραφίζω, απεικονίζω || *(house etc)* μπογιατίζω, χρωματίζω || ~**brush** n χρωστήρας, πινέλο || ~**er** n *(ART)* ζωγράφος m/f || *(decorator)* χρωματιστής, μπογιατζής || ~**ing** n *(action)* ζωγραφική || *(picture)* πίνακας, ζωγραφιά.

pair [peə*] n ζευγάρι || *(of shoes)* ζεύγος nt || ~ **of scissors** n ψαλίδι || ~ **of trousers** n παντελόνι.

pajamas [pə'dʒɑːməz] npl *(US)* πυτζάμες fpl.

pal [pæl] n *(col)* σύντροφος, φίλος.

palace ['pælɪs] n ανάκτορο, παλάτι.

palatable ['pælətəbl] a εύγευστος, νόστιμος.

palate ['pælɪt] n υπερώα, ουρανίσκος || *(taste)* γεύση.

pale [peɪl] a *(face)* ωχρός, χλωμός || *(colour)* ανοιχτός.

palette ['pælɪt] n παλέτα.

palisade [pælɪ'seɪd] n φράκτης από πασσάλους.

pall [pɔːl] n *(of smoke)* σύννεφο ♦ vi κουράζω, βαριέμαι.

pally ['pælɪ] a *(col)* που πιάνει εύκολα φιλίες.

palm [pɑːm] n *(tree)* φοίνικας || *(of hand)* παλάμη || ~**ist** n χειρομάντις/ισσα m/f || **P~ Sunday** n Κυριακή των Βαΐων || ~ **tree** n φοινικιά, χουρμαδιά.

palpable ['pælpəbl] a *(obvious)* φανερός, καταφανής.

palpitation [pælpɪ'teɪʃən] n παλμός, σπαρτάρισμα nt.

paltry ['pɔːltrɪ] a μηδαμινός, τιποτένιος, άθλιος.

pamper ['pæmpə*] vt *(παρα)*χαϊδεύω.

pamphlet ['pæmflɪt] n φυλλάδιο.

pan [pæn] n τηγάνι, κατσαρόλα ♦ vi *(+ out)* επιτυγχάνω, αποδίδω.

panacea [pænə'sɪə] n *(fig)* πανάκεια.

pancake ['pænkeɪk] n τηγανίτα.

panda ['pændə] n πάντα.

pandemonium [pændɪ'məunɪəm] n πανδαιμόνιο.

pander ['pændə*] vi *(+ to)* κάνω το ρουφιάνο, κολακεύω πρόστυχα.

pane [peɪn] n τζάμι.

panel ['pænl] n *(of wood)* φάτνωμα nt, φύλλο || *(of people)* επιτροπή || ~**ling,** ~**ing** *(US)* n ξυλεπένδυση.

pang [pæŋ] n δυνατός πόνος || *(pain)* αγωνία.

panic ['pænɪk] n πανικός ♦ a *(reaction)* πανικόβλητος ♦ vi πανικοβάλλομαι || ~**ky** a *(person)* πανικόβλητος, έντρομος, φοβισμένος.

pannier ['pænɪə*] n κοφίνι, πανέρι.

panorama [pænə'rɑːmə] n πανόραμα nt.

pansy ['pænzɪ] n *(flower)* πανσές m.

pant [pænt] vi λαχανιάζω.

panther ['pænθə*] n πάνθηρας.

panties ['pæntɪz] npl *(woman's)* κυλότα.

pantomime ['pæntəmaɪm] n παντομίμα.

pantry ['pæntrɪ] n κελάρι || *(butler's)* κάβα.

pants [pænts] npl *(woman's)* κυλότα || *(man's)* σώβρακο || *(US: trousers)* παντελόνι.

papal ['peɪpəl] a παπικός.

paper ['peɪpə*] n *(material)* χαρτί || *(newspaper)* εφημερίδα || *(essay)* μελέτη, διατριβή, υπόμνημα nt ♦ a χάρτινος ♦ vt σκεπάζω με χαρτί, στολίζω με χαρτί || ~**s** npl *(identity)* πιστοποιητικά nt || *(documents)* έγγραφα ntpl || ~**back** n χαρτόδετο (βιβλίο) || ~ **bag** n χαρτοσακούλα || ~ **clip** n συνδετήρας || ~**weight** n πρες παπιέ nt inv || ~ **work** n γραφική εργασία.

papier-mâché ['pæpɪeɪ'mæʃeɪ] n πιεσμένο χαρτί.

par [pɑː*] n *(COMM)* ισοτιμία, άρτιο, ισότητα || **on a ~ with** ίσος με, ίση αξία με.

parable ['pærəbl] n παραβολή.

parachute ['pærəʃuːt] n αλεξίπτωτο ♦ vi πέφτω με αλεξίπτωτο.

parade [pə'reɪd] n *(procession)* παρέλαση

P

|| *(review)* παράταξη, παρέλαση ♦ *vt* επιδεικνύω, κάνω παρέλαση ♦ *vi* παρελαύνω.

paradise ['pærədais] *n* παράδεισος.

paradox ['pærədɒks] *n* παράδοξο, παραδοξολογία || ~**ical** *a* παράδοξος.

paraffin ['pærəfin] *n* παραφίνη.

paragraph ['pærəgra:f] *n* παράγραφος *f.*

parallel ['pærəlel] *a* παράλληλος || *(similar)* όμοιος, παράλληλος, ανάλογος ♦ *n* παράλληλος.

paralysis [pə'rælisis] *n* παράλυση.

paralyze ['pærəlaiz] *vt* παραλύω.

paramount ['pærəmaunt] *a* ύψιστος, υπέρτατος, εξαίρετος.

paranoia [pærə'nɔiə] *n* παράνοια.

paraphernalia [pærəfə'neiliə] *n* διάφορα *ntpl*, καλαμπαλίκια *ntpl*.

paraphrase ['pærəfreiz] *vt* παραφράζω.

paraplegic [pærə'pli:dʒik] *a* παραπληγικός.

parasite ['pærəsait] *n* παράσιτο.

parasol [pærə'sɒl] *n* ομπρέλα του ήλιου.

paratrooper ['pærətru:pə*] *n* αλεξιπτωτιστής.

parcel ['pa:sl] *n* δέμα *nt*, πακέτο ♦ *vt* *(also:* ~ **up)** πακετάρω.

parch [pa:tʃ] *vt* ξηραίνω, καψαλίζω, ψήνω || ~**ed** *a* ξηρός, στεγνός, άνυδρος.

parchment ['pa:tʃmənt] *n* περγαμηνή.

pardon ['pa:dn] *n* συγγνώμη, συγχώρηση ♦ *vt (free from punishment)* δίνω χάρη σε || ~! συγγνώμη! || ~ **me!** με συγχωρείτε! || **I beg your** ~! συγγνώμη! || **I beg your** ~? παρακαλώ;.

parent ['pεərənt] *n* γονέας || ~**al** *a* πατρικός, μητρικός.

parenthesis [pə'renθisis] *n* παρένθεση.

parish ['pæriʃ] *n* ενορία, κοινότητα || ~**ioner** *n* ενορίτης/ισσα *m/f.*

park [pa:k] *n* πάρκο || *(cars)* χώρος σταθμεύσεως ♦ *vti* σταθμεύω, παρκάρω || ~**ing** *n* στάθμευση, παρκάρισμα *nt*, πάρκιγκ *nt inv* || 'no ~**ing**' 'απαγορεύεται η στάθμευση' || ~**ing lot** *n (US)* χώρος σταθμεύσεως || ~**ing meter** *n* παρκόμετρο || ~**ing place** *n* θέση σταθμεύσεως.

parliament ['pa:ləmənt] *n* κοινοβούλιο || *(in Britain)* κοινοβούλιο, βουλή || ~**ary** *a* κοινοβουλευτικός.

parody ['pærədi] *n* παρωδία.

parole [pə'rəul] *n:* **on** ~ ελεύθερος (προσωρινά) επί λόγου.

parquet ['pa:kei] *n* παρκέτο.

parrot ['pærət] *n* παπαγάλος || ~ **fashion** *ad (learn)* παπαγαλίστικα.

parry ['pæri] *vt* αποκρούω, αποφεύγω, ξεφεύγω.

parsimonious [pa:si'məuniəs] *a* φειδωλός, σφιχτός, τσιγγούνης || ~**ly** *ad* με φειδωλότητα, μετρημένα.

parsley ['pa:sli] *n* μαϊντανός.

parsnip ['pa:snip] *n* δαυκί.

parson ['pa:sn] *n* εφημέριος, παπάς.

part [pa:t] *n* μέρος *nt*, κομμάτι || *(in play)* ρόλος || *(of machine)* τμήμα *nt*, μέρος *nt*, εξάρτημα *nt*, κομμάτι ♦ *a* μερικό, ημι-, μισο- ♦ *ad* =**partly** ♦ *vt* χωρίζω, διαιρώ, κόβω ♦ *vi (people)* χωρίζομαι || *(roads)* παρεκκλίνω, χωρίζομαι || **for my** ~ όσο για μένα || **for the most** ~ ως επί το πλείστον || **to** ~ **with** *vt* εγκαταλείπω, παραδίδω || ~**ial** ['pa:ʃəl] *a* μερικός || *(favouring)* μεροληπτικός || *(+ to)* έχω συμπάθεια σε, έχω προτίμηση σε || ~**ially** *ad* μερικά, εν μέρει.

participate [pa:'tisipeit] *vi (+ in)* συμμετέχω, παίρνω μέρος.

participation [pa:tisi'peiʃən] *n* συμμετοχή.

participle ['pa:tisipl] *n* μετοχή.

particular [pə'tikjulə*] *a* συγκεκριμένος || *(single)* ιδιαίτερος || *(hard to please)* ιδιότροπος, ακριβολόγος ♦ *n* λεπτομέρεια, ιδιομορφία || ~**s** *npl (details)* χαρακτηριστικά *ntpl*, περιγραφή || ~**ly** *ad* ιδιαίτερα, ειδικά, συγκεκριμένα.

parting ['pa:tiŋ] *n (separation)* αναχώρηση, χωρισμός || *(of hair)* χωρίστρα ♦ *a* διαχωριστικός.

partisan [pa:ti'zæn] *n* οπαδός, παρτιζάνος ♦ *a* μεροληπτικός.

partition [pa:'tiʃən] *n (wall)* χώρισμα *nt*, μεσότοιχος.

partly ['pa:tli] *ad* εν μέρει.

partner ['pa:tnə*] *n* εταίρος, συνέταιρος || *(in dance etc)* καβαλιέρος, ντάμα ♦ *vt* συνεταιρίζομαι, συμπράττω || ~**ship** *n* συνεταιρισμός, συνεργασία.

partridge ['pa:tridʒ] *n* πέρδικα.

part-time ['pa:t'taim] *ad* για λίγες ώρες, μερικώς απασχολούμενος.

party ['pa:ti] *n (POL)* κόμμα *nt* || *(group)* ομάδα, συντροφιά || *(lawsuit)* διάδικος || μέτοχος || *(agreement)* πρόσωπο || *(celebration)* πάρτυ *nt inv* ♦ *a (dress)* του πάρτυ, της διασκεδάσεως || *(POL)* του κόμματος, κομματικός.

pass [pa:s] *vt* περνώ, διαβαίνω || *(surpass)* υπερβαίνω, ξεπερνώ, προσπερνώ || *(move one to another)* μεταβιβάζω, διαβιβάζω, δίνω || *(spend time)* περνώ || *(be successful)* επιτυγχάνω, περνώ || *(approve)* εγκρίνω ♦ *vi* μεταβαίνω, διαβαίνω, διέρχομαι ♦ *n (passage)* στενό, πέρασμα *nt* || *(permission)* άδεια || *(success)* περνώ || *(SPORT)* πάσα || **to** ~ **away** *vi (die)* πεθαίνω || *(disappear)* εξαφανίζομαι || **to** ~ **by** *vi* περνώ || παραμελώ || **to** ~ **for** *vt* περνώ για || **to** ~ **out** *vi (faint)* λιποθυμώ || ~**able** *a* διαβατός || *(fairly good)* υποφερτός, καλούτσικος.

passage ['pæsidʒ] *n (corridor)* διάδρομος || *(part of book etc)* απόσπασμα *nt*, κομμάτι || *(crossing)* διάβαση, δίοδος *f*, διάβα *nt* || ~**way** *n* δίοδος *f*, πέρασμα *nt* || *(sidestreet)* πάροδος *f.*

passenger ['pæsindʒə*] *n* επιβάτης/ρια *m/f.*

passer-by ['pa:sə'bai] *n* διαβάτης, περαστικός.

passing ['pɑːsiŋ] n (death) θάνατος ♦ a (car) διερχόμενος, διαβατικός || in ~ παρεμπιπτόντως.

passion ['pæʃən] n πάθος nt, θέρμη, μανία || (love) έρωτας, πάθος nt || ~ate a σφοδρός, φλογερός, βίαιος || ~ately ad παράφορα, θερμά.

passive ['pæsiv] a (GRAM) παθητικός.

Passover ['pɑːsəuvə*] n Λαμπρή, Πάσχα nt.

passport ['pɑːspɔːt] n διαβατήριο.

password ['pɑːswɜːd] n σύνθημα nt, παρασύνθημα nt.

past [pɑːst] ad, prep (beyond) πέρα, πέρα από || (with numbers) περασμένος || (with time) μετά, περασμένα ♦ a (years) περασμένος, τον παλιό καιρό || (president etc) τέως, πρώην.

paste [peist] n (for paper) κόλλα || (for cooking) πάστα, ζυμάρι.

pastel ['pæstəl] a (colour) ναστέλ.

pasteurized ['pæstəraizd] a παστεριωμένος.

pastille ['pæstil] n παστίλια.

pastime ['pɑːstaim] n διασκέδαση, παιχνίδι.

pastor ['pɑːstə*] n πάστορας, παπάς.

pastry ['peistri] n ζύμη, πάστα || (pies, tarts etc) γλυκό.

pasture ['pɑːstʃə*] n (ground) βοσκότόπι.

pasty ['pæsti] n κρεατόπιτα ♦ ['peisti] a ζυμαρένιος, ωχρός.

pat [pæt] n ελαφρό κτύπημα nt, χάδι ♦ vt κτυπώ ελαφρά, χαϊδεύω.

patch [pætʃ] n μπάλωμα nt || (stain) λεκές m ♦ vt μπαλώνω || ~work n σύρραμα nt, συνονθύλευμα nt || ~y a (irregular) ανομοιόμορφος.

patent ['peitənt] n προνόμιο, πατέντα ♦ vt πατεντάρω ♦ a προφανής, απλός, προνομιακός, πρωτότυπος || ~ leather n λουστρίνι.

paternal [pə'tɜːnl] a πατρικός.

path [pɑːθ] n δρομάκος, μονοπάτι || (of sun etc) διαδρομή, πορεία γραμμή.

pathetic [pə'θetik] a συγκινητικός, αξιολύπητος || ~ally ad παθητικά, συγκινητικά.

pathologist [pə'θɒlədʒist] n παθολόγος.

pathology [pə'θɒlədʒi] n παθολογία.

pathos ['peiθɒs] n πάθος nt, συγκίνηση.

pathway ['pɑːθwei] n μονοπάτι, πέρασμα nt.

patience ['peiʃəns] n υπομονή.

patient ['peiʃənt] n νοσηλευόμενος/n m/f, άρρωστος/n m/f ♦ a υπομονητικός.

patio ['pætiəu] n πλακόστρωτη αυλή.

patriotic [pætri'ɒtik] a πατριωτικός.

patrol [pə'trəul] n περίπολος f, περιπολία ♦ vti περιπολώ || on ~ σε περιπολία || ~ car n περιπολικό || ~man n (US) αστυφύλακας.

patron ['peitrən] n πάτρωνας, προστάτης/ρια m/f, υποστηρικτής/ίκτρια m/f || (COMM) τακτικός πελάτης || ~age ['pætrənidʒ] n προστασία, υποστήριξη || ~ize

['pætrənaiz] vt υποστηρίζω || (manner) μεταχειρίζομαι συγκαταβατικά || ~izing a (attitude) συγκαταβατικός || ~ saint n προστάτης/ρια m/f, άγιος/a m/f.

patter ['pætə*] n (sound) ελαφρά συνεχή χτυπήματα ntpl || (sales talk) φλυαρία, κορακίστικα ntpl ♦ vi χτυπώ ελαφρά και συνεχώς.

pattern ['pætən] n υπόδειγμα nt, πρότυπο, μοντέλο || (design) σχέδιο, τύπος, μοντέλο.

paunch [pɔːntʃ] n κοιλιά.

pauper ['pɔːpə*] n άπορος/n m/f, πτωχός/ή m/f.

pause [pɔːz] n παύση, διακοπή, ανάπαυλα, διάλειμμα nt ♦ vi σταματώ, διστάζω, κοντοστέκομαι.

pave [peiv] vt επιστρώνω || to ~ the way for ανοίγω το δρόμο, προετοιμάζω το έδαφος.

pavement ['peivmənt] n (Brit) πεζοδρόμιο.

pavilion [pə'viliən] n (building) περίπτερο, υπόστεγο.

paving ['peiviŋ] n στρώσιμο.

paw [pɔː] n πέλμα nt ζώου, πόδι ♦ vt χτυπώ με το πόδι || (person) πασπατεύω.

pawn [pɔːn] n ενέχυρο ♦ vt ενεχυριάζω, βάζω ενέχυρο || ~broker n ενεχυροδανειστής || ~shop n ενεχυροδανειστήριο.

pay [pei] (irreg v) n πληρωμή, μισθός ♦ vt πληρώνω, καταβάλλω, ξοδεύω || (be profitable to) συμφέρω, αποδίδω ♦ vi πληρώνομαι, είναι συμφέρον || to ~ attention (to) προσέχω || to ~ for vt πληρώνω, κερνώ || to ~ up vi εξοφλώ || ~able a πληρωτέος || ~ day n μέρα πληρωμής || ~ee n δικαιούχος || ~ing a επικερδής, αποδοτικός || ~ment n πληρωμή || (compensation) αποζημίωση, ανταπόδοση || ~roll n μισθοδοτική κατάσταση.

p.c. abbr of **per cent**.

pea [piː] n (seed) μπιζέλι.

peace [piːs] n ειρήνη, ησυχία || ~ful a γαλήνιος, ήσυχος || ~ offering n δώρο συμφιλιώσεως.

peach [piːtʃ] n ροδάκινο.

peacock ['piːkɒk] n παγώνι.

peak [piːk] n κορυφή || (of cap) γείσος.

peal [piːl] n κωδωνοκρουσία, κτύπημα nt.

peanut ['piːnʌt] n αράπικο φυστίκι.

pear [peə*] n απίδι, αχλάδι.

pearl [pɜːl] n μαργαριτάρι.

peasant ['pezənt] n χωρικός/ή m/f, χωριάτης/ισσα m/f, αγρότης/ισσα m/f.

peat [piːt] n τύρφη, ποάνθρακας.

pebble ['pebl] n χαλίκι.

peck [pek] vti ραμφίζω, τσιμπώ ♦ n (with beak) ραμφισμός, τσίμπημα nt || (kiss) φιλάκι.

peckish ['pekiʃ] a (col): to feel ~ νοιώθω το στομάχι άδειο.

peculiar [pi'kjuːliə*] a (interest) ειδικός, ιδιαίτερος || (+ to) ιδιαίτερο χαρακτηριστικό, ιδιάζων || ~ity n ιδιομορφία, ιδιορρυθμία || (oddness) παραξενιά.

pedal ['pedl] n ποδωστήριο, πεντάλ nt inv ♦ vti χρησιμοποιώ πεντάλ, ποδηλατώ.

pedantic [pɪ'dæntɪk] a σχολαστικός.

peddle ['pedl] vt κάνω το μικροπωλητή, πουλώ στους δρόμους.

pedestal ['pedɪstl] n βάθρο, βάση αγάλματος.

pedestrian [pɪ'destrɪən] n πεζός, διαβάτης ♦ a με τα πόδια, πεζός || (humdrum) μονότονος, πεζός || ~ crossing n διάβαση πεζών.

pediatrics [pi:dɪ'ætrɪks] n (US) = **paediatrics**.

pedigree ['pedigri:] n γενεαλογικό δέντρο, καταγωγή ♦ a (animal) καθαρόαιμος.

pee [pi:] (col) n ούρα ntpl ♦ vi κατουρώ, κάνω πιπί.

peek [pi:k] n ματιά ♦ vi κρυφοκοιτάζω, ξεπροβάλλω.

peel [pi:l] n φλούδα ♦ vi (paint etc) ξεφλουδίζομαι, φεύγω.

peep [pi:p] n (look) φευγαλέο βλέμμα nt, ματιά || (sound) τιτίβισμα nt, σκούξιμο, τσίριγμα nt ♦ vi (look) κρυφοκοιτάζω.

peer [pɪə*] vi κοιτάζω με προσοχή || (+ at) κοιτάζω προσεκτικά || (peep) κρυφοκοιτάζω ♦ n (nobleman) λόρδος, ευγενής || (equal) ισάξιος, ίσος, ταίρι || ~age n τάξη ευγενών || ~less a απαράμιλλος, ασύγκριτος.

peeve [pi:v] vt (col) εκνευρίζω || ~d a εκνευρισμένος.

peevish ['pi:vɪʃ] a ευερέθιστος, δύστροπος.

peg [peg] n γόμφος, πάσσαλος, κρεμάστρα || **to buy clothes off the ~** αγοράζω έτοιμα ρούχα.

pekinese ['pi:kɪ'ni:z] n πεκινουά nt inv.

pelican ['pelɪkən] n πελεκάνος.

pellet ['pelɪt] n (of paper, bread etc) σφαιρίδιο, σβώλος || (pill) δισκίο.

pelt [pelt] vt πετροβολώ, πετώ, κτυπώ ♦ vi (fall heavily) πέφτω με δύναμη ♦ n δορά, δέρμα nt, προβειά.

pelvis ['pelvɪs] n λεκάνη.

pen [pen] n (for writing) γραφίδα, πένα, στυλό || (for sheep) μάντρα.

penal ['pi:nl] a ποινικός || ~ize vt επιβάλλω ποινή σε, τιμωρώ || ~ty ['penəltɪ] n ποινή, τιμωρία || ~ty kick n πέναλτυ nt inv.

penance ['penəns] n αυτοτιμωρία, μετάνοια.

pence [pens] npl πένες fpl.

pencil ['pensl] n μολύβι || (of light) δέσμη || ~ sharpener n ξύστρα.

pendant ['pendənt] n κρεμαστό κόσμημα nt.

pending ['pendɪŋ] prep κατά τη διάρκεια του, μέχρι ♦ a εκκρεμής.

pendulum ['pendjuləm] n εκκρεμές nt.

penetrate ['penɪtreɪt] vt εισχωρώ σε,

διεισδύω || (pierce) διαπερνώ, τρυπώ || **penetrating** a διαπεραστικός, οξύς.

penetration [penɪ'treɪʃən] n (lit) διείσδυση.

penfriend ['penfrend] n φίλος από αλληλογραφία.

penguin ['peŋgwɪn] n πιγκουίνος.

penicillin [penɪ'sɪlɪn] n πενικιλίνη.

peninsula [pɪ'nɪnsjulə] n χερσόνησος f.

penis ['pi:nɪs] n πέος nt.

penitence ['penɪtəns] n μετάνοια.

penitent ['penɪtənt] a μετανοημένος.

penitentiary [penɪ'tenʃərɪ] n (US) σωφρονιστήριο.

penknife ['pennaɪf] n σουγιάς.

pen name ['penneɪm] n ψευδώνυμο (φιλολογικό).

pennant ['penənt] n τριγωνικό σημαία.

penniless ['penɪlɪs] a απένταρος.

penny ['penɪ] n πένα.

pension ['penʃən] n (from job) σύνταξη || ~er n συνταξιούχος.

pensive ['pensɪv] a σκεπτικός, συλλογισμένος.

pentagon ['pentəgən] n πεντάγωνο.

Pentecost ['pentɪkɒst] n Πεντηκοστή.

penthouse ['penthaus] n ρετιρέ nt inv, υπόστεγο.

pent-up ['pentʌp] a (feelings) συγκρατημένη συγκίνηση.

penultimate [pɪ'nʌltɪmɪt] a προτελευταίος.

people ['pi:pl] n άνθρωποι mpl, κόσμος || (nation) λαός, έθνος nt ♦ vt κατοικώ, οικίζω.

pep [pep] n (col) κέφι, ζωή || **to ~ up** vt ενθαρρύνω, δίνω κέφι σε.

pepper ['pepə*] n πιπέρι || (green) πιπεριά ♦ vt (pelt) κοπανίζω, βομβαρδίζω || ~mint n (plant) δυόσμος, μέντα || (sweet) μέντα (καραμέλα).

per [pɜ:*] prep κατά, ανά, διά || ~ cent τοις εκατό || ~ annum το χρόνο.

perceive [pə'si:v] vt διακρίνω, βλέπω || (understand) αντιλαμβάνομαι, καταλαβαίνω.

percentage [pə'sentɪdʒ] n ποσοστό, τοις εκατό.

perception [pə'sepʃən] n αντίληψη, αίσθηση.

perceptive [pə'septɪv] a αντιληπτικός.

perch [pɜ:tʃ] n κούρνια, ξύλο || (fish) πέρκα ♦ vi κουρνιάζω, τοποθετώ ψηλά.

percolator ['pɜ:kəleɪtə*] n καφετιέρα με φίλτρο.

percussion [pə'kʌʃən] n (MUS) κρουστά όργανα ntpl.

peremptory [pə'remptərɪ] a τελικός, αμετάκλητος, αποφασιστικός.

perennial [pə'renɪəl] a αιώνιος, μόνιμος, πολυετής ♦ n πολυετές φυτό.

perfect ['pɜ:fɪkt] a τέλειος, πλήρης, τελειωμένος || (GRAM) τετελεσμένος ♦ n (GRAM) παρακείμενος ♦ [pə'fekt] vt τελειοποιώ, συμπληρώνω || ~ion [pə'fekʃən] n τελειότητα, εντέλεια, τελειοποίηση || ~ly ad τελείως, τέλεια.

perforate ['pɜːfəreɪt] vt διατρυπώ, διαπερνώ || ~**d** a διάτρητος.

perforation [pɜːfə'reɪʃən] n διάτρηση, τρύπα.

perform [pə'fɔːm] vt εκτελώ, εκπληρώ, επιτελώ || (THEAT) παριστάνω, παίζω ♦ vi (THEAT) παίζω || ~**ance** n εκτέλεση, κατόρθωμα ntl || (THEAT) παράσταση || ~**er** n εκτελεστής, ηθοποιός m/f|| ~**ing** a (animal) γυμνασμένο (ζώο).

perfume ['pɜːfjuːm] n οσμή, μυρωδιά || (scent) άρωμα nt, μυρωδικό.

perhaps [pə'hæps] ad ίσως.

peril ['peril] n κίνδυνος || ~**ous** a επικίνδυνος || ~**ously** ad επικίνδυνα.

perimeter [pə'rimitə*] n περίμετρος f.

period ['piəriəd] n εποχή, περίοδος f|| (stop) τελεία || (MED) στάδιο, φάση, περίοδος f ♦ a (costume) της εποχής || ~**ic** a περιοδικός || ~**ical** a περιοδικός ♦ n περιοδικό || ~**ically** ad κατά περιόδους.

peripheral [pə'rifərəl] a περιφερειακός, περιμετρικός ♦ n (COMPUT) περιφερειακή μονάδα.

periphery [pə'rifəri] n περιφέρεια, περίμετρος f.

periscope ['periskəup] n περισκόπιο.

perish ['periʃ] vi χάνομαι, αφανίζομαι, πεθαίνω || ~**able** a φθαρτός || ~**ing** a (col: cold) τρομερό κρύο.

perjury ['pɜːdʒəri] n επιορκία, ψευδομαρτυρία.

perk [pɜːk]: **to** ~ **up** vi ξανακάνω κέφι, ξαναζωντανεύω || ~**y** a (cheerful) ζωηρός, εύθυμος.

perm [pɜːm] n περμανάντ f inv.

permanent ['pɜːmənənt] a μόνιμος, διαρκής || ~**ly** ad μόνιμα.

permissible [pə'misəbl] a επιτρεπόμενος, ανεκτός.

permission [pə'miʃən] n άδεια, έγκριση.

permissive [pə'misiv] a επιτρεπτικός.

permit ['pɜːmit] n άδεια ♦ [pə'mit] vt επιτρέπω.

permutation [pɜːmjuː'teiʃən] n (αντι)μετάθεση, αντιμετάταξη.

pernicious [pɜː'niʃəs] a ολέθριος, καταστρεπτικός.

perpendicular [pɜːpən'dikjulə*] a κάθετος, κατακόρυφος.

perpetrate ['pɜːpitreit] vt διαπράττω.

perpetual [pə'petjuəl] a αδιάκοπος, συνεχής, παντοτεινός.

perpetuate [pə'petjueit] vt διαιωνίζω, αποθανατίζω.

perplex [pə'pleks] vt περιπλέκω, φέρνω σε αμηχανία, μπερδεύω || ~**ed** a σε αμηχανία || ~**ing** a μπερδεμένος || ~**ity** n αμηχανία, παραζάλη, δίλημμα nt.

persecute ['pɜːsikjuːt] vt (oppress) καταδιώκω, διώκω.

persecution [pɜːsi'kjuːʃən] n διωγμός, καταδίωξη.

perseverance [pɜːsi'viərəns] n καρτερία, εμμονή, επιμονή.

persevere [pɜːsi'viə*] vi εμμένω, επιμένω.

Persia ['pɜːʃə] n Περσία || ~**n** a περσικός ♦ n (person) Πέρσης/ίδα m/f|| (LING) Περσικά ntpl|| ~**n Gulf** n Περσικός Κόλπος.

persist [pə'sist] vi επιμένω, μένω, σταθερός || (keep saying) επιμένω, εμμένω || ~**ence** n επιμονή, εμμονή || ~**ent** a επίμονος, διαρκής.

person ['pɜːsn] n πρόσωπο, άνθρωπος, άτομο || ~**able** a ευπαρουσίαστος, ωραίος || ~**al** a προσωπικός, ατομικός || (of body) σωματικός || ~**ality** n προσωπικότητα || ~**ally** ad προσωπικά || ~**ify** vt προσωποποιώ.

personnel [pɜːsə'nel] n προσωπικό || ~ **manager** n διευθυντής προσωπικού.

perspective [pə'spektiv] n προοπτική || (view) άποψη, θέα.

perspex ['pɜːspeks] n (R) άθραυστο γυαλί, περσπέξ nt inv.

perspiration [pɜːspə'reiʃən] n εφίδρωση, ιδρώτας.

perspire [pəs'paiə*] vi ιδρώνω.

persuade [pə'sweid] vt πείθω, καταφέρνω.

persuasion [pə'sweiʒən] n πειθώ f, πειστικότητα || (belief) πεποίθηση, θρήσκευμα nt.

persuasive [pə'sweisiv] a πειστικός.

pert [pɜːt] a αναιδής, αυθάδης, τσαχπίνης.

pertaining [pɜː'teiniŋ]: ~ **to** prep σχετικά με.

pertinent ['pɜːtinənt] a σχετικός, κατάλληλος, σωστός.

perturb [pə'tɜːb] vt διαταράσσω, προκαλώ ανησυχία.

perusal [pə'ruːzəl] n ανάγνωση, διάβασμα nt.

pervade [pɜː'veid] vt εμποτίζω, διαπερνώ, επικρατώ.

perverse [pə'vɜːs] a διεστραμμένος, κακότροπος.

perversion [pə'vɜːʃən] n διαστροφή, ανωμαλία.

pervert ['pɜːvɜːt] n διεστραμμένος, ανώμαλος τύπος, εκφυλισμένος ♦ [pə'vɜːt] vt διαστρέφω, στρεβλώνω, διαφθείρω.

pessimism ['pesimizəm] n απαισιοδοξία.

pessimist ['pesimist] n απαισιόδοξος/η nt|| ~**ic** a απαισιόδοξος.

pest [pest] n επιβλαβές φυτό (ή έντομο) || (fig: person, thing) ενοχλητικός/ή m/f, πληγή.

pester ['pestə*] vt ενοχλώ, πειράζω.

pestle ['pesl] n κόπανος, γουδοχέρι.

pet [pet] n χαϊδεμένος/η m/f|| (animal) ζώο του σπιτιού ♦ vt χαϊδεύω.

petal ['petl] n πέταλο.

peter ['piːtə*]: **to** ~ **out** vi εξαφανίζομαι, σβήνω.

petition [pə'tiʃən] n αίτηση, αναφορά.

petrified ['petrifaid] a απολιθωμένος.

petrol ['petrəl] n (Brit) βενζίνη || ~ **engine** n βενζινομηχανή.
petroleum [pɪ'trəulɪəm] n πετρέλαιο.
petrol: ~ **pump** n (in car) αντλία βενζίνης || ~ **station** n πρατήριο βενζίνης || ~ **tank** n δεξαμενή || (car) ρεζερβουάρ nt inv βενζίνης.
petticoat ['petɪkəut] n μεσοφόρι.
petty ['petɪ] a μικρός, ασήμαντος, κατώτερος || (mean) μικρόχους, στενοκέφαλος || ~ **cash** n μικροέξοδα ntpl, πρόχειρο ταμείο || ~ **officer** n υπαξιωματικός, υποκελευστής.
petulant ['petjulənt] a οξύθυμος, ευερέθιστος.
pew [pjuː] n στασίδι.
pewter ['pjuːtə*] n κράμα nt κασσιτέρου και μολύβδου.
phantom ['fæntəm] n φάντασμα nt.
Pharaoh ['feərəu] n Φαραώ m.
pharmacist ['fɑːməsɪst] n φαρμακοποιός m/f.
pharmacy ['fɑːməsɪ] n (shop) φαρμακείο || (science) φαρμακευτική.
phase [feɪz] n φάση.
Ph.D. (abbr = Doctor of Philosophy) = διδακτορικό δίπλωμα nt.
pheasant ['feznt] n φασιανός.
phenomenon [fɪ'nɒmɪnən] n φαινόμενο.
philanthropist [fɪ'lænθrəpɪst] n φιλάνθρωπος.
philately [fɪ'lætəlɪ] n φιλοτελισμός.
philosopher [fɪ'lɒsəfə*] n φιλόσοφος.
philosophical [fɪlə'sɒfɪkəl] a φιλοσοφικός.
philosophy [fɪ'lɒsəfɪ] n φιλοσοφία.
phlegm [flem] n φλέγμα nt.
phobia ['fəubɪə] n φοβία, φοβοπάθεια.
phone [fəun] (abbr of **telephone**) n τηλέφωνο ♦ vt τηλεφωνώ.
phonetics [fəu'netɪks] n φωνολογία, φωνητική.
phon(e)y ['fəunɪ] (col) a ψεύτικος ♦ n απατεώνας.
phosphate ['fɒsfeɪt] n φωσφορικό αλάτι.
phosphorus ['fɒsfərəs] n φωσφόρος.
photo ['fəutəu] n φωτογραφία.
photocopier ['fəutəu'kɒpɪə*] n φωτοτυπική μηχανή.
photocopy ['fəutəukɒpɪ] n φωτοαντίτυπο, φωτοτυπία ♦ vt κάνω φωτοτυπία.
photogenic [fəutəu'dʒenɪk] a φωτογενής.
photograph ['fəutəgrɑːf] n φωτογραφία ♦ vt φωτογραφίζω, βγάζω φωτογραφίες || ~ **er** [fə'tɒgrəfə*] n φωτογράφος || ~ **ic** a φωτογραφικός || ~ **y** n φωτογραφική τέχνη, φωτογράφιση.
photostat ['fəutəustæt] n φωτοστατικό αντίτυπο.
phrase [freɪz] n φράση ♦ vt διατυπώνω || ~ **book** n συλλογή εκφράσεων.
physical ['fɪzɪkəl] a φυσικός || (of the

body) σωματικός || ~ **ly** ad φυσικά, σωματικά.
physician [fɪ'zɪʃən] n γιατρός m/f.
physicist ['fɪzɪsɪst] n φυσικός m/f.
physics ['fɪzɪks] n φυσική.
physiology [fɪzɪ'ɒlədʒɪ] n φυσιολογία.
physiotherapy [fɪzɪə'θerəpɪ] n φυσιοθεραπεία.
physique [fɪ'ziːk] n σωματική διάπλαση.
pianist ['pɪənɪst] n πιανίστας/ρια m/f.
piano ['pjɑːnəu] n πιάνο.
pick [pɪk] n (tool) αξίνα, κασμάς, σκαπάνη || (choice) εκλογή || (best) ότι εκλεκτό, αφρόκρεμα ♦ vti μαζεύω, κόβω, συλλέγω || (choose) εκλέγω, διαλέγω || I ~ **a pocket** βουτώ από την τσέπη, κλέβω το πορτοφόλι || **to** ~ **out** vt διαλέγω || **to** ~ **up** vi (improve) βελτιώνομαι ♦ vt (arrest) συλλαμβάνω, πιάνω || (from ground) σηκώνω, μαζεύω || (in car etc) παίρνω || ~ **axe** n σκαπάνη, κασμάς.
picket ['pɪkɪt] n (stake) πάσσαλος, παλούκι || (strikers) σκοπός απεργών ♦ vt βάζω σκοπούς.
pickle ['pɪkl] n (also: ~ **s**: as condiment) τουρσί, άλμη ♦ vt διατηρώ σε άλμη, παστώνω.
pickpocket ['pɪkpɒkɪt] n πορτοφολάς.
pickup ['pɪkʌp] n (on record player) φωνολήπτης, πικάπ nt inv || (small truck) μικρό φορτηγό || (casual acquaintance) ψάρεμα nt, τσίμπημα nt πελάτου.
picnic ['pɪknɪk] n εκδρομή, πικνίκ nt inv ♦ vi τρώγω στην εξοχή || ~ **ker** n εκδρομέας.
pictorial [pɪk'tɔːrɪəl] a εικονογραφικός || (graphic) γραφικός || (illustrated) εικονογραφημένος.
picture ['pɪktʃə*] n εικόνα, ζωγραφιά, προσωποποίηση ♦ vt ζωγραφίζω, απεικονίζω, φαντάζομαι || **the** ~ **s** npl κινηματογράφος || ~ **book** n βιβλίο με εικόνες.
picturesque [pɪktʃə'resk] a γραφικός.
pie [paɪ] n πίτα.
piece [piːs] n κομμάτι || **in** ~ **s** (broken) (σε) κομματάκια || (taken apart) σε κομμάτια || ~ **meal** ad λίγο-λίγο, κομματιαστά || ~ **work** n εργασία με το κομμάτι.
pier [pɪə*] n (landing place) προκυμαία, αποβάθρα.
pierce [pɪəs] vt τρυπώ, διεισδύω, εισχωρώ.
piercing ['pɪəsɪŋ] a (cry) διαπεραστικός.
piety ['paɪətɪ] n ευσέβεια, θρησκοληψία.
pig [pɪg] n γουρούνι || (person) παλιάνθρωπος, γουρούνι.
pigeon ['pɪdʒən] n περιστέρι || ~ **hole** n (compartment) θυρίδα, γραμματοθήκη ♦ vt βάζω στο αρχείο.
piggy bank ['pɪgɪbæŋk] n κουμπαράς.
pigheaded ['pɪg'hedɪd] a πεισματάρης, ξεροκέφαλος.
piglet ['pɪglɪt] n γουρουνόπουλο.
pigment ['pɪgmənt] n χρώμα nt, βαφή.

pigmy ['pɪgmɪ] n = **pygmy**.

pigskin ['pɪgskɪn] n γουρουνόδερμα nt.

pigsty ['pɪgstaɪ] n χοιροστάσιο.

pigtail ['pɪgteɪl] n κοτσίδα.

pilchard ['pɪltʃəd] n μεγάλη σαρδέλα.

pile [paɪl] n (of books) σωρός, στοίβα || (in ground) πάσσαλος, παλούκι, κολώνα || (on carpet) τρίχα, χνούδι ♦ vti (also: ~ up) συσσωρεύω, στοιβάζω.

piles [paɪlz] npl αιμορροΐδες fpl, ζοχάδες fpl.

pilfer ['pɪlfə*] vt κλέβω, βουτώ, σουφρώνω.

pilgrim ['pɪlgrɪm] n προσκυνητής/ήτρια m/f|| ~**age** n προσκύνημα nt.

pill [pɪl] n χάπι || the P~ n χάπι αντισυλληπτικό.

pillage ['pɪlɪdʒ] vt λεηλατώ.

pillar ['pɪlə*] n κίονας, κολώνα, στύλος || (fig) στύλος || ~ **box** n (Brit) ταχυδρομικό κουτί.

pillion ['pɪljən] n πισινό κάθισμα nt.

pillory ['pɪlərɪ] vt διαπομπεύω, στηλιτεύω.

pillow ['pɪləʊ] n προσκέφαλο, μαξιλάρι || ~**case** n μαξιλαροθήκη.

pilot ['paɪlət] n πλοηγός, πιλότος || (AVIAT) χειριστής, πιλότος ♦ vt (AVIAT) οδηγώ, πιλοτάρω || ~ **light** n καυστήρας (θερμάστρας φωταερίου).

pimp [pɪmp] n μαστρωπός, ρουφιάνος.

pimple ['pɪmpl] n εξάνθημα nt, σπυρί.

pin [pɪn] n καρφίτσα || (peg) περόνη ♦ vt καρφιτσώνω || (hold fast) καρφώνω, πλακώνομαι || (on) ~**s and needles** στα κάρβουνα || to ~ **down** vt (fig: person) καθηλώνω.

pinafore ['pɪnəfɔː*] n ποδιά.

pincers ['pɪnsəz] npl τανάλια.

pinch [pɪntʃ] n μικρή ποσότητα, πρέζα || (nip) τσίμπημα nt, τσιμπιά ♦ vt (with fingers) τσιμπώ || (col: steal) αποσπώ, σουφρώνω, βουτώ ♦ vi (shoe) στενεύω, σφίγγω || at a ~ στην ανάγκη, σε ώρα ανάγκης.

pincushion ['pɪnkʊʃən] n μαξιλαράκι για καρφίτσες.

pine [paɪn] n (also: ~ **tree**) πεύκο ♦ vi: to ~ **for** ποθώ, μαραζώνω.

pineapple ['paɪnæpl] n ανανάς.

ping [pɪŋ] n (noise) σφύριγμα nt, κουδούνισμα nt|| ~-**pong** n πινγκ-πονγκ nt inv.

pink [pɪŋk] n (plant) γαρουφαλιά || (pale red) ρόζ ♦ a ρόζ, ρόδινος.

pin money n χαρτζιλίκι.

pinnacle ['pɪnəkl] n (highest point) κορυφή, κολοφώνας.

pinpoint ['pɪnpɔɪnt] vi υποδεικνύω ακριβώς.

pint [paɪnt] n πίντα (.567 λ.).

pioneer [paɪə'nɪə*] n πρωτοπόρος/α m/f.

pious ['paɪəs] a ευσεβής, θρήσκος.

pip [pɪp] n (seed) κουκούτσι || (on uniform) άστρο (επωμίδας).

pipe [paɪp] n σωλήνας, οχετός || (smoking) πίπα, τσιμπούκι || (instrument) αυλός || (of bird) κελάδημα nt|| to ~ **down** vi (be quiet) το βουλώνω || ~ **dream** n μάταιη ελπίδα || ~**line** n αγωγός || ~**r** n αυλητής, παίκτης γκάιντας || ~ **tobacco** n καπνός πίπας.

piping ['paɪpɪŋ] ad: ~ **hot** καυτερός, ζεματιστός, αχνιστός.

piquant ['piːkənt] a πικάντικος.

pique [piːk] n μνησικακία, φούρκα.

piracy ['paɪərəsɪ] n πειρατεία.

pirate ['paɪərɪt] n πειρατής || ~ **radio** n πειρατικός σταθμός.

pirouette [pɪruːˈet] n πιρουέτα ♦ vi κάνω πιρουέτες, περιστρέφομαι.

pissed [pɪst] a (col) μεθυσμένος.

pistol ['pɪstl] n πιστόλι.

piston ['pɪstən] n έμβολο, πιστόνι.

pit [pɪt] n λάκκος, ανθρακωρυχείο ♦ vt σημαδεύω, κόβω || (put to test) έχω κάποιον σαν αντίπαλο.

pitch [pɪtʃ] n (way of throwing) βολή, ριξιά || (ground) γήπεδο || (degree) βαθμός, κλίση || (of note) ύψος τόνου, διαπασών nt|| (tar) πίσσα, κατράμι ♦ vt (throw) πετώ || (tent) στήνω (σκηνή) ♦ vi (fall headlong) πέφτω || (of ship) σκαμπανεβάζω || ~-**black** a μαύρος σαν κατράμι || ~**ed battle** n μάχη εκ του συστάδην.

pitcher ['pɪtʃə*] n στάμνα, κανάτα.

pitchfork ['pɪtʃfɔːk] n δίκρανο, τσουγκράνα, φούρκα ♦ vt φορτώνω με δικράνι.

pitfall ['pɪtfɔːl] n (trap) παγίδα.

pith [pɪθ] n (essence) ουσία, σθένος nt.

pithy ['pɪθɪ] a (concise) με ουσία, ουσιαστικός.

pitiable ['pɪtɪəbl] a αξιολύπητος, αξιοθρήνητος, οικτρός.

pitiful ['pɪtɪful] a αξιολύπητος || (mean) ελεεινός || ~**ly** ad θλιβερά, ελεεινά.

pitiless ['pɪtɪlɪs] a ανελέητος, άσπλαχνος, άκαρδος || ~**ly** ad σκληρά, ανελέητα.

pittance ['pɪtəns] n εξευτελιστικός μισθός.

pity ['pɪtɪ] n έλεος, οίκτος, λύπηση || (of regret) κρίμα nt|| **what a** ~! τι κρίμα!

pivot ['pɪvət] n άξονας, κέντρο περιστροφής, κεντρικό σημείο ♦ vi (turn) περιστρέφομαι.

pixie ['pɪksɪ] n ξωτικό, νεράιδα.

placard ['plækɑːd] n τοιχοκόλληση, ταμπέλα, πινακίδα.

placate [pləˈkeɪt] vt κατευνάζω.

place [pleɪs] n τόπος, μέρος nt, τοποθεσία || (position) σημείο, μέρος nt|| (location) τοποθεσία || (town etc) τόπος || (employment, rank) θέση, υπηρεσία, βαθμός || (seat) θέση, κάθισμα nt ♦ vt (object) τοποθετώ, βάζω || (order) τοποθετώ, πουλώ || (in race) έρχομαι πλασέ || **in** ~ στη σωστή θέση || **out of** ~ άτοπος || **in the first** ~ εν πρώτοις.

placid ['plæsɪd] a γαλήνιος, ήρεμος, ατάραχος.

plagiarism ['pleɪdʒərɪzəm] n λογοκλοπή, λογοκλοπία.

plague [pleɪg] n πληγή, μάστιγα, λοιμός, πανούκλα.

plaice [pleɪs] n γλώσσα (ψάρι).

plaid [plæd] n καρώ ύφασμα nt.

plain [pleɪn] a (clear) σαφής, φανερός || (simple) απλός, λιτός || (not beautiful) κοινός, όχι ωραίος ♦ ad καθαρά, ευδιακρίτως, ειλικρινά ♦ n πεδιάδα, κάμπος || in ~ clothes (police) με πολιτικά || ~ly ad προφανώς, ολοφάνερα || (simply) απλά.

plaintiff ['pleɪntɪf] n ενάγων/ουσα m/f, μηνυτής/ύτρια m/f.

plait [plæt] n πλόκαμος, πλεξούδα ♦ vt πλέκω.

plan [plæn] n σχέδιο, προσχέδιο, πρόγραμμα nt || (of house etc) σχέδιο, πλάνο, σχεδιάγραμμα nt || (POL, ECON) σχέδιο ♦ vt (holiday etc) σχεδιάζω ♦ vi (make a plan) καταστρώνω, σχεδιαγραφώ.

plane [pleɪn] n (tree) πλάτανος || (tool) πλάνη, ροκάνι, πλάνια || (level) επίπεδο, επίπεδος (επιφάνεια) || (AVIAT) αεροπλάνο ♦ a επίπεδος ♦ vt (with tool) ροκανίζω, πλανίζω.

planet ['plænɪt] n πλανήτης.

plank [plæŋk] n σανίδα, μαδέρι.

planner ['plænə*] n προγραμματιστής m/f, σχεδιαστής/άστρια m/f.

planning ['plænɪŋ] n χάραξη (σχεδίου), κατάστρωση, προγραμματισμός.

plant [plɑ:nt] n φυτό || (factory) εγκατάσταση, εργοστάσιο, μηχανήματα ntpl ♦ vt φυτεύω || (set firmly) καρφώνω, εγκαθιστώ.

plantation [plæn'teɪʃən] n φυτεία.

plaque [plæk] n (on wall) πλάκα (αναμνηστική) || (on teeth) πέτρα.

plasma ['plæzmə] n πλάσμα nt, πρωτόπλασμα nt.

plaster ['plɑ:stə*] n σουβάς, κονίαμα nt, γύψος || (for wounds) έμπλαστρο, τσιρότο ♦ vt σοβατίζω || φορτώνω, σκεπάζω || in ~ (leg etc) σε γύψο || ~ed a (col) μεθυσμένος || ~er n σουβατζής.

plastic ['plæstɪk] n πλαστική ύλη ♦ a πλαστικός || (easily shaped) εύπλαστος || P~ine n (R) πλαστολίνη || ~ surgery n πλαστική εγχείρηση.

plate [pleɪt] n πιάτο, δίσκος || (table utensils) χρυσά ή αργυρά επιτραπέζια σκεύη ntpl, ασημικά ntpl || (flat sheet) πλάκα, λάμα, φύλλο.

plateau ['plætəʊ] n υψίπεδο, οροπέδιο.

plateful ['pleɪtfʊl] n πιάτο γεμάτο.

plate glass ['pleɪt'glɑ:s] n κρύσταλλο, υαλοπίνακας.

platform ['plætfɔ:m] n (at meeting) εξέδρα, βήμα nt || (RAIL) αποβάθρα, εξέδρα.

platinum ['plætɪnəm] n λευκόχρυσος, πλατίνη.

platitude ['plætɪtju:d] n κοινοτοπία.

platoon [plə'tu:n] n διμοιρία, ουλαμός.

platter ['plætə*] n πιατέλα.

plausible ['plɔ:zəbl] a εύλογος, πιθανός.

play [pleɪ] n παιχνίδι, διασκέδαση || (stage) έργο || (of shadows etc) παίξιμο || (MECH) ανοχή, παίξιμο ♦ vt παίζω, διασκεδάζω || (trick) παιχνιδιάζω, κάνω αστείο || (part) παίζω, υποδύομαι ρόλο, ερμηνεύω || (instrument) παίζω ♦ vi (amuse o.s.) διασκεδάζω, παίζω || (of light etc) σπιθοβολώ, παίζω, χοροπηδώ || ~boy n γλεντζές m, έκλυτος νέος || ~ed-out a εξαντλημένος, αποκαμωμένος || ~er n παίκτης/ρια m/f, ηθοποιός m/f|| ~ful a παιχνιδιάρικος, παιχνιδιάρης || ~ground n προαύλιο, τόπος διασκεδάσεως || ~ing card n τραπουλόχαρτο || ~ing field n γήπεδο || ~mate n συμπαίκτης, σύντροφος στο παιχνίδι || ~thing n παιχνίδι, παιχνιδάκι || ~wright n θεατρικός συγγραφέας m/f.

plea [pli:] n (LAW) έκκληση, αγωγή.

plead [pli:d] vt επικαλούμαι, προβάλλω ♦ vi παρακαλώ, ικετεύω || (LAW) υποστηρίζω, υπερασπίζω, απολογούμαι.

pleasant ['plɛznt] a ευχάριστος || ~ry n ευθυμία, κέφι, χιούμορ.

please [pli:z] vt αρέσω, ευχαριστώ || ~! παρακαλώ! || my bill, ~ το λογαριασμό, παρακαλώ || ~ yourself! κάνε το κέφι σου! || ~d a (happy, glad) ευχαριστημένος, ικανοποιημένος.

pleasing ['pli:zɪŋ] a ευχάριστος.

pleasurable ['plɛʒərəbl] a ευχάριστος, τερπνός.

pleasure ['plɛʒə*] n τέρψη, ευχαρίστηση, χαρά || (amusement) απολαύσεις fpl, ηδονές fpl, χαρές || it's a ~! χαίρομαι!, παρακαλώ!

pleat [pli:t] n πτυχή, πιέτα.

plebs [plɛbz] npl λαουτζίκος.

plectrum ['plɛktrəm] n πλήκτρο.

pledge [plɛdʒ] n ενέχυρο, δεσμευτική υπόσχεση, τεκμήριο ♦ vi δίνω το λόγο μου, υπόσχομαι.

plentiful ['plɛntɪfʊl] a άφθονος, πλουσιοπάροχος.

plenty ['plɛntɪ] n αφθονία, πλήθος nt || (enough) αρκετό ♦ ad (col) πάρα πολύ || ~ of άφθονα, με το τσουβάλι.

plethora ['plɛθərə] n πληθώρα.

pleurisy ['plʊərɪsɪ] n πλευρίτιδα.

pliable ['plaɪəbl] a εύκαμπτος, ευλύγιστος.

pliers ['plaɪəz] npl τανάλια, λαβίδα.

plight [plaɪt] n κατάσταση, θέση.

plinth [plɪnθ] n πλίνθος, πλινθίο.

plod [plɒd] vi περπατώ βαρειά, σέρνομαι || ~der n φιλόπονος, ευσυνείδητος.

plot [plɒt] n (conspiracy) συνωμοσία || (of story) πλοκή, υπόθεση || (land) οικόπεδο, χωράφι ♦ vt χαράσσω, σχεδιάζω ♦ vt (plan secretly) συνωμοτώ, μηχανορραφώ.

plough, plow (US) [plaʊ] n άροτρο, αλέτρι ♦ vt (earth) αροτριώ, αλετρίζω || (col: exam candidate) απορρίπτω (μαθητή) || to ~ back vt (COMM) επενδύω (τα κέρδη) στην ίδια επιχείρηση || to ~ **through** vt (book) διαβάζω με κόπο || ~**ing** η άροση, αλέτρισμα nt.

pluck [plʌk] vt (fruit) κόβω || (feathers) μαδώ ♦ n (col) κουράγιο, θάρρος nt || to ~ **up courage** παίρνω κουράγιο || ~**y** a θαρραλέος, παλικάρι.

plug [plʌg] n (for hole) πώμα nt, βούλωμα nt, τάπα || (wall socket) πρίζα || (col: publicity) διαφήμιση, προβολή || (AUT) μπουζί ♦ vt (hole) βουλώνω, ταπώνω || (col: advertise) διαφημίζω, προβάλλω.

plum [plʌm] n (fruit) δαμάσκηνο ♦ a (choice) εκλεκτό πράμα, καλύτερη θέση.

plumage ['pluːmɪdʒ] n φτέρωμα nt, φτερά ntpl.

plumb [plʌm] a κατακόρυφος || πλήρης, αληθής ♦ ad (exactly) ακριβώς || (wholly) τελείως ♦ vt βυθομετρώ, σταθμίζω.

plumber ['plʌmə*] n υδραυλικός.

plumbing ['plʌmɪŋ] n (craft) υδραυλική τέχνη || (piping) σωληνώσεις fpl, υδραυλικά ntpl.

plume [pluːm] n λοφίο, φτερό.

plump [plʌmp] a στρογγυλός, παχουλός, αφράτος ♦ vi σωριάζομαι, πέφτω βαριά ♦ vt πετώ απότομα || to ~ **for** vt (col: choose) υποστηρίζω, ψηφίζω υπέρ.

plunder ['plʌndə*] n λεία, λεπλασία, πλιάτσικο ♦ vt λεπλατώ, λαφυραγωγώ.

plunge [plʌndʒ] n κατάδυση, βουτιά ♦ vt (κατα)βυθίζω, βουτώ, χώνω ♦ vi καταδύομαι, βουτώ.

plunging ['plʌndʒɪŋ] a (neckline) μεγάλο (ντεκολτέ).

pluperfect ['pluː'pɜːfɪkt] n υπερουντέλικος.

plural ['pluərəl] a πληθυντικός, πολλαπλός ♦ n πληθυντικός.

plus [plʌs] prep πλέον, συν, μαζί με ♦ a θετικός.

plush [plʌʃ] a (col: luxurious) πολυτελής, πλούσιος.

ply [plaɪ] n (layer) φύλλο, φλοίωμα nt || **three-~ wool** τρίκλωνο μαλλί ♦ vt (with questions) ταλαιπωρώ (με ερωτήσεις) || to ~ **a trade** ασκώ επάγγελνα ♦ vi ταξιδεύω, εκτελώ γραμμή || ~**wood** n κοντραπλακέ nt inv.

P.M. abbr see **prime**.

p.m. ad (abbr of post meridiem) μ.μ. (μετά το μεσημέρι).

pneumatic [njuːˈmætɪk] a πνευματικός, του πεπιεσμένου αέρα.

pneumonia [njuːˈməʊnɪə] n πνευμονία.

P.O. abbr see **post office**.

poach [pəʊtʃ] vt (cook) βράζω ξεφλουδισμένα αυγό, ποσάρω || (steal) κλέβω ♦ vi λαθροθηρώ || ~**ed** a (egg) (αυγό) ποσέ || ~**er** n λαθροθήρας || ~**ing** n λαθροθηρία, κλοπή.

pocket ['pɒkɪt] n τσέπη || (hollow) θύλακας, λάκκος || (of resistance) νησίδα αντιστάσεως ♦ vt τσεπώνω, βάζω στην τσέπη || **out of** ~ ζημιωμένος, βγαίνω χαμένος || ~**book** n (US: wallet)

πορτοφόλι || (notebook) σημειωματάριο (της τσέπης) || (small book) βιβλίο τσέπης || ~**ful** n όσο χωρεί μια τσέπη || ~ **knife** n σουγιάς (της τσέπης) || ~ **money** n χαρτζιλίκι.

pod [pɒd] n περικάρπιο.

podgy ['pɒdʒɪ] a κοντόχονδρος, χοντρός.

poem ['pəʊɪm] n ποίημα nt.

poet ['pəʊɪt] n ποιητής/ήτρια m/f || ~**ic** [pəʊˈetɪk] a ποιητικός || ~ **laureate** n επίσημος ποιητής || ~**ry** n ποίηση.

poignant ['pɔɪnjənt] a οξύς, δριμύς, τσουχτερός, δυνατός.

point [pɔɪnt] n (sharp end) ακίδα, άκρα, αιχμή, μύτη || (dot) στίξη, σημείο || (moment) στιγμή, σημείο || (detail) λεπτομέρεια, στοιχείο, σημείο || (headland) ακρωτήριο || (RAIL) κλειδί, διασταύρωση || (of compass) ρόμβος πυξίδας, κάρτα || (degree) βαθμός, σημείο || (decimal point) κόμμα nt ♦ vt στρέφω, κατευθύνω, δείχνω || (gun etc) σκοπεύω με, σημαδεύω ♦ vi δείχνω, δακτυλοδεικτώ || ~**s** npl κλειδί || ~ **of view** n άποψη || **what's the** ~? τι το όφελος; || to ~ **out** vt δείχνω, επισύρω την προσοχή, υπογραμμίζω || to ~ **to** vt δείχνω, δακτυλοδεικτώ || ~**-blank** ad κατ' ευθείαν, απερίτροφος || ~ **duty** n υπηρεσία τροχαίας || ~**ed** a (shape) αιχμηρός, μυτερός || (remark) δηκτικός, καυστικός, τσουχτερός || ~**er** n δείκτης || ~**less** a άσκοπος, μάταιος.

poise [pɔɪz] n παρουσιαστικό, κορμοστασιά ♦ vti ισορροπώ, σταθμίζω.

poison ['pɔɪzn] n δηλητήριο ♦ vt δηλητηριάζω, μολύνω || ~**ous** a δηλητηριώδης, φαρμακερός.

poke [pəʊk] vt (stick into) κτυπώ, χώνω || (fire) συδαυλίζω, σκαλίζω ♦ n (jab) κτύπημα nt, σπρωξιά || to ~ **one's nose into** ανακατεύομαι σε || to ~ **about** vi ψηλαφώ, ψάχνω || ~**r** n σκαλιστήρι || (CARDS) πόκερ nt inv.

poky ['pəʊkɪ] a μικρός, στενόχωρος.

Poland ['pəʊlənd] n Πολωνία.

polar ['pəʊlə*] a πολικός || ~ **bear** n πολική άρκτος || ~**ize** vt πολώνω ♦ vi πολούμαι.

pole [pəʊl] n (of wood) στύλος, ιστός, κοντάρι || (ELEC) στύλος || (GEOG) πόλος || ~**-cat** n (US) είδος νυφίτσας || ~ **star** n πολικό αστέρι || ~ **vault** n άλμα nt επί κοντώ.

police [pəˈliːs] n αστυνομία ♦ vt αστυνομεύω, ελέγχω, τηρώ (την τάξη) || ~ **car** n αστυνομικό (αυτοκίνητο) || ~**man** n αστυφύλακας, αστυνομικός, πολισμάνος || ~ **state** n αστυνομικό κράτος nt || ~ **station** n αστυνομικό τμήμα nt || ~**woman** n n αστυνομικός, αστυνομικίνα.

policy ['pɒlɪsɪ] n πολιτική || (prudence) φρόνηση || (insurance) ασφαλιστήριο.

polio ['pəʊlɪəʊ] n πολυομυελίτιδα.

Polish ['pəʊlɪʃ] a πολωνικός ♦ n (LING) Πολωνικά ntpl.

polish ['pɒlɪʃ] n βερνίκι || (surface) γυαλάδα, στιλπνότητα, λούστρο || (fig: refinement) ευγένεια, καλοί τρόποι mpl ♦ vt στιλβώνω, γυαλίζω, λουστράρω || (refine) εξευγενίζω || **to ~ off** vt (work) τελειώνω βιαστικά || (food) αδειάζω, κατεβάζω, καθαρίζω || **~ed** a (fig) ευγενικός, λεπτός || εκλεπτισμένος.

polite [pə'laɪt] a ευγενής, φιλόφρονας || **~ness** n ευγένεια, λεπτότητα.

politic ['pɒlɪtɪk] a (wise) συνετός, προνοητικός || **~al** [pə'lɪtɪkəl] a πολιτικός || **~ian** [pɒlɪ'tɪʃən] n πολιτικός, πολιτικάντης || **~s** npl (n) πολιτική || (US) πολιτικολογία.

polka [pɒlkə] n πόλκα || **~ dot** (φόρεμα) με πίκες fpl, με βούλες fpl.

poll [pəʊl] n ψηφοφορία, αριθμός ψήφων ♦ vt συγκεντρώνω ψήφους, ψηφίζω.

pollen ['pɒlən] n γύρη (λουλουδιού).

pollination [pɒlɪ'neɪʃən] n επικονίαση, γονιμοποίηση.

polling booth ['pəʊlɪŋbuːð] n απομονωτήριο εκλογικού τμήματος.

polling day ['pəʊlɪŋdeɪ] n μέρα εκλογών.

polling station ['pəʊlɪŋsteɪʃən] n εκλογικό τμήμα nt.

pollute [pə'luːt] vt μολύνω, βρωμίζω.

pollution [pə'luːʃən] n μίανση, μόλυνση.

polo ['pəʊləʊ] n πόλο nt inv.

poly- ['pɒlɪ] prefix πολυ-.

polygamy [pɒ'lɪɡəmɪ] n πολυγαμία.

polytechnic [pɒlɪ'teknɪk] n πολυτεχνείο.

polythene ['pɒlɪθiːn] n πολυθένιο.

pomegranate ['pɒmɪɡrænɪt] n ρόδι.

pommel ['pʌml] vt γρονθοκοπώ, κοπανίζω.

pomp [pɒmp] n λαμπρότητα, επίδειξη.

pompous ['pɒmpəs] a πομπώδης, φανφαρόνος || **~ly** ad με επιδεικτικότητα, με στόμφο.

ponce [pɒns] n (col) σωματέμπορος.

pond [pɒnd] n δεξαμενή, λιμνούλα.

ponder ['pɒndə*] vti ξανασκέφτομαι, μελετώ, ζυγίζω || **~ous** a βαρύς, βραδύς, ανιαρός.

pontificate [pɒn'tɪfɪkeɪt] vi (fig) μιλώ με ύφος ποντιφηκό.

pontoon [pɒn'tuːn] n πλωτό στήριγμα nt γέφυρας || (CARDS) είκοσι ένα.

pony ['pəʊnɪ] n αλογάκι || **~tail** n αλογοουρά.

poodle ['puːdl] n σγουρόμαλλο σκυλάκι.

pool [puːl] n (of liquid) λιμνούλα, νερόλακκος || (at cards) πόστα, πότ || (billiards) μπάτσικα || **~s** (football) προ-πο nt inv ♦ vt (money etc) ενώνω, συγκεντρώνω.

poor [pʊə*] a φτωχός, δυστυχισμένος || (feeble) αδύνατος, άθλιος || (pitied) κακόμοιρος, αξιολύπητος ♦ n: **the ~** οι φτωχοί mpl || **~ly** ad φτωχικά, άθλια ♦ a αδιάθετος.

pop [pɒp] n (noise) ξηρός κρότος || (MUS) μουσική ποπ || (col US: father) μπαμπάς ♦ vt (put suddenly) θέτω απότομα ♦ vi (explode) κάνω ποπ, κροτώ || (come suddenly) μπαίνω ξαφνικά, βγαίνω || **~ concert** n λαϊκή συναυλία (ποπ) || **~corn** n ψημένο καλαμπόκι, ποπ-κορν nt inv.

Pope [pəʊp] n Πάπας.

poplar ['pɒplə*] n λεύκη.

poppy ['pɒpɪ] n παπαρούνα.

populace ['pɒpjʊlɪs] n λαός, το πλήθος.

popular ['pɒpjʊlə*] a δημοφιλής, κοσμοαγάπητος || (of the people) λαϊκός || **~ity** n δημοτικότητα, δημοφιλία || **~ize** vt εκλαϊκεύω.

populate ['pɒpjʊleɪt] vt (συν)οικίζω, κατοικώ.

population [pɒpjʊ'leɪʃən] n πληθυσμός.

porcelain ['pɔːslɪn] n πορσελάνη.

porch [pɔːtʃ] n προστέγασμα nt || (US) βεράντα.

porcupine ['pɔːkjʊpaɪn] n ακανθόχοιρος.

pore [pɔː*] n πόρος || **to ~ over** vt προσηλώνομαι.

pork [pɔːk] n χοιρινό.

pornographic [pɔːnə'ɡræfɪk] a πορνογραφικός.

pornography [pɔː'nɒɡrəfɪ] n πορνογραφία.

porous ['pɔːrəs] a πορώδης.

porpoise ['pɔːpəs] n φώκαινα.

porridge ['pɒrɪdʒ] n χυλός (βρώμης).

port [pɔːt] n λιμένας, λιμάνι || (town) πόρτο || (COMPUT) σύνδεση εισόδου/εξόδου || (NAUT: left side) αριστερή πλευρά || (wine) πορτό, οίνος Πορτογαλίας.

portable ['pɔːtəbl] a φορητός.

portal ['pɔːtl] n είσοδος, πύλη.

portcullis [pɔːt'kʌlɪs] n καταραχτή θύρα, καταραχτή.

portent ['pɔːtent] n κακός οιωνός || (good) θαυμάσιο πράγμα nt, οιωνός.

porter ['pɔːtə*] n αχθοφόρος, χαμάλης || (doorkeeper) θυρωρός.

porthole ['pɔːthəʊl] n (NAUT) φινιστρίνι.

portion ['pɔːʃən] n μερίδα, μερίδιο.

portly ['pɔːtlɪ] a παχύς, επιβλητικός.

portrait ['pɔːtrɪt] n προσωπογραφία, πορτραίτο.

portray [pɔː'treɪ] vt (describe) περιγράφω || **~al** n απεικόνιση, περιγραφή.

Portugal ['pɔːtjʊɡəl] n Πορτογαλία.

Portuguese ['pɔːtjʊ'ɡiːz] a πορτογαλικός ♦ n (person) Πορτογάλος/ίδα m/f || (LING) Πορτογαλικά ntpl.

pose [pəʊz] n (position) στάση || (affectation) προσποίηση, πόζα ♦ vi (take up attitude) ποζάρω || (assume false pose) εμφανίζομαι, παριστάνω ♦ vt (put *question*) θέτω || ~r n (*problem*) δύσκολο πρόβλημα nt.

posh [pɒʃ] a (*col*) πλούσιος.

position [pə'zɪʃən] n θέση, στάση || (*place*) θέση, σειρά || (*location*) τοποθεσία || (*attitude*) θέση, πρόταση || (*rank*) θέση, βαθμός || (*job*) θέση, εργασία.

positive ['pɒzɪtɪv] a θετικός, καταφατικός || (*confident*) βέβαιος, σίγουρος || (*real*) πραγματικός, αληθινός || (*character*) θετικός.

posse ['pɒsɪ] n (*US*) απόσπασμα nt (αστυνομικών).

possess [pə'zes] vt (κατ)έχω, διατηρώ || ~ion n κατοχή, κτήμα nt || (*owning*) κατοχή || ~ive a κτητικός, παθολογικά στοργικός || (*GRAM*) κτητικό.

possibility [pɒsə'bɪlɪtɪ] n (*chance*) πιθανότητα || (*event*) δυνατότητα.

possible ['pɒsəbl] a δυνατός, ενδεχόμενος, λογικός || **if** ~ αν μπορώ, αν είναι δυνατόν.

possibly ['pɒsəblɪ] ad κατά το δυνατό, πιθανό, ίσως.

post [pəʊst] n (*pole*) στύλος, πάσσαλος, κολώνα || (*mail*) ταχυδρομείο || (*man*) ταχυδρόμος || (*station*) θέση, φυλακή, πόστο || (*job*) θέση, πόστο ♦ vt (*notice*) τοιχοκολλώ || (*letters*) ταχυδρομώ || (*station*) εγκαθιστώ, τοποθετώ || ~**age** n ταχυδρομικά ntpl, γραμματόσημα ntpl || ~**al** a ταχυδρομικός || ~**al order** n ταχυδρομική επιταγή || ~**box** n ταχυδρομικό κουτί || ~**card** n καρτποστάλ f inv, κάρτα.

postdate ['pəʊst'deɪt] vt (*cheque*) μεταχρονολογώ, επιχρονολογώ.

poster ['pəʊstə*] n διαφήμιση, αφίσα.

poste restante [pəʊst'restɑ:nt] n ποστ-ρεστάντ.

posterior [pɒs'tɪərɪə*] n (*col*) ο πισινός, κώλος.

posterity [pɒs'terɪtɪ] n (οι) μεταγενέστεροι.

postgraduate ['pəʊst'grædjuɪt] n μεταπτυχιακός σπουδαστής.

posthumous ['pɒstjuməs] a (*works*) κατάλοιπα ntpl.

postman ['pəʊstmən] n ταχυδρόμος.

postmark ['pəʊstmɑ:k] n ταχυδρομική σφραγίδα.

postmaster ['pəʊstmɑ:stə*] n διευθυντής ταχυδρομείου.

post-mortem ['pəʊst'mɔːtem] n (*examination*) νεκροψία.

post office ['pəʊstɒfɪs] n ταχυδρομείο || ~ **box** (**P.O. Box**) n ταχυδρομική θυρίδα (Τ.Θ.), ταχυδρομικό κιβώτιο.

postpone [pəʊst'pəʊn] vt αναβάλλω.

postscript ['pəʊsskrɪpt] n υστερόγραφο.

postulate ['pɒstjuleɪt] vt απαιτώ, αξιώνω.

posture ['pɒstʃə*] n στάση, θέση, κατάσταση ♦ vi τοποθετώ, στήνω, ποζάρω.

postwar ['pəʊst'wɔː*] a μεταπολεμικός.

posy ['pəʊzɪ] n μπουκέτο (από λουλούδια), ανθοδέσμη.

pot [pɒt] n (*for cooking*) χύτρα, δοχείο, γλάστρα || (*sl: marijuana*) ναρκωτικά ntpl ♦ vt (*plant*) βάζω σε γλάστρα, φυτεύω σε γλάστρα.

potash ['pɒtæʃ] n ποτάσσα.

potato [pə'teɪtəʊ] n πατάτα.

potent ['pəʊtənt] a ισχυρός, πειστικός.

potential [pəʊ'tenʃəl] a δυνητικός, λανθάνων, πιθανός, δυνατός ♦ n δυναμικό || ~**ly** ad ενδεχομένως, πιθανώς.

pothole ['pɒthəʊl] n πηγάδι, σπήλαιο || (*in road*) λακκούβα, λάκκος.

potholing ['pɒthəʊlɪŋ] n σπηλαιολογία.

potion ['pəʊʃən] n δόση (φαρμάκου).

potted ['pɒtɪd] a (*food*) διατηρημένος || (*plant*) στη γλάστρα, της γλάστρας.

potter ['pɒtə*] n κεραμοποιός, τσουκαλάς ♦ vi χασομερώ, ψευδοδουλεύω || ~**y** n αγγειοπλαστική, κεραμεική || (*place*) κεραμοποιείο.

potty ['pɒtɪ] a (*mad*) λοξός, τρελός ♦ n (*child's*) δοχείο (μωρού).

pouch [paʊtʃ] n (*ZOOL*) θύλακας || (*tobacco*) ταμπακιέρα.

poultice ['pəʊltɪs] n κατάπλασμα nt.

poultry ['pəʊltrɪ] n πουλερικά ntpl || ~ **farm** n ορνιθοτροφείο.

pounce [paʊns] vi (+ on) εφορμώ, πηδώ πάνω σε, χυμώ ♦ n πήδημα nt, εφόρμηση.

pound [paʊnd] n (*weight*) λίμπρα (435 γρ), λίβρα, λίτρα || (*sterling*) λίρα (Αγγλίας) || (*area*) περίβολος, μάντρα ♦ vt κτυπώ, κοπανίζω || (*crush to powder*) λειοτριβώ, κονιοποιώ, κοπανίζω || ~**ing** n σφυροκόπημα nt.

pour [pɔː*] vt (*cause*) χύνω ♦ vi μπαίνω σαν ποτάμι, τρέχω, χύνομαι || **to** ~ **away or off** vt χύνω (έξω), ξεχύνομαι || **to** ~ **in** vi (*people*) μπαίνω κατά κύματα || ~**ing rain** n βροχή με το τουλούμι, καταρρακτώδης βροχή.

pout [paʊt] n κατσούφιασμα nt ♦ vi κατσουφιάζω, στραβομουριάζω.

poverty ['pɒvətɪ] n φτώχεια || ~-**stricken** a φτωχός, άπορος.

powder ['paʊdə*] n σκόνη || (*medicine*) σκόνη || (*cosmetic*) πούδρα ♦ vt (*make into powder*) κονιοποιώ, τρίβω || (*put on powder*) πουδράρομαι || **to** ~ **one's nose** πουδράρομαι || (*fig*) πάω στη τουαλέτα || ~ **room** n τουαλέτα || ~**y** a κονιώδης, σαν σκόνη.

power [paʊə*] n (*ability to act*) εξουσία, δύναμη, ικανότητα || (*strength*) δύναμη || (*mighty nation*) (μεγάλη) δύναμη || (*mental*) ικανότητα, ιδιοφυΐα, ταλέντο || (*ELEC*) ενέργεια, δύναμη || (*POL: of party or leader*) εξουσία, επιρροή, ισχύς ♦ vt παρέχω ενέργεια σε, κινώ || ~ **cut** n διακοπή ρεύματος || ~**ful** a (*person*) ρωμαλέος, μεγάλος, δυνατός || (*government*) ισχυρός || (*engine*) ισχυρός, αποδοτικός || ~**less** a ανίσχυρος,

αδύναμος || ~ **line** n γραμμή
μεταφοράς || ~ **station** n εργοστάσιο
παραγωγής ρεύματος.

p.p. abbr: ~ P. Smith Δια τον κον Π.
Σμιθ.

P.R. abbr of **public relations**.

practicable ['præktikəbl] a δυνατός,
κατορθωτός, εφαρμόσιμος.

practical ['præktikəl] a πρακτικός,
θετικός, εφαρμόσιμος || ~ **joke** n βαρύ
αστείο, φάρσα || ~ **ly** ad (almost) σχεδόν,
ουσιαστικά.

practice ['præktis] n άσκηση, εξάσκηση
|| (habit) συνήθεια, έθιμο || (business)
άσκηση, εξάσκηση || (clients) πελατεία ||
in~ (in reality) στην πραγματικότητα ||
to be out of ~ (SPORT) ξεσυνηθίζω, δεν
είμαι σε φόρμα.

practicing ['præktisiŋ] a (US) =
practising.

practise, practice (US) ['præktis] vt
ασκώ, εφαρμόζω, ακολουθώ, συνηθίζω ||
(SPORT) εκγυμνάζω || (piano) μελετώ,
κάνω ασκήσεις || (profession)
επαγγέλλομαι, (εξ)ασκώ.

practising ['præktisiŋ] a (Christian etc)
που ασκεί τα θρησκευτικά του
καθήκοντα.

practitioner [præk'tiʃənə*] n
επαγγελματίας.

pragmatic [præg'mætik] a πρακτικός,
πραγματικός.

prairie ['prɛəri] n λιβάδι, κάμπος.

praise [preiz] n έπαινος, εγκώμι ♦ vt
επαινώ, εξυμνώ || (worship) δοξάζω ||
~ **worthy** a αξιέπαινος.

pram [præm] n καροτσάκι μωρού.

prance [prɑːns] vi ανασκιρτώ, αναπηδώ
|| (strut) κορδώνομαι, καμαρώνω.

prank [præŋk] n ζαβολιά, κατεργαριά,
κόλπο.

prattle ['prætl] vi φλυαρώ.

prawn [prɔːn] n είδος nt γαρίδας.

pray [prei] vi προσεύχομαι, παρακαλώ ||
~ **er** n προσευχή || (praying) παράκληση ||
~ **er book** n ευχολόγιο, προσευχητήριο.

pre- [priː] prefix προ-.

preach [priːtʃ] vi κηρύσσω || ~ **er** n
ιεροκήρυκας.

preamble [priː'æmbl] n προοίμιο,
εισαγωγή.

prearranged ['priːə'reindʒd] a
προκαθορισμένος, συμφωνημένος από
πριν.

precarious [pri'kɛəriəs] a επισφαλής,
επικίνδυνος, αβέβαιος.

precaution [pri'kɔːʃən] n προφύλαξη.

precede [pri'siːd] vti προηγούμαι,
προπορεύομαι || ~ **nt** ['presidənt] n
προηγούμενο.

preceding [pri'siːdiŋ] a προηγούμενος.

precept ['priːsept] n κανόνας, δίδαγμα
nt, διαταγή.

precinct ['priːsiŋkt] n περίβολος,
περιοχή.

precious ['preʃəs] a πολύτιμος ||
(affected) επιτηδευμένος, προσποιητός.

precipice ['presipis] n γκρεμός.

precipitate [pri'sipitit] a (hasty)
βιαστικός, εσπευσμένος || ~ **ly** ad
βιαστικά.

precipitous [pri'sipitəs] a (steep)
κρημνώδης || ~ **ly** ad απότομα.

precise [pri'sais] a ακριβής, ορισμένος,
συγκεκριμένος || (careful) ακριβολόγος,
τυπικός.

preclude [pri'kluːd] vt αποκλείω,
προλαμβάνω.

precocious [pri'kəuʃəs] a πρόωρος.

preconceived ['priːkən'siːvd] a (idea)
προκαταληπτικός.

precondition [priːkən'diʃən] n
προϋπόθεση.

precursor [priː'kɜːsə*] n πρόδρομος.

predator ['predətə*] n ληστής,
αρπακτικό || (animal) ζώο.

predecessor ['priːdisesə*] n
προκάτοχος.

predestination [priːdesti'neiʃən] n
προκαθορισμός.

predetermine ['priːdi'tɜːmin] vt
προκαθορίζω, προαποφασίζω.

predicament [pri'dikəmənt] n δύσκολη
θέση, δυσχέρεια.

predicate ['predikit] n βεβαιώνω,
υποδηλώ.

predict [pri'dikt] vt προλέγω,
προφητεύω || ~ **ion** n πρόβλεψη,
προφητεία.

predominance [pri'dominəns] n
επικράτηση, υπεροχή.

predominant [pri'dominənt] a
υπερισχύων, επικρατών.

predominate [pri'domineit] vi
επικρατώ, υπερισχύω.

pre-eminent [priː'eminənt] a
διαπρεπής, υπερέχων.

pre-empt [priː'empt] vt αποκτώ
πρώτος.

preen [priːn] vt: **to** ~ **o.s.** στολίζομαι,
καμαρώνω.

prefabricated ['priː'fæbrikeitid] a
προκατασκευασμένος.

preface ['prefis] n πρόλογος, εισαγωγή,
προοίμιο.

prefect ['priːfekt] n (of school)
επιμελητής/ήτρια m/f.

prefer [pri'fɜː*] vt προτιμώ, υποβάλλω,
προάγω || ~ **able** ['prefərəbl] a (+to)
προτιμότερος, καλύτερος (από) ||
~ **ence** n προτίμηση || ~ **ential** a
προνομιακός, προνομιούχος.

prefix ['priːfiks] n πρόθεμα nt.

pregnancy ['pregnənsi] n εγκυμοσύνη.

pregnant ['pregnənt] a έγκυος || (of
ideas) γόνιμος (σε), γεμάτος συνέπειες.

prehistoric ['priːhis'tɒrik] a
προϊστορικός.

prehistory ['priː'histəri] n προϊστορία.

prejudice ['predʒudis] n προκατάληψη,
πρόληψη || (harm) ζημιά, βλάβη ♦ vt
ζημιώνω, επηρεάζω || ~ **d** a
προκατειλημμένος, προδιατεθειμένος.

prelate ['prelit] n ιεράρχης.

preliminary [prɪ'lɪmɪnərɪ] *a* προκαταρκτικός.

prelude ['prelju:d] *n* πρόλογος, προοίμιο || *(MUS)* προανάκρουσμα *nt*, πρελούντιο.

premarital ['pri:'mærɪtl] *a* προγαμιαίος.

premature ['prematʃʊə*] *a* πρόωρος || ~**ly** *ad* πρόωρα.

premeditated [pri:'medɪteɪtɪd] *a* προεσκεμμένος, εκ προμελέτης.

premier ['premɪə*] *a* πρώτος, κύριος ♦ *n (head of country)* πρωθυπουργός *m/f* || ~**e** [premɪ'ɛə*] *n* πρεμιέρα.

premise ['premɪs] *n* πρόταση || ~**s** *npl* οίκημα *nt*, κτίριο.

premium ['pri:mɪəm] *n (insurance)* ασφάλιστρο.

premonition [pri:mə'nɪʃən] *n* προαίσθημα *nt*.

preoccupied [pri:'ɒkjʊpaɪd] *a* απορροφημένος, αφηρημένος.

prep [prep] *n (SCH: study)* βραδυνή, μελέτη.

preparation [prepə'reɪʃən] *n* προπαρασκευή, προετοιμασία.

preparatory [prɪ'pærətərɪ] *a (SCH)* προπαρασκευαστικός, προεισαγωγικός.

prepare [prɪ'pɛə*] *vt* προετοιμάζω, προπαρασκευάζω ♦ *vi* προετοιμάζομαι, προπαρασκευάζομαι || ~**d for** είμαι έτοιμος για || ~**d to** είμαι διατεθειμένος να.

preponderance [prɪ'pɒndərəns] *n* υπεροχή, επικράτηση.

preposition [prepə'zɪʃən] *n* πρόθεση.

preposterous [prɪ'pɒstərəs] *a* παράλογος, γελοίος.

prerequisite [pri:'rekwɪzɪt] *n* προϋπόθεση, αναγκαίος όρος.

prerogative [prɪ'rɒgətɪv] *n* προνόμιο.

Presbyterian [prezbɪ'tɪərɪən] *a, n* Πρεσβυτεριανός.

preschool ['pri:'sku:l] *a* προσχολικός.

prescribe [prɪs'kraɪb] *vt* ορίζω, παραγγέλλω || *(medicine)* δίνω συνταγή.

prescription [prɪs'krɪpʃən] *n (for medicine)* συνταγή.

presence ['prezns] *n* παρουσία || *(bearing)* ύφος *nt*, παρουσιαστικό, εμφάνιση || ~ **of mind** ψυχραιμία, ετοιμότητα πνεύματος.

present ['preznt] *a* παρών || *(time)* σημερινός ♦ *n (time)* το παρόν, το σήμερα || *(gift)* δώρο || *(GRAM)* ενεστώτας ♦ [prɪ'zent] *vt* παρουσιάζω, παρουσιάζομαι || *(introduce)* συστήνω, παρουσιάζω || *(offer, give)* κατάθετω, προσφέρω, δίνω || **at** ~ τώρα, προς το παρόν || ~**able** *a* παρουσιάσιμος || ~**ation** *n* παρουσίαση, παράσταση || ~-**day** *a* σημερινός || ~**ly** *ad (soon)* σε λίγο, αμέσως, σύντομα || *(at present)* τώρα.

preservation [prezə'veɪʃən] *n* διατήρηση, διαφύλαξη.

preservative [prɪ'zɜ:vətɪv] *n* συντηρητικό ♦ *a* α διατηρητικός.

preserve [prɪ'zɜ:v] *vt* διαφυλάσσω || *(keep up)* συντηρώ ♦ *n* μέρος *nt* διατηρήσεως ζώων || *(jam)* γλυκό κουταλιού, μαρμελάδα.

preside [prɪ'zaɪd] *vi* προεδρεύω.

presidency ['prezɪdənsɪ] *n* προεδρία.

president ['prezɪdənt] *n* πρόεδρος || *(of university)* πρύτανης || *(of a country)* πρόεδρος || ~**ial** *a* προεδρικός.

press [pres] *n (machine)* πιεστήριο, πρέσσα || *(printing house)* (τυπογραφικό) πιεστήριο, τυπογραφείο || *(newspapers)* τύπος, εφημερίδες *fpl* || *(journalists)* τύπος, δημοσιογράφοι *mpl* ♦ *vt* πιέζω, συνθλίβω || *(urge)* πιέζω, επιμένω || *(clothes)* σιδερώνω ♦ *vi* πιέζομαι, σφίγγομαι || **to be** ~**ed for** δεν έχω αρκετά, πιέζομαι για || **to** ~ **for** αξιώνω, επιμένω σε, ασκώ πίεση για || **to** ~ **on** *vi* σπεύδω, επισπεύδω, συνεχίζω || ~ **agency** *n* πρακτορείο ειδήσεων || ~ **conference** *n* δημοσιογραφική συνέντευξη || ~ **cutting** απόκομμα *nt* εφημερίδας || ~**ing** *a (urgent)* επείγων || *(persistent)* επίμονος, πιεστικός || ~ **stud** *n* κουμπί με πίεση.

pressure ['preʃə*] *n* πίεση || ~ **cooker** *n* χύτρα ταχύτητας, κατσαρόλα ταχύτητας || ~ **gauge** *n* θλιβόμετρο, πιεζόμετρο, μανόμετρο || ~ **group** *n* ομάδα με ισχυρή επιρροή.

pressurized ['preʃəraɪzd] *a* πιεζόμενος, υπό πίεσι.

prestige [pres'ti:ʒ] *n* γόητρο.

presumably [prɪ'zju:məblɪ] *ad* κατά το φαινόμενο, πιθανώς.

presume [prɪ'zju:m] *vti* υποθέτω, προϋποθέτω || *(venture)* τολμώ, παίρνω το θάρρος.

presumption [prɪ'zʌmpʃən] *n* υπόθεση, παραδοχή || *(impudence)* αναίδεια.

presuppose [pri:sə'pəʊz] *vt* προϋποθέτω.

pretence [prɪ'tens] *n* προσποίηση || *(false excuse)* πρόσχημα *nt*, πρόφαση.

pretend [prɪ'tend] *vt (feign)* προσποιούμαι, υποκρίνομαι ♦ *vi* προσποιούμαι.

pretense [prɪ'tens] *n (US)* = **pretence**.

pretension [prɪ'tenʃən] *n (claim to merit)* αξίωση, απαίτηση.

pretentious [prɪ'tenʃəs] *a* απαιτητικός, επιδεικτικός.

pretext ['pri:tekst] *n* πρόφαση, πρόσχημα *nt*.

pretty ['prɪtɪ] *a* χαριτωμένος, ωραίος.

prevail [prɪ'veɪl] *vi* επικρατώ, υπερισχύω || *(succeed)* επιβάλλω, πείθω || ~**ing** *a (current)* επικρατών, ισχύων.

prevalent ['prevələnt] *a* διαδεδομένος, επικρατών.

prevent [prɪ'vent] *vt* αποτρέπω, προλαμβάνω || *(hinder)* εμποδίζω, (παρα)κωλύω || ~**able** *a* αποφεύξιμος || ~**ative** *n* προληπτικό (φάρμακο) ||

~ion n πρόληψη, εμπόδιση || ~ive a προληπτικός, προφυλακτικός.

preview ['pri:vju:] n προκαταρκτική προβολή, δοκιμαστική προβολή.

previous ['pri:viəs] a προηγούμενος || ~ly ad προηγουμένως, πρωτύτερα.

prewar ['pri:'wɔ:*] a προπολεμικός.

prey [prei] n λεία, βορά, θύμα nt || to ~ on vt (chase) κυνηγώ || (eat) τρώγω || (mind) βασανίζω.

price [prais] n τιμή, τίμημα nt || (value) αξία ♦ vt διατιμώ, καθορίζω τιμή || ~less a ανεκτίμητος.

prick [prik] n τσίμπημα nt ♦ vt τσιμπώ, κεντρώ, τρυπώ.

prickle ['prikl] n αγκάθι.

prickly ['prikli] a (lit) αγκαθωτός, τσουχτερός || (fig: person) δύσκολος.

pride [praid] n (self-respect) φιλότιμο || (something to be proud of) υπερηφάνεια, καμάρι || (conceit) αλαζονεία, υπεροψία || to ~ o.s. on sth υπερηφανεύομαι, καμαρώνω για κάτι.

priest [pri:st] n ιερέας, παπάς || ~ess n ιέρεια || ~hood n ιερωσύνη, ιερείς mpl.

prig [prig] n φαντασμένος, ξιπασμένος.

prim [prim] a ακριβής, τυπικός, μαζεμένος.

primarily ['praimərili] ad πρωτίστως, κυρίως || (at first) αρχικά, πρώτα-πρώτα.

primary ['praiməri] a πρώτος, αρχικός || (basic) βασικός || (first in importance) πρωτεύων, κύριος, ουσιώδης || (education) στοιχειώδης || (election) προκριματική εκλογή || ~ colours npl πρωτεύοντα χρώματα ntpl || ~ school n δημοτικό σχολείο.

primate ['praimit] n αρχιεπίσκοπος, πριμάτος || ['praimeit] (ZOOL) πρωτεύον θηλαστικό.

prime [praim] a πρώτος, πρώτιστος, κύριος || (excellent) εξαίρετος, πρώτης ποιότητας ♦ vt κατηχώ, δασκαλεύω || (gun, pump) γεμίζω || ~ minister n πρωθυπουργός m/f || ~r n αλφαβητάριο, πρώτον βιβλίο.

primeval [prai'mi:vəl] a πρωτόγονος, αρχέγονος.

primitive ['primitiv] a πρωτόγονος.

primrose ['primrəuz] n πράνθεμο, δακράκι, πασχαλούδα.

primula ['primjulə] n πριμούλη.

primus (stove) ['praiməs(stəuv)] n (R) γκαζιέρα.

prince [prins] n (of royal family) πρίγκηπας, βασιλόπουλο || ~ss n πριγκήπισσα.

principal ['prinsipəl] a κύριος, κυριότερος ♦ n (capital) κεφάλαιο || (of school) προϊστάμενος/n m/f, διευθυντής/ύντρια m/f || ~ly ad κυρίως, προπαντός, κατά το πλείστον.

principle ['prinsipl] n αρχή.

print [print] n σφραγίδα, τύπος || (fingerprint) αποτύπωμα nt || (PHOT) αντίτυπο, κόπια || (picture) εικόνα || (pattern) εμπριμέ nt inv ♦ vt τυπώνω,

εκτυπώνω || to ~ out (text) τυπώνω || ~ed matter n έντυπα ntpl || ~er n τυπογράφος || ~ing n (εκ)τύπωση, τυπογραφία || ~ing press n πιεστήριο (τυπογραφείου).

prior ['praiə*] a προγενέστερος, προηγούμενος ♦ n (ECCL) ηγούμενος.

priority [prai'ɒriti] n προτεραιότητα.

priory ['praiəri] n μοναστήρι, κοινόβιο.

prise [praiz] vt: to ~ open ανοίγω με μοχλό.

prism ['prizəm] n πρίσμα nt.

prison ['prizn] n φυλακή || ~er n φυλακισμένος/n m/f, υπόδικος/n m/f, κατάδικος m/f || (of war) αιχμάλωτος/n m/f.

pristine ['pristain] a πρωτόγονος, αρχικός.

privacy ['privəsi] n μοναξιά || (secrecy) μυστικότητα.

private ['praivit] a ιδιωτικός, ιδιαίτερος || (secret) μυστικός ♦ n (MIL) φαντάρος || '~' (sign) 'ιδιωτικό', 'ιδιαίτερον' || in ~ ιδιαιτέρως, μυστικά || ~ eye n ιδιωτικός αστυνομικός || ~ly ad ιδιωτικά || (in confidence) εμπιστευτικά.

privet ['privit] n λιγούστρο, αγριομυρτιά.

privilege ['privilidʒ] n προνόμιο || ~d a προνομιούχος.

privy ['privi] a: ~ council ανακτοβούλιο.

prize [praiz] n βραβείο, έπαθλο ♦ a (example) λαμπρό υπόδειγμα || (idiot) υπόδειγμα ηλιθίου ♦ vt εκτιμώ, τιμώ || ~fight n πυγμαχικός αγώνας || ~giving n βράβευση || ~winner n βραβευμένος/n m/f.

pro- [prəu] prefix (in favour) υπέρ-, αντί- || the pros and cons τα υπέρ και τα κατά.

pro [prəu] n (professional) επαγγελματίας.

probability [prɒbə'biliti] n πιθανότητα.

probable ['prɒbəbl] a ενδεχόμενος, πιθανός.

probably ['prɒbəbli] ad πιθανώς, πιθανόν.

probation [prə'beiʃən] n δοκιμασία || (in court etc) αστυνομική επιτήρηση || on ~ υπό δοκιμασία || ~er n δόκιμος.

probe [prəub] n (MED) καθετήρας, μήλη || (enquiry) εξερεύνηση, διερεύνηση ♦ vti (εξ)ερευνώ, διερευνώ.

probity ['prəubiti] n τιμιότητα, ακεραιότητα.

problem ['prɒbləm] n πρόβλημα nt || ~atic a προβληματικός.

procedure [prə'si:dʒə*] n διαδικασία, μέθοδος f.

proceed [prə'si:d] vi προχωρώ, συνεχίζω || (begin) προβαίνω || ~ings npl συζητήσεις fpl, πρακτικά ntpl || (LAW) δικαστική ενέργεια, δίκη || ~s ['prəusi:dz] npl εισπράξεις fpl.

process ['prəuses] n πορεία, εξέλιξη || (method) μέθοδος f, τρόπος ♦ vt επεξεργάζω, κατεργάζω.

procession [prə'seʃən] n πομπή,

παρέλαση || *(orderly progress)* παράταξη, σειρά, συνοδεία.

proclaim [prə'kleɪm] *vt* κηρύσσω, ανακηρύσσω, αναγορεύω || *(show)* φανερώνω, δείχνω.

procure [prə'kjuə*] *vt* προμηθεύω, προμηθεύομαι.

prod [prɒd] *vt* σκαλίζω, κεντρίζω, εξάπτω ♦ *n (push, jab)* μπήξιμο, κέντρισμα *nt*.

prodigal ['prɒdɪgəl] *a* άσωτος.

prodigious [prə'dɪdʒəs] *a* τεράστιος, καταπληκτικός.

prodigy ['prɒdɪdʒɪ] *n* φαινόμενο, θαύμα *nt*.

produce ['prɒdjuːs] *n (AGR)* προϊόν, καρπός ♦ [prə'djuːs] *vt (show)* παρουσιάζω, δείχνω || *(make)* παράγω, γεννώ, προξενώ || *(play)* ανεβάζω, παρουσιάζω || ~**r** *n* παραγωγός || *(THEAT)* σκηνοθέτης, παραγωγός.

product ['prɒdʌkt] *n* προϊόν || *(result)* αποτέλεσμα *nt*.

production [prə'dʌkʃən] *n* παραγωγή, κατασκευή || *(THEAT)* σκηνοθέτηση, παράσταση, ανέβασμα *nt* || ~ **line** *n* γραμμή παραγωγής.

productive [prə'dʌktɪv] *a* παραγωγικός || *(fertile)* γόνιμος.

productivity [prɒdʌk'tɪvɪtɪ] *n* παραγωγικότητα || *(fertility)* γονιμότητα.

profane [prə'feɪn] *a* βέβηλος || *(language)* βλάσφημος.

profess [prə'fes] *vt* διακηρύττω || *(confess)* ομολογώ || *(claim)* προσποιούμαι.

profession [prə'feʃən] *n* επάγγελμα *nt* || *(declaration)* ομολογία, διακήρυξη || ~**al** *n* επαγγελματίας ♦ *a* επαγγελματικός || ~**alism** *n* επαγγελματισμός.

professor [prə'fesə*] *n* καθηγητής/ήτρια *m/f*.

proficient [prə'fɪʃənt] *a* ικανός, ειδικός.

profile ['prəʊfaɪl] *n (of face)* κατατομή, προφίλ *nt inv* || *(fig report)* σύντομη βιογραφία.

profit ['prɒfɪt] *n* κέρδος *nt*, όφελος *nt*, ωφέλεια ♦ *vi (+ by, from)* ωφελούμαι (από) επωφελούμαι || ~**able** *a* επικερδής, επωφελής || ~**ably** *ad* επωφελώς, επικερδώς, ωφέλιμα.

profiteering [prɒfɪ'tɪərɪŋ] *n* κερδοσκοπία.

profound [prə'faʊnd] *a* βαθύς || *(mysterious)* μυστηριώδης.

profuse [prə'fjuːs] *a* άφθονος, γενναιόδωρος.

programing ['prəʊgræmɪŋ] *n* = **programming.**

programme, program *(US, COMPUT)* ['prəʊgræm] *n* πρόγραμμα *nt*.

programmer ['prəʊgræmə*] *n* προγραμματιστής *m/f*.

programming ['prəʊgræmɪŋ] *n* προγραμματισμός || ~ **language** *n* γλώσσα προγραμματισμού.

progress ['prəʊgres] *n* πρόοδος *f*,

εξέλιξη ♦ [prə'gres] *vi* προοδεύω, προχωρώ, εξελίσσομαι || **to make** ~ σημειώνω πρόοδο, προκόβω || ~**ion** *n* πρόοδος *f* || ~**ive** *a* προοδευτικός.

prohibit [prə'hɪbɪt] *vt* απαγορεύω || ~**ion** *n* απαγόρευση || *(US: of alcohol)* ποταπαγόρευση || ~**ive** *a (price etc)* απαγορευτικός, απλησίαστος.

project ['prɒdʒekt] *n (plan)* σχέδιο || *(study)* μελέτη ♦ [prə'dʒekt] *vt (throw)* εκτοξεύω, εξακοντίζω || *(extend)* προεκτείνω || *(film etc)* προβάλλω ♦ *vi* (προ)εξέχω, προβάλλω.

projectile [prə'dʒektaɪl] *n* βλήμα *nt*.

projection [prə'dʒekʃən] *n* προεξοχή, προβολή.

projector [prə'dʒektə*] *n (film)* προβολέας, μηχάνημα *nt* προβολής.

proletariat [prəʊlə'teərɪət] *n* προλεταριάτο.

proliferate [prə'lɪfəreɪt] *vi* πολλαπλασιάζομαι.

prolific [prə'lɪfɪk] *a* γόνιμος || *(plentiful)* άφθονος.

prologue ['prəʊlɒg] *n* πρόλογος.

prolong [prə'lɒŋ] *vt* παρατείνω || *(extend)* προεκτείνω.

prom [prɒm] *n abbr of* **promenade** || *abbr of* **promenade concert** || *(US: college ball)* συναυλία με λαϊκές τιμές.

promenade [prɒmɪ'naːd] *n* περίπατος || *(place)* τόπος περιπάτου || ~ **concert** *n* συναυλία || ~ **deck** *n (NAUT)* κατάστρωμα *nt* περιπάτου.

prominent ['prɒmɪnənt] *a* περίφημος, διακεκριμένος.

promiscuity [prɒmɪs'kjuːɪtɪ] *n* σμίξιμο, ανακάτεμα *nt*, ελεύθερες ερωτικές σχέσεις.

promise ['prɒmɪs] *n* υπόσχεση, τάξιμο || *(hope)* υπόσχεση ♦ *vti* υπόσχομαι, δίνω υποσχέσεις, προμηνύω.

promising ['prɒmɪsɪŋ] *a* γεμάτος υποσχέσεις, ενθαρρυντικός.

promote [prə'məʊt] *vt* προάγω, προβιβάζω || *(support)* υποστηρίζω || ~**r** *n* υποστηρικτής, υποκινητής || *(organiser)* διοργανωτής.

promotion [prə'məʊʃən] *n (of sales etc)* διαφήμιση, προαγωγή || *(in rank)* προαγωγή, προβιβασμός.

prompt [prɒmpt] *a* άμεσος, σύντομος, πρόθυμος, ταχύς ♦ *ad (punctually)* στην ώρα ♦ *vt (inaugurate)* || *(remind)* υποβάλλω || ~**er** *n (THEAT)* υποβολέας || ~**ness** *n* ταχύτητα, ετοιμότητα, προθυμία.

prone [prəʊn] *a* πεσμένος μπρούμυτα || *(inclined)* (+ *to*) επιρρεπής *(τιρος)*, αυτός που έχει τάση *(τιρος)*.

prong [prɒŋ] *n* δόντι πηρουνιού, πηρούνα, διχάλα.

pronoun ['prəʊnaʊn] *n* αντωνυμία.

pronounce [prə'naʊns] *vt (GRAM)* προφέρω || *(LAW)* εκδίδω, επιβάλλω, γνωματεύω || ~**d** *a (marked)* έντονος, ζωηρός.

pronto ['prɒntəʊ] ad (col) αμέσως, γρήγορα.

pronunciation [prənʌnsɪ'eɪʃən] n προφορά.

proof [pru:f] n απόδειξη, τεκμήριο || (test) δοκιμή, δοκιμασία || (copy) δοκίμιο ♦ a αδιαπέραστος, στεγανός || (resistant) ανθεκτικός.

prop [prɒp] n στήριγμα nt, έρεισμα nt, υποστήριγμα nt || (THEAT) βοηθητικά ntpl, αξεσουάρ nt inv ♦ vt (also: ~ up) (υπο)στηρίζω, στηλώνω.

propaganda [prɒpə'gændə] n προπαγάνδα.

propagation [prɒpə'geɪʃən] n (of plants) αναπαραγωγή, πολλαπλασιασμός || (of knowledge) διάδοση.

propel [prə'pɛl] vt προωθώ || ~ler n έλικας, προπέλα.

proper ['prɒpə*] a πρέπων, αρμόζων || ~ly ad καλά, καταλλήλως, σωστά || ~ noun n κύριο όνομα nt.

property ['prɒpətɪ] n ιδιοκτησία, περιουσία || (quality) ιδιότητα, χαρακτηριστικό || (THEAT) βοηθητικό, αξεσουάρ nt inv|| (land) κτήμα nt, ακίνητο || ~ owner n ιδιοκτήτης/ρια m/f.

prophecy ['prɒfɪsɪ] n (prediction) προφητεία.

prophesy ['prɒfɪsaɪ] vt προφητεύω, προλέγω.

prophet ['prɒfɪt] n προφήτης || ~ic a προφητικός.

proportion [prə'pɔ:ʃən] n σχέση, αναλογία || (share) μέρος, τμήμα nt ♦ vt ρυθμίζω, μοιράζω κατ' αναλογία || ~al a ανάλογος, συμμετρικός, αναλογικός || ~ate a ανάλογος.

proposal [prə'pəʊzl] n πρόταση, εισήγηση || (of marriage) πρόταση γάμου.

propose [prə'pəʊz] vt προτείνω, σκοπεύω ♦ vi (marriage) κάνω πρόταση γάμου.

proposition [prɒpə'zɪʃən] n πρόταση, σχέδιο, υπόθεση.

proprietary [prə'praɪətərɪ] a της ιδιοκτησίας, της κυριότητας.

proprietor [prə'praɪətə*] n ιδιοκτήτης/τρια m/f.

propulsion [prə'pʌlʃən] n (προ)ώθηση.

prorata [prəʊ'rɑ:tə] ad κατ' αναλογία.

prosaic [prəʊ'zeɪk] a (ordinary) πεζός.

prose [prəʊz] n πεζός λόγος, πεζογραφία, πρόζα.

prosecute ['prɒsɪkju:t] vt υποβάλλω μήνυση.

prosecution [prɒsɪ'kju:ʃən] n (ποινική) δίωξη || (people bringing action) κατηγορία, μηνυτής.

prosecutor ['prɒsɪkju:tə*] n εισαγγελέας.

prospect ['prɒspɛkt] n (expectation) προσδοκία || (hope) ελπίδα || ~ing n (for minerals) αναζήτηση (μεταλλευμάτων) || ~ive a πιθανός, μελλοντικός || ~or n μεταλλοδίφης || (for gold) χρυσοθήρας.

prospectus [prə'spɛktəs] n αγγελία, πρόγραμμα nt.

prosper ['prɒspə*] vi ευδοκιμώ, ακμάζω, ευημερώ || ~ity n ευημερία, ευδαιμονία || ~ous a ευημερών, ακμάζων || (successful) επιτυχής.

prostitute ['prɒstɪtju:t] n πόρνη, πουτάνα.

prostrate ['prɒstreɪt] a (lying flat) πρηνής, μπρούμυτος.

protagonist [prəʊ'tægənɪst] n πρωταγωνιστής/ίστρια m/f.

protect [prə'tɛkt] vt προστατεύω, προφυλάσσω, υπερασπίζω, καλύπτω || ~ion n προστασία, υπεράσπιση, άμυνα || (shelter) σκέπαστρο, προστατευτικό μέσο || ~ive a προστατευτικός || ~or n προστάτης, προφυλακτήρας.

protégé ['prɒtɛʒeɪ] n προστατευόμενος || ~e προστατευόμενη.

protein ['prəʊti:n] n πρωτεΐνη.

protest ['prəʊtɛst] n διαμαρτυρία ♦ [prə'tɛst] vi (+ against) διαμαρτύρομαι.

Protestant ['prɒtɪstənt] a, n Διαμαρτυρόμενος, Προτεστάντης.

protocol ['prəʊtəkɒl] n πρωτόκολλο.

prototype ['prəʊtəʊtaɪp] n πρωτότυπο.

protractor [prə'træktə*] n μοιρογνωμόνιο.

protrude [prə'tru:d] vi προεξέχω, βγαίνω έξω.

proud [praʊd] a περήφανος || (snobbish) φαντασμένος || (condescending) ακατάδεκτος.

prove [pru:v] vt (show) αποδεικνύω, επαληθεύω || (turn out) δείχνομαι.

proverb ['prɒvɜ:b] n παροιμία.

provide [prə'vaɪd] vt προμηθεύω, χορηγώ || ~d cj εφόσον, αρκεί να.

province ['prɒvɪns] n επαρχία || (fig) αρμοδιότητα.

provincial [prə'vɪnʃəl] a επαρχιακός.

provision [prə'vɪʒən] n (supply) προμήθεια || (condition) όρος || ~s npl (food) τρόφιμα ntpl || (equipment) εφόδια ntpl || ~al a προσωρινός.

provocation [prɒvə'keɪʃən] n πρόκληση.

provocative [prə'vɒkətɪv] a προκλητικός, ερεθιστικός.

provoke [prə'vəʊk] vt προκαλώ, διεγείρω, εξερεθίζω.

prow [praʊ] n πρώρα, πλώρη.

prowess ['praʊɪs] n γενναιότητα || (bravery) ανδρεία, παλικαριά.

prowl [praʊl] vt (streets) περιφέρομαι, τριγυρίζω ♦ n: on the ~ ψάχνω διαρκώς || ~er n νυχτοπάτης, τριγυριστής.

proximity [prɒk'sɪmɪtɪ] n εγγύτητα, αμεσότητα.

proxy ['prɒksɪ] n πληρεξούσιος, αντιπρόσωπος || by ~ δι' αντιπροσώπου.

prudent ['pru:dənt] a συνετός, φρόνιμος.

prudish ['pru:dɪʃ] a σεμνότυφος || ~ness n σεμνοτυφία.

prune [pru:n] n ξερό δαμάσκηνο ♦ vt κλαδεύω.

pry [praɪ] vi (+ into) ψάχνω, χώνω τη μύτη (σε).

psalm [sa:m] n ψαλμός.

pseudo- ['sju:dəʊ] prefix ψεύτικος, κίβδηλος || (in compds) ψευδο-.

pseudonym ['sju:dəʊnɪm] n ψευδώνυμο.

psyche ['saɪkɪ] n (soul, mind, intelligence) ψυχή.

psychiatric [saɪkɪ'ætrɪk] a ψυχιατρικός.

psychiatrist [saɪ'kaɪətrɪst] n ψυχίατρος m/f.

psychiatry [saɪ'kaɪətrɪ] n ψυχιατρική.

psychic(al) ['saɪkɪk(əl)] a ψυχικός.

psychoanalyst [saɪkəʊ'ænəlɪst] n ψυχαναλυτής/ύτρια m/f.

psychological [saɪkə'lɒdʒɪkəl] a ψυχολογικός || ~ly ad ψυχολογικά.

psychologist [saɪ'kɒlədʒɪst] n ψυχολόγος m/f.

psychology [saɪ'kɒlədʒɪ] n ψυχολογία.

psychopath ['saɪkəʊpæθ] n ψυχοπαθής m/f.

psychosomatic ['saɪkəʊsəʊ'mætɪk] a ψυχοσωματικός.

psychotherapy ['saɪkəʊ'θerəpɪ] n ψυχοθεραπεία.

psychotic [saɪ'kɒtɪk] a, n ψυχωτικός.

p.t.o. abbr of please turn over.

pub [pʌb] n (Brit) = public house || see public.

puberty ['pju:bətɪ] n ήβη, εφηβεία.

public ['pʌblɪk] a δημόσιος || (generally known) πασίγνωστος ♦ n (also: the general ~) το κοινό || ~ house n ταβέρνα.

publican ['pʌblɪkən] n (innkeeper) ταβερνιάρης, κάπελας.

publication [pʌblɪ'keɪʃən] n (something published) δημοσίευση, έκδοση || (making known) κοινοποίηση, δημοσίευση.

publicity [pʌb'lɪsɪtɪ] n δημοσιότητα || (advertising) διαφήμιση.

publicly ['pʌblɪklɪ] ad δημόσια, ολοφάνερα.

public: ~ **opinion** n κοινή γνώμη || ~ **relations** n δημόσιες σχέσεις fpl || ~ **school** n (Brit) ιδιωτικό σχολείο (Αγγλίας) || ~-**spirited** a ενδιαφερόμενος για το κοινό καλό.

publish ['pʌblɪʃ] vt εκδίδω, δημοσιεύω || (figures etc) αναγγέλω, δημοσιεύω || ~**er** n εκδότης/ρια m/f || ~**ing** n έκδοση, δημοσίευση.

pucker ['pʌkə*] vt ζαρώνω.

pudding ['pʊdɪŋ] n πουτίγκα.

puddle ['pʌdl] n (pool) λακκούβα, λιμνούλα.

puff [pʌf] n ξεφύσημα nt, φύσημα nt ♦ vt ξεφυσώ, βγάζω καπνό ♦ vi φυσώ, λαχανιάζω || ~**ed** a (col: out of breath) λαχανιασμένος.

puff pastry ['pʌf'peɪstrɪ] n, **puff paste** (US) ['pʌf'peɪst] n γλύκισμα με φύλλο.

puffy ['pʌfɪ] a φουσκωμένος, φουσκωτός.

pull [pʊl] n (tug) έλξη, τράβηγμα nt || (fig) επιρροή, μέσο ♦ vt (trolley) σύρω, έλκω, τραβώ, σέρνω || (hair) τραβώ || (trigger) πατώ, τραβώ ♦ vi (on rope etc) τραβώ, σύρω || '~' (sign) 'σύρατε' || to ~ **a face** κάνω μούτρα, μορφάζω || to ~ **to pieces** τραβώ και κομματιάζω, κάνω κομμάτια || to ~ **o.s. together** συνέρχομαι || to ~ **apart** vt (break) σχίζω στα δυο, αποχωρίζω || (dismantle) λύω || to ~ **down** vt (house) κατεδαφίζω, γκρεμίζω || to ~ **in** vi (RAIL) μπαίνω (στο σταθμό) || to ~ **off** vt (deal etc) επιτυγχάνω (κάτι) || to ~ **out** vi φεύγω, ξεκινώ, ανακωρώ || (vehicle) βγαίνω από τη λωρίδα ♦ vt αφαιρώ, βγάζω, τραβώ || to ~ **round** or **through** vi συνέρχομαι, γλυτώνω || (from illness) αναρρώνω || to ~ **up** vi σταματώ.

pulley ['pʊlɪ] n τροχαλία.

pullover ['pʊləʊvə*] n πουλόβερ nt inv.

pulp [pʌlp] n πολτός, σάρκωμα nt.

pulpit ['pʊlpɪt] n άμβωνας.

pulsate [pʌl'seɪt] vi πάλλομαι, πάλλω, σφύζω.

pulse [pʌls] n σφυγμός, παλμός || (vegetable) όσπρια ntpl.

pulverize ['pʌlvəraɪz] vt κάνω σκόνη, κονιοποιώ.

pummel ['pʌml] vt γρονθοκοπώ.

pump [pʌmp] n αντλία || (bicycle) τρόμπα ♦ vt αντλώ || to ~ **up** vt (tyre) φουσκώνω (λάστιχο).

pumpkin ['pʌmpkɪn] n κολοκύθα.

pun [pʌn] n λογοπαίγνιο.

punch [pʌntʃ] n τρυπητήρι, ζουμπάς || (blow) γροθιά || (drink) πόντς nt inv, πόντσι ♦ vt γρονθοκοπώ, δίνω μια γροθιά || (a hole) τρυπώ, ανοίγω.

punctual ['pʌŋktjʊəl] a ακριβής.

punctuate ['pʌŋktjʊeɪt] vt στίζω || (fig) τονίζω, υπογραμμίζω.

punctuation [pʌŋktjʊ'eɪʃən] n στίξη.

puncture ['pʌŋktʃə*] n (παρα)κέντηση || (tyre) σκάσιμο, τρύπημα σε λάστιχο ♦ vt παρακεντώ, τρυπώ, σπάζω.

pungent ['pʌndʒənt] a δριμύς, σουβλερός, οξύς.

punish ['pʌnɪʃ] vt τιμωρώ, δέρνω || (in boxing etc) δίνω άγριο ξύλο, μαστιγώνω || ~**able** a αξιόποινος, τιμωρητέος || ~**ment** n τιμωρία.

punitive ['pju:nɪtɪv] a τιμωρητικός || (MIL.) ~ **expedition** n εκστρατεία αντιποίνων.

punt [pʌnt] n πλοιάρι, ρηχή βάρκα.

punter ['pʌntə*] n (gambler) παίκτης.

puny ['pju:nɪ] a μικροκαμωμένος, αδύνατος, ασήμαντος.

pup [pʌp] n σκυλάκι, κουτάβι.

pupil ['pju:pɪl] n μαθητής/ήτρια m/f || (of eye) κόρη (οφθαλμού).

puppet ['pʌpɪt] n μαριονέτα || (person) ανδρείκελο.

puppy ['pʌpɪ] n σκυλάκι.

purchase ['pɜːtʃɪs] n ψώνισμα, ψώνιο || (buying) αγορά, ψώνισμα nt ♦ vt αγοράζω, ψωνίζω || ~r n αγοραστής.

pure [pjuə*] a καθαρός || (innocent) άδολος, αγνός || (unmixed) αμιγής, ανόθευτος.

purée ['pjuəreι] n πουρές m inv.

purge [pɜːdʒ] n κάθαρσιο || (POL) εκκαθάριση ♦ vt (εκ)καθαρίζω.

purify ['pjuərɪfaι] vt καθαρίζω, εξαγνίζω.

purist ['pjuərɪst] n: Greek language ~ καθαρευουσιάνος, καθαρολόγος.

puritan ['pjuərɪtən] n πουριτανός || ~ical a πουριτανικός.

purity ['pjuərɪtι] n καθαρότητα || (authenticity) γνησιότητα.

purl [pɜːl] n ανάποδη βελονιά ♦ vt πλέκω ανάποδες.

purple ['pɜːpl] (colour) a πορφυρός ♦ n πορφύρα, πορφυρό (χρώμα).

purpose ['pɜːpəs] n σκοπός, πρόθεση || on ~ σκόπιμα || ~ful a (προ)εσκεμμένος, σκόπιμος || ~ly ad επίτηδες, σκόπιμα.

purr [pɜː*] vi (of cat) ρουθουνίζω, κάνω ρουρό ♦ n γουργούρισμα.

purse [pɜːs] n πορτοφόλι ♦ vt ζαρώνω.

purser ['pɜːsə*] n λογιστής (πλοίου).

pursue [pə'sjuː] vt (κατα)διώκω, κυνηγώ || (carry on) συνεχίζω, ακολουθώ || ~r n διώκτης.

pursuit [pə'sjuːt] n (κατα)δίωξη, κυνήγημα nt || (occupation) επιδίωξη, επάγγελμα nt.

purveyor [pɜː'veιə*] n προμηθευτής (τροφίμων).

pus [pʌs] n πύο.

push [pʊʃ] n ώθηση, σκούντημα nt, σπρωξιά || (MIL) προώθηση ♦ vt σπρώχνω, σκουντώ || (forward) προχωρώ, προοδεύω || vi σπρώχνω, ωθώ, ασκώ πίεση || (make one's way) προχωρώ (με δυσκολία) || ~' (sign) 'ωθήσετε' || at a ~ (if necessary) στην ανάγκη || to ~ aside vt απωθώ, παραμερίζω || to ~ off vi (col) φεύγω, ξεκινώ || to ~ on vi (continue) προχωρώ, συνεχίζω, επισπεύδω || to ~ through vt (measure) περνώ (νομοσχέδιο κτλ) || ~ chair n καροτσάκι, παιδικό αμαξάκι || ~ing a δραστήριος, επίμονος || ~over n (col) εύκολο πράμα nt, εύκολη κατάκτηση.

puss [pʊs] n (also: pussy cat) γατάκι, ψιψίνα.

put [pʊt] (irreg v) vt θέτω, τοποθετώ, βάζω || (express) εκφράζω, εξηγώ, υποβάλλω || to ~ about vi στρέφομαι, αναστρέφω ♦ vt διαδίδω, θέτω σε κυκλοφορία || to ~ across vt (succeed) επιτυγχάνω, βγάζω πέρα || (meaning) δίνω να καταλάβει || to ~ away vt (store) βάζω κατά μέρος, φυλάω || to ~ back vt (replace) βάζω πίσω || (postpone) αναβάλλω || to ~ by vt (money) αποταμιεύω || to ~ down vt (lit) κατεβάζω || (in writing) γράφω, σημειώνω || to ~ forward vt (idea) αναπτύσσω,

εισηγούμαι, προτείνω || (date) αναβάλλω || to ~ off vt (postpone) αναβάλλω || (discourage) μεταπείθω, εμποδίζω, αποθαρρύνω || to ~ on vt (clothes etc) φορώ || (light etc) ανάβω || (play etc) ανεβάζω || (brake) φρενάρω || (false air) προσποιούμαι || to ~ out vt (hand etc) εκτείνω, απλώνω || (news, rumour) διαδίδω || (light etc) σβήνω || (person: inconvenience) στενοχωρώ, ενοχλώ || to ~ up vt (raise) σηκώνω, υψώνω || (guest) φιλοξενώ || to ~ up with vt ανέχομαι.

putrid ['pjuːtrɪd] a σαπρός, σάπιος.

putt [pʌt] vt σέρνω (τη μπάλα) ♦ n συρτό χτύπημα nt, πάτιγκ nt inv.

putty ['pʌtι] n στόκος.

put-up ['pʊtʌp] a: ~ job δουλειά σκαρωμένη, στημένη μηχανή.

puzzle ['pʌzl] n αίνιγμα nt, δύσκολο πρόβλημα nt, μπέρδεμα nt || (toy) παιχνίδι συναρμολογήσεως, γρίφος ♦ vt (perplex) περιπλέκω, συγχίζω ♦ vi σπάζω το κεφάλι μου.

puzzling ['pʌzlιŋ] a πολύπλοκος, δύσκολος, μπλεγμένος.

pygmy ['pιgmι] n πυγμαίος.

pyjamas [pι'dʒɑːməz] npl πυζάμες fpl.

pylon ['paιlən] n στύλος.

pyramid ['pιrəmιd] n πυραμίδα.

python ['paιθən] n πύθωνας.

Q

quack [kwæk] n κραυγή πάπιας || (dishonest person) κομπογιαννίτης.

quad [kwɒd] n abbr of **quadrangle, quadruple, quadruplet.**

quadrangle ['kwɒdræŋgl] n (court) τετράγωνη αυλή.

quadruped ['kwɒdruped] n τετράποδο.

quadruple ['kwɒdrʊpl] a τετραπλός, τετραπλάσιος, τετράπλετος ♦ [kwɒ'druːpl] vti τετραπλασιάζω, τετραπλασιάζομαι.

quadruplet [kwɒ'druːplιt] n τετράδυμο.

quaint [kweιnt] a παράξενος, αλλόκοτος.

quake [kweιk] vi τρέμω, σείομαι || Q~r n Κουάκερος.

qualification [kwɒlιfι'keιʃən] n ικανότητα, προσόν nt || (reservation) επιφύλαξη, όρος, περιορισμός.

qualified ['kwɒlιfaιd] a έχων τα προσόντα, κατάλληλος || (reserved) επιφυλακτικός, περιωρισμένος, μετριασμένος.

qualify ['kwɒlιfaι] vt καθιστώ κατάλληλο, αποκτώ τα προσόντα || (limit) τροποποιώ, προσδιορίζω ♦ vi (acquire degree) λαμβάνω δίπλωμα.

quality ['kwɒlιtι] n (kind) ποιότητα || (of person) ιδιότητα, χαρακτηριστικό, ικανότητα ♦ a καλής ποιότητας.

qualm [kwɑːm] n (misgiving) τύψη, ενδοιασμός.

quandary ['kwɒndərɪ] n αμηχανία, δίλημμα nt.

quantity ['kwɒntɪtɪ] n ποσότητα || (large amount) μεγάλη ποσότητα, πολύ, με το σωρό.

quarantine ['kwɒrəntiːn] n καραντίνα.

quarrel ['kwɒrəl] n (argument) φιλονεικία, διένεξη, καυγάς, τσακωμός ♦ vi (argue) φιλονεικώ, τσακώνομαι || ~some a ευέξαπτος, καυγατζής.

quarry ['kwɒrɪ] n (of stone) λατομείο || (animal) θήραμα nt, κυνήγι.

quart [kwɔːt] n τέταρτο του γαλονιού.

quarter ['kwɔːtə*] n τέταρτο || (of year) τριμηνία ♦ vt κόβω στα τέσσερα || (MIL) στρατωνίζω || ~s npl (esp MIL) κατάλυμα nt, στρατώνας || (accommodation) στέγαση || ~ of an hour ένα τέταρτο (της ώρας) || ~ past three τρεις και τέταρτο || ~ to three τρεις παρά τέταρτο || ~-deck n πρυμναίο κατάστρωμα nt, κάσαρο || ~ly a τριμηνιαίος || ~master n (NAUT) υποναύκληρος || (MIL) επιμελητής.

quartet(te) [kwɔː'tet] n τετραφωνία, κουαρτέτο.

quartz [kwɔːts] n χαλαζίας.

quash [kwɒʃ] vt (verdict) αναιρώ, ακυρώνω.

quasi ['kwɑːzɪ] a σαν, σχεδόν, τρόπον τινά.

quaver ['kweɪvə*] n (MUS) όγδοο ♦ vi τρέμω, κάνω τρίλιες.

quay [kiː] n αποβάθρα, προκυμαία.

queasy ['kwiːzɪ] a ευαίσθητος, απδιαστικός.

queen [kwiːn] n βασίλισσα || (CARDS) ντάμα || ~ mother n βασιλομήτωρ f.

queer [kwɪə*] a αλλόκοτος, παράξενος ♦ n (col: homosexual) 'τοιούτος'.

quell [kwel] vt καταπνίγω, καταβάλλω, κατευνάζω.

quench [kwentʃ] vt κόβω (τη δίψα μου), κατευνάζω || (fire etc) σβήνω.

query ['kwɪərɪ] n ερώτηση, ερώτημα nt ♦ vt ερωτώ, ερευνώ.

quest [kwest] n αναζήτηση, έρευνα.

question ['kwestʃən] n ερώτηση, ερώτημα nt || (problem) ζήτημα nt, θέμα nt || (doubt) αμφιβολία, αμφισβήτηση ♦ vt ρωτώ, εξετάζω || (doubt) αμφισβητώ || beyond ~ αναμφισβήτητα || out of the ~ εκτός συζητήσεως, απαράδεκτος || ~able a αμφίβολος, αμφισβητήσιμος || ~er n εξεταστής, ανακριτής || ~ing a ερώτηση, ανάκριση || ~ mark n ερωτηματικό.

questionnaire [kwestʃə'nɛə*] n ερωτηματολόγιο.

queue [kjuː] n (line) ουρά ♦ vi μπαίνω στην ουρά, σχηματίζω ουρά.

quibble ['kwɪbl] n (petty objection) υπεκφυγή.

quick [kwɪk] a (fast) ταχύς, γρήγορος, γοργός || (impatient) βιαστικός, ευέξαπτος || (keen) ζωηρός, ζωντανός, έξυπνος ♦ ad γρήγορα ♦ n (ANAT) ευαίσθητο σημείο, σάρκα, κρέας nt || (old:

the living) οι ζωντανοί || ~en vt (hasten) επιταχύνω || (rouse) (ανα)ζωογονώ, ζωντανεύω ♦ vi (ξανα)ζωντανεύω, αναζωπυρούμαι || ~ly ad γρήγορα || ~sand n κινητή άμμος f || ~step n (MUSIC) ταχύς ρυθμός || ~-witted a ξύπνιος, ατσίδα.

quid [kwɪd] n (Brit col: £1) λίρα (Αγγλίας).

quiet ['kwaɪət] a (without noise) σιωπηλός, ήσυχος, αθόρυβος || (still) ήρεμος, γαλήνιος, ήσυχος || (peaceful) ήρεμος, ατάραχος ♦ n ησυχία, ηρεμία || ~en vti (also: ~en down) (καθ)ησυχάζω, καλμάρω || ~ly ad ήρεμα, απαλά, σιγαλά, σιωπηλά || ~ness n ηρεμία, γαλήνη, κάλμα.

quill [kwɪl] n (pen) πένα από φτερό.

quilt [kwɪlt] n πάπλωμα nt, εφάπλωμα nt.

quin [kwɪn] n abbr of **quintuplet.**

quince [kwɪns] n κυδώνι.

quinine [kwɪ'niːn] n κινίνη.

quintet(te) [kwɪn'tet] n κουιντέτο.

quintuplet [kwɪn'tjuːplɪt] n πεντάδυμο.

quip [kwɪp] n ευφυολόγημα nt, πείραγμα nt, σαρκασμός ♦ vi ευφυολογώ.

quit [kwɪt] (irreg v) vt εγκαταλείπω, φεύγω ♦ vi (give up) παραιτούμαι, εγκαταλείπω.

quite [kwaɪt] ad τελείως, εντελώς || (fairly) μάλλον, πολύ || ~ (so)! σωστά!, σύμφωνοι!

quits [kwɪts] ad στα ίσια, πάτσι.

quiver ['kwɪvə*] vi τρέμω, τρεμουλιάζω ♦ n (for arrows) φαρέτρα, σαϊτοθήκη.

quiz [kwɪz] n στροβοκοίταγμα nt || (test) προφορική εξέταση ♦ vt (question) εξετάζω || ~zical a αινιγματώδης, ερωτηματικός.

quorum ['kwɔːrəm] n απαρτία.

quota ['kwəʊtə] n ανάλογο μερίδιο, μερίδα.

quotation [kwəʊ'teɪʃən] n (from book) απόσπασμα nt || (price) προσφορά || ~ marks npl εισαγωγικά ntpl.

quote [kwəʊt] n (quotation) απόσπασμα nt ♦ vti (price) καθορίζω, δίνω τιμή || (cite) παραθέτω, αναφέρω.

quotient ['kwəʊʃənt] n πηλίκο nt.

Q

R

R

rabbi ['ræbaɪ] n ραββίνος.

rabbit ['ræbɪt] n κουνέλι || ~ hutch n κλουβί κουνελιού.

rabble ['ræbl] n όχλος.

rabid ['ræbɪd] a (fig) μανιασμένος, αδιάλακτος.

rabies ['reɪbiːz] n λύσσα.

R.A.C. abbr of Royal Automobile Club.

race [reɪs] n (people) ράτσα, φυλή || (generation) γενιά || (animals) ράτσα || (competition) αγώνας δρόμου || (rush) βία, γρηγοράδα ♦ vt κάνω αγώνα δρόμου ♦ vi τρέχω || (compete) συναγωνίζομαι || ~course n (for horses) ιππόδρομος || ~horse n άλογο ιπποδρομιών || ~

meeting n (for horses) ιπποδρομία || ~
relations npl φυλετικές σχέσεις fpl || ~
~track n (for cars etc) πίστα (αγώνων).

racial ['reιʃəl] a φυλετικός || ~ism n
φυλετισμός, ρα(τ)σισμός || ~ist a
ρα(τ)σιστικός.

racing ['reιsιŋ] n αγώνες mpl, συμμετοχή
σε αγώνες || ~ car n αυτοκίνητο
αγώνων || ~ driver n οδηγός
αυτοκινήτου αγώνων.

racist ['reιsιst] a ρατσιστής.

rack [ræk] n (clothes etc) κρεμάστρα ♦ vt
βασανίζω || ~ and ruin καταστροφή,
κατά διαβόλου.

racket ['rækιt] n θόρυβος, φασαρία ||
(dishonest scheme) κομπίνα || (for tennis)
ρακέτα.

racquet ['rækιt] n ρακέτα.

racy ['reιsι] a (spirited) ζωηρός, κεφάτος.

radar ['reιda:*] n ραντάρ nt inv.

radiant ['reιdιənt] a λαμπερός || (giving
out rays) ακτινοβόλος.

radiate ['reιdιeιt] vt (of heat)
ακτινοβολώ, εκπέμπω ♦ vi (lines) εκτείνω
ακτινοειδώς.

radiation [reιdι'eιʃən] n ακτινοβολία.

radiator ['reιdιeιtə*] n σώμα nt
καλοριφέρ || (AUT) ψυγείο.

radical ['rædιkəl] a ριζικός || (POL)
ριζοσπαστικός.

radio ['reιdιəυ] n ραδιόφωνο.

radio... ['reιdιəυ] prefix: ~active a
ραδιενεργός || ~activity n ραδιενέργεια
|| ~grapher n ακτινογράφος ||
~telephone n ασύρματο τηλέφωνο ||
~ telescope n ραδιοτηλεσκόπιο ||
~therapist n ακτινολόγος ιατρός.

radish ['rædιʃ] n ρεπανάκι.

radium ['reιdιəm] n ράδιο.

radius ['reιdιəs] n ακτίνα.

raffia ['ræfιə] n ραφία.

raffle ['ræfl] n λαχείο, λοταρία.

raft [ra:ft] n σχεδία.

rafter ['ra:ftə*] n δοκάρι, καδρόνι.

rag [ræg] n (of cloth) ράκος nt, κουρέλι ||
(col: newspaper) εφημερίδα ♦ vt κάνω
φάρσα, κάνω καζούρα || ~bag n (fig)
κακοντυμένη γυναίκα.

rage [reιdʒ] n (fury) λύσσα, μανία ||
(fashion) μανία της μόδας ♦ vi (person)
μαίνομαι, είμαι έξω φρενών || (storm)
μαίνομαι, είμαι αγριεμένος.

ragged ['rægιd] a (edge) τραχύς,
απότομος.

raging ['reιdʒιŋ] a μαινόμενος,
αγριεμένος.

raid [reιd] n (MIL) επιδρομή || (invasion)
εισβολή || (criminal) επιδρομή, γιουρούσι
|| (by police) επιδρομή, μπλόκος ♦ vt
εισβάλλω σε, κάνω μπλόκο || ~er n
επιδρομέας.

rail [reιl] n (on stair) κάγκελο, κιγκλίδωμα
nt || (of ship) κουπαστή, || (RAIL)
σιδηροτροχιά, γραμμή || ~s npl (RAIL)
τροχιά, γραμμές fpl || by ~
σιδηροδρομικώς, με τραίνο || ~ings npl
κάγκελα ntpl, φράκτης || ~road n (US),

~way n (Brit) σιδηρόδρομος,
σιδηροδρομική γραμμή || ~road or
~way station n σιδηροδρομικός
σταθμός.

rain [reιn] n βροχή ♦ vti βρέχω || ~bow
n ουράνιο τόξο || ~coat n αδιάβροχο ||
~drop n σταγόνα βροχής || ~storm n
καταιγίδα (flood) κατακλυσμός || ~y a
(region) βροχερός || (day) βροχερή (μέρα)
|| (fig) ώρα ανάγκης || (season) εποχή των
βροχών.

raise [reιz] n (esp US: increase) αύξηση
(μισθού) ♦ vt (build) κτίζω, στήνω || (lift)
σηκώνω, υψώνω, ανεβάζω || (a question)
προβάλλω, θέτω || (doubts) προκαλώ,
γεννώ || (collect) μαζεύω, συλλέγω || (bring
up) ανατρέφω, τρέφω.

raisin ['reιzən] n σταφίδα.

rake [reιk] n τσουγκράνα || (dissolute
person) έκλυτος, ακόλαστος ♦ vt (AGR)
μαζεύω με τσουγκράνα, σκαλίζω || (with
shots) γαζώνω || (search keenly) εξετάζω,
ερευνώ || to ~ in or together etc vt
μαζεύω.

rally ['rælι] n (POL etc) συγκέντρωση,
συναγερμός || (AUT) ράλλυ nt inv ||
(improvement) ανάκτηση, βελτίωση ♦ vt
συναθροίζω, συγκεντρώνω ♦ vi (health)
συνέρχομαι, αναρρώνω || to ~ round
vti συσπειρώνομαι.

ram [ræm] n κριάρι || (beam) έμβολο,
κριός ♦ vt εμβολίζω, μπήγω || (strike)
κτυπώ || (stuff) παραγεμίζω, χώνω.

ramble ['ræmbl] n περίπατος,
περιπλάνηση ♦ vi κάνω βόλτες,
περιφέρομαι || (be delirious) μιλώ
ασυνάρτητα.

rambling ['ræmblιŋ] a (plant)
αναρριχητικός || (speech) ασύνδετος,
ασυνάρτητος.

ramification [ræmιfι'keιʃən] n
διακλάδωση.

ramp [ræmp] n (incline) κεκλιμένο
επίπεδο, ανωφέρεια.

rampage [ræm'peιdʒ] n: to be on the
~ vi (also: ~) συμπεριφέρομαι βίαια.

rampant ['ræmpənt] a (unchecked)
αχαλίνωτος, ξαπλωμένος || (on hind legs)
όρθιος.

rampart ['ræmpa:t] n έπαλξη,
προμαχώνας, ντάπια.

ramshackle ['ræmʃækl] a
ετοιμόρροπος, ερειπωμένος, ρημάδι.

ran [ræn] pt of run.

ranch [ra:ntʃ] n αγρόκτημα nt, ράντσο.

rancid ['rænsιd] a ταγγός, τσαγγός.

rancour, rancor (US) ['ræŋkə*] n
μνησικακία, έχθρα.

random ['rændəm] a τυχαίος ♦ n: at ~
στην τύχη, στα κουτουρού.

randy ['rændι] a (col) ασελγής, λάγνος.

rang [ræŋ] pt of ring.

range [reιndʒ] n (in row, line) σειρά,
οροσειρά || (extent, series) έκταση, σειχά,
περιοχή || (of gun) βεληνεκές nt, εμβέλεια
|| (for shooting) πεδίο βολής, σκοπευτήριο
|| (cooking stove) κουζίνα, μαγειρική

συσκευή ♦ vt παρατάσσω, βάζω στη σειρά || (roam) περιπλανώμαι, περιφέρομαι ♦ vi (extend) εκτείνομαι, απλώνομαι || ~r n (of forest) δασάρχης, δασονόμος.

rank [ræŋk] n (row, line) στοίχος, γραμμή || (social position) (κοινωνική) τάξη || (high position) ανώτερη θέση, βαθμός ♦ vi (of place) κατατάσσομαι, έρχομαι ♦ a (bad smelling) δύσοσμος, τσαγγός || (extreme) πλήρης, τέλειος, απόλυτος || the ~s npl (MIL) οι στρατιώτες, φαντάροι mpl || the ~ and file (fig) ο απλός λαός.

ransack ['rænsæk] vt λεηλατώ, κάνω άνω-κάτω, ψάχνω καλά.

ransom ['rænsəm] n λύτρα ntpl || to hold to ~ ζητώ λύτρα.

rant [rænt] vi κομπάζω || ~ing n στόμφος.

rap [ræp] n κτύπημα nt, κτύπος, κρότος ♦ vt κρούω, κτυπώ.

rape [reɪp] n βιασμός ♦ vt βιάζω.

rapid ['ræpɪd] a ταχύς, γρήγορος || ~s npl μικρός καταρράκτης || ~ly ad γρήγορα, γοργά.

rapist ['reɪpɪst] n βιαστής.

rapture ['ræptʃə*] n έκσταση, μεγάλη χαρά.

rapturous ['ræptʃərəs] a εκστατικός, ενθουσιασμένος.

rare [rɛə*] a σπάνιος, ασυνήθιστος || αραιός || (air) αραιός || (especially good) θαυμάσιος, σπουδαίος || (in cooking) μισοψημένος.

rarity ['rɛərɪtɪ] n σπάνιο πράγμα nt || (scarcity) σπανιότητα.

rascal ['rɑːskəl] n παλιάνθρωπος, μασκαράς.

rash [ræʃ] a παράτολμος, απερίσκεπτος ♦ n εξάνθημα nt.

rasher ['ræʃə*] n ψιλή φέτα μπέικον.

raspberry ['rɑːzbərɪ] n σμέουρο, φραμπουάζ nt inv, βατόμουρο.

rasping ['rɑːspɪŋ] a (noise) οξύς, στριγγός.

rat [ræt] n (animal) αρουραίος, μεγάλος ποντικός.

ratable ['reɪtəbl] a: ~ value φορολογήσιμο τεκμαρτό ενοίκιο (ακινήτου).

ratchet ['rætʃɪt] n οδοντωτός τροχός, καστάνια ntpl.

rate [reɪt] n (proportion) αναλογία, ανάλογο ποσό, ανάλογος αριθμός || (price) ποσοστό, τόκος || (speed) ρυθμός, ταχύτητα ♦ vt εκτιμώ, ταξινομώ || ~s npl (Brit) τοπικός φόρος ♦ a ~ οπωσδήποτε, εν πάσει περιπτώσει || at this ~ έτσι || ~ of exchange n τιμή συναλλάγματος || ~payer n φορολογούμενος || see first.

rather ['rɑːðə*] ad μάλλον, καλύτερα, παρά || (somewhat) λίγο, κάπως, μάλλον, σχετικά.

ratify ['rætɪfaɪ] vt επικυρώνω, εγκρίνω.

rating ['reɪtɪŋ] n (classification) εκτίμηση,

τάξη || (NAUT) μέλος πληρώματος, ειδικότητα.

ratio ['reɪʃɪəʊ] n λόγος, αναλογία.

ration ['ræʃən] n μερίδα || (usually pl, food) σιτηρέσιο, τροφη ♦ vt περιορίζω, επιβάλλω μερίδες.

rational ['ræʃənl] a λογικός || **rationale** [ræʃə'nɑːl] n λογική εξήγηση, λογική βάση || ~ize vt ορθολογίζομαι, οργανώνω ορθολογικά.

rationing ['ræʃnɪŋ] n καθορισμός μερίδων, διανομή με δελτίο.

rattle ['rætl] n κρότος, κροταλισμός || (toy) ροκάνα, κρόταλο ♦ vi κροταλίζω, κροτώ || ~snake n κροταλίας.

raucous ['rɔːkəs] a βραχνός.

ravage ['rævɪdʒ] vt ερημώνω, αφανίζω, ρημάζω || ~s npl (of time etc) φθορά του χρόνου.

rave [reɪv] vi παραληρώ, παραμιλώ || (rage) μαίνομαι, ουρλιάζω.

raven ['reɪvn] n κοράκι, κόρακας.

ravenous ['rævənəs] a (hungry) πεινασμένος, λιμασμένος.

ravine [rə'viːn] n φαράγγι.

raving ['reɪvɪŋ] a: ~ lunatic μανιακός, παράφρονας.

ravioli [rævɪ'əʊlɪ] n ραβιόλια ntpl.

ravish ['rævɪʃ] vt απάγω, κλέβω || (rape) βιάζω || ~ing a γοητευτικός, μαγευτικός.

raw [rɔː] a (uncooked) ωμός, άψητος || (not manufactured) ακατέργαστος || (tender) ευαίσθητος, ματωμένος || (inexperienced) άξεστος, ατζαμής || ~ material n πρώτες ύλες fpl.

ray [reɪ] n ακτίδα.

raze [reɪz] vt ισοπεδώνω, κατεδαφίζω, γκρεμίζω.

razor ['reɪzə*] n ξυράφι || ~ blade n ξυριστική λεπίδα.

Rd abbr of **road.**

re- [riː] prefix αντι-, ανά-, ξανά-.

reach [riːtʃ] n έκταση, άπλωμα nt, τέντωμα nt (χεριού) || (distance) εντός βολής, κοντά ♦ vt απλώνω, τεντώνω || (arrive at) φθάνω ♦ vi (επ)εκτείνομαι || to ~ out vi απλώνω (το χέρι). ·

react [riː'ækt] vi αντιδρώ || ~ion n αντίδραση || ~ionary a αντιδραστικός.

reactor [riː'æktə*] n αντιδραστήρας.

read [riːd] n (irreg v) n ανάγνωση, διάβασμα nt ♦ vti διαβάζω || (aloud) διαβάζω δυνατά || (understand) ερμηνεύω, δείχνω || (find in book) διαβάζομαι || (COMPUT) διαβάζω || ~able a αναγνώσιμος, που διαβάζεται || ~er n αναγνώστης/ρια m/f || (book) αναγνωστικό || ~ership n (of newspaper etc) αναγνωστικό κοινό.

readily ['redɪlɪ] ad πρόθυμα, αδίστακτα, εύκολα.

readiness ['redɪnɪs] n προθυμία || (being ready) ετοιμότητα.

reading ['riːdɪŋ] n ανάγνωση, διάβασμα nt || ~ lamp n λάμπα του τραπεζιού || ~ room n αναγνωστήριο.

readjust ['riːə'dʒʌst] vt
αναπροσαρμόζω, διορθώνω, σιάζω.

ready ['redɪ] a έτοιμος || (willing)
πρόθυμος, διατεθειμένος || (condition)
έτοιμος || (quick, facile) γρήγορος,
εύκολος || (available) πρόχειρος ♦ ad
τελείως ♦ n: at the ~ έτοιμος || ~-
made a έτοιμος.

real [rɪəl] a πραγματικός, αληθινός || ~
estate n ακίνητος περιουσία, οικόπεδα
ntpl || ~ism n πραγματισμός, ρεαλισμός
|| ~ist n πραγματιστής,
ρεαλιστής/ίστρια m/f || ~istic a
ρεαλιστικός.

reality [riː'ælɪtɪ] n πραγματικότητα,
αλήθεια || in ~ πράγματι, πραγματικά.

realization [rɪəlaɪ'zeɪʃən] n
συνειδητοποίηση || (fulfilment)
πραγματοποίηση.

realize ['rɪəlaɪz] vt (understand) κατανοώ,
αντιλαμβάνομαι, καταλαβαίνω || (bring
about) πραγματοποιώ.

really ['rɪəlɪ] ad πραγματικά, αληθινά,
όχι δα.

realm [rɛlm] n σφαίρα, δικαιοδοσία ||
(kingdom) βασίλειο.

reap [riːp] vt θερίζω || (harvest)
συγκομίζω, μαζεύω || ~er n (machine)
θεριστική μηχανή.

reappear ['riːə'pɪə*] vi
επανεμφανίζομαι, ξαναφαίνομαι ||
~ance n επανεμφάνιση, επάνοδος f.

reapply ['riːə'plaɪ] vi (+ to, for)
ξαναϋποβάλλω (αίτηση).

reappoint ['riːə'pɔɪnt] vt επαναδιορίζω.

rear [rɪə*] a οπίσθιος, πισινός ♦ n νώτα
ntpl, οπίσθια ntpl, οπισθοφυλακή ♦ vt
(bring up) (ανα)τρέφω ♦ vi ανορθούμαι,
σηκώνομαι σούζα || ~guard n
οπισθοφυλακή.

rearm [riː'ɑːm] vti επανεξοπλίζω,
επανεξοπλίζομαι || ~ament n
επανεξοπλισμός.

rearrange ['riːə'reɪndʒ] vt τακτοποιώ
πάλι, αναδιαρρυθμίζω.

rear-view ['rɪəvjuː] a: ~ mirror
καθρέφτης οδήγησης.

reason ['riːzn] n (cause) λόγος, αιτία ||
(ability to think) λογικό, λογική ||
(judgment) κρίση ♦ vi σκέφτομαι,
συλλογίζομαι, συμπεραίνω || ~able a
λογικός || (fair) μετριοπαθής, μέτριος ||
~ably ad λογικά || ~ed a (argument)
αιτιολογημένος, δικαιολογημένος ||
~ing n συλλογισμός, επιχείρημα nt.

reassert ['riːə'sɜːt] vt επαναβεβαιώνω.

reassure [riːə'ʃuə*] vt ενθαρρύνω
καθησυχάζω.

reassuring [riːə'ʃuərɪŋ] a
καθησυχαστικός || (encouraging)
ενθαρρυντικός.

rebate ['riːbeɪt] n έκπτωση.

rebel ['rɛbl] n αντάρτης/ισσα m/f,
επαναστάτης/ρια m/f ♦ a
επαναστατημένος, ανταρτικός || ~lion
[rɪ'bɛljən] n ανταρσία || ~lious a
ανταρτικός, ανυπότακτος.

rebirth ['riː'bɜːθ] n αναγέννηση.

rebound [rɪ'baund] vi αναπηδώ ♦
['riːbaund] n αναπήδηση.

rebuff [rɪ'bʌf] n απόκρουση, άρνηση ♦
vt αποκρούω, αρνούμαι.

rebuild [riː'bɪld] vt ανοικοδομώ || ~ing
n ανοικοδόμηση.

rebuke [rɪ'bjuːk] n επίπληξη, μομφή ♦
vt επιπλήττω, επιτιμώ.

recalcitrant [rɪ'kælsɪtrənt] a
ανυπάκουος, δύστροπος.

recall [rɪ'kɔːl] vt (call back) ανακαλώ ||
(remember) ξαναθυμίζω, ξαναθυμάμαι ||
(withdraw) ανακαλώ.

recant [rɪ'kænt] vi ανακαλώ, αναιρώ,
αναθεωρώ.

recap ['riːkæp] vti ξαναβουλώνω.

recede [rɪ'siːd] vi αποσύρομαι,
υποχωρώ, τραβιέμαι.

receipt [rɪ'siːt] n απόδειξη παραλαβής ||
(receiving) λήψη, παραλαβή || ~s npl
εισπράξεις fpl, έσοδα ntpl.

receive [rɪ'siːv] vt λαμβάνω || (welcome)
(υπο)δέχομαι || ~r n (TEL) ακουστικό.

recent ['riːsnt] a πρόσφατος, νέος ||
~ly ad τελευταία, πρόσφατα.

receptacle [rɪ'sɛptəkl] n δοχείο.

reception [rɪ'sɛpʃən] n (welcome)
υποδοχή || (party) δεξίωση || (at hotel etc)
γραφείο υποδοχής || ~ist n υπάλληλος
m/f επί της υποδοχής.

receptive [rɪ'sɛptɪv] a δεκτικός.

recess [rɪ'sɛs] n (interval) διακοπή,
διάλειμμα nt || (in wall) εσοχή,
βαθούλωμα nt || (inner place) μυστικό
μέρος nt.

recharge ['riː'tʃɑːdʒ] vt (battery)
αναφορτίζω, ξαναγεμίζω.

recipe ['rɛsɪpɪ] n συνταγή.

recipient [rɪ'sɪpɪənt] n δέκτης, λήπτης,
παραλήπτης.

reciprocal [rɪ'sɪprəkəl] a αμοιβαίος,
αντίστροφος.

recital [rɪ'saɪtl] n (MUS) ρεσιτάλ nt inv.

recite [rɪ'saɪt] vt απαγγέλλω,
αποστηθίζω || (tell one by one) εξιστορώ,
απαριθμώ.

reckless ['rɛklɪs] a αδιάφορος,
απρόσεκτος, απερίσκεπτος || ~ly ad
απερίσκεπτα, παράτολμα.

reckon ['rɛkən] vt (count) υπολογίζω,
λογαριάζω, μετρώ || (consider) εκτιμώ,
λογαριάζω ♦ vi υπολογίζω || to ~ on vt
στηρίζομαι σε, υπολογίζω σε || ~ing n
υπολογισμός.

reclaim [rɪ'kleɪm] vi (land) εκκερσώνω,
αποξηραίνω.

recline [rɪ'klaɪn] vi ξαπλώνω, πλαγιάζω,
ακουμπώ.

reclining [rɪ'klaɪnɪŋ] a πλαγιαστός,
ξαπλωμένος.

recluse [rɪ'kluːs] n ερημίτης.

recognition [rɛkəg'nɪʃən] n
αναγνώριση.

recognize ['rɛkəgnaɪz] vt αναγνωρίζω ||
(admit) ομολογώ, παραδέχομαι.

recoil [rɪ'kɔɪl] vi οπισθοδρομώ, μαζεύομαι || (spring) αναπηδώ.

recollect [rekə'lekt] vt θυμούμαι, αναπολώ || ~ion n ανάμνηση || (memory) μνημονικό.

recommend [rekə'mend] vt συνιστώ || ~ation n σύσταση || (qualification) προσόν nt.

recompense ['rekəmpens] n ανταμοιβή, αποζημίωση ♦ vt ανταμείβω, αποζημιώνω.

reconcile ['rekənsaɪl] vt (make agree) συμβιβάζω || (make friendly) συμφιλιώνω.

reconciliation [rekənsɪlɪ'eɪʃən] n συμφιλίωση, συμβιβασμός.

reconditioned ['riːkən'dɪʃənd] a επισκευασμένος, ανακαινισθείς.

reconnoitre, reconnoiter (US) [rekə'nɔɪtə*] vti κάνω αναγνώριση, εξερευνώ.

reconsider ['riːkən'sɪdə*] vti αναθεωρώ, επανεξετάζω.

reconstitute [riː'kɒnstɪtjuːt] vt επαναφέρω στη φυσική κατάσταση.

reconstruct ['riːkən'strʌkt] vt ανοικοδομώ, ανασυγκροτώ || ~ion n ανοικοδόμηση, ανασυγκρότηση.

record ['rekɔːd] n αναγραφή, καταγραφή, σημείωση || (disc) δίσκος, πλάκα || (best performance) πρωτάθλημα nt, ρεκόρ nt inv, επίδοση || (COMPUT) εγγραφή ♦ a (time) με μεγάλη ταχύτητα, σε διάστημα του σημειώνει ρεκόρ ♦ [rɪ'kɔːd] vt (set down) καταγράφω, αναγράφω || (music etc) πχογραφώ, εγγράφω || ~ed a (music) πχογραφημένος || ~er n μηχάνημα nt εγγραφής || (tape recorder) μαγνητόφωνο || ~ holder n (SPORT) πρωταθλητής/ήτρια m/f || ~ing n (music) πχογράφηση || ~ player n πικάπ nt inv.

recount [rɪ'kaunt] vt (tell in detail) αφηγούμαι, εξιστορώ.

re-count ['riː'kaunt] n νέα καταμέτρηση ♦ [riː'kaunt] vt ξαναμετρώ.

recoup [rɪ'kuːp] vt αποζημιώνω, ξαναπέρνω.

recourse [rɪ'kɔːs] n καταφυγή, προσφυγή.

recover [rɪ'kʌvə*] vt ανακτώ, ξαναβρίσκω ♦ vi ανακτώ (την υγεία μου), θεραπεύομαι || ~y n ανάκτηση, ανεύρεση || (from illness) ανάρρωση.

recreation [rekrɪ'eɪʃən] n αναψυχή, διασκέδαση || ~al a διασκεδαστικός.

recrimination [rɪkrɪmɪ'neɪʃən] n αντέγκληση, αντικατηγορία.

recruit [rɪ'kruːt] n νεοσύλλεκτος ♦ vt στρατολογώ || ~ment n στρατολογία.

rectangle ['rektæŋgl] n ορθογώνιο.

rectangular [rek'tæŋgjulə*] a ορθογώνιος.

rectify ['rektɪfaɪ] vt επανορθώνω, διορθώνω.

rectory ['rektərɪ] n (ECCL) πρεσβυτέριο, εφημερείο.

recuperate [rɪ'kuːpəreɪt] vi αναλαμβάνω, αναρρώνω.

recur [rɪ'kɜː*] vi επανέρχομαι, ξανασυμβαίνω || ~rence n επανάληψη.

red [red] n (colour) κόκκινο || (Communist) κομουνιστής/ίστρια m/f, αριστερός/ή m/f ♦ a κόκκινος, ερυθρός || to be in the ~ έχω έλλειμα nt || R~ Cross n Ερυθρός Σταυρός || ~den vti κοκκινίζω || ~dish a κοκκινωπός.

redeem [rɪ'diːm] vt αντισταθμίζω, εξοφλώ, εξαγοράζω.

red-haired ['red'heəd] a κοκκινομάλλης.

red-handed ['red'hændɪd] a επ' αυτοφώρω, στα πράσα.

redhead ['redhed] n κοκκινομάλλα.

red herring ['red'herɪŋ] n (fig) ξεγέλασμα nt, άσχετο θέμα nt.

red-hot ['red'hɒt] a ερυθροπυρωμένος || (fig) φανατικός, ένθερμος.

redirect [riːdaɪ'rekt] vt (mail) απευθύνω σε νέα διεύθυνση.

rediscovery ['riːdɪs'kʌvərɪ] n εκ νέου ανακάλυψη.

red-letter ['red'letə*] a: ~ day μέρα ευτυχισμένων γεγονότων, αξιομνημόνευτη μέρα.

redness ['rednɪs] n κοκκινίλα, κοκκινάδα.

redo ['riː'duː] vt ξανακάνω.

redouble [riː'dʌbl] vt αναδιπλασιάζω.

red tape ['red'teɪp] n γραφειοκρατία.

reduce [rɪ'djuːs] vt (decrease) ελαττώνω, μικραίνω, περιορίζω || (in strength) αδυνατίζω || (lower) υποβιβάζω, κατεβάζω || (change state) μεταβάλλω || ~d a (price) μειωμένη (τιμή).

reduction [rɪ'dʌkʃən] n ελάττωση || (in size) σμίκρυνση || (in price) έκπτωση.

redundancy [rɪ'dʌndənsɪ] n περίσσευμα nt, πλεόνασμα nt.

redundant [rɪ'dʌndənt] a πλεονάζων, περιττός.

reed [riːd] n καλάμι || (of clarinet etc) γλωσσίδι.

reef [riːf] n (at sea) ύφαλος, ξέρα.

reek [riːk] vi αναδίδω κακή μυρωδιά, βρομάω.

reel [riːl] n (for rope) ανέμη || (for cotton, film etc) πηνίο, καρούλι, μασούρι || (dance) ζωηρός (σκωτικός) χορός ♦ vt τυλίγω || (stagger) τρικλίζω, ζαλίζομαι.

re-election [riː'lekʃən] n επανεκλογή.

re-entry [riː'entrɪ] n επάνοδος f, ξαναμπάσιμο.

re-examine ['riːɪg'zæmɪn] vt επανεξετάζω.

ref [ref] n (col: abbr of referee) διαιτητής.

refectory [rɪ'fektərɪ] n τραπεζαρία μοναστηριού ή κολλεγίου.

refer [rɪ'fɜː*] vt παραπέμπω || to ~ to vt αναφέρομαι σε || (consult) συμβουλεύομαι.

referee [refə'riː] n διαιτητής || (for job application) υπέγγυος, εγγυητής ♦ vt (SPORT) διαιτητεύω.

reference ['refrəns] n αναφορά || (in book etc) παραπομπή || (of character) πιστοποιητικό, σύσταση || (person referred to) αυτός που δίνει τη σύσταση, ο εγγυητής || (allusion) μνεία, υπαινιγμός || ~ **book** n βιβλίο οδηγός, σύμβουλος.

referendum [refə'rendəm] n δημοψήφισμα nt.

refill ['ri:fil] n (for pen etc) ανταλλακτικό.

refine [ri'fain] vt καθαρίζω, διυλίζω, ραφινάρω || (make finer) εκλεπτύνω, εξευγενίζω || ~**d** a (person) λεπτός, καλλιεργημένος || ~**ment** n εξευγενισμός, λεπτή διάκριση || ~**ry** n διϋλιστήριο.

reflect [ri'flekt] vt αντανακλώ ♦ vi (meditate) σκέφτομαι, συλλογίζομαι, μελετώ || ~**ion** n αντανάκλαση || (thought) σκέψη || ~**or** n ανακλαστήρας, καθρέφτης.

reflex ['ri:fleks] a (involuntary) αντανακλαστικός || ~**ive** a (GRAM) αυτοπαθής.

reform [ri'fɔ:m] n μεταρρύθμιση, αποκατάσταση, ανασχηματισμός ♦ vt μεταρρυθμίζω, αποκαθιστώ, αναμορφώνω.

reformat [ri:'fɔ:mæt] vt (COMPUT) ανασχηματίζω.

refrain [ri'frein] vi (+ from) απέχω, συγκρατούμαι.

refresh [ri'freʃ] vt αναζωογονώ, δροσίζω, φρεσκάρω || ~**er course** n επανάληψη, μετεκπαίδευση || ~**ing** a ευχάριστος, ζωογόνος, δροσιστικός || ~**ments** npl (food, drink) αναψυκτικά ntpl.

refrigerator [ri'fridʒəreitə*] n ψυγείο.

refuel ['ri:fjuəl] vti ανεφοδιάζομαι (με καύσιμα).

refuge ['refju:dʒ] n καταφύγιο, καταφυγή, προστασία || **refugee** [refju'dʒi:] n πρόσφυγας.

refund ['ri:fʌnd] n επιστροφή χρημάτων, απόδοση ♦ [ri'fʌnd] vt επιστρέφω (χρήματα).

refurbish [ri:'fɜ:biʃ] vt (decorate) ανακαινίζω, φρεσκάρω.

refusal [ri'fju:zəl] n άρνηση.

refuse ['refju:s] n απορρίμματα ntpl, σκουπίδια ntpl ♦ [ri'fju:z] vti αρνούμαι, απορρίπτω.

refute [ri'fju:t] vt ανασκευάζω, ανατρέπω.

regain [ri'gein] vt επανακτώ.

regal ['ri:gəl] a βασιλικός.

regard [ri'ga:d] n (respect) εκτίμηση, σεβασμός ♦ vt (consider) θεωρώ || ~**s** npl (greetings) χαιρετισμοί mpl, χαιρετίσματα ntpl || ~**ing**, as ~**s** όσον αφορά, σχετικά με || as ~**s, with** ~ **to** ως προς, όσο για || ~**less** a (+ of) αδιάφορος, άσχετος ♦ ad αδιάφορος, αδιαφορώντας.

regatta [ri'gætə] n λεμβοδρομία.

régime [rei'ʒi:m] n καθεστώς nt.

regiment ['redʒimənt] n σύνταγμα nt || ~**al** a του συντάγματος.

region ['ri:dʒən] n περιοχή || ~**al** a τοπικός, περιφερειακός.

register ['redʒistə*] n κατάλογος, ληξιαρχικό βιβλίο, μητρώο ♦ vt καταγράφω, εγγράφω || (write down) σημειώνω ♦ vi (at hotel) εγγράφομαι || (make impression) δείχνω || ~**ed** a (design) κατατεθειμένος || (letter) συστημένο γράμμα.

registrar [redʒis'tra:*] n ληξίαρχος, γραμματέας m/f.

registration [redʒis'treiʃən] n (act) καταγραφή, εγγραφή || (number) αριθμός εγγραφής.

registry ['redʒistri] n ληξιαρχείο || ~ **office** n (for civil marriage) ληξιαρχείο.

regret [ri'gret] n λύπη, μετάνοια ♦ vt λυπούμαι, μετανοώ || ~**fully** ad με λύπη, με πόνο || ~**table** a δυσάρεστος, λυπηρός.

regular ['regjulə*] a τακτικός, κανονικός, συνηθισμένος || (not varying) ομαλός ♦ n (client etc) τακτικός (πελάτης) || ~**ity** n κανονικότητα, ομαλότητα.

regulate ['regjuleit] vt κανονίζω, τακτοποιώ, ρυθμίζω.

regulation [regju'leiʃən] n κανονισμός || (control) ρύθμιση.

rehabilitation ['ri:əbili'teiʃən] n αποκατάσταση, παλινόρθωση.

rehash [ri:'hæʃ] vt (col) ξαναδουλεύω, διασκευάζω.

rehearsal [ri'hɜːsəl] n δοκιμή, πρόβα.

rehearse [ri'hɜːs] vt (practise) κάνω δοκιμές, κάνω πρόβα.

reign [rein] n (period) βασιλεία ♦ vi βασιλεύω.

reimburse [ri:im'bɜːs] vt επιστρέφω (χρήματα), αποζημιώνω.

rein [rein] n ηνία ntpl, χαλινάρι.

reindeer ['reindiə*] n τάρανδος.

reinforce [ri:in'fɔːs] vt ενισχύω, δυναμώνω || ~**d concrete** n μπετό αρμέ nt inv || ~**ment** n ενίσχυση || ~**ments** npl (MIL) ενισχύσεις fpl.

reinstate ['ri:in'steit] vt επαναφέρω στη θέση του, αποκαθιστώ, επανεγκαθιστώ.

reiterate [ri:'itəreit] vt επαναλαμβάνω.

reject [ri'dʒekt] vt απορρίπτω, αποκρούω ♦ ['ri:dʒekt] n απόρριμμα nt, σκάρτο || ~**ion** n απόρριψη.

rejoice [ri'dʒɔis] vi χαίρομαι, χαίρω.

relapse [ri'læps] n υποτροπή.

relate [ri'leit] vt διηγούμαι, εξιστορώ || (connect) συσχετίζω || ~**d** a (subjects) σχετιζόμενος, σχετικά με || (people) (+ to) συγγενής.

relating [ri'leitiŋ] prep: ~ **to** σχετικός με, ότι αφορά.

relation [ri'leiʃən] n (of family) συγγενής m/f || (connection) σχέση, συγγένεια || ~**ship** n συγγένεια, σχέση.

relative ['relətiv] n συγγενής m/f ♦ a αναφορικός, σχετικός || ~**ly** ad σχετικά || ~ **pronoun** n αναφορική αντωνυμία.

relax [rɪˈlæks] vi χαλαρώνω, λασκάρω || (rest) ανακουφίζω ♦ vt χαλαρούμαι, αναπαύομαι, ξεκουράζομαι || ~ation n αναψυχή, διασκέδαση || ~ed a χαλαρός, λάσκος || ~ing a ξεκουραστικός.

relay [ˈriːleɪ] n (SPORT) σκυταλοδρομία ♦ vt (message) αναμεταδίδω.

release [rɪˈliːs] n (relief) απαλλαγή, απόλυση || (from prison) αποφυλάκιση || (device) διακόπτης ♦ vt απελευθερώνω || (prisoner) απολύω, αποφυλακίζω || (grip) χαλαρώνω, λασκάρω, απομπλέκω || (report, news) θέτω σε κυκλοφορία, επιτρέπω δημοσίευση.

relegate [ˈrelɪgeɪt] vt (put down) υποβιβάζω.

relent [rɪˈlent] vi κάμπτομαι, μαλακώνω || ~less a αδιάλλακτος, αμείλικτος, ανελέητος.

relevant [ˈreləvənt] a σχετικός

reliable [rɪˈlaɪəbl] a αξιόπιστος.

reliably [rɪˈlaɪəblɪ] ad μ'εμπιστοσύνη, σίγουρα.

reliance [rɪˈlaɪəns] n εμπιστοσύνη, πεποίθηση.

relic [ˈrelɪk] n απομεινάρι, ενθύμιο || (of saint) λείψανο.

relief [rɪˈliːf] n (from pain etc) ανακούφιση, ξελάφρωμα nt || (help) βοήθεια || (from duty) αντικατάσταση, αλλαγή || (design) ανάγλυφο || (distinctness) προβολή, ευδιακρισία.

relieve [rɪˈliːv] vt (pain etc) ανακουφίζω, ξαλαφρώνω || (bring help) βοηθώ, περιθάλπω || (take place of) αντικαθιστώ, απαλλάσσω || to ~ of παίρνω, απαλλάσσω.

religion [rɪˈlɪdʒən] n θρησκεία, θρήσκευμα nt.

religious [rɪˈlɪdʒəs] a θρησκευτικός || (pious) ευσεβής.

relinquish [rɪˈlɪŋkwɪʃ] vt παραιτούμαι, εγκαταλείπω.

relish [ˈrelɪʃ] n (sauce) καρύκευμα nt, σάλτσα ♦ vt απολαμβάνω, τρώγω ευχάριστα.

relive [ˈriːˈlɪv] vt ξαναζώ.

reluctant [rɪˈlʌktənt] a απρόθυμος || ~ly ad με το ζόρι, με το στανιό.

rely [rɪˈlaɪ]: to ~ on vt βασίζομαι, στηρίζομαι, εμπιστεύομαι.

remain [rɪˈmeɪn] vi (be left) απομένω || (stay) παραμένω, μένω || ~der n υπόλοιπο || ~ing a υπόλοιπος || ~s npl υπολείμματα ntpl || (corpse) λείψανα ntpl.

remand [rɪˈmɑːnd] n: on ~ παραπομπή (κατηγορουμένου) ♦ vt: to ~ in custody προφυλακίζω.

remark [rɪˈmɑːk] n παρατήρηση, σημείωση ♦ vt (say) λέγω || (notice) παρατηρώ || ~able a αξιοσημείωτος || (unusual) ασυνήθιστος || ~ably ad αξιόλογα, εξαιρετικά.

remarry [ˈriːˈmærɪ] vi ξαναπαντρεύομαι.

remedial [rɪˈmiːdɪəl] a θεραπευτικός.

remedy [ˈremədɪ] n θεραπεία || (MED)

φάρμακο, γιατρικό ♦ vt θεραπεύω, διορθώνω.

remember [rɪˈmembə*] vt θυμούμαι || (give regards) δίνω χαιρετισμούς σε.

remembrance [rɪˈmembrəns] n ανάμνηση, μνήμη.

remind [rɪˈmaɪnd] vt υπενθυμίζω, θυμίζω || ~er n κάτι που θυμίζει, ενθύμημα nt.

reminisce [remɪˈnɪs] vi αναπολώ, ξαναθυμάμαι.

reminiscences [remɪˈnɪsnsɪz] npl αναμνήσεις fpl, απομνημονεύματα ntpl.

reminiscent [remɪˈnɪsnt] a (+ of) που θυμίζει κάτι.

remission [rɪˈmɪʃən] n (from sins) άφεση, ελάττωση || (release) χάρη, μείωση (ποινής).

remit [rɪˈmɪt] vt (send money) εμβάζω, μεταβιβάζω || ~tance n έμβασμα nt (χρηματικό).

remnant [ˈremnənt] n υπόλειμμα nt.

remorse [rɪˈmɔːs] n τύψη, μεταμέλεια || ~ful a γεμάτος τύψεις, μετανοιωμένος || ~less a άσπλαγχνος, αμετανόητος.

remote [rɪˈməʊt] a μακρινός, απομονωμένος, απόμερος || (slight) αμυδρός, ελαφρός || (vague) αόριστος || ~ control a τηλερρυθμιστής || ~ly ad αόριστα, μακριά.

remould [ˈriːˈməʊld] vt (tyre) ξαναφορμάρω.

removable [rɪˈmuːvəbl] a μεταθέσιμος, κινητός, φορητός.

removal [rɪˈmuːvəl] n αφαίρεση, βγάλσιμο || (from house) μετακόμιση, μετακίνηση || (from office) απόλυση, ανάκληση || ~ van n φορτηγό μετακομίσεων.

remove [rɪˈmuːv] vt αφαιρώ, βγάζω, μεταφέρω || (dismiss) απολύω, απομακρύνω || ~r (for paint etc) εξαλειπτικό μέσο || ~rs npl (company) εταιρεία μεταφορών οικοσκευών.

remuneration [rɪmjuːnəˈreɪʃən] n αμοιβή, πληρωμή.

rend [rend] (irreg v) vt σχίζω, αποσπώ.

render [ˈrendə*] vt (make) καθιστώ, κάνω || (translate) μεταφράζω || ~ing n (MUS) ερμηνεία, απόδοση.

rendezvous [ˈrɒndɪvuː] n συνάντηση, ραντεβού nt inv.

renew [rɪˈnjuː] vt (make new) ανανεώνω || (begin again) ανασυνδέω, ξαναπιάνω || (negotiations) επαναλαμβάνω || ~al n ανανέωση, ανασύνδεση.

renounce [rɪˈnaʊns] vt (give up) εγκαταλείπω, αποκηρύσσω || (disown) αρνούμαι, αποποιούμαι.

renovate [ˈrenəʊveɪt] vt ανακαινίζω || (repair) επισκευάζω.

renovation [renəʊˈveɪʃən] n ανακαίνιση || (repair) επισκευή.

renown [rɪˈnaʊn] n φήμη || ~ed a φημισμένος, ονομαστός.

rent [rent] n (of dwelling) ενοίκιο || (hiring) μίσθωμα, νοίκι ♦ vt ενοικιάζω || (hire)

μισθώνω || (AUT etc) ενοικιάζω
(αυτοκίνητο) || ~al η μίσθωμα, νοίκι.

renunciation [rɪnʌnsɪ'eɪʃən] n
απάρνηση.

reorganize ['riː'ɔːgənaɪz] vt
αναδιοργανώνω.

rep [rεp] n (COMM: abbr of
representative) αντιπρόσωπος ||
(THEAT: abbr of **repertory**) ρεπερτόριο.

repair [rɪ'pεə*] n επισκευή, επιδιόρθωση
|| (in good condition) σε καλή κατάσταση ♦
vt επισκευάζω, επιδιορθώνω || ~ **kit** n
σύνεργα ntpl επισκευή || ~**man** n
επισκευαστής, επιδιορθωτής.

repartee [rεpɑː'tiː] n ετοιμολογία,
εύστοχη απάντηση.

repay [riː'peɪ] vt (pay back) ανταποδίδω
|| (money) ξεπληρώνω || ~**ment** n
ανταπόδοση.

repeal [rɪ'piːl] n ανάκληση, ακύρωση ♦
vt ανακαλώ, ακυρώνω.

repeat [rɪ'piːt] n (RAD, TV) επανάληψη ♦
vt επαναλαμβάνω || ~**edly** ad
επανειλημμένα, πολλές φορές.

repel [rɪ'pεl] vt αποκρούω, απωθώ ||
~**lent** a αποκρουστικός, απωθητικός ♦
n: **insect** ~**lent** εντομοαπωθητική
λοσιόν f inv.

repent [rɪ'pεnt] vi μετανοιώνω,
μεταμελούμαι || ~**ance** n μετάνοια,
μεταμέλεια.

repercussion [riːpə'kʌʃən] n (effect)
αντίδραση, αντίκτυπος.

repertoire ['rεpətwɑː*] n
δραματολόγιο, ρεπερτόριο.

repertory ['rεpətərɪ] n (THEAT)
ρεπερτόριο.

repetition [rεpɪ'tɪʃən] n επανάληψη.

repetitive [rɪ'pεtɪtɪv] a επαναληπτικός.

replace [rɪ'pleɪs] vt αντικαθιστώ || (put
back) ξαναβάζω || ~**ment** n
αντικατάσταση || (person)
αντικαταστάτης.

replenish [rɪ'plεnɪʃ] vt ξαναγεμίζω,
συμπληρώνω.

replica ['rεplɪkə] n πανομοιότυπο,
αντίγραφο έργου τέχνης.

reply [rɪ'plaɪ] n απάντηση ♦ vi απαντώ,
αποκρίνομαι.

report [rɪ'pɔːt] n (account) έκθεση,
εξιστόρηση, αναφορά || (bang) κρότος,
πυροβολισμός || vt αναφέρω || (give
account of) εξιστορώ || (news) κάνω
ρεπορτάζ ♦ vi (make a report) εκθέτω,
αναφέρω, κάνω αναφορά || (present o.s.)
παρουσιάζομαι || ~**er** n
δημοσιογράφος.

reprehensible [rεprɪ'hεnsɪbl] a
αξιόμεμπτος.

represent [rεprɪ'zεnt] vt (describe)
παριστάνω, παρουσιάζω || (act)
αντιπροσωπεύω || ~**ation** n παράσταση,
αναπαράσταση || (in parliament)
αντιπροσώπευση, αντιπροσωπεία ||
~**ative** n αντιπρόσωπος ♦ a
αντιπροσωπευτικός, παραστατικός.

repress [rɪ'prεs] vt καταβάλλω,

καταστέλλω, καταπνίγω || ~**ion** n
καταστολή, κατάπνιξη || ~**ive** a
κατασταλτικός, καταπιεστικός.

reprieve [rɪ'priːv] n αναστολή
(θανατικής ποινής), αναβολή ♦ vt
αναστέλλω, ανακουφίζω.

reprimand ['rεprɪmɑːnd] n επιτίμηση,
επίπληξη ♦ vt επιτιμώ, επιπλήττω.

reprint ['riːprɪnt] n ανατύπωση ♦
[riː'prɪnt] vt ανατυπώνω.

reprisal [rɪ'praɪzəl] n αντεκδίκηση,
αντίποινο.

reproach [rɪ'prəʊtʃ] n επίπληξη, μομφή
♦ vt επιπλήττω, μέμφομαι, ψέγω.

reproduce [riːprə'djuːs] vt αναπαράγω
|| (make copy) ανατυπώνω ♦ vi
αναπαράγομαι, πολλαπλασιάζομαι.

reproduction [riːprə'dʌkʃən] n (copy)
αναπαράσταση, αντίγραφο || (breeding)
αναπαραγωγή.

reproductive [riːprə'dʌktɪv] a
αναπαραγωγικός.

reproving [rɪ'pruːvɪŋ] a επικριτικός,
επιτιμητικός.

reptile ['rεptaɪl] n ερπετό.

republic [rɪ'pʌblɪk] n δημοκρατία || ~**an**
a δημοκρατικός || (party: US)
ρεπουμπλικανικός ♦ n δημοκράτης ||
(US) ρεπουμπλικάνος.

repudiate [rɪ'pjuːdɪeɪt] vt απαρνούμαι,
αποκρούω, αποκηρύσσω.

repugnant [rɪ'pʌgnənt] a απεχθής,
απδιαστικός, σιχαμερός.

repulse [rɪ'pʌls] vt απωθώ, αποκρούω ||
(reject) αποκρούω, απορρίπτω.

repulsive [rɪ'pʌlsɪv] a αποκρουστικός,
σιχαμερός.

reputable ['rεpjutəbl] a έντιμος,
αξιοπρεπής.

reputation [rεpju'teɪʃən] n φήμη,
υπόληψη || (good name) όνομα nt.

repute [rɪ'pjuːt] n εκτίμηση, υπόληψη ||
~**d** a φημισμένος, υποτιθέμενος || ~**dly**
ad κατά την κοινή γνώμη.

request [rɪ'kwεst] n αίτηση, παράκληση
|| (demand) ζήτηση ♦ vt ζητώ, παρακαλώ.

requiem ['rεkwɪεm] n μνημόσυνο.

require [rɪ'kwaɪə*] vt (oblige) απαιτώ ||
(oblige) χρειάζομαι || ~**ment** n απαίτηση,
ανάγκη.

requisite ['rεkwɪzɪt] n απαιτούμενο
πράγμα nt, προϋπόθεση ♦ a
απαιτούμενος.

requisition [rεkwɪ'zɪʃən] n επίταξη,
απαίτηση ♦ vt απαιτώ, επιτάσσω.

reroute ['riː'ruːt] vt χαράσσω νέα
πορεία, κάνω άλλο δρόμο.

resale ['riː'seɪl] n μεταπώληση,
ξαναπούλημα nt.

rescue ['rεskjuː] n διάσωση,
απολύτρωση ♦ vt (save) σώζω, λυτρώνω
|| ~**r** n σωτήρας, λυτρωτής.

research [rɪ'sɜːtʃ] n έρευνα ♦ vi (+ into)
κάνω έρευνα ♦ vt ερευνώ || ~**er** n
ερευνητής.

resemblance [rɪ'zεmbləns] n
ομοιότητα.

resemble [rɪ'zɛmbl] vt μοιάζω.

resent [rɪ'zɛnt] vt φέρω βαρέως, θίγομαι από || ~ful a μνησίκακος, πειραγμένος || ~ment n μνησικακία, έχθρα, πίκρα.

reservation [rɛzə'veɪʃən] n επιφύλαξη || (place) εξασφάλιση, κλείσιμο || (doubt) επιφύλαξη.

reserve [rɪ'zɜːv] n απόθεμα nt, αποθεματικό || (self-restraint) επιφύλαξη, συντηρητικότητα || (area of land) επιφυλασσόμενη περιοχή || (SPORT) εφεδρικός παίκτης ♦ vt (seats etc) κρατώ, αγκαζάρω, κλείνω || ~s npl (MIL) εφεδρείες fpl || in ~ κατά μέρος, για ρεζέρβα || ~d a επιφυλακτικός, συγκρατημένος || '~d' (notice) 'κλεισμένος', 'κρατημένος'.

reservoir ['rɛzəvwɑː*] n δεξαμενή, ντεπόζιτο, ρεζερβουάρ nt inv || (store) απόθεμα nt.

reshape ['riː'ʃeɪp] vt μεταπλάθω, τροποποιώ, αναπλάθω.

reshuffle ['riː'ʃʌfl] n (POL) ανασχηματισμός.

reside [rɪ'zaɪd] vi διαμένω, ανήκω || **residence** ['rɛzɪdəns] n κατοικία, σπίτι || (living) διαμονή, παραμονή || **resident** n κάτοικος ♦ a εγκατεστημένος || **residential** a της μόνιμης διαμονής, με ιδιωτικές κατοικίες.

residue ['rɛzɪdjuː] n υπόλοιπο, υπόλειμμα nt, κατάλοιπο.

resign [rɪ'zaɪn] vt παραιτούμαι || (submit) υποτάσσομαι, εγκαταλείπομαι || **resignation** [rɛzɪg'neɪʃən] n παραίτηση || (submission) υποταγή, υπομονή || ~ed a ανεχόμενος, υποτακτικός.

resilient [rɪ'zɪlɪənt] a ελαστικός.

resin ['rɛzɪn] n ρητίνη, ρετσίνη.

resist [rɪ'zɪst] vt ανθίσταμαι σε, αντιδρώ κατά || ~ance n αντίσταση.

resolute ['rɛzəluːt] a αποφασιστικός, σταθερός.

resolution [rɛzə'luːʃən] n αποφασιστικότητα || (decision) απόφαση.

resolve [rɪ'zɔlv] n απόφαση ♦ vt αναλύω, διαλύω, λύω || vi διαλύομαι, αναλύομαι || (decide) αποφασίζω || ~d a αποφασισμένος.

resonant ['rɛzənənt] a αντηχών, αντηχητικός.

resort [rɪ'zɔːt] n τόπος διαμονής, θέρετρο || (help) καταφυγή, μέσο, βοήθεια ♦ vi (+ to) προσφεύγω, καταφεύγω (σε) || in the last ~ σαν τελευταία λύση.

resound [rɪ'zaund] vi αντηχώ, απηχώ || ~ing a απηχών, ηχηρός.

resource [rɪ'sɔːs] n καταφύγιο, μέσο, βοήθημα nt || ~s npl (of fuel) πλούτος (σε καύσιμα) || (of a country etc) οι πόροι mpl, πλούτος || ~ful a εφευρετικός.

respect [rɪs'pɛkt] n σεβασμός || (way) αναφορά ♦ vt σέβομαι || (treat with consideration) προσέχω || ~s npl (greetings) σέβη ntpl, χαιρετίσματα ntpl ||

with ~ to όσον αφορά || in ~ of σχετικά με || in this ~ ως προς αυτό το σημείο || ~able a έντιμος, ευυπόληπτος || (fairly good) υποφερτός, αρκετά καλός || ~ed a σεβαστός || ~ful a γεμάτος σεβασμό || ~ive a σχετικός, αμοιβαίος, αντίστοιχος || ~ively ad αντιστοίχως.

respiration [rɛspɪ'reɪʃən] n αναπνοή.

respite ['rɛspaɪt] n ανάπαυλα, διακοπή.

resplendent [rɪs'plɛndənt] a (bright) λαμπρός || (magnificent) μεγαλοπρεπής.

respond [rɪs'pɔnd] vi απαντώ, αποκρίνομαι || (act in answer) ανταποκρίνομαι, ανταποδίδω.

response [rɪs'pɔns] n απάντηση, αντανόκριση.

responsibility [rɪspɔnsə'bɪlɪtɪ] n ευθύνη.

responsible [rɪs'pɔnsəbl] a υπεύθυνος, υπόλογος || (reliable) αξιόπιστος.

responsive [rɪs'pɔnsɪv] a ευαίσθητος, που ανταποκρίνεται.

rest [rɛst] n ανάπαυση, ξεκούραση || (pause) πτώση, ανάπαυλα || (remainder) υπόλοιπο ♦ vi αναπαύομαι, ξεκουράζομαι || (be supported) στηρίζομαι, ακουμπώ || (remain) στηρίζομαι, βασίζομαι || the ~ of them οι υπόλοιποι.

restaurant ['rɛstərɜːŋ] n εστιατόριο || ~ car n βαγκόν-ρεστωράν nt inv.

rest cure ['rɛstkjuə*] n θεραπεία αναπαύσεως.

restful ['rɛstful] a ξεκούραστος, ήσυχος, αναπαυτικός.

rest home ['rɛsthəum] n πρεβαντόριο, αναρρωτήριο.

restive ['rɛstɪv] a ατίθασος, ανήσυχος.

restless ['rɛstlɪs] a ανήσυχος, αεικίνητος, άυπνος || ~ly ad ανήσυχα, νευρικά, ταραγμένα.

restore [rɪs'tɔː*] vt επιστρέφω, αποκαθιστώ || (repair) επισκευάζω, ανασπλώνω.

restrain [rɪs'treɪn] vt αναχαιτίζω, συγκρατώ || ~ed a (style etc) ήρεμος, συγκρατημένος, μετρημένος || ~t n περιορισμός, περιστολή || (self-control) συγκράτηση.

restrict [rɪs'trɪkt] vt περιορίζω || ~ed a περιορισμένος || ~ion n περιορισμός || ~ive a περιοριστικός.

rest room ['rɛstrum] n (US) αποχωρητήριο, τουαλέτα.

result [rɪ'zʌlt] n αποτέλεσμα nt, συνέπεια || (of test) αποτέλεσμα ntpl ♦ vi (+ in) καταλήγω, απολήγω.

resume [rɪ'zjuːm] vt επαναρχίζω, ξαναρχίζω.

résumé ['reɪzjuːmeɪ] n περίληψη.

resumption [rɪ'zʌmpʃən] n (επ)ανάληψη, συνέχιση.

resurgence [rɪ'sɜːdʒəns] n αναζωογόνηση, ανανέωση || (uprising) ξεσήκωμα nt.

resurrection [rɛzə'rɛkʃən] n ανάσταση, ανανέωση.

resuscitate [rɪ'sʌsɪteɪt] *vt* ανασταίνω, επαναφέρω στη ζωή.

resuscitation [rɪsʌsɪ'teɪʃən] *n* αναζωογόνηση, ανάσταση.

retail ['riːteɪl] *n* λιανική πώληση ♦ *a* λιανικός ♦ [riː'teɪl] *vt* πουλώ λιανικά || ~**er** *n* μεταπωλητής, λιανέμπορος || ~ **price** *n* τιμή λιανικής πωλήσεως.

retain [rɪ'teɪn] *vt* διατηρώ, συγκρατώ, κρατώ || ~**er** *n* υπηρέτης || *(fee)* προκαταβολή δικηγόρου.

retaliate [rɪ'tælieɪt] *vi* αντεκδικούμαι, ανταποδίδω.

retarded [rɪ'taːdɪd] *a* καθυστερημένος.

retention [rɪ'tenʃən] *n* διατήρηση, συγκράτηση.

retentive [rɪ'tentɪv] *a* συνεκτικός, ισχυρός.

rethink [riː'θɪŋk] *vt* ξανασκέπτομαι.

reticent ['retɪsənt] *a* λιγομίλητος, επιφυλακτικός.

retina ['retɪnə] *n* αμφιβληστροειδής (χιτών).

retinue ['retɪnjuː] *n* ακολουθία, συνοδεία.

retire [rɪ'taɪə*] *vi* αποχωρώ, γίνομαι συνταξιούχος || *(withdraw, retreat)* υποχωρώ, αποσύρομαι || *(go to bed)* πάω για ύπνο || ~**d** *a (person)* συνταξιούχος || ~**ment** *n* αποχώρηση, συνταξιοδότηση.

retiring [rɪ'taɪərɪŋ] *a* επιφυλακτικός, ακοινώνητος || *(shy)* ντροπαλός.

retort [rɪ'tɔːt] *n (reply)* οξεία απάντηση, έξυπνη απάντηση ♦ *vi* ανταπαντώ, αποκρίνομαι.

retrace [rɪ'treɪs] *vt* ανατρέχω, ξαναγυρίζω.

retract [rɪ'trækt] *vti* ανακαλώ, παίρνω πίσω || ~**able** *a (aerial)* εισελκόμενος.

retread [riː'tred] *vt (AUT: tyre)* ανεπιστρώνω, ξαναφορμάρω.

retreat [rɪ'triːt] *n* υποχώρηση, οπισθοχώρηση || *(escape)* καταφύγιο ♦ *vi* υποχωρώ, οπισθοχωρώ.

retribution [retrɪ'bjuːʃən] *n* τιμωρία, ανταπόδοση, εκδίκηση.

retrieve [rɪ'triːv] *vt* επανακτώ, αποδίδω || *(rescue)* επανορθώνω, σώζω || ~**r** *n* κυνηγετικός σκύλος, ριτρίβερ.

retrograde ['retrəʊgreɪd] *a (step, action)* οπισθοδρομικός, παλινδρομικός.

retrospect ['retrəʊspekt] *n*: **in** ~ σε ανασκόπηση, όταν το σκέφτομαι || ~**ive** *a (LAW)* αναδρομικός.

return [rɪ'tɜːn] *n* επιστροφή, επάνοδος *f*, γύρισμα || *(arrival)* ερχομός || *(profits)* κέρδος, εισπράξεις *fpl* || *(rail ticket etc)* εισιτήριο μετ' επιστροφής || *(journey)* ταξίδι επιστροφής || *(match)* αγώνας ανταποδόσεως || ~**s** *npl (report)* έκθεση, δήλωση || *(statistics)* στατιστική ♦ *vi* επιστρέφω, γυρίζω, επανέρχομαι ♦ *vt* *(give back)* επιστρέφω, δίνω πίσω, γυρίζω || *(pay back)* επιστρέφω, πληρώνω || *(elect)* εκλέγω || ~**able** *a (bottle etc)* επιστρεφόμενος, επιστρεπτός || ~ **key** *n (COMPUT)* πλήκτρο επαναφοράς.

reunion [riː'juːnjən] *n* συνάντηση, συγκέντρωση.

reunite ['riːjuː'naɪt] *vt* ξανασμίγω, συναντώμαι.

rev [rev] *n (AUT)* στροφές *fpl* ♦ *vti (also:* ~ **up)** φουλάρω.

reveal [rɪ'viːl] *vt* αποκαλύπτω, φανερώνω || ~**ing** *a* αποκαλυπτικός.

reveille [rɪ'vælɪ] *n* εγερτήριο σάλπισμα *nt*.

revel ['revl] *vi (+ in)* διασκεδάζω, γλεντώ.

revelation [revə'leɪʃən] *n* αποκάλυψη.

reveller ['revlə*] *n* γλεντζές *m*.

revelry ['revlrɪ] *n* διασκέδαση, γλέντι.

revenge [rɪ'vendʒ] *n* εκδίκηση ♦ *vt* εκδικούμαι.

revenue ['revənjuː] *n* πρόσοδος *f*, έσοδα *ntpl*, εισόδημα *nt*.

reverberate [rɪ'vɜːbəreɪt] *vi* αντηχώ, αντανακλώμαι.

revere [rɪ'vɪə*] *vt* σέβομαι, τιμώ || ~**nce** ['revərəns] *n* σέβας *nt*, σεβασμός || **the R~nd Smith** ο αιδεσιμώτατος Σμιθ || ~**nt** *a* ευσεβής.

reversal [rɪ'vɜːsəl] *n* αντιστροφή, αναστροφή.

reverse [rɪ'vɜːs] *n* αντίστροφο || *(defeat)* ήττα || *(misfortune)* ατυχία || *(AUT: gear)* όπισθεν *f inv* ♦ *a (order, direction)* αντίθετος, αντίστροφος ♦ *vt (put upside down)* αναστρέφω || *(change)* αντιστρέφω ♦ *vi* βάζω την όπισθεν.

revert [rɪ'vɜːt] *vi* επανέρχομαι, επιστρέφω.

review [rɪ'vjuː] *n* επιθεώρηση || *(of critic)* κριτική (βιβλίου) || *(magazine)* επιθεώρηση, περιοδικό ♦ *vt (look back on)* ανασκοπώ, εξετάζω || *(troops)* επιθεωρώ || *(a book)* γράφω κριτική || ~**er** *n (critic)* κριτικογράφος, κριτικός.

revise [rɪ'vaɪz] *vt* αναθεωρώ, ξανακοιτάζω || *(correct)* διορθώνω.

revision [rɪ'vɪʒən] *n* αναθεώρηση || *(correct)* επανεξέταση.

revitalize [riː'vaɪtəlaɪz] *vt* αναζωογονώ.

revival [rɪ'vaɪvəl] *n* αναγέννηση || *(of play)* επανάληψη.

revive [rɪ'vaɪv] *vt* αναζωογονώ, ανασταίνω, ξαναζωντανεύω ♦ *vi* αναζωογονούμαι, ξαναζωντανεύω, αναζωπυρούμαι.

revoke [rɪ'vəʊk] *vt* ανακαλώ, ακυρώνω.

revolt [rɪ'vəʊlt] *n* στάση, επανάσταση ♦ *vi* επαναστατώ || ~**ing** *a* απδιαστικός, σκανδαλώδης.

revolution [revə'luːʃən] *n (of wheel)* περιστροφή || *(change, POL)* επανάσταση || ~**ary** *a* επαναστατικός, ανατρεπτικός, *n* επανάσταση || ~**ize** *vt* αλλάζω οριστικά.

revolve [rɪ'vɒlv] *vi* περιστρέφομαι.

revolver [rɪ'vɒlvə*] *n* περίστροφο.

revue [rɪ'vjuː] *n* επιθεώρηση (θεατρική).

revulsion [rɪ'vʌlʃən] *n* μεταστροφή.

reward [rɪ'wɔːd] *n (αντ)*αμοιβή ♦ *vt*

ανταμείβω || ~ing a ανταμειπτικός || (fig) που αξίζει τον κόπο.

rewind ['ri:'waɪnd] vt ξανατυλίγω, ξανακουρδίζω.

rewire ['ri:'waɪə*] vt (house) αλλάζω τα σύρματα (σπιτιού).

reword ['ri:'wɜːd] vt ανασυντάσσω, ξαναγράφω με άλλες λέξεις.

rewrite ['ri:'raɪt] vt ξαναγράφω.

rhapsody ['ræpsədɪ] n ραψωδία.

rhetoric ['rɛtərɪk] n ρητορική, ρητορία || ~al a ρητορικός.

rheumatic [ru:'mætɪk] a ρευματικός.

rheumatism ['ru:mətɪzəm] n ρευματισμός.

rhinoceros [raɪ'nɒsərəs] n ρινόκερως m.

rhododendron [rəʊdə'dɛndrən] n ροδόδεντρο.

rhubarb ['ru:bɑ:b] n ραβέντι, ρουμπάρμπαρο.

rhyme [raɪm] n ομοιοκαταληξία, ρίμα.

rhythm ['rɪðəm] n ρυθμός, μέτρο || ~ic(al) a ρυθμικός || ~ically ad ρυθμικά, με ρυθμό.

rib [rɪb] n πλευρά, πλευρό ♦ vt (mock) εμπαίζω, κοροϊδεύω.

ribald ['rɪbəld] a αισχρός, πρόστυχος, σόκιν.

ribbed [rɪbd] a ραβδωτός, με νευρώσεις.

ribbon ['rɪbən] n ταινία, κορδέλα.

rice [raɪs] n ρύζι || ~ pudding n ρυζόγαλο.

rich [rɪtʃ] a πλούσιος || (fertile) εύφορος, πλούσιος, γόνιμος || (splendid) πολυτελής, λαμπρός, υπέροχος || (of food) παχύς, από εκλεκτά συστατικά || the ~ οι πλούσιοι || ~es npl πλούτη ntpl, αφθονία || ~ly a πλούσια || ~ness n πλούτος || (abundance) αφθονία.

rickety ['rɪkɪtɪ] a (unsteady) που τρέμει, σαθρός, σαραβαλιασμένος.

rickshaw ['rɪkʃɔː] n δίτροχη άμαξα συρόμενη από άνθρωπο.

ricochet ['rɪkəʃeɪ] n εποστρακισμός ♦ vi εποστρακίζω, αναπηδώ.

rid [rɪd] (irreg v) vt απαλλάσσω, ελευθερώνω || to get ~ of απαλλάσσομαι από || good riddance! καλά ξεκουμπίδια!, ας πάει στο καλό!

riddle ['rɪdl] n (puzzle) αίνιγμα nt ♦ vt (esp passive) κάνω κόσκινο.

ride [raɪd] (irreg v) n διαδρομή, περίπατος, ταξίδι ♦ vt τρέχω, διασχίζω || (horse, bicycle) καβαλικεύω ♦ vi πάω καβάλα, καβαλικεύω, πηγαίνω με αμάξι || (NAUT) είμαι αγκυροβολημένος || ~r n ιππέας, καβαλάρης || (in contract etc) προσθήκη, παράρτημα nt, συμπληρωματική διάταξη.

ridge [rɪdʒ] n (hill) κορυφογραμμή, ράχη || (of roof) κολοφώνας, καβελαριά, κορφιάς || (narrow raised strip) πτυχή, ζάρα, προεξοχή.

ridicule ['rɪdɪkju:l] n περίγελος, εμπαιγμός, κοροϊδία ♦ vt κοροϊδεύω, γελοποιώ.

ridiculous [rɪ'dɪkjʊləs] a γελοίος.

riding ['raɪdɪŋ] n: to go ~ πηγαίνω ιππασία || ~ school n σχολή ιππασίας.

rife [raɪf] a: ~ with μεστός, γεμάτος από.

riffraff ['rɪfræf] n αλητεία, σκυλολόι.

rifle ['raɪfl] n όπλο, τουφέκι ♦ vt (rob) αδειάζω, διαρπάζω || ~ range n πεδίο βολής, σκοπευτήριο.

rift [rɪft] n σχισμή, ρωγμή.

rig [rɪg] n (outfit) φορεσιά, στόλισμα nt || (oil rig) γεωτρύπανο ♦ vt (election etc) νοθεύω τις εκλογές || ~ging n ξάρτια ntpl || to ~ out vt ντύνω, στολίζω || to ~ up vt στήνω, μαντάρω.

right [raɪt] a (correct, proper) ορθός, σωστός, κανονικός || (just, good) ευθύς, δίκαιος, έντιμος || (on right side) στα δεξιά ♦ n (what is just or true) το δίκαιο, n δικαιοσύνη || (title, claim) δικαίωμα nt, προνόμιο || (not left) δεξιά (πλευρά), το δεξιό || (POL) n Δεξιά ♦ ad (straight) κατευθείαν, ίσια || (completely, thoroughly) ακριβώς, κατευθείαν, τελείως ♦ vt ανορθώνω, ισορροπώ, ξαναφέρνω στα ίσια ♦ excl σωστά!, σύμφωνοι!, έχεις δίκιο! || to be ~ έχω δίκαιο || all ~! εντάξει! || ~ now αμέσως || by ~s δικαιωματικά, νομίμως || on the ~ στα δεξιά || ~ angle n ορθή γωνία || ~eous a ευθύς, ηθικός || ~eousness n ορθότητα, τιμιότητα || ~ful a νόμιμος, δίκαιος || ~-hand drive n με δεξιό τιμόνι || ~-handed a δεξιόχειρας, δεξιόστροφος || ~-hand man n το δεξί χέρι || ~-hand side n τα δεξιά || ~ly ad δίκαια, ορθά || ~-minded a λογικός, ορθοφρονών || ~ of way n προτεραιότητα || ~-winger n δεξιός.

rigid ['rɪdʒɪd] a άκαμπτος, αλύγιστος || (strict) αυστηρός || ~ity n ακαμψία, αλυγισία || ~ly ad άκαμπτα, αλύγιστα, αυστηρά.

rigmarole ['rɪgmərəʊl] n ασυναρτησίες fpl, κουραφέξαλα ntpl.

rigor ['rɪgə*] n (US) = rigour.

rigorous ['rɪgərəs] a αυστηρός, τραχύς.

rigour ['rɪgə*] n αυστηρότητα, δριμύτητα.

rim [rɪm] n στεφάνη, χείλος nt || (of wheel) στεφάνι, ζάντα || ~less a χωρίς σκελετό, χωρίς γείσο || ~med a με στεφάνη, με σκελετό.

rind [raɪnd] n φλοιός, φλούδα.

ring [rɪŋ] n (irreg v) n δακτύλιος, δακτυλίδι || (of people) συντροφιά, φατρία, συμμορία || (arena) παλαίστρα, στίβος, πίστα, αρένα, ρίγκ nt inv || (TEL) τηλεφώνημα nt, κτύπημα nt τηλεφώνου ♦ vt κτυπώ το κουδούνι ♦ vi (TEL) (also: ~ up) τηλεφωνώ || (resound) αντηχώ, κτυπώ || (bell) κουδουνίζω || to ~ off vi διακόπτω τη συνομιλία, κλείνω το τηλέφωνο || ~leader n (of gang) αρχηγός συμμορίας.

ringlets ['rɪŋlɪts] npl (hair) μπούκλες fpl.

ring road ['rɪŋrəʊd] n περιφεριακή οδός f.

rink [rɪŋk] n πίστα πατινάζ.

rinse [rɪns] n ξέπλυμα nt ♦ vt ξεπλένω, ξεβγάζω.

riot ['raɪət] n στάση, οχλαγωγία ♦ vi οχλαγωγώ, θορυβώ || ~ous a ταραχώδης, οχλαγωγικός, οργιαστικός.

rip [rɪp] n σχισμή, σχίσιμο ♦ vti σχίζω, ξεσχίζω.

ripcord ['rɪpkɔːd] n σχοινί ανοίγματος.

ripe [raɪp] a ώριμος, γινομένος || ~n vti ωριμάζω, γίνομαι || ~ness n ωριμότητα.

ripple ['rɪpl] n κυματισμός, ρυτίδα ♦ vti κυματίζω, ρυτιδώνω.

rise [raɪz] (irreg v) n ύψωμα nt, ανήφορος, κλίση || (esp in wages) αύξηση, άνοδος f ♦ vi (from chair) σηκώνομαι όρθιος || (from bed) ξυπνώ, σηκώνομαι || (sun) ανατέλλω, βγαίνω || (smoke, prices) υψώνομαι, ανεβαίνω || (mountain) υψώνομαι || (ground) ανηφορίζω, υψώνομαι || (revolt) εξεγείρομαι, ξεσηκώνομαι, επαναστατώ || to give ~ to προκαλώ || to ~ to the occasion φαίνομαι αντάξιος των περιστάσεων.

risk [rɪsk] n κίνδυνος, ριψοκινδύνευση ♦ vt ριψοκινδυνεύω || ~y a επικίνδυνος, ριψοκίνδυνος.

risqué ['riːskeɪ] a τολμηρό.

rissole ['rɪsəʊl] n κεφτές m, κροκέτα.

rite [raɪt] n ιεροτελεστία, εκκλησιαστική τελετή.

ritual ['rɪtjʊəl] n τυπικό, λειτουργικό ♦ a τυπικός, καθιερωμένος.

rival ['raɪvəl] n, a αντίπαλος, αντίζηλος, ανταγωνιστής ♦ vt ανταγωνίζομαι, συναγωνίζομαι || ~ry n ανταγωνισμός, συναγωνισμός.

river ['rɪvə*] n ποταμός, ποτάμι || ~bank n όχθη (ποταμού) || ~bed n κοίτη ποταμού || ~side n όχθη ♦ a της όχθης.

rivet ['rɪvɪt] n καρφωτό, καρφί ♦ vt καθηλώνω, καρφώνω || (fix) προσηλώνω, καρφώνω.

Riviera [rɪvɪ'ɛərə] n: the ~ n Ριβιέρα.

R.N. abbr of Royal Navy.

road [rəʊd] n οδός f, δρόμος || ~block n οδόφραγμα nt || ~hog n κακός οδηγός || ~map n οδικός χάρτης || ~side n άκρη του δρόμου, δίπλα στο δρόμο ♦ a στο δρόμο, του δρόμου || ~sign n πινακίδα δρόμου || ~way n αμαξητή οδός || ~worthy a κατάλληλος για κυκλοφορία.

roam [rəʊm] vi περιπλανώμαι, περιφέρομαι ♦ vt διασχίζω, διατρέχω, τριγυρίζω.

roar [rɔː*] n βρυχηθμός, μουγγρητό ♦ vi βρυχώμαι, ωρύομαι || ~ing a (fire) γερή (φωτιά), δυνατή (φωτιά) || (trade) ακμάζων (εμπόριο), καλές (δουλειές).

roast [rəʊst] n ψητό κρέας nt, ψητό ♦ vt ψήνω || (coffee beans) καβουρντίζω.

rob [rɒb] vt κλέβω, ληστεύω, αποστερώ ||

~ber n ληστής, κλέφτης || ~bery n ληστεία.

robe [rəʊb] n ρόμπα, φόρεμα nt || (of office) στολή, τήβεννος ♦ vt περιβάλλω, ντύνω.

robin ['rɒbɪn] n κοκκινολαίμης, κομπογιάννης.

robot ['rəʊbɒt] n αυτόματο, ρομπότ nt inv.

robust [rəʊ'bʌst] a εύρωστος, ρωμαλέος.

rock [rɒk] n βράχος || (GEOL) πέτρωμα nt || (candy) είδος καραμέλας ♦ vti λικνίζω, κουνώ, κουνιέμαι || on the ~s (drink) με πάγο, χωρίς νερό || (ship) νέφτω στα βράχια || (marriage etc) υπό διάλυση, σε δύσκολη θέση || ~-bottom n (fig) κατώτερο σημείο || ~ climber n ορειβάτης βράχων || ~ery n τεχνητοί βράχοι mpl.

rocket ['rɒkɪt] n ρουκέτα, πύραυλος, βολίδα.

rock fall ['rɒkfɔːl] n πτώση βράχων.

rocking chair ['rɒkɪŋtʃɛə*] n κουνιστή πολυθρόνα.

rocking horse ['rɒkɪŋhɔːs] n αλογάκι (παιδικό).

rocky ['rɒkɪ] a βραχώδης.

rod [rɒd] n (bar) ράβδος f, βέργα.

rode [rəʊd] pt of ride.

rodent ['rəʊdənt] n τρωκτικό.

rodeo ['rəʊdɪəʊ] n διαγωνισμός (καουμπόιδων).

roe [rəʊ] n (deer) δορκάδα, ζαρκάδι || (of fish) αυγά ntpl ψαριών.

rogue [rəʊg] n παλιάνθρωπος || (mischievous) κατεργάρης, πειραχτήριο, πονηρός.

roguish ['rəʊgɪʃ] a (playful) κατεργάρικος, τσαχπίνικος || (cheating) δόλιος, πανούργος.

role [rəʊl] n ρόλος.

roll [rəʊl] n (paper, meat etc) κύλινδρος, ρολό, τόπι || (bread) φραντζολάκι, κουλουράκι || (list) κατάλογος, λίστα || (of drum) συνεχής τυμπανοκρουσία ♦ vt (over) περιστρέφω, κυλώ || (wind round) τυλίγω, κάνω ρολό || (smooth out) ισοπεδώνω, πατώ, στρώνω ♦ vi (swing) στριφογυρίζω, κουνώ || (make deep sound) ηχώ, βροντώ || to ~ by vi (time) περνώ γρήγορα || to ~ in vi (mail) φθάνω σε μεγάλες ποσότητες || to ~ over vi ανατρέπομαι, κυλιέμαι || to ~ up vi (arrive) φθάνω, κουβαλιέμαι ♦ vt (carpet) τυλίγω || ~ call n ονομαστική κλήση, προσκλητήριο || ~ed a (umbrella) τυλιγμένος || ~er n κύλινδρος, τροχός || ~er skates npl πατίνια ntpl με ρόδες.

rolling ['rəʊlɪŋ] a (landscape) ανώμαλο έδαφος || ~ pin n πλάστης (για άνοιγμα φύλλου) || ~ stock n τροχαίο υλικό.

roly-poly ['rəʊlɪ'pəʊlɪ] n (pudding) πουτίγγια ρολό με φρούτα.

ROM abbr of read only memory μνήμη ROM, μνήμη που μόνο διαβάζεται.

Roman ['rəʊmən] a ρωμαϊκός ♦ n

Ρωμαίος || ~ **Catholic** a, n ρωμαιοκαθολικός.

romance [rəʊˈmæns] n ρομάντζο || (story) ρομαντική ιστορία ♦ vi υπερβάλλω, φαντασιολογώ.

Romanesque [rəʊməˈnɛsk] a ρωμανικός (ρυθμός).

romantic [rəʊˈmæntɪk] a ρομαντικός.

romp [rɒmp] n εύθυμο παιχνίδι, φασαρία ♦ vi (also: ~ **about**) θορυβώ, κάνω φασαρία, ατακτώ || ~**ers** npl μπλούζα, ποδιά παιδιών, φόρμα.

rondo [ˈrɒndəʊ] n (MUS) ροντό nt inv, ρόντο nt inv.

roof [ruːf] n στέγη, σκεπή || (of car etc) σκεπή || (of mouth) ουρανίσκος ♦ vt στεγάζω, σκεπάζω || ~ **garden** n κήπος σε ταράτσα || ~**ing** n στέγαση, ταβάνωμα.

rook [rʊk] n (bird) κορώνη, κουρούνα, χαβαρώνι || (thief) κλέφτης, λωποδύτης ♦ vt (cheat) κλέβω.

room [rʊm] n (in house) δωμάτιο, κάμαρα || (space) χώρος, τόπος || (opportunity) περιθώριο || ~**s** npl (flat) δωμάτια ntpl, διαμέρισμα nt || (lodgings) δωμάτια ntpl με φαγητό || ~**iness** n ευρυχωρία || ~**ing house** n οικία ενοικιάζουσα επιπλωμένα δωμάτια || ~**mate** n συγκάτοικος || ~ **service** n υπηρεσία || ~**y** a ευρύχωρος.

roost [ruːst] n κούρνια, κοτέτσι ♦ vi κουρνιάζω.

root [ruːt] n ρίζα || (source) πηγή, αιτία, ρίζα ♦ vt ριζώνω || **to ~ about** vi (fig) ψάχνω || **to ~ for** vt υποστηρίζω, ενθαρρύνω || **to ~ out** vt ξεριζώνω.

rope [rəʊp] n σχοινί ♦ vt δένω με σχοινί || **to ~ in** vt περικλείω, προσηλυτίζω, παρασύρω || **to know the ~s** ξέρω τη δουλειά μου, είμαι μπασμένος || ~ **ladder** n ανεμόσκαλα.

rosary [ˈrəʊzərɪ] n κομβολόι.

rose [rəʊz] pt of **rise** || (flower) n τριαντάφυλλο, ρόδο ♦ a ροδόχρους, ρόζ.

rosé [ˈrəʊzeɪ] n (wine) κοκκινέλι.

rosebed [ˈrəʊzbɛd] n ροδωνιά, βραγιά με τριανταφυλλιές.

rosebud [ˈrəʊzbʌd] n μπουμπούκι τριανταφύλλου.

rosebush [ˈrəʊzbʊʃ] n τριανταφυλλιά.

rosemary [ˈrəʊzmərɪ] n δενδρολίβανο.

rosette [rəʊˈzɛt] n ροζέτα.

roster [ˈrɒstə*] n κατάλογος, κατάσταση.

rostrum [ˈrɒstrəm] n άμβωνας, βήμα nt.

rosy [ˈrəʊzɪ] a (colour) ροδόχρους, ρόδινος, ρόζ || (hopeful) ρόδινα.

rot [rɒt] n σήψη, σαπίλα, σάπισμα nt || (nonsense) ανονσία, μπούρδα ♦ vti αποσυντίθεμαι, σαπίζω.

rota [ˈrəʊtə] n κατάλογος, πίνακας.

rotary [ˈrəʊtərɪ] a περιστροφικός.

rotate [rəʊˈteɪt] vt (two or more things in order) εναλλάσσω, εκτελώ εκ περιτροπής ♦ vi περιστρέφομαι, γυρίζω (γύρω από).

rotating [rəʊˈteɪtɪŋ] a περιστρεφόμενος, περιστροφικός.

rotation [rəʊˈteɪʃən] n περιστροφή.

rotor [ˈrəʊtə*] n στροφείο, ρώτωρ m inv, ρότορ m inv.

rotten [ˈrɒtn] a σαθρός, σάπιος, σαπισμένος || (dishonest) πρόστυχος, κακής ποιότητας.

rotund [rəʊˈtʌnd] a στρογγυλός, παχουλός.

rouble [ˈruːbl] n ρούβλι.

rouge [ruːʒ] n κοκκινάδι, βαφή.

rough [rʌf] a (uneven) ανώμαλος, τραχύς || (violent, coarse) χονδροειδής, πρόστυχος, τραχύς, απότομος || (stormy, wild) άγριος, σφοδρός, τρικυμιώδης || (without comforts) πρόχειρος, στοιχειώδης || (unfinished drawing) πρόχειρο, του προσχέδιο || (stones) ακατέργαστος || (makeshift) βιαστικός, πρόχειρος || (approximate) κατά προσέγγιση ♦ n (uncut grass) ψηλό χορτάρι || (violent person) μάγκας, κουτσαβάκης ♦ vt **to ~ it** στερούμαι τις ανέσεις, αντιμετωπίζω δυσκολίες || **to play ~** παίζω σκληρό παιχνίδι || **to ~ out** vt (draft) προσχεδιάζω, κάνω πρόχειρα || ~**en** vt τραχύνω || ~**ly** ad δυνατά || (draft) πρόχειρα || (approximately) περίπου || ~**ness** τραχύτητα, σκληρότητα.

roulette [ruːˈlɛt] n ρουλέτα.

Roumania [ruːˈmeɪnɪə] n Ρουμανία || ~ n (person) Ρουμάνος/α m/f ♦ a ρουμανικός.

round [raʊnd] a στρογγυλός, σφαιρικός, κυκλικός || (rough) στρογγυλός ♦ ad γύρω, τριγύρω ♦ prep γύρω από, περί ♦ n κύκλος, γύρος || (duty) γύρος, βόλτα, περιοδεία, καθημερινή δουλειά || (SPORT) γύρος ♦ vt (corner) κάμπτω, στρίβω, κάνω στροφή, παίρνω τη στροφή || **to ~ off** vt στρογγυλεύω, τελειώνω || **to ~ up** vt συγκεντρώνω, μαζεύω, πιάνω, περικυκλώνω || ~ **of ammunition** n φυσίγγι || ~ **of applause** n ομοβροντία χειροκροτημάτων || ~ **of drinks** n ένας γύρος ποτών || ~**about** n κυκλική διασταύρωση δρόμων || (merry-go-round) περιστρεφόμενα ξύλινα αλογάκια ntpl ♦ a κυκλικός, περιφερειακός || ~**ed** a στρογγυλεμένος || ~**ly** ad (fig) τέλεια, ολοσχερώς, πλήρως || ~**-shouldered** a με κυρτούς ώμους, σκυφτός || ~**up** n περίμάζεμα nt.

rouse [raʊz] vt σηκώνω || (stir up) προκαλώ, διεγείρω, ξεσηκώνω.

rousing [ˈraʊzɪŋ] a (welcome) θορυβώδης, ζωηρός.

rout [raʊt] n φυγή, άτακτη φυγή ♦ vt κατατροπώνω, τρέπω σε φυγή.

route [ruːt] n δρομολόγιο, δρόμος, πορεία || ~ **map** n οδικός χάρτης.

routine [ruːˈtiːn] n ρουτίνα, στερεότυπη πορεία ♦ a κανονικός, τακτικός.

roving [ˈrəʊvɪŋ] a περιφερόμενος, περιπλανώμενος.

row [rəʊ] n (line) σειρά, στοίχος, γραμμή, αράδα ♦ vt (boat) κινώ με κουπί, μεταφέρω με τα κουπιά ♦ vi (in boat) κωπηλατώ, τραβώ κουπί ♦ [raʊ] n (noise) θόρυβος, φασαρία, σαματάς || (dispute) φιλονεικία, καυγάς, σκηνή || (scolding) επίπληξη, κατσάδα, λούσιμο ♦ vi φιλονεικώ, καυγαδίζω, αρπάζομαι.

rowdy ['raʊdɪ] a θορυβώδης, που κάνει σαματά ♦ n (person) θορυβοποιός, καυγατζής.

rowing ['rəʊɪŋ] n κωπηλασία, κουπί || ~ **boat** n βάρκα με κουπιά.

rowlock ['rɒlək] n σκαλμός.

royal ['rɔɪəl] a βασιλικός || ~**ist** n βασιλόφρων m, βασιλικός ♦ a βασιλικός.

royalty ['rɔɪəltɪ] n (royal family) βασιλική οικογένεια || (payment: to inventor) δικαιώματα ntpl εφευρέτου || (: to author) συγγραφικά δικαιώματα ntpl.

r.p.m. abbr (= revs per minute) στρ./λεπ., σ.α.λ. (στροφές ανά λεπτό).

R.S.V.P. abbr (= répondez s'il vous plaît) R.S.V.P.

Rt. Hon. abbr (= Right Honourable) Εντιμότατος.

rub [rʌb] n (polish, with cloth) τρίψιμο, σφούγγισμα nt ♦ vt τρίβω, επαλείφω, προστρίβω || (clean) στεγνώνω, σκουπίζω || **to** ~ **off** vi τρίβω, σβήνω.

rubber ['rʌbə*] n (substance) καουτσούκ nt inv || (Brit) γομμολάστιχα || ~ **band** n λάστιχο || ~ **plant** n εβέα, δέντρο καουτσούκ || ~ **stamp** n (lit) σφραγίδα || (fig) ο εγκρίνων τυφλιά.

rubbish ['rʌbɪʃ] n σκουπίδια ntpl, απορρίμματα ntpl || (nonsense) ανοησίες fpl, κολοκύθια ntpl || ~ **dump** n τόπος απορρίψεως σκουπιδιών || ~**y** a άχρηστος, της πεντάρας.

rubble ['rʌbl] n χαλίκι, σκύρο.

ruble ['ruːbl] n (US) = **rouble**.

ruby ['ruːbɪ] n ρουμπίνι ♦ a κόκκινο, ρουμπινί.

rucksack ['rʌksæk] n σακκίδιο.

rudder ['rʌdə*] n πηδάλιο, τιμόνι.

ruddy ['rʌdɪ] a (colour) ροδοκόκκινος, ερυθρωπός || (col: bloody) τρομερός.

rude [ruːd] a (vulgar) πρόστυχος || (impolite) βάναυσος, απολίτιστος, αγενής || (rough) τραχύς, πρωτόγονος || ~**ly** ad πρωτόγονα, απότομα || ~**ness** n χοντροκοπιά, αγένεια.

rudiment ['ruːdɪmənt] n στοιχείο, υποτυπώδης αρχή || ~**ary** a στοιχειώδης.

ruff [rʌf] n τραχηλιά.

ruffian ['rʌfɪən] n παλιάνθρωπος, κακούργος.

ruffle ['rʌfl] vt ρυτιδώνω, τσαλακώνω, ανακατεύω.

rug [rʌg] n τάπης, χαλί || (for knees) κουβέρτα, κάπα.

rugby ['rʌgbɪ] n ράγκμπυ nt inv.

rugged ['rʌgɪd] a τραχύς || (surface) ανώμαλος.

rugger ['rʌgə*] n ράγκμπυ nt inv.

ruin ['ruːɪn] n καταστροφή, συμφορά, αφανισμός ♦ vt καταστρέφω, αφανίζω || ~**s** npl ερείπια ntpl || ~**ation** n καταστροφή, όλεθρος, ρήμαγμα nt.

rule [ruːl] n (guide) κανόνας || (what is usual) συνήθεια, το κανονικό || (government) εξουσία, αρχή, κυριαρχία || (stick) κανόνας ♦ vt κυβερνώ, διοικώ || (pervade) διέπω || (lines) χαρακώνω || **as a** ~ κατά κανόνα, συνήθως || ~**d** a (paper) ριγωτός, χαρακωμένος || ~**r** n κυβερνήτης, άρχοντας || (straight edge) χάρακας, ρίγα, μέτρο.

ruling ['ruːlɪŋ] a (party) άρχοντας, διευθύνων, κυβερνών || (class) άρχουσα (τάξη).

rum [rʌm] n ρούμι ♦ a (col) παράξενος, αλλόκοτος.

rumble ['rʌmbl] n υπόκωφος βοή, βροντή ♦ vi βροντώ, βουίζω, γουργουρίζω.

rummage ['rʌmɪdʒ] n έρευνα, ψάξιμο ♦ vt ερευνώ, ψάχνω.

rumour, rumor (US) ['ruːmə*] n φήμη, διάδοση ♦ vt: **it is** ~**ed that** λέγεται ότι, διαδίδεται ότι, φημολογείται ότι.

rump [rʌmp] n γλουτός, οπίσθια ntpl || ~**steak** n κόντρα φιλέτο.

rumpus ['rʌmpəs] n θόρυβος, ταραχή || (col) καυγάς, σαματάς.

run [rʌn] (irreg v) n (running) δρόμος, τρέξιμο || (AUT) διαδρομή, βόλτα || (series) σειρά, συνέχεια || (sudden demand) ζήτηση || (enclosed space) χώρος κλειστός || (ski run) πίστα του σκι, κατήφορος για σκι ♦ vt (cause to run) κατευθύνω, λειτουργώ || (train, bus) κυκλοφορώ, κάνω διαδρομή || (manage) διευθύνω || (compete in race) τρέχω σε αγώνα || (stand for election) βάζω υποψηφιότητα || (force) περνώ || (pass: hand, eye) περνώ || (COMPUT: program) τρέχω ♦ vi (move quickly) τρέχω, το βάζω στα πόδια || (in election) θέτω υποψηφιότητα || (in race) τρέχω σε αγώνες || (machine) λειτουργώ || (flow) ρέω, κυλώ, τρέχω || (colours) ξεβάφω, βγαίνω, τρέχω || **on the** ~ σε φυγή || **to** ~ **riot** οργιάζω || **to** ~ **a risk** ριψοκινδυνεύω || **to** ~ **about** vi (children) τρέχω εδώ και κει || ~ **to** ~ **across** vt (find) συναντώ τυχαία || **to** ~ **away** vi δραπετεύω || **to** ~ **down** vi (clock) ξεκουρδίζω ♦ vt (run over) κτυπώ, πατώ (κάποιον), πλακώνω || (talk against) δυσφημώ, κατηγορώ || **to be** ~-**down** είμαι εξαντλημένος, είμαι τσακισμένος || **to** ~ **off** vi φεύγω, τρέπομαι σε φυγή, το σκάω || **to** ~ **out** vi (person) βγαίνω τρέχοντας || (liquid) χύνομαι, τρέχω, στάζω || (lease) λήγω || (money) τελειώνω, εξαντλούμαι || **to** ~ **out of** vt εξαντλώ, τελειώνω, μένω από || **to** ~ **over** vt κτυπώ, πλακώνω, πατώ || (read) ρίχνω μια ματιά || **to** ~ **through** vt (instructions) διαβάζω γρήγορα, εξετάζω βιαστικά || ~ **up** vt (debt) αφήνω να ανέβει, χρεώνομαι περισσότερα || (dress) ράβω γρήγορα-γρήγορα || **to** ~ **up against** vt

(difficulties) συναντώ, αντιμετωπίζω ||
~about n (small car) αυτοκίνητο δύο
θέσεων || ~away a (horse) αφηνιασμένο
(άλογο) || (person) ο δραπέτης.

rung [rʌŋ] pp of ring ♦ n βαθμίδα || (of
rope ladder) σκαλί ανεμόσκαλας.

runner ['rʌnə*] n (messenger)
αγγελιαφόρος || (of sleigh) πατίνι || ~-up
n ο επιλαχών, ο δεύτερος (νικητής).

running ['rʌnɪŋ] n (of business)
διεύθυνση || (of machine) λειτουργία,
κίνηση ♦ a (water) τρεχούμενος || ~
commentary n σύγχρονη περιγραφή,
(ραδιο) ρεπορτάζ nt inv.

run-of-the-mill ['rʌnəvðə'mɪl] a
κοινός, συνηθισμένος.

runt [rʌnt] n κοντοστούμπης.

run-through ['rʌnθru:] n γρήγορο
διάβασμα nt, γρήγορη επανάληψη.

runway ['rʌnweɪ] n διάδρομος
απογειώσεως.

rupture ['rʌptʃə*] n (MED) ρήξη,
διάρρηξη ♦ vt: to ~ o.s. πάσχω από
κήλη.

rural ['ruərəl] a αγροτικός, υπαίθριος.

ruse [ru:z] n τέχνασμα nt, πανουργία,
κόλπο.

rush [rʌʃ] n (dash) βιασύνη || (sudden
demand) μεγάλη ζήτηση || (current)
εκτόξευση, εισροή ♦ vt ορμώ, τρέχω
επειγόντως || (attack) κάνω έφοδο || (col:
overcharge) υδέρνω ♦ vi (dash) (εξ)ορμώ,
εφορμώ, σπεύδω, τρέχω || ~es npl (BOT)
βούρλο, σπάρτο || ~ hour n ώρα
συνωστισμού, ώρα πολλής δουλειάς.

rusk [rʌsk] n παξιμάδι.

Russia ['rʌʃə] n Ρωσία || ~n n
Ρώσος/ίδα m/f ♦ a ρωσικός, ρούσικος.

rust [rʌst] n σκουριά, σκουριά ♦ vi
σκουριάζω.

rustic ['rʌstɪk] a (of the country)
αγροτικός, χωριάτικος || (roughly made)
χοντροκαμωμένος.

rustle ['rʌsl] n ψίθυρος, τρίξιμο,
μουρμούρισμα nt ♦ vi θροΐζω,
μουρμουρίζω ♦ vt (US: animals) κλέβω,
είμαι ζωοκλέπτης.

rustproof ['rʌstpru:f] a ανοξείδωτος.

rusty ['rʌstɪ] a σκουριασμένος.

rut [rʌt] n (track) αυλάκι, τροχιά, ροδιά ||
(routine) ρουτίνα, μονοτονία.

ruthless ['ru:θlɪs] a ανελέητος,
άσπλαχνος, ωμός || ~ly ad χωρίς οίκτο,
αλύπητα || ~ness n ασπλαχνία,
σκληρότητα.

rye [raɪ] n σίκαλη || ~ bread n ψωμί από
σίκαλη.

S

sabbath ['sæbəθ] n (Jewish) Σάββατο ||
(Christian) Κυριακή.

sabbatical [sə'bætɪkəl] a: ~ year άδεια
ενός χρόνου (καθηγητού).

saber ['seɪbə*] n (US) = sabre.

sabotage ['sæbətɑ:ʒ] n σαμποτάζ nt inv.

sabre ['seɪbə*] n σπαθί.

saccharin(e) ['sækərɪn] n σακχαρίνη.

sack [sæk] n σάκος, τσουβάλι || (dismissal)
απόλυση ♦ vt απολύω || (town) λεηλατώ ||
~ful n σακιά, τσουβάλι || ~ing n
(material) σακόπανο || (dismissal)
απόλυση, παύση.

sacrament ['sækrəmənt] n μυστήριο,
μετάληψη.

sacred ['seɪkrɪd] a ιερός, άγιος || (duty
etc) απαραβίαστος.

sacrifice ['sækrɪfaɪs] n θυσία ♦ vt
θυσιάζω.

sacrilege ['sækrɪlɪdʒ] n ιεροσυλία ||
βεβήλωση.

sacrosanct ['sækrəusæŋkt] a ιερός και
απαραβίαστος.

sad [sæd] a λυπημένος, θλιμένος || (dull)
θλιβερός || ~den vt λυπώ, θλίβω.

saddle ['sædl] n σέλα ♦ vt (burden)
φορτώνω || ~bag n σακίδιο.

sadism ['seɪdɪzəm] n σαδισμός.

sadist ['seɪdɪst] n σαδιστής/ίστρια m/f ||
~ic [sə'dɪstɪk] a σαδιστικός.

sadness ['sædnɪs] n θλίψη, μελαγχολία.

safari [sə'fɑ:rɪ] n σαφάρι.

safe [seɪf] a ασφαλής, σώος || (cautious)
προσεκτικός, σίγουρος || (sure)
ασφαλής, ακίνδυνος ♦ n
χρηματοκιβώτιο || ~guard n
εξασφάλιση, προστασία ♦ vt
προστατεύω || ~keeping n ασφάλεια ||
~ly ad ασφαλώς, σίγουρα.

safety ['seɪftɪ] n ασφάλεια, σιγουριά || ~
belt n ζώνη ασφαλείας || ~ curtain n
αυλαία ασφαλείας || ~ pin n παραμάνα.

sag [sæg] vi κάμπτομαι, βουλιάζω.

sage [seɪdʒ] n (herb) φασκομηλιά,
αλιφασκιά || (man) σοφός.

sago ['seɪgəu] n (food) σάγος.

said [sɛd] pt, pp of say || a λεγόμενος,
λεχθείς.

sail [seɪl] n ιστίο, πανί || (trip) ταξίδι,
απόπλους ♦ vt κυβερνώ (πλοίο) ♦ vi
πλέω, πάω με το πανί || (depart) αποπλέω
|| (fig: cloud etc) τρέχω, περνώ || ~boat n
(US) βάρκα με πανί || ~ing n (SPORT)
ιστιοδρομία || to go ~ing κάνω
ιστιοδρομίες || ~ing ship n ιστιοφόρο
πλοίο || ~or n ναύτης, ναυτικός.

saint [seɪnt] n άγιος/α m/f.

sake [seɪk] n: for the ~ of για χάρη του
|| for your ~ για το καλό σου.

salad ['sæləd] n σαλάτα || ~ dressing n
είδος nt μαγιονέζας || ~ oil n λάδι για
σαλάτα.

salary ['sælərɪ] n μισθός.

sale [seɪl] n πώληση, πούλημα nt || (for
short periods) ξεπούλημα ntpl, εκπτώσεις
fpl || ~room n δημοπρατήριο ||
salesman n πωλητής || saleswoman n
πωλήτρια.

salient ['seɪlɪənt] a προεξέχων,
εντυπωσιακός.

saliva [sə'laɪvə] n σάλιο.

sallow ['sæləu] a ωχρός, χλωμός.

salmon ['sæmən] n σολομός.

S

salon ['sælɔ̃:ŋ] n κομμωτήριο.

saloon [sə'luːn] n (AUT) κλειστό (αυτοκίνητο) || (ship's lounge) σαλόνι.

salt [sɔːlt] n άλας nt, αλάτι || (CHEM) άλας nt ♦ vt (cure) αλατίζω, παστώνω || (flavour) αλατίζω || ~-cellar n αλατιέρα || ~y a αλμυρός.

salutary ['sæljutəri] a ωφέλιμος, σωτήριος.

salute [sə'luːt] n (MIL) χαιρετισμός ♦ vt (MIL) χαιρετίζω, αποδίδω χαιρετισμό.

salvage ['sælvidʒ] n διάσωση || (property saved) διασωθέν, υλικό ♦ vt διασώζω.

salvation [sæl'veiʃən] n σωτηρία || **S~ Army** n o Στρατός της Σωτηρίας.

salver ['sælvə*] n δίσκος.

salvo ['sælvəʊ] n κανονιοβολισμός, ομοβροντία.

same [seim] a ίδιος || **all the ~** παρ' όλα αυτά.

sample ['saːmpl] n δείγμα nt ♦ vt (test) δοκιμάζω.

sanatorium [sænə'tɔːriəm] n σανατόριο.

sanctimonious [sæŋkti'məʊniəs] a ψευτοθεοφοβούμενος, υποκριτής.

sanction ['sæŋkʃən] n (POL, ECON) (επι)κύρωση.

sanctity ['sæŋktiti] n αγιότητα, αγιοσύνη || (sacredness) ιερότητα, το απαράβιαστο.

sanctuary ['sæŋktjuəri] n ιερό, άδυτο || (for fugitive) άσυλο || (refuge) καταφύγιο.

sand [sænd] n άμμος f ♦ vt στρώνω με άμμο || ~s npl αμμουδιά.

sandal ['sændl] n σανδάλι, πέδιλο.

sandbag ['sændbæg] n σάκος άμμου.

sand dune ['sænddjuːn] n αμμόλοφος.

sandpaper ['sændpeipə*] n γυαλόχαρτο.

sandpit ['sændpit] n (for children) αμμόκουτο.

sandstone ['sændstəʊn] n ψαμμίτης, ψαμμόλιθος.

sandwich ['sænwidʒ] n σάντουιτς ♦ vt παρεμβάλλω, στριμώχνω.

sandy ['sændi] a (with sand) αμμώδης, αμμουδερός || (colour) πυρόξανθος.

sane [sein] a συνετός || (sensible) λογικός.

sang [sæŋ] pt of **sing**.

sanitarium [sæni'tɛəriəm] n (US) = **sanatorium**.

sanitary ['sænitəri] a υγιεινός || (protective) υγιειονομικός || ~ **napkin** (US), ~ **towel** n πετσέτα υγείας.

sanitation [sæni'teiʃən] n υγιεινή.

sanity ['sæniti] n πνευματική υγεία, υγιής νούς || (good sense) λογική.

sank [sæŋk] pt of **sink**.

Santa Claus [sæntə'klɔːz] n 'Αη Βασίλης.

sap [sæp] n (of plants) χυμός, οπός ♦ vt (wear away) υπονομεύω, υποσκάπτω.

sapling ['sæpliŋ] n δενδρύλιο.

sapphire ['sæfaiə*] n σάπφειρος.

sarcasm ['saːkæzəm] n σαρκασμός.

sarcastic [saː'kæstik] a σαρκαστικός.

sardine [saː'diːn] n σαρδέλα.

sash [sæʃ] n (MIL) ζώνη αξιωματικών.

sat [sæt] pt, pp of **sit**.

Satan ['seitn] n Σατανάς || ~ic [sə'tænik] a σατανικός.

satchel ['sætʃəl] n (SCH) τσάντα, σάκα.

satellite ['sætəlait] n δορυφόρος ♦ a δορυφορικός.

satin ['sætin] n σατέν nt inv ♦ a σατινέ, από σατέν.

satire ['sætaiə*] n σάτυρα.

satirical [sə'tirikəl] a σατυρικός.

satisfaction [sætis'fækʃən] n ικανοποίηση || ευχαρίστηση.

satisfactory [sætis'fæktəri] a ικανοποιητικός.

satisfy ['sætisfai] vt ικανοποιώ || (convince) πείθω, διαβεβαιώ || ~ing a ικανοποιητικός.

saturate ['sætʃəreit] vt διαβρέχω, διαποτίζω, μουσκεύω.

Saturday ['sætədi] n Σάββατο.

sauce [sɔːs] n σάλτσα || ~pan n κατσαρόλα.

saucer ['sɔːsə*] n πιατάκι.

saucy ['sɔːsi] a αναιδής, αυθάδης.

saunter ['sɔːntə*] vi σουλατσάρω, περπατώ άσκοπα ♦ n βόλτα.

sausage ['sɒsidʒ] n λουκάνικο || ~ **roll** n λουκάνικο με ζύμη.

savage ['sævidʒ] a άγριος, θηριώδης || (uncivilized) απολίτιστος, βάρβαρος ♦ n άγριος ♦ vt (fig) επιτίθεμαι άγρια || ~ry n αγριότητα, βαρβαρότητα.

save [seiv] vt σώζω, γλυτώνω || (store up) (εξ)οικονομώ, αποταμιεύω, μαζεύω || (avoid using up) αποφεύγω || (COMPUT) φυλάω ♦ prep, cj εκτός από εκτός, εξαιρουμένου.

saving ['seiviŋ] a (redeeming) σωτήριος ♦ n οικονομία || ~s npl αποταμιεύσεις fpl, καταθέσεις fpl, οικονομίες fpl || ~s **bank** n ταμιευτήριο.

saviour ['seivjə*] n σωτήρας.

savour, savor (US) ['seivə*] n ουσία, γεύση, γούστο ♦ vt γεύομαι || (enjoy) απολαμβάνω || ~y a γευστικός, νόστιμος, ορεκτικός.

saw [sɔː] (irreg v) n (tool) πριόνι ♦ vt πριονίζω || pt of **see** || ~dust n πριονίδια ntpl || ~mill n πριονιστήριο.

saxophone ['sæksəfəʊn] n σαξόφωνο.

say [sei] (irreg v) n λόγος ♦ vt (tell) λέγω || (suppose) υποθέτω || ~ing n ρητό.

scab [skæb] n κάρκαδο || (pej: industry) απεργοσπάστης.

scabby ['skæbi] a ψωριάρης.

scaffold ['skæfəld] n ικρίωμα nt || ~ing n σκαλωσιά.

scald [skɔːld] n ζεμάτισμα nt ♦ vt ζεματίζω.

scale [skeil] n (of fish) λέπι || (MUS) κλίμακα, σκάλα || (for measuring) κλίμακα, διαβάθμιση || (on map) κλίμακα || (size) κλίμακα ♦ vt (climb) αναρριχώμαι, σκαρφαλώνω || ~s npl (balance) ζυγός, ζυγαριά || **on a large ~** σε μεγάλη κλίμακα || ~ drawing n σχέδιο υπό κλίμακα.

scallop ['skɒləp] n (shellfish) χτένι.

scalp [skælp] n τριχωτό δέρμα nt κεφαλής ♦ vt γδέρνω το κρανίο.

scalpel ['skælpəl] n νυστέρι.

scamper ['skæmpə*] vi τρέχω τρελά, το στρίβω.

scan [skæn] vt εξουνιχίζω, διερευνώ || (POET) διαβάζω μετρικά.

scandal ['skændl] n σκάνδαλο || (gossip) κακολογία, κουτσομπολιό || ~ize vt σκανδαλίζω || ~ous a σκανδαλώδης.

Scandinavia [skændı'neıvıə] n Σκανδιναβία || ~n a σκανδιναβικός ♦ n Σκανδιναβός/ή m/f.

scant [skænt] a πενιχρός, ανεπαρκής, λιγοστός || ~y a ανεπαρκής, λιγοστός.

scapegoat ['skeıpgəʊt] n αποδιοπομπαίος τράγος.

scar [ska:*] n ουλή, σημάδι ♦ vt αφήνω σημάδι.

scarce [skɛəs] a σπάνιος || ~ly ad μόλις, σχεδόν καθόλου || ~ness n σπανιότητα έλλειψη.

scarcity ['skɛəsıtı] n σπανιότητα, έλλειψη.

scare [skɛə*] n εκφόβιση, τρομάρα ♦ vt φοβίζω, τρομάζω || ~crow n σκιάχτρο.

scarf [ska:f] n σάρπα, κασκόλ nt inv.

scarlet ['ska:lıt] a (colour) κατακόκκινος ♦ n κτυπητό κόκκινο || ~ fever n οστρακιά, σκαρλατίνα.

scarves [ska:vz] npl of scarf.

scathing ['skeıðıŋ] a καυστικός, δηκτικός.

scatter ['skætə*] n διασπορά, σκόρπισμα nt ♦ vt (sprinkle) σκορπίζω || (an enemy) διασκορπίζω ♦ vi διαλύομαι, σκορπίζω || ~brained a άμυαλος, ξεμυαλισμένος || ~ing n μικρή ποσότητα, σκόρπισμα nt.

scavenger ['skævındʒə*] n (animal) ζώο που τρώει ψοφίμια.

scene [si:n] n (of accident etc) τόπος, θέατρο || (of play) σκηνή || (division of play) σκηνή || (view) τοπείο, άποψη, θέα || (fuss) σκηνή, φασαρία, επεισόδιο || (incident) σκηνή || on the ~ στον τόπο, επί σκηνής || ~ry n σκηνικό, σκηνογραφία, σκηνή || (view) τοπίο, θέα.

scenic ['si:nık] a σκηνικός, θεαματικός.

scent [sent] n οσμή, άρωμα nt, μυρουδιά || (sense of smell) όσφρηση ♦ vt (make fragrant) αρωματίζω, μοσχοβολώ.

scepter ['septə*] n (US) = sceptre.

sceptic ['skeptık] n σκεπτικιστής || ~al a σκεπτικός, δύσπιστος || ~ism n σκεπτικισμός.

sceptre ['septə*] n σκήπτρο.

schedule ['ʃedju:l, (US) 'skedju:l] n πρόγραμμα, nt || (of trains) δρομολόγιο || (of prices) κατάλογος ♦ vt καταγράφω, προγραμματίζω || on ~ στην ώρα || σύμφωνα με το πρόγραμμα || behind ~ καθυστερημένος.

scheme [ski:m] n διάταξη || (plan)

σχέδιο || (plot) μηχανορραφία, δολοπλοκία ♦ vti (plot) μηχανορραφώ || (plan) σχεδιάζω.

scheming ['ski:mıŋ] a δολοπλόκος, κομπιναδόρος.

schism ['sızəm] n σχίσμα nt.

schizophrenic [skıtsəʊ'frenık] a σχιζοφρενικός.

scholar ['skɒlə*] n μελετητής, μορφωμένος || (with scholarship) υπότροφος || ~ly a μορφωμένος || ~ship n υποτροφία || (learning) μόρφωση.

school [sku:l] n σχολείο || (group) σχολή || (department) σχολή ♦ attr a σχολικό, του σχολείου ♦ vt διδάσκω, γυμνάζω, μορφώνω || ~book n σχολικό βιβλίο || ~boy n μαθητής || ~days npl σχολικά χρόνια ntpl || ~girl n μαθήτρια || ~ing n εκπαίδευση, μόρφωση δάσκαλος, καθηγητής || ~mistress n δασκάλα, καθηγήτρια || ~teacher n δημοδιδάσκαλος/ισσα m/f.

schooner ['sku:nə*] n (ship) σκούνα || (glass for sherry etc) ποτηράκι.

sciatica [saı'ætıkə] n ισχιαλγία.

science ['saıəns] n επιστήμη.

scientific [saıən'tıfık] a επιστημονικός.

scientist ['saıəntıst] n επιστήμονας m/f.

scintillating ['sıntıleıtıŋ] a σπινθηρβόλος, αστραφτερός.

scissors ['sızəz] npl (also: a pair of ~) ψαλίδι.

scoff [skɒf] vt (eat) τρώγω, καταβροχθίζω ♦ vi (mock) (+at) σκόπτω, κοροϊδεύω.

scold [skəʊld] vt επιπλήττω, μαλώνω.

scone [skɒn] n είδος nt κέικ.

scoop [sku:p] n φτυάρι, σέσουλα ♦ vt: to ~ out αδειάζω || to ~ up vt βγάζω.

scooter ['sku:tə*] n (motorcycle) βέσπα || (child's toy) πατίνι.

scope [skəʊp] n αντίληψη, γνώση || (opportunity) ευκαιρία || (margin) περιθώριο.

scorch [skɔ:tʃ] n καψάλισμα nt, κάψιμο ♦ vt καψαλίζω, τσουρουφλίζω || (wither) ψήνω, ξεραίνω || ~ing a καφτερός.

score [skɔ:*] n (points) σκορ nt inv || (MUS) παρτιτούρα || (reason) σημείο || (twenty) εικοσάρα, εικοσαριά ♦ vt (win points) σημειώνω, κάνω πόντους || (mark) χαράσσω, χαρακώνω ♦ vi (keep record) κρατώ σκόρ || ~board n πίνακας των σκορ || ~r n (player) ο επιτυχών τέρμα || (recorder) μαρκαδόρος.

scorn ['skɔ:n] n περιφρόνηση ♦ vt περιφρονώ.

scorpion ['skɔ:pıən] n σκορπιός.

Scot [skɒt] n Σκωτσέζος/α m/f || **Scotch** n (whisky) (σκωτσέζικο) ουίσκυ.

scotch [skɒtʃ] vt (terminate) αποτρέπω, καταπνίγω.

Scotland ['skɒtlənd] n Σκωτία.

Scots [skɒts] npl Σκωτσέζοι mpl ♦ a σκωτσέζος || ~man n Σκωτσέζος || ~woman n Σκωτίδα, Σκωτσέζα.

Scottish ['skɒtɪʃ] a σκωτικός, σκωτσέζικος.

scoundrel ['skaundrəl] n παλιάνθρωπος.

scour ['skauə*] vt (search) διατρέχω, ερευνώ || (clean) καθαρίζω || ~ er n (for pans) σύρμα nt.

scourge [skɜːdʒ] n (plague) πληγή.

scout [skaut] n ανιχνευτής || (boy scout) πρόσκοπος ♦ vi (reconnoitre) ανιχνεύω, κάνω αναγνώριση.

scowl [skaul] n συνοφρύωση, σκυθρωπότητα ♦ vi συνοφρυούμαι, κατσουφιάζω.

scraggy ['skrægɪ] a ισχνός, κοκκαλιάρης.

scram [skræm] vi (col) στρίβω, το βάζω στα πόδια || ~! στρίβε!, δίνε του!

scramble ['skræmbl] n σκαρφάλωμα nt || (struggle) αγώνας, πάλη ♦ vi: to ~ for αγωνίζομαι || ~d eggs npl αυγά χτυπητά ntpl.

scrap [skræp] n κομματάκι, απόρριμμα nt, ψίχουλο || (fight) συμπλοκή, καυγάς || (scrap iron) παλιοσίδερα ntpl ♦ a για πέταμα, άχρηστος ♦ vt πετώ σαν άχρηστο, απορρίπτω ♦ vi (fight) πιάνομαι στα χέρια || ~s npl (waste) απομεινάρια ntpl, απορρίμματα ntpl || ~book n λεύκωμα nt αποκομμάτων.

scrape [skreip] n απόξεση, ξύσιμο || (awkward position) αμηχανία, μπελάς ♦ vt ξύνω, ξεγδέρνω || (clean) καθαρίζω, τρίβω ♦ vi ξύνω || ~r n ξύστρα, ξυστήρι.

scrap heap ['skræphiːp] n σωρός παλιοσιδερικών.

scrap merchant ['skræpmɜːtʃənt] n έμπορος παλιοσιδερικών.

scrappy ['skræpɪ] a ασύνδετος, ασυνάρτητος, ανακατεμένος.

scratch ['skrætʃ] n νυχιά, αμυχή, γρατσουνιά || (itch) ξύσιμο ♦ a πρόχειρος ♦ vt ξύνω, τρίβω || (wound) γρατσουνίζω, ξεγδέρνω ♦ vi (rub) ξύνομαι.

scrawl [skrɔːl] n ορνιθοσκαλίσματα ntpl ♦ vti κακογράφω, ορνιθοσκαλίζω.

scream [skriːm] n κραυγή, ξεφωνητό, στριγγλιά ♦ vi ξεφωνίζω || (speak loudly) στριγγλίζω.

screech [skriːtʃ] n κραυγή, στριγγλιά ♦ vi σκούζω, στριγγλίζω, ουρλιάζω.

screen [skriːn] n παραπέτασμα nt, προπέτασμα nt, παραβάν nt inv || (for films) οθόνη, πανί || (church) κιγκλίδωμα nt ♦ vt προφυλάσσω, προστατεύω || (film) κινηματογραφώ, γυρίζω.

screw [skruː] n κοχλίας, βίδα || (NAUT) έλικας, προπέλα ♦ vt βιδώνω, σφίγγω || (col) καταπιέζω || ~ driver n κατσαβίδι || ~y a (col) μουρλός, ξεβιδωμένος.

scribble ['skrɪbl] n κακογραφία ♦ vt γράφω βιαστικά, ορνιθοσκαλίζω.

script [skrɪpt] n χειρόγραφο || (of play) κείμενο, σενάριο.

Scripture ['skrɪptʃə*] n n Αγία Γραφή.

scriptwriter ['skrɪptraitə*] n σεναριογράφος.

scroll [skrəul] n κύλινδρος, ρόλος (περγαμηνής) ♦ vt (COMPUT) μετακινώ τα περιεχόμενα της οθόνης πάνω/κάτω.

scrounge [skraundʒ] vt (col) διακονεύω ♦ n: on the ~ πάω τσάρκα.

scrub [skrʌb] n (clean) τριβή, τρίψιμο, βούρτσισμα nt || (countryside) χαμόκλαδα ntpl, αγριμιά ♦ vt πλένω, βουρτσίζω, τρίβω || (erase) ακυρώνω, σβήνω.

scruff [skrʌf] n σβέρκο.

scrum(mage) ['skrʌm(ɪdʒ)] n συμπλοκή.

scruple ['skruːpl] n ενδοιασμός, δισταγμός της συνείδησης.

scrupulous ['skruːpjuləs] a ευσυνείδητος || ~ly ad ευσυνείδητα.

scrutinize ['skruːtɪnaɪz] vt εξετάζω προσεκτικά, διερευνώ.

scrutiny ['skruːtɪnɪ] n αυστηρός έλεγχος, διερεύνηση.

scuff [skʌf] vt (shoes) σέρνω.

scuffle ['skʌfl] n συμπλοκή, καυγάς.

scullery ['skʌlərɪ] n πλυντήριο μαγειρίου, λάντσα.

sculptor ['skʌlptə*] n γλύπτης/τρια n/f.

sculpture ['skʌlptʃə*] n γλυπτική || (statue) γλυπτό.

scum [skʌm] n βρώμικος αφρός, βρωμιά || (people) κατακάθια ntpl, αποβράσματα ntpl.

scurrilous ['skʌrɪləs] a υβριστικός, αχρείος, βρώμικος.

scurry ['skʌrɪ] vi τρέχω, σπεύδω.

scurvy ['skɜːvɪ] n σκορβούτο.

scuttle ['skʌtl] vt (plans) εγκαταλείπω, υποχωρώ ♦ vi (scamper) τρέχω βιαστικά, το στρίβω.

scythe [saɪð] n δρεπάνι.

sea [siː] n θάλασσα || (broad stretch) ωκεανός, θάλασσα ♦ a θαλάσσιος, της θάλασσας || ~ bird n θαλασσοπούλι || ~board n ακτή, παραλία || ~ breeze n θαλασσινή αύρα, μπάτης || ~farer n θαλασσινός, θαλασσοπόρος || ~food n θαλασσινά ntpl || ~ front n παραλία, προκυμαία || ~going a ποντοπόρος || ~gull n γλάρος.

seal [siːl] n (animal) φώκια || (stamp) σφραγίδα, βούλα || (impression) σφραγίδα ♦ vt σφραγίζω || (close) κλείνω, σφραγίζω, βουλώνω.

sea level ['siːlevl] n επιφάνεια της θάλασσας.

sealing wax ['siːlɪŋwæks] n βουλοκέρι.

sea lion ['siːlaɪən] n είδος φώκιας.

seam [siːm] n ραφή || (joining) ένωση, ραφή || (of coal etc) φλέβα.

seaman ['siːmən] n ναυτικός, ναύτης.

seamy ['siːmɪ] a ανάποδος, άσχημος.

seaport ['siːpɔːt] n λιμάνι.

search [sɜːtʃ] n έρευνα, αναζήτηση ♦ vt ερευνώ, αναζητώ || (COMPUT) διερευνώ || ~ing a ερευνητικός, προσεκτικός || ~light n προβολέας || ~ party n απόσπασμα nt έρευνας.

seashore ['siːʃɔː*] n ακτή, παραλία.

seasick ['siːsɪk] *a* αυτός που έχει ναυτία || ~**ness** *n* ναυτία.

seaside ['siːsaɪd] *n* παραλία, γιαλός.

season ['siːzn] *n* εποχή ♦ *vt* αρτύω, καρυκεύω || ~**al** *a* εποχιακός || ~**ing** *n* καρύκευμα, άρτυμα *nt*, μπαχαρικό || ~ **ticket** *n* διαρκές εισιτήριο.

seat [siːt] *n* κάθισμα *nt*, καρέκλα || *(PARL etc)* έδρα || *(manner of sitting)* κάθισμα *nt*, θέση || *(bottom)* πισινός, οπίσθια *ntpl* ♦ *vt* καθίζω || **it** ~**s 20 people** είναι 20 θέσεων || ~ **belt** *n* ζώνη ασφαλείας.

sea water ['siːwɔːtə*] *n* θαλασσινό νερό.

seaweed ['siːwiːd] *n* φύκι, φύκια *ntpl*.

seaworthy ['siːwɜːðɪ] *a* πλόιμος, ικανός να πλεύσει.

sec. *abbr of* **second(s).**

secluded [sɪ'kluːdɪd] *a* παράμερος, απομονωμένος.

seclusion [sɪ'kluːʒən] *n* απομόνωση.

second ['sɛkənd] *a* δεύτερος ♦ *ad (in second position)* δεύτερος || *(RAIL)* δεύτερη (θέση) ♦ *n (of time)* δευτερόλεπτο || *(COMM: imperfect)* δεύτερο χέρι ♦ *vt* υποστηρίζω, βοηθώ || ~**ary** *a* δευτερεύων, ασήμαντος || ~**ary education** είναι εκπαίδευση || ~**ary school** *n* σχολείο μέσης εκπαιδεύσεως || ~**er** *n* υποστηρικτής/ίκτρια *m/f* || ~**hand** *a* μεταχειρισμένος, δεύτερο χέρι || *(not original)* μη πρωτότυπος || ~**ly** *ad* κατά δεύτερο λόγο || ~**-rate** *a* μέτριος, δευτέρας ποιότητας || ~ **thoughts** *npl* δεύτερες σκέψεις *fpl*.

secrecy ['siːkrəsɪ] *n* μυστικότητα, εχεμύθεια.

secret ['siːkrɪt] *n* μυστικό ♦ *a* μυστικός, κρυφός, απόρρητος.

secretariat [sɛkrə'tɛərɪət] *n* γραμματεία.

secretary ['sɛkrɪtrɪ] *n* γραμματέας *m/f* || *(minister etc)* υπουργός *m/f.*

secretive ['siːkrətɪv] *a* κρυψίνους.

sect [sɛkt] *n* αίρεση || ~**arian** *a* αιρετικός, στενοκέφαλος, κομματικός.

section ['sɛkʃən] *n* χωρισμός, κόψιμο || *(piece)* τμήμα *nt*, μέρος *nt*, τομή || ~**al** *a* τμηματικός, τοπικός.

sector ['sɛktə*] *n (private or public sector)* τομέας.

secular ['sɛkjulə*] *a* λαϊκός, κοσμικός.

secure [sɪ'kjuə*] *a* βέβαιος, ακίνδυνος || *(fixed)* ασφαλής ♦ *vt (fix)* στερεώνω, σφίγγω || *(obtain)* εξασφαλίζω.

security [sɪ'kjuərɪtɪ] *n* ασφάλεια, σιγουριά || *(bond)* εγγύηση, χρεώγραφο || *(national security)* ασφάλεια || *see* **social.**

sedate [sɪ'deɪt] *a* ατάραχος, ήρεμος.

sedation [sɪ'deɪʃən] *n (MED)* καταπράυνση.

sedative ['sɛdətɪv] *n* καταπραϋντικό ♦ *a* καταπραϋντικός.

sedentary ['sɛdntrɪ] *a* αδρανής, καθιστικός.

sediment ['sɛdɪmənt] *n* κατακάθι, ίζημα.

seduce [sɪ'djuːs] *vt (general)* δελεάζω, παρασύρω || *(sexually)* διαφθείρω, αποπλανώ.

seduction [sɪ'dʌkʃən] *n* αποπλάνηση, δελεασμός.

seductive [sɪ'dʌktɪv] *a* γοητευτικός, αποπλανητικός.

see [siː] *(irreg v) vt* βλέπω || *(find out)* κοιτάζω || *(understand)* καταλαβαίνω || *(make sure)* φροντίζω || *(accompany)* συνοδεύω || *(visit)* πηγαίνω, βλέπω, επισκέπτομαι ♦ *vi (understand)* αντιλαμβάνομαι ♦ *n (bishop's)* επισκοπή || **to** ~ **through** *vt* φροντίζω μέχρι τέλους, παρακολουθώ || **to** ~ **to** *vt* φροντίζω για || **to** ~ **off** *vt* συνοδεύω, ξεπροβοδίζω.

seed [siːd] *n* σπόρος || *(grain)* κόκκος, σπειρί || ~**ling** *n* νεαρό φυτό || ~**y** *a (ill)* αδιάθετος, τσακισμένος || *(shabby)* κουρελιασμένος.

seeing ['siːɪŋ] *cj:* ~ **(that)** εφόσον, αφού, δεδομένου ότι.

seek [siːk] *(irreg v) vt* αναζητώ, ψάχνω, ζητώ.

seem [siːm] *vi* φαίνομαι, μοιάζω || ~**ingly** *ad* φαινομενικά, κατά τα φαινόμενα.

seen [siːn] *pp of* **see.**

seep [siːp] *vi* διαρρέω, περνώ από.

seesaw ['siːsɔː] *n (plank)* τραμπάλα.

seethe [siːð] *vi (be agitated)* αναταράσσομαι, βράζω.

segment ['sɛgmənt] *n* τμήμα *nt.*

segregate ['sɛgrɪgeɪt] *vt* απομονώνω, χωρίζω.

segregation [sɛgrɪ'geɪʃən] *n* απομόνωση, χωρισμός.

seismic ['saɪzmɪk] *a* σεισμικός.

seize [siːz] *vt* αρπάζω, πιάνω || *(take possession of)* κατάσχω || *(understand)* αντιλαμβάνομαι, συλλαμβάνω || **to** ~ **up** *vi (MECH)* σφηνώνομαι, μαγκώνω, κολλώ.

seizure ['siːʒə*] *n (illness)* απότομη προσβολή.

seldom ['sɛldəm] *ad* σπανίως, σπάνια.

select [sɪ'lɛkt] *a* εκλεκτός, διαλεκτός ♦ *vt* εκλέγω, διαλέγω || ~**ion** *n* εκλογή, διαλογή, επιλογή || ~**ive** *a* εκλεκτικός || ~**or** *n (person)* επιλογέας, εκλέκτωρ *m* || *(TECH)* επιλογέας.

self [sɛlf] *n* εαυτός, το πρόσωπο, το άτομο || ~**-appointed** *a* αυτοδιορισμένος || ~**-assured** *a* επηρμένος, γεμάτος αυτοπεποίθηση || ~**-confidence** *n* αυτοπεποίθηση || ~**-conscious** *a* δειλός, ενσυνείδητος || ~**-contained** *a* αυτοτελής, ανεξάρτητος || *(reserved)* επιφυλακτικός || ~**-defence** *n* αυτοάμυνα || ~**-evident** *a* αυταπόδεικτος || ~**-indulgent** *a* αυτεντρύφηλος, τρυφηλός || ~**-interest** *n* ιδιοτέλεια || ~**-ish** *a* εγωιστικός, ιδιοτελής || ~**-ishness** *n* εγωισμός, ιδιοτέλεια || ~**-lessly** *ad* αλτρουϊστικά || ~**-portrait** *n* αυτοπροσωπογραφία || ~**-reliant** *a*

ανεξάρτητος || ~-**respect** n
αυτοσεβασμός || ~-**righteous** a
υποκριτικός || ~-**satisfied** a
αυτάρεσκος, ικανοποιημένος από τον
εαυτό του || ~-**service** a
αυτοσερβίρισμα || ~-**sufficient** a
αυτάρκης || ~-**supporting** a (FIN)
αυτοσυντήρητος, αυτάρκης.
sell [sɛl] (irreg v) vt πουλώ ♦ vi (COMM)
πωλούμαι || ~**er** n πωλητής/τρια m/f||
~**ing price** n τιμή πωλήσεως.
selves [sɛlvz] pl of **self.**
semaphore ['sɛməfɔ:*] n (system)
σηματοφόρος.
semi ['sɛmɪ] prefix ημι- || ~**circle** n
ημικύκλιο || ~**colon** n άνω τελεία || ~-
conscious a ημιαναίσθητος ||
~**detached house** n οριζόντιος
διπλοκατοικία || ~**final** n ημιτελικός.
seminar ['sɛmɪnɑ:*] n σεμινάριο.
semitone ['sɛmɪtəun] n (MUS) ημιτόνιο.
semolina [sɛmə'li:nə] n σιμιγδάλι.
senate ['sɛnɪt] n σύγκλητος f|| (US)
γερουσία.
senator ['sɛnɪtə*] n γερουσιαστής.
send [sɛnd] (irreg v) vt πέμπω, στέλνω,
αποστέλλω || (col: inspire) ενθουσιάζω,
τρελαίνω || to ~ **away** vt απολύω,
διώχνω || to ~ **back** vt στέλνω πίσω,
επιστρέφω || to ~ **for** vt στέλνω να
φωνάξω, καλώ || to ~ **off** vt (goods)
αποστέλνω, στέλνω || (player) αποβάλλω
|| to ~ **out** vi (invitation) στέλνω || to ~
up (general) ανεβάζω, στέλνω,
ανυψώνω || ~**er** n αποστολέας || ~-**off**
n αποχαιρετισμός.
senile ['si:naɪl] a γεροντικός.
senility [sɪ'nɪlɪtɪ] n γεράματα ntpl,
ξεμωράματα ntpl.
senior ['si:nɪə*] a μεγαλύτερος,
πρεσβύτερος || (rank) αρχαιότερος,
ανώτερος ♦ n πρεσβύτερος,
γηραιότερος, μεγαλύτερος || (US)
τελειόφοιτος/η m/f|| ~**ity** n αρχαιότητα
(βαθμού).
sensation [sɛn'seɪʃən] n αίσθηση,
αίσθημα nt|| (state of excitement) αίσθηση,
εντύπωση || ~**al** a εντυπωσιακός.
sense [sɛns] n αίσθηση || (understanding)
λογική, λογικό || (meaning) έννοια, νόημα
nt|| (feeling) (συν)αίσθημα nt ♦ vt
(δι)αισθάνομαι || ~**less** a ανόητος,
παράλογος || (unconscious) αναίσθητος.
sensibility [sɛnsɪ'bɪlɪtɪ] n ευαισθησία,
ευπάθεια.
sensible ['sɛnsəbl] a λογικός.
sensitive ['sɛnsɪtɪv] a (+ to) ευαίσθητος,
ευπαθής || (easily hurt) ευσυγκίνητος,
εύθικτος.
sensitivity [sɛnsɪ'tɪvɪtɪ] n ευαισθησία,
ευπάθεια.
sensual ['sɛnsjuəl] a αισθησιακός,
σαρκικός, φιλήδονος.
sensuous ['sɛnsjuəs] a ηδυπαθής,
αισθησιακός.
sent [sɛnt] pt, pp of **send.**

sentence ['sɛntəns] n (GRAM) πρόταση ||
(LAW) απόφαση, ποινή.
sentiment ['sɛntɪmənt] n αίσθημα nt,
αισθηματικότητα || (thought) γνώμη,
άποψη || ~**al** a αισθηματικός || ~**ality** n
αισθηματισμός.
sentry ['sɛntrɪ] n σκοπός, φρουρός.
separate ['sɛprɪt] a χωριστός ♦
['sɛpəreɪt] vt χωρίζω, ξεχωρίζω || ~**ly** ad
ξεχωριστά.
separation [sɛpə'reɪʃən] n χωρισμός,
διαχώριση.
September [sɛp'tɛmbə*] n
Σεπτέμβριος.
septic ['sɛptɪk] a σηπτικός.
sequel ['si:kwəl] n συνέχεια,
αποτέλεσμα nt|| (continuation) συνέχεια.
sequence ['si:kwəns] n διαδοχή,
συνέχεια, ακολουθία.
sequin ['si:kwɪn] n πούλι nt.
serenade [sɛrə'neɪd] n σερενάτα ♦ vt
κάνω σερενάτα.
serene [sə'ri:n] a γαλήνιος, ατάραχος ||
~**ly** ad ήρεμα, γαλήνια.
serenity [sɪ'rɛnɪtɪ] n γαλήνη, ηρεμία.
sergeant ['sɑːdʒənt] n λοχίας || (police)
ενωμοτάρχης.
serial ['sɪərɪəl] n ιστορία σε συνέχειες ||
~ **number** n αύξοντας αριθμός || ~**ize**
vt δημοσιεύω σε συνεχείες.
series ['sɪərɪz] n σειρά.
serious ['sɪərɪəs] a σοβαρός || ~**ly** ad
σοβαρά || ~**ness** n σοβαρότητα.
sermon ['sɜːmən] n κήρυγμα nt, ομιλία.
serrated [sɛ'reɪtɪd] a οδοντωτός,
πριονωτός.
serum ['sɪərəm] n ορός.
servant ['sɜːvənt] n υπηρέτης/έτρια m/f
|| see civil.
serve [sɜːv] vt υπηρετώ || (do work of)
εξυπηρετώ, εκτελώ || (supply) προμηθεύω
♦ vi (be useful) χρησιμεύω για || (in army)
υπηρετώ || (wait at table, tennis) σερβίρω ♦
n (tennis) σερβίρισμα nt|| it ~s him
right καλά να πάθει || to ~ out or up vt
(food) σερβίρω, διανέμω.
service ['sɜːvɪs] n υπηρεσία || (work done)
εξυπηρέτηση || (government department)
υπηρεσία || (civil etc) υπηρεσία, εργασία ||
(help) διάθεση, χρησιμότητα || (REL)
λειτουργία || (set of dishes) σερβίτσιο ||
(tennis) σερβίς nt inv || (AUT: maintenance)
συντήρηση, επισκευή ♦ vt (AUT, MECH)
συντηρώ, επισκευάζω || the S~s npl
(armed forces) τα όπλα ntpl, οι ένοπλες
δυνάμεις fpl|| ~**able** a εύχρηστος,
ανθεκτικός, χρήσιμος || ~**men** npl
(soldier etc) άντρες των ενόπλων
δυνάμεων || ~ **station** n γκαράζ nt inv.
serviette [sɜːvɪ'ɛt] n πετσέτα
(φαγητού).
servile ['sɜːvaɪl] a δουλικός,
δουλοπρεπής.
session ['sɛʃən] n συνεδρίαση,
συνεδρία.
set [sɛt] (irreg v) n (of things) σειρά,
συλλογή || (RAD, TV) συσκευή || (tennis)

γύρος, σέτ *nt inv* || *(group of people)* ομάδα, κατηγορία, συντροφία, κόσμος || *(CINE)* συσκευή || *(THEAT)* διάκοσμος, σκηνικό ♦ *a (specified)* καθωρισμένος || *(determined)* αποφασισμένος ♦ *vt* θέτω, τοποθετώ, βάζω || *(arrange)* κανονίζω || *(adjust)* ρυθμίζω, βάζω, κανονίζω || *(exam)* δίδω τα θέματα ♦ *vi (of sun)* δύω, βασιλεύω || *(fix)* σκληρύνομαι, σφίγγω, πιάνω || to ~ on fire καίω, πυρπολώ, βάζω φωτιά || to ~ free ελευθερώνω || to ~ going ξεκινώ || to ~ sail αποπλέω || to ~ about *vt (task)* αρχίζω || to ~ aside *vt* ξεχωρίζω, βάζω κατά μέρος, απορρίπτω || to ~ back *vt (in time)* επιβραδύνω, καθυστερώ || *(cost)* κοστίζω || to ~ off *vi* ξεκινώ, φεύγω ♦ *vt (explode)* εκτοξεύω, ρίχνω, εκρηγνύω || *(show up well)* εξαίρω, αναδεικνύω, τονίζω, υπογραμμίζω || to ~ out *vi* ξεκινώ, φεύγω ♦ *vt (arrange)* ρυθμίζω, κανονίζω, σιάζω || *(state)* (καθ)ορίζω || to ~ up *vt (organization)* ιδρύω, οργανώνω || ~back *n (reverse)* αποτυχία, ατυχία, αναποδιά.

settee [se'tiː] *n* καναπές *m*.

setting ['setiŋ] *n (scenery)* τοποθεσία, πλαίσιο || *(MUS)* μελοποίηση, μουσική τραγουδιού.

settle ['setl] *vt (MED: calm)* καθησυχάζω, καταπραύνω || *(pay)* εξοφλώ, πληρώνω || *(agree)* ρυθμίζω κανονίζω ♦ *vi (also: ~ down)* εγκαθίσταμαι || *(person)* σοβαρεύω || ~ment *n (payment)* εξόφληση || *(colony)* εποικισμός || ~r *n* άποικος.

setup ['setʌp] *n (arrangement)* τοποθέτηση, οργάνωση || *(situation)* κατάσταση.

seven ['sevn] *num* επτά || ~teen *num* δεκαεπτά || ~th *n* έβδομος || ~ty *num* εβδομήντα.

sever ['sevə*] *vt* κόβω || *(fig)* διακόπτω.

several ['sevrəl] *a* διάφορος, ξεχωριστός ♦ *pron* μερικοί.

severance ['sevərəns] *n* διαχωρισμός || *(fig)* (δια)κοπή.

severe [si'viə*] *a* αυστηρός, σκληρός || *(serious)* σοβαρός || *(hard, rigorous)* δριμύς, σκληρός, άγριος || *(unadorned)* αυστηρός, απέριττος, λιτός || ~ly *ad* αυστηρά, σκληρά.

severity [si'veriti] *n* αυστηρότητα, σκληρότητα, δριμύτητα.

sew [səu] *(irreg v) vti* ράβω || to ~ up *vt* ράβω.

sewage ['sjuːidʒ] *n* ακαθαρσίες *ftpl* υπονόμων, βρωμόνερα *ntpl*.

sewer ['sjuə*] *n* οχετός, υπόνομος.

sewing ['səuiŋ]n ράψιμο || ~ machine *n* ραπτομηχανή.

sewn [səun] *pp of* sew.

sex [seks] *n* φύλο, σεξ *nt inv* || *(activity)* γενετήσιο ορμή || ~ act *n* συνουσία.

sexual ['seksjuəl] *a* γενετήσιος, σεξουαλικός || ~ly *ad* σεξουαλικά.

sexy ['seksi] *a* ελκυστικός, σεξρυαλικός.

shabby ['ʃæbi] *a* κουρελιασμένος,

σαραβαλιασμένος || *(mean)* μικροπρεπής, αχρείας.

shack [ʃæk] *n* καλύβα.

shackles ['ʃæklz] *npl* δεσμά, χειροπέδες *fpl*.

shade [ʃeid] *n* σκιά, ίσκιος || *(for lamp)* αμπαζούρ *nt inv* || *(of colour)* απόχρωση || *(small quantity)* ίχνος *m*, μικρή ποσότητα ♦ *vt* σκιάζω.

shadow ['ʃædəu] *n* σκιά, σκοτάδι ♦ *vt (follow)* παρακολουθώ || ~y *a* σκιερός, σκιασμένος || *(dim)* ασαφής, θαμπός.

shady ['ʃeidi] *a* σκιερός || *(dubious)* ύποπτος.

shaft [ʃɑːft] *n* κοντάρι, στέλεχος, λαβή || *(of mine)* φρέαρ *nt* || *(of machine)* άξονας, άτρακτος *f* || *(of light)* αχτίδα.

shaggy ['ʃægi] *a* τραχύς, τριχωτός.

shake [ʃeik] *(irreg v) vt* σείω, κουνώ, τινάζω || *(fist etc)* απειλώ με τη γροθιά μου || *(rock) (συγ)κλονίζω, κουνώ, τραντάζω || *(weaken)* κλονίζω || *(alarm)* συγκλονίζω, αναστατώνω ♦ *vi* τρέμω, κλονίζομαι, τραντάζομαι ♦ *n* τίναγμα *nt*, κούνημα *nt*, δόνηση || to ~ off *vt* τινάζω || *(fig)* απαλλάσσομαι από || to ~ up *vt (lit)* ταράζω, κουνώ || *(fig)* ξυπνώ || ~-up *n* πρόχειρο πράμα.

shaky ['ʃeiki] *a* ασταθής, τρεμουλιαστός || *(weak)* κλονισμένος, αδύνατος.

shall [ʃæl] *auxiliary v*: I ~ go θα φύγω, θα πάω || you ~ do it! θα το κάμεις.

shallot [ʃə'lɔt] *n* μικρό κρεμμύδι.

shallow ['ʃæləu] *a (lit)* ρηχός || *(fig)* επιπόλαιος.

sham [ʃæm] *n* προσποίηση, απομίμηση, ψευτιά ♦ *a* προσποιητός, ψεύτικος.

shambles ['ʃæmblz] *n sing* χάος *nt*.

shame [ʃeim] *n* ντροπή || *(disgrace)* αίσχος *nt* || *(pity)* ντροπή, αμαρτία, κρίμα *nt* ♦ *vt (humiliate)* ντροπιάζω || **what a ~**! τι κρίμα! || ~faced *a* ντροπιασμένος || ~ful *a* ντροπιασμένος || ~less *a* αναίσχυντος, αδιάντροπος.

shampoo [ʃæm'puː] *n* σαμπουάν *nt inv* ♦ *vt* λούζω (τα μαλλιά μου).

shamrock ['ʃæmrɔk] *n* τριφύλλι.

shandy ['ʃændi] *n (beer and lemonade)* μπύρα με λεμονάδα.

shan't [ʃɑːnt] = shall not | *see* shall.

shanty ['ʃænti] *n* καλύβα, παράγγα || ~ town *n* παραγγούπολη.

shape [ʃeip] *n* σχήμα *nt*, μορφή, φόρμα, καλούπι ♦ *vt* σχηματίζω, διαμορφώνω, διαπλάθω || to take ~ διαμορφούμαι, παίρνω μορφή || ~less *a* άμορφος, ακανόνιστος || ~ly *a* καλοσχηματισμένος, όμορφος.

share [ʃeə*] *n (thing received)* μερίδιο || *(contribution)* μετοχή, μερίδιο || *(FIN)* μετοχή, τίτλος, αξία ♦ *vt* μοιράζω, διανέμω || *(in common)* (συμ)μετέχω || ~holder *n* μέτοχος.

shark [ʃɑːk] *n (fish)* σκυλόψαρο, καρχαρίας.

sharp [ʃɑːp] *a (razor, knife)* κοφτερός || *(distinct)* ξεχωριστός, έντονος, καθαρός ||

shatter *(biting)* δριμύς, διαπεραστικός || *(quick-witted)* οξύνους, έξυπνος || *(unscrupulous)* πονηρός, κατεργάρης ♦ *n (MUS)* δίεση ♦ *ad* ακριβώς, εντονα, καθαρά || **look** ~! κάνε γρήγορα!, κουνήσου! || ~**en** *vt* ακονίζω, τροχίζω, ξεμυτίζω || ~**ener** *n* ξύστρα || ~**-eyed** *a* που κόβει το μάτι του || ~**ness** *n* κόψη || ~**-witted** *a* οξύνους, ευφυής.

shatter ['ʃætə*] *vt* θρυμματίζω, σπάζω, κάνω κομμάτια || *(fig)* συντρίβω, κλονίζω ♦ *vi* συντρίβομαι, σπάω.

shave [ʃeɪv] *(irreg v)* *n* ξύρισμα *nt* ♦ *vt* ξυρίζω || *(fig)* περνώ ξυστά ♦ *vi* ξυρίζομαι || ~**r** *n (ELEC)* ξυριστική μηχανή.

shaving ['ʃeɪvɪŋ] *n (action)* ξύρισμα *nt* || ~**s** *npl (of wood etc)* ροκανίδια *ntpl*, ρινίσματα *ntpl* || ~ **brush** *n* πινέλο του ξυρίσματος || ~ **cream** *n* κρέμα ξυρίσματος.

shawl [ʃɔːl] *n* σάλι.

she [ʃiː] *pron* αυτή ♦ *a* θηλυκός.

sheaf [ʃiːf] *n* δέσμη, δεμάτι.

shear [ʃɪə*] *(irreg v)* *vt (sheep etc)* κουρεύω || **to** ~ **off** *vt* κόβω || ~**s** *npl (for hedge)* ψαλίδα.

sheath [ʃiːθ] *n* θήκη, κολεός, θηκάρι.

shed [ʃed] *(irreg v)* *n* υπόστεγο ♦ *vt* αποβάλλω, βγάζω || *(pour out)* χύνω.

she'd [ʃiːd] = **she had, she would** || *see* **have, would.**

sheep [ʃiːp] *n* πρόβατο || ~**dog** *n* τσοπανόσκυλο || ~**ish** *a* δειλός, ντροπαλός || ~**skin** *n* προβιά.

sheer [ʃɪə*] *a* καθαρός πραγματικός, γνήσιος || *(steep)* κατακόρυφος, απότομος || *(almost transparent)* διαφανής, λεπτός ♦ *ad* τελείως, πλήρως, απολύτως.

sheet [ʃiːt] *n* σεντόνι || *(thin piece)* έλασμα *nt*, φύλλο, λαμαρίνα || *(paper)* φύλλο, κόλλα.

sheik(h) [ʃeɪk] *n* σεΐχης.

shelf [ʃelf] *n* ράφι.

she'll [ʃiːl] = **she will, she shall** || *see* **will, shall.**

shell [ʃel] *n* κέλυφος *nt*, τσόφλι, φλοιός || *(explosive)* οβίδα, βλήμα *nt* || *(of building)* σκελετός ♦ *vt* ξεφλουδίζω || *(MIL)* βομβαρδίζω.

shellfish ['ʃelfɪʃ] *n (ZOOL)* οστρακοειδές *nt* || *(as food)* θαλασσινά *ntpl*.

shelter ['ʃeltə*] *n* καταφύγιο || *(protection)* προστασία ♦ *vt* προφυλάσσω, προστατεύω, στεγάζω ♦ *vi* προφυλάσσομαι, φυλάγομαι || ~**ed** *a (life)* αποτραβηγμένος, περιορισμένος || *(spot)* προφυλαγμένος, προστατευμένος.

shelve [ʃelv] *vt (put aside)* βάζω στο ράφι || ~**s** *npl of* **shelf.**

shepherd ['ʃepəd] *n* ποιμένας, βοσκός ♦ *vt (guide)* οδηγώ, συνοδεύω || ~**ess** *n* βοσκοπούλα || ~'**s pie** *n* κιμάς σκεπασμένος με πουρέ και ψημένος στο φούρνο.

sheriff ['ʃerɪf] *n* σερίφης.

sherry ['ʃerɪ] *n* σέρυ *nt inv.*

she's [ʃiːz] = **she is, she has** || *see* **be, have.**

shield [ʃiːld] *n* ασπίδα, σκουτάρι || *(protection)* προστατευτικό κάλυμμα *nt* ♦ *vt* προασπίζω, προστατεύω || καλύπτω.

shift [ʃɪft] *n (change)* αλλαγή || *(group of workers, period)* βάρδια ♦ *vt* μετατοπίζω, μεταθέτω, μετακινώ || *(remove)* αλλάζω, μεταβάλλω ♦ *vi* μετακινούμαι, μετατοπίζομαι || ~**y** *a* πονηρός, ύπουλος.

shilling ['ʃɪlɪŋ] *n (old)* σελίνι.

shimmer ['ʃɪmə*] *n* ανταύγεια, μαρμαρυγή ♦ *vi* σπιθοβολώ, λαμπυρίζω, γυαλίζω.

shin [ʃɪn] *n* αντικνήμιο, καλάμι (ποδιού).

shine [ʃaɪn] *(irreg v)* *n (gleam)* γυάλισμα *nt*, στιλπνότητα, γυαλάδα ♦ *vt (polish)* στίλβω, λουστράρω, γυαλίζω || *(torch)* ακτινοβολώ, λάμπω ♦ *vi* λάμπω, αστράφτω, γυαλίζω || *(excel)* διακρίνομαι, ξεπροβάλλω.

shingle ['ʃɪŋgl] *n* ξυλοκέραμος, ταβανοσάνιδο || *(on beach)* βότσαλα *ntpl*, κροκάλες *fpl* || ~**s** *npl (MED)* έρπης, ζωστήρ *m*.

shiny ['ʃaɪnɪ] *a* λαμπερός, γυαλιστερός.

ship [ʃɪp] *n* πλοίο, σκάφος *nt* ♦ *vt* επιβιβάζω, μπαρκάρω || *(transport as cargo)* φορτώνω, αποστέλλω || ~**building** *n* ναυπηγική || ~**ment** *n* φόρτωση || *(goods)* φορτίο, εμπόρευμα *nt* || ~**per** *n (sender)* αποστολέας || ~**ping** *n (act)* φόρτωση || *(ships)* πλοία *ntpl*, ναυτιλία || *(ships of country)* εμπορική ναυτιλία || ~**shape** *a* περίφημος, εξαιρετικός || ~**wreck** *n* ναυάγιο || ~**yard** *n* ναυπηγείο.

shire ['ʃaɪə*] *n* κομητεία.

shirk [ʃɜːk] *vt* αποφεύγω, ξεφεύγω, φυγοπονώ.

shirt [ʃɜːt] *n (man's shirt)* πουκάμισο.

shiver ['ʃɪvə*] *n* ρίγος *nt*, τρεμούλα ♦ *vi (with cold)* τρέμω, τουρτουρίζω.

shoal [ʃəʊl] *n (of fish)* κοπάδι (ψαριών).

shock [ʃɒk] *n* δόνηση, σύγκρουση, τίναγμα *nt* || *(ELEC)* ηλεκτρικό σόκ *nt inv*, ηλεκτροπληξία || *(emotional)* συγκλονισμός, ταραχή || *(MED)* καταπληξία, σόκ ♦ *vt* σκανδαλίζω, σοκάρω || ~ **absorber** *n* αποσβεστήρας κρούσεων, αμορτισέρ *nt inv* || ~**ing** *a* σκανδαλώδης || συγκλονιστικός || ~**proof** *a (watch)* προφυλαγμένος από δόνηση.

shod [ʃɒd] *pt, pp of* **shoe.**

shoddiness ['ʃɒdɪnɪs] *n* κακή ποιότητα.

shoddy ['ʃɒdɪ] *a* κακής ποιότητας, της πεντάρας.

shoe [ʃuː] *(irreg v)* *n* υπόδημα *nt*, παπούτσι || *(of horse)* πέταλο ♦ *vt* πεταλώνω (άλογο) || ~**brush** *n* βούρτσα των παπουτσιών || ~**horn** *n* κόκκαλο των παπουτσιών || ~**lace** *n* κορδόνι || ~**shop** *n* παπουτσάδικο υποδηματοποιείο.

shone [ʃɒn] *pt, pp of* **shine.**

shook [ʃuk] *pt of* **shake.**

shoot [ʃuːt] *(irreg v)* n *(branch)* βλαστός, βλαστάρι ♦ *vt (gun)* πυροβολώ, εκκενώνω || *(kill)* σκοτώνω || *(film)* τραβώ, γυρίζω *(ταινία)* ♦ *vi (move swiftly)* (εξ)ορμώ, τρέχω, πετώ || *(let off gun)* πυροβολώ, κτυπώ || **to ~ down** *vt (plane)* καταρρίπτω || **~ing** *n (shots)* πυροβολισμός, πόλεμος || *(hunting)* κυνήγι || **~ing star** *n* διάττων αστέρας.

shop [ʃɒp] *n* κατάστημα *nt,* μαγαζί || *(workshop)* εργαστήριο, μαγαζί *nt* ♦ *vi (also:* **go ~ping)** ψωνίζω || **~ assistant** *n* υπάλληλος *m/f* καταστήματος || **~keeper** *n* καταστηματάρχης, μικροέμπορος || **~lifter** *n* κλέφτης καταστημάτων || **~lifting** *n* κλοπή καταστημάτων || **~per** *n* πελάτης/τρια *m/f,* αγοραστής/άστρια *m/f* || **~ping** *n* αγορές *fpl,* ψώνια *ntpl* || **~ping bag** *n* τσάντα για τα ψώνια || **~ping centre, ~ping center** *(US)* n αγορά, εμπορικό κέντρο || **~soiled** *a* στραπατσαρισμένος || **~ steward** *n (industry)* αντιπρόσωπος του συνδικάτου || **~ window** *n* προθήκη, βιτρίνα || *see* **talk.**

shore [ʃɔː*] *n (of sea, lake)* ακτή, παραλία ♦ *vt:* **to ~ up** υποστηρίζω, στηλώνω.

shorn [ʃɔːn] *pp of* **shear.**

short [ʃɔːt] *a (branch,* κοντός || *(not tall)* κοντός || *(soon finished)* βραχύς, σύντομος || *(curt)* απότομος, κοφτός || *(in measure)* λιποβαρής, ελλειπής, λειψός || *(ELEC: short-circuit)* βραχύς (βραχυκύκλωμα *nt)* ♦ *ad* απότομα || **~ of** εκτός ♦ *vti (ELEC)* βραχυκυκλώνω, βραχυκυκλούμαι || **to cut ~** τερματίζω απότομα, συντομεύω, διακόπτω || **to fall ~** πέφτω κοντά, δεν πετυχαίνω || **to stop ~** σταματώ ξαφνικά || **~age** *n* ανεπάρκεια, έλλειψη || **~bread** *n* είδος *nt* κέικ || **~-circuit** *n* βραχυκύκλωμα *nt* ♦ *vi* βραχυκυκλούμαι || **~coming** *n* ελάττωμα *nt,* ατέλεια, μειονέκτημα *nt* || **~ cut** *n* συντομότερος δρόμος || **~en** *vt* μικραίνω, κονταίνω || **~hand** *n* στενογραφία || **~hand typist** *n* στενογράφος-δακτυλογράφος *m/f* || **~-lived** *a* βραχύβιος, εφήμερος || **~ly** *ad (soon)* προσεχώς, σύντομα, σε λίγο || **~ness** *n* βραχύτητα, συντομία || **~-sighted** *a (lit)* μυωπικός || *(fig)* μη προνοητικός, κοντόφθαλμος || **~ story** *n* διήγημα *nt* || **~-tempered** *a* απότομος, ευέξαπτος || **~-term** *a (FIN)* βραχυπρόθεσμος || **~wave** *n (RAD)* βραχύ κύμα *nt.*

shot [ʃɒt] *pt, pp of* **shoot** ♦ *n (firing etc)* πυροβολισμός, τουφεκιά || *(person)* σκοπευτής || *(attempt)* δοκιμή, προσπάθεια, απόπειρα || *(injection)* ένεση || *(PHOT)* λήψη φωτογραφία || **like a ~** *(very readily)* αμέσως, πρόθυμα || **~gun** *n* κυνηγετικό όπλο.

should [ʃud] *auxiliary v:* **I ~ go now** πρέπει να φύγω τώρα || **he ~ be there now** πρέπει να έχει φθάσει τώρα || **I ~ like** θα ήθελα.

shoulder [ˈʃəʊldə*] *n* ώμος ♦ *vt* επωμίζομαι || **~ blade** *n* ωμοπλάτη.

shouldn't [ˈʃudnt] = **should not** || *see* **should.**

shout [ʃaut] *n* κραυγή, φωνή ♦ *vt* κραυγάζω ♦ *vi* κραυγάζω, φωνάζω || **~ing** *n* φωνές *fpl,* κραυγές *fpl.*

shove [ʃʌv] *n* ώθηση, σπρωξιά, σπρώξιμο ♦ *vt* σπρώχνω || **to ~ off** *vi (NAUT)* απωθώ || *(fig, col)* φεύγω, ξεκινώ.

shovel [ˈʃʌvl] *n* φτυάρι ♦ *vt* φτυαρίζω.

show [ʃəu] *(irreg v)* n επίδειξη, προβολή || *(appearance)* εμφάνιση, όψη || *(exhibition)* έκθεση, θέαμα *nt* || *(THEAT, CINE)* θέατρο, σινεμά *nt inv,* παράσταση ♦ *vt* δείχνω, οδηγώ || *(demonstrate)* παρουσιάζω, αποδεικνύω || *(explain)* δείχνω, εξηγώ || *(give)* δείχνω ♦ *vi (be visible)* εμφανίζομαι, φαίνομαι, ξεπροβάλλω || **to ~ in** *vi* πες να μπει || **to ~ out** *vi* συνοδεύω στην έξοδο || **to ~ off** *vi (pej)* επιδεικνύομαι, καμαρώνω ♦ *vt (display)* επιδεικνύω, δείχνω, διαφημίζω || **to ~ up** *vi (appear)* εμφανίζομαι, παρουσιάζομαι ♦ *vt* δείχνω || **~down** *n* αναμέτρηση, διακήρυξη προθέσεων.

shower [ˈʃauə*] *n* μπόρα || *(stones etc)* βροχή από πέτρες κτλ || *(shower bath)* ντους *nt inv* ♦ *vt (fig only)* δίνω άφθονα || **~y** *a (weather)* βροχερός.

showing [ˈʃəuiŋ] *n (of film)* εμφάνιση, προβολή.

shown [ʃəun] *pp of* **show.**

show-off [ˈʃəuɒf] *n (col: person)* κορδωμένος.

showroom [ˈʃəurum] *n* αίθουσα εκθέσεων.

shrank [ʃræŋk] *pt of* **shrink.**

shrapnel [ˈʃræpnl] *n* βολιδοφόρο βλήμα *nt.*

shred [ʃred] *n (generally pl)* κομμάτι, λουρίδα, κουρέλι ♦ *vt* κομματιάζω, σχίζω σε λουρίδες || **in ~s** ξεσχισμένος, κουρελιασμένος.

shrewd [ʃruːd] *a* διορατικός, επιδέξιος || **~ness** *n* ευφυΐα, εξυπνάδα.

shriek [ʃriːk] *n* ξεφωνητό, στριγγλιά ♦ *vti* ξεφωνίζω, στριγγλίζω.

shrill [ʃril] *a* οξύς, διαπεραστικός.

shrimp [ʃrimp] *n* γαρίδα.

shrine [ʃrain] *n* λειψανοθήκη, βωμός, ιερός τόπος.

shrink [ʃriŋk] *(irreg v)* vi συστέλλομαι, μαζεύομαι ♦ *vt (make smaller)* ζαρώνω, συστέλλω, κάνω να μαζέψει || **~age** *n* συστολή, μπάσιμο, μάζεμα *nt.*

shrivel [ˈʃrivl] *vti (also: ~ up)* μαραίνομαι, ζαρώνω, ξεραίνομαι.

shroud [ʃraud] *n* σάβανο ♦ *vt* σκεπάζω, καλύπτω.

Shrove Tuesday [ˈʃrəuvˈtjuːzdi] *n* Καθαρή Τρίτη.

shrub [ʃrʌb] *n* θάμνος, χαμόδενρο || **~bery** *n* θαμνώνας, λόγγος.

shrug [ʃrʌg] *n* σήκωμα *nt* των ώμων || **to ~ off** *vt* αφηνώ, απορρίπτω.

shrunk [ʃrʌŋk] *pp of* **shrink.**

shudder ['ʃʌdə*] n ρίγος nt, φρικίαση, τρεμούλα ♦ vi τρέμω.

shuffle ['ʃʌfl] n (CARDS) ανακάτεμα nt (τράπουλας) ♦ vt ανακατεύω ♦ vi σέρνω τα πόδια.

shun [ʃʌn] vt αποφεύγω.

shush [ʃuʃ] excl (col) σουτ!

shut [ʃʌt] (irreg v) vt κλείνω ♦ vi κλείομαι, κλείνω || **to ~ down** vti κλείνω, σταματώ εργασίες || **to ~ off** vt (supply) διακόπτω, αποκόπτω, αποκλείω || **to ~ up** vi (keep quiet) σωπαίνω, βουλώνω ♦ vt (close) κλείνω καλά, κλειδώνω || (silence) αποστομώνω, κλείνω το στόμα || **~ up!** σκασμός! || **~ter** n παραθυρόφυλλο, παντζούρι || (of camera) φωτοφράκτης.

shuttlecock ['ʃʌtlkɔk] n φτερωτή σφαίρα, βολάν nt inv.

shy [ʃaɪ] a ντροπαλός, δειλός || **~ly** ad ντροπαλά, δειλά || **~ness** n δειλία, ντροπαλότητα.

Siamese [saɪə'miːz] a: **~ cat** Σιαμαία γάτα.

sick [sɪk] a ασθενής, άρρωστος || (inclined to vomit) έχω τάση προς εμετό || (disgusting) αηδιαστικός, σιχαμερός || **~ bay** n νοσοκομείο πλοίου || **~en** vt αρρωσταίνω, αηδιάζω ♦ vi αηδιάζω || **~ening** a (fig) αηδιαστικός.

sickle ['sɪkl] n δρεπάνι.

sick leave ['sɪkliːv] n αναρρωτική άδεια.

sickly ['sɪklɪ] a αρρωστιάρης, ωχρός, ασθενικός || (nauseating) που προκαλεί αναγούλα.

sickness ['sɪknɪs] n ασθένεια, αρρώστεια, νόσος f || (vomiting) ναυτία, αναγούλα, εμετός.

sick pay ['sɪkpeɪ] n επίδομα nt ασθενείας.

side [saɪd] n πλευρά, πλευρό, μέρος nt, μεριά || (of body) πλευρά, μεριά || (of lake) όχθη || (aspect) πλευρά, όψη, άποψη ♦ a (door, entrance) πλάγια (είσοδος), πλαϊνή (είσοδος f) ♦ vi: **to ~ with** πάω με, παίρνω το μέρος του || **by the ~ of** στο πλευρό του, σε σύγκριση με || **on all ~s** από παντού || **to take ~s (with)** υποστηρίζω, μεροληπτώ || **~board** n μπουφές m inv || **~boards, ~burns** npl (whiskers) φαβορίτες fpl || **~ effect** n (MED) παρενέργεια || **~light** n (AUT) πλευρικός φανός || **~line** n (RAIL) δευτερεύουσα γραμμή || (fig: hobby) πάρεργο || **~ road** n πάροδος f || **~show** n δευτερεύον θέαμα nt || **~track** vt (fig) παραμερίζω || **~walk** n (US) πεζοδρόμιο || **~ways** ad πλάγια, λοξά.

siding ['saɪdɪŋ] n πλευρική διακλάδωση.

sidle ['saɪdl] vi: **to ~ up** πλησιάζω δειλά και πλάγια.

siege [siːdʒ] n πολιορκία.

sieve [sɪv] n κόσκινο ♦ vt κοσκινίζω.

sift [sɪft] vt κοσκινίζω || (examine) ξεχωρίζω, εξονυχίζω.

sigh [saɪ] n αναστεναγμός ♦ vi (ανα)στενάζω.

sight [saɪt] n όραση || (scene) θέα, θέαμα nt || (of rifle) κλισιοσκόπιο, στόχαστρο ♦ vt αντικρύζω, βλέπω, παρατηρώ || **in ~** φαίνομαι, γίνομαι ορατός || **out of ~** δε φαίνομαι || **~seeing** n επίσκεψη αξιοθέατων || **to go ~seeing** επισκέπτομαι τα αξιοθέατα.

sign [saɪn] n (with hand) νεύμα nt, νόημα nt || (indication) ένδειξη, σημάδι || (notice, road etc) σήμα nt, ταμπέλα, πινακίδα || (written symbol) σημείο, σημάδι ♦ vt υπογράφω || **to ~ off** vi ξεμπαρκάρω || **to ~ up** vti (MIL) κατατάσσομαι.

signal ['sɪgnl] n σύνθημα nt, σημείο, σήμα nt ♦ vt σηματοδοτώ, στέλνω με σήματα.

signature ['sɪgnətʃə*] n υπογραφή.

significance [sɪg'nɪfɪkəns] n σημασία, έννοια, νόημα nt || (importance) σπουδαιότητα, σημαντικότητα.

significant [sɪg'nɪfɪkənt] a με σημασία, σημαντικός || (important) σημαντικός, σπουδαίος, σημαίνων || **~ly** ad με έννοια, με σημασία.

signify ['sɪgnɪfaɪ] vt σημαίνω, εννοώ || (express) είμαι ένδειξη, (εκ)δηλώνω.

sign language ['saɪnlæŋgwɪdʒ] n γλώσσα με νεύματα.

signpost ['saɪnpəust] n σήμα nt κυκλοφορίας, πινακίδα της τροχαίας.

silence ['saɪləns] n σιγή, σιωπή, ησυχία ♦ vt σωπαίνω, ησυχάζω || **~r** n σιγαστήρας, σιλανσιέ nt inv.

silent ['saɪlənt] a σιωπηλός, αθόρυβος, σιγαλός || (saying nothing) άφωνος, αμίλητος.

silhouette [sɪlu:'et] n (outline) σιλουέτα ♦ vt διαγράφομαι σα σιλουέτα.

silk [sɪlk] n μετάξι ♦ a μεταξωτός || **~y** a μεταξένιος, απαλός, στιλπνός.

silliness ['sɪlɪnɪs] n μωρία, ανονσία, χαζομάρα.

silly ['sɪlɪ] a ανόητος, μωρός.

silt [sɪlt] n βόρβορος, λάσπη.

silver ['sɪlvə*] n άργυρος, ασήμι ntpl || (coins) αργυρά νομίσματα ntpl || (objects) ασημικά ntpl ♦ a αργυρός, ασημένιος || **~ paper** n ασημόχαρτο || **~-plated** a επάργυρος || **~smith** n αργυροχόος || **~y** a ασημένιος.

similar ['sɪmɪlə*] a (+ to) όμοιος (με) || **~ity** n ομοιότητα || **~ly** ad παρόμοια, όμοια.

simile ['sɪmɪlɪ] n παρομοίωση.

simmer ['sɪmə*] vi σιγοβράζω.

simple ['sɪmpl] a (easy) απλός, εύκολος || (natural) απλός, απλοϊκός || (plain) απλός, απλοϊκός || (of one kind) απλός || (weak-minded) αφελής, μωρόπιστος || **~-minded** a αφελής, απλοϊκός.

simplicity [sɪm'plɪsɪtɪ] n απλότητα.

simplify ['sɪmplɪfaɪ] vt απλουστεύω, απλοποιώ.

simulation [sɪmju'leɪʃən] n (imitation) απομίμηση, προσποίηση.

simultaneous [sɪməl'teɪnɪəs] a

ταυτόχρονος || ~ly ad ταυτόχρονα, σύγχρονα με.

sin [sɪn] n αμάρτημα nt, αμαρτία ♦ vi αμαρτάνω.

since [sɪns] ad έκτοτε, από τότε ♦ prep από ♦ cj (time) αφότου, από τότε που || (because) αφού, εφόσον.

sincere [sɪnˈsɪə*] a ειλικρινής || ~ly ad ειλικρινά.

sincerity [sɪnˈsɛrɪtɪ] n ειλικρίνεια.

sinful [ˈsɪnful] a αμαρτωλός.

sing [sɪŋ] (irreg v) vt (song) τραγουδώ ♦ vi (gen) τραγουδώ || (bird) κελαηδώ || (ears) βουΐζω.

singe [sɪndʒ] vt τσουρουφλίζω, καψαλίζω.

singer [ˈsɪŋə*] n αοιδός m/f, τραγουδιστής/ίστρια m/f.

singing [ˈsɪŋɪŋ] n τραγούδι.

single [ˈsɪŋgl] a μόνος, μοναδικός || (bed, room) μονό (κρεββάτι, δωμάτιο) || (unmarried) άγαμος || (ticket) απλό (εισιτήριο) || (one part) απλός, ένας ♦ n (ticket) απλό εισιτήριο || ~s npl (tennis) απλό παιχνίδι, σύγκλ nt inv || to ~ out vt διαλέγω, επιλέγω, ξεχωρίζω || in ~ file κατ' άνδρα, στη γραμμή, ένας-ένας || ~-handed a ολομόναχος, αβοήθητος, μόνος || ~-minded a που έχει ένα μόνο σκοπό || ~-sided disk n (COMPUT) δίσκος μιας όψεως.

singlet [ˈsɪŋglɪt] n φανελίτσα.

singular [ˈsɪŋgjulə*] a ενικός || (odd) παράξενος, σπάνιος, μοναδικός ♦ n (GRAM) ενικός αριθμός.

sinister [ˈsɪnɪstə*] a απαίσιος, δυσοίωνος, μοχθηρός.

sink [sɪŋk] (irreg v) n νεροχύτης ♦ vt (put under) καταβυθίζω, βουλιάζω || (dig) σκάβω, ανοίγω ♦ vi (fall slowly) καταβυθίζομαι, βουλιάζω, καθίζω || to ~ in vi (news etc) χαράσσομαι στο μυαλό || ~ing a (feeling) απογοητευτικός || with ~ing heart με σφιγμένη καρδιά.

sinner [ˈsɪnə*] n αμαρτωλός.

sinus [ˈsaɪnəs] n (ANAT) κόλπος.

sip [sɪp] n ρουφηξιά, γουλιά ♦ vt πίνω γουλιά-γουλιά, ρουφώ.

siphon [ˈsaɪfən] n σιφόνι || to ~ off vt αναρρροφώ, σιφωνίζω.

sir [sɜ:*] n κύριε || (title) κύριος || yes S~ μάλιστα, κύριε.

siren [ˈsaɪərən] n σειρήνα.

sirloin [ˈsɜ:lɔɪn] n κόντρα φιλέτο.

sister [ˈsɪstə*] n αδελφή || (MED) αρχινοσοκόμος || (nun) μοναχή, καλογρηά, αδελφή || ~-in-law n κουνιάδα, νύφη.

sit [sɪt] (irreg v) vi κάθομαι || (at session) συνεδριάζω ♦ vt (exam) δίνω εξετάσεις, εξετάζομαι || to ~ tight δεν το κουνώ, βάζω τα δυνατά μου || to ~ down vi κάθομαι || to ~ up vi (after lying) ανασηκώνομαι || (at night) αγρυπνώ, ξενυχτώ.

site [saɪt] n τοποθεσία, θέση ♦ vt τοποθετώ, εγκαθιστώ.

sit-in [ˈsɪtɪn] n (demonstration) καταλαμβάνω σαν ένδειξη διαμαρτυρίας.

sitting [ˈsɪtɪŋ] n συνεδρίαση || ~ room n σαλόνι.

situated [ˈsɪtjueɪtɪd] a κείμενος, ευρισκόμενος.

situation [sɪtjuˈeɪʃən] n (state of affairs) κατάσταση || (place) τοποθεσία, θέση || (post) θέση, εργασία, δουλειά.

six [sɪks] num έξι || ~teen num δεκαέξι || ~th a έκτος || ~ty num εξήντα.

size [saɪz] n μέγεθος, διάσταση, έκταση, όγκος || (glue) κόλλα || (of clothing) νούμερο || to ~ up vt (assess) εκτιμώ (το μέγεθος), σχηματίζω γνώμη για || ~able a αρκετά μεγάλος, μεγαλούτσικος.

sizzle [ˈsɪzl] n σφύριγμα nt, τσιτσίρισμα nt ♦ vi τσιτσιρίζω, σφυρίζω.

skate [skeɪt] n πέδιλο, πατίνι ♦ vi πατινάρω, παγοδρομώ || ~r n πατινέρ m/f inv, παγοδρόμος.

skating [ˈskeɪtɪŋ] n: to go ~ πηγαίνω για πατινάζ || ~ rink n παγοδρόμιο, αίθουσα πατινάζ.

skeleton [ˈskelɪtn] n σκελετός.

skeptic [ˈskeptɪk] n (US) = sceptic.

sketch [sketʃ] n σκαρίφημα nt, σκιαγραφία || (play) σκίτσο, σκετς nt inv ♦ vt σκιαγραφώ, σκιτσάρω || ~book n σημειωματάριο || ~ pad n καρνέ nt inv για σκίτσα || ~y a ατελής, ασαφής, ακαθόριστος.

skewer [ˈskjuə*] n σούβλα.

ski [ski:] n σκι ♦ vi κάνω σκι || ~ boot n παπούτσι του σκι.

skid [skɪd] n (skid-pan) τροχοπέδη ♦ vi γλυστρώ πλαγίως, ντεραπάρω.

skidmark [ˈskɪdmɑːk] n ίχνη ntpl ντεραπαρίσματος.

skier [ˈskiːə*] n σκιέρ m/f inv.

skiing [ˈskiːɪŋ] n: to go ~ πάω για σκι.

skijump [ˈskiːdʒʌmp] n πήδημα nt με σκι.

skilful [ˈskɪlful] a ικανός, επιδέξιος, επιτήδειος.

skill [skɪl] n ικανότητα, επιδεξιότητα || ~ed a επιδέξιος || (trained) ειδικευμένος.

skim [skɪm] vt ξαφρίζω, βγάζω || (read) ξεφυλλίζω || (glide over) περνώ ξυστά.

skimp [skɪmp] vt τσιγγουνεύομαι || (do carelessly) εκτελώ γρήγορα και επιπόλαια || ~y a (work, dress) ανεπαρκής || (meal) φτωχός.

skin [skɪn] n δέρμα nt, πετσί, τομάρι || (peel, rind) φλοιός, φλούδα || (on milk) πέτσα ♦ vt γδέρνω, ξεφλουδίζω || ~-deep a επιπόλαιος, επιφανειακός || ~-diving n υποβρύχιο κολύμπι || ~ny a αδύνατος, κοκκαλιάρης, τσίρος || ~tight a (dress etc) (φόρεμα) εφαρμοστό.

skip [skɪp] n (ανα)πήδημα nt, σκίρτημα nt ♦ vi σκιρτώ, πηδώ, πετάγομαι ♦ vt παραλείπω, πηδώ.

ski pants [ˈskiːpænts] npl παντελόνι του σκι.

skipper ['skɪpə*] n (NAUT, SPORT) καπετάνιος.

skipping rope ['skɪpɪŋrəup] n σχοινάκι.

skirmish ['skɜːmɪʃ] n αψιμαχία.

skirt [skɜːt] n φούστα ♦ vt περιτρέχω, φέρνω βόλτα.

skit [skɪt] n ευθυμογράφημα nt, παρωδία, νούμερο.

skittle ['skɪtl] n (one pin) τσούνι || ~s n (game) τσούνια.

skull [skʌl] n κρανίο.

skunk [skʌŋk] n μεφίτη, είδος ασβού.

sky [skaɪ] n ουρανός || ~-**blue** a ανοιχτό μπλε|| ~ **blue** n ουρανί (χρώμα) || ~light n φεγγίτης || ~scraper n ουρανοξύστης.

slab [slæb] n πλάκα.

slack [slæk] a χαλαρός, λάσκος || (slow, dull) πεσμένος, νεκρή (εποχή) || (careless) αμελής, αδρανής ♦ vi ατονώ, τεμπελιάζω ♦ n (in rope etc) χαλαρότητα || ~s npl σπορ παντελόνι || ~en (also: ~en off) vi χαλαρούμαι, μειούμαι, πέφτω ♦ vt χαλαρώνω, μετριάζω, επιβραδύνω, λασκάρω.

slag [slæg] n σκουριά || ~ **heap** n σωρός σκουριάς.

slam [slæm] n κρότος, κτύπημα nt πόρτας ♦ vt (door) κλείνω απότομα, κτυπώ || (throw down) πετάω με δύναμη ♦ vi κλείνω με κρότο.

slander ['slɑːndə*] n κακολογία, διαβολή, συκοφαντία ♦ vt συκοφαντώ, κακολογώ, διαβάλλω || ~ous a συκοφαντικός.

slang [slæŋ] n μάγκικη γλώσσα, λαϊκό, ιδίωμα nt.

slant [slɑːnt] n (lit) κλίση, γέρσιμο || (fig) άποψη, αντίληψη ♦ vti κλίνω, γέρνω || ~ing a λοξός, πλάγιος.

slap [slæp] n κτύπημα nt, χαστούκι, μπάτσος, καρπαζιά ♦ vt ραπίζω, μπατσίζω, καρπαζώνω ♦ ad (directly) κατευθείαν || ~dash ad ξένοιαστα, απρόσεκτα || ~stick n (comedy) φάρσα.

slash [slæʃ] n δυνατό κτύπημα nt, σχίσιμο ♦ vt κόβω, σχίζω, πετσοκόβω.

slate [sleɪt] n σχιστόλιθος || (piece of slate) αβάκια, πλάκα ♦ vt (criticize) επικρίνω, κουρελιάζω.

slaughter ['slɔːtə*] n σφαγή, σφάξιμο ♦ vt σφάζω.

Slav [slɑːv] n (person) Σλάβος/α m/f ♦ a σλαβικός.

slave [sleɪv] n σκλάβος, δούλος ♦ vi δουλεύω σκληρά, μοχθώ || ~ry n δουλεία, σκλαβιά.

slavish ['sleɪvɪʃ] a δουλικός || ~ly ad δουλικά.

sledge [sledʒ] n έλκηθρο || ~hammer n βαριά, μεγάλο σφυρί.

sleek [sliːk] a λείος, απαλός, προσποιητός.

sleep [sliːp] n (irreg v) n ύπνος ♦ vi κοιμούμαι, πλαγιάζω || to go to ~ αποκοιμούμαι || to ~ in vi (late) ξυπνώ αργά || ~er n υπναράς || (RAIL)

κλινάμαξα || ~ily ad κοιμισμένα|| ~iness n υπνηλία, νυσταγμός, νύστα ||~ing bag n σάκκος ύπνου || ~ing car n κλινάμαξα, βαγκόν-λι nt inv|| ~ing pill n υπνωτικό χάπι || ~lessness n αϋπνία, αγρυπνία || ~walker n υπνοβάτης/άτρια m/f|| ~y a νυσταλέος, νυσταγμένος.

sleet [sliːt] n χιονόνερο.

sleeve [sliːv] n μανίκι || ~less a (garment) χωρίς μανίκια.

sleigh [sleɪ] n έλκηθρο.

sleight [slaɪt] n: ~ of hand ταχυδακτυλουργία.

slender ['slendə*] a λεπτός, λιγνός || (small) ισχνός, ασθενής.

slept [slept] pt, pp of **sleep**.

slice [slaɪs] n (of bread) φέτα || (of cake, cheese etc) κομμάτι ♦ vt τεμαχίζω, κόβω σέ φέτες.

slick [slɪk] a (smart) γλυστερός, δόλιος, επιτήδειος.

slid [slɪd] pt, pp of **slide**.

slide [slaɪd] n (irreg v) n τσουλήθρα, ολισθητήριο, στίβος || (PHOT: transparency) διαφάνεια, σλάιντ nt inv|| (brooch) τσιμπιδάκι || (fall in prices) πτώση τιμών ♦ vt παρακάμπτω, ξεφεύγω ♦ vi γλυστρώ.

sliding ['slaɪdɪŋ] a (door) συρτή (πόρτα).

slight [slaɪt] a λεπτός || (trivial) ελαφρός, ασήμαντος || (small) μικροκαμωμένος, μικρούλης ♦ n υποτίμηση, περιφρόνηση ♦ vt (offend) προσβάλλω, θίγω || ~ly ad ελαφρά, κάπως, λιγάκι.

slim [slɪm] a λεπτός, μικρός ♦ vi κάνω δίαιτα.

slime [slaɪm] n λάσπη, βούρκος.

slimming ['slɪmɪŋ] n αδυνάτισμα nt.

slimy ['slaɪmɪ] a βορβορώδης, γλοιώδης.

sling [slɪŋ] n (irreg v) n (bandage) ανωμίτης, κρεμαστάρι ♦ vt εκσφενδονίζω, ρίχνω.

slip [slɪp] n (slipping) ολίσθημα nt, γλύστρημα nt || (petticoat) μισοφόρι || (of paper) φύλλο, χαρτί ♦ vt γλυστρώ αθόρυβα, μπαίνω || (escape from) ξεφεύγω από ♦ vi (lose balance) γλυστρώ || (move smoothly) κινούμαι αθόρυβα || (make mistake) κάνω γκάφα, σφάλλω || (decline) παρεκτρέπομαι, παραστρατώ || to ~ away vi γλιστρώ, φεύγω απαρατήρητα || to ~ in vt βάζω, χώνω || to ~ out vi βγαίνω (κρυφά).

slipper ['slɪpə*] n παντούφλα.

slippery ['slɪpərɪ] a ολισθηρός, γλυστερός || (tricky) πανούργος, πονηρός.

slipshod ['slɪpʃɒd] a ακατάστατος, απρόσεκτος.

slip-up ['slɪpʌp] n (mistake) σφάλμα nt, γκάφα.

slipway ['slɪpweɪ] n ναυπηγική κλίνη.

slit [slɪt] n (irreg v) n σχίσιμο, σχισμή ♦ vt κόβω, σχίζω, σχίζομαι.

slither ['slɪðə*] vi σέρνομαι, γλιστρώ.

slob [slɒb] n (col: unpleasant person) ατζαμής.

slog [slɒg] n (great effort) αγγαρεία, βαρειά δουλειά ♦ vi (work hard) δουλεύω σκληρά.

slogan ['sləʊgən] n (catchword) σύνθημα nt.

slop [slɒp] vi ξεχειλίζω, χύνομαι ♦ vt χύνω.

slope [sləʊp] n κατηφοριά, πλαγιά || (slant) κλίση ♦ vi: to ~ down κατηφορίζω || to ~ up vi ανηφορίζω.

sloping ['sləʊpɪŋ] a λοξός, πλάγιος.

sloppy ['slɒpɪ] a λασπωμένος, λασπώδης || (untidy) πρόχειρος, ακατάστατος || (weak, silly) άτονος, σαχλός.

slot [slɒt] n σχισμή, χαραμάδα ♦ vt: to ~ in βάζω, τοποθετώ || ~ machine n αυτόματος πωλητής || μηχάνημα τυχερών παιχνιδιών.

slouch [slaʊtʃ] vi κινούμαι αδέξια.

slovenly ['slʌvnlɪ] a ακατάστατος, απρόσεκτος.

slow [sləʊ] a βραδύς, αργός || (of clock) πάω, πίσω || (stupid) βραδύνους, χοντροκέφαλος ♦ ad σιγά, αργά || '~' (roadsign) 'αργά' || to ~ down vi επιβραδύνω, μειώνω, κόβω (ταχύτητα) ♦ vt επιβραδύνω || to ~ up vi σταματώ, φρενάρω ♦ vt επιβραδύνω || ~ly ad σιγά, αργά || in ~ motion σε αργό ρυθμό, ρελαντί.

sludge [slʌdʒ] n λάσπη, βούρκος.

slug [slʌg] n γυμνοσάλιαγκας || (bullet) μικρή σφαίρα || ~gish a αδρανής, τεμπέλης, νωθρός || ~gishly ad νωθρά, τεμπέλικα || ~gishness n νωθρότητα, βραδύτητα.

sluice [sluːs] n υδροφράκτης, φράγμα nt.

slum [slʌm] n φτωχογειτονιά.

slumber ['slʌmbə*] n γαλήνιος ύπνος.

slump [slʌmp] n πτώση, ελάττωση ζητήσεως ♦ vi πέφτω απότομα.

slung [slʌŋ] pt, pp of sling.

slur [slɜː*] n βιαστική προφορά, τραύλισμα nt || (insult) στίγμα nt προσβολή ♦ vt (also: ~ over) κακοπροφέρω, τραυλίζω.

slush [slʌʃ] n λασπωμένο χιόνι || ~y a (lit) λασπωμένος || (fig: sentimental) σαχλός, γλυκανάλατος.

slut [slʌt] n τσούλα, παλιοθήλυκο.

sly [slaɪ] a πονηρός, πανούργος, ύπουλος.

smack [smæk] n (slap) κτύπημα nt, χαστούκι, μπάτσος ♦ vt (slap) ραπίζω, καρπαζώνω || to ~ one's lips κτυπώ τα χείλη.

small [smɔːl] a μικρός, λίγος || ~holding n μικρό κτήμα nt || ~ hours npl πολύ πρωϊνές ώρες fpl || ~ish a μάλλον μικρός, μικρούτσικος || ~pox n ευλογιά, βλογιά || ~ talk n φλυαρία.

smart [smɑːt] a (well-dressed) κομψός, μοντέρνος || (clever) έξυπνος, επιδέξιος ||

(sharp, quick) σβέλτος, γρήγορος, ζωηρός ♦ vi πονώ, τσούζω, υποφέρω || to ~ en up vi ζωηρεύω, κάνω κέφι || κομψεύομαι ♦ vt επισπεύδω.

smash [smæʃ] n (collision) σύγκρουση ♦ vt τσακίζω, θρυμματίζω, κομματιάζω || (destroy) καταστρέφω, συντρίβω ♦ vi θραύομαι, κομματιάζομαι || ~ing a (col) σπουδαίος, περίφημος.

smattering ['smætərɪŋ] n επιπόλαια γνώση, πασάλειμα nt.

smear [smɪə*] n κηλίδα, λεκές m || επίχρισμα nt ♦ vt λερώνω, μουντζουρώνω.

smell [smɛl] (irreg v) n όσφρηση || (odour) οσμή, μυρωδιά ♦ vt (breathe in) μυρίζω || vi μυρίζω, παίρνω μυρωδιά || (give out smell) μυρίζω, βρωμάω || ~y a (unpleasant) δύσοσμος, βρωμερός.

smile [smaɪl] n χαμόγελο ♦ vi χαμογελώ.

smiling ['smaɪlɪŋ] a χαμογελαστός, γελαστός.

smirk [smɜːk] n ψεύτικο χαμόγελο ♦ vi χαμογελώ ψεύτικα.

smith [smɪθ] n σιδηρουργός, σιδεράς || ~y ['smɪðɪ] n σιδηρουργείο, σιδεράδικο.

smock [smɒk] n μπλούζα, φόρμα.

smoke [sməʊk] n καπνός, καπνίλα || (tobacco) κάπνισμα nt, τσιγάρο ♦ vt (puff) καπνίζω || (dry food) καπνίζω ♦ vi αναδίδω καπνούς, καπνίζω || (of cigarette) καπνίζω || ~d a (bacon etc) καπνιστός || ~r n (person) καπνιστής || (RAIL) όχημα nt καπνιστών.

smoking ['sməʊkɪŋ] n κάπνισμα nt || 'no ~' (sign) 'απαγορεύεται το κάπνισμα'.

smoky ['sməʊkɪ] a γεμάτος καπνό, καπνισμένος.

smolder ['sməʊldə*] vi (US) = smoulder.

smooth [smuːð] a (in consistency) απαλός || (wine) γλυκόπιοτος || (movement) ομαλός, μαλακός, αθόρυβος || (person) γλυκομίλητος, γαλίφης ♦ vt (also: ~ out) λειαίνω, εξομαλύνω, ισιώνω.

smother ['smʌðə*] vt πνίγω, καταπνίγω.

smoulder ['sməʊldə*] vi σιγοκαίω, υποβόσκω.

smudge [smʌdʒ] n κηλίδα, λεκές m, βρωμιά ♦ vt λεκιάζω, λερώνω, βρωμίζω.

smug [smʌg] a αυτάρεσκος, καμαρωτός.

smuggle ['smʌgl] vt κάνω λαθρεμπόριο, περνώ λαθραία || ~r n λαθρέμπορος, κοντραμπαντζής.

smuggling ['smʌglɪŋ] n λαθρεμπόριο, κοντραμπάντο.

smutty ['smʌtɪ] a (fig: obscene) αισχρός, βρώμικος, πρόστυχος.

snack [snæk] n ελαφρό φαγητό, κολατσιό || ~ bar n σνακ-μπαρ nt inv.

snag [snæg] n (obstacle) εμπόδιο, κώλυμα nt || (in stocking) τράβηγμα nt κλωστής.

snail [sneɪl] n σαλιγκάρι.

snake [sneɪk] n φίδι.

snap [snæp] n (sound) ψαλιδιά, κρακ nt inv, ξηρός κρότος || (photograph) στιγμιότυπο, ενσταντανέ nt inv, φωτογραφία ♦ a βιαστικός || *(unexpected)* απροσδόκητος ♦ *vt (make sound)* κροταλίζω || *(break)* θραύω, σπάζω, τσακίζω || *(photograph)* φωτογραφίζω, τραβώ, πέρνω ♦ *vi (break)* σπάω || to ~ off *vt (break)* σπάω || to ~ up *vt* αρπάζω, βουτώ || ~py a δηκτικός, απότομος, ζωηρός || ~shot n φωτογραφία ενσταντανέ.

snare [snɛə*] n παγίδα ♦ *vt* παγιδεύω, πιάνω.

snarl [snɑːl] n γρυλισμός, μούγγρισμα nt ♦ *vi (also person)* γρυλίζω.

snatch [snætʃ] n άρπαγμα nt || *(small amount)* κομμάτι ♦ *vt* αρπάζω, βουτώ.

sneak [sniːk] *vi* κινούμαι κρυφά.

sneer [snɪə*] n καγχασμός, σαρκασμός ♦ *vi* κοροϊδεύω, σαρκάζω, χλευάζω.

sneeze [sniːz] n φτέρνισμα nt ♦ *vi* φτερνίζομαι.

sniff [snɪf] n εισπνοή, ρούφηγμα nt ♦ *vi* ξερνώ, είμαι συναχωμένος ♦ *vt (smell)* μυρίζω, ρουφώ.

snigger [ˈsnɪgə*] n πνιχτό γέλιο, πονηρό γέλιο ♦ *vi* κρυφογελώ, ξερογελώ.

snip [snɪp] n ψαλίδισμα nt, κομματάκι || *(bargain)* ευκαιρία, καλή δουλειά ♦ *vt* ψαλιδίζω, κόβω.

sniper [ˈsnaɪpə*] n *(marksman)* ελεύθερος σκοπευτής.

snippet [ˈsnɪpɪt] n κομματάκι, απόσπασμα nt.

snivelling [ˈsnɪvlɪŋ] a *(whimpering)* κλαψιάρικος.

snob [snɒb] n σνόμπ m inv, ψωροπερήφανος/η m/f || ~bery n σνομπισμός || ~bish a σνόμπ, φαντασμένος, ποζάτος.

snooker [ˈsnuːkə*] n είδος nt μπιλιάρδο.

snoop [snuːp] *vi*: to ~ about χώνω τη μύτη, παραφυλάω.

snooty [ˈsnuːtɪ] a *(col: snobbish)* υπερόπτης, ψηλομύτης.

snooze [snuːz] n υπνάκος ♦ *vi* παίρνω έναν υπνάκο, μισοκοιμάμαι.

snore [snɔː*] *vi* ροχαλίζω.

snorkel [ˈsnɔːkl] n αναπνευστικός σωλήνας.

snort [snɔːt] n φρίμασμα nt, ξεφύσημα nt, ρουθούνισμα nt ♦ *vi* ρουθουνίζω, φριμάζω, ξεφυσώ.

snout [snaut] n ρύγχος nt, μουσούδα, μύτη.

snow [snəʊ] n χιόνι ♦ *vi* χιονίζω, ρίχνω χιόνι || ~ball n μπάλα χιόνι, χιονόσφαιρα || ~bound a (απο)κλεισμένος από τα χιόνια || ~drift n χιονοστιβάδα || ~drop n γάλανθος ο χιονώδης || ~fall n χιονόπτωση || ~flake n νιφάδα || ~man n χιονάνθρωπος || ~plough, ~plow (US) n εκχιονιστήρας || ~storm n χιονοθύελλα.

snub [snʌb] *vt* αποκρούω, προσβάλλω, κόβω ♦ n επίπληξη, προσβολή, κατσάδα.

snuff [snʌf] n ταμπάκο, πρέζα.

snug [snʌg] a άνετος, βολικός, ζεστός, αναπαυτικός.

so [səʊ] *ad (extent)* τόσο(ν) || *(in such manner)* έτσι || *(thus)* μ' αυτόν τον τρόπο || *(to such an extent)* τόσο ♦ *cj* επομένως, γι αυτό, έτσι λοιπόν || or ~ περίπου, πάνω κάτω || ~ long! *(goodbye)* γεια σου!, αντίο!! || ~ many, ~ much τόσος || ~ that ούτως ώστε.

soak [səʊk] *vt* διαβρέχω, μουσκεύω || *(leave in liquid)* διαποτίζω, μουσκεύω || to ~ in *vi* διεισδύω, διαποτίζω, ποτίζω.

soap [səʊp] n σαπούνι || ~flakes npl τριμμένο σαπούνι || ~powder n σαπούνι σε σκόνη || ~y a γεμάτος σαπούνι.

soar [sɔː*] *vi* πετώ ψηλά, ανυψώνομαι.

sob [sɒb] n λυγμός, αναφυλλητό ♦ *vi* κλαίω με αναφιλητά.

sober [ˈsəʊbə*] a νηφάλιος, ξεμέθυστος || *(calm)* σοβαρός, εγκρατής, ήρεμος || to ~ up *vi* συνέρχομαι, ξεμεθάω.

Soc. abbr of **society**.

so-called [ˈsəʊˈkɔːld] a δήθεν, λεγόμενος.

soccer [ˈsɒkə*] n ποδόσφαιρο.

sociable [ˈsəʊʃəbl] a κοινωνικός, φιλικός, ομιλητικός.

social [ˈsəʊʃəl] a κοινωνικός || ~ism n σοσιαλισμός || ~ist n σοσιαλιστής/ίστρια m/f ♦ a σοσιαλιστικός || ~ly ad κοινωνικώς || ~ science n κοινωνική επιστήμη || ~ security n κοινωνική ασφάλεια || ~ work n κοινωνική εργασία || ~ worker n κοινωνικός λειτουργός m/f.

society [səˈsaɪətɪ] n *(people and customs)* κοινωνία || *(club)* εταιρεία || *(fashionable life)* κοσμική ζωή, καλός κόσμος.

sociologist [səʊsɪˈɒlədʒɪst] n κοινωνιολόγος.

sociology [səʊsɪˈɒlədʒɪ] n κοινωνιολογία.

sock [sɒk] n *(κοντή)* κάλτσα ♦ *vt (hit)* δίνω γροθιά.

socket [ˈsɒkɪt] n ντουί, πρίζα.

sod [sɒd] n *(of earth)* χορταριασμένο χώμα || *(col: term of abuse)* παλιάνθρωπος.

soda [ˈsəʊdə] n *(CHEM)* νάτριο, σόδα || *(drink)* σόδα || ~ water n αεριούχο νερό, σόδα.

sodden [ˈsɒdn] a βρεγμένος, μουσκεμένος || *(moist and heavy)* λασπωμένος.

sofa [ˈsəʊfə] n σοφάς, καναπές m.

soft [sɒft] a μαλακός, απαλός || *(not loud)* απαλός, γλυκός, ελαφρός || *(kind)* τρυφερός, καλός || *(weak, silly)* ανόητος, χαζός || ~ drink n αναψυκτικό || ~en *vt* μαλακώνω ♦ *vi* μαλακύνω, γίνομαι μαλακός || ~-hearted a ευαίσθητος, με τρυφερή καρδιά || ~ly ad απαλά, μαλακά, αθόρυβα || ~ness n μαλακότητα, απαλότητα.

soggy [ˈsɒgɪ] a υγρός, μουσκεμένος.

soil [sɔɪl] n *(earth)* έδαφος nt, χώμα nt ♦ *vt*

λερώνω || ~ed a λερωμένος,
ακάθαρτος.

solar ['səʊlə*] a ηλιακός.

sold [səʊld] pt, pp of **sell.**

solder ['səʊldə*] vt (συγ)κολλώ ♦ n
συγκόλληση || (material) καλάι.

soldier ['səʊldʒə*] n στρατιώτης.

sole [səʊl] n πέλμα nt, πατούσα || (of shoe)
σόλα || (fish) γλώσσα ♦ a μόνος,
μοναδικός || ~ly ad (only) μόνο,
μοναδικά.

solemn ['sɔləm] a σοβαρός || (formal)
επίσημος, σεμνός.

solicitor [sɔlisitə*] n δικηγόρος m/f,
σύμβουλος, συνήγορος.

solid ['sɔlid] a στερεός, συμπαγής ||
(hard) στερεός, γερός, σκληρός ||
(reliable) σοβαρός, βάσιμος || (meal)
γερός, ολόκληρος ♦ n στερεό || ~arity
n ενότητα, αλληλεγγύη || ~ify [sɔ'lidifai]
vi στερεοποιούμαι, πήζω ♦ vt
στερεοποιώ, πήζω, παγώνω || ~ity n
στερεότητα.

solitaire [sɔli'tɛə*] n (game) πασιέντσα ||
(gem) μονό διαμάντι, μονόπετρο.

solitary ['sɔlitəri] a μόνος || (lonely)
ολομόναχος, μοναχικός.

solitude ['sɔlitjuːd] n μοναξιά, ερημιά.

solo ['səʊləʊ] n σόλο || ~ist n σολίστας
m, σολίστ m/f.

soluble ['sɔljubl] a διαλυτός,
ευδιάλυτος || (able to be solved)
επιδεικτικός λύσεως.

solution [sə'luːʃən] n λύση, λύσιμο ||
(explanation) λύση, εξήγηση || (in liquid)
διάλυση, διάλυμα nt.

solve [sɔlv] vt λύω, εξηγώ.

solvent ['sɔlvənt] a αξιόχρεος.

sombre, somber (US) ['sɔmbə*] a
σκοτεινός, μελαγχολικός || ~ly ad
μελαγχολικά.

some [sʌm] a (uncertain number) λίγος,
λίγοι, μερικοί || (indefinite) κάποιος ||
(remarkable) σπουδαίος, περίφημος ||
(partitive) μερικός ♦ pron μερικοί, κάτι ♦
ad περίπου || ~body pron κάποιος ♦ n
κάποιος || ~day ad (μιά) κάποια μέρα ||
~how ad κάπως, κατά κάποιο τρόπο ||
~one pron = **somebody** || ~place ad
(US) = **somewhere.**

somersault ['sʌməsɔːlt] n τούμπα,
κουτρουβάλα ♦ vi κάνω τούμπα.

something ['sʌmθiŋ] pron κάτι,
οτιδήποτε.

sometime ['sʌmtaim] ad κάποτε || ~s
ad μερικές φορές, κάπου-πάπου.

somewhat ['sʌmwɔt] ad κάπως.

somewhere ['sʌmwɛə*] ad κάπου.

son [sʌn] n γιός.

song [sɔŋ] n τραγούδι || ~writer n
(μουσικο)συνθέτης.

sonic ['sɔnik] a ηχητικός.

son-in-law ['sʌninlɔ:] n γαμπρός.

sonnet ['sɔnit] n σονέτο.

soon [su:n] ad γρήγορα || (early)
σύντομα, νωρίς || as ~ as **possible** το
συντομότερο δυνατό || ~er ad (time)

γρηγορότερα || (of preference) καλύτερα,
κάλιο.

soot [sut] n αιθάλη, φούμο, καπνιά.

soothe [su:ð] vt καταπραΰνω,
παρηγορώ.

sophisticated [sə'fistikeitid] a (person)
κοσμικός, μοντέρνος || (machinery) πιο
σύγχρονος.

soporific [sɔpə'rifik] a υπνωτικός,
ναρκωτικός.

sopping ['sɔpiŋ] a (very wet)
καταβρεγμένος, μουσκεμένος.

soppy ['sɔpi] a (col: sentimental)
δακρύβρεκτος, σαχλός.

soprano [sə'pra:nəʊ] n υψίφωνος f,
σοπράνο f.

sordid ['sɔ:did] a ακάθαρτος, ρυπαρός ||
(mean) άθλιος, χυδαίος.

sore [sɔ:*] a πονεμένος, ερεθισμένος nt
|| (offended) πειραγμένος, θυμωμένος ♦ n
πληγή, τραύμα || ~ly ad (tempted) βαθειά,
σοβαρά.

sorrow ['sɔrəʊ] n λύπη, θλίψη, μετάνοια
|| ~ful a θλιμμένος, λυπημένος.

sorry ['sɔri] a λυπημένος, πονεμένος ||
(pitiable) θλιος, αξιολύπιτος.

sort [sɔ:t] n είδος, τάξη ♦ vt (COMPUT)
ταξινομώ || (also: ~ out) (papers)
ταξινομώ, ξεκαθαρίζω || (problems)
τακτοποιώ, (ξε)χωρίζω.

so-so ['səʊsəʊ] ad έτσι κι έτσι.

soufflé ['su:flei] n σουφλέ nt inv.

sought [sɔ:t] pt, pp of **seek.**

soul [səʊl] n ψυχή || ~-destroying a
ψυχοφθόρος, αποκτηνωτικός || ~ful a
αισθηματικός, συγκινητικός || ~less a
άψυχος, άκαρδος.

sound [saʊnd] a (healthy) υγιής, γερός ||
(safe) στερεός, ασφαλής, σίγουρος ||
(reasonable) λογικός || (deep, hearty) γερός
♦ n (noise) ήχος, θόρυβος || (GEOG) στενό,
πορθμός ♦ vt (alarm) κτυπώ ♦ vi (find
depth) βυθομετρώ || (seem) φαίνομαι,
μοιάζω || to ~ out vt (opinions)
βολιδοσκοπώ || ~ barrier n φράγμα του
ήχου || ~ing n (NAUT etc) βυθομέτρηση,
βολιδοσκόπηση || ~ly ad (sleep) βαθειά,
καλά, ήσυχα || (beat) γερά, τελείως ||
~proof a (room) ηχομονωτικός ♦ vt
κάνω αδιαπέραστο από ήχο || ~track n
(of film) ηχητική ζώνη (ταινίας).

soup [su:p] n σούπα, ζωμός || in the ~
σε δύσκολη θέση || ~spoon n κουτάλι
της σούπας.

sour ['saʊə*] a ξινός || (milk) ξυνός ||
(bad-tempered) στριφνός, γκρινιάρης.

source [sɔ:s] n πηγή, προέλευση.

south [saʊθ] n νότος ♦ a νότιος ♦ ad
προς νότο, νοτίως || ~-east n το
νοτιοανατολικό || ~-easterly a
νοτιοανατολικός || ~ern a νότιος,
μεσημβρινός || S~ **Pole** n Νότιος Πόλος
|| ~ward(s) ad πρός νότο || ~-west n
το νοτιοδυτικό.

souvenir [su:və'niə*] n ενθύμιο,
σουβενίρ nt inv.

sovereign ['sɔvrin] n μονάρχης

βασιλέας ♦ a (independent) κυρίαρχος ||
~ty η ηγεμονία, κυριαρχία.
soviet ['sɔʊvɪət] a σοβιετικός.
sow [sɔʊ] η γουρούνα || [sɔʊ] (irreg v) vt
σπέρνω || (spread abroad) ενσπείρω.
soya bean ['sɔɪə'biːn] η σόγια.
spa [spɑː] η ιαματική πηγή || (place)
λουτρόπολη.
space [speɪs] η χώρος, τόπος || (distance)
απόσταση || (length of time) διάστημα nt ||
(universe) διάστημα nt || to ~ out vt
αραιώνω, τοποθετώ κατ' αποστάσεις ||
~craft η διαστημόπλοιο || ~man η
κοσμοναύτης.
spacing ['speɪsɪŋ] η αραίωση.
spacious ['speɪʃəs] a ευρύς, ευρύχωρος,
απλόχωρος.
spade [speɪd] η (tool) φτυάρι, τσάπα,
τσαπί || ~s npl (CARDS) μπαστούνι, πίκα.
spaghetti [spə'gɛtɪ] η σπαγέτο,
μακαρονάδα.
Spain [speɪn] η Ισπανία.
span [spæn] η (of arch) άνοιγμα nt,
απόσταση || (of time) διάρκεια (ζωής) ♦
vt απλώνω, καλύπτω.
Spaniard ['spænjəd] η Ισπανός.
spaniel ['spænjəl] η σπάνιελ η inv.
Spanish ['spænɪʃ] η (LING) Ισπανικά ntpl
♦ a ισπανικός.
spank [spæŋk] vt δέρνω (στον πισινό).
spanner ['spænə*] η κλειδί
(υδραυλικού).
spare [spɛə*] a περίσσιος, λιτός, ισχνός ||
η = ~ part || vt (do without) οικονομώ,
φυλάγω || (save from hurt) λυπούμαι,
χαρίζω, φείδομαι || (lend, give)
περισσεύω, δίνω, παραχωρώ, διαθέτω ||
to ~ περισσεύω || ~ part η
ανταλλακτικό, εξάρτημα nt || ~ wheel η
ρεζέρβα || ~ time η ελεύθερες ώρες.
spark [spɑːk] η σπινθήρας, σπίθα || (fig)
ίχνος, σπίθα || ~ plug η σπινθηριστής,
μπουζί nt inv.
sparkle ['spɑːkl] η σπινθήρας, σπίθα,
λάμψη || (gaiety) σπιρτάδα ♦ vi
σπινθηρίζω, σπιθοβολώ, αστράφτω.
sparkling ['spɑːklɪŋ] a (lit)
αστραφτερός, σπινθηροβόλος || (wine)
αφρώδης || (conversation) πνευματώδης
(ομιλία).
sparrow ['spærəʊ] η σπουργίτης.
sparse [spɑːs] a αραιός, σποραδικός.
spasm ['spæzəm] η σπασμός,
σπαρτάρισμα nt || (short spell) κρίση,
έξαψη || ~odic [-'mɔdɪk] a
σπασμωδικός, σπαστικός.
spastic ['spæstɪk] η σπαστικός.
spat [spæt] pt, pp of **spit**.
spate [speɪt] η (fig) πλημμύρα,
πλημμύρισμα nt || in ~ (river)
φουσκωμένος, πλημμυρισμένος.
spatter ['spætə*] η πιτσίλισμα nt,
ράντισμα nt ♦ vt πιτσιλίζω, ραντίζω ♦ vi
αναπηδώ, (ξε)πετιέμαι, στάζω.
spatula ['spætjʊlə] η σπάτουλα.
spawn [spɔːn] vt αφηνω αυγά || (fig)
γεννώ.

speak [spiːk] (irreg v) vt λέγω, προφέρω,
εκφράζω || (truth) λέγω, λέω || (language)
μιλώ ♦ vi (+ to) μιλώ (σε) || μιλώ, συζητώ
|| (make speech) αγορεύω, μιλώ || to ~ for
vt συνηγορώ, μιλώ για || to ~ up vi
υψώνω τη φωνή μιλώ σε κάποιο || ~er η
ομιλητής/ήτρια m/f, συνομιλητής/ήτρια
m/f || (chairman) πρόεδρος || (loudspeaker:
on record player) μεγάφωνο.
spear [spɪə*] η ακόντιο, δόρυ nt, κοντάρι
♦ vt τρυπώ με κοντάρι, πιάνω με
κοντάρι.
special ['spɛʃəl] a ειδικός, ίδιος ||
(particular kind) εξαιρετικός,
ασυνήθιστος || (particular purpose)
ιδιαίτερος, ξεχωριστός ♦ η (RAIL) ειδική
αμαξοστοιχία || (cooking) ειδικός,
ιδιαίτερος || ~ist η ειδικός || ~ity η
ειδικότητα || (food) σπεσιαλιτέ nt inv ||
~ize vi (+ in) ειδικεύομαι σε || ~ly ad
ειδικά, ιδιαίτερα, προ παντός, πάνω απ'
όλα.
species ['spiːʃiːz] η είδος nt.
specific [spə'sɪfɪk] a ειδικός, ορισμένος,
ακριβής, σαφής || ~ally ad ειδικά,
συγκεκριμένα || ~ation [spɛsɪfɪ'keɪʃən] η
περιγραφή, καθορισμός, προδιαγραφή.
specify ['spɛsɪfaɪ] vt καθορίζω,
προσδιορίζω.
specimen ['spɛsɪmɪn] η δείγμα nt.
speck [spɛk] η κηλίδα, σταγόνα ||
(particle) κόκκος, μόριο.
speckled ['spɛkld] a διάστικτος,
πιτσιλισμένος.
specs [spɛks] npl (col) γυαλιά ntpl.
spectacle ['spɛktəkl] η θέαμα nt || ~s
npl ματογυάλια ntpl, γυαλιά ntpl.
spectacular [spɛk'tækjʊlə*] a
θεαματικός.
spectator [spɛk'teɪtə*] η θεατής.
spectre, (US) **specter** ['spɛktə*] η
φάντασμα nt, σκιάκτρο.
spectrum ['spɛktrəm] η φάσμα nt.
speculate ['spɛkjʊleɪt] vi κάνω
υποθέσεις || (FIN) κερδοσκοπώ.
speculation [spɛkjʊ'leɪʃən] η (FIN)
κερδοσκοπία.
sped [spɛd] pt, pp of **speed**.
speech [spiːtʃ] η λόγος, λαλιά || (talk)
λόγος, αγόρευση, ομιλία || ~ day η (SCH)
απονομή των πτυχίων || ~less a άλαλος,
βουβός, άφωνος || ~ therapy η
θεραπευτική αγωγή λόγου.
speed [spiːd] (irreg v) η ταχύτητα,
σπουδή || (gear) ταχύτητα ♦ vi σπεύδω,
κάνω γρήγορα, τρέχω || to ~ up vi
επιταχύνω ♦ vt επισπεύδω, επιταχύνω ||
~boat η εξακυλβιος || ~ily ad γρήγορα,
εσπευσμένα, βιαστικά || ~ing η
υπερβολική ταχύτητα || ~ limit η όριο
ταχύτητας || ~ometer η ταχύμετρο,
κοντέρ nt inv || ~way η
αυτοκινητόδρομος || ~y a ταχύς,
γρήγορος.
spell [spɛl] (irreg v) η (magic) γοητεία,
μαγεία, μάγια ntpl || (period of time)
διάστημα nt, χρονική περίοδος ♦ vt

ορθογραφώ || (word) συλλαβίζω || (mean) σημαίνω || ~bound a γοητευμένος, μαγεμένος || ~ing n συλλαβισμός, ορθογραφία.

spelt [spɛlt] pt, pp of **spell**.

spend [spɛnd] (irreg v) vt ξοδεύω, δαπανώ || (use up) εξαντλώ, χρησιμοποιώ.

spent [spɛnt] pt, pp of **spend** ♦ a (patience) εξαντλημένος.

sperm [spɜːm] n (BIOL) σπέρμα nt.

spew [spjuː] vt ξερνώ, κάνω εμετό.

sphere [sfɪəʳ] n σφαίρα, υδρόγειος.

spherical ['sfɛrɪkəl] a σφαιρικός.

sphinx [sfɪŋks] n σφίγγα.

spice [spaɪs] n καρύκευμα nt, μπαχαρικό ♦ vt καρυκεύω.

spicy ['spaɪsɪ] a αρωματισμένος, πικάντικος.

spider ['spaɪdəʳ] n αράχνη || ~y a αράχνινος.

spike [spaɪk] n αιχμή, καρφί, στάχυ nt, νάσσαλος.

spill [spɪl] (irreg v) vt (upset) ανατρέπω, αναποδογυρίζω || (pour out) χύνω ♦ vi (flow over) χύνομαι.

spin [spɪn] (irreg v) n (revolution of wheel) περιστροφή, στριφογύρισμα || (trip in car) περίπατος, βόλτα || (AVIAT) σπινάρισμα nt ♦ vt (wool etc) κλώθω, γνέθω || (turn) γυρίζω ♦ vi περιστρέφομαι, (στριφο)γυρίζω||to ~ out vi (of money etc) οικονομώ (τα λεφτά μου) ♦ vt παρατείνω, παρατραβώ.

spinach ['spɪnɪdʒ] n σπανάκι.

spinal ['spaɪnl] a νωτιαίος, ραχιαίος, σπονδυλικός || ~ cord n νωτιαίος μυελός.

spindly ['spɪndlɪ] a λιγνός.

spin-drier ['spɪn'draɪəʳ] n στεγνωτήριο.

spine [spaɪn] n σπονδυλική στήλη, ραχοκοκκαλιά || (thorn) αγκάθι || ~less a (fig) δειλός, άβολος.

spinning ['spɪnɪŋ] n (of thread) κλώσιμο, στρίψιμο || ~ wheel n ροδάνι, ανέμη.

spinster ['spɪnstəʳ] n γεροντοκόρη.

spiral ['spaɪərəl] n σπείρα, έλικα ♦ a ελικοειδής, σπειροειδής ♦ vi κινούμαι σπειροειδώς || ~ staircase n γυριστή σκάλα, στριφτή σκάλα.

spire ['spaɪəʳ] n κορυφή κωδωνοστασίου.

spirit ['spɪrɪt] n πνεύμα nt, ψυχή || (ghost) φάντασμα nt || (humour, mood) διάθεση, κέφι || (courage) κουράγιο, θάρρος nt || (alcoholic) οινοπνευματώδες ποτό, οπίρτο || in good ~s κεφάτος, καλόκεφος || ~ed a ζωηρός, έντονος, θαρραλέος || ~ level n αλφάδι.

spiritual ['spɪrɪtjuəl] n πνευματικός, ψυχικός ♦ n θρησκευτικό τραγούδι || ~ism n πνευματισμός.

spit [spɪt] (irreg v) n (for roasting) σούβλα || (saliva) φτύσιμο, σάλιο || vi φτύνω || (of motor) ρετάρω.

spite [spaɪt] n μίσος, έχθρα, κακία ♦ vt ενοχλώ, πεισμώνω, φουρκίζω || in ~ of

παρά το, παρ' όλα || ~ful a μοχθηρός, εκδικητικός.

splash [splæʃ] n πιτσίλισμα nt, πλατσούλισμα nt, λεκές || (of colour) πολυχρωμία ♦ vti πλατσουλίζω, πιτσιλίζω.

spleen [spliːn] n σπλήνα.

splendid ['splɛndɪd] a λαμπρός, μεγαλοπρεπής || (fine) εξαίσιος, περίφημος.

splendour, (US) splendor ['splɛndəʳ] n λαμπρότητα, λάμψη || (glory) μεγαλοπρέπεια.

splint [splɪnt] n νάρθηκας.

splinter ['splɪntəʳ] n θραύσμα nt ♦ vi θραύομαι, σπάζω.

split [splɪt] (irreg v) n σχισμή, σχίσιμο, ρωγμή, διαίρεση ♦ vt σχίζω, θραύω, σπάζω ♦ vi (divide) διασπώ || (col: depart) αναχωρώ || to ~ up vi διαιρούμαι ♦ vt διαιρώ, χωρίζω, διασπώ.

splutter ['splʌtəʳ] vi τραυλίγω || (of motor) ρετάρω.

spoil [spɔɪl] (irreg v) vt χαλώ || ~s npl λεία, λάφυρα ntpl || ~sport n αυτός που χαλάει το κέφι.

spoke [spəʊk] n ακτίνα (τροχού) || pt of **speak** || ~n pp of **speak** || ~sman n εκπρόσωπος.

sponge [spʌndʒ] n σφουγγάρι ♦ vt πλένω, σφουγγίζω ♦ vi (+ on) ζω σε βάρος κάποιου || ~ bag n σάκκος για σφουγγάρι || ~ cake n παντεσπάνι.

spongy ['spʌndʒɪ] a σφουγγώδης.

sponsor ['spɒnsəʳ] n ανάδοχος, εγγυητής/ήτρια m/f, εισηγητής/ήτρια m/f ♦ vt υποστηρίζω, εισηγούμαι || ~ship n υποστήριξη.

spontaneous [spɒn'teɪnɪəs] a αυτόματος || (natural) αυθόρμητος.

spool [spuːl] n καρούλα, μασούρι.

spoon [spuːn] n κουτάλι || ~-feed vt (lit) ταΐζω με το κουτάλι || (fig) επιχορηγώ || ~ful n κουταλιά.

sporadic [spə'rædɪk] a σποραδικός.

sport [spɔːt] n (games) αθλητισμός, σπόρ nt inv || (fun) διασκέδαση, παιχνίδι || (good-humoured person) καλός άνθρωπος || ~ing a (fair) τίμιος || ~s car n αυτοκίνητο σπόρ || ~(s) coat n, ~(s) jacket n σακκάκι σπόρ || ~sman n φίλαθλος, τίμιος παίκτης || ~smanship n τιμιότητα στο σπόρ || ~swear n είδη ntpl αθλητισμού || ~swoman n αθλήτρια.

spot [spɒt] n στίγμα nt, κηλίδα, λεκές m || (place) τόπος, μέρος nt, τοποθεσία || (small amount) στάλα, λίγο ♦ vt (notice) διακρίνω, σημειώνω || (make spots on) λεκιάζω || ~ check n αιφνιδιαστικός έλεγχος || ~less a άσπιλος, ακηλίδωτος, καθαρός || ~light n προβολέας θεάτρου || (position) το προσκήνιο, κέντρο || ~ted a διάστικτος, πιτσιλωτός || ~ty a (face) με πανάδες, με σπειριά.

spouse [spauz] n σύζυγος m/f.

spout [spaut] n στόμιο, σωλήνας || (jet)

εκροή, πίδακας ♦ vi ξεπηδώ, αναπηδώ, ξεχύνομαι.

sprain [spreɪn] n διάστρεμμα nt, στραμπούλισμα nt ♦ vt στραμπουλίζω.

sprang [spræŋ] pt of **spring**.

sprawl [sprɔːl] vi εκτείνομαι, ξαπλώνομαι.

spray [spreɪ] n (sprinkle) πιτσιλίσματα ntpl || (of sea) αφρός || (instrument) ψεκαστήρας, βαποριζατέρ nt inv || (branch) κλωνάρι ♦ vt ψεκάζω, καταβρέχω.

spread [spred] (irreg v) n (extent) επέκταση, διάδοση || (col) τραπέζι, πλούσιο γεύμα nt ♦ vt απλώνω, στρώνω || (scatter) σκορπίζω, στρώνω, διαδίδω || (smear) αλείφω, χύνω.

spree [spriː] n διασκέδαση, ξεφάντωμα nt, γλέντι.

sprightly [ˈspraɪtlɪ] a ζωηρός, κεφάτος.

spring [sprɪŋ] (irreg v) n (leap) πήδημα nt || (of water) πηγή || (coil) ελατήριο || (season) άνοιξη ♦ vi (ανα)πηδώ, ξεπετάγομαι || **to ~ up** vi (problem) δημιουργούμαι, εμφανίζομαι || **~board** n βατήρας, τραμπλέν nt inv || **~-clean** n γενικός καθαρισμός ♦ vt κάνω γενικό καθαρισμό || **~-cleaning** n γενικός καθαρισμός (ανοιξιάτικος) || **~iness** n ελαστικότητα || **~time** n άνοιξη || **~y** a ελαστικός, εύκαμπτος.

sprinkle [ˈsprɪŋkl] n ράντισμα nt ♦ vt ραντίζω, ραίνω.

sprint [sprɪnt] n δρόμος ταχύτητας ♦ vi τρέχω σε δρόμο ταχύτητας || **~er** n δρομέας ταχύτητας.

sprite [spraɪt] n ξωτικό, στοιχειό.

sprout [spraut] vi βλαστάνω, φυτρώνω || see **Brussels sprout**.

spruce [spruːs] n έλατο ♦ a κομψός, περιποιημένος.

sprung [sprʌŋ] pp of **spring**.

spry [spraɪ] a ζωηρός, ενεργητικός.

spun [spʌn] pt, pp of **spin**.

spur [spɜː*] n σπηρούνι || (fig) κίνητρο, ελατήριο ♦ vt (also: ~ **on**) κεντρίζω, παρακινώ || **on the ~ of the moment** χωρίς σκέψη, αυθόρμητα.

spurn [spɜːn] vt περιφρονώ, αποκρούω.

spurt [spɜːt] n (effort) σφίξιμο, φουλάρισμα nt, ξέσπασμα nt || (jet) ανάβλυση, πίδακας ♦ vti ξεχύνομαι, φουλάρω.

spy [spaɪ] n κατάσκοπος m/f ♦ vi κατασκοπεύω ♦ vt διακρίνω, βλέπω, παρατηρώ || **~ing** n (espionage) κατασκοπεία.

sq. (MATH), **Sq.** (in address) abbr of **square**.

squabble [ˈskwɒbl] n φιλονεικία, καυγάς ♦ vi φιλονεικώ, καυγαδίζω, πιάνομαι (με).

squad [skwɒd] n (MIL) απόσπασμα nt, ουλαμός || (police) υπηρεσία διώξεως.

squadron [ˈskwɒdrən] n μοίρα.

squalid [ˈskwɒlɪd] a βρώμικος, βρωμερός, άθλιος.

squall [skwɔːl] n (scream) κραυγή, στριγγλιά.

squalor [ˈskwɒlə*] n ακαθαρσία, βρώμα, αθλιότητα.

squander [ˈskwɒndə*] vt σπαταλώ.

square [skwɛə*] n (figure) τετράγωνο || (of town) πλατεία || (instrument) γωνία, γνώμονας || (product) τετράγωνο || (col: person) ανίαρος, ατάιριαστος ♦ a τετραγωνικός || (honest) τίμιος, καθαρός, δίκαιος || (ample) ικανοποιητικός, άφθονος ♦ ad (exactly) ακριβώς, κάθετα ♦ vt (arrange) ρυθμίζω, κανονίζω, τακτοποιώ || (MATH) τετραγωνίζω ♦ vi (agree) (+ **with**) συμφωνώ, συμβιβάζομαι || **all ~** στα ίσια, πάτσι || **2 metres ~** 4 τετραγωνικά μέτρα || **1 ~ metre** 1 τετραγωνικό μέτρο || **~ly** ad τίμια, ντόμπρα.

squash [skwɒʃ] n (drink) χυμός (φρούτων) ♦ vt συνθλίβω, ζουλώ, στύβω.

squat [skwɒt] n κοντόχοντρος ♦ vi κάθομαι σταυροπόδι || **~ter** n σφετεριστής γης.

squawk [skwɔːk] n κράξιμο, βραχνή κραυγή ♦ vi κράζω, φωνάζω, κραυγάζω.

squeak [skwiːk] n τσιριχτή φωνή, σκούξιμο ♦ vi σκούζω, τσιρίζω, τρίζω.

squeal [skwiːl] n διαπεραστικός ήχος, κραυγή, στριγγλιά ♦ vi στριγγλίζω, σκούζω.

squeamish [ˈskwiːmɪʃ] a ευαίσθητος, με τάση στον εμετό || (easily shocked) σιχασιάρης, δύστροπος.

squeeze [skwiːz] n (lit) σύνθλιψη, σφίξιμο, στρίμωγμα nt || (ECON) πίεση ♦ vt συνθλίβω, σφίγγω, στύβω || **to ~ out** vt στύβω.

squid [skwɪd] n σουπιά.

squint [skwɪnt] n αλλοιθωρισμός, στραβισμός ♦ vi αλλοιθωρίζω, στραβοκοιτάζω.

squirm [skwɜːm] vi συστρέφω το σώμα, στενοχωριέμαι, ντρέπομαι.

squirrel [ˈskwɪrəl] n σκίουρος.

squirt [skwɜːt] n εκτόξευση, πιτσίλισμα nt, ριπή ♦ vi αναβλύζω, πετάγομαι, εκτοξεύω.

Sr abbr of **senior**.

St abbr of **saint, street**.

stab [stæb] n (blow) κτύπημα nt, μπαμπεσιά || (col: try) **to have a ~** δοκιμάζω.

stability [stəˈbɪlɪtɪ] n σταθερότητα.

stabilize [ˈsteɪbəlaɪz] vt σταθεροποιώ || **~r** n ζυγοσταθμιστής, σταθεροποιητής.

stable [ˈsteɪbl] n στάβλος ♦ vt σταβλίζω ♦ a σταθερός, μόνιμος.

stack [stæk] n θημωνιά, σωρός ♦ vt συσσωρεύω, στοιβάζω.

stadium [ˈsteɪdɪəm] n στάδιο.

staff [staːf] n (stick) ράβδος f, μπαστούνι, κοντάκι || (people) προσωπικό, επιτελείο ♦ vt (with people) καταρτίζω προσωπικό.

stag [stæg] n ελάφι.

stage [steɪdʒ] n (theatre) σκηνή || (actors)

θέατρο || (degree) στάδιο ♦ vt (play)
ανεβάζω, σκηνοθετώ || (demonstration)
οργανώνω, σκηνοθετώ || in ~s
βαθμηδόν, κατά στάδια || ~coach n
ταχυδρομική άμαξα || ~ door n είσοδος
f ηθοποιών || ~ manager n σκηνοθέτης.

stagger ['stægə'] vi κλονίζομαι,
τρικλίζω, παραπατώ ♦ vt (person) ζαλίζω,
συγκλονίζω, κάνω να τα χάσει || (hours)
κλιμακώνω (τις ώρες) || ~ing a (amazing)
καταπληκτικός, συγκλονιστικός.

stagnant ['stægnənt] a στάσιμος,
λιμνασμένος || (dull) αδρανής, άγονος.

stagnate [stæg'neit] vi είμαι στάσιμος,
αδρανώ.

staid [steid] a θετικός, σοβαρός.

stain [stein] n λεκές m, κηλίδα ||
(colouring) χρώμα nt, βαφή, μπογιά ♦ vt
λεκιάζω, λερώνω || ~ed glass n
χρωματιστό γυαλί || ~less a (steel)
ανοξείδωτος.

stair [stɛə'] n (one step) σκαλοπάτι, σκαλί
|| ~case n κλίμακα, σκάλα || ~s npl
σκάλα || ~way n σκάλα.

stake [steik] n πάσσαλος, παλούκι ||
(gambling) στοίχημα nt, μίζα, ποντάρισμα
nt ♦ vt ποντάρω || (fig) παίζω.

stalactite ['stæləktait] n σταλακτίτης.

stalagmite ['stæləgmait] n
σταλαγμίτης.

stale [steil] a μπαγιάτικος || ~mate n
αδιέξοδο.

stalk [stɔːk] n κοτσάνι, στέλεχος nt,
μίσχος ♦ vt παρακολουθώ αθέατος ♦ vi
(walk stiffly) βαδίζω με μεγάλα βήματα.

stall [stɔːl] n παράπηγμα nt στάβλου,
παχνί || (stand) υπάγκος, περίπτερο ♦ vt
(AUT) κολλώ, μπλοκάρω ♦ vi (AUT) κολλώ
|| (delay) αναβάλλω, χρονοτριβώ || ~s npl
(THEAT) καθίσματα ntpl (ορχήστρας).

stallion ['stæliən] n επιβήτορας,
βαρβάτο αλογο.

stalwart ['stɔːlwət] a ρωμαλέος,
σταθερός ♦ n παλληκάρι.

stamina ['stæminə] n σφρίγος nt, ζωτική
δύναμη.

stammer ['stæmə'] n τραύλισμα nt,
τσέβδισμα nt ♦ vi τραυλίζω, ψευδίζω,
ψελλίζω.

stamp [stæmp] n (postage)
γραμματόσημο || (official) ένσημο || (of
foot) κτήπημα nt του ποδιού,
ποδοβολητό || (on document) σφραγίδα,
βούλα, στάμπα ♦ vi κτυπώ το πόδι,
περπατώ βαρειά ♦ vt (make mark)
σφραγίζω, μαρκάρω, σταμπάρω || (fix
postage) κολλώ γραμματόσημο || ~
album n συλλογή γραμματοσήμων || ~
collecting n φιλοτελισμός.

stampede [stæm'piːd] n εσπευσμένη
φυγή, πανικός.

stance [stæns] n (posture) στάση.

stand [stænd] (irreg v) n (position) στάση ||
(MIL) αντίσταση || (rest) υποστήριγμα nt,
πόδι, στήριγμα nt || (seats) εξέδρα ♦ vi
(erect) στέκομαι || (rise) σπκώνομαι ||
(place, set) κείμαι, βρίσκομαι, είμαι || (halt,

stop) σταματώ, στέκομαι ♦ vt (place)
τοποθετώ, βάζω, κουμπώ (όρθιο) ||
(endure) υποφέρω, αντέχω, υπομένω || to
make a ~ αντιστέκομαι, αντιτάσσομαι
|| **it ~s to reason** είναι λογικό || to ~
by vi (be ready) είμαι έτοιμος, είμαι σε
επιφυλακή ♦ vt (opinion) μένω πιστός σε
|| to ~ **for** vt (defend) υπερασπίζομαι,
υποστηρίζω || (signify) αντιπροσωπεύω ||
(permit, tolerate) υπομένω, ανέχομαι || to
~ **in for** vt αντικαθιστώ || to ~ **out** vi
(be prominent) (προ)εξέχω, ξεχωρίζω || to
~ **up** vi (rise) σπκώνομαι || to ~ **up for**
vt υποστηρίζω.

standard ['stændəd] n (measure)
υπόδειγμα nt, κανόνας, μέτρο || (flag)
σημαία, λάβαρο ♦ a (size etc) πρότυπος,
κανονικός, συνηθισμένος || ~ize vt
τυποποιώ || ~ of living n βιωτικό
επίπεδο.

standby ['stændbai] n (person)
αντικαταστάτης/τρια m/f.

stand-in ['stændin] n
αντικαταστάτης/τρια m/f,
αναπληρωτής/ώτρια m/f.

standing ['stændiŋ] a όρθιος || (lasting)
μόνιμος, διαρκής ♦ n διάρκεια ||
(reputation) κοινωνική θέση, υπόληψη ||
~ **orders** npl (MIL) μόνιμες διατάξεις fpl,
κανονισμοί mpl || ~ **room only** μόνο
όρθιοι.

stand-offish ['stænd'ɒfiʃ] a
υπεροπτικός.

standpoint ['stændpɔint] n άποψη,
σκοπιά.

standstill ['stændstil] n: at a ~
στασιμότητα, νεκρό σημείο || to come
to a ~ καταλήγω σε αδιέξοδο,
σταματώ.

stank [stæŋk] pt of stink.

stanza ['stænzə] n στροφή, στάντσα.

staple ['steipl] n άγκιστρο, συνδετήρας
|| (product) κύριο προϊόν ♦ a κύριος,
πρωτεύων ♦ vt στερεώνω, συνδέω || ~r
n συνδετήρας.

star [staː'] n άστρο, αστέρι || (actor)
αστέρας, πρωταγωνιστής/ίστρια m/f,
στάρ m/f inv || (shape) αστέρι ♦ vi (in film)
πρωταγωνιστώ, παίζω σε ταινία ♦ vt (to
star an actor) παρουσιάζω σαν
πρωταγωνιστή.

starboard ['staːbəd] n δεξιά πλευρά, ♦
a δεξιά.

starch [staːtʃ] n άμυλο || ~ed a (collar)
κολλαριστός || ~y a αμυλώδης,
αμυλούχος || (formal) υπεροπτικός,
ποζάτος.

stardom ['staːdəm] n θέση αστέρα.

stare [stɛə'] n στενές βλέμμα nt,
καρφωτή ματιά ♦ vi (+ at) ατενίζω,
καρφώνω με το μάτι.

starfish ['staːfiʃ] n αστερίας.

stark [staːk] a ψυχρός, σκληρός ♦ ad: ~
naked ολόγυμνος, θεόγυμνος,
τσίτσιδος.

starlight ['staːlait] n αστροφεγγιά.

starling ['staːliŋ] n ψαρώνι, καραβέλι.

starry ['stɑːrɪ] a έναστρος, αστερόφεγγος, λαμπερός || **~-eyed** a (innocent) ονειροπαρμένος αφελής.

start [stɑːt] n αρχή, σημείο εκκινήσεως, εκκίνηση || (beginning) αρχή, αρχίνισμα nt || (sudden movement) ξάφνιασμα nt, ανατίναγμα nt ♦ vt (set going) αρχίζω, ανοίγω, βγάζω ♦ vi (begin journey) αρχίζω, ξεκινώ || (make sudden movement) αναπηδώ, ξαφνίζομαι || to ~ doing αρχίζω με, πιάνομαι με || to ~ off vi (begin) αρχίζω, ξεκινώ || to ~ up vi βάζω μπρος || ~er n (AUT) εκκινητήρας, μίζα || (for race) αφέτης || ~ing point n αφετηρία, σημείο εκκινήσεως.

startle ['stɑːtl] vt ξαφνιάζω, φοβίζω, εκπλήσσω.

startling ['stɑːtlɪŋ] a καταπληκτικός, εντυπωσιακός, χτυπητός.

starvation [stɑːˈveɪʃən] n λιμός, λιμοκτονία, ασιτία, πείνα.

starve [stɑːv] vi (die of hunger) πεθαίνω από πείνα || (suffer from hunger) ψοφώ της πείνας, πεινώ ♦ vt (keep without food) στερώ τροφής.

starving ['stɑːvɪŋ] a πεινασμένος, λιμασμένος, ψόφιος της πείνας.

state [steɪt] n κατάσταση, θέση || (government) κράτος nt, πολιτεία || (anxiety) αναστάτωση ♦ vt δηλώνω, λέγω, ανακοινώνω || ~ly a μεγαλοπρεπής, αξιοπρεπής || ~ment n δήλωση, έκθεση || ~sman n πολιτικός.

static ['stætɪk] n στατική ♦ a ακίνητος, αδρανής || (PHYS) στατικός || ~ electricity n στατικός ηλεκτρισμός.

station ['steɪʃən] n (RAIL) σταθμός || (post) σταθμός, θέση || (position in life) κοινωνική θέση, βαθμός ♦ vt τοποθετώ, βάζω.

stationary ['steɪʃənərɪ] a στάσιμος, ακίνητος.

stationer ['steɪʃənə*] n χαρτοπώλης || ~'s (shop) n χαρτοπωλείο || ~y n χαρτικά είδη ntpl.

station master ['steɪʃənmɑːstə*] n σταθμάρχης.

station wagon ['steɪʃənwægən] n (US AUT) στέισον-βάγκον nt inv.

statistic [stəˈtɪstɪk] n στατιστικό (στοιχείο) || ~al a στατιστικός || ~s npl στατιστική.

statue ['stætjuː] n άγαλμα nt.

stature ['stætʃə] n ανάστημα nt.

status ['steɪtəs] n θέση, κατάσταση || the ~ quo n καθεστώς nt, στάτους κβο nt inv.

statute ['stætjuːt] n νόμος, θέσπισμα nt.

statutory ['stætjutərɪ] a νομοθετημένος, θεσπισμένος.

staunch [stɔːntʃ] a αξιόπιστος, πιστός, δυνατός.

stave [steɪv] vt: to ~ off (attack) αποκρούω, απωθώ || (threat) αποτρέπω, αποφεύγω.

stay [steɪ] n διαμονή, παραμονή ♦ vi (παρα)μένω || (at place) διαμένω || to ~ put μένω στην ίδια θέση || to ~ with friends μένω με φίλους || to ~ the night μένω το βράδυ || to ~ behind vi παρακολουθώ από πίσω || μένω πίσω || to ~ in vi (at home) μένω (στο σπίτι) || to ~ on vi (continue) παραμένω || to ~ out vi (of house) μένω έξω, δεν επιστρέφω || to ~ up vi (at night) αγρυπνώ, ξενυχτώ.

STD n (abbr of Subscriber Trunk Dialling) τηλεφωνικός κώδικας (Τηλ. Κωδ.).

steadfast ['stedfəst] a σταθερός.

steadily ['stedɪlɪ] ad σταθερά.

steady ['stedɪ] a σταθερός, στερεός || (regular) κανονικός, συνεχής, σταθερός || (reliable) σταθερός, συνεπής, τακτικός ♦ vt σταθεροποιώ, στερεώνω || to ~ o.s. σταθεροποιούμαι, καθησυχάζω.

steak [steɪk] n (meat) μπριζόλα, μπιφτέκι || (fish) φέτα.

steal [stiːl] (irreg v) vt κλέβω, βουτώ, σουφρώνω ♦ vi φεύγω κλεφτά || ~th ['stelθ] n: by ~th κρυφά, κλεφτά, μυστικά || ~thy a κρυφός, φευγαλέος, προσεκτικός.

steam [stiːm] n ατμός ♦ vt βράζω στον ατμό ♦ vi αναδίνω ατμό, αχνίζω || (ship) κινούμαι, πλέω (με ατμό) || ~ engine n ατμομηχανή || ~er n ατμόπλοιο, βαπόρι || ~roller n οδοστρωτήρας || ~y a θολός, γεμάτος ατμού.

steel [stiːl] n χάλυβας, ατσάλι ♦ a χαλύβδινος, ατσάλινος || ~works n χαλυβδουργείο.

steep [stiːp] a απότομος, απόκρημνος || (price) εξωφρενική ♦ vt διαποτίζω, μουσκεύω, βουτώ.

steeple ['stiːpl] n κωδωνοστάσιο || ~chase n ιπποδρομία με εμπόδια || ~jack n επιδιορθωτής καπνοδόχων.

steeply ['stiːplɪ] ad απότομα, κατηφορικά.

steepness ['stiːpnɪs] n το απότομο, το απόκρημνο.

steer [stɪə*] n μικρός ταύρος ♦ vt (car) οδηγώ || (boat) πηδαλιουχώ ♦ vi κατευθύνομαι, βάζω πλώρη για || ~ing n (AUT) σύστημα nt διεύθυνσης || ~ing wheel n βολάν nt inv, τιμόνι.

stem [stem] n στέλεχος nt, κορμός ♦ vt. σταματώ, ανακόπτω || to ~ from vt προέρχομαι από.

stench [stentʃ] n δυσοσμία, δυσωδία.

stencil ['stensl] n μεμβράνη ♦ vt γράφω μεμβράνες, πολυγραφώ.

stenographer [steˈnɒɡrəfə*] n στενογράφος m/f.

step [step] n βήμα nt, πάτημα nt || (stair) βαθμίδα, σκαλοπάτι, σκαλί || (action) διάβημα nt, ενέργεια || (sound) βήμα nt, βάδισμα nt ♦ vi βηματίζω, βαδίζω || ~s npl = stepladder || to ~ down vi (fig) παραιτούμαι || to ~ up vt αυξάνω, ανεβάζω || ~brother n ετεροθαλής αδελφός || ~child n προγονός, προγονή m/f || ~father n πατριός || ~ladder n σκάλα (φορητή) || ~mother n μητριά.

stepping stone ['stɛpɪŋstəʊn] n σκαλοπάτι, ενδιάμεσος σταθμός.

stereo ['stɪərɪəʊ] n (RAD) στερεοφωνικό ραδιόφωνο || ~**phonic** a στερεοφωνικό || ~**type** n στερεοτυπία ♦ vt τυπώνω διά στερεοτυπίας.

sterile ['stɛraɪl] a στείρος, άγονος, άκαρπος || (free from germs) αποστειρωμένος.

sterility [stɛ'rɪlɪtɪ] n στειρότητα, αγονία.

sterilization [stɛrɪlaɪ'zeɪʃən] n αποστείρωση.

sterilize ['stɛrɪlaɪz] vt στειρώνω || (from germs) αποστειρώνω.

sterling ['stɜːlɪŋ] a στερλίνα || (top quality) αμιγής, καλής ποιότητας.

stern [stɜːn] a αυστηρός, βλοσυρός ♦ n πρύμνη, πρύμη.

stethoscope ['stɛθəskəʊp] n στηθοσκόπιο.

stevedore ['stiːvɪdɔː*] n φορτοεκφορτωτής.

stew [stjuː] n κρέας nt με χορταρικά ♦ vt κάνω κρέας στην κατσαρόλα ♦ vi σιγοβράζω.

steward ['stjuːəd] n (AVIAT, NAUT, RAIL, in club etc) φροντιστής, οικονόμος, καμαρότος || ~**ess** n (AVIAT) αεροσυνοδός.

stick [stɪk] (irreg v) n βέργα, ράβδος f || (cane) μπαστούνι ♦ vt (πήγω, χώνω, καρφώνω) || (gum) κολλώ || (col: tolerate) ανέχομαι, υποφέρω ♦ vi (stop) πιάνομαι, κολλώ, φρακάρω || (hold fast) κολλιέμαι, κολλώ || to ~ out vi (project) κρατώ μέχρι τέλους, επιμένω || to ~ up vi (project) υψώνομαι, στήνω || to ~ up for vt (defend) υπερασπίζομαι, παίρνω το μέρος || ~**er** n ετικέτα.

stickler ['stɪklə*] n (+ for) άκαμπτος, στενοκέφαλος (OE).

stick-up ['stɪkʌp] n (col: robbery) ληστεία.

sticky ['stɪkɪ] a κολλώδης, γλοιώδης.

stiff [stɪf] a δύσκαμπτος, σκληρός, άκαμπτος || (examination etc) δύσκολος || (paste) σκληρός, σφιχτός || (formal) επιτηδευμένος, τυπικός, ψυχρός || (strong) ισχυρός, δυνατός || ~**en** vt σκληραίνω, δυναμώνω ♦ vi σκληραίνομαι, γίνομαι άκαμπτος || ~**ness** n σκληρότητα, πιάσιμο.

stifle ['staɪfl] vt (keep back) καταπνίγω, συγκρατώ.

stifling ['staɪflɪŋ] a (atmosphere) αποπνικτικός, ασφυκτικός.

stigma ['stɪgmə] n στίγμα nt, κηλίδα.

stile [staɪl] n στύλος.

still [stɪl] a ακίνητος, αθόρυβος, σιωπηλός ♦ ad (yet) ακόμη || (even) ακόμη (περισσότερα) || ~**born** a θνησιγενής || ~ **life** n νεκρή φύση.

stilt [stɪlt] n ξυλοπόδαρο.

stilted ['stɪltɪd] a άκαμπτος, τυπικός, τεχνητός.

stimulant ['stɪmjʊlənt] n διεγερτικό, τονωτικό.

stimulate ['stɪmjʊleɪt] vt διεγείρω, εξάπτω.

stimulating ['stɪmjʊleɪtɪŋ] a διεγερτικός, τονωτικός.

stimulation [stɪmjʊ'leɪʃən] n διέγερση, τόνωση.

stimulus ['stɪmjʊləs] n κίνητρο.

sting [stɪŋ] (irreg v) n δήγμα nt, κέντρισμα nt ♦ vt κεντρίζω, τσιμπώ.

stingy ['stɪndʒɪ] a φιλάργυρος, τσιγγούνης, σφιχτοχέρης.

stink [stɪŋk] (irreg v) n δυσοσμία, βρώμα ♦ vi βρωμώ, βρωμάω || ~**ing** a (fig) τρομερός.

stint [stɪnt] n όριο, καθήκον ♦ vt στερώ, περιορίζω.

stipend ['staɪpɛnd] n (to vicar etc) μισθός, επίδομα nt.

stipulate ['stɪpjʊleɪt] vt αποφαίνομαι, συμφωνώ, συνομολογώ.

stipulation [stɪpjʊ'leɪʃən] n όρος, διάταξη, συμφωνία.

stir [stɜː*] n ταραχή, σάλεμα nt, κούνημα nt, κίνηση ♦ vt (mix) ανακατώνω, αναδεύω ♦ vi (move) κουνιέμαι, σαλεύω || to ~ up vt υποκινώ, υποδαυλίζω || ~**ring** a συγκλονιστικός, συγκινητικός.

stirrup ['stɪrəp] n αναβολέας, σκάλα.

stitch [stɪtʃ] n βελονιά, ραφή || (sudden pain) σουβλιά πόνου, σουβλιά ♦ vt ράβω, κάνω βελονιές.

stock [stɒk] n (supply) απόθεμα nt, στοκ nt inv, προμήθεια || (trader's goods) εμπορεύματα ntpl, στοκ nt inv || (farm animals) κτήνη ntpl, ζώα ntpl || (liquid) ζωμός, κονσομέ nt inv || (ECON) χρεώγραφο, τίτλος, αξία ♦ a της σειράς, κανονικός, συνηθισμένος ♦ vt εφοδιάζω, έχω παρακαταθήκη από || to take ~ κάνω απογραφή || (+ of) κρίνω, εκτιμώ || to ~ up with vt αποθηκεύω.

stockade [stɒ'keɪd] n πασσαλόπηγμα nt, φράκτης.

stockbroker ['stɒkbrəʊkə*] n χρηματομεσίτης, χρηματιστής.

stock exchange ['stɒkɪkstʃeɪndʒ] n χρηματιστήριο.

stocking ['stɒkɪŋ] n κάλτσα.

stock market ['stɒkmɑːkɪt] n αγορά χρεωγράφων.

stockpile ['stɒkpaɪl] n αποθέματα ntpl ♦ vt δημιουργώ αποθέματα.

stocktaking ['stɒkteɪkɪŋ] n (COMM) απογραφή.

stocky ['stɒkɪ] a κοντόχοντρος.

stodgy ['stɒdʒɪ] a βαρύς, ανιαρός.

stoical ['stəʊɪkəl] n a στωικός.

stoke [stəʊk] vt τροφοδοτώ φωτιά, διατηρώ φωτιά.

stole [stəʊl] pt of steal ♦ n (fur) γούνα, σάρπα || ~n pp of steal ♦ a κλεμμένος.

stomach ['stʌmək] n στομάχι || (inclination) όρεξη, διάθεση ♦ vt ανέχομαι, χωνεύω || ~ ache n στομαχόπονος.

stone [stəʊn] n λίθος, πέτρα || (gem) πολύτιμος λίθος, πετράδι, κόσμημα nt ||

(of fruit) πυρήνας, κουκούτσι || *(weight)* βάρος 14 λιβρών ♦ a από λίθους, πέτρινος ♦ vt βγάζω κουκούτσια από || ~-**cold** a κρύος σαν μάρμαρο || ~-**deaf** a θεόκουφος || ~-**work** n λιθοδομή.

stony ['stəʊnɪ] a πετρώδης, γεμάτος πέτρες.

stood [stʊd] pt, pp of **stand**.

stool [stu:l] n σκαμνί.

stoop [stu:p] vi σκύβω.

stop [stɒp] n στάση || *(punctuation)* σημείο στίξεως ♦ vt *(prevent)* σταματώ || *(bring to end)* διακόπτω, σταματώ ♦ vi *(cease)* παύω, σταματώ, διακόπτομαι || *(remain)* παραμένω, πηγαίνω || **to ~ doing sth** παύω να κάνω κάτι, σταματώ || ~ **it!** σταμάτα!, φτάνει! || **to ~ dead** vi σταματώ απότομα || **to ~ in** vi *(at home)* περνώ από, επισκέπτομαι || **to ~ off** vi κατεβαίνω, διακόπτω το ταξίδι μου ♦ vt *(hole)* φράζω, βουλώνω, κλείνω || ~**lights** npl *(AUT)* κόκκινα φανάρια ntpl, κόκκινα φώτα npl || ~**over** n *(on journey)* σταθμός, στάθμευση.

stoppage ['stɒpɪdʒ] n σταμάτημα nt, παύση, διακοπή.

stopper ['stɒpə*] n πώμα nt, βούλωμα nt.

stopwatch ['stɒpwɒtʃ] n χρονόμετρο.

storage ['stɔ:rɪdʒ] n (εν)αποθήκευση, αποθήκη.

store [stɔ:*] n παρακαταθήκη, εφόδιο || *(place)* αποθήκη || *(large shop)* κατάστημα nt, μαγαζί ♦ vt εφοδιάζω, αποθηκεύω || *(COMPUT)* αποθηκεύω || **to ~ up** vt συσσωρεύω, συγκεντρώνω, μαζεύω || ~**room** n αποθήκη, κελάρι.

storey ['stɔ:rɪ] n *(Brit)* όροφος, πάτωμα nt.

stork [stɔ:k] n πελαργός, λελέκι.

storm [stɔ:m] n θύελλα, καταιγίδα, φουρτούνα || *(disturbance)* θύελλα, καταιγισμός ♦ vi μαίνομαι ♦ vt *(attack)* εξαπολύω έφοδο || **to take by ~** *(lit)* καταλαμβάνω με έφοδο || *(fig)* κατακτώ, παρασύρω || ~ **cloud** n μαύρο σύννεφο || ~**y** a *(weather)* θυελλώδης.

story ['stɔ:rɪ] n *(account)* ιστορία, αφήγηση, διήγημα nt || *(lie)* παραμύθι, ψέμα nt || *(US: storey)* όροφος, πάτωμα nt || ~**book** n βιβλίο διηγημάτων || ~**teller** n αφηγητής, παραμυθάς.

stout [staʊt] a *(bold)* δυνατός, γερός, θαρραλέος || *(too fat)* χονδρός, σωματώδης, παχύς, ναχύς ♦ n είδος μπύρας.

stove [stəʊv] n *(for cooking)* κουζίνα, συσκευή μαγειρεύματος || *(for heating)* θερμάστρα, σόμπα.

stow [stəʊ] vt στοιβάζω, αποθηκεύω || ~**away** n λαθρεπιβάτης.

straddle ['strædl] vt κάθομαι καβαλικευτά, καβαλικεύω.

straggle ['strægl] vi σκορπίζω, βραδυπορώ || ~**r** n παραπλανημένος, ο βραδυπορών.

straight [streɪt] a ευθύς, ευθύγραμμος, ίσιος || *(honest)* δίκαιος, ευθύς, τίμιος,

ντόμπρος || *(in order)* τακτικός, τακτοποιημένος, σιαγμένος ♦ ad ίσια, κατευθείαν, αμέσως || *(drink)* σκέτο ♦ n ευθεία || ~ **away** ad *(at once)* αμέσως || ~ **off** ad *(without stopping)* στη στιγμή, αυτοστιγμεί || ~**en** vt *(also: ~ out)* ισιώνω || *(fig)* τακτοποιώ || ~**forward** a *(simple)* χωρίς περιστροφές, ντόμπρος, ειλικρινής.

strain [streɪn] n *(mental)* ένταση, κούραση || *(streak, trace)* φυσική διάθεση, κλίση, τάση ♦ vt *(stretch)* εντείνω, τεντώνω || *(filter)* διυλίζω, φιλτράρω ♦ vi *(make effort)* μοχθώ, κοπιάζω, εντείνω || ~**s** npl *(MUS)* τόνος, ύφος nt || ~**ed** a *(laugh)* βιασμένος, ψεύτικος || *(relations)* τεταμένος || ~**er** n σουρωτήρι, φίλτρο, τρυπητό.

strait [streɪt] n *(GEOG)* στενό, πορθμός || ~ **jacket** n ζουρλομανδύας || ~-**laced** a ηθικολόγος, σεμνότυφος.

strand [strænd] n *(thread)* κλώνος, κλωνί, κλωστή ♦ vt εξοκέλλω || ~**ed** a εγκαταλειμμένος, αφισμένος πίσω.

strange [streɪndʒ] a ξένος || *(unusual)* ασυνήθιστος, παράξενος || ~**ness** n το περίεργο, παράξενο || ~**r** n ξένος/n m/f, άγνωστος/n m/f || *(new to a place)* νεοαρχικθείς/είσα m/f, καινούργιος/a m/f.

strangle ['stræŋgl] vt στραγγαλίζω, πνίγω, καταπνίγω.

strangulation [stræŋgjʊ'leɪʃən] n στραγγαλισμός.

strap [stræp] n λωρίδα, λουρί ♦ vt δένω με λουρί || *(beat)* δέρνω με λουρί || ~**ping** a γεροδεμένος.

strata ['strɑ:tə] npl of **stratum**.

stratagem ['strætɪdʒəm] n στρατήγημα nt, κόλπο.

strategic [strə'ti:dʒɪk] a στρατηγικός || ~**ally** ad στρατηγικά.

strategy ['strætɪdʒɪ] n στρατηγική, τέχνασμα nt.

stratum ['strɑ:təm] n στρώμα nt.

straw [strɔ:] n *(AGR)* άχυρο, ψάθα || *(drinking straw)* καλάμι, καλαμάκι ♦ a *(hat, basket)* ψάθινος, αχυρένιος.

strawberry ['strɔ:bərɪ] n φράουλα.

stray [streɪ] n χαμένος, ζώο που έχει ξεκόψει από το κοπάδι ♦ vi περιπλανώμαι, απομακρύνομαι ♦ a *(animal)* περιπλανώμενος, αδέσποτος || *(thought)* ξεκάρφωτος, σκόρπιος, ξεκόλλητος.

streak [stri:k] n γραμμή, λωρίδα, ρίγα || *(strain)* δόση ♦ vt χαράσσω, ριγώνω, σχηματίζω ραβδώσεις || ~**y** a ραβδωτός, γραμμωτός, ριγωτός.

stream [stri:m] n ποτάμι, ρυάκι, ρέμα nt || *(flow)* ροή, ρούς m, χείμαρρος || *(crowd)* κύματα ntpl, αδιάκοπη σειρά ♦ vi ρέω, τρέχω, κυλώ.

streamer ['stri:mə*] n σερπαντίνα, ταινία, σημαία.

streamlined ['stri:mlaɪnd] a αεροδυναμικός.

street [striːt] n οδός f, δρόμος || ~**car** n (US: tram) τράμ nt inv || ~ **lamp** n φανοστάτης.

strength [streŋθ] n (lit) δύναμη, ισχύς f || (fig) **on the** ~**of** βασιζόμενος σε, στηριζόμενος σε || ~**en** vt ενισχύω, δυναμώνω.

strenuous ['strenjuəs] a κουραστικός, δραστήριος || (requiring effort) επίπονος, σκληρός.

stress [stres] n (force, pressure) πίεση, καταναγκασμός || (mental strain) ένταση || (accent) τόνος ♦ vt τονίζω.

stretch [stretʃ] n (area) έκταση ♦ vt τεντώνω, απλώνω ♦ vi εκτείνομαι, πλαταίνω || **at a** ~ (continuously) χωρίς διακοπή || **to** ~ **out** vi επεκτείνομαι, αραιώνω ♦ vt τείνω, απλώνω || ~**er** n φορείο.

stricken ['strikən] a (person) χτυπημένος, λιμμένος || (city, country) χτυπημένος.

strict [strikt] a ακριβής, αυστηρός || δριμύς || ~**ly** ad αυστηρά, ακριβώς || ~**ly speaking** κυριολεκτικώς, για να πούμε την αλήθεια || ~**ness** n αυστηρότητα.

stride [straid] (irreg v) n μεγάλο βήμα n, δρασκελιά ♦ vi δρασκελίζω, βηματίζω.

strident ['straidənt] a οξύς, στριγγός, στρίγγλικος.

strife [straif] n αγώνας, πάλη, σύγκρουση.

strike [straik] (irreg v) n απεργία || (discovery) ανακάλυψη, συνάντηση || (attack) επιχείρηση, πλήγμα nt ♦ vt κτυπώ, προσκρούω, σκουντώ || (come into mind) έρχομαι (στο μυαλό), μου φαίνεται || (find gold) ανακαλύπτω, βρίσκω ♦ vi (stop work) κηρύσσω απεργία, απεργώ || (attack) χτυπώ || (clock) ηχώ, κτυπώ, σημαίνω || **to** ~ **down** vt (lay low) ρίχνω χάμω || **to** ~ **out** vt (cross out) εξαλείφω, διαγράφω, σβήνω || **to** ~ **up** vt (music) αρχίζω (να παίζω) || (friendship) πιάνω φιλία || ~**r** n απεργός.

striking ['straikiŋ] a κτυπητός, ελκυστικός, ενδιαφέρων || ~**ly** ad εντυπωσιακά, κτυπητά.

string [striŋ] n σπάγγος, κορδόνι || (series) σειρά || (MUS) χορδή || (COMPUT) διατεταγμένη σειρά χαρακτήρων || ~ **bean** n φρέσκο φασολάκι.

stringent ['strindʒənt] a αυστηρός, στενός.

strip [strip] n λουρίδα, ταινία ♦ vt γυμνώνω, γδύνω, βγάζω || (machine etc) αποσυνθέτω ♦ vi γδύνομαι, γυμνώνομαι || ~ **cartoon** n σειρά εύθυμων σκίτσων.

stripe [straip] n γραμμή, λουρίδα, ράβδωση || ~**d** a ραβδωτός, ριγωτός.

stripper ['stripə*] n στριπτηζέ f inv.

striptease ['striptiːz] n στριπτήζ nt inv.

strive [straiv] (irreg v) vi (+ for) αγωνίζομαι (για), προσπαθώ || ~**n** ['strivn] pp of strive.

strode [strəud] pt, pp of stride.

stroke [strəuk] n κτύπημα nt, πλήγμα nt ||

(TECH) κίνηση, διαδρομή, ρυθμός || (sudden attack) προσβολή || (caress) θωπεία, χάδι, χάιδεμα nt ♦ vt χαϊδεύω, τρίβω, σιάζω || **at a** ~ μ' ένα κτύπημα, με μιας || **on the** ~ **of 5** στις 5 ακριβώς.

stroll [strəul] n περίπατος, βόλτα ♦ vi κάνω περίπατο, κάνω βόλτες.

strong [stroŋ] a δυνατός, ισχυρός, γερός || (firm) στερεός, γερός || (flavour) δυνατός, έντονος || (protest) έντονος || (wind) ισχυρός, δυνατός || **they are 50** ~ δυνάμεως 50 ανδρών || ~**hold** n φρούριο, οχυρό, προπύργιο || ~**ly** ad δυνατά, γερά || ~**room** n αίθουσα χρηματοκιβωτίων.

strove [strəuv] pt of strive.

struck [strʌk] pt, pp of strike.

structural ['strʌktʃərəl] a δομικός.

structure ['strʌktʃə*] n κατασκευή, δομή || (building) οικοδόμημα nt, κτίριο, κτίσμα nt.

struggle ['strʌgl] n αγώνας, πάλη, σκληρή προσπάθεια ♦ vi (+ to) αγωνίζομαι, παλεύω.

strum [strʌm] vt (guitar) παίζω αδέξια, παίζω άτεχνα.

strut [strʌt] n (support) στήριγμα nt, υποστήριγμα nt ♦ vi περιφέρομαι καμαρωτός, κορδώνομαι.

stub [stʌb] n (cigarette etc) υπόλειμμα nt, γόπα.

stubble ['stʌbl] n καλαμιά, ρίζες fpl || (on face) γένια ntpl ημερών.

stubborn ['stʌbən] a επίμονος, πεισματάρης, ξεροκέφαλος || ~**ly** ad πεισματικά, επίμονα.

stubby ['stʌbi] a κοντόχοντρος.

stuck [stʌk] pt, pp of stick || ~**-up** a υπεροπτικός, φαντασμένος.

stud [stʌd] n πλατυκέφαλο καρφί || (of shirt) κουμπί, ξενόκουμπο || (of horses) στάβλος αλόγων, ιπποστάσιο ♦ vt διαστίζω, κοσμώ με καρφιά.

student ['stjuːdənt] n φοιτητής/ήτρια m/f, σπουδαστής/άστρια m/f, μελετητής.

studio ['stjuːdiəu] n εργαστήριο, ατελιέ nt inv || (also TV) στούντιο.

studious ['stjuːdiəs] a μελετηρός, φιλομαθής || (careful) προσεκτικός || ~**ly** ad (carefully) vt επιμελώς.

study ['stʌdi] n σπουδή, μελέτη || (something studied) μελέτη, έρευνα || (room) σπουδαστήριο, αναγνωστήριο ♦ vt σπουδάζω, μελετώ || (examine) μελετώ, παρατηρώ ♦ vi επιμελούμαι, μελετώ.

stuff [stʌf] n ύλη, υλικό, ουσία ♦ vt (παρα)γεμίζω || ~**ing** n παραγέμισμα nt, γέμιση || (of fowl etc) γέμισμα nt || ~**y** a (room) πνιγηρός, χωρίς αέρα || (ideas: old-fashioned) σεμνότυφος.

stumble ['stʌmbl] vi σκοντάφτω, προσκρούω || **to** ~ **on** vt ανακαλύπτω αναπάντεχα.

stumbling block ['stʌmbliŋblɒk] n εμπόδιο.

stump [stʌmp] n κούτσουρο, στέλεχος nt ♦ vt (puzzle) μπερδεύω, τα χάνω.

stun [stʌŋ] vt ζαλίζω, ταράζω.

stung [stʌŋ] pt, pp of **sting**.

stunk [stʌŋk] pp of **stink**.

stunning ['stʌnɪŋ] a εξαίσιος, κοταπλυκτικός.

stunt [stʌnt] n εκπληκτική παράσταση, άθλος ♦ vt περιστέλλω, εμποδίζω την ανάπτυξη || ~ed a κατοισασμένος.

stupefy ['stjuːpɪfaɪ] vt καταπλήσσω.

stupendous [stjuːˈpɛndəs] a τεράστιος, πελώριος, καταπληκτικός || ~ly ad καταπληκτικά.

stupid ['stjuːpɪd] a ηλίθιος, βλάκας, κουτός || ~ity n βλακεία, κουταμάρα || ~ly ad ηλίθια, βλακωδώς.

stupor ['stjuːpə*] n νάρκη, λήθαργος, χαύνωση.

sturdy ['stɜːdɪ] a δυνατός, σθεναρός, γεροδεμένος.

stutter ['stʌtə*] n ψέλλισμα nt, τραύλισμα nt ♦ vi τραυλίζω, τσεβδίζω.

sty [staɪ] n χοιροστάσιο, γουρνοστάσι.

stye [staɪ] n χαλάζιο, κριθαράκι.

style [staɪl] n στύλ nt inv, τεχνοτροπία, ύφος nt || (fashion) ρυθμός, στύλ nt inv, μόδα || (distinction) επιδεξιότητα, μεγαλοπρέπεια.

stylish ['staɪlɪʃ] a μοντέρνος, κομψός || ~ly ad κομψά, με σικ.

stylus ['staɪləs] n στύλος, γραφίδα.

suave [swaːv] a ευγενικός, απαλός, ευχάριστος.

sub- [sʌb] prefix υπο-.

subconscious ['sʌbˈkɒnʃəs] a υποσυνείδητος ♦ n: the ~ το υποσυνείδητο.

subdivide ['sʌbdɪˈvaɪd] vt υποδιαιρώ.

subdivision ['sʌbdɪvɪʒən] n υποδιαίρεση.

subdue [səbˈdjuː] vt κατακτώ, υποτάσσω, μαλακώνω || ~d a συντριμμένος, μαλακωμένος.

subject ['sʌbdʒɪkt] n υπήκοος m/f || (theme) θέμα nt, αντικείμενο || (GRAM) υποκείμενο ♦ [səbˈdʒɛkt] vt: to ~ s.o. to sth υποβάλλω κάποιον σε κάτι || to be ~ to υπόκειμαι σε, εξαρτώμαι από || ~ion n καθυποτάξη, υποταγή || ~ive a υποκειμενικός || ~ matter n θέμα nt, περιεχόμενο.

sublet ['sʌbˈlɛt] vt υπενοικιάζω.

sublime [səˈblaɪm] a θείος, ανώτερος, υπέροχος, έξοχος.

submarine [sʌbməˈriːn] n υποβρύχιο.

submerge [səbˈmɜːdʒ] vt βυθίζω, χώνω στο νερό ♦ vi καταδύομαι, βυθίζομαι, βουλιάζω.

submission [səbˈmɪʃən] n υποταγή, υπακοή || (presentation) υποβολή.

submit [səbˈmɪt] vt υποβάλλω ♦ vi υποτάσσομαι, υποβάλλομαι.

subnormal ['sʌbˈnɔːməl] a κάτω του κανονικού.

subordinate [səˈbɔːdnɪt] a κατώτερος, εξαρτημένος ♦ n υφιστάμενος.

subpoena [səbˈpiːnə] n κλήση (μορτύρων) ♦ vt καλώ, αποστέλλω κλήση.

subscribe [səbˈskraɪb] vi (pay contribution) εγγράφομαι, συνεισφέρω || (+ to) επιδοκιμάζω, αποδέχομαι, παραδέχομαι || ~r n (to periodical, TEL) συνδρομητής/ήτρια m/f.

subscription [səbˈskrɪpʃən] n συνεισφορά, συνδρομή.

subsequent ['sʌbsɪkwənt] a επακόλουθος, μεταγενέστερος || ~ly ad έπειτα, αργότερα.

subside [səbˈsaɪd] vi κατακαθίζω, υποχωρώ, κοπάζω || ~nce n καθίζηση, κόπαση.

subsidiary [səbˈsɪdɪərɪ] a βοηθητικός, δευτερεύων ♦ n θυγατρική εταιρεία.

subsidize ['sʌbsɪdaɪz] vt επιχορηγώ, επιδοτώ.

subsidy ['sʌbsɪdɪ] n επιχορήγηση, βοήθημα nt, επίδομα nt.

subsistence [səbˈsɪstəns] n ύπαρξη, συντήρηση, επιβίωση.

substance ['sʌbstəns] n ουσία || (wealth) περιουσία, αξία.

substandard ['sʌbˈstændəd] a κάτω του μέσου όρου, κακής ποιότητας.

substantial [səbˈstænʃəl] a (strong) στερεός, γερός || (important) σημαντικός, ουσιώδης || ~ly ad ουσιαστικά, πραγματικά.

substantiate [səbˈstænʃɪeɪt] vt επαληθεύω, αποδεικνύω, αιτιολογώ.

substitute ['sʌbstɪtjuːt] n αντικαταστάτης, υποκατάστατο ♦ vt υποκαθιστώ, αντικαθιστώ.

substitution [sʌbstɪˈtjuːʃən] n αντικατάσταση, υποκατάσταση.

subterfuge ['sʌbtəfjuːdʒ] n υπεκφυγή, τέχνασμα nt, πρόφαση.

subterranean [sʌbtəˈreɪnɪən] a υπόγειος.

subtitle ['sʌbtaɪtl] n (CINE) υπότιτλος.

subtle ['sʌtl] a (faint) λεπτός, διακριτικός || (clever, sly) έξυπνος, πανούργος || ~ty n λεπτότητα.

subtly ['sʌtlɪ] ad διακριτικά, με λεπτότητα.

subtract [səbˈtrækt] vt αφαιρώ || ~ion n αφαίρεση.

subtropical ['sʌbˈtrɒpɪkəl] a υποτροπικός.

suburb ['sʌbɜːb] n προάστειο || ~an a των προαστείων.

subversive [səbˈvɜːsɪv] a ανατρεπτικός.

subway ['sʌbweɪ] n (US) υπόγειος σιδηρόδρομος.

succeed [səkˈsiːd] vi επιτυγχάνω, πετυχαίνω ♦ vt διαδέχομαι || ~ing a (following) επόμενος, μελλοντικός.

success [səkˈsɛs] n επιτυχία, ευτυχής έκβαση || (person) επιτυχημένος άνθρωπος || ~ful a επιτυχής, επιτυχημένος || ~fully ad επιτυχώς, με επιτυχία.

succession [səkˈsɛʃən] n διαδοχή.

successive [sək'sɛsiv] a διαδοχικός, συνεχής, αλλεπάλληλος.

successor [sək'sɛsə*] n διάδοχος.

succinct [sək'sɪŋkt] a σύντομος και σαφής.

succulent ['sʌkjulənt] a εύχυμος, ζουμερός, νόστιμος.

succumb [sə'kʌm] vi (+ to) υποκύπτω, υποτάσσομαι, ενδίδω.

such [sʌtʃ] a (of that kind) τέτοιος, τέτοιου είδους || (so great etc) τόσος ♦ pron αυτός, αυτοί, τέτοιος.

suck [sʌk] vt (toffee) πιπιλίζω || ~er n (col) κορόιδο.

suction ['sʌkʃən] n αναρρόφηση, άντληση.

sudden ['sʌdn] a ξαφνικός, αιφνίδιος || **all of a** ~ αιφνιδίως, ξαφνικά || ~ly ad ξαφνικά.

sue [su:] vt ενάγω, κάνω αγωγή.

suede [sweid] n καστόρι, σουέντ nt inv.

suet [suɪt] n λίπος nt, ξύγγι.

suffer ['sʌfə*] vt (death) θανατούμαι, εκτελούμαι || (permit) υποφέρω, ανέχομαι, δέχομαι ♦ vi υποφέρω, πάσχω || ~er n υποφέρων, πάσχων || ~ing n πόνος, βάσανα ntpl, πάθη ntpl.

suffice [sə'fais] vi (επ)αρκώ, φθάνω.

sufficient [sə'fiʃənt] a επαρκής, αρκετός || ~ly ad αρκετά.

suffix ['sʌfiks] n κατάληξη, πρόσφυμα nt.

suffocate ['sʌfəkeit] vi πνίγομαι, ασφυκτιώ.

suffocation [sʌfə'keiʃən] n ασφυξία, πνίξιμο.

sugar ['ʃugə*] n ζάχαρη ♦ vt ζαχαρώνω, βάζω ζάχαρη |! ~ **beet** n ζαχαρότευτλο || ~ **cane** n ζαχαροκάλαμο || ~y a ζαχαρένιος, ζαχαρωμένος, γλυκύτατος.

suggest [sə'dʒɛst] vt εισηγούμαι, προτείνω || (show indirectly) υπαινίσσομαι, υπονοώ || (propose) προτείνω, υποβάλλω, υποδεικνύω || ~ion n πρόταση, υποβολή || ~ive a υπαινισσόμενος, υποβλητικός, με υπονοούμενα.

suicidal [sui'saidl] a της αυτοκτονίας.

suicide ['suisaid] n αυτοκτονία || (person) αυτόχειρας.

suit [su:t] n (of clothes) κοστούμι || (in cards) τα τέσσερα χρώματα ♦ vt ταιριάζω, πηγαίνω || (satisfy) ικανοποιώ, βολεύω || (adapt) προσαρμόζω || ~able a κατάλληλος, αρμόζων, ταιριαστός || ~ably ad καταλλήλως, όπως πρέπει.

suitcase ['su:tkeis] n βαλίτσα.

suite [swi:t] n (of rooms) διαμέρισμα nt, σουίτα || (MUS) σουίτα.

sulfur ['sʌlfə*] n (US) = sulphur.

sulk [sʌlk] vi κάνω μούτρα, κατσουφιάζω || ~y a κακόκεφος, κατσούφης.

sullen ['sʌlən] a (gloomy) κατηφής, μελαγχολικός || (bad-tempered) κακόκεφος, κατσούφης.

sulphur ['sʌlfə*] n θείο, θειάφι.

sultan ['sʌltən] n σουλτάνος || ~a n σουλτάνα || (raisin) σουλτανίνα.

sultry ['sʌltri] a αποπνικτικός, πνιγηρός.

sum [sʌm] n (total) σύνολο || (calculation) άθροισμα nt || (of money) ποσό (χρημάτων) || **to** ~ **up** vt συνοψίζω, ανακεφαλαιώνω ♦ vi κρίνω, εκτιμώ.

summarize ['sʌmərarz] vt συνοψίζω, συγκεφαλαιώνω.

summary ['sʌməri] n (συνοπτική) περίληψη, σύνοψη.

summer ['sʌmə*] n καλοκαίρι ♦ attr a (clothing) καλοκαιρινός || ~house n (in garden) περίπτερο κήπου || ~time n καλοκαίρι, θερινή ώρα.

summit ['sʌmit] n κορυφή || ~ **conference** n συνεδρίαση κορυφής.

summon ['sʌmən] vt (συγ)καλώ, προσκαλώ || (gather up) συγκεντρώνω, μαζεύω || ~s n κλήση ♦ vt κλητεύω, καλώ.

sump [sʌmp] n λεκάνη αποστραγγίσεως, κάρτερ nt inv.

sumptuous ['sʌmptjuəs] a πολυτελής, πολυδάπανος.

sun [sʌn] n ήλιος || (sunshine) λιακάδα || ~**bathe** vi κάνω ηλιοθεραπεία || ~**burn** n έγκαυμα nt από τον ήλιο || ~**burnt** a ηλιοκαμμένος, μαυρισμένος.

Sunday ['sʌndi] n Κυριακή.

sundial ['sʌndaiəl] n ηλιακό ρολόι.

sundry ['sʌndri] a διάφορος || **sundries** npl διάφορα είδη ntpl.

sunflower ['sʌnflauə*] n ήλιος, ηλίανθος.

sung [sʌŋ] pp of sing.

sunglasses ['sʌngla:siz] npl γυαλιά ntpl του ήλιου.

sunk [sʌŋk] pp of sink.

sunlight ['sʌnlait] n ηλιακό φως, λιακάδα.

sunlit ['sʌnlit] a ηλιόλουστος.

sunny ['sʌni] a εύήλιος, ηλιόλουστος || (cheerful) χαρωπός, γελαστός.

sunrise ['sʌnraiz] n ανατολή του ηλίου.

sunset ['sʌnset] n ηλιοβασίλεμα nt.

sunshade ['sʌnʃeid] n (over table) αλεξήλιο, ομπρέλα του ήλιου.

sunshine ['sʌnʃain] n λιακάδα.

sunspot ['sʌnspɒt] n ηλιακή κηλίδα.

sunstroke ['sʌnstrəuk] n ηλίαση.

suntan ['sʌntæn] n μαύρισμα nt από τον ήλιο.

super ['su:pə*] a (col) υπέροχος, περίφημος, σπουδαίος || prefix υπερ-.

superannuation [su:pərænju'eiʃən] n συνταξιοδότηση.

superb [su:'pɜ:b] a υπέροχος, έξοχος, εξαίσιος || ~ly ad υπέροχα, έξοχα, λαμπρά.

supercilious [su:pə'siliəs] a αγέρωχος, υπεροπτικός.

superficial [su:pə'fiʃl] a επιφανειακός || (shallow) επιπόλαιος, επιφανειακός.

superfluous [su'pɜ:fluəs] a περιττός.

superhuman [su:pə'hju:mən] a (effort) υπεράνθρωπος.

superimpose ['su:pərim'pəuz] vt βάζω από πάνω, υπερθέτω.

superintendent [su:pərin'tendənt] n (police) αξιωματικός της αστυνομίας.

superior [su'piəriə*] a ανώτερος, υπέρτερος, εξαιρετικός || (proud) υπεροπτικός, ακατάδεχτος ♦ n προϊστάμενος, ανώτερος || ~ity n υπεροχή, ανωτερότητα.

superlative [su'pə:lətiv] a ανώτατος, υπερθετικός ♦ n (το) υπερθετικό.

superman ['su:pəmæn] n υπεράνθρωπος.

supermarket ['su:pəmɑ:kit] n σουπερμάρκετ f inv, υπεραγορά.

supernatural [su:pə'nætʃərəl] a υπερφυσικός.

superpower ['su:pəpauə*] n (POL) υπερδύναμη.

supersede [su:pə'si:d] vt αντικαθιστώ, παραμερίζω.

supersonic ['su:pə'sɒnik] a υπερηχητικός.

superstition [su:pə'stiʃən] n δεισιδαιμονία, πρόληψη.

superstitious [su:pə'stiʃəs] a δεισιδαίμονας, προληπτικός.

supertanker ['su:pətæŋkə*] n υπερδεξαμενόπλοιο.

supervise ['su:pəvaiz] vt επιβλέπω, εποπτεύω, διευθύνω.

supervision [su:pə'viʒən] n εποπτεία, επιθεώρηση, διεύθυνση.

supervisor ['su:pəvaizə*] n επιθεωρητής/ήτρια m/f, επόπτης/όπτρια m/f, επιστάτης/άτρια m/f.

supper ['sʌpə*] n δείπνο.

supple ['sʌpl] a εύκαμπτος, ευλύγιστος, λυγερός.

supplement ['sʌplimənt] n συμπλήρωμα nt || (newspaper) παράρτημα nt ♦ [sʌpli'ment] vt συμπληρώνω || ~ary a συμπληρωματικός, πρόσθετος.

supplier [sə'plaiə*] n προμηθευτής.

supply [sə'plai] vt παρέχω, εφοδιάζω, προμηθεύω ♦ n εφόδιο, απόθεμα nt, προμήθεια || (supplying) εφοδιασμός, τροφοδότηση || **supplies** npl (food) τρόφιμα ntpl || (MIL) εφόδια ntpl || ~ **and demand** προσφορά και ζήτηση.

support [sə'pɔ:t] n (moral, financial etc) υποστήριξη, ενίσχυση || (TECH) στήριγμα nt, υποστήριγμα nt, έρεισμα nt ♦ vt (υπο)στηρίζω, ενισχύω || (speak for) υποστηρίζω, ενισχύω || (endure) υπομένω, υποφέρω || ~er n (POL etc) οπαδός, υπερασπιστής/ίστρια m/f || (SPORT) οπαδός, υποστηρικτής/ίκτρια m/f || ~ing a (programme, role) βοηθητικός, δευτερεύων.

suppose [sə'pəuz] vti υποθέτω, προϋποθέτω || (think, imagine) φαντάζομαι, νομίζω || ~ **he comes ...** αν έρθει ... || ~dly ad υποθετικά, δήθεν.

supposing [sə'pəuziŋ] cj εάν, ας υποθέσουμε ότι.

supposition [sʌpə'ziʃən] n υπόθεση, γνώμη.

suppress [sə'pres] vt καταπνίγω, καταστέλλω || (hold back) συγκρατώ, σκεπάζω || ~ion n κατάπνιξη, συγκράτηση, απόκρυψη.

supremacy [su'preməsi] n υπεροχή, ανώτατη εξουσία.

supreme [su'pri:m] a υπέρτατος, ανώτατος, ύψιστος.

surcharge ['sə:tʃɑːdʒ] n πρόσθετη επιβάρυνση.

sure [ʃuə*] a βέβαιος, ασφαλής, σίγουρος ♦ ad βεβαίως, ασφαλώς || ~! (of course) βέβαια!, ασφαλώς! || **to make ~ of** βεβαιώνω || ~-footed a με σίγουρο πόδι || ~ly ad ασφαλώς, βεβαίως || (firmly) αναμφίβολα || (gladly) βεβαίως, μετά χαράς.

surf [sə:f] n κύμα nt, αφρός.

surface ['sə:fis] n (top side) επιφάνεια || (outward appearance) εξωτερικό, εμφάνιση ♦ vt (roadway) επιστρώνω, στρώνω ♦ vi βγαίνω στην επιφάνεια || ~ **mail** n τακτικό ταχυδρομείο.

surfboard ['sə:fbɔ:d] n σανίδα κυματοδρομίας, σέρφμπορντ nt inv.

surfeit ['sə:fit] n υπεραφθονία, πληθώρα, κόρος.

surge [sə:dʒ] n μεγάλο κύμα nt || (fig) μεγάλη αύξηση ♦ vi ορμώ, ξεχύνομαι.

surgeon ['sə:dʒən] n χειρούργος.

surgery ['sə:dʒəri] n χειρουργική || (room) ιατρείο, χειρουργείο.

surgical ['sə:dʒikəl] a χειρουργικός.

surly ['sə:li] a αγροίκος, κατσούφης, αγενής.

surmise [sə:'maiz] vt εικάζω, υποθέτω, μαντεύω.

surmount [sə:'maunt] vt (difficulty) υπερνικώ, ξεπερνώ.

surname ['sə:neim] n επώνυμο.

surpass [sə:'pɑːs] vt υπερτερώ, υπερβαίνω, ξεπερνώ.

surplus ['sə:pləs] n περίσσευμα nt, πλεόνασμα nt ♦ a πλεονάζων, υπεράριθμος.

surprise [sə'praiz] n έκπληξη, κατάπληξη, ξάφνισμα nt ♦ vt αιφνιδιάζω || (astonish) εκπλήσσω, καταπλήσσω, ξαφνίζω.

surprising [sə'praiziŋ] a εκπληκτικός, καταπληκτικός.

surrender [sə'rendə*] n παράδοση, εγκατάλειψη ♦ vi παραδίδομαι, παραδίδω, παραχωρώ.

surreptitious [sʌrəp'tiʃəs] a λαθραίος, κρυφός.

surround [sə'raund] vt περιβάλλω, περικυκλώνω || ~ing a (countryside) περιβάλλων, εξοχικός || ~ings npl περιβάλλον, περίχωρα ntpl.

surveillance [sə:'veiləns] n (observation) επιτήρηση, εποπτεία.

survey ['sə:vei] n (inquiry) επισκόπηση || (of land) χωρογράφηση, τοπογράφηση ♦ [sə:'vei] vt επισκοπώ, εξετάζω || (measure

land) χωρογραφώ, τοπογραφώ || ~**ing** *n*
(*of land*) χωρογράφηση, τοπογραφία ||
~**or** *n* (*of land*) τοπογράφος.

survival [sə'vaivəl] *n* επιβίωση || (*from
past*) υπόλειμμα, επιβίωμα *nt*.

survive [sə'vaiv] *vi* επιζώ ♦ *vt* επιζώ || (*a
shipwreck etc*) σώζομαι, γλυτώνω.

survivor [sə'vaivə*] *n* επιζών,
διασωθείς.

susceptible [sə'sεptəbl] *a* (+ *to*)
επιδεκτικός, τρωτός.

suspect ['sʌspεkt] *n* ύποπτος ♦ *a*
ύποπτος ♦ [səs'pεkt] *vt* υποπτεύομαι,
υποψιάζομαι || (*think likely*) υποψιάζομαι,
φαντάζομαι.

suspend [səs'pεnd] *vt* αναστέλλω,
διακόπτω || (*hang up*) αναρτώ, κρεμώ ||
~**ers** *npl* καλτοδέτες *fpl* || (*US*) τιράντες
fpl.

suspense [səs'pεns] *n* εκκρεμότητα,
ανησυχία, αβεβαιότητα.

suspension [səs'pεnʃən] *n* αναστολή,
ανακοπή || (*being suspended*) απόλυση ||
(*AUT*) ανάρτηση || ~ **bridge** *n* κρεμαστή
γέφυρα.

suspicion [səs'piʃən] *n* υποψία, υπόνοια
|| (*small amount*) μικρή δόση.

suspicious [səs'piʃəs] *a* ύποπτος,
καχύποπτος || ~**ly** *ad* ύποπτα, δύσπιστα.

sustain [səs'tein] *vt* υποστηρίζω,
στηρίζω, βαστάζω || (*confirm*)
αποδέχομαι || (*injury*) υφίσταμαι,
παθαίνω, δέχομαι || ~**ed** *a* (*effort*)
επίμονος, συνεχής.

sustenance ['sʌstinəns] *n* συντήρηση,
τροφή.

swab [swɒb] *n* (*pad*) ξέστρο.

swagger ['swægə*] *vi* περπατώ
καμαρωτός, επιδεικνύομαι.

swallow ['swɒləu] *n* (*bird*) χελιδόνι || (*of
food etc*) μπουκιά ♦ *vt* καταπίνω, χάφτω ||
to ~ **up** *vt* καταπίνω, καταβροχθίζω.

swam [swæm] *pt of* **swim**.

swamp [swɒmp] *n* έλος *nt*, βάλτος ♦ *vt*
(*overwhelm*) συντρίβω, σαρώνω.

swan [swɒn] *n* κύκνος.

swap [swɒp] *n* (*exchange*) ανταλλαγή ♦
vt (+ *for*) ανταλλάσσω, αλλάζω.

swarm [swɔːm] *n* (*of bees*) σμήνος *nt*,
πλήθος *nt* || (*of insects*) σύννεφο || (*of
people*) μπουλούκι, τσούρμο ♦ *vt* (*crowd*)
συρρέω, συγκεντρώνομαι.

swarthy ['swɔːði] *a* μελαψός,
μελαχροινός.

swastika ['swɒstikə] *n* αγκυλωτός
σταυρός.

swat [swɒt] *vt* κτυπώ, βαρώ.

sway [swei] *vi* ταλαντεύομαι, κουνιέμαι,
τρικλίζω ♦ *vt* ταλαντεύω, κουνώ ||
(*influence*) διευθύνω, επηρεάζω,
παρασύρω.

swear [swεə*] (*irreg v*) *vi* ορκίζομαι ||
(*curse*) βλαστημώ, βρίζω || to ~ to
ορκίζομαι σε, βεβαιώ || ~**word** *n*
βλαστήμια, βρισιά.

sweat [swεt] *n* ιδρώτας || (*MED*) ίδρωμα

nt ♦ *vi* ιδρώνω || (*toil*) μοχθώ, σπάω στη
δουλειά.

sweater ['swεtə*] *n* πουλόβερ *nt inv*.

sweaty ['swεti] *a* ιδρωμένος.

Swede [swiːd] *n* Σουηδός/ή *m/f*.

swede [swiːd] *n* (*turnip*) ραπίτσα.

Sweden ['swiːdn] *n* Σουηδία.

Swedish ['swiːdiʃ] *a* σουηδικός ♦ *n*
(*LING*) Σουηδικά *ntpl*.

sweep [swiːp] (*irreg v*) *n* σκούπισμα *nt*,
σάρωμα *nt* || (*wide curve*) κυκλική κίνηση,
καμπή || (*range*) άνοιγμα *nt*, ευρύτητα ||
(*of chimney*) καπνοδοχοκαθαριστής ♦ *vt*
σκουπίζω, καθαρίζω, σαρώνω ♦ *vi* (*move
in curve*) εκτείνομαι, απλώνομαι ||
προχωρώ μεγαλόπρεπα || to ~ **away** *vt*
σκουπίζω, σαρώνω || to ~ **past** *vi* περνώ
γρήγορα || to ~ **up** *vi* φθάνω, ανεβαίνω
♦ *vt* σκουπίζω, μαζεύω || ~**ing** *a* (*gesture*)
πλατειά (χειρονομία) || (*statement*)
γενικός, ριζικός.

sweet [swiːt] *n* γλυκό || (*candy*)
ζαχαρωτό, καραμέλα ♦ *a* γλυκός || (*fresh*)
δροσερός, φρέσκος || (*gentle, pretty*)
χαριτωμένος, γλυκός, συμπαθητικός ||
~**breads** *npl* γλυκάδια *ntpl* || ~**en** *vt*
γλυκαίνω || ~**heart** *n* αγαπητικός,
αγαπημένος || ~**ly** *ad* γλυκά, μελωδικά,
ευχάριστα || ~**ness** *n* γλυκύτητα, γλύκα
|| ~ **pea** *n* λάθυρος, μοσχομπίζελο || ~
tooth *n* αδυναμία για γλυκά.

swell [swεl] (*irreg v*) *n* (*wave*) μεγάλο
κύμα *nt* ♦ *a* (*col: excellent*) εξαιρετικός,
πρώτης τάξης ♦ *vt* (*numbers*) εξογκώνω,
αυξάνω ♦ *vi* (*also:* ~ *up*) εξογκούμαι,
φουσκώνω || (*become louder*) δυναμώνω ||
(*MED*) πρήζομαι || ~**ing** *n* εξόγκωση,
πρήξιμο.

sweltering ['swεltəriŋ] *a* ιδρωμένος,
αποπνυκτικός.

swept [swεpt] *pt, pp of* **sweep**.

swerve [swɜːv] *n* παρέκκλιση,
παρατιμονιά ♦ *vti* παρεκκλίνω,
παραστρατίζω, στρίβω.

swift [swift] *n* (*bird*) κλαδευτήρα,
πετροχελίδονο ♦ *a* ταχύς, γρήγορος,
άμεσος.

swig [swig] *n* (*col: of drink*) μεγάλη
ρουφηξιά.

swill [swil] *n* (*for pigs*) τροφή χοίρων ♦ *vt*
(*also:* ~ *out,* ~ *down*) ξεπλένω.

swim [swim] (*irreg v*) *n* κολύμπι ♦ *vi*
(*person*) κολυμπώ || (*be flooded*)
πλημμυρίζω, είμαι πλημμυρισμένος ||
(*feel dizzy*) ιλιγγιώ, ζαλίζομαι ♦ *vt* (*cross by
swimming*) περνώ κολυμπώντας || ~**mer**
n κολυμβητής/ήτρια *m/f* || ~**ming** *n*
κολύμπι || to go ~**ming** πάω κολύμπι ||
~**ming baths** *npl* κολυμβητικές
δεξαμενές *fpl* || ~**ming cap** *n* σκουφί ||
~**ming costume** *n* μαγιό || ~**ming pool**
n πισίνα || ~**suit** *n* μαγιό.

swindle ['swindl] *n* απάτη ♦ *vt*
(εξ)απατώ || ~**r** *n* απατεώνας,
κατεργάρης.

swine [swain] *n* χοίρος, γουρούνι ||
(*person*) γουρούνι, παλιάνθρωπος.

swing [swɪŋ] (irreg v) n κούνια ||
(swinging) αιώρηση, ταλάντευση || (music)
ρυθμός ♦ vt ταλαντεύω, κουνώ || (move
round) περιστρέφω, στρέφω ♦ vi
αιωρούμαι, κουνιέμαι || (move round)
στρέφομαι, κάνω μεταβολή || in full ~
σε πλήρη δράση || ~ bridge n
περιστρεφόμενη γέφυρα || ~ door n
περιστρεφόμενη πόρτα.

swipe [swaɪp] n δυνατό κτύπημα nt ♦ vt
(hit) κτυπώ δυνατά || (col: steal) κλέβω,
βουτώ.

swish [swɪʃ] a (col: smart) κομψός,
μοντέρνος ♦ vt θροΐζω.

Swiss [swɪs] a ελβετικός ♦ n (person)
Ελβετός/ίδα m/f.

switch [swɪtʃ] n (for light, radio etc)
διακόπτης || (change) αλλαγή ♦ vti
διακόπτω || (turn) γυρίζω απότομα || to
~ off vt πραίνω που ανεβοκατεβαίνει
διακόπτω, σβήνω || to ~ on vt ανάβω,
ανοίγω || ~back n (at fair) σε λούνα
παρκ || ~board n πίνακας διανομής,
τηλεφωνικό κέντρο.

Switzerland ['swɪtsələnd] n Ελβετία.

swivel ['swɪvl] vti (also: ~ round)
(περι)στρέφομαι, στρέφω.

swollen ['swəulən] pp of swell ♦ a (ankle
etc) πρησμένος, διογκωμένος.

swoon [swu:n] vi λιποθυμώ.

swoop [swu:p] n (esp by police) ξαφνική
επίθεση, εφόρμηση ♦ vi (also: ~ down)
εφορμώ, πέφτω.

swop [swɒp] = swap.

sword [sɔːd] n ξίφος nt, σπαθί || ~fish n
ξιφίας.

swore [swɔː*] pt of swear.

sworn [swɔːn] pp of swear.

swum [swʌm] pp of swim.

swung [swʌŋ] pt, pp of swing.

sycamore ['sɪkəmɔː*] n συκομουριά.

syllable ['sɪləbl] n συλλαβή.

syllabus ['sɪləbəs] n διδακτέα ύλη.

symbol ['sɪmbəl] n σύμβολο, σημείο ||
~ic(al) [sɪm'bɒlɪk(əl)] a συμβολικός ||
~ism n συμβολισμός || ~ize vt
συμβολίζω, παριστάνω.

symmetrical [sɪ'mɛtrɪkəl] a
συμμετρικός.

symmetry ['sɪmɪtrɪ] n συμμετρία.

sympathetic [sɪmpə'θɛtɪk] a
συμπαθητικός || (agreeing) ευνοϊκός με.

sympathize ['sɪmpəθaɪz] vi (+ with)
συμπάσχω με, συμπονώ, συμπαθώ || ~r
n οπαδός.

sympathy ['sɪmpəθɪ] n συμπάθεια,
συμπόνια.

symphony ['sɪmfənɪ] n (composition)
συμφωνία || ~ orchestra n συμφωνική
ορχήστρα.

symposium [sɪm'pəʊzɪəm] n (meeting for
discussion) συγκέντρωση, συμπόσιο.

symptom ['sɪmptəm] n σύμπτωμα nt ||
~atic a συμπτωματικός.

synagogue ['sɪnəgɒg] n συναγωγή.

synchronize ['sɪŋkrənaɪz] vt
συγχρονίζω ♦ vi (+ with) γίνομαι
ταυτοχρόνως.

syndicate ['sɪndɪkɪt] n συνδικάτο.

syndrome ['sɪndrəʊm] n (MED)
σύνδρομο.

synonym ['sɪnənɪm] n συνώνυμο ||
~ous [sɪ'nɒnɪməs] a συνώνυμος.

synopsis [sɪ'nɒpsɪs] n σύνοψη,
περίληψη.

syntax ['sɪntæks] n σύνταξη, συντακτικό
|| ~ error n (COMPUT) συντακτικό λάθος
nt.

synthesis ['sɪnθəsɪs] n σύνθεση.

synthetic [sɪn'θɛtɪk] a (artificial)
συνθετικός.

syphilis ['sɪfɪlɪs] n σύφιλη.

syphon ['saɪfən] = siphon.

syringe [sɪ'rɪndʒ] n σύριγγα.

syrup ['sɪrəp] n σιρόπι || ~y a
σιροποιασμένος.

system ['sɪstəm] n σύστημα nt || (railway
etc) δίκτυο || (method) σύστημα nt,
μέθοδος f || ~atic a συστηματικός,
μεθοδικός.

T

tab [tæb] n θηλειά.

tabby ['tæbɪ] n (cat) γάτα.

table ['teɪbl] n τραπέζι || (list) πίνακας.

tablecloth ['teɪblklɒθ] n
τραπεζομάντηλο.

table d'hôte ['tɑːbl'dəʊt] a ταμπλ ν'
τοτ.

table lamp ['teɪbllæmp] n πορτατίφ nt
inv.

tablemat ['teɪblmæt] n ψάθα για ζεστά
πιάτα.

tablespoon ['teɪblspuːn] n κουτάλι του
σερβιρίσματος || ~ful n κουταλιά του
σερβιρίσματος.

tablet ['tæblɪt] n πλάκα || (notebook)
σημειωματάριο || (pellet) δισκίο, χάπι.

table tennis ['teɪbltɛnɪs] n πιγκ πογκ nt
inv.

table wine ['teɪblwaɪn] n επιτραπέζιο
κρασί.

taboo [tə'buː] n ταμπού nt inv ♦ a
απαγορευμένος, ταμπού.

tacit ['tæsɪt] a σιωπηρός,
υπονοούμενος.

taciturn ['tæsɪtɜːn] a σιωπηλός,
λιγόλογος.

tack [tæk] n πινέζα || (stitch) μεγάλη
βελονιά, τρύπωμα nt || (NAUT)
αναστροφή, διαδρομή || (course) πορεία.

tackle ['tækl] n (for lifting) πτροχαλία,
παλάγκο || fishing ~ σύνεργα ntpl
ψαρικής ♦ vt αντιμετωπίζω,
καταπιάνομαι με || (a player) κάνω τάκελ.

tacky ['tækɪ] a κολλώδης.

tact [tækt] n τάκτ nt inv, λεπτότητα ||
~ful a με τάκτ, διακριτικός.

tactical ['tæktɪkəl] a τακτικός.

tactics ['tæktɪks] npl τακτική.

tactless ['tæktlıs] a στερούμενος τάκτ, αδέξιος.

tadpole ['tædpəʊl] n γυρίνος.

taffeta ['tæfıtə] n ταφτάς.

tag [tæg] n (label) ετικέτα.

tail [teıl] n ουρά || to ~ off vi (in size, quality etc) ελαττώνομαι, αραιώνω || ~ **end** n τελευταίο τμήμα nt, ουρά, τέλος nt.

tailor ['teılə*] n ράφτης || ~ing n ραπτική || ~-made a καμωμένο ειδικά.

tailwind ['teılwınd] n ούριος άνεμος.

tainted ['teıntıd] a μολυσμένος, χαλασμένος.

take [teık] (irreg v) vt παίρνω, βγάζω || (seize) πιάνω, παίρνω, καταλαμβάνω || (require) απαιτώ, χρειάζομαι || (hire) παίρνω, νοικιάζω || (understand) δέχομαι, παραδέχομαι, συμπεραίνω || (choose) διαλέγω || (PHOT) φωτογραφίζω, φωτογραφίζομαι || to ~ part in συμμετέχω || to ~ place συμβαίνω || to ~ after vt μοιάζω || to ~ back vt (return) φέρνω πίσω, παίρνω πίσω || to ~ down vt κατεβάζω, ξεκρεμώ || (demolish) κατεδαφίζω || (write) σημειώνω καταγράφω || to ~ in vt (deceive) εξαπατώ, ξεγελώ || (understand) καταλαβαίνω, αντιλαμβάνομαι || (include) περιλαμβάνω || to ~ off vi (aeroplane) απογειούμαι, ξεκινώ ♦ vt (remove) αφαιρώ, βγάζω, παίρνω || (imitate) μιμούμαι, παρωδώ || to ~ on vt (undertake) αναλαμβάνω || (engage) μισθώνω, προσλαμβάνω || (accept as opponent) δέχομαι την πρόσκληση || to ~ out vt (licence etc) βγάζω, κάνω || (stain) βγάζω || to ~ over vt αναλαμβάνω || (succeed) διαδέχομαι || to ~ to vt (person) συμπαθώ || (sport, hobby) επιδίδομαι σε, μ' αρέσει να || to ~ up vt (raise) σηκώνω, μαζεύω || (occupy) καταλαμβάνω, πιάνω || (absorb) απορροφώ, τραβώ || (engage in) απασχολούμαι σε || ~off n (AVIAT) απογείωση || (imitation) μίμηση || ~over n (COMM) ανάληψη επιχειρήσεως, κτήση.

takings ['teıkıŋz] npl (COMM) εισπράξεις fpl.

talc [tælk] n (also: ~um powder) τάλκ nt inv.

tale [teıl] n αφήγηση, παραμύθι, ιστορία.

talent ['tælənt] n ταλέντο || ~ed a με ταλέντο.

talk [tɔːk] n συζήτηση, συνομιλία, κουβέντα || (rumour) φλυαρία, διάδοση || (speech) λόγος, ομιλία || to ~ shop συζητώ για την εργασία μου || to ~ over vt συζητώ || ~ative a φλύαρος.

tall [tɔːl] a ψηλός || ~boy n (furniture) ψηλό κομμό, ψηλός καθρέφτης || ~ story n μπούρδα, αρλούμπα.

tally ['tælı] n (account) λογαριασμός ♦ vi συμφωνώ, αντιστοιχώ.

tambourine [tæmbə'riːn] n ντέφι.

tame [teım] a ήμερος, δαμασμένος || (dull) άτονος || ~ness ημερότητα.

tamper ['tæmpə*] : to ~ with vt ανακατεύομαι με || (falsify) παραποιώ.

tan [tæn] n (colour) (also: sun ~) μελαχροινό χρώμα, μαύρισμα nt ♦ a (colour) φαιοκίτρινος, καφέ.

tandem ['tændəm] n διπλό ποδήλατο.

tang [tæŋ] n οξεία γεύση, δυνατή οσμή.

tangent ['tændʒənt] n εφαπτομένη.

tangerine [tændʒə'riːn] n μανταρίνι.

tangible ['tændʒəbl] a απτός, ψηλαφητός || (real) πραγματικός, αισθητός.

tangle ['tæŋgl] n μπέρδεμα nt, ανακάτωμα nt || (complication) περιπλοκή ♦ vti μπερδεύομαι || (complicate) περιπλέκω.

tango ['tæŋgəʊ] n ταγκό nt inv.

tank [tæŋk] n δεξαμενή, ντεπόζιτο || (MIL) τάνκ nt inv, άρμα μάχης.

tankard ['tæŋkəd] n κύπελλο, μαστραπάς.

tanker ['tæŋkə*] n (ship) δεξαμενόπλοιο, τάνκερ nt inv || (truck) βυτιοφόρο.

tankful ['tæŋkful] n γεμάτο δοχείο.

tantalizing ['tæntəlaızıŋ] a προκλητικός, βασανιστικός.

tantrum ['tæntrəm] n έκρηξη οργής, ξέσπασμα nt, παράφορα.

tap [tæp] n βρύση || (on barrel) κάνουλα || (gentle blow) ελαφρό κτύπημα nt ♦ vt (strike) κτυπώ ελαφρά || (supply) παίρνω, τροφοδοτώ, ανοίγω.

tap-dance ['tæpdɑːns] vi χορεύω με κλακέτες.

tape [teıp] n ταινία || **magnetic** ~ μαγνητοταινία ♦ vt (to record) μαγνητογραφώ, ηχογραφώ || ~ **measure** n μετρική ταινία, μέτρο.

taper ['teıpə*] n λαμπάδα, κερί ♦ vi λεπτύνομαι, λιγοστεύω.

tape recorder ['teıprıkɔːdə*] n μαγνητόφωνο.

tapestry ['tæpıstrı] n ταπέτο τοίχου, ταπετσαρία.

tar [tɑː*] n πίσσα.

tardy ['tɑːdı] a βραδύς, αργός.

target ['tɑːgıt] n στόχος.

tariff ['tærıf] n (list of charges) τιμολόγιο || (duty) δασμός, δασμολόγιο.

tarmac ['tɑːmæk] n (AVIAT) διάδρομος απογειώσεως.

tarnish ['tɑːnıʃ] vt (lit) θαμπώνω, σκοτεινιάζω || (fig) μαυρίζω, κηλιδώνω.

tarpaulin [tɑː'pɔːlın] n κηρόπανο, μουσαμάς.

tart [tɑːt] n (pie) τούρτα, τάρτα || (col: low woman) τσούλα ♦ a ξυνός, οξύς, δριμύς.

tartan ['tɑːtən] n σκωτσέζικο ύφασμα nt.

tartar ['tɑːtə*] n τρυγία, πουρί.

task [tɑːsk] n καθήκον, έργο, δουλειά, αποστολή.

tassel ['tæsəl] n θύσανος, φούντα.

taste [teıst] n γεύση, γούστο || (preference) προτίμηση ♦ vti γεύομαι, δοκιμάζω || ~ful a κομψός, με γούστο, καλαίσθητος || ~less a άγευστος, άνοστος || (bad taste) χωρίς γούστο, κακόγουστος.

tasty ['teɪstɪ] a γευστικός, νόστιμος.

tatters ['tætəz] npl: in ~ (also : tattered) κουρελιασμένος.

tattoo [tə'tuː] n (νυκτερινή) στρατιωτική επίδειξη || (on skin) δερματοστιξία, τατουάζ nt inv ♦ vt διαστίζω, τατουάρω.

tatty ['tætɪ] a (col: cheap, of poor quality) φτηνός, πρόστυχος.

taught [tɔːt] pt, pp of **teach**.

taunt [tɔːnt] n χλευασμός, λοιδορία, κοροϊδία ♦ vt χλευάζω, κοροϊδεύω.

taut [tɔːt] a τεντωμένος, τεταμένος.

tavern ['tævən] n ταβέρνα.

tawdry ['tɔːdrɪ] a φανταχτερός, φτηνός, τιποτένιος.

tawny ['tɔːnɪ] a φαιοκίτρινος.

tax [tæks] n φόρος ♦ vt φορολογώ || (burden) εξαντλώ, βάζω σε δοκιμασία || ~ation n φορολογία || ~ collector n εισπράκτορας φόρων || ~-free a αφορολόγητος.

taxi ['tæksɪ] n ταξί ♦ vi (AVIAT) τροχοδρομώ || ~ driver n οδηγός ταξί, ταξιτζής || ~ rank n, ~ stand n στάση ταξί, πιάτσα.

taxpayer ['tækspeɪə*] n φορολογούμενος.

T.B. abbr of **tuberculosis.**

tea [tiː] n τέιο, τσάι || (drink) τσάι || (meal) απογευματινό τσάι, γεύμα nt με τσάι || ~ bag n σακκουλάκι τσαγιού || ~ break n διάλειμμα nt για τσάι.

teach [tiːtʃ] (irreg v) vti διδάσκω, μαθαίνω || ~er n δάσκαλος/δασκάλα m/f || ~ing n διδασκαλία.

tea cosy ['tiːkəʊzɪ] n σκέπασμα nt τσαγιέρας.

teacup ['tiːkʌp] n φλυτζάνι τσαγιού.

teak [tiːk] n τικ, τεκ ♦ a από τικ.

tea leaves ['tiːliːvz] npl φύλλα ntpl τσαγιού.

team [tiːm] n ομάδα, συνεργείο || (of animals) ζευγάρι || ~work n ομαδικό παίξιμο, συνεργασία.

tea party ['tiːpɑːtɪ] n δεξίωση με τσάι.

teapot ['tiːpɒt] n τσαγιέρα.

tear [tɛə*] n (rip) σχίσιμο, σχισμή δάκρυ nt ♦ (irreg v) vt ανοίγω τρύπα || (pull apart) σχίζω, σπαράσσω ♦ vi (become torn) σχίζομαι || (rush) τρέχω, ορμώ ♦ [ˈtɪə*] n (cry) δάκρυ || in ~s δακρυσμένος, βουτηγμένος στα δάκρυα || ~ful a δακρυσμένος, κλαμένος || ~ gas n δακρυγόνο αέριο.

tearoom ['tiːrʊm] n αίθουσα τεΐου.

tease [tiːz] n πειραχτήριο, πείραγμα nt ♦ vt πειράζω, κοροϊδεύω.

tea set ['tiːset] n σερβίτσιο τσαγιού.

teaspoon ['tiːspuːn] n κουταλάκι του τσαγιού || ~ful n κουταλιά του τσαγιού.

tea strainer ['tiːstreɪnə*] n σουρωτήρι του τσαγιού.

teat [tiːt] n θηλή, ρώγα.

teatime ['tiːtaɪm] n ώρα του τσαγιού.

technical ['tɛknɪkəl] a τεχνικός || ~ity n τεχνική λεπτομέρεια.

technician [tɛk'nɪʃən] n (craftsman) τεχνίτης, τεχνικός || (specialist) ειδικός.

technique [tɛk'niːk] n τεχνική, ειδική μέθοδος f.

technological [tɛknə'lɒdʒɪkəl] a τεχνολογικός.

technology [tɛk'nɒlədʒɪ] n τεχνολογία.

teddy (bear) ['tɛdɪ(bɛə*)] n αρκουδάκι (παιχνίδι).

tedious ['tiːdɪəs] a ανιαρός, βαρετός.

tedium ['tiːdɪəm] n ανιαρότητα, μονοτονία, ανία.

tee [tiː] n υψωματάκι, σωρός (άμμου).

teem [tiːm] vi βρίθω, αφθονώ || (pour) πέφτω καταρρακτωδώς.

teenage ['tiːneɪdʒ] a εφηβικός, μεταξύ 13 και 20 || ~r n έφηβος.

teens [tiːnz] npl ηλικία μεταξύ 13 και 20 χρονών.

teeth [tiːθ] npl of **tooth**.

teethe [tiːð] vi βγάζω δόντια.

teething ring ['tiːðɪŋrɪŋ] n ροδέλα μωρού (για οδοντοφνΐα).

teetotal ['tiː'təʊtl] a αντιαλκοολικός || ~ler, ~er (US) n απέχων από οινοπνευματώδη ποτά.

telecommunication ['tɛlɪkəmjuːnɪ'keɪʃən] n τηλεπικοινωνία.

telegram ['tɛlɪgræm] n τηλεγράφημα nt.

telegraph ['tɛlɪgrɑːf] n τηλέγραφος || ~ic a (address) τηλεγραφικός || ~ pole n τηλεγραφικός στύλος.

telepathic [tɛlɪ'pæθɪk] a τηλεπαθητικός.

telepathy [tɪ'lɛpəθɪ] n τηλεπάθεια.

telephone ['tɛlɪfəʊn] n τηλέφωνο ♦ vt τηλεφωνώ || ~ booth, ~ box n τηλεφωνικός θάλαμος || ~ call n τηλεφώνημα nt, κλήση || ~ directory n τηλεφωνικός κατάλογος || ~ exchange n κέντρο || ~ number n αριθμός τηλεφώνου.

telephonist [tɪ'lɛfənɪst] n τηλεφωνήτρια.

telephoto ['tɛlɪ'fəʊtəʊ] a: ~ lens n τηλεφακός.

teleprinter ['tɛlɪprɪntə*] n τηλέτυπο.

telescope ['tɛlɪskəʊp] n τηλεσκόπιο ♦ vt (compress) συμπτύσσω.

telescopic [tɛlɪs'kɒpɪk] a τηλεσκοπικός.

televise ['tɛlɪvaɪz] vt μεταδίδω τηλεοπτικά.

television ['tɛlɪvɪʒən] n τηλεόραση || ~ set n δέκτης τηλεοράσεως.

telex ['tɛlɛks] n τέλεξ nt inv, τηλέτυπος ♦ vt στέλλω με τον τηλέτυπο.

tell [tɛl] (irreg v) vt λέγω, λέω || (make known) αφηγούμαι, γνωστοποιώ || (order) διατάσσω, παραγγέλλω, λέω σε || (person of sth) λέω κάτι, ανακοινώνω ♦ vi (have effect) αποφέρω, συνεπάγομαι, έχω || to ~ on (inform against) προδίδω, κατάδίδω, προδίδω || to ~ off vt μαλώνω, κατσαδιάζω || ~er n (in bank) ταμίας ||

~ing a αποτελεσματικός || ~tale a μαρτυριάρης, κουτσομπόλης.

telly ['tɛlɪ] n (col) abbr of **television**.

temerity [tɪ'mɛrɪtɪ] n θάρρος nt, τόλμη.

temper ['tɛmpə*] n (disposition) διάθεση, τεμπεραμέντο || (burst of anger) οργή, θυμός ♦ vt (moderate) απαλύνω, μαλακώνω, συγκρατώ.

temperament ['tɛmprəmənt] n διάθεση, ιδιοσυγκρασία, τεμπεραμέντο || ~al a (moody) ιδιότροπος || (fig) γεμάτος βίδες.

temperance ['tɛmpərəns] n (in drinking) αποφυγή οινοπνευματωδών ποτών || (moderation) εγκράτεια, μετριοπάθεια.

temperate ['tɛmpərɪt] a μετριοπαθής, εύκρατος.

temperature ['tɛmprətʃə*] n θερμοκρασία.

tempered ['tɛmpəd] a (steel) εσκληρυμένος, βαμμένος.

tempest ['tɛmpɪst] n θύελλα, τρικυμία, φουρτούνα.

temple ['tɛmpl] n (building) ναός || (ANAT) κρόταφος, μηλίγγι.

tempo ['tɛmpəʊ] n ρυθμός, τέμπο || (of movement) ρυθμός, μέτρο.

temporal ['tɛmpərəl] a (of time) χρονικός, του χρόνου || (worldly) εγκόσμιος, κοσμικός.

temporarily ['tɛmpərərɪlɪ] ad προσωρινά, για λίγο.

temporary ['tɛmpərərɪ] a προσωρινός, πρόσκαιρος.

tempt [tɛmpt] vt (persuade) παροτρύνω, προτρέπω || (attract) δελεάζω || ~ation n πειρασμός, δελεασμός || ~ing a δελεαστικός.

ten [tɛn] num δέκα.

tenable ['tɛnəbl] a υπερασπίσιμος, υποστηρίξιμος, λογικός.

tenacious [tə'neɪʃəs] a εμμένων, επίμονος.

tenacity [tə'næsɪtɪ] n εμμονή, επιμονή.

tenancy ['tɛnənsɪ] n ενοίκιαση, μίσθωση.

tenant ['tɛnənt] n ενοικιαστής/ ενοικιάστρια m/f, μισθωτής/ μισθώτρια m/f.

tend [tɛnd] vt (look after) περιποιούμαι ♦ vi (incline, lean) ρέπω, κλίνω.

tendency ['tɛndənsɪ] n τάση, κλίση, ροπή.

tender ['tɛndə*] a τρυφερός, μαλακός || (delicate) λεπτός, ευπαθής, τρυφερός || (loving) στοργικός, ευαίσθητος, πονετικός ♦ n (COMM: offer) προσφορά || ~ness n τρυφερότητα, λεπτότητα, στοργικότητα.

tendon ['tɛndən] n τένων m.

tenement ['tɛnɪmənt] n λαϊκή πολυκατοικία.

tenet ['tɛnɛt] n αρχή, αξίωμα nt, δόγμα nt.

tennis ['tɛnɪs] n τένις nt inv, αντισφαίριση || ~ ball n μπάλα του τένις

|| ~ court n γήπεδο του τένις || ~ racket n ρακέτα του τένις.

tenor ['tɛnə*] n (male voice) οξύφωνος, τενόρος || (singer) τενόρος.

tense [tɛns] a (fig) σε υπερένταση, τεταμένος || (taut) τεντωμένος ♦ n χρόνος || ~ness n ένταση, τεταμένη κατάσταση.

tension ['tɛnʃən] n ένταση || (stretching) τάση, τέντωμα nt.

tent [tɛnt] n σκηνή, τέντα.

tentacle ['tɛntəkl] n κεραία, πλόκαμος.

tentative ['tɛntətɪv] a δοκιμαστικός, προσωρινός.

tenterhooks ['tɛntəhʊks] npl: on ~ ανήσυχος, ανυπόμονος.

tenth [tɛnθ] a δέκατος, δέκατο.

tent peg ['tɛntpɛg] n πάσσαλος σκηνής.

tent pole ['tɛntpəʊl] n ορθοστάτης σκηνής.

tenuous ['tɛnjʊəs] a λεπτός, αραιός, ελαφρός.

tenure ['tɛnjʊə*] n κατοχή, κτήση.

tepid ['tɛpɪd] a χλιαρός.

term ['tɜːm] n όριο || (fixed time) περίοδος f, διάρκεια, χρόνος || (word) όρος, έκφραση, λέξη ♦ vt ονομάζω, καλώ || ~s npl όροι mpl, διατάξεις fpl || (relationship) σχέσεις fpl.

terminal ['tɜːmɪnl] a τελικός, άκρος ♦ n (ELEC) ακροδέκτης, πόλος || (for oil, ore etc) ακραίος σταθμός || (COMPUT) τερματικό.

terminate ['tɜːmɪneɪt] vi (+ in) τερματίζω, τελειώνω.

termination [tɜːmɪ'neɪʃən] n τερματισμός, περάτωση, κατάληξη.

terminology [tɜːmɪ'nɒlədʒɪ] n ορολογία.

terminus ['tɜːmɪnəs] n ακραίος, σταθμός, τέρμα nt.

termite ['tɜːmaɪt] n τερμίτης.

terrace ['tɛrəs] n σειρά σπιτιών || (in garden etc) επιπέδωμα nt, ταράτσα || ~d a (garden) σε βαθμίδες, κλιμακωτός || (house) ίδιου ρυθμού.

terrain [tɛ'reɪn] n έδαφος nt, πεδίο, έκταση.

terrible ['tɛrəbl] a (causing fear) τρομερός, τρομακτικός, φοβερός || (inferior) φοβερός, κατώτερος || (very great) απερίγραπτος, υπερβολικός.

terribly ['tɛrəblɪ] ad τρομερά, φρικτά, τρομακτικά.

terrier ['tɛrɪə*] n σκυλί τερριέ.

terrific [tə'rɪfɪk] a τρομερός, καταπληκτικός.

terrify ['tɛrɪfaɪ] vt τρομάζω, τρομοκρατώ.

territorial [tɛrɪ'tɔːrɪəl] a εδαφικός, τοπικός, κτηματικός.

territory ['tɛrɪtərɪ] n γη, περιοχή, έδαφος nt.

terror ['tɛrə*] n τρόμος, φρίκη, φόβος, τρομάρα || ~ism n τρομοκρατία || ~ist n τρομοκράτης || ~ize vt τρομοκρατώ.

terse [tɜ:s] a σύντομος, βραχύς || (concise) περιληπτικός.

test [test] n δοκιμή, δοκιμασία || (examination) εξέταση, ανάλυση ♦ vt δοκιμάζω || (examine) εξετάζω.

testament ['testəmənt] n διαθήκη.

testicle ['testikl] n όρχις m, αρχίδι.

testify ['testifai] vi καταθέτω (ενόρκως).

testimonial [testi'məuniəl] n πιστοποιητικό, βεβαίωση || (gift) δώρο ευγνωμοσύνης.

testimony ['testiməni] n μαρτυρία, κατάθεση || (proof) απόδειξη.

test match ['testmætʃ] n (cricket, rugby) μεγάλη διεθνής συνάντηση.

test pilot ['testpailət] n πιλότος δοκιμών.

test tube ['testtju:b] n δοκιμαστικός σωλήνας.

testy ['testi] a (short-tempered) ευέξαπτος, δύστροπος.

tetanus ['tetənəs] n τέτανος.

tether ['teðə*] vt δένω.

text [tekst] n κείμενο || ~book n εγχειρίδιο, διδακτικό βιβλίο.

textiles ['tekstailz] npl υφαντά ntpl, υφάσματα ntpl.

texture ['tekstʃə*] n (of surface) υφή.

than [ðæn] prep, cj ή, παρά, από.

thank [θæŋk] vt ευχαριστώ || ~ful a ευγνώμων || ~fully ad με ευγνωμοσύνη || ~less a αχάριστος || ~s excl ευχαριστώ || (gratitude) ευγνωμοσύνη, ευχαριστίες fpl || T~sgiving n (US: festival) Ημέρα των Ευχαριστιών.

that [ðæt] a αυτός, εκείνος ♦ pron εκείνος, ο οποίος, που ♦ cj ότι, ώστε, διότι, να ♦ ad πόσο, έτσι.

thatched [θætʃt] a (cottage) αχυροστρωμένος.

thaw [θɔ:] n τήξη, λυώσιμο ♦ vi τήκομαι, λυώνω.

the [ði:, ðə] definite article o, η, το || (pl) οι, τα.

theatre, theater (US) ['θiətə*] n θέατρο || (drama) θεατρική τέχνη, δραματική τέχνη || (MED) αμφιθέατρο || ~goer n θεατρόφιλος.

theatrical [θi'ætrikəl] a θεατρικός, θεαματικός || (showy) θεατρινίστικος, προσποιητός.

theft [θeft] n κλοπή, κλεψιά.

their [ðeə*] poss a δικός τους, δική τους || ~s poss pron δικός τους, δικοί τους.

them [ðem, ðəm] pron αυτούς, αυτές, αυτά.

theme [θi:m] n θέμα nt, υπόθεση || (melody) θέμα, μοτίβο || ~ song n (of film etc) κύρια μελωδία.

themselves [ðəm'selvz] pl pron τους εαυτούς τους || (they themselves) αυτοί οι ίδιοι.

then [ðen] ad τότε || (next) κατόπιν, έπειτα || cj λοιπόν, τότε, επί πλέον ♦ n τότε.

theological [θiə'lodʒikəl] a θεολογικός.

theology [θi'olədʒi] n θεολογία.

theorem ['θiərəm] n θεώρημα nt.

theoretical [θiə'retikəl] a θεωρητικός.

theorize ['θiəraiz] vi κάνω θεωρίες.

theory ['θiəri] n θεωρία || (idea) ιδέα.

therapeutic(al) [θerə'pju:tik(l)] a θεραπευτικός.

therapist ['θerəpist] n θεραπευτής/ύτρια m/f.

therapy ['θerəpi] n θεραπεία.

there [ðeə*] ad εκεί, να, έλα ♦ n εκείνος εκεί || (interj) να || (never mind) έλα, έλα || ~ is υπάρχει || ~ are υπάρχουν || ~abouts ad εκεί κοντά, περίπου || ~after ad έπειτα, κατόπιν || ~fore ad γι'αυτό το λόγο, επομένως || ~'s = there is, there has.

Thermos ['θɜ:məs] n (R) (flask) θέρμο(ς).

thermostat ['θɜ:məstæt] n θερμοστάτης.

thesaurus [θi'sɔ:rəs] n θησαυρός, συλλογή λέξεων.

these [ði:z] pl pron αυτοί, αυτές, αυτά.

thesis ['θi:sis] n θέμα, θέση || (UNIV) διατριβή.

they [ðei] pl pron αυτοί, αυτές, αυτά.

thick [θik] a χοντρός, παχύς, πυκνός, πηχτός || (person: slow, stupid) κουτός, χοντροκέφαλος ♦ n: in the ~ of στη φούρια, στο οξύτερο σημείο || ~en vi (fog) πυκνώνω, γίνομαι πυκνότερο ♦ vt (sauce etc) πήζω, πυκνώνω, δένω || ~ness n (of object) πάχος, πυκνότητα || (of voice) βραχνάδα || ~set a κοντόχοντρος || ~skinned a παχύδερμος, χοντρόπετσος.

thief [θi:f] n κλέφτης, λωποδύτης.

thieves [θi:vz] npl of thief.

thieving ['θi:viŋ] n κλοπή, κλεψιά.

thigh [θai] n μηρός, μπούτι.

thimble ['θimbl] n δακτυλήθρα.

thin [θin] a λεπτός, ψιλός, αδύνατος || (not abundant) αραιός, διεσπαρμένος || (person) ισχνός, λιγνός, αδύνατος || (crowd) αραιός, λιγοστός.

thing [θiŋ] n πράγμα nt, αντικείμενο.

think [θiŋk] (irreg v) vi σκέπτομαι || (believe) νομίζω || (have in mind) σκοπεύω || to ~ over vt σκέπτομαι, συλλογίζομαι || to ~ up vt σκέπτομαι, καταστρώνω.

thinly ['θinli] ad (disguised) μόλις.

thinness ['θinnis] n λεπτότητα, αδυναμία || (of liquids, crowds) αραιότητα.

third [θɜ:d] a τρίτος ♦ n τρίτος, τρίτο || ~ly ad κατά τρίτο λόγο, τρίτο || ~-party insurance n ασφάλιση τρίτων || ~-rate a τρίτης τάξεως, κακής ποιότητας.

thirst [θɜ:st] n δίψα || (strong desire) δυνατή επιθυμία, πόθος || ~y a διψασμένος.

thirteen [θɜ:'ti:n] num δεκατρία.

thirty ['θɜ:ti] num τριάντα.

this [ðis] pron, a αυτός, αυτή, αυτό || (this much) τόσος.

thistle ['θisl] n γαϊδουράγκαθο.

thorn [θɔ:n] n αγκάθι || (plant) ακανθώδης θάμνος, αγκάθι || ~y a αγκαθωτός || (problem) ακανθώδης.

thorough ['θʌrə] a πλήρης, τέλειος || (accurate) λεπτομερής, εξονυχιστικός || ~**bred** n καθαρόαιμος, από ράτσα ♦ a καθαρόαιμος || ~**fare** n οδός f, διάβαση, αρτηρία || (main street) κεντρική λεωφόρος || ~**ly** ad τέλεια, πλήρως, κατά βάθος.

those [δəuz] pl pron αυτές, αυτοί, αυτά ♦ a τούτοι, εκείνοι.

though [δəu] cj άνκαι, μολονότι ♦ ad παρ' όλα αυτά, ωστόσο.

thought [θɔːt] n ιδέα, σκέψη || (thinking) σκέψη, συλλογισμός || pt, pp of **think** || ~**ful** a σοβαρός, σκεπτικός || (also kind) διακριτικός, ευγενικός || ~**less** a απερίσκεπτος, απρόσεκτος, αδιάκριτος.

thousand ['θauzənd] num χίλιοι, χίλιες, χίλια || ~**th** a χιλιοστός.

thrash [θræʃ] vt (lit) κτυπώ, δέρνω, ξυλοφορτώνω || (fig) νικώ.

thread [θrɛd] n (of cotton, silk etc) νήμα nt, κλωστή || (of screw) σπείρωμα nt, βήμα nt || (of story) συνέχεια, ειρμός ♦ vt (needle) βάζω κλωστή σε, περνώ ♦ vi (pick one's way) περνώ με δυσκολία || ~**bare** a ξεφτισμένος, παλιός.

threat [θrɛt] n φοβέρα, φοβέρισμα nt || (sign of danger) απειλή || ~**en** vti (person) απειλώ, φοβερίζω || (storm) απειλώ.

three [θriː] num τρεις, τρία || ~-**dimensional** a τρισδιάστατος || ~**fold** a τριπλός, τρίδιπλος || ~-**piece suit** n (clothes) τρουαπιές nt inv || ~-**ply** a (wool) τρίκλωνος.

thresh [θrɛʃ] vt αλωνίζω.

threshold ['θrɛʃhəuld] n (beginning) κατώφλι, αρχή || (doorway) κατώφλι.

threw [θruː] pt of **throw.**

thrift [θrift] n (economy) οικονομία, αποταμίευση || ~**y** a οικονόμος, μετρημένος.

thrill [θril] n ρίγος nt, ανατριχίλα, σύγκρυο, τρεμούλα ♦ vt προκαλώ ρίγος σε, συγκινώ, ηλεκτρίζω ♦ vi φρικιώ, ριγώ, τρέμω. αγωνιώ || ~**er** n μυθιστόρημα nt αγωνίας.

thrive [θraiv] vi (+ on) (plants) ευδοκιμώ || (business) ευημερώ || (children) αναπτύσσομαι.

thriving ['θraiviŋ] a ακμαίος, ρωμαλέος, ακμάζων || (successful) επιτυχής.

throat [θrəut] n λαιμός || (internal passages) φάρυγγας, λάρυγγας, λαρύγγι.

throb [θrɔb] n κτύπημα nt, παλμός, δόνηση ♦ vi κτυπώ, πάλλομαι.

throes [θrəuz] npl οδύνες fpl, πόνοι ntpl || in the ~ of αγωνιζόμενος με.

thrombosis [θrɔm'bəusis] n θρόμβωση.

throne [θrəun] n θρόνος.

throttle ['θrɔtl] n ρυθμιστική βαλβίδα μηχανής, δικλείδα ♦ vt (choke) στραγγαλίζω.

through [θruː] prep διαμέσου, καθ' όλην τη διάρκεια του || (because of) λόγω του, εξαιτίας του ♦ ad εξ ολοκλήρου, κατευθείαν, από την αρχή μέχρι το τέλος ♦ a (without a stop) κατευθείαν ||

(end to end) πέρα για πέρα || (ticket) ολοκλήρου διαδρομής (εισιτήριο) || (finished) τελειωμένος || ~**out** prep σε ολόκληρο, σ' όλο, παντού ♦ ad παντού, ολόκληρα.

throw [θrəu] (irreg v) n ρίξη, ρίξιμο, πέταγμα nt, βολή ♦ vt ρίχνω, πετώ || to ~ **out** vt (lit) πετώ έξω || (reject) απορρίπτω, αποκρούω || to ~ **up** vi (vomit) ξερνώ, κάνω εμετό || ~-**in** n (SPORT) δίνω επιπλέον.

thru [θruː] (US) = **through.**

thrush [θrʌʃ] n κίχλη, τσίχλα.

thrust [θrʌst] (irreg v) n (TECH) ώθηση, σπρωξιά ♦ vti σπρώχνω, μπήγω || (push one's way) διαπερνώ, διασχίζω, περνώ.

thud [θʌd] n γδούπος.

thug [θʌg] n γκάγκστερ m inv, μπράβος.

thumb [θʌm] n αντίχειρας ♦ vt (book) φυλλομετρώ || to ~ **a lift** κάνω ωτοστόπ || ~-**tack** n (US) πινέζα.

thump [θʌmp] n βαρύ κτύπημα nt, γροθιά ♦ vti κτυπώ δυνατά, γρονθοκοπώ.

thunder ['θʌndə*] n βροντή ♦ vi βροντώ, βροντοφωνώ || ~**storm** n καταιγίδα, θύελλα || ~**struck** a εμβρόντητος, κατάπληκτος || ~**y** a (weather, sky) θυελλώδης.

Thursday ['θɜːzdi] n Πέμπτη.

thus [δʌs] ad έτσι || (therefore) έτσι, λοιπόν.

thwart [θwɔːt] vt ματαιώνω, ανατρέπω, εμποδίζω.

thyme [taim] n θυμάρι.

thyroid ['θairɔid] n θυρεοειδής (αδένας).

tiara [ti'ɑːrə] n διάδημα nt, τιάρα.

tic [tik] n (nervous) τικ, σπάσμα nt, σπασμός.

tick [tik] n τικ (ρολογιού), λεπτό || (small mark) σημείο ελέγχου, τσεκάρισμα ♦ vi κτυπώ, κάνω τικ ♦ vt σημειώνω, τσεκάρω.

ticket ['tikit] n (for travel etc) εισητήριο, δελτίο || (label) σημείωση, ετικέτα || ~ **collector** n ελεγκτής εισητηρίων || ~ **holder** n κάτοχος εισητηρίου || ~ **office** n γραφείο εκδόσεως εισητηρίων.

tickle ['tikl] n γαργάλισμα nt ♦ vt γαργαλίζω, γαργαλώ || (amuse) διασκεδάζω.

ticklish ['tikliʃ] a που γαργαλιέται εύκολα || (difficult) λεπτός, δύσκολος.

tidal ['taidl] a παλιρροιακός.

tide [taid] n παλίρροια, ρεύμα nt || (season) εποχή.

tidiness ['taidinis] n τάξη, συγύρισμα.

tidy ['taidi] a συγυρισμένος, τακτοποιημένος, σιαγμένος ♦ vt τακτοποιώ, σιάζω, συγυρίζω.

tie [tai] n (necktie) γραβάτα, λαιμοδέτης || (connection) δεσμός || (SPORT) ισοπαλία ♦ vt προσδένω, δένω || (into knot) δένω, κάνω κόμπο ♦ vi έρχομαι ισόπαλος, ισοψηφώ || to ~ **down** vt (lit) στερεώνω, δένω καλά || (fig) δεσμεύω || to ~ up vt (dog) προσδένω, δένω || (boat) δένω.

tier [tɪə*] n σειρά.

tiff [tɪf] n μικροτσακωμός, καυγαδάκι.

tiger ['taɪgə*] n τίγρη.

tight [taɪt] a σφικτός, στερεός || (stretched) τεντωμένος || (close) στεγανός, ερμητικός || (col) πιωμένος, σκνίπα || (miserly) τσιγγούνης || ~ npl καλτσόν nt inv || ~en vti σφίγγω, σφίγγομαι || ~-fisted a σφιχτοχέρης, σπαγγοραμμένος || ~ly ad σφιχτοκλεισμένα, σφιχτά, γερά || ~rope n τεντωμένο σχοινί.

tile [taɪl] n (in roof) κεραμίδι || (on wall or floor) πλακάκι || ~d a (roof) με κεραμίδια.

till [tɪl] n συρτάρι ταμείου ♦ vt καλλιεργώ ♦ prep ως, μέχρι ♦ cj έως ότου, ως που.

tilt [tɪlt] vti γέρνω, κλίνω.

timber ['tɪmbə*] n ξυλεία || (trees) δάσος nt, ψηλά δέντρα ntpl.

time [taɪm] n χρόνος || (period) καιρός || (hour) ώρα || (point in time) στιγμή, φορά || (occasion) καιρός, εποχή || (rhythm, speed) χρόνος, ρυθμός ♦ vt ρυθμίζω, χρονομετρώ || in ~ έγκαιρα || (MUS) μέτρο, χρόνος || on ~ στην ώρα || five ~s πέντε φορές || local ~ τοπική ώρα || what ~ is it? τι ώρα είναι; || ~keeper n (SPORT) χρονομετρητής || ~less a (beauty) αιώνιος, άφθαρτος || ~ limit n χρονικό όριο, προθεσμία || ~ly a έγκαιρος, επίκαιρος || ~ switch n χρονοδιακόπτης || ~table n (travel) δρομολόγιο || (schools) ωρολόγιο πρόγραμμα nt || ~ zone n άτρακτος χρόνου, ωριαία ζώνη.

timid ['tɪmɪd] a δειλός, φοβιτσιάρης.

timing ['taɪmɪŋ] n ρύθμιση, χρονισμός, χρονομέτρηση.

timpani ['tɪmpənɪ] npl τύμπανα ntpl.

tin [tɪn] n κασσίτερος, καλάι || (container) τενεκές m, κουτί κονσέρβας || ~foil n ασημόχαρτο, αλουμινόχαρτο, χρυσόχαρτο.

tinge [tɪndʒ] n χροιά, απόχρωση, δόση ♦ vt χρωματίζω, βάφω.

tingle ['tɪŋgl] n τσούξιμο, έξαψη ♦ vi τσούζω, τσιμπώ.

tinker ['tɪŋkə*] n γανωματάς || to ~ with vt σκαλίζω, φτιάχνω αδέξια.

tinkle ['tɪŋkl] vi κουδουνίζω, ηχώ.

tinned [tɪnd] a (food) κονσέρβα, του κουτιού.

tin opener ['tɪnəʊpnə*] n ανοιχτήρι.

tinsel ['tɪnsəl] n γυαλιστερές κορδέλες fpl μετάλλου, ασημένια βροχή.

tint [tɪnt] n χροιά, απόχρωση.

tiny ['taɪnɪ] a μικροσκοπικός, μικρούτσικος.

tip [tɪp] n άκρη, άκρο, μύτη || (for protection) σιδηρά άκρα ntpl, οίδερο, πετράκι || (of money) φιλοδώρημα nt, νουρμπουάρ nt inv || (useful hint) υπαινιγμός, μυστική πληροφορία ♦ vt (put end on) προσθέτω άκρη σε || (tip over) γέρνω αναποδογυρίζω || (waiter) φιλοδωρώ, δίνω νουρμπουάρ || ~-off n

(hint) πληροφορία, υπαινιγμός || ~ped a (cigarette) με φίλτρο.

tipsy ['tɪpsɪ] a μεθυσμένος, πιωμένος.

tiptoe ['tɪptəʊ] n: on ~ ακροποδητί, στα νύχια.

tiptop ['tɪp'tɒp] a: in ~ condition σε καλή φόρμα, πρώτης τάξεως.

tire ['taɪə*] n (US) = tyre ♦ vti κουράζω, εξαντλώ, κουράζομαι, βαριέμαι || ~d a κουρασμένος, εξαντλημένος || ~d of βαριέμαι || ~dness n κόπωση, κούραση || ~less a ακούραστος, ακαταπόντος.

tiring ['taɪərɪŋ] a κουραστικός || (boring) πληκτικός, ανιαρός.

tissue ['tɪʃuː] n (BIOL) ιστός, υφή || (paper handkerchief) χαρτομάντηλο || ~ paper n τσιγαρόχαρτο.

tit [tɪt] n (bird) αιγίθαλος, || (col: breast) βυζί, μαστός || ~ for tat οφθαλμόν αντί οφθαλμού.

titbit ['tɪtbɪt] n μεζές m.

title ['taɪtl] n τίτλος, επικεφαλίδα || (rank etc) τίτλος || (legal) τίτλος, δικαίωμα nt || (SPORT) (παγκόσμιος) τίτλος || ~ deed n τίτλος κυριότητας, τίτλος ιδιοκτησίας || ~ role n πρώτος ρόλος, ρόλος που δίνει το τίτλο του έργου.

titter ['tɪtə*] vi γελώ ανόητα, κρυφογελώ.

titular ['tɪtjʊlə*] a επίτιμος.

to [tuː, tə] prep (towards) προς, στο || (as far as) μέχρι || (comparison) προς το, έναντι || (for infin) για να || ~ and fro πάνω κάτω, πηγαινοέλα, ανεβοκατέβασμα.

toad [təʊd] n φρύνος, βάτραχος || (fig) μπούφος || ~stool n βωλίτης ο δηλητηριώδης (μανιτάρι).

toast [təʊst] n φρυγανιά || (drink) πρόποση ♦ vt (drink) κάνω πρόποση || (brown) ψήνω, φρυγανίζω || (warm) ζεσταίνω || ~er n φρυγανιέρα.

tobacco [tə'bækəʊ] n καπνός || ~nist n καπνοπώλης || ~nist's (shop) n καπνοπωλείο.

toboggan [tə'bɒgən] n έλκηθρο, τόμπογκαν nt inv.

today [tə'deɪ] n το σήμερα ♦ ad σήμερα || (present time) σήμερα, τώρα.

toddy ['tɒdɪ] n (warm, alcoholic drink) ζεστό γκρόγκ nt inv.

toe [təʊ] n δάκτυλο του ποδιού ♦ vt: to ~ the line (fig) υπακούω, υποτάσσομαι || ~nail n νύχι του ποδιού.

toffee ['tɒfɪ] n καραμέλα με βούτυρο || ~ apple n ζαχαρωμένο μήλο.

together [tə'gɛðə*] ad μαζί, μόνοι, ο ένας με τον άλλο || (at the same time) μαζί, συγχρόνως || ~ness n πνεύμα συνεργασίας.

toggle switch ['tɒglswɪtʃ] n (COMPUT) διακόπτης με σκαλιάκο.

toil [tɔɪl] n μόχθος, κόπος, σκληρή δουλειά ♦ vi μοχθώ, εργάζομαι σκληρά.

toilet ['tɔɪlɪt] n (lavatory) αποχωρητήριο, μέρος nt ♦ a τουαλέτα || ~ paper n χαρτί τουαλέτας, χάρτης υγείας || ~ries *npl* είδη *ntpl* τουαλέτας || ~ **roll** *n* ρολό χαρτιού τουαλέτας || ~ **water** *n* κολώνια.

token ['təʊkən] *n* ένδειξη, τεκμήριο, σημείο.

told [təʊld] *pt, pp of* **tell**.

tolerable ['tɔlərəbl] *a* ανεκτός, υποφερτός || *(moderate)* καλούτσικος.

tolerance ['tɔlərəns] *n* ανοχή, ανεκτικότητα || *(engineering)* ανοχή.

tolerant ['tɔlərənt] *a* ανεκτικός.

tolerate ['tɔləreɪt] *vt* ανέχομαι, υποφέρω.

toleration [tɔlə'reɪʃən] *n* ανοχή, ανεκτικότητα.

toll [təʊl] *n (tax, charge)* διόδια, φόρος ♦ *vi (bell)* κτυπώ (καμπάνα), καμπανίζω || ~**bridge** *n* γέφυρα με διόδια *ntpl*.

tomato [tə'mɑːtəʊ] *n* ντομάτα.

tomb [tuːm] *n* τύμβος, τάφος.

tomboy ['tɔmbɔɪ] *n* αγοροκόριτσο.

tombstone ['tuːmstəʊn] *n* επιτύμβιος λίθος.

tomcat ['tɔmkæt] *n* γάτος.

tomorrow [tə'mɔrəʊ] *n* αύριο, αυριανή μέρα ♦ *ad* αύριο.

ton [tʌn] *n* τόνος (2240 λίμπρες) || *(US)* τόνος (2000 λίμπρες) || ~**s of** *(col)* μεγάλη ποσότητα, πολλές φορές.

tone [təʊn] *n* τόνος, ήχος || *(character)* τόνος, πνεύμα *nt*, τάση || *(colour)* τόνος, απόχρωση ♦ *vi* συντονίζομαι, ταιριάζω ♦ *vt* τονίζω, τονώνω, ρυθμίζω || **to** ~ **down** *vi* απαλύνω, μαλακώνω, μετριάζω.

tongs [tɔŋz] *npl* λαβίδα, τσιμπίδα, μασιά.

tongue [tʌŋ] *n* γλώσσα || *(ox tongue: food)* βοδινή γλώσσα || **with** ~ **in cheek** ειρωνικά || ~-**tied** *a* άφωνος, βουβός (από κατάπληξη) || ~-**twister** *n* γλωσσοδέτης.

tonic ['tɔnɪk] *n* τονωτικό, δυναμωτικό || *(MUS)* τονική, βασική νότα || ~ **water** *n* τόνικ.

tonight [tə'naɪt] *n* σήμερα το βράδυ ♦ *ad* απόψε.

tonnage ['tʌnɪdʒ] *n* χωρητικότητα, τοννάζ *nt inv*.

tonsil ['tɔnsl] *n* αμυγδαλή || ~**litis** *a* αμυγδαλίτιδα.

too [tuː] *ad* πολύ, πάρα πολύ, υπερβολικά || *(also)* επίσης.

took [tʊk] *pt of* **take**.

tool [tuːl] *n* εργαλείο || ~**box** *n* κιβώτιο εργαλείων.

toot [tuːt] *n* κορνάρισμα *nt* ♦ *vi* κορνάρω.

tooth [tuːθ] *n* δόντι || *(on gearwheel)* δόντι || ~**ache** *n* πονόδοντος, οδοντόπονος || ~**brush** *n* οδοντόβουρτσα || ~**paste** *n* οδοντόπαστα || ~**pick** *n* οδοντογλυφίδα.

top [tɔp] *n* κορυφή, κορφή, απάνω (μέρος) || *(at school)* πρώτος, καλύτερος || *(spinning toy)* σβούρα ♦ *a* ανώτερος, ψηλότερος ♦ *vt (list)* είμαι επικεφαλής, είμαι πρώτος || **from** ~ **to toe** από την κορυφή ως τα νύχια || ~ **coat** *n* παλτό ||

~ **hat** *n* ψηλό καπέλο || ~-**heavy** *a* ασταθής, βαρύς στην κορυφή.

topic ['tɔpɪk] *n* θέμα *nt*, ζήτημα *nt* || ~**al** *a* επίκαιρος.

top-level ['tɔp'levl] *a* υψηλού επιπέδου.

topmost ['tɔpməʊst] *a* υψηλότερτος, κορυφαίος, ύψιστος.

topple ['tɔpl] *vti* κλονίζομαι, πέφτω || *(overturn)* αναποδογυρίζω.

topsy-turvy ['tɔpsɪ'tɜːvɪ] *a, ad* άνω κάτω.

torch [tɔːtʃ] *n (electric)* φακός, φανάρι || *(Olympic)* πυρσός, λαμπάδα, δαυλί.

tore ['tɔː*] *pt of* **tear**.

torment ['tɔːment] *n* βασανιστήριο, μαρτύριο ♦ [tɔː'ment] *vt* ενοχλώ, πειράζω || *(distress)* βασανίζω, τυραννώ.

torn [tɔːn] *pp of* **tear** || *a (undecided) (between)* ταλαντευόμενος, αναποφάσιστος.

tornado [tɔː'neɪdəʊ] *n* ανεμοστρόβιλος, λαίλαπα.

torpedo [tɔː'piːdəʊ] *n* τορπίλη.

torrent ['tɔrənt] *n* χείμαρρος || ~**ial** *a* χειμαρρώδης.

torso ['tɔːsəʊ] *n* κορμός, τόρσο.

tortoise ['tɔːtəs] *n* χελώνα.

tortuous ['tɔːtjʊəs] *a* ελικοειδής, στρεβλός || *(deceitful)* ανέντιμος, δόλιος.

torture ['tɔːtʃə*] *n* βασανιστήριο, βασανισμός, μαρτύριο ♦ *vt* βασανίζω.

Tory ['tɔːrɪ] *n* συντηρητικός ♦ *a* συντηρητικός.

toss [tɔs] *vt* πετώ, τραντάζω || *(in the air)* ρίχνω, πετώ ♦ *n (of coin to decide)* στρίψιμο || **to** ~ **a coin, to** ~ **up for** ρίχνω κορώνα-γράμματα.

tot [tɔt] *n* ποτηράκι, γουλιά || *(child)* παιδάκι, μωρό, μπέμπης.

total ['təʊtl] *n* σύνολο, όλο, άθροισμα *nt*, σούμα ♦ *a (συν)ολικός, ολόκληρος, πλήρης ♦ *vt* προσθέτω, αθροίζω || *(amount to)* ανέρχομαι σε, φθάνω.

totem pole ['təʊtəmpəʊl] *n* στήλη του τότεμ.

totter ['tɔtə*] *vi* παραπατώ, τρικλίζω.

touch [tʌtʃ] *n* αφή, επαφή, άγγιγμα *nt* || *(sense)* επαφή, αφή || *(small amount)* μικρή δόση, ίχνος *nt*, υποψία || *(style)* πινελιά, μολυβιά, ύφος *nt* ♦ *vt* αγγίζω || *(come against)* εφάπτομαι, ακουμπώ || *(move)* θίγω, συγκινώ || **in** ~ **with** σ' επαφή με, διατηρώ επαφή || **to** ~ **on** *(topic)* θίγω (θέμα) || **to** ~ **up** *vt (paint)* ρετουσάρω, επισκευάζω || ~-**and-go** *a* επικίνδυνος, αβέβαιος, επισφαλής || ~**down** *n* προσγείωση || ~**ing** *a* συγκινητικός || ~**line** *n* γραμμή του τέρματος || ~**y** *a* ευαίσθητος, εύθικτος.

tough [tʌf] *a* σκληρός, στερεός || *(difficult)* δυσχερής, σκληρός, δύσκολος || *(meat)* σκληρός ♦ *n (gangster etc)* κακοποιός, μπράβος || ~**en** *vti* σκληραίνω, σκληρύνομαι || ~**ness** *n* σκληρότητα || *(resilience)* αντοχή.

toupee ['tuːpeɪ] *n (wig)* περούκα.

tour ['tuə*] *n* περιοδεία, περιήγηση ♦ *vi* περιηγούμαι, περιοδεύω || ~**ing** *n* περιοδεία.

tourism ['tuərɪzəm] *n* τουρισμός.

tourist ['tuərɪst] *n* τουρίστας/τουρίστρια *m/f*, περιηγητής/περιηγήτρια *m/f* || ~ **office** *n* τουριστικό γραφείο.

tournament ['tuənəmənt] *n* πρωτάθλημα *nt*, τουρνουά *nt inv*.

tousled ['tauzld] *a* (*hair*) αναστατωμένος, ξεχτένιστος.

tow [təu] *n* (*pull*) ρυμούλκηση ♦ *vt* (*pull*) ρυμουλκώ.

toward(s) [tə'wɔːd(z)] *prep* προς, κατά, για.

towel ['tauəl] *n* πετσέτα.

tower ['tauə*] *n* πύργος || ~**ing** *a* πανύψηλος || (*rage*) βίαιος, άγριος.

town [taun] *n* πόλη, πολιτεία, χώρα || ~ **clerk** *n* γραμματέας δημαρχίας || ~ **hall** *n* δημαρχείο || ~ **planning** *n* πολεοδομία.

towrope ['təurəup] *n* σχοινί ρυμούλκησης.

toxic ['tɒksɪk] *a* τοξικός.

toy [tɔɪ] *n* παιχνίδι, παιχνιδάκι || **to** ~ **with** *vt* παίζω με, σκέπτομαι να.

trace [treɪs] *n* ίχνος *nt* || (*small amount*) ίχνος *nt*, υπόλειμμα *nt*, τεκμήριο ♦ *vt* παρακολουθώ || (*find out*) ανιχνεύω, διακρίνω || (*copy*) χαράσσω, αντιγράφω, ξεσηκώνω.

track [træk] *n* ίχνη *ntpl*, πέρασμα *nt*, πατημασιές *fpl* || (*path*) μονοπάτι || (*road*) δρομάκος || (*racing*) διάδρομος αγώνων, στίβος, πίστα || (*RAIL*) (σιδηροδρομική) γραμμή ♦ *vt* παρακολουθώ || (*persecute*) καταδιώκω || **to keep** ~ **of** παρακολουθώ, βρίσκομαι σε επαφή με || **to** ~ **down** *vt* ανακαλύπτω, βρίσκω || ~**er dog** *n* κυνηγόσκυλο.

tract [trækt] *n* περιοχή, έκταση || (*book*) φυλλάδιο.

tractor ['træktə*] *n* ελκυστήρας, τρακτέρ *nt inv*.

trade [treɪd] *n* εμπόριο || (*business*) επάγγελμα *nt*, δουλειά || (*people*) συντεχνία, κλάδος ♦ *vi* (+ *in*) εμπορεύομαι, συναλλάσσομαι, κάνω δουλειές || ~**mark** *n* σήμα *nt* (κατατεθέν) || ~ **name** *n* εμπορική επωνυμία, φίρμα || ~ *r n* έμπορος || ~**sman** *n* καταστηματάρχης, λιανέμπορος || (*skilled workman*) τεχνίτης || ~ **union** *n* εργατική ένωση, συνδικάτο.

trading ['treɪdɪŋ] *n* εμπόριο.

tradition [trə'dɪʃən] *n* παράδοση || ~**al** *a* παραδοσιακός, πατροπαράδοτος.

traffic ['træfɪk] *n* κίνηση, κυκλοφορία || (*esp in drugs*) εμπόριο, συναλλαγή ♦ *vt* (*esp drugs*) εμπορεύομαι (κάτι) || ~ **circle** *n* (*US: roundabout*) κυκλοφοριακός δρόμος || ~ **jam** *n* μποτιλιάρισμα || ~ **lights** *npl* φανάρια *ntpl*, φώτα *ntpl* κυκλοφορίας.

tragedy ['trædʒɪdɪ] *n* τραγωδία, δράμα *nt*.

tragic ['trædʒɪk] *a* τραγικός.

trail [treɪl] *n* ίχνος *nt* || (*footsteps*) πατήματα *ntpl* || (*something trailing*) γραμμή (καπνού), ουρά || (*rough road*) μονοπάτι ♦ *vi* (*follow*) σέρνομαι πίσω || (*hang loosely*) σέρνομαι, σέρνω || **to** ~ **behind** *vi* σέρνομαι πίσω || ~**er** *n* (*truck*) ρυμουλκούμενο όχημα *nt* || (*film*) απόσπασμα *nt* ταινίας || (*US: caravan*) τροχόσπιτο.

train [treɪn] *n* συρμός αμαξοστοιχίας, τραίνο || (*of gown*) ουρά || (*series*) σειρά, αλληλουχία, ειρμός ♦ *vt* εκπαιδεύω, διδάσκω, μαθαίνω || (*plant*) κατευθύνω, οδηγώ || (*point gun*) σκοπεύω ♦ *vi* (*exercise*) προπονώ, προγυμνάζω || ~**ed** *a* εκγυμνασμένος, εξασκημένος || ~**ee** *n* ασκούμενος μαθητής || ~**er** *n* εκπαιδευτής || (*sport*) προπονητής, γυμναστής/ γυμνάστρια *m/f* || ~**ing** *n* εκπαίδευση, εξάσκηση || (*sport*) προπόνηση || **in** ~**ing** σε φόρμα || ~**ing college** *n* παιδαγωγική ακαδημία.

traipse [treɪps] *vi* (*wander*) σέρνομαι εδώ και κει, τριγυρίζω κουρασμένα.

trait [treɪt] *n* χαρακτηριστικό.

traitor ['treɪtə*] *n* προδότης/τρια *m/f*.

tram(car) ['træm(kaː*)] *n* τράμ *nt inv*.

tramp [træmp] *n* (*vagabond*) αλήτης/αλήτισσα *m/f* ♦ *vi* περπατώ βαριά, βηματίζω βαριά || (*by foot*) πεζοπορώ, πηγαίνω πεζή.

trample ['træmpl] *vt* ποδοπατώ, καταπατώ.

trampoline ['træmpəliːn] *n* τραμπολίνο.

trance [traːns] *n* έκσταση, ύπνωση, όραμα *nt*.

tranquil ['træŋkwɪl] *a* ήρεμος, ήσυχος || ~**lity** *n* ηρεμία || ~**lizer** *n* (*drug*) καταπραϋντικό.

transact [træn'zækt] *vt* εκτελώ, διεξάγω, διεκπεραιώνω || ~**ion** *n* διεκπεραίωση, διεξαγωγή, συναλλαγή.

transatlantic ['trænzət'læntɪk] *a* υπερατλαντικός.

transcend [træn'sɛnd] *vt* υπερέχω, υπερβαίνω.

transcript ['trænskrɪpt] *n* αντίγραφο, αντιγραφή || ~**ion** *n* αντιγραφή, αντίγραφο.

transept ['trænsɛpt] *n* πτέρυγα ναού, εγκάρσιο κλίτος *nt*.

transfer ['trænsfə*] *n* μεταφορά, (*job*) μετάθεση || (*legal*) μεταβίβαση, εκχώρηση, μεταγραφή || (*design*) χαλκομανία, στάμπα, αντιγραφή || (*SPORT*) μεταβίβαση, μεταφορά ♦ [træns'fɜː*] *vt* μεταφέρω, μεταθέτω, αλλάζω || ~**able** *a* μεταβιβάσιμος, μεταφερτός || 'not ~**able**' (*on ticket*) 'προσωπικό'.

transform [træns'fɔːm] *vt* μετασχηματίζω, μεταβάλλω, μεταμορφώνω || ~**ation** *n* μετασχηματισμός, μεταβολή, μεταμόρφωση || ~ er n (ELEC) μετασχηματιστής.

transfusion [træns'fjuːʒən] n μετάγγιση.

transient ['trænzıənt] a παροδικός.

transistor [træn'zɪstə*] n κρυσταλλικός πολλαπλασιαστής || (radio) τρανσίστορ nt inv, φορητό ραδιόφωνο.

transit ['trænzıt] n: in ~ κατά τη μεταφορά, υπό μεταφορά.

transition [træn'zıʃn] n μετάβαση, μεταβολή, αλλαγή || ~al a μεταβατικός.

transitive ['trænzıtıv] a μεταβατικό (ρήμα).

transitory ['trænzıtərı] a παροδικός, βραχύς, εφήμερος.

translate [trænz'leıt] vt μεταφράζω.

translation [trænz'leıʃən] n μετάφραση.

translator [trænz'leıtə*] n μεταφραστής/άστρια m/f.

transmission [trænz'mıʃən] n (of information) μεταβίβαση, διαβίβαση || (AUT) μετάδοση || (RAD) εκπομπή, μετάδοση.

transmit [trænz'mıt] vt μεταδίδω, μεταβιβάζω, διαβιβάζω || ~ter n πομπός.

transparency [træns'pɛərənsı] n (PHOT: slide) διαφάνεια, σλάιντ nt inv.

transparent [træns'pɛərənt] a διαφανής, διαυγής || (clear) καθαρός.

transplant [træns'plaːnt] vt μεταφυτεύω, μεταφέρω ♦ ['trænsplaːnt] n (also MED) μεταφύτευση, μεταμόσχευση.

transport [træns'pɔːt] n μεταφορά ♦ [træns'pɔːt] vt μεταφέρω || ~able a μετακομιστός, φορητός || ~ation n μεταφορά.

transverse ['trænzvɜːs] a εγκάρσιος.

trap [træp] n (trick) παγίδα, απάτη || (snare) παγίδα, φάκα || (carriage) δίτροχη άμαξα || (col: mouth) στόμα nt ♦ vt παγιδεύω, πιάνω στην παγίδα || ~door n καταπακτή.

trapeze [trə'piːz] n τραπέζιο.

trappings ['træpıηz] npl διακόσμηση, στολίδια ntpl.

trash [træʃ] n σκουπίδια ntpl, χωρίς αξία || (nonsense) μπούρδες fpl, τρίχες fpl || ~ can n (US) σκουπιδοτενεκές m.

trauma ['trɔːmə] n τραύμα nt || ~tic a τραυματικός.

travel ['trævl] n ταξίδι, περίηγηση ♦ vi ταξιδεύω, κάνω ταξίδια ♦ vt (distance) πηγαίνω, βαδίζω, προχωρώ, μετακινούμαι || ~ler, ~er (US) n ταξιδιώτης/τισσα m/f || (salesman) πλασιέ m inv, αντιπρόσωπος || ~ler's cheque, ~er's check (US) n ταξιδιωτική επιταγή, τράβελερς τσεκ nt inv || ~ling, ~ing (US) n τα ταξίδια ♦ attr a ταξιδιωτικός, του ταξιδιού || ~ sickness n ναυτία.

traverse ['trævəs] vt διασχίζω, διαβαίνω, περνώ.

travesty ['trævıstı] n διακωμώδηση, παρωδία.

trawler ['trɔːlə*] n αλιευτικό, τράτα.

tray [treı] n δίσκος.

treacherous ['tretʃərəs] a (person) δόλιος, ύπουλος || (road: dangerous, icy etc) επικίνδυνος, άστατος.

treachery ['tretʃərı] n δολιότητα, προδοσία, απιστία.

treacle ['triːkl] n μελάσσα, πετιμέζι.

tread [tred] (irreg v) n περπάτημα nt || (way of walking) βήμα nt, βηματισμός || (stair, tyre) βαθμίδα, πάτημα nt, πέλμα nt ελαστικού ♦ vi βαδίζω, περπατώ || to ~ on vt (πόδι)πατώ.

treason ['triːzn] n προδοσία.

treasure ['trɛʒə*] n θησαυρός ♦ vt αποθησαυρίζω || (value highly) εκτιμώ, θεωρώ πολύτιμο || ~ hunt n θησαυροθηρία || ~r n ταμίας.

treasury ['trɛʒərı] n θησαυροφυλάκειο, ταμείο.

treat [triːt] n ευχαρίστηση, απόλαυση ♦ vt μεταχειρίζομαι, φέρομαι || (entertain) κερνώ, προσφέρω.

treatise ['triːtız] n πραγματεία, διατριβή.

treatment ['triːtmənt] n μεταχείρηση, περιποίηση || (MED) κούρα, θεραπεία.

treaty ['triːtı] n συνθήκη.

treble ['trebl] a τριπλός, τριπλάσιος ♦ vt τριπλασιάζω ♦ n πρίμο || (voice) υψίφωνος, σοπράνο f inv.

tree [triː] n δέντρο || ~ trunk n κορμός δέντρου.

trek [trek] n ταξίδι, μετανάστευση ♦ vi (migrate) μετοικώ, μεταναστεύω.

trellis ['trelıs] n δικτυωτό πλέγμα nt, καφασωτό πλαίσιο.

tremble ['trembl] vi τρέμω, δονούμαι.

trembling ['tremblıη] n τρόμος, τρεμούλα ♦ a τρεμάμενος, τρεμουλιάρης.

tremendous [trə'mendəs] a (vast) πελώριος, τρομερός.

tremor ['tremə*] n τρεμούλιασμα nt.

trench [trentʃ] n τάφρος f, αυλάκι, χαντάκι || (of war) χαράκωμα nt.

trend [trend] n τάση, πορεία ♦ vi τείνω.

trepidation [trepı'deıʃən] n φόβος, ανυσηχία, τρεμούλα.

trespass ['trespəs] vi καταπατώ.

tress [tres] n βόστρυχος, πλεξούδα, κοτσίδα, μπούκλα.

trestle ['tresl] n υπόβαθρο, υποστήριγμα nt, καβαλέτο || ~ table n τραπέζι σε καβαλέτο.

trial ['traıəl] n (in court) δίκη, κρίση || (test) δοκιμή || (hardship) δοκιμασία, βάσανο || by ~ and error με τη μέθοδο της δοκιμής και πλάνης, εμπειρικά.

triangle ['traıæηgl] n τρίγωνο.

triangular [traı'æηgjulə*] a τριγωνικός.

tribal ['traıbəl] a φυλετικός.

tribe [traıb] n φυλή || ~sman n μέλος m φυλής.

tribulation [trɪbjʊ'leɪʃən] n δοκιμασία, συμφορά, πάθημα nt.

tribunal [traɪ'bjuːnl] n δικαστήριο.

tributary ['trɪbjutərɪ] n παραπόταμος.

tribute ['trɪbjuːt] n (respect) φόρος τιμής.

trice [traɪs] n: in a ~ στη στιγμή.

trick [trɪk] n τέχνασμα nt, κόλπο, κατεργαριά || (clever act) δεξιοτεχνία, ταχυδακτυλουργία || (habit) συνήθεια || (CARDS) κόλπο, πιάσιμο, λεβέ nt inv ♦ vt εξαπατώ || ~ery n απάτη, κοροϊδία.

trickle ['trɪkl] n λεπτή ροή, στάξιμο, στάλα (νερού) ♦ vi σταλάζω, στάζω.

tricky ['trɪkɪ] a (problem, situation) περίπλοκος, δύσκολος.

tricycle ['traɪsɪkl] n τρίκυκλο.

trifle ['traɪfl] n είδος nt τούρτας || (of little importance) μικροπράγματα ntpl, ασήμαντο γεγονός, μηδαμινό ποσό.

trifling ['traɪflɪŋ] a ασήμαντος, τιποτένιος.

trigger ['trɪgə*] n σκανδάλη.

trigonometry [trɪgə'nɒmɪtrɪ] n τριγωνομετρία.

trim [trɪm] a κομψός, ευπρεπής ♦ n τάξη, φόρμα, ευπρεπής κατάσταση || (haircut etc) κόψιμο, φρεσκάρισμα nt (μαλλιών) ♦ vt κόβω, κουρεύω, κλαδεύω || (decorate) γαρνίρω || ~mings npl γαρνιτούρες fpl.

Trinity ['trɪnɪtɪ] n: the ~ (REL) Αγία Τριάδα.

trinket ['trɪŋkɪt] n μικρό κόσμημα nt, μπιμπελό nt inv.

trio ['trɪəʊ] n τριάδα || (MUS) τρίο.

trip [trɪp] n εκδρομή, ταξίδι || (stumble) παραπάτημα nt, τρικλοποδιά ♦ vi περπατώ ελαφρά, αλαφροπατώ || (stumble) σκοντάφτω, παραπατώ || to ~ up vi ανεβαίνω ελαφροπατώντας ♦ vt βάζω τρικλοποδιά σε.

tripe [traɪp] n (food) νατσάς || (rubbish) ανοησίες fpl, μπούρδες fpl.

triple ['trɪpl] a τριπλός, τρίδιπλος.

triplets ['trɪplɪts] npl τρίδυμα ntpl.

triplicate ['trɪplɪkɪt] n: in ~ σε τριπλούν.

tripod ['traɪpɒd] n τρίποδο.

trite [traɪt] a τριμμένος, κοινός, συνηθισμένος.

triumph ['traɪəmf] n θρίαμβος ♦ vi θριαμβεύω || ~ant a θριαμβευτικός.

trivial ['trɪvɪəl] a ασήμαντος, τιποτένιος || ~ity n ασημαντότητα, κοινοτοπία.

trod [trɒd] pt of tread || ~den pp of tread.

trolley ['trɒlɪ] n (small truck) καροτσάκι || ~ bus n τρόλλεϋ nt inv.

trombone [trɒm'bəʊn] n τρομπόνι.

troop [truːp] n ομάδα, όμιλος || ~s npl στρατεύματα ntpl || to ~ in/out vi μπαίνω/βγαίνω ομαδικά || ~er n ιππέας, έφιππος αστυνομικός.

trophy ['trəʊfɪ] n τρόπαιο, έπαθλο.

tropic ['trɒpɪk] n τροπικός || ~al a τροπικός.

trot [trɒt] n τριποδισμός, ελαφρό τρέξιμο ♦ vi τρέχω σιγά.

trouble ['trʌbl] n στενοχώρια, ανησυχία, σκοτούρα || (effort, care) κόπος ♦ vt ενοχλώ, ανησυχώ || ~d a ανήσυχος, ταραγμένος || ~-free a χωρίς σκοτούρες || ~maker n ταραχοποιός, ταραξίας || ~some a ενοχλητικός, δύσκολος.

trough [trɒf] n σκάφη, ποτίστρα || (channel) τάφρος f || (meteorology) σφήνα υφέσεως.

troupe [truːp] n θίασος.

trousers ['trauzəz] npl πανταλόνι.

trousseau ['truːsəʊ] n προίκα (ασπρόρουχα και φορέματα).

trout [traut] n πέστροφα.

trowel ['trauəl] n μυστρί.

truant ['truːənt] n: to play ~ το σκάω, απουσιάζω αδικαιολόγητα.

truce [truːs] n ανακωχή.

truck [trʌk] n φορτηγό αμάξι, καμιόνι || (RAIL) φορείο || (barrow) χειράμαξα αχθοφόρου || ~ driver n οδηγός φορτηγού || ~ farm n (US) αγρόκτημα nt λαχανικών, περιβόλι.

truculent ['trʌkjulənt] a βίαιος, άγριος, επιθετικός.

trudge [trʌdʒ] vi βαδίζω με δυσκολία, σέρνομαι.

true [truː] a αληθινός || (precise) ακριβής || (genuine) πραγματικός, αυθεντικός, γνήσιος || (friend) πιστός, τίμιος, αληθινός.

truffle ['trʌfl] n τρούφα.

truly ['truːlɪ] ad ειλικρινά, πιστά, αληθινά || (exactly) με ακρίβεια, ακριβώς, ορθά || yours ~ όλως υμέτερος.

trump [trʌmp] n (CARDS) ατού nt inv || ~ed-up a ψεύτικος, σκαρωμένος.

trumpet ['trʌmpɪt] n σάλπιγα, τρουμπέτα.

truncheon ['trʌntʃən] n ρόπαλο, αστυνομικό γκλόμπ nt inv.

trundle ['trʌndl] vti: to ~ along κυλώ, τρέχω, τσουλώ.

trunk [trʌŋk] n κορμός, κούτσουρο || (body) κορμός, τόρσο nt inv || (box) κιβώτιο, μπαούλο || (of elephant) προβοσκίδα || ~s npl μαγιό || ~ call n υπεραστική κλήση.

truss [trʌs] n (MED) κοιλεπίδεσμος, ζώνη.

trust [trʌst] n πίστη, εμπιστοσύνη || (property) καταπίστευμα nt ♦ vt εμπιστεύομαι σε || ~ed a έμπιστος, της εμπιστοσύνης || ~ee n επίτροπος, κηδεμόνας, έφορος || ~ful a γεμάτος εμπιστοσύνη, ευκολόπιστος || ~ing a πλήρης εμπιστοσύνης || ~worthy a αξιόπιστος || ~y a πιστός, αξιόπιστος.

truth [truːθ] n αλήθεια || ~ful a φιλαλήθης, αληθινός || ~fully ad αληθινά, ειλικρινά, πιστά || ~fulness n φιλαλήθεια, ειλικρίνεια.

try [traɪ] (irreg v) n προσπάθεια || (test) δοκιμή, απόπειρα ♦ vt δοκιμάζω, κάνω

δοκιμή || *(in court)* δικάζω || *(strain)*
κουράζω ♦ *vi (attempt)* προσπαθώ, ζητώ
να || to ~ on *vt* δοκιμάζω, προβάρω || to
~ out *vt* δοκιμάζω || ~ing *a* δύσκολος,
κουραστικός, σκληρός.

tsar [zɑː*] *n* τσάρος.

T-shirt ['tiːʃɜːt] *n* φανέλα (αθλητική).

tub [tʌb] *n* μεγάλη λεκάνη, σκάφη,
κάδος.

tuba ['tjuːbə] *n* μεγάλη κορνέτα,
κοντραμπάσο.

tubby ['tʌbɪ] *a (fat)* στρογγυλός σαν
βαρέλι, κοντοπίθαρος.

tube [tjuːb] *n* σωλήνας, αγωγός, αυλός ||
(also for toothpaste etc) σωληνάριο || *(in
London)* υπόγειος σιδηρόδρομος || *(AUT:
for tyre)* σαμπρέλα || ~less *a (AUT)* χωρίς
σαμπρέλα.

tuber ['tjuːbə*] *n* βολβός, γογγύλι.

tuberculosis [tjuːbɜːkjuˈləʊsɪs] *n*
φυματίωση.

tube station ['tjuːbsteɪʃən] *n* σταθμός
του υπόγειου τραίνου.

tubing ['tjuːbɪŋ] *n* σωλήν(ωση).

tubular ['tjuːbjʊlə*] *a (steel, furniture)*
σωληνοειδής, σωληνωτός.

TUC *n (abbr of Trades Union Congress)*
Συμβούλιο Αγγλικών Εργατικών
Συνδικάτων.

tuck [tʌk] *n (pleat)* πιέτα, πτυχή ♦ *vt
(gather)* διπλώνω, μαζεύω || to ~ away
vt χώνω || to ~ in *vt* μαζεύω, χώνω ♦ *vi
(food)* πέφτω με τα μούτρα στο φαΐ || to
~ up *vt (child)* σκεπάζω, τακτοποιώ.

Tuesday ['tjuːzdɪ] *n* Τρίτη.

tuft [tʌft] *n* θύσανος, φούντα.

tug [tʌg] *n* απότομο τράβηγμα *nt* ||
(steamship) ρυμουλκό (πλοίο) ♦ *vti* σύρω,
τραβώ δυνατά || ~-of-war *n*
διελκυστίνδα.

tuition [tjuːˈɪʃən] *n* διδασκαλία || *(fees)*
δίδακτρα *ntpl*.

tulip ['tjuːlɪp] *n* τουλίπα.

tumble ['tʌmbl] *n* πέσιμο, τούμπα,
κουτρουβάλα ♦ *vi* πέφτω, τουμπάρω ||
(somersault) κάνω τούμπες,
αναποδογυρίζω ♦ *vt (toss about)*
κατρακυλώ, σωριάζομαι || to ~ to *vt*
συλλαμβάνω, αντιλαμβάνομαι || ~down
a ετοιμόρροπος, σαραβαλιασμένος ||
~r *n (acrobat)* ακροβάτης/τρια *m/f* ||
(glass) ποτήρι.

tummy ['tʌmɪ] *n (col: stomach, belly)*
στομάκι, κοιλιά.

tumour ['tjuːmə*] *n* όγκος.

tumult ['tjuːmʌlt] *n* θόρυβος, σαματάς,
φασαρία || ~uous *a* θορυβώδης,
ταραχώδης, θυελλώδης.

tuna ['tjuːnə] *n* τόνος.

tune [tjuːn] *n* μελωδία, σκοπός || *(pitch)*
τόνος, συντονισμός ♦ *vt* κουρδίζω,
συντονίζω || *(motorcar)* ρυθμίζω,
εναρμονίζω, || in ~ μελωδικός,
συντονισμένος || out of ~ παραφωνία,
έξω από το τόνο || to ~ up *vi (MUS)*
συντονίζομαι, βρίσκω τον τόνο || ~ful *a*
μελωδικός, αρμονικός.

tunic ['tjuːnɪk] *n* χιτώνιο, αμπέχονο.

tuning ['tjuːnɪŋ] *n (RAD)* συντονισμός ||
(AUT) ρύθμιση.

Tunisia [tjuˈnɪzɪə] Τυνησία || ~n *a*
τψησιακός ♦ *n* Τυνήσιος.

tunnel ['tʌnl] *n* σήραγγα, τουνέλι ♦ *vi*
ανοίγω σήραγγα.

tunny ['tʌnɪ] *n* τόνος.

turban ['tɜːbən] *n* σαρίκι, τουρμπάνι.

turbine ['tɜːbaɪn] *n* στρόβιλος,
τουρμπίνα.

turbulence ['tɜːbjʊləns] *n (AVIAT)*
στροβιλισμός, αναταραχή.

turbulent ['tɜːbjʊlənt] *a* ταραγμένος,
βίαιος, άτακτος.

turf [tɜːf] *n* χλόη, γρασίδι || *(sod)*
χορταριασμένος βώλος.

turgid ['tɜːdʒɪd] *a (pompous)* στομφώδης,
πομπώδης.

Turk [tɜːk] *n* Τούρκος.

turkey ['tɜːkɪ] *n* γαλοπούλα, ινδιάνος ||
T~ *n* Τουρκία.

Turkish ['tɜːkɪʃ] *a* τουρκικός || *(LING)*
Τουρκική || ~ bath *n* χαμάμ *nt inv.*

turmoil ['tɜːmɔɪl] *n* αναταραχή,
αναστάτωση, πατιρντί.

turn [tɜːn] *n* περιστροφή, γύρισμα *nt* ||
(turning) στροφή || *(performance)* σειρά ||
(shape, manner) νοοτροπία, διάθεση ||
(chance) σειρά || *(MED)* κρίση ♦ *vt
(peri)στρέφω, γυρίζω, στρίβω || *(change
position)* αλλάζω, γυρίζω || *(of colour)*
αλλάζω χρώμα *nt* ♦ *vi* περιστρέφομαι,
γυρίζω || *(change direction)* στρέφομαι,
στρίβω || *(become sour)* ξυνίζω || to ~
back *vti* γυρίζω πίσω || to ~ down *vt
(refuse)* απορρίπτω || *(fold down)* διπλώνω,
τσακίζω || to ~ in *vi (go to bed)* πάω για
ύπνο ♦ *vt (fold)* γυρίζω (μέσα), στριφώνω
|| to ~ off *vi (from road)* αλλάζω δρόμο,
στρίβω ♦ *vt (light)* κλείνω, σβήνω || *(RAD)*
κλείνω, σβήνω || to ~ on *vt (light)*
ανοίγω, ανάβω || *(RAD)* ανοίγω || to ~
out *vt* εξελίσσομαι, πάω || *(extinguish)*
κλείνω, σβήνω || to ~ up *vi (person)*
εμφανίζομαι, φθάνω ξαφνικά || *(lost
object)* ξαναβρίσκω ♦ *vt (collar)*
ανασηκώνω || *(RAD: increase volume)*
ανεβάζω, δυναμώνω || ~ing *n (in road)*
καμπή, στροφή || ~ing point *n* κρίσιμο
σημείο, αποφασιστικό σημείο.

turnip ['tɜːnɪp] *n* γογγύλι.

turnout ['tɜːnaʊt] *n* συνάθροιση,
ακροατήριο.

turnover ['tɜːnəʊvə*] *n* τζίρος.

turnpike ['tɜːnpaɪk] *n (US: toll highway)*
οδός *f* με διόδια.

turnstile ['tɜːnstaɪl] *n* περιστροφική
είσοδος *f.*

turntable ['tɜːnteɪbl] *n* περιστροφική
εξέδρα, περιστροφική βάση.

turn-up ['tɜːnʌp] *n (on trousers)* ρεβέρ *nt
inv.*

turpentine ['tɜːpəntaɪn] *n* νέφτι.

turquoise ['tɜːkwɔɪz] *n* τουρκουάζ *nt inv*
♦ *a (colour)* κυανοπράσινος.

turret ['tʌrɪt] *n* πυργίσκος.

turtle ['tɜːtl] n χελώνα.

tusk [tʌsk] n χαυλιόδοντο.

tussle ['tʌsl] n τσακωμός, καυγάς.

tutor ['tjuːtə*] n ιδιαίτερος καθηγητής, οικοδιδάσκαλος || (at college) υφηγητής || ~**ial** n (UNIV) ιδιαίτερο μάθημα από καθηγητή.

TV [tiː'viː] n (abbr of **television**) TV f, τηλεόραση.

twaddle ['twɒdl] n (col) μωρολογία, φλυαρία, μπούρδες fpl.

twang [twæŋ] n οξύς ήχος χορδής, ένρινος τόνος, σβούρισμα nt ♦ vti αφήνω τεντωμένη χορδή, αντηχώ, κρούω.

tweed [twiːd] n τουήντ nt inv.

tweezers ['twiːzəz] npl τσιμπίδα.

twelfth [twelfθ] a δωδέκατος || T~ **Night** n παραμονή των Φώτων.

twelve [twelv] num δώδεκα.

twentieth ['twentiiθ] a εικοστός.

twenty ['twenti] num είκοσι.

twerp [twɜːp] n (col: fool) βλάκας.

twice [twais] ad δυό φορές, διπλάσιος.

twig [twig] n κλαδί, κλωνάρι ♦ vt (understand, realize) αντιλαμβάνομαι, μπαίνω, πιάνω.

twilight ['twailait] n λυκόφως nt, λυκαυγές nt.

twin [twin] n δίδυμος ♦ a δίδυμος.

twine [twain] n σπάγγος, χοντρή κλωστή ♦ vi τυλίγομαι.

twinge [twindʒ] n δυνατός πόνος, σουβλιά.

twinkle ['twiŋkl] n σπινθηρισμός, σπίθισμα nt ♦ vi σπινθηροβολώ, σπιθίζω || (star) τρεμοσβήνω.

twirl [twɜːl] n περιστροφή, στρίψιμο ♦ vti περιστρέφω, στρίβω.

twist [twist] n συστροφή, στρίψιμο, στραμπούληγμα nt ♦ vt συστρέφω, πλέκω, στρίβω || (distort) στρεβλώνω, στραβώνω || (cheat) εξαπατώ ♦ vi συστρέφομαι, στρίβομαι || (curve) στρίβω.

twit [twit] n (col: fool) κορόιδο, βλάκας.

twitch [twitʃ] n σύσπαση, τίναγμα nt ♦ vi συσπώμαι νευρικά.

two [tuː] num δύο, δυο || ~-**door** a (AUT) με δύο πόρτες || ~-**faced** a (pej: person) διπρόσωπος || ~**fold** ad δύο φορές, διπλά ♦ a διπλός || ~-**piece** a (suit) ντετπιές || (swimsuit) κοστούμι μπάνιου ντετπιές || ~-**seater** n (plane) διθέσιο || (car) διθέσιο || ~-**some** n ζευγάρι || ~-**way** a (traffic) διπλής κυκλοφορίας.

tycoon [tai'kuːn] n μεγιστάνας των επιχειρήσεων.

type [taip] n τύπος || (example) είδος nt, τάξη || (printing) χαρακτήρες mpl, στοιχεία ntpl ♦ vt δακτυλογραφώ || ~**face** n τύπος γραφής || ~**script** n δακτυλογραφημένο κείμενο || ~**writer** n γραφομηχανή || ~**written** a δακτυλογραφημένος.

typhoid ['taifɔid] n τυφοειδής.

typhoon [tai'fuːn] n τυφώνας.

typhus ['taifəs] n τύφος.

typical ['tipikəl] a τυπικός, χαρακτηριστικός.

typify ['tipifai] vt αντιπροσωπεύω, συμβολίζω.

typing ['taipiŋ] n δακτυλογράφηση.

typist ['taipist] n δακτυλογράφος m/f.

tyranny ['tirəni] n τυραννία.

tyrant ['taiərənt] n τύραννος.

tyre ['taiə*] n (AUT) ρόδα, λάστιχο.

U

udder ['ʌdə*] n μαστός, μαστάρι.

UFO ['juːfəu] n (abbr of **unidentified flying object**) αντικείμενο αγνώστου ταυτότητας.

ugliness ['ʌglinis] n ασχήμια.

ugly ['ʌgli] a άσχημος, άσκημος || (bad) άσχημος, κακός || (dangerous) δυσάρεστος, επικίνδυνος, άσχημος.

UHF abbr of ultra-high frequency υπερηψηλή συχνότητα, UHF.

UK n abbr see **united**.

ulcer ['ʌlsə*] n (in mouth, stomach) έλκος nt.

ulterior [ʌl'tiəriə*] a (hidden) υστερόβουλος, κρυφός.

ultimate ['ʌltimit] a τελευταίος, τελικός, ύστατος, βασικός || ~**ly** ad τελικά, βασικά.

ultimatum [ʌlti'meitəm] n τελεσίγραφο.

ultraviolet ['ʌltrə'vaiəlit] a: ~ **light** υπεριώδες φώς nt.

umbilical [ʌmbi'laikəl] a: ~ **cord** ομφάλιος λώρος, ομφάλιος.

umbrella [ʌm'brelə] n ομπρέλα.

umpire ['ʌmpaiə*] n διαιτητής ♦ vti διαιτητεύω.

umpteen ['ʌmptiːn] num (col) ένα σωρό, δεν ξέρω πόσοι.

UN abbr see **united**.

unable [ʌn'eibl] a ανίκανος, μη δυνάμενος.

unaccompanied [ʌnə'kʌmpənid] a (child, lady) ασυνόδευτος, μόνος.

unaccountably [ʌnə'kauntəbli] ad ανεξήγητα.

unaccustomed [ʌnə'kʌstəmd] a ασυνήθιστος || (+ to) ασυνήθιστος (σε, να).

unaided [ʌn'eidid] a χωρίς βοήθεια, αβοήθητος.

unanimous [juː'næniməs] a ομόθυμος, ομόφωνος || ~**ly** ad ομόφωνα, παμψηφεί.

unattached [ʌnə'tætʃt] a (single) ελεύθερος, εργένης.

unattended [ʌnə'tendid] a χωρίς συνοδεία, παραμελυμένος.

unattractive [ʌnə'træktiv] a μη συμπαθητικός.

unauthorized [ʌn'ɔːθəraizd] a χωρίς άδεια, μη εξουσιοδοτημένος.

unavoidable [ʌnə'vɔidəbl] a αναπόφευκτος.

unaware [ʌnə'weə*] a ανίδεος, αγνοών || ~**s** ad ξαφνικά, χωρίς προειδοποίηση.

unbalanced [ʌn'bælənst] a μη ισορροπημένος, ανισόρροπος.

unbearable [ʌn'bɛərəbl] a ανυπόφορος, αφόρητος.

unbeatable [ʌn'biːtəbl] a (team) αήττητος, ακατανίκητος.

unbeaten [ʌn'biːtn] a (team, record) αήττητος, αχτύπητο ρεκόρ.

unbeknown [ʌnbɪ'nəun] ad (+ to) εν αγνοία του.

unbelievable [ʌnbɪ'liːvəbl] a απίστευτος.

unbend [ʌn'bend] vi ευθυγραμμίζομαι, σιάζω ♦ vt χαλαρώνω, ξετεντώνω.

unbounded [ʌn'baundid] a απεριόριστος, απέραντος.

unbreakable [ʌn'breikəbl] a άθραυστος.

unbridled [ʌn'braidld] a αχαλίνωτος, ασυγκράτητος.

unbroken [ʌn'brəukən] a (inviolate) άθραυστος, άσπαστος, || (undisturbed) απαράβατος, αδιατάρακτος.

unburden [ʌn'bɜːdn] vt: to ~ o.s. ανακουφίζω, ξαλαφρώνω.

unbutton [ʌn'bʌtn] vt ξεκουμπώνω.

uncalled-for [ʌn'kɔːldfɔː*] a άκαιρος, αδικαιολόγητος.

uncanny [ʌn'kæni] a παράξενος, αφύσικος, μυστηριώδης.

unceasing [ʌn'siːsiŋ] a ακατάπαυστος.

uncertain [ʌn'sɜːtn] a αβέβαιος, αμφίβολος || (weather etc) ασταθής || (vague) ακαθόριστος || ~**ty** n αβεβαιότητα, αμφιβολία, αστάθεια.

unchanged [ʌn'tʃeindʒd] a αμετάβλητος.

uncharitable [ʌn'tʃæritəbl] a άσπλαχνος, αφιλάνθρωπος.

uncharted [ʌn'tʃaːtid] a ανεξερεύνητος.

unchecked [ʌn'tʃekt] a (unhindered) ανεμπόδιστος, ασταμάτητος || (not confirmed) ανεξέλεγκτος.

uncivil [ʌn'sivil] a αγενής, άξεστος, κακότροπος.

uncle [ʌŋkl] n θείος, μπάρμπας.

uncomfortable [ʌn'kʌmfətəbl] a (uneasy) ανήσυχος, δυσάρεστος.

unconscious [ʌn'kɔnʃəs] a ασυνείδητος || (not aware) αναίσθητος ♦ n: the ~ το ασυνείδητο || ~**ly** ad ασυνείδητα, χωρίς να το καταλάβω.

uncontrollable [ʌnkən'trəuləbl] a αχαλίνωτος, ακατάσχετος, ασυγκράτητος.

uncouth [ʌn'kuːθ] a αδέξιος, άξεστος.

uncover [ʌn'kʌvə*] vt ξεσκεπάζω || (expose) αποκαλύπτω, εκθέτω.

undecided [ʌndɪ'saidid] a αναποφάσιστος || (pending) εκκρεμής.

undeniable [ʌndɪ'naiəbl] a αναμφισβήτητος.

under [ʌndə*] prep υπό, κάτω από || (in time of) επί, στην εποχή του ♦ ad κάτω, από κάτω || ~ **age** a ανήλικος || ~ **repair** υπό επισκευή.

undercarriage [ʌndəkæridʒ] n, **undercart** [ʌndəkaːt] n σύστημα nt, προσγειώσεως.

underclothes [ʌndəkləuðz] npl εσώρουχα ntpl.

undercoat [ʌndəkəut] n (paint) βασικό χρώμα nt.

undercover [ʌndəkʌvə] a μυστικός, κρυφός.

undercurrent [ʌndəkʌrənt] n ρεύμα nt, κάτω από την επιφάνεια.

undercut [ʌndəkʌt] n (cooking) φιλέτο κρέατος ♦ vt πουλάω φθηνότερα από.

underdeveloped [ʌndədi'veləpt] a (country) υποανάπτυκτος.

underdog [ʌndədɔg] n ο πιο αδύνατος.

underdone [ʌndə'dʌn] a (cooking) μισοψημένος.

underestimate [ʌndər'estimeit] vt υποτιμώ.

underfed [ʌndə'fed] a υποσιτιζόμενος.

underfoot [ʌndə'fut] ad κάτω από τα πόδια.

undergo [ʌndə'gəu] vt υφίσταμαι, παθαίνω.

undergraduate [ʌndə'grædjuit] n φοιτητής/τήτρια m/f.

underground [ʌndəgraund] n υπόγειος σιδηρόδρομος ♦ a (press etc) μυστικός, κρυφός || (movement) της αντιστάσεως.

undergrowth [ʌndəgrəuθ] n θάμνοι mpl, χαμόκλαδα.

underhand [ʌndəhænd] a πανούργος, ύπουλος.

underlie [ʌndə'lai] vt υπόκειμαι, είμαι n βάση.

underline [ʌndə'lain] vt υπογραμμίζω || (draw attention to) υπογραμμίζω, τονίζω.

underling [ʌndəliŋ] n υφιστάμενος, παραγιός, υποτακτικός.

undermine [ʌndə'main] vt υπονομεύω, υποσκάβω.

underneath [ʌndə'niːθ] ad κάτω από, από κάτω ♦ prep κάτω από, υπό.

underpaid [ʌndə'peid] a κακοπληρωμένος.

underpass [ʌndəpaːs] n υπόγεια διάβαση.

underprivileged [ʌndə'privilidʒd] a με μειωμένα προνόμοια, αδικημένος.

underrate [ʌndə'reit] vt υποτιμώ.

underside [ʌndəsaid] n κάτω πλευρά, το αποκάτω.

underskirt [ʌndəskɜːt] n κομπιναιζόν nt inv, μεσοφόρι.

understand [ʌndə'stænd] vt αντιλαμβάνομαι || (know) γνωρίζω, καταλαβαίνω || (hear, believe) μαθαίνω, πιστεύω, νομίζω || (GRAM) υπονοώ || ~**able** a (κατα) νοητός, καταληπτός, ευνόητος || ~**ing** n συνεννόηση, κατανόηση || (agreement) συμφωνία.

U

understatement ['ʌndəsteitmənt] n δήλωση κάτω από την πραγματικότητα.

understudy ['ʌndəstʌdɪ] n αντικαταστάτης/τρια m/f.

undertake [ʌndə'teik] vt αναλαμβάνω || ~r n εργολάβος κηδειών.

undertaking [ʌndə'teikiŋ] n επιχείρηση || (promise) δέσμευση, υποχρέωση.

underwater [ʌndə'wɔːtə*] ad υποβρυχίως ♦ a υποβρύχιος.

underwear ['ʌndəwɛə*] n εσώρουχα ntpl.

underweight [ʌndə'weit] a λιποβαρής, αδύνατος.

underworld ['ʌndəwɜːld] n (of crime) υπόκοσμος.

underwriter ['ʌndəraitə*] n (insurance) ασφαλιστής.

undesirable [ʌndɪ'zaiərəbl] a ανεπιθύμητος.

undies ['ʌndɪz] npl (col) εσώρουχα (γυναικεία).

undisputed [ʌndɪs'pjuːtɪd] a αδιαφιλονίκητος, αδιαμφισβήτητος.

undo [ʌn'duː] vt λύνω, ξεκουμπώνω, ανοίγω || (work) καταστρέφω, χαλώ || ~ing n καταστροφή, αφανισμός.

undoubted [ʌn'dautid] a αναμφισβήτητος, αναμφίβολος || ~ly ad αναμφισβήτητα.

undress [ʌn'dres] vti γδύνομαι, γδύνω.

undue [ʌn'djuː] a υπερβολικός, αδικαιολόγητος.

undulating ['ʌndjuleitiŋ] a κυμαινόμενος, ταλαντευόμενος.

unduly [ʌn'djuːlɪ] ad υπερβολικά, άπρεπα.

unearth [ʌn'ɜːθ] vt ξεθάβω, ανακαλύπτω || ~ly a υπερφυσικός, απόκοσμος.

uneasy [ʌn'iːzɪ] a ανήσυχος, στενοχωρημένος.

uneconomic(al) ['ʌniːkə'nomɪk(əl)] a ανοικονομικός, σπάταλος, ασύμφορος.

uneducated [ʌn'edjukeitid] a ασπούδαστος, αμόρφωτος.

unemployed [ʌnɪm'plɔid] a άνεργος, αχρησιμοποίητος || npl: the ~ οι άνεργοι.

unemployment [ʌnɪm'plɔimənt] n ανεργία.

unending [ʌn'endiŋ] a ατελείωτος.

unerring [ʌn'ɜːriŋ] a αλάνθαστος, ακριβής.

uneven [ʌn'iːvən] a (surface) ανώμαλος || (quality) άνισος, ακανόνιστος.

unfair [ʌn'fɛə*] a (unkind, unreasonable) άδικος || ~ly ad άδικα, άτιμα.

unfaithful [ʌn'feiθful] a (to spouse) άπιστος.

unfasten [ʌn'faːsn] vt λύνω || (clothes) ξεκουμπώνω || (open) ξεκλειδώνω.

unfavourable, (US) **unfavorable** [ʌn'feivərəbl] a δυσμενής, δυσοίωνος.

unfeeling [ʌn'fiːliŋ] a σκληρόκαρδος, αναίσθητος.

unfinished [ʌn'finiʃt] a ατέλειωτος, ασυμπλήρωτος.

unfit [ʌn'fit] a (in health) ανίκανος, αδιάθετος || (+ for) ακατάλληλος (για).

unflagging [ʌn'flægiŋ] a ακλόνητος, ακατάπαυστος, αλύγιστος.

unfold [ʌn'fəuld] vt ξεδιπλώνω, ξετυλίγω, απλώνω || (reveal) αποκαλύπτω || (develop) αναπτύσσω || (explain) εξηγώ ♦ vi (develop) αναπτύσσομαι, εκτυλίσσομαι.

unforeseen ['ʌnfɔː'siːn] a απρόβλεπτος, αηροσδόκητος.

unforgivable [ʌnfə'givəbl] a ασυγχώρητος.

unfortunate [ʌn'fɔːtʃnit] a άτυχος, κακότυχος || ~ly ad δυστυχώς.

unfounded [ʌn'faundid] a (rumour) αβάσιμος.

unfriendly [ʌn'frendli] a δυσμενής, εχθρικός.

unfurnished [ʌn'fɜːniʃt] a (flat) χωρίς έπιπλα.

ungainly [ʌn'geinli] a αδέξιος.

unhappiness [ʌn'hæpinis] n δυστυχία, στενοχώρια.

unhappy [ʌn'hæpi] a δυστυχισμένος, στενοχωρημένος.

unharmed [ʌn'haːmd] a σώος, αβλαβής, απείραχτος.

unhealthy [ʌn'helθi] a (lit) ανθυγιεινός, αρρωστιάρης || (fig) νοσηρός.

unheard-off [ʌn'hɜːdɒv] a πρωτάκουστος, ανήκουστος.

unhurt [ʌn'hɜːt] a χωρίς τραύμα, σώος και αβλαβής.

unidentified [ʌnai'dentifaid] a μη αναγνωρισθείς, άγνωστος.

uniform ['juːnifɔːm] n στολή ♦ a ομοιόμορφος, ίδιος || ~ity n ομοιομορφία.

unify ['juːnifai] vt ενοποιώ.

unilateral [juːni'lætərəl] a μονόπλευρος.

unintentional [ʌnin'tenʃənl] a ακούσιος, αθέλητος.

union ['juːnjən] n ένωση || (alliance) ένωση || (agreement) ένωση || (of workers) εργατικό σωματείο, συνδικάτο || U~ Jack n Αγγλική σημαία.

unique [juː'niːk] a μοναδικός, ιδιόρρυθμος, ασυνήθιστος.

unison ['juːnisn] n: in ~ ομόφωνα, από κοινού || (MUS) αρμονία, μονοφωνία, ομονχία.

unit ['juːnit] n μονάδα || (team, squad) ομάδα, συγκρότημα nt.

unite [juː'nait] vt ενώνω ♦ vi ενώνομαι (με) || ~d a ενωμένος, συνδυασμένος || U~d Kingdom (UK) n Ηνωμένο Βασίλειο (H.B) || U~d Nations (UN) npl Ηνωμένα Έθνη (O.H.E.) m || U~d States (of America) (US, USA) npl Ηνωμένες Πολιτείες (Αμερικής) (Η.Π.Α.) fpl.

unity ['juːniti] n ενότητα, αρμονία, σύμπνοια, μονάδα.

universal [juːnɪˈvɜːsəl] a οικουμενικός, καθολικός || (general) γενικός || (of the world) παγκόσμιος.

universe [ˈjuːnɪvɜːs] n σύμπαν nt, οικουμένη.

university [juːnɪˈvɜːsɪtɪ] n πανεπιστήμιο.

unjust [ʌnˈdʒʌst] a άδικος.

unkempt [ʌnˈkɛmpt] a ατημέλητος, ακτένιστος.

unkind [ʌnˈkaɪnd] a αγενής, άστοργος, σκληρός.

unknown [ʌnˈnəʊn] a (+ to) άγνωστος (σε), αγνοούμενος από.

unladen [ʌnˈleɪdn] a (col: weight) χωρίς φορτίο, κενός.

unleash [ʌnˈliːʃ] vt λύνω, ελευθερώνω.

unless [ʌnˈlɛs] cj εκτός εάν, εκτός αν.

unlike [ʌnˈlaɪk] a ανόμοιος, διαφορετικός από.

unlimited [ʌnˈlɪmɪtɪd] a απεριόριστος.

unload [ʌnˈləʊd] vt εκφορτώνω, ξεφορτώνω.

unlock [ʌnˈlɒk] vt ξεκλειδώνω.

unmarried [ʌnˈmærɪd] a άγαμος.

unmask [ʌnˈmɑːsk] vt (expose) αποκαλύπτω || αφαιρώ προσωπείο από.

unmistakable [ʌnmɪsˈteɪkəbl] a αλάθητος, ολοφάνερος, σαφής.

unmitigated [ʌnˈmɪtɪɡeɪtɪd] a αμετρίαστος, απόλυτος.

unnecessary [ʌnˈnɛsɪsərɪ] a περιττός, άσκοπος, μάταιος.

unobtainable [ʌnəbˈteɪnəbl] a ανεπίτευκτος.

unoccupied [ʌnˈɒkjʊpaɪd] a (seat etc) ελεύθερος, διαθέσιμος.

unorthodox [ʌnˈɔːθədɒks] a ανορθόδοξος.

unpack [ʌnˈpæk] vti ξεπακετάρω, βγάζω από βαλίτσες.

unparalleled [ʌnˈpærəleld] a απαράμιλλος.

unpleasant [ʌnˈplɛznt] a δυσάρεστος.

unplug [ʌnˈplʌg] vt ξεβουλώνω || (ELEC) βγάζω την πρίζα.

unpopular [ʌnˈpɒpjʊlə*] a αντιδημοτικός.

unprecedented [ʌnˈprɛsɪdəntɪd] a χωρίς προηγούμενο.

unqualified [ʌnˈkwɒlɪfaɪd] a αναρμόδιος, ακατάλληλος || (success) αμετρίαστος, απόλυτος.

unravel [ʌnˈrævəl] vt ξεφτώ, ξηλώνω, ξετυλίγω || (clarify) διευκρινίζω || (solve) λύνω, διαλύω.

unreal [ʌnˈrɪəl] a απατηλός, φανταστικός.

unreasonable [ʌnˈriːznəbl] a (unfair) παράλογος.

unrelenting [ʌnrɪˈlɛntɪŋ] a αδυσώπητος, ανελέητος.

unrelieved [ʌnrɪˈliːvd] a (monotony) χωρίς ποικιλία, μονότονος.

unrepeatable [ʌnrɪˈpiːtəbl] a (offer) που δεν επαναλαμβάνεται.

unrest [ʌnˈrɛst] n (discontent, trouble) ανησυχία, ταραχή.

unroll [ʌnˈrəʊl] vt ξετυλίγω.

unruly [ʌnˈruːlɪ] a ανυπότακτος, ατίθασος, άτακτος.

unsafe [ʌnˈseɪf] a επικίνδυνος, ανασφαλής.

unsaid [ʌnˈsɛd] a: to leave sth ~ αποσιωπώ κάτι.

unsatisfactory [ˈʌnsætɪsˈfæktərɪ] a μη ικανοποιητικός, ανεπαρκής.

unsavoury, (US) **unsavory** [ʌnˈseɪvərɪ] a (of bad character) ύποπτος, σκοτεινός.

unscrew [ʌnˈskruː] vt ξεβιδώνω.

unscrupulous [ʌnˈskruːpjʊləs] a ασυνείδητος, ανενδοίαστος.

unsettled [ʌnˈsɛtld] a ανήσυχος, αβέβαιος || (weather) ευμετάβλητος, αβέβαιος.

unshaven [ʌnˈʃeɪvn] a αξύριστος.

unsightly [ʌnˈsaɪtlɪ] a άσχημος, δύσμορφος.

unskilled [ʌnˈskɪld] a (workman) ανειδίκευτος.

unspeakable [ʌnˈspiːkəbl] a απερίγραπτος, ανείπωτος, ανέκφραστος || (very bad) αποκρουστικός, απδιαστικός, σιχαμερός.

unstuck [ʌnˈstʌk] a: to come ~ ξεκολλώ || (lit) ξεκολλώ, ξεκολλιέμαι || (fig) καταρρέω, γκρεμίζομαι.

unsuitable [ʌnˈsuːtəbl] a ακατάλληλος.

unsuspecting [ʌnsəsˈpɛktɪŋ] a ανυποψίαστος.

unswerving [ʌnˈswɜːvɪŋ] a (loyalty) σταθερός, πιστός.

untangle [ʌnˈtæŋgl] vt ξεχωρίζω, ξεμπλέκω.

untapped [ʌnˈtæpt] a (resources) ανεκμετάλλευτος.

unthinkable [ʌnˈθɪŋkəbl] a ασύλληπτος, πολύ απίθανος.

untidy [ʌnˈtaɪdɪ] a ακατάστατος.

untie [ʌnˈtaɪ] vt λύνω.

until [ənˈtɪl] prep μέχρι, έως || cj μέχρς ότου, έως ότου.

untimely [ʌnˈtaɪmlɪ] a (death) πρόωρος.

untold [ʌnˈtəʊld] a (countless) αμέτρητος, ανυπολόγιστος.

untoward [ʌntəˈwɔːd] a δυσάρεστος, δυσμενής.

unused [ʌnˈjuːzd] a αμεταχείριστος.

unusual [ʌnˈjuːʒʊəl] a ασυνήθιστος, σπάνιος || ~ly ad εξαιρετικά, αφάνταστα, ασυνήθιστα.

unveil [ʌnˈveɪl] vt αποκαλύπτω, ξεσκεπάζω.

unwell [ʌnˈwɛl] a αδιάθετος, άρρωστος.

unwieldy [ʌnˈwiːldɪ] a δυσκίνητος, βαρύς, αδέξιος.

unwilling [ʌnˈwɪlɪŋ] a απρόθυμος, ακούσιος.

unwind [ʌnˈwaɪnd] vt (lit) ξετυλίγω, ξεκουρδίζω ♦ vi (relax) χαλαρώνομαι.

unwitting [ʌn'wɪtɪŋ] *a* χωρίς πρόθεση, ακούσιος.

unwrap [ʌn'ræp] *vt* ξετυλίγω.

unwritten [ʌn'rɪtn] *a (law)* άγραφος, προφορικός.

up [ʌp] *prep* προς τα πάνω, αντίθετα με το ρεύμα ♦ *ad* επάνω, άνω, τελείως || it is ~ to you εξαρτάται από σένα || what is he ~ to? τι επιδιώκει; τι θέλει; || he is not ~ to it δεν έχει την ικανότητα (να) ||~-and-coming *a* εξαιρετικά δραστήριος, ανερχόμενος ♦ *n*: ~s and downs διακυμάνσεις *fpl*, μεταβολές *fpl* της τύχης.

upbringing ['ʌpbrɪŋɪŋ] *n* ανατροφή.

update [ʌp'deɪt] *vt* ενημερώνω, εκσυγχρονίζω.

upheaval [ʌp'hiːvəl] *n (violent disturbance)* αναστάτωση, αναταραχή.

uphill [ʌp'hɪl] *a* ανηφορικός ♦ *ad* προς τα άνω.

uphold [ʌp'həʊld] *vt (maintain)* υποστηρίζω.

upholstery [ʌp'həʊlstərɪ] *n* ταπετσαρία.

upkeep ['ʌpkiːp] *n* συντήρηση, έξοδα *ntpl* συντηρήσεως.

upon [ə'pɒn] *prep* πάνω, σε.

upper ['ʌpə*] *a* ανώτερος, άνω, από πάνω || the ~ class *n* η ανωτέρα τάξη, η καλή κοινωνία || ~-class *a* της ανωτέρας τάξεως || ~most *a* υπέρτατος, ανώτατος.

upright ['ʌpraɪt] *a* όρθιος, κατακόρυφος, κάθετος || *(honest)* ευθύς, δίκαιος, τίμιος ♦ *n* ορθοστάτης.

uprising [ʌp'raɪzɪŋ] *n* εξέγερση, ξεσήκωμα *nt*.

uproar ['ʌprɔː*] *n* θόρυβος, φασαρία, αναστάτωση.

uproot [ʌp'ruːt] *vt* ξεριζώνω.

upset ['ʌpset] *n* αναστάτωση, ανατροπή, αναποδογύρισμα *nt* ♦ [ʌp'set] *vt (overturn)* ανατρέπω, αναποδογυρίζω || *(distress)* ταράσσω, αναστατώνω.

upshot ['ʌpʃɒt] *n* αποτέλεσμα *nt*, έκβαση, κατάληξη.

upside ['ʌpsaɪd]: ~ down *ad* άνω-κάτω, ανάποδα, φύρδην-μύγδην.

upstairs ['ʌp'stɛəz] *ad* στο επάνω πάτωμα *nt* ♦ *a (room)* επάνω, του άνω ορόφου ♦ *n* επάνω.

upstart ['ʌpstɑːt] *n* νεόπλουτος, αναιδής άνθρωπος.

upstream [ʌp'striːm] *ad* αντίθετα με το ρεύμα.

uptake ['ʌpteɪk] *n* αντίληψη || to be quick, (slow) on the ~ (δεν) παίρνω, (δεν) αρπάζω.

up-to-date ['ʌptə'deɪt] *a* σύγχρονος, μοντέρνος || *(fashionable)* της μόδας.

upturn ['ʌptɜːn] *n (in luck)* βελτίωση, άνοδος *f*.

upward ['ʌpwəd] *a* προς τα άνω || ~(s) *ad* προς τα άνω.

uranium [juə'reɪnɪəm] *n* ουράνιο.

urban ['ɜːbən] *a* αστικός.

urbane [ɜː'beɪn] *a* ευγενικός, αβρός, ραφιναρισμένος.

urchin ['ɜːtʃɪn] *n (boy)* αλητάκι || sea ~ αχινός.

urge [ɜːdʒ] *n (desire)* επίμονη επιθυμία, ώθηση ♦ *vt (entreat)* παροτρύνω.

urgency ['ɜːdʒənsɪ] *n* επείγουσα ανάγκη, επιμονή, πίεση.

urgent ['ɜːdʒənt] *a* επείγων, πιεστικός, άμεσος || ~ly *ad* επειγόντως.

urinal ['juərɪnl] *n* ουρητήριο.

urine ['juərɪn] *n* ούρα *ntpl*.

urn [ɜːn] *n* υδρία, δοχείο, αγγείο || *(teapot)* σαμοβάρι.

us [ʌs] *pron* εμάς, μας.

US, USA *n* *abbr see* **united.**

usage ['juːzɪdʒ] *n* μεταχείριση, έθιμο, συνήθειο || *(esp LING)* χρήση.

use [juːs] *n* χρήση || *(custom)* συνήθεια, έθιμο || *(employment)* χρήση, χρησιμοποίηση || *(value)* χρησιμότητα ♦ [juːz] *vt* χρησιμοποιώ, μεταχειρίζομαι || *(make most of)* χρησιμεύω || in ~ εν χρήσει || out of ~ εν αχρηστία || ~d to συνηθίζω να || she ~d to do do it συνήθιζε να το κάνει || to ~ up *vt* καταναλίσκω, εξαντλώ || ~d *a (car)* μεταχειρισμένος, δεύτερο χέρι || ~ful *a* χρήσιμος || ~less *a* άχρηστος || ~r *n* χρήστης.

usher ['ʌʃə*] *n (at wedding)* παράνυμφος || ~ette *n (at cinema)* ταξιθέτρια.

USSR *n*: the ~ Ε.Σ.Σ.Δ ('Ενωση Σοσιαλιστικών Σοβιετικών Δημοκρατιών).

usual ['juːʒʊəl] *a* συνηθισμένος || ~ly *ad* συνήθως.

usurp [juː'zɜːp] *vt* σφετερίζομαι, αρπάζω.

utensil [juː'tensl] *n* σκεύος *nt*, εργαλείο.

uterus ['juːtərəs] *n* μήτρα.

utilitarian [juːtɪlɪ'tɛərɪən] *a* κοινωφελής, ωφελιμιστικός.

utility [juː'tɪlɪtɪ] *n* χρησιμότητα, ευχρηστία || *(useful thing)* χρήσιμο πράγμα *nt* || *(also public utility: electricity supply industry)* δημοσία υπηρεσία, κοινωφελής επιχείρηση.

utilize ['juːtɪlaɪz] *vt* χρησιμοποιώ, εκμεταλλεύομαι.

utmost ['ʌtməʊst] *a* ακρότατος, απότατος, έσχατος || *n*: to do one's ~ κάνω ότι μπορώ.

utter ['ʌtə*] *a* πλήρης, ολοσχερής ♦ *vt* αρθρώνω, εκστομίζω, προφέρω, λέω || ~ly *ad* τελείως, εξ ολοκλήρου.

U-turn ['juː'tɜːn] *n (AUT)* στροφή 180 μοιρών.

V

v. *(abbr of verse)* ποιητ. (ποιητικός) || *abbr of* versus || *(abbr of vide)* βλ (βλέπετε) || *abbr of* volt.

vacancy ['veɪkənsɪ] *n* κενό, κενή θέση || *(room)* δωμάτιο.

vacant ['veikənt] a κενός || (not occupied) άδειος, ελεύθερος || (stupid) αφηρημένος, ανέκφραστος || '~' (on door) 'δωμάτια'.

vacate [və'keit] vt εκκενώνω, αδειάζω, εγκαταλείπω.

vacation [və'keiʃən] n διακοπή, αργία.

vaccinate ['væksineit] vt εμβολιάζω, μπολιάζω.

vaccination [væksi'neiʃən] n εμβολιασμός, μπόλιασμα nt.

vaccine ['væksi:n] n εμβόλιο, βατσίνα.

vacuum ['vækjum] n κενό || ~ bottle n (US) φιάλη κενού, θερμός nt|| ~ cleaner n ηλεκτρική σκούπα || ~ flask n (Brit) φιάλη κενού, θερμός nt.

vagina [və'dʒainə] n κόλπος (γυναίκας).

vagrant ['veigrənt] n περιπλανώμενος, αλήτης.

vague [veig] a ασαφής, αμυδρός, ακαθόριστος || ~ly ad αόριστα, ασαφώς.

vain [vein] a μάταιος, άκαρπος || (conceited) ματαιόδοξος || in ~ μάταια.

vale [veil] n κοιλάδα, λαγκαδιά.

valid ['vælid] a έγκυρος, βάσιμος, νόμιμος, λογικός || ~ity n εγκυρότητα, ισχύς f.

valise [və'li:z] n (suitcase) βαλίτσα.

valley ['væli] n κοιλάδα, λαγκάδι.

valuable ['væljuəbl] a πολύτιμος || ~s npl αντικείμενα αξίας ntpl.

valuation [vælju'eiʃən] n εκτίμηση, αξία.

value ['vælju:] n αξία, τιμή, σημασία, έννοια ♦ vt εκτιμώ || ~ added tax (VAT) n Φόρος Προστιθέμενης Αξίας (Φ.Π.Α.) m|| ~d a (appreciated) εκτιμώμενος.

valve [vælv] n βαλβίδα, δικλείδα, λυχνία.

vampire ['væmpaiə*] n βρυκόλακας.

van [væn] n φορτηγό, σκευοφόρος.

vandal ['vændəl] n βάνδαλος || ~ism n βανδαλισμός.

vanilla [və'nilə] n βανίλια ♦ attr a (ice cream) παγωτό.

vanish ['væniʃ] vi εξαφανίζομαι, χάνομαι.

vanity ['væniti] n ματαιοδοξία, εγωισμός || ~ case n γυναικείο τσαντάκι.

vantage ['va:ntidʒ] n: ~ point (good viewpoint) πλεονεκτική θέση.

vapour, (US) vapor ['veipə*] n αχνός, πάχνη || (gas) ατμός, υδρατμός.

variable ['vεəriəbl] a μεταβλητός, ευμετάβλητος.

variance ['vεəriəns] n: at ~ σε διάσταση, σε διαφωνία.

variation [vεəri'eiʃən] n παραλλαγή, παρέκκλιση, μεταβολή.

varicose ['værikəus] a: ~ veins κιρσώδες φλέβες fpl.

varied ['vεərid] a διάφορος, ποικίλος, μεταβαλλόμενος.

variety [və'raiəti] n ποικιλία, διαφορά || (varied collection) ποικιλία, πολλά και διάφορα || (kind) ποικιλία || ~ show n (THEAT) επιθεώρηση.

various ['vεəriəs] a ποικίλος, διάφορος.

varnish ['va:niʃ] n βερνίκι, στιλβωμένη επιφάνεια ♦ vt βερνικώνω, στιλβώνω.

vary ['vεəri] vt διαφοροποιώ, ποικίλω ♦ vi αλλάζω, μεταβάλλομαι, διαφέρω || ~ing a μεταβαλλόμενος, μεταβλητός, ποικίλος.

vase [va:z] n βάζο, αγγείο.

vast [va:st] a πελώριος, εκτεταμένος, απέραντος.

vat [væt] n κάδος, βούτα, δεξαμενή.

VAT [væt] n abbr see value.

Vatican ['vætikən] n: the ~ το Βατικανό.

vault [vɔ:lt] n θόλος, καμάρα || (cellar) υπόγειο || (tomb) θολωτός τάφος || (leap) πήδημα nt, άλμα nt ♦ vt πηδώ, κάνω άλμα επί κοντώ.

VD n abbr see venereal.

VDU n abbr see visual.

veal [vi:l] n μοσχάρι.

veer [viə*] vi στρέφω, αλλάζω κατεύθυνση, γυρίζω.

vegetable ['vedʒitəbl] n φυτό, λαχανικό, χορταρικό.

vegetarian [vedʒi'tεəriən] a, n (people) χορτοφάγος || (animal) φυτοφάγος.

vegetate ['vedʒiteit] vi φυτοζωώ.

vegetation [vedʒi'teiʃən] n βλάστηση.

vehement ['vi:imənt] a βίαιος, ορμητικός.

vehicle ['vi:ikl] n όχημα nt, αμάξι.

veil [veil] n πέπλος, βέλο || (fig) κάλυμμα nt ♦ vt καλύπτω, κρύβω.

vein [vein] n φλέβα || (of ore) φλέβα, στρώμα nt|| (streak) διάθεση, ταλέντο || (mood) πνεύμα nt, διάθεση, κέφι.

velocity [vi'lɒsiti] n ταχύτητα.

velvet ['velvit] n βελούδο.

vendetta [ven'detə] n βεντέτα, εκδίκηση.

vending machine ['vendiŋməʃi:n] n μηχάνημα nt πωλήσεως.

vendor ['vendɔ:*] n πωλητής.

veneer [və'niə*] n (lit) καπλαμάς, επίστρωση, επένδυση || (fig) επίχρισμα nt, επίστρωμα nt|| (lustre) λούστρο.

venerable ['venərəbl] a αξιοσέβαστος, σεβάσμιος.

venereal [vi'niəriəl] a (disease) αφροδίσιος || ~ disease (VD) n αφροδίσιο νόσημα.

venetian [vi'ni:ʃən] a: ~ blind παντζούρι.

vengeance ['vendʒəns] n εκδίκηση.

venison ['venisn] n κρέας nt ελαφιού.

venom ['venəm] n δηλητήριο, φαρμάκι || ~ous a φαρμακερός.

vent [vent] n τρύπα εξαερισμού, διέξοδος f, άνοιγμα nt ♦ vt ξεσπώ, ξεθυμαίνω.

ventilate ['ventileit] vt αερίζω.

ventilation [venti'leiʃən] n (εξ)αερισμός.

ventilator ['ventileitə*] n εξαεριστήρας, ανεμιστήρας.

ventriloquist [ven'triləkwist] n εγγαστρίμυθος.

V

venture ['ventʃə*] n τόλμημα nt,
εγχείρημα nt|| (COMM) επιχείρηση ♦ vt
ριψοκινδυνεύω, ρισκάρω ♦ vi
αποτολμώ, τολμώ.

venue ['venju:] n τόπος συναντήσεως,
τόπος δίκης.

veranda(h) [və'rændə] n βεράντα.

verb [vɜ:b] n ρήμα nt|| ~al a λεκτικός,
προφορικός.

verbose [vɜ:'bəʊs] a πολύλογος,
μακροσκελής.

verdict ['vɜ:dikt] n κρίση, γνώμη|| (of
jury) ετυμηγορία, απόφαση.

verge [vɜ:dʒ] n (of road) άκρη (του
δρόμου) || on the ~ of doing έτοιμος
να ♦ vi: to ~ on πλησιάζω, τείνω προς.

verger ['vɜ:dʒə*] n νεωκόρος.

verify ['verifai] vt επιβεβαιώνω,
αποδεικνύω.

vermin ['vɜ:min] npl βλαβερά ζωύφια
ntpl.

vermouth ['vɜ:məθ] n βερμούτ nt inv.

vernacular [və'nækjulə*] n τοπική
διάλεκτος f, κοινή γλώσσα.

versatile ['vɜ:sətail] a πολύπλευρος,
εύστροφος.

verse [vɜːs] n ποίηση, ποιήματα ntpl||
(line) στίχος|| (of poem, song) στροφή|| (of
Bible) εδάφιο|| ~d a (+ in) μυημένος,
πεπειραμένος, μορφωμένος.

version ['vɜ:ʃən] n (account) έκδοση,
ερμηνεία.

versus ['vɜ:səs] prep κατά, εναντίον.

vertebra ['vɜ:tibrə] n σπόνδυλος,
ραχοκόκκαλο.

vertebrate ['vɜ:tibrit] a σπονδυλωτός.

vertical ['vɜ:tikəl] a κάθετος,
κατακόρυφος.

vertigo ['vɜ:tigəʊ] n ίλιγγος, ζάλη.

very ['veri] ad πολύ || (precisely) ακριβώς
♦ a (identical) ίδιος || (mere) και μόνο.

vespers ['vespəz] npl εσπερινός.

vessel ['vesl] n πλοίο, σκάφος nt||
(container) αγγείο, σκεύος nt.

vest [vest] n φανελάκι || (US: waistcoat)
γιλέκο ♦ vt περιβάλλω, παραχωρώ,
παρέχω || ~ed a (interest) κεκτημένος.

vestibule ['vestibju:l] n (of house)
προθάλαμος, χωλ nt inv.

vestige ['vestidʒ] n υπόλειμμα nt, ίχνος
nt.

vestry ['vestri] n ιεροφυλάκειο,
σκευοφυλάκιο, βεστιάριο.

vet [vet] n (abbr of veterinary surgeon)
κτηνίατρος ♦ vt εξετάζω.

veteran ['vetərən] n παλαίμαχος,
βετεράνος ♦ a του παλαιμάχου,
πεπειραμένος.

veterinary ['vetərinəri] a κτηνιατρικός ||
~ surgeon n κτηνίατρος.

veto ['vi:təʊ] n δικαίωμα nt
αρνησικυρίας, βέτο || (prohibition)
απαγόρευση ♦ vt προβάλλω βέτο (σε).

vex [veks] vt ενοχλώ, ερεθίζω, ταράσσω
|| ~ed a θυμωμένος, πειραγμένος.

VHF n (abbr of very high frequency) πολύ
υψηλή συχνότητα (Λ.Υ.Σ.).

via ['vaiə] prep μέσω, διά μέσου.

viable ['vaiəbl] a βιώσιμος.

viaduct ['vaiədʌkt] n οδογέφυρα,
αψιδωτή γέφυρα.

vibrate [vai'breit] vi πάλλομαι,
δονούμαι, ταλαντεύομαι || (resound) ηχώ.

vibration [vai'breiʃən] n ταλάντευση,
δόνηση, κούνημα nt.

vicar ['vikə*] n εφημέριος || ~age n
πρεσβυτέριο, οικία εφημερίου.

vice [vais] n (evil) εκφυλισμός, ακολασία,
αμάρτημα nt|| (TECH) μέγγενη.

vice- [vais] prefix αντί-, υπό ||
~chairman n αντιπρόεδρος.

vice versa ['vaisi'vɜ:sə] ad αντίστροφα.

vicinity [vi'siniti] n γειτονιά, εγγύτητα,
περιοχή.

vicious ['viʃəs] a (also cruel) κακός,
κακοήθης.

victim ['viktim] n θύμα nt|| ~ization n
καταπίεση, αντίποινα ntpl|| ~ize vt
καταπιέζω, μεταχειρίζομαι σαν θύμα.

victor ['viktə*] n νικητής/ήτρια m/f.

Victorian [vik'tɔ:riən] a βικτωριανός.

victorious [vik'tɔ:riəs] a νικηφόρος,
θριαμβευτής.

victory ['viktəri] n νίκη.

video ['vidiəʊ] n βίντεο.

vie [vai] vi (compete) (+ with) αμιλλώμαι,
ανταγωνίζομαι.

view [vju:] n όψη, ματιά, βλέμμα nt||
(scene) θέα, προοπτική, όψη || (opinion)
άποψη, έκθεση || (intention) πρόθεση,
βλέψη, σκοπός ♦ vt (situation) κυττάζω,
επιθεωρώ, εξετάζω || ~er n (viewfinder)
σκόπευτρο || (PHOT: small projector) μικρό
μηχάνημα nt προβολής || (TV) θεατής ||
~finder n σκόπευτρο, εικονοσκόπιο ||
~point n σημείο με καλή θέα || (attitude)
άποψη.

vigil ['vidʒil] n αγρυπνία, ξενύχτι,
ολονυχτία || ~ant a άγρυπνος,
προσεκτικός.

vigor ['vigə*] n (US) = **vigour**.

vigorous ['vigərəs] a ρωμαλέος,
σθεναρός, ζωηρός || ~ly ad γερά,
δυνατά.

vigour ['vigə*] n σθένος nt, σφρίγος nt,
ζωτικότητα, ζωηρότητα.

vile [vail] a ανήθικος, αχρείος, αισχρός ||
(foul) ακάθαρτος, βρωμερός, σιχαμερός.

villa ['vilə] n έπαυλη, βίλα.

village ['vilidʒ] n χωριό || ~r n
χωριάτης/άτισσα m/f.

villain ['vilən] n ο κακός, παλιάνθρωπος.

vindicate ['vindikeit] vt δικαιώνω,
υπερασπίζω.

vindictive [vin'diktiv] a εκδικητικός.

vine [vain] n αμπέλι, κλήμα nt.

vinegar ['vinigə*] n ξύδι.

vineyard ['vinjəd] n αμπελώνας, αμπέλι.

vintage ['vintidʒ] n (wine) κρασί
ωρισμένου έτους || (gathering) τρυγητός,
τρύγος.

vinyl ['vainl] n βινύλιο.

viola [vi'əʊlə] n (MUS) βιόλα.

violate ['vaiəleit] vt (break promise)

αθετώ, καταπατώ || (disturb) παραβιάζω || (desecrate) βεβηλώνω.

violation [vaɪə'leɪʃən] n παράβαση, παράβαση, αθέτηση.

violence ['vaɪələns] n σφοδρότητα, ένταση || (rough treatment) βία, βιαιότητα.

violent ['vaɪələnt] a βίαιος, ορμητικός || (extreme) ζωηρός, έντονος, οξύς, ισχυρός || ~ly ad βίαια, απότομα, εξαιρετικά, πολύ.

violet ['vaɪəlɪt] n βιολέτα, μενεξές m ♦ a μενεξεδένιος, μώβ.

violin [vaɪə'lɪn] n βιολί.

VIP n (abbr of very important person) ≈ Επίσημος/n m/f.

viper ['vaɪpə*] n έχιδνα, οχιά.

virgin ['vɜːdʒɪn] n παρθένα ♦ a παρθένος, παρθενικός, καθαρός || ~ity n παρθενία.

virile ['vɪraɪl] a ανδρικός, δυνατός, σθεναρός.

virility [vɪ'rɪlɪtɪ] n ανδρισμός, ανδροπρέπεια, αρρενωπότητα.

virtually ['vɜːtjʊəlɪ] ad (in fact) ουσιαστικά || (almost) σχεδόν.

virtue ['vɜːtjuː] n αρετή || (good quality) ικανότητα, δραστικότητα || by ~ of δυνάμει, συνεπεία, λόγω, εξαιτίας.

virtuoso [vɜːtjʊ'əʊzəʊ] n δεξιοτέχνης μουσικός, βιρτουόζος.

virtuous ['vɜːtjʊəs] a ενάρετος.

virulent ['vɪrʊlənt] a τοξικός, θανατηφόρος || (bitter) εχθρικός, κακεντρεχής, φαρμακερός.

virus ['vaɪərəs] n ιός, μικρόβιο.

visa ['viːzə] n θεώρηση, βίζα.

vis-à-vis ['viːzəviː] prep απέναντι, αντίκρυ.

viscount ['vaɪkaʊnt] n υποκόμης.

visibility [vɪzɪ'bɪlɪtɪ] n ορατότητα.

visible ['vɪzəbl] a ορατός, εμφανής, φαλερός || **visibly** ad καταφανώς, προφανώς, ολοφάνερα.

vision ['vɪʒən] n όραση || (imagination) διορατικότητα || (dream) όραμα nt, οπτασία || ~ary n οραματιστής, ονειροπόλος.

visit ['vɪzɪt] n επίσκεψη ♦ vt επισκέπτομαι || (stay with) κάνω βίζιτα, φιλοξενούμαι || ~or n επισκέπτης/ρια m/f || ~ors' book n βιβλίο επισκεπτών.

visor ['vaɪzə*] n προσωπίδα.

vista ['vɪstə] n θέα, άνοιγμα nt, προοπτική, άποψη.

visual ['vɪzjʊəl] a οπτικός, ορατός, πραγματικός || ~ display unit (VDU) n μονάδα οφόνης βίντεο || ~ize vt φαντάζομαι, οραματίζομαι.

vital ['vaɪtl] a ουσιώδης, κεφαλαιώδης, ζωτικός || (necessary to life) ζωτικός, ουσιώδης || ~ity n ζωτικότητα, ανθεκτικότητα, ζωή.

vitamin ['vɪtəmɪn] n βιταμίνη.

vivacious [vɪ'veɪʃəs] a ζωηρός, εύθυμος, κεφάτος.

vivid ['vɪvɪd] a ζωντανός, ζωηρός || (bright, clear) ζωηρός, λαμπρός.

vivisection [vɪvɪ'sɛkʃən] n ζωοτομία.

vocabulary [vəʊ'kæbjʊlərɪ] n λεξιλόγιο.

vocal ['vəʊkəl] a φωνητικός, ηχητικός || ~ cord n φωνητική χορδή || ~ist n αοιδός m/f, τραγουδιστής/ίστρια m/f.

vocation [vəʊ'keɪʃən] n (calling) προορισμός, κλήση || (profession) επάγγελμα nt, τέχνη.

vociferous [vəʊ'sɪfərəs] a κραυγαλέος, φωνακλάς.

vodka ['vɒdkə] n βότκα.

vogue [vəʊg] n μόδα || (popularity) δημοτικότητα.

voice [vɔɪs] n φωνή || (right of opinion) ψήφος, γνώμη || (GRAM) φωνή (του ρήματος) ♦ vt εκφράζω || with one ~ ομόφωνα.

void [vɔɪd] n κενό ♦ a (of meaning) κενός, άδειος.

volatile ['vɒlətaɪl] a άστατος, ευμετάβολος, ασταθής || (evaporating quickly) πτητικός.

volcanic [vɒl'kænɪk] a ηφαιστειώδης, εκρυκτικός.

volcano [vɒl'keɪnəʊ] n ηφαίστειο.

volition [və'lɪʃən] n: of one's own ~ με τη θέλησή μου.

volley ['vɒlɪ] n ομοβροντία || (shower) καταιγισμός, θύελλα || (TENNIS) βολλέ nt inv, κατευθείαν κτύπημα nt || ~ball n χειροσφαίρηση, βόλλεϋ-μπωλ nt inv.

volt [vəʊlt] n βόλτ || ~age n τάση, βολτάζ nt inv.

volume ['vɒljuːm] n τόμος βιβλίων || (amount) μεγάλη ποσότητα || (space) όγκος || (loudness of sound) ένταση, όγκος.

voluntarily ['vɒləntərɪlɪ] ad εκουσίως, αυθόρμητα, εθελοντικά.

voluntary ['vɒləntərɪ] a εθελοντικός, εκούσιος.

volunteer [vɒlən'tɪə*] n εθελοντής/όντρια m/f ♦ vi προσφέρομαι.

voluptuous [və'lʌptjʊəs] a φιλήδονος, ηδυπαθής.

vomit ['vɒmɪt] n εμετός, ξέρασμα nt ♦ vti κάνω εμετό, ξερνώ.

vote [vəʊt] n ψηφοφορία, ψήφος || (right) δικαίωμα nt ψήφου || (result) αποτέλεσμα nt ψηφοφορίας ♦ vt ψηφίζω, ♦ vi ψηφίζω || ~r n ψηφοφόρος m/f, εκλογέας.

voting ['vəʊtɪŋ] n ψηφοφορία.

vouch [vaʊtʃ] : to ~ for vt υποστηρίζω, εγγυώμαι για.

voucher ['vaʊtʃə*] n απόδειξη πληρωμής, δικαιολογητικό.

vow [vaʊ] n όρκος, τάξιμο, τάμα nt ♦ vt ορκίζομαι, διακηρύττω.

vowel ['vaʊəl] n φωνήεν nt.

voyage ['vɔɪɪdʒ] n ταξίδι.

vulgar ['vʌlgə*] a χυδαίος, πρόστυχος, άξεστος || (of common people) κοινός, λαϊκός || ~ity n χυδαιότητα, προστυχιά.

vulnerable ['vʌlnərəbl] a τρωτός, εύτρωτος, ευπρόσβλητος.

vulture ['vʌltʃə*] n γύπας, όρνιο.

W

wad [wɒd] n (bundle) δέσμη, μάτσο.

wade [weɪd] vi βαδίζω στο νερό.

wafer ['weɪfə*] n λεπτό μπισκότο.

waffle ['wɒfl] n (food) είδος nt τηγανίτα || (col: empty talk) φλυαρία ♦ vi (col) φλυαρώ.

waft [wɑ:ft] vti μεταφέρω, σκορπίζω.

wag [wæg] vti κινώ, κουνώ, κινούμαι.

wage [weɪdʒ] n ημερομίσθιο, μισθός, αμοιβή, μεροκάματο ♦ vt διεξάγω, διενεργώ || ~s npl μισθός || ~ **earner** n μισθωτός || ~ **freeze** n παγίωση μισθών.

wager ['weɪdʒə*] n στοίχημα nt.

waggle ['wægl] vti (tail) κουνώ, ταλαντεύομαι.

wag(g)on ['wægən] n (road, rail) άμαξα, βαγόνι.

wail [weɪl] n θρήνος, ολοφυρμός ♦ vi θρηνώ, κλαίω, ολοφύρομαι.

waist [weɪst] n μέση, ζώνη || ~**coat** n γιλέκο || ~**line** n μέση.

wait [weɪt] n αναμονή, στάση ♦ vi περιμένω, αναμένω, σερβίρω || **to ~ for** vt περιμένω, αναμένω, καρτερώ || ~**er** n σερβιτόρος, γκαρσόνι || ~**ing room** n αίθουσα αναμονής, προθάλαμος || ~**ress** n σερβιτόρα.

wake [weɪk] (irreg v) vt ξυπνώ ♦ vi αγρυπνώ, είμαι άυπνος ♦ n ξενύχτι νεκρού || ~**n** vt αφυπνίζω, ξυπνώ.

Wales [weɪlz] n Ουαλία.

walk [wɔ:k] n περπάτημα nt, βόλτα, περίπατος || (way of walking) βάδισμα nt, περπατησιά || (path, route) περίπατος, δρόμος, πεζοδρόμιο || (walk of life) επάγγελμα nt ♦ vi περπατώ, βαδίζω || ~**er** n πεζοπόρος/α m/f, περπατητής m/f || ~**ie-talkie** n φορητός ασύρματος || ~**ing** n πεζοπορία, περπάτημα nt ♦ attr a (holiday) με τα πόδια || ~**ing shoes** παπούτσια ntpl πεζοπορίας || ~**ing stick** n μπαστούνι || ~**out** n (of workers) απεργία || ~**over** n (col) εύκολη νίκη, εύκολη δουλειά.

wall [wɔ:l] n (of house) τοίχος || (of city) τείχος nt.

wallet ['wɒlɪt] n πορτοφόλι.

wallop ['wɒləp] n δυνατό χτύπημα.

wallow ['wɒləʊ] vi (+ in) κυλιέμαι (σε), πλέω (σε) || (in money) κολυμπώ στο χρήμα.

wallpaper ['wɔ:lpeɪpə*] n τοιχόχαρτο, χαρτί ταπετσαρίας.

walnut ['wɔ:lnʌt] n καρύδι || (tree) καρυδιά.

walrus ['wɔ:lrəs] n θαλάσσιος ίππος.

waltz [wɔ:lts] n βαλς nt inv ♦ vi χορεύω βαλς.

wand [wɒnd] n ράβδος f, ραβδί.

wander ['wɒndə*] vi περιπλανώμαι, περιφέρομαι, τριγυρίζω || ~**ing** a πλανόδιος, περιπλανώμενος.

want [wɒnt] vt θέλω, επιθυμώ || (need)

χρειάζομαι, έχω ανάγκη ♦ n: **for ~ of** ελλείψει || ~**s** npl (needs) ανάγκες fpl.

wanton ['wɒntən] a ακόλαστος, λάγνος.

war [wɔ:*] n πόλεμος.

ward [wɔ:d] n (division) περιφέρεια, συνοικία || (hospital) θάλαμος ♦ vt: **to ~ off** αποκρούω, αποφεύγω.

warden ['wɔ:dn] n διευθυντής, φύλακας.

warder ['wɔ:də*] n φύλακας, δεσμοφύλακας.

wardrobe ['wɔ:drəʊb] n ντουλάπα || (clothing) γκαρνταρόμπα, τα ρούχα ntpl.

warehouse ['wɛəhaʊs] n αποθήκη.

wares [wɛəz] npl εμπορεύματα ntpl.

warfare ['wɔ:fɛə*] n πόλεμος.

warhead ['wɔ:hɛd] n κώνος βλήματος.

warily ['wɛərɪlɪ] ad προσεκτικά, επιφυλακτικά.

warlike ['wɔ:laɪk] a πολεμικός, πολεμοχαρής, φιλοπόλεμος.

warm [wɔ:m] a θερμός || (fire) ζεστός || (welcome) θερμός, ζωηρός || **to ~ up** vti ζεσταίνω, ζωηρεύω, ενθουσιάζομαι || ~**-hearted** a με ζεστή καρδιά, συμπονετικός || ~**ly** ad θερμά, ενθουσιωδώς || ~**th** n θερμότητα, ζεστασιά, ενθουσιασμός.

warn [wɔ:n] vt προειδοποιώ || ~**ing** n προειδοποίηση || (caution) ειδοποίηση.

warp [wɔ:p] vt σκεβρώνω ♦ n παραμόρφωση || (in meaning) στημώνι.

warrant ['wɒrənt] n (police) ένταλμα nt.

warranty ['wɒrəntɪ] n εξουσιοδότηση, εγγύηση.

warrior ['wɒrɪə*] n πολεμιστής.

warship ['wɔ:ʃɪp] n πολεμικό πλοίο.

wart [wɔ:t] n κρεατοελιά.

wartime ['wɔ:taɪm] n πολεμική εποχή, πολεμική περίοδος f.

wary ['wɛərɪ] a προσεκτικός, πονηρός, επιφυλακτικός.

was [wɒz, wəz] pt of **be**.

wash [wɒʃ] n πλύση, πλύσιμο || (face, hands) νίψιμο || (clothes) μπουγάδα ♦ vt πλένω ♦ vi πλένομαι || **to ~ away** vt παρασύρω, παίρνω || ~**able** a που πλένεται || ~**basin** n λεκάνη (νιπτήρα) || ~**er** n ροδέλα || (person) πλύστρα || ~**ing** n (linen etc) ρούχα ntpl για πλύσιμο, πλύση, πλύσιμο || ~**ing machine** n πλυντήριο || ~**ing powder** n σκόνη πλυσίματος || ~**ing-up** n πλύσιμο των πιάτων || ~**-out** n (col) αποτυχία, φιάσκο || ~**room** n τουαλέτα.

wasn't ['wɒznt] = **was not** || see **be**.

wasp [wɒsp] n σφήκα.

wastage ['weɪstɪdʒ] n σπατάλη.

waste [weɪst] n σπατάλη || (what is wasted) άχρηστα υλικά ntpl, σκουπίδια ntpl, απορρίμματα ntpl || (wilderness) έρημος f ♦ a άχρηστος || (land) χέρσος, ερημωμένος ♦ vt (object) σπαταλώ, καταστρέφω || (time) σπαταλώ, χάνω ♦ vi: **to ~ away** φθίνω, αδυνατίζω || ~**ful**

a σπάταλος || ~paper basket n
κάλαθος αχρήστων.

watch [wɔtʃ] n επίβλεψη, επιτήρηση ||
(vigilance) επαγρύπνηση || (guard)
φυλακή, φρουρός || (NAUT) φυλακή,
βάρδια || (timepiece) ρολόι ♦ vt
παρατηρώ, παρακολουθώ ♦ vi αγρυπνώ,
προσέχω, φρουρώ || ~dog n (fig)
επιστάτης/ρια m/f, φύλακας || ~ful a
άγρυπνος, προσεκτικός || ~maker n
ωρολογοποιός, ρολογάς || ~man
(νυκτο)φύλακας || ~ strap n λουρίδα
ρολογιού.

water ['wɔːtə*] n νερό ♦ vt ποτίζω ||
(wet) βρέχω, καταβρέχω || (soak)
διαβρέχω || to ~ down vt απαλύνω
(έκφραση), εξασθενίζω || ~ closet n
αποχωρητήριο, απόπατος, μέρος nt ||
~colour, (US) ~color n πίνακας με
νερομπογιά, ακουαρέλα || (paint)
υδρόχρωμα nt, νερομπογιά || ~cress n
νεροκάρδαμο || ~fall n καταρράκτης ||
~ hole n νερόλακκος || ~ing can n
ποτιστήρι || ~ lily n νούφαρο || ~line n
ίσαλος (γραμμή) || ~logged a
πλημμυρισμένος, διάβροχος,
μουσκεμένος || ~melon n καρπούζι ||
~proof a αδιάβροχος, υδατοστεγής ||
~shed n γραμμή διαχωρισμού υδάτων ||
~-skiing n θαλάσσιο σκί || ~tight a
υδατοστεγής, στεγανός, αδιάβροχος ||
~works npl μηχανοστάσιο υδρεύσεως
|| ~y a (colour) ξεπλυμένος, άτονος.

watt [wɔt] n βάτ(τ) nt inv.

wave [weiv] n κύμα nt || (of hand)
κούνημα nt του χεριού || (RAD) κύμα nt ||
(in hair) κυμάτωση, κατσάρωμα nt ♦ vt
(hand) χαιρετώ με το χέρι, κουνώ το χέρι
|| (shape in curves) κατσαρώνω ♦ vi (flag)
κυματίζω, ανεμίζω || ~length n μήκος
nt, κύματος.

waver ['weivə*] vi ταλαντεύομαι,
κυμαίνομαι || (weaken) κλονίζομαι.

wavy ['weivi] a κυματώδης, κυματιστός.

wax [wæks] n κερί ♦ vt (floors) κερώνω,
παρκετάρω ♦ vi (moon) μεγαλώνω,
γίνομαι.

way [wei] n οδός f, δρόμος || (manner)
τρόπος || (direction) κατεύθυνση, δρόμος
|| (habit) τρόπος, συνήθεια, έθιμο || in the
~ φράζω, εμποδίζω, κόβω (το δρόμο) ||
by the ~ με την ευκαιρία || '~ in'
'είσοδος' || '~ out' 'έξοδος'.

waylay ['wei'lei] vt ενεδρεύω,
καιροφυλακτώ.

wayward ['weiwəd] a δύστροπος,
πεισματάρης.

W.C. ['dʌbljuːsiː] n τουαλέτα.

we [wiː] pl pron εμείς.

weak [wiːk] a αδύνατος, ασθενικός ||
(not powerful) ανίσχυρος || (diluted)
αδύνατος, ελαφρός || ~en vti
εξασθενίζω, αδυνατίζω, εξασθενώ ||
~ling n ασθενικό ανθρωπος, ασθενικό
πλάσμα nt || ~ness n αδυναμία || (fault)
ελάττωμα nt || (fondness) προτίμηση,
αδυναμία.

wealth [wɛlθ] n πλούτος || (abundance)
αφθονία || (things having value) περιουσία
|| ~y a πλούσιος.

wean [wiːn] vt απογαλακτίζω, αποκόβω.

weapon ['wɛpən] n όπλο.

wear [wɛə*] (irreg v) n ρούχα ntpl,
ρουχισμός, φόρεμα nt || (use) χρήση ||
(decay) φθορά ♦ vt φέρω, φορώ || (show)
δείχνω, κρατιέμαι || (use) φθείρω, λυώνω
♦ vi (last long) αντέχω, διατηρούμαι || ~
and tear φθορά, χρήσεως || to ~ away
vti φθείρω, φθείρομαι, τρώγω, τρίβω || to
~ down vt φθείρω, τρώγω || to ~ off vi
εξαφανίζω, περνώ || to ~ out vt φθείρω,
τρίβω, λυώνω || ~er n φορών.

weariness ['wiərinis] n κόπωση,
κούρασιν.

weary ['wiəri] a κουρασμένος,
αποκαμωμένος || (tiring) κουραστικός,
πληκτικός, ανιαρός ♦ vti κουράζω,
κουράζομαι.

weasel ['wiːzl] n νυφίτσα, κουνάβι.

weather ['wɛðə*] n καιρός ♦ vt
αντιμετωπίζω || (season) εκθέτω στον
καιρό || ~-beaten a ανεμοδαρμένος,
ηλιοκαμμένος, μαυρισμένος || ~cock n
ανεμοδείκτης || ~forecast n πρόβλεψη
καιρού.

weave [wiːv] (irreg v) vt υφαίνω, πλέκω,
συνθέτω || ~r n υφαντής/άντρια m/f.

weaving ['wiːviŋ] n υφανση, πλέξιμο.

web [wɛb] n ύφασμα nt, μεμβράνη || (of
spider) ιστός αράχνης || ~bed a
μεμβρανώδης || ~bing n ύφασμα nt
λωρίδων || (for reinforcement) ενισχυτική
ταινία.

wed [wɛd] vt νυμφεύω, νυμφεύομαι,
παντρεύομαι.

we'd [wiːd] = we had, we would ||
see have, would.

wedding ['wɛdiŋ] n γάμος, παντρειά ||
~ day n μέρα των γάμων, επέτειος f των
γάμων || ~ present n γαμήλιο δώρο || ~
ring n αρραβώνας, βέρα.

wedge [wɛdʒ] n σφήνα || vt ενσφηνώνω,
χώνω, μπήγω || (pack tightly) σφηνώνω,
στριμώγνω.

Wednesday ['wɛnzdi] n Τετάρτη.

wee [wiː] a (Scottish col) μικρούλης,
λιγάκι, τόσος δα.

weed [wiːd] n ζιζάνιο, αγριόχορτο ♦ vt
ξεχορταριάζω, σκαλίζω, βγάζω,
καθαρίζω || ~killer n ζιζανιοκτόνο.

week [wiːk] n βδομάδα || ~day n
καθημερινή || ~end n Σαββατοκύριακο
|| ~ly ad εβδομαδιαίως ♦ a
εβδομαδιαίος.

weep [wiːp] (irreg v) vi κλαίω, χύνω
δάκρυα, δακρύζω.

weigh [wei] vt σταθμίζω, ζυγίζω || (have
weight) ζυγίζω ♦ vi (be important) ζυγίζω ||
to ~ down vt (υπερ)φορτώνω,
βαραίνω, πιέζω || to ~ up vt εκτιμώ,
ζυγίζω || ~bridge n γεφυροπλάστιγγα.

weight [weit] n βαρύτητα || (something
used on scales) σταθμό, μέτρο, ζύγι || (load)
βάρος nt, φορτίο || (importance) κύρος nt,

επιρροή, αξία || ~ **lifting** n άρση βαρών || ~γ a βαρύς.

weir [wɪə*] n φράγμα nt ποταμού.

weird [wɪəd] a υπερφυσικός, παράξενος.

welcome ['wɛlkəm] n υποδοχή || (reception) δεξίωση ♦ vt καλωσορίζω, (υπο) δέχομαι.

welcoming ['wɛlkəmɪŋ] a καλής υποδοχής.

weld [wɛld] n συγκόλληση, κόλληση ♦ vt (συγ)κολλώ, ενώνω || ~er n συγκολλητής.

welfare ['wɛlfɛə*] n ευμέρεια, κοινωνική πρόνοια || ~ **state** n κράτος nt κοινωνικής πρόνοιας.

well [wɛl] n πηγάδι, πηγή, πετρελαιοπηγή ♦ ad καλά || (to considerable extent) αρκετά, σχεδόν || (thoroughly) καλά, τελείως ♦ a υγιής, καλά || (satisfactory) καλός, καλά || interj (beginning conversation) λοιπόν, ίσως, καλά || (surprise) αδύνατο, μπά || **as** ~ (also) επίσης, ομοίως.

we'll [wi:l] = **we will, we shall** || see **will, shall.**

well-behaved ['wɛlbɪ'heɪvd] a φρόνιμος, πειθαρχημένος.

well-being ['wɛlbi:ɪŋ] n ευμέρεια.

well-earned ['wɛl'ɜːnd] a (rest) δίκαιος, καλοκερδισμένος.

wellingtons ['wɛlɪŋtənz] npl ψηλές μπότες fpl.

well-known ['wɛl'nəʊn] a (person) πασίγνωστος, φημισμένος.

well-meaning ['wɛl'mi:nɪŋ] a καλοπροαίρετος.

well-off ['wɛl'ɒf] a εύπορος, πλούσιος.

well-read ['wɛl'rɛd] a μορφωμένος, πολυδιαβασμένος.

well-to-do ['wɛltə'du:] a εύπορος.

well-wisher ['wɛlwɪʃə*] n καλοθελητής/ήτρα m/f.

Welsh [wɛlʃ] a ουαλικός ♦ n (LING) Ουαλικά || ~**man** n Ουαλαός.

went [wɛnt] pt of **go.**

wept [wɛpt] pt, pp of **weep.**

were [wɜː*] pt, pl of **be.**

we're [wɪə*] = **we are** || see **be.**

weren't ['wɜːnt] = **were not** || see **be.**

west [wɛst] n δύση || (country) δύση, δυτικά ♦ a δυτικός ♦ ad δυτικά, προς δυσμάς || the **W**~ n n Δύση || ~**erly** a δυτικός (άνεμος) || ~**ern** a δυτικός ♦ n (CINE) ταινία με καουμπόης || **W**~ **Indies** npl Οι Αντίλλες || ~**ward(s)** ad προς τα δυτικά.

wet [wɛt] a υγρός, βρε(γ)μένος, μουσκεμένος || (rainy) βροχερός || '~ paint' 'προσοχή χρώμα' || ~ **blanket** n (fig) άνθρωπος που χαλάει το κέφι, κρύος.

we've [wi:v] = **we have** || see **have.**

whack [wæk] vt κτυπώ, δέρνω στα ψαχνά.

whale [weɪl] n φάλαινα.

wharf [wɔːf] n αποβάθρα, προκυμαία.

what [wɒt] a (relative) ότι, όσος || (quantity) όσος, πόσος || (interrogative) τι, πώς; ποιος || interj τι, πώς; || ~**ever** a όποιος...και, ό τι... και, οποιοσδήποτε.

wheat [wi:t] n σιτάρι, στάρι.

wheel [wi:l] n τροχός, ρόδα ♦ vt (περι)στρέφω, σπρώχνω ♦ vi περιστρέφομαι, γυρίζω γύρω-γύρω || ~**barrow** n χειράμαξα || ~**chair** n αναπηρική καρέκλα.

wheeze [wi:z] vi αναπνέω δύσκολα, ασθμαίνω, σφυρίζω.

when [wɛn] ad πότε || (relative) όταν || cj όταν, που || ~**ever** ad οποτεδήποτε.

where [wɛə*] ad πού; || (relative) (εκεί) που, όπου || ~**abouts** ad πού; || (λοιπόν) || πού περίπου; ♦ n θέση, διαμονή, κατατόπια ntpl || ~**as** cj εφόσον, ενώ.

wherever [wɛə*'ɛvə*] ad οπουδήποτε.

whet [wɛt] vt (appetite) διεγείρω, ανοίγω (την όρεξη).

whether ['wɛðə*] cj εάν, αν, είτε.

which [wɪtʃ] a ποιος ♦ pron (interrogative) ποιο || (relative) ο' οποίος, στο οποίο, του οποίου || ~**ever** a όποιος, απ' όπου ♦ pron οποσδήποτε.

whiff [wɪf] n πνοή, φύσημα nt, ρουφηξιά.

while [waɪl] n χρονική περίοδος f, καιρός, χρόνος || cj ενώ.

whim [wɪm] n παραξενιά, ιδιοτροπία, καπρίτσιο.

whimper ['wɪmpə*] vi κλαυθμηρίζω, βογγώ.

whimsical ['wɪmzɪkəl] a ιδιότροπος, παράξενος.

whine [waɪn] vi κλαυθμηρίζω, μεμψιμοιρώ.

whip [wɪp] n μαστίγιο, καμτσίκι || (PARL) κοινοβουλευτικός ηγέτης ♦ vt μαστιγώνω, δέρνω, κτυπώ || (snatch) κινώ απότομα, αρπάζω || ~-**round** n έρανος, συνεισφορά.

whirl [wɜːl] n στροβιλισμός, στριφογύρισμα nt, γύρισμα nt ♦ vti στροβιλίζω, στριφογυρίζω, περιστρέφομαι || ~**pool** n δίνη, ρουφήχτρα || ~**wind** n ανεμοστρόβιλος.

whirr [wɜː*] vi βουίζω, αβουρίζω.

whisk [wɪsk] n (for eggs) χτυπητήρι ♦ vt (cream etc) κτυπώ, ανακατεύω.

whisker ['wɪskə*] n φαβορίτα || (of cat) μουστάκι.

whisk(e)y ['wɪskɪ] n ουίσκυ.

whisper ['wɪspə*] n ψίθυρος, θρόισμα nt, ψιθύρισμα ♦ vi ψιθυρίζω, μουρμουρίζω ♦ vt (secretly) ψιθυρίζω, σφυρίζω.

whist [wɪst] n ουίστ nt inv.

whistle ['wɪsl] n σφύριγμα nt || (instrument) σφυρίχτρα ♦ vi σφυρίζω.

white [waɪt] n λευκό, άσπρο || (of egg, eye) λεύκωμα nt, ασπράδι ♦ a λευκός, άσπρος || (with fear) άσπρος, χλωμός || ~-**collar worker** n υπάλληλος m/f σε γραφείο || ~ **lie** n αθώο ψέμα nt || ~**wash** n (paint) ασβεστόνερο, ασβεστόχρωμα *nt* ♦ *vt* ασβεστώνω, ασπρίζω || *(fig)* αποκαθιστώ, δικαιολογώ.

Whitsun ['wɪtsn] *n (also Whit Sunday)* Πεντηκοστή.

whittle ['wɪtl] *vt:* to ~ **away** *or* **down** ελαττώνω, περιορίζω.

whizz [wɪz] *vi* σφυρίζω, περνώ γρήγορα || ~ **kid** *n (col)* σπουδαίο παιδί.

who [hu:] *pron* ποιος || *(relative)* όποιος, που || ~**ever** *pron* οποιοσδήποτε, οιοσδήποτε.

WHO *n (abbr of World Health Organization)* Παγκόσμιος Οργανισμός Υγείας (WHO).

whole [həʊl] *a (complete)* ολόκληρος, όλος, πλήρης || *(uninjured)* αβλαβής, σώος ♦ *n* σύνολο || *(not broken)* σύνολο, ακέραιο || ~**hearted** *a* ολόψυχος || ~**sale** *n* χοντρική πώληση, χοντρεμπόριο || *attr a (trade)* χοντρικός || *(destruction)* ολοκληρωτικός || ~**saler** *n* χοντρέμπορος, κατάστημα *nt* χοντρικής πωλήσεως || ~**some** *a* υγιεινός, υγιής.

wholly ['həʊlɪ] *ad* πλήρως, τελείως.

whom [hu:m] *pron (object)* ποιον.

whooping cough ['hu:pɪŋkɒf] *n* κοκκύτης.

whore ['hɔ:*] *n* πόρνη, πουτάνα.

whose [hu:z] *pron* ποιου, τίνος ποιανού || *(of whom)* του οποίου.

why [waɪ] *ad* γιατί || *(relative)* που, γιατί || *interj* μπα || ε.

wick [wɪk] *n* φυτίλι.

wicked ['wɪkɪd] *a* κακός, διεστραμμένος, κακόηθης.

wicker ['wɪkə*] *n* λυγαριά.

wicket ['wɪkɪt] *n (cricket)* φράκτης, στυλίσκοι *mpl* του κρίκετ.

wide [waɪd] *a* ευρύς, πλατύς, φαρδύς, εκτενής || *(mouth)* ορθάνοικτος || *(in firing)* έξω *(από το στόχο)* άστοχος ♦ *ad (opening)* διάπλατα || ~-**angle lens** *n* ευρυγώνιος φακός || ~-**awake** *a* εντελώς ξύπνιος || ~**ly** *ad* ευρύτατα, πλατειά || ~**n** *vt (road)* ευρύνω, πλαταίνω, διευρύνω || ~ **open** *a (lit)* ορθάνοικτος, ακάλυπτος || ~**spread** *a* εκτεταμένος || *(rumour etc)* διαδεδομένος, γενικός.

widow ['wɪdəʊ] *n* χήρα || ~**ed** *a* χηρεύσας, χηρεύσασα || ~**er** *n* χήρος.

width [wɪdθ] *n* εύρος *nt*, πλάτος *nt*, φάρδος *nt*.

wield [wi:ld] *vt* χειρίζομαι, ελέγχω, εξασκώ.

wife [waɪf] *n* η σύζυγος, γυναίκα.

wig [wɪg] *n* περούκα.

wiggle ['wɪgl] *vti* κινώ νευρικά, κουνώ, κουνιέμαι.

wild [waɪld] *a* άγριος || *(not cultivated)* σε άγρια κατάσταση || *(excited)* αχαλίνωτος, ξετρελαμένος, τρελός || ~**erness** ['wɪldənɪs] *n* έρημος, αγριότοπος || ~-**goose chase** *n* μάταιη αναζήτηση, άσκοπη κυνήγι || ~**life** *n* άγρια ζώα *ntpl* || ~**ly** *ad* άγρια, σαν τρελός.

wilful ['wɪlful] *a* εσκεμμένος, εκ

προμελέτης || *(obstinate)* ξεροκέφαλος, πεισματάρης.

will [wɪl] *auxiliary v:* **he** ~ **come** θα έρθει || **I** ~ **do it!** θα το κάνω! ♦ *n* βούληση, θέληση || *(purpose)* απόφαση, βούληση, θέλημα *nt* || *(inheritance)* διαθήκη ♦ *vt* θέλω, αποφασίζω || ~**ing** *a* πρόθυμος.

willow ['wɪləʊ] *n* ιτιά.

will power ['wɪlpaʊə*] *n* θέληση, αυτοέλεγχος.

wilt [wɪlt] *vi* μαραίνομαι.

wily ['waɪlɪ] *a* πανούργος.

win [wɪn] *(irreg v) n* νίκη, επιτυχία ♦ *vt* νικώ, κερδίζω ♦ *vi* επιτυγχάνω || to ~ **over** *vt* κατακτώ, αποκτώ.

wince [wɪns] *n* σύσπαση, τρεμούλιασμα *nt* ♦ *vi* μορφάζω, σφίγγομαι.

winch [wɪntʃ] *n* βαρούλκο, βίντσι.

wind [waɪnd] *(irreg v) vt (wrap)* τυλίγω || *(tighten)* σφίγγω, κουρδίζω ♦ *vi* στρέφω, στρέφομαι, ελίσσομαι, τυλίγομαι || to ~ **up** *vt (clock)* κουρδίζω || *(debate)* κλείνω, τερματίζω.

wind [wɪnd] *n* άνεμος, αέρας || *(MED)* αέρια *ntpl*, τυμπανισμός || ~**fall** *n (good luck)* κελεπούρι.

winding ['waɪndɪŋ] *a (road)* ελισσόμενος, φιδίσιος, με κορδέλες, στριφτός.

wind instrument ['wɪndɪnstrumənt] *n (MUS)* πνευστό *(όργανο)*.

windmill ['wɪndmɪl] *n* ανεμόμυλος.

window ['wɪndəʊ] *n* παράθυρο, βιτρίνα || *(COMPUT)* παράθυρο || ~ **box** *n* κιβώτιο λουλουδιών || ~ **cleaner** *n (man)* καθαριστής παραθύρων || ~-**frame** *n* πλαίσιο παραθύρου, κούφωμα *nt* || ~ **ledge** *n* περβάζι παραθύρου || ~-**pane** *n* τζάμι || ~-**sill** *n* περβάζι παραθύρου.

windpipe ['wɪndpaɪp] *n* τραχεία, λαρύγγι.

windscreen ['wɪndskri:n], *(US)* **windshield** ['wɪndʃi:ld] *n* παρμπρίζ *nt inv*|| ~ **wiper** *n* υαλοκαθαριστήρας.

windswept ['wɪndswɛpt] *a* ανεμοδαρμένος.

windy ['wɪndɪ] *a* ανεμώδης, εκτεθειμένος στους ανέμους.

wine [waɪn] *n* οίνος, κρασί || ~ **cellar** *n* κάβα || ~-**glass** *n* ποτήρι του κρασιού || ~ **list** *n* κατάλογος κρασιών || ~ **merchant** *n* κρασέμπορος || ~ **tasting** *n* δοκιμή κρασιών || ~ **waiter** *n* σερβιτόρος για τα κρασιά.

wing [wɪŋ] *n (of bird, plane)* φτερούγα, φτερό || *(of building)* πτέρυγα *(κτιρίου)* || *(MIL* πτέρυγα || ~**s** *npl (THEAT)* παρασκήνια *ntpl*.

wink [wɪŋk] *n* ανοιγοκλείσιμο του ματιού, νεύμα *nt* ♦ *vi* κλείνω το μάτι, νεύω.

winner ['wɪnə*] *n* νικητής/ήτρια *m/f*.

winning ['wɪnɪŋ] *a (team)* κερδίζων, νικήτρια *(ομάδα)* || *(goal)* κερδίζων γκολ || ~**s** *npl* κέρδη *ntpl* || ~ **post** *n* τέρμα *nt*.

winter ['wɪntə*] *n* χειμώνας ♦ *attr a*

(clothes) χειμωνιάτικα ♦ *vi* περνώ το χειμώνα (σε) || ~ **sports** *npl* χειμωνιάτικα σπόρ *nt inv.*

wintry ['wintri] *a* χειμωνιάτικος, ψυχρός.

wipe [waip] *n* σκούπισμα *nt*, στέγνωμα *nt*, σφούγγισμα *nt* ♦ *vt* σκουπίζω, στεγνώνω, σφουγγίζω || to ~ out *vt* *(debt)* σβήνω, εξοφλώ || *(destroy)* εξολοθρεύω, σαρώνω.

wire ['waiə*] *n* σύρμα *nt* || *(cable)* τηλεγράφημα *nt* ♦ *vt* ενώνω με σύρμα, τοποθετώ τα καλώδια.

wireless ['waiəlis] *n* ασύρματος || *(radio)* ραδιόφωνο.

wiry ['waiəri] *a* σαν σύρμα, νευρώδης, δυνατός.

wisdom ['wizdəm] *n* σοφία, φρόνηση || *(good judgment)* σωφροσύνη || *(prudence)* φρονιμάδα, γνώση || ~ **tooth** *n* φρονιμίτης.

wise [waiz] *a* σοφός, φρόνιμος, συνετός || -**wise** *suffix* κατά κάποιο τρόπο, σαν || ~**crack** *n* ευφυολόγημα *nt*, καλαμπούρι.

wish [wiʃ] *n (desire)* επιθυμία, ευχή ♦ *vt (desire)* εύχομαι, επιθυμώ || **with best** ~**es** με τις καλύτερες ευχές || to ~ **good-bye** εύχομαι καλό ταξίδι || to ~ **to do** επιθυμώ, θέλω να || ~**ful thinking** *n* ευσεβείς πόθοι *mpl.*

wisp [wisp] *n (of hair)* τσουλούφι, τολύπη.

wistful ['wistful] *a* συλλογισμένος, πικραμένος.

wit [wit] *n (sense)* αντίληψη, κατανόηση, νους *m*, μυαλό || *(cleverness)* πνεύμα *nt*, ευφυΐα || *(person)* πνευματώδης άνθρωπος, ευφυής, σπίρτο || ~**s** *npl* μυαλό, εξυπνάδα.

witch [witʃ] *n* μάγισσα || ~**craft** *n* μαγεία.

with [wið, wɪθ] *prep* μετά, μαζί, με || *(by means of)* με, από || *(concerning)* μαζί με, μετά || *(notwithstanding)* παρά, παρ όλο.

withdraw [wɪð'drɔ:] *vt* αποσύρω, σύρω, τραβώ, σέρνω ♦ *vi* αποσύρομαι, αποτραβιέμαι, τραβιέμαι || ~**al** *n* αποχώρηση, ανάκληση.

wither ['wiðə*] *vi* μαραίνομαι, ξεραίνομαι || ~**ed** *a* μαραμένος.

withhold [wɪθ'həʊld] *vt* αναστέλλω, κατακρατώ.

within [wɪð'ɪn] *prep* εντός, μέσα σε.

without [wɪð'aut] *prep* εκτός, χωρίς, δίχως.

withstand [wɪθ'stænd] *vt* αντιστέκομαι σε, αντέχω σε.

witness ['witnis] *n* μαρτυρία || *(LAW)* μάρτυρας ♦ *vt (see)* παρίσταμαι μάρτυς, βλέπω || *(sign documents)* επικυρώνω, βεβαιώνω, υπογράφω || ~ **box**, *(US)* ~ **stand** *n* θέση του εξεταζόμενου μάρτυρα.

witticism ['witisizəm] *n* ευφυολογία, ευφυολόγημα *nt*, εξυπνάδα, αστείο.

wittily ['witili] *ad* πνευματωδώς, έξυπνα, σπιρτόζικα.

witty ['witi] *a* πνευματώδης, σπιρτόζικος, έξυπνος.

wives [waivz] *npl of* **wife.**

wizard ['wizəd] *n* μάγος.

wk *abbr of* **week.**

wobble ['wɒbl] *vi* παραπατώ, ταλαντεύομαι, τρέμω.

woe [wəʊ] *n* συμφορά, δυστυχία, λύπη, θλίψη.

woke [wəʊk] *pt, pp of* **wake.**

wolf [wulf] *n* λύκος.

wolves [wulvz] *npl of* **wolf.**

woman ['wumən] *n* γυναίκα ♦ *attr a (doctor)* (η) γιατρός.

womb [wu:m] *n* μήτρα.

women ['wimin] *npl of* **woman.**

won [wʌn] *pt, pp of* **win.**

wonder ['wʌndə*] *n* θαύμα *nt* || *(feeling)* θαυμασμός, κατάπληξη ♦ *vi (want to know)* απορώ, διερωτώμαι || ~**ful** *a* θαυμάσιος, εκπληκτικός.

won't [wəʊnt] = **will not** || *see* **will.**

wood [wud] *n* ξύλο, ξυλεία || *(forest)* δάσος *nt*, δρυμός, άλσος *nt* || ~ **carving** *n* ξυλογλυπτική || ~**en** *a* ξύλινος || *(stiff)* αδέξιος, άκαμπτος || ~**pecker** *n* δρυοκολάπτης || ~**wind** *n* ξύλινα πνευστά *ntpl* ~**work** *n* ξυλουργική || ~**worm** *n* σκουλήκι του ξύλου.

wool [wul] *n* μαλλί || *(material)* μάλλινο ύφασμα *nt* || ~**len**, *(US)* ~**en** *a* μάλλινος || *(industry)* υφαντουργική || ~**ly**, *(US)* ~**y** *a* σαν μαλλί, σκεπασμένος με μαλλί.

word [wɜːd] *n* λέξη || *(talk, speech)* λόγος, παρατήρηση || *(news)* είδηση, ειδοποίηση, μήνυμα *nt*, νέο || *(promise)* λόγος ♦ *vt* διατυπώνω, εκφράζω με λέξεις || ~**ing** *n* διατύπωση, φρασεολογία || ~ **processing** *n* επεξεργασία κειμένου || ~ **processor** *n* επεξεργαστής κειμένου.

wore [wɔː*] *pt of* **wear.**

work [wɜːk] *n* έργο || *(task)* εργασία, δουλειά, απασχόληση || *(ART, LITER)* έργο, προϊόν εργασίας ♦ *vi* εργάζομαι, δουλεύω || *(have occupation)* εργάζομαι, ασχολούμαι με, δουλεύω || *(cause to act)* λειτουργώ, επιτυγχάνω || ~**s** *n (factory)* εργοστάσιο || to ~ **on** *vt* συνεχίζω || *(influence)* επηρεάζω || to ~ **out** *vi (sum)* υπολογίζομαι, ανέρχομαι σε ♦ *vt (problem)* λύνω, αναπτύσσω || *(plan)* επεξεργάζομαι || to ~ **up to** *vt* ανέρχομαι || to **get** ~**ed up** εξάπτομαι, θυμώνω || ~**able** *a* επεξεργάσιμος, εκμεταλλεύσιμος, εφαρμόσιμος || ~**er** *n* εργάτης/ρια *m/f*, εργαζόμενος/η *m/f* || ~**ing class** *n* εργατική τάξη, εργαζόμενοι *mpl* || ~**ing-class** *a* της εργατικής τάξη || ~**ing man** *n* εργάτης, δουλευτής || ~**man** *n* εργάτης, τεχνίτης || ~**manship** *n* εκτέλεση, δούλεμα *nt*, επεξεργασία || ~**shop** *n* εργαστήριο.

world [wɜːld] *n* σύμπαν *nt*, υφήλιος *f*, κόσμος || *(the earth)* γη, κόσμος || *(mankind)* κόσμος, ανθρωπότητα || *(society)* κοινωνία, κόσμος || *(sphere)*

κόσμος || attr a (champion) παγκόσμιος, διεθνής || out of this ~ απίστευτος, περίφημος || ~-famous a παγκοσμίου φήμης || ~ly a εγκόσμιος, του κόσμου || ~-wide a παγκόσμιος, διεθνής.
worm [wɜːm] n σκουλήκι.
worn [wɔːn] pp of **wear** || a εφθαρμένος, φορεμένος || ~-out a (object) τριμμένος, φαγωμένος || (person) εξαντλημένος, τσακισμένος.
worried ['wʌrɪd] a στενοχωρημένος, ανήσυχος.
worry ['wʌrɪ] n ανησυχία, σκοτούρα ♦ vt βασανίζω, στενοχωρώ ♦ vi ανησυχώ, στενοχωρούμαι || ~ing a ενοχλητικός, βασανιστικός.
worse [wɜːs] a comp of **bad** ♦ ad comp of **badly** ♦ n κάτι χειρότερο, πιο κακό || ~n vt επιδεινώνω, χειροτερεύω ♦ vi επιδεινούμαι.
worship ['wɜːʃɪp] n λατρεία, προσκύνηση || (religious service) λατρεία, εκκλησίασμα nt || (title) n αυτού εντιμότης ♦ vt λατρεύω || (adore) αγαπώ, λατρεύω.
worst [wɜːst] a sup of **bad** ♦ ad sup of **badly** ♦ n ο χειρότερος, ο πιό κακός.
worsted ['wustid] n υφάσματα πενιέ, μαλλί πενιέ.
worth [wɜːθ] n αξία ♦ a άξιος || ~less a χωρίς αξία || (useless) άχρηστος || ~while a αξιόλογος.
worthy ['wɜːðɪ] a άξιος || (+ of) αντάξιος.
would [wud] auxiliary v: **she** ~ **come** ερχόταν || **if you asked he** ~ **come** άν παρακαλούσες θα 'ρχότανε || ~ **you like a drink?** θέλεις κανένα ποτό; || ~- **be** a δήθεν || ~**n't** = ~ **not**.
wound [waund] pt, pp of **wind** ♦ [wuːnd] n τραύμα nt, πληγή ♦ vt τραυματίζω, πληγώνω.
wove [wəuv] pt of **weave** || ~n pp of **weave**.
wpm n (abbr of words per minute) λεξ./λεπ., λ.α.λ. (λέξεις ανά λεπτό).
wrangle ['ræŋgl] n καυγάς, τσακωμός, λογομαχία ♦ vi καυγαδίζω, λογομαχώ, τσακώνομαι.
wrap [ræp] n σκέπασμα nt, σάλι ♦ vt (also: ~ **up**) τυλίγω, περιβάλλω, καλύπτω || ~**per** n περιτύλιγμα nt, κάλυμμα nt || (gown) ρόμπα || ~**ping paper** n χαρτί περιτυλίγματος.
wreath [riːθ] n στεφάνι.
wreck [rɛk] n ερείπιο, καταστροφή || (NAUT) ναυάγιο || (ruin) καταστροφή ♦ vt καταστρέφω || (NAUT) προκαλώ ναυάγιο || ~**age** n ναυάγιο, συντρίμματα ntpl.
wren [rɛn] n τρόχιλος, τρυποκαρύδα.
wrench [rɛntʃ] n (γαλλικό) κλειδί || (violent twist) βίαιη κίνηση στρέψεως, στρέβλωση ♦ vt στρεβλώνω, στραμπουλίζω.
wrestle ['rɛsl] vi (+ with) αγωνίζομαι || (SPORT) παλεύω.
wrestling ['rɛslɪŋ] n πάλη, πάλεμα nt || ~ **match** n αγώνισμα nt πάλης.

wretched ['rɛtʃɪd] a πολύ δυστυχισμένος άθλιος || (bad, poor) άθλιος, θλιβερός, αξιοθρήνητος.
wriggle ['rɪgl] n συστροφή στριφογύρισμα ♦ vi συστρέφομαι, σπαρταρώ στριφογυρίζω, γλιστρώ.
wring [rɪŋ] (irreg v) vt συστρέφω, στρίβω.
wrinkle ['rɪŋkl] n (on face) ρυτίδα || (in cloth) πτυχή ♦ vt ρυτιδώνω, ζαρώνω ♦ vi ρυτιδούμαι, ζαρώνω.
wrist [rɪst] n καρπός (του χεριού) || ~ **watch** n ρολόι του χεριού.
writ [rɪt] n (LAW) δικαστική πράξη, ένταλμα nt.
write [raɪt] (irreg v) vt γράφω || (book) συντάσσω, γράφω ♦ vi (send letter) γράφω, στέλνω γράμμα || **to** ~ **down** vt διατυπώνω, (κατα) γράφω, σημειώνω, περιγράφω || **to** ~ **off** vt (dismiss) ακυρώνω, διαγράφω, ξεγράφω || **to** ~ **out** vt καθαρογράφω, αντιγράφω, συντάσσω || **to** ~ **up** vt (report) συντάσσω, γράφω || ~-**off** n (smashed car) τελείως κατεστραμμένο || ~**r** n συγγραφέας, συντάκτης.
writing ['raɪtɪŋ] n γράψιμο, γραφή || (books etc) λογοτεχνικό έργο || ~ **paper** n κόλλα, χαρτί γραψίματος.
written ['rɪtn] pp of **write**.
wrong [rɒŋ] a κακός, άδικος || (incorrect) ανακριβής, λανθασμένος || (to be mistaken) κάνω λάθος.
wrote [rəut] pt of **write**.
wrought [rɔːt] a: ~ **iron** κατεργασμένος σίδηρος.
wrung [rʌŋ] pt, pp of **wring**.
wry [raɪ] a στρεβλός, στριμμένος, στραβός.
wt. abbr of **weight**.

X

Xmas ['ɛksməs] n (col: Christmas) Χριστούγεννα ntpl.
X-ray ['ɛks'reɪ] n ακτινογραφία, ακτινοσκόπηση.
xylophone ['zaɪləfəun] n ξυλόφωνο.

Y

yacht [jɒt] n θαλαμηγός f, γιώτ nt inv, κότερο || ~ing n ενασχόληση με γιωτ, γιώτσιγκ nt inv || ~**sman** n άνθρωπος ασχολούμενος με γιώτ.
Yank [jæŋk] n (col: American) Αμερικάνος, Γιάγκης.
yap [jæp] vi (dog) γαυγίζω.
yard [jɑːd] n (of house etc) αυλή, προαύλιο, μάντρα || (measure) υάρδα (0.914 μ).
yarn [jɑːn] n νήμα nt, κλωστή || (tale) ιστορία φανταστική.
yawn [jɔːn] n χασμούρημα nt, χασμουρητό ♦ vi χασμουριέμαι.

yd. *abbr of* **yard(s).**

year ['jiə*] *n* έτος *nt*, χρόνος || ~**ly** *a* ετήσιος ♦ *ad* ετησίως, κάθε χρόνο.

yearn [jз:n] *vi* (+ *for*) ποθώ, λαχταρώ || ~**ing** *n* πόθος, λαχτάρα.

yeast [ji:st] *n* προζύμι, μαγιά.

yell [jɛl] *n* κραυγή, σκούξιμο ♦ *vi* ωρύομαι, φωνάζω δυνατά, σκούζω.

yellow ['jɛləʊ] *a* κίτρινος ♦ *n* κίτρινο.

yelp [jɛlp] *vi* γαυγίζω.

yes [jɛs] *ad* ναι, μάλιστα.

yesterday ['jɛstədei] *ad* χθες, χτες.

yet [jɛt] *ad* (*by now*) ακόμη, τώρα || (*still*) ακόμη || (*by that time*) κι όμως, παρ' όλα αυτά || *cj* κι όμως, εντούτοις.

yew [ju:] *n* τάξος.

Yiddish ['jidiʃ] *n* (*LING*) γερμανοεβραϊκά.

yield [ji:ld] *n* παραγωγή, απόδοση ♦ *vt* αποδίδω, αποφέρω ♦ *vi* (*surrender*) υποτάσσομαι, παραδίδομαι.

yodel ['jəʊdl] *vi* τραγουδώ (τυρολέζικα).

yoga ['jəʊgə] *n* γιόγκα *nt inv.*

yogurt ['jəʊgət] *n* γιαούρτι *nt.*

yoke [jəʊk] *n* ζυγός, ζευγάρι || (*servitude*) ζυγός.

yolk [jəʊk] *n* κρόκος, κροκάδι.

you [ju:] *pron* (ε)σείς, (ε)σύ.

you'd [ju:d] = **you had, you would** || *see* **have, would.**

you'll [ju:l] = **you will, you shall** || *see* **will, shall.**

young [jʌŋ] *a* νέος, νεαρός, μικρός || **the** ~ οι νέοι *mpl*, η νεολαία || ~**ish** *a* μάλλον νέος, νεούτσικος || ~**ster** *n* νεαρός, νέος, αγόρι.

your ['juə*] *poss a* σου, σας.

you're ['juə*] = **you are** || *see* **be.**

yours ['juəz] *poss pron* (δικός) σου, (δικός) σας || ~ **faithfully** υμέτερος || ~ **sincerely** όλως υμέτερος.

yourself [jə'sɛlf] *pron* συ (ο ίδιος), τον εαυτόν σας, χωρίς βοήθεια.

yourselves [jə'sɛlvz] *pron pl* σεις (οι ίδιοι), μόνοι σας.

youth [ju:θ] *n* νεότητα, νιάτα, νιότη || (*young man*) νέος, νεαρός, έφηβος || (*young people*) νέοι *mpl*, νεολαία || ~**ful** *a* νεανικός, νεαρός || ~ **hostel** *n* ξενώνας νεότητας.

you've [ju:v] = **you have** || *see* **have.**

Yugoslav ['ju:gəʊ'slɑ:v] *a* γιουγκοσλαβικός ♦ *n* (*person*) Γιουγκοσλάβος/α *m/f* || (*LING*) Γιουγκοσλαβικά *ntpl* || ~**ia** *n* Γιουγκοσλαβία.

Z

zany ['zeini] *a* ηλίθιος, βλάκας.

zeal [zi:l] *n* ζήλος || ~**ous** *a* γεμάτος ζήλο.

zebra ['zi:brə] *n* ζέβρα || ~ **crossing** *n* διάβαση (πεζών).

zero ['ziərəʊ] *n* μηδέν *nt*, μηδενικό || ~ **hour** *n* ώρα μηδέν, ώρα (επιθέσεως).

zest [zɛst] *n* ζέση, ενθουσιασμός, όρεξη.

zigzag ['zigzæg] *n* ζιγκ-ζαγκ *nt inv* ♦ *vi* κάνω ζιγκ-ζαγκ.

zinc [ziŋk] *n* ψευδάργυρος, τσίγκος.

Zionism ['zaiənizəm] *n* σιωνισμός.

zip [zip] *n* (*also:* ~ **fastener,** ~**per**) φερμουάρ *nt inv* ♦ *vt* (*also:* ~ **up**) κλείνω (με φερμουάρ).

zodiac ['zəʊdiæk] *n* ζωδιακός κύκλος.

zone [zəʊn] *n* ζώνη.

zoo [zu:] *n* ζωολογικός κήπος || ~**logical** *a* ζωολογικός || ~**logist** *n* ζωολόγος || ~**logy** *n* ζωολογία.

zoom [zu:m] *vi* βομβώ, βουίζω || ~ **lens** *n* φακός μεταβλητής εστιακής αποστάσεως, ζούμ *nt inv.*

ΑΓΓΛΙΚΑ ΑΝΩΜΑΛΑ ΡΗΜΑΤΑ

present	pt	pp	present	pt	pp
arise	arose	arisen	eat	ate	eaten
awake	awoke	awaked	fall	fell	fallen
be (am,	was,	been	feed	fed	fed
is, are;	were		feel	felt	felt
being)			fight	fought	fought
bear	bore	born(e)	find	found	found
beat	beat	beaten	flee	fled	fled
become	became	become	fling	flung	flung
befall	befell	befallen	fly	flew	flown
begin	began	begun	forbid	forbade	forbidden
behold	beheld	beheld	forecast	forecast	forecast
bend	bent	bent	forget	forgot	forgotten
beset	beset	beset	forgive	forgave	forgiven
bet	bet,	bet,	forsake	forsook	forsaken
	betted	betted	freeze	froze	frozen
bid	bid	bid	get	got	got, (US)
bind	bound	bound			gotten
bite	bit	bitten	give	gave	given
bleed	bled	bled	go	went	gone
blow	blew	blown	(goes)		
break	broke	broken	grind	ground	ground
breed	bred	bred	grow	grew	grown
bring	brought	brought	hang	hung,	hung,
build	built	built		hanged	hanged
burn	burnt,	burnt,	have	had	had
	burned	burned	hear	heard	heard
burst	burst	burst	hide	hid	hidden
buy	bought	bought	hit	hit	hit
can	could	(been able)	hold	held	held
cast	cast	cast	hurt	hurt	hurt
catch	caught	caught	keep	kept	kept
choose	chose	chosen	kneel	knelt,	knelt,
cling	clung	clung		kneeled	kneeled
come	came	come	know	knew	known
cost	cost	cost	lay	laid	laid
creep	crept	crept	lead	led	led
cut	cut	cut	lean	leant,	leant,
deal	dealt	dealt		leaned	leaned
dig	dug	dug	leap	leapt,	leapt,
do (3rd	did	done		leaped	leaped
person;			learn	learnt,	learnt,
he/she/				learned	learned
it does)			leave	left	left
draw	drew	drawn	lend	lent	lent
dream	dreamed,	dreamed,	let	let	let
	dreamt	dreamt	lie	lay	lain
drink	drank	drunk	(lying)		
drive	drove	driven	light	lit,	lit,
dwell	dwelt	dwelt		lighted	lighted

209

Z

present	pt	pp	present	pt	pp
lose	lost	lost	speed	sped,	sped,
make	made	made		speeded	speeded
may	might	—	spell	spelt,	spelt,
mean	meant	meant		spelled	spelled
meet	met	met	spend	spent	spent
mistake	mistook	mistaken	spill	spilt,	spilt,
mow	mowed	mown,		spilled	spilled
		mowed	spin	spun	spun
must	(had to)	(had to)	spit	spat	spat
pay	paid	paid	split	split	split
put	put	put	spoil	spoiled,	spoiled,
quit	quit,	quit,		spoilt	spoilt
	quitted	quitted	spread	spread	spread
read	read	read	spring	sprang	sprung
rend	rent	rent	stand	stood	stood
rid	rid	rid	steal	stole	stolen
ride	rode	ridden	stick	stuck	stuck
ring	rang	rung	sting	stung	stung
rise	rose	risen	stink	stank	stunk
run	ran	run	stride	strode	stridden
saw	sawed	sawn	strike	struck	struck,
say	said	said			stricken
see	saw	seen	strive	strove	striven
seek	sought	sought	swear	swore	sworn
sell	sold	sold	sweep	swept	swept
send	sent	sent	swell	swelled	swollen,
set	set	set			swelled
shake	shook	shaken	swim	swam	swum
shall	should	—	swing	swung	swung
shear	sheared	shorn,	take	took	taken
		sheared	teach	taught	taught
shed	shed	shed			
shine	shone	shone	tear	tore	torn
shoot	shot	shot	tell	told	told
show	showed	shown	think	thought	thought
shrink	shrank	shrunk	throw	threw	thrown
shut	shut	shut	thrust	thrust	thrust
sing	sang	sung	tread	trod	trodden
sink	sank	sunk	wake	woke,	woken,
sit	sat	sat		waked	waked
slay	slew	slain	wear	wore	worn
sleep	slept	slept	weave	wove,	woven,
slide	slid	slid		weaved	weaved
sling	slung	slung	wed	wedded,	wedded,
slit	slit	slit		wed	wed
smell	smelt,	smelt,	weep	wept	wept
	smelled	smelled	win	won	won
sow	sowed	sown,	wind	wound	wound
		sowed	wring	wrung	wrung
speak	spoke	spoken	write	wrote	written

ΑΠΟΛΥΑ   CARDINAL NUMBERS

μηδέν	0	zero
ένας, μία (μια), ένα	1	one
δύο	2	two
τρεις, τρία	3	three
τέσσερις, τέσσερα	4	four
πέντε	5	five
έξι	6	six
επτά (εφτά)	7	seven
οκτώ (οχτώ)	8	eight
εννέα (εννιά)	9	nine
δέκα	10	ten
έντεκα	11	eleven
δώδεκα	12	twelve
δεκατρείς, δεκατρία	13	thirteen
δεκατέσσερις, δεκατέσσερα	14	fourteen
δεκαπέντε	15	fifteen
δεκαέξι	16	sixteen
δεκαεπτά (δεκαεφτά)	17	seventeen
δεκαοκτώ (δεκαοχτώ)	18	eighteen
δεκαεννέα (δεκαεννιά)	19	nineteen
είκοσι	20	twenty
είκοσι ένας, μία, ένα	21	twenty-one
είκοσι δύο	22	twenty-two
είκοσι τρεις, τρία	23	twenty-three
τριάντα	30	thirty
σαράντα	40	forty
πενήντα	50	fifty
εξήντα	60	sixty
εβδομήντα	70	seventy
ογδόντα	80	eighty
ενενήντα	90	ninety
εκατό	100	one hundred
εκατόν ένας, εκατό μία, εκατόν ένα	101	one hundred and one
εκατόν πενήντα έξι	156	one hundred and fifty-six
διακόσιοι,ες,α	200	two hundred
τριακόσιοι,ες,α	300	three hundred
τετρακόσιοι,ες,α	400	four hundred
πεντακόσιοι,ες,α	500	five hundred
εξακόσιοι,ες,α	600	six hundred
επτακόσιοι,ες,α (εφτακόσιοι,ες,α)	700	seven hundred
οκτακόσιοι,ες,α (οχτακόσιοι,ες,α)	800	eight hundred
εννιακόσιοι,ες,α	900	nine hundred
χίλιοι, χίλιες, χίλια	1,000	one thousand
δύο χιλιάδες	2,000	two thousand
τρεις χιλιάδες	3,000	three thousand
ένα εκατομμύριο	1,000,000	one million
ένα δισεκατομμύριο	1,000,000,000	one billion

TAKTIKA

ORDINAL NUMBERS

πρώτος, πρώτη, πρώτο	1st	first
δεύτερος	2nd	second
τρίτος	3rd	third
τέταρτος	4th	fourth
πέμπτος	5th	fifth
έκτος	6th	sixth
έβδομος	7th	seventh
όγδοος	8th	eighth
ένατος	9th	ninth
δέκατος	10th	tenth
ενδέκατος (εντέκατος)	11th	eleventh
δωδέκατος	12th	twelfth
δέκατος τρίτος	13th	thirteenth
δέκατος τέταρτος	14th	fourteenth
δέκατος πέμπτος	15th	fifteenth
δέκατος έκτος	16th	sixteenth
δέκατος έβδομος	17th	seventeenth
δέκατος όγδοος	18th	eighteenth
δέκατος ένατος	19th	nineteenth
εικοστός	20th	twentieth
εικοστός πρώτος	21st	twenty-first
εικοστός δεύτερος	22nd	twenty-second
εικοστός τρίτος	23rd	twenty-third
τριακοστός	30th	thirtieth
τεσσερακοστός	40th	fortieth
πεντηκοστός	50th	fiftieth
εξηκοστός	60th	sixtieth
εβδομηκοστός	70th	seventieth
ογδοηκοστός	80th	eightieth
ενενηκοστός	90th	ninetieth
εκατοστός	100th	(one) hundredth
διακοσιοστός	200th	two hundredth
τριακοσιοστός	300th	three hundredth
τειρακοσιοστός	400th	four hundredth
πεντακοσιοστός	500th	five hundredth
εξακοσιοστός	600th	six hundredth
επτακοσιοστός (εφτακοσιοστός)	700th	seven hundredth
οκτακοσιοστός (οχτακοσιοστός)	800th	eight hundredth
εννιακοσιοστός	900th	nine hundredth
χιλιοστός	1,000th	(one) thousandth
εκατομμυριοστός	1,000,000th	millionth
δισεκατομμυριοστός	1,000,000,000th	billionth

THE TIME

what time is it?	τι ώρα είναι;
it is ...	είναι ...
at what time?	τι ώρα;
at 8	στις οκτώ
at midnight	τα μεσάνυχτα
at one p.m.	στη μία μετά το μεσημέρι

00.00	midnight	μεσάνυχτα, δώδεκα τα μεσάνυχτα
00.10	ten past midnight, ten past twelve a.m.	δώδεκα και δέκα μετά τα μεσάνυχτα
00.15	a quarter past midnight, twelve fifteen a.m.	δώδεκα και τέταρτο μετά τα μεσάνυχτα, δώδεκα και δεκαπέντε π.μ.
00.30	half past twelve, twelve thirty a.m.	δώδεκα και μισή, δώδεκα και τριάντα π.μ.
01.10	ten past one, one ten	μία (μια) και δέκα
01.15	a quarter past one, one fifteen	μία (μια) και τέταρτο, μία και δεκαπέντε
01.30	half past one, one thirty	μία (μια) και μισή, μία και τριάντα
01.45	a quarter to two, one forty-five	δύο παρά τέταρτο, μία και σαράντα πέντε
01.50	ten to two, one fifty	δύο παρά δέκα, μία και πενήντα
12.00	midday	μεσημέρι, δώδεκα το μεσημέρι
12.30	half past twelve, twelve thirty p.m.	δώδεκα και μισή, δώδεκα και τριάντα μ.μ.
13.00	one (o'clock) (in the afternoon), one p.m.	μία (μια) η ώρα (το απόγευμα ή μ.μ.)
19.00	seven (o'clock) (in the evening), seven p.m.	επτά η ώρα (το βράδυ ή μ.μ.)
21.30	nine thirty (p.m. *or* at night)	εννέα και μισή (μ.μ. ή το βράδυ)
23.45	a quarter to twelve, eleven forty-five p.m.	δώδεκα παρά τέταρτο, έντεκα και σαράντα πέντε μ.μ.

in 20 minutes	σε είκοσι λεπτά
20 minutes ago	πριν από είκοσι λεπτά
wake me up at 7	ξυπνήστε με στις επτά
20 km.p.h.	είκοσι χιλιόμετρα την ώρα

DATES AND NUMBERS

1. The date

what's the date today?	τι ημερομηνία είναι σήμερα;
it's the ...	είναι η ...
1st of February	πρώτη Φεβρουαρίου
2nd of February	δευτέρα Φεβρουαρίου
28th of February	εικοστή ογδόη Φεβρουαρίου
he's coming on the 7th of May	θα φθάσει στις επτά Μαΐου
I was born in 1945	γεννήθηκα το χίλια εννιακόσια σαράντα πέντε
I was born on the 15th of July 19 ...	γεννήθηκα στις δεκαπέντε Ιουλίου χίλια εννιακόσια...
during the sixties	στη δεκαετία του εξήντα
in the twentieth century	στον εικοστό αιώνα
in May	το Μάιο
on Monday (the 15th)	τη Δευτέρα (στις δεκαπέντε)
on Mondays	κάθε Δευτέρα
next/last Monday	την επόμενη/την περασμένη Δευτέρα
in 10 days' time	σε δέκα μέρες

2. Telephone numbers

I would like Athens 24 35 56

    θα ήθελα Αθήνα είκοσι τέσσερα/ τριάντα πέντε/ πενήντα έξι

could you get me Athens 22 00 79, extension 2233

    μπορείτε να μου πάρετε Αθήνα είκοσι δύο/ μηδέν μηδέν/ εβδομήντα εννέα, εσωτερική γραμμή είκοσι δύο/ τριάντα τρία

the Athens prefix is 01

    ο κωδικός της Αθήνας είναι μηδέν ένα

3. Using numbers

he lives at number 10	μένει στον αριθμό δέκα
it's in chapter 7, on page 7	είναι στο έβδομο κεφάλαιο, στη σελίδα επτά
he lives on the 3rd floor	μένει στο τρίτο πάτωμα
he came in 4th	ήρθε τέταρτος
a share of one seventh	μερίδιο ένα έβδομο
scale 1:25,000	κλίμακα ένα στις είκοσι πέντε χιλιάδες